e Orders and Tractates of the Talmud

SEDER ZERA'IM *1 volume*

Pe'ah, Demai, Kil'ayim, Shebi'ith, Terumoth,
oth, Ma'aser Sheni, Ḥallah, 'Orlah, Bikkurim

SEDER MO'ED *4 volumes*

1: Shabbath
2: 'Erubin, Pesaḥim
3: Yoma, Sukkah, Bezah
Ta'anith, Sheḳalim, Megillah, Mo'ed Ḳaṭan, Ḥagigah

SEDER NASHIM *4 volumes*

1: Yebamoth
2: Kethuboth
3: Nedarim, Nazir, Soṭah
4: Giṭṭin, Ḳiddushin

SEDER NEZIḲIN *4 volumes*

1: Baba Ḳamma, Baba Meẓi'a
2: Baba Bathra
3: Sanhedrin
Horayoth, Shebu'oth, Makkoth, 'Eduyyoth, Aboth

EDER ḲODASHIM *3 volumes*

1: Zebaḥim, Menaḥoth
2: Ḥullin
Temurah, Kerithoth, Me'ilah, Tamid, Middoth, Ḳinnim

DER ṬOHOROTH *1 volume*

Oholoth, Nega'im, Parah, Ṭohoroth, Miḳwaoth,
n, Zabim, Ṭebul Yom, Yadayim, 'Uḳẓin

INDEX *1 volume*

THIS SPECIAL LIMITED ANNIVERSARY EDITION OF

THE BABYLONIAN TALMUD IN ENGLISH

HAS BEEN PUBLISHED BY THE SONCINO PRESS

AND PRINTED AND BOUND AT THE

OXFORD UNIVERSITY PRESS

COINCIDING WITH THE QUINCENTENARY OF

BOTH HOUSES

THE BABYLONIAN TALMUD

SEDER NASHIM

VOLUME III

NEDARIM

★

NAZIR

★

SOṬAH

THE BABYLONIAN TALMUD

SEDER NASHIM

IN FOUR VOLUMES

III

TRANSLATED INTO ENGLISH
WITH NOTES / GLOSSARY AND INDICES
UNDER THE EDITORSHIP OF

RABBI DR I. EPSTEIN

B.A., Ph. D., D. Lit.

THE SONCINO PRESS
LONDON

FIRST PUBLISHED 1936

Printed in Great Britain
at the University Press, Oxford
by Eric Buckley
Printer to the University

NEDARIM

TRANSLATED INTO ENGLISH
WITH NOTES, GLOSSARY
AND INDICES

BY

RABBI DR H. FREEDMAN, B. A., PH. D.

PREFATORY NOTE BY THE EDITOR

The Editor desires to state that the translation of the several Tractates, and the notes thereon, are the work of the individual contributors and that he has not attempted to secure general uniformity in style or mode of rendering. He has, nevertheless, revised and supplemented, at his own discretion, their interpretation and elucidation of the original text, and has himself added the footnotes in square brackets containing alternative explanations and matter of historical and geographical interest.

ISIDORE EPSTEIN

CONTENTS

INTRODUCTION

Nedarim, 'Vows' is generally regarded as the third Tractate of Nashim, 'Women',[1] though the order of the Tractates is not uniform in all editions. The first nine chapters have no particular connection with women, yet the tractate is included in this Order on account of the last two chapters, which treat of the husband's power to annul the vows of his wife and the father's power to annul those of his daughter. According to Maimonides in the Introduction to his commentary on the Mishnah, this Tractate immediately follows Kethuboth because once a woman has entered under the *ḥuppah* (bridal canopy) and the provisions of the *kethubah* (marriage settlement) are operative, her husband has the right to annul her vows.

The making of vows would appear to have been a frequent practice in ancient life. People voluntarily denied themselves permitted pleasures, though the Rabbis frowned upon unnecessary asceticism, holding it a sin to abstain from legitimate enjoyment. Again, to express anger or resentment, vows were made whereby one forbade himself to benefit from the object of his displeasure, or forbade the latter to benefit from him. It may be remarked in this connection that the Rabbis disapproved of the whole practice of vowing, so much so that one might rightly speak of the vows of the wicked, but not of the vows of the righteous (Mishnah, 9*a*). And in making vows of abstinence people, as a rule, did not say, 'I vow that So-and-so shall be forbidden to me,' for a definite technique of vowing had in course of time been evolved. Generally speaking, they related their vow to the Temple Service, as the religious centre of their lives, and would declare, 'Let So-and-so be to me as a *ḳorban*, sacrifice,' which meant that it was to be prohibited. Yet there was a tendency to avoid the actual use of the word *ḳorban*, and similar sounding substitutes were employed instead. The first two chapters deal with this technique of vowing:

1) V. Soṭah 2*a*.

which formulas were valid (chapter 1) and which were not (chapter 2).

The third chapter treats of vows which for certain reasons were not recognised as vows at all, but merely as rhetorical means of emphasizing one's determination, such as vows taken in business transactions to enhance or depress the value of merchandise. An excursus at the end of the chapter gives definitions of the persons to be understood by particular terms, as when e.g., one vows not to benefit from land-dwellers, seafarers, the children of Noah, the seed of Abraham, etc. In this connection a definition of 'circumcised' is given, and this is made the opportunity for a digression on the vital importance of circumcision in Judaism. These definitions may be regarded as a fitting introduction to the subject-matter of chapter 4, which is to define the scope of vows, such as the extent to which one is forbidden when he is under a vow not to eat aught of his neighbour, and when he is under a vow not to benefit from his neighbour.

Chapter 5 deals with partners in property who subject one another to vows, and how their partnership rights are thereby affected. It is characteristic of the high place kindliness and pity hold in Judaism that the chapter proceeds to discuss how one who may not confer benefit upon his neighbour as a result of a vow may nevertheless help him in distress. Some of the expedients permitted may appear to be and are in fact mere evasions; but they correspond to the finer instincts of the true ethical values of religion.

Chapters 6 and 7 contain a further series of definitions. But whereas the excursus at the end of chapter 3 treats of definitions of persons, we have here definitions of common terms used in vowing, e.g., what is understood when one vows to abstain from boiled food, food prepared in a pot, roast, milk, various fruits, vegetables, house, etc. In the following chapter time-definitions form the main subject: what is meant by day, month, year, etc., when one sets these as limits to his vow, and how they are affected by the intercalation of the month or the year.

The frequency and possibly light-hearted spirit with which vows were made, only to be regretted later in calmer moments, made it necessary to provide for their remission, when this was desired. Nevertheless, absolution could not be granted at one's mere request, but some grounds for regret had to be found. For it was presumed that had these grounds been present to the mind of the vower at the time, he would have refrained from vowing. This presumption sufficed to render it a vow made in error and thereby warrant its nullification. The ninth chapter deals with the grounds upon which absolution may be granted.

As has already been stated, it is to the 10th and 11th chapters that this Tractate owes its inclusion in the present Order. The former deals with the persons who can annul a woman's vows, viz., her father and her husband, and under what conditions. Finally the last chapter discusses which vows a husband can annul. It may be observed that though a woman's vows were thus subject to annulment by her father or husband (in the latter case only where they affected him), neither had the power to *impose* vows upon her, such as was recognised in some ancient non-Jewish legal systems.

The text, particularly in the *halachic* portion, is in some disorder, far more so than is the case of other Tractates of the Talmud. A great number of readings differing from those of the cur. edd. are preserved in the standard commentaries of Rashi, Ran, Asheri and Tosafoth. These variants are not merely linguistic, but in many cases materially affect the thread of the discussion. Naturally, interpretation is affected too, and the necessary changes consequent upon the changes in the text have been indicated in the notes.

There is very little *Aggada* in this Tractate. The most noteworthy passages and *Aggadic* sayings are those dealing with the great importance of circumcision; the emphasis that learning must be free; the enumeration of the things created before the Creation of the world; the importance of sick visiting; the story of R. Akiba's rise from a poor shepherd to a great teacher in Israel, bound up, in true romantic fashion, with a tender love-story; the warning against selfish motives in study — 'he who makes use of the crown of the law is uprooted from the world'; and the exhortation: 'Take heed of the sons of the poor, for from them cometh Torah'—a democratic assertion fitting for a cultural and religious system which always strives to assess a man's worth not by his material wealth and possessions but by the higher standard of piety and knowledge.

H. FREEDMAN

The Indices of this Tractate have been compiled by Judah J. Slotki, M. A.

NEDARIM

CHAPTER I

MISHNAH. [2*a*] ALL THE SUBSTITUTES FOR [THE FORMULAS OF] VOWS HAVE THE VALIDITY OF VOWS.[1] THOSE FOR ḤARAMIM ARE LIKE ḤARAMIM,[2] THOSE FOR OATHS ARE LIKE OATHS, AND THOSE FOR NEZIROTH ARE LIKE NEZIROTH.[3] IF ONE SAYS TO HIS NEIGHBOUR, 'I AM DEBARRED FROM YOU BY A VOW, [OR] I AM SEPARATED FROM YOU,' [OR] 'I AM REMOVED FROM YOU, IN RESPECT OF AUGHT[4] THAT I MIGHT EAT OF YOURS OR THAT I MIGHT TASTE OF YOURS,' HE IS PROHIBITED. IF HE SAYS: 'I AM BANNED TO YOU,' THEN R. AKIBA WAS INCLINED TO GIVE A STRINGENT RULING.[5]

GEMARA. [2*b*] ALL THE SUBSTITUTES FOR [THE FORMULAS OF] VOWS HAVE THE VALIDITY OF VOWS: Why are the other clauses[6] not stated in [the Mishnah of] Nazir,[7] whilst [our Mishnah of] Nedarim includes them all?—Because oaths and vows are written side by side [in the Bible][8] they are both stated, and since the two are mentioned, the others are stated also. Then let OATHS be taught immediately after VOWS?—Because he states vows in which the *article* is forbidden to the person, he follows it up with

(1) The principal form of a vow to abstain from anything is: 'This shall be to me as a *ḳorban* (Heb. sacrifice); *ḳorban* was sometimes substituted by *ḳonam* or *ḳonas*. (2) *Ḥerem* (plural *ḥaramim*): a vow dedicating something to the Temple or the priests. (3) *Neziroth*: the vow of a nazirite. A nazirite had to abstain from grapes and intoxicating liquors and refrain from cutting his hair and defiling himself through the dead. (4) [Reading שֶׁאֲנִי. *Var. lec.* שֶׁאֵינִי 'for I will eat naught of yours'.] (5) I.e., declared the vow binding. [According to Maimonides, provided he adds: 'for I will eat naught of yours'. Tosaf., however, (*infra* 7*a*) holds that the phrase by itself implies a vow to abstain from aught belonging to the other person.] (6) Viz., ḤARAMIM, OATHS, AND VOWS. (7) The tractate Nazir commences likewise: All substitutes for the nazirite vow are binding. (8) Num. XXX, 3: *If a man vow a vow unto the Lord, or swear an oath.*

HARAMIM, where likewise the *article* is forbidden to the person. OATHS, however, are excluded [from the category of vows], since oaths bind the *person* to abstain from a thing;[1] [hence they cannot immediately follow vows].

The Mishnah commences with substitutes: ALL THE SUBSTITUTES FOR [THE FORMULAS OF] VOWS etc., yet proceeds to explain the laws of abbreviations of vows: IF ONE SAYS TO HIS NEIGHBOUR: 'I AM DEBARRED FROM YOU BY A VOW' . . . WITH HIS VOW;[2] moreover, [the Tanna] has altogether omitted to state that abbreviations [are binding]?—[The Tanna does] speak of them, but our text is defective,[3] and this is what was really meant: ALL SUBSTITUTES and abbreviations OF VOWS HAVE THE VALIDITY OF VOWS. Then let substitutes be first explained?—The clause to which [the Tanna] has last referred is generally first explained, as we have learned: Wherewith may [the Sabbath lights] be kindled, and wherewith may they not be kindled? They may not be kindled etc.[4] Wherein may food be put away [to be kept hot for the Sabbath], and wherein may it not be put away? It may not be put away [etc.].[5] Wherewith may a woman go out [from her house on the Sabbath], and wherewith may she not go out? She may not go out from etc.[6] [Is it then a universal rule] that the first clause is never explained first? But we have learnt: Some relations inherit from and transmit [their estate] to others; some inherit but do not transmit. Now, these relations inherit from and transmit to each other etc.[7] Some women are permitted to their husbands but forbidden to their husbands' brothers;[8] others

(1) A vow is thus taken: 'This shall be forbidden to me,' the prohibition falling upon the *thing*. An oath, however, is thus taken: 'I *swear* to abstain from a certain thing,' the prohibition falling upon the *person*. (2) Since the principal way of making a vow is to declare a thing to be as a *ḳorban*, the omission of such a declaration renders the vow merely an abbreviation or suggestion (lit., 'a handle') of a vow, v. Nazir (Sonc. ed.) p. 2. (3) This may mean either that there is actually a lacuna in the text, words having fallen out, or that though it is correct in itself something has to be supplied to complete the sense; v. Weiss, *Dor.* III, p. 6, n. 14. The former is the most probable here. (4) Shab. 20*b*. (5) Ibid. 47*b*. (6) Ibid. 57*a*.—In all these examples the second clause is first discussed. (7) B.B. 108*a*. (8) In Levirate marriage, v. Deut. XXV, 5 *seq*.

are the reverse. Now, these are permitted to their husbands but forbidden to their husbands' brothers etc.[1] Some meal offerings require oil and frankincense; others require oil but no frankincense. Now, these require both oil and frankincense etc.[2] Some meal-offerings must be taken [by the priest to the south-west corner of the altar], but do not need waving;[3] others are the reverse. Now, these must be taken to the altar etc.[4] Some are treated as first-borns in respect of inheritance[5] but not in respect of the priest;[6] others are treated as first-borns in respect of the priest but not in respect of inheritance. Now who is regarded as a first-born in respect of inheritance but not in respect of the priest etc.?[7]—In these examples [the first clause is explained first] because it contains numerous instances [to which its law applies]. But, 'Wherewith may a beast go out on the Sabbath, and wherewith may it not go out?' where [the first clause does] not contain numerous instances, yet it is explained [first], viz., a camel may go out, etc.? [3*a*] Hence there is no fixed rule: sometimes the first clause is explained first, at others the last clause is first explained. Alternatively: abbreviations are explained first, because they [*sc.* their validity] are deduced by exegesis.[8] Then let these be stated first?—He [the Tanna] commences indeed with substitutes, since these are Scriptural,[9] and proceeds to explain abbreviations, which are inferred by interpretation only.[10] This harmonises with the view that substitutes are merely the foreign equivalents [of the word *ḳorban*].[11] But what can be said on the view that they are forms expressly invented by the

(1) Yeb. 84*a*. (2) Men. 59*a*. (3) A ceremony in which the priest put his hands under those of the person bringing the offering and waved them to and fro in front of the altar. (4) Ibid. 60*a*. (5) I.e., they receive a double share of their patrimony; v. Deut. XXI, 17. (6) They do not need redemption; v. Ex. XIII, 13. (7) Bek. 46*a*.—In all these examples the first clause is discussed first. (8) But not explicitly stated in the Bible. (9) I.e., their validity is explicitly stated in the Bible. (10) When stating the law in general terms there is a preference for that which is best known; hence, substitutes, being explicitly taught, are first mentioned. But when going into details, the Tanna prefers to deal first with the lesser known. (11) Hence their validity may be regarded as explicitly stated in the Bible, since it obviously does not matter in which language a vow is taken.

Sages for the purpose of making vows?[1]—Now, are abbreviations mentioned at all; were you not compelled to assume a defective text? Then indeed place abbreviations first. Thus: All abbreviations of vows have the validity of vows, and ALL SUBSTITUTES FOR VOWS HAVE THE VALIDITY OF VOWS. These are the abbreviations: IF ONE SAYS TO HIS NEIGHBOUR . . . And these are the substitutes: *Ḳonam, ḳonas, ḳonaḥ*.[2]

Now, where are abbreviations written?—*When either a man or a woman shall separate themselves to vow a vow* [lindor neder] *of a nazirite* [nazir le-hazzir];[3] and it has been taught: *Nazir le-hazzir* is to render substitutes and abbreviations of *neziroth* as *neziroth*.[4] From this I may infer only the law of *neziroth;* whence do we know that it applies to other vows too? This is taught by the verse: *When either a man or a woman shall separate themselves to vow a vow of a nazirite to the Lord:*[5] here ordinary vows are compared to *neziroth* and *vice versa*.[6] Just as in *neziroth* abbreviations are equally binding, so in the case of other vows; and just as in other vows, he who does not fulfil them violates the injunctions: *He shall not break his word,*[7] and *Thou shalt not delay to pay it,*[8] so in *neziroth*. And just as in other vows, the father can annul those of his daughter and the husband those of his wife, so with *neziroth*.

Wherein does *neziroth* differ? Because it is written *nazir le-hazzir!* But [in the case of] vows too it is written, *lindor neder;*[9] then what need is there of analogy?—If the text were *neder lindor* just as '*nazir le-hazzir*', it would be as you say, and the analogy would be *unnecessary;* since however, '*lindor neder*' is written,—the Torah spoke in the language of men.[10] This agrees with the view that the Torah spoke in the language of men; but he who maintains that the Torah did not speak in the language

(1) V. *infra*, 10a. (2) V. *infra* 9a. (3) Num. VI, 2. (4) *Sc.* equally binding. (5) Ibid. (6) Since they are coupled together. This method of exegesis is known as *heḳḳesh*. (7) Ibid. XXX, 3. (8) Deut. XXIII, 22. (9) Lit., 'to vow a vow'—likewise a pleonastic form. (10) The point is this: The usual grammatical form is for the verb to precede its cognate object. Hence, when this order is reversed, as in *nazir le-hazzir*, one may directly infer something from the unusual order. When it is observed, however, nothing can be inferred.

of men,[1] to what purpose does he put this '*lindor neder*'?—He interprets it to deduce that abbreviations of vows are as vows, and then *neziroth* is compared to vows; and as to '*nazir le-hazzir*' he interprets it as teaching [3*b*] that one nazirite vow falls upon another.[2] Then he who maintains that the Torah spoke in the language of men, and interprets '*nazir le-hazzir*' as teaching the validity of abbreviations of *neziroth*, whence does he learn that a nazirite vow can fall upon another? If he agrees with the view that a nazirite vow does not fall upon another, it is well; but if he agrees with the view that it does, whence does he know it?—Let Scripture say, *li-zor* [the *ḳal* form]; why '*le-hazzir*' [the causative]? That you may infer both from it.[3] In the West[4] it was said: One Tanna deduces [the validity of] abbreviations from '*lindor neder*'; whilst another deduces it from [the phrase], *he shall do according to all that proceedeth out of his mouth*.[5]

The Master said: 'And just as in other vows, he who does not fulfil them violates the injunctions, *he shall not break his word*, and *thou shalt not delay to pay it*, so in *neziroth*.' Now, as for '*he shall not break his word*' as applying to [ordinary] vows, it is well: it is possible *e.g.*, if one says, 'I vow to eat this loaf', and does not eat it; he violates the injunction, '*he shall not break his word*'. But how is, '*he shall not break* [*his word*],' possible in the case of *neziroth*? For, as soon as one says, 'Behold, I am a *nazir*,' he is one; if he eats [grapes], he is liable for, *nor eat moist grapes or dried*;[6] if he drinks [wine], he violates, *he . . . shall drink no vinegar of wine, or vinegar of strong drink, neither shall he drink any liquor of grapes*.[7]—Raba answered: It is to

(1) So that every pleonasm, even if in accordance with the general idiom, gives an additional teaching. (2) A nazirite vow for an unspecified period means for thirty days. If one who is already a *nazir* takes a nazirite vow, it is binding, and becomes operative when the first ends. Thus he translates: a *nazir* can take a vow *le-hazzir*, to become a *nazir* after his present vow terminates, v. *infra* 18*a*. (3) The heavier form *le-hazzir* implies intensity, therefore it is interpreted as meaning something additional to what might be inferred from the *ḳal li-zor*, which itself being pleonastic allows us to infer something not explicit in the verse. (4) I.e., the Palestinian academies. (5) Num. XXX, 3: this embraces every form in which a vow can be made. (6) Ibid. VI, 3. (7) Ibid. [It is assumed that the injunction '*he shall not break his word*' can apply only to a case

transgress two [injunctions].[1] How is *'thou shalt not delay to pay it,'* referring to *neziroth*, conceivable? [For] as soon as one says 'Behold, I am a *nazir*', he is one; if he eats [grapes], he transgresses, *'neither shall he . . . eat moist grapes or dried?'* — When one says: 'when I wish, I will be a *nazir*'.[2] But if he says, 'when I *wish*', the injunction *'thou shalt not delay'* does not apply?[3] — Said Raba: E.g., if he says, 'I must not depart this world before having been a *nazir*,' for he becomes a *nazir* from that moment.[4] For this is similar to one who says to his wife: 'Here is your divorce, [to take effect] one hour before my death,' where she is immediately forbidden to eat *terumah*.[5] Thus we see that we fear[6] that he may die at any moment: so here[7] too, he becomes a *nazir* immediately, for we say, Perchance he will die now.

[4*a*] R. Aḥa b. Jacob said: E.g., if one takes a nazirite vow whilst in a cemetery.[8] This agrees with the view that the naziriteship is not immediately binding. But on the view that it is immediately valid, is then, *'he shall not delay,'* applicable?[9] Moreover, Mar, son of R. Ashi, said: The vow is immediately valid, and they differ[10] only on the question of flagellation? — Nevertheless he violates, *'thou shalt not delay,'* because the [ritually] clean naziriteship is delayed. R. Ashi said: Since this is so, [it follows that] if a *nazir* intentionally defiles himself, he transgresses *thou shalt not delay* in respect to [the recommencement of] the *clean* naziriteship.

where the vow is nullified by his action, e.g., where he vows to eat and he does not eat, but not where he, for instance, vows *not* to eat and he does eat, where the vow has not been nullified but transgressed; and similarly in the case of a *nazir*.]

(1) [Raba extends the scope of the injunction to include cases where the oath is transgressed; and thus by drinking wine he transgresses *'he shall not drink'*, in addition to *'he shall not break his word'*.] (2) If he postpones becoming a *nazir*, he violates, *'thou shalt not delay* etc'. (3) Since there is no vow until he so desires. (4) Not actually, but in the sense that he must assume his naziriteship without delay lest he dies the next moment. (5) V. Glos. (6) Lit., 'we say'. (7) In the case of a nazirite. (8) A *nazir* may not defile himself through the dead. Consequently the vow does not become immediately operative, but he must not *delay* to leave the cemetery so that it shall become binding. (9) Surely not, for he is an actual *nazir*, subject to all the provisions of a *nazir*. (10) *Sc.* R. Joḥanan and Resh Laḳish, in Nazir 16*b*.

R. Aḥa, the son of R. Iḳa, said: He[1] might transgress *'thou shalt not delay'* in respect to shaving.[2] Now, this goes without saying according to the view that shaving is indispensable;[3] but even on the view that the shaving is not a bar [to the sacrifices], nevertheless he does not observe the precept of shaving. Mar Zuṭra the son of R. Mari said: He might violate *'Thou shalt not delay'* in respect to his sacrifices. Is this deduced from here; surely, it is rather inferred from elsewhere: [*When thou shalt vow a vow unto the Lord, thou shalt not slack to pay it, for the Lord thy* God] *will surely require it of thee:*[4] this refers to sin-offerings and trespass-offerings?[5]—I might say that the Torah set up an anomaly[6] in the case of *nazir*.[7] What is the anomaly? Shall we say, the fact that a vow to bring the sin-offering of a *nazir*[8] is invalid; but a sin-offering for *ḥeleb*[9] cannot be made obligatory by a vow,[10] yet one transgresses, *'thou shalt not delay'?* But the anomaly is this: I might have thought, since even if one says, 'I will be a *nazir* only with respect to the kernels of grapes,'[11] he is a *nazir* in all respects, I would think that he does not violate, *'Thou shalt not delay'*; therefore we are told [otherwise].[12] Now, this is well according to the opinion that a vow of naziriteship in respect of the kernels of grapes makes one a *nazir* in all respects; but on the view of R. Simeon, viz., that one is not a *nazir* unless he separates himself from all, what can be said? Moreover, this is an anomaly in the direction of greater stringency?[13]—But the anomaly is this: I might have thought, since [4b] if he shaves himself for one

(1) The nazirite. (2) After the completion of his naziriteship; v. Num. VI, 9, and thus violate the injunction *'thou shalt not delay'*. (3) Lit., 'hinders'—the offering of the sacrifices on the completion of naziriteship; hence delay in shaving involves a delay in sacrifices. (4) Deut. XXIII, 22. (5) And this would cover the case of a nazirite. For what purpose then the application of the verse *'thou shalt not delay'* to the nazirite? (6) Lit., 'a novelty'—as such it cannot be included in other general laws, as it is a principle of exegesis that an anomaly stands in a class by itself. (7) Which includes a *nazir's* sacrifices. (8) By one who is not nazirite. (9) Forbidden fat. (10) A vow to bring a sin-offering which is normally due for eating *ḥeleb* is not binding if the vower is not actually liable. (11) V. Num. VI, 4. (12) By the coupling of the nazirite vow with other vows in the same sentence. (13) How then would we think that the injunction does not apply, so that it is more lenient?

[sacrifice] of the three, he fulfils his duty,[1] therefore he should not be subject to, '*Thou shalt not delay*'; hence we are told [that it is not so]. An alternative answer is this: the anomaly is that it cannot be vowed; but as to your difficulty of the sin-offering for *ḥeleb*,[2]—the sin-offering for *ḥeleb* comes for atonement,[3] but for what does the sin-offering of a *nazir* come?[4] But the sin-offering of a woman who gave birth,[5] which does not come for an atonement, yet one violates, '*thou shalt not delay*' on account thereof?—That permits her to eat of sacrifices.[6]

The Master said: 'And just as in other vows, the father can annul those of his daughter and the husband those of his wife, so in the case of *neziroth*, the father can annul the *neziroth* of his daughter and the husband that of his wife'. But what need is there of analogy; let us infer it from vows by general similarity?[7]—Perhaps he can annul only in the case of other vows, because their duration is unlimited; but with respect to *neziroth*, the duration of which is limited—for an unspecified vow of *neziroth* is for thirty days,—I might say that it is not so.[8] Hence we are informed [otherwise].[9]

IF ONE SAYS TO HIS NEIGHBOUR, 'I AM DEBARRED FROM YOU BY A VOW' etc. Samuel said: In all these instances he must say, 'in respect of aught that I might eat of yours or that I might taste of yours'. An objection is raised: [If one says to his neighbour], 'I am debarred from you by a vow,' [or] 'I am separated from you,'

(1) A *nazir* at the termination of his vow is bound to bring three sacrifices, viz., a burnt-offering, a sin-offering, and a peace-offering. Yet if he shaves and brings only one, the prohibitions of a *nazir*, such as the drinking of wine, etc., are lifted. This is a unique law, and in the direction of greater leniency. (2) *Supra* p. 7, n. 10. (3) Hence one violates the injunction by delaying to make atonement. (4) Though technically a sin-offering, it is, in fact, merely part of a larger vow. Hence it is an anomaly that it cannot be vowed separately. (5) V. Lev. XII, 6ff. (6) Which may be an obligation, e.g., the eating of the Passover sacrifice. Hence '*thou shalt not delay*' is applicable. (7) Since naziriteship is a form of vow. [מה מצינו. Lit., 'as we find concerning', a method of hermeneutics whereby an analogy is drawn from one case for one *single* similar case, as distinct from *hekkesh* (*supra* p. 4, n. 6) where the analogy is based on the close connection of the two subjects in one and the same context.] (8) Since the vow will automatically lapse. (9) By the analogy.

[or] 'I am removed from you', he is forbidden [to derive any benefit from him]. [If he says,] 'That which I might eat or taste of yours' [shall be to me prohibited], he is forbidden![1]—This is what is taught: When is this? If he adds 'in respect of aught that I might eat or taste of yours.' But the reverse was taught: [If one says to his neighbour,] 'That which I might eat or taste of yours' [shall be prohibited to me], he is forbidden; 'I am debarred from you by a vow', [or] 'I am separated from you', [or] 'I am removed from you,' he is [likewise] forbidden!—Read thus: Providing that he had first said, 'I am debarred from you, etc.'[2] If so, it is identical with the first [Baraitha]?[3] Moreover, why teach further, 'he is forbidden' twice?[4]—But this is what Samuel really said: Because he said, 'in respect of aught that I might eat of yours or that I might taste of yours', the maker of the vow alone is forbidden while his neighbour is permitted;[5] [5*a*] but if he merely says, 'I am debarred from you by a vow,' both are forbidden. Just as R. Jose son of R. Ḥanina said: [If one says to his neighbour] 'I am debarred from you by a vow,' both are forbidden.

We learnt: [If one says to his neighbour,] 'Behold! I am *ḥerem*[6] to you,' the *muddar*[7] is forbidden.[8] But the *maddir*[7] is not [forbidden]?[9]—*E.g.*, if he explicitly states, 'but you are not [*ḥerem*] to me'. [But does it not continue,] 'You are *ḥerem* to me', the *maddir* is forbidden, [implying,] but not the *muddar?*—*E.g.*, if he explicitly states, 'but you are not [*ḥerem*] to me.' But what if it is not explicit: both are forbidden? But since the final clause teaches, 'I am [*ḥerem*] to you and you are [*ḥerem*] to me,' both are forbidden, it is only in

(1) The first clause proves that the vow is valid without the addition. (2) According to this rendering, the bracketed 'shall be prohibited to me' must be deleted. (3) Why then is the order reversed? This difficulty arises in any case. But if each clause is independent, it can be answered that the second Baraitha *intentionally* reverses the clauses, so as to make their independence obvious, since the interpretation 'providing that he had first said' is forced; whilst in the first Baraitha the assumption that the second clause is an addition to the first is quite feasible. (4) Seeing that the whole refers to one vow. (5) To benefit from him. (6) V. Glos. (7) *Muddar* is the object of the vow; *maddir* is the man who makes the vow. (8) *Infra* 47*b*. (9) This contradicts Samuel's dictum that without the addition the incidence of the vow is reciprocal.

that case that both are forbidden, but in general he is forbidden while his neighbour is permitted?[1] But this is how R. Jose son of R. Ḥanina's [dictum] was stated: [If one says to his neighbour,] 'I am under a vow in respect of you,' both are forbidden; 'I am debarred from you by a vow,' *he* is forbidden but his neighbour is permitted. But our Mishnah teaches, 'FROM YOU,' yet our Mishnah was explained according to Samuel that in all cases he must say, 'in respect of aught that I might eat of yours or that I might taste of yours'—only then is he [alone] forbidden while his neighbour is permitted, but in the case of, 'I am debarred from you by a vow,' both are forbidden? But this is what was originally stated in Samuel's name: It is only because he said, 'in respect of aught that I might eat of yours or that I might taste of yours,' that he is forbidden only in respect of eating. But [if he only said,] 'I am debarred from you by a vow,' he is forbidden even benefit. If so, let Samuel state thus: But if he did not say, 'In respect of aught that I might eat of yours or that I might taste of yours,' even benefit is forbidden to him?[2]—But this is what was stated: Only if he says, 'in respect of aught that I might eat of yours or that I might taste of yours', is he forbidden; but if he [merely] says, 'I am debarred from you by a vow,' it does not imply a prohibition at all. What is the reason? 'I am debarred from you,' [implies] 'I am not to speak to you'; 'I am separated from you' [implies] 'I am to do no business with you'; 'I am removed from you' implies, 'I am not to stand within four cubits of you'.

[5*b*] Shall we say Samuel holds the opinion that inexplicit abbreviations are not abbreviations?[3]—Yes. Samuel makes the Mishnah agree with R. Judah, who maintained: Inexplicit abbreviations are not abbreviations. For we learnt: The essential part of a *Get*[4] is, 'Behold, thou art free unto all men'. R. Judah said: [To this must be added] 'and this [document] shall be unto thee from me a deed of dismissal and a document of release.'[5] Now, what forced Samuel

(1) Which contradicts R. Jose b. R. Ḥanina. (2) So the text as amended by BaḤ. (3) I.e., invalid. For the above forms are such, and Samuel maintains that they impose no prohibition at all without the explanatory clauses. (4) V. Glos. (5) Otherwise it is not clear that the divorce is to be

to thus interpret the Mishnah, so as to make it agree with R. Judah: let him make it agree with the Rabbis, that even inexplicit abbreviations [are binding]?[1] —Said Raba: The Mishnah presents a difficulty to him: Why state, IN RESPECT OF AUGHT THAT I MIGHT EAT OF YOURS OR THAT I MIGHT TASTE OF YOURS; let him teach, IN RESPECT OF AUGHT THAT I MIGHT EAT OR THAT I MIGHT TASTE [and no more]? This proves that we require explicit abbreviations.

It was stated: Inexplicit abbreviations—Abaye maintained: They are [valid] abbreviations; while Raba said: They are not [valid] abbreviations. Raba said: R. Idi explained the matter to me. Scripture says, [*When either a man or a woman shall*] explicitly *vow a vow of a nazirite, to separate themselves unto the Lord:* abbreviations of *neziroth* are compared to *neziroth:* just as *neziroth* must be explicit in meaning, so must their abbreviations be too.

Are we to say that they differ in the dispute of R. Judah and the Rabbis? For we learnt: The essential part of a *Get* is the words, 'Behold, thou art free unto all men.' R. Judah said: [To this must be added,] 'and this [document] shall be unto thee from me a deed of dismissal and a document of discharge and a letter of release': [Thus] Abaye rules as the Rabbis, and Raba as R. Judah?—[No.] Abaye may assert: My opinion agrees even with R. Judah's. Only in divorce does R. Judah insist that abbreviations shall be explicit, because 'cutting off'[2] is necessary, and this is lacking;[3] but do you know him to require it elsewhere too? Whilst Raba can maintain, My view agrees even with that of the Rabbis. Only in the case of divorce do they say that explicit abbreviations are not essential, [6a] because no man divorces his neighbour's wife;[4] but do you know them [to rule thus] elsewhere?[5]

effected by the *Get*. Thus he holds that inexplicit abbreviations are invalid.

(1) [For unless Samuel had cogent reasons to make the Mishnah agree only with R. Judah, he himself would not have accepted the view of R. Judah in preference to that of the majority of Rabbis (Ran).] (2) [Referring to Deut. XXIV, 3: '*And he shall write unto her a writ of cutting off*' (so literally).] (3) If the abbreviation is inexplicit the severance is not complete. (4) I.e., even if the wording is inexplicit, the whole transaction makes its meaning perfectly clear.

An objection is raised: [If one says,] 'That is to me,' [or] 'this is to me,' he is forbidden,[1] because it is an abbreviation of ['that is as a] *ḳorban* [to me].'[2] Thus, the reason is that he said, 'unto me,' but if he did not say, 'unto me,' it is not so:[3] this refutes Abaye? —Abaye replies thus: It is only because he said, 'to me,' that he is forbidden; but if he [merely] said, 'behold, that is,' without adding 'to me' he might have meant, 'behold, that is *hefḳer*,'[4] or 'that is for charity.'[5] But is it not stated, 'because it is an abbreviation of, "a *ḳorban?*"'[6]—But answer thus: Because he said, 'to me,' he [alone] is forbidden, but his neighbour is permitted; but if he said, 'behold, that is', both are forbidden, because he may have meant,[7] 'behold that is *heḳdesh*.[8]

An objection is raised: [If one says,] 'Behold, this [animal] is a sin-offering,' 'this is a trespass-offering,' though he is liable to a sin-offering or a trespass-offering, his words are of no effect. [But if he says,] 'Behold, this animal is *my* sin-offering,' or '*my* trespass-offering,' his declaration is effectual if he was liable. Now, this is a refutation of Abaye![9]—Abaye answers: This agrees with R. Judah.[10] But Abaye said, My ruling agrees even with R. Judah?[10] —Abaye retracted. Are we to say [then] that Raba's ruling agrees [*only*] with R. Judah's?[11]—No. Raba may maintain: My view agrees even with that of the Rabbis. Only in the case of

[This argument makes it evident that the point at issue between R. Judah and the Rabbis is mainly concerning the phrase '*from me*', the Rabbis being of the opinion that since no man divorces his neighbour's wife, it is clear that the *Get* comes 'from him' (Ran); v. Giṭ. 85*b*.] (5) Elsewhere they may agree that inexplicit allusions are invalid.

(1) To benefit from it. (2) So Rashi and Asheri. [Alternatively: Because it is an abbreviation valid for a *ḳorban* (an offering), and therefore also valid in case of a vow.] (3) Because it is an inexplicit abbreviation. (4) Ownerless property. V. Glos. (5) Hence it is not an abbreviation of a vow at all. (6) [This is difficult. The meaning apparently is that the reason that it is an abbreviation valid for a *ḳorban*, (v. n. 2) ought to apply also to the declaration 'that is' by itself, since such a declaration too is valid for a *ḳorban;* v. Ran.] (7) [Where the object vowed was not fit for sacrifice; v. n. 6.] (8) Sanctified property. V. Glos. (9) Since in the first clause the abbreviation is invalid because it is inexplicit. (10) V. *supra* 5*b*. (11) Since Abaye's view agrees only with that of the Rabbis.

divorce do they say that explicit abbreviations are not essential, because no man divorces his neighbour's wife; but elsewhere explicit abbreviations are required.

[6*b*] R. Papa enquired: Are abbreviations valid in the case of *kiddushin*,[1] or not? Now, how does this problem arise? Shall we say thus: If one said to a woman, 'Behold, thou art betrothed unto me,' and said to her companion, 'and thou *too*,' it is obvious that this is actual *kiddushin*?[2]—But e.g., If one said to a woman, 'Behold, thou art betrothed unto me,' and then to her companion, 'and thou'. Do we assume that he meant 'and thou *too*,' and so the second is betrothed;[3] or perhaps he said to her companion, 'and do thou witness it', and so she is not betrothed?

But is R. Papa really in doubt? But since he said to Abaye, Does Samuel hold that inexplicit abbreviations are valid?[4] it follows that he [R. Papa] holds that abbreviations are valid in the case of *kiddushin*?—R. Papa's question to Abaye was based on Samuel's opinion.[5]

R. Papa enquired: Are abbreviations binding in respect of *pe'ah*[6] or not? What are the circumstances? Shall we say that one said, 'Let this furrow be *pe'ah*, and this one too'—that is a complete [declaration of] *pe'ah*?—His problem arises, e.g., if he [merely] said, 'and this,' without adding 'too'.[7] (Hence it follows that if one says, 'Let the entire field be *pe'ah*', it is so?[8]—Yes. And it was taught likewise: Whence do we know that if one wishes to render his whole field *pe'ah*, he can do so? From the verse, [*And when ye reap the harvest of thy land, thou shalt not wholly reap*] *the corner of*

(1) Betrothals. V. Glos. (2) Not an abbreviation. (3) Lit., '*kiddushin* takes hold on her companion'. (4) In reference to *kiddushin*, v. Kid. 5*b*. (5) Recognising that Samuel held abbreviations to be valid in the case of *kiddushin*. (6) *Pe'ah*—the corner of the field, which was left for the poor, v. Lev. XIX, 9. (7) [Asheri seems to have read: Did he then mean 'and this too is for *pe'ah*' or 'and this is for personal expenses'.] (8) The presumption is that R. Papa's problem arises only if the first furrow alone contained the necessary minimum, for otherwise the second would certainly be *pe'ah*; therefore the second furrow is *in addition* to the requisite minimum, and becomes *pe'ah*, if abbreviations are binding. But if more than the minimum can be *pe'ah*, it follows that even the whole field can be *pe'ah*.

the field.)[1]—Do we say, Since it [*sc. pe'ah*] is compared to sacrifices, just as abbreviations are binding in the case of sacrifices, so in the case of *pe'ah* too; or perhaps, the analogy holds good only in respect of [the injunction,] *thou shalt not delay?*[2] Now, where is the analogy found?—For it was taught: [7a] [*When thou shalt vow a vow unto the Lord thy God, thou shalt not delay to pay it, for the Lord will surely require it*] *of thee:*[3] this refers to gleanings, forgotten sheaves, and *pe'ah*.[4]

Are abbreviations binding in the case of charity or not? How does this arise? Shall we say, that one said, 'This *zuz*[5] is for charity, and this one too,' that is a complete [declaration of] charity!—But, e.g., if one said, '[And] this,' omitting 'too'. What then: did he mean, 'and this *too* is for charity,' or, 'and this is for my personal expenditure,' his statement being incomplete?[6] Do we say, Since this is likened to sacrifices, as it is written: [*That which is gone out of thy lips thou shalt keep and perform; even a free-will offering according as thou hast vowed unto the Lord thy God, which thou hast promised*] *with thy mouth*, which refers to charity:[7] hence, just as abbreviations are valid for sacrifices, so with charity; or possibly the comparison is in respect of '*Thou shalt not delay*' only?

Are abbreviations valid in respect of *hefker* or not? But that is charity?[8]—This problem is based on a presupposition:[9] Should you rule, abbreviations are valid in the case of charity, because there

(1) And not 'the corner *in* thy field'. Lev. XIX, 9. (2) I.e., if *pe'ah* is not given within the fixed period, this injunction is violated. (3) Deut. XXIII, 22. (4) Whilst *he will surely require it* refers to sacrifices, *supra* 4a. Hence they are assimilated to each other, being coupled in the same verse. The Hebrew for *of thee* is מעמך, which can be rendered 'of that which is with thee', the reference being to the gleanings etc., which are to be left for those that are '*with thee*', i.e., the poor; Ex. XXII, 24. (5) *Zuz*, a silver coin, one fourth of a *shekel*. (6) This alternative may apply to the query on *pe'ah* too: i.e., did he mean, 'and this furrow *too*', or, 'and this furrow be for my personal use?' V. p. 13, n. 7. (7) This is deduced from the verse: *the promise of charity is gone out of my mouth* (Isa. XLV, 23, so translated here), where a promise by mouth refers to charity. (8) Renunciation of one's property is the equivalent of giving it to charity. Thus the problem has already been stated. (9) Lit., 'he says, "if you should say".'

is no analogy by halves,[1] [what of] *hefker?* Do we say: *Hefker* is charity; or possibly charity differs, charity being for the poor only, whilst *hefker* is both for the rich and the poor?

Rabina propounded: Are abbreviations effective in respect of a privy or not?[2] How does this arise? Shall we say, that he declared, 'Let this place be for a privy, and this one too,' then obviously it is one?—But *e.g.*, if he declared, 'and this,' omitting 'too'. What then? Does '[and] this' mean 'and this too shall be a privy,' or perhaps, what is meant by 'and this'? In respect of general use? Now, this proves that it is certain to Rabina that designation is valid for a privy. But Rabina propounded: What if one designates a place for a privy or for baths; is designation effective or not?[3]—Rabina propounded this problem on an assumption. [Thus:] Is designation effective or not; should you answer, Designation is effective, are abbreviations valid or not?[4]—This question remains.

'I AM BANNED TO YOU,' etc. Abaye said: R. Akiba admits in respect to lashes, that he is not flagellated;[5] for otherwise, let [the Mishnah] state, R. Akiba gave a stringent ruling.[6] R. Papa said: With respect to, 'I am isolated [*nedinah*] from you,' all agree that he is forbidden; 'I am accursed [*meshamatna*] from you,' all agree that he is permitted. Wherein do they differ? [7*b*] In the case of, 'I am banned to you,' R. Akiba maintaining that it is the equivalent of 'isolated' [*nedinah*]; whilst the Rabbis hold that it means 'accursed' [*meshamatna*]. Now, this conflicts with R. Ḥisda's view. For a certain man, who declared, 'I am accursed in respect of the property of the son of R. Jeremiah b. Abba' went before R. Ḥisda.

(1) I.e., it cannot be confined to certain aspects only. (2) A place so appointed may not be used for reciting prayers, even before it was used as a privy. (3) In the sense that this place may not be used henceforth for reciting prayers. (4) In all the foregoing problems on *kiddushin*, *pe'ah*, charity etc., the abbreviations, though apparently not clear in meaning, since alternatives are given, are regarded as explicit, since the alternatives are, in every case, of a remote character, and the question then arises whether abbreviations, though explicit enough, are effective in these cases, v. Ran. 6*b*, s.v. בעי. (5) If he breaks the vow. (6) 'WAS INCLINED' shews that he entertained some doubt, and would therefore not inflict the penalty of lashes.

Said he to him, 'None pay regard to this [ruling] of R. Akiba'. [Thus] he holds that they differ in respect to, 'I am accursed' [*meshamatna*].

R. Elai said in the name of Rab. If [a Rabbi] places a person under a ban in his presence, the ban can be revoked *only* in his presence; if in his absence, it can be revoked both in his presence and in his absence. R. Ḥanin said in Rab's name. One who hears his neighbour utter God's name in vain[1] must place him under a ban; otherwise he himself must be under a ban,[2] because the unnecessary utterance of the Divine Name always leads to poverty, and poverty leads to death, as it is written, [*And the Lord said unto Moses in Midian, Go, return unto Egypt*]. *For all the men are dead* [*which sought thy life*];[3] and it was taught: Wherever the Sages cast their eyes [in disapproval] death or poverty has resulted.

R. Abba said: I was standing in the presence of R. Huna, when he heard a woman utter God's name in vain. Thereupon he banned her, but immediately lifted the ban in her presence. This proves three things: [i] He who hears his neighbour utter the Divine Name unnecessarily must excommunicate him; [ii] If [a Rabbi] bans a person in his presence, the ban must be lifted in his presence too. [iii] No time need elapse between the imposition and the lifting of a ban.[4]

R. Giddal said in Rab's name: A scholar may utter a ban against

(1) Lit., the mentioning of the Name from his neighbour's mouth. (2) [I.e., deserves to be placed under a ban, (Ran).] (3) Ex. IV, 19. It is stated *infra* 64*b* that the reference is to Dathan and Abiram, who in fact were alive at Korah's rebellion, but had become poverty-stricken. Four are regarded as dead: a poor man, a leper, a blind person, and one who has no children. They were not blind, for it is written, *wilt thou put out the eyes of these men?* (Num. XVI, 14). Again, they were not lepers, for we find that they had not been excluded from the congregation: *in the* midst *of all Israel* (Deut. XI, 6). Even if they had been childless, they still could have been a source of danger to Moses before Pharaoh. Hence when God assured Moses that the danger was past, He meant that they were now poor and without influence (Ran). (4) Hence, the ban may be merely a nominal punishment. V. *J.E.* art. Anathema. The term used here is *niddui*, and though it is stated there (p. 560, 2) that *niddui* is for seven days (M.Ḳ. 16*a*, 17*b*), it is evident from this passage that there was a formal ban too of no particular duration.

himself, and lift it himself. But is this not obvious?—I would think that a prisoner cannot free himself from prison; hence we are taught otherwise. Now, how can such a thing occur?—As in the case of Mar Zuṭra the Pious:[1] when a disciple incurred a ban,[2] [Mar Zuṭra] first excommunicated himself and then the disciple.[3] On arriving home, he lifted the ban from himself and then from the disciple.

R. Giddal also said in Rab's name: [8*a*] Whence do we know that an oath may be taken to fulfil a precept? From the verse, *I have sworn, and I will perform it, that I will keep thy righteous judgments.*[4] But is he not under a perpetual oath from Mount Sinai?[5]—But what [R. Giddal] teaches us is that one may stimulate himself.[6] R. Giddal also said in Rab's name: He who says, 'I will rise early to study this chapter or this tractate,' has vowed a great vow to the God of Israel. But he is under a perpetual oath from Mount Sinai, and an oath cannot fall upon another?[7] Then [again] if he informs us that a person may thus stimulate himself, it is identical with R. Giddal's first [statement]?—This is what R. Giddal teaches: The oath is binding, since one can free [i.e., acquit] himself by the reading of the *Shema'* morning or evening.[8] R. Giddal said in Rab's name: If one says to his neighbour, 'Let us rise early and study this chapter,' it is *his* [the former's] duty to rise early, as it is written, *And he said unto me, arise, go forth into the plain, and there I will talk with thee. Then*

(1) Heb. *ḥasida*, (*ḥasid*). In Rabbinic literature the term is a title of respect denoting the type of an ideal Jew; (cf. Ta'an. 8*a*; Tem. 15*b*). (2) [Here the term used is *shamta*, 'desolation', 'curse'. According to Rashi, '*shamta*' is a less severe form of ban than '*niddui*'; Maimonides, *Yad, Talmud Torah*, VII, 2, equates them. Naḥmanides, *Mishpat ha-Ḥerem*, considers *shamta* to be a general term for the more severe form of excommunication, the *Ḥerem*, and the less severe, the *Niddui*.] (3) This was done to safeguard the honour of his disciple. (4) Ps. CXIX, 106. (5) Every Jew is regarded as having sworn at Sinai to observe God's precepts. (6) By an oath, to do what he is in any case bound to do. (7) I.e., an oath is not valid when referring to that which is already subject to an oath. (8) The passage commencing: *Hear O Israel* etc. (Deut. VI, 4 *seq.*). There is a definite obligation to study day and night, which is derived either from Deut. VI, 7 (*and thou shalt teach them*, etc.) or from Josh. I, 8 (*This book of the law shall not depart out of thy mouth*). But it is stated in Men. 95*b* that the obligation is fulfilled by the reading of the *Shema'* morning and evening.

I arose and went forth into the plain, and behold, the glory of the Lord stood there.[1]

R. Joseph said: If one was placed under a ban in a dream, ten persons are necessary for lifting the ban.[2] They must have studied *halachah*;[3] but if they had only learnt [Mishnah],[4] they cannot lift the ban; but if such as have studied *halachah* are unavailable, then even those who have only learnt [Mishnah], but had not studied [*halachah*] will do. But if even such are unavailable, let him go and sit at the cross-roads, and extend greetings[5] to ten men, until he finds ten men who have studied *halachah*.[6] Rabina asked R. Ashi: If he knew [in his dream] the person who placed him under a ban, can this person lift the ban?—He answered: He might have been appointed [God's] messenger to ban him, but not to revoke it. R. Aḥa asked R. Ashi: What if one was both banned and readmitted[7] in his dream?—Said he to him: Just as grain is impossible without straw,[8] [8*b*] so is there no dream without meaningless matter.[9]

Rabina's wife was under a vow; he then came before R. Ashi, asking, Can the husband become an agent for his wife's regret?[10]—He replied: If they [the three scholars] are ready assembled, he can do so: but not otherwise.[11] Three things may be inferred from

(1) Ezek. III, 22, 23. The Lord, having instructed him to go forth, had preceded him. (2) Dreams were widely held to have a positive significance; indeed, as almost partaking of the nature of prophecy. As we see here, a definite quality of reality was ascribed to them. V. *J.E. s.v.* 'Dreams'. (3) Heb., *hilketha*, v. next note. (4) So Rashi and Ran on the basis of our text. Mishnah is the law in broad outline, which characterises the whole of our present Mishnah, as compiled by R. Judah I. *Hilketha* (*halachah*) (law, rule) would appear to connote here the Talmudic discussion thereon, i.e., the amoraic development of the Mishnah. For *tanu* (תנו) referring to *amoraic* teaching instead of *Tannaitic*, cf. Kaplan, *Redaction of the Talmud*, pp. 209 *seq*. Ran, Asheri, and Tosaf. offer another interpretation, based on a slightly different reading: They must have *taught* law, but not merely learnt it (themselves). (5) Lit., 'give peace'—the usual form of a Jewish greeting. (6) Tosaf.: the greetings of ten men at the cross-roads will remove his grief; but ten *scholars* are necessary for the removal of the ban. (7) Lit., 'it was loosened for him'. (8) Cf. Jer. XXIII, 28. (9) I.e., the ban is not lifted. (10) So as to have the vow cancelled. On regret (*haraṭah*), v. *infra* 21*b*, *a.l.* (11) Because having troubled to assemble three scholars, he may be

this incident: [i] A husband can become an agent for his wife's regret. [ii] It is not seemly[1] for a scholar to revoke a vow in his teacher's town.[2] [iii] If they [the necessary scholars] are already assembled, it is well. But a scholar may lift a ban even in the vicinity of his master, and even a *single* ordained scholar[3] may lift a ban.

R. Simeon b. Zebid said in the name of R. Isaac b. Ṭabla, in the name of R. Ḥiyya Areka of the school of R. Aḥa, in the name of R. Zera in the name of R. Eleazar in the name of R. Ḥanania in the name of R. Mi'asha on the authority of R. Judah b. Il'ai: What is the meaning of, *But unto you that fear my name shall the sun of righteousness arise with healing in its wings?*[4]—This refers to those people who fear to utter the Divine name in vain.[5] *'The sun of righteousness with healing in its wings'*: Said Abaye, This proves that the motes dancing in the sun's rays have healing power. Now, he differs from R. Simeon b. Laḳish, who said: There is no Gehinnom[6] in the world to come,[7] but the Holy One, blessed be He, will draw forth the sun from its sheath: the righteous shall be healed, and the wicked shall be judged and punished thereby. As it is written, *But unto you that fear my name shall the sun of righteousness arise with healing in its wings.*[8] Moreover, they shall be rejuvenated by it, as it is written, *And ye shall go forth and grow up as calves of the stall.*[9] But the wicked shall be punished thereby, as it is written, *Behold, the day cometh that shall burn as an oven, and all the proud, yea, and all*

anxious that his trouble should not be unrewarded and so exceed his wife's instructions as to the grounds on which she desired absolution.

(1) This is the reading of Ran. Cur. edd. (quoted by Rashi too): a scholar is not permitted. (2) Since Rabina, himself a Rabbi, did not act in the town of R. Ashi, his teacher. (3) *Mumḥe*, v. Glos. (4) Mal. III, 20. (5) The name of God represents the Divine nature and the relation of God to His people. As such it was understood as the equivalent of the Divine Presence, hence the awe with which it was surrounded; cf. Ḳid. 71*a*, Sanh. 99*a*. (6) Gehinnom (Gehenna) as an equivalent of hell, purgatory, takes its name from the place where children were once sacrificed to Moloch, viz., *ge ben Hinnom*, the valley of the son of Hinnom, to the south of Jerusalem (Josh. XV, 8; II Kings XXIII, 10; Jer. VII, 31-32; XIX, 6, 13-14). (7) ['*Olam ha-ba*. Here, as it is clear from the context, the reference is to the Messianic days.] (8) Thus, unlike Abaye, he applies the verse to the future world. (9) Mal. III, 20.

that do wickedly, shall be stubble; and the day that cometh shall burn them up, saith the Lord of Hosts, that it shall leave them neither root nor branch.[1]

MISHNAH. [9a] [IF ONE SAYS] 'AS THE VOWS OF THE WICKED,' HE HAS VOWED IN RESPECT OF NEZIROTH, A SACRIFICE, AND AN OATH.[2] [IF HE SAYS:] 'AS THE VOWS OF THE RIGHTEOUS,' HIS WORDS ARE OF NO EFFECT. [BUT IF HE SAID,] 'AS THEIR FREEWILL-OFFERINGS,' HE HAS VOWED IN RESPECT OF A NAZIRITE VOW AND A SACRIFICE.[2]

GEMARA. But perhaps he meant thus: 'I do *not* vow as the vows of the wicked?'—Samuel answered: The Mishnah refers to one who said, 'As the vows of the wicked behold I am,' [or] '[I take] upon myself,' [or] '[I am debarred] from it': [which means,] 'Behold, I am a *nazir,*' [or] 'I take upon myself [the obligation] to offer a sacrifice,' [or] 'I [am debarred] by an oath [to derive any benefit] therefrom. Behold, I am a *nazir*': but perhaps he meant, 'Behold, I am to fast'?—Said Samuel: That is if a *nazir* was passing in front of him.[3] 'I am [debarred] by an oath [to derive any benefit] therefrom.' But perhaps [*hemennu*] [*from* or *of it*] means 'that I am to eat of it'?—Said Raba: It means that he said, '[I am debarred] from it *not* to eat it.' If so, why state it?[4]—I would argue, But he has not *explicitly* taken an oath![5] Hence we are informed [otherwise].[6]

[IF HE SAYS], 'AS THE VOWS OF THE RIGHTEOUS,' etc. Which Tanna recognises a distinction between a vow and a freewill-

(1) Mal. III, 19. (2) I.e., his vow is valid in respect of these. This will be explained in the Gemara. (3) So he meant, 'such as he'. (4) Since it is obvious. (5) Hence it is not an oath. (6) [The meaning of the Mishnah would be accordingly: If a nazirite is passing by and a man noticing him says, 'Behold, I am as he who makes the vows of the wicked', (meaning the nazirite, who in a sense is regarded as a sinner; *v. infra* 10*a*); or if a man with a beast before him says, 'I take upon myself as the vows of the wicked', or, with a loaf of bread before him, says, 'From it as the vows of the wicked', he becomes respectively a nazirite; is obliged to bring a sacrifice; and is forbidden to eat of the loaf, each utterance being treated as an abbreviation of a vow (Ran).]

offering:[1] shall we say, neither R. Meir nor R. Judah? For it was taught: *Better it is that thou shouldst not vow, than that thou shouldst vow and not pay.*[2] Better than both is not to vow at all: thus said R. Meir. R. Judah said: Better than both is to vow and repay.[3] —You may even say that it is R. Meir: [9*b*] R. Meir spoke only of *a vow*, but not of a freewill-offering. But the Mishnah states: AS THEIR FREEWILL-OFFERINGS, HE HAS VOWED IN RESPECT OF NAZIR AND A SACRIFICE?[4]—Learn: HE HAS made a *freewill-offering* IN RESPECT OF NAZIR AND A SACRIFICE. Now, wherein does a vower differ, that he is not [approved]: because he may thereby come to a stumbling-block?[5] But a freewill-offering too can become a stumbling-block?[6]—[He does as] Hillel the Elder.[7] For it was taught: It was said of Hillel the Elder that no man ever trespassed through his burnt-offering;[8] he would bring it as *hullin*[9] to the Temple court, then sanctify it, and put his hand upon it[10] and slaughter it. That is well in respect of a freewill-offering of sacrifices; but what can be said of a freewill-offering of *neziroth?*[11]—It is as Simeon the Just.[12] For it was taught:

(1) In making a *vow* to offer a sacrifice, one says, 'Behold, I will bring a sacrifice'; since he may forget to do so, it is considered wrong to make a vow. But a freewill donation is declared thus: 'Behold, this animal is for a sacrifice'. Since the animal has already been put aside for the purpose, there is no fear of forgetfulness. (2) Eccl. V, 4. (3) Thus neither draw a distinction between a vow and a freewill-offering. (4) Rashi: this implies that it is stated as a vow. Asheri: the use of both terms together, FREEWILL-OFFERINGS and HE HAS VOWED proves that the Tanna of our Mishnah recognises no difference between them. (5) By forgetting to fulfil his vow. (6) Because when an animal has been dedicated, it may not be put to any use; in a momentary forgetfulness, however, one may use it. (7) 'Elder' (Heb. *zaḳen*) does not necessarily refer to age, but was a title of scholarship; cf. Ḳid. 32*b*; Yoma 28*b*; J.M.Ḳ. III, beginning of 81*c*. (8) By putting it to secular use after dedication. (9) Non-holy, v. Glos. (10) Lev. I, 4: *And he shall put his hand upon the head of the burnt-offering.* (11) Since the possibility of violating one of the laws of *neziroth* constitutes a stumbling-block. (12) So the text as emended by Ran.—One who takes the vow of a nazirite in such circumstances as those related by Simeon the Just need not fear a stumbling-block. Scholars differ whether he is identical with Simeon I (310-291 or 300-270 B.C.E.) or Simeon II (219-199 B.C.E.), v. Ab. (Sonc. ed.) p. 2, n. 1.

Simeon the Just said: Only once in my life have I eaten of the trespass-offering brought by a defiled *nazir*. On one occasion a *nazir* came from the South country, and I saw that he had beautiful eyes, was of handsome appearance, and with thick locks of hair symmetrically arranged. Said I to him: 'My son, what [reason] didst thou see to destroy this beautiful hair of thine?'[1] He replied: 'I was a shepherd for my father in my town. [Once] I went to draw water from a well, gazed upon my reflection in the water, whereupon my evil desires rushed upon me and sought to drive me from the world [through sin]. But I said unto it [my lust]: "Wretch! why dost thou vaunt thyself in a world that is not thine, with one who is destined to become worms and dust?[2] I swear[3] that I will shave thee off [his beautiful hair] for the sake of Heaven."' I immediately arose and kissed his head, saying: 'My son, may there be many nazirites such as thou in Israel! Of thee saith the Holy Writ, *When either a man or a woman shall separate themselves to vow a vow of a nazirite, to separate themselves* unto the Lord.[4]

R. Mani demurred: Wherein does the trespass-offering of an unclean nazirite differ, that he did not eat [thereof]: because it comes on account of sin? Then he should not have partaken [of] *all* trespass-offerings, since they come on account of sin?—Said R. Jonah to him, This is the reason: When they regret [their evil deeds], they become nazirites, but when they become defiled, and the period of *neziroth* is lengthened,[5] they regret their vow, and thus *hullin* is brought to the Temple court.[6] If so, it is the same even with an undefiled *nazir* too?[7]—A clean *nazir* is not so, for he [previ-

(1) V. Num. VI, 18. (2) Meaning himself. In thus apostrophising his lust he did not ascribe any personal, independent identity to it, as is evident from the context. (3) Lit., 'by the service' (of the Temple). (4) Num. VI, 2. A nazirite vow made for such reasons may be regarded as the vow of the righteous. Simeon the Just's refusal to partake of these sacrifices must be regarded as a protest against the growing ascetic practice of taking vows to be a nazirite, —usually a sign of unhappy times; Weiss, *Dor*, I, 85, v. Nazir (Sonc. ed.) p. 13. (5) Since they must recommence their *neziroth*; v. Num. VI, 12. (6) Actually, of course, the animal would be consecrated; but it is as though it were *hullin*, since their *neziroth*, on account of which the sacrifice is brought, was not whole-hearted. (7) He may regret the vow before the expiration of his term.

ously] estimates his will-power, [and decides] that he can vow.

Alternatively: [10a] You may even say that it [the Mishnah] agrees with R. Judah, for R. Judah said this[1] only of a freewill-offering, but not of a vow. But he teaches: Better than both is to *vow* and repay?—Learn: To make a *freewill*-offering and repay. Now, why is a vow objectional: because one may come thereby to a stumbling-block.[2] [Does not] the same apply to a free-will offering whereby too he may come to a stumbling-block?—R. Judah conforms to his other view, viz., that a person may bring his lamb to the Temple-court, consecrate and lay [hands] upon it, and slaughter it.[3] This answer suffices for a freewill-offering of a sacrifice; but what can be said of a free-will offering of *neziroth?* —R. Judah follows his view [there too]. For it was taught: R. Judah said: The early *hasidim*[4] were eager to bring a sin-offering, because the Holy One, blessed be He, never caused them to stumble. What did they do? They arose and made a free-will vow of *neziroth* to the Omnipresent, so as to be liable to a sin-offering to the Omnipresent.[5] R. Simeon said: They did not vow *neziroth*. But he who wished to bring a burnt-offering donated it freely, and brought it; if a peace-offering, he donated it freely and brought it; or if a thanks-offering and the four kinds of loaves,[6] donated it freely and brought it. But they did not take *neziroth* upon themselves, so as not to be designated sinners, as it is written, *And [the priest] shall make atonement for him, for that he sinned against a soul.*[7]

Abaye said: Simeon the Just, R. Simeon, and R. Eleazar ha-Ḳappar, are all of the same opinion, viz., that a *nazir* is a sinner. Simeon the Just and R. Simeon, as we have stated. R. Eleazar ha-Ḳappar Berabbi,[8] as it was taught: *And he shall make atonement*

(1) That it is better to vow and repay. (2) V. p. 21, nn. 1 & 6. (3) It cannot become a stumbling-block, because it is *hullin* practically until it is killed. (4) *Ḥasid*, pl. *ḥasidim;* lit., 'pious ones'. The *ḥasidim* referred to here are definitely not the Essenes (Weiss, *Dor*, I, p. 110). [Büchler, *Types*, p. 78, makes these early *ḥasidim* contemporaries of Shammai and Hillel.] (5) V. Num. VI, 14. (6) A thanks-offering was accompanied by forty loaves of bread, divided into four different kinds. (7) Num. VI, 11. (8) [Or, Berebi, designation by which Bar Ḳappara is known to distinguish him from his father who bore the same name, v. Nazir, (Sonc. ed.) p. 64, n. 1.]

for him, for that he sinned against a soul. Against which *'soul'* then has he sinned? But it is because he afflicted himself through abstention from wine. Now, does not this afford an argument from the minor to the major? If one, who afflicted himself only in respect of wine, is called a sinner: how much more so one who ascetically refrains from everything. Hence, one who fasts is called a sinner. But this verse refers to an *unclean nazir?*[1] — That is because he doubly sinned.[2]

MISHNAH. ONE WHO SAYS, 'ḲONAM,' 'ḲONAḤ,' OR 'ḲONAS,'[3] THESE ARE THE SUBSTITUTES FOR ḲORBAN.[4] 'ḤEREḲ,' 'ḤEREK,' [OR] 'ḤEREF,' THESE ARE SUBSTITUTES FOR ḤEREM.[5] 'NAZIḲ,' 'NAZIAḤ,' 'PAZIAḤ,' THESE ARE SUBSTITUTES FOR NEZIROTH;[6] 'SHEBUTHAH,' 'SHEḲUḲAH,' OR ONE WHO VOWS BY MOHI,[7] THESE ARE SUBSTITUTES FOR SHEBU'AH.[8]

GEMARA. It was stated: Substitutes: R. Joḥanan said: They

(1) How then can one deduce that a *nazir* in general is a sinner? (2) The verse shews that a double sin is referred to, because *'for that he sinned'* alone would have sufficed; *'against a soul'* is superfluous, and teaches that he is a sinner in two respects: (i) by becoming a *nazir* at all; (ii) by defiling his *neziroth* (Ran). — The whole passage shows the Jewish opposition to asceticism, for Judaism rejects the doctrine of the wickedness of this life and the inherent corruption of the body, which is the basis of asceticism. Whilst the community as a whole fasted in times of trouble (cf. Esth. IV, 16; Ta'an. 10a, 15a), and certain Rabbis too were addicted to it (e.g. R. Ze'ira, B.M. 85a), yet individual fasting was discouraged, as here; v. Maim. *Yad, De'oth*, III, 1; VI, 1; Lazarus, *Ethics of Judaism*, §§ 246-256. (3) [Its derivation is probably from *ḳenum*, 'self', 'person', and then the object in an elliptical sentence, 'I pledge (myself) my person with So-and-so (that I will not do this or that)', v. Cooke, *North Semitic Inscriptions*, p. 34. This is a substitute for *ḳorban* vow, in which he declares 'this may be forbidden to me as is a sacrifice'. No satisfactory explanation has been given so far for the other terms, which seem to be corruptions of *ḳonam*.] (4) Heb. for sacrifice. (5) Ban. (6) The vow of a *nazir*: 'Behold, I will be a *nazir*'. These words may be substituted for *nazir*. (7) This is explained in the Gemara. [The Mishnayoth text reads 'BY MOTHA', an abbreviation of *Momatha*, the Aramaic equivalent of Shebu'ah.] (8) Heb. for oath.

are foreign equivalents [of the Hebrew]; R. Simeon b. Laḳish said: They are forms devised by the Sages for the purpose of making vows; (and thus it is written, *in the month which he had devised of his own heart*).[1] And why did the Rabbis institute substitutes?—That one should not say *ḳorban*. Then let him say, *ḳorban?*—Lest he say *ḳorban la-adonai* [a sacrifice to the Lord]. And why not say *ḳorban la-adonai?*—Lest one say *la-adonai* without *ḳorban*, and thus utter the Divine Name in vain.[2] And it was taught: R. Simeon said: [10*b*] Whence do we know that one must not say, 'Unto the Lord a burnt-offering,' 'unto the Lord a meal-offering,' 'unto the Lord a thanks-offering,' or 'unto the Lord a peace-offering'?[3] Because it is written, [*If any man of you bring*] *an offering to the Lord*.[4] And from the minor we may deduce the major: If concerning one who intended uttering the Divine Name only in connection with a sacrifice, the Torah taught, *an offering to the Lord*;[5] how much more [care must one take against its deliberate utterance] in vain!

Shall we say that this [conflict] is dependent on Tannaim? For it was taught: Beth Shammai maintain: Substitutes of substitutes are binding; whilst Beth Hillel say: They are not.[6] Surely, the ruling that secondary substitutes are valid is based on the view that substitutes are foreign equivalents;[7] whilst he who says that they are invalid holds that they are forms devised by the Sages?[8]—No. All agree that substitutes are foreign words; but Beth Shammai hold that Gentiles speak in these [terms] too,[9] whilst Beth Hillel

(1) I Kings XII, 33, referring to the unauthorised festival instituted by Jeroboam in the eighth instead of the seventh month. [The Heb. for 'devised', בדה is the same as used by R. Joḥanan in his definition. The bracketed words appear to be a copyist's gloss that has crept into the text. They do not occur in MS.M.] (2) This machinery for vows, regulating the manner in which they were to be made, points to the practice as being very prevalent. V. Weiss, *Dor*, I, 85. (3) In this order, the Divine Name preceding. (4) Lev. I, 1; thus the *offering* must precede. (5) But not the reverse, lest one utter the Name in vain. (6) Lit., 'they are permitted'. (7) Hence, the first modifications are correct foreign words, the substitutes thereof are corrupt, but also used, and hence valid for oaths. (8) Hence secondary substitutes, not having been assigned by the Sages to that purpose, are invalid. (9) Sc. secondary substitutes; hence they are valid.

hold that they do not speak in these [terms]. Alternatively Beth Shammai hold: Secondary substitutes [are declared valid] as a precautionary measure on account of substitutes themselves;[1] but Beth Hillel maintain: We do not enact a precautionary measure for secondary substitutes on account of the substitutes themselves.

What forms do double modifications of vows take?—R. Joseph recited: *Meḳanamana, meḳanehana, meḳanesana*. What are the secondary substitutes of *ḥerem?*—Mafash'ah taught: *ḥarakim, ḥarakim, ḥarafim*. Secondary substitutes of *neziroth?*—R. Joseph learnt: *meḥazaḳana, menazaḥana, mepḥana*.[2] The scholars inquired: What of *mipaḥazna, mithḥazana, mith'azana?*[3] Rabina asked R. Ashi: What of *ḳinema:* does it mean *ḳonam,*[4] or perhaps, *ḳinemon besem* [sweet cinnamon]?[5] R. Aḥa, the son of R. Ḥiyya, asked R. Ashi: What of *ḳinah:* does it mean a fowl's sty,[6] or *ḳonam?* These remain questions.[7]

What are secondary substitutes of oaths?—*Shebuel, shebuthiel, sheḳuḳeel*. But *shebuel* may simply mean Shebhuel the son of Gershon? But say thus: *Shebubiel, shebuthiel, sheḳuḳeel*.[8] Samuel said: If one says *ashbithah,* he says nothing: *ashḳiḳah,* he says nothing; *ḳarinsha,* he says nothing.[9]

OR ONE WHO VOWS BY MOHI, THESE ARE SUBSTITUTES [FOR SHEBU'A]. It was taught: R. Simeon b. Gamaliel said: One who says 'by Mohi' [*Moses*][10] says nothing; 'by Momtha which *Mohi* said,'[11] these are substitutes for an oath.

(1) Which would otherwise be treated as invalid by the masses. (2) [Read *Menazaḳna . . . mepazaḥna*, each of which consists of the three consonantal letters of the substitutes with prefix and suffix; v. Strashun]. (3) [Strashun reads: *Mepaḥazna, menaḥazna, menaḳazna*, the last consonantal letters of the substitutes being transposed. This receives support from MS.M.]. Are they binding or not? (4) Hence it is valid. (5) Ex. XXX, 23; i.e., it is not a vow-form at all. (6) I.e., the fem. of קֵן (*kin*), a bird's nest. (7) In all these doubtful forms the question arises when they were actually used to express vows, the question being whether they imply vows or something else—notwithstanding the intention of their user. (8) מהו 'What is the law' in cur. edd. is to be deleted; BaḤ. (9) These forms are ineffective for expressing oaths. (10) ['By Moses', was one of the common forms of asseveration, cf. Beẓ. 38*b*; Shab. 101*b*. V. Chajes, Notes.] (11) By the oath which Moses uttered. [The allusion is to Ex. II, 21, where ויואל משה is rendered, 'Moses swore'. (Ran).]

MISHNAH. IF ONE SAYS [TO HIS NEIGHBOUR], 'THAT WHICH I MIGHT EAT OF YOURS BE NOT[1] ḤULLIN,'[2] 'BE NOT KASHER,'[3] 'BE NOT PURE,' 'BE CLEAN OR UNCLEAN,'[4] 'BE NOTHAR,'[5] OR PIGGUL,[6] HE IS FORBIDDEN.[7] 'AS THE LAMB,'[8] 'AS THE TEMPLE SHEDS OF CATTLE OR WOOD,'[9] 'AS THE WOOD' [ON THE ALTAR], 'AS THE FIRE [ON THE ALTAR],'[10] 'AS THE ALTAR,' 'AS THE TEMPLE,' 'AS JERUSALEM;' [OR] IF ONE VOWED BY REFERENCE TO THE ALTAR UTENSILS,[11] THOUGH HE DID NOT MENTION ḲORBAN, IT IS AS THOUGH HE HAD VOWED BY ḲORBAN.[12] R. JUDAH SAID: HE WHO SAYS JERUSALEM[13] HAS SAID NOTHING.

GEMARA. [11*a*] The scholars presumed. What does *la-ḥullin* mean: Let it *not* be as *ḥullin*, [implying] but as a sacrifice. Who is the authority of our Mishnah? If R. Meir: but he does not hold that the positive may be inferred from the negative?[14] For we learnt, R. Meir said: Every stipulation which is not like the stipulation of the children of Gad and Reuben is invalid.[15] Hence it must be R. Judah.[16] Then consider the conclusion: R. JUDAH

(1) The Hebrew is *la-ḥullin*, here regarded as meaning: not *ḥullin*. V. also p. 28, n. 8. (2) V. Glos. (3) Lit., 'fit'; ritually permitted for consumption. (4) So cur. edd. Asheri explains: be as sacrifices, to which the laws of cleanliness and uncleanness apply—i.e., forbidden. Rashi's text reads simply: be not clean, be unclean, etc. (5) Lit., 'left over'. The flesh of an offering which remains over after the period in which it must be eaten, v. Ex. XXIX, 34, and Lev., VII, 17. (6) Lit., 'abomination'. The flesh of an animal sacrificed with the deliberate intention of eating it after the permitted period; it is then forbidden even *within* the period, v. Lev. VII, 18. (7) To eat aught of his neighbour. (8) I.e., the lamb of the daily sacrifice. (9) The alternative is implied by the use of the plural in the Mishnah (Tosaf.). (10) [So T. J. Others: Fire-offerings, cf. Lev. XXI, 6. (V. Asheri and Tosaf.)] (11) I.e., your food be as the altar utensils unto me, hence, forbidden. (12) V. Mishnah 10*a*. (13) Without 'as', i.e., 'Your food be Jerusalem to me'. (14) To render it legally binding. Thus, if one says, 'let it *not* be as *ḥullin*', we may not infer that he meant, 'but let it be as a *ḳorban*', and so declare it forbidden. (15) Num. XXXII, 20-23; 29-30, q.v. We see there that Moses stipulated what was to happen in each case, and did not rely on one clause only, from which the reverse might be deduced, v. Ḳid. 61*a*. (16) That the positive is inferred from the negative, and is then legally binding.

SAID: HE WHO SAYS JERUSALEM HAS SAID NOTHING. Now, since the conclusion is R. Judah, the former clause is *not* R. Judah?[1] —The whole Mishnah gives R. Judah's ruling, but this is what is stated: for R. JUDAH SAID: HE WHO SAYS JERUSALEM HAS SAID NOTHING.[2]

But if one says, 'as Jerusalem,' is he forbidden according to R. Judah? But it was taught: R. Judah said: He who says, 'as Jerusalem,' has said nothing, unless he vows by what is sacrificed in Jerusalem!—It is all R. Judah, and two Tannaim conflict as to his views.[3]

[11*b*] It was taught: [If one says,] 'That which I might eat of yours,' or 'that which I might *not* eat of yours, be *ḥullin*,' or, 'be the *ḥullin*,' or, 'be as *ḥullin*,' he is permitted.[4] [If he says,] 'That which I might eat of yours be not *ḥullin*,' he is forbidden;[5] 'that which I might not eat of yours be *not ḥullin*,' he is permitted. Now with whom does the first clause agree? With R. Meir, viz., who does not hold that the positive may be inferred from the negative.[6] Then consider the latter clause: 'That which I might *not* eat of yours be *not ḥullin*,' he is permitted. But we learnt: [If one says,] 'That which I might not eat of yours be not for *ḳorban*': R. Meir forbids [him]. Now we raised the difficulty: but he does not rule that the positive may be inferred from the negative?[7] And R. Abba replied: It is as though he said, 'Let it [i.e., your food] be for the *ḳorban*, therefore I will not eat of yours.'[8] Then here too,

(1) Since it is specifically pointed out that the second clause is R. Judah. (2) For that reason 'as' is specified in all the previous expressions. (3) The Tanna of the Mishnah holding R. Judah's view to be that 'as Jerusalem' is a binding form, and the Tanna of the Baraitha that it is not. (4) To eat or benefit from his neighbour. (5) Rashi. Ran is inclined to delete the clause, since, as the Talmud shews, this Baraitha is taught according to R. Meir, who holds that the positive may not be inferred from the negative. (6) Hence, when he says, 'That which I might *not* eat of yours be *ḥullin*', we may not infer that that which he *might* eat should *not* be *ḥullin*, and so prohibited. (7) The hypothesis being that he is forbidden on account of this inference. (8) The Hebrew form is *la-ḳorban:* in popular speech *la* 'to the' may be a hurried utterance of *la'* 'not'; therefore on the first assumption what he said was: 'shall *not* be a *ḳorban*'; in the answer the preposition is given its normal meaning, viz., shall be *for the ḳorban*.

perhaps, he meant, 'Let it *not* be *ḥullin;* therefore I may *not* eat of yours'?—This Tanna agrees with R. Meir on one point, but disagrees with him on another. He agrees with him on one point, that the positive may not be inferred from the negative; but disagrees with him on another, [viz.,] on [the interpretation of] *la-ḳorban*. R. Ashi said: In the one case he said *le-ḥullin;*[1] in the other[2] he said, '*la-hullin*', which might mean, 'let it *not* be *ḥullin,*[3] but as a *ḳorban*'.

'BE CLEAN OR UNCLEAN,' 'AS NOTHAR,' 'AS PIGGUL,' HE IS FORBIDDEN. Rami b. Ḥama asked: What if one said: 'This be unto me as the flesh of a peace-offering after the sprinkling of the blood'? But if he vowed thus, he related [his vow] to what is *permissible!*[4]—But [the question arises thus]: E.g., if there lay flesh of a peace-offering before him and permitted food lay beside it, and he said, 'This be like this'. What then: did he relate it to its *original* state,[5] or to its present [permitted] condition?—Raba answered: Come and hear: [We learnt:] IF ONE SAYS ... AS NOTHAR, [OR] AS PIGGUL, [HE IS FORBIDDEN]. [12*a*] Now, *nothar* and *piggul*[6] are [possible only] *after* the sprinkling of the blood!—[7] R. Huna the son of R. Nathan said to him, This refers to *nothar* of a burnt-offering.[8] Said he to him, If so, let him [the Tanna] teach: As the *flesh* of the burnt-offering?[9]—He

(1) Meaning as (or, for) *ḥullin*. [This can by no means be taken to denote 'not', and since R. Meir does not infer the positive from the negative, he does not consider it a vow.] (2) The case interpreted by R. Abba. (3) [So Ran. curr. edd. *lo-ḥullin*, 'not *ḥullin*']. (4) His words imply no prohibition. (5) Before the sprinkling of the blood, when it was forbidden. (6) Some delete *piggul*, since at no time was it permitted. If retained in the text, it is so because *nothar* and *piggul* are generally coupled; but Raba's deductions are from *nothar* only. (7) The proof is this. A sacrifice is forbidden because at some time it was consecrated by a vow. With the sprinkling of its blood it loses its forbidden character until it becomes *nothar*, when it resumes it. But a direct reference to *nothar* itself is inadmissible in a vow, because *nothar* is *Divinely* forbidden, and not the result of a vow (v. text, and p. 30, n. 2). Hence the reference must have been to the condition of the flesh before the sprinkling of the blood. (8) The flesh of which is not permitted even after the sprinkling of the blood; hence it proves nothing. (9) Without reference to *nothar* at all.

proceeds to a climax.[1] [Thus:] It is unnecessary [to teach that if one relates his vow to] the flesh of a burnt-offering, that he is forbidden, since he referred it to a sacrifice. But it is necessary for him [to teach the case of] *nothar* and *piggul* of a burnt-offering. For I would think that he referred it to the *prohibitions* of *nothar* and *piggul*, so that it counts as a reference to what is inherently forbidden, and he is not prohibited;[2] hence he informs us [otherwise].

An objection is raised: Which is the bond mentioned in the Torah?[3] If one says, 'Behold! I am not to eat meat or drink wine, as on the day that my father or teacher died,' [or] 'as on the day when Gedaliah the son of Ahikam was slain,'[4] [or] 'as on the day that I saw Jerusalem in ruins.' Now Samuel commented thereon: Providing that he was under a vow in respect to that very day.[5] What does this mean? Surely that e.g., he stood thus on a Sunday, on which day his father had died, and though there were many *permitted* Sundays, it is taught that he is forbidden; this proves that the original [Sunday] is referred to.[6]—Samuel's dictum was

(1) Lit., he states, 'it is unnecessary'. (2) When a man imposes a prohibition by referring one thing to another, the latter must be also *artificially* forbidden, e.g., a sacrifice, which was originally permitted, and then forbidden through consecration. But if it is *Divinely* forbidden, without the agency of man, the vow is invalid. Thus, if one says, 'This be to me as the flesh of the swine', it is not forbidden. Now, the prohibition of *piggul* and *nothar* are Divine; therefore, if the reference was in point of that particular prohibition, the vow would be invalid. (3) Num. XXX, 3: *If a man vow a vow unto the Lord, or swear an oath to bind his soul with a* bond, *he shall not break his word.* (4) After the destruction of the first Temple by Nebuchadnezzar in 586 B.C.E. and the deportation of the nobles and the upper classes to Babylon, Gedaliah the son of Ahikam was appointed governor of the small community that was left. As a result of a conspiracy he was slain on the second day of Tishri. Jer. XL-XLI. (5) The assumed meaning is: he had vowed on the day of his father's death, or had once vowed not to eat meat on the day that Gedaliah the son of Ahikam was slain, and now he vowed a second time, 'I am not to eat meat, etc. as on the day when I am forbidden by my previous vow'; thus the second vow was related to an interdict which was itself the result of a vow (Ran.). (6) I.e., the first Sunday distinguished by his former vow.

thus stated: Samuel said, Providing that he was under a vow uninterruptedly since that day.[1]

Rabina said, Come and hear: [If one says, 'This be unto me] as Aaron's dough[2] or as his *terumah*', he is permitted.[3] Hence, [if he vowed,] 'as the *terumah* of the loaves of the thanksgiving-offering,'[4] he would be forbidden.[5] [12b] But the *terumah* of the thanksgiving loaves is [forbidden] only *after* the sprinkling of the blood![6]—[No.] Infer thus: [If he vows,] 'as the *terumah* of the *shekel*-chamber,'[7] he is forbidden. But what if [he said,] 'as the *terumah* of the thanksgiving loaves,' he is permitted? Then let him [the Tanna] state the *terumah* of the thanksgiving loaves, then how much more so 'his *terumah*'![8]—He teaches us this: The *terumah* of the thanksgiving loaves is 'his *terumah*'.[9] Alternatively, the *terumah* of the thanksgiving loaves may also mean *before* the sprinkling of the blood,[10] e.g., if it was separated during the kneading [of the dough].[11] Even as R. Ṭobi b. Ḳisna said in Samuel's name: If the thanksgiving loaves are baked as four loaves [instead of forty],

(1) I.e., he had been under a vow *every* Sunday until this present vow. Hence nothing can be proved, v. Shebu. (Sonc. ed.) p. 105. (2) Num. XV, 20-21. *Ye shall offer up a cake of the first of your dough for an heave offering*. This, and *terumah* (v. Glos.) belonged to Aaron, i.e., the priest, and was prohibited to a *zar* (i.e., a non-priest). (3) To benefit therefrom. The vow is invalid, because the dough and the *terumah*, not being prohibited to all, are regarded as Divinely forbidden; v. p. 30, n. 2. (4) V. Lev. VII, 22ff. Of the forty loaves brought (p. 32, n. 1) one out of each set of ten was *terumah*, and belonged to the priest. (5) Because the prohibition of these is evidently due to a vow. (6) This itself is disputed. The view of R. Eliezer b. Simon is adopted here. Since, by deduction, this vow is binding, we evidently regard the reference as being to the present state. (7) This refers to a special fund kept in the Temple for various purposes, mainly congregational sacrifices; Sheḳ. III, 2; IV, 1.—This is the deduction to be made, not the previous one. (8) If a vow referring to the *terumah* of the loaves of a thanks-offering is invalid, though in their origin their own prohibition is due to a vow, how much more will a vow referring to other *terumah*, which is Divinely forbidden, be valid. Also, it is a general rule that there is a preference for teaching the less likely, so that the more likely may be deduced therefrom *a minori*. (9) I.e., the word '*terumah*' embraces all forms of *terumah*. (10) It is even then forbidden to a *zar*, v. Glos. (11) Although the loaves become sanctified only by the sprinkling of the blood, according to our premise, yet if the *terumah* was separated in the dough, it is consecrated.

it suffices. But does not the Writ state forty?[1]—As a meritorious deed. But *terumah* has to be taken therefrom?[2] And should you answer that one loaf is taken for all,—but we learnt: [*And of it he shall offer*] *one out of each oblation:*[3] 'one' teaches that *terumah* is not to be taken from one oblation for another?[4] And should you say that a *piece* is taken from each,—but we learnt: *'One'* teaches that a piece is not to be taken? But it must be that he separates it during kneading, taking one [part] of the leaven, one of the unleavened cakes, one of the unleavened wafer, and one of the fried cake;[5] [so here too].

Shall we say that this is dependent on Tannaim? [For it was taught: If one says,] 'This be unto me as a firstling,'[6] R. Jacob forbids it, while R. Jose permits it. Now, how is this meant? If we say, *before* the sprinkling of the blood:[7] what is the reason of him who permits it? If *after,* on what grounds does the other forbid it? But it surely [means] [13*a*] that flesh of a firstling lay before him, and this other flesh lay at its side, and he declared, 'this be as this,' and [thus] it is a controversy of Tannaim?[8]—No. All treat of before the sprinkling of the blood; and what is the reason of him who permits it? The Writ states, *If a man vow,*[9] [teaching] that one must vow by that which is [itself] forbidden through a vow; thus excluding a firstling, which is an interdicted thing. And he who forbids it?[10]—The Writ states, *'unto the Lord,'*[9] to include an interdicted thing.[11] Then he who permits it, how does he interpret *'unto the Lord'?*—He employs it in respect of relating [a vow] to a sin-offering or a guilt-offering.[12] Now, what [reason] do you see to include a sin-offering and a guilt-offering and exclude

(1) Not actually. But since the Writ speaks of four species, and *terumah* (i.e., one in ten) was to be given from each, it follows that forty had to be made. (2) One from each ten. (3) Lev. VII, 14. (4) Each kind of loaf is here referred to as an oblation. (5) V. Lev. VII, 12. (6) V. Num. XVIII, 15. (7) Of the firstling, when it is definitely forbidden. (8) Whether the reference is to its present (permitted) state or to its original (forbidden) condition. (9) Num. XXX, 3. (10) What is his reason? (11) This will not apply to all Divinely forbidden things, but only to such as the firstling, as the Talmud proceeds to explain. (12) That the vow is valid.

the firstling?—I include the sin-offering and the guilt-offering which one sanctifies[1] by a vow,[2] but exclude the firstling, which is holy from its mother's womb. But he who forbids?[3] A firstling too one sanctifies by a vow. For it was taught: It was said on the authority of Rabbi, Whence do we know that one is bidden to consecrate the firstling born in one's house?—From the verse, [*All*] *the firstling males* [*that come of thy herd and thy flock*] *thou shalt sanctify* [*unto the lord*].[4] But he who permits it [argues thus]: If he does not consecrate it, is it not holy?[5]

... AS THE LAMB, AS THE TEMPLE SHEDS etc. It was taught: A lamb, *for* a lamb, *as* a lamb; [or] sheds, *for* sheds, *as* sheds; [or] wood, *for* wood, *as* wood; [or] fire, *for* fire, *as* fire; [or] the altar, *for* the altar, *as* the altar; [or] the temple, *for* the temple, *as* the temple; or Jerusalem, *for* Jerusalem, *as* Jerusalem,—in all these cases, [if he says,] 'what I might eat of yours,' he is forbidden; 'what I might not eat of yours,' he is permitted.

Now which Tanna do we know draws no distinction between a lamb, *for* a lamb and *as* a lamb?—R. Meir.[6] Then consider the second clause: and in all these cases, [if he says], 'that which I might not eat of yours [be so],' he is permitted. But we learnt: [If one says to his neighbour,] 'That which I might *not* eat of yours be not for *korban*, R. Meir forbids [him]. Now R. Abba commented thereon: It is as though he said, 'Let it [i.e., your food] be for *korban*, therefore I may not eat of yours'?—This is no difficulty: in the one case he said, *'lo le-imra'*;[7] in the other he said, *'le-imra'*.[8]

(1) Lit., 'seizes'. (2) Though one *cannot* offer these as vows, without having incurred the obligation, the actual animal is forbidden as a result of the vow of consecration, since another could equally well have been sacrificed. (3) How will he meet this argument? (4) Deut. XV, 19. Thus, though Divinely consecrated, yet its owner must formally declare it holy, and hence it may be regarded as subject to a vow. (5) Of course it is! Hence its interdict is not the result of a vow. (6) Since R. Judah rules that if one says Jerusalem, without 'for' or 'as', the vow is invalid. (7) 'Let it *not* be for the lamb'—hence it is permitted. [So cur. edd. MS.M. and Ran read: In one case he said *la'-imra;* 'let it not be the lamb'. V. *supra*, p. 28, n. 8.] (8) 'Let it be for the lamb'—there he is forbidden.

MISHNAH. IF ONE SAYS [TO HIS NEIGHBOUR], 'THAT WHICH I MIGHT EAT OF YOURS BE ḲORBAN', [OR] 'A BURNT-OFFERING',[1] [OR] 'A MEAL-OFFERING', [OR] 'A SIN-OFFERING', [OR] 'A THANKSGIVING-OFFERING', [OR] 'A PEACE-OFFERING', —HE IS FORBIDDEN.[2] R. JUDAH PERMITTED [HIM].[3] [IF HE SAYS,] 'THE ḲORBAN,' [OR] 'AS A ḲORBAN,' [OR] 'ḲORBAN,[4] BE THAT WHICH I MIGHT EAT OF YOURS,' HE IS FORBIDDEN.[5] IF HE SAYS: 'THAT WHICH I MIGHT NOT EAT OF YOURS BE FOR A ḲORBAN,'[6] R. MEIR FORBIDS [HIM].

GEMARA. Now, the Mishnah teaches, [IF HE SAYS,] 'THE ḲORBAN,' [OR] 'AS ḲORBAN,' [OR] 'A ḲORBAN BE THAT WHICH I MIGHT EAT OF YOURS,' HE IS FORBIDDEN. Thus, it is anonymously taught as R. Meir, who recognises no distinction between '*a* sheep' and '*for* a sheep'.[7] But if so, then as to what he [the Tanna] teaches: 'THE ḲORBAN . . . [BE] THAT WHICH I MIGHT EAT OF YOURS,' HE IS FORBIDDEN. But it was taught: The Sages concede to R. Judah that if one says, 'Oh, *ḳorban*,' or 'Oh, burnt-offering,' 'Oh, meal-offering,' 'Oh, sin-offering, what I will eat this of thine,' he is permitted, because he merely vowed by the life of the *ḳorban!*[8]—[13*b*] This is no difficulty: Here he said *ha ḳorban;*[9] there he said *ha-ḳorban.*[10] What is the reason?[11] He meant, '[I swear] by the life of the sacrifice.'[12] He [the Tanna] teaches: THAT WHICH I MIGHT NOT EAT OF YOURS BE NOT FOR

(1) [The two may also be taken together and thus rendered 'a sacrifice of a burnt-offering'.] (2) To eat aught of his neighbour's. (3) Because he did not say, '*as* a sacrifice', etc. (4) In this last case *ḳorban* is used as an oath: I swear by the sacrifice to eat naught of thine. (5) Vowing by means of *ḳorban* formula was a specifically Jewish practice; v. Josephus, *Contra Apionem*, 1, § 22, Halevy, *Doroth* I, 3, pp. 314 f. (6) In the Gemara these words are subsequently otherwise interpreted, but in the premise they are thus translated. (7) V. *supra* p. 33, n. 6. (8) That he *would* eat. Then why not assume the same in our Mishnah? (9) The *ha* being a separate word, and thus an interjection expressing an affirmative oath—I will eat. [The vowel of the *ha* as interjection is, in addition, of a longer quality than that of *ha* as definite article.] (10) Here the *ha* is an inseparate def. art.; hence he must have meant, 'What I might eat of yours *be* a sacrifice', and therefore he is forbidden. (11) Of the Baraitha, that he is permitted. (12) That I will eat of yours.

ḲORBAN, R. MEIR FORBIDS HIM. But R. Meir does not rule
that the positive may be inferred from the negative?[1]—R. Abba
answered: It is as though he said: 'Let it be for *ḳorban*, therefore
I will not eat of yours'.[2]

MISHNAH. IF ONE SAYS TO HIS NEIGHBOUR, 'ḲONAM BE
MY MOUTH SPEAKING WITH YOU,' [OR] 'MY HANDS WORKING
FOR YOU,' [OR] 'MY FEET WALKING WITH YOU,' HE IS FOR-
BIDDEN.[3]

GEMARA. But a contradiction is shewn: There is greater
stringency in oaths than in vows, and greater stringency in vows
than in oaths. There is greater stringency in vows, for vows apply
to obligatory as to optional matters,[4] which is not so in the case
of oaths.[5] And there is greater stringency in oaths, for oaths are
valid with respect to things both abstract and concrete, but vows
are not so?[6]—Said Rab Judah: It means that he says,[7] 'let my
mouth be forbidden in respect of my speech,' or 'my hands in
respect of their work', or 'my feet in respect of their walking'.[8]
This may be inferred too, for he [the Tanna] teaches: 'MY MOUTH
SPEAKING WITH YOU,' not, ['*ḳonam*] if I speak with you'.[9]

---

(1) And according to our premise the reason for R. Meir's ruling is that we
deduce the opposite from his words, thus: 'but that which I *might* eat of thine be
for *ḳorban*. (2) V. p. 28, n. 8. (3) According to the terms of his vow. (4) I.e.,
if one said, 'I am forbidden by a vow to erect a *sukkah* (v. Glos.), or put on
tefillin', (v. Glos.) the vow is binding, although he is bound to do these things,
and if he does them, he violates the injunction *he shall not break his word*. (5) I.e.,
if he said, 'I swear not to erect a *sukkah*, his oath is invalid. (6) Vows being
applicable to concrete things only. Walking, talking and working are regarded
here as abstractions (by contrast with the vow that a loaf of bread etc. shall be
as a sacrifice and forbidden), yet the Mishnah states that the vows are valid.
(7) I.e., it is regarded as though he says. (8) The reason for this assumption is
this: the *ḳonam* of the Mishnah may refer either to *my mouth* (concrete) or to *my
talking* (abstract). In the former case the vow would be valid, but not in the
latter. Since it is not clear which, we adopt the more rigorous interpretation.
(9) In which case the *speaking* would be the object of the vow; the speaking
being abstract, the vow would be invalid.

NEDARIM

CHAPTER II

MISHNAH. NOW THESE ARE PERMITTED:[1] [HE WHO SAYS,] 'WHAT I MIGHT EAT OF YOURS BE ḤULLIN,' 'AS THE FLESH OF THE SWINE,' 'AS THE OBJECT OF IDOLATROUS WORSHIP,'[2] 'AS PERFORATED HIDES,'[3] 'AS NEBELOTH AND ṬEREFOTH',[4] 'AS ABOMINATIONS AND REPTILES', 'AS AARON'S DOUGH OR HIS TERUMAH',[5]—[IN ALL THESE CASES] HE IS PERMITTED. IF ONE SAYS TO HIS WIFE, 'BEHOLD! THOU ART UNTO ME AS MY MOTHER,'[6] HE MUST BE GIVEN AN OPENING ON OTHER GROUNDS,[7] IN ORDER THAT HE SHOULD NOT ACT FRIVOLOUSLY IN SUCH MATTERS.[8]

GEMARA. Now, the reason is because he said, 'WHAT I MIGHT EAT OF YOURS BE ḤULLIN'; but if he said, 'What I might eat of yours be le*ḥullin*,' it would imply: let it not be *ḥullin* but a *ḳorban*.[9] Whose view is taught in our Mishnah? If R. Meir's, but he does not hold [14*a*] that the positive may be inferred from the negative? But if R. Judah's, it is identical with the earlier Mishnah?[10] —Because he [the Tanna] teaches, 'AS THE FLESH OF THE SWINE, AS THE OBJECT OF IDOLATROUS WORSHIP,' he teaches *ḥullin*

(1) I.e., invalid. (2) Lit., 'as the worship of stars'. (3) The hide was perforated opposite the heart, which was cut out from the living animal and offered to the idol. Cf. 'A.Z. 29*b* and 32*a*. (4) V. Glos. s.v. *nebelah* (pl. *nebeloth*) and *ṭerefah* (pl. *ṭerefoth*). (5) V. *supra* 12*a, a.l.* (6) I.e., forbidden. (7) Lit., 'from another place'. I.e., when he wishes his vow to be annulled, the Rabbi, who must find for him some grounds of regret to invalidate his vow, must not do so by pointing out that such a vow is derogatory to his mother's dignity. (8) His mother's honour is too easy a ground for regret, and if the vow is invalidated on that score it is an encouragement to make such vows lightly, since they can easily be annulled. The making of vows was discouraged: cf. 9*a*. (9) And the vow would be binding. (10) *Supra* 10*b*.

too.[1] Rabina said: This is what he teaches: NOW THESE ARE PERMITTED as [if he said WHAT I MIGHT EAT OF YOURS BE] ḤULLIN, viz., [IF ONE SAYS,] 'AS THE FLESH OF THE SWINE', 'AS THE OBJECT OF IDOLATROUS WORSHIP'; and if ḤULLIN were not stated, I would have thought that absolution[2] is required. But could I possibly think so? Since the last clause teaches: IF ONE SAYS TO HIS WIFE, 'BEHOLD! THOU ART UNTO ME AS MY MOTHER,' HE MUST BE GIVEN AN OPENING ON OTHER GROUNDS, it follows that in the first clause absolution is unnecessary? But it is clear that ḤULLIN is mentioned incidentally.

Whence do we know it?[3]—Scripture states, *If a man vow a vow unto the Lord:*[4] This teaches that one must vow by what is [itself] forbidden through a vow.[5] If so, even [if one vows] by a [Divinely] interdicted object too, since it is written, *to bind his soul with a bond?*[6]—That is necessary for what was taught: Which is the bond referred to in the Torah etc.[7]

HE WHO SAYS TO HIS WIFE, 'BEHOLD! THOU ART UNTO ME AS MY MOTHER', etc. But a contradiction is shewn: If one says to his wife, 'Behold! thou art unto me as the flesh of my mother, as the flesh of my sister, as *'orlah,*[8] as *kil'ayim*[9] of the vineyard, his words are of no effect.[10]—Said Abaye: His words are of no effect by Biblical law, yet absolution is required by Rabbinical law. Raba answered: One refers to a scholar; the other refers to an *'am ha-areẓ.*[11] And it was taught even so: If one vows by the Torah,[12] his words are of no effect. Yet R. Joḥanan commented: He must retract [his vow] before a Sage; while R. Naḥman observed: A scholar does not need absolution.

(1) I.e., *ḥullin* is unnecessary in itself, but mentioned merely for the sake of completeness. (2) Lit., 'a request' (for revocation). (3) That these vows are not binding. (4) Num. XXX, 3. (5) Translating: if a man vow by referring to a vow. (6) Ibid. This may also be interpreted: to bind his soul by that which is already a bond, viz. something Divinely interdicted. (7) V. *supra* 12a. (8) V. Glos. (9) V. Glos. Deut. XXII, 9. (10) Because all these objects are forbidden by the Law. (11) Lit., 'people of the earth'—an ignoramus; v. *J.E.* s.v. In the first case the vow is entirely invalid; but an ignoramus will treat vows too lightly if shewn leniency, and therefore needs absolution. (12) [E.g., 'I vow by the Torah not to eat of this loaf'—in reality a kind of oath. V. *infra* (Ran).]

[14b] It was taught: If one vows by the Torah, his words are of no effect; by what is written therein, his vow is binding; by it *and* by what is written therein, his vow is binding. Since he states, 'by what is written therein, his vow is binding,' is it necessary to mention, 'by it *and* by what is written therein?'—R. Naḥman answered: There is no difficulty: one means that a Torah is lying on the ground; the other, that [the vower] holds a Torah in his hand. If it is lying on the ground, his thoughts are of the parchment; if he holds it in his hand, his thoughts are of the Divine Names therein.[1] Alternatively, [both clauses mean] that it is lying on the ground, and we are informed this: even when it is lying on the ground, since he vows, 'by what is written therein,' his vow is valid;[2] and an anti-climax is taught.[3] A further alternative: the whole [Baraitha] indeed means that he holds it in his hand, and we are informed this:[4] Since he holds it in his hand, even if he merely says, 'by it,' it is as though he said, 'by what is written therein'.[5]

MISHNAH. [IF ONE SAYS,] 'ḲONAM IF I SLEEP', 'IF I

(1) The Heb. *bamah shekathuw bah* may mean either, by what is written therein, or, by that whereon it (the Law) is written. Now if the Scroll is lying on the ground, and one says, '*bamah shekathuw bah*', we assume that he thought that it was a mere scroll not written upon, since it had been irreverently placed on the ground, and his words refer to the actual parchment, unless he says '*bah u-bamah shekathuw bah*', which can only mean by the scroll and by what is written therein. A reference to the parchment is invalid; to the Divine Names, is binding. (2) I.e., we assume the Heb. *bamah shekathuw bah* to bear that meaning, not, 'by that whereon it is written'. (3) In the clause: 'By it and by what is written therein.' Lit., 'this, and the other goes without saying'. (4) BaḤ. [Cur. ed.: 'the whole also, the middle clause etc.'. Ran: 'the final clause informs us this'. All of which shows the text is in disorder. An attempt may be made to restore the text on the basis of MS.M. and Ran: 'The first clause (refers to the case) where it lies on the ground (MS.M.), the final clause (Ran) where he holds it in his hand (MS.M.). Such a text is also implied in the Ran on the passage.] (5) I.e., *bah u-bamah shekathuw bah* are now translated 'by it *or* by what is written therein', the copulative sometimes meaning *or*. The text is not quite clear; that of the Ran has been adopted as giving the most plausible rendering.

SPEAK', OR 'IF I WALK';[1] OR IF ONE SAYS TO HIS WIFE, 'ḲONAM IF I COHABIT WITH YOU,' HE IS LIABLE TO [THE INJUNCTION] HE SHALL NOT BREAK HIS WORD.[2]

GEMARA. It was stated: [If one says,] '*Ḳonam* be my eyes sleeping to-day, if I sleep to-morrow'—Rab Judah said in Rab's name: He must not sleep that day, lest he sleep on the morrow. But R. Naḥman said: He may sleep on that day, and we do not fear that he may sleep on the morrow. Yet Rab Judah agrees that if one says, '*Ḳonam* be my eyes sleeping to-morrow, if I sleep to-day,' he may sleep that day; [15*a*] a person may be lax with respect to a *condition*, but he is observant of an actual prohibition.[3] We learnt: [IF ONE SAYS,] 'ḲONAM IF I SLEEP, IF I WALK, IF I SPEAK, etc. How is it meant? If literally, 'if I sleep,' is such a vow valid? But it was taught: There is greater stringency in oaths than in vows, for oaths are valid with respect to things both abstract and concrete, but vows are not so; and sleep is an abstract thing! But if he said, '*Ḳonam* be *my eyes* sleeping,'[4] then, if he states no time-limit, is he permitted to go on until he violates the injunction, *he shall not break his word?*[2] But R. Joḥanan said: [If one says,] 'I swear not to sleep for three days', he is flagellated and may sleep immediately.[5] But if it means that he says, '*Ḳonam* be my eyes sleeping tomorrow, if I sleep to-day[6]—surely

(1) I.e., I am forbidden by a vow to sleep, etc. [Lit., '*ḳonam* be that which I sleep'. V. Laible, *MGWJ*. 1916, pp. 29ff.] (2) Num. XXX, 3. (3) Thus, where the second day is merely a condition for the first, we fear that even after having slept on the first, he may do so on the second too; but where the second day is the subject of the actual vow, we do not fear that having slept on the first he will disregard the prohibition of the second. (4) Since the *ḳonam* falls upon the eyes, the vow is valid, eyes being concrete. (5) Because it is impossible to keep awake three consecutive days. Therefore his oath is inherently vain (v. Shebu. 25*a*); hence he is punished, and the oath is invalid. (6) It cannot mean that he simply said, '*ḳonam* be my eyes sleeping to-day', as in that case it is obvious; hence the stipulation must be assumed, and the meaning of the Mishnah will be that he must take heed not to sleep on the *first* day, lest he sleep on the second too, and thereby violate the injunction; for on any other meaning the Mishnah is superfluous.

you say that a person is observant in respect of an actual prohibition?[1] Hence it is obvious that he says, '*Konam* be my eyes sleeping *to-day*, if I sleep tomorrow.' Now, if he did *not* sleep that first day, how can the injunction, *he shall not break his word*[2] apply, even if he slept on the second? Hence it surely means that he *did* sleep, thus proving that he is permitted to do so. This refutes Rab Judah!—When is this stated? If he happened to sleep on the first day.[3] Rabina said: After all, it is as taught,[4] yet how can *he shall not break his word* apply?—By Rabbinical law.[5] But can the *Biblical* injunction apply by *Rabbinical* law?[6]—Yes. Even as it was taught: Things which are permitted, yet some treat them as forbidden, you must not permit them in their presence, because it is written, *he shall not break his word.*[7]

We learnt: [If one says to his wife, '*Konam* be] that which you benefit from me until Passover, if you go to your father's house until the Festival',[8] if she went before Passover, she may not benefit from him until Passover. Now, only if she went before Passover is she forbidden, but not otherwise?[9]—R. Abba answered: If she went before Passover, she is forbidden and is flagellated;[10] if she did not go, she is merely forbidden. Then consider the second clause: After Passover, she is subject to *he shall not break his word.* Now if she did not benefit before Passover, how can the injunction apply? Hence it is obvious that she *did* benefit, which proves that this is permitted, [15*b*] thus refuting Rab Judah!—[No.] That Mishnah

(1) So there is no reason for refraining from sleeping that day, since he will observe his oath on the next. (2) Num. XXX, 3. (3) Despite the prohibition for which very reason he may not sleep on the first. (4) Literally, viz., '*konam* if I sleep'. (5) Though by Biblical law the vow is invalid, since sleep is abstract, the Rabbis declared it binding, and therefore the injunction holds good. (6) Lit., 'is there (the transgression) *he shall not break* in a Rabbinic (law)'. (7) When one is accustomed to treat a thing as forbidden, it is as though it were subject to a vow. Thus, though the prohibitive force of custom is Rabbinical only, the Biblical injunction applies to it. (8) 'The Festival', without any further determinant, always refers to Tabernacles, six months after Passover. (9) Though the condition extends to Tabernacles, we do not fear that she may yet violate it *after* Passover: this refutes Rab Judah. (10) If she benefits from him.

teaches that *if* she benefited, she is involved in, '*he shall not break his word*'.

We learnt: [If one says to his wife, '*Konam* be] that which you benefit from me until the Festival, if you go to your father's house before Passover': if she goes before Passover, she may not benefit from him until the Festival, but is permitted to go after Passover. [Thus,] if she goes, she is forbidden, but not otherwise?[1]—Raba answered: The same law applies that even without going she is forbidden. But if she goes, she is forbidden [to benefit], and receives lashes [if she does]; if she does not go, she is merely forbidden.

An objection is raised: [If he says,] 'This loaf [of bread be forbidden] to me to-day, if I go to such and such a place to-morrow': if he eats it, he is liable to an injunction, 'he shall not go'![2]—Does he [the Tanna] teach: he *may* eat it—[surely] he teaches, '*if* he eats it' so that if he eats it he is under the injunction not to go.[3] [The Baraitha continues:] If he goes, he violates the injunction, *he shall not break his word*.[4] But there is no [clause] teaching that he goes [on the second day]: this contradicts Rab Judah![5]—R. Judah answers you: In truth, he could teach, he goes: but since the first clause teaches, '*if* he eats', not being able to teach, 'he eats',[6] the second clause too teaches, '*if* he goes'.

IF ONE SAYS TO HIS WIFE, 'KONAM IF I COHABIT WITH YOU,' HE IS LIABLE TO [THE INJUNCTION,] HE SHALL NOT BREAK HIS WORD. But he is obligated to her by Biblical law, as it is written, *her food, her raiment, and her marriage rights he shall not* diminish?[7]—It means that he vows, 'The pleasure of cohabitation with you be forbidden me': thus he surely denies himself the enjoyment of cohabitation.[8] For R. Kahana said: [If a woman

(1) Though by going any time before Passover, subsequent to having benefited from her husband, the vow is violated. This contradicts Rab Judah. (2) This too refutes Rab Judah, since he may eat the loaf on the first day. (3) But actually this is forbidden. (4) Num. XXX, 3. (5) For if he may not eat the loaf on the first day, the Baraitha should teach such a clause on the assumption that he did not eat it. (6) For it cannot be taught that he may eat—this being Rab Judah's opinion. (7) Ex. XXI, 10. How then can he free himself by a vow? (8) Hence his vow is valid, since it falls primarily upon *himself*.

says to her husband,] 'Cohabitation with me be forbidden to you,' she is compelled to grant it, since she is under an obligation to him. [But if she says,] 'The pleasure of cohabitation with you be forbidden *me*,' he is forbidden [to cohabit], since one may not be fed with what is prohibited to him.[1]

MISHNAH. [IF HE SAYS,] '[I SWEAR] AN OATH NOT TO SLEEP,' OR, 'TALK,' OR, 'WALK,' HE IS FORBIDDEN [TO DO SO]. [IF HE SAYS,] 'A ḲORBAN BE WHAT I MIGHT NOT EAT OF YOURS,'[2] [OR] 'OH ḲORBAN! IF I EAT OF YOURS,' [OR] 'WHAT I MIGHT NOT EAT OF YOURS BE NOT A ḲORBAN UNTO ME,' HE IS PERMITTED [TO EAT OF HIS NEIGHBOURS'].

GEMARA. [16a] Whose view is taught in our Mishnah?—R. Meir's; for if R. Judah's, he recognises no distinction between a *ḳorban* and Oh, *ḳorban*.[3] Then consider the latter clause [IF HE SAYS,], 'WHAT I MIGHT NOT EAT OF YOURS BE NOT A ḲORBAN UNTO ME,' HE IS PERMITTED. But we learnt: [If one says,] 'That which I might not eat of yours be not for a *ḳorban* unto me': R. Meir forbids [him]. And R. Abba observed thereon: It is as though he said, 'Let it [i.e., your food] be for a *ḳorban*, therefore I may not eat of yours.[4]—There is no difficulty: in the latter case he said, 'le-*ḳorban*' [*for* a *ḳorban*]; but here [in our Mishnah] he said, '*la'-ḳorban*,'[5] which means: let it *not* be a *ḳorban*.

(1) So here too. Where the husband or wife make a vow, depriving the *other* of his or her rights, it is invalid. But if the vow deprives its *maker* from the enjoyment of his or her privileges, it is valid, though the other is affected thereby too. (2) An alternative is: 'By the sacrifice (i.e., I swear by the sacrifice) I will not eat of yours.' [On this interpretation, the declaration is a form of oath taken by the life of the *ḳorban*, which is not binding. V. *supra* 13*a*, (Ran).] (3) This is argued from the fact the Mishnah does not include the form '*ḳorban* be what *I might eat* of yours', as permissible, as it does in the case of 'Oh, *ḳorban*', which could be included according to R. Judah's opinion that the particle '*as*' is necessary to render the oath binding, v. *supra* 10*a*. (4) Then why not assume the same here? (5) So Ran. cur. edd. *lo le-ḳorban*.

MISHNAH. [IF HE SAYS, 'I TAKE] AN OATH [THAT] I WILL NOT EAT OF YOURS,' [OR] 'OH OATH THAT[1] I EAT OF YOURS,' [OR 'I TAKE] NO OATH [THAT] I WILL NOT EAT OF YOURS,'[2] HE IS FORBIDDEN.

GEMARA. This proves that 'Oh oath that I eat of yours' implies that I will *not* eat. Now this contradicts the following: Oaths are of two categories, which are extended to four, viz., '[I swear] that I will eat,' 'that I will not eat,' 'that I have eaten,' 'that I have not eaten'.[3] Now, since he enumerates, 'that I will eat,' 'that I will not eat,' 'that I have eaten,' 'that I have not eaten,' it follows that [the phrase,] 'that I eat of yours' implies, 'I *will* eat'?—Abaye answered: 'That I eat' has two meanings. If one was being urged to eat, and he replied: 'I will eat, I will eat, moreover, [I take] an oath that I eat,' it implies, 'I *will* eat.' But if he said, 'I will not eat, I will not eat,' and then added: '[I take] an oath that I eat,' it implies, 'I will not eat'.[4] R. Ashi answered: 'That I eat,' in connection with an oath,[5] really means that he [actually] said, 'I will *not* eat'.[6] If so, it is obvious: why state it?—I might think it is a mispronunciation[7] which caused him to stumble;[8] we are therefore taught [otherwise].

(1) V. Gemara. (2) This even according to R. Meir, for the Talmud states (Shebu'oth 36a) that R. Meir holds that the positive may be inferred from the negative in oaths. (3) The two categories are affirmative and negative oaths referring to the future, which are extended to include similar oaths in the past. (4) The Heb. then means: 'I swear in this matter of eating'—viz., that I will not eat. [The whole turns on the meaning attached to שאוכל. The particle שֶׁ may denote 'that' or 'if' (or 'that which'). In the first instance, the circumstance favours the former interpretation: 'An oath that I eat', i.e., 'I swear *that* I eat'. In the latter, he probably meant: 'An oath *if* (or *that which*) I eat; i.e., 'I swear not to eat', (or, 'By oath be forbidden that which I eat); cf. Shebu. 19b.] (5) I.e., the Mishnah, when employing this phrase in connection with oaths. (6) I.e., the Mishnah merely indicates that his oath bore reference to eating, but actually it was a negative one. (7) Lit., 'a twisting of the tongue'. (8) Saying *she-i-'okel* instead of *she-'okel*, the difference in Hebrew being very slight.—This answer, as well as the discussion *supra et passim* on *le-korban* and *lo korban*, implies that the vows and oaths, as hypothetically posited in the Mishnah, were actually taken in Hebrew, not in another language. Thus Hebrew was generally spoken

Abaye does not give R. Ashi's reason, because it is not stated, 'That I will *not* eat.' R. Ashi rejects Abaye's interpretation: he holds, 'that I will *not* eat' may also bear two meanings. [Thus:—] if one was being urged to eat, and he said, 'I will not eat, I will not eat,' and then added, 'I [swear by] an oath', whether [he concluded] 'that I eat,' or, 'that I do not eat,' it implies, 'I will eat'. While the language, 'An oath that I will not eat,' may also be explained as meaning, 'I swear [indeed] that I will not eat.'[1] But the Tanna[2] states a general rule: *she-'okel* [always] means that I will eat, and *she-lo 'okel,* that I will not eat.[3]

when the Mishnah was composed, and the Hebrew employed in the Mishnah would appear a natural, not an artificial language. V. M.H. Segal, *Mishnaic Hebrew Grammar*, Introduction.

(1) The text is not quite clear, but the general meaning appears to be this: When he says, '*lo akilna, lo akilna* (I will not eat),' he may mean it positively, 'I will certainly not eat'; when he further adds, 'I swear that I will eat (*she-'okel*)' or 'that I will not eat' he is strengthening his first statement, for 'I swear that I will eat (*she-'okel*)' may mean, 'I swear in respect of this matter of eating'. On the other hand, his first words may mean, 'I will not eat'?—of course I will! Hence the subsequent oath confirms this, for 'I swear that I will not eat (*she-lo 'okel*)' may mean, 'An oath may be imposed upon what I will *not* eat, but not upon what I will eat' Hence, if Abaye's explanation is correct, that the Tanna teaches that *she-'okel* may imply a negative, he should also teach that *she-lo 'okel* may imply an affirmative. [MS.M. preserves a better reading: . . . if one was being urged to eat . . . whether (he concluded) 'that I eat' or 'that I do not eat' he means 'I shall *not* eat', while the language 'An oath that I will not eat' may be explained 'An oath that I *do* eat'. The meaning is thus clearer: When he first says 'I will not eat', his subsequent statement, whatever it is, will, on Abaye's explanation, be taken as confirming the first: If it is 'An oath that I eat' the particle שֶ (v. *supra* p. 43, n. 4) denotes 'if' or ('that which') and he means 'I swear . . . if I eat'; if it is 'An oath that I do not eat' the particle is simply taken in the sense of 'that'. And thus similarly on Abaye's view, the phrase 'that I do not eat' could also be explained in a positive sense: 'I swear . . . if I do not eat', viz., where it was preceded by the statement 'I will eat'. This however, is impossible, in view of the Mishnah in Shebu'oth, which draws a distinction between 'that I will eat' and 'that I will not eat' and not between the circumstances that produced the oath.] (2) Of the Mishnah in Shebu'oth. (3) Disregarding the special cases where the general tenor of a person's speech or the inflection of his voice reverses the literal meaning of his oath.

MISHNAH. IN THESE INSTANCES OATHS ARE MORE RIGOROUS THAN VOWS.[1] YET THERE IS [ALSO] GREATER STRINGENCY IN VOWS THAN IN OATHS. E.G., IF ONE SAYS, 'KONAM BE THE SUKKAH THAT I MAKE,' OR, 'THE LULAB THAT I TAKE,' OR, 'THE TEFILLIN[2] THAT I PUT ON:' [WHEN EXPRESSED] AS VOWS THEY ARE BINDING, BUT AS OATHS THEY ARE NOT, BECAUSE ONE CANNOT SWEAR TO TRANSGRESS THE PRECEPTS.

GEMARA. [16b] MORE RIGOROUS? That implies that they are [valid] vows;[3] but it is taught, He is permitted?[4]—This is taught in reference to the second clause of the other section: [viz.,] [If one says,] ['I swear] on oath not to sleep,' or, 'talk,' or 'walk,' he is forbidden [to do so]: IN THESE INSTANCES OATHS ARE MORE RIGOROUS THAN VOWS.[5]

YET THERE IS GREATER STRINGENCY IN VOWS THAN IN OATHS etc. R. Kahana recited, R. Giddal said in Rab's name, and R. Ṭabyomi recited, R. Giddal said in Samuel's name: Whence do we know that one cannot swear [a valid oath] to violate the precepts? From the verse, *When a man . . . swear an oath . . . he shall not break* his *word;*[6] [this implies,] he may not break *his* word,[7] but he must break a word [i.e., an oath] in respect of Heavenly matters.[8] Now, why are vows different: because it is written, *When a man vow a vow* unto the Lord . . . *he shall not break his word?*[9] But [of] oaths too it is written, *or swear an oath* unto the Lord *he shall not break his word?*[10]—Abaye answered: In that case [vows]

(1) Since the Mishnah (15*b*) states that a vow in these terms is not binding. (2) V. Glos. for these words. (3) Save that their binding character is not so rigid as that of oaths; but if not binding at all, the term is inapplicable. (4) V. Mishnah 15*b*; that indicates that these vows are quite invalid. (5) For as stated in the Mishnah on 14*b*, such *vows* are indeed binding, but as explained by Rabina (v. 15*a*), only by Rabbinical Law; whereas oaths of a similar nature are Biblically valid. (6) Num. XXX, 3. (7) I.e., when it refers to human, optional matters. (8) I.e. when the subject of the vow is obligatory. (9) Ibid. Implying that it is binding even when referring to Divine, non-optional matters. This is inferred by regarding unto (ל) as meaning against: i.e., when a man vows contrary to the Lord's precepts. (10) Ibid. Not actually; but as *to the Lord* immediately precedes *or swear an oath*, it may be regarded as referring to it.

one says: 'The pleasure of the *sukkah* be forbidden me';[1] but in this case [oaths] one says: 'I swear that I shall not benefit from the *sukkah*'.[2] Raba objected: Were the precepts then given for enjoyment?[3] But Raba answered: There [in the case of vows] one says, 'The sitting in the *sukkah* be forbidden me';[4] but here [oaths] one says, 'I swear not to sit in the *sukkah*'.

Now, do we learn that one cannot swear to transgress the precepts from this verse: do we not rather deduce it from elsewhere? For it was taught: If one swears to annul a precept, and does not, I might think that he is liable;[5] [17a] hence the Bible teaches, [*or if a soul swear, pronouncing with his lips*] *to do evil, or to do good* etc.:[6] just as doing good refers to something optional,[7] so doing evil refers [only] to something optional. This excludes one who swears to annul a precept, and did not annul it,[8] because it is not optional!—One verse is to exempt him from the sacrifice due for [violating] an oath, and the other is to exempt him [from punishment[9] for having violated] the injunction concerning an oath.

MISHNAH. A VOW WITHIN A VOW IS VALID,[10] BUT NOT AN OATH WITHIN AN OATH. E.G., IF ONE DECLARES, 'BEHOLD, I WILL BE A NAZIR IF I EAT [THIS LOAF],' 'I WILL BE A NAZIR

(1) Hence it is binding, as one may not enjoy that which he has vowed not to enjoy. (2) I.e., the oath falls primarily upon the person, v. *supra* 2b; but one cannot free himself from a Biblical obligation. (3) Technically speaking, one cannot be said to derive physical enjoyment from the fulfilment of a precept, and therefore a vow in these terms would not be binding. One's highest enjoyment should be in obedience to God's word. [Apart from its *halachic* implications, the object of this saying was to keep the ethical principle free from any admixture of the idea of utility V. Lazarus, M. *Ethics of Judaism*, I, p. 284.] (4) Thus the vow falls upon the *sukkah*, which is rendered forbidden, and not upon the person; therefore it is valid. (5) For swearing falsely. (6) Lev. V, 4. (7) V. Shebu. (Sonc. ed.) p. 147 for notes. (8) Teaching that no penalty is incurred. (9) [I.e., the penalty of lashes for transgressing '*he shall not break his word*'. He is however lashed for uttering a vain oath; v. Shebu. 29a (Tosaf).] (10) Lit., 'there is a vow within a vow'.

IF I EAT [THIS LOAF],' AND THEN EATS [IT], HE IS LIABLE IN RESPECT OF EACH [VOW].[1] BUT IF HE SAYS, 'I SWEAR THAT I WILL NOT EAT [THIS LOAF],' 'I SWEAR THAT I WILL NOT EAT [THIS LOAF],' AND THEN EATS [IT], HE IS LIABLE [TO PUNISHMENT] FOR ONE [OATH] ONLY.

GEMARA. R. Huna said: This holds good only if one says, 'Behold, I will be a *nazir* to-day [if I eat this loaf]; I will be a *nazir* to-morrow [if I eat this loaf]', since an extra day is added, the [second] *neziruth*[2] is binding in addition to the first.[3] But if he says, 'Behold, I will be a *nazir* to-day, I will be a *nazir* to-day,' the second *neziruth* is not valid in addition to the first. But Samuel said: Even if one declares, 'Behold, I will be a *nazir* to-day, I will be a *nazir* to-day,' the second *neziruth* is binding. Now, according to R. Huna, [the Mishnah,] instead of teaching, BUT NOT AN OATH WITHIN AN OATH, should teach, Sometimes A VOW WITHIN A VOW IS VALID, and sometimes not. [If one says,] 'Behold, I will be a *nazir* to-day; behold, I will be a *nazir* to-morrow,' the vow within the vow is binding. But if he says, 'Behold, I will be a *nazir* to-day, I will be a *nazir* to-day,' [17b] the second is not binding?[4]—This is a difficulty.

We learnt: A VOW WITHIN A VOW IS VALID, BUT NOT AN OATH WITHIN AN OATH. How is this? Shall we say that one declared, 'Behold, I will be a *nazir* to-day, Behold, I will be a *nazir* to-morrow':[5] then an analogous oath is: 'I swear not to eat figs, I swear not to eat grapes;' why should this second oath be invalid? But the invalidity of an oath within an oath arises thus: 'I swear not to eat figs, I swear not to eat figs.' Then an analogous vow in respect of *neziruth* is: 'Behold, I will be a *nazir* to-day; Behold, I will

(1) And he must observe two periods of *neziroth* of thirty days each. This double vow relating to the same thing is called a vow within a vow. (2) Abstract noun from *nazir*, 'naziriteship'. (3) And the full statutory period of thirty days must be observed for the second *neziruth*. (4) The point of the difficulty is that the Tanna should not draw a distinction between vows and oaths, when it can be drawn between vows themselves. (5) The second vow being a real addition to the first.

be a *nazir* to-day; and it is stated, A VOW WITHIN A VOW IS VALID. This refutes R. Huna?—R. Huna answers you: The Mishnah applies to one who said: 'Behold, I will be a *nazir* to-day, Behold, I will be a *nazir* to-morrow;'[1] and an analogous oath is: 'I swear not to eat figs, I swear not to eat figs and grapes,'[2] the second oath being invalid. But did not Rabbah say: [If one says,] 'I swear not to eat figs,' and then adds, 'I swear not to eat figs and grapes'; if he eats figs, sets aside [an animal for] a sacrifice and then eats grapes, the grapes constitute [only] half the extent [of his second oath],[3] and a sacrifice is not brought for [the violation of] such. From this we see that if one declares, 'I swear not to eat figs,' and then adds, 'I swear not to eat figs and grapes': since the [second] oath is valid in respect of grapes, it is valid in respect of figs too?—R. Huna does not agree with Rabbah.

An objection is raised: If one made two vows of *neziruth*, observed[4] the first, set aside a sacrifice,[5] and then had himself absolved thereof [*sc.* the first vow], the second is accounted to him in [the observance of] the first.[6] How is this? Shall we say that he declared, 'Behold, I will be a *nazir* to-day; Behold, I will be a *nazir* to-morrow', why does the second replace the first; surely there is an additional day? But it is obvious that he said: 'Behold, I will be a *nazir* to-day; Behold, I will be a *nazir* to-day.' [18*a*] This contradicts R. Huna!—No. After all, [it means that he said,] 'Behold, I will be a *nazir* to-day; Behold, I will be a *nazir* to morrow'; and how is it accounted to him? With the exception of that additional day. Alternatively, [it means], e.g., that one undertook two periods of *neziruth* simultaneously.[7]

R. Hamnuna objected: *To vow a vow of a Nazirite, declaring themselves a Nazirite* [*unto the Lord*]:[8] teaches hence [we learn] that *neziruth* falls upon *neziruth*.[9] For I would think, does it [the reverse]

(1) So that the second vow is identical with the first, save that a day is added. (2) The second oath thus included the first, and added thereto. (3) Which embraces grapes and figs. (4) Lit., 'counted'—the days of his vow. (5) Due on the expiration of *neziroth*. (6) I.e., the term of *neziroth* already observed is accounted to the second vow, since the first was revoked. (7) Declaring, 'I vow two periods of *neziroth*'. (8) Num. VI, 2. (9) I.e., a vow of *neziruth* is

not follow *a fortiori:* If an oath, which is [more] stringent, is not binding upon another oath; how much more so *neziruth,* which is less rigorous![1] Therefore it is stated, *'a nazirite, declaring himself a nazirite to the Lord';* from which [we learnt] that *neziroth* falls upon *neziroth.* Now how is this? Shall we say, that one said, 'Behold, I will be a *nazir* to-day; Behold, I will be a *nazir* to-morrow,'—is a verse necessary? But presumably it applies to one who said, 'Behold, I will be a *nazir* to day, Behold, I will be a *nazir* to-day;' and it is stated that the second [vow of] *neziruth* is binding in addition to the first?[2]—No. This refers to one who undertook two [periods of] *neziruth* simultaneously.

Now, wherein is an oath more rigorous than a vow? Shall we say in so far that it is applicable even to the abstract:[3] but a vow too is more stringent, since it is as valid in respect to a precept as in respect to anything optional?[4]—But it is because it is written in reference thereto, *he shall not be held guiltless [that taketh my name in vain].*[5]

BUT IF HE SAYS, 'I SWEAR THAT I WILL NOT EAT [THIS LOAF],' 'I SWEAR THAT I WILL NOT EAT [THIS LOAF],' AND THEN EATS IT, HE IS LIABLE [TO PUNISHMENT] FOR ONE [OATH] ONLY. Raba said: If he was absolved of the first, the second becomes binding. How is this deduced? Since it is not stated, It is only one [oath], but, HE IS LIABLE [TO PUNISHMENT] FOR ONE [OATH] ONLY: thus, there is no room for it;[6] but if the first is revoked, the second becomes binding. A different version [of Raba's dictum] is this: There is no *penalty* [for the second], yet it is an oath. For what purpose is it so?[7]—For Raba's dictum. For Raba said: If he was absolved of the first, the second

binding upon one who is already a *nazir,* translating thus: . . . *of a nazirite, when he is already a nazirite to the Lord.*

(1) The greater stringency of oaths is explained below. To shew that the second is binding—surely it is obvious! (2) This contradicts R. Huna. (3) V. *supra* 13*b*, *a.l.* (4) V. Mishnah on 16*a*. (5) Ex. XX, 7. (6) I.e., for the second to impose a penalty, since that is incurred on account of the first. (7) Since he is not punished for violating the second, whilst he is already bound by the first, what does it matter whether we regard the second as an oath or not?

takes its place. Shall we say that the following supports him: If one made two vows of *neziruth*, observed the first, set aside a sacrifice, and was then absolved thereof, the second [vow] is fulfilled in [the observance of] the first?[1]—[No.] This refers e.g., to one who vowed two periods of *neziruth* simultaneously.[2]

MISHNAH. [18*b*] UNSPECIFIED VOWS ARE INTERPRETED STRICTLY, BUT IF SPECIFIED,[3] LENIENTLY. E.G., IF ONE VOWS, 'BEHOLD! THIS BE TO ME AS SALTED MEAT,' OR, 'AS WINE OF LIBATION': NOW, IF HE VOWED BY ALLUSION TO A PEACE-OFFERING,[4] HE IS FORBIDDEN;[5] IF BY AN IDOLATROUS SACRIFICE, HE IS PERMITTED, BUT IF IT WAS UNSPECIFIED, HE IS FORBIDDEN. [IF ONE DECLARES], 'BEHOLD! THIS BE TO ME AS ḤEREM': IF AS A ḤEREM TO THE LORD,[6] HE IS FORBIDDEN; IF AS A ḤEREM TO THE PRIESTS, HE IS PERMITTED.[7] IF IT IS UNSPECIFIED, HE IS FORBIDDEN. 'BEHOLD! THIS BE TO ME AS TITHE': IF HE VOWED, AS CATTLE TITHES, HE IS FORBIDDEN; IF AS CORN TITHES, HE IS PERMITTED; IF UNSPECIFIED, HE IS FORBIDDEN.[8] 'BEHOLD! THIS BE TO ME AS

(1) This proves that the second is actually valid. (2) Hence the second is binding; but if one declares, 'I swear not to eat this loaf, I swear not to eat this loaf', it may be that his second statement has no validity at all. For further notes on this passage v. Shebu. (Sonc. ed.) pp. 150ff. (3) After the vow is made in general terms (Ran). (4) [*Var. lec.* 'TO HEAVEN', v. next note.] (5) To benefit from the object of his vow—i.e., his vow is valid. (6) Lit., 'of Heaven'. For 'Heaven' as a synonym of God cf. I Macc. III, 18 (though some ancient authorities read there 'the God of heaven'); Matt. XXI, 25; v. A. Marmorstein, *The Old Rabbinic doctrine of God*, I, pp. 14 and 105-106. (7) That which was devoted (*ḥerem*) to the Lord, i.e., to be utilized in or sold for Temple purposes, could not be redeemed, and hence was definitely forbidden for secular use (Lev. XXVII, 28); but if devoted to the priests, it might be so used once they had taken possession of it (Num. XVIII, 14); it is therefore regarded as permitted, and a reference to it in a vow has no validity. (8) The cattle tithe had to be formally designated, hence it is regarded as *humanly* forbidden, and a reference to it is valid; but the corn tithe belonged automatically to the Levite, even if not formally designated; therefore it is regarded as *Divinely* forbidden; v. *supra* 13*b*.

TERUMAH':[1] IF HE VOWED, AS THE TERUMAH OF THE TEMPLE-CHAMBER,[2] HE IS FORBIDDEN; IF AS THE TERUMAH OF THE THRESHING-FLOOR [I.E., OF CORN], HE IS PERMITTED;[3] IF UNSPECIFIED, HE IS FORBIDDEN: THIS IS THE VIEW OF R. MEIR. R. JUDAH SAID: AN UNSPECIFIED REFERENCE TO TERUMAH IN JUDEA[4] IS BINDING, BUT NOT IN GALILEE, BECAUSE THE GALILEANS ARE UNFAMILIAR WITH THE TERUMAH OF THE TEMPLE-CHAMBER.[5] UNQUALIFIED ALLUSIONS TO ḤARAMIM IN JUDEA ARE NOT BINDING, BUT IN GALILEE THEY ARE, BECAUSE THE GALILEANS ARE UNFAMILIAR WITH PRIESTLY ḤARAMIM.[6]

GEMARA. But we learnt: A doubt in *neziruth* is treated leniently?[7]—R. Zera answered: There is no difficulty: This [our Mishnah] agrees with the Rabbis; the other, with R. Eliezer. For it was taught: If one consecrates [all] his beasts and his cattle,[8] the *koy*[9] is included. R. Eliezer said: He has not consecrated the *koy*.[10] He who maintains that one permits doubt to extend to his chattels,[11]

(1) V. Glos. (2) For congregational sacrifices; v. Sheḳ. III, 2; IV, 1. (3) V. p. 50, n. 8. The *terumah* of the Temple fund had to be formally designated, but that of corn was regarded as Divinely and automatically forbidden. (4) I.e., the southern portion of Palestine. (5) The Galileans, living at some distance from the Temple, did not think much about the Temple fund; consequently, when they spoke of *terumah* without any further qualification, they meant *terumah* of corn. (6) As the priests lived mainly in Judea, priestly *ḥaramim* were unusual in Galilee; hence a Divine *Ḥerem* must have been meant. (7) Ṭoho. IV, 12. E.g., if one vows, 'Behold! I will be a *nazir* if the man who is just passing is one', and that person disappeared before it could be ascertained whether he was or not, the vow is not binding. This contradicts the Mishnah that an unspecified vow, the meaning of which is doubtful, is rigorously interpreted. (8) So Rashi and Asheri. Ran: his beasts *or* his cattle; Tosaf. maintains that it refers to both cases. The term 'cattle' (*behemah*) refers to domesticated animals; 'beasts' (*ḥayyah*) to wild or semi-wild animals. (9) Probably a kind of bearded deer or antelope. It is doubtful whether this belongs to the genus of cattle or of beasts. This view is that the *koy* must be included in the one or the other. Or, according to the interpretation of the Ran, we are strict because of our doubt. (10) Because his vow embraced animals of *certain*, but not of *uncertain* genus. (11) I.e., in consecrating his cattle or his beasts, he meant it to include the *koy*, though aware that it is of doubtful genus.

maintains likewise that he permits it to extend to himself too.[1] But he who holds that one does not permit doubt to extend to his chattels, will maintain this all the more of one's own person. [19a] Abaye said to him: How have you explained [the Mishnah] 'A doubt in *neziruth* is ruled leniently'—as being R. Eliezer's view? Then consider the latter clause: Doubtful first-borns, whether of man[2] or beast,[3] whether clean or unclean—the claimant must furnish proof [that they are first-borns].[4] And it was taught thereon: They may neither be sheared nor put to service![5]—He replied: Why do you compare innate sanctity[6] with man-made sanctity?[7] But if there is a difficulty, it is this: Doubtful fluids,[8] in respect of becoming unclean [themselves], are unclean; in respect of defiling others, they are clean:[9] this is R. Meir's view, and R. Eliezer agreed with him. But is it R. Eliezer's opinion that in respect of becoming unclean [themselves] they are unclean? But it was taught, R. Eliezer said: Liquids have no uncleanness at all [by Scriptural law]; the proof is that Jose b. Joezer of Ẓeredah[10] testified[11] that the stag-

(1) Thus, having subjected himself to an unspecified vow, his intention is that the most rigorous interpretation of his words shall apply. (2) If, e.g., a woman gave birth to twins, a male and a female, and it is not known the head of which appeared first (this being legally regarded as birth). If of the male, he is a first-born; but if of the female, the male is not a first-born even if he subsequently issued first. (3) If, e.g., two cows calved, one a male and one a female, one a firstling and one not; and it is not known whether the male is the firstling. Only male firstlings belong to the priest. (4) I.e., if the priest claims the firstling or redemption money for the first-born. (5) Just as certain firstlings, (v. Deut. XV, 19). How then can this be the view of R. Eliezer, who holds that when in doubt the animal is not regarded as consecrated? (6) Lit., 'sanctity that comes of itself', v. B.M. (Sonc. ed.) pp. 26ff. (7) In the former case a rigorous view is naturally taken. But when man consecrates, he has in mind only that which certainly comes within the terms of his consecration. (8) E.g., if an unclean person, whose touch defiles liquids, put his hand into a vessel, and it is not known whether he actually touched the liquid there or not. (9) They do not defile them. (10) I Kings XI, 26. (11) On the historic occasion, when as a result of a dispute between R. Gamaliel and R. Joshua, the former was temporarily deposed from the Patriarchate, and R. Eliezer b. 'Azariah appointed in his stead. An examination was then made of scholars' traditions, which were investigated and declared valid or otherwise, v. 'Ed. (Sonc. ed.) Introduction, XI.

locust[1] is clean [i.e., fit for food], and that the fluids[2] in the [temple] slaughter-house are clean?[3] Now, there is no difficulty according to Samuel's interpretation that they are clean [only] insofar that they cannot defile other liquids, but that nevertheless they are unclean in themselves; but according to Rab, who maintained that they are literally clean [even in respect of themselves], what can be said?[4] But [answer thus]: One [the Mishnah in Ṭoharoth] teaches R. Judah's view; the other [our Mishnah] gives R. Simeon's. For it was taught: [If one says,] 'Behold! I will be a *nazir;* if this stack contains a hundred *kor,*'[5] and he goes and finds it stolen or destroyed: R. Judah ruled that he is not a *nazir:* R. Simeon, that he is.[6]

Now, R. Judah is self-contradictory. Did he say that one does not place himself in a doubtful position?[7] Then a contradiction is shewn: R. JUDAH SAID: AN UNSPECIFIED REFERENCE TO TERUMAH IN JUDEA IS BINDING, BUT NOT IN GALILEE, BECAUSE THE GALILEANS ARE UNFAMILIAR WITH THE TERUMAH OF THE TEMPLE-CHAMBER. Thus the reason is that they are unfamiliar, [19b] but if they were familiar [therewith], it would be binding?[8]—Raba answered: In the case of the stack he holds that since doubt is graver than certainty, one will not put himself into that doubtful position. For if he is a certain *nazir,* he may

(1) Heb. *Ayil,* of doubtful meaning. (2) The flow of blood and water. (3) Even by Rabbinical law. Since the general uncleanliness of liquids is rabbinical only, it was not imposed upon liquids in the temple slaughter house, so as not to defile the flesh of sacrifices. The language of this testimony is Aramaic, whereas all other laws in the Mishnah are couched in Hebrew. Weiss, *Dor,* I, 105, sees in this a proof of its extreme antiquity; v. A.Z. (Sonc. ed.) pp. 181ff for further notes. (4) It may appear that this difficulty arises in any case. But if the Mishnah, 'an uncertain vow of *neziruth*', is *not* R. Eliezer's ruling, it can be answered that though the entire law of the uncleanness of liquids is rabbinical only, he is nevertheless stringent in a case of doubt. But if the Mishnah agrees with R. Eliezer, so that though *neziruth* and vows in general are Biblically binding, he is lenient in case of doubt, how can he treat liquids strictly, when the law is merely rabbinical? (5) A measure of capacity: 36.44 litres in dry measure; 364.4 litres in liquid measure. *J.E.* 'Weights and Measures'. (6) Lit., 'R. Judah permits, R. Simeon forbids'. (7) I.e., he meant to be a *nazir* only if it *certainly* contained that measure. (8) Though it would still be doubtful to which he referred.

shave[1] and offer his sacrifice, which may be eaten; but if he is a doubtful *nazir*, he may never shave.[2] R. Huna b. Judah asked Raba: But what if he said, 'Behold! I will be a lifelong *nazir*'?[3]—He replied: Even then, a lifelong *nazir*, his doubt is graver than his certainty: for a certain *nazir* lightens the burden of his hair and offers three animals,[4] but not so a doubtful *nazir*. But what if he said, 'Behold! I will be a Samson nazirite'?[5]—He replied: A Samson nazirite was not included.[6] Said he to him: But R. Adda b. Ahabah said: A Samson Nazirite was taught?[7]—He replied: If it was taught, it was taught.[8]

R. Ashi said: That [the Mishnah in Ṭoharoth] gives the view of R. Judah quoting R. Tarfon.[9] For it was taught: R. Judah said on the authority of R. Tarfon: Neither is a *nazir*, because *neziroth* must be expressed with certainty.[10] If so, why particularly if the stack was stolen or destroyed?[11]—To shew how far-reaching is R. Simeon's view, that even if it was stolen or destroyed, he still maintains that one places himself in a doubtful position.

R. JUDAH SAID: AN UNSPECIFIED REFERENCE TO TERUMAH IN JUDEA etc. But if they *were* familiar therewith, it would be binding, which shews that the doubt is ruled stringently. Then consider the last clause: UNQUALIFIED ALLUSIONS TO ḤARA-

(1) On the expiration of his term of *neziroth*. (2) Because this must follow his sacrifices. But being a doubtful *nazir*, he cannot offer any at all, lest he be not one, in which case the animal, having been wrongfully designated as a *nazir's* sacrifice, is *ḥullin* (q.v. Glos.), which may not be brought to the Temple Court. (3) Here the doubt cannot be more stringent than the certainty, as the term never expires; and since R. Judah draws no distinction in *neziroth*, his ruling must apply even to such. (4) V. Nazir, 4*a*. (5) V. ibid. In which case his hair may never be cut. (6) The term *nazir* may include a lifelong *nazir*, but not a Samson *nazir*, which would require special mention. (7) [I.e., that R. Judah declares that he is not a *nazir* even in the case of a Samson nazirite vow (Ran).] (8) I cannot answer it. (9) But not his own view. (10) This refers to the following case: If two persons were walking together, and one said: 'I will be a *nazir*, if the man who is coming towards us is one'; whereupon the other said: 'I will be a *nazir* if he is *not*', the vow is binding upon neither, because of the element of doubt in each when it was made, v. Naz. 34*a*. (11) Even if the stack is intact and contains the stipulated measure, the vow of *neziruth* is invalid, since when it was taken it was unknown.

MIM IN JUDEA ARE NOT BINDING BUT IN GALILEE THEY ARE, BECAUSE THE GALILEANS ARE UNFAMILIAR WITH PRIESTLY ḤARAMIM. But if they *were* familiar, they would be invalid: thus in doubt we are lenient?—Abaye answered: The last clause is the view of R. Eleazar b. R. Zadok. For it was taught: R. Judah said: An unspecified [reference to] *terumah* in Judah is binding. R. Eleazar son of R. Zadok said: Unspecified [references to] *ḥaramim* in Galilee are binding.

MISHNAH. [20*a*] IF ONE VOWS BY ḤEREM,[1] AND THEN SAYS, 'I VOWED ONLY BY A FISHING NET';[2] BY ḲORBAN, AND THEN SAYS, 'I VOWED ONLY BY ROYAL GIFTS';[3] [IF HE SAYS] 'BEHOLD! [I MYSELF] 'AẒMI BE A ḲORBAN',[4] AND THEN STATES, 'I VOWED ONLY BY THE EẒEM [BONE] WHICH I KEEP FOR THE PURPOSE OF VOWING';[5] [IF ONE SAYS,] 'ḲONAM BE ANY BENEFIT MY WIFE HAS OF ME', AND THEN DECLARES, 'I SPOKE ONLY OF MY FIRST WIFE, WHOM I HAVE DIVORCED': OF NONE OF THESE [VOWS] DO THEY REQUIRE TO SEEK ABSOLUTION.[6] BUT IF A REQUEST FOR ABSOLUTION IS PREFERRED, THEY ARE PUNISHED AND TREATED STRICTLY: THIS IS THE VIEW OF R. MEIR, BUT THE SAGES SAY: THEY ARE GIVEN AN OPENING [FOR REGRET] ON OTHER GROUNDS.[7] AND THEY ARE ADMONISHED SO THAT THEY DO NOT TREAT VOWS WITH LEVITY.

GEMARA. This is self-contradictory: You say, OF NONE OF THESE VOWS DO THEY REQUIRE TO SEEK ABSOLUTION;

(1) Viz., 'This be *ḥerem* unto me'. (2) *Ḥerem* meaning net too; i.e., 'I did not vow at all'. (3) *Ḳorban* meaning an offering, and hence applicable to gifts or tribute to the king. (4) Implying that he had consecrated himself to the Lord and needed redemption; v. Lev. XXVII, 1-8. (Rashi). [Or: May I myself be forbidden to you as *ḳorban* (Ran).] (5) [In order to give the impression to the hearer that I am making a vow.] (6) Being invalid, according to the meaning assigned to them. (7) Lit., 'from another place'. I.e., they cannot obtain absolution on the plea that they had attached an unusual significance to their words; for the phrase cf. *supra* 13*b*.

and then you continue: IF A REQUEST FOR ABSOLUTION IS PREFERRED, THEY ARE PUNISHED AND TREATED STRICTLY?[1] —Said Rab Judah, This is its meaning: OF NONE OF THESE VOWS DO THEY REQUIRE TO SEEK ABSOLUTION. This applies however only to a scholar;[2] and when *'am ha-areẓ*[3] applies for absolution, he is punished and treated strictly. Now 'TREATED STRICTLY' is well: it means that we do not suggest an opening for regret.[4] But how are they punished?—As it was taught: If one vowed *neziroth* and then violated his vow: his case is not examined unless he observes his vow for the full period that he had violated it: this is the view of R. Judah. R. Jose said: This applies only to short *neziroth* [i.e., thirty days]; but in the case of a long period of *neziroth*, thirty days are sufficient.[5] R. Joseph said: Since the Rabbis have decreed, his case is not to be examined, if a Beth din[6] does attend to it [before time], it does not act right [and must be reprimanded]. R. Aḥa b. Jacob said: It is banned.[7]

BUT THE SAGES SAY: THEY ARE GIVEN AN OPENING [FOR] REGRET etc. It was taught: Never make a practice of vowing, for ultimately you will trespass in the matter of oaths,[8] and do not frequent an *'am ha-areẓ*, for eventually he will give you *ṭebalim*;[9] and do not associate with a priest, an *'am ha-areẓ*, for ultimately he will give you *terumah* to eat;[10] and do not converse much with

(1) The first implies that they are altogether invalid, whereas the second implies that they are valid vows. (2) Who is careful about making vows. (3) V. Glos. (4) When one desired absolution, the Rabbi usually suggested grounds for granting it; here, however, such aid was to be withheld. (5) E.g., if he had vowed to be a *nazir* a hundred days, violated his vow for fifty days, and then desired absolution, it is enough to observe thirty days only, and then he is absolved. Here too he is punished in this way. (6) Lit., 'house of law': Jewish court of law. Any three persons could constitute themselves a Beth din, by request, and it is to such a constituted body of laymen that this dictum probably refers. [Absolution could be granted either by one Rabbi or by three laymen; *infra*.] (7) On the term used *shamta*, v. *supra* p. 17, n. 2. (8) Which are more stringent. (9) *Ṭebel*, pl. *ṭebalim*, produce from which no tithes have been set aside. (10) According to this reading the exhortation is to a *zar*. The Ran however reads: '*unclean* terumah', which was forbidden even to a priest, in which case the exhortation is to a priest.

women, as this will ultimately lead you to unchastity.[1] R. Aḥa of the school of[2] R. Josiah said: He who gazes at a woman eventually comes to sin, and he who looks even at a woman's heel will beget degenerate children. R. Joseph said: This applies even to one's own wife when she is a *niddah*.[3] R. Simeon b. Laḳish said: 'Heel' that is stated means the unclean part, which is directly opposite the heel.

It was taught: [*And Moses said unto the people, fear not: for God is come to prove you,*] *that his fear may be before your faces:*[4] By this is meant shamefacedness; *that ye sin not*[5]—this teaches that shamefacedness leads to fear of sin: hence it was said[6] that it is a good sign if a man is shamefaced.[7] Others say: No man who experiences shame[8] will easily sin; and he who is not shamefaced—it is certain that his ancestors were not present at Mount Sinai.

R. Joḥanan b. Dahabai said: The Ministering Angels told me four things: People are born lame because they [*sc.* their parents] overturned their table [i.e., practised unnatural cohabitation]; dumb, because they kiss 'that place'; deaf, because they converse during cohabitation; blind, because they look at 'that place'. But this contradicts the following: Imma Shalom[9] was asked: Why are [20*b*] thy children so exceedingly beautiful? She replied: [Because] he [my husband] 'converses' with me neither at the beginning nor at the end of the night, but [only] at midnight; and when he 'converses', he uncovers a handbreadth and covers a hand-

(1) The present statement is not meant to be derogatory to women, who were held in high esteem, but conditioned by the prevailing laxity in sexual matters which characterised many of the ancient peoples. V. Herford *Talmud and Apocrypha*, pp. 163ff. (2) Berabbi or Beribbi is a contraction of Be Rab, belonging to the school of an eminent teacher (Jast.). (3) A woman during her period of menstruation and seven days following. (4) Ex. XX, 17. (5) Ibid. (6) This indicates a very ancient tradition; v. Frankel, Z.: *Darke ha-Mishnah*, p. 305; Bacher, *Tradition und Tradenten*, pp. 160, 171 seqq. (7) Cf. Yeb. 79*a*, where a sense of shame is said to be one of the characteristics of the Jew; also Ab. V, 20, where 'shamefacedness' is contrasted with 'bold-facedness', i.e., impudence or insolence. (8) I.e., who is not hardened or callous, but feels humiliated when he does wrong. (9) The wife of R. Eliezer b. Hyrḳanos, a sister of Gamaliel II.

breadth, and is as though he were compelled by a demon. And when I asked him, What is the reason for this [for choosing midnight], he replied, So that I may not think of another woman,[1] lest my children be as bastards.[2]—There is no difficulty: this refers to conjugal matters;[3] the other refers to other matters.

R. Joḥanan said: The above is the view of R. Joḥanan b. Dahabai; but our Sages said: The *halachah* is not as R. Joḥanan b. Dahabai, but a man may do whatever he pleases with his wife [at intercourse]: A parable: Meat which comes from the abattoir, may be eaten salted, roasted, cooked or seethed; so with fish from the fishmonger.[4] Amemar said: Who are the 'Ministering Angels'? The Rabbis. For should you maintain it literally, why did R. Joḥanan say that the *halachah* is not as R. Joḥanan b. Dahabai, seeing that the angels know more about the formation of the fetus than we? And why are they designated 'Ministering Angels'?—Because they are as distinguished as they.[5]

A woman once came before Rabbi and said, 'Rabbi! I set a table before my husband, but he overturned it.' Rabbi replied: 'My daughter! the Torah hath permitted thee to him—what then can *I* do for thee?' A woman once came before Rab and complained, 'Rabbi! I set a table before my husband, but he overturned it.' Rab replied: Wherein does it differ from a fish?[6]

And that ye seek not after your own heart.[7] [Deducing] from this Rabbi taught: One may not drink out of one goblet and think of another.[8] Rabina said: This is necessary only when both are his wives.

And I will purge out from among you the rebels, and them that transgress

(1) At the beginning of the night women are still going about in the streets; at the end, before morning, they are abroad again. (2) Figuratively, of course. This shews that they did converse. (3) That are permitted. (4) [This parable serves to express the absence of reserve that may characterise the mutual and intimate relationship of husband and wife without offending the laws of chastity.] (5) Rashi (in Ḳid. 71*a*): they are distinguished in dress, being robed in white and turbaned; cf. passage *a.l.*; Shab. 25*b*. (6) V. *supra*. (7) Num. XV, 39. (8) Whilst cohabiting with one woman to think of another.

against me.[1] R. Levi said: This refers to children belonging to the following nine categories: children of fear,[2] of outrage, of a hated wife, one under a ban,[3] of a woman mistaken for another,[4] of strife,[5] of intoxication [during intercourse], of a mentally divorced wife,[6] of promiscuity, and of a brazen woman.[7] But that is not so: for did not R. Samuel b. Naḥmani say in the name of R. Jonathan: One who is summoned to his marital duty by his wife will beget children such as were not to be found even in the generation of Moses? For it is said, *Take you wise men, and* understanding [*and known among your tribes, and I will make them rulers over you*];[8] and it is written, *So I took the chiefs of your tribes, wise men and known*[9] but 'understanding' is not mentioned.[10] But it is also written, *Issachar is a large-boned ass;*[11] whilst elsewhere it is written, *And of the children of Issachar, which were men that had understanding of the times?*[12]—[It is virtuous] only when the wife ingratiates herself [with her husband].[13]

(1) Ezek. XX, 38. (2) When a husband imposes himself upon his wife by force; Asheri reads: children of a maidservant (אמה instead of אימה); v. *MGWJ* 1934 p. 136, n. 1. (3) A person under a ban was forbidden to cohabit. (4) Having intended to cohabit with one of his wives, he cohabited with another. (5) Not a hated wife, but one with whom he had just then quarrelled. (6) I.e., when her husband has decided to divorce her. (7) One who openly demands her conjugal rights. (8) Deut. I, 13. (9) Ibid. I, 15. (10) The Heb. נבונים is here taken to denote the highest degree of wisdom—but such could not be found. (11) Gen. XLIX, 14; cf. Gen. XXX, 16-18. The allusion is to the legend that Leah heard the braying of Jacob's ass, and so came out of the tent and said to Jacob, *thou must come in unto me*. She had thus demanded her conjugal rights. (12) I Chron. XII, 33; though such men were not to be found in the days of Moses. This was Leah's reward; thus proving that it is meritorious for a woman to demand her rights. (13) She may shew her desires, as did Leah, who merely invited Jacob into her tent, but not explicitly demand their gratification.

NEDARIM

CHAPTER III

MISHNAH. FOUR TYPES OF VOWS HAVE THE SAGES INVALIDATED;[1] VIZ., VOWS INCENTIVE, VOWS OF EXAGGERATION, VOWS IN ERROR, AND VOWS [BROKEN] UNDER PRESSURE.[2] VOWS INCENTIVE: E.G., IF ONE WAS SELLING AN ARTICLE AND SAID, 'ḲONAM THAT I DO NOT LET YOU HAVE IT FOR LESS THAN A SELA''; AND THE OTHER REPLIED, 'ḲONAM THAT I DO NOT GIVE YOU MORE THAN A SHEḲEL' —[21*a*] BOTH ARE AGREED UPON THREE DENARII.[3]

GEMARA. FOUR VOWS HAVE THE RABBIS INVALIDATED etc. R. Abba b. Memel said to R. Ammi: You have told us in the name of R. Judah Nesi'ah:[4] Which Tanna holds this view?— R. Judah, who said on the authority of R. Ṭarfon: Neither is a *nazir*, because *neziroth* must be expressed with certainty.[5] Raba said: You may even say, The Rabbis. Does the Mishnah teach, both [*subsequently*] agreed—it teaches, BOTH ARE AGREED.[6]

Rabina asked R. Ashi: If he demanded more than a *sela'*, and the other offered less than a *sheḳel*,[7] is it a [valid] vow, or still a matter of incitement?[8]—He replied, We have learnt this. If one was urging his neighbour to eat in his house, and he answered: '*Ḳonam* if I enter your house,' or 'if I drink a drop of cold water', he may enter his house and drink cold water, because he only meant

(1) Lit., 'permitted'. (2) This is explained *infra* 27*a*. (3) A *sela'* = two *sheḳels* = four *denarii*. (4) R. Judah, the Prince II. (5) 19*b*. Thus here too, in the case of the incentive vow, since the two parties are dependent upon another, the vow is invalid. (6) Thus, neither meant the vow seriously at all; but the conditional vow of *neziroth* was really meant. (7) [I.e., the vendor demanded a *sela'* and a *peruṭah* (v. Glos.) and the buyer offered a *sheḳel* minus a *peruṭah* (Ran).] (8) Since each was so exact, it may be that the sum was literally meant by both, and the vow likewise.

eating and drinking in general.[1] But why? Did he not state, a *drop* of cold water? Hence this is the usual manner of speech.[2] Thus here too: this is the usual manner of speech![3]—He said to him: [21*b*] How compare? In the case of cold water, 'the righteous promise little and perform much';[4] but here, it is really doubtful whether he [the vendor] implied that he would take less than a *sela'*, and [the buyer] that he would give more than a *shekel*,[5] and it is [a vow of] incitement, or perhaps, each spoke literally, and it is a valid [vow]? This problem remains unsolved.

Rab Judah said in R. Assi's name: For these four vows [formal] absolution must be sought from a Sage. When I stated this before Samuel, he observed: The Tanna teaches, FOUR VOWS HAVE THE SAGES INVALIDATED,[6] yet you say, absolution must be sought from a Sage! R. Joseph reported this discussion in the following version: Rab Judah said in R. Assi's name: A Sage may remit only such [vows] as are similar to these four. Thus in his view mere regret is not given as an opening [for absolution].[7] A man once came before R. Huna [for absolution]. He asked him: 'Are you still of the same mind?' and he replied 'No!' Thereupon he absolved him. A man once came before Rabbah son of R. Huna, who asked him: 'Had ten men been present to appease you just then, would you have vowed?' On his replying 'No!' he absolved him. It was taught: R. Judah said: We ask him, 'Are you still of the same mind?' If he answers, 'No!' he is absolved. R. Ishmael son of R. Jose said on his father's authority: We say to him: 'Had ten men been

(1) But did not intend his words literally. (2) For emphasis stating 'a drop of water', when in reality something substantial was meant. (3) For emphasis: but neither meant his words literally, hence the vow is invalid. (4) When the would-be host urged him to partake just a little, he understood that a full meal was intended, and therefore made the vow in the terms he did, meaning, however, to debar himself only from a substantial meal. (5) Both intending to compromise on three *denarii*. (6) I.e., they have no binding power at all. (7) A definite reason for absolution is necessary, based on a fact which was unknown when the vow was made; consequently, it may be regarded as having been made in error. But if the only reason for cancellation is that the vower regrets it, absolution cannot be granted, v. *infra* 77*b*.

present to appease you just then, would you have vowed?' If he replies in the negative, absolution is granted.

(Mnemonic: *Assi and Eleazar, Johanan and Jannai*).[1]

A man once came before R. Assi. He asked him: 'Do you now regret [that you ever vowed]?' and he replied, 'Do I not?' Thereupon he absolved him.[2] A man once came before R. Eleazar. He said to him, 'Do you desire your vow?'[3] He replied: 'Had I not been provoked, I certainly would not have desired aught.' 'Let it be as you wish,' answered he. A woman who had subjected her daughter to a vow[4] came before R. Johanan. Said he to her, 'Had you known that your neighbours would say of your daughter, [22a] "If her mother had not seen something shameful[5] in her [behaviour], she would not have put her under a vow without cause"—would you have vowed?' On her replying in the negative, he absolved her. The grandson of R. Jannai the Elder[6] came before him. Said he to him, 'Had you known that [when you vow] your ledger[7] is opened [in heaven] and your deeds examined—would you have vowed?' On his giving a negative reply, he absolved him. R. Abba said: Which verse [teaches this]? *After vows*

(1) A mnemonic is a short phrase or a string of words or letters each consisting of catchwords of statements or incidents, strung together as an aid to the memory. (2) [He holds that mere regret is accepted as ground for revoking a vow, contrary to the view of Rab Assi in the name of Rab Judah, the author of this ruling here being Rabbi Assi, a Palestinian Amora as distinct from the former, who was a Babylonian. (Ran).] (3) Ran: I.e., have you no regret that you ever made the vow except that you wish that it be no longer valid from now, in which case absolution cannot be granted. Rashi: 'Did you fully desire to vow, i.e., were you calm and composed, vowing with full deliberation'—this seems more plausible. (4) Not to benefit from her mother. (5) Lit., 'something best left alone'. (6) Lit., 'the son of the daughter'. *Var. lec.*: Jannai Rabbah, the Great. He was a Palestinian amora of the first generation (second and third generation); to be distinguished from Jannai the Younger, a Palestinian amora of the fourth generation. (7) The notion that there is a Heavenly ledger in which man's doings are recorded (cf. Aboth, III, 20) is probably connected with the idea of the Book of Life, in which are inscribed on the Judgment Day of New Year those who are to be granted life for the ensuing year (cf. R.H. 15*b*). The *Sefer Hasidim* (13th century) observes that God is in no need of a book of records: 'the Torah speaks the language of man', i.e., figuratively. Cf. Aboth, (Sonc. ed.,) p. 12, n. 9.

cometh examination.[1] But though R. Jannai proposed this as a ground for absolution, we may not do so.[2] Nor do we suggest the following, which Rabbah b. Bar Ḥanah related in R. Joḥanan's name: What opening did R. Gamaliel give to a certain old man? *There is that speaketh like the piercings of a sword; but the tongue of the wise is health.*[3] He who speaketh [a vow] is worthy of being pierced by the sword, but that the tongue of the wise [i.e., absolution] healeth. Nor do we suggest the following, viz., what was taught, R. Nathan said: One who vows is as though he built a high place,[4] and he who fulfils it is as though he sacrificed thereon. Now the first [half] may be given as an opening,[5] but as for the second,—Abaye maintained: We suggest [it]; Raba said: We do not suggest [it]. This is the version of the discussion as recited by R. Kahana. R. Ṭabyomi reported it thus: We may not suggest the latter half;[6] but as for the first,—Abaye maintained: We suggest [it]; Raba said: We do not. The law is that neither the first [half] nor the second may be proposed.

Nor do we suggest the following dictum of Samuel, viz., Even when one fulfils his vow he is called wicked. R. Abba said: Which verse [teaches this]? *But if thou shalt* forbear *to vow, it shall be no sin in thee.*[7] And [the meaning of] forbearance is learnt from forbearance as expressed elsewhere. Here it is written, *But if thou shalt* forbear *to vow;* and there it is written, *There the wicked* forbear *from insolence.*[8] R. Joseph said: We too have learnt so. [If one says:] 'As the vows of the righteous,' his words are of no effect. [But if he says:] 'As the vows of the wicked,' he has vowed in respect of a nazirite vow and a sacrifice.[9]

R. Samuel b. Naḥmani said in the name of R. Jonathan: He who

(1) Prov. XX, 25. (2) Because it terrifies one too much, and makes him ready to express a regret which he may not feel. (3) Ibid. XII, 18. (4) For sacrifice—this being forbidden since the building of Solomon's Temple. (5) Merely building a high place without sacrificing is not so heinous an offence, and therefore the suggestion is not so terrifying. (6) All agreeing that it is too frightening. (7) Deut. XXIII, 23. (8) Job III, 17. Thus forbearing being employed of the wicked in the latter verse, its use in the former shews that he who vows is also so dubbed. (9) *Supra* 9a.

loses his temper is exposed to all the torments of Gehenna,[1] for it is written, *Therefore remove anger from thy heart; thus wilt thou put away evil from thy flesh.*[2] Now 'evil' can only mean Gehenna, as it is written, *The Lord hath made all things for himself; yea, even the wicked for the day of evil.*[3] Moreover, he is made to suffer from abdominal troubles, as it is written, *But the Lord shall give thee there a trembling heart, and failing of eyes, and sorrow of mind.*[4] Now what causes failing eyes and a sorrowful mind? Abdominal troubles.

When 'Ulla went up to Palestine,[5] he was joined by two inhabitants of Ḥozai,[6] one of whom arose and slew the other. The murderer asked of 'Ulla: 'Did I do well?' 'Yes,' he replied; 'moreover, cut his throat clean across.'[7] When he came before R. Joḥanan, he asked him, 'Maybe, God forbid, I have strengthened the hands of transgressors?' He replied, 'You have saved your life.'[8] Then R. Joḥanan wondered: *The Lord shall give them there an infuriated heart*[9] refers to Babylon?[10]—'Ulla replied, 'We had not yet [22b] crossed the Jordan [into Palestine].'

Rabbah son of R. Huna said: He who loses his temper, even the Divine Presence is unimportant in his eyes, as it is written, *The wicked, through the pride of his countenance, will not seek God; God is not in all his thoughts.*[11] R. Jeremiah of Difti[12] said: He forgets his learning and waxes ever more stupid, as it is written, *For anger resteth in the bosom of fools;*[13] and it is written, *But the fool layeth open his folly.*[14] R. Naḥman b. Isaac said: It is certain that his sins out-

(1) V. p. 19, n. 6. (2) Ecc. XI, 10. (3) Prov. XVI, 4. This is understood to mean Gehenna. (4) Deut. XXVIII, 65. (5) 'Ulla was a prominent Palestinian amora of the latter part of the third century and the beginning of the fourth. He frequently visited Babylonia, in pursuance of the general policy of maintaining intellectual intercourse between these two great centres, and his learning was very highly esteemed there; Bacher, *Ag. Bab. Amor.* pp. 93-97. (6) [Or Be-Ḥozae, the modern Khuzistan, province S.W. Persia, Obermeyer, *Die Landschaft Babylonien*, pp. 204ff.] (7) Fearing that disapproval would endanger his own life; moreover, he wished to hasten his death. (8) The action was excusable, being in self-defence. (9) Ibid. (10) How then could one Jew become so angry with another in Palestine as to slay him? (11) Ps. X, 4. (12) V. p. 214, n. 2. (13) Ecc. VII, 9. (14) Prov. XIII, 16.

number his merits, as it is written, *And a furious man aboundeth in transgressions.*[1]

R. Adda son of R. Ḥanina said: Had not Israel sinned, only the Pentateuch and the Book of Joshua would have been given them, [the latter] because it records the disposition of Palestine [among the tribes].[2] Whence is this known? *For much wisdom proceedeth from much anger.*[3]

R. Assi said: Absolution is not granted for[4] [a vow in the name of] the God of Israel, except [the following]: '*Ḳonam* be any benefit [by the God of Israel] my wife has of me, because she stole my purse or beat my child'; and it was subsequently learnt that she had done neither.[5]

A woman once came before R. Assi. He asked her, 'How did you vow?' She replied, 'By the God of Israel.' Said he to her, 'Had you vowed by *mohi*, which is a mere substitute,[6] I would absolve you. Now that you did not vow by *mohi*, but by the God of Israel, I will not absolve you.'

R. Kahana visited[7] R. Joseph's home. The latter said to him, 'Eat something'; to which he replied, 'No, by the Master of all, I will not taste anything.' R. Joseph answered, 'No, by the Master of all, you may not eat.' Now R. Kahana rightly said, 'No, by the Master of all, etc.' [to strengthen his vow]; but why did R. Joseph repeat this?—This is what he said: 'Since you have said, "No, by the Master of all", you may not eat.'[8]

Raba said in R. Naḥman's name: The law is: Regret may be made an opening [for absolution], and absolution is granted for [a vow made in the name of] the God of Israel.

Raba was praising R. Seḥorah to R. Naḥman as a great man.

(1) Prov. XXIX, 22. (2) But the other books, consisting mostly of the rebukings of the prophets, would have been unnecessary. (3) Ecc. I, 18; i.e., the anger of God caused Him to send many prophets with their wise teachings.—We learn through error, and sin becomes the occasion of a fuller Revelation by God. (4) Lit., 'no (request for absolution) is attended to in the case of'. (5) [This exception is made for the sake of restoring peace in the home.] (6) V. Mishnah, *supra* 10*a*. (7) Lit., 'happened (to be) at'. (8) I.e., Even if you desire, because one cannot be absolved from such an oath.

Thereupon R. Naḥman said: 'When he comes to you, bring him to me.' Now he [R. Seḥorah] had a vow for absolution, so he went before R. Naḥman, who asked him: 'Did you vow bearing this[1] in mind?' 'Yes,' he replied. 'Or this?' 'Yes.' This being repeated a number of times, R. Naḥman became angry and exclaimed, 'Go to your room!'[2] R. Seḥorah departed, and found an opening for himself: Rabbi said: Which is the right course that man should choose for himself? That which he feels to be honourable to himself, and brings him honour from mankind.[3] But now, since R. Naḥman has become angry, I did not vow on this understanding. He thus absolved himself.

R. Simeon son of Rabbi had a vow for absolution. He went before the Rabbis, who asked him, 'Did you vow bearing this in mind?' He replied, 'Yes.' 'Or this?' 'Yes.' [This was repeated] several times, [23a] and the Rabbis passed wearily to and fro 'twixt sun and shade.[4] Said Boṭnith, the son of Abba Saul b. Boṭnith, to him, 'Did you vow in order that the Rabbis should thus wearily pass from sun to shade and from shade to sun?' 'No,' replied he. Thereupon they absolved him.

R. Ishmael son of R. Jose had a vow for absolution. He went before the Rabbis, who asked him, 'Did you vow bearing this in mind?' 'Even so,' replied he. 'Or this?' 'Yes.' This was repeated several times. A fuller, seeing that he was paining the Rabbis, smote him with his basket.[5] Said he, 'I did not vow to be beaten by a fuller,' and so he absolved himself. R. Aḥa of Difti objected to Rabina: But this was an unexpected fact, as it had not occurred to him that a fuller would smite him, and we learnt: An unexpected fact may not be given as an opening?[6]—He replied: This is not unexpected, because scoffers[7] are common who vex the Rabbis.[8]

(1) Some fact mentioned. (2) I cannot absolve you. (3) V. Aboth II, 1 (Sonc. ed.) p. 11, n. 2 and 5. (4) In an endeavour to find grounds for absolution. (5) The Rabbis appear to have held open session. (6) V. *infra* 64*a*. The fact must have been in existence, when the vow was made, but overlooked. If, however, it occurred only subsequently, it cannot be a ground for absolution. (7) *Apiḳora* (*paḳar*) etymologically should mean a loose, unbridled person. Its phonetic similarity to Epicurus, the philosopher, stamped it with the meaning

Abaye's wife had a daughter. *He* declared, '[She must marry] one of *my* relations,' and *she* maintained, 'one of *mine*'. So he said to her: '[All] benefit from me be forbidden to you if you disregard my wish and marry her to one of your relations.' She went, ignored his desire, and married her to her relation. [Subsequently Abaye] went before R. Joseph [for absolution], who asked him: 'Had you known that she would disregard your wish and marry her to her relation, would you have vowed?' He answered, 'No,' and R. Joseph absolved him. But is such permitted?[1]—Yes; and it was taught: A man once imposed a vow on his wife not to make the festival pilgrimage [to Jerusalem]; but she disregarded his wish, and did go. He went to R. Jose [for absolution], who said to him, 'Had you known that she would disregard your wish and make the journey, would you have imposed the vow on her?' He answered, 'No,' and R. Jose absolved him.

MISHNAH. R. ELIEZER B. JACOB SAID: ALSO HE[2] WHO WISHES TO SUBJECT HIS FRIEND TO A VOW TO EAT WITH HIM, SHOULD DECLARE: 'EVERY VOW WHICH I MAY MAKE IN THE FUTURE SHALL BE NULL'. [HIS VOWS ARE THEN INVALID,] PROVIDING THAT HE REMEMBERS THIS AT THE TIME OF THE VOW.

GEMARA. But since he says, 'Every vow which I may make in the future shall be null,' he will surely not listen to him[3] and not come to [eat with] him?—[23*b*] The text is defective, and this is what was taught: He who desires his friend to eat with him, and

of sceptic, heretic, and that is its probable meaning in Sanh. XI, 1, where an *apikoros* is excluded from the world to come. The definition given in the Gemara, 99*b*, viz., one who is scornful of the Rabbis, which is the same as it bears here, was in all probability an extension of its meaning, due to feuds between the Rabbis and some sections of the people. (8) And as their adherents naturally try to punish them, the incident could have been anticipated, and therefore is not regarded as unexpected

(1) The vow itself providing cause for absolution. (2) The friend. (3) This too is an example of a vow of incitement; v. Gemara.

after urging him, imposes a vow upon him, it is 'a vow of incitement' [and hence invalid]. And he who desires that none of his vows made during the year shall be valid, let him stand at the beginning of the year and declare, 'Every vow which I may make in the future shall be null.[1] [HIS VOWS ARE THEN INVALID,] PROVIDING THAT HE REMEMBERS THIS AT THE TIME OF THE VOW. But if he remembers, he has cancelled the declaration and confirmed the vow?[2]—Abaye answered: Read: providing that it is *not* remembered at the time of the vow. Raba said, After all, it is as we said originally.[3] Here the circumstances are e.g., that one stipulated at the beginning of the year, but does not know in reference to what. Now he vows. Hence, if he remembers [the stipulation] and he declares: 'I vow in accordance with my original intention', his vow has no reality. But if he does not declare thus, he has cancelled his stipulation and confirmed his vow.

R. Huna b. Ḥinena wished to lecture thereon [*sc.* anticipatory cancellation] at the public session. But Raba remonstrated with him: The Tanna has *intentionally* obscured the law,[4] in order that vows should not be lightly treated, whilst you desire to teach it publicly!

The scholars propounded: Do the Rabbis disagree with R. Eliezer b. Jacob or not?[5] And should you say that they differ, is the *halachah* like him or not?[6]—Come and hear: For we learnt: If one

(1) This may have provided a support for the custom of reciting *Kol Nidre* (a formula for dispensation of vows) prior to the Evening Service of the Day of Atonement (Ran.). The context makes it perfectly obvious that only vows, where the maker abjures benefit from aught, or imposes an interdict of his own property upon his neighbour, are referred to. V. *J.E.* s.v. *Kol Nidre.* Though the beginning of the year (New Year) is mentioned here, the Day of Atonement was probably chosen on account of its great solemnity. But *Kol Nidre* as part of the ritual is later than the Talmud, and, as seen from the following statement about R. Huna b. Ḥinena, the law of revocation in advance was not made public. (2) Since, when vowing, he knows of his previous declaration, he obviously disregards it, as otherwise he would not vow at all. (3) The received text is correct. (4) By giving a defective text. This implies that here, at least, the lacuna is not accidental, due to faulty transmission, but deliberate; cf. p. 2, n. 3. (5) But regard this as a binding vow. (6) Since the Mishnah teaches it as an individual opinion.

says to his neighbour, [24a] '*Ḳonam* that I do not benefit from you, if you do not accept for your son a *kor* of wheat and two barrels of wine,'—his neighbour may annul his vow without [recourse to] a Sage, by saying: 'Did you vow for any other purpose but to honour me? *This* [non-acceptance] is my honour.' Thus, it is only because he asserts, 'This is my honour'; but otherwise, it is [a binding] vow. Whose view is this? If R. Eliezer b. Jacob's,—it is a vow of incitement?[1] Hence it must be the Rabbis,[2] thus proving that they disagree with R. Eliezer!—[No.] After all, it may be R. Eliezer b. Jacob's view: he admits that this is a [real] vow, for he [who makes it] says [in effect], 'I am not a dog, that I should benefit from you without your benefiting from me.'

Come and hear: If one says to his neighbour, '*Ḳonam* that you benefit not from me, if you do not give my son a *kor* of wheat and two barrels of wine,'—R. Meir rules: He is [so] forbidden until he gives; but the Rabbis maintain: He too can annul his vow without a Sage by declaring: 'I regard it as though I have received it.' Thus, it is only because he says, 'I regard it as though I have received it'; but otherwise it is [a valid] vow. Whose view is this? If R. Eliezer b. Jacob's,—but it is a vow of incitement. Hence it must be the Rabbis'; thus proving that they disagree with him!—[No.] Verily, it may be R. Eliezer b. Jacob's view: he admits that this is a [real] vow, for he [who makes it] says, 'I am not a king to benefit you without your benefiting me.'

Mar Ḳashisha son of R. Ḥisda said to R. Ashi, Come and hear: VOWS [BROKEN] UNDER PRESSURE: If one subjected his neighbour to a vow to dine with him,[3] and then he or his son fell sick, or a river prevented him [from coming to him]. But otherwise the vow is binding. Whose view is this? If R. Eliezer b. Jacob's,—but it is [a vow of] incitement. Hence it must be the Rabbis', which proves that they disagree with him!—[No.] This may be R. Eliezer b. Jacob's view. Do you think that the inviter imposed the vow upon the invited? On the contrary, the invited imposed

(1) Which is invalid in any case. (2) The text is thus emended by BaḤ. (3) Saying, 'You are forbidden to benefit from me if you do not eat with me'.

the vow upon the inviter. Thus: He said to his neighbour, 'Do you invite me to your banquet?' 'Yes,' replied he. 'Then make a vow to that effect.' So he vowed, and then he [the person invited] or his son fell sick, or was kept back by a river; such are vows [broken] under pressure.

Come and hear: R. Eliezer b. Jacob went even further [in his definition of vows of incitement]: If one says to his neighbour, '*Ḳonam* that I do not benefit from you if you will not be my guest and partake of fresh bread and a hot drink with me'; and the latter remonstrated in his turn—such too are vows of incitement.[1] But the Sages did not admit this. Now, to what does this disagreement refer? Surely, [24*b*] even to the first [illustration given by R. Eliezer b. Jacob]! This proves that the Rabbis dispute his ruling [in its entirety]. This proves it.[2] What is our final conclusion on the matter?[3]—Come and hear: For R. Huna said: The *halachah* is like R. Eliezer b. Jacob.[4]

MISHNAH. VOWS OF EXAGGERATION: WHEN ONE SAYS, 'ḲONAM, IF I DID NOT SEE ON THIS ROAD AS MANY AS DEPARTED FROM EGYPT,' OR 'IF I DID NOT SEE A SERPENT LIKE THE BEAM OF AN OLIVE PRESS.'

GEMARA. It was taught: Vows of exaggeration are invalid,

(1) [Although the fact that the invitation was so carefully worded, and that the other remonstrated would tend to indicate that the vower was in earnest.] (2) So cur. edd. Asheri: No. The disagreement refers only to the latter example. Accordingly, the next question: what is our final conclusion, still refers to the same problem, whether the Rabbis disagree or not. (3) Having proved that they disagree, whose view is law? V. preceding note. (4) Ran: The answerer knew that R. Huna referred to the first too, or assumed that he would be referring to the Mishnah, which was well known by all, rather than the Baraitha, which was not so well known. Alternatively, the whole point of the question whether the Rabbis disagree is to know the correct *halachah*, for since they are in the majority it may not be as R. Eliezer b. Jacob. Now, however, that R. Huna gave his ruling that the *halachah* is as R. Eliezer b. Jacob in the whole matter, it makes no difference whether the Rabbis disagree with him or not.

but oaths of such a nature are binding. How are such oaths possible? Shall we say that one said, 'I swear [so and so] if I have not seen etc.'—he said nothing![1]—Abaye answered: When one declares, 'I swear that I did see' etc.[2] Raba objected: If so, why teach it?[3] Moreover, it is taught parallel to vows![4] But, said Raba: When one says, 'May [all] the fruit in the world be forbidden me on oath if I did not see on this road as many as departed from Egypt.' Rabina said to R. Ashi: Perhaps this man saw an ant nest and designated them[5] 'those who left Egypt', his oath thus being genuine?—[25*a*] He replied, One who swears, swears in our sense, and we do not think of an ant nest. Now, does one never swear in his own sense? But it was taught: When an oath is administered, he [the man swearing] is admonished: 'Know that we do not adjure you according to your own mind, but according to our mind[6] and the mind of the Court.' Now, what does this exclude? Surely the case of one who gave [his creditor] checkers [tokens in game] and [mentally] dubbed them coins; and since he is admonished, 'according to our intention,' it follows that [otherwise] one may swear in his own sense?—No. It excludes such an incident as Raba's cane. A man with a monetary claim upon his neighbour once came before Raba, demanding of the debtor, 'Come and pay me.' 'I have repaid you,' pleaded he. 'If so,' said Raba to him, 'go and swear to him that you have repaid.' Thereupon he went and brought a [hollow] cane, placed the money therein, and came before the Court, walking and leaning on it. [Before swearing] he said to the plaintiff: 'Hold the cane in your hand'. He then took a scroll of the Law and swore that he had repaid him all that he [the creditor] held in his hand.[7] The creditor thereupon broke the cane in his rage and the money poured out on the ground; it was thus seen that he had [literally] sworn to the truth.[8]

(1) He did not complete his sentence. (2) It is then not regarded as an intentionally false oath, meriting punishment, but as an oath of exaggeration. (3) It is obvious. (4) Just as vows seek to impose an interdict, so do these oaths too. (5) On account of their large number. (6) [In Shebu. 29*b*. the reading is 'the mind of the Omnipresent'.] (7) In his (the debtor's) possession i.e., all that he claimed of him. (8) Hence the exhortation is needed to exclude such oaths, as

But even so, does one never swear in his own sense? But it was taught: Thus we find that when Moses adjured the children of Israel in the plains of Moab, he said unto them, 'Know that I do not adjure you in your sense, but in mine, and in that of the Omnipresent', as it is written, *Neither with you only* etc.[1] Now what did Moses say to Israel? Surely this: Lest you transgress my words[2] and then say, 'We swore in our own sense'; therefore he exhorted them: [swear] in my sense. What does this exclude: surely the naming of idols 'god'? This proves that one does sometimes swear in his own sense.—No. Idols too are called 'god', as it is written, *And against all the gods of Egypt I will execute judgment.*[3] Then let him adjure them to fulfil the commands?—That might imply the commands of the King. Then let him adjure them to fulfil *all* the commands?—That might imply [the precept of] fringes,[4] for a Master said, The precept of fringes is equal to all the [other] precepts of the Torah.[5] But why did not Moses simply adjure the Israelites to fulfil the Torah?[6]—Because that would imply one Torah only.[7] Then why not adjure them to fulfil the Toroth?[8]—That might mean the Torah of the meal-offering, the Torah of the sin-offering, the Torah of the trespass-offering.[9] Then why not impose an oath to fulfil the *whole* Torah?—The whole Torah might mean merely to refrain from idolatry, as it was taught: Idolatry is so

the defendant may really believe that he is swearing truly. But no person regards his oath as true when he mentally attaches a particular meaning to his words.

(1) Deut. XXIX, 13; i.e., not merely according to your thoughts. (2) [So BaḤ. cur. edd. 'lest you do something'.] (3) Ex. XII, 12. (4) Num. XV, 38. (5) Because it is written, *and it shall be unto you for a fringe, that ye may look upon it, and remember* all *the commandments of the Lord.* Ibid. 39. (6) Instead of imposing an oath against idol-worship, which, as shewn, is ambiguous. (7) The written Law, but not the Oral law. The former is the Bible, more especially the Pentateuch, while the latter is the whole body of tradition and Rabbinical development thereof. It is generally assumed that the Oral Law was the matter in dispute between the Pharisees, who accepted it, and the Sadducees, who rejected it. Weiss, *Dor,* I, 116 *seq.*; Halevy, *Doroth,* I, 3, 360 *seq.* denies this *in toto,* and maintains that the Sadducees were purely a political party that rejected religious teaching altogether, and only later, through force of circumstances, attempted some interpretation of Scripture. (8) Pl. of Torah. (9) Each of which is referred to a 'torah': Lev. VI, 7, 18; VII, 1.

grave a sin that the rejection thereof is as the fulfilment of the whole Torah. Then why not impose an oath to observe the prohibition against idolatry and the whole Torah; or to fulfil the 613 precepts? —Moses used a general expression without troubling [to enumerate details].[1]

OR IF I DID NOT SEE A SERPENT LIKE THE BEAMS OF AN OLIVE-PRESS. Is this impossible? Was there not a serpent in the days of King Shapur[2] before which thirteen stables of straw were placed, and it swallowed them all?[3]—Samuel answered: He meant 'as *smooth* as a beam etc.' But are not all serpents smooth?—We speak [of one who declared that] its *back* was smooth [not only the neck].[4] Then let him [the Tanna] state 'smooth'?—He thereby informs us in passing that the beams of the olive-press must be smooth. How does this affect the law?—In respect of buying and selling: to tell you that if one sells the beams of an olive-press, the sale is valid only if they are smooth, but not otherwise.[5]

MISHNAH. [25*b*] VOWS IN ERROR: [IF ONE SAYS, 'ḲONAM,] IF I ATE OR DRANK,' AND THEN REMEMBERED THAT HE HAD; OR, 'IF I EAT OR DRINK,' AND THEN FORGOT [HIS VOW] AND ATE OR DRANK; [OR] 'ḲONAM BE ANY BENEFIT WHICH MY WIFE HAS OF ME, BECAUSE SHE STOLE MY PURSE OR BEAT MY CHILD,' AND IT WAS SUBSEQUENTLY LEARNT THAT SHE HAD NOT BEATEN HIM NOR STOLEN; ALL THESE

(1) The text of the whole passage is in some disorder; the translation is of the text as emended by BaḤ; for further notes v. Shebu. (Sonc. ed.) pp. 159ff. (2) Shapur I, a contemporary of Samuel and King of Persia. (3) This question assumes that the comparison is in point of size.—Aruch reads: thirteen hides full of straw. Rashi in Shebu. 29*b* explains that it was a man-eating serpent; hot coals were concealed in the straw, and these killed it. [This is reminiscent of the Apocryphal story of Daniel and the Dragon.] (4) The backs of serpents are not smooth but somewhat scaly, caused by hard folds of skin; v. Lewysohn, *Zoologie*, p. 234. (5) A number of other interpretations have been given to the whole passage. Rashi translates: *spotted* like a beam. Ran: *incised* like a beam; and an alternative, based on the Jerusalemi: *square* like a beam, instead of circular. Asheri inclines to the last interpretation.

ARE VOWS IN ERROR. IF A MAN SAW PEOPLE EATING [HIS] FIGS AND SAID TO THEM, 'LET THE FIGS BE A KORBAN TO YOU,' AND THEN DISCOVERED THEM TO BE HIS FATHER OR HIS BROTHERS,[1] WHILE OTHERS WERE WITH THEM TOO—BETH SHAMMAI MAINTAIN: HIS FATHER AND BROTHERS ARE PERMITTED, BUT THE REST ARE FORBIDDEN. BETH HILLEL RULE: ALL ARE PERMITTED.

GEMARA. It was taught: Just as vows in error are permitted, so are oaths in error.[2] What are oaths in error?—E.g., those of R. Kahana and R. Assi. One said, I swear that Rab taught this, whilst the other asserted, I swear that he taught this: thus each swore truthfully according to his belief.

IF A MAN SAW PEOPLE EATING [HIS] FIGS. We learnt elsewhere: The Sabbaths and festivals are suggested as an opening [for regret].[3] Before then the ruling was that for those days the vow is cancelled, but for others it is binding; until R. Akiba taught: A vow which is partially annulled is *entirely* annulled.

Rabbah said: All agree that if he said, 'Had I known that my father was among you I would have declared, "You are all forbidden except my father",' all are forbidden but his father is permitted. They differ only if he asserted, 'Had I known that my father was among you, I would have said, "So-and-so are forbidden and my father is permitted".'[4] [26a] But Raba maintained: All agree that

(1) Whom he would not have prohibited. (2) V. Shebu. 28*b*. (3) E.g., if one made a self-denying vow, the Rabbi may ask him, 'Had you known that this is forbidden on Sabbaths and Festivals, would you have vowed?' Should he answer 'No', he is absolved. (4) In the former instance, the second declaration, apart from excluding his father, does not alter the vow at all, since just as he first vowed 'you are all forbidden', so now too. Therefore it is not regarded as even *partially* annulled. But in the second case, the actual form of the vow is changed from the inclusive 'you are *all* forbidden' to the detailed enumeration 'So-and-so are forbidden', even if the enumeration covered all. Because of these two factors, viz., the exclusion of his father and the change in form in respect to the rest, it is regarded as partially annulled. Thus the view of Beth Hillel is in accordance with R. Akiba's dictum, whilst Beth Shammai's decision agrees with the earlier ruling. In many cases we find Beth Shammai adhering to the older view; cf. Weiss, *Dor*, I, 183.

if he declared, 'Had I known that my father was among you I would have said, "So-and-so are forbidden but my father is permitted",' all are permitted.[1] They are in dispute only if he declared, 'Had I known that my father was among you, I would have said, "You are all forbidden except my father".' Beth Shammai agree with R. Meir, who maintains, one's *first* words are to be reckoned with, and Beth Hillel agree with R. Jose who said, one's last words count.[2]

R. Papa objected to Raba: In what instance did R. Akiba rule that a vow which is *partially* annulled is *entirely* annulled? E.g., [If one said,] '*Ḳonam*, that I do not benefit from any of you,' if one was [subsequently] permitted [to afford him benefit], they are all permitted. [But if he said,] '*Ḳonam* that I do not benefit from A, B, C,' etc.: if the first was [subsequently] permitted, all are permitted; but if the last-named was permitted, he alone is permitted, but the rest are forbidden. As for Rabbah, it is well, [for] he can apply the first clause[3] to one who [in the first instance] enumerated A, B, C, etc.;[4] while the second clause[5] refers to one who [in the first instance] declared, 'to any of you.'[6] But as for yourself:

(1) Even Beth Shammai regard such as a partially annulled vow, and accept R. Akiba's dictum. (2) The dispute refers to his *second* declaration, which is divided into 'first words' and 'last words'. The first words are, 'you are all forbidden'; since these are identical with his earlier declaration, Beth Shammai maintain that his vow has not even been partially annulled. His last words are 'except my father'; since these definitely limit the scope of the earlier declaration, Beth Hillel maintain that the vow has thereby been partially, and consequently entirely, annulled. (3) Viz., '*ḳonam* that I do not benefit from all of you'. (4) Subsequently altering it to the form given in the Mishnah. (5) '*Ḳonam* that I do not benefit from A, B, C', etc. (6) Hence the actual forms given refer to the second declaration. Now, Rabbah maintains that the dispute of Beth Hillel and Beth Shammai, as that of R. Akiba and his predecessors, refers to a case where the second declaration, besides excluding a particular person, differs in form from the first. Hence in the two instances dealt with here it is the view *only* of R. Akiba (and Beth Hillel) that that absolution extends to all; but his predecessors hold that even in these instances absolution is limited to the person definitely excluded. This explanation does not allow for the distinction drawn in the two subdivisions of the second clause, and Raba draws attention to it in his reply.—A number of varying

granted that you can apply the first clause to one who [in his second statement] declared, 'to any of you.'[1] [26b] But as for the second clause, where one enumerated, A, B, C—is this R. Akiba's view [only]: why do the Rabbis disagree therewith? But you say that all agree that the vow is entirely annulled?—Raba answered: Even according to Rabbah, is R. Akiba's ruling satisfactory? How have you explained it: that he said, 'any of you': who then is the '*first*', and who is the '*last*'? But [explain it thus]: The first clause means that he said, 'any of you'; but the second refers e.g., to one who made each dependent on the preceding, vowing, B be as A, C be as B, etc.[2] This may be proved too, for it is taught: if the middle person was permitted, those mentioned after him are [also] permitted, but not those named before.

R. Adda b. Ahaba objected to Raba: '*Ḳonam*, if I taste onions, because they are injurious to the heart': then one said to him, But the wild onion[3] is good for the heart—he is permitted to partake of wild onions, and not only of these, but of all onions. Such a case happened before R. Meir, who gave absolution in respect of all onions. Does it not mean that he declared, 'Had I known that wild onions are good for the heart, I would have vowed: "all onions be forbidden me, but wild onions be permitted"'?[4] —No. This refers to one who declared, 'Had I known that wild onions are good for the heart, I would have vowed, "Such and such onions be forbidden me, but wild onions be permitted"'; and therefore R. Meir's ruling agrees with both R. Akiba and the Rabbis.

interpretations have been given to this passage. The one adopted here is that of Tosaf.

(1) Hence, as explained by Raba above, this ruling is disputed by R. Akiba's predecessors; therefore it is given as an illustration of R. Akiba's view *only*, implying that his predecessors disagree. (2) Therefore if by his second statement A is excluded, the rest are likewise excluded. But if the last-named is excluded, the vow remains in full force with respect to those mentioned earlier. (3) Rashi: the name of a place—probably Cyprus. (4) This contradicts Raba's view that Beth Shammai's ruling, confining absolution only to that explicitly excluded, is in agreement with R. Meir. Here we see that R. Meir himself granted complete absolution.

Rabina objected to Raba: R. Nathan said: A vow may be partly permitted and partly binding. E.g., if one vowed not to eat a basket [of figs], [27a] among which were *shuaḥ*[1] figs, and then declared, 'Had I known that *shuaḥ* figs were among them, I would not have vowed'—the basket of figs is forbidden, but the *shuaḥ* figs are permitted. Then R. Akiba came and taught: A vow which is *partially* annulled is *entirely* annulled. Does it not mean that he declared, 'Had I known that *shuaḥ* figs were among them, I would have vowed: "The black figs and white figs be forbidden, but the *shuaḥ* figs be permitted"?' Yet it is R. Akiba's view only, but the Rabbis dispute it.[2]—No. This refers to one who declared, 'Had I known that *shuaḥ* figs were among them, I would have vowed, "Let the whole basket [of figs] be forbidden, but the *shuaḥ* figs permitted."'

Which Tanna is the authority for the following dictum of the Rabbis? If one vowed simultaneously not to benefit from five men, if he is absolved in respect of one of them, he is absolved in respect of all; but [if he stated,] 'Except one of them,' that one is permitted, but the others are forbidden [to him]. According to Rabbah, the first clause agrees with R. Akiba [only], and the second clause with all.[3] According to Raba, the second clause agrees with the Rabbis [only], and the first clause with all.

MISHNAH. VOWS [BROKEN] UNDER PRESSURE: IF ONE SUBJECTED HIS NEIGHBOUR TO A VOW, TO DINE WITH HIM,[4] AND THEN HE OR HIS SON FELL SICK, OR A RIVER PREVENTED HIM [FROM COMING TO HIM]—SUCH IS A VOW [BROKEN] UNDER PRESSURE.

(1) A species of white figs. (2) This contradicts Raba's view that in such a case there is no dispute. (3) In the first clause it is assumed that his partially revoking statement was, 'Had I known that X was in the group, I would have said, "A, B, C, etc. be forbidden, but X be permitted".' This assumption is based on the *contrast* with the second clause, where *one* was excluded, from which it is assumed that his revoking statement was, 'Had I known . . . I would have declared, "All of you be forbidden etc."' (4) Saying, 'You are forbidden to benefit from me if you do not eat with me'.

GEMARA. A man once deposited his rights[1] at Beth din, and declared: 'If I do not appear within thirty days, these rights shall be void.' Subsequently he was unavoidably prevented from appearing. Thereupon R. Huna ruled: His rights are void. But Rabbah said to him, He was unavoidably prevented, and the Divine Law exempts such, for it is written, *But unto the damsel shalt thou do nothing*.[2] And should you answer, the death penalty is different,[3] but we learnt: VOWS [BROKEN] UNDER PRESSURE: IF ONE SUBJECTED HIS NEIGHBOUR TO A VOW TO DINE WITH HIM, AND THEN HE OR HIS SON FELL SICK, OR A RIVER PREVENTED HIM [FROM COMING TO HIM]—SUCH IS A VOW [BROKEN] UNDER PRESSURE![4]

Now, according to Rabbah, wherein does this differ from what we learnt: [If one said to his wife,] 'Behold! this is thy divorce, [to be effective] from now, if I do not come back within twelve months', and he died within the twelve months, the divorce is valid?[5] Yet why so? was he not forcibly prevented!—I will tell you. There it may be different, [27*b*] because had he known that he would die, he would have decided and given the divorce so as to take effect *immediately*.[6] And how does it differ from the case of the man who declared, 'If I do not come within thirty days from now, let it be a divorce.' He came [on the last day], but was cut off through [the lack of] a ferry. [Yet though] he cried out, 'See! I have come; see! I have come!' Samuel ruled, That is not called coming[7]. But why: surely he was unavoidably prevented?—Perhaps an accident that can be foreseen is different, and [the lack of] a ferry could be foreseen.[8]

Now according to R. Huna, let us see: it is an *asmakta*,[9] and

(1) A document embodying his rights (Tosaf.). (2) Deut. XXII, 26. This refers to a betrothed maiden who was violated against her will; but if she was a consenting party, she was punished with death. (3) Because of its gravity. (4) Proving that such exemption holds good in all cases. (5) And if she is childless she is free from Levirate marriage or the ceremony of loosening the shoe (v. Deut. XXV, 5, *seq*.), because she is not the deceased's widow. (6) So that the result would be the same. (7) Because he had stipulated to come at a particular time. (8) But the Mishnah refers to a river abnormally swollen by the rains and melting snow. (9) V. Glos.

an *asmakta* gives no title?[1]—Here it is different, because he had *deposited* his rights.[2] And where they are deposited, is it not an *asmakta?* But we learnt: If one repaid a portion of his debt, and then placed the bond in the hands of a third party, and declared, 'If I do not repay [the balance] within thirty days, return the bill to the creditor,'[3] and the time came and he did not repay, R. Jose maintained: He [the third party] must surrender the bond to the [creditor]; R. Judah maintained: He must not surrender it. And R. Naḥman said in the name of Rabbah b. Abbahu in Rab's name: The *halachah* is not as R. Jose, who ruled that an *asmakta* gives a legal claim.[4]—Here it is different, because he had declared, 'These rights shall be *void*.'[5] Now the law is: an *asmakta* does give a legal claim, providing that no unavoidable accident supervened, and that a formal acquisition was made[6] at an authoritative Beth din.[7]

MISHNAH. ONE MAY VOW TO MURDERERS,[8] ROBBERS,[9] AND PUBLICANS THAT IT [THE PRODUCE WHICH THEY DEMAND] IS TERUMAH, EVEN IF IT IS NOT,[10] OR THAT IT BELONGS TO THE ROYAL HOUSE, EVEN IF IT DOES NOT. BETH SHAMMAI MAINTAIN: ONE MAY MAKE ANY FORM OF VOW, [28*a*] EXCEPTING THAT SUSTAINED BY AN OATH;[11] BUT

(1) I.e., gives the claimant no rights, because it is presumed that such a promise was not meant seriously, but made only in order to give the transaction the character of good faith and solemnity. (2) Not merely promised them. (3) Who will thus be able to demand the full sum. (4) V. B.B. (Sonc. ed.) p. 734. (5) This is a stronger declaration than e.g., 'I will not claim my rights'; hence it is valid. (6) The conceding party formally ceded his rights. This was symbolically effected by one giving an article, e.g., a scarf, to the other. (7) Rashi and Maim.: an *ordained* Beth din; Ran: a Beth din with the power to enforce its decisions. (8) I.e., robbers who kill if their demands are not granted. (9) Rashi, Ran, Rosh and Tosaf. all interpret this as private robbers. Jast.: official oppressors. These are less desperate than murderers, and do not kill if their demands are refused. (10) This vow is to save it from their hands, as *terumah* is forbidden to a *zar*, q.v. Glos.—It is remarkable that even murderers and robbers are assumed to respect the prohibition of *terumah!* (11) I.e. one may not vow, 'may this corn be forbidden me by an oath if' etc.

BETH HILLEL MAINTAIN: EVEN SUCH ARE PERMISSIBLE.[1] BETH SHAMMAI RULE: HE MUST NOT VOLUNTEER TO VOW;[2] BETH HILLEL RULE: HE MAY DO SO. BETH SHAMMAI SAY: [HE MAY VOW] ONLY AS FAR AS HE [THE MURDERER, etc.] MAKES HIM VOW; BETH HILLEL SAY: EVEN IN RESPECT OF WHAT HE DOES NOT MAKE HIM VOW. E.G., IF HE [THE ROBBER] SAID TO HIM, SAY: 'ḲONAM BE ANY BENEFIT MY WIFE HAS OF ME'; AND HE DECLARED, 'ḲONAM BE ANY BENEFIT MY WIFE AND CHILDREN HAVE OF ME,'—BETH SHAMMAI RULE: HIS WIFE IS PERMITTED, BUT HIS CHILDREN ARE FORBIDDEN; BETH HILLEL RULE: BOTH ARE PERMITTED.

GEMARA. But Samuel said, The law of the country is law?[3] —R. Ḥinena said in the name of R. Kahana in the name of Samuel: The Mishnah refers to a publican who is not limited to a legal due.[4] The School of R. Jannai answered: This refers to an unauthorised collector.

OR THAT IT BELONGS TO THE ROYAL HOUSE, EVEN IF IT DOES NOT. How does he vow?—R. Amram said in Rab's name: By saying, 'May all the fruits of the world be forbidden me, if this does not belong to the royal house.' But if he said, 'may they be forbidden,' all the fruits of the world are forbidden to him.[5] —He adds, to-day. But if so, the publican will not accept it!—He *mentally* stipulates 'to-day,' but makes no explicit reservation; and though we [normally] rule that an unexpressed stipulation is invalid,[6] it is different when made under duress.

BETH SHAMMAI MAINTAIN: ONE MAY MAKE ANY FORM OF VOW . . . BUT BETH HILLEL RULE THAT EVEN SUCH ARE PER-

(1) Weiss, *Dor* I, p. 185, conjectures that this controversy arose out of Herod's demand that all the members of the nation should swear loyalty to him (Joseph. *Ant.* 15, § 10). (2) If the murderer does not demand a vow as an assurance, he must not offer to vow of his own accord. (3) Therefore the publican has a legal claim: why then is the owner permitted to evade payment by a false vow? (4) Under the Roman Procurators there was a tremendous amount of illegal extortion, particularly of octroi tolls, v. Sanh. (Sonc. ed.) p. 148. (5) For if the vow contains no sort of evasion, it is binding whatever its purpose. (6) Lit., 'words that are in the heart are no words'.

MISSIBLE. BETH SHAMMAI RULE: THE OWNER MUST NOT VOLUNTEER TO VOW; BETH HILLEL RULE: HE MAY DO SO. BETH SHAMMAI SAY: HE MAY VOW ONLY AS FAR AS HE [THE MURDERER] MAKES HIM VOW; BETH HILLEL SAY: EVEN IN RESPECT OF WHAT HE DOES NOT MAKE HIM VOW. E.G., IF HE [THE ROBBER] SAID TO HIM, SAY: 'ḲONAM BE ANY BENEFIT MY WIFE HAS OF ME'; AND THE OWNER DECLARED, 'ḲONAM BE ANY BENEFIT MY WIFE AND CHILDREN HAVE OF ME'—BETH SHAMMAI RULE: HIS WIFE IS PERMITTED, BUT HIS CHILDREN ARE FORBIDDEN; BETH HILLEL RULE: BOTH ARE PERMITTED.

R. Huna said: A Tanna taught: Beth Shammai maintain: He must not volunteer with an oath; Beth Hillel say: He may volunteer even with an oath. Now, in the view of Beth Shammai, only with an *oath* may he not volunteer, but he may volunteer a vow. But we learnt: BETH SHAMMAI RULE: THE OWNER MUST NOT VOLUNTEER TO VOW. Moreover, he may merely not *volunteer* an oath, but he may vow with an oath [if requested]; but we learnt, BETH SHAMMAI MAINTAIN: ONE MAY MAKE ANY FORM OF VOW, EXCEPTING THAT SUSTAINED BY AN OATH?—The Mishnah deals with a *vow*, to shew how far-reaching is Beth Shammai's ruling;[1] whilst the Baraitha treats of an oath, to shew the full extent of Beth Hillel's view.[2]

R. Ashi answered, This is what is taught: Beth Shammai say, There is no absolution for an oath; and Beth Hillel say, There is absolution for an oath.[3]

MISHNAH. [IF ONE SAYS,] 'LET THESE SAPLINGS BE ḲORBAN [I.E., CONSECRATED] IF THEY ARE NOT CUT DOWN'; OR, 'LET THIS GARMENT BE ḲORBAN IF IT IS NOT BURNT':

(1) I.e., one may not volunteer even a vow, which is not as grave as an oath.
(2) That one may volunteer even an oath, in spite of its greater gravity.
(3) According to this, the Baraitha does not treat of vows under pressure at all. The Heb. *lo yiftaḥ* (rendered 'he may not volunteer') will mean: He (the rabbi) must not give an opening for regret, i.e., must not grant absolution.

THEY CAN BE REDEEMED.[1] [IF HE SAYS,] 'LET THESE SAPLINGS BE ḲORBAN UNTIL THEY ARE CUT DOWN'; OR, 'LET THIS GARMENT BE ḲORBAN UNTIL IT IS BURNT', [28b] THEY CANNOT BE REDEEMED.[2]

GEMARA. Let [the Mishnah] teach 'they are consecrated!'[3] —Because the second clause must state 'THEY CANNOT BE REDEEMED,'[4] the first clause also states, 'THEY CAN BE REDEEMED.'

How was the vow made?[5]—Amemar answered: By saying, '. . . if they are not cut down to-day'; and the day passed without their being cut down. If so, why teach it: is it not obvious?—The need for teaching it arises e.g., when a strong wind is blowing.[6] But the same is taught with respect to a garment: and does a garment stand to be burnt?—Even so; e.g., when a fire has broken out. So here too [in respect of plants], a strong wind is blowing; and I might think that he thought that they would not be saved, and therefore vowed.[7] Hence the Mishnah informs us [that the vow is binding].

'LET THESE SAPLINGS BE ḲORBAN etc.' [Can they] never

(1) They are duly consecrated, and must be redeemed before they are permitted for secular use. (2) Because a definite limit having been set, even if they are redeemed, they revert to their consecrated state. (3) Instead of the unusual 'they can be redeemed'. This is the reading of Ran, Asheri, and one view of Tosaf. Rashi's reading, which is that of cur. edd. is, 'let the Mishnah teach "they are consecrated" (in one respect) "and unconsecrated" (in another)'; the meaning of which is, they are consecrated in accordance with his vow, but not so strongly that they cannot be redeemed. This aspect of non-consecration is merely by contrast with the case of the second clause, where, even if redeemed, they revert to their consecrated state. [Tosaf. in name of R. Isaac of Dampierre (Ri.) gives a more satisfactory interpretation to this reading: 'They are consecrated' as long as they are not cut down, and 'unconsecrated' when they are cut down.] (4) It would be insufficient merely to state that they are consecrated, as the emphasis lies on the fact that redemption cannot release them. (5) Since ultimately they have to be cut down, how and when can they become consecrated? (6) In which case it might be assumed that he never for a moment thought it possible for the saplings to be spared and did not consecrate them with a perfect heart. (7) But not really meaning it, and so the vow is invalid.

[be redeemed]?[1]—Said Bar Pada: If he redeems them, they revert to their sanctity; if he redeems them again, they again revert to their sanctity, until they are cut down.[2] When cut down, he redeems them once,[3] and that suffices. 'Ulla said: Having been cut down, they require no further redemption.[4] [29a] Said R. Hamnuna to him: Whither then has their sanctity departed? What if one said to a woman, 'Be thou my wife to-day, but to-morrow thou art no longer my wife': would she be free without a divorce?[5]—Raba replied: Can you compare monetary consecration to bodily consecration?[6] Monetary sanctity may automatically end; but bodily consecration cannot end thus. Abaye objected to him: Cannot bodily consecration automatically cease? But it was taught: [If one says,] 'Let this ox be a burnt-offering for thirty days, and after that a peace-offering':[7] it is a burnt-offering for thirty days, and after that a peace-offering. Now why? it has bodily sanctity, yet it loses it automatically![8]—This deals with one who consecrated its value.[9] If so, consider the second clause: [If he says,] 'Let it be a burnt-offering after thirty days, but a peace-offering from now' [it is so]. Now, if you agree that one clause refers to bodily sanctity, and the other to monetary sanctity, [29b] hence the Tanna must teach both [clauses], because I would think that monetary consecration can automatically cease, but not so bodily sanctity; hence both are rightly taught. But if

(1) Surely that is impossible, since the vow set a limit to their period of sanctity! (2) V. p. 82, n. 3. (3) V. *infra*. (4) Since by the term of the vow their consecration lasts only until then. (5) Notwithstanding that he had married her for a limited period. So here too, though he had declared, 'let them be *korban* until they are cut down'; yet when they are, they do not *automatically* lose their sanctity, but must be redeemed. (6) The plants have only a *monetary* consecration, i.e., they cannot themselves be offered in the Temple, but must be redeemed, and their redemption money is utilized in the Temple service. But a married woman is herself consecrated to her husband. (7) I.e., if sacrificed within thirty days, it must be a burnt-offering; if after, a peace-offering. (8) Its sanctity as a *burnt*-offering has automatically ceased, though it retains the sanctity of a peace-offering. (9) I.e., the value of this ox be consecrated as a burnt-offering for thirty days, viz., that if redeemed within thirty days, a burnt-offering must be bought for the money; if after, a peace-offering.

you maintain that the two refer to monetary consecration, why teach them both? If a higher sanctity can automatically give way to a lower sanctity, surely it is superfluous to state that a lower sanctity can be replaced by a higher one?[1] Shall we say that this is a refutation of Bar Pada, who maintained that sanctity cannot cease automatically?—Said R. Papa, Bar Pada can answer thus: The text is defective,[2] and this is its meaning: If he did not say, 'let this be a peace-offering from now,' it remains a burnt-offering after thirty days.[3] This may be compared to the case of one who says to a woman, 'Be thou betrothed unto me after thirty days'; she becomes betrothed [then], even though the money [of betrothal] has been consumed [in the meanwhile].[4] But is this not obvious?[5]—This is necessary only [to teach that] where he supplemented his first declaration [it is still ineffective].[6] Now that is

(1) The burnt-offering has a higher sanctity than a peace-offering. (2) This is Rashi's reading, but is absent from the versions of Asheri, Ran, and Tosaf. (3) The text is thus to be reconstructed: If one says, 'Let this ox be a burnt-offering for thirty days, and *from now* and after thirty days a peace-offering': it is a burnt-offering for the first thirty days, and a peace-offering after that. But if he did not say, 'Let it be a peace-offering *from now* and after thirty days', but merely, 'let it be a burnt-offering for thirty days; and a peace-offering afterwards'; it remains a burnt-offering after thirty days. In the former case, the sanctity pertaining to the burnt-offering automatically ceases, because that of the peace-offering is potentially concurrent therewith and extends beyond it; but in the latter case, the sanctity cannot automatically cease (Rashi). Ran, Asheri and Tosaf. explain it differently. (4) So here too. When the second sanctity is *not* imposed concurrently with the first, the latter, on the completion of the thirty days, is similar to the money, which though consumed in the meanwhile, is nevertheless effective in betrothing the woman; so also the first sanctity remains though the period has been 'consumed'. (5) Since it is taught that only when the second sanctity runs concurrently with the first does it take effect after thirty days, it is self-evident that if it is not imposed concurrently, the first sanctity remains after the period. (6) I.e., if after declaring, 'this ox be a burnt-offering for thirty days and after that let it be a peace-offering' (in which case, as we have seen, it remains a burnt-offering), he made a supplementary statement, 'let it be a peace-offering *from now* and after thirty days', it will still remain a burnt-offering after that period, because this statement *'from now'* must be made at the outset. Now, if only the first clause had been taught, viz., that if he imposed the second sanctity concurrently with

well on the view that she [the woman] cannot retract;[1] but on the view that she can retract, what can be said?[2]—Even according to that view, this case is different, because a verbal promise to God is as actual delivery in secular transactions.[3]

R. Abin and R. Isaac b. Rabbi[4] were sitting before R. Jeremiah, who was dozing. Now they sat and stated: According to Bar Pada, who maintained that they revert to their sanctity, [30a] you may solve the problem of R. Hoshaia. Viz., what if one gives two *peruṭahs* to a woman, saying to her, 'Be thou betrothed unto me for one of these to-day, and for the other be thou betrothed unto me after I divorce thee'?[5] [Now, from Bar Pada's ruling you may deduce that the second] is indeed [valid] *ḳiddushin*.[6] This

the first the former is duly effective, I would think that it is so even if this concurrent sanctity was imposed only in a supplementary statement. Hence the need for the second clause, viz., that if the second sanctity was not (at the very outset) imposed concurrently with the first, it cannot come into effect.

(1) During the interval and become betrothed to another man. So here too, unless the second sanctity was at the outset imposed concurrently with the first, the force of the latter remains. (2) So here too by analogy, even if the second sanctity was not imposed concurrently with the first, it should cancel the first after the thirty days. (3) I.e., the declaration, 'this ox be a burnt-offering for thirty days', has more force than a normal promise affecting the interests of man only, but is regarded as though thereby the animal had actually been made into a burnt-offering, and therefore that sanctity, even though imposed for a limited period, remains after it, unless another was imposed concurrently therewith. (4) [Read with MS.M. 'b. Joseph'.] (5) Is the second betrothal valid? (6) For, just as the plants after redemption revert to their sanctity in virtue of an earlier declaration, so the woman, after being freed by a divorce, will revert to her betrothed state in virtue of the declaration prior thereto—Ran and Asheri. Rashi: For, when the plants are cut down, they should, according to the terms of the vow, lose their sanctity; yet in virtue of the first declaration they retain it until they are redeemed. So here too: though the divorce sets the woman free, the prior declaration is valid insofar as she becomes betrothed again. This interpretation is rather strained. Moreover, it would appear that the deduction is made from the fact that *before* being cut down the plants revert to their sanctity after being redeemed, and not because they require redemption even after being cut down. In Rashi's favour, however, it may be observed that this law of consecration after redemption is that of the Mishnah as explained both by Bar Pada and by 'Ulla. So that the particular reference to Bar Pada may indicate that the solution

roused R. Jeremiah, and he said to them, Why do you compare redemption by the owner to redemption by others? Thus did R. Johanan say: If he himself redeems them, they revert to their sanctity; but if others redeem them, they do not.[1] Now a [divorced] woman may be compared to the case of redemption by others.[2] It was stated likewise: R. Ammi said in R. Johanan's name: Only if he himself redeems them was this taught [that they revert to their sanctity]; but when others redeem them, they do not revert to their sanctity.

MISHNAH. HE WHO VOWS [NOT TO BENEFIT] FROM SEAFARERS, MAY BENEFIT FROM LAND-DWELLERS; FROM LAND-DWELLERS, HE IS FORBIDDEN [TO BENEFIT] EVEN FROM SEAFARERS, BECAUSE SEAFARERS ARE INCLUDED IN THE TERM 'LAND-DWELLERS'; NOT THOSE WHO MERELY TRAVEL FROM ACCO TO JAFFA,[3] BUT THOSE WHO SAIL AWAY GREAT DISTANCES [FROM LAND].

GEMARA. R. Papa and R. Aḥa son of R. Iḳa—one referred it [the last statement] to the first clause, and the other to the second. Now, he who referred it to the first clause learnt thus: HE WHO VOWS [NOT TO BENEFIT] FROM SEAFARERS MAY BENEFIT FROM LAND-DWELLERS. Hence, he may not benefit from seafarers; NOT THOSE WHO MERELY [30b] TRAVEL FROM ACCO TO JAFFA, as these are land-dwellers, BUT THOSE WHO SAIL AWAY GREAT DISTANCES [FROM LAND]. He who referred it

is deduced from the continued sanctity of the saplings after they are cut down, which is maintained by Bar Pada only.

(1) For since they are redeemed by others, they are no longer under the authority of their first owner, therefore his first declaration is no longer valid. (2) Because once divorced, she is no longer under her husband's authority, just as the plants, when redeemed by others, are not under the authority of their first owner. (3) Acco (also called Acre). A city and seaport of Phoenicia on a promontory at the foot of mount Carmel (Cf. Josephus, *Ant*, II, 10, 2). Jaffa. A city of Palestine and a Mediterranean port, 35 miles northwest of Jerusalem.

to the second clause learnt thus: [IF ONE VOWS NOT TO BENEFIT] FROM LAND-DWELLERS, HE MAY NOT BENEFIT FROM SEA-FARERS; [this applies] NOT ONLY TO THOSE WHO TRAVEL MERELY FROM ACCO TO JAFFA, BUT even TO THOSE WHO TRAVEL GREAT DISTANCES, since they eventually land.

MISHNAH. HE WHO VOWS [NOT TO BENEFIT] FROM THE SEERS OF THE SUN, IS FORBIDDEN FROM THE BLIND TOO, BECAUSE HE MEANT 'THOSE WHOM THE SUN SEES'.[1]

GEMARA. What is the reason?—Since he did not say 'from those who see,' he meant to exclude only fish and embryos.[1]

MISHNAH. HE WHO VOWS [NOT TO BENEFIT] FROM THE BLACK-HAIRED MAY NOT [BENEFIT] FROM THE BALD AND THE GREY-HAIRED, BUT MAY [BENEFIT] FROM WOMEN AND CHILDREN, BECAUSE ONLY MEN ARE CALLED 'BLACK-HAIRED'.

GEMARA. What is the reason?—Since he did not say 'from those who possess hair'.[2]

BUT MAY [BENEFIT] FROM WOMEN AND CHILDREN, BECAUSE ONLY MEN ARE CALLED 'BLACK-HAIRED'. What is the reason? —Men sometimes cover their heads and sometimes not; but women's hair is always covered, and children are always bareheaded.[3]

(1) [I.e., he might have intended the phrase 'those who see the sun' as an euphemism for 'those whom the sun sees', i.e., the blind (cf. Bek. VIII, 3, סכי שמש, 'looking to the sun' used euphemistically for 'squinting'). But since with vows we adopt the more rigorous interpretation, he is forbidden to benefit from those who see as well as from the blind (cf. Rabinowitz, M. *Graber Otzar ha-Safruth* II, 137ff.).] (2) Therefore bald and grey-haired people are included, since they were once black-haired. (3) Hence women would be referred to as 'those of covered hair', and children as 'the bare-headed'.—Ran. In Mishnaic times it was the universal practise for women's hair to be covered, and its violation was deemed sufficient ground for divorce without payment of the *kethubah*

MISHNAH. ONE WHO VOWS [NOT TO BENEFIT] FROM YILLODIM [THOSE BORN] MAY [BENEFIT] FROM NOLADIM [THOSE TO BE BORN]; FROM NOLADIM, HE MAY NOT [BENEFIT] FROM YILLODIM. R. MEIR PERMITTED [HIM TO BENEFIT] EVEN FROM YILLODIM; BUT THE SAGES SAY: HE MEANT ALL WHOSE NATURE IT IS TO BE BORN.[1]

GEMARA. Now, according to R. Meir, *noladim* go without saying;[2] who then is forbidden to him?—The text is defective, and thus to be reconstructed: ONE WHO VOWS [NOT TO BENEFIT] FROM YILLODIM MAY [BENEFIT] FROM NOLADIM; FROM NOLADIM, YILLODIM ARE FORBIDDEN TO HIM. R. MEIR SAID: ALSO HE WHO VOWS [NOT TO BENEFIT] FROM NOLADIM MAY [BENEFIT] FROM YILLODIM, JUST AS HE WHO VOWS NOT TO BENEFIT FROM YILLODIM MAY [BENEFIT] FROM NOLADIM.[3]

R. Papa said to Abaye: Are we to conclude that *noladim* implies those about to be born? If so, does the verse, *thy two sons, which* noladim *unto thee in the land of Egypt,*[4]—mean 'who are to be born'?[5]—What then will you say: that it implies who were born? If so, what of the verse, *behold a child* nolad *unto the house of David Josiah by name:*[6] will you say that he was [already born]? but even Menasseh [Josiah's grandfather] was not yet born![7] But *nolad* implies both,[8] and in vows, we follow general usage.[9]

(Keth. 72*a* Mishnah.) From the present passage it appears that no distinction was drawn between married and unmarried women, but later on custom became more lenient with respect to unmarried women (*Shulhan 'Aruk*, O.Ḥ. 75, 2; cf. Sanh. (Sonc. ed.) p. 398, n. 1, referring to Gentiles). As for men, it was considered a sign of reverence and piety to cover the head (Ḳid. 31*a*, Shab. 118*b*); nevertheless only in the case of great scholars was it held to be indispensable (cf. Ḳid. 8*a*.

(1) I.e., not hatched, and therefore including both those already born and those to be born. (2) That they are permitted, since the Mishnah states, R. MEIR PERMITTED (HIM TO BENEFIT) EVEN FROM YILLODIM. (3) I.e. in each case his words are taken literally. (4) Gen. XLVIII, 5. (5) The reference being to Ephraim and Manasseh, who were already born. (6) I Kings XIII, 2. (7) This verse was spoken in the reign of Jeroboam I. (8) Biblically. *Sc.* 'born' and 'to be born'. (9) Lit., 'the language of the sons of men', which applies *nolad* to those who are yet to be born.

BUT THE SAGES SAY: HE MEANT ALL WHOSE NATURE IT IS TO BE BORN. Excluding what?—It excludes fish and fowl.[1]

MISHNAH. [31a] HE WHO VOWS [NOT TO BENEFIT] FROM THOSE WHO REST ON THE SABBATH, IS FORBIDDEN [TO BENEFIT] BOTH FROM ISRAELITES AND CUTHEANS.[2] IF HE VOWS [NOT TO BENEFIT] FROM GARLIC EATERS, HE MAY NOT BENEFIT FROM ISRAELITES AND CUTHEANS;[3] FROM THOSE WHO GO UP[4] TO JERUSALEM, HE IS FORBIDDEN [TO BENEFIT] FROM ISRAELITES BUT FROM CUTHEANS HE IS PERMITTED.[5]

GEMARA. What is meant by 'THOSE WHO REST ON THE SABBATH'? Shall we say, 'those who observe the Sabbath,' why particularly Cutheans: even heathens [if they observe the Sabbath] too? Hence it must mean 'those who are *commanded* to observe the Sabbath.' If so, consider the last clause: FROM THOSE WHO GO UP TO JERUSALEM, HE IS FORBIDDEN [TO BENEFIT] FROM ISRAELITES BUT FROM CUTHEANS HE IS PERMITTED. But why so: are they not commanded too?[6]—Said Abaye: In both clauses the reference is to those who are commanded *and fulfil* [their obligations]. Hence, in the first clause, both Israelites and

(1) Which are spawned and hatched respectively. (2) Lit., 'men of Cuth or Cuthah'; this was one of the five cities from which Sargon, King of Assyria, brought settlers for the depopulated Northern Palestine, after it had been conquered and its inhabitants deported (II Kings XVII, 24, 30). During the period of its depopulation the land had become overrun by lions, who now attacked the settlers; they took this as a sign of the wrath of the local deity, and so, after instruction, they became Jews, though continuing some of their heathen practices. The religious status of the Cutheans (also called Samaritans) was of rather a vacillating nature. The Cutheans observed the Sabbath. (3) It was customary for these to eat garlic on Friday evenings. B.Ḳ. 82*a*. (4) For the three Festivals v. Deut. XVI, 16. (5) The Cutheans built a temple upon mount Gerizim, and though this was destroyed by John Hyrcanus, they continued to reverence the site and make pilgrimages thereto, instead of to Jerusalem. (6) Since they regarded themselves as true Jews and had formally become converts.

Cutheans are commanded and observe [the Sabbath]; but those heathens who rest on the Sabbath do so without being obliged to. As for making pilgrimages to Jerusalem, Jews are commanded and observe it; but Cutheans, though commanded, do not.

MISHNAH. [IF ONE SAYS,] 'ḲONAM THAT I DO NOT BENEFIT FROM THE CHILDREN OF NOAH,' HE MAY BENEFIT FROM ISRAELITES, BUT NOT FROM HEATHENS.

GEMARA. But are then Israelites excluded from the children of Noah?—Since Abraham was sanctified, they are called by *his* name.[1]

MISHNAH. [IF ONE SAYS, 'ḲONAM] THAT I DO NOT BENEFIT FROM THE SEED OF ABRAHAM,' HE IS FORBIDDEN [TO BENEFIT] FROM ISRAELITES, BUT PERMITTED [TO BENEFIT] FROM HEATHENS.

GEMARA. But there is Ishmael?[2]—It is written, *for in* Isaac *shall thy seed be called.*[3] But there is Esau?—'In *Isaac*',[4] but not *all* [the descendants of] Isaac.

MISHNAH. [IF ONE SAYS, 'ḲONAM] THAT I DO NOT BENEFIT FROM ISRAELITES', HE MUST BUY THINGS FROM THEM FOR MORE [THAN THEIR WORTH] AND SELL THEM FOR LESS.[5] [IF HE SAYS, 'ḲONAM] IF ISRAELITES BENEFIT FROM ME,' HE MUST BUY FROM THEM FOR LESS AND SELL FOR MORE [THAN THEIR WORTH], BUT NONE NEED CONSENT TO THIS.[6]

(1) I.e., they are referred to as descendants of *Abraham*, not of Noah. (2) Hence his descendants, who are heathens, should be included in the vow. (3) Gen. XXI, 12. (4) I.e., only a portion of his descendants. (5) Because if he trades on ordinary terms, he is benefiting from them. (6) I.e., since others are not likely to trade on such terms, in practice he may not trade with them at all.

'THAT I MAY NOT BENEFIT FROM THEM, NOR THEY FROM ME,' HE MAY BENEFIT ONLY FROM HEATHENS.[1]

GEMARA. Samuel said: If one takes an article from an artisan[2] on approval, and whilst in his possession it is accidentally damaged, he is liable for it. Hence we see that in his view the benefit is on the side of the buyer.[3] We learnt: [IF ONE SAYS, 'ḲONAM] THAT I DO NOT BENEFIT FROM ISRAELITES,' HE MUST ... SELL THEM FOR LESS. Hence he may not sell at its actual worth: but if the *purchaser* benefits [not the vendor], why not sell at its actual worth?—The Mishnah refers to an unsaleable article.[4] If so, consider the first statement: HE MUST BUY FOR MORE THAN THEIR WORTH.[5] Moreover, consider the second clause: [IF HE SAYS, 'ḲONAM] IF ISRAELITES BENEFIT FROM ME,' HE MUST BUY FROM THEM FOR LESS AND SELL FOR MORE THAN THEIR WORTH. But if this refers to unsaleable merchandise, even [to sell] at its actual worth [should be permitted]?[6]—The second clause refers to 'keen' merchandise.[7] If so, why must he purchase at a lesser [price]; he may even pay the full value?[8]—[31b] But the Mishnah refers to average merchandise;[9] whilst Samuel refers to an article that is eagerly sought.

It was taught in agreement with Samuel: If one takes articles

(1) The point is this. One might think that since it is almost impossible for such a vow to be kept, it is by its very nature invalid; hence it is taught that its observance is not impossible, as he can fall back upon heathens. (2) Ran reads: from a tradesman. (3) Trustees are divided into various categories, according to their degrees of responsibility, depending upon the benefit they derive from their trust. Only one who *borrows* an article is liable for accidental damage, because all the benefit is on his side, the lender receiving nothing in return. Since Samuel rules that the prospective purchaser is liable for accidental damage, it is evident that he puts him in the same category as a borrower, who is the only one to derive benefit. (4) I.e., something for which there are no buyers. Hence the vendor benefits from the transaction, unless he sells below market price. (5) But if it is unsaleable, even if he pays no more than its market value, he is not benefiting. (6) Since the purchaser does not thereby benefit from him. (7) Goods in keen demand. (8) As the vendor does not benefit, since he can easily sell it to someone else. (9) Which is neither a drag on the market nor in keen demand.

from a tradesman [on approval] to send them [as a gift] to his father-in-law's house, and stipulates: 'if they are accepted, I will pay you their value, but if not, I will pay you for their goodwill benefit':[1] if they were accidentally damaged on the outward journey, he is liable;[2] if on their return journey, he is not liable, because he is regarded as a paid trustee.[3]

A middleman [once] took an ass[4] to sell, but could not sell it. On his way back it was accidentally injured, [whereupon] R. Naḥman held him liable to make it good. Raba objected: 'if they were damaged on the outward journey, he is liable; if on their return journey, he is not!'—Said he to him: The return journey of a middleman counts as an outward journey, for if he finds a purchaser even at his doorstep, will he not sell [it] to him?

MISHNAH. [IF ONE SAYS,] 'ḲONAM THAT I DO NOT BENEFIT FROM THE UNCIRCUMCISED,' HE MAY BENEFIT FROM UNCIRCUMCISED ISRAELITES BUT NOT FROM CIRCUMCISED HEATHENS; 'THAT I DO NOT BENEFIT FROM THE CIRCUMCISED,' HE IS FORBIDDEN TO BENEFIT FROM UNCIRCUMCISED ISRAELITES BUT NOT FROM CIRCUMCISED HEATHENS, BECAUSE 'UNCIRCUMCISED' IS A TERM APPLICABLE ONLY TO HEATHENS, AS IT IS WRITTEN, FOR ALL THE NATIONS ARE UNCIRCUMCISED AND ALL THE HOUSE OF ISRAEL ARE UNCIRCUMCISED IN THE HEART.[5] AND IT IS FURTHER SAID, AND THIS UNCIRCUMCISED PHILISTINE

(1) Which he would derive from his father-in-law's knowing that he wished to make him a present. Although only a matter of goodwill a monetary value could be set upon it. (2) This supports Samuel's ruling. (3) Who is not liable for accidental damage; this is because he has derived some benefit through having had it in his charge; but he cannot be considered as a simple borrower, the *sole* benefit being his, since this benefit has by now ceased, B.M. (Sonc. ed.) p. 460. (4) המרא. The word may also mean 'wine'. (5) Jer. IX, 25. Thus, though there may be some circumcised among the heathens, they are collectively termed 'uncircumcised'; similarly, when the Israelites are rebuked for their leanings to paganism, they are denounced as 'uncircumcised of heart'.

SHALL BE [AS ONE OF THEM].[1] AND IT IS FURTHER SAID, LEST THE DAUGHTERS OF THE PHILISTINES REJOICE, LEST THE DAUGHTERS OF THE UNCIRCUMCISED TRIUMPH.[2] R. ELEAZAR B. 'AZARIAH SAID: THE FORESKIN IS LOATHSOME, SINCE IT IS A TERM OF OPPROBRIUM FOR THE WICKED, AS IT IS WRITTEN, 'FOR ALL THE NATIONS ARE UNCIRCUMCISED'. R. ISHMAEL SAID, GREAT IS [THE PRECEPT] OF CIRCUMCISION, SINCE THIRTEEN COVENANTS WERE MADE THEREON.[3] R. JOSE SAID, CIRCUMCISION IS A GREAT PRECEPT, FOR IT OVERRIDES [THE SEVERITY OF] THE SABBATH.[4] R. JOSHUA B. ḲARḤA SAID: GREAT IS [THE PRECEPT OF] CIRCUMCISION, FOR [NEGLECTING] WHICH MOSES DID NOT HAVE [HIS PUNISHMENT] SUSPENDED EVEN FOR A SINGLE HOUR[5]. R. NEHEMIAH SAID, GREAT IS [THE PRECEPT OF] CIRCUMCISION, SINCE IT SUPERSEDES THE LAWS OF LEPROSY.[6] RABBI SAID, GREAT IS CIRCUMCISION, FOR [NOTWITHSTANDING] ALL THE PRECEPTS WHICH ABRAHAM FULFILLED HE WAS NOT DESIGNATED PERFECT UNTIL HE CIRCUMCISED HIMSELF, AS IT IS WRITTEN, WALK BEFORE ME, AND BE THOU PERFECT.[7] ANOTHER EXPLANATION: GREAT IS CIRCUMCISION, SINCE BUT FOR THAT, THE HOLY ONE, BLESSED BE HE, WOULD NOT HAVE CREATED THE UNIVERSE, AS IT IS WRITTEN, BUT FOR MY COVENANT BY DAY AND NIGHT,[8] I WOULD NOT HAVE APPOINTED THE ORDINANCES OF HEAVEN AND EARTH.[9]

(1) I Sam. XVII, 36, though he did not know whether Goliath was uncircumcised or not. (2) II Sam. I, 20. (3) In the passage dealing with God's command to Abraham to circumcise himself, the word 'covenant' occurs thirteen times. Gen. XVII. (4) Circumcision, though entailing work, is performed on the Sabbath. (5) This is discussed in the Gemara. (6) A leprous spot, such as a swelling etc., may not be cut off (Deut. XXIV, 8 is so interpreted); but if it is on the foreskin, it may be removed together with it. (7) Gen. XVII, 1. (8) This is taken to refer to circumcision, which, as shown above, is frequently designated as such. (9) Jer. XXXIII, 25. This is the end of the Mishnah in our text, but other versions, including that of Ran and Tosaf., add the following:— Great is circumcision, for it counterbalances all other precepts put together, as it is written, *behold the blood of the covenant, which the Lord hath made with you concerning*

GEMARA. It was taught: R. Joshua b. Ḳarḥa said, Great is circumcision, for all the meritorious deeds performed by Moses our teacher did not stand him in stead when he displayed apathy towards circumcision, as it is written, *and the Lord met him, and sought to kill him.*[1] R. Jose said, God forbid that Moses should have been apathetic towards circumcision, but he reasoned thus: 'If I circumcise [my son] and [straightway] go forth [on my mission to Pharaoh], I will endanger his life, as it is written, *and it came to pass on the third day, when they were sore.*[2] If I circumcise him, and tarry three days,—but the Holy One, blessed be He, has commanded: *Go, return unto Egypt.*[3] Why then was Moses punished? [32a] Because he busied himself first with the inn,[4] as it is written, *And it came to pass by the way, in the inn.*[5] R. Simeon b. Gamaliel said: Satan[6] did not seek to slay Moses but the child, for it is written, [*Then Zipporah took a sharp stone, and cut off the foreskin of her son, and cast it as his feet, and said,*] *Surely a bloody* ḥathan *art thou to me.*[7] Go forth and see: who is called a *ḥathan?* Surely the infant [to be circumcised].[8]

R. Judah b. Bizna lectured: When Moses was lax in the perform-

all these words (Ex. XXIV, 8). *All these words* are understood to mean all God's precepts: and '*the blood of the covenant*', though referring in its context to sacrifice, is applied to circumcision, on account of its frequent designation as covenant. Part of this reading is quoted in the Gemara as a *Baraitha*.—Weiss, *Dor*, II, 9. regards all these dicta as called forth by Christianity's abrogation of circumcision.

(1) Ex. IV, 24. (2) Gen. XXXIV, 25. This refers to the inhabitants of the city of Shechem, who underwent circumcision. Moses considered it dangerous to take his son on a journey within the first three days of circumcision. (3) Ex. IV, 19, implying without delay. (4) Instead of with circumcision. (5) Ibid. IV, 24. This implies that as soon as he left the road he turned his attention to the inn, arranging his baggage, quarters, etc., instead of immediately circumcising his son. (6) *Var. lec.* 'that angel'. Generally speaking, Satan was regarded as man's adversary and accuser, but without independent power, which he must derive from God. (Cf. Job I, 7 seq., Zech. III, 1 f.) In the older Talmudic literature Satan is seldom mentioned, but his name is found more frequently in the amoraic period, and it may well be that the variant reading here (angel) is the original one. V. also Ḳid. (Sonc. ed.) p. 142, n. 5. (7) Ex. IV, 25. (8) *Ḥathan* generally means bridegroom, son-in-law: but in connection with circumcision it refers to the infant to be circumcised.

ance of circumcision, Af and Ḥemah[1] came and swallowed him up, leaving nought but his legs. Thereupon immediately *Zipporah 'took a sharp stone and cut off the foreskin of her son';*[2] straightway *he let him alone.*[3] In that moment Moses desired to slay them, as it is written, *Cease from* Af *and forsake* Ḥemah.[4] Some say that he did slay Ḥemah, as it is written, *I have not* Ḥemah.[5] But is it not written, *for I was afraid of* Af *and* Ḥemah?[6]—There were two [angels named] Ḥemah. An alternative answer is this: [he slew] the troop commanded by Ḥemah, [but not Ḥemah himself].

It was taught: Rabbi said, Great is circumcision, for none so ardently busied himself with [God's] precepts as our Father Abraham, yet he was called perfect only in virtue of circumcision, as it is written, *Walk before me and be thou perfect,*[7] and it is written, *And I will make my covenant between me and thee.*[8] Another version [of Rabbi's teaching] is this: Great is circumcision, for it counterbalances all the [other] precepts of the Torah, as it is written, *For after the tenor of these words I have made a covenant with thee and with Israel.*[9] Another version is: Great is circumcision, since but for it heaven and earth would not endure, as it is written, [*Thus saith the*

(1) Wrath and anger personified. (2) As the whole body was swallowed up save the legs, Zipporah understood that this was a punishment for neglecting the circumcision of the foreskin. (3) Ex. IV, 26. (4) Ps. XXXVII, 8. Af and Ḥemah are regarded here as proper nouns. (5) Isa. XXVII, 4. Spoken by God, and according to this interpretation, because Ḥemah had been slain. (6) Deut. IX, 19. This refers to the sin of the Golden Calf, which was subsequent to the incident under discussion. (7) Gen. XVII, 1, in reference to circumcision. (8) Ibid. XVII, 2. [Indicating that Abraham was to attain perfection through the covenant of circumcision.] Rashi, without pointing out any incorrectness in the text, relates this verse to the next passage; v. next note. (9) Ex. XXXIV, 27. *After the tenor of these words* is taken to refer to all God's precepts; by a 'covenant', 'circumcision' is understood; thus the two—all God's precepts and circumcision—are equated. Rashi appears to have the following reading: As it is written, *Behold the blood of the* covenant, *which the Lord hath made with you concerning all these words* (Ex. XXIV, 8); and it is also written, *And I will make my covenant between me and thee* (Gen. XVII, 2). Just as 'covenant' in the latter verse refers to circumcision, so also in the former; whilst the end of that verse, '*concerning all these words*', shews that circumcision is equal in importance to '*all these words*', i.e., all God's commandments.

Lord,] *But for my covenant by day and night,*[1] *I would not have appointed the ordinances of Heaven and earth.*[2] Now this [statement][3] conflicts with R. Eleazar's: for R. Eleazar[4] said, Great is the Torah, since but for it heaven and earth could not endure, as it is written, *But for my covenant by day and night, I would not have appointed the ordinances of heaven and earth.*[5]

Rab Judah said in Rab's name: When the Holy One, blessed be He, said to our Father Abraham, '*Walk before me and be thou perfect*',[6] he was seized with trembling. 'Perhaps,' he said, 'there is still aught shameful in me!' But when He added, '*And I will make my covenant between me and thee*', his mind was appeased.[7]

And he brought him forth abroad.[8] Now Abraham had said unto him, 'Sovereign of the Universe! I have gazed at the constellation which rules my destiny, and seen that I am not fated to beget children.' To which [God] replied: '*Go forth* from thy astrological speculations: Israel is not subject to planetary influences.'

R. Isaac said: He who perfects himself, the Holy One, blessed be He, deals uprightly with him, as it is written, *With the merciful thou wilt shew thyself merciful, and with the upright thou wilt shew thyself upright.*[9] R. Hoshaia said: If one perfects himself, good fortune will be his,[10] as it is written, *Walk before me and be thou perfect;*[11] and it is further written, *And thou shalt be a father of many nations.*[12]

Rabbi[13] said: He who practises enchantment will be harassed by witchcraft, as it is written, *For against him, of [the seed of] Jacob, there is enchantment.*[14] But surely it is written with *lamed aleph?*[15]—But he is thus punished as measure for measure.[16]

(1) V. p. 93, n. 8. (2) Jer. XXXIII, 25. (3) Which identifies 'covenant' here with circumcision. (4) [So Pes. 68*b*. Cur. edd. R. Eliezer.] (5) Thus, according to him, 'covenant' in this verse refers to the Torah, not to circumcision. (6) Gen. XVII, 1. (7) For he then understood that the imperfection was not in himself, but in the lack of a formal covenant between him and the Almighty. (8) Gen. XV, 5. (9) II Sam. XXII, 26. (10) Lit., 'the hour will stand by him'. (11) Gen. XVII, 1. (12) Ibid. XVII, 4. This should be his good fortune, as a reward for perfecting himself. (13) *Var. lec.*: R. Levi. (14) Num. XXIII, 23. (15) *Lo*=*not*, so that the verse reads, *Surely there is* no *enchantment in Jacob*. (16) I.e., this is not deduced from a Scriptural verse, but from the general axiom that punishment corresponds to the crime. Though the Jewish Sages attributed

Ahabah the son of R. Zera learnt: He who does not practice enchantment is brought within a barrier [i.e., in proximity to God] which not even the Ministering Angels may enter, as it is written, *For there is no enchantment in Jacob, neither is there any divination in Israel: now it shall be asked* [by the angels] *of Jacob and Israel, What hath God wrought?*[1]

R. Abbahu said in R. Eleazar's name: Why was our Father Abraham punished and his children doomed to Egyptian servitude for two hundred and ten years? Because he pressed scholars into his service, as it is written, *He armed his dedicated servants*[2] *born in his own house.*[3] Samuel[4] said: Because he went too far in testing the attributes [i.e., the promises] of the Lord, as it is written, [*And he said, Lord God,*] *whereby shall I know that I shall inherit it?*[5] R. Joḥanan said: Because he prevented men from entering beneath the wings of the *Shechinah*, as it is written, [*And the king of Sodom said unto Abraham,*] *Give me the persons, and take the goods to thyself.*[6]

And he armed his trained servants, born in his own house.[7] Rab said, he equipped them[8] by [teaching them] the Torah.[9] Samuel said, he made them bright with gold [i.e., rewarded them for accompanying him]. *Three hundred and eighteen:*[10] R. Ammi b. Abba said: Eliezer outweighed them all. Others say, It was Eliezer, for this is the numerical value of his name.[11]

reality to supernatural agencies in general, they nevertheless sought to discourage superstitious practices; v. M. Joseph, *Judaism as Creed and Life*, pp. 79-81.

(1) Num. XXIII, 23. The Israelites, through not practising enchantments, are brought into such close contact with God, that they know secrets not entrusted to the angels. (2) I.e., scholars dedicated to the study of the Torah. The word is treated as a derivative of *ḥanok*, to educate, dedicate. (3) Gen. XIV, 14. (4) *Var. lec.*: R. Samuel b. Naḥmani. (5) Gen. XV, 8. (6) Ibid. XIV, 21. Abraham, by permitting this, instead of taking the persons himself, and teaching them to know God, is said to have prevented them from coming beneath the wings of the Divine Presence. This dictum seems to indicate that R. Joḥanan was in favour of proselytes. (7) Ibid. XIV, 14. (8) A variant reading is *heriḳan;* he emptied them from the Torah, i.e., disregarded their learning and forced them into service, or perhaps, withdrew them from their studies. (9) *Wa-yareḳ* is here connected with *yaraḳ* to make shine; cf. *yeraḳraḳ*, yellow (shining). (10) Ibid. (11) Hebrew letters are also used as numbers, and the numerical value of אליעזר is 318.

R. Ammi b. Abba also said: Abraham was three years old when he acknowledged the Creator, for it is written, *Because* [Heb. *'ekeb*] *that Abraham obeyed my voice:*[1] the numerical value of *'ekeb* is 172.[2] R. Ammi b. Abba also said: [32*b*] The numerical value of *ha-saṭan* [Satan] is 364.[3]

R. Ammi b. Abba also said: [First] Abram is written, then Abraham:[4] at first God gave him mastery over 243 limbs, and later over 248, the additional ones being the two eyes, two ears, and the membrum.[5]

R. Ammi b. Abba also said: What is the meaning of, *There is a little city, etc.?*[6] '*A little city*' refers to the body; and '*a few men within*' to the limbs; '*and there came a great king against it and besieged* [it]' to the Evil Urge;[7] '*and built great bulwarks aganst it*', to sin; '*Now there was found in it a poor wise man,*' to the Good Urge; *and he by his wisdom delivered the city,* to repentance and good deeds; *yet no man remembered that same poor man,* for when the Evil Urge gains dominion, none remember the Good Urge.

Wisdom strengtheneth the wise more than ten mighty ones which are in the city.[8] '*Wisdom strengtheneth the wise*' refers to repentance and good deeds; '*more than ten mighty ones,*' viz., the two eyes, two ears, two hands, two feet, membrum and mouth.[9]

R. Zechariah said on R. Ishmael's authority: The Holy One, blessed be He, intended to bring forth the priesthood from Shem,

(1) Gen. XXVI, 5. (2) The verse is therefore thus interpreted: 172 years hath Abraham obeyed my voice. As he lived 175 years in all, he was three years old when he acknowledged the Creator. (3) This indicates that his seductive powers over mankind are only for 364 days of the year. On the 365th, viz., the Day of Atonement, he has no power over man. (4) The original name of Abram, whose numerical value is 243, was changed to Abraham, with the value 248, the numbers of members of man's body. V. Mak. (Sonc. ed.) p. 109, n. 5. (5) As a reward for his undergoing circumcision he was given mastery over those limbs, which, through hearing and seeing, entice one to immorality; but now he was enabled by his will-power to forbid them to look upon or listen to sin. The last mentioned, of course, refers to the control of the sex-lust. Cf. Maim. '*Guide*', III, ch. 49. (6) Eccl. IX, 14 f. (7) One's evil inclinations personified; in B.B. 16*a* he is identified with Satan. (8) Ibid. VII, 19. (9) I.e., by repentance and good deeds one can conquer the evil desires of all these.

as it is written, *And he* [sc. Melchizedek] *was the priest of the most high God.*[1] But because he gave precedence in his blessing to Abraham over God, He brought it forth from Abraham; as it is written, *And he blessed him and said, Blessed be Abram of the most high God, possessor of heaven and earth, and blessed be the most high God.*[2] Said Abraham to him, 'Is the blessing of a servant to be given precedence over that of his master?' Straightway it [the priesthood] was given to Abraham, as it is written, *The Lord said unto my Lord,*[3] *Sit thou at my right hand, until I make thine enemies thy footstool;*[4] which is followed by, *The Lord hath sworn, and will not repent, Thou art a priest for ever, after the order of Melchizedek;*[5] meaning, 'because of the words of Melchizedek.'[6] Hence it is written, *And* he *was a priest of the most High God,* [implying that] *he* was a priest, but not his seed.[7]

1) Gen. XIV, 18. The Midrash identifies him with Shem, the son of Noah, Abraham's eighth ancestor. (2) Ibid. 19f. (3) Here taken as referring to Abraham; cf. Ber. 7*b*, where *my Lord* is explicitly so explained. (4) Ps. CX, 1. (5) Ibid. CX, 4. (6) I.e., because of his giving precedence to Abraham. (7) Though Abraham was a descendant of Melchizedek, and thus the priesthood was inherited by the latter's seed, yet this was through the merit of Abraham, not of Melchizedek.—Ran.

NEDARIM

CHAPTER IV

MISHNAH. THE ONLY DIFFERENCE BETWEEN ONE WHO IS UNDER A VOW NOT TO BENEFIT AUGHT FROM HIS NEIGHBOUR, AND ONE WHO IS FORBIDDEN TO EAT OF HIS FOOD, IS IN RESPECT OF WALKING [OVER HIS PROPERTY] AND [THE USE OF] UTENSILS NOT EMPLOYED IN THE PREPARATION OF FOOD.[1] IF A MAN IS UNDER A VOW [NOT TO EAT] OF HIS NEIGHBOUR'S FOOD, THE LATTER MAY NOT LEND HIM A SIFTER, SIEVE, MILL-STONE OR OVEN,[2] BUT HE MAY LEND HIM A SHIRT, RING, CLOAK, AND EAR-RINGS.[3]

GEMARA. Which Tanna [is the authority of the Mishnah]?[4]—R. Adda b. Ahabah said, It is R. Eliezer. For it was taught: R. Eliezer said: Even the extra [given by a vendor to his customer] is forbidden to him who is under a vow not to benefit [by his neighbour].[5]

IF A MAN IS UNDER A VOW NOT TO [EAT] OF HIS NEIGHBOUR'S FOOD, THE LATTER MAY NOT LEND HIM etc. [33*a*] But he vowed in respect of *food?*[6]—Said R. Simeon b. Lakish: This refers to one who said, 'The benefit of your food be forbidden me.'[7] But may it not mean that he is not to chew wheat [to a pulp]

(1) If he is forbidden *all* benefit, these are forbidden; but if the vow is only in respect of food, these are permitted. (2) This teaches that not only are those utensils prohibited which are used in the immediate preparation of food *for eating*, such as a cooking pot, but even those employed in the early stages only. (3) [Or 'nose-rings']. (4) That even such a trifling benefit as walking over his property is forbidden. (5) Since R. Eliezer held that the vow applied even to such trifles, he is the authority of our Mishnah. (6) Which does not include these utensils. (7) Instead of simply 'Your food be forbidden me'. The additional words, 'b. etc.' are understood to include something besides actual food, viz., utensils for its preparation.

and apply it to his wound?[1]—Raba replied: The Mishnah refers to one who said: 'Any benefit from you *leading* to the enjoyment of food be forbidden me.' R. Papa said: A sack for bringing fruit, an ass for bringing fruit, and even a mere basket, all lead to the enjoyment of food. R. Papa propounded: What of a horse for travelling [to a banquet] or a ring to appear in;[2] or, what of passing over his land?[3]—Come and hear: BUT HE MAY LEND HIM A SHIRT, RING, CLOAK AND EAR-RINGS. How is this to be understood? Shall I say it is not to appear in them, need this be stated?[4] Hence it must mean to be seen in them, and it is taught that he *may* lend them to him!—No. After all, it does not mean to appear in them; but because the first clause teaches THE LATTER MAY NOT LEND HIM,[5] the second clause teaches HE MAY LEND HIM.[6]

MISHNAH. AND WHATEVER IS NOT EMPLOYED IN THE PREPARATION OF FOOD, WHERE SUCH ARE HIRED OUT, IT IS FORBIDDEN.[7]

GEMARA. Hence the first clause applies even where such things are not hired. Which Tanna [rules thus]?[8]—Said R. Adda b. Ahabah: It is R. Eliezer.[9]

MISHNAH. IF ONE IS UNDER A VOW NOT TO BENEFIT FROM HIS NEIGHBOUR, THE LATTER MAY PAY HIS SHEKEL,[10]

(1) I.e., the longer form may imply that food is forbidden no matter how used, yet still be confined to actual foodstuffs. (2) So as to be treated as an honoured guest. (3) On the way to a feast. (4) For then he does not benefit at all, and it is obvious that he may lend them to him. (5) This must be taught; v. p. 100, n. 2. (6) I.e., it is merely to round off the Mishnah, though it is self-evident. (7) Even to one who is under a vow in respect of *food* as explained in the Gemara above, for the remission of the hiring fee is a benefit leading to the enjoyment of food. (8) That even where the benefit is so trifling, since it can be borrowed without a fee, it is forbidden. (9) V. p. 100, n. 5. (10) There was an annual tax of half a *shekel* for the upkeep of the Temple; v. Shek. I, 1; Ex. XXX, 13.

SETTLE HIS DEBTS, AND RETURN A LOST ARTICLE TO HIM. WHERE PAYMENT IS TAKEN FOR THIS,[1] THE BENEFIT MUST ACCRUE TO HEKDESH.[2]

GEMARA. Thus we see that it is merely driving away a lion [from his neighbour's property],[3] and permitted. Which Tanna [rules thus]?—Said R. Hoshaia: This is [33*b*] Ḥanan's view.[4] Raba said: You may even say that it agrees with all: [We suppose that] the man who is interdicted by vow not to benefit from his neighbour was lent [money] without obligation to repay.[5]

What is [the ruling of] Ḥanan?—We learnt: If a man departed overseas, and another arose and supported his wife: Ḥanan said: He has lost his money.[6] But the sons of the High Priests[7] disputed this and maintained: He must swear how much he expended and is reimbursed [by the husband]. R. Dosa b. Harkinas ruled as they did; whilst R. Joḥanan b. Zakkai said: Ḥanan has ruled well—it is as though he had placed his money upon a deer's horn.[8]

Now, Raba did not say as R. Hoshaia, because he interpreted our Mishnah to harmonize with all views. R. Hoshaia did not say as Raba: [to settle a debt] that need not be repaid is forbidden as a preventive measure on account of [a debt] that must be repaid.[9]

AND RETURN A LOST ARTICLE TO HIM. R. Ammi and R. Assi [differ thereon]—one said: This is only when the property of the finder[10] is forbidden to the loser, so that in returning it to him, he

(1) E.g., if he lost work through returning the article; v. B.M. 30*b*. (2) V. Glos. This is discussed in the Gemara. (3) I.e., he is merely performing a neighbourly action, without bestowing real benefit, for even if the other man does not pay the *shekel*, he still shares in the public sacrifices; also, when his debts are settled, the debtor *personally* receives nothing. (4) This is explained further on. (5) The creditor having lent it to be repaid at the debtor's leisure (Ran). Therefore, when his neighbour repays his debt, he confers no benefit upon him. Similarly, he may pay his *shekel* only when he is not bound to pay it himself, e.g., if he had already sent it and it was lost on the road. (6) He has no claim upon the husband. (7) There was a special court of priests, and this may be referred to here; v. Keth. 104*b*. (8) I.e., he cannot expect its return. (9) Lest it be thought that the latter too may be settled. (10) Lit., 'restorer'.

returns what is his own.[1] But if the property of the loser is forbidden to the finder, he may not return it, because he benefits him by R. Joseph's *peruṭah.*[2] But the other maintained: Even if the finder may not benefit from the loser's property, he may return it, and as for R. Joseph's *peruṭah,* this is rare.[3] [34a] We learnt: WHERE PAYMENT IS TAKEN FOR THIS, THE BENEFIT MUST ACCRUE TO HEKDESH. Now, that is well on the view that even if the finder must not benefit from the loser's property, he may also return it: hence it is taught: WHERE PAYMENT IS MADE FOR THIS, THE BENEFIT MUST ACCRUE TO HEKDESH.[4] But on the view that if the finder may not benefit from the loser he must not return it, why should the benefit accrue to *hekdesh?*[5] —This law refers to one case only.[6]

Others report it in the following version: R. Ammi and R. Assi differ thereon: one said: This was taught only if the finder may not benefit from the loser's property, R. Joseph's *peruṭah* being rare;

(1) So that the loser is not benefiting. (2) Since when a person is engaged in the performance of one precept, he is exempt from another, the finder, when fulfilling this precept, may decline to give a *peruṭah* of charity to a poor man. This is referred to as R. Joseph's *peruṭah,* because he based a certain ruling upon this fact. B.K. 56*b*. (3) One rarely avails himself of that privilege, hence the finder gains nothing. (4) For since the finder cannot benefit from the loser, he cannot receive his fee from him; on the other hand, the loser is liable for it; therefore it goes to *hekdesh;* v. p. 104, n. 2, for the reverse case. (5) Since he may not return it, there is no fee. (6) I.e., where the loser may not benefit from the finder. This is the interpretation of the passage according to our text. But the text of Ran is reversed, and (with its explanation) is as follows: This is well on the view that only if the loser may not benefit from the finder it may be returned, but not in the reverse case. Hence, the fee must go to the Temple treasury, if it is beneath the finder's dignity to accept it, for were the loser to retain it, he would be benefiting from the finder. But on the view that even if the finder must not benefit from the loser it may be returned, why must the fee go to the Temple treasury? If the finder declines it, the loser may retain it, since here is no prohibition upon *him.* If on the other hand the finder wishes to accept it, why may he not do so: in accepting it he is not benefiting from the loser, but merely being paid for lost time? The Talmud replies that though the law permitting the return of the lost article applies to both cases, the statement that the fee must go to the sanctuary applies only to one, viz., where the loser may not benefit from the finder.

but if the loser may not benefit from the finder's property, he may not return it, because he [the finder] benefits him. While the other maintained: Even if the loser may not benefit from the finder's property, he may return it, for he is only returning his own.

We learnt: WHERE PAYMENT IS TAKEN FOR THIS, THE BENEFIT MUST ACCRUE TO HEḲDESH. Now that is well on the view that even if the loser may not benefit from the finder, he may also return it: thus he justifies WHERE [etc.],[1] but on the view that if the loser may not benefit from the finder, he may not return it, how is WHERE [etc.] explained?[2] This is a difficulty.

[34b] Raba said: If a *hefḳer* loaf[3] lies before a man, and he declares, 'This loaf be *heḳdesh*', and he takes it to eat it, he trespasses in respect of its entire value; if to leave it to his children, he trespasses in respect of its goodwill value only.[4] R. Ḥiyya b. Abin asked Raba: [What if one says to his neighbour,] 'My loaf [be forbidden] to you,' and then gifts it to him: now, he said, '*my* loaf,' meaning only so long as it is in his own possession;[5] or perhaps, having said '[be forbidden] to you,' he has rendered it to him *heḳdesh*?[6]—He replied: It is obvious that even if he gifted it to him, it is forbidden. For what was it [his vow] to exclude? Surely not the case where

(1) The law referring to this case, as explained above, where it is beneath the finder's dignity to accept the fee. (2) For then it may be returned only if the loser may benefit from the finder; but in that case, why must the fee be given to *heḳdesh*? If the finder does not accept it, the loser may retain it for himself. (3) V. Glos. (4) A *Zar* (i.e., not a priest) is forbidden to eat consecrated food; if he does, he is guilty of trespass, and bound to make restitution of its value plus a fifth (Lev. XXII, 14). Now as soon as he takes this consecrated loaf, with the intent of eating it, he withdraws it from the possession of *heḳdesh* into his own. Hence he has trespassed in respect of the whole of it. But if he merely intends leaving it to his children, he merely benefits by its goodwill value (i.e., the benefit he enjoys through his children's knowing that he wishes to leave it to them) and hence liable for that only. [Had, however, the loaf been his own, he would not have been guilty of a trespass by taking it up with the intent of eating it. Since it was all the time in his possession, both before and after the consecration, he would be treated in regard to it as a Temple Treasurer, to whom the law of trespass does not apply, v. B.Ḳ. (Sonc. ed.) p. 103.] (5) Therefore now that he gave it to him, it is no longer his; hence permitted. (6) So that the prohibition always remains.

it would be stolen from him?[1] —He replied, No: It excludes the case
where he invites him for it.[2]

[35a] He objected: If A says to B, 'Lend me your cow,' and B
replies, '*Konam* be [this] cow if I possess [another] for you,'[3] or,
'my property be forbidden you if I possess any cow but this': [or,]
'Lend me your spade,' and he replies, 'This spade be forbidden
me if I possess [another];' or 'my property be forbidden me, if
I possess any spade but this', and it is discovered that he possesses
[another]. During his [B's] lifetime it is forbidden [him]; but if
he dies, or it is given to him,[4] it is permitted?[5] —Said R. Aḥa son
of R. Iḳa: That is if it was given to him through another.[6] R. Ashi
said: This may be proved too, for it is stated, 'it is given to him,'
not 'he gives it to him.'[7]

Raba asked R. Naḥman: Does the law of trespass apply to
Konamoth?[8] —He replied, We have learnt this: WHERE PAYMENT
IS TAKEN FOR THIS, THE BENEFIT MUST ACCRUE TO HEĶ-
DESH. This teaches that it is as *hekdesh:* just as the law of trespass
applies to *hekdesh*, so it applies to *Konamoth*.

---

(1) When A says to B, 'My loaf be forbidden to you', thus excluding B from
its enjoyment, what is his purpose? Obviously, as long as it is in A's possession it is forbidden to B in any case, since it does not belong to him. Surely
A did not intend his vow only in the unlikely event of the loaf being stolen?
Hence he must have meant, 'Even if I give you this loaf, which is now mine,
it shall be forbidden to you.'   (2) I.e., if A should invite B to dine with him
off that loaf of bread, it should be forbidden to him; but not if he gives it to
him. This interpretation follows Ran. Others explain the passage differently.
According to all versions, לאו must be deleted from the text.   (3) The actual
wording is difficult, and the commentators attempt various explanations. The
literal translation is given here.   (4) V. *infra*.   (5) This contradicts Raba.
(6) B gave it to C, who gave it to A. Since B *voluntarily* (in contradistinction
to theft) let it out of his possession, his vow loses its validity.   (7) Though
the Hebrew word is the same for both, by tradition it was to be read as a
niphal, not as a *kal*.   (8) A *terminus technicus* for things interdicted by a vow,
usually introduced with the formula *konam*. Since *konam* is a *korban* (a sacrifice)
when one vows that a thing shall be *konam*, he declares it to be virtually
consecrated, and hence if the vow is violated, it is as though trespass has been
committed. Or it may be argued that in spite of its origin, *konam* is used
without the suggestion of consecration, but merely to imply prohibition.

This is dependent on Tannaim: If one says, '*Ḳonam,* this loaf
is *heḳdesh,*'¹ then whosoever eats it, whether he or his neighbour,
commits trespass; therefore the law of redemption applies to it.²
[But if he says,] 'This loaf is *heḳdesh* to me'; [by eating it] he commits
trespass; but his neighbour does not commit a trespass; therefore
the law of redemption does not apply:³ this is the view of R. Meir.
But the Sages maintain: In both cases no trespass is involved, because the law of trespass does not apply to *Ḳonamoth.*

R. Aḥa son of R. Avi asked R. Ashi: [If A says to B,] 'My loaf
be forbidden to you,'⁴ and then makes a gift of it to him, who is
liable for trespass? Shall the giver incur it — but it is not forbidden
to him? Is the receiver to incur it — but he can say, 'I desired to
accept what is permitted, not what is forbidden?'⁵ — He replied:
The receiver incurs the liability when he uses it, for whoever
converts money of *heḳdesh* into *ḥullin,*⁶ thinks that it is *ḥullin,* yet
he is involved in trespass;⁷ so this one too is liable for trespass.

MISHNAH. [35b] AND HE MAY SEPARATE HIS TERUMAH
AND HIS TITHES WITH HIS CONSENT.⁸ HE MAY OFFER UP FOR
HIM THE BIRD SACRIFICES OF ZABIM AND ZABOTH⁹ AND
THE BIRD SACRIFICES OF WOMEN AFTER CHILDBIRTH, SIN-
OFFERINGS AND GUILT-OFFERINGS.¹⁰ HE MAY TEACH HIM
MIDRASH, HALACHOTH AND AGGADOTH,¹¹ BUT NOT

(1) Not specifying to whom, and therefore applying it to all, including himself.
[Read with MS.M.: 'This loaf is *heḳdesh*', omitting *ḳonam;* v. also Shebu. 22a.]
(2) Since it is so much regarded as consecrated that by eating it one commits
trespass, it is also so in respect of redemption, whereby it reverts to *ḥullin*
(non-consecrated), whilst the redemption money becomes consecrated. (3) Since
it is not regarded as consecrated in respect of all. (4) Using the formula '*ḳonam*'.
(5) The receiver not knowing that this was the forbidden loaf. (6) V. Glos.
(7) Because the law of trespass applies only to unwitting misuse of *heḳdesh.*
(8) If A is forbidden to benefit from B, B (the *maddir*) may separate *terumah* on
the produce of the former (called the *muddar*). The Gemara discusses whose
consent is meant. (9) V. Glos. (10) Lev. XV, 14f, 29f, XII, 6-8. i.e., the
maddir, if a priest, may offer these sacrifices for the *muddar.* (11) The three
branches of Jewish learning. *Midrash* (from *darash,* to study, investigate) means

SCRIPTURE.[1] YET HE MAY TEACH SCRIPTURE TO HIS SONS AND DAUGHTERS.[2]

GEMARA. The scholars propounded: Are the priests [in sacrificing] our agents or agents of the All-Merciful? What is the practical difference?—In respect of one who is forbidden to benefit [from a priest]: if you say that they are our agents, surely he [the priest] benefits him [by offering up his sacrifices]; hence it is prohibited. But if you say that they are the agents of the All-Merciful, it is permitted. What [then is the ruling]?—Come and hear: We learnt: HE MAY OFFER UP FOR HIM THE BIRD SACRIFICES [etc.]. Now if you say that they are our agents, does he not benefit him? Then on your view, let him [the Tanna] teach, HE MAY OFFER UP SACRIFICES FOR HIM?[3] But those who lack atonement are different.[4] For R. Johanan said: All [sacrifices]

any kind of Biblical hermeneutics. In contradistinction to the *peshaṭ* (literal interpretation) it denotes the deeper investigation into the text of the Bible in order to derive interpretations and laws not obvious on the surface. *Halachoth* is a term referring to religious law (embracing both civil and ritual law) whether based on Biblical exposition, (and thus arrived at by *Midrash*) or not. By *Aggadah* (or *Haggadah*, from *higgid*, to narrate) is meant the whole of the non-legal portion of the Talmud. Thus it includes narratives, homiletical exegesis of the Bible (which inculcate morals, beliefs, etc. but no actual laws) medicine, astronomy, dreams, legends and folklore in general.

(1) Lit., 'that which is (to be) read' *sc.* from a written text. The Pentateuch with its literal interpretations in contradistinction to Midrash, v. Aboth (Sonc. ed.) p. 75, n. 1. As will be seen on 37*a*, Scripture was generally regarded as the study of children only, adults usually investigating the deeper meaning too. (2) From this we see that it was usual to teach the Bible to girls, in spite of the Talmudic deduction that daughters need not be educated (Ḳid. 30*a*). The opposition of R. Eliezer to teaching Torah to one's daughter (Soṭ. 20*a*: He who teaches his daughter Torah is as though he taught her lewdness) was probably directed against the teaching of the Oral Law, and the higher branches of study. [V. Maim. *Yad. Talmud Torah*, I, 13.] Yet even in respect of this, his view was not universally accepted, and Ben 'Azzai (*a.l.*) regarded it as a positive duty to teach Torah to one's daughters. The context shows that the reference is to the higher knowledge of Biblical law. In point of fact, there were learned women in Talmudic times e.g., Beruriah, wife of R. Meir (Pes. 62*b*). (3) Sacrifices, in general, not just these. (4) I.e., those who are unclean, and not

require [the owner's] consent,[1] save for those lacking atonement; since a man brings a sacrifice for his sons and daughters when minors, for it is said, *This is the law of him that hath issue,*[2] [implying] both for a minor or an adult.[3] If so, according to R. Johanan, does, *This is the law for her that hath born [a male or a female]*[4] imply both an adult or a minor? Is a minor capable of childbirth? But R. Bibi recited in R. Naḥman's presence: Three women use a resorbent [to prevent conception]: a minor, a pregnant woman, and a woman giving suck: a minor, lest she conceive and die?[5]—That verse, '*This is the law for her that hath born*', [teaches,] that it is all one whether the woman be sane or an imbecile, since one must offer a sacrifice for his wife, if an imbecile, in accordance with R. Judah's dictum. For it was taught: R. Judah said: A man must offer a rich man's sacrifice[6] for his wife, and all other sacrifices which are incumbent upon her; since he writes thus for her [in her marriage settlement]: [I shall pay] every claim you may have against me from before up to now.[7] [36a] R. Simi b. Abba objected: If he [the

permitted to eat holy food (e.g., the flesh of sacrifices) or enter the Sanctuary until their sacrifices have been offered up. This term however does not refer to sinners, whose sacrifice makes atonement for them. The sin- and guilt-offerings mentioned in the Mishnah will also refer to the former.

(1) Before the priest may offer them. (2) Lev. XV, 32, referring to the sacrifices. (3) The expression '*this is the law*' is emphatic, and hence extends its provisions to include those who might otherwise not have been included. Since a minor cannot bring a sacrifice himself, his father must do so for him. Moreover, a minor has no legal consent. Thus, we see that these sacrifices can be brought without their owner's (i.e., those on whose behalf it is offered) consent. Since their consent is unnecessary, the priests do not act as their agents, and on that account it is permitted. (4) Ibid. XII, 7. (5) V. Yeb. 12*b*. Thus we see that a minor is incapable of childbirth.—Of course, the same might have been stated simply on physiological grounds. (6) Certain sacrifices were variable, depending on their owner's financial position (v. Lev. V, 1-13; XII, 1-8). Now in a strictly legal sense every married woman is poor, since she has no proprietary rights, everything belonging to her husband. Nevertheless, if he is wealthy, he must bring the sacrifice of a rich person. (7) [This clause is taken as referring to sacrifices for which she may have become liable after the betrothal.] So curr. edd. Ran omits 'R. Judah said' from the beginning of the Baraitha, and adds at this point: R. Judah said: Therefore, if he divorced her, he is free from this liability, for thus she writes (in the document acknowledging

maddir][1] is a priest, he may sprinkle for him the blood of his sin-offering and his guilt-offering?[2] — This refers to the blood of a leper's sin-offering and of a leper's guilt-offering [who lack atonement], as it is written, *This shall be the law of the leper:*[3] both an adult and a minor.[4]

We learnt: If priests render a sacrifice *piggul*[5] in the Temple, and do so intentionally, they are liable;[6] This implies [that if they do so] unwittingly, they are exempt, though it was taught thereon:[7] Yet their *piggul* stands.[8] Now, it is well if you say that they are the agents of the All-Merciful: hence their *piggul* stands. But if you say that they are our agents, why is it so; let him say to him, 'I appointed you an agent for my advantage, not for my hurt'?[9] — I will tell you: *Piggul* is different, because the Writ saith, *neither shall it be imputed unto him:*[10] [implying that it is *piggul*] in spite of everything.[11]

The [above] text [states]: 'R. Johanan said: All require [the owner's] consent, save for those lacking atonement, since one brings a sacrifice for his sons and daughters when minors.' If so, let one offer a sin-offering on behalf of his neighbour for [eating]

receipt of settlements due to her on divorce): (I free you) from all the liabilities hitherto borne by you in respect of me. From the Rashi in B.M. 104*a*, it appears that his version there was the same as the Ran's here. Now, reverting to the argument, since R. Judah (and the first Tanna) taught that a husband is liable for his wife's obligatory sacrifices, '*this is the law*' may be interpreted as applying to an imbecile too, the liability resting with her husband. For if this principle of the husband's liability were not admitted, this interpretation would be impossible, since an imbecile herself is not a responsible person.

(1) V. Glos. (2) Now, since these offerings are unspecified, they must refer to all, even of those who do not lack atonement. (3) Lev. XIV, 2, referring to his purificatory sacrifices. (4) Therefore the same reasoning applies as in the case of a *zab*. (5) V. Glos. Such a sacrifice is 'not acceptable' and does not acquit its owner of his liability, so that he is bound to offer another. (6) To compensate the owner of the sacrifice. (7) This is absent in our text, but supplied from Men. 49*a*. (8) Though committed unwittingly, the sacrifice remains *piggul*. (9) I.e., such an act committed on behalf of someone else can be repudiated. (10) Lev. VII, 18. (11) I.e., the priest is the owner's agent, yet the latter cannot repudiate him, because his power of rendering a sacrifice *piggul* is absolute and unconditional.

ḥeleb,[1] since one brings [a sin-offering] for his insane wife?[2] Why then did R. Eleazar say: If a man set aside a sin-offering for *ḥeleb* on his neighbour's behalf, his action is invalid?[3]—[Now consider:] In respect to his insane wife, what are the circumstances? If she ate [*ḥeleb*] whilst insane, she is not liable to a sacrifice;[4] while if she ate it when sane, subsequently becoming insane, [there is the ruling of] R. Jeremiah who said in the name of R. Abbahu in R. Joḥanan's name: If a man ate *ḥeleb*, set aside an offering, became insane, and then regained his sanity, it [the sacrifice] is unfit: having been once rejected, it remains so.[5]

Yet if so,[6] a man should be able to offer the Passover sacrifice for his neighbour,[7] since he brings it for his sons and daughters, who are minors. Why then did R. Eleazar say: If a man sets aside a Passover sacrifice for his neighbour his action[7] is null?—Said R. Zera: [The law, *And they shall take to them every man*] *a lamb, according to the house of their fathers*, [*a lamb for a house*],[8] is not Biblically incumbent [upon minors].[9] And how do we know this?—Because we learnt: If a man says to his sons [who are not of age], 'I will slaughter the Passover sacrifice for whomever of you first enters Jerusalem', then as soon as the first of them enters with his

(1) Forbidden fat. The objection is not particularly in regard to this sin-offering, but to all sin-offerings brought on account of transgression. The addition of *ḥeleb* merely illustrates the type of offering referred to, and is frequently used as the general designation of a sin-offering. (2) Who also has neither legal consent nor knowledge. (3) The animal not becoming sanctified. (4) Not being responsible for her actions. (5) I.e., when the transgressor lost his reason, his sacrifice became unfit for offering, because an insane person cannot offer, and it remains unfit even if he regains his sanity. Thus we see that even if a sane person sinned, he is not liable to a sacrifice on becoming insane. Therefore, one cannot bring a sin-offering for his insane wife for actual transgression; hence the proposed analogy cannot be drawn. (6) Still objecting to R. Joḥanan's first ruling. (7) Without his knowledge. (8) Ex. XII, 3. (9) The Passover sacrifice had to be definitely assigned (before the animal was slain) to a number of persons and anyone not so appointed was subsequently forbidden to eat thereof. But this assignment does not, by Scriptural law, apply to minors at all. For this reason the father could slaughter for them, since they did not need to be appointed. Hence, one cannot argue from this to an adult, to whom the law of appointment applies.

head and the greater part of his body, he acquires his portion, and assigns a part thereof to his brothers with him. Now, if you maintain that *'a lamb, according to the house of their fathers'* is Biblically applicable [to minors], then standing over the flesh, can he transfer a portion to his brethren?[1] If so, why did their father speak thus to them?—In order to stimulate them in [the performance of] precepts. It was taught likewise: It once happened [after their father had spoken thus] that the daughters entered [the city] before the sons, so that the daughters shewed themselves zealous, and the sons indolent.[2]

HE MAY SEPARATE HIS TERUMAH [etc.] [36*b*] The scholars propounded: If one gives *terumah* of his own for his neighbour's produce, does he require his consent or not? Do we say, since it is a benefit for him, his consent is unnecessary;[3] or perhaps, [the privilege of performing] the precept is his, and he prefers to perform it himself? Come and hear! HE MAY SEPARATE HIS TERUMAH AND HIS TITHES WITH HIS CONSENT. How is this meant: Shall we say, his own corn is used?[4] Then with whose consent? If with his own, who appointed him an agent?[5] But if it means with the owner's consent—does he not benefit him by acting as his agent?[6] Hence it must mean that he separates his own [i.e., the *maddir's*] produce for the owner's. Now, with whose consent? If with the owner's, does he not benefit him? Hence it must mean with his own knowledge [without informing the owner].[7] Now if you say that he requires his consent, does he not benefit him?[8]

(1) For the assignment of the sacrifice can be made only before it is slain, not after (Pes. 89*a*). How then can one son assign a portion of the sacrifice to his brothers after it is killed? Therefore we must conclude that by Biblical law they are not bound to be appointed for the eating of the sacrifice at all. (2) But it is not stated that they lost their portion, proving that assignment is not Biblically incumbent upon them. (3) As it may be taken for granted. (4) Lit., '(produce) of the owner of the stack (is separated as *terumah*, etc.) for produce belonging to the owner of the stack.' (5) I.e., surely A cannot separate *terumah* for B, using B's produce, without the latter's consent. (6) Whereas his vow forbids him to benefit him. (7) [This is not regarded as a direct benefit, since he does not give him aught; v. Ran.] (8) For by consenting he shews that he regards it as a benefit.

—[No.] After all, it means the owner's [produce] for the owner's produce; and it is as Raba said [elsewhere], That the owner had announced, 'Whoever wishes to separate, let him do so;' here, too, the owner had announced etc.[1]

R. Jeremiah asked R. Zera: If one separates of his own for his neighbour's [produce], to whom does the goodwill [value] belong?[2] Do we say, but for this man's produce, would the other's stack have been made fit to use?[3] Or perhaps, but for this man's stack, the other man's produce would not be *terumah*?[4]—He replied, Scripture saith, *all the increase of thy seed .... and thou shalt give.*[5]

He objected: HE MAY SEPARATE HIS TERUMAH AND HIS TITHES WITH HIS CONSENT. Now if you say that the goodwill belongs to the owner, surely he [the *maddir*] benefits him? Hence this proves that the goodwill is his![6]—I will tell you: it is not so. This means that the *terumah* belongs to the owner; 'HIS CONSENT' also referring to the owner, who had announced, 'Whoever wishes to separate, let him do so.'

Come and hear: R. Abbahu said in R. Joḥanan's name: He who sanctifies the animal must add the fifth, whilst only he for whom atonement is made sanctifies a substitute;[7] and he who gives

(1) Though such an announcement is a sufficient authorisation, the *maddir* is not thereby specially appointed an agent, and so does not directly benefit him. (2) I.e., if another Israelite paid him something to give the *terumah* to a particular friend of his, to whom does that thing belong? (3) Therefore the goodwill should belong to him who renders the *terumah*. (4) Produce can be declared *terumah* only on account of other produce. But one cannot take some corn and declare it *terumah*. (5) Deut. XIV, 25. In its context, *thou shalt give* refers to the changing of produce into money; but it is here taken out of its context and related to *all the increase of thy seed*, shewing that the goodwill belongs to the owner of the corn, no matter who actually separates the tithe. This is the reading of our text, and also that of Ran. But such forcible disregard of the context is not very plausible. Asheri prefers a preferable reading: (*When thou hast made an end of tithing*) *All the tithes of thine increase . . . and thou shalt give it to the Levite;* (Deut. XXVI, 12). (6) This of course is on the assumption that the *maddir* gives his own corn as *terumah*. (7) If A dedicates an animal for B's sacrifice and it subsequently receives a blemish and must be redeemed, then if A, who sanctified it, redeems it himself, he must add a fifth to its value, but not if B redeems it (this is deduced from Lev. XXVII, 15). Again,

terumah of his own for another man's produce, the goodwill is his.[1]

HE MAY TEACH HIM MIDRASH, HALACHOTH, AND AGGA-
DOTH, BUT NOT SCRIPTURE. Why not Scripture—because he
benefits him? But [by] Midrash too he benefits him?—Said Samuel:
This refers to a place where the teaching of Scripture is remuner-
ated, but not that of Midrash. How state this definitely?[2]—[37a]
He [the Tanna] informs us this: that even where a fee is taken, it
may be accepted only for Scripture, but not for Midrash. Now, why
does Midrash differ, that remuneration is forbidden: because it is
written, *And the Lord commanded me at that time to teach you;*[3] and it
is also written, *Behold I have taught you statutes and judgments, even
as the Lord my God commanded me*[4] just as I [taught you] gratuitously,
so you must teach gratuitously? Then should not Scripture too
be unremunerated?—Rab said: The fee is for guarding [the
children]. R. Joḥanan maintained: The fee is for the teaching of
accentuation.[5]

We learnt: HE MAY NOT TEACH HIM SCRIPTURE. Now that is
well on the view that remuneration is for the teaching of accentuation. But on the view that payment is for acting as guardian—does

if another animal is substituted for the first, both the original and its substitute
are holy (ibid. 10). R. Joḥanan rules that this is only if B, on whose behalf the
animal was sanctified, made the substitution, but not if A did so.

(1) Sc. the man who gives it. (2) Seeing that the statement in the Mishnah
is unqualified. (3) Deut. IV, 14. (4) Ibid. 5. (5) The whole system of
punctuation and accentuation being post-Biblical, Moses' prohibition does not
apply to it. The meaning of the phrase *pisuk ṭe' ammim* is not altogether clear.
Jastrow translates: 'the division of words into clauses in accordance with the
sense, punctuation'. Be that as it may, it must at least refer to a particular
manner of dividing the Biblical text with or without signs, over and above that
which would naturally suggest itself by the subject matter. This conclusion
must be drawn from the fact that it is regarded by Rab as non-Sinaitic: yet the
clearly natural division, corresponding to *peshaṭ,* could not have been thought
of as introduced after Moses; what sense then did it make otherwise? There is
mention of chanting in Meg. 32a, but there the reference is to the Mishnah as
well as the Bible, the former being studied in a sort of chant, and the phrase
pisuk ṭe'ammim is not used there. [Berliner, A., however, in *Bertr. z. hebr. Gram.*
p. 29, n. 1, quotes Rashi on Gen. Rab. XXXVI, (according to a München MS.)
as explaining *pisuk ṭe'ammim* as *Tropen,* cantillation.]

an adult need one?[1]—It refers to a child. If so, consider the last clause: BUT HE MAY TEACH SCRIPTURE TO HIS SONS: can a child have children?—It is defective, and teaches thus: HE MAY NOT TEACH HIM SCRIPTURE in the case of a minor: but if he is an adult, HE MAY TEACH SCRIPTURE BOTH TO him and HIS SONS.

An objection is raised: Children are not to study a new portion of Bible on the Sabbath; but they may make a first revision on the Sabbath.[2] This is well on the view that remuneration is for the teaching of accentuation: hence a passage may not be read for the first time on the Sabbath;[3] but on the view that payment is for acting as guardian, why is it forbidden to teach a passage for the first time on the Sabbath, yet permitted to give a first revision on the Sabbath; surely there is pay for guardianship on the Sabbath?[4] —Now, even according to your reasoning: is remuneration for teaching the accentuation on the Sabbath forbidden? Is it not included [in the weekly or monthly fee], which is permitted? For it was taught: If one engages a [day] labourer to look after a child,[5] or the heifer,[6] or to watch over the crops,[7] he may not pay him for the Sabbath:[8] therefore [37*b*] if they are lost [or harmed] [on the Sabbath], he is not responsible. But if he was engaged by the week, month, year or septennate, he is paid for the Sabbath;

(1) Hence, Bible teaching to an adult should be unremunerated, in which case it should be permitted in the Mishnah. (2) I.e., having studied it before, they may revise it even for the first time on the Sabbath. (3) Because remuneration is made chiefly for teaching a passage for the first time, as that is the most difficult part of instruction. Hence, if a new passage is thus taught on the Sabbath, the teacher is paid chiefly for Sabbath labour, which is forbidden. (4) What does it matter whether the passage is a new one or not? The guardianship is the same in both cases, and remuneration for such work on the Sabbath is forbidden. (5) That he should not ritually defile himself. It was customary for a child to draw the water from a well to mix with the ashes of the red heifer; this child had to be ritually clean. (6) This refers to the red heifer. The guardian was to take care that '*no yoke came upon it*' (Num. XIX, 2). (7) This refers to the barley specially sown seventy days before Passover (Men. 85*a*) for the ceremony of 'sheaf waving' (v. Lev. XXIII, 11) and to the wheat of which were made the '*two wave-loaves*' on Pentecost (ibid. 17). These crops were specially guarded. (8) Since each day is separately paid for, and payment for the Sabbath *per se* is forbidden.

consequently, if they are lost, he is responsible.[1] But in the matter of the Sabbath a new passage may not be studied for the first time for this reason: that the parents of the children may be free for the observance of the Sabbath. An alternative answer is this: because on the Sabbath they eat and drink [more than on week-days] and feel sluggish;[2] as Samuel said: The change in one's regular diet is the beginning of digestive trouble.[3]

Now, he who maintains that remuneration is for the teaching of accentuation,—why does he reject the view that it is for acting as guardian?—He reasons: Do daughters then need guarding?[4] And

(1) Thus we see that the Sabbath may be paid for providing it is included in the general weekly agreement. Hence, though the main work in teaching lies in the first reading, this should be permitted on the Sabbath, since the fee is included in the general arrangements. (2) Hence are not fit to study a portion for the first time. (3) Lit., 'disease of the bowels'. The Sabbath being a day of delight, the parents naturally wish to play and amuse themselves with their children thereon. But if the children study a new passage on that day, since this requires great concentration, the parents may be afraid of distracting their attention. It is interesting to observe from actual life what the Sabbath meant to the people. In spite of the innumerable restrictions pertaining to that day, and on account of which the Sabbath has been severely criticised as an intolerable burden, right from the New Testament times down to the present day, this simple statement, teaching no doctrine or view of the Sabbath, but recording a simple fact, vividly illustrates the utter shallowness of all that misinformed criticism. Cf. Schechter, *Studies in Judaism* ('The Law and Recent Criticism, pp. 296f).—'On the one side, we hear the opinions of so many learned professors, proclaiming *ex cathedra* that the Law was a most terrible burden, and the life under it the most unbearable slavery . . . On the other side we have the testimony of a literature extending over about twenty-five centuries, and including all sorts and conditions of men, scholars, poets, mystics, lawyers . . . schoolmen, tradesmen, workmen, women, simpletons, who all . . . give unanimous evidence in favour of this Law, and of the bliss and happiness of living and dying under it,—and this, the testimony of people who were actually living under the Law, not merely theorising upon it'. (4) Girls are generally at home and do not venture into the streets; hence require no guarding. Now the Mishnah states in general terms that he may not teach Scripture. Though this, as explained, refers to a minor, yet even so the law holds good both of boys and of girls, since no limitations are given. But if payment is for guardianship, he should be permitted to teach girls, who do not need it.—Another reading is: does an adult need guarding? According to this, the

he who maintains that the fee is for guardianship,—why does he reject the view that it is for teaching accents?—He holds that accents are also Biblical;[1] for R. Iḳa b. Abin said in the name of R. Ḥananel in Rab's name: What is the meaning of, *And they read in the book, in the law of God, distinctly, and they gave the sense, so that they understood the reading?*[2] '*They read in the book, in the law of God,*' refers to Scripture; '*distinctly,*' to *Targum;*[3] '*and they gave the sense*', to the division of sentences; '*so that they understood the reading,*' to the accentuation; others say, to the *masoroth.*[4]

R. Isaac said: The textual reading,[5] as transmitted by the Soferim, their stylistic embellishments, [words] read [in the text] but not written, and words written but omitted in the reading, are all *halachah* from Moses at Sinai.[6] By textual reading is meant words

explanation that the Mishnah refers to a minor is rejected as being too far-fetched.

(1) I.e., the system of accentuations goes back to Moses: consequently it was included in Moses' prohibition. (2) Neh. VIII, 8. (3) Targum, 'translation', generally refers to the Aramaic translation of the Bible. In Mishnaic phraseology it might refer to a translation from Hebrew or the Bible into any language, (v. J. Ḳid. 59*a*, where it denotes a Greek version of Aquila; Meg. II, 1; Shab. 115*a*), but the word Targum by itself was restricted to the Aramaic version of the Bible. This Aramaic translation was publically read in the synagogue, along with the original text, and rules for reading it were formulated (v. Meg. II, 1; Tosef. Meg. II, V). This practice was an ancient institution, dating back to the Second Temple, and according to Rab, going back to Ezra, v. *J.E.*, XII, p. 57. (4) *Masoroth:* Tosaf. and Asheri refer this to the plene and defective readings, e.g., where the 'o' is represented by waw (plene) and where it is missing (defective); where the 'i' is shewn by *yod*, and where not. Ran simply states: the traditional readings. The term '*masorah*' occurs in Ezek. XX, 37, and means 'fetter'. Thus the masorah is a fetter upon the text, i.e., it fixes its reading. In course of time it was connected with *masar* (to hand down), and thus came to mean traditional reading. The old Hebrew text was in all probability written without any breaks. It was the work of the Masorites to make the divisions into words, books, sections, paragraphs, etc., and fix the orthography and pronunciation. The traditionally fixed text, especially with a view to its orthography, was called *masoreth;* the division into sense-clauses, *pisuḳ ṭe'ammim;* the traditional pronunciation, *miḳra*. V. *J.E.* s.v. Masorah. (5) V. preceding note. (6) I.e., though these were established by the Soferim (v. Glos.) they are based on usage going back to Moses.

as *erez, shamayim, mizraim.*[1] Stylistic embellishments: e.g., [*and comfort ye your hearts;*] after *that ye shall pass on.*[2] [*Let the damsel abide with us a few days, at least ten:*] after *that she shall go.* [*Avenge the children of Israel of the Midianites;*] afterwards, *shalt thou be gathered unto thy people.*[3] [*The singers went before,*] *the players on instruments followed after.*[4] *Thy righteousness is* like *the great mountains.*[5]

[Words] read [in the text] but not written: [the word] '*Euphrates*' in [the verse] *as he went to recover his border at the river* [*Euphrates*];[6] [the word] '*man*' in [the verse] *And the counsel of Ahitophel . . . was as if a* [*man*] *had enquired of the oracle of God;*[7] [the word] '*come*' in [the verse] *Behold, the days* [*come*], *saith the Lord, the city shall be built etc.;*[8] '*for it*' in [the verse] *let there be no escape* [*for it*];[9] '*unto me*' in [the verse] *All that thou sayest* [*unto me*] *I will do;* '*to me*' [in the verse] *And she went down unto the floor;*[10] '*to me*' in [the verse] *And she said, These six measures of barley gave he unto me; for he said* [*to me*].[11] All these [words] are read but not written.[12] The following are written

(1) In pause (viz., an *ethnaḥta* or *sof pasuḳ*) the tone-vowels are lengthened. Since there is nothing in the lettering to indicate this grammatical change, it was the work of the Soferim to teach it. (2) Gen. XVIII, 5. (3) Num. XXXI, 2. (4) Ps. LXVIII, 26. (5) Ps. XXXVI, 7. In all these examples '*after*' is strictly speaking superfluous, for the verses would have made the same sense without it (presumably by the use of the copulative). In the last example, the comparative *kaf* (like) is also unnecessary, being omitted in the parallel stich: *thy judgments are a great deep.* But they are inserted in the text in order to give it a smoother flow. Ran: In all these cases, '*after*' (Heb. *aḥar*), and in the last example, '*like* the mountains' (Heb. *keharere*) bear a disjunctive accent, so as to elucidate the meaning. E.g., the first example (disregarding the accents) might read, 'and comfort ye your hearts after ye shall have passed', and so the other examples. The last example, owing to the disjunctive of *ke-harere*, is according to Ran to be translated: *Thy righteousness, O God, is as* (*manifest as*) *the mountains.* These disjunctives are referred to as the embellishments of the Soferim. Goldschmidt, Nedarim a.l. (p. 442, n. 84) observes that a copulative word has been omitted in all these texts, as is shewn by the Samaritan text and some MSS. (6) II Sam. VIII, 3. (7) Ibid. XVI, 23. (8) Jer. XXXI, 38. (9) Jer. L, 29. (10) Ruth III, 5. (11) Ibid. 17. (12) Wilna Gaon adds the following examples, given in some editions, and also in Soferim VI, 8: *But* (*the children of*) *Benjamin would not hearken* (Jud. XX, 13); *Because* (Heb. *Ki 'al ken: ken* is read but not written) *the king's son is dead* (II Sam. XVIII, 20); *The zeal of the Lord of* (*hosts*) (II Kings XIX, 31); *Adrammelech and Sharaezer* (*his sons*) *smote him* (Ibid. 37).

but not read: [the word] '*pray*' in *forgive;*[1] [38a] '*these*' in *Now* [*these*] *are the commandments.*[2] '*let him bend*' in *Against him that bendeth* [*let him bend*] *the bow;*[3] '*five*' in *and on the south side, four thousand and five* [*five*] *hundred;*[4] '*if*' in *it is time that* [*if*] *I am thy near kinsman.*[5] The foregoing are written but not read.[6]

R. Aḥa b. Adda said: In the West [i.e., Palestine] the following verse is divided into three verses, viz., *And the Lord said unto Moses, Lo, I come unto thee in a thick cloud etc.*[7]

R. Ḥama b. R. Ḥanina said: Moses became wealthy but from the chippings of the tablets, for it is written, *Hew* thee *two tablets of stone like unto the first:*[8] their chips be thine.

R. Jose son of R. Ḥanina said: The Torah was given only to Moses and his seed, for it is written, *write thee these words*[9] [and] *Hew thee:*[10] just as the chips are thine so is the writing thine.[11] But Moses in his generosity gave it to Israel, and concerning him it is said, *He that hath a bountiful eye shall be blessed, etc.*[12] R. Ḥisda objected: *And the Lord commanded me at that time to teach you statutes and judgments?*[13] —He commanded me, and I [passed it on] to you.[14] [A further objection:] *Behold, I have taught you statutes and judgments, even as the Lord my God commanded me?*[15] —He commanded me, and I taught you. *Now, therefore, write this song for you!*[16]—This refers to the song

(1) II Kings V, 18. (2) Deut. VI, 1. Wilna Gaon deletes this example, as in fact '*these*' is read. He substitutes '*eth* in *As the Lord liveth* ('*eth*—sign of the accusative) that *made us this soul* (Jer. XXXVIII, 16). In Heb. *Zoth* (this) and '*eth* are similar, differing only in one letter, and this may have caused the error in the text. (3) Jer. LI, 3. (4) Ezek. XLVIII, 16. (5) Ruth III, 12. (6) Wilna Gaon adds the following examples: Ibid. XV, 21 Jer. XXXIX. These are given in Soferim VI. (7) Ex. XIX, 9. [This is not to imply that in Palestine where the whole of the Pentateuch was read in three years, most verses were divided in two or three (v. Rappaport, *Halichoth Kedem* pp. 10 and 17). It only means that this was one of the few passages in which there existed a difference of division between the Palestinians and Babylonians; v. Blau, *JQR*, 1896, p. 143.] (8) Ex. XXXIV, 1. (9) Ibid. 27. (10) Ibid. 1. (11) The Torah is thy property. (12) Prov. XXII, 9. (13) Deut. IV, 14. This proves that it was not given to Moses for himself. (14) This is the answer, which interprets the verse thus: And the Lord commanded me at that time, (and I determined) to teach you etc. (15) Ibid. 5. (16) Ibid. XXXI, 19. '*For you*' shews that it was given to the Israelites in the first place.

alone.[1] *That this song be a witness for me against the children of Israel?*[2] —But only the [Scripture] dialectics [were given to Moses alone].[3]

R. Joḥanan said: The Holy One, blessed be He, causes His Divine Presence to rest only upon him who is strong, wealthy, wise and meek;[4] and all these [qualifications] are deduced from Moses. Strong, for it is written, *And he spread abroad the tent over the tabernacle;*[5] and a Master said, Moses our teacher spread it; and it is also written, *Ten cubits shall be the length of the board.*[6] Yet perhaps it was long and thin?[7]—But [it is derived] from this verse: *And I took the two tables, and cast them out of my two hands, and broke them.*[8] Now, it was taught: The tablss were six [handbreadths] in length, six in breadth, and three in thickness.[9] Wealthy, [as it is written] *Hew thee,* [interpreted] the chips be thine. Wise: for Rab and Samuel both said, Fifty gates of understanding were created in the world, and all but one were given to Moses, for it is said, *For thou hast made him* [*sc.* Moses] *a little lower than God.*[10] Meek, for it is written, *Now the man Moses was very meek.*[11]

R. Joḥanan said: All the prophets were wealthy. Whence do we derive this? From Moses, Samuel, Amos and Jonah. Moses, because it is written, *I have not taken one ass from them.*[11] Now, if he

(1) But the rest of the Torah was originally given to Moses alone. (2) Deut. XXXI, 19. If the reference is to the song alone, how can that testify against Israel? (3) And he taught them to the people. (4) Cf. Maim. *Guide,* II, ch. 32. It seems strange that wealth should be regarded as a necessary qualification for prophecy. Poverty was not regarded as a fault, many of the Rabbis being poor (e.g., Hillel, before he became *nasi;* R. Joshua, the opponent of R. Gamaliel; R. Judah), yet were not thought of any the less. Cf. also Aboth, VI, 4. Is it possible that 'wealthy' was included in order to oppose the N.T. teachings which imply that poverty in itself is a virtue? [According to Asheri these qualifications are deemed necessary for the gift of permanent prophecy. This would explain the inclusion of wealth, which dowers its possessor with the sense of independence, the better to proclaim the word of God and which commands greater respect.] (5) Ex. XL, 19. (6) Ex. XXVI, 16. This then was the height of the tabernacle: to have spread the tent over it he must have been extremely tall, and presumably correspondingly strong. (7) In which case he would not necessarily be strong. (8) Deut. IX, 17. (9) These would be extremely heavy and require great strength to handle. (10) Ps. VIII, 6. (11) Num. XII, 3. (11) Num. XVI, 15.

meant without a hiring fee—did he then merely claim not to be one of those who take without a fee?[1] He must hence have meant, even with a fee.[2] But perhaps it was because of his poverty?[3]—But [it is derived] from the verse, *Hew thee etc.*: the chips be thine. Samuel, because it is written, *Behold here I am: witness against me before the Lord, and before his anointed: whose ox have I taken, or whose ass have I taken?*[4] Now, if he meant for nothing—did he then merely claim not to be one of those who take without payment? Hence he must have meant, even for payment. But perhaps it was due to poverty?—Rather from this verse, *And his return was to Ramah: for there was his house.*[5] Whereupon Raba observed, wherever he went, his house went with him.[6] (Raba said: A greater thing is said of Samuel than of Moses: for in the case of Moses it is stated, *'I have not taken one ass from them,'* implying even for a fee;[7] but in the case of Samuel, he did not hire it even with their consent, for it is written, *And they said, thou hast not defrauded us, nor taken advantage of our willingness.*)[8] Amos, because it is written, *Then answered Amos and said to Amaziah, I was no prophet, neither was I a prophet's son; but I was a herdman and a gatherer of sycamore fruit;*[9] which R. Joseph translated: Behold, I am the owner of flocks, and possess sycamore trees in the valley.[10] Jonah, as it is written [*and he found a ship going to Tarshish:*] *so he paid the fare thereof, and went down into it.*[11] And R. Joḥanan observed: He paid for the hire of the whole ship. R. Romanus said: The hire of the ship was four thousand gold *denarii*.

R. Joḥanan also said: At first Moses used to study the Torah

(1) Surely he did not pride himself on not being a thief! (2) I.e., he had no need to hire an animal, possessing so many himself. Therefore he must have been wealthy. (3) I.e., having so few possessions that he did not need one. (4) I Sam. XII, 3. (5) Ibid. VII, 17. (6) I.e., he travelled about with all the retinue and baggage of his house: this could be done only by a wealthy man. (7) This implies that he did not compel them to hire him an ass. Yet even when he merely requested it, they might have dissimulated their unwillingness through shame and hired it to him. (8) Ibid. XII, 4. (9) Amos VII, 14. (10) Hence I have no need to turn my prophecy to professional uses. *Boker*, rendered in the A.V. '*herdman*', is here translated 'owner of flocks'. [This is the rendering of Targum Pseudo-Jonathan; v. B.Ḳ. (Sonc. ed.) p. 9, n. 9.] (11) Jon. I, 3.

and forget it, until it was given to him as a gift, for it is said, *And he gave unto Moses, when he had made an end of communing with him [. . . two tables of testimony].*[1]

MISHNAH. AND HE MAY SUPPORT HIS WIFE AND CHILDREN, THOUGH HE [THE MUDDAR] IS LIABLE FOR THEIR MAINTENANCE.[2] BUT HE MAY NOT FEED HIS BEASTS, WHETHER CLEAN OR UNCLEAN.[3] R. ELIEZER SAID: HE MAY FEED AN UNCLEAN BEAST OF HIS, BUT NOT A CLEAN ONE. THEY [THE SAGES] SAID TO HIM, WHAT IS THE DIFFERENCE BETWEEN AN UNCLEAN AND A CLEAN BEAST? HE REPLIED TO THEM, THE LIFE OF A CLEAN BEAST BELONGS TO HEAVEN, BUT THE BODY IS HIS OWN;[4] BUT AN UNCLEAN ANIMAL [38b] BELONGS BODY AND LIFE TO HEAVEN.[5] SAID THEY TO HIM, THE LIFE OF AN UNCLEAN BEAST TOO BELONGS TO HEAVEN AND THE BODY IS HIS. FOR IF HE WISHES, HE CAN SELL IT TO A HEATHEN OR FEED DOGS WITH IT.

GEMARA. R. Isaac b. Ḥananiah said in R. Huna's name: He who is under a vow not to benefit from his neighbour may give him his daughter in marriage. R. Zera pondered thereon: What are the circumstances? If the property of the bride's father is forbidden to the bridegroom,—is he not giving him a servant to serve him?[6] If again the bridegroom's property is forbidden to the father of the bride[7]—but even a greater thing was said: HE MAY

(1) Ex. XXXI, 18. This shews that the two tables (i.e., the Torah) were made a gift to him. (2) This continues the preceding Mishnahs. Tosaf.: this applies, according to the Rabbis *supra* 33*b*, to maintenance above the minimum necessities, which is all a husband is liable for. (3) Because a fattened animal has more value than otherwise; hence it is a direct benefit to the *muddar*. (4) I.e., since it may be eaten, he directly benefits by its fattening. (5) Since it may not be eaten, he does not benefit through its fattening. (6) Why is it then permitted? This is on the assumption that the reference is to a *na'arah*, (v. Glos.), whose labour belongs to her father, and who in turn transfers it to her husband. (7) And R. Huna teaches that he may marry his daughter, though by maintaining her he indirectly benefits her father.

SUPPORT HIS WIFE AND CHILDREN, THOUGH HE [THE MUDDAR] IS LIABLE FOR THEIR MAINTENANCE;[1] then you say, He may give him his daughter in marriage!—After all, this refers to the case where the property of the father of the bride is forbidden to the bridegroom, but this treats of his daughter, a *bogereth*,[2] [who marries] at her own desire. It was taught likewise: He who is under a vow not to benefit from his neighbour may not give him his daughter in marriage; but he may permit his daughter, a *bogereth*, to marry him at her own desire.

R. Jacob said: If a man imposes a vow on his son [to do no service for him], in order that his son may study,[3] the latter may fill a barrel of water and light the lamp for him.[4] R. Isaac said: He is permitted to broil him a small fish.

R. Jeremiah said in R. Joḥanan's name: If a man is under a vow not to benefit from his neighbour, the latter may offer him the cup of peace. What is that?—Here [in Babylon] it has been interpreted, the cup drunk in the house of mourning.[5] In the West [Palestine] it was said: the cup of the baths.[6]

BUT HE MAY NOT FEED HIS BEASTS, WHETHER etc. It was taught: Joshua of 'Uzza said: He may feed his Canaanitish [i.e., heathen] bondmen and bondwomen, but not his beasts, whether clean or unclean. Why so? Because slaves are for service;[7] beasts are for fattening.

MISHNAH. IF ONE IS FORBIDDEN TO BENEFIT FROM

(1) So that he could support his daughter even when under her father's roof, and he is not considered as thereby benefiting her father. Surely then it is only too obvious that he may marry her. (2) Over twelve years and six months and one day of age. She is no longer under her father's authority, and the profits of her labour belong to herself. (3) Without interruption. (4) For presumably his vow was not directed against such trifling services, which require very little time. (5) It was customary to drink a special mourner's cup at the meals in a mourner's house. Keth. 8*b*. (6) It was the custom to drink a cup of some beverage after a hot bath. (7) Consequently their master does not gain anything when one feeds them. This refers to extra food over the slave's requirements.—Ran.

HIS NEIGHBOUR, AND HE PAYS HIM A VISIT [IN SICKNESS] HE MUST STAND, BUT NOT SIT; HE MAY AFFORD HIM A CURE OF LIFE, BUT NOT A CURE OF MONEY.[1]

GEMARA. [39*a*] What are the circumstances? If the visitor's property is forbidden to the invalid, he may even sit? Whilst if the invalid's property is forbidden to the visitor, he may not even stand?[2]—Said Samuel: In truth, it means that the visitor's property is forbidden to the invalid, and applies to a place where a fee is received for sitting [with an invalid], but not for standing.[3] How state this definitely?[4]—He [the Tanna] teaches us thus: that even where it is customary to take a fee for visiting, one may receive it only for sitting, but not for standing.[5] An alternative answer is this: Just as R. Simeon maintained [elsewhere] that it is feared that he may tarry a long time whilst standing,[6] so here too it is feared that he may stay a long time if he sits.[7] 'Ulla said: After all it means that the invalid's property is forbidden to the visitor, for[8] he did not vow where it affects his health.[9] If so, he may sit too?—Because he can stand.[10]

An objection is raised: If he fell sick, he may enter to visit him; if his son became ill, he may inquire [after his health] in the street.[11] Now this is well according to 'Ulla, who maintains that it means that the invalid's property is forbidden to the visitor, for he did

(1) The meaning of this is discussed on 42*b*. (2) For by standing in his house he is regarded as benefiting. (3) It was customary to have companions or visitors for invalids, to cheer them up. Therefore if the visitor gives the invalid his company without accepting a fee, he is benefiting him. (4) That money is paid for sitting and not for standing. (5) One who sits presumably stays a long time; but one who stands pays only a fleeting visit, and hence may not receive a fee. (6) V. 42*b*. (7) I.e., the Mishnah refers to an invalid who is forbidden to benefit from the visitor. The visitor may not sit, lest he stay a long time, which is certainly a benefit to the invalid. (8) Generally the Heb. *kegon* states a particular instance. Here, however, it introduces a general statement.—Rashi, Ran, and Asheri. (9) The invalid never intended that his neighbour should be so stringently forbidden to benefit from him as not even to stand in his house to cheer him up in his illness. (10) For the invalid would not have the visitor benefit from him more than is strictly necessary. (11) But not enter his house.

not vow where it affects his own health.[1] But on Samuel's explanation, that the visitor's property is forbidden to the invalid, what is the difference between himself and his son?—He can answer you: Our Mishnah means that the invalid may not benefit from the visitor; in the Baraitha, the case is reversed. How state this definitely?[2]—Said Raba: [39b] Our Mishnah presents a difficulty to Samuel: Why particularly teach that he may stand but not sit? Hence it must refer to a case where the invalid is forbidden to benefit from his visitor.[3]

Resh Lakish said: Where is visiting the sick indicated in the Torah? In the verse, *If these men die the common death of all men, or if they be visited after the visitation of all men etc.*[4] How is it implied?—Raba answered: [The verse means this:] If these men die the common death of all men, who lie sick a-bed and men come in and visit them, what will people say? *The Lord hath not sent me*[5] for this [task]. Raba expounded: *But if the Lord make a new thing:*[6] if the Gehenna[7] is already created, 'tis well: if not, let the Lord create it. But that is not so, for it was taught: Seven things were created before the world, viz., The Torah, repentance, the Garden of Eden, Gehenna, the Throne of Glory, the Temple, and the name of the Messiah. The Torah, for it is written, *The Lord possessed me* [*sc.* the Torah] *in the beginning of his way, before his works of old.*[8] Repentance, for it is written, *Before the mountains were brought forth, or ever thou hadst formed the earth and the world . . . Thou turnest man to destruction, and sayest, Repent, ye sons of men.*[9] The Garden of Eden, as it is written, *And the Lord God planted a garden in Eden from aforetime.*[10] Gehenna, as it is written, *For Tophet*[11] *is ordained of old.*[12] The

(1) Therefore, if his son fell sick, the visitor may not enter his house, because it is to be assumed that the question of his son's health did not come into consideration at the time of the vow. (2) On what grounds is this difference based? (3) It is certainly true that one who forbids his neighbour to benefit from him does not do so at the cost of his own health. But then he would draw no distinction between standing and sitting, and would desire the visitor to have the benefit of sitting in his house too. Hence on 'Ulla's interpretation the distinction in the Mishnah is wrong; therefore Samuel reverses it. (4) Num. XVI, 29. (5) Ibid. (6) Ibid. 30. (7) V. p. 19, n. 6. (8) Prov. VIII, 22. (9) Ps. XC, 2f. 'Before', etc. applies to 'Repent'. (10) Gen. II, 8. (11) Another name for Gehenna. (12) Isa. XXX, 33.

Throne of Glory, as it is written, *Thy Throne is established from of old.*[1] The Temple, as it is written, *A glorious high throne from the beginning is the place of our sanctuary.*[2] The name of the Messiah, as it is written, *His name* [*sc.* of Messiah] *shall endure for ever, and* [*has existed*] *before the sun!*[3] —But Moses said thus: If a mouth has already been created for it [*sc.* Gehenna], 'tis well; if not, let the Lord create one. But is it not written, *There is no new thing under the sun?*[4] —He said thus: If the mouth is not near to this spot, let it draw near.

Raba, or as others say, R. Isaac, lectured: What is meant by, *The sun and the moon stood still in their* zebul?[5] What were they doing in the *zebul*, seeing that they were set in the *raḳi'a?*[6] This teaches that the sun and the moon ascended from the *raḳi'a* to the *zebul* and exclaimed before Him, 'Sovereign of the Universe! If thou wilt execute judgment for Amram's son,[7] we will give forth our light; if not, we will not shine.' In that moment He shot spears and arrows at them. 'Every day,' He rebuked them, 'men worship you, and yet you give your light. For My honour you do not protest, yet you protest for the honour of flesh and blood.' [Since then,] spears and arrows are shot at them every day before they consent to shine,[8] as it is written, *And at the light of thy arrows they go, etc.*[9]

(1) Ps. XCIII, 2. (2) Jer. XVII, 12. (3) Ps. LXXII, 17. Now, according to this, Gehenna was definitely created before the world; how then could Moses be doubtful?—The general idea of this Baraitha is that these things are the indispensable prerequisites for the orderly progress of mankind upon earth. The Torah, the supreme source of instruction, the concept of repentance, in recognition that 'to err is human', and hence, if man falls, he needs the opportunity to rise again; the garden of Eden and the Gehenna symbolising reward and punishment, which, without conceding a purely utilitarian basis for ethical striving, are nevertheless powerful incentives thereto; the Throne of Glory and the Temple, indicating that the goal of creation is that the kingdom of God (represented by the Temple) should be established on earth as it is in Heaven; and finally, the name of Messiah, the assurance that God's purpose shall be eventually achieved. (4) Ecc. I, 9. (5) Hab. III, 11. (6) According to tradition, there are seven heavens, *zebul* being one. (7) By punishing Korah and his confederates. (8) Accepting the Almighty's rebuke, they refuse to shine, because of the insult to His glory, until they are forced to. (9) Ibid.

It was taught: There is no measure for visiting the sick. What is meant by, 'there is no measure for visiting the sick?' R. Joseph thought to explain it: its reward is unlimited. Said Abaye to him: Is there a definite measure of reward for any precept? But we learnt: Be as heedful of a light precept as of a serious one, for thou knowest not the grant of reward for precepts? But Abaye explained it: Even a great person must visit a humble one. Raba said: [One must visit] even a hundred times a day. R. Abba son of R. Ḥanina said: He who visits an invalid takes away a sixtieth of his pain.[1] Said they to him: If so, let sixty people visit him and restore him to health?—He replied: The sixtieth is as the tenth spoken of in the school of Rabbi, and [providing further that] he [the visitor] is of his affinity.[2] For it was taught: Rabbi said: A daughter who enjoys maintenance from her brothers' estate receives a tenth of the estate.[3] Said they to Rabbi: If so, if a man leaves ten daughters and one son, the latter receives nothing! He replied: The first [to marry] receives a tenth of the estate; the second, a tenth of the residue; the third, a tenth of what remains. [Now, if they all married at the same time], they redivide equally.[4]

R. Ḥelbo fell ill. Thereupon R. Kahana went and proclaimed: [40a] R. Ḥelbo is sick. But none visited him. He rebuked them [*sc.* the scholars], saying, 'Did it not once happen that one of R. Akiba's disciples fell sick, and the Sages did not visit him? So R. Akiba himself entered [his house] to visit him, and because they swept and sprinkled the ground before him,[5] he recovered. 'My master,' said he, 'you have revived me!' [Straightway] R. Akiba went forth and lectured: He who does not visit the sick is like a shedder of blood.

(1) A variant: his sickness. (2) As the invalid. Born under the same planetary influence, Asheri; Rashi (and Jast.) 'of the same age'. (3) She can, on marriage, demand a tenth of the estate for a dowry and trousseau. V. Keth. 68*a*. (4) I.e., after taking one tenth of the estate, and another a tenth of what is left, and a third likewise, etc., they pool the lot together, and divide it equally.—Thus here too, the first visitor with the same affinity takes away a sixtieth of the sickness; the second a sixtieth of the remainder, and so on. Hence he would not be completely cured. (5) Asheri: R. Akiba, finding the chamber neglected, gave the necessary orders.

When R. Dimi came,[1] he said: He who visits the sick causes him to live, whilst he who does not causes him to die. How does he cause [this]? Shall we say that he who visits the sick prays[2] that he may live, whilst he who does not prays that he should die, —'that he should die!' can you really think so? But [say thus:] He who does not visit the sick prays neither that he may live nor die.[3]

Whenever Raba fell sick, on the first day he would ask that his sickness should not be made known to any one lest his fortune be impaired.[4] But after that, he said to them [his servants], 'Go, proclaim my illness in the market place, so that whoever is my enemy may rejoice, and it is written, *Rejoice not when thine* enemy *falleth . . . Lest the Lord see it, and it displeases him, and he turn away his wrath from him.*[5] whilst he who loves me will pray for me.

Rab said: He who visits the sick will be delivered from the punishments of Gehenna, for it is written, *Blessed is he that considereth the poor: the Lord will deliver him in the day of evil.*[6] '*The poor*' [dal] means none but the sick, as it is written, *He will cut me off from pining sickness* [mi-dalah];[7] or from this verse: *Why art thou so poorly* [dal], *thou son of the King?*[8] Whilst 'evil' refers to Gehenna, for it is written, *The Lord hath made all things for himself: Yea, even the wicked for the day of evil.*[9] Now, if one does visit, what is his reward? [You ask,] 'what is his reward?' Even as hath been said: 'he will be delivered from the punishment of Gehenna!'—But what is his reward in this world?—*The Lord will preserve him, and keep him alive, and he shall be blessed upon the earth; and thou wilt not deliver him unto the will of his enemies.*[10] '*The Lord will preserve him*', —from the Evil Urge, '*and keep him alive*'—[saving him] from sufferings; '*and he shall be blessed upon the earth,*'—that all will take pride in him;[11] '*and thou wilt not deliver him unto the will of his enemies*',—that he may procure friends like Naaman's, who healed

(1) From Palestine. (2) Lit., 'begs mercy for him'. (3) Through the lack of his prayers, which might have been accepted, he is said to cause his death. (4) If his illness became known, people might talk about it and thus affect his fate (Rashi). (5) Prov. XXIV, 17f. (6) Ps. XLI, 2. (7) Isa. XXXVIII, 12. (8) II Sam. XIII, 4. (9) Prov. XVI, 4. (10) Ps. XLI, 3. (11) Lit., 'all will be honoured in him'—he will be a source of pride to all.

his leprosy; and not chance upon friends like Rehoboam's, who divided his kingdom.

It was taught: R. Simeon b. Eleazar said: If the young tell you to build, and the old to destroy, hearken to the elders, but hearken not to the young, for the building of youth is destruction, whilst the destruction of the old is building. And a sign for the matter is Rehoboam the son of Solomon.[1]

R. Shisha son of R. Idi said: One should not visit the sick during the first three or the last three hours [of the day], lest he thereby omit to pray[2] for him. During the first three hours of the day his [the invalid's] illness is alleviated; in the last three hours his sickness is most virulent.[3]

Rabin said in Rab's name: Whence do we know that the Almighty sustains the sick? From the verse, *The Lord will strengthen him upon the bed of languishing.*[4] Rabin also said in Rab's name: Whence do we know that the Divine Presence rests above an invalid's bed? From the verse, *The Lord doth set himself upon the bed of languishing.*[5] It was taught likewise: He who visits the sick must not sit upon the bed, or on a stool or a chair, but must [reverently] robe himself and sit upon the ground, because the Divine Presence rests above an invalid's bed, as it is written, *The Lord doth set himself upon the bed of languishing.*

Rabin also said in Rab's name: [The swelling of] the Euphrates testifies abundantly to rain in the West.[6] Now, he disagrees with

(1) His elder councillors advised him to submit to the malcontents, thus apparently weakening his authority; whilst his young friends advised him to strengthen his rule by rejecting their demands. As a result of listening to the young men his kingdom was split. Kings XII. (2) Lit., 'dismiss' his mind from mercies. (3) Consequently, a visitor in the first three hours may think him on the road to recovery, and consider prayer unnecessary; in the last three hours, on the other hand, he may feel that prayer is hopeless. (4) Ps. XLI, 4. (5) This is another rendering of the same verse. Rashi suggests another interpretation; for *yisa'denu*, meaning 'he will strengthen him', read *yesharenu*, 'he will abide with him'. (6) Palestine. When it rains in Palestine, which is higher than Babylon, the water flows down and causes the swelling of the Euphrates. This is another way of saying that the rise of a river is due to the rains. The practical bearing of this on ritual law is discussed below.

Samuel, who said: A river increases [in volume] from its bed.[1] Now, Samuel is self-contradictory. For Samuel said: Running water does not purify, [40b] except the Euphrates in Tishri.[2] Samuel's father made *mikwaoth* for his daughters in Nisan[3] and had mats set for them in the days of Tishri.[4]

R. Ammi said in Rab's name: What is meant by the verse, *Therefore, thou son of man, prepare thee stuff for removing?*[5] This is a lamp, plate and [41a] a rug.[6]

[*And thou shalt serve thine enemies ...*] *in want of all things.*[7] R. Ammi said in Rab's name: This means without a lamp or table. R. Ḥisda said: Without a wife; R. Shesheth said: Without an attendant; R. Naḥman said: Without knowledge. A Tanna taught: Without salt or fat. Abaye said: We have it on tradition that no one is poor save he who lacks knowledge. In the West [Palestine] there is a proverb: He who has this, has everything; he who lacks this,

(1) Lit., 'from its rock': though it appears to swell through the rains, actually more water gushes upwards from the river bed than is added by the rain. (2) Tishri is the seventh month of the Jewish year, generally coinciding with September-October. If a *mikweh* (ritual bath) is made of collected rain water, it is efficacious only if its water is still, not running or flowing. On the other hand, a well or spring with its water gushing forth from its source is efficacious even when it flows onward. Now, during the whole year, the river may contain more rain water or melted snow than its own natural waters; consequently, it is all considered as rain water, which does not cleanse when in a running state. But in Tishri the rains have ceased, nor is there any melted snow in the river. Then it is like a well or spring, and even though running its water is efficacious for ritual cleansing. Now, according to this, the river's rise is caused mainly by rain. This conflicts with the view that at all times the water from its source is more. (3) Nisan, the first Jewish month, corresponding to March-April. As the river is then swollen by rain, he did not permit them to take their ritual bath in the running river, but made special enclosed baths for them. (4) In Tishri they performed their ablutions in the river. Now the bed of the river is miry, and should the feet sink into it, the water cannot reach them and the immersion is invalid; he therefore placed mats in the river bed for them to stand on. Ran gives another explanation: He hung up mats on the shore to serve as a screen, for modesty. [Obermeyer *op. cit.* p. 278: he set up for them tents made of reeds]. On both explanations this story is mentioned here in support of Samuel's second dictum. (5) Ezek. XII, 3. (6) These are the minimum requisites of a wanderer. (7) Deut. XXVIII, 48.

what has he? Has one acquired this, what does he lack? Has he not acquired this, what does he possess?

R. Alexandri said in the name of R. Ḥiyya b. Abba: A sick man does not recover from his sickness until all his sins are forgiven him, as it is written, *Who forgiveth all thine iniquities; who healeth all thy diseases.*[1] R. Hamnuna said: He [then] returns to the days of his youth, for it is written, *His flesh shall be fresher than a child's: he shall return to the days of his youth.*[2]

Thou hast turned his bed in his sickness:[3] R. Joseph said: This means that he forgets his learning. R. Joseph fell ill and forgot his learning; but Abaye restored it to him. Hence it is frequently stated that R. Joseph said, 'I have not heard this law,' and Abaye reminded him, 'You yourself did teach it to us and did deduce it from this particular Baraitha.'

When Rabbi had studied his teaching in thirteen different interpretations, he taught R. Ḥiyya only seven of them. Eventually Rabbi fell sick [and forgot his learning]. Thereupon R. Ḥiyya restored to him the seven versions which he had taught him, but the other six were lost. Now, there was a certain fuller who had overheard Rabbi when he was studying them himself; so R. Ḥiyya went and learned them from the fuller, and then repeated these before Rabbi. When Rabbi met him, he said to him, 'Thou hast taught[4] both R. Ḥiyya and myself'. Others say that he spoke thus to him: 'Thou hast taught R. Ḥiyya, and he has taught me.'

R. Alexandri also said in the name of R. Ḥiyya b. Abba: Greater is the miracle wrought for the sick than for Hananiah, Mishael and Azariah. [For] that of Hananiah, Mishael and Azariah [concerned] a fire kindled by man, which all can extinguish; whilst that of a sick person is [in connection with] a heavenly fire,[5] and who can extinguish that?

R. Alexandri also said in the name of R. Ḥiyya b. Abba,—others state, R. Joshua b. Levi said: When a man's end has come, all have dominion over him, for it is written, *And it will be that whosoever*

(1) Ps. CIII, 3. (2) Job XXXIII, 25. (3) Ps. XLI, 4. (4) Lit., 'made'. (5) I.e., his temperature rises.

findeth me will slay me.[1] Rab deduced it from this verse: *They stand forth this day to receive thy judgments: for all are thy servants.*[2]

Rabbah b. Shila was told that a tall man had died. [Now it happened thus:] This man was riding on a little mule and when he came to a bridge, the mule shied and threw the man, and he was killed. Thereupon Rabbah applied to him the verse, *They stand forth this day to receive thy judgments etc.*

Samuel saw a scorpion borne by a frog across a river, and then stung a man, so that he died. Thereupon Samuel quoted, *They stand forth this day to receive thy judgments etc.*[3]

Samuel said: Only a sick person who is feverish[4] may be visited. What does this exclude? It excludes those concerning whom it has been taught by R. Jose b. Parṭa in R. Eliezer's name, viz., One must not visit those suffering with bowel [trouble], or with eye disease, or from headaches. Now the first is well, the reason being through embarrassment;[5] but what is the reason of the other two?—On account of Rab Judah's dictum, viz., Speech is injurious to the eyes and to [people suffering from] headaches.[6]

Raba said: Feverishness, were it not a forerunner of the angel of death,[7] it would be as salutary [41*b*] once in thirty days as thorns which surround [and protect] a palm tree, and as theriak[8]

(1) Gen. IV, 14; thus Cain, thinking that his end had arrived, recognised that everything would have power to slay him. (2) Ps. CXIX, 91. I.e., all become servants to carry out God's judgment of doom. (3) Though a scorpion cannot swim, he was carried across by the frog, in order to fulfil God's judgment. (4) Lit., 'when he is wrapped in heat'. (5) He has his bowels frequently moved. (6) This is the reading of Asheri; cur. edd. add, 'and is good for fever' and Wilna Gaon amends likewise. (7) Both in the Bible and in the Talmud death is regarded as coming to man through an angel. Thus we find mention of the 'angel of the Lord' destroying 185,000 men in the Assyrian camp (II Kings XIX, 35); the destroying angel (II Sam. XXIV, 15); 'the angel of the Lord' whom David saw standing 'between the earth and the heaven, having a drawn sword in his hand stretched out over Jerusalem' (I Chron. XXI, 15). In the Talmud this angel is frequently referred to, and he was conceived as causing death by dropping gall into the mouth of the victim; 'A.Z. 20*b*; v. *J.E.* IV, 480ff. (8) A certain compound believed to be an antidote against poisonous bites.

to the body.[1] R. Naḥman b. Isaac said: [I want] neither it nor its theriak.

Rabbah b. Jonathan said in R. Jeḥiel's name: *'Arsan* is beneficial for healing the sick. What is *'arsan?*—Said R. Jonathan: Old peeled barley which sticks to the sieve.[2] Abaye observed: They require boiling as the flesh of an ox. R. Joseph said: It is fine barley flour which sticks to the sieve; [whereupon] Abaye remarked: It needs as much boiling as the flesh of an ox.

R. Joḥanan said: We must not visit one afflicted with *burdam,*[3] nor mention its [real] name. What is the reason?—R. Eleazar said: Because it is like a gushing well.[4] R. Eleazar also said: Why is it called *burdam?* Because it is a gushing well.[5]

THE LATTER MAY AFFORD HIM A CURE OF LIFE BUT NOT A CURE OF MONEY. What does this mean? Shall we say that 'A CURE OF LIFE' means without payment, and 'A CURE OF MONEY' is for a fee?[6] Then let him [the Tanna] state: He may heal him without payment, but not for a fee?—But by 'A CURE OF LIFE' his own person is meant: whilst 'A CURE OF MONEY' refers to his cattle.[7] R. Zuṭra b. Ṭobiah said in Rab's name: Nevertheless he may tell him: this drug is beneficial for it, that drug is injurious for it.

MISHNAH. HE MAY BATHE TOGETHER WITH HIM IN A

(1) I.e., the fever has a purging and purifying effect on the body. (2) On account of its fatness. Lit., 'of the top of the sieve'. (3) Dysentery, bloody flux; Rashi quotes a version *burdas.* (4) Not to shame the one afflicted with it. (5) The word is a compound; *bor dam,* a well of blood. (6) LIFE, Heb. *nefesh,* will then be the equivalent of desire (*nefesh* in Heb. sometimes bears that meaning, e.g., Gen. XXIII, 8: *If it be your desire,* Heb. *nafshekem*), i.e., of his own free will. The Mishnah then will refer to the doctor being a *muddar* (v. Glos.), who may not accept a fee from the invalid. (7) Hence, *nefesh* in the Mishnah is translated 'his soul', i.e., himself, whilst *mamon* (money) refers to his chattels. According to this interpretation the invalid is the *muddar:* nevertheless, the saving of life overrules other considerations. This is so, even if another doctor is available, for the skill of the first may be greater. In fact, the prohibition to heal his cattle holds good only if another doctor can be obtained.—Ran.

LARGE BATH, BUT NOT IN A SMALL ONE,[1] HE MAY SLEEP IN A BED WITH HIM. R. JUDAH SAID: [ONLY] IN SUMMER, BUT NOT IN WINTER, BECAUSE HE [THEREBY] BENEFITS HIM.[2] HE MAY RECLINE ON A COUCH[3] OR EAT AT THE SAME TABLE WITH HIM[4] BUT NOT OUT OF THE SAME DISH;[5] BUT HE MAY DINE WITH HIM OUT OF A BOWL WHICH RETURNS.[6]

GEMARA. It was taught: He may not bathe together with him in a bath, or sleep in a bed with him, whether large or small: this is R. Meir's ruling. R. Judah said: A large one in winter, and a small one in summer are permitted.[7] He may bathe with him in a large bath, and may take a hot air bath with him [even] in a small one.[8] He may recline on a couch with him, and eat at the same table, but not out of the same dish. Yet he may eat out of the same bowl that returns. R. Jose b. Ḥanina said: that means the bowl that returns to the host.[9]

MISHNAH. HE MAY NOT EAT WITH HIM OUT OF THE BOWL PUT BEFORE WORKMEN,[10] NOR MAY HE WORK WITH HIM ON THE SAME FURROW: THIS IS R. MEIR'S VIEW. BUT THE SAGES SAY: HE MAY WORK, PROVIDED HE IS AT A DISTANCE.

GEMARA. There is no dispute at all that they may not work

(1) In a small one his own body perceptibly raises the level of the water, and also adds to its heat; he thereby benefits him. (2) By adding warmth. (3) Even in winter, as no benefit is gained. (4) This is not forbidden lest he eat of the other's portion. (5) A large bowl was sometimes placed on the table, from which all ate. The *maddir* and the *muddar* may not eat out of the same bowl, lest the former take too little from it and thereby benefit the latter. (6) This is explained in the Gemara. (7) In the first case the warmth is not appreciably increased, whilst in the second the increase is of no advantage. (8) The addition of heat there being of no benefit. (9) I.e., there is so much in it that it goes back to the host unemptied. Another meaning: that continually goes back to the host to be replenished. In that case the *maddir* does not benefit the *muddar* by taking a small portion. (10) The employer used to provide a large bowl of food for his workmen, out of which they all ate.

near [each other]. They differ only in reference to [working at] a distance. R. Meir maintains: We forbid at a distance as a preventive measure on account of nearby, for he [the *maddir*] softens the ground before him; while the Rabbis hold: We do not enact a preventive measure.

MISHNAH. [42*a*] HE WHO IS FORBIDDEN BY VOW TO BENEFIT FROM HIS NEIGHBOUR, [IF THE VOW WAS IMPOSED] BEFORE THE SEVENTH YEAR,[1] MAY NOT ENTER HIS FIELD [IN THE SEVENTH YEAR][2] NOR TAKE OF THE OVERHANGING [FRUIT].[3] BUT IF [THE VOW WAS IMPOSED] IN THE SEVENTH YEAR, HE MAY NOT ENTER HIS FIELD, BUT MAY EAT OF THE OVERHANGING BRANCHES.[4] IF HE WAS [MERELY] FORBIDDEN IN RESPECT OF FOOD [BUT NOT ALL BENEFIT], [AND THE VOW WAS IMPOSED] BEFORE THE SEVENTH YEAR, HE MAY ENTER HIS FIELD, BUT MAY NOT EAT OF ITS FRUITS; BUT [IF IT WAS IMPOSED] IN THE SEVENTH YEAR, HE MAY ENTER [HIS FIELD] AND EAT [OF ITS FRUITS].

GEMARA. Rab and Samuel both ruled: [If one says to his neighbour], 'This my property [be forbidden] to you', [if he vowed] before the seventh year, he may not enter his field or take of the overhanging [fruits] even when the seventh year arrives. But if he vowed in the seventh year, he may not enter his field, yet may enjoy the overhanging [fruits]. R. Joḥanan and Resh Laḳish both maintained· [If one says to his neighbour,] 'This my property [be forbidden] to you'; [if he vowed] before the seventh year he may neither enter his field nor eat of the overhanging [fruits]; when

(1) Lev. XXV, 1-7. The seventh year was called the year of release. The land was not to be ploughed or sowed, and its crops, with certain reservations, were free to all. (2) To gather of its crops, since he is forbidden 'the treading of the foot'. Cf. Mishnah on 32*b*. (3) I.e., if the *maddir* has a tree close to his boundary, and the fruit overhangs the *muddar's* field, so that it is possible for the *muddar* to take of the fruit without entering the *maddir's* land, he is still forbidden to do so. (4) [Omitted in the printed Mishnayoth version].

the seventh year arrives, he may not enter his field, yet may eat of the overhanging [fruits].

Shall we say that they differ in this: Rab and Samuel hold that a man can prohibit [unto others] that which is in his ownership, [for the prohibition to be effective] even after it passes out of his ownership;[1] whilst R. Joḥanan and Resh Laḳish maintain: One cannot prohibit [unto others] that which is in his ownership [for the prohibition to continue even] after it leaves his ownership? Now can you reason so? Does anyone rule that a person cannot declare prohibited that which is his, even after it passes out of his ownership? If so, let them differ with reference to 'this property [be forbidden etc.],' and how much more so would it apply to 'this *my* property!'[2] Moreover, we have learnt that a person can declare prohibited that which is in his ownership for even after it leaves his ownership. For we learnt: If one says to his son, '*Ḳonam*, if you benefit from me,'—if he dies, he inherits him.[3] [But if he explicitly stipulates] during his lifetime and after his death, [42*b*] if he dies he does not succeed him!—Here it is different, because he [explicitly] stated during his lifetime and after his death.[4] Yet at all events there is a difficulty?[5]—But [explain the dispute thus:] There is no dispute at all in respect of 'this property etc.'[6] They differ [only] in respect of 'My property etc.' Rab and Samuel maintain: There is no difference between 'This property' or 'my property': one can prohibit [for all time]. But R. Joḥanan and Resh Laḳish maintain: [By saying,] 'This property,' he can prohibit; 'my property,' he cannot prohibit. But does anyone maintain that

(1) Consequently, though in the seventh year the crops do not belong exclusively to their owner, being free to all, yet the vow made before retains its validity, forbidding the *muddar* to take even of the overhanging fruits. (2) I.e., even if one says, 'This property be forbidden to you', R. Joḥanan and Resh Laḳish maintain that the vow is ineffective for the seventh year, when the crops are no longer his. The same will hold good with even greater force, if he vows 'this my property' etc., for in that case he appears to limit the incidence of the vow to the period in which it is his. (3) For it is his by right. (4) But otherwise it may well be that the validity of a vow ceases when its subject is no longer under the control of the *maddir*. (5) *Sc.* the first. (6) The vow remains valid even in the seventh year.

there is no difference between 'this property' and 'my property'? But we learnt: If one says to his neighbour, '*Ḳonam*, if I enter *your* house,' or 'if I purchase *your* field,' and then the owner dies or sells it, he is permitted [to enter or buy it]. [But if he says, '*Ḳonam*], if I enter *this* house', or 'if I purchase *this* field,' and the owner dies or sells it, he is forbidden!—But [explain thus:] R. Joḥanan and Resh Laḳish refer to 'my property'; Rab and Samuel to 'this property': and they do not differ.

BUT [IF THE VOW WAS IMPOSED] IN THE SEVENTH YEAR, HE MAY NOT ENTER HIS FIELD etc. Why may he eat of the overhanging [fruits]—because they are [now] ownerless? But the land too is ownerless.[1]—Said 'Ulla: This refers to trees standing on the border.[2] R. Simeon b. Eliakim said: It is forbidden lest he stand and linger there.[3]

MISHNAH. HE WHO IS FORBIDDEN BY VOW TO BENEFIT FROM HIS NEIGHBOUR MAY NEITHER LEND TO HIM NOR BORROW FROM HIM NOR ADVANCE HIM OR RECEIVE FROM HIM A LOAN.[4] HE MAY NEITHER SELL TO NOR PURCHASE FROM HIM.

GEMARA. [43a] As for 'HE MUST NOT LEND TO HIM,' that is well, since he [thereby] benefits him. But 'HE MUST NOT BORROW FROM HIM'—how does he benefit him? Further, [even] 'HE MUST NOT RECEIVE A LOAN FROM HIM' and 'HE MUST NOT PURCHASE FROM HIM' are well, since he [the *muddar*] may benefit.[5] But 'HE MUST NOT BORROW FROM HIM': how does he [the

(1) In the sense that every person has the right to enter and take of its crops. (2) Therefore, since it is unnecessary to enter the field, it is not ownerless. (3) The land is ownerless only in respect of entering and taking its crops: this done, it reverts to its real owner. But we fear that the *muddar*, having eaten his fill, may tarry there, which is forbidden to him. (4) *Yalwenu* (*lawah*) and *yash'ilenu* (*sha'al*) refer to money and utensils respectively. (5) For the *maddir* may borrow worn coins, and return new ones. As the value of coins depended to some extent on their weight, the *muddar* would benefit. Likewise, the *maddir* may not purchase an article for which there is no demand, and for the same reason.

muddar] benefit?—Said R. Jose son of R. Ḥanina: It means e.g., that they made a vow not to benefit from one another. Abaye answered: He is forbidden to borrow, lest he also lend, and the same applies to the other clauses.[1]

MISHNAH. IF ONE SAYS TO ANOTHER, 'LEND ME YOUR COW,' TO WHICH THE OTHER REPLIES, 'IT IS NOT FREE'; WHEREUPON HE EXCLAIMS, 'ḲONAM, IF I EVER PLOUGH MY FIELD WITH IT', IF HE GENERALLY PLOUGHED HIMSELF, HE IS FORBIDDEN,[2] BUT OTHERS ARE PERMITTED. BUT IF HE DID NOT GENERALLY PLOUGH HIMSELF, HE AND ALL MEN ARE FORBIDDEN.[3] IF ONE IS FORBIDDEN BY VOW TO BENEFIT AUGHT FROM HIS NEIGHBOUR, AND HE HAS NAUGHT TO EAT, HE [THE MADDIR] CAN GO TO THE SHOPKEEPER AND SAY, 'SO-AND-SO IS FORBIDDEN BY VOW TO BENEFIT AUGHT FROM ME, AND I DO NOT KNOW WHAT TO DO'. THE SHOPKEEPER MAY THEN SUPPLY HIM, AND COME AND RECEIVE PAYMENT FROM HIM [THE MADDIR]. IF HE HAD HIS [THE MUDDAR'S] HOUSE TO BUILD, OR HIS FENCE TO ERECT, OR HIS FIELD TO REAP, HE [THE MADDIR] MAY GO TO LABOURERS, AND SAY, 'SO-AND-SO IS FORBIDDEN BY VOW TO BENEFIT AUGHT FROM ME, AND I DO NOT KNOW WHAT TO DO.' THEREUPON THEY WORK FOR HIM [THE MUDDAR], AND COME AND RECEIVE WAGES FROM HIM [THE MADDIR]. IF THEY ARE WALKING TOGETHER ON THE ROAD, AND HE [THE MUDDAR] HAS NOTHING TO EAT, HE [THE MADDIR] CAN MAKE A GIFT TO A THIRD PERSON, AND HE [THE MUDDAR] IS PERMITTED [TO HAVE] IT. IF THERE IS NO OTHER WITH THEM, HE PLACES IT ON A STONE OR A WALL, SAYING, 'THIS IS FREE TO WHOMEVER DESIRES IT'; AND THE OTHER TAKES AND EATS IT. BUT R. JOSE FORBIDS THIS.

(1) By 'other clauses' the reference is only to borrowing money.—Asheri. (2) To plough the field with that cow, if it is subsequently lent to him. (3) For his vow must have referred to others.

GEMARA. R. Johanan said, what is R. Jose's reason? He maintains that *hefker*[1] is like a gift: just as a gift [is not valid] until it passes from the possession of the giver into that of the receiver, so *hefker* too [is not valid] until it passes into the ownership of him who acquires it.[2] R. Abba objected: And the other [the *muddar*] takes and eats it; but R. Jose forbids this. Said R. Jose: When is that? If the vow preceded his renunciation; [43*b*] but if his renunciation preceded his vow, it is permitted. Now if you say [that it belongs to the first owner] until it comes into the possession of him who acquires it, what does it matter whether his vow preceded his renunciation or the reverse?—He raised the objection and answered it himself: He who vows has no thought of what he has renounced.

Raba objected: [If the dying person assigned] part [of his property] to the first, and all of it to the second, [and then recovered,] the first acquires, but not the second![3] But Raba said,

(1) V. Glos. (2) I.e., when a person declares a thing to be *hefker*, it does not immediately cease to be his, but remains his property until taken. Thus the *muddar* takes the *maddir's* food. (3) V. B.B. 148*b*. The law of a sick person likely to die is this: If he assigns all his property to anyone, and then recovers, his gift is invalid, it being assumed that it was made only on account of expected death. But if he leaves part for himself, it is valid; for, we argue, were it on account of approaching death, he would have left nothing for himself. Here, when he made the first assignation, part was still left for himself: hence it remains valid on his recovery. But after the assignation of the second nothing is left: consequently, on his recovery, it is null. Now, if it is maintained that a gift is not valid until the recipient actually takes possession, why is it more valid for the first than for the second: just as the portion assigned to the second is the residue left by the first, so that assigned to the first may be regarded as the residue left by the second?—So Rashi. On this interpretation, 'all of it' means 'the rest of it'. Asheri and Tosaf., however, point out that in such a case *both* gifts would be null on recovery, since he leaves after all nothing for himself. Accordingly, they explain thus: He assigned part of his property to A, then *all* to B, meaning also that already assigned to A. Consequently his gift to B was the result of a new intention, not borne in mind when making his first gift. Now, just as in making a gift, the donor intends it to apply even to that which he has already given away, as shewn, so when one vows, the vow is made even with respect to that which he has previously declared *hefker*. This refutes the distinction drawn by R. Abba.—Ran has a variant reading of this passage.

This is R. Jose's reason: It is a preventive measure, on account of the gift of Beth Horon.[1]

It was taught: If one declares his field *hefker:* he can retract within the first three days, but not after.[2] [44*a*] If he declares, 'Let this field be *hefker* for one day, one week, one year, or one septennate';[3] before possession has been taken thereof, whether by himself or by a stranger, he can retract. But if it has [already] been acquired by himself or by a stranger, he cannot retract. [Must we assume that] the first clause agrees with the Rabbis, and the second with R. Jose?[4]—Said 'Ulla: The second clause too agrees with the Rabbis. If so, why 'before possession has been taken thereof, whether by himself or by a stranger, he can retract?'— [*Hefker* for] a year or a septennate is different, being unusual.[5] Resh Lakish

(1) V. 48*a*. There it is a case of a gift being an obvious evasion; so here too, his declaration of *hefker* does not appear genuine but as a mere evasion of his vow. (2) This is in reference to the tithe. No tithe was due on produce taken from ownerless fields. Now, if he either revokes his declaration within the first three days, or takes possession without a formal retraction, his declaration is null: consequently, it has never been ownerless, and the crops must be tithed. But after three days, the declaration has legal force. Naturally, if no one else takes possession thereof, he can do so himself, but whether he or another, it is free from tithe. (3) After the end of which it is to revert to himself, if no one has taken possession in the meanwhile. (4) For since he cannot retract after three days even though no person has taken possession, it is evident that *hefker* is legally valid even before it reaches another. This agrees with the view of the Sages that the *maddir* can declare his property *hefker* and the *muddar* acquire it without its being regarded as passing direct from one to the other. But the second clause, stating that he can retract so long as no one has taken possession, shews that until then it is legally his. This agrees with R. Jose, that the *maddir* cannot declare his property *hefker* for the *muddar* to acquire it. (5) 'Ulla interprets the whole Baraitha on the view of the Rabbis. Consequently, if one declares his property *hefker*, it immediately becomes so, and should the first owner take possession thereof, even immediately, the law of *hefker* applies thereto, rendering it free from tithe. That it is by Biblical law. Since, however, this is manifestly exposed to abuse, for by a legal fiction everyone could thus evade the tithe, the Rabbis enacted that the law of *hefker* should apply only after three days, during which a stranger can take possession. So Rashi and Asheri appear to interpret it, though according to the latter, if the first owner resumes possession within three days, explicitly declaring that he is acquiring *hefker* but not retracting, the crops are exempt

said, Since the second clause agrees with R. Jose,[1] the first too must agree with him. But this is the reason of the first clause:[2] that the law of *hefker* may not be forgotten.[3] If so, let it be *hefker* even from the first day?—Said Rabbah, This is on account of evaders, who may declare their property *hefker*, and then reacquire it.[4] [Will you maintain] that by Biblical law it is not *hefker*:[5] [44*b*] but perhaps he will come to tithe from [produce] that is liable for [produce] that is exempt, or vice versa?[6]—He is told, 'When you tithe, tithe for it out of itself.'[7]

from tithe. Ran and Tosaf. explain that within the first three days he can retract even if a stranger has already taken possession thereof. In Ḥ.M. 273, 9 the first interpretation is accepted. But in the second clause, the declaration itself is weak, being limited to a certain period. Consequently the Rabbis admit that it is not valid until one has actually taken possession.—It may be asked, if it is *hefker* even if re-acquired by the first owner, of what use is the enactment? The answer is that to acquire *hefker* it is insufficient to make a mere declaration of acquisition, but some work must be done in the field. Before the owner has time to do this, he may be forestalled: that is regarded as a sufficient check to evasion (v. Rashi).

(1) Resh Laḳish accepts the obvious implications. (2) That 'after three days, the declaration is binding', even if no one has taken possession thereof. (3) For if we rule that whenever the owner resumes possession, it is not regarded as *hefker*, it will be forgotten altogether that *hefker* is exempt from tithe. Therefore the Rabbis ruled that after three days the declaration is binding. Nevertheless, since on this view it is not, Biblically, *hefker* even after three days if no stranger has taken possession, the crops are not free from tithe on the first owner re-acquiring them, for the Rabbis have no power to exempt crops which by Biblical law are liable, as is explained *infra*. (4) V. p. 139, n. 5. (5) V. n. 3. (6) The tithe could be separated from one lot of produce upon another (of the same species), providing that both bore the same liability. E.g., if one harvests his two fields, he can take from one the tenth of the combined produce. If, however, he separates a tithe of one field, thus freeing the rest, he cannot take another tithe from the same for the second field. Similarly, if he has two lots of corn, one liable to tithe by Biblical law, and the other only by Rabbinical law, so that by Biblical law it is really exempt, he may not separate from the one for the other. Now it has been explained here that according to R. Jose, so long as no stranger has taken possession, it is not *hefker* by Biblical law even after three days, and consequently Biblically liable. But by Rabbinical law it is *hefker*, even if the original owner re-acquires it. Nevertheless, as explained on p. 139, n. 5, the Rabbis ordered that he shall tithe it. Thus, in this respect, the Rabbis restored it to Biblical law. But the owner, being told that it is *hefker*, may

An objection is raised: If a man declares his vineyard *hefker* and rises early on the following morning and vintages it,[1] he is liable to *peret*,[2] *'oleloth*,[3] the forgotten sheaves,[4] and *pe'ah*,[5] but he is exempt from tithe. Now as for 'Ulla, it is well: it states the rabbinic law, and states the Biblical law.[6] But on the view of Resh Lakish, why is he free from tithe?[7]—He answers you thus: My statement is based on R. Jose; whilst this accords with the Rabbis.[8] [45a] Alternatively: One case refers to *hefker* declared in the presence of two; the other, if declared before three. For R. Johanan said in the name of R. Simeon b. Jehozadak: *Hefker* declared in the presence of three is valid, but not in the presence of two.[9] R. Joshua b. Levi said: By the Torah, it is *hefker* even if declared in the presence of one: why then are three required? So that one can take possession, and the other two attest it.[10]

regard the liability to tithe as merely a Rabbinical measure, and therefore, if he has any other corn which is only Rabbinically liable, separate from the one, which is really Biblically exempt, for the Biblically liable, or vice versa. (7) Only in this respect is it regarded as *hefker* even if the first owner resumes possession.

(1) Thus he resumed possession thereof. (2) Single grapes fallen off during the cutting, which must be left for the poor.—Lev. XIX, 10. (3) *'Olelah*, *'oleleth*, pl. *'oleloth*, gleanings reserved for the poor; in general, a small single bunch on a single branch. Ibid. and Deut. XXIV, 21. (4) Sheaves (here grapes) forgotten in the course of ingathering, which had to be left for the poor.—Deut. XXIV, 19. (5) *Pe'ah*—corner; the corner of the field left for the poor.—Lev. XIX, 9. (6) 'Ulla maintains that the Baraitha in stating that he can retract within the first three days, teaches the Rabbinical law, whereas this Baraitha states the Biblical law according to which it is *hefker* immediately. (7) Since he maintains that within the first three days it is not *hefker* even by Biblical law, and hence subject to tithes, and even after that it is *hefker* only by Rabbinical law, why is it taught here that on the very next day it is free from tithe? (8) Who maintain in the Mishnah that it is *hefker* immediately, hence free from tithe. (9) Until one actually takes possession. Therefore, in the Mishnah, since no person is present, R. Jose maintains that if the *maddir* declares the food *hefker*, and the *muddar* takes it, he receives it directly from the *maddir*. But the vineyard, we assume, was renounced in the presence of three; therefore even R. Jose agrees that the renunciation is immediately valid. Hence, if he re-acquires it, it is exempt from tithe. The stronger validity of *hefker* in the presence of three is due to its greater publicity. (10) For otherwise the first owner can deny his renunciation.

NEDARIM

CHAPTER V

MISHNAH. [45*b*] IF [TWO] JOINT OWNERS MADE A VOW NOT TO BENEFIT FROM ONE ANOTHER, THEY MAY NOT ENTER THE COURTYARD.[1] R. ELIEZER B. JACOB SAID: EACH ENTERS INTO HIS OWN.[2] [46*a*] AND BOTH ARE FORBIDDEN TO SET UP A MILL-STONE OR AN OVEN OR BREED FOWLS THEREIN.[3] IF [ONLY] ONE WAS FORBIDDEN BY VOW TO BENEFIT FROM THE OTHER, HE MAY NOT ENTER THE COURT. R. ELIEZER B. JACOB SAID: HE CAN MAINTAIN, 'I AM ENTERING INTO MY OWN, NOT INTO YOURS.' HE WHO THUS VOWED IS FORCED TO SELL HIS SHARE [OF THE COURT].[4] IF A MAN FROM THE STREET WAS FORBIDDEN BY VOW TO BENEFIT FROM ONE OF THEM, HE MAY NOT ENTER THE COURT. R. ELIEZER B. JACOB SAID: HE CAN MAINTAIN, 'I ENTER YOUR NEIGHBOUR'S PORTION, AND I DO NOT ENTER INTO YOURS.' IF ONE IS FORBIDDEN BY VOW TO BENEFIT FROM HIS NEIGHBOUR, AND THE LATTER POSSESSES A BATH-HOUSE OR AN OLIVE PRESS LEASED TO SOMEONE IN THE TOWN, AND HE HAS AN INTEREST THEREIN, HE [THE MUDDAR] IS FORBIDDEN [TO MAKE USE OF THEM]; IF NOT, HE IS PERMITTED. IF A MAN SAYS TO HIS NEIGHBOUR, 'ḲONAM, IF I ENTER YOUR HOUSE', OR 'IF I PURCHASE YOUR FIELD,' AND THEN [THE OWNER] DIES OR SELLS IT TO ANOTHER, HE IS PERMITTED [TO ENTER OR BUY

(1) Which belongs to both. (2) He maintains that it is as though it had been stipulated when jointly acquiring the property, that it should belong to each partner separately for his entering therein. Consequently, when he enters, he is not benefiting from the other. The Sages do not accept this view. (3) R. Eliezer b. Jacob admits this, for joint owners can object to this. Consequently, if they do not, each benefits by the permission of the other. (4) For since he may enter, but not the other (this being taught on the view of the Sages), the second, in resentment, might enter none the less in disregard of the vow.

IT]; [BUT IF HE SAYS,] 'KONAM, IF I ENTER THIS HOUSE,' OR 'IF I PURCHASE THIS FIELD,' AND [THE OWNER] DIES OR SELLS IT TO ANOTHER, HE IS FORBIDDEN.

GEMARA. The scholars propounded: They differ when they interdicted themselves by vow. But what if each imposed a vow upon the other? Do we say, they differ [only] in the former case, but that in the latter the Rabbis agree with R. Eliezer b. Jacob, since they are involuntarily prohibited;[1] or perhaps the Rabbis dispute even in the latter case?[2] Come and hear: IF [ONLY] ONE WAS FORBIDDEN BY VOW[3] TO BENEFIT FROM THE OTHER ... and the Rabbis dispute it!—Learn, forbade himself from his neighbour.[4] This is logical too, for the second clause states: NOW, HE WHO THUS VOWED IS FORCED TO SELL HIS SHARE OF THE COURT. Now, this is reasonable if the vow was self-imposed: hence he is compelled. But if you say that a vow was imposed against him, why is he compelled, seeing that the position is not of his making?[5]

Rabbah said in Ze'iri's name: [46b] The dispute is only if it [the court] is large enough to be divided; but if not, all agree that they are permitted.[6] Said R. Joseph to him: But what of a synagogue

(1) For if they voluntarily interdict themselves of all benefit, it may be maintained that each thereby renounces also his share, which is inseparable from his partner's. But when each forbids the other, it may be argued that neither can prohibit that which the other enjoys in his own right. (2) For the prohibition arises because in their opinion it is impossible to distinguish between the portions belonging to each. (3) *Muddar* is the *hofal*, and implies that the vow was imposed upon him by another. (4) *Nadur*, passive *Kal*. implies self-imposed. No emendation is really made in the Mishnah, but the Talmud answers that *muddar* may be synonymous with *nadur*, self-imposed. (5) Lit., 'surely he is under constraint'. I.e., it is equitable to force him to sell, if as a result of his own vow he may come to transgression, but not otherwise. (6) The smallest area of a court to be of any use as such is four square cubits. Now, only if it contains at least eight square cubits do the Rabbis maintain that each is forbidden to enter, since it is possible for them to divide, and yet each portion shall be large enough itself for a court; for then it cannot be said that when they purchased it jointly, each was entitled to the whole of it, as explained on p. 142, n. 2. But a lesser area cannot be

which is as a thing which cannot be divided,[1] yet we learnt, Both are forbidden [the use of] the [common] property of the town?[2] —But, said R. Joseph in Ze'iri's name, The controversy is only when it is not [large] enough to divide;[3] but if it is, all agree that both are forbidden. R. Huna said: The *halachah* is as R. Eliezer b. Jacob; and R. Eleazar said likewise: The *halachah* is as R. Eliezer b. Jacob.

IF ONE IS FORBIDDEN BY VOW TO BENEFIT FROM HIS NEIGHBOUR, AND THE LATTER POSSESSES A BATH-HOUSE etc. How much is meant by AN INTEREST THEREIN?—R. Naḥman said: A half, third, or a quarter, but not less.[4] Abaye said, Even for less, he is forbidden. Under what conditions is he permitted? If he [the lessee] rents it in return for [the payment of] the land-tax.[5]

[47*a*] IF ONE SAYS TO HIS NEIGHBOUR etc. Abimi[6] propounded: What [if one says to his neighbour,] '*Ḳonam*, if you enter this house,' and then he sells it or dies: Can one prohibit that which he owns [for the prohibition] to be effective even when it leaves his ownership, or not?—Said Raba, Come and hear: If one says to his son, '*Ḳonam* that you benefit not from me,' and he dies, he is his heir. [But if he explicitly stipulates] during his lifetime and he dies, he does not succeed him. This proves that one

divided, and therefore the original condition of purchase must have been that the whole belongs to each.

(1) Since its essential use is *joint* worship, and should it be divided, it ceases to be a synagogue. (2) *Infra* 48*a*. (3) Yet even then the Rabbis maintain that each is forbidden to enter. (4) Less than a quarter is regarded as negligible. And the *muddar* is not forbidden to use it on its account. [*Var. lec.*, 'but for eggs it is permitted'. בבצים for בבציר, the reference being to the egg-shaped forms of clay which are placed in the oven of the bath-house for drying. If his interest consists in the use he makes of the bath-house for that purpose, it is not regarded of any consequence.] (5) The tax must have been very high if the owner was prepared to forego any possible profit.—*Ṭaska* was the Persian land tax. (v. Obermeyer, p. 221, n. 3), and the Mishnah, which was produced in Palestine, cannot actually refer to this tax. Abaye's interpretation must therefore be regarded merely as an illustration. [*Aliter:* If he (the lessee) obtained it on a rental; retaining all the profit to himself.] (6) *Var. lec.*: Abaye.

can prohibit that which he owns [for the prohibition] to hold good when it leaves his ownership. The proof is conclusive.

We learnt elsewhere: [If one says,] '*Ḳonam* be these fruits to me,' or, 'Be they *ḳonam* for my mouth,' or, 'Be they *ḳonam* to my mouth': he is forbidden [to benefit] from what has been exchanged for them or grown from them.[1] Rami b. Hama propounded. If he vows, '*Ḳonam* be these fruits to So-and-so', what of their exchange? Do we say, With respect to *oneself*, since he can forbid to himself [even] his neighbour's property, he can [likewise] forbid to himself what is not yet in existence;[2] but as for his *neighbour*, since one cannot prohibit another's produce to his neighbour, he likewise cannot prohibit what is non-existent; [47*b*] or perhaps since what is taken in exchange is the same as what grows from its seed, there is no difference between oneself and his neighbour?[3]—Said R. Aḥa b. Manyumi, Come and hear: If a man says to his wife, '*Ḳonam*, if I benefit thee,' she may borrow [money], and the creditors come and exact it from him. Why can the creditors collect it [from him]: surely because what is taken in exchange is not the same as what grows from them?[4] Said Raba, Possibly it is forbidden [to make an exchange] in the first place only, but if it has been done, it is valid.[5] But come and hear: If a man betroths [a woman] with '*orlah*,[6] she is not betrothed; but if he sells it and betroths her with the money thereof, she is betrothed![7]—[No.] Here too it may be forbidden in the first place only, but if done it is valid.

(1) *Infra* 57*a*. (2) What may be given for the produce subsequent to the vow is regarded as non-existent when the vow is made. (3) For it is obvious that the fruit which grows is forbidden to his neighbour, and possibly what is given in exchange is the same. (4) Thus, in this case, the money she receives is not the same that is repaid. (5) I.e., it can be maintained that the problem regarding what is exchanged for them, is whether one may *deliberately* exchange these fruits for something else, so that it shall be permitted to the *muddar*. But if they were exchanged, they certainly are permitted. Hence, in this case, since the wife receives the money before the creditors exact it from her husband, it is regarded as a *fait accompli*, the legality of which is not in doubt. (The explanation follows Asheri. Ran gives a different interpretation). (6) 'Fruit of uncircumcision'. V. Lev. XIX, 23. (7) This proves that the prohibition does not remain upon what has been exchanged for something forbidden.

MISHNAH. [IF A MAN SAYS TO HIS NEIGHBOUR,] 'I AM ḤEREM TO YOU,' THE MUDDAR IS FORBIDDEN [TO DERIVE BENEFIT]. 'YOU ARE ḤEREM TO ME,' THE MADDIR IS FORBIDDEN. I AM [ḤEREM] TO YOU, AND YOU ARE [ḤEREM] TO ME,' BOTH ARE PROHIBITED. BOTH ARE PERMITTED [TO ENJOY THE USE OF] THOSE THINGS WHICH BELONG TO THOSE WHO CAME UP FROM BABYLON [TO PALESTINE],[1] BUT ARE FORBIDDEN [THE USE OF] THINGS THAT BELONG TO THAT TOWN.[2] [48a] NOW, WHAT ARE THE THINGS THAT BELONG TO THEM THAT CAME UP FROM BABYLON? E.G., THE TEMPLE MOUNT, THE COURTS OF THE TEMPLE AND THE WELL ON THE MIDROAD.[3] WHAT ARE THE THINGS THAT BELONG TO THAT TOWN? E.G., THE PUBLIC SQUARE, THE BATH-HOUSE, THE SYNAGOGUE, THE ARK [IN WHICH THE SACRED SCROLLS WERE KEPT] AND THE BOOKS [OF THE LAW],[4] AND [THE ESTATE OF] HIM WHO ASSIGNS HIS PORTION TO THE NASI.[5] R. JUDAH SAID: IT IS THE SAME WHETHER HE ASSIGNS IT TO THE NASI OR TO A PRIVATE INDIVIDUAL, BUT WHAT IS THE DIFFERENCE? IF HE ASSIGNS IT TO THE NASI, HE NEED NOT [FORMALLY] CONFER TITLE;[6] WHILST IN THE CASE OF AN INDIVIDUAL IT IS NECESSARY TO CONFER TITLE.[7] BUT THE SAGES MAINTAIN: FORMAL GRANT OF TITLE IS NECESSARY IN BOTH CASES; THEY MENTIONED THE NASI IN PARTICULAR AS THIS IS USUAL.[8] R. JUDAH SAID: THE GALILEANS NEED

(1) I.e., the band of immigrants who returned to Palestine under Zerubbabel, and later under Ezra and Nehemiah, who declared certain things inalienable property which can be deemed ownerless. (2) In which each citizen has a share. (3) Between Babylon and Palestine, for the supply of water to the pilgrims, v. 'Erub. 104*b*. These things were declared the property of all Israel. (4) [Rashi. Asheri: Books purchased by the congregation for the reading of the general public.] (5) The head of the Sanhedrin in Jerusalem and subsequent places. According to this reading, this portion too would be forbidden. But the Gemara amends the text of the Mishnah. (6) I.e., by the mere documentary assignation it becomes the Nasi's property. (7) E.g., one of the recognised methods of acquisition. (8) For one would fear to assign his portion in communal property to an individual, lest he then forbid it to him. V. also Halevy, *Doroth*, I, 3, p. 61 and general discussion *a.l.*

NOT ASSIGN [THEIR PORTION], BECAUSE THEIR ANCESTORS HAVE ALREADY DONE SO FOR THEM.

GEMARA. Why is it forbidden?[1]—Said R. Shesheth, The Mishnah teaches thus: How can they repair their position?[2] Let them assign their portion to the *nasi.*[3]

R. JUDAH SAID: THE GALILEANS NEED NOT ASSIGN [THEIR PORTION], BECAUSE THEIR ANCESTORS HAVE ALREADY DONE SO FOR THEM. It was taught: R. Judah said: the Galileans were quarrelsome and wont to make vows not to benefit from each other: so their fathers arose and assigned their portions to the *nasi.*

MISHNAH. IF ONE IS FORBIDDEN BY VOW TO BENEFIT FROM HIS NEIGHBOUR AND HAS NOTHING TO EAT, THE LATTER CAN GIVE IT [FOOD] TO A THIRD PARTY, AND THE FORMER IS PERMITTED TO USE IT. IT HAPPENED TO ONE IN BETH HORON[4] THAT HIS FATHER WAS FORBIDDEN TO BENEFIT FROM HIM. NOW HE [THE SON] WAS GIVING HIS SON IN MARRIAGE,[5] SO HE SAID TO HIS NEIGHBOUR, 'THE COURTYARD AND THE BANQUET BE A GIFT TO YOU, BUT THEY ARE YOURS ONLY THAT MY FATHER MAY COME AND FEAST WITH US AT THE BANQUET.' THEREUPON HE ANSWERED, 'IF THEY ARE MINE, LET THEM BE CONSECRATED TO HEAVEN!' 'BUT I DID NOT GIVE YOU MY PROPERTY TO CONSECRATE IT TO HEAVEN,' HE PROTESTED. 'YOU GAVE ME YOURS SO THAT YOU AND YOUR FATHER MIGHT EAT AND DRINK TOGETHER AND BECOME RECONCILED TO ONE ANOTHER, WHILST THE SIN [OF

(1) This question is based on the assumption that if the *maddir* assigns his portion to the *nasi*, the *muddar* is still forbidden. (2) Since the use of communal property as defined in the Mishnah is essential to them. (3) In cur. edd. a portion of the Mishnah is here reproduced in brackets, viz., 'R. Judah said, It is the same . . . this is usual'. But the quotation is pointless, and should be deleted. (4) A border town between Benjamin and Ephraim. (5) And desired his father's presence.

A BROKEN VOW] SHOULD DEVOLVE UPON HIS HEAD,'[1] HE RETORTED. [WHEN THE MATTER CAME BEFORE] THE SAGES, THEY RULED: EVERY GIFT WHICH IS NOT [SO GIVEN] THAT IF HE [THE RECIPIENT] CONSECRATES IT, IT IS CONSECRATED, IS NO GIFT [AT ALL].

GEMARA. [Does the Mishnah adduce] a story to contradict [its ruling]?[2]—The text is defective, and was thus taught: But if the end proves [his intention] at the beginning,[3] it is forbidden, and so it happened in Beth Horon, in the case of one whose last action demonstrated his first [as a mere evasion].

Raba said: They [the Sages] taught [that it is forbidden] only if he said, 'They are yours *only* in order that my father may come [etc.].' But if he said, 'They are yours so that my father may come,' he meant, 'It depends on your will.'[4] A different version is this: Raba said: Do not think that he is forbidden only if he said, 'And they are yours *only* in order that my father may come', but if he said, 'They are yours so that my father may come' it is permitted. [That is not so,] for even if he said, 'They are yours: let my father come,' it is forbidden. What is the reason? Because the banquet proves his intention.

[48*b*] A certain man had a son who used to carry off bundles of flax. Thereupon his father forbade his property to him.[5] 'But,' said others to him, 'what if the son of your son is a scholar?'[6] He replied, 'Let him acquire it, and if my[7] grandson be a scholar, it shall be his.'[8] Now, what is the law?—The Pumbedithans[9] ruled,

(1) [Probably a euphemism for 'my head'. J. reads 'my head'.] (2) Surely not! For the Mishnah states that the *maddir* may make a gift for the *muddar* to benefit thereby, and then quotes a case where this was forbidden. (3) That it was a mere device. (4) Hence it is permitted. (5) Though, as stated above, (*supra* 47*a*) his son would still inherit it, this story may be explained on the supposition that he had two sons, and wished to give the whole of his estate to the second (Ran). (6) At the time he had no grandson yet. (7) This is Rashi's reading. Cur. edd.: and if . . . . [*Var. lec.* 'let him not acquire, and if . . .' v. BaḤ.] (8) But if not, it reverts to my other son.—Ran. (9) A great academy town in Babylonia, at the mouth of the Beditha (which is the meaning of the name), a canal of the Euphrates.

This is a case of 'Acquire, in order to give possession,' and such does not give a legal title. R. Naḥman said: He [the son] acquires [it], for [the giving of] a *sudarium* too is a case of 'Acquire, in order to give possession.'[1] R. Ashi demurred: But in the case of a *sudarium*, who tells you that if he retains it, it is not his?[2] Moreover, the *sudarium* is a case of 'Acquire in order to give possession,' and 'Acquire [it] from *now*.'[3] But as for this property,—when shall he acquire it? When his grandson is a scholar: [but] by then the *sudarium* [whereby the transference was made] has been returned to its owner.[4] Raba [also] questioned R. Naḥman: But the gift of Beth Horon was a case of 'Acquire, in order to give possession,' yet it was invalid?—Sometimes he answered, Because his banquet proves his intention;[5] sometimes he answered, This is taught in accordance with R. Eliezer, who maintained that even the extra [given by the vendor to a customer] is forbidden to one who is interdicted by vow to benefit.[6]

We learnt, THE SAGES RULED, EVERY GIFT WHICH IS NOT [SO GIVEN] THAT IF HE [THE BENEFICIARY] CONSECRATES IT, IT IS CONSECRATED, IS NOT A GIFT [AT ALL]. Now, what

(1) One of the methods of acquisition was by exchange (*ḥalifin*), in which an object (a *sudarium*, kerchief) was given by the purchaser or recipient to the vendor or donor as a symbolical substitute v. B.M. 47*a*. Now, actually, this was given merely in order that the latter might give legal possession to the former, and was generally returned, yet it was valid. (2) I.e., though in fact it was only a symbol, and usually returned, yet it may be retained; but here it was not intended that the son should have possession at all but merely to be the medium of transference, for if his grandson would not be a scholar, the estate was to revert to his second son. (3) [Ran reads: Acquire in order to give possession from now.] As soon as the vendor acquires the scarf, the purchaser is the legal owner of his purchase. (4) [At the time when the title was granted the grandson was not yet in existence, and when he is ripe enough to receive the legacy the act of transference had long been a matter of the past, and no longer effective.] (5) I.e., it was not a genuine gift at all. (6) On account of this he ruled that he may not even walk over his field (32*b*), though ordinarily walking over another person's field is not accounted an encroachment of rights. Thus R. Eliezer treats vows far more stringently than other matters. Consequently, here too he rules the gift invalid. But the Sages, who disagree with him, would regard the gift of Beth Horon valid.

does EVERY include? Surely it includes such as this case of stealing flax?[1]—No. It includes the case of the second version of Raba's ruling.[2]

(1) That such a gift is invalid, not merely because of the greater stringency of vows, but because 'Acquire in order to give possession' confers no title. [This is the reading of Ran. Rashi and Asheri: Where the condition was repeated or cast in two forms (v. *supra* p. 149 n. 3). Our text presents a conflation of the two readings.] (2) V. *supra*.

NEDARIM

CHAPTER VI

MISHNAH. [49*a*] HE WHO VOWS [NOT TO EAT] WHAT IS COOKED [MEBUSHAL] IS PERMITTED WHAT IS ROASTED OR SEETHED.[1] IF HE SAYS, 'ḲONAM THAT I TASTE ANY COOKED DISH [TABSHIL]' HE IS FORBIDDEN [TO EAT] FOOD LOOSELY COOKED IN A POT, BUT IS PERMITTED [TO PARTAKE] OF WHAT IS SOLIDLY PREPARED.[2] HE MAY ALSO EAT A HARD BOILED EGG[3] AND REMUẒIAN CUCUMBERS.[4] HE WHO VOWS ABSTINENCE FROM FOOD PREPARED IN A POT, IS FORBIDDEN ONLY BOILED DISHES; BUT IF HE SAYS, 'ḲONAM THAT I TASTE NOT WHATEVER DESCENDS INTO A POT,' HE IS FORBIDDEN EVERYTHING PREPARED IN A POT.[5]

GEMARA. It was taught: R. Josiah forbids [them].[6] And though there is no proof of this,[7] there is some indication, for it is said, *And they boiled*[8] *the Passover in fire, according to the law.*[9] Shall we say that they differ in this: That R. Josiah holds: Follow Biblical usage; whilst our Tanna maintains: In vows follow the popular usage?—No. All agree that in vows we must follow popular usage: but each [rules] according to [the usage] in his district. In the district of our Tanna roast is called roast, and cooked, cooked. But in R. Josiah's, even

(1) Seethed, Heb. *shaluḳ* שלוק, denotes more thoroughly boiled than cooked (*mebushal*). (2) Because *tabshil* is only applicable to a loose liquid-like substance, but not to a dense mass. (3) [טורמוטא, Gr. τρομητόν trembling, hence shrivelled up; v. Gemara. J. explains it as lightly boiled egg; cf. Krauss. *T.A.* I. pp. 125 and 515.] (4) This is discussed on 51*a*. (5) Both liquids and solids. (6) *Sc.* what is roasted or seethed. This refers to the first clause of the Mishnah. (7) That מבושל includes these. (8) Heb. ויבשלו, impf. of בשל, of which מבושל is a pass. part. (9) II Chron. XXXV, 13. But the Passover Sacrifice had to be *roasted;* hence מבושל is applicable to roasts too. Yet this is not actual proof, because as stated *infra*, in vows the popular usage is the norm.

roast is called cooked. But he adduces a verse?—That is a mere support.[1]

[IF HE SAYS,] 'KONAM THAT I TASTE NOT ANY COOKED DISH [TABSHIL]. But he vowed [abstinence] from a *tabshil?*[2]—Said Abaye: This Tanna designates everything with which bread is eaten a *tabshil.*[3] And it was taught [likewise], He who vows [abstinence] from a *tabshil* is forbidden all cooked food [*tabshil*], and whatsoever is roasted, seethed, or boiled; he is also forbidden soft preserves of gourds with which the sick eat their bread. But this is not so. For R. Jeremiah fell sick. When the doctor called to heal him, he saw a pumpkin lying in the house. Thereupon he left the house, saying. 'The angel of death is in that house,[4] yet I am to cure him'![5]—That is no difficulty: the former refers to soft preserves; the latter to hard.[6] Raba b. 'Ulla said: The latter refers to the pumpkin itself;[7] the former to its inner contents.[8] For Rab Judah said: The soft part of a pumpkin [should be eaten] with beet; the soft part of linseed is good with *kutah.*[9] But this may not be told to the ignorant.[10]

Raba said: By 'the sick', scholars are meant.[11] This agrees with another dictum of his. For Raba said: [49*b*] In accordance with whom is it that we pray for the invalid and the sick?[12] In accordance with R. Jose.[13] Since he said, 'the invalid *and* the sick,' it follows

(1) His ruling, however, is not based thereon. (2) Which implies both loosely cooked and a dense mass. (3) But not otherwise; a dense mass cannot be eaten with bread. (4) I.e., the pumpkin is like poison for him. (5) This shows that they are injurious to invalids. (7) The soft are beneficial; the hard, injurious. (7) I.e., the outer portion, which is hard and injurious. (8) Its heart, which is soft and beneficial. (9) A preserve consisting of sour milk, bread-crusts and salt.—Jast. (10) Lest they tear up the growing flax to obtain the seed (Ran). Because it will appear absurd to them (Tosaf.). (11) I.e., in the Baraitha stating that 'the sick' eat their bread with soft preserves of gourds, the Rabbis and students are meant, not the literally sick. Hence there is no contradiction between that and the story of R. Jeremiah. (12) In our daily prayers; v. *P.B.* p. 47. (13) V. R.H. 16*a*. The Rabbis there maintain that a man is judged on New Year, and once he is sentenced, whether to life or death, the verdict cannot be reversed. Consequently, in their opinion it would be futile to pray for the recovery of the sick during the year. Hence the practice of praying for them accords with R. Jose's view, that man is judged every day.

that 'invalid' is literal, and 'the sick' [metaphorically] means the Rabbis.[1]

BUT IS PERMITTED [TO PARTAKE] OF A DISH SOLIDLY PREPARED. Our Mishnah does not agree with the Babylonians, for R. Zera said: The Babylonians are fools, eating bread with bread.[2]

R. Ḥisda said: There is none[3] to make enquiries of the epicureans[4] of Huẓal[5] how porridge is best eaten, whether a wheat porridge with wheaten bread, and a barley porridge with barley bread, or perhaps [they are best reversed,] wheat with barley, and barley with wheat. Raba ate it with stunted [parched] grains. Rabbah son of R. Huna found R. Huna eating porridge with his fingers. So he said to him, 'Why do you eat with your hands?' He replied, Thus did Rab say, [To eat] porridge with [one] finger is well: how much more so with two or three! Rab said to his son Ḥiyya, and R. Huna said the same to his son Rabbah, 'If you are invited to eat porridge, [you may even go] a parasang[6] for it; to eat beef, even three parasangs. Rab said to his son Ḥiyya, and R. Huna said likewise to his son Rabbah: You must never expectorate before your teacher, save [after eating] a pumpkin or porridge, because they are like lead pellets:[7] expectorate this even in the presence of King Shapur.[8]

R. Jose and R. Judah,—one ate porridge with his fingers, and one with a prick.[9] He who was eating with the prick said to him who was eating with the fingers, 'How long will you make me eat your filth?'[10] The other replied, 'How long will you feed me with your saliva?'[11]

(1) Who are weakened by their intensive studies. (2) I.e., even food solidly prepared is eaten by them with bread, consequently such would be included in the term '*tabhshil*' and forbidden. (3) So the text as emended by BaḤ. Asheri reads: is there any one etc. (4) Lit., 'those who are very careful in their eating', Rashi and one version of the Ran. Others: the fastidious. (5) A very old town lying below Nehardea, but nearer to Sura and belonging to the judicial circuit of the latter; Obermeyer, p. 299. (6) V. Glos. (7) I.e., it is dangerous to swallow the saliva left in the mouth after eating these. (8) Known otherwise as Shapur I. He was King of Persia and a friend of Samuel; Ber. 56*a* (9) Used as a fork. (10) They were both eating out of the same dish. (11) Because the thorn was not wiped each time after being put into his mouth.

Lesbian figs[1] were placed before R. Judah and R. Simeon. R. Judah ate; R. Simeon did not. [Whereupon] R. Judah asked him, 'Why are [you], Sir, not eating?' He replied, 'These never pass out at all from the stomach.' But R. Judah retorted, 'All the more [reason for eating them], as they will sustain us to-morrow.'[2]

R. Judah was sitting before R. Tarfon, who remarked to him, 'Your face shines to-day.' He replied, 'Your servants went out to the fields yesterday and brought us beets, which we ate unsalted; had we salted them, my face would have shone even more.'

A certain matron[3] said to R. Judah, 'A teacher and drunkard!'[4] He replied, 'You may well believe me that[5] I taste [no wine] but that of *Kiddush* and *Habdalah*[6] and the four cups of Passover,[7] on account of which I have to bind my temples from Passover until Pentecost;[8] but *a man's wisdom maketh his face shine*.[9] A *Min*[10] said to R. Judah, 'Your face is like that of a moneylender or pig breeder.'[11] He replied, 'Both of these are forbidden to Jews; but there are twenty-four conveniences between my house and the school, and every hour I visit one of them.'

When R. Judah went to the Beth ha-Midrash,[12] he used to take a pitcher on his shoulders [to sit on], saying, 'Great is labour, for it honours the worker.'[13] R. Simeon used to carry a basket upon

(1) So Jast. These are very difficult to digest. (2) As seen below, R. Judah was extremely poor; hence this was a consideration to him, though there is probably an element of humour in his retort. (3) This is mostly used of Roman ladies of noble birth. (4) מורה ורוי I.e., you are a Sage, yet you are drunk! His face was always red and shining, giving that impression. (5) Lit., 'My faith in the hand of this woman if . . .' (6) *Kiddush:* a short blessing of sanctification, recited at the commencement of Sabbaths and festivals. *Habdalah*, lit., 'separation', a benediction said at the end of Sabbaths and festivals, thanking God for the distinction He created between holy and non-holy days. Both are recited over wine, which is drunk. (7) Four cups of wine are drunk at the meals on the first evening (without Palestine, two evenings) of Passover. (8) They gave him such a headache! Doubtlessly a metaphorical exaggeration. (9) Ecc. VIII, 1. (10) [So MS.M. (v. Glos.), cur. edd. 'Sadducee'.] (11) Their faces are always shining because of their great profits! (12) School House. (13) Lit., 'its master'. Otherwise he would have had to sit on the floor. It is not clear whether the school was so deficient in equipment that this was really necessary, or he himself wished to shew his appreciation of labour. In the story of the

his shoulders, saying likewise, 'Great is labour, for it honours the worker.'

R. Judah's wife went out, brought wool, and made an embroidered cloak. On going to market she used to put it on, whilst when R. Judah went [to synagogue] to pray he used to wear it. When he donned it, he uttered the benediction, Blessed be He who hath robed me with a robe.[1] Now, it happened once that R. Simeon b. Gamaliel proclaimed a fast,[2] but R. Judah did not attend the fast-service.[3] Being informed that he had nothing to wear, he [R. Simeon b. Gamaliel] sent him a robe, which he did not accept. [50*a*] Lifting up the mat [upon which he was sitting], he exclaimed to the messengers, 'See what I have here,[4] but I do not wish to benefit from this world.'[5]

The daughter of Kalba Shebu'a[6] betrothed herself to R. Akiba.[7] When her father heard thereof, he vowed that she was not to benefit from aught of his property. Then she went and married him in winter.[8] They slept on straw, and he had to pick out the straw from his hair. 'If only I could afford it,' said he to her, 'I would present you with a golden Jerusalem.'[9] [Later] Elijah came to them in the guise of a mortal,[10] and cried out at the door, 'Give

deposition of R. Gamaliel (Ber. 27*b*-28*a*.), it is stated that many additional seats were placed for the great accretion of new disciples, proving that it was not customary to sit on the floor. R. Judah belonged to the following generation.

(1) There is no such benediction in the statutory liturgy, and R. Judah probably uttered this without the use of the Divine Name and without mention of God's sovereignty. Through the omission of these it is not really a benediction at all, hence R. Judah might recite it. (Real benedictions may not be uttered save where the Rabbis have prescribed them). (2) Over and above the statutory fasts special fasts were proclaimed in times of drought or on account of national disasters, such as pestilence, evil decrees, etc.; Ta'an. 19*a*. (3) A special service was held; Ta'an. 15*a*. (4) By a miracle, upon which he had relied, the place was filled with gold. (5) This story shows that R. Judah, i.e., R. Judah b. Ila'i, was extremely poor. In general the scholars of that generation lived in great poverty, as a result of the Hadrianic persecutions. V. A. Büchler, *The Jewish Community of Sepphoris*, pp. 67 *seq*. (6) V. Giṭ. 56*a*. (7) Then a poor shepherd. (8) An interval generally elapsed between betrothal (*kiddushin*) and marriage (*nesu'in*). (9) A golden ornament with Jerusalem engraved thereon. V. 'Ed. II. 7. (10) Cf. Sanh. 109*a*, 113*b*; v. Tosaf. Ḥul. 6*a*. *s.v.* אשכחיה.

me some straw, for my wife is in confinement and I have nothing for her to lie on.' 'See!' R. Akiba observed to his wife, 'there is a man who lacks even straw.' [Subsequently] she counselled him, 'Go, and become a scholar.' So he left her, and spent twelve years [studying] under R. Eliezer and R. Joshua. At the end of this period, he was returning home, when from the back of the house he heard a wicked man jeering at his wife, 'Your father did well to you. Firstly, because he is your inferior; and secondly, he has abandoned you to living widowhood all these years.' She replied, 'Yet were he to hear my desires, he would be absent another twelve years.' 'Seeing that she has thus given me permission,' he said, 'I will go back.' So he went back, and was absent for another twelve years, [at the end of which] he returned with twenty four thousand disciples.[1] Everyone flocked to welcome him, including her [his wife] too. But that wicked man said to her, 'And whither art *thou* going?'[2] '*A righteous man knoweth the life of his beast,*'[3] she retorted. So she went to see him, but the disciples wished to repulse her. 'Make way for her,' he told them, 'for my [learning] and yours are hers.' When Kalba Shebu'a heard thereof, he came [before R. Akiba] and asked for the remission of his vow and he annulled it for him.

From six incidents did R. Akiba become rich: [i] From Kalba Shebu'a.[4] [ii] From a ship's ram. For every ship is provided with the figurehead of an animal. Once this [a wooden ram] was forgotten on the sea shore, and R. Akiba found it.[5] [iii] From a hollowed out trunk.[6] For he once gave four *zuz* to sailors, and told them to bring him something [that he needed]. But they found only a hollow log on the sea shore, which they brought to him, saying, 'Sit on this and wait'.[7] It was found to be full of *denarii*.

(1) Cur. edd.: 'pairs of disciples'. But 'pairs' is absent in the version of Ket. 62*b*, and should be deleted here. (2) Taunting her that she was too humble to be observed by so great a scholar. (3) Prov. XII, 10. (4) Who shared his wealth with him. (5) It contained money. (6) גמוזא < גזע, a stem, trunk; Rashi translates: a ship's coffer, from גנז to hide, and גזא, treasure. (7) [Lit., 'make this a tarrying place' (Goldschmidt); or, 'Let our master make this (a tarrying place)', Rashi.]

For it once happened that a ship sunk and all the treasures thereof were placed in that log, and it was found at that time. [iv] From the *seroḳita*.[1] [v] From a matron.[2] [vi] [50b] The wife of Turnus-rufus.[3] [vi] From Ḳeti'a b. Shalom.[4]

R. Gamada gave four *zuz* to sailors to bring him something. But as they could not obtain it, they brought him a monkey for it. The monkey escaped, and made his way into a hole. In searching for it, they found it lying on precious stones, and brought them all to him.

The Emperor's[5] daughter said to R. Joshua b. Ḥananiah: 'Such comely wisdom in an ugly vessel!'[6] He replied, 'Learn from thy father's palace. In what is the wine stored?' 'In earthern jars,' she answered. 'But all [common] people store [wine] in earthern vessels, and thou too likewise! Thou shouldst keep it in jars of gold and silver!' So she went and had the wine replaced in vessels of gold and silver, and it turned sour. 'Thus,' said he to her, 'The Torah is likewise!' 'But are there not handsome people who are learned too?' 'Were they ugly they would be even more learned,' he retorted.

A certain woman of Nehardea came before Rab Judah[7] for a

(1) '*Aruch* translates: Ishmaelite traders. The phrase is missing in 'En Jacob and unnoticed by the commentaries, and is obviously a corrupt dittography of ומן מטרוניתא (Jast.) (2) A large sum of money was once needed for the school house. R. Akiba borrowed it from a matron, and at her request gave the Almighty and the sea as sureties for its punctual repayment. But when the money fell due, R. Akiba was unwell. Thereupon the matron stood at the edge of the sea and exclaimed, 'Sovereign of the Universe! Thou knowest that to Thee and to the sea have I entrusted my money'. In reply, He inspired the Emperor's daughter with a mad fit, in the course of which she threw a chest full of treasures into the sea, which was washed up at the matron's feet. On his recovery, he brought her the money, with apologies for the delay; but she told him what had happened, and sent him away with many gifts. (3) Tineius Rufus, a Roman governor of Judea. After her husband's death she became a convert and married R. Akiba, bringing him in much wealth. V. 'A.Z. 20*a*. (4) Ḳeti'a b. Shalom was condemned to death by a Roman emperor—probably Hadrian—for giving counsel against the emperor and in favour of the Jews. He made R. Akiba his heir.—'A.Z. (Sonc. ed.) 10*b*, pp. 53ff. (5) [Hadrian; v. *J.E.* VII, 291.] (6) He was very ugly. (7) [At Pumbeditha where he had his school.]

lawsuit, and was declared guilty by the court. 'Would your teacher Samuel[1] have judged thus?' she said. 'Do you know him then?' he asked. 'Yes. He is short and big-stomached, black and large teethed.' 'What, you have come to insult him! Let that woman be under the ban!' he exclaimed. She burst and died.

HE MAY ALSO EAT A WELL-BOILED EGG [BEẒA ṬURMIṬA]. What is *beẓa ṭurmiṭa?*—Samuel said: The slave who can prepare one is worth a thousand *denarii*. For it must be placed a thousand times in hot water and a thousand times in cold, until small enough to be swallowed whole. If one is ulcerated, it attracts the matter to itself, and when it passes out the doctor knows what medicine is required and how to treat him. Samuel used to examine himself with *Kulḥa*,[2] [which weakened him so] that his household tore their hair [in despair].

We have learnt elsewhere: If one is working among *kelusfin*, [Lesbian figs], he may not eat of *benoth sheba'*;[3] among *benoth sheba'*, he may not eat of *kelusfin*. What are *kelusfin?*—A species of figs of which pap is made. A certain man once gave his slave to his friend to teach him a thousand different ways of making pap, but he taught him only eight hundred. So he summoned him to a lawsuit before Rabbi. Rabbi remarked, 'Our *fathers* said, "*We have* forgotten *prosperity*,"[4] but *we* have never even seen it!'[5]

Rabbi made a wedding feast for his son Simeon, (and did not invite Bar Ḳappara).[6] He wrote above the banqueting-hall,[7] 'Twenty four thousand myriad *denarii* have been expended on these festivities.' Thereupon Bar Ḳappara said, 'If it is thus with

(1) [R. Judah was for a short time a pupil of Samuel, after the death of Rab and R. Assi; v. Yeb. 18*a*.] (2) A stalk of some plant, which acted in the same way as the *beẓa ṭurmiṭa*. (3) A different species of figs. The reference is to Deut. XXIII, 25: *When thou comest into thy neighbour's vineyard, then thou mayest eat grapes until thy fill at thine own pleasure*. The Rabbis interpret this as referring to workers, who may eat any of the fruit—not particularly grapes—upon which they are engaged, but must confine themselves thereto. (4) Cf. Lam. III, 17, implying that they had once known it. (5) I.e., it is extraordinary that in these bad times he should know as many as he did. (6) The bracketed phrase is transposed in our editions. (7) Where the festivities took place.

those who transgress His will[1], how much more so with those who do His will!' When he [subsequently] invited him, he observed, 'If it is thus with those who do His will in this world, how much more so [will it be] in the world to come!'

On the day that Rabbi laughed, punishment would come upon the world.[2] So he said to Bar Ḳappara [who was a humorist], 'Do not make me laugh, and I will give you forty measures of wheat.' He replied, 'But let the Master see [51*a*] that I may take whatever measure I desire.' So he took a large basket, pitched it over,[3] placed it on his head, went [to Rabbi] and said to him, 'Fill me the forty measures of wheat which I may demand from you.' Thereupon Rabbi burst into laughter, and said to him, 'Did I not warn you not to jest?' He replied, 'I wish but to take the wheat which I may [justly] demand.'

Bar Ḳappara [once] said to Rabbi's daughter, 'To-morrow I will drink wine to your father's dancing and your mother's singing.'[4]

Ben Eleasa, a very wealthy man, was Rabbi's son-in-law, and he was invited to the wedding of R. Simeon b. Rabbi. [At the wedding] Bar Ḳappara asked Rabbi, What is meant by *to'ebah?*[5] Now, every explanation offered by Rabbi was refuted by him, so he said to him, 'Explain it yourself.' He replied, 'Let your housewife come and fill me a cup.' She came and did so, upon which he said to Rabbi, 'Arise, and dance for me, that I may tell it to you.' Thus saith the Divine Law, *'to'ebah': to'eh attah bah.*[6] At his second cup he asked him, 'What is meant by *ṭebel?*'[7] He replied in the same manner as before, [until] he remarked, 'Do [something] for me, and I will tell you.' On his complying, he said *'ṭebel hu'* means: Is there *tablin* [perfume] in it [the animal]? Is intimacy therewith

(1) A reference to the wrong done in not inviting him. (2) Rabbi suffered internal pains for thirteen years, during which there was never a drought.—B.M. 85*a*. (3) That it should retain the wheat. (4) Jast. lit., 'croaking', connecting קירקני with קירקור the croaking of frogs. Asheri, Rosh and Tosaf: 'in the rounds', perhaps connecting it with κίρκος circus, (Goldschmidt). Rashi: when she fills my cup. (5) Abomination. Lev. XX, 13, referring to unnatural vice. (6) Thou errest in respect of her, i.e., by forsaking the permitted and indulging in the forbidden. (7) Disgrace, Lev. XVIII, 23, referring to bestiality; E.V.: *'confusion'*.

sweeter than all other intimacies?[1] Then he further questioned, 'And what is meant by *zimmah?*'[2] 'Do as before, [and I will tell you.'] When he did so, he said, '*zimmah*' means *zu mah hi*'.[3] Now, Ben Eleasa could not endure all this, so he and his wife left.

What is [known of] Ben Eleasa?—It was taught: Ben Eleasa did not disburse his money for nothing, but that he might achieve thereby the High Priest's style of hair-dressing, as it is written, *They shall only poll their heads.*[4] It was taught: [That means] in the Lulian fashion.[5] What was the Lulian style?—Rab Judah said: A unique style of hairdressing. How is that?—Raba said: The end [of one row of hair] reaching the roots of the other, and such was the hairdressing fashion of the High Priest.[6]

AND REMUZIAN CUCUMBERS [DELA'ATH HA-REMUẒAH]. What is DELA'ATH HA-REMUẒAH?—Samuel said, Karkuz pumpkins.[7] R. Ashi said, Cucumbers baked in ashes. Rabina objected to R. Ashi: R. Nehemiah said: Syrian cucumbers, i.e., Egyptian cucumbers, are *kil'ayim*[8] in respect of Greek and Remuẓian [cucumbers!][9] This refutation is unanswerable.

MISHNAH. HE WHO VOWS [ABSTINENCE] FROM FOOD PREPARED IN A POT IS FORBIDDEN ONLY BOILED DISHES. BUT IF ONE SAYS, 'ḲONAM, IF I TASTE AUGHT THAT DESCENDS INTO A POT', HE IS FORBIDDEN EVERYTHING PREPARED IN A POT.[10]

(1) Lit., 'different from'. That thou leavest thine own kind for it. (2) Wickedness, Ibid. 17, referring to incest with a wife's daughter. (3) Who is she, i.e., through promiscuous intercourse the parentage is unknown, and thus a father might marry his daughter. (4) Ezek. XLIV, 20. (5) Lulianus was a popular corruption of Julianus. V. Sanh. (Sonc. ed.) p. 128 n. 2. (6) Eleasa expended huge sums to have his hair so dressed. Presumably it was a costly process known only to a few experts. (7) That do not improve in cooking כרכוז. Obermeyer, *op. cit.* pp. 35f., identifies it with Circesium on the Euphrates, some 73 parasangs from Pumbeditha on the way to Palestine. (8) V. Glos. (9) And may not be sown together with them, v. Deut. XXII, 9, which applies to all diverse species; cf. Kil. I, 5.—This Baraitha proves that *remuẓah* indicates the place of origin, not the manner of its preparation. Obermeyer *a.l.* regards הרמוצא as a form of הרמאס, the river Hirmas which rises by Nisibis. (10) This is repeated exactly in VI, 1. From Ran it would appear that it was absent in

GEMARA. It was taught: He who vows [abstinence] from what goes into a boiling pot, may not eat of what goes into a stew pot, because it has already entered the boiling pot before going into the stew pot; from what goes into a stew pot, he may eat of what goes into a boiling pot; from what is [wholly] prepared in a boiling pot, he may eat of what is prepared in a stew pot; from what is wholly prepared in a boiling pot, he may eat what is [partially] prepared in a stew pot. If he vows [abstinence] from what goes into an oven, only bread is forbidden him. But if he declares, 'Everything made in an oven be forbidden me,' he is forbidden everything that is made in an oven.

MISHNAH. [51b] [IF HE VOWS ABSTINENCE] FROM THE PRESERVE, HE IS FORBIDDEN ONLY PRESERVED VEGETABLES;[1] [IF HE SAYS, 'ḲONAM,] IF I TASTE PRESERVE', HE IS FORBIDDEN ALL PRESERVES. 'FROM THE SEETHED,' HE IS FORBIDDEN ONLY SEETHED MEAT; 'ḲONAM, IF I TASTE SEETHED [FOOD]', HE IS FORBIDDEN EVERYTHING SEETHED.

GEMARA. R. Aḥa the son of R. Awia asked R. Ashi: If one said, 'That which is preserved,' 'that which is roasted,' 'that which is salted', what do these terms imply?[2]—This remains a problem.

MISHNAH. [IF ONE VOWS ABSTINENCE] 'FROM THE ROAST,' HE IS FORBIDDEN ONLY ROAST MEAT: THIS IS R. JUDAH'S OPINION. '[ḲONAM,] IF I TASTE ROAST', HE IS FOR-

VI, 1, in his edition, its correct place being here. Rashi, on the other hand, comments upon it in both places. It is possible that the words MISHNAH and GEMARA should be deleted, the whole being a quotation from the first Mishnah serving as a caption for the discussion in the Gemara (Marginal Gloss to Wilna ed.).—As to the difference between 'boiled dishes' and 'food prepared in a pot', the first term applies to dishes completely boiled therein, the second to food only partially prepared therein and finished elsewhere.

(1) The use of the def. art. limits the vow to the most common form of preserve. (2) Are they the equivalent of the definite art. and so limited, or not?

BIDDEN [TO PARTAKE] OF ALL FORMS OF ROAST. 'FROM THE SALTED', HE IS FORBIDDEN ONLY SALTED FISH; '[KONAM, IF I TASTE] SALTED [FOOD],' HE IS FORBIDDEN [TO PARTAKE] OF EVERYTHING PRESERVED IN SALT. '[KONAM,] IF I TASTE FISH OR FISHES,'[1] HE IS FORBIDDEN [TO EAT] THEM, BOTH LARGE AND SMALL, SALTED AND UNSALTED, RAW AND COOKED. YET HE MAY EAT HASHED ṬERITH,[2] BRINE, AND FISH PICKLE.[3] HE WHO VOWS [ABSTINENCE] FROM ẒAḤANAH,[4] IS FORBIDDEN HASHED ṬERITH, BUT MAY PARTAKE OF BRINE AND FISH PICKLE. HE WHO VOWS [ABSTINENCE] FROM HASHED ṬERITH MAY NOT[5] PARTAKE OF BRINE AND FISH PICKLE.

GEMARA. It was taught: R. Simeon b. Eleazar said: [If he vows] '[*Ḳonam*, If I taste] fish [*dag*],' he is forbidden large ones but permitted small ones. '[*Ḳonam*] if I taste *dagah*,'[6] he is forbidden small ones, but permitted large ones. '[*Ḳonam*,] if I taste *dag* [and] *dagah*,' he is forbidden both large and small ones. R. Papa said to Abaye: How do we know that '[*Ḳonam*, If I taste] *dag*' implies large ones only? because it is written, *Now the Lord had prepared a great fish* [dag] *to swallow up Jonah?*[7] But is it not written, *Then Jonah prayed unto the Lord his God out of the fish's* [dagah] *belly?*[8]—This is no difficulty: perhaps he was vomited forth by the large fish and swallowed again by a smaller one. But [what of the verse] *And the fish* [dagah] *that was in the river died?*[9] did only the small fish die, not the large?—Hence *dagah* implies both large and small, but in vows human speech is followed.[10]

HE WHO VOWS [ABSTINENCE] FROM ẒAḤANAH, etc. Rabina

(1) 'Fish' refers to large ones, 'fishes' to small, which are sold in quantities. (2) A certain fish. This is sold in slices, whereas his vow related to whole ones only. (3) This is absent from cur. edd., but is inserted by BaḤ. (4) Mud-fish, small fish preserved in brine, similar to *ṭerith* (Jast.). (5) This is the reading of Rashi and Asheri. Other editions, likewise Ran, read 'may'. (6) Fem. of *dag* used in the collective. (7) Jon. II, 1. (8) Ibid. 2, shewing that *dagah* too refers to large fish. (9) Ex. VII, 21. (10) In *general* usage, *dag* refers to large fish, *dagah* to small.

asked R. Ashi: What if one says, '*Ẓiḥin* be forbidden me'?[1] The problem remains.

MISHNAH. HE WHO VOWS [ABSTINENCE] FROM MILK MAY PARTAKE OF CURD.[2] BUT R. JOSE FORBIDS IT. 'FROM CURD,' HE IS PERMITTED MILK. ABBA SAUL SAID: HE WHO VOWS [TO ABSTAIN] FROM CHEESE, IS INTERDICTED THEREFROM, WHETHER SALTED OR UNSALTED. 'FROM MEAT,' [52*a*] HE MAY PARTAKE OF BROTH AND THE SEDIMENTS OF BOILED MEAT;[3] BUT R. JUDAH FORBIDS [THEM]. R. JUDAH SAID: IT ONCE HAPPENED THAT [IN SUCH A CASE] R. TARFON FORBADE US[4] [EVEN] EGGS BOILED THEREWITH. THEY REPLIED, THAT IS SO, BUT ONLY IF HE VOWS, 'THIS MEAT BE FORBIDDEN ME.' FOR IF HE VOWS [TO ABSTAIN] FROM SOMETHING, AND IT IS MIXED UP WITH ANOTHER, IF IT [THE FORBIDDEN FOOD] IS SUFFICIENT TO IMPART ITS TASTE [TO THE OTHER], IT[5] IS FORBIDDEN.[6] IF HE VOWS [TO ABSTAIN] FROM WINE, HE IS PERMITTED [TO EAT] FOOD WHICH CONTAINS THE TASTE OF WINE; BUT IF HE SAYS, 'ḲONAM, IF I TASTE THIS WINE', AND IT FALLS INTO FOOD, IF IT IS SUFFICIENT TO IMPART ITS TASTE [TO THE FOOD], IT IS FORBIDDEN.

GEMARA. [52*b*] But the following contradicts this. [If one vows abstinence] from lentils, lentil cakes are forbidden him; R. Jose permits them![7]—There is no difficulty: each Master [rules] according to [the usage] of his locality. In that of the Rabbis, milk is called milk, and curd, curd; but in that of R. Jose, curd too is called curd of milk.

(1) *Ziḥin*, a preparation of small fish, is analogous to *ẓaḥanah*. The problem is whether he is allowed brine and fish pickle (*muries*). (2) Maim: whey. (3) Bits of meat that fall away from the piece in boiling and form a jelly. (4) *Var. lec.* me. (5) That other food. (6) But if one vows abstinence from meat *in general*, the eggs boiled therewith, likewise the soup and meat sediment, are permitted. (7) *Infra* 53*b*. Thus R. Jose permits what is made from the forbidden substance, whilst in the Mishnah he declares curd forbidden under the term milk.

It was taught: He who vows [abstinence] from milk, is permitted curd; from curd, is permitted milk; from milk, is permitted cheese; from cheese, is permitted milk; from broth, is permitted meat sediment; from meat sediment, is permitted broth. If he says, 'This meat be forbidden me,' the meat itself, its broth and its sediment, are forbidden him. If he vows [to abstain] from wine, he may partake of food which contains the taste of wine; but if he says, '*Ḳonam* that I taste not this wine,' and it falls into food, if the taste of wine is [perceptible] therein, it is forbidden.

MISHNAH. HE WHO VOWS [ABSTINENCE] FROM GRAPES IS PERMITTED WINE; FROM OLIVES, IS PERMITTED OIL. IF HE SAYS, 'ḲONAM, THAT I TASTE NOT THESE OLIVES AND GRAPES', BOTH THEY AND THEIR JUICE[1] ARE FORBIDDEN.

GEMARA. Rami b. Ḥama propounded: Is 'these' essential, or 'that I taste not' essential?[2] (But, if you can think that 'these' is essential, why add 'that I taste not'?—He [the Tanna] may teach this [by the addition]: even if he says, 'that I taste not,' yet only if he declares, 'these' is he prohibited, but not otherwise.)—Raba said, Come and hear: [If one says,] '*Ḳonam* be *these* fruits to me,'[3] 'Be they *ḳonam* to my mouth,' he is forbidden [to benefit] from what is exchanged for them or what grows of their seeds. This implies that he may benefit from their juice![4]—In truth, even their juice is forbidden; but he [the Tanna] prefers to teach that what is exchanged for them is the same as what grows from their seeds.[5]

(1) Lit., 'what comes from them'. (2) Since an ordinary vow does not interdict the juice of grapes and olives, whilst in the second clause this is forbidden, the question arises, on account of which particular phrase are they prohibited? Is it because he vowed 'these grapes', or because he added 'that I taste not', superfluous in itself, being implied in *ḳonam*, and therefore perhaps extending the vow to oil and wine? (3) *Infra* 57a. (4) Though he said 'these'. This proves that the essential clause in the Mishnah is 'that I taste not'. (5) Though the former is an entirely different thing: how much more so that which actually issues therefrom!

Come and hear: 'That I eat not or taste not of them,' he is permitted [to benefit] from what is exchanged for them or what grows of their seeds.[1] This implies that their juice is forbidden![2] —Because the first clause does not mention their juice, the second clause omits it too.[3]

Come and hear: R. Judah said: It once happened that [in such a case] R. Tarfon forbade us [even] eggs boiled therewith. They replied, that is so. But only if he vows, 'This meat be forbidden me.' For if he vows [to abstain] from something, and it is mixed up with another, if it [the forbidden food] is sufficient to impart its taste [to the other], it is forbidden![4]—There is no question about 'these': that is certainly essential.[5] The problem is with respect to 'that I taste not': is that essential or not?[6]—Come and hear: ['*Ḳonam* that I taste not fish or fishes'], he is forbidden [to eat] them, both large and small, salted and unsalted, raw and cooked. Yet he may eat hashed ṭerith and brine![7]—Raba said: Providing it [the brine] had already issued from them [before the vow].[8]

MISHNAH. [53a] HE WHO VOWS [ABSTINENCE] FROM DATES IS PERMITTED DATE HONEY; FROM WINTER GRAPES,[9] HE IS PERMITTED VINEGAR MADE FROM WINTER GRAPES. R. JUDAH B. BATHYRA SAID: IF IT BEARS THE NAME OF ITS ORIGIN,[10] AND HE VOWS [TO ABSTAIN] FROM IT,[11] HE IS FOR-

(1) This continues the quotation. (2) For, according to the last answer, this is more likely to be forbidden than the others. Hence, were this permitted, it would be explicitly stated. This too proves that the essential clause is 'that I taste not'. (3) For the sake of uniformity. But actually it may be permitted. (4) This definitely proves that 'this' is essential. (5) I.e., it is certain that 'these' alone extends the vow as indicated. (6) Is that phrase alone sufficient to extend its scope? (7) Brine is the juice that issues from the fish, yet it is permitted, though he said, 'that I taste not'. This proves that that alone is insufficient. (8) But the brine which issues thereafter may be forbidden: hence the problem remains. (9) סתוניות < סתוא winter, remaining on the tree till winter. (10) As here, the vinegar being called 'winter grapes vinegar'. (11) *Sc.* the article of its origin, i.e., winter grapes.

BIDDEN [TO BENEFIT] FROM WHAT COMES FROM IT. BUT THE SAGES PERMIT IT.

GEMARA. But the Sages are identical with the first Tanna?—They differ in respect of the following which was taught: R. Simeon b. Eleazar laid down this general rule: Whatever is eaten itself, and what comes from it too is eaten, e.g., dates and the honey of dates, and he vowed [abstinence] from the substance itself, he is forbidden that which comes from it;[1] but if he vows [abstinence] from what comes from it, he is also forbidden the substance itself.[2] But if the substance is not eaten itself, whilst what comes from it is,[3] and he vowed [abstinence] from the substance itself, he is forbidden only what comes from it,[4] because he meant nought else but what comes from it.[5]

MISHNAH. HE WHO VOWS [ABSTINENCE] FROM WINE MAY PARTAKE OF APPLE-WINE [CIDER]; FROM OIL, HE IS PERMITTED SESAME OIL;[6] FROM HONEY, HE IS PERMITTED DATE HONEY; FROM VINEGAR, HE IS PERMITTED THE VINEGAR OF WINTER GRAPES; FROM LEEKS, HE IS PERMITTED PORRET;[7] FROM VEGETABLES, HE IS PERMITTED FIELD HERBS,[8] BECAUSE IT IS A QUALIFYING EPITHET.[9]

GEMARA. It was taught: He who vows [to abstain] from oil: in Palestine sesame oil is permitted him, but he is forbidden olive

(1) T. J. has 'permitted', which Wilna Gaon regards as correct. (2) V. preceding note. (3) E.g., winter grapes. (4) If the substance is foresworn. (5) The first Tanna, who rules that vinegar of winter grapes is permitted, disagrees with R. Simeon b. Eleazar, whilst the Sages agree with him. Hence, 'the Sages permit it', refers to the substance itself, when not usually eaten, but not to what comes from it (6) שומשום (pl. שומשמין) probably fr. שמש (sun-flower), sesame. (7) קפלוט pl. קפלוטות (κεφάλωτον), is a species of leek with a head (*porrum capitatum*). (8) Wild vegetables. (9) The reason of all these is that where a qualifying epithet is normally added to the name of the substance it is not included in the unspecified term: thus, in speaking of wine (unspecified), grape wine is meant, not apple wine; and so the rest.

oil; in Babylon, he is forbidden sesame oil but permitted olive oil. In the place where they are both commonly used, both are forbidden. But that is obvious?—It is necessary to teach it only when most people use one: I might think that the majority must be followed. We are therefore taught that a doubtful prohibition is [resolved] stringently.[1]

He who vows [abstinence] from vegetables, in normal years is forbidden garden vegetables but permitted wild vegetables; in the seventh year, he is forbidden wild vegetables but permitted garden vegetables.[2] R. Abbahu said on the authority of R. Ḥanina b. Gamaliel: [53*b*] This was taught only where vegetables are not imported into Palestine from abroad;[3] but where they are imported into Palestine from abroad, [garden vegetables] are forbidden. This is dependent on Tannaim: Vegetables may not be imported from abroad into Palestine; R. Ḥanina b. Gamaliel said: We may import them. What is the reason of him who prohibits it?—R. Jeremiah said: On account of the clods of earth.[4]

MISHNAH. [HE WHO VOWS TO ABSTAIN] FROM CABBAGE IS FORBIDDEN ASPARAGUS;[5] FROM ASPARAGUS, HE IS PERMITTED CABBAGE;[6] FROM POUNDED BEANS, HE IS FORBIDDEN MIKPEH:[7] R. JOSE PERMITS IT. [IF ONE VOWS TO ABSTAIN] FROM MIKPEH, HE IS FORBIDDEN GARLIC. R. JOSE PERMITS IT; FROM GARLIC, HE IS PERMITTED MIKPEH. FROM LENTILS, LENTIL CAKES ARE FORBIDDEN HIM. R. JOSE PERMITS THEM. FROM LENTIL CAKES, LENTILS ARE PERMITTED HIM. [IF ONE

(1) Consequently, though a particular oil is used by a minority only, yet if its usage is sufficiently prevalent to warrant the assumption that the vow may have been meant to include it, it is forbidden. (2) Since none are planted then, by the unspecified term wild vegetables are meant. (3) Lit., 'outside the Land (of Israel)'. (4) Which may adhere to the roots when they are brought: these clods were considered unclean; v. Shab. 15*b*. (5) Being considered a species of the genus 'cabbage' (Jast.). (6) The part is included in the whole, but the whole is not included in the part. (7) A stiff mass of oil, grist, and onions (Jast.).

SAYS] 'ḲONAM, IF I TASTE ḤIṬṬAH, ḤIṬṬIN',[1] BOTH THE FLOUR THEREOF AND THE [BAKED] BREAD ARE FORBIDDEN TO HIM: 'IF I TASTE GERIS, GERISSIN',[2] HE IS FORBIDDEN [TO PARTAKE] OF THEM WHETHER RAW OR COOKED. R. JUDAH SAID: [IF ONE DECLARES], 'ḲONAM, IF I TASTE ḤIṬṬAH OR GERIS,' HE MAY CHEW THEM RAW.

GEMARA. It was taught: R. Simeon b. Gamaliel said: [If one vows '*Ḳonam*,] if I taste *ḥiṭṭah* [wheat]', baked wheat [i.e., flour] is forbidden him, but he may chew it raw; '[*Ḳonam*,] if I taste *ḥiṭṭin*,'[3] he may not chew them raw, but if baked, they are permitted;[4] 'If I taste *ḥiṭṭah, ḥiṭṭin*', he may neither eat them baked nor chew them raw. [If he says, '*Ḳonam*,] if I taste *geris*', it is forbidden cooked, but may be chewed [raw]; '[*Ḳonam*], if I taste *gerissin*', he is forbidden either to cook them or chew them raw.

(1) *Ḥiṭṭah*, a grain of wheat, also (generically) wheat; pl. *ḥiṭṭim* (in popular speech the Aramaic plural *ḥiṭṭin*, was used). (2) *Geris*, a pounded bean, also used collectively; pl. *gerissim*. (3) Wheat, but plural in form. (4) Such are the respective meanings assigned in common speech to *ḥiṭṭah* and *ḥiṭṭin*: the same difference occurs in *geris* and *gerissin*.

NEDARIM

CHAPTER VII

MISHNAH. [54*a*] HE WHO VOWS [TO ABSTAIN] FROM VEGETABLES IS PERMITTED GOURDS. R. AKIBA FORBIDS THEM. THE [SAGES] SAID TO HIM, BUT WHEN A MAN SAYS TO HIS AGENT 'FETCH ME VEGETABLES,' HE REPLIES, 'I COULD OBTAIN ONLY GOURDS.' HE ANSWERED, EXACTLY: BUT WOULD HE SAY, 'I COULD OBTAIN ONLY PULSE?'[1] BUT THAT GOURDS ARE INCLUDED IN VEGETABLES, WHILST PULSE IS [DEFINITELY] NOT. HE IS [ALSO] FORBIDDEN FRESH EGYPTIAN BEANS, BUT PERMITTED THE DRY [SPECIES].[2]

GEMARA. HE WHO VOWS [TO ABSTAIN] FROM VEGETABLES etc. But he vowed [to abstain] from vegetables![3]—Said 'Ulla: This refers to one who vows, 'The vegetables of the pot [be forbidden] to me.'[4] But perhaps he meant vegetables which are eaten [with food cooked] in a pot?[5]—He said: 'Vegetables that are cooked in a pot [be forbidden] to me.'[6]

Wherein do they differ?—The Rabbis maintain: Whatever an agent must inquire about does not belong to the same species;[7] but R. Akiba maintains, Whatever the agent needs inquire about is of the same species.[8] Abaye said: R. Akiba admits in respect to punishment that he is not flagellated.[9]

(1) If only pulse were obtainable, he would simply report that vegetables were unobtainable. (2) These are two different species, the fresh regarded as a vegetable, the dry a cereal, because it is ground into flour. (3) Which gourds are certainly not. (4) And since gourds are boiled in pots, R. Akiba maintains that they are included. (5) E.g., onions, which are put in a pot for seasoning. (6) This must refer to something prepared for itself, and not mere seasoning. (7) A servant, being told to buy vegetables and finding only gourds, would ask his master whether these would do. (8) For if not, he would reject them immediately. (9) For eating them. Though he forbids them, it is not certain that they are vegetables.

We learnt elsewhere: If the agent carried out his commission, the principal[1] is guilty of a trespass; if he did not carry out his commission, he himself is guilty of a trespass.[2] With which Tanna does this agree?—R. Ḥisda said: Our Mishnah does not agree with R. Akiba. For we learnt:[3] Thus, if he said to him, 'Give the guests meat,' and he gave them liver; '[give them] liver,' and he gave them meat, the agent is guilty of a trespass.[4] But if this agrees with R. Akiba: did he not say, Whatever an agent must inquire about, belongs to that species? In that case, the principal, and not the agent, should be liable to a trespass- [offering]?[5] Abaye said, This may agree even with R. Akiba: [54b] does not R. Akiba admit that he must consult [his principal]?[6] When this discussion was repeated before Raba, he remarked, Naḥmani hath said well.[7]

Which Tanna disagrees with R. Akiba?—R. Simeon b. Gamaliel. For it was taught: He who vows [to abstain] from meat, is forbidden every kind of meat; he is also forbidden the head, feet, windpipe, liver, heart, and fowl; but he is permitted the flesh of fish and locusts. R. Simeon b. Gamaliel said: He who vows [to abstain] from meat is forbidden every kind of meat, but permitted the head, feet, windpipe, liver, heart and fowl, and it is superfluous

(1) Lit., 'householder'. (2) V. Me'il, 20a. The reference is to *ḥekdesh* (q.v. Glos.), which must not be appropriated for secular use; if it is (unwittingly), a trespass-offering must be brought, v. Lev. V, 14. Now, if one instructs his agent to do this, and his instructions are exactly carried out, he is responsible; if not, the agent is held to have acted of his own accord, and is himself responsible. (3) Continuing the Mishnah quoted. (4) It should be observed that by offering this *ḥekdesh* to the guests the agent has already misappropriated it by withdrawing it from sacred to secular ownership. The sacrifice is due for that withdrawal; hence when the guests eat it, it is no longer sacred, and no obligation rests upon them. (5) For if one is sent to buy meat and finds only liver, he would certainly consult his master about it. Therefore, if the servant gave liver when ordered to give meat, on R. Akiba's view he carried out his master's instructions. (6) Though maintaining that it is of the same species, R. Akiba agrees that a servant would not take meat when ordered to get liver without further instructions. Consequently his action is regarded as his own. (7) Abaye was an orphan brought up in the house of Rabbah b. Naḥmani, who called him by the name of his father, v. Giṭ. (Sonc. ed.) p. 140, n. 6.

to mention the flesh of fish and locusts.[1] And thus R. Simeon b. Gamaliel used to say: The entrails are not meat, and he who eats them is no man. In respect of what is this said?[2] [To teach that] he who eats them as meat is no man in respect of purchase.[3]

Why does the first Tanna declare fowl forbidden? Because the agent is wont to inquire about it! But the same applies to flesh of fish in regard to which the agent too, if he can obtain no meat, consults [his master] saying, 'If I cannot obtain meat, shall I bring fish?' Hence it should be forbidden?—Said Abaye: This refers to one who was bled [just before his vow] who [consequently] would not eat fish.[4] If so, he would not eat fowl either, for Samuel said: If one is bled, and then eats fowl, his heart will palpitate like a fowl's. And it was taught: One must not be bled and eat fish, fowl, or pickled meat. And it was taught: If one is bled, he must not eat milk, cheese, eggs, cress, fowl, or pickled meat!—Fowl is different, because it may be eaten after being thoroughly boiled. Abaye [also] said:[5] It refers to one whose eyes ache, fish being injurious to the eyes, If so, he *should* eat fish, for Samuel said, *Nun, Samek, 'Ayin*[6] [read] *Nuna* [fish] *sama* [are a healing] *la-'enayim* [to the eyes]!—That is at the end of the illness.[7]

MISHNAH. [55*a*] HE WHO VOWS [TO ABSTAIN] FROM DAGAN [GRAIN] IS FORBIDDEN DRY EGYPTIAN BEANS: THIS

(1) Thus he maintains that liver is not included in meat, and so differs from R. Akiba. (2) Thus the reading as emended by BaḤ. Since R. Simeon does not exclude the entrails from the things forbidden, in what respect are they not meat? (3) I.e., If one likes them as much as other meat and is prepared to pay the same price, he is regarded as irrational (Rashi). Tosaf. in Meil. 20*b* s.v. קרביים explains thus: If one buys an animal and finds that the entrails are unfit for food, he cannot demand that the sale be nullified on that account, since they are not meant for human consumption. (4) It was considered unhealthy to eat fish after being bled. Since then he would not have eaten fish in any case, his vow was not directed against it. (5) 'Also' must be added if this reading be retained, since the first answer was also Abaye's. In Me'il. *loc. cit.*, however, the reading is 'R. Papa'. (6) Three letters of the Hebrew alphabet in order. (7) When the eyes are recovering, fish is beneficial, but at the beginning of the ailment fish is injurious.

IS R. MEIR'S VIEW, BUT THE SAGES SAY: ONLY THE FIVE SPECIES ARE FORBIDDEN HIM.[1] R. MEIR SAID: IF HE VOWS [TO ABSTAIN] FROM TEBU'AH,[2] HE IS FORBIDDEN ONLY THE FIVE SPECIES; BUT ONE WHO VOWS [ABSTINENCE] FROM DAGAN, IS FORBIDDEN ALL; YET HE IS PERMITTED THE FRUITS OF THE TREE AND VEGETABLES.

GEMARA. Shall we say that DAGAN implies anything that can be heaped up?[3] To this R. Joseph objected: *And as soon as the commandment came abroad, the children of Israel brought in abundance the first-fruits of corn* [dagan] *wine and oil, and honey, and of all the increase of the field; and the tithe of all things brought they in abundantly.*[4] But should you say that DAGAN implies everything that can be heaped up, what is meant by, *And as soon as the commandment came abroad they brought in abundance?*[5]—Abaye answered: It is to include the fruits of the tree and vegetables.

R. MEIR SAID: IF ONE VOWS [TO ABSTAIN] FROM TEBU'AH, etc. R. Johanan said: All agree that if one vows [to abstain] from *tebu'ah*, the five species only are forbidden to him. It was taught likewise: And both[6] agree that if one vows [abstinence] from *tebu'ah*, only the five species are forbidden. But that is obvious?—I might argue, *tebu'ah* implies everything: therefore he teaches that it does not imply everything. R. Joseph objected: *And as soon as the commandment came abroad, they brought in abundance etc.?*[7]—Raba answered: *Tebu'ah* is one thing: *tebuath sadeh* is another.[8]

(1) Viz., Wheat, barley, rye, oats, and spelt. (2) Field produce. (3) Heb. *midgan:* this being the reason that R. Meir forbids dry Egyptian beans under the term DAGAN. (4) II Chron. XXXI, 5: the emphasis laid upon the abundance of their offering implies that they brought more tithes than required by Biblical law. (5) Since they were obliged to tithe DAGAN by Biblical law, and DAGAN includes all things that can be heaped up, what did they add to the Biblical ordinance? (Rashi). Asheri explains: since DAGAN includes all things that can be heaped up, what else be implied by the phrase *'and all the increase of the field'?* (6) R. Meir and the Sages. (7) *'And all the increase of the field'* (*tebu'ath sadeh*) is not confined there to the five species only (Rashi). Tosaf. remarks: And Abaye has already interpreted it as referring to vegetables and fruit. (8) I.e. *tebu'ah* does mean the five species only: but *tebu'ath sadeh*, lit., 'that which is brought

The Son of Mar Samuel ordered that thirteen thousand *zuz* worth of *'allalta*[1] from Nehar Pania[2] should be given to Raba. So Raba sent [an enquiry] to R. Joseph: what is meant by *'allalta?* —R. Joseph replied, It is [taught in] a Baraitha: And all agree that if he vows [abstinence] from *tebu'ah*, the five species only are forbidden him. Said Abaye to him, How compare? *Tebu'ah* implies only the five species, [whereas] *'allalta* implies everything. When this was repeated before Raba, he observed, I am in no doubt that *'allalta* means everything. My problem is this: What of the rent of houses and the hire of ships? Shall we say, Since they depreciate, they are not included in *'allalta;* or perhaps since the depreciation is imperceptible, they [too] are termed *'allalta?*[3] The scholars narrated this to R. Joseph, 'Since he does not need us!' he exclaimed, 'why did he send to us?' And so R. Joseph was annoyed. When Raba learnt this, he went before him on the eve of the Day of Atonement, and found his attendant mixing him a cup of wine.[4] 'Let me prepare it for him,' said he. So he gave it to him, and he mixed the cup of wine. On drinking it he observed, 'This mixture is like that of Raba the son of R. Joseph b. Ḥama. 'It is indeed he,' was his reply. He then said to him. 'Do not take your seat[5] until you have explained this verse to me. [Viz.,] What is meant by, '*And from the wilderness, Mattanah; and from Mattanah, Nahaliel; and from Nahaliel, Bamoth*'?[6]—He replied, When one makes himself as the wilderness, which is free to all,[7] the Torah is presented to

in from the field', is wider in scope, and applies to everything brought in from the field, even fruit and vegetables.

(1) *'Allalta*, connected with Heb. עלל (cf. Lam. I, 22: *and do unto them, as thou has done unto me* ועולל למו כאשר עוללת לי) denotes that which is produced (in the fields), and is the Aramaic equivalent of *tebu'ah*. (2) [Ḥarpania, a rich agricultural town in the Mesene district S. of Babylon situated on a hill and canal. Obermeyer (*op. cit.*) p. 198ff.] (3) *'Allalta*, perhaps derived by popular etymology from עלל to enter, to come in (as revenue), applies to that which appreciates, not depreciates, viz., field produce, which from the time of sowing until it is ready for food appreciates in value. Once ready, it cannot depreciate as food, whereas a house, even when still fit for its purpose, continuously depreciates. (4) Wine was not drunk raw, but had to be diluted with water. (5) Lit., 'sit on your legs'. V. Nazir (Sonc. ed.) p. 87, n. 7. (6) Num. XXI, 19f. (7) I.e., is prepared truly to teach the Torah to all.

him as a gift [*mattanah*] as it is written, '*And from the wilderness, Mattanah*'. And once he has it as a gift, God gives it to him as an inheritance [*nahaliel*],[1] as it is written, '*And from Mattanah, Nahaliel;*' And when God gives it him as an inheritance, he ascends to greatness, as it is written, '*And from Nahaliel, Bamoth* [heights']. But if he exalts himself, the Holy One, blessed be He, casts him down, as it is written, '*And from Bamoth, the valley*'.[2] Moreover, he is made to sink[3] into the earth, as it is written, *Which is pressed down*[4] *into the desolate soil.* But should he repent, the Holy One, blessed be He, will raise him again, [55*b*] as it is written, *Every valley shall be exalted.*[5]

It was taught: He who vows [to abstain] from *dagan* is also forbidden dry Egyptian beans; yet moist ones are permitted. He is also permitted rice, grist, groats and pearl-barley. He who vows [to abstain] from the fruits of that year, is forbidden all the fruit of that year, but is permitted goats, lambs, milk, eggs, and fledglings [of that year].[6] But if he vows, 'The growths of this year [be forbidden] to me,' all these are forbidden. He who vows [abstinence] from the fruits of the earth is forbidden all the fruits of the earth, yet is permitted mushrooms and truffles; but if he vows, 'that which grows from the earth [be forbidden] to me,' all these are forbidden him. But this contradicts the following: For that which does not grow from the earth, one must recite the benediction, 'by whose word all things exist.'[7] And it was taught: For salt, brine mushrooms, and truffles, 'by whose word all things exist' is said![8]—Abaye answered, They do indeed grow out of the earth, but draw their sustenance from the air,[9]

(1) I.e., it becomes his safe possession. (2) From the heights he is hurled down into the valley. (3) *Var. lec.* pressed down—שוקפין—which has a more obvious connection with the verse adduced. (4) ונשקפה E.V. '*which looketh*', is here connected with שקף to strike (down). (5) Isa. XL, 4. (6) Though metaphorically they too might be regarded as the fruits of the year, the vow must be understood literally. (7) This deals with the blessings to be recited before partaking of food or drink. (8) The combination of these two statements proves that mushrooms and truffles are not earth-grown, and thus contradicts the ruling that a vow to abstain from what grows from the earth includes them. (9) Therefore they are included in the vow, 'growths of the earth'; yet since their sustenance

and not from the earth. But he [the Tanna] states: For that which does not *grow* out of the earth?[1] —Read: For that which does not draw its sustenance from the earth.[2]

MISHNAH. HE WHO VOWS [NOT TO BENEFIT] FROM GARMENTS IS PERMITTED SACK-CLOTH,[3] CURTAIN,[4] AND BLANKET WRAPPING. IF HE SAYS, 'ḲONAM, IF WOOL COMES UPON ME,' HE MAY COVER HIMSELF WITH WOOL FLEECES;[5] '[ḲONAM,] IF FLAX COMES UPON ME', HE MAY COVER HIMSELF WITH FLAX BUNDLES.[6] R. JUDAH SAID: IT ALL DEPENDS UPON THE PERSON WHO VOWS, [THUS:] IF HE IS LADEN [WITH WOOL OR FLAX] AND PERSPIRES AND HIS ODOUR IS OPPRESSIVE, AND HE VOWS 'ḲONAM' IF WOOL OR FLAX COME UPON ME,' HE MAY WEAR THEM, BUT NOT THROW THEM [AS A BUNDLE] OVER HIS BACK.[7]

GEMARA. It was taught: He who vows [not to benefit] from garments is permitted sack-cloth, curtain, and blanket wrapping. But he is forbidden a belt,[8] *fascia*,[9] *scortea*, a leather spread, shoes,[10] knee breeches, breeches and a hat. What is a *scortea*?—Rabbah b. Bar Huna said: a leather coat.

It was taught: One may go out [on the Sabbath] wearing a thick sack-cloth, a coarse blanket, a curtain, and a blanket wrap, to keep off the rain;[11] but not with a box, basket[12] or matting for the

is drawn chiefly from the air, they are not regarded as earth grown in respect of a benediction.

(1) Whilst according to Abaye they do. (2) This is hardly an emendation, but rather an interpretation; cf. p. 3, n. 2. (3) [Of goats-hair, v. Kel. XXVII, 1.] (4) Some kind of rough, ready garment, which was not a garment proper. (5) Because the vow implies garments which can be worn. (6) אניצי פשתן flax—stalks after they are soaked, beaten and baked (Jast.). (7) For in the circumstances it is evident that his vow referred to it as a load, not as a garment. (8) The פונדא was a hollow belt used as a pouch. (9) A band or sash; Lat. *fascia*. (10) The word is the plural of εμπιλιον, *impilia* (pair of) felt shoes (Jast.). (11) These, though not actually garments, are nevertheless counted as such, and hence permissible on the Sabbath. (12) Placed over the head to ward off the rains.

same purpose. Shepherds may go out with sacks;[1] not only shepherds, but all men, but that the Sages spoke of what is usual.

R. JUDAH SAID, IT ALL DEPENDS UPON THE PERSON WHO VOWED, etc. It was taught: How did R. Judah say, It all depends upon the person who vows? If he is wearing wool, and he is irritated and he vows, '*Ḳonam,* if wool comes upon me,' he is forbidden to wear, but permitted to carry it; if he is laden with flax and perspires and vows, '*Ḳonam,* if flax comes upon me,' he may wear but must not carry it.

MISHNAH. [56a] ONE WHO VOWS [NOT TO BENEFIT] FROM A HOUSE IS PERMITTED THE UPPER STOREY:[2] THIS IS R. MEIR'S VIEW. BUT THE SAGES SAY: THE UPPER STOREY IS INCLUDED IN 'HOUSE'. HE WHO VOWS [NOT TO HAVE THE USE OF] THE UPPER STOREY IS PERMITTED [THE USE OF] THE HOUSE.

GEMARA. Which Tanna taught: [*And I put a plague of leprosy*] *in a house* [*of the land of your possession*]:[3] this includes the side-chambers;[4] '*in a house*', this includes the upper storey?—R. Ḥisda said, It is R. Meir's teaching. For if the Rabbis', why require '*in a house*' to include the upper storey, since they say that an upper storey is an integral part of the house? Abaye said, it may agree even with the Rabbis, yet a verse is necessary. For you might think, [since] it is written, '*in a house of the land of your possession*': that which is [directly] attached to the 'land'[5] is called 'house', but the upper storey, not being attached to the land, [is not called

(1) In the first clause, 'sack-cloth' would seem to refer to a rough garment; in the second, 'sacks' is probably to be understood literally, put over one's head to ward off the rain. (2) These were quite distinct, often belonging to separate owners; cf. B.M. 116*b*. (3) Lev. XIV, 34. (4) יציע, V. B.B. 61*a*. So curr. edd. Ran and Wilna Gaon emend it to צבוע painted walls, because side chambers are excluded in the Sifra from the laws of leprosy, and the teaching is that even these are subject to the laws of house leprosy. This is necessary, because leprosy in garments only applies to undyed materials.—Neg. XI, 3. (5) This soil.

'house']. With whom does the following dictum of R. Huna b. Ḥiyya in 'Ulla's name agree? Viz., [If one says,] 'I sell you a house[1] within my house,' he can offer him an upper storey. Hence it is only because he says, 'I sell you a house within my house';[2] but in the case of 'house' without definition he cannot offer him the upper storey. Shall we say, It agrees with R. Meir?—You may even say, It agrees with the Rabbis: by *'aliyyah*, the best[3] of his houses is meant.[4]

MISHNAH. ONE WHO VOWS [ABSTINENCE] FROM A BED IS PERMITTED A DARGESH:[5] THIS IS R. MEIR'S VIEW. BUT THE SAGES SAY: DARGESH IS INCLUDED IN 'BED'. IF HE VOWS [ABSTINENCE] FROM A DARGESH, HE IS ALLOWED [THE USE OF] A BED.

GEMARA. What is *dargesh?*—'Ulla said: A bed reserved for the domestic genius.[6] Said the Rabbis to 'Ulla: But we learnt, When he [*sc.* the High Priest] was given the mourner's meal,[7] all the people sat on the ground, whilst he reclined on the *dargesh*. Now, in normal times[8] he does not sit upon it, yet on that day he does! Rabina demurred to this: Let it be analogous to meat and wine, of which at other times[8] he partakes or not, as he pleases, whereas on that day we give them to him?[9] But this is the difficulty,

(1) [בית may mean either an apartment or a whole house, v. B.B. (Sonc. ed.) p. 247, n. 6.] (2) 'Apartment'. (3) מעולה fr. עלה, lit., 'the highest'. (4) I.e., the purchaser can demand the best of his houses, the phrase in Hebrew בית שבביתי denoting the superlative. But if he simply sold him a בית, he could give him an upper storey. (5) V. Gemara. (6) I.e., one not put to any use, but to bring good luck to the house. (7) The first meal eaten by mourners after the funeral was called the סעודת הבראה meal of comfort or restoration, v. Sanh. 20*a*. (8) Lit., 'the whole year'. (9) [On the wine drunk at the house of the mourner, v. Keth. 8*a*. There is however no law stated anywhere else that meat had to form part of the mourner's meal of comfort. The only reference in Sem. XIV speaks merely of a local custom (cf. Tur *Yoreh De'ah*, 282). It should however be noted that the parallel passages (Sanh. 20*a* and M.Ḳ. 27*a*) read: 'Let it be analogous to eating and drinking', and this is also the reading of MS.M. here.]

for it was taught: The *dargesh* was not lowered[1] but stood up [on its legs]. Now if you say that it is the bed of the domestic genius, has it not been taught: He who lowers his bed, lowers not merely his own bed [as mourner], but all the beds of the house?—This is no difficulty: [56*b*] for it may be similar to the trestle[2] reserved for utensils. For it was taught, If there was a trestle reserved for utensils [in the house], he need not lower it. But if there is a difficulty, it is this: For it was taught: R. Simeon b. Gamaliel said: As for the *dargesh*, its thongs are untied and it automatically collapses;[3] but if the *dargesh* is the bed of the domestic genius, has it then thongs? When Rabin came,[4] he said, I consulted one of the scholars named R. Taḥlifa b. Taḥlifa of the West,[5] who frequented the leather-workers' market, and he told me, What is *dargesh?* A leather bed.[6] It has been stated: What is a *miṭṭah*, and what a *dargesh?*—R. Jeremiah said, [In] a *miṭṭah* [a bedstead] the strapwork is drawn on top; a *dargesh* has the strapwork inside.[7]

An objection is raised: From when are wooden articles ready to receive uncleanliness?[8] A *miṭṭah* and a cradle from when they are smoothed [by being rubbed] with fish skin.[9] Now if the *miṭṭah* has its strapwork drawn up on top, why must it be smoothed with fish skin?[10] But both [the *miṭṭah* and the *dargesh*] have their strappings drawn inside: a *miṭṭah* has its straps drawn in and out through slits [in the boards]; those of a *dargesh* go in and out through loops.

R. Jacob b. Aḥa said in Rabbi's name: A *miṭṭah* whose poles[11]

(1) As is the rule with all other stools and beds in a house of mourning. (2) מטה *miṭṭah*, lit., 'bed'; this trestle must have been similar in shape to a bed. (3) This too refers to a house of mourning. (4) From Palestine. (5) The Palestinian. (6) Its strapping consisted of leather instead of ropes. Not being supported by long legs it stood very low. For this reason it is disputed in the Mishnah whether it is included in bed or not, and also whether it needs lowering during mourning, v. Sanh. (Sonc. ed.) p. 107, n. 1. (7) The straps are attached on the inside through slits in the frame. (8) An article cannot become unclean unless it is completely finished for use. (9) To polish the surface, v. Kel. XXI, 1. (10) By the *miṭṭah* the bedstead itself, i.e., the framework, is understood. If this framework is always overlaid with straps, why need it be smoothed at all? (11) נקליטין, two poles fixed at the head and foot of the bedstead, in the centre

protrude [downwards][1] is set up [on its side], and that is sufficient.[2] R. Jacob b. Idi said in R. Joshua b. Levi's name: The *halachah* is as R. Simeon b. Gamaliel.[3]

MISHNAH. ONE WHO VOWS [NOT TO BENEFIT] FROM A TOWN, MAY ENTER THE TOWN TEḤUM[4] BUT MAY NOT ENTER ITS OUTSKIRTS.[5] BUT ONE WHO VOWS [ABSTINENCE] FROM A HOUSE, IS FORBIDDEN FROM THE DOOR-STOP[6] AND WITHIN.

GEMARA. Whence do we know that the outskirts of a town are as the town itself?—R. Johanan said, Because it is written, *and it came to pass, when Joshua was in Jericho etc.*[7] Now, what is meant by '*in Jericho*'? Shall we say, actually in Jericho: but is it not written, *Now Jericho was straitly shut up because of the children of Israel?*[8] Hence it must mean in its outskirts.[9] Then say that it means even in the *teḥum?*[10]—But with respect to the *teḥum* it is written, *And ye shall measure* without *the city* [*in the east side two thousand cubits etc.*].[11]

BUT ONE WHO VOWS [ABSTINENCE] FROM A HOUSE IS FORBIDDEN FROM THE DOOR-STOP AND WITHIN. But not from the door-stop and without.[12] R. Mari objected: *Then the priest shall go out of the house;*[13] I might think that he goes home and then has it

probably of the width. To these a cross-piece was attached, the whole forming a frame over which a net or curtain was slung.

(1) I.e., below the level of the bedding to the space underneath. (2) The reference is to a house of mourning. Such a bed, if actually lowered, may appear to be standing in its usual position, since then the poles protrude upwards. (3) That the thongs of a *dargesh* must be untied in a house of mourning. (4) A distance of two thousand cubits right round the town boundaries. (5) $70\frac{2}{3}$ cubits from the town borders. The two thousand cubits which is the permitted journey outside the town on the Sabbath, are calculated from the outer edge of these $70\frac{2}{3}$ cubits, v. 'Er. 52*b*. (6) The moulding of the door frame against which the door shuts. (7) Josh. V, 13. (8) Ibid. VI, 1. (9) Which are referred to as the town itself. (10) Perhaps Joshua was stationed within the *teḥum* of Jericho which is spoken of as '*in Jericho*'. (11) Num. XXXV, 5. (12) I.e., the steps or threshold up to the doorstep are permitted. (13) Lev. XIV, 38, The priest, after inspecting the leprous house for the first time, was to go out and have it sealed up for a week.

shut up; therefore it is taught, *to the* door *of the house.*[1] If [I had only to go by] *'to the door of the house,'* I might think that he stands under the lintel and closes it; therefore, it is written, [*'Then the priest shall go*] out *of the house'*, implying that he must go right out of it. How so? He must stand at the side of the lintel and close it. Yet how do we know that if he goes home and has it closed, or stands under the lintel and shuts it, that it is validly shut? From the verse, *And shut up the house,*[2] implying no matter how it be done.[3]—In the case of the [*leprous*] house it is different, because it is written 'out *of the house*', implying that he must go right out of the house.

MISHNAH. [57a] [IF A MAN SAYS], 'ḲONAM BE THESE FRUITS TO ME,' 'BE THEY ḲONAM FOR MY MOUTH,' OR 'BE THEY ḲONAM TO MY MOUTH,' HE IS FORBIDDEN [TO BENEFIT] FROM WHAT IS EXCHANGED FOR THEM OR WHAT GROWS FROM THEM. [IF HE SAYS 'ḲONAM] IF I EAT OR TASTE OF THEM,' HE IS PERMITTED [TO BENEFIT] FROM WHAT IS EXCHANGED FOR THEM OR WHAT GROWS OF THEM, [THAT IS] IN A THING OF WHICH THE SEED ITSELF PERISHES; BUT IF THE SEED DOES NOT PERISH,[4] EVEN THAT WHICH GROWS OUT OF THAT WHICH [FIRST] GREW FROM IT IS FORBIDDEN. IF HE SAYS TO HIS WIFE, 'ḲONAM BE THE WORK OF YOUR HANDS TO ME,' 'ḲONAM BE THEY FOR MY MOUTH,' OR 'ḲONAM BE THEY TO MY MOUTH':[5] HE IS FORBIDDEN THAT WHICH IS EXCHANGED FOR THEM OR GROWN FROM THEM. [IF HE SAID, 'ḲONAM] IF I EAT OR TASTE [THEREOF]', HE IS PERMITTED WHAT IS EXCHANGED FOR THEM OR WHAT IS GROWN FROM

(1) Lev. XIV, 38. (2) Ibid. (3) Now, when one is outside the lintel, he is also, of course, outside the door-stop; yet he is not regarded here as being right out of the house, thus contradicting the implication of the Mishnah that without the door-stop is not part of the house. (4) E.g., garlic or onions; these, when placed in the soil, do not rot away, but grow so that their growths always contain part of the original. (5) And she was paid by means of agricultural produce.

THEM, THAT IS IN A THING OF WHICH PERISHES THE SEED ITSELF; BUT IF THE SEED DOES PERISH, EVEN THAT WHICH GROWS OUT OF THAT WHICH [FIRST] GREW FROM IT IS FORBIDDEN. [IF HE SAYS TO HIS WIFE, 'ḲONAM THAT] WHAT YOU WILL PRODUCE I WILL NOT EAT THEREOF UNTIL PASSOVER' OR 'THAT WHAT YOU WILL PRODUCE, I WILL NOT WEAR UNTIL PASSOVER', HE MAY EAT OR WEAR AFTER PASSOVER OF WHAT SHE PRODUCES BEFORE PASSOVER. '[THAT] WHAT YOU PRODUCE UNTIL PASSOVER I WILL NOT EAT', OR '[THAT] WHAT YOU PRODUCE UNTIL PASSOVER I WILL NOT WEAR', HE MAY NOT EAT OR WEAR AFTER PASSOVER WHAT SHE PRODUCED BEFORE PASSOVER.[1] [IF HE SAYS, 'ḲONAM] BE ANY BENEFIT YOU HAVE FROM ME UNTIL PASSOVER, IF YOU GO TO YOUR FATHER'S HOUSE UNTIL THE FESTIVAL',[2] IF SHE GOES BEFORE PASSOVER SHE MAY NOT BENEFIT FROM HIM UNTIL PASSOVER; [57*b*] IF SHE GOES AFTER PASSOVER[3] SHE IS SUBJECT TO, HE SHALL NOT BREAK HIS WORD.[4] ['ḲONAM] BE ANY BENEFIT YOU HAVE FROM ME UNTIL THE FESTIVAL IF YOU GO TO YOUR FATHER'S HOUSE BEFORE PASSOVER', IF SHE GOES BEFORE PASSOVER, SHE MAY NOT BENEFIT FROM HIM UNTIL THE FESTIVAL, BUT IS PERMITTED TO GO AFTER PASSOVER.

GEMARA. IF A MAN SAYS TO HIS WIFE, 'ḲONAM BE THE WORK OF YOUR HANDS TO ME,' 'FOR MY MOUTH,' OR 'TO MY MOUTH, etc.' Ishmael, of Kefar yama,[5] — others say, Kefar Dima[6] — propounded[7] the case of an onion that has been pulled up in the seventh year and planted in the eighth, and its growth exceeds the stock. And this is what he asked: The growth is permitted, whilst the stock is forbidden;[8] but since the growth

(1) The reference is to her earnings in general, which he may not expend on food or clothing. (2) [החג where unspecified denotes generally the Festival of Succoth, cf. 1 Kings VIII, 2.] (3) After having enjoyed benefit from him. (4) Num. XXX, 3. (5) [The former and modern Jabneel near Tiberias. V. Horowitz, *Palestine*, pp. 322ff.] (6) In the original the difference is denoted by the single letter. (7) Lit., 'brought up in his hand'. (8) The produce of the

exceeds the stock, the permitted growth comes and annuls what is forbidden;[1] or is it not so?[2] He came before R. Ammi, and he could not solve it. He then went before R. Isaac the smith,[3] who solved it from the following dictum of R. Ḥanina of Torata[4] in R. Jannai's name: If one plants an onion of *terumah*, and its increase exceeds the stock, it is [all] permitted.[5] Said R. Jeremiah, others state, R. Zeriḳa, to him, Do you abandon two and follow one? Now who are the two?—[i] R. Abbahu, who said in R. Joḥanan's name: If a young tree[6] already with fruit is grafted on an old one, even if it multiplies two hundredfold, it [the original fruit] is forbidden.[7] [ii] R. Samuel son of R. Naḥmani said in R. Jonathan's name: If an onion is planted in a vineyard and the vineyard is [subsequently] removed, it [the onion] is forbidden.[8]

Then he [Ishmael] again went before R. Ammi, who solved it from the following: For R. Isaac said in R. Joḥanan's name: If a *liṭra*[9] of onions was tithed[10] and then planted, the whole of it must

seventh year, if retained for private use after a certain period, were forbidden for use. V. p. 183, n. 16.

(1) If something forbidden becomes mixed up with something permitted, the latter exceeding the former (the ratio of excess differs: generally it must be sixty times as much), the latter annuls the former, and it is all permitted. Here too, the stock is used with the increase. (2) Rashi, Tosaf. and Asheri regard the problem as referring only to annulment, but that it is certain that the increase itself is permitted. Ran, however, interprets the problem as relating to the increase: either it is permitted, in which case it also annuls the stock, or all is forbidden since it grew from prohibited stock. (3) The Rabbinate being unpaid (cf. *supra* 37a), many Rabbis were tradesmen or workers. E.g., Hillel was a woodcutter before he became *nasi;* R. Joshua was a charcoal maker, and there was a R. Joḥanan who was a sandal maker. (4) This is the conjectured meaning of תריתאה otherwise תורתייה. (5) To a lay Israelite. So likewise in our problem. (6) I.e., less than three years old, the fruit of which, called *'orlah*, is forbidden. (7) Though elsewhere *'orlah* is nullified by such an increase. (8) For when growing there together, they were 'forbidden mixture', (Deut. XXII, 9) and hence the onion was forbidden. Though the vines were removed, and the further growth of the onion permitted, yet the original remains forbidden. (Ran.: yet it is all, including the increase, forbidden). Both these statements are opposed to the first in R. Jannai's name. (9) λίτρα, the Roman Libra, a pound. (10) I.e., all the priestly dues were separated from it.

be re-tithed.[1] This proves that the yield nullifies the stock.[2] Perhaps, however, this is different, being in the direction of greater stringency![3]—But [it can be solved] from the following: For it was taught: R. Simeon said: [58a] For everything [forbidden] which can become permitted, e.g., *ṭebel*,[4] second tithe,[5] *hekdesh*,[6] and *ḥadash*,[7] the Sages declared no limit.[8] But for everything which cannot become permitted, e.g., *terumah, the terumah* of the tithe,[9] *ḥallah*,[10] *'orlah*,[11] and *kil'ayim* of the vineyard,[12] the Sages declared a limit.[13] Said they to him, But seventh year produce cannot become permitted, yet the Sages set no limit to it. For we learnt: Seventh year produce of no matter what quality renders its own kind forbidden![14] He replied, my[15] ruling too is only in respect of removal; but as for eating, [it renders it forbidden] only if sufficient to impart its taste thereto.[16] But perhaps this too is different, since [the

(1) I.e., both the stock and the increase. (2) Though the stock had been tithed once, the whole must be re-tithed, the original being assimilated to the increase. (3) I.e., whereby assimilating the original to the increase the law is more stringent, it is so assimilated. But the problem is whether the original is regarded as nullified though thereby a prohibition is raised. (4) V. Glos. This is forbidden for use, but becomes permitted on payment of the priestly dues. (5) A tithe which had to be eaten in Jerusalem, but forbidden elsewhere. It could, however, be redeemed, by allocating its value, plus a fifth, to be expended in Jerusalem, after which it might be enjoyed anywhere. (6) Anything dedicated to the Temple which cannot be offered as sacrifice may be put to secular use after it is redeemed. (7) Lit., 'new'. The new crops which are forbidden until the offering of the *'Omer*, v. Lev. XXIII, 10-14. (8) If these are mixed up with permitted food, the Sages do not rule that if the latter exceeds the former by a certain ratio the whole is permitted, as in the next clause. The reason is, since it is possible to cancel the prohibition in itself, there is no need to have recourse to nullification through excess. (9) Of the tithe which the Levite received from the Israelite, he had to give one tenth to the priest. (10) V. Glos. The last three are forbidden to a lay Israelite, and the prohibition itself cannot be cancelled. (11) V. Glos. (12) V. Glos. (13) If these became mixed with other permitted substances, the latter nullifies them, providing they exceed them by certain fixed amounts. (14) If mixed with other produce of the same kind, not of the seventh year, the latter is forbidden. (15) So cur. edd., also Rashi and Asheri. Ran.: their ruling, which is more suitable to the context. (16) The seventh year produce might be kept by its owner for his personal use only as long as like produce is still growing in the fields, and available to wild

nullification] is in the direction of greater stringency. But solve it from the following: We learnt: Onions [of the sixth year] upon which rain fell, and which grew [in the seventh],—if the leaves are blackish, they are forbidden; if greenish, they are permitted.[1] R. Ḥanina b. Antigonus said: If they can be pulled up by their leaves, they are forbidden.[2] Conversely, on the termination of the seventh year they are permitted.[3] This proves that the increase,

beasts. Once the produce has ceased from the fields the gathered species of the same produce must be 'removed'. That time, the exact limits of which are given in Sheb. IX. 2 *et seqq*. is called the time of removal. Now R. Simeon answers the difficulty thus: If seventh year produce, of no matter what quality, is mixed with other produce before the time of removal, it all becomes as the former, and must be eaten before the time of removal. For, since it is permitted until then, there is no need to have recourse to nullification by excess. But if after the time of removal (and this has not been removed, so that it may not be eaten), the permitted produce is forbidden only if there is sufficient of the prohibited to impart its taste to the whole mixture. Of course, where they are both of the same kind, this is strictly speaking impossible, but it is calculated on the basis of two different kinds. Now what has been said with respect to a mixture of two lots of produce, seventh year and non-seventh year, also applies to a single plant which is partly seventh and partly non-seventh year produce. E.g., if a sixth year onion is planted and grows no matter how slightly in the seventh, the addition, even if but the smallest fraction of the original, renders the whole as seventh year produce, which is subject to the law of removal. Thus we see that the increase, though grown out of that which is permitted, is reckoned as distinct from the original, and can render it forbidden. Hence, contrariwise, if the increase is permitted and of sufficient quantity, it can nullify the prohibition attaching to the original.

(1) Whilst the onion is growing naturally from the soil, its leaves have a blackish tint. But sometimes, after its natural growth has ceased, the rain inflates it, giving it a sort of over-ripeness. Then its leaves bear a greenish and faded appearance. Hence in this case, if the leaves are blackish, it is a sign that the onion has naturally grown in the seventh year, and therefore the addition renders it all forbidden, i.e., imposes upon the whole the law of seventh year produce. But if they are greenish, it has grown of itself, and hence permitted. (2) Even if the leaves are not blackish, yet if they are strong enough for the whole onion to be pulled up by them without their breaking off, it is a sign of normal growth, and so forbidden. (3) If seventh year onions were left in the soil and grew in the eighth, if the leaves go blackish, it is a sign of natural growth in the eighth, and therefore the whole onion is permitted.—Asheri observes that the two cases are not exactly similar. For the sixth year onion is

which is permitted, nullifies that which is forbidden.[1] But perhaps it refers to crushed [onions]?[2]—But [it may be solved] from the following. For it was taught: [58b] If [a workman] is engaged in weeding leek plants[3] for a Cuthean,[4] he may make a light meal of them and must separate the tithes from them as certain.[5] R. Simeon b. Eleazar said: If [the labourer is employed by] an Israelite suspected of violating the laws of the seventh year,[6] he may make a light meal thereof [if working] in the eighth year.[7] This proves that the growth, which is permitted, nullifies [the original stock], which is

rendered forbidden even by a slight increase in the seventh, whereas the seventh under the same conditions is rendered permitted only by an increase in the eighth at least greater than the original. Nevertheless, the general principle, that blackishness of the leaves indicates natural growth, is the same in both.

(1) And thus solves the problem. (2) I.e., if the onions were crushed and grated, so that the forbidden part no longer preserves its separate identity; in that case it is nullified by excess. But the problem arises only if the onion is intact. (3) The Talmud explains below what this is. (4) V. Glos. (5) If he wishes to make of them a regular meal. The obligation of tithing vegetables is Rabbinical only, not Biblical. When crops are tithed, and then resown, the new produce is again liable to the priestly dues. Nevertheless, a labourer engaged in working on crops may make a light meal of them. If, however, the crops originally sown were *ṭebel* (v. Glos.) one may not even make a light meal of their produce whilst working on them. Now, this Baraitha is to some extent self-contradictory, but in reality represents a compromise. Thus, the Cutheans disregarded their tithe obligations. Consequently, it must be assumed with certainty that they have not set aside the tithes from their produce, of which no regular meal may be made without tithing. This is not regarded as a doubtful tithe, viz., that it is not known whether the Cuthean fulfilled his obligations or not, but as a certain tithe. Yet since the entire obligation is Rabbinical only, the Rabbis did not carry through this assumption to its extreme logical conclusion and forbid a labourer engaged thereon to enjoy even a snack, but permitted it, as ordinary tithed plants which are resown. This leniency is based on another possible assumption, viz., only if crops are taken in through the front of the house they are *ṭebel* in the sense that one may not even make a light meal thereof before the priestly dues are rendered. Here it is possible that these crops were never thus taken in (Tosaf.). (6) I.e., that he planted them in the seventh year. (7) Lit., 'the termination of the Sabbatical year'. Though the original is forbidden as seventh year produce, the increase nullifies it, and hence it is permitted to the labourer.

forbidden. But perhaps it refers to a plant whose seed perishes [in the soil]?—But it is taught: The following are leek plants: The *lof*,[1] garlic and onions.[2] But perhaps it refers to crushed plants?[3]—This teaches of one who is suspected of violating the Sabbatical year.[4] But perhaps it refers to a mixture?[5]—This teaches of one who is engaged in weeding.[6] Now, shall we say that this refutes R. Joḥanan and R. Jonathan?[7]—Said R. Isaac: The Sabbatical year produce is different; since the interdict is through the soil,[8] its nullification too is through the soil.[9] But the prohibition of the tithe is likewise through the soil,[10] yet it is not nullified by the soil. For it was taught: If a *liṭra* of tithe, itself *ṭebel*,[11] is sown in the soil and it improves [i.e., increases], and is the equivalent of ten *liṭras*, it [*sc*. the whole] is liable to tithes[12] and [is subject to the laws of] the Sabbatical year,[13] whilst as for the [original] *liṭra*, a tithe thereof must be seperated from elsewhere,[14] according to calculation.[15] [59*a*]—I will tell you: The tithe obligation is caused by the storing up [of the grain].[16]

(1) A plant similar to colocasin, with edible leaves and roots, and bearing beans; and it is classified with onions and garlic (Jast.). (2) Thus proving that it applies even to those plants whose original stock remain. (3) The crushing obliterates the original stock. (4) He would not trouble to crush it in order to evade the prohibition. (5) I.e., the labourer may eat it only when it is mixed up with other plants, the excess of which nullifies the original forbidden stock. (6) The labourer may eat while engaged in the act of weeding, though there is no mixture. Thus this definitely proves that the increase nullifies the original. (7) V. *supra* 57*b*. (8) Lev. XXV, 2: *Then* the land *shall keep a sabbath unto the Lord.* (9) But *'orlah* is prohibited through immaturity, and 'diverse seeds' (*kil'ayim*) through mixture. (10) I.e., by replanting. For if one sows tithed grain the produce is *ṭebel:* thus, by putting it into soil, it becomes prohibited. (11) I.e., the tithe of which had not been given, v. p. 183, n. 9. (12) Although itself a tithe, the ordinary law of *ṭebel* applies to it, and it must be retithed (and *terumah* too must be given). (13) If it grew in that year. (14) I.e., a tithe—the *terumah* of the tithe due in the first place—must be given to the priest. This tithe must not be taken out of the resultant crop, but from the previous year's, of which the *liṭra* was part, because one must not tithe one year's grain with another's. (15) This proves that the forbidden nature of the untithed tithe remains, in spite of the fact that it was sown in the soil. (16) Until the grain is harvested and actually piled up in a stack, there is no obligation for the priestly dues. Thus it is not an obligation caused by the soil.

Rami b. Ḥama objected: [If a man says,] 'KONAM BE THESE FRUITS TO ME,' 'BE THEY ḲONAM FOR MY MOUTH,' OR 'BE THEY ḲONAM TO MY MOUTH,' HE IS FORBIDDEN [TO BENEFIT] FROM WHAT IS EXCHANGED FOR THEM OR WHAT GROWS FROM THEM. [IF HE SAYS, 'ḲONAM] IF I EAT OR TASTE OF THEM,' HE IS PERMITTED [TO BENEFIT] FROM WHAT IS EXCHANGED FOR THEM OR WHAT GROWS OF THEM, [THAT IS] IN A THING OF WHICH THE SEED ITSELF PERISHES; BUT IF THE SEED DOES NOT PERISH, EVEN THAT WHICH GROWS OF THAT WHICH [FIRST] GREW FROM IT IS FORBIDDEN![1]—Said R. Abba: Vows[2] are different: since if he wishes he can demand absolution from tithes, they are as [forbidden] things that may become permitted, and [hence] are not nullified by excess.[3] But with *terumah* likewise he may, if he wishes, demand absolution from it,[4] and yet it can be nullified?[5] For we learnt: If a *se'ah*[6] of unclean *terumah* falls into less than a hundred of *ḥullin* it must [all] rot.[7] [This implies, but if it falls] into a hundred [*se'ahs* of *ḥullin*], it is nullified?—I will tell you: This refers to *terumah* in the priest's hands, in regard to which he can demand no absolution.[8] If so, consider the second clause: If it was undefiled, it should [all] be sold to a priest.[9] But this refers to [*terumah* in the hands of] an Israelite, who inherited it from his maternal grandfather, a priest.[10] But the second clause teaches, It must be sold to a priest, save for the value of that *se'ah*?[11]—But answer thus: As for vows, it is well, since it is meritorious to seek

(1) This proves that the increase does not nullify the original, thus refuting R. Ammi's view. (2) *Ḳonamoth*, Lit., 'Vows expressed by *Ḳonam*'. (3) V. p. 183, n. 8. (4) If one declares certain grain *terumah* in error, he can have this declaration nullified, and the grain reverts to its former state. (5) Cur. edd. add 'by mere excess'. Wilna Gaon deletes this, since mere excess is insufficient, a hundred times its quantity being required. (6) V. Glos. (7) Unclean *terumah* may not be eaten by anyone, and therefore nothing can be done with the mixture. (8) The Israelite who declares it *terumah* can have his declaration nullified only before it reaches the hands of the priest but not after. (9) Obviously then it was still in the hands of an Israelite. (10) Thus it had already belonged to a priest, and cannot be revoked. (11) Which belongs to the priest as *terumah*. But under the circumstances here posited, even that *se'ah* too belongs to the Israelite.

absolution from them on account of R. Nathan's dictum, viz., He who vows, is as though he built a high place; and he who fulfils it, is as though he burned incense thereon. But what merit is there in seeking absolution from *terumah?*[1]

The text [above] states: 'R. Joḥanan said: If a *liṭra* of onions was tithed and then planted, the whole of it must be retithed'. Now Rabbah[2] was sitting and stating this law, whereupon R. Ḥisda said to him: Who will obey you and R. Joḥanan your teacher: whither has the permitted portion in them departed? He replied: But did we not learn something similar? Viz., 'Onions [of the sixth year] upon which rain fell, and which grew [in the seventh],—[59*b*] if the leaves are blackish, they are forbidden; if greenish, they are permitted.'[3] But even if blackish, why are they forbidden? Let us say, whither has the permitted portion in them departed?—He replied: Do you think that it refers to the original stock? [Only] with respect to the increase is it taught, They are forbidden. If so, what does R. Simeon b. Gamaliel come to teach? For it was taught [thereon:] R. Simeon b. Gamaliel said: That which grew under the obligation [of removal][4] is under that obligation: that which grew in a state of exemption is exempt. Surely the first Tanna too says thus?—The whole Mishnah is stated by R. Simeon b. Gamaliel.[5] Yet you learn R. Simeon b. Gamaliel's view [to be thus] only where he took no trouble;[6] but where one takes trouble,[7] it [the stock] is nullified by the excess [of the increase].[8] Now, where one takes trouble, is it nullified by the excess? But what of the case of the *liṭra* of tithe, itself *ṭebel*, where he took trouble, yet it is taught, 'whilst as for the original *liṭra*, a tithe thereof must be separated from elsewhere according to calculation'?[9]—The tithe

(1) Therefore something prohibited by a vow is treated as that which can become permitted, since it ought to be revoked; but this does not apply to *terumah*. (2) *Var. lec.:* Raba. (3) V. 58*a*. (4) Viz., in the Sabbatical year. (5) The second clause is merely stating a reason for the ruling in the first. (6) As in this case, the sixth year onions having been left in the earth during the seventh year. (7) Where he plants the onions. (8) This is Rabbah's remark: though it would appear that R. Simeon b. Gamaliel's view is opposed to his, in reality it is not. (9) V. *supra* 58*b*.

is different, because Scripture saith, *Thou shalt surely tithe all the increase of thy sowing;*[1] and people sow what is permitted, but do not sow what is forbidden.[2]

The text [above states:] 'R. Ḥanina of Torata said in R. Jannai's name: If one plants an onion of *terumah*, and its increase exceeds the stock, it is [all] permitted.' Shall we say that the permitted increase [60*a*] nullifies the forbidden [stock]? But we learnt: What grows from *terumah* is [likewise] *terumah?*—He [R. Ḥaninah] refers to the second growth.[3] But we learnt this too: The second growth [of *terumah*] is *ḥullin?*[4]—He teaches us this: [this is so] even where the stock does not perish in the earth. But we learnt: The growth of *ṭebel* is permitted in the case where the seed thereof [which is *ṭebel*] perishes [in the earth], but if it does not perish, [even] its second growth is forbidden!—He teaches us [that the second growth is permitted] when it exceeds the original.[5]

(1) Deut. XIV, 22. (2) I.e., we oblige him to give *terumah* on the original tithe, since he did wrong in sowing it without rendering the *terumah*. It is thus in the nature of a fine, that he should not profit by his neglect. But normally the original stock is nullified, when labour is required to produce the excess. (3) I.e., an onion of *terumah* having been planted and its yield replanted, the second crop is permitted, but the first is *terumah*. (4) Then what does R. Ḥanina teach? (5) Whilst the Mishnah stating that it is forbidden holds good only if the growth does not exceed the original.

NEDARIM

CHAPTER VIII

MISHNAH. [IF ONE VOWS,] 'ḲONAM, IF I TASTE WINE TO-DAY,' HE IS FORBIDDEN ONLY UNTIL IT GETS DARK; [IF HE SAYS] 'THIS SABBATH,'[1] HE IS FORBIDDEN THE WHOLE WEEK AND THE SABBATH BELONGS TO THE PAST;[2] 'THIS MONTH,' HE IS FORBIDDEN THE WHOLE OF THAT MONTH, BUT THE BEGINNING OF THE [FOLLOWING] MONTH BELONGS TO THE FUTURE;[3] 'THIS YEAR,' HE IS FORBIDDEN THE WHOLE YEAR, WHILST THE BEGINNING OF THE [FOLLOWING] YEAR BELONGS TO THE FUTURE; 'THIS SEPTENNATE,'[4] HE IS FORBIDDEN THE WHOLE OF THAT SEPTENNATE, AND THE [FOLLOWING] SABBATICAL YEAR BELONGS TO THE PAST.[5] BUT

(1) 'Sabbath' denotes both the Sabbath day and a calendar week. (2) I.e., the Sabbath following his vow, belongs to the current week, not the following. (3) And hence permitted. (4) I.e., the seven-year cycle. (5) I.e., it ends the Septennate in which the vow was made, and hence is included. An alternate rendering of the whole passage is this: 'This Sabbath' (that is the actual word of the Mishnah; v. n. 1): e.g., if one vows on the Sabbath day, the whole week is forbidden, and the Sabbath of the past week too, i.e., the day of his vow, though belonging to the past week, while the vow obviously refers to the coming one, is nevertheless included. 'This month', e.g., if he vows on new moon (*Rosh ḥodesh*), the whole of the following month is forbidden, and the new moon itself is also accounted to the next month. 'This year', i.e., if one vows on new year's day, the whole of the year is forbidden, including that day, which belongs to the future. 'This septennate', i.e., if one vows in the Sabbatical year, the following septennate is forbidden, and the Sabbatical year itself in which he vows, though really belonging to the past Septennate.—On this interpretation, if a vow is made on the Sabbath, New Moon, New Year's day or in a Sabbatical year, for a Sabbath (i.e., calendar week), month, year, or septennate respectively, the day itself on which the vow is made, and in the last case, the Sabbatical year itself, are forbidden. The different phraseology used to indicate this, reference being made to the *future* in two cases and to the *past* in two others, intimates the law if one vows in the *middle* of the week, etc. Thus, if in the middle of the week or septennate, the following Sabbath

IF HE SAYS, 'ONE DAY,' 'ONE SABBATH,' 'ONE MONTH,' 'ONE YEAR,' [OR] 'ONE SEPTENNATE,' HE IS FORBIDDEN FROM DAY TO DAY.[1] [IF ONE VOWS,] 'UNTIL PASSOVER,' HE IS FORBIDDEN UNTIL IT ARRIVES; 'UNTIL IT BE' [PASSOVER], HE IS FORBIDDEN UNTIL IT GOES;[2] 'UNTIL PENE[3] PASSOVER,' R. MEIR SAID: HE IS FORBIDDEN UNTIL IT ARRIVES; R. JOSE SAID: UNTIL IT GOES.

GEMARA. 'ḲONAM, IF I TASTE WINE' etc. R. Jeremiah[4] said: At nightfall he must obtain absolution from a Sage.[5] What is the reason?—R. Joseph said: 'To-day' is forbidden as a precautionary measure on account of 'one day'.[6] [60*b*] Said Abaye to him: If so, let 'one day' be forbidden on account of 'to-day'?[7] —He replied: 'To-day' may be mistaken for 'one day', but 'one day' cannot be mistaken for 'to-day'.[8]

Rabina said: Meremar told me: Thus said your father in R. Joseph's name: With whom does this statement of R. Jeremiah b. Abba agree?—With R. Nathan. For it was taught: R. Nathan said: Whoever vows is as though he built a high place, and who fulfils it, is as though he burnt incense thereon.[9]

and Sabbatical year are forbidden; in the middle of the month or year, the following New Moon or New Year's day are permitted. Ran, Asheri and Tosaf. prefer the former interpretation: Rashi the latter.

(1) I.e., a day of twenty-four hours; likewise a month of thirty days, a year of twelve months, and a septennate of seven years. (2) I.e., the future tense is regarded as future perfect. (3) [*Var. lec.: lifene.* Either word may denote (*a*) the turn of; (*b*) the face of; (*c*) until before.] (4) Asheri in his '*Pesaḳim*' reads: R. Jeremiah b. Abba. (5) But the vow is not lifted automatically. (6) If when one vows 'to-day', he is told that the vow *automatically* ends at nightfall, he may think the same of 'one day', which binds him, however, twenty-four hours. (7) I.e., if he vows 'one day', let him be forbidden until the nightfall of the following day. Otherwise, if he terminates his vow in the middle of the day, twenty-four hours after its commencement, he may think that had he stated 'to-day', he could likewise end it in the middle of the day of his vow. (8) I.e , if he vows 'one day', he may think that it ends at nightfall, just as 'to-day'; but if he vows 'to-day', he cannot possibly think that it ends before the nightfall of the same day, since in 'one day' the vow lasts beyond nightfall and includes part of the following day too. (9) I.e., because one does wrong in vowing at all, he is

'THIS SABBATH,' HE IS FORBIDDEN THE WHOLE WEEK [AND THE SABBATH BELONGS TO THE PAST]. This is obvious?—I might think that he meant the [week] days of the Sabbath:[1] we are therefore taught [otherwise].

'THIS MONTH,' HE IS FORBIDDEN THE WHOLE OF THAT MONTH, BUT THE BEGINNING OF THE [FOLLOWING] MONTH BELONGS TO THE FUTURE. This is obvious?—It is necessary only when the [following] month is defective: I might think that the new moon belongs to the past, and is forbidden: it is therefore intimated that people call it new moon.[2]

'THIS YEAR,' HE IS FORBIDDEN THE WHOLE YEAR. The scholars propounded: What if one vows, '*Ḳonam,* if I taste wine a day'? is its law as 'to-day' or 'one day'?—Come and hear [a solution] from our Mishnah. 'ḲONAM, IF I TASTE WINE TO DAY', HE IS FORBIDDEN WINE ONLY UNTIL IT GETS DARK; hence 'a day' is as 'one day'! Then consider the second clause: IF HE

treated stringently and ordered to obtain absolution for his vow when it should lapse automatically. In Rashi's opinion, this conflicts with the reason given by R. Joseph. But Asheri regards it as complementary thereto: whilst accepting the reasoning, he regards the fear of mistaking 'to-day' for 'one day' as insufficient in itself to justify this precautionary measure; hence he adds the reason drawn from R. Nathan's dictum.

(1) The Sabbath being a day of delight, it might be assumed that he never intended to deny himself wine on that day, since week-days too are implied in that term. (2) The months of the Jewish year consist of either twenty-nine or thirty days and generally alternate. Hence, if the following month is defective (i.e., of twenty-nine days), this one is full. In the month following a full one, the first two days are designated 'new moon', the first being really the thirtieth day of the past full month. Hence, if one vowed in a full month, it might be thought that he is bound on the first new moon day of the next. Therefore the Mishnah teaches that since it is called new moon, people generally regard it as part of the next month, and hence he is permitted thereon.—This is the reading of Asheri, Ran and Tosaf. But our editions, and Rashi too, have: I might think that the new moon belongs to the past, and should *not* be forbidden. This reading cannot be reconciled with the first interpretation of the Mishnah, but agrees with the second (q.v. p. 190, n. 5). If he vowed 'this month' on the first new moon day, I might think that since it actually belongs to the past month he is not forbidden thereon. Therefore it is taught that since it is designated new moon, he must have meant to include it.

SAYS, 'ONE DAY,' HE IS FORBIDDEN FROM DAY TO DAY: hence 'a day' is as 'to-day'?[1] Thus nothing can be deduced from this.

R. Ashi said, Come and hear: '*Konam*, if I taste wine this year,'[2] if the year was intercalated, he is forbidden for the year and the extra month. How is this meant? [61*a*] Shall we say, [literally,] as taught? [Then] why state it?[3] Hence it must surely mean that he vowed 'a year':[4] this proves that 'a year' is as 'this year', and [consequently], 'a day' as 'to-day'!—No! In truth, it means that he vowed, 'this year'; yet I might think that the majority of years should be followed, which have no intercalated months;[5] therefore we are taught [otherwise].

The scholars propounded: What if one vows, '*Konam*, if I taste wine a Jubilee':[6] Is the fiftieth year [counted] as before the fiftieth or as after?[7] Come and hear: For a conflict of R. Judah and the Rabbis has been taught: *And ye shall hallow the fiftieth year:*[8] you must count it as the fiftieth year, but not as the fiftieth and as the first year [of the following jubilee].[9] Hence they [the Sages] said: The Jubilee is not part of the [following] septennate. R. Judah maintained: The Jubilee is counted as part of the septennate. Said they to R. Judah, But Scripture saith, *six years shalt thou sow thy field,*[10] whereas here there are only five![11] He replied: But on your view, surely it is said, *and it shall bring forth fruit for three years:*[12]

(1) In Heb. 'one' is expressed by אחד, but the indef. 'a' is unexpressed, lit., 'day', and hence the problem, and the differentiation between 'a day' and one day'. (2) Lit., 'the year'. (3) It is obvious, since the addition is an integral part of the year. (4) Only then is it necessary to state that the addition is forbidden him, i.e., 'a year' is as 'this year'; for if it implied 'one year', he should be forbidden exactly twelve months. (5) Hence the intercalated month is permitted. (6) Ran observes that since the former problem is left unsolved, 'a day' would be the equivalent of 'one day' (since when in doubt the more stringent interpretation is adopted), and consequently a jubilee as one jubilee, and the problem cannot arise. Therefore he must have vowed 'this (the) jubilee'. (7) On the former supposition it is forbidden; on the latter it is permitted. (8) Lev. XXV, 10. (9) I.e., that year is the fiftieth, the jubilee, and it cannot be counted also as the first of the following fifty and seven year-cycles. (10) Ibid. 3. (11) Since there is no sowing in the jubilee year. (12) Ibid. 21.

whereas here there are four![1] But it can be referred to other Sabbatical years; hence mine too[2] must be thus explained.

'UNTIL PASSOVER', HE IS FORBIDDEN etc. Shall we say that R. Meir holds that a man does not place himself. [61b] in a doubtful position, whilst R. Jose maintains that he does place himself in a doubtful position?[3] But the following contradicts it: If a man has two groups of daughters by two wives, and he declares, 'I have given one of my elder daughters in betrothal,[4] but do not know whether it was the eldest of the senior[5] group or of the junior group, or the youngest of the senior group, who is older than the eldest of the junior group': they are all forbidden,[6] except the youngest of the junior group:[7] this is R. Meir's view. R. Jose said: They are all permitted except the eldest of the senior group.[8] —Said R. Ḥanina b. Abdimi in Rab's name: The passage must be reversed.[9] And it was taught [even so]: This is a general principle: That which has a fixed time, and one vows, until the turn [*pene*] thereof,—R. Meir said: It means, until it goes; R. Jose maintained: Until it arrives.

MISHNAH. [IF HE VOWS,] 'UNTIL THE HARVEST,' 'UNTIL

(1) The forty-eighth year produce must suffice for itself, the forty-ninth, which is a Sabbatical year, the fiftieth, which is Jubilee, and until the harvesting of the fifty-first. This is a difficulty on any view, R. Judah's included: he posits it merely to prove that the Biblical statements about the Sabbatical year do not in any case apply to the Jubilee period, even on the view of the Rabbis. (2) I.e., the verse by which you desire to refute me. (3) The expression until *pene*—or *lifene*—is a doubtful one, v. *supra* p. 191, n. 3. R. Meir, on this hypothesis, holds that when one vows he intends his words to bear only that meaning which can with certainty be attributed to them, not desiring to be in a position of doubt; while R. Jose controverts it. (4) A father could betroth his daughter, if a minor, even without her knowledge; though v. Ḳid. 41*a*. (5) I.e., by his first wife. (6) Both to the groom, since they may be sisters of the betrothed, and to others, being possibly betrothed themselves. (7) Who is permitted to strangers, since she is definitely not 'the elder'. (8) This shews that in R. Meir's view one intends his words or actions to bear even a meaning which can be attributed to it only with doubt, and R. Jose holds the opposite. (9) I.e., the authorities of our Mishnah.

THE VINTAGE,' OR, 'UNTIL THE OLIVE HARVEST,' HE IS FORBIDDEN ONLY UNTIL IT ARRIVES. THIS IS A GENERAL RULE: WHATEVER HAS A FIXED TIME AND ONE VOWS, 'UNTIL IT ARRIVES,' HE IS FORBIDDEN UNTIL IT ARRIVES; IF HE DECLARES, 'UNTIL IT BE', HE IS FORBIDDEN UNTIL IT GOES. BUT WHATEVER HAS NO FIXED TIME, WHETHER ONE VOWS, 'UNTIL IT BE,' OR 'UNTIL IT ARRIVES,' HE IS FORBIDDEN ONLY UNTIL IT ARRIVES. [IF HE SAYS,] 'UNTIL THE SUMMER [HARVEST],'[1] OR, 'UNTIL THE SUMMER [HARVEST] SHALL BE,' [HE IS FORBIDDEN] UNTIL PEOPLE BEGIN TO BRING [THE FIGS] HOME IN BASKETS; 'UNTIL THE SUMMER [HARVEST] IS PAST,' [IT MEANS] UNTIL THE KNIVES[2] ARE FOLDED UP [AND LAID AWAY].[3]

GEMARA. A Tanna taught: The basket referred to is the basket of figs, not of grapes.[4] It was taught: He who vows [abstinence] from summer fruits, is forbidden only figs. R. Simeon b. Gamaliel said: Grapes are included in figs.[5] What is the reason of the first Tanna? He holds that figs are plucked off by hand, whilst grapes are not plucked off by hand;[6] whereas R. Simeon b. Gamaliel maintains, Grapes too are plucked off by hand when quite ripe.[7]

'UNTIL THE SUMMER [HARVEST] IS PAST,' [IT MEANS] UNTIL THE KNIVES ARE FOLDED UP [AND LAID AWAY]. A Tanna taught: Until *most* of the knives have been put away. [62a] A Tanna taught: If most of the knives have been put away, they [the remaining figs] are permitted [to strangers] as far as theft is concerned, and are exempt from tithes.[8]

(1) The time for this is not fixed. (2) Used for cutting off the figs from the tree. (3) Other meanings: until the figs are arranged in layers; until the matting, on which the figs are dried, is folded up. (4) I.e., he is forbidden only until the figs are brought in in baskets, not the grapes, which are gathered in slightly later. (5) I.e., in summer fruits. (6) קייץ, the Heb. for summer (fruits), denotes the gathering or plucking (of the fruit). But as grapes are *cut* off from the vine with a pruning knife, the term is inapplicable in their case. (7) Lit., 'when about to be detached' (from the tree). Asheri. [Rashi: 'overripe'. Jast: 'when their stems are thin', cf. Ran.] (8) Because once the knives are put away, the owner has, in effect, shewn that the remaining figs are unwanted by him and free to all, i.e., *hefker*, from which there are no priestly dues; cf. p. 139, n. 2.

Rabbi and R. Jose son of R. Judah came to a certain place when most of the knives had been folded. Rabbi ate;[1] R. Jose son of R. Judah did not. Their owner came and said to them, 'Why do the Rabbis not eat? most of the knives have been folded!' Nevertheless R. Jose son of R. Judah did not eat, believing that the man had spoken [sarcastically] in a grudging spirit.

R. Ḥama son of R. Ḥanina came to a place when most of the knives had been folded. He ate; but [when] he offered [some] to his attendant, he would not eat. 'Eat,' said he; 'thus did R. Ishmael son of R. Jose tell me on his father's authority: When most of the knives have been folded, they [the remaining figs] are permitted [to strangers] as far as theft is concerned, and are exempt from tithes'.

R. Tarfon was found by a man eating [of the figs] when most of the knives had been folded, [whereupon] he threw him into a sack and carried him, to cast him in the river. 'Woe to Tarfon,' he cried out, 'whom this man is about to murder!' When the man heard this,[2] he abandoned him and fled. R. Abbahu said on the authority of R. Ḥananiah b. Gamaliel: All his lifetime that pious man grieved over this, saying, 'Woe is me that I made [profane] use of the crown of the Torah!'[3] For Rabbah b. Bar Ḥanah said in R. Joḥanan's name: Whoever puts the crown of the Torah to [profane] use, is uprooted from the world.[4] This follows *a fortiori*. If Belshazzar, who used the holy vessels which had become profaned, as it is written, *For the robbers shall enter into it, and profane it:*[5] [teaching], since they had broken in, they were profaned; yet he was uprooted from the world, as it is written, *In that night was Belshazzar slain:*[6] how much more so he who makes [profane] use of the crown of the Torah, which endureth for ever!

Now since R. Tarfon ate when most of the knives were folded, why did that man ill-treat him?—Because someone had been stealing his grapes all the year round, and when he found R.

(1) Of the figs left on the fields. (2) That he was R. Tarfon. (3) I.e., over saving his life by revealing his identity. (4) This is in accordance with the general view held that one should derive no benefit whatsoever from the Torah. Cf. *supra* 37a and Aboth, IV, 5, (Sonc. ed.) p. 47, n. 3. (5) Ezek. VII, 22. (6) Dan. V, 30.

Tarfon, he thought that it was he. If so, why was he grieved [at revealing his identity]?[1]—Because R. Tarfon, being very wealthy, should have pacified him with money.[2]

It was taught: *That thou mayest love the Lord thy God and that thou mayest obey his voice, and that thou mayest cleave unto him:*[3] [This means] that one should not say, I will read Scripture that I may be called a Sage; I will study, that I may be called Rabbi; I will study,[4] to be an Elder, and sit in the assembly [of elders];[5] but learn out of love, and honour will come in the end, as it is written, *Bind them upon thy fingers, write them upon the table of thine heart;*[6] and it is also said, *Her ways are ways of pleasantness;*[7] also, *She is a tree of life to them that lay hold upon her: and happy is everyone that retaineth her.*[8]

R. Eliezer son of R. Ẓadoḳ said: Do [good] deeds for the sake of their Maker,[9] and speak of them[10] for their own sake. Make not of them a crown wherewith to magnify thyself, nor a spade to dig with.[11] And this follows *a fortiori*. If Belshazzar, who merely used the holy vessels which had been profaned, was driven from the world; how much more so one who makes use of the crown of the Torah!

Raba said: A man may reveal his identity where he is unknown, as it is said, *but I thy servant fear the Lord from my youth.*[12] But as for the

(1) His grief would have been justified had the keeper been angry on account of R. Tarfon's action alone; for instead of saving himself by disclosing his name, he should have told him the law on the subject and offered to pay for what he had eaten. But if he was mistaken for an habitual thief, what else could he have done: should he have offered to make good the depredations of the whole year! (2) Precisely so. (3) Deut. XXX, 20. (4) [So BaḤ. cur. edd.: אשנן 'I will teach.' I.e. he teaches others, so that his fame may spread and he may obtain a seat in the Academy.] (5) 'Elder' may simply mean scholar (cf. Ḳid. 32b), or more exactly a member of the Sanhedrin; cf. Joseph. *Ant.* XII, 111, p. 3. (6) Prov. VII, 3: i.e., make it an integral part of thyself, not as something outside thee, cherished only for its worldly advantages. (7) Ibid. III, 17. (8) Ibid. 18: this is quoted to shew that honour comes eventually. (9) I.e., God Who decreed them (Ran.). [Or, 'the performance of them', i.e., for the sake of doing good (Baḥja Ibn Paḳuda, *Duties of the Heart, Introduction*.] (10) Viz., the words of the Torah. (11) In I Sam. XIII, 20, and Ps. LXXIV, 5, *kardom* means an axe. Possibly it was a two-sided tool, one side serving as a spade and the other as an axe. (12) I Kings XVIII, 12.

difficulty of R. Tarfon,[1]—he was very wealthy, and should have pacified him with money.

Raba opposed [two verses]: It is written, *But I thy servant fear the Lord from my youth;* whilst it is also written, *Let another man praise thee, and not thine own mouth?*[2] One refers to a place where he is known; the other, to where he is unknown.

Raba said: A rabbinical scholar may assert, I am a rabbinical scholar; let my business receive first attention;[3] as it is written, *And David's sons were priests:*[4] just as a priest receives [his portion] first, so does the scholar too. And whence do we know this of a priest?—Because it is written, *Thou shalt sanctify him therefore, for he offereth the bread of thy God:*[5] whereon the School of R. Ishmael taught: *'Thou shalt sanctify him'*—in all matters pertaining to holiness: [62*b*] to be the first to commence [the reading of the Law],[6] the first to pronounce the blessing,[7] and first to receive a good portion.[8]

Raba said: A rabbinical scholar may declare, I will not pay poll-tax, for it is written, [*also we certify to you, that touching any of the priests . . . or ministers of this house of God,*] *it shall not be lawful to impose mindah* [*tribute,*] *belo* [*custom,*] *or halak* [*toll,*] *upon them:*[9] whereon Rab Judah said: *'mindah'* is the king's portion [of the crops]; *'belo'* is a capitation tax, and *'halak'* is *arnona.*[10] Raba also said: A Rabbinical scholar may assert, 'I am a servant of fire, and will not pay poll-tax.'[11] What is the reason? Because it is [only] said in order

(1) V. *supra.* (2) Prov. XXVII, 2. (3) Lit., 'dismiss my case first'. E.g., in a shop or market place; cf. the story in Ḳid. 70*a*. (4) II Sam. VIII, 18. They were not priests, of course; hence the verse means that as scholars they were entitled to certain priestly privileges. (5) Lev. XXI, 8. (6) In ancient times the public reading of the Law was done by those 'called up'. The priest was to be called to read the first portion; v. Giṭ. 59*a*. (7) I.e., the blessing for bread prior to the meal, and grace after the meal. (8) At a meal he must be served first.—Asheri: when sharing anything with an Israelite, the latter must divide the thing to be shared in two equal portions and give choice of pick to the priest. (9) Ezra VII, 24. (10) Or *'annona'*, produce tax. Jast. conjectures that הלך probably means a tax for the sustenance of marching troops. (11) To the Persian it would suggest a fire worshipper, who was free from poll-tax. But the scholar making this assertion would mean that he worships the Lord, who is designated

to drive away a lion.[1] R. Ashi owned a forest, which he sold to a fire-temple. Said Rabina to R. Ashi: But there is [the injunction], *Thou shalt not put a stumbling-block before the blind!*[2] —He replied: Most wood is used for [ordinary] heating.[3]

MISHNAH. [IF HE VOWS,] 'UNTIL THE HARVEST,' [IT MEANS] UNTIL THE PEOPLE BEGIN REAPING THE WHEAT HARVEST, BUT NOT THE BARLEY HARVEST.[4] IT ALL DEPENDS ON THE PLACE WHERE HE VOWED:[5] IF IN A HILL-COUNTRY, THE HILL-COUNTRY [HARVEST]; IF IN THE PLAIN, [THE HARVEST OF] THE PLAIN [IS MEANT].[6] [IF HE VOWS,] 'UNTIL THE RAINS,' [OR], 'UNTIL THE RAINS SHALL BE', [IT MEANS] UNTIL THE SECOND RAINFALL DESCENDS.[7] R. SIMEON B. GAMALIEL SAID: UNTIL THE [NORMAL] TIME FOR THE [FIRST] RAINFALL IS REACHED.[8] [IF HE VOWS,] 'UNTIL THE RAINS CEASE,' [IT MEANS] UNTIL THE END OF NISAN:[9] THIS IS R. MEIR'S VIEW. R. JUDAH SAID: UNTIL PASSOVER IS PAST.

GEMARA. It was taught: He who vows in Galilee, 'until the

'consuming fire' in Deut. IV, 24. (Under Shapur II, fire worship became the national and state-aided religion of the Persians, and in order to win converts to that religion fire worshippers enjoyed exemption from poll-tax; v. Funk, S. *Die Juden in Babylonien* II. p. 3.)

(1) I.e., in self-defence, against irregular extortion. Ran states that Raba's dictum means that *even* a Rabbinical student may act thus, and it is not regarded as an untruth; the ordinary person may certainly do so. (2) Lev. XIX, 14: i.e., nothing must be done to aid idolatry. (3) Not for idolatrous service, (4) Which is earlier. (5) I.e., though normally 'harvest', unspecified, means the wheat harvest, if in a particular place one refers thus to the barley harvest it means until then. Likewise, as the Mishnah proceeds to explain. (6) Harvesting is later in a hill-country than in a plain. (7) I.e., until it commences. There are three winter rainfalls in Palestine. Their times are discussed on 63*a*. When he states, 'until the rainfall', without specifying which, it is assumed that he means the middle one, as he would have defined the first or last by name. (8) Even if it does not rain then. Since the times of the rainfalls are not exact, he must have meant when the rainfall commences. (9) The first month in the Jewish year, corresponding to March-April.

fruit-harvest,' and then descends to the valleys, though the fruit harvest has begun in the valley, he is forbidden [by his vow] until the fruit-harvest in Galilee.

[IF HE VOWS,] 'UNTIL THE RAINS,' [OR] 'UNTIL THE RAINS SHALL BE,' [IT MEANS] UNTIL THE SECOND RAINFALL DESCENDS. R. SIMEON B. GAMALIEL SAID, etc. R. Zera said: The dispute is only if he said, 'until the rains';[1] but if he declared, 'until the rain,' he [certainly] meant, until the time of the [first] rain.[2]

[63a] An objection is raised: What is the time of the rainfall?[3] The earliest is on the third [of Marḥeshwan],[4] the middle [i.e., the second] on the seventh, and the last on the twenty-third: this is R. Meir's view. R. Judah said: The seventh, the seventeenth, and the twenty-third. R. Jose said: The seventeenth, the twenty-third, and the new moon of Kislew.[5] And R. Jose used likewise to rule that individuals must not fast [for rain] until Kislew has commenced.[6] Now we observed thereon: As for the first rainfall, it is well: [they differ] in respect of petitioning;[7] the third [likewise] is in respect of fasting.[8] But [as for] the second, in respect of what [is the controversy]?—And R. Zera answered: In respect of one who vows.[9] Whereon we observed: With whom does the following Baraitha agree: R. Simeon b. Gamaliel said: If the rain descends for seven days in succession, it is counted as the first and second

(1) The first Tanna maintains that the plural implies, until there shall have been at least two rainfalls; whilst in R. Simeon b. Gamaliel's opinion the terms of the vow are fulfilled when the *time* for the second rainfall comes, even though it did not actually rain. (2) So Rashi. (3) *Sc.* the winter rain, which generally came in three periods, as explained here. There was also, of course, the Spring rain. V. Ta'an. 6*a*. (4) Marḥeshwan is the eighth month of the year, corresponding to October-November. (5) Kislew is the ninth month of the year, corresponding to November-December. (6) And rain has not yet fallen. (7) For rain. A short prayer for rain—טל ומטר '(give) dew and rain', called *she'elah*, request or petition, is inserted in the eighth benediction of the *'amidah* when the first rainfall is due. V. Ta'an. 10*a*. (8) A public fast was proclaimed if the drought continued after the time of the third rainfall had arrived. V. Ta'an. I, 4-7; II, 1. (9) I.e., if one vows, 'until the rains', it means until the second rainfall: hence the controversy as to when it is due.

rainfall?[1] With whom does this agree? With R. Jose![2]—That refers to one who vows, 'Until the rains.'

MISHNAH. [IF HE VOWS,] 'KONAM THAT I TASTE NOT WINE FOR A YEAR', IF THE YEAR IS INTERCALATED,[3] HE IS FORBIDDEN DURING THE YEAR AND ITS EXTENSION. [IF HE SAYS,] 'UNTIL THE BEGINNING OF ADAR,'[4] [IT MEANS] UNTIL THE BEGINNING OF THE FIRST ADAR; 'UNTIL THE END OF ADAR,' UNTIL THE END OF THE FIRST ADAR.[5]

GEMARA. Thus we see that by stating Adar, without qualification, the first is meant. Shall we say that our Mishnah reflects R. Judah's views? For it was taught: For the first Adar, one writes 'The first Adar'; for the second, simply 'Adar': this is R. Meir's view. R. Judah said: For the first Adar, one writes 'Adar'; for the second, one writes 'the second Adar'![6]—Abaye said: You may say that it agrees even with R. Meir: the latter is where he knew that it was a leap year; the former [i.e., the Mishnah], if he did not know.[7] [63*b*] And it was taught even so: [If one writes,] 'until the

(1) As we have seen, R. Simeon b. Gamaliel's own view is that the *time* of the rainfall is the deciding factor, whether it actually rains or not. But since the Rabbis maintain that the vow means until it rains, R. Simeon argued that even on their view, if it rains for seven days in succession, it should be considered as two rainfalls, and hence terminates the vow. It is now assumed that no dictinction is here made how he expressed his vow. But on R. Zera's view, that they all agree that where he says 'until the rain', the *time* of the first rainfall is the deciding factor, R. Simeon b. Gamaliel's remark is irrelevant. (2) For in R. Meir's view there are only four days between the two rain-falls, and in R. Judah's there are ten. (3) The Jewish year being lunar, an extra month is periodically intercalated to make it agree with the Solar year; v. *J.E.* art. 'Calendar'. (4) The twelfth month of the year = February-March. (5) *Var. lec.:* SECOND ADAR. When a year is intercalated, a month is added after Adar, which is called the second Adar. (6) This is in reference to the dating of documents. (7) If he knew and stated Adar, without qualification, the second is meant, in R. Meir's view. But if he did not know, he must have meant the first, since he does not wish to be in doubt as to the length of his vow, that he should include the second Adar if the year is subsequently intercalated.

new moon of Adar,' [it means] until the new moon of the first Adar; but if it was a leap year, until the new moon of the second Adar. Now, this proves that the first clause does not refer to a leap year?[1] Hence the latter clause means, if he knew that it was a leap year; the former, if he did not know.

MISHNAH. R. JUDAH SAID: [IF ONE VOWS,] 'ḲONAM THAT I TASTE NO WINE UNTIL PASSOVER SHALL BE,' HE IS FORBIDDEN ONLY UNTIL THE PASSOVER NIGHT,[2] FOR HE MERELY MEANT, UNTIL THE EVENING OF PASSOVER, UNTIL THE HOUR WHEN MEN ARE WONT TO DRINK WINE.[3] IF HE VOWS, 'ḲONAM THAT I TASTE NO MEAT UNTIL THE FAST [I.E., THE DAY OF ATONEMENT] SHALL BE,' HE IS FORBIDDEN ONLY UNTIL THE EVE OF THE FAST, FOR HE MERELY MEANT, UNTIL PEOPLE USUALLY EAT MEAT.[4] R. JOSE, HIS SON, SAID: [IF HE VOWS,] 'ḲONAM, IF I TASTE GARLIC UNTIL THE SABBATH', HE IS FORBIDDEN ONLY UNTIL SABBATH EVE [I.E., FRIDAY NIGHT], FOR HE MEANT, UNTIL IT IS CUSTOMARY FOR PEOPLE TO EAT GARLIC.[5] IF HE SAYS TO HIS NEIGHBOUR, 'ḲONAM, IF I BENEFIT FROM YOU, IF YOU DO NOT COME AND ACCEPT FOR YOUR SONS A KOR OF WHEAT AND TWO BARRELS OF WINE,' THE LATTER MAY ANNUL HIS VOW WITHOUT RECOURSE TO A SAGE, BY DECLARING, 'DID YOU VOW FOR ANY OTHER PURPOSE BUT TO HONOUR ME? THIS [NON-ACCEPTANCE] IS MY HONOUR.' LIKEWISE, IF HE SAYS TO HIS NEIGHBOUR, 'ḲONAM, IF YOU BENEFIT FROM ME, IF YOU DO NOT GIVE

(1) That is obviously impossible, since in that case 'until the new moon of the first Adar' is meaningless. (2) So in Mishnayoth edd. (3) This is the reading as amended by BaḤ. (4) It was a widespread custom to eat meat on the eve of Atonement day. The point of these two rulings, as of the next too, is that although the expression might mean until Passover shall have been, etc., the imperfect being intended as a fut. perfect, yet since it is customary to drink wine on the first evening, he is assumed to have meant until it comes, which is also a possible rendering of his words. And the same applies to the vow regarding meat. (5) I.e., on the eve of Sabbath; the institution thereof is ascribed to Ezra; v. B.Ḳ. 82*a* and *supra* 31*a*.

MY SON A KOR OF WHEAT AND TWO BARRELS OF WINE'—R. MEIR RULES: HE IS FORBIDDEN UNTIL HE GIVES; BUT THE SAGES MAINTAIN: HE TOO CAN ANNUL HIS VOW WITHOUT A SAGE, BY DECLARING, 'I REGARD IT AS THOUGH I HAVE RECEIVED IT.' IF HE WAS URGING HIS NEIGHBOUR TO MARRY HIS SISTER'S DAUGHTER, AND HE EXCLAIMED, 'ḲONAM, IF SHE EVER BENEFITS FROM ME'; LIKEWISE, IF HE IS DIVORCING HIS WIFE AND VOWS, 'ḲONAM, IF MY WIFE HAS EVER BENEFIT FROM ME,'—THEY ARE PERMITTED TO BENEFIT FROM HIM, BECAUSE HE MEANT ONLY MARRIAGE. IF HE WAS URGING HIS NEIGHBOUR TO EAT IN HIS HOUSE, AND HE REPLIED, 'ḲONAM, IF I ENTER,' OR, 'THE DROP OF WATER THAT I DRINK,' HE MAY ENTER HIS HOUSE AND DRINK COLD WATER, BECAUSE HE ONLY MEANT EATING AND DRINKING IN GENERAL.[1]

(1) But did not mean the expression to be taken literally.

NEDARIM

CHAPTER IX

MISHNAH. [64*a*] R. ELIEZER SAID: ONE MAY SUGGEST TO A MAN AS AN OPENING [FOR ABSOLUTION][1] THE HONOUR OF HIS FATHER AND MOTHER BUT THE SAGES FORBID.[2] SAID R. ZADOK: INSTEAD OF GIVING THE HONOUR OF HIS FATHER AND MOTHER, LET US SUGGEST THE HONOUR OF THE ALMIGHTY AS AN OPENING.[3] IF SO, THERE ARE NO VOWS.[4] BUT THE SAGES ADMIT TO R. ELIEZER THAT IN A MATTER CONCERNING HIMSELF AND HIS FATHER AND MOTHER THEIR HONOUR IS SUGGESTED AS AN OPENING. R. ELIEZER ALSO RULED: A NEW FACT[5] MAY BE GIVEN AS AN OPENING; BUT THE SAGES FORBID IT. E.G., IF A MAN SAID, 'ḲONAM THAT I BENEFIT NOT FROM SO AND SO,' AND HE [THE LATTER] THEN BECAME A SCRIBE,[6] OR WAS ABOUT TO GIVE HIS SON IN MARRIAGE,[7] AND HE DECLARED, 'HAD I KNOWN THAT HE WOULD BECOME A SCRIBE OR WAS ABOUT TO GIVE HIS SON IN MARRIAGE, I WOULD NOT HAVE VOWED;' [OR IF HE SAID,] 'ḲONAM, IF I ENTER NOT THIS HOUSE,' AND IT BECAME A SYNAGOGUE, AND HE DECLARED, 'HAD I KNOWN THAT IT

(1) Lit., 'open for man'. (2) V. p. 61, n. 7. Since vows are discreditable (v. *supra* 9*a*), to make them is to cast a reflection upon one's parents. (3) One dishonours God by committing anything unworthy. (4) The Talmud discusses the meaning of this. According to our text, this is still R. Zadok's speech, and a refutation of R. Eliezer. But Ran, Tosaf. and Asheri read: They (the Sages) said to him: If so, there are no vows. On this reading, R. Zadok agrees with R. Eliezer, but goes beyond him, whilst the Sages maintain that even on R. Eliezer's view, one could not go so far as to suggest the honour of God as an opening, for if so, there are no vows. But, as is evident from the Mishnah, they disagree with R. Eliezer too. (5) Lit., 'newly-born', 'unexpected'. (6) I.e., a school teacher, whose services the *maddir* might require for his child; others: a notary, whose services might be essential to him. (7) And the *maddir* wished to take part in the festivities.

WOULD BECOME A SYNAGOGUE, I WOULD NOT HAVE VOWED': R. ELIEZER PERMITS IT,[1] BUT THE SAGES FORBID IT.

GEMARA. What is meant by THERE ARE NO VOWS?—Abaye said: If so, vows are not properly revoked.[2] [64b] Raba explained: If so, no one will seek a Sage's absolution for his vow.[3]

We learnt: BUT THE SAGES ADMIT TO R. ELIEZER THAT IN A MATTER CONCERNING HIMSELF AND HIS FATHER AND MOTHER, THEIR HONOUR IS SUGGESTED AS AN OPENING. Now, as for Abaye, who explains [it as meaning], if so, vows are not properly revoked, it is well: here, since he has been [so] impudent, he is impudent.[4] But on Raba's explanation, viz., if so, none will seek a Sage's absolution for his vow, why is such an opening suggested to him here?[5]—I will tell you. Since all [other] vows cannot be annulled without a Sage,[6] it may be offered as an opening here too.[7]

R. ELIEZER ALSO RULED: A NEW FACT MAY BE GIVEN AS AN OPENING, etc. What is R. Eliezer's reason?—R. Ḥisda said: Because Scripture saith, [*And the Lord said unto Moses in Midian, Go, return into Egypt:*] *for all the men are dead* [*which sought thy life*].[8]

(1) As an opening for absolution. (2) Because a vow can be annulled only on grounds, which, when suggested, need not necessarily make him regret his vow, in which case when he is moved to repent, it is to be assumed that his repentance is genuine. But when it is suggested to him that by vowing he dishonoured God, no person is so impudent as to maintain that he would have vowed notwithstanding, even if he would have done so; consequently, his vow is not properly revoked. (3) Since God's honour may apply to all vows, if such is suggested, every person will annul his vow himself, and thus the solemnity of vows be destroyed. (4) For obviously, if he has been so impudent as to make such a vow, he is sufficiently brazen not to offer regard for his parents' honour as a ground for absolution, unless he has genuinely repented of having acted so contumaciously toward them. (5) Since one can thus annul his own vow. (6) This not being accepted as a ground in other vows. (7) On account of other vows, it will be the practice to apply for absolution to a Sage, and that will be adhered to even in such an isolated case as this, which is an exception to the general rule. (8) Ex. IV, 19: the Talmud states below that Moses had vowed to Jethro not to return to Egypt, on account of the men who sought his life, and now God absolved Moses of his vow on the grounds that they were dead.

But death was a new fact:[1] this proves that a new fact is given as an opening. What then is the reason of the Rabbis?—They argue thus: Did these men die? Surely R. Johanan said on the authority of R. Simeon b. Yohai: Wherever *nizzim* [quarrelling] or *nizzawim* [standing] is mentioned, the reference is to none but Dathan and Abiram?[2] But, said Resh Lakish, they had become poor.[3]

R. Joshua b. Levi said: A man who is childless is accounted as dead, for it is written, *Give me children, or else I am dead.*[4] And it was taught: Four are accounted as dead: A poor man, a leper, a blind person, and one who is childless. A poor man, as it is written, *for all the men are dead* [*which sought thy life*].[5] A leper, as it is written, [*And Aaron looked upon Miriam, and behold, she was leprous. And Aaron said unto Moses . . .*] *let her not be as one dead.*[6] The blind, as it is written, *He hath set me in dark places, as they that be dead of old.*[7] And he who is childless, as it is written, *Give me children, or else I am dead.*[8]

[65*a*] It was taught: He who is forbidden to benefit from his neighbour can have the vow absolved only in his [neighbour's] presence.[9]

(1) I.e., one that arose subsequent to Moses' vow. (2) Cf. Ex. II, 13: *And when he went out on the second day, behold, two men of the Hebrews strove together* (*nizzim*), with: *That is that Dathan and Abiram, which were famous in the congregation, who strove against* (*hizzu*, of which *nizzim* is a participle) *Moses against Aaron*. Cf. also Ex. V, 20: *And they met Moses and Aaron, who* (*sc.* they) *stood* (*nizzawim*) *in the way*, with Num. XVI, 27: *And Dathan and Abiram came out, and stood* (*nizzawim*) *etc.* The similarity of language leads to the assumption that the same people are referred to in all cases, viz., Dathan and Abiram. Now, it was on their account that Moses fled from Egypt, and God told him that they were dead. But they reappear in Korah's rebellion. Hence the statement that they were dead cannot be taken literally. (3) Lit., 'they had descended from their property'. V. *supra* p. 16, n. 3. Now, though impoverishment was also a new fact, yet since it is of common occurrence (here regarded as more likely than death, as he left them, presumably, in good health), the Rabbis regard it as one which might be foreseen, and therefore a legitimate ground for absolution. (4) Gen. XXX, 1. (5) V. n. 2. (6) Num. XII, 10-12. (7) Lam. III, 6: this is interpreted: he hath set me in dark places, just as the blind, who are accounted as long since dead. (8) Possibly the inclusion of the poor and childless was directed against the early Christian exaltation of poverty and celibacy. (9) If A vowed not to benefit from B, A cannot have his vow absolved except in the presence of B. In the Jerusalem Talmud two reasons are given for this: (i) if his neighbour does not know of his absolution, he may

Whence do we know this?—R. Naḥman said: Because it is written, *And the Lord said unto Moses, In Midian, go, return into Egypt: for all the men are dead which sought thy life.*[1] He said [thus] to him: 'In Midian thou didst vow; go and annul thy vow in Midian.' [How do we know that he vowed in Midian?]— Because it is written, *And Moses was content* [wa-yo'el] *to dwell with the man;*[2] now *alah*[3] can only mean an oath, as it is written, *and hath taken an* [alah] *oath of him.*[4]

And also against King Nebuchadnezzar he rebelled, who had adjured him by the living God.[5] What was [the nature of] his rebellion?—Zedekiah found Nebuchadnezzar eating a live rabbit.[6] 'Swear to me,' exclaimed he, 'not to reveal this, that it may not leak out!' He swore. Subsequently he grieved thereat, and had his vow absolved and disclosed it. When Nebuchadnezzar learned that they were deriding him, he had the Sanhedrin[7] and Zedekiah brought before him, and said to them, 'Have ye seen what Zedekiah has done? Did he not swear by the name of Heaven not to reveal it?' They answered him, 'He was absolved of his oath.' 'Can then one be absolved of an oath?' he asked them. 'Yes,' they returned. 'In his presence or even not in his presence?'[8]—'[Only] in his presence,' was their reply. 'How then did ye act?' said he to them: 'why did ye not say this to Zedekiah?' Immediately, '*The elders of the daughter of Zion sit upon the ground, and keep silence.*'[9] R. Isaac said: This teaches that they removed the cushions from under them.[10]

MISHNAH. R. MEIR SAID: SOME THINGS APPEAR AS NEW

suspect him of breaking his vow, (ii) he who vowed not to benefit from his neighbour—presumably for his neighbour's benefit—he should be put to shame for his niggardly spirit and be made to seek absolution in his presence. Therefore it is insisted upon.

(1) Ex. IV, 19. (2) Ibid. II, 21. (3) The root of *wa-yo'el*. (4) Ezek. XVII, 13. (5) II Chron. XXXVI, 13. (6) Other: a raw rabbit. (7) The Jewish court. (8) *Sc.* of the person to whom the oath was sworn. (9) Lam. II, 10. (10) A sign of their unworthiness and deposition.

FACTS, AND YET ARE NOT [TREATED] AS NEW;[1] BUT THE SAGES DO NOT AGREE WITH HIM.[2] E.G., IF ONE SAYS, 'ḲONAM THAT I DO NOT MARRY SO AND SO, BECAUSE HER FATHER IS WICKED,' AND HE IS [THEN] TOLD, HE IS DEAD, OR, HE HAS REPENTED; 'ḲONAM, IF I ENTER THIS HOUSE, BECAUSE IT CONTAINS A WILD DOG,' OR, 'BECAUSE IT CONTAINS A SERPENT,' AND HE IS [THEN] INFORMED, THE DOG IS DEAD, OR, THE SERPENT HAS BEEN KILLED, THESE ARE AS NEW FACTS, YET ACTUALLY NOT [TREATED] AS NEW FACTS. BUT THE SAGES DO NOT AGREE WITH HIM.[3]

GEMARA. 'ḲONAM, IF I ENTER THIS HOUSE, BECAUSE IT CONTAINS A WILD DOG, etc.' But if it died, it really is a new fact?[4] —Said R. Huna: It is as though he conditioned his vow by this fact. R. Joḥanan said: He was told, 'He has already died,' or, 'already repented.'[5]

[65*b*] R. Abba objected: [If one vows,] '*Ḳonam* that I do not marry that ugly woman,' whereas she is beautiful; 'that black-[skinned] woman,' whereas she is fair; 'that short woman,' who in fact is tall, he is permitted to marry her. Not because she was ugly and became beautiful [after the vow], black and turned fair, short and grew tall, but because the vow was made in error. Now, as for R. Huna, who explained it, It is as though he conditioned his vow by this fact, it is well: he [the Tanna] teaches the case of one who makes his vow dependent upon a fact, and the case of an erroneous vow. But according to R. Joḥanan, who explained [this Mishnah as meaning] that he had already died or repented,[6] why teach [two instances of erroneous vows]?—This is a difficulty.

(1) I.e., though occurring after the vow, they might have been anticipated. (2) *Var. lec.*: and the Sages agree with him. (3) *Var. lec.*: and the Sages agree with him. (4) Not only in appearance. (5) I.e., before the vow, and the vow was thus made in error. Therefore R. Meir teaches that in the former it is not treated as a novel occurrence and absolution may be granted on that score. The Sages disagree, holding that it may not be granted, as a precautionary measure. (6) So that it was a vow in error.

MISHNAH. R. MEIR ALSO SAID: AN OPENING [FOR ABSOLUTION], MAY BE GIVEN FROM WHAT IS WRITTEN IN THE TORAH, AND WE SAY TO HIM, 'HAD YOU KNOWN THAT YOU WERE VIOLATING [THE INJUNCTIONS], THOU SHALT NOT AVENGE, THOU SHALT NOT BEAR A GRUDGE AGAINST THE CHILDREN OF THY PEOPLE, THOU SHALT LOVE THY NEIGHBOUR AS THYSELF,[1] OR THAT THY BROTHER MAY LIVE WITH THEE;[2] OR THAT HE MIGHT BECOME POOR AND YOU WOULD NOT BE ABLE TO PROVIDE FOR HIM,[3] [WOULD YOU HAVE VOWED]?' SHOULD HE REPLY, 'HAD I KNOWN THAT IT IS SO, I WOULD NOT HAVE VOWED,' HE IS ABSOLVED.

GEMARA. R. Huna son of R. Ḳaṭṭina said to the Rabbis:[4] But he can reply, Not all who become poor fall upon me [for support]; and as for my share of the [general] obligations, I can provide for him together with everyone else?[5]—He replied: I maintain, He who falls [upon the community] does not fall at the beginning into the hands of the charity overseer.[6]

MISHNAH. A WIFE'S KETHUBAH[7] MAY BE GIVEN AS AN OPENING [FOR ABSOLUTION]. AND THUS IT ONCE HAPPENED THAT A MAN VOWED NOT TO BENEFIT FROM HIS WIFE,[8] AND HER KETHUBAH AMOUNTED TO FOUR HUNDRED DENARII.[9] HE WENT BEFORE R. AKIBA, WHO ORDERED HIM TO PAY HER THE KETHUBAH [IN FULL]. SAID HE TO HIM, 'RABBI, MY FATHER LEFT EIGHT HUNDRED DENARII, OF WHICH MY BROTHER TOOK FOUR HUNDRED AND I TOOK FOUR HUNDRED:

(1) Lev. XIX, 18. (2) Ibid. XXV, 36; e.g., when one forbids another to benefit from him. (3) So the reading in Ran and Asheri. (4) Asheri reads: Rabbah. (5) I.e., I can still give my share through the communal charitable institutions, since it is not directly for him. (6) Only as a last resource does one apply for communal relief. But in the first place one seeks private relief, which the man who made the vow is debarred from affording. (7) Marriage settlement. (8) He, being unable to live without benefiting from her, must divorce her and pay her marriage settlement. (9) The *kethubah* was variable. The minima are two hundred *denarii* and one hundred *denarii* for a virgin and a widow respectively; Keth. 10*b*.

IS IT NOT ENOUGH THAT SHE SHOULD RECEIVE TWO HUNDRED AND I TWO HUNDRED?'—R. AKIBA REPLIED: 'EVEN IF YOU SELL THE HAIR OF YOUR HEAD, YOU MUST PAY HER HER KETHUBAH.' 'HAD I KNOWN THAT IT IS SO,' HE ANSWERED, 'I WOULD NOT HAVE VOWED.' THEREUPON R. AKIBA PERMITTED HER [TO HIM].[1]

GEMARA. Is then movable property under a lien for the *kethubah?*[2]—Abaye said: [It refers to] real estate worth eight hundred *denarii*. But the hair of his head is mentioned, which is movable property! —It means thus: Even if you must sell the hair of your head for your keep.[3] This proves that the debtor's means are not assessed?[4]—Said R. Naḥman son of R. Isaac: [No]. [66a] It means that the *kethubah* deed is not torn up.[5]

MISHNAH. THE SABBATHS AND FESTIVALS[6] ARE GIVEN AS AN OPENING. THE EARLIER RULING WAS THAT FOR THESE DAYS THE VOW IS CANCELLED, BUT FOR OTHERS IT IS BINDING; UNTIL R. AKIBA CAME AND TAUGHT: A VOW WHICH IS PARTIALLY ANNULLED IS ENTIRELY ANNULLED. E.G., IF ONE SAID, 'ḲONAM THAT I DO NOT BENEFIT FROM ANY OF YOU,' IF ONE WAS [SUBSEQUENTLY] PERMITTED [TO BENEFIT HIM], THEY ARE ALL PERMITTED. [BUT IF HE SAID, 'ḲONAM] THAT I DO NOT BENEFIT FROM A, B, C, ETC.', IF THE FIRST WAS PERMITTED, ALL ARE PERMITTED; BUT IF THE LAST-NAMED WAS PERMITTED, HE ALONE IS PERMITTED, BUT THE REST

(1) Thus annulling the vow. (2) This is the subject of a dispute between R. Meir and the Rabbis in Keth. 81*b*.—It is now assumed that the eight hundred *denarii* were in the form of movables. (3) Lit., 'and eat'. Even so, you are bound to hand over your real estate in payment of the *kethubah*. (4) For the purpose of exempting him of payment, in whole or in part. This is disputed in B.M. 114*a*. (5) I.e., though the debtor may be exempted of part payment *now*, the debt always remains, in case his prospects improve later. Thus R. Akiba merely meant that the debt of the *kethubah* would always hang over him. (6) Here the reading is, The Festivals and the Sabbaths; but on 25*b* it is quoted in the order given here, and Asheri gives the same reading here too.

ARE FORBIDDEN. (IF THE MIDDLE PERSON WAS PERMITTED, THOSE MENTIONED AFTER HIM ARE [ALSO] PERMITTED, BUT THOSE MENTIONED BEFORE HIM ARE FORBIDDEN.)[1] [IF ONE VOWS,] 'ĶORBAN BE WHAT I BENEFIT FROM THIS [MAN], ĶORBAN BE WHAT I BENEFIT FROM THAT [MAN],' AN OPENING [FOR ABSOLUTION] IS NEEDED FOR EACH ONE INDIVIDUALLY. [IF ONE VOWS,] 'ĶONAM, IF I TASTE WINE, BECAUSE IT IS INJURIOUS TO THE STOMACH': WHEREUPON HE WAS TOLD, 'BUT WELL-MATURED WINE IS BENEFICIAL TO THE STOMACH,' HE IS ABSOLVED IN RESPECT OF WELL-MATURED WINE, AND NOT ONLY IN RESPECT OF WELL-MATURED WINE, BUT OF ALL WINE. 'ĶONAM, IF I TASTE ONIONS, BECAUSE THEY ARE INJURIOUS TO THE HEART'; THEN HE WAS TOLD, 'BUT THE WILD ONION[2] IS GOOD FOR THE HEART,'—HE IS PERMITTED TO PARTAKE OF WILD ONIONS, AND NOT ONLY OF WILD ONIONS, BUT OF ALL ONIONS. SUCH A CASE HAPPENED BEFORE R. MEIR, AND HE GAVE ABSOLUTION IN RESPECT OF ALL ONIONS.

GEMARA. IF THE LAST-NAMED WAS PERMITTED, HE ALONE IS PERMITTED, BUT THE REST ARE FORBIDDEN. Which Tanna [ruled thus]?—Raba said: It is R. Simeon, who maintained, unless he declared 'I swear' to each one separately.[3]

(1) This is quoted on 26b, but as part of a Baraitha, not a Mishnah; hence it should be omitted, and Asheri too omits it. (2) Or, Cyprus onions. (3) V. Shebu. 38a. If a man is dunned by a number of creditors, and he takes a false oath, saying, 'I swear that I owe nothing to you, nor to you, nor to you etc.,' he is liable only to one sacrifice, as for one false oath; unless he declares, 'I swear that I owe nothing to you', 'I swear that I owe nothing to you', 'I swear that I owe nothing to you', etc., in which case he is liable to a sacrifice for each false oath—this is R. Simeon's view. Thus here too, if he declared, 'Ķorban be what I benefit from A', 'Ķorban be what I benefit from B', etc., mentioning 'Ķorban' in the case of each separately, each is regarded as a separate vow. Otherwise they would all be forbidden or permitted alike by the same vow, or its absolution. (The earlier clause in which 'Ķorban' was not mentioned in the case of each refers to an enumeration in which each person was made dependent upon the preceding). Although the caption of this passage is, IF THE LAST-NAMED, ETC., it appears from Ran, Asheri and

'ḲONAM, IF I TASTE WINE,' etc. But let it follow [from the fact] that it is not injurious?[1] — R. Abba said: It means: Moreover, it is beneficial.[2]

'ḲONAM, IF I TASTE ONIONS,' etc. But let it follow [from the fact] that they are not injurious? — Said R. Abba: It means: Moreover, they are beneficial.

MISHNAH. A MAN'S OWN HONOUR, AND THE HONOUR OF HIS CHILDREN, MAY BE GIVEN AS AN OPENING. [THUS:] WE SAY TO HIM, 'HAD YOU KNOWN THAT TO-MORROW IT WILL BE SAID OF YOU, "THAT IS HIS REGULAR HABIT TO DIVORCE HIS WIFE"; AND OF YOUR DAUGHTERS THEY WILL SAY, "THEY ARE THE DAUGHTERS OF A DIVORCED WOMAN. WHAT FAULT DID HE FIND IN THIS WOMAN TO DIVORCE HER?"'[3] IF HE REPLIES, 'HAD I KNOWN THAT IT IS SO, I WOULD NOT HAVE VOWED,' HE IS ABSOLVED.

[IF ONE VOWS,] 'ḲONAM IF I MARRY THAT UGLY WOMAN,' WHEREAS SHE IS BEAUTIFUL; 'THAT BLACK [-SKINNED] WOMAN,' WHEREAS SHE IS FAIR; 'THAT SHORT WOMAN,' WHO IN FACT IS TALL, HE IS PERMITTED TO MARRY HER, NOT BECAUSE SHE WAS UGLY, AND BECAME BEAUTIFUL, OR BLACK AND TURNED FAIR, SHORT AND GREW TALL, BUT BECAUSE THE VOW WAS MADE IN ERROR. AND THUS IT HAPPENED WITH ONE WHO VOWED NOT TO BENEFIT FROM HIS SISTER'S DAUGHTER, AND SHE WAS TAKEN INTO R. ISHMAEL'S HOUSE AND MADE BEAUTIFUL. 'MY SON,' EXCLAIMED R. ISHMAEL TO HIM, 'DID YOU VOW NOT TO BENEFIT FROM THIS ONE!' 'NO,' HE REPLIED, WHEREUPON R. ISHMAEL PERMITTED HER [TO HIM]. IN THAT HOUR R. ISHMAEL WEPT AND SAID, 'THE DAUGH-

Tosaf. that the deduction as to authorship is based on 'ḲORBAN BE WHAT I BENEFIT FROM THIS (MAN).

(1) Even if not beneficial, that is sufficient to annul the vow.   (2) I.e., firstly, it is not injurious, which itself is sufficient; but what is more, it is even beneficial. (3) I.e., there must be something wrong with her, and her daughters probably follow in her footsteps. This refers to a vow to divorce one's wife.

TERS OF ISRAEL ARE BEAUTIFUL, BUT POVERTY DISFIGURES THEM.'[1] AND WHEN R. ISHMAEL DIED, THE DAUGHTERS OF ISRAEL RAISED A LAMENT, SAYING, YE DAUGHTERS OF ISRAEL WEEP FOR R. ISHMAEL. AND THUS IT IS SAID TOO OF SAUL, YE DAUGHTERS OF ISRAEL, WEEP OVER SAUL.[2]

GEMARA. A story [is quoted] contradicting [the ruling]![3] —The text is defective[4] and was thus taught: R. Ishmael said: Even if she was ugly and became beautiful, black and turned fair, or short and grew tall. AND THUS IT HAPPENED WITH ONE WHO VOWED NOT TO BENEFIT FROM HIS SISTER'S DAUGHTER: SHE WAS TAKEN INTO R. ISHMAEL'S HOUSE AND MADE BEAUTIFUL, etc. [66*b*] A Tanna taught: She had a false[5] tooth, and R. Ishmael made her a gold tooth at his own cost. When R. Ishmael died, a professional mourner commenced [the funeral eulogy] thus: Ye daughters of Israel, weep over R. Ishmael, who clothed you etc.[6]

A man once said to his wife, '*Ḳonam* that you benefit not from me, until you make R. Judah and R. Simeon taste of your cooking.' R. Judah tasted thereof, observing, 'It is but logical:[7] If, in order to make peace between husband and wife, the Torah commanded, Let My Name, written in sanctity, be dissolved in "*the waters that curse*",[8] though 'tis but doubtful,[9] how much more so I!' R. Simeon did not taste thereof, exclaiming, 'Let all the widows' children perish,[10] rather than that Simeon be moved from his standpoint, lest they fall into the habit of vowing.'

(1) R. Ishmael flourished during the latter portion of the first century and the early part of the second C.E. This period, falling roughly between the destruction of the Temple and the Bar Cochba revolt, and extending some time beyond the fall of Bethar in 135 C.E., must have been one of hardship and poverty for many Jews. (2) II Sam. I, 24.—In ancient days women were professional mourners, and chanted dirges in chorus at the bier of the dead. (3) The Mishnah, after ruling that the vow is annulled only if she was actually beautiful when it was made, then quotes a story in which R. Ishmael annulled it in respect of a woman who was *subsequently* made beautiful. (4) Cf. p. 2, n. 3. (5) Lit., 'An inserted tooth'. (6) Continuing as in II Sam. I, 24, q.v. (7) Lit., '(it follows) *a fortiori*' (that I should do so). (8) V. Num. V, 23. (9) Whether the wife was guilty of adultery. (10) I.e., let the husband die, so that she becomes a widow, and all her children—of course, hardly to be taken literally.

A man once said to his wife, '*Konam* that you benefit not from me until you expectorate on R. Simeon b. Gamaliel.' She went and spat upon his garment, and he [R. Simeon b. Gamaliel] absolved her.[1] R. Aḥa of Difti[2] said to Rabina: But his aim was to insult him!—He replied: To expectorate upon the garments of R. Simeon b. Gamaliel is a great insult.

A man once said to his wife, '*Konam* that you benefit not from me, until you shew aught beautiful[3] in yourself to R. Ishmael son of R. Jose.' Said he to them:[4] 'Perhaps her head is beautiful?'—'It is round,' they replied.[5] 'Perhaps her hair is beautiful?'—'It is like stalks of flax.' 'Perhaps her eyes are beautiful?'—'They are bleared.' 'Perhaps her nose is beautiful?'—'It is swollen.' 'Perhaps her lips are beautiful?'—'They are thick.' 'Perhaps her neck is beautiful?'—'It is squat.' 'Perhaps her abdomen is beautiful?'—'It protrudes.' 'Perhaps her feet are beautiful?'—'They are as broad as those of a duck.' 'Perhaps her name is beautiful?'—'It is *liklukith*.'[6] Said he to them, 'She is fittingly called *liklukith*, since she is repulsive through her defects'; and so he permitted her [to her husband].

A certain Babylonian went up to the Land of Israel and took a wife [there]. 'Boil me two [cows'] feet,' he ordered, and she boiled him two lentils,[7] which infuriated him with her. The next day he said, 'Boil me a *griwa*';[8] so he boiled him a *griwa*. 'Go and bring me two *bezuni*';[9] so she went and brought him two candles.[9] 'Go and break them on the head of the *baba*.'[10] Now Baba b. Buṭa was sitting

(1) So emended by BaḤ. (2) Identified with Dibtha in the vicinity of Wasiṭ on the lower reaches of the Tigris; Obermeyer, *op. cit.*, p. 197. (3) So BaḤ. [Cur. ed. 'a becoming defect'.] (4) Either to the husband and wife, or to those who reported the matter to him. (5) Perhaps it was Esquimaux-shaped, which both in the East and in the West would hardly be considered beautiful. (6) Which means repulsive. (7) Misunderstanding his Babylonian pronunciation, and mistaking *ṭelafe* (feet) for *ṭelafḥe* (lentils) Rashi. Another version: Boil me two (meaning 'some') lentils, and she boiled him (just) two lentils, taking him literally. (8) A large measure (of lentils). Thinking that she had intentionally boiled only two the previous day through laziness or meanness, he asked for an extraordinary large quantity, believing that she would scale it down. (9) Denoting either 'melons' or 'candles'. (10) Threshold; i.e., break them on the top of the threshold.

on the threshold, engaged in judging in a lawsuit. So she went and broke them on his head. Said he to her, 'What is the meaning of this that thou hast done?'—She replied, 'Thus my husband did order me.' 'Thou hast performed thy husband's will,' he rejoined; 'may the Almighty bring forth from thee two sons like Baba b. Buṭa.'

NEDARIM

CHAPTER X

MISHNAH. IN THE CASE OF A BETROTHED MAIDEN,[1] HER FATHER AND HER BETROTHED HUSBAND ANNUL HER VOWS.[2] [67*a*] IF HER FATHER ANNULLED [HER VOW] BUT NOT THE HUSBAND, OR IF THE HUSBAND ANNULLED [IT] BUT NOT THE FATHER, IT IS NOT ANNULLED; AND IT GOES WITHOUT SAYING IF ONE OF THEM CONFIRMED [IT].

GEMARA. But that[3] is the same as the first clause, HER FATHER AND HUSBAND ANNUL HER VOWS!—I might think that either her father or her husband is meant;[4] therefore we are taught [otherwise].

AND IT GOES WITHOUT SAYING IF ONE OF THEM CONFIRMED [IT]. Then why teach it? If we say that annulment by one without the other is invalid, what need is there to state 'IF ONE OF THEM CONFIRMED [IT]?'—It is necessary, in the case where one of them annulled it and the other confirmed it, and then the latter sought absolution of his confirmation.[5] I might think, that which he confirmed, he has surely overthrown;[6] there-

(1) There were two stages of marriage: (i) *erusin*, betrothal, and (ii) *nissu'in*, home-taking. The betrothed maiden was called *arusah*, and her husband *arus*. *Erusin* was as binding as marriage, and could be annulled only by divorce, but cohabitation was forbidden, and the *arusah* remained in her father's house until the *nissu'in*. By maiden—*na'arah*—a girl between twelve years and one day and twelve and a half years plus one day old is meant, after which she becomes a *bogereth*. The reference to a maiden here is to exclude a *bogereth*, not a minor. (2) V. Num. XXX, 3ff. But not separately, because she is partly under the authority of both. A *bogereth* is not under her father's authority, and is therefore excluded. (3) Viz., IF HER FATHER ANNULLED, etc. (4) The 'and', Heb. ו, having the disjunctive force of 'or'. (5) By a Rabbi, who granted it to him just as he would for a vow. (6) Either that the very revoking of his confirmation is in itself the equivalent of nullification, or, having revoked his confirmation, he is now free to nullify the vow.

fore we are taught that they must both annul simultaneously.[1]

IN THE CASE OF A BETROTHED MAIDEN, HER FATHER AND HER HUSBAND ANNUL HER VOWS. Whence do we know this?[2] —Rabbah[3] said: The Writ saith, *And if she be to an husband, when she vowed* [. . . *then he shall make her vow . . . of no effect*]:[4] hence it follows that a betrothed maiden, her father and her husband annul her vows.[5] But perhaps this verse refers to a *nesu'ah?*—In respect to a *nesu'ah* there is a different verse, viz., *And if she vowed in her husband's house, etc.*[6] But perhaps both refer to a *nesu'ah*,[7] and should you object, what need of two verses relating to a *nesu'ah?* It is to teach that a husband cannot annul pre-marriage vows? [67*b*] —But does that not follow in any case?[8] Alternatively, I might say '*to be*' implies *kiddushin*.[9] But perhaps the father himself can annul?[10]

(1) Not literally, for even if one annulled in the morning, and the other in the evening, it is valid. But there must be no invalidating act between the two nullifications, and here, since one confirmed it, the nullification of the other previous thereto is void. (2) That her husband may annul her vows, though she has not yet entered his home. (3) Yalkuṭ reads: Raba. (4) Num. XXX, 7-9. (5) This verse is preceded by, *But if her father disallow her in the day that he heareth; not any of her vows . . . shall stand . . . because her father disallowed her.* Then follows: *And if she be etc.* Now, Rabbah reasons thus: Since we have a different verse for a *nesu'ah* (a married woman, v. Glos.), as explained below, this verse must refer to an *arusah*, and consequently, the copulative '*and*' must mark a continuation of the preceding verse; i.e., if in her father's house, the father has power to annul her vow, and if at the same time she is married, viz., an *arusah*, her husband too, in conjunction with her father, exercises this authority. For if the '*and*' introduces a separate law, namely, that the husband of an *arusah* can disallow her vows without her father, the verse referring to a *nesu'ah* is superfluous: if the husband can himself annul the vows of an *arusah*, surely it goes without saying that he can do so for a *nesu'ah!* Now this reasoning is implicit in the first verse quoted, but the Talmud proceeds to elucidate it by means of question and answer. (6) Ibid. II. (7) But in the case of an *arusah* the father alone can annul her vows. (8) Rashi, Ran, and one alternative in Asheri explain: '*And if she vowed in her husband's house*', which obviously refers to a *nesu'ah*, teaches at the same time that the vow must have been made in her husband's house, and not before marriage. So that '*and if she be, etc.*', must refer to an *arusah*. (9) The phrase '*if she be*' denotes mere betrothal; it therefore refers to an *arusah*. (10) Though it has been shewn that the husband can annul only in conjunction with the father, the latter, on the other hand, can perhaps act alone.

—If so, what is the need of, *'and bind himself by a bond, being in the father's house . . . if her father disallow . . . not any of her vows shall stand . . . because her father disallowed her'?*[1] If the father can annul them alone even when there is an *arus,* surely he can do so when there is no *arus!* But perhaps the father needs the *arus,* but the *arus* can annul alone? And should you reply, If so, why does Scripture mention the father?[2] It is to shew that if he confirmed, the confirmation is valid![3]—If so, why write, *'and if she vowed in her husband's house':* [since] it follows *a fortiori:* if the *arus* can annul alone even where there is a father,[4] is it necessary [to state it] when she is no longer under her father's control! But perhaps, *'and if she vowed in her husband's house',* teaches that he cannot annul pre-marriage vows?[5]—From that fact itself [it is proved. That] an *arus* can annul pre-marriage vows: surely, that is [only] because of his partnership with the father.[6]

[68a] The School of R. Ishmael taught: [*These are the statutes which the Lord commanded Moses*] *between a man and his wife, between the father and his daughter,* [*being yet in her youth in her father's house*]:[7] this teaches that in the case of a betrothed maiden both her father and her husband annul her vows.[8] Now, according to the Tanna

(1) Num. XXX, 4-6. (2) I.e., why is *and if she be at all to an husband* coupled with *because her father disallowed her*; as explained p. 217, n. 5, that the *and* combines the two. But why combine them, if the *arus* can annul entirely without the father? (3) I.e., the father still retains that authority. But if he is neutral, the *arus* alone can annul. (4) I.e., when she is still under the paternal roof and to some extent under his authority; e.g., her earnings belong to her father. (5) The question here is not the same as on 67*a*. There it was suggested that both *'and if she be to an husband'* and, *'and if she vowed in her husband's house'* refer to a *nesu'ah,* the latter verse teaching that the husband cannot annul pre-marriage vows. Here the question is: perhaps the first verse refers to an *arus,* and means that he can annul alone, and the second to a husband (after *nissu'in*)? But it does not teach that in the second case too he can annul, since this is obvious from the first *a fortiori,* but implies a limitation: that he cannot annul pre-marriage vows. (6) It is obvious that an *arus* alone cannot wield greater authority than a husband. Hence, when we find that in one respect his power is greater, it must be because he does not exercise it alone, but in conjunction with the father, who can disallow his daughter's vows whenever made under his authority. (7) Num. XXX, 17. (8) The verse is interpreted as referring to one and the same woman;

of the School of Ishmael, what is the purpose of *'and if she be to an husband'?*[1]—He utilizes it for Rabbah's other dictum.[2] Now, how does Raba utilize the verse adduced by the Tanna of the School of Ishmael?[3]—It is necessary to teach that the husband can annul vows which concern himself and his wife.[4]

The scholars propounded: Does the husband cut [the vow] or weaken [it]?[5] How does this problem arise? E.g., If she [the betrothed maiden] vowed not to eat the size of two olives [of anything],[6] and the *arus* heard of it and annulled the vow, and she ate them. Now, if we say that he cuts the vow apart, she is flagellated; but if he weakens it, it is merely forbidden.[7] What [is the law]?—Come and hear: When was it said that if the husband died, his authority passes over[8] to the father? In the case where the husband did not hear [the vow] before he died, or heard and annulled it, or heard it and was silent,[9] and died on the same day: this is what we learnt: If the husband died, his authority passes over to the father;[10] [68*b*] but if he heard and confirmed it, or heard it and was silent, and died on the following day,[11] he [the father] cannot annul it.[12] If the father heard and annulled it, and died before the husband managed to hear of it,—this is what we learnt: If the

hence it states that her father and her husband have authority over her, and that is possible only in the case of a betrothed maiden.

(1) Which was utilized on 67*a* for this teaching. (2) V. 70*a*. (3) Since he deduces this from *'and if she be etc'*. (4) Deduced from *'between a man and his wife'*, i.e., only such vows as concern them and their mutual relationship. (5) Does he completely nullify half the vow, leaving the other half for the father, or does he weaken the whole vow, whilst actually nullifying nothing of it? [The same question applies equally to the father (Ran).] (6) Nothing whatsoever may be eaten of that which is forbidden, but the size of an olive is the smallest quantity for which punishment is imposed. (7) If he cuts the vow in two, then the size of one olive remains forbidden in its full stringency, and therefore she is flagellated for the violation of her vow. But if he weakens the whole of the vow, though leaving it all forbidden, the prohibition is not so stringent that punishment should be imposed. (8) Lit., 'emptied out'. (9) So emended by BaḤ. (10) In all these cases the husband had no actually confirmed the vow; therefore the father is left with the full authority to annul it. (11) Having thus *ipso facto* confirmed it. (12) Once the husband has confirmed, the father cannot annul it, even after the former's death.

father died, his authority does not pass over to the husband.[1] If the husband heard and annulled it, and died before the father managed to hear of it,—in this case we learnt: If the husband died, his authority passes over to the father.[2] If the husband heard and annulled it, and the father died before he managed to hear of it, the husband cannot annul it,[3] because the husband can annul only in partnership. [69a] If the father heard and annulled it, and the husband died before he managed to hear of it, the father can again annul the husband's portion. R. Nathan said: That is the view of Beth Shammai; but Beth Hillel maintain: He cannot annul it [a second time]. This proves that according to Beth Shammai, he cuts it apart, whilst in the view of Beth Hillel he weakens it.[4] This proves it.[5]

Raba propounded: Can absolution be sought from confirmation,[6] or not? Should you say, no absolution can be sought from confirmation, is there absolution from annulment, or not?[7]—Come

(1) *Infra* 70a. With his death his annulment is void, and the husband is not empowered to nullify the vow himself, though in the reverse case the father could do so. (2) The first clause of the Mishnah means that the father heard it before the husband's death; this clause, that the husband died before the father heard it. Now I might think that only if he had heard it in the husband's lifetime, and so could have annulled it together with him, does he inherit his authority, but if he had not heard of it in her husband's lifetime, his authority is not transmitted. Therefore this clause teaches otherwise. (3) I.e., act in lieu of her father. (4) Hence, according to Beth Shammai, when the father annulled it, the husband's portion remains, as it were, intact in all its stringency. The husband's right to annul the other half is sufficiently tangible, since that half is as stringent in itself as the whole, to be transmitted to the father. But in the view of Beth Hillel annulment by the father, as by the husband, merely weakens it; hence the husband's right to wipe off entirely a prohibition that is already weakened is too intangible to be transmitted to the father.—But in the first clause, where without the father having annulled his share, the husband annuls it and then dies, since the father can annul his own share he can annul too the weakened share of the husband (Asheri). (5) And since in all disputes between Beth Shammai and Beth Hillel the *halachah* is in the latter, the final ruling is that the husband weakens the incidence of the whole vow. (6) By a Sage, after expressing 'regret'. (7) The confirmation of a vow is as a vow; hence the question whether it can be revoked. The revocation of the annulment of a vow should not be in question, since it might be assumed that one cannot

and hear: For R. Joḥanan said: One can seek absolution from confirmation but not from annulment.

Rabbah propounded: What if [he said], 'It is confirmed to thee, it is confirmed to thee,' and then sought absolution of his first confirmation?—Come and hear: For Raba said: If he obtained absolution from the first, the second becomes binding upon him.[1]

Rabbah propounded: What if [he declares], 'It be confirmed unto thee and annulled unto thee, but the confirmation be not valid unless the annulment had operated?'[2] [69*b*]—Come and hear [a solution] from the controversy of R. Meir and R. Jose: For we learnt: [If one declares,] 'This [animal] be a substitute for a burnt-offering, a substitute for a peace-offering,' it is a substitute for a burnt-offering [only]; this is R. Meir's view. But R. Jose ruled: If that was his original intention,[3] since it is impossible to pronounce both designations simultaneously, his declarations are valid.[4] Now, even R. Meir asserted [that the second statement is disregarded] only because he did not say, 'Let the first not be valid unless the second take effect'; but here that he declared, 'but the confirmation be not valid unless the annulment has operated,' even R. Meir admits that the annulment is valid.

revoke in order to *impose* a prohibition, but that elsewhere (76*b*) we find the two likened to each other.

(1) V. *supra* 18*a*: just as there, so here too, and hence the second confirmation retains its full force. (2) Without the stipulation it is obvious that the annulment is invalid, for a vow once confirmed cannot be annulled. Since, however, one is made dependent upon the other, the question arises whether the annulment cancels the confirmation or not. (3) To declare it a substitute for both. (4) V. Lev. XXVII, 33: *He shall not search whether it be good or bad, neither shall he change it: and if he change it at all, then both it and the change thereof shall be holy.* This is interpreted as meaning that if an animal be dedicated for a particular sacrifice, e.g., a peace-offering, and then a second substituted for it, both are holy, the second having exactly the same holiness as the first. Now, R. Meir rules that if he declares it a substitute for two other consecrated animals in succession, only the first declaration is valid, and the second disregarded. But R. Jose maintains that if the second statement was not added as an afterthought, but formed part of the original intention, the whole is valid. Consequently, the animal must be sold, and the money expended half for a burnt-offering and half for a peace-offering.

Rabbah propounded: What [if he declares], 'It be confirmed unto thee and annulled to thee simultaneously?' [1]—Come and hear: For Rabbah said: Whatever is not [valid] consecutively, is not valid even simultaneously. [2]

Rabbah propounded: What [if he declares], 'It be confirmed to thee to-day? Do we rule, it is as though he had said to her, 'but it be annulled unto thee to-morrow' [by implication], or perhaps he in fact did not declare thus? [70a] Now, if you say, he did not in fact declare thus, what if he declares, 'It be confirmed unto thee to-morrow'; [3] do we rule, he is unable to annul it for to-morrow, since [by implication] he confirmed it for to-day; [4] or perhaps, since he did not state, 'It be confirmed unto thee to-day,' by declaring, 'It be annulled unto thee to-morrow,' he really meant from to-day? Now, should you say that even so, since he [implicitly] confirmed it to-day, [5] it is as though in force to-morrow too, [6] what if he declares, 'It be confirmed unto thee for an hour?' Do we say, It is as though he declared, 'It be annulled unto thee thereafter'; or perhaps, he in fact did not say thus to her? Should you rule, he did not in fact declare thus, what if he did explicitly annul it? [7] Do we say, Since he confirmed it, he confirmed it [for good]; or perhaps, as he is empowered to confirm and annul it the whole day, if he says, 'It be annulled unto thee after an hour,' his statement is efficacious?—Come and hear: [If a woman vows], 'Behold, I will be a nazirite'; and her husband on hearing it, exclaimed 'And I'; he cannot [subsequently] annul it. [8] But why so? Let us say that

(1) [Or, if he said at one and the same time 'It be confirmed and annulled to thee']. (2) If one marries two sisters in succession, the second marriage is obviously invalid; hence, if one makes a simultaneous declaration of marriage to two sisters, such declaration is entirely null, v. Ḳid. 50*b*. Thus here too, since they could not *both* take effect if pronounced in succession, they are null when pronounced simultaneously. It is therefore as though he has not spoken at all, and he remains at liberty to confirm or annul the vow, as he pleases. (3) Without first asserting, 'It be disallowed thee to-day'. (4) A vow can be annulled only on the day the husband or father hears of it.—Num. XXX, 6-9, 13. (5) Accepting the first alternative. (6) Having confirmed it for the first day, he no longer has the power to annul it; hence his nullification from the morrow is invalid. (7) I.e., it be confirmed to thee for an hour and thereafter annulled. (8) Mishnah, Nazir 20*b*.

his exclamation, 'And I,' referred to himself only [viz.,] that he would be a nazirite, but as for her vow, 'Behold, I will be a nazirite,' he confirmed it [but] for one hour;[1] whilst thereafter, if he wishes to annul it, why cannot he do so? Surely it is because having confirmed it, he confirmed it [for good]!—No. He [the Tanna of that Mishnah] holds that every 'And I' is as though one declares, 'It be permanently confirmed unto thee.'

MISHNAH. IF THE FATHER DIES, HIS AUTHORITY DOES NOT PASS OVER TO THE HUSBAND: BUT IF THE HUSBAND DIES, HIS AUTHORITY PASSES OVER TO THE FATHER. IN THIS RESPECT, THE FATHER'S POWER IS GREATER THAN THE HUSBAND'S. BUT IN ANOTHER, THE HUSBAND'S POWER IS GREATER THAN THAT OF THE FATHER, FOR THE HUSBAND CAN ANNUL [HER VOWS] AS BOGERETH[2] BUT THE FATHER CANNOT ANNUL HER VOWS AS BOGERETH.[3]

GEMARA. What is the reason?[4]—Because the Writ saith, *In her youth, she is in her father's house.*[5]

IF THE HUSBAND DIES, HIS AUTHORITY PASSES OVER TO HER FATHER. Whence do we know this?[6]—Said Rabbah:[7] Because it is written, *And if she be at all to an husband and her vows be upon her:*[8]

(1) Since he merely attached his vow to that of his wife, he must have meant momentarily to confirm the vow. (2) V. Glos. (3) The father can annul his daughter's vow only if a *na'arah* (v. Glos.) (4) That the father's authority is not transmitted to the husband, as it is in the reverse case. (5) Num. XXX, 17: i.e., as long as she is in her youth, she is under parental control. Hence if her father dies, his authority is not transferable. (6) The first question was 'what is the reason thereof', because, granted that the husband's authority is transmitted, as stated in the second clause, why is the father's not? But now the Talmud asks, how do we know that the husband's authority is transmitted? (7) This is alluded to in 68*a*, where the reading is Raba. (8) Ibid. 7. The word for 'being' is repeated, from which it is deduced that two betrothals are referred to. This is preceded by a verse dealing with the father's powers of annulment, and as stated above (p. 217, n. 5), the '*And*' commencing v. 7 combines the two verses, teaching that even in the case of marriage the father may still retain his authority.

[70*b*] hence the [vows made by her] previously to her second betrothal are assimilated to [those made] previously to her first betrothal;[1] just as those made before the first betrothal, the father can annul alone, so also those made before the second betrothal, the father can annul alone. But perhaps this is only in the case of vows which were unknown to the *arus*,[2] but those which were known to the *arus* the father is not able to annul?[3]—As to vows unknown to the *arus*, these[4] follow from *'in her youth, she is in her father's house'*.[5]

IN THIS RESPECT, THE FATHER'S POWER IS GREATER THAN THE HUSBAND'S etc. How is this meant?[6] Shall we say, that he betrothed her[7] whilst a *na'arah*, and then she became a *bogereth?* But consider: [her father's] death frees her from her father's authority, and the *bogereth* stage frees her from her father's authority; then just as at death, his authority does not pass over to her husband, so on puberty, his authority should not pass over to her husband?[8] Again, if he betrothed her as a *bogereth*, surely that has already been taught once, viz., A *bogereth* who tarried twelve months?[9] (Now this is self-contradictory. You say, 'a *bogereth* who tarried twelve months': in the case of a *bogereth*, why twelve months? thirty days are sufficient?[10]—Read: A *bogereth* and one [viz., a *na'arah*] who

(1) I.e., since the verse implies a reference to two betrothals, they are equalized, and therefore the periods preceding them too. The period preceding the second betrothal is of course after the first husband's death. (2) Lit., 'which were not seen by the *arus*'. I.e., the first *arus* died before becoming aware of them. (3) Just as the vows made *prior* to her first betrothal. (4) *Sc.* that the father can annul these alone after the death of the *arus*. (5) Which implies that as long as there is no other authority over her, her father is in authority, and the very least to which this can be applied is to vows of which the *arus* was not aware, hence the deduction from, *'and if she be at all to an husband'* must apply even to vows known to the *arus* before his death. (6) That the husband (*arus*) can annul the vows of a *bogereth*. (7) I.e., by *kiddushin*, making her an *arusah*. (8) Since she was under parental control when she made the vow. (9) V. *infra* 73*b*: there it is seen that the *arus* can annul the vows of a *bogereth*. (10) V. p. 216, n. 1; in the case of a *na'arah* the interval between *kiddushin* (*erusin*) and *nissu'in* might not be more than twelve months; in the case of a *bogereth*, not more than thirty days. After that, even if the *nissu'in* were not celebrated, the *arus* is responsible for her maintenance, though she is still in her father's house.

tarried twelve months.) But still the difficulty remains?[1]—I can answer either that *here* it is specifically taught, whilst there *bogereth* is mentioned because it is desired to state the controversy between R. Eliezer and the Rabbis. Or, alternatively, *bogereth* [there] is specifically taught; but [here], because the first clause states 'IN THIS RESPECT etc.,' a second [contrary] clause IN THIS RESPECT, is added.[2]

MISHNAH. [71a] IF ONE VOWED AS AN ARUSAH, WAS DIVORCED ON THAT DAY AND BETROTHED [AGAIN] ON THE SAME DAY, EVEN A HUNDRED TIMES,[3] HER FATHER AND LAST BETROTHED HUSBAND CAN ANNUL HER VOWS. THIS IS THE GENERAL RULE: AS LONG AS SHE HAS NOT PASSED OUT INTO HER OWN CONTROL FOR [BUT] ONE HOUR, HER FATHER AND LAST HUSBAND CAN ANNUL HER VOWS.[4]

GEMARA. Whence do we know that the last *arus* can annul vows known[5] to the *first arus?*—Said Samuel: Because it is written, *And if she be at all to an husband, and her vows are upon her:*[6] this implies, the vows that were already *'upon her'*.[7] But perhaps that is only where they [*sc.* her vows] were not known to her first *arus,* but those which were known to her first *arus,* the last *arus* cannot annul?—*'Upon her'* is a superfluous word.[8]

(1) Viz., that we know from elsewhere that the *arus* can annul the vows of a *bogereth.* (2) Though really unnecessary here. (3) To a hundred. (4) I.e., that she has never been completely married (with *nissu'in*) and divorced, in which case she would be her own mistress. (5) Lit., 'seen by'. (6) Num. XXX, 7. (7) I.e., before she was betrothed. (8) Because Scripture could state, *now if she be at all to an husband,* then as for her vows, or the utterance of her lips etc. Hence *'upon her'* is added to intimate that the last *arus* can annul vows made during the first betrothal. Now actually the Mishnah may simply mean that if she was betrothed a number of times, the power of annulment always lies with her father and her last husband, and does not necessarily refer to vows made during an earlier betrothal; whilst the phrase *'on that day'* may be due to her father, who of course can annul only on the day he heard her vow. But Samuel assumed that it does in fact refer to such vows, and therefore the

It was taught in accordance with Samuel: A betrothed maiden, her father and her husband annul her vows. How so? If her father heard and disallowed her, and the husband died before he managed to hear, and she became betrothed [again] on the same day, even a hundred times, her father and her last husband can annul her vows. If her husband heard and disallowed her, and before the father heard it the husband died, the father must again annul the husband's portion.[1] R. Nathan said: That is the view of Beth Shammai; but Beth Hillel maintain: He cannot re-annul.[2] Wherein do they differ? [71*b*]—Beth Shammai maintain that even in respect to vows known to the *arus*, his [the husband's] authority passes over to the father; also he [the husband] cuts [the vow] apart;[3] whilst Beth Hillel maintain: Her father and second husband [together] must annul her vow, and the husband does not cut it apart.[4]

The scholars propounded: Is divorce as silence or as confirmation?[5] What is the practical difference? E.g., if she vowed, her husband heard it, divorced and remarried her on the same day:

passage may be understood as though it read, Samuel said: Whence do we know, etc.? Hence this law is ascribed to Samuel rather than to the Mishnah, and consequently the Talmud proceeds to quote a Baraitha in support of Samuel's ruling.

(1) It goes without saying that he must annul his own portion. But the Baraitha teaches that he must also annul the husband's portion, because the latter's action is rendered void by his death. (2) Without the co-operation of the second *arus*. Thus, according to Beth Hillel the second *arus* has a right of annulment over the vows known to the first *arus*, which is in support of Samuel. (3) V. p. 220, n. 4; because he cuts the vow apart, therefore his powers therein are finished when he has annulled it, and consequently, even if she remarries, the father can annul the vow entirely alone, without the co-operation of the second *arus*. (4) Therefore the husband only weakens it; hence he is not finished with it, and so, on remarriage, his authority is transmitted to the second husband (Ran). Asheri, however, explains that the question whether the father needs the co-operation of the second husband is independent of whether the husband cuts the vow apart or weakens the stringency of the whole: it is mentioned here merely because, as was stated on 69*a*, they do differ on this question too. (5) If a woman made a vow, and her husband heard it and divorced her on that day, without first annulling the vow.

now, if you say, it is as silence, he can now disallow her; but should you rule that it is as confirmation, he can not? [72a]—Come and hear: When was it said that if the husband dies his authority passes over to the father? If the husband did not hear [the vow], or heard and annulled it, or heard it, was silent, and died on the same day.[1] Now, should you say that divorce is as silence, let him [the Tanna] also teach, 'or heard it and divorced her'? Since it is not taught thus, it follows that divorce is as confirmation!—Then consider the second clause: But if he heard and confirmed it, or heard it, was silent, and died on the following day, he [the father] cannot annul it.[2] But if you maintain that divorce [too] is as confirmation, let him also state, 'or if he heard it and divorced her.' But since this is omitted, it proves that divorce is tantamount to silence! Hence no deductions can be made from this: if the first clause is exact, the second clause is stated [in that form] on account of the first; if the second is exact, the first is so taught on account of the second.[3]

Come and hear: IF SHE VOWED AS AN ARUSAH, WAS DIVORCED ON THAT DAY AND BETROTHED [AGAIN] ON THE SAME DAY, EVEN A HUNDRED TIMES, HER FATHER AND HER LAST HUSBAND CAN ANNUL HER VOWS: this proves that divorce is the equivalent of silence, for if it is as confirmation, can the second *arus* annul vows which the first *arus* confirmed?[4]—No. This refers to a case where the first *arus* did not hear thereof. If so, why particularly state ON THE SAME DAY? The same holds good even after a hundred days!—This refers to a case where the *arus* did not hear thereof, but her father did; so that he can annul only on the same day, but not afterwards.

Come and hear: If she vowed on one day, and he divorced her on the same day and took her back on the same day, he cannot annul it.[5] This proves that divorce is as confirmation!—I will tell

(1) V. 68*a*, *b*, and notes. (2) The silence of a whole day is the equivalent of confirmation. (3) I.e., one clause must have been taught with exactitude, and the omission of divorce is intentional; but the other has been stated inexactly, for though divorce could have been included therein, it was omitted for the sake of parallelism. (4) Surely not! (5) Now it is assumed that it refers to mere betrothal.

you. This refers to a *nesu'ah*,[1] and the reason that he cannot annul is because a husband cannot annul pre-marriage vows.[2]

MISHNAH. [72*b*] IT IS THE PRACTICE OF SCHOLARS,[3] BEFORE THE DAUGHTER OF ONE OF THEM DEPARTS FROM HIM [FOR NISSU'IN], TO DECLARE TO HER, 'ALL THE VOWS WHICH THOU DIDST VOW IN MY HOUSE ARE ANNULLED'. LIKEWISE THE HUSBAND, BEFORE SHE ENTERS INTO HIS CONTROL [FOR NISSU'IN] WOULD SAY TO HER, 'ALL VOWS WHICH THOU DIDST VOW BEFORE THOU ENTERST INTO MY CONTROL ARE ANNULLED'; BECAUSE ONCE SHE ENTERS INTO HIS CONTROL HE CANNOT ANNUL THEM.[4]

GEMARA. Rami b. Ḥama propounded: Can a husband annul [a vow] without hearing [it]:[5] is, *and her husband heard it*,[6] expressly stated,[7] or not?—Said Raba: Come and hear: IT IS THE PRACTICE OF SCHOLARS, BEFORE THE DAUGHTER OF ONE OF THEM DEPARTS FROM HIM, TO DECLARE TO HER, 'ALL THE VOWS WHICH THOU DIDST VOW IN MY HOUSE ARE ANNULLED'. But he did not hear them![8]—Only when he hears them does he annul them. If so, why make a declaration before he hears?[9]—He [the Tanna] informs us this: that it is the practice of scholars to go over such matters.[10] Come and hear, from the second clause: LIKEWISE THE HUSBAND, BEFORE SHE ENTERS INTO HIS CONTROL, WOULD SAY TO HER [etc.]!—Here too it means that he said, 'When I hear them.'[11]

(1) I.e., when she finally becomes married to him. (2) I.e., in the case of a *nesu'ah*: v. *supra* 67*a*. (3) Lit., 'disciples of the Sages'. (4) Because they are pre-*nissu'in* vows. (5) I.e., can he declare that if his wife has vowed, he vetoes her vows? (6) Num. XXX, 8. (7) That he can annul only if he heard it. (8) The fact that he generalises, 'ALL THE VOWS' proves this. (9) Since his present annulment is, on this hypothesis, invalid. (10) I.e., to mention this at frequent intervals: the daughter, on hearing this, may confess that she has vowed so and so, and then the father really annuls it. (11) According to the reading of our text, this answer differs from the previous. There it was stated that the father can annul the vows only when he hears them, his purpose in generalizing

Come and hear: If one says to his wife, 'All vows which thou mayest vow until I return from such and such a place are confirmed,' his statement is valueless;[1] [If he said] 'Behold, they are annulled,' R. Eliezer ruled: They are annulled. But he has not heard them![2]—Here too [it means] that he said, 'When I hear them.' Why then state it now? Let him disallow her when he hears it?—He fears, I may then be busily occupied.[3]

Come and hear: If one says to a guardian,[4] 'Annul all the vows which my wife may make between now and my return from such and such a place', and he does so: I might think that they are void, therefore Scripture teaches, her husband *may establish it, or* her husband *may make it void.*[5] This is the view of R. Josiah. Said R. Jonathan to him: But we find in the whole Torah that a man's agent is as himself![6] Now, even R. Josiah ruled thus only because it is a Scriptural decree, 'her husband *may establish it, or* her husband *may make it void'*: but both agree that a man's agent is as himself;[7] but he [the husband] did not hear the vows![8] [73a]—Here too it means that he said, 'When I hear of it, annul it.' But when he hears it, let him annul it himself?—He fears, I may then be busily occupied.

Rami b. Ḥama propounded: Can a deaf man disallow [the vows of] his wife? Now, should you rule that a husband can annul without hearing, that is because he is capable of hearing; but a deaf man, who is incapable of hearing, falls within R. Zera's dictum, viz.,

being to induce his daughter to reveal that she had vowed. Here, however, the answer is that this general annulment will *automatically* become valid when the husband hears the vow, and another declaration is unnecessary. The reason for the difference is this: since she became a *nesu'ah,* and entirely freed from parental control, the father will not be in a position to annul her vows when he hears them; hence he cannot annul them in anticipation either. The husband, on the contrary, will have her even more under his authority when she actually vows; therefore his anticipatory veto is valid.

(1) So that he can subsequently annul them. (2) Proving that this is unnecessary. (3) And overlook it; hence the annulment is made now. (4) I.e., one appointed to be in charge of his household in his absence. (5) Num. XXX, 14. (6) Hence the guardian's annulment is valid. (7) So that but for the decree, the annulment would be valid. (8) And if it were necessary for him to hear them before making them void, his authorisation to the guardian would be invalid, since a man cannot invest an agent with authority which he himself lacks.

That which is eligible for mixing, [the lack of] mixing does not hinder its validity; whilst that which is not eligible for mixing, [the lack of] mixing hinders its validity?[1] Or perhaps, *'and her husband heard it'*[2] is not indispensable?—Said Raba, Come and hear: *'And her husband heard'*,—this excludes the wife of a deaf man. This proves it.

The scholars propounded: Can a husband disallow [the vows of] his two wives simultaneously: is the word *'her'* particularly stated, or not?[3]—Said Rabina, Come and hear: Two suspected wives are not made to drink[4] simultaneously, because each is emboldened[5] by her companion.[6] R. Judah said: It is not [forbidden] on that score, but because it is written, *and he shall make* her *drink*:[7] implying, *her* alone.[8]

MISHNAH. [73b] [IN THE CASE OF] A BOGERETH WHO TARRIED TWELVE MONTHS, AND A WIDOW [WHO TARRIED] THIRTY DAYS,[9]—R. ELIEZER SAID: SINCE HER [BETROTHED]

(1) The reference is to a meal-offering, in which the flour was mixed with oil. Not more than sixty *'esronim* (*'isaron*, pl. *'esronim*, is the tenth part of an ephah) could be thoroughly mixed with oil in the vessels used for that purpose. Hence, if a person vowed a meal-offering of sixty-one *'esronim*, sixty were brought in one vessel, and one in another. Whereon R. Zera observed, though the meal-offering is in fact valid even if not mixed with oil at all, it must be capable of being mixed, and therefore sixty-one *'esronim* in one utensil would be invalid. So here too, though it may be unnecessary for the husband actually to hear the vow, he must be physically able to hear it. (2) I.e., the hearing of the husband. (3) Num. XXX, 9, *'but if her husband disallow her'*. I.e., when Scripture uses the singular *'her'* in this connection, does it expressly teach that only one wife can be disallowed at a time, or is no particular emphasis to be laid thereon, the singular being the usual mode of expression? (4) V. Num. V, 2 ff. (5) Lit., 'her heart swells'. (6) The consciousness that another is undergoing the same ordeal emboldens each not to confess. (7) Ibid. 27; In Tosef. Neg. the verse quoted is, *and the Priest shall bring* her *near*, ibid. 16. [MS.M. reads: because it is written *'her'*, the reference either to verse 16 or 19, *'The priest shall cause* her *to swear'*. V. Soṭ. (Sonc. ed.) p. 32. n. 2.] (8) Hence the same applies to vows: in R. Judah's view, two wives cannot have their vows disallowed simultaneously; in the opinion of the first Tanna, they can. (9) V. *supra* 70b.

HUSBAND IS RESPONSIBLE FOR HER MAINTENANCE, HE MAY ANNUL [HER VOWS]. BUT THE SAGES SAY: THE HUSBAND CANNOT ANNUL UNTIL SHE ENTERS INTO HIS CONTROL.[1]

GEMARA. Rabbah said: R. Eliezer and the early Mishnah[2] taught the same thing. For we learnt: A virgin is given twelve months to provide for herself.[3] When the twelve months expire,[4] she must be supported by him [i.e., her *arus*] and may eat *terumah*.[5] But the *yabam*[6] does not authorize her to eat *terumah*.[7] If she spent six months in the lifetime of[8] her husband [the *arus*], and six months in that of the *yabam*,[9] or even the whole period less one day in the lifetime of her husband, or the whole period less one day in that of the *yabam*, she may not eat *terumah*: this is the early Mishnah. But a subsequent Beth din[10] rules: No woman can partake of *terumah*

(1) V. *supra*, 70*b*. (2) 'Early Mishnah' bears various connotations. Sometimes it simply means the earlier view of a particular school, which subsequently gave a different ruling (v. Ḥag. 2*a*, where, however, the term does not occur in the Mishnah itself but is used by an Amora to differentiate between the earlier and the later views of Beth Hillel). Elsewhere it may denote the collection of Mishnaic material made by the 'elders of Beth Shammai and Beth Hillel'; as such it is brought into contrast with the rulings of later Rabbis, e.g., R. Akiba; v. Sanh. III, 4; 'Ed. VII, 2. But it is also used to differentiate between the views of earlier and later Rabbis. Thus, in the present instance, the term connotes the views of R. Tarfon and R. Akiba (v. Keth. 57*a*), with which 'a later Beth din' (v. text *infra*) differed; here, too, the term is so used by an Amora. (3) I.e., to make the necessary preparations for marriage, such as acquiring a trousseau; the reference is to an *arusah*, and twelve months is the maximum that may elapse before the *nissu'in* without either side having legal cause for complaint. (4) While *nissu'in* was still postponed. (5) If the daughter of an Israelite is betrothed to a priest, she may eat *terumah*, as is deduced from Lev. XXII, 11. By a Rabbinical law, however, she is forbidden until after the *nissu'in*: but if twelve months have elapsed, she is permitted. (6) The levir, v. Glos. (7) V. n. 5: on the priest's death she reverts to her former status, and even if there is no issue, so that she is bound to marry the *yabam*, this tie does not permit her to eat *terumah*. (8) Lit., 'in the presence of'. (9) I.e., the *arus* having died within the twelve months. (10) 'Beth din', which is now generally taken to mean a court of law, was originally the court or college which decided on civil and religious questions; (v. *J.E.*, s.v. Beth din.)

until she enters the *ḥuppah.*[1] Said Abaye to him, Perhaps it is not so. The early Mishnah informs us in respect of [her] eating *terumah,* which is [forbidden merely by] a Rabbinical enactment;[2] but as for vows, which are Biblically binding, I may say that it is not so. And you know R. Eliezer's view[3] only in respect to vows for the reason which R. Phinehas said in Raba's name, viz.: Every [woman] who vows, vows conditionally upon her husband's assent.[4] But as for *terumah,* it may well be that though [forbidden only by] a Rabbinical precept,[5] she may not eat thereof.

MISHNAH. [74a] IF A WOMAN WAITS FOR A YABAM,[6] WHETHER FOR ONE OR FOR TWO,[7]—R. ELIEZER RULED: HE [THE YABAM] CAN ANNUL [HER VOWS]. R. JOSHUA SAID: [ONLY IF SHE WAITS] FOR ONE, BUT NOT FOR TWO. R. AKIBA SAID: NEITHER FOR ONE NOR FOR TWO. R. ELIEZER ARGUED: IF A MAN CAN ANNUL THE VOWS OF A WOMAN WHOM HE ACQUIRED HIMSELF, HOW MUCH THE MORE CAN HE ANNUL THOSE OF A WOMAN GIVEN TO HIM BY GOD![8] SAID R. AKIBA TO HIM: IT IS NOT SO; IF YOU SPEAK OF A WOMAN WHOM HE ACQUIRES HIMSELF, THAT IS BECAUSE OTHERS HAVE NO RIGHTS IN HER; WILL YOU SAY [THE SAME] OF A WOMAN GRANTED TO HIM BY GOD, IN WHOM OTHERS TOO HAVE RIGHTS![9] R. JOSHUA SAID TO HIM: AKIBA, YOUR WORDS APPLY

(1) V. Glos. i.e., until the home-taking, v. Keth. 57*a*..—Thus both R. Eliezer in our Mishnah and the early Mishnah maintain that after twelve months they are regarded as completely married: R. Eliezer, in that the husband can annul her vows; the early Mishnah, in that his wife may eat *terumah*. (2) V. p. 231, n. 5. (3) That the period of twelve months establishes *quasi nissu'in*. (4) Though the stipulation is not expressed, in recognition of her dependence upon him, since he maintains her. Hence the same holds good of an *arus* after twelve months, who also must provide for her. (5) This interpretation of the phrase *terumah* of the Rabbis follows Asheri. (6) This is the designation of the widow between the death of her husband and her union with or rejection by the *yabam*. (7) If there is more than one, she waits for all, as anyone may marry or free her. (8) Lit., 'heaven'. The *yabam* acquires his sister-in-law through a Biblical precept. (9) I.e., all the brothers of the deceased have the same rights in her.

TO TWO YEBAMIM: BUT WHAT WILL YOU ANSWER IF THERE IS ONLY ONE YABAM? HE REPLIED, THE YEBAMAH IS NOT AS COMPLETELY UNITED TO THE YABAM[1] AS AN ARUSAH IS TO HER [BETROTHED] HUSBAND.[2]

GEMARA. It is well according to R. Akiba, for he maintains that the bond [wherewith she is bound to the *yabam*] involves no legal consequences;[3] also according to R. Joshua, who maintains that the tie is a real one.[4] But what is R. Eliezer's reason? Even if the tie is a real one, selection is not retrospective?[5]—R. Ammi answered: [The circumstances are] e.g., that he [the *yabam*] made a [betrothal] declaration,[6] R. Eliezer ruling with Beth Shammai that a declaration completely acquires.[7] But R. Joshua says thus: That applies only to one *yabam*, but not to two *yebamin;* for can there be such a case that though when his brother comes he can prohibit her to him by cohabitation or divorce, and yet he [the first] can annul![8] Whilst R. Akiba maintains that the bond

(1) [MS.M.: HER HUSBAND v. *infra* p. 236, n. 3.] (2) The meaning of this is discussed below. (3) Lit., 'there is no real tie'. E.g., in respect of vows this tie gives him no right of veto. (4) Hence, if there is only one *yabam*, he can annul her vows, but not if there are two, since it is not clear which will take her. (5) *Bererah*, a term denoting retrospective validity of a subsequent selection. Cf. *supra* Mishnah 45*b*, v. Glos. Thus, here, when she vows, it is not clear which *yabam* will eventually marry her. [Unlike, however, elsewhere in the Talmud where this principle is debated and gives rise to difference of opinion, its application here would not be retro-active, as we are not considering whether the annulment by one *yabam* before marriage becomes effective *after* marriage, but whether it takes effect immediately. And in regard to this it is taken as axiomatic that there is no *bererah*, as in the case of two *yebamim* it cannot be stated with certainty which of the two will be her husband (cf. Adereth. S. *Ḳiddushin*). The term *bererah* is accordingly used here in a loose sense and in fact does not occur in the parallel passage, Yeb. 29*b*; v. *a.l.*] (6) מאמר in reference to a *yabam* means a formal declaration, 'be thou betrothed to me'. (7) I.e., by means of this declaration she is his wife in all legal respects; hence that *yabam* can annul her vows.—The view of Beth Hillel is that only cohabitation effects this. (8) I.e., even in Beth Shammai's view a declaration is a legal betrothal only if there is but one *yabam*, but not if there are two. Because even after the declaration, if the other cohabited with her or divorced her, she is forbidden to the first.

carries with it no legal consequences. Now, according to R. Eleazar,[1] who maintained that in the opinion of Beth Shammai a declaration is binding only in that it renders her co-wife[2] ineligible,[3] what can be said?[4]—The reference here is to one who had come before Court and been ordered to support her;[5] and [the law] is in accordance with the dictum of R. Phineas in Raba's name: Every woman who vows, vows conditionally upon her husband's assent.

[74b] We learnt: R. ELIEZER ARGUED, IF HE CAN ANNUL THE VOWS OF A WOMAN WHOM HE ACQUIRED HIMSELF, SURELY HE CAN ANNUL THOSE OF A WOMAN GIVEN TO HIM BY GOD! But if it means that he made her a declaration, it is [also] a case of acquiring her himself?—It means that he acquired her himself through the instrumentality of Heaven.[6]

You may [now] solve Rabbah's problem? [Viz.,] in the view of Beth Shammai, does a declaration effect *erusin* or *nissu'in?* You can solve it that it effects *nissu'in;* for if it effects *erusin,* surely we learnt, [In the case of] a betrothed maiden, her father and [betrothed] husband [jointly] annul her vows?[8] Said R. Naḥman b. Isaac: What is meant by 'He can annul [her vows]'? He can annul [them] in conjunction with her father.[9]

(1) An amora; the Tanna in the Mishnah is R. Eliezer. (2) Two or more wives of the same husband are co-wives (*Ẓaroth*) to each other. (3) Lit., 'to reject the co-wife'. In the following case: A, B and C, are three brothers, A and B being married to X and Y, two sisters. If A dies childless and C makes a declaration to X (but does not consummate the marriage), and then B dies childless too, Beth Shammai rule that X, A's widow, remains C's wife; hence Y, B's wife and the would-be co-wife of X, is ineligible to him, since one cannot take in marriage a *yebamah* who is also his wife's sister. Thus we see that Beth Shammai rule that the declaration made by C is *Biblically* valid as betrothal, for otherwise he would be regarded as having become the *yabam* of two sisters *simultaneously,* in which case a different law applies. Thereon R. Eleazar observed, only in this respect did Beth Shammai hold a declaration to be Biblically binding; but should he subsequently desire to free her, a divorce is not sufficient (as it would be had the marriage been consummated), but *ḥaliẓah* too is needed. (4) Since then she is not his wife in *all* respects, why can he annul her vows? (5) If the *yabam* delayed to marry or free her, she could claim support from him. V. Yeb. 41*b*. (6) Scripture in the first place giving him a unique right in her. (7) On the hypothesis that the Mishnah refers to a *yabam* who made a declaration. (8) Whilst this Mishnah merely mentions the *yabam*. (9) Though the Mishnah

It was taught likewise as R. Ammi: If a woman waits for a *yabam*, whether for one or for two,—R. Eliezer ruled: he can annul [her vows]; R. Joshua said: [Only if she waits] for one, but not for two; R. Akiba said, Neither for one nor for two. R. Eliezer argued: If a woman, in whom he has no portion at all until she comes under his authority [by marriage], yet once she comes under his authority, she is completely his;[1] then a woman in whom he has a portion even before she comes under his authority,[2] when she does come under his authority, she is surely completely his! Said R. Akiba, No. If you say this in the case of a woman whom he acquires himself, that is because just as he has no portion in her [before marriage], so have others no portion in her; will you say [the same] of a woman gifted to him by God, in whom, just as he has a portion, so have others too a portion in her! Thereupon R. Joshua said to him: Akiba, your words apply to two *yebamim:* what will you answer in respect of one *yabam?* He replied: Have we then drawn a distinction [in other respects] between one *yabam* and two *yebamim*, whether he makes her a declaration or not? and just as it is in reference to other matters, so it is in reference to vows.[3] Thus did Ben 'Azzai lament, 'Woe to thee, Ben 'Azzai, that thou didst not study under R. Akiba.'[4] How [75a] does this Baraitha support R. Ammi? —Because it states, 'whether he made her a declaration or not.'[5]

does not state it, that is merely because it deals only with the question whether a *yabam* has annulment rights at all, without inquiring into the extent of such rights.

(1) That he may annul her vows either alone (after *nissu'in*) or in conjunction with her father. (2) The *yabam* has a presumptive claim upon her as soon as her husband dies childless. (3) The reference is explained on 75*a*;—hence, since one of two *yebamim* cannot annul, one himself is also unable to annul. Lit., 'wait in attendance upon R. Akiba'. (4) He was so impressed with the keen intellect displayed by R. Akiba in this controversy, that he voiced his regret at not having studied under him.—Ben 'Azzai was a younger contemporary of Akiba, and in spite of this lament he followed R. Akiba in *halachah* and exegesis; whilst his tone towards him is that of a pupil to his teacher. For that reason the amoraim concluded that he was a disciple-colleague. V. Weiss, *Dor.* II, 112. Jer. B.B. IX, 17*b*; Bab. ibid. 158*b*; Jer. Shek. III, 47*b*. (5) Which proves that the former is the case here, as otherwise this is irrelevant.

Alternately, [it follows] from the first clause, which states, 'then when she does come under his authority, she is surely completely his': but if he did not betroth her, how is she completely his? Hence it follows that he had made a declaration to her.

What is meant by 'and just as it is in reference to other matters, so it is in reference to vows'?—Said Raba, It means this: Do you not admit that one is not stoned for [violating] her, as in the case of a betrothed maiden?[1] R. Ashi said, The Mishnah too supports [this interpretation]:[2] THE YEBAMAH IS NOT AS COMPLETELY UNITED TO HER [BETROTHED] HUSBAND AS AN ARUSAH TO HER [BETROTHED] HUSBAND.[3]

MISHNAH. IF A MAN SAYS TO HIS WIFE, 'ALL VOWS WHICH YOU MAY VOW FROM NOW UNTIL I RETURN FROM SUCH AND SUCH A PLACE ARE CONFIRMED,' THE STATEMENT IS VALUELESS; [IF HE SAID] 'BEHOLD, THEY ARE ANNULLED,'—R. ELIEZER RULES, THEY ARE ANNULLED; THE SAGES MAINTAINED, THEY ARE NOT ANNULLED. SAID R. ELIEZER: IF HE CAN ANNUL VOWS WHICH HAVE ALREADY HAD THE FORCE OF A PROHIBITION,[4] SURELY HE CAN ANNUL THOSE WHICH HAVE NOT HAD THE FORCE OF PROHIBITION! THEY SAID TO HIM: BEHOLD, IT IS SAID, HER HUSBAND MAY ESTABLISH IT, AND HER HUSBAND MAY ANNUL IT:[5] THAT WHICH HAS ENTERED THE CATEGORY OF CONFIRMATION, HAS ENTERED THE CATEGORY OF ANNULMENT;[6] BUT THAT WHICH HAS NOT ENTERED THE CATEGORY OF

(1) Even if a declaration was made, her seducer is not stoned: this proves that she is not yet his wife, and therefore the same is true of vows. (2) [That R. Akiba based his argument on the penalty for violation, and consequently that the Mishnah deals with the case where a declaration was made, (cf. Rashi).] (3) [Since he is designated as her husband, this shows that we deal with a case where he made a declaration (Rashi); v. *supra* p. 233, n. 1.] And the reference can only be to the penalty for violation. (4) I.e., after they are made. (5) Num. XXX, 14. (6) Having been made, it can be confirmed, and hence annulled too.

CONFIRMATION, HAS NOT ENTERED THE CATEGORY OF ANNULMENT.

GEMARA. The scholars propounded: In R. Eliezer's view, do they take effect and [then] become annulled, or do they take no effect at all? What is the practical difference? [75*b*]—E.g., if another man makes a vow dependent on this.[1] Now, if you say that [the wife's vows] take effect, the dependence is a real one;[2] but if you say that they take no effect, there is no substantiality in it.[3] What [is the law]?—Come and hear: SAID R. ELIEZER, IF HE CAN ANNUL VOWS WHICH HAVE ALREADY HAD THE FORCE OF A PROHIBITION, SURELY HE CAN ANNUL VOWS WHICH HAVE NOT HAD THE FORCE OF PROHIBITION! This proves that they take no effect at all.—[No.] Is it then stated, which *do* not have the force etc.: WHICH HAVE NOT HAD THE FORCE OF PROHIBITION is taught, [meaning], which have not yet had the force of a prohibition.[4]

Come and hear: R. Eliezer said to them, If where a man cannot annul his own vows, once he has vowed,[5] he can nevertheless annul his own vows before making them;[6] then where he can annul his wife's vows after she vowed, how much the more should he be able to annul them before she vows! Now, surely this means that his wife's [vows] are like his: just as his vows take no effect at all,[7] so his wife's vows too would take no effect at all!—No: each is governed by its own laws.[8]

(1) Lit., 'attached to them'. I.e., if the wife vowed, 'Behold, I will be a nazirite'; and another person exclaimed, 'And I likewise'. (2) Hence the second vow is valid. (3) And the vow made dependent upon the wife's vow is invalid. (4) Yet they may take effect only, however, to be immediately made void. (5) I.e., every person excepting a married woman. (6) By an anticipatory declaration of annulment; v. *supra* 23*b*. (7) If preceded by a declaration of annulment; for if they did take effect, only a Rabbi could grant absolution. Moreover, the anticipatory annulment, forgotten at the time of actual vowing, renders it a vow made in error, which *ab initio* is no vow. Cf. *supra* 23*b*. (8) Though one is deduced from the other, it is not necessary to assume similarity in all respects. An anticipatory annulment of one's own vows prevents them from taking effect at all, whilst if applied to his wife's, they may take effect and become void.

Come and hear: They answered R. Eliezer: If a *miḳweh*,[1] though it raises the unclean from their uncleanness, cannot nevertheless save the clean from becoming unclean;[2] then a man, who cannot raise the unclean from their uncleanness,[3] how much the more can he not save the clean from becoming unclean.[4] This proves that they[5] take no effect at all.[6] [76a] Then consider the second clause: They [the Rabbis] said to R. Eliezer: If an unclean utensil is immersed in order to purify it, shall a clean utensil be immersed, so that on [subsequently] becoming defiled it shall [simultaneously] become clean![7] This proves that they do take effect.[8]—I will tell you: The Rabbis were not clear as to R. Eliezer's standpoint. Hence they said thus to him: What is your opinion? If you maintain that they [the vows] take effect, but are annulled, you are refuted by [the analogy of] a utensil; whilst if you do not hold that they take effect, the *miḳweh* is your refutation.

Come and hear: R. Eliezer said to them: If defiled seeds are rendered clean by being sown in the soil, how much more so if [already] sown and rooted [in the soil]![9] This proves that they do not take effect at all.

(1) A ritual bath, by immersion in which unclean persons or things are purified. (2) I.e., one cannot take a ritual bath to be kept clean, should he subsequently come into contact with defiling matter. (3) Rashi: if a man swallowed an unclean ring and then took a ritual bath, the ring, since it is within him, is not purified, but remains defiled after excretion. (4) If he swallows a clean ring, and then comes in contact with the dead, the ring ought to become unclean, whereas the law is that it remains clean (Ran), v. Ḥul. 71a.—So also, though a husband can annul a vow when made, he cannot before. So cur. edd. and Rashi. Asheri and Ran have a simpler and more effective reading: They replied to R. Eliezer, Let the *miḳweh* prove it, which frees the unclean from their uncleanness, yet cannot prevent the clean from becoming unclean. So also, a husband may annul his wife's vow *after* it has become binding, but not before. (5) Sc. the wife's vows annulled in anticipation. (6) Since they draw an analogy from a *miḳweh*, which cannot prevent a clean man from becoming unclean, it follows that in R. Eliezer's view the husband's annulment prevents the vow from taking effect at all. (7) Surely not. (8) Since they compare it to the prior immersion of a utensil to render it clean *after* it has become defiled. (9) That they certainly cannot be defiled. Thus also vows: if a vow can be annulled when already in force, surely the annulment can operate to prevent it from coming into force!

Now, do not the Rabbis admit the validity of [such] an *ad majus* conclusion? Surely it was taught: I might think that a man can *sell* his daughter when a *na'arah:*[1]—But you can argue *a minori:* if she who was already sold goes free,[2] is it not logical that if not sold yet, she cannot be sold [now]![3] [76*b*]—Yes: elsewhere they do draw an *ad majus* conclusion, but here it is different, because Scripture writes, ***Her husband may confirm it, and her husband may annul it:***[4] [teaching], that which has entered the category of confirmation, has entered the category of annulment; but that which has not entered the category of confirmation, has not entered the category of annulment.

MISHNAH. [THE PERIOD ALLOWED FOR] THE ANNULMENT OF VOWS IS THE WHOLE DAY:[5] THIS MAY RESULT IN GREATER STRINGENCY OR GREATER LENIENCY.[6] THUS, IF SHE VOWED ON THE NIGHT OF THE SABBATH, HE CAN ANNUL ON THE NIGHT OF THE SABBATH AND ON THE SABBATH DAY UNTIL NIGHTFALL. IF SHE VOWED JUST BEFORE NIGHTFALL,[7] HE CAN ANNUL ONLY UNTIL NIGHTFALL: FOR IF NIGHT FELL AND HE HAD NOT ANNULLED IT, HE CAN NO LONGER ANNUL IT.

GEMARA. It was taught: [The period allowed for] the annulment of vows is the whole day. R. Jose son of R. Judah and R. Eliezer son of R. Simeon maintained: Twenty-four hours.[8] What is the reason of the first Tanna?—Scripture saith, [*But if her husband disallowed her*] *on the* day *that he heard it.*[9] And what is the reason

(1) The reference is to Ex. XXI, 7. (2) On attaining the *na'arah* stage. (3) V. Ḳid. 4*a*. This reasoning is exactly analogous to R. Eliezer's. The Talmud interposes that no verse is required. (4) Num. XXX, 14. (5) In which the husband or father learns of the vow. (6) 'Stringency' and 'leniency' are not quite relevant in this connection, the meaning being that by thus fixing a calendar day, i.e., a night and a day, the period for annulment may be shorter or longer, as the case might be. (7) At the close of the Sabbath. (8) Lit., 'from time to time', from the hour the vow is made until the same hour the following day. (9) Num. XXX, 9. By 'day' a calendar day is understood: V. n. 6.

of the Rabbis?—Because it is written, [*But if her husband altogether holds his peace at her*] *from day to day*.[1] But on the view of the first Tanna, surely it is written, *'from day to day'*?—That is necessary. For were [only] *'on the day that he heard it'* [written], I would say, only by day,[2] but not by night; therefore it is written, *'from day to day'*.[3] Now, according to him who cites *'from day to day'*, is it not written, *'on the day that he heard it'*?—That is necessary. For were only *'from day to day'* written, I would think that he can annul her vows from [e.g.,] the first day of one week to the first day of the following;[4] therefore it is written, *'on the day that he heard it'*.

R. Simon b. Pazzi said in the name of R. Joshua b. Levi: The *halachah* is not in accordance with that pair.[5] Levi wished to give a practical decision in accordance with these Tannaim; whereupon Rab said to him, Thus said my dear relative,[6] The *halachah* is not in accordance with that pair. Ḥiyya b. Rab used to shoot arrows and at the same time examine [a person] desirous of absolution;[7] Rabbah b. R. Huna would [repeatedly] sit down and stand up.[8]

[77*a*] We learnt elsewhere: Vows may be annulled[9] on the Sabbath, and absolution from vows[10] may be sought where it is necessary for the Sabbath.[11] The scholars propounded: May vows be annulled on the Sabbath only if it is needed for the Sabbath, or perhaps, even if it is unnecessary?[12] Come and hear: For R. Zuṭi, of the school of R. Papi, learnt: Vows may be annulled [on the Sabbath] only if necessary for the Sabbath. Said R. Ashi: But we did

(1) Num. XXX, 15: v. p. 239, n. 8: the same is implied in *'from day to day.'* (2) I.e., he can annul the vow. (3) Which naturally includes the night. (4) So interpreting the phrase. (5) Viz., R. Jose b. R. Judah and R. Eliezer b. R. Simeon. (6) *Sc.* Ḥiyya b. Rab, his uncle. (7) Ḥiyya b. Rab just having been mentioned, another thing is stated about him, viz., that he took absolution very lightly, granting it even whilst engaged in other pursuits. (8) In the earnestness of his examination, he could not keep in his place. [Cf. *supra* 23*a*. Ran: 'would keep seated or standing', not taking the matter too seriously.] (9) By a husband or father, as the case may be. (10) From a sage. (11) I.e., where the absolution is necessary for the Sabbath. E.g., if one vowed not to eat, which clashes with the joyous spirit of the Sabbath. (12) I.e., does the last condition, 'where it is necessary for the Sabbath,' refer to the whole Mishnah, or only to absolution?—By 'annulment' the annulment by a father or husband is meant.

not learn thus: IF SHE VOWED JUST BEFORE NIGHTFALL, HE CAN ANNUL ONLY UNTIL NIGHTFALL. But if you rule [that he can annul] only when it is necessary for the Sabbath, but not otherwise, why say, UNTIL NIGHTFALL; he cannot annul even by day,[1] since it is unnecessary for the Sabbath?[2]—It is a controversy of Tannaim: [The period allowed for] the annulment of vows is the whole day. R. Jose son of R. Judah and R. Eliezer son of R. Simeon maintained: Twenty-four hours. Now, on the view that [they can be annulled only] the whole of that day, but not thereafter, [it follows that] he can annul them even if unnecessary for the Sabbath;[3] but on the view [that he has] twenty-four hours, [he can annul] only if it is necessary for the Sabbath, but not otherwise.

'And absolution from vows may be sought where it is necessary for the Sabbath'. The scholars propounded: Is that only if one had no time [to seek absolution before the Sabbath], or perhaps even if he had time?—Come and hear: For the Rabbis gave a hearing to the son of R. Zuṭra son of R. Ze'ira [to grant him absolution] even for vows for which there was time before the Sabbath.[4]

Now, R. Joseph thought to rule that absolution may be granted[5] on the Sabbath only by a single ordained scholar, but not by three laymen, because it would look like a lawsuit.[6] Said Abaye to him: Since we hold that [those who grant it] may stand, be relatives, and [absolve] even at night, it does not look like a lawsuit.[7]

R. Abba said in the name of R. Huna in the name of Rab: The *halachah* is that vows may be annulled on the Sabbath. But this is [explicitly taught in] our Mishnah: IF SHE VOWED ON THE NIGHT OF THE SABBATH [ETC.]?[8]—But say thus: The *halachah* is that *absolution*[9] may be sought at night. R. Abba said to R. Huna,

(1) The reference being to a vow made on the Sabbath; v. Mishnah. (2) The vow having been made just before nightfall, it cannot be necessary for the sake of the Sabbath to annul it. (3) Since we cannot abrogate his right of annulment altogether. (4) Lit., 'whilst yet day.' (5) Lit., 'sought'. (6) Three judges are necessary for that, and it must not take place on the Sabbath. (7) Because in a lawsuit the judges must be seated, may not be relatives of the litigants, and it may not take place at night. (8) Which shows that the husband can annul vows on Sabbath. (9) From a Sage.

Did Rab really say thus? Said he, He was silent.[1] Do you say, 'He was silent', or, 'he was drinking'? asked he.[2]—R. Iḳa b. Abin said: Rab gave a hearing to Rabbah [to grant him absolution] [77b] in a chamber of the College, whilst standing, alone, and at night.[3]

Raba said in R. Naḥman's name: The *halachah* is that absolution from vows may be granted standing, alone, and at night, on the Sabbath, by relatives, and even if there was time before the Sabbath [to seek absolution]. 'Standing'? But it was taught: R. Gamaliel descended from the ass, wrapped himself [in his robe], sat down, and absolved him?[4]—R. Gamaliel held that [the Rabbi] must give an 'opening' for regret, so that the vow may be revoked *ab initio;* this requires deep thought; therefore he sat down.[5] But in R. Naḥman's opinion no opening for regret is necessary;[6] therefore he [the Rabbi] can stand.[7]

(1) Heb. אישתיק; this bears a close resemblance to drinking, and R. Abba seems not to have quite caught his reply. (2) So Rashi: Do you mean that you stated this *halachah* before him and that he remained silent, which you interpreted as assent: or that he was drinking at the time, and could make no comment? Other versions, based on different readings: R. Huna asked, Would you offer me a drink, or do you say that he was silent, i.e., do you question me because you agree, and desire Rab's authority for it, or do you disagree, and suggest that Rab was silent when I stated this law, deeming it unworthy even of refutation? Or: do you offer me a drink (in approval), or silence me (in disapproval)? —In all these cases, the alternatives are expressed by words very similar to each other. (3) The former question is left unanswered, but this incident is quoted to show that Rab himself acted on this ruling.—So cur. edd. But other readings introduce this by 'come and hear.' (4) This happened once when R. Gamaliel was travelling from Acco to Chezib. On the way he was accosted by a man who demanded to be absolved from a vow. (5) The Rabbi must find grounds sufficiently strong to make him regret his vow (v. *supra* 21*b*). Such grounds are not easily found. But sitting is not essential for the actual granting of absolution. (6) [Even if he expresses no regret for ever having made the vow, but merely wishes to be absolved from it from now on, the Sage may revoke it; (v. Rashi 'Er. 64*a*).] (7) So cur. edd. and Rashi. Ran and Asheri reverse the reading, though the final result remains unaltered. Thus: R. Gamaliel held that mere (present) regret does not afford an 'opening', i.e., grounds for absolution, but some fact, which, had it been present to the mind of the person vowing, would have caused him to desist, so that the vow may be voided from its very beginning, etc.

Raba said to R. Naḥman: Behold, Master, a scholar, who came from the west [i.e., Palestine], and related that the Rabbis gave a hearing to the son of R. Huna b. Abin and absolved him of his vow, and then said to him, 'Go, and pray for mercy, for you have sinned. For R. Dimi, the brother of R. Safra, learnt: He who vows, even though he fulfils it, is designated a sinner.' R. Zebid said: What verse [teaches this]?—*But if thou shalt forbear to vow, it shall be no sin in thee;*[1] hence, if thou hast not forborne, there is sin.

It was taught: If a man says to his wife, '[In respect to] all vows which you may make, I object to your vowing,' or, 'they are no vows,' the declaration is valueless.[2] [If he says,] 'You have done well,' or, 'there is none like you,'[3] or, 'had you not vowed, I myself would have imposed a vow upon you,'[4]—these declarations are effective.[5]

A man should not say to his wife on the Sabbath, 'It is annulled for you,' or, 'made void for you,' as he would say on week-days, but, 'Take and eat it,' 'Take and drink it,'[6] and the vow becomes automatically void.[7] R. Joḥanan observed: Yet he must annul it in his heart.[8] It was taught: Beth Shammai say: On the Sabbath he must annul it in his heart; on week-days he must express [his

(1) Deut. XXIII, 23. (2) Because it is not the correct way of annulment.—So Rashi, on the basis of our reading, and likewise one version of Ran. (3) An expression of satisfaction. (4) This must not be taken that in Talmudic times the husband could impose a vow upon his wife, the expression merely being one of approval. In the chapter dealing with vows (Num. XXX) the husband is merely given powers of annulment, not to impose vows; in fact, no person is empowered to impose vows upon another; but v. Weiss, *Dor.* 1, p. 15. (5) I.e., they are perfect confirmations, which cannot be withdrawn by subsequent annulment.—'Effective' is followed by two dots(:), which denotes the completion of a subject, the next word commencing a new one. As, however, the next passage is not preceded in our text by 'It was taught' nor by any other word which generally introduces a new passage, it is possible that the dots have crept into the editions in error. But in the version of Ran the next passage is preceded by 'It has been taught' (v. Marginal Glosses to Wilna edition). (6) If she vowed not to eat or drink. (7) To preserve the sanctity of the Sabbath one should not use the same phraseology as of week-days. (8) Formally: 'it is annulled for thee.'

annulment] with his lips. But Beth Hillel say: In both cases he may annul it in his heart, and need not express it with his lips.[1]

R. Johanan said: If a Sage employs a husband's phraseology, or a husband that of a Sage, their pronouncements are invalid.[2] For it was taught: *This is the thing* [*which the Lord hath* commanded]:[3] [this teaches], only a Sage may absolve, but a husband cannot absolve.[4] For I might think, If a Sage, who cannot annul, can absolve, surely a husband, who may annul, can also absolve! Therefore it is stated, [78*a*] '*This is the thing*', [implying] only a Sage can absolve, but a husband cannot absolve. Another [Baraitha] taught: '*This is the thing*', [teaches,] [only] a husband may annul, but a Sage cannot annul. For I might think, If a husband, who cannot absolve, can annul; surely a Sage, who may absolve, can also annul! Therefore it is stated, '*This is the thing*', [implying,] a husband can annul, but a Sage cannot annul. [Further:] It is here stated, *This is the thing;* whilst elsewhere, in connection with [sacrifices] slaughtered without [the Temple Court], it is also written, *This is the thing* [*which the Lord hath commanded*]:[5] just as in the latter case, Aaron, his sons, and all Israel [are included in the law],[6] so does the chapter on vows relate to Aaron, his sons, and all Israel; and just as here, the heads of the tribes [are particularly addressed],[7] so there too [the reference is] to the heads of the tribes. In respect of what law [is this deduced] in the chapter of vows?—Said R. Aha b. Jacob: To teach that three laymen are qualified [to grant absolution]. But is not '*the* heads *of the tribes*' stated?[8]—R. Ḥisda,—others state R. Johanan—answered: [That intimates that] a single

(1) Of annulment, it being sufficient to say 'Take and eat it.' (2) A husband must say, מופר לך 'It is annulled for thee'; a Sage, מותר לך 'It is permitted thee'. [The difference in the phraseology employed by Sage and husband is determined by the distinct function of each. The Sage revokes the vow, rendering it void *ab initio*, whereas the husband annuls it that it may not be binding for the future (Ran).] (3) Num. XXX, 2. '*This is the thing*' implies that the following enactments must be exactly carried out. (4) Absolution by a Sage is deduced from the next verse. (5) Lev. XVII, 2. (6) The verse commences, *Speak unto Aaron, and unto his sons, and unto all the children of Israel.* (7) Num. XXX, 2: *And Moses spake unto the heads of the tribes concerning the children of Israel.* (8) This, in the case of vows, implies the ordained scholars.

ordained scholar [can absolve].[1] For what purpose are the heads of the tribes related to [sacrifices] slaughtered without?—R. Shesheth said: To teach that the law of revocation applies to *hekdesh*.[2] But according to Beth Shammai, who maintained that *hekdesh* cannot be revoked, for what purpose are the heads of the tribes related to [sacrifices] slaughtered without?—Beth Shammai do not admit [the validity of] *this gezerah shawah*. Now, for what purpose is *'this is the thing'* written in the chapter on vows?—To teach that only a Sage may absolve, but a husband cannot absolve; and that only a husband can annul, but a Sage cannot annul. Why is *'this is the thing'* related to [sacrifices] slaughtered without?—To teach that one incurs guilt only for slaughtering [without the prescribed place], but not for wringing [a bird's neck outside].[3]

Then on the view of Beth Shammai, whence do we know that three laymen are valid?[4]—They deduce it from [the teaching reported by] R. Assi b. Nathan. For it is written, *And Moses declared unto the children of Israel the set feasts of the Lord*.[5] Whereon it was taught, R. Jose the Galilean said: The festivals were stated, but not the Sabbath of the Creation[6] with them: Ben 'Azzai said: The festivals were stated, but not the chapter on vows with them. Now, this Baraitha was unintelligible to R. Assi b. Nathan, so he went to Nehardea, before R. Shesheth. Not finding him there, he followed him to Mahuza,[7] and said to him: 'The festivals were

(1) For since the *gezerah shawah* (v. Glos.) based on *'this is the thing'* relates all Israel to vows, whilst *'the heads of the tribes'* specifies scholars, the discrepancy can be reconciled only by assuming that either one ordained scholar or three laymen may absolve.—One layman being insufficient, three (not two) are required, as in the case of a Beth din. (2) V. Glos. I.e., if one consecrates an animal, which is really a form of vow, and then slaughters it without the Temple court, he can be absolved of his vow, thus revoking his consecration, whereby he is found to have slaughtered an unconsecrated animal. (3) The passage reads: *This is the thing which the Lord hath commanded . . . what man that slaughtered an ox . . . and bringeth it not unto the door of the tabernacle of the congregation, etc.; yishhat ('slaughtered')*, implies cutting the throat (cf. *shehitah*). A bird sacrifice was killed by its neck being wrung, Lev. I, 15. (4) Since they reject the *gezerah shawah* by which it is deduced in the Baraitha. (5) Lev. XXIII, 44. (6) Lit., 'the Sabbath of the beginning'. I.e., the Sabbath, so called because God rested on the seventh day. (7) A large Jewish town on the Tigris, where Raba had his academy.

stated, but not the Sabbath of the Creation with them': but the Sabbath is written together with them![1] Furthermore, the festivals were stated, but not the chapter on vows with them, but that is written alongside thereof![2]—Said he to him, It means this: [78*b*] [only] the festivals of the Lord need sanctification by Beth din,[3] but not the Sabbath of the Creation;[4] [further] the festivals of the Lord require an ordained scholar,[5] but absolution of vows requires no ordained scholar, for even a Beth din of laymen [may grant it]. But in the chapter on vows '*the* heads *of the tribes*' is stated!—R. Ḥisda, others state, R. Joḥanan, said: That refers to a single ordained scholar.

R. Ḥanina said: He who keeps silence [when his wife vows] in order to provoke her[6] can annul even after ten days. Raba objected: When was it said that if the husband dies his authority is transferred to the father? If the husband did not hear [the vow], or heard it and was silent, or heard and annulled it and died on the same day. But if he heard and confirmed it, or heard it, was silent, and died on the following day, he [the father] cannot annul.[7] Now, surely it means that he kept his silence in order to vex her?[8]—No. It means that he was silent in order to confirm it. If so, it is tantamount to 'or if he heard and confirmed it?'[9]—But it means that he kept silent without specifying [his intentions].

R. Ḥisda objected: Confirmation is more stringent than annulment, and annulment is more stringent than confirmation. [Thus:] Confirmation is more stringent, [79*a*] since silence confirms, but does not annul;[10] and if he confirms in his heart, he has confirmed it, [whereas] if he annuls in his heart, it is not annulled; [moreover],

(1) At the beginning of Lev. XXIII, v. 3 and also in v. 38. (2) Num. XXVIII-XXIX deal with the festivals, and XXX treats of vows. (3) Beth din must declare which day is new moon, and thereby sanctify it, and thence the festival was calculated. (4) The seventh day of the week is automatically sacred. (5) To declare the sanctification of the New Moon, which cannot be done by a layman. (6) Intending to annul the vow eventually, but keeping silence in the meantime to vex his wife, who may wish to be freed. (7) V. *supra* 68*a*. (8) And yet if he died the following day, his silence is regarded as confirmation. (9) Why teach it in two clauses? (10) Which is viewed as greater stringency.

if he confirmed, he cannot annul, and if he annulled, he cannot confirm.[1] Now, this teaches that silence confirms. Surely it means silence in order to provoke?—No; [it means] that he was silent in order to confirm. If so, it is identical with 'if he confirms in his heart?'—But it means that he was silent with no specified intention.

Now we have seen that confirmation is more stringent than annulment; where do we find that annulment is more [stringent] than confirmation?—Said R. Johanan: One may seek absolution from confirmation, but not from annulment.

R. Kahana objected: *But if her husband altogether hold his peace at her from day to day:*[2] Scripture refers to silence in order to vex. You say, in order to vex. Perhaps this is not so, the reference being to silence with intention to confirm? Now, when it is said, *because he held his peace at her,*[3] Scripture already refers to silence in order to confirm; hence, to what can I apply the phrase, *'but if the husband altogether hold his peace at her'?* To silence in order to vex. That is indeed a refutation.[4] But let one [verse] be applied to silence in order to confirm, and the other to silence without specified intentions?—Additional verses are written.[5]

Raba objected: IF SHE VOWED JUST BEFORE NIGHTFALL, HE CAN ANNUL ONLY UNTIL NIGHTFALL: FOR IF NIGHT FELL AND HE HAD NOT ANNULLED IT, HE CAN NO LONGER DO SO: but why? Let it [at least] be counted as though he were silent in order to provoke her! This is a refutation.

R. Ashi objected: [If the husband declares,] 'I know that there were vows, but did not know that they could be annulled,' he may annul them [now].[6] 'I knew that they could be annulled,

(1) This is not stated as an aspect of greater stringency in one or the other, but merely teaches a law. (2) Num. XXX, 15. (3) Ibid. (4) Of R. Ḥanina. (5) The idea of silence is expressed three times in that verse, *But if her husband altogether keep silence*—expressed in Heb. by החרש יחריש, which is a double expression, and, *because he has kept silence*—a third time; therefore every form of silence is meant. (6) Because only when he knows his authority is the day regarded as *'the day on which he heard it.'*

but did not know that this is a vow,'[1] R. Meir ruled: He cannot annul [now];[2] whilst the Sages maintain: He can annul. But why [not, according to R. Meir]; let it [at least] be as though he were silent in order to provoke! This is a refutation.

(1) Rashi: of a binding nature; Ran· such as the husband may annul, (v. next Mishnah). (2) For since he knew that the husband could annul vows, the day that he first learnt of his wife's vow is the day that he heard it.

NEDARIM

CHAPTER XI

MISHNAH. NOW THESE ARE THE VOWS WHICH HE[1] CAN ANNUL: VOWS WHICH INVOLVE SELF-DENIAL.[2] [E.G.,]. 'IF I BATHE,' OR, 'IF I DO NOT BATHE,' 'IF I ADORN MYSELF,' OR, 'IF I DO NOT ADORN MYSELF.' [79*b*] R. JOSE SAID: THESE ARE NOT VOWS OF SELF-DENIAL, BUT THE FOLLOWING ARE VOWS OF SELF-DENIAL: VIZ., IF SHE SAYS, 'ḲONAM BE THE PRODUCE OF THE [WHOLE] WORLD TO ME', HE CAN ANNUL; 'ḲONAM BE THE PRODUCE OF THIS COUNTRY TO ME,' HE CAN BRING HER THAT OF A DIFFERENT COUNTRY;[3] '[ḲONAM BE] THE FRUITS OF THIS SHOP-KEEPER TO ME', HE CANNOT ANNUL; BUT IF HE CAN OBTAIN HIS SUSTENANCE ONLY FROM HIM,[4] HE CAN ANNUL: THIS IS R. JOSE'S OPINION.

GEMARA. [He can annul] only vows of self-denial, but not if they involve no self-denial? But it was taught: *Between a man and his wife, between the father and his daughter:*[5] this teaches that a husband can annul vows which [affect the relationship] between himself and his wife?—I will tell you: He can annul both; but vows of self-denial he can permanently annul;[6] but if they involve no self-denial, annulment is valid only so long as she is under him, but if he divorces her, the vow becomes effective. [This refers however] to matters affecting their mutual relationship but involving no self-denial; but if they involve self-denial, the vow does not become effective. Now, do vows involving no self-denial become effective if he divorces her? But we learnt: R. Joḥanan b. Nuri said: He must

(1) The husband. (2) Cf. Num. XXX, 13. (3) Hence it is not a vow of self-deprival. (4) E.g., if he must buy on credit, and no other tradesman trusts him. (5) Num. XXX, 17. (6) Even if he subsequently divorces her.

annul it, lest he divorce her and she thereby be forbidden to him.[1] This proves that if he divorces her after first having annulled the vow, the annulment remains valid?—I will tell you: in both cases the annulment stands; but vows of self-denial he can annul in respect of both himself and strangers,[2] whereas if they involve no self-denial, he can annul in respect of himself only, not of others;[3] and it is thus meant: THESE ARE THE VOWS WHICH HE CAN ANNUL in respect of both himself and others, viz., VOWS THAT INVOLVE SELF-DENIAL.

'IF I BATHE.' What does this mean? Shall we say, that she declared, '*Ḳonam* be the fruit of the world to me, if I bathe'? then why annul it? Let her not bathe, and so the fruit of the world will not be prohibited to her! Moreover, could R. Jose maintain in this case that THESE ARE NOT VOWS OF SELF-DENIAL: perhaps she bathes, and the fruit of the world become forbidden to her? [80*a*] Again, if she said, '*Ḳonam* be the pleasure of bathing to me for ever, if I bathe [once]', and the reason he can annul is because what can she do? if she bathes [once], the pleasure of [subsequent] bathing is forbidden her; if not, she becomes repulsive; whilst R. Jose maintains that she need not bathe, her repulsiveness being of no concern to us. But if so, it should be taught thus: R. Jose said: This *condition* involves no self-denial?—Hence she must have vowed, '*Ḳonam* be the pleasure of bathing to me for ever, if I bathe to-day,' R. Jose maintaining that the disfigurement of one day's [neglect of bathing] is not disfigurement.

[80*b*] You have explained, 'IF I BATHE': how is 'IF I DO NOT BATHE' meant? Shall we say that she vowed, 'The pleasure of bathing be forbidden me forever, if I do not bathe *to-day*,' why does she need annulment—let her bathe!—Said Rab Judah: [It means]

(1) If a woman vows that the work of her hands be forbidden to her husband, though the vow, through seeking to deprive the husband of his legal due, is invalid, R. Joḥanan b. Nuri ruled that the husband should nevertheless annul it. For, should he divorce her, the vow becomes valid, and therefore he could not remarry her, v. *infra* 85*a*. (2) I.e., even if she marries another, the annulment holds good. (3) I.e. if he divorces her and she marries another, the vow resumes its force.

that she said, 'The pleasure of bathing be forbidden me for ever, if I do not bathe in the water of steeping.'[1] Then by analogy, 'IF I DO NOT ADORN MYSELF' means, 'If I do not adorn myself with naphtha': but that renders her filthy![2]—Said Rab Judah, She vowed, 'The pleasure of bathing be forbidden me for ever, if I bathe to-day, and I swear not to bathe [to-day]'; 'the pleasure of adornment be forbidden me for ever, if I adorn myself to-day, and I swear not to adorn myself [to-day]'. Rabina said to R. Ashi: If so, the Mishnah should state, THESE ARE THE VOWS and oaths!—He replied: Learn, THESE ARE THE VOWS and oaths. Alternatively, oaths too are included in vows, for we learnt, [if one says,] As the vows of the wicked, he has vowed in respect of a nazirite vow, a sacrifice and an oath.[3]

Now, did the Rabbis rule that bathing involves self-denial when one refrains therefrom? But the following contradicts it: Though all these are forbidden,[4] *kareth*[5] is incurred only for eating, drinking and performing work. But if you maintain that in refraining from bathing there is self-denial, then if one bathes on the Day of Atonement he should be liable to *kareth*?[6]—Raba answered: In each case our ruling is based on the Scriptural context. In reference to the Day of Atonement, where it is written, *Ye shall afflict your souls*,[7] something whereby affliction is there and then perceptible [is implied];[8] whereas [to refrain from] bathing is not an immediately perceptible affliction. But of vows, where it is written, *Every vow and every binding oath to afflict the soul*,[9] something which *leads* to affliction [is indicated],[10] and not to bathe [for a long time] results in affliction.

One ruling of R. Jose contradicts another of his: With respect to a well belonging to townspeople, when it is a question of their

(1) I.e., the water in which flax was steeped; such water is foul and noisome, and it is an act of mortification to bathe therein. (2) Surely 'adorn' would not be used in that sense! (3) V. *supra* 9*a*. (4) Viz., eating, drinking, etc., on the Day of Atonement. (5) V. Glos. (6) Since *kareth* is the penalty for not '*afflicting one's soul*'—i.e., undergoing mortification; Lev. XXIII, 29. (7) Ibid. XVI, 29. (8) E.g., abstention from food. (9) Num. XXX, 14. (10) That follows from the infinitive.

own lives or the lives of strangers,[1] their own lives take precedence;[2] their cattle or the cattle of strangers, their cattle take precedence over those of strangers; their laundering or that of strangers,[3] their laundering takes precedence over that of strangers. But if the choice lies between the lives of strangers and their own laundering, the lives of the strangers take precedence over their own laundering. R. Jose ruled: Their laundering takes precedence over the lives of strangers.[4] Now, if to [refrain merely from] washing one's garment is a hardship in R. Jose's view, [81*a*] how much more so with respect to the body?—I will tell you: In R. Jose's opinion laundering is indeed of greater importance than bathing. For Samuel said: Scabs of the head [caused by not washing] lead to blindness; scabs [arising through the wearing] of [unclean] garments cause madness; scabs [due to neglect] of the body cause boils and ulcers.[5]

They sent word from there [*sc.* Palestine]:[6] Be on guard against scabs; take good care [to study] in company,[7] and be heedful [not to neglect] the children of the poor,[8] for from them Torah goeth forth, as it is written, *The water shall flow out of his buckets* [*mi-dalyaw*]:[9] [meaning], from the *dallim* [poor] amongst them goeth forth Torah.[10] And why is it not usual for scholars to give birth to sons who are scholars?—Said R. Joseph, That it might not be maintained, The Torah is their legacy.[11] R. Shisha, the son of R. Idi, said: That they should not be arrogant towards the community. Mar Zuṭra said: Because they act high-handedly against the community.[12] R. Ashi said: Because they call people asses.[13]

(1) The well being the sole source of supply, sufficient only for the townspeople or for strangers, but not for both. (2) They have a prior right thereto. (3) The water being used for laundering purposes. (4) In his opinion there is great self-denial in wearing unlaundered linen. (5) Madness is the worst of the lot. (6) This always refers to R. Eleazer b. Pedath—Sanh. 17*b*. (7) This ensures greater keeness and understanding than studying alone. (8) Or, not to neglect their teaching (Ran). (9) Num. XXIV, 7. (10) Adopting reading of *'En Yaḳob*. Water being symbolic of Torah: cf. Is. LV, 1. (11) I.e., others should not complain that it is useless for them to study, or that they themselves should not think study unnecessary. (12) *Var. lec.*: because they are arrogant etc. (13) These observations shew that there was a mutual antipathy between

Rabina said: Because they do not first utter a blessing over the Torah.[1] For Rab Judah said in Rab's name: What is meant by, *Who is the wise man, that he may understand this [. . . for what is the land destroyed etc.]*?[2] Now, this question was put to the Sages, Prophets, and Ministering Angels,[3] but they could not answer it, until the Almighty Himself did so, as it is written, *And the Lord said, Because they have forsaken my law which I set before them, and have not obeyed my voice, neither walked therein:*[4] but is not *'have not obeyed my voice'* identical with, *'neither walked therein'?* — Rab Judah said in Rab's name: [It means] that they did not first recite a benediction over the Torah.[5]

Isi b. Judah did not come for three days to the college of R. Jose. Wardimus, the son of R. Jose, met him and asked, 'Why have you Sir, not been for these last three days at my father's school?' He replied, 'Seeing that I do not know your father's grounds [for his rulings], why should I attend?' 'Please repeat, Sir, what he told you,' he urged; 'perhaps I may know the reason.' Said he, 'As to what was taught, R. Jose said: Their laundering takes precedence over the lives of strangers, whence do we know a verse [to support this]? Said he, Because it is written, *And the suburbs of them shall be for their cattle, and for their goods, and for all their beasts [ḥayyatham]*.[6] Now, what is meant by *ḥayyatham:* Shall we say, 'beasts' — but beasts are included in cattle? But if *ḥayyatham* means literally 'their lives', is it not obvious?[7] Hence it must surely refer to laundering,[8] since [neglect of one's clothes] causes the pains of scabs.[9]

the scholars and the masses. Cf. Graetz, *Gesch.* IV, p. 361. It is noteworthy however that, as evidenced by this passage, many Rabbis themselves criticised the attitude of scholars.

(1) As required. (2) Jer. IX, 11. (3) 'And ministering angels' is absent from our text, but added from the parallel passage in B.M. 85*a*. (4) Ibid. 10. (5) This follows since the Almighty Himself had to answer; had they neglected it altogether, the reason would have been patent to all. Hence it must mean that though they studied it, their motives were selfish, and not based on an appreciation of its own intrinsic worth. This is expressed by saying that they did not recite a benediction over it, i.e., they did not value it for itself. Ran. (6) Num. XXXV, 3. (7) That they use it to benefit their own lives. (8) I.e., wells in their suburbs shall be put to this use. (9) And as it is expressed by

R. JOSE SAID: THESE ARE NOT VOWS OF SELF-DENIAL. The scholars propounded: In the view of R. Jose, can he [the husband] annul them as matters affecting their mutual relationship?[1]—Come and hear: R. JOSE SAID: THESE ARE NOT VOWS OF SELF-DENIAL, implying however that they are matters affecting their mutual relationship.[2]—[No.] Perhaps he argues to them on their view. [Thus:] In my opinion they are not even matters affecting their mutual relationship: but you who maintain that they are vows of self-denial, should at least concede to me that these are not vows of self-denial.[3] What [is our decision on the matter]?—R. Adda b. Ahabah said: He can annul them, R. Huna said: He cannot annul, [81*b*] because no fox dies in the earth of its own lair.[4]

It was taught in accordance with R. Adda b. Ahabah: Vows involving self-denial he [the husband] can annul in respect of both himself and herself, and in respect to herself and strangers;[5] but if they involve no self-denial, he can annul in respect of himself and herself, but not in respect to herself and strangers. E.g., if she vows, '*Ḳonam* be fruit unto me'? he can annul: '*Ḳonam* that I prepare nought for my father,' 'for your brother,' 'for your father,' 'for my brother,' or 'that I place no straw before your cattle,' or, 'water before your herds,' he cannot annul.[6] '[*Ḳonam*] that I may not paint or rouge or cohabit,' he can annul as a matter affecting their mutual relationship; 'that I do not make your bed,' or, 'prepare[7] you drink,' or, 'wash your hands or feet,' he need not annul.[8] R. Gamaliel said: He must annul [them], as it is written,

a word meaning life, we deduce that its importance is so great that it takes precedence over the lives of strangers.

(1) For the husband may assert that he personally is affected by his wife's refusal to bathe or adorn herself. On the difference between the grounds of annulment, v. *supra*, 79*b*. (2) For otherwise he should simply state that the husband cannot annul them (Ran and Asheri). (3) So that if you persist in conceding the husband the right to annul, it should be on the grounds of mutual concern, not mortification. (4) I.e., being accustomed to it, he cannot be harmed thereby. Likewise, the husband, being accustomed to his wife, is unaffected by her refusal to bathe. (5) V. 79*b*. (6) Because it is not a vow of mortification, nor is she under any obligation to do these things. (7) Lit., 'mix the cup' (of wine with water). (8) Such vows are automatically invalid, since she is under an obligation to do these things.

he shall not break his word.[1] Alternatively, '*he shall not break his word*' teaches that a Sage cannot absolve himself from his own vows. Now, whom do we know to regard [a vow], 'that I paint not nor rouge' as matters affecting their mutual relationship [and not of self-denial]? R. Jose;[2] yet it is stated that he can annul them as matters affecting their mutual relationship.

The Master said: ' . . . "or cohabit," he can annul as a matter affecting their mutual relationship.' How so? If she vows, 'The pleasure of cohabitation with me [be forbidden] to you', why annul it, seeing that she is bound to afford it to him?[3]—But it means that she vowed, 'the pleasure of cohabitation with you be forbidden me,' and it accords with R. Kahana's dictum, viz., [If she vows,] 'The pleasure of cohabitation with me [be forbidden] to you,' she is compelled to grant it; but if she vows, 'The pleasure of cohabitation with you [be forbidden] to me,' he must annul it, because no person may be fed with what is forbidden to him. Who is the author of what was taught: Things that are in themselves permissible, and yet are treated by others as forbidden, you may not treat them as permitted in order to nullify them? Who is the author?—R. Gamaliel. For it was taught: R. Gamaliel said: He must annul them, as it is written, *he shall not break his word;*[4] alternatively, '*he shall not break his word*' teaches that a Sage cannot absolve himself from his own vows.[5]

Raba asked R. Naḥman: In the Rabbis' view, is [a vow to refrain from] cohabitation [a vow of] self-denial or a matter affecting their mutual relationship?—He replied, We have learnt this: [If she vows,] 'May I be removed from all Jews,'[6] [82*a*] he must annul his own part, and she shall minister to him, whilst remaining removed from all Jews.[7] But if you say that this is a vow of self-denial, why

(1) Num. XXX, 3; i.e., by a Rabbinical decree he must annul it, that she may not treat vows lightly. The law is not deduced from the verse, which is cited merely to shew the solemnity of vows. (2) For the Rabbis of the Mishnah hold it to be a vow of mortification. (3) Hence it is automatically invalid. (4) Just as there, a self-imposed prohibition may not be lightly treated, so here too. (5) Thus the text as amended by BaḤ. (6) That no Jew shall cohabit with me. (7) I.e., if he divorces her.

does she remain forbidden to all Jews?[1] This proves that it is [only] a matter affecting their mutual relationship!—[No.] This is asked according to the Rabbis, whereas 'May I be removed from the Jews' is the teaching of R. Jose [only]. For R. Huna said: This entire chapter states the ruling of R. Jose. Whence is this deduced? Since the Mishnah teaches, R. JOSE SAID: THESE ARE NOT VOWS OF SELF-DENIAL, why state again HE CAN ANNUL: THIS IS R. JOSE'S OPINION? It therefore follows that from this onward [the author] is R. Jose.[2]

Samuel said on Levi's authority: All vows the husband can annul to his wife, except 'my benefit [be forbidden] to so and so,' which he cannot annul.[3] But he can annul [the vow], 'the benefit of so and so [be forbidden] to me.'[4]

We learnt: '[ḲONAM] BE THE FRUIT OF THIS COUNTRY TO ME,' HE CAN BRING HER THAT OF A DIFFERENT COUNTRY?[5] —Said R. Joseph: It means that she vowed, '[ḲONAM BE THE FRUIT OF THIS COUNTRY TO ME] which *you* may bring'.[6] Come and hear: 'ḲONAM BE THE FRUIT OF THIS SHOP-KEEPER TO ME,' HE CANNOT ANNUL?—Here too it means that she said, 'which *you* may bring.' [But does it not state:] BUT IF HE CAN OBTAIN SUSTENANCE ONLY FROM THIS SHOP-KEEPER, HE CAN ANNUL. Now if you maintain that she vowed, 'which *you* may bring,' why can he annul it?[7] Hence, since the second clause must mean [even] those not brought by the husband, the first clause [too must refer to even] what she herself brings?—But in the first clause he cannot annul, though [her vow forbade even what] she herself brings; [82*b*] and our Mishnah states R. Jose's view. For R. Huna said:

(1) Since the husband can annul vows of self-denial. (2) The Talmud leaves the problem unsolved and proceeds to another subject. (3) Not being a vow of mortification; this is self-evident, but is mentioned as a contrast to the next clause. (4) Though she may not be immediately in need thereof, she may need it later, and therefore it is a vow of mortification. (5) If abstention from the produce of an entire country is no mortification, surely to be forbidden benefit from a single person is none! (6) Hence there is no self-denial. But had she entirely forbidden them, it would certainly entail deprivation, and the same holds good if she forbids benefit from a single person. (7) Let some other person, or herself, obtain supplies.

This entire chapter states the ruling of R. Jose. And what is meant by HE CANNOT ANNUL? On the score of self-denial, but he can annul it as a vow affecting their mutual relationship.[1]

Rab Judah said in Rab's name: If she vows [to abstain] from two loaves, [abstention from] one of which is self-denial, but not from the other:[2] since he [the husband] can annul in respect of that which causes self-denial, he can also annul in respect of the other. R. Assi said in R. Joḥanan's name: He can annul only in respect of that which causes self-denial, but not in respect of the other. Others say, R. Assi asked R. Joḥanan: What if she vows [to abstain] from two loaves, [abstention from] one of which is self-denial, but not from the other?—He answered: He can annul in respect of that which causes self-denial, but not in respect of the other. He objected: If a woman made a vow of a nazirite, and drank wine or defiled herself through the dead,[3] [83*a*] she receives forty [lashes].[4] If her husband disallowed her and she did not know that he disallowed her, and she drank wine and defiled herself through the dead, she does not receive forty [lashes]. But if you maintain, He can annul [only] in respect of that which

(1) Because he may find it necessary to maintain his wife with the provisions of that particular tradesman, and by forbidding benefit from him, his wife puts him to inconvenience.—Now, to revert to the subject, since this is the view of R. Jose only, in the Rabbis' opinion he could annul it as a vow of self-denial, in which case the annulment is wider in scope, as stated on 79*b*, and Samuel's dictum is in accordance with the Rabbis (Rashi and Ran). Asheri and Tosaf. explain that there may be two different answers here. Thus: (i) The Mishnah is taught according to R. Jose, whereas Samuel's dictum agrees with the Rabbis. Alternatively, (ii) by HE CANNOT ANNUL is meant that he cannot annul it as a vow of self-denial, but as a vow affecting them both. But Asheri and Tosaf. disagree on the interpretation of (ii). Asheri: and therefore Samuel's dictum may agree even with R. Jose, for Samuel too meant that he can annul it only as a vow affecting their mutual interests. Tosaf.: alternatively, the first clause could accord even with the Rabbis, who agree with R. Jose that this is no vow of mortification, being so limited in scope, yet it may be annulled as a vow of mutual concern, and Samuel too meant it in the same way. (2) E.g., if one loaf was of fine flour and the other of coarse. (3) Both of which are forbidden to a nazirite, Num. VI, 3, 6. (4) The usual punishment for violating a negative injunction. Actually only thirty-nine lashes were given.

causes self-denial, but not in respect of that which does not, perhaps he annulled her vow only in respect of wine, since [abstention therefrom] is a deprivation, but not of the kernels or husks [of grapes], abstention from which is no deprivation; hence let her receive forty?[1]—R. Joseph replied: There is [no state of] semi-*neziruth*.[2] Said Abaye to him: Does that imply that there is a sacrifice for semi-*neziruth*?[3] But, said Abaye, there is no semi-*neziruth*,[4] nor is there a sacrifice for semi-*neziruth*.

An objection is raised: If a woman made a vow of *neziruth*, set aside an animal, and then her husband disallowed her: she must bring the sin-offering of a bird, but not burnt-offering of a bird.[5] But if you say, a sacrifice is not incurred for half [the period of] *neziruth*, why must she bring the sin-offering of a bird?—What then: a sacrifice *is* incurred for half [the period of] *neziruth*—then she should bring *three* animals, [viz.,] a sin-offering, a burnt-

(1) For 'she goes unpunished' implies for no matter which injunction of a nazirite she transgresses. By 'perhaps' etc., 'surely can annul only' is meant. (2) One is either completely a nazirite or not at all. But the vow to abstain from two loaves is divisible. (3) Surely not! Since R. Joseph replied that there is no *state* of semi-*neziruth*, it follows that there may be a *sacrifice* for semi-*neziruth*. E.g., if a woman vowed to become a nazirite, whose duration, if unspecified, is thirty days, and after fifteen her husband learnt of her vow and annulled it. Now, his annulment cancels the following fifteen days, but not the previous, and Abaye expresses his surprise that, as is implied in R. Joseph's answer, the sacrifices are to be offered for half the period of *neziruth*. (4) I.e., that some provisions of *neziruth* shall apply whilst others do not. (5) On the expiration of the *neziruth*, three sacrifices are due, a burnt-offering, a sin-offering, and a peace-offering; Num. VI, 14. If, however, a *nazir* becomes defiled through the dead within his period, he must bring one animal as guilt-offering and two turtle-doves or young pigeons, one as a sin-offering and the other as a burnt-offering, and then recommence the full period afresh; ibid. 10f. Now, this is the meaning of the Baraitha. If a woman made the vow of a nazirite, and separated the animal for a guilt-offering, became defiled, and then had the vow annulled, she must offer only the pigeon sin-offering, but not the pigeon burnt-offering. Tosaf. and Asheri both question the purpose of the clause 'and set aside her animal,' which is apparently irrelevant, and leave the difficulty unresolved. Ran explains that its purpose is to shew that even if she had gone so far as to dedicate her guilt-offering, annulment cancels the *neziruth* retrospectively.

offering and a peace-offering?[1] But after all no sacrifice is incurred for half *neziruth;* whilst, as for the sin-offering of a bird which she must bring, that is because such is due even in case of doubt.[2]

He [further] objected: If a woman made a vow of a nazirite and became defiled, and then her husband disallowed her, she must bring the sin-offering of a bird, but not the burnt-offering of a bird. But if you rule, he can annul [only] in respect of what involves self-denial, but cannot annul that which involves no self-denial, [83*b*] perhaps he disallowed her [only] in respect of wine, [abstention from] which is a real hardship, but not in respect of defilement through the dead, since no hardship is involved?[3]—I will tell you: [The prohibition of] defilement through the dead too involves hardship, for it is written, *and the living will lay it to his heart;*[4] whereon it was taught: R. Meir used to say, What is meant by, *and the living will lay it to his heart?* He who laments will be lamented; he who weeps will be wept for; he who buries will be buried.[5]

(1) Since the annulment by the husband is not retrospective (v. *supra* p. 244, n. 1) the short period in which she practised *neziruth* stands and is for her regarded as the whole, at the termination of which the three animals enumerated above are due. Cf. Num. VI, 13: *And this is the law of the nazirite, when the days of his separation are fulfilled* etc. Since her husband annulled the vow, her days are fulfilled by whatever period she observed. (2) E.g., if a pregnant woman miscarried, and it is unknown whether the fetus had attained viability, in which case the sacrifices of childbirth are due, or not, she must bring a fowl sin-offering. Since this sacrifice is brought even for a doubtful liability, she must also bring it here for the sin of having vowed to be a nazirite; cf. 10*a*. (3) On 'perhaps etc.' v. p. 258, n. 1. Hence in spite of the annulment she ought to complete the full period and then offer the usual sacrifices. Tosaf. objects that the same answer could be given here as above, viz., there is no state of semi-*neziruth;* and replies that this perhaps holds good only of the kernels and husks of grapes, and everything appertaining thereto. But the prohibition of defilement is quite distinct from that of wine, (as is illustrated by a Samson nazirite. V. Nazir 4*a*) and therefore one may exist without the other. (4) Ecc. VII, 2. (5) I.e., one who pays the last respects to the dead will be similarly honoured, and, by implication, he who refrains will be likewise treated with contempt. It is therefore a matter of self-denial to abstain from death defilement, since thereby one forfeits the respects of his fellow-men at his own death.

MISHNAH. [IF SHE VOWS], 'ḲONAM, IF I MIGHT BENEFIT FROM MANKIND,'[1] HE CANNOT ANNUL,[2] AND SHE CAN BENEFIT FROM THE GLEANINGS, FORGOTTEN SHEAVES, AND PE'AH.[3] [IF A MAN SAYS] 'ḲONAM BE THE BENEFIT WHICH PRIESTS AND LEVITES HAVE FROM ME,' THEY CAN SEIZE [THEIR DUES] AGAINST HIS WILL.[4] [BUT IF HE VOWS,] 'ḲONAM BE THE BENEFIT THESE PRIESTS AND LEVITES HAVE FROM ME,' OTHERS TAKE [THE DUES].

GEMARA. Thus we see that she may derive her sustenance from his [her husband's goods],[5] thus proving that her husband is not included in 'MANKIND' [in the sense of her vow]. Then consider the second clause: AND SHE CAN BENEFIT FROM THE GLEANINGS, FORGOTTEN SHEAVES, AND PE'AH; but she may not eat of her husband's, which proves that he is included in 'MANKIND'?—Said 'Ulla: After all, the husband is not included, and [the Mishnah] teaches thus: *moreover,* he cannot annul because SHE CAN BENEFIT FROM THE GLEANINGS, FORGOTTEN SHEAVES, AND PE'AH.[6] Raba said: In truth, the husband is included in 'mankind', and [the second clause] states a reason. [Thus:] Why cannot he annul?[7] Because SHE CAN BENEFIT FROM THE GLEANINGS, FORGOTTEN SHEAVES, AND PE'AH.[8]

(1) Lit., 'creatures'. (2) Discussed in the Gemara. (3) These are free to all. Since these are *hefḳer* (v. Glos.), she does not benefit from mankind in taking them. (4) Since these belong to them, he cannot prohibit them. (5) As otherwise it is certainly a vow of self-denial, which he may annul. It is now assumed that 'AND SHE CAN .... PE'AH' does not give the reason why he cannot annul, but is an independent statement. For surely abstention from all mankind, including her husband, is no less deprivation than abstention from a tradesman from whom alone the husband can obtain supplies, which is regarded as mortification (v. *supra 79b*), though there too recourse might be had to gleanings, etc.! (Ran.). (6) I.e., in the first place he cannot annul because his own substance is available to her, but an additional reason is that SHE CAN, etc. This furnishes a reason only when taken in conjunction with the first, but not independently (Ran. v. n. 5). (7) Seeing that she cannot benefit even from her husband. (8) As for the argument in n. 5, Raba will maintain that abstention from a tradesman from whom alone the husband can obtain supplies constitutes mortification only in winter, when gleanings, etc. are not available (Ran).

R. Naḥman said: In truth, the husband is not included in 'MANKIND', and the Mishnah teaches thus: if she was divorced, SHE CAN BENEFIT FROM THE GLEANINGS, FORGOTTEN SHEAVES, AND PE'AH.[1] [84a] Raba objected before R. Naḥman: Now, is the husband not included in the term 'MANKIND'? But we learnt: [If she vows,] 'May I be removed from all Jews,' he must annul his own portion therein, and she shall minister unto him, whilst remaining removed from all Jews.[2] But if you say that the husband is not included in MANKIND,[3] it is a vow of self-denial, which he should permanently annul?[4]—Here it is different, because it is obvious that she forbids to herself [primarily] what is [normally] permitted.[5]

SHE CAN BENEFIT FROM THE GLEANINGS, FORGOTTEN SHEAVES, AND PE'AH. Now the poor tithe is not included;[6] but it was taught in the Baraitha: And [she can benefit] from the poor tithe?—Said R. Joseph: That is no difficulty: one [teaching] agrees with R. Eliezer, the other with the Rabbis. For we learnt, R. Eliezer said: One need not designate the poor-tithe of *demai*;[7] [84b] whilst the Sages say: He must designate [it], but need not separate it.[8] Now surely he who maintains that the doubt[9] renders it

(1) I.e., though the husband is not included when she vows, he *is* after divorcing her, and then she must have recourse to gleanings, etc. (2) If she is divorced or becomes a widow. *Infra* 90a. (3) [The terms 'Jews' and 'mankind' are taken to denote the same thing in relation to the husband.] (4) For if the husband is not included in 'mankind', her vow cannot refer to cohabitation, which is forbidden in any case, but to benefit in general, and hence is a vow of mortification, which he can permanently annul (as stated on 79b); why then state 'whilst remaining removed from all Jews,' which, on this hypothesis, means that she may never benefit from them. So cur. edd. and as rendered by Asheri. Ran, Tosaf. and the chief reading of Asheri are much simpler: But if the husband is not included in mankind, why annul his own portion therein, seeing that the vow never referred to him? (5) Hence she must have meant her husband too, it being altogether unlikely that her vow bore reference to after divorce. But normally the term does not include her husband. (6) In the third and sixth years of the septennate a tithe was separated for the poor, the owner of the field giving it directly to whomsoever of the poor he pleased. (7) V. next note. (8) *Demai*, lit., 'of what (nature),' 'dubious' is the technical term for produce bought from a person who is not trusted to render the tithes, generally the *'am ha-areẓ*; (v. Glos.) such produce had to be tithed by the

tebel,[1] also holds that he [the owner] possesses the goodwill thereof,[2] and that being so, he may not benefit [her].[3] Whilst he who maintains that no designation is necessary, is of the view that the doubt does not render it *tebel;*[4] and wherever the doubt does not render it *tebel*, he [the owner] enjoys no goodwill therein,[5] and therefore she may benefit therefrom.[6] Said Abaye to him: [No.] All agree that the doubt renders it *tebel*, but R. Eliezer and the Rabbis differ in this: R. Eliezer maintains that the *'amme ha-arez* are not suspected of withholding the poor tithe, since should he renounce the title to his property and thus become a poor man, he may take [the tithe] himself; hence he suffers no loss.[7] But the Rabbis hold that no one will renounce ownership of his property, for he fears that another may acquire it;[8] therefore they are suspected.[9] Raba said: Here

purchaser. R. Eliezer maintains that it is unnecessary to designate any portion thereof as the poor tithe, because even if the first owner has definitely not separated the poor tithe the produce is permitted. But the Sages hold that as long as the poor tithe has not been separated the produce may not be eaten; therefore, since the original owner is under suspicion, he must designate the poor tithe himself, i.e., declare, 'this part of the produce is the poor tithe.' On the other hand, he is not compelled to give it to the poor, as he can challenge them, 'Prove that the first owner did not render the poor tithe.' (9) Whether the poor tithe has been set aside or not.

(1) V. Glos. (2) I.e., the owner can give the poor tithe to whomsoever of the poor he wishes. (3) For the owner confers a definite benefit upon the person of his choice, since he could have given it to some other. Consequently, if a woman vows not to benefit from all mankind, she cannot take the poor tithe. (4) Actually, according to this view, even if the poor tithe has definitely not been separated, it is not *tebel;* but since the discussion refers to *demai*, the doubt is mentioned. (5) But *must* give it to the first poor man who applies. The interdependence of goodwill and *tebel* is deduced from Scripture. (6) Lit., 'one'. For she does not benefit from the owner, but takes it in virtue of her own right. (7) It is assumed that no person transgresses a law which he can observe without loss to himself. Hence there is no fear that the *'am ha-arez* does not separate the poor-tithe. For he can designate part of the produce as poor tithe, formally renounce ownership of all his possessions, acquire the tithe, and then reacquire their possessions. Therefore when one purchases cereals from an *'am ha-arez*, he may assume that the poor tithe has been separated, or that by formally renouncing ownership the peasant has exempted it. (8) For such renunciation had to be in the presence of witnesses, *supra* 45*a*, one of whom might forestall the first owner and acquire it himself. (9) Since Abaye had

[the Mishnah] refers to the poor tithe distributed in the [owner's] house,[1] in connection wherewith 'giving' is mentioned, [viz.,] *and thou shalt give it unto the Levite, the stranger, etc.;*[2] therefore one [who vows not to benefit from mankind] may not benefit therefrom.[3] Whilst there [in the Baraitha] the reference is to the poor tithe distributed in the threshing floor; since it is written thereof, *And thou shalt leave it at thy gates,*[4] one may benefit therefrom.

'KONAM BE THE BENEFIT PRIESTS AND LEVITES HAVE FROM ME,' THEY CAN SEIZE, ETC. Thus we see that goodwill benefit has no monetary value.[5] Then consider the last clause: [BUT IF HE VOWS]. 'KONAM BE THE BENEFIT THESE PRIESTS AND LEVITES HAVE FROM ME,' OTHERS TAKE [THE DUES]: but not these, thus proving that goodwill benefit has monetary value?—Said R. Hoshaia:[6] There is no difficulty: the one [clause] accords with Rabbi, the other with R. Jose son of R. Judah. For it was taught: If one steals his neighbour's *ṭebel* and consumes it, he must pay him the value of the *ṭebel*:[7] that is Rabbi's ruling. R. Jose son of R. Judah said: He must pay him only for the value of its *ḥullin*. Now presumably they differ in this: [85a] Rabbi holds that goodwill benefit has money value, whilst R. Jose son of R. Judah holds that goodwill benefit has no money value.[8]—No. All agree that goodwill benefit has no monetary value, but here they disagree over unseparated [priestly] dues.[9] But since goodwill benefit has

refuted R. Joseph's answer, the difficulty remains, and Raba proceeds to dispose of it.

(1) If for any reason the poor tithe was not distributed in the threshing floor, as it should have been, it must be done in the house. (2) Deut. XXVI, 12. (3) For '*thou shalt give*' implies that the owner possesses disposal rights therein. (4) Ibid. XIV, 28; this implies that it must be left for whomever wishes to take it, and that the owner cannot allot it to any one in particular. (5) Since the priest and Levites, who may not benefit from him, can seize the dues against his wishes, though he possesses the right of disposing of them at will. (6) *Var. lec.*: Joseph. (7) I.e., the value of the *ḥullin* (v. Glos.) it contains and the monetary value of his disposal rights over the *terumah* and tithes therein. (8) Hence the first clause of the Mishnah under discussion agrees with R. Jose b. R. Judah, and the second with Rabbi. (9) Rabbi regards the whole as *ḥullin*, whilst R. Jose b. R. Judah maintains that since they would have had to be separated eventually, they are regarded as though already removed from the whole, and therefore he must pay only for its *ḥullin*.

no monetary value, what does it matter whether they have been separated or not?[1]—But this is Rabbi's reason: the Rabbis penalised the thief, that he may not steal; whereas R. Jose son of R. Judah maintains that the Rabbis penalised the owner, that he should not delay with his *ṭebel*.[2] Raba said:[3] *Terumah* is different, this being the reason that they can take it against his will: for *terumah* is fit only for priests, and since he came and forbade it to them, he rendered it just like dust.[4]

MISHNAH. [IF SHE VOWS,] 'ḲONAM THAT I DO NOT AUGHT FOR[5] MY FATHER,' 'YOUR FATHER,' 'MY BROTHER,' OR, 'YOUR BROTHER,' [THE HUSBAND] CANNOT ANNUL IT. 'THAT I DO NOT AUGHT FOR YOU,' HE NEED NOT ANNUL.[6] R. AKIBA SAID: HE MUST ANNUL IT, LEST SHE EXCEED HER OBLIGATIONS.[7] R. JOḤANAN B. NURI SAID: HE MUST ANNUL IT, LEST HE DIVORCE HER AND SHE THEREBY BE FORBIDDEN TO HIM.

GEMARA. Samuel said: The *halachah* is as R. Joḥanan b. Nuri. Shall we say that in Samuel's opinion a man can consecrate that which is non-existent?[8] But the following contradicts it: If a man consecrates his wife's handiwork [which she *will* produce], [85*b*]

(1) Since they must eventually be separated. (2) But render its dues immediately after harvesting. He therefore receives a payment only for its *ḥullin*. Presumably he is nevertheless required to render the priestly dues or their value on the stolen produce. (3) In reconciling the discrepancy between the two clauses. (4) I.e., entirely valueless, as far as he is concerned, and therefore the priests can take it. (5) Lit., 'for the mouth'. (6) Since she is bound to work for him. (7) The amount of work she is obliged to do for him is prescribed in Keth. 64*b*. Her vow is valid in respect of everything above that, and therefore the husband must annul the vow. (8) Lit., 'a thing that has not come into the world'. For the prohibition of a vow is a manner of consecration, v. p. 105, n. 8. Now, according to R. Joḥanan b. Nuri that prohibition is effective in respect of anything she may do after he divorces her, though as yet she is neither divorced nor has she produced anything: hence, just as a vow is valid in respect of the non-existent, so is consecration too, and since Samuel accepts this ruling as the *halachah*, it must be his view too.

she may work and provide for herself, and as for the surplus, R. Meir[1] rules that it is *hekdesh*.[2] R. Johanan the sandal-maker ruled that it is *hullin*.[3] Whereon Samuel said: The *halachah* is as R. Johanan the sandal-maker, thus proving that a man cannot consecrate the non-existent. And should you reply that he ruled that the *halachah* is as R. Johanan b. Nuri only in respect of the excess;[4] then he should have said, The *halachah* is as R. Johanan b. Nuri in respect of the excess, or, the *halachah* is as the first Tanna,[5] or, the *halachah* is not as R. Akiba?—But, said R. Joseph, *konamoth*[6] are different: since a man can interdict his neighbour's fruit to himself, he can prohibit to himself the non-existent.[7] Said Abaye to him: It is proper that one may prohibit his neighbour's fruit to himself, since he can forbid his own fruit to his neighbour: but shall he forbid the non-existent to his neighbour, seeing that he cannot interdict his neighbour's fruit to his neighbour![8]—But, said R. Huna the son of R. Joshua, it means that she vowed, 'My hands be consecrated in respect of what they may produce';[9] [the vow is valid even after divorce,] because her hands are already in existence. But if she vowed thus, would they be consecrated [and forbidden]? surely her hands are pledged to her husband.[10] She vowed, 'When he divorces me.' But now at least she is not divorced: how then do you know that such a declaration is valid? [86*a*]—Said R. Elai: What if a man declares to his neighbour, 'Let

(1) *Var. lec.*: Tarfon. (2) Because one can consecrate the non-existent. (3) He holds that one cannot consecrate the non-existent. (4) For since R. Johanan b. Nuri rejects R. Akiba's reason, it follows that in his opinion the surplus belongs to the husband, not to the wife. (5) Who also holds that the excess belongs to the husband, since he maintains he need not annul. (6) I.e., prohibitions, arising as a result of vows, v. *supra* p. 105, n. 8. (7) For in real consecration one cannot consecrate his neighbour's property. (8) Abaye objects that the analogy is defective. For in both cases cited by R. Joseph, viz., prohibiting his neighbour's produce and prohibiting the non-existent to himself, there is when vowing one element of the vow under his control—himself. But if a woman interdicts her earnings to her husband, neither her husband nor her future earnings are in her control when she vows. (9) So that whatever my hands produce shall be forbidden. (10) And since the vow cannot take immediate effect, it cannot become effective after divorce.

this field which I am selling you be consecrated when I buy it back from you',—is it not consecrated?[1] R. Jeremiah demurred to this: How compare! [In the case of] 'Let this field which I sell you [etc.],' it is *now* in his possession; but is it in a woman's power to consecrate the work of her hands?[2] This is [rather] to be compared only to a man who says to his neighbour, 'Let this field, which I have sold to you, be consecrated when I repurchase it from you,'—is it consecrated?[3] R. Papa demurred to this: How compare! In the case of purchase the matter is definitely closed;[4] but as for a woman, is the matter definitely closed?[5] This can only be compared to a man who declares to his neighbour, 'Let this field, which I have mortgaged to you, be consecrated when I redeem it from you',—is it not consecrated? R. Shisha the son of R. Idi demurred to this: How compare! As for the field, it is in his power to redeem it; but does it lie with a woman to be divorced? This is [rather] to be compared to one who says to his neighbour, 'Let this field, which I have mortgaged to you for ten years, be consecrated on its redemption,' —is it not consecrated?[6] R. Ashi demurred to this: How compare! There is a definite term [for redemption]; has then a woman a definite term [when she can encompass her divorce]?[7] [86*b*] But, said R. Ashi, *ḳonamoth* are different, since they have the force of intrinsic sanctity;[8] and [it is] in accordance with Raba's dictum,

(1) Surely it is! So here too the vow is valid in respect of a future state though it is not valid when made. (2) Obviously not. (3) Surely not. Thus, he argued, this analogy proves on the contrary that the woman's vow is invalid. (4) Neither the field nor its produce belongs, for the time being, to the vower. (5) For her body at least still belongs to herself. (6) Surely it is, though it cannot be redeemed before a certain date; so in the case of a woman too, though she cannot procure her divorce. As far as actual law is concerned this Rabbi agrees with the preceding: he merely varies the analogy for the sake of greater accuracy, though the result is the same. (7) Obviously not; hence it should follow that her vow is invalid. (8) Lit., 'bodily sanctity'. I.e., of objects consecrated in themselves, and which are offered on the altar; these are irredeemable. The term is opposed to 'monetary consecration,' i.e., objects which are consecrated so that they may be redeemed and their redemption money dedicated to Temple Service. As seen above (p. 105, n. 8), *ḳonam* is really a form of consecration, and it is here stated that its prohibition is as strong as that which is intrinsically consecrated.

For Raba said: *Hekdesh*,[1] [the prohibition of] leaven, and manumission [of a slave] release from [the burden of] mortgage.[2] If so, why state LEST HE DIVORCE HER?[3]—Learn: *moreover*, LEST HE DIVORCE HER.[4]

MISHNAH. IF HIS WIFE VOWED, AND HE TOUGHT THAT HIS DAUGHTER HAD VOWED, OR IF HIS DAUGHTER VOWED AND HE THOUGHT THAT HIS WIFE HAD VOWED; IF SHE TOOK THE VOW OF A NAZIRITE, AND HE THOUGHT THAT SHE HAD VOWED [TO OFFER] A SACRIFICE, OR IF SHE VOWED [TO OFFER] A SACRIFICE, AND HE THOUGHT THAT SHE VOWED A NAZIRITE VOW; IF SHE VOWED [TO ABSTAIN] FROM FIGS, AND HE THOUGHT THAT SHE VOWED FROM GRAPES, OR IF SHE VOWED [TO ABSTAIN] FROM GRAPES AND HE THOUGHT THAT SHE VOWED FROM FIGS,[5] HE MUST ANNUL [THE VOW] AGAIN.

GEMARA. Shall we say that ['*if her husband*] *disallow her*'[6] is

(1) V. Glos. (2) If one pledges an unblemished animal for repayment of a debt, and then consecrates it, the intrinsic sanctity it acquires liberates it from the bond and the creditor cannot seize it in payment. Similarly, if one pledges leaven to a Gentile, the advent of Passover and the resultant prohibition cancels the pledge, and the Jew is bound to destroy it, like any other leaven. Likewise, if one mortgages a slave and then manumits him, he is released from the pledge, and the creditor cannot take him on payment. Hence, if a woman declares her hands *konam*, she thereby destroys their pledged character, and the vow is valid. (3) For according to this the vow is valid even before. (4) I.e., actually the vow is valid even now, since *konam* has the force of intrinsic consecration. But should you dispute this, for the Rabbis strengthened the husband's rights, so that not even *konam* may cancel them, the husband must still annul the vow, lest he divorce her. The objections raised above to the assumption that the vow has after-divorce validity are now inapplicable. Since in fact the vow should be valid immediately, but that the Rabbis, by a special decree, strengthened the husband's rights and rendered it valid, it follows that on divorce the law is restored to its proper basis.—In Keth. 59*b* the text reads: 'the Rabbis strengthened the husband's rights, so that the consecration should not be valid from now'; and the reading of Rashi, Tosaf. and Asheri is the same here too. Cur. edd., however, and also Ran, have the reading as given. (5) And on these assumptions he annulled the vow. (6) Num. XXX, 9.

precisely meant?[1] [87a] But what of the rents [for the dead], concerning which, *for* . . . *for* . . . is written, viz., [*Then David took hold on his clothes and rent them* . . .] for *Saul and* for *Jonathan his son:*[2] yet it was taught: If he was informed that his father had died, and he rent [his garments], and then it was discovered that it was his son, he has fulfilled the duty of rending?[3]—I will tell you: there is no difficulty. The one [teaching] refers to an unspecified action; the other to a specified one.[4] And it was taught [likewise]:[5] If he was informed that his father had died, and he rent his garments, and then it was discovered to be his son, he did not fulfil the duty of rending. If he was told that a relation of his had died, and thinking that it was his father, he rent [his garments], and then it was discovered to be his son, he fulfilled the duty of rending.[6] R. Ashi said: The one means [that he realised his error] within the period of an utterance;[7] the other, [that he realised it] after the period of an utterance. ([Thus:] Your ruling that his duty of rending is fulfilled holds good when it is discovered to be his son within the period of an utterance, whilst your ruling that his obligation remains unfulfilled is [if he learnt it] after such period of an utterance.)[8] And it was taught likewise: If one has an invalid

(1) I.e., he must intend to disallow *her*, not a different person. (2) II Sam. I, 11f. The repetition of '*for*' implies that he made a rent for each specifically. (3) Though it appears from the verse quoted that the rent must be for a particular person; the same then should hold good of annulment of vows. (4) I.e., the Baraitha means that he rent his garment without specifying for whom (v. Tosaf.), but in the Mishnah he explicitly designated the wrong person. (5) והתניא, v. note 6. (6) Thus if he had explicitly rent his garments for the wrong person, his obligation is unfulfilled; but not if his error was a mental one only. [Some texts omit the last clause. The Baraitha just cited is thus regarded as contradictory to the first. On this reading והתניא (v. n. 5) introduces a question and is to be rendered 'But was it not taught'. V. Asheri, 4a.) (7) I.e., almost immediately after he rent his garments, within the time that it would take to make an utterance, e.g., a greeting, v. Nazir 20b. (8) [On this reading, which is that of cur. edd., R. Ashi's main object is to reconcile the two Baraithas (v. n. 6), though his distinction in regard to the time when the error was discovered might serve also to explain our Mishnah (Ran). Some texts; however, omit the bracketed passage. On this latter reading R. Ashi's reply is intended solely to reconcile our Mishnah and the first cited Baraitha; v. Asheri, cur. edd. which

in his house, who falls into a swoon and appears to be dead, and he rends his garments, and then he [the invalid] dies, his duty of rending is unfulfilled.[1] Said R. Simeon b. Pazzi in the name of R. Joshua b. Levi on the authority of Bar Ḳappara. This was taught only if he died after the period of an utterance; but [if he died] within the period of an utterance, he need not rend his garments again.[2] Now, the law is that [that which follows an action] within the period of an utterance is as [though it were simultaneous with] the utterance,[3] except in the case of blasphemy, idolatry, betrothal and divorce.[4]

MISHNAH. IF SHE VOWS, 'ḲONAM, IF I TASTE THESE FIGS AND GRAPES,' AND HE [THE HUSBAND] CONFIRMS [THE VOW] IN RESPECT OF FIGS, THE WHOLE [VOW] IS CONFIRMED; IF HE ANNULS IT IN RESPECT OF FIGS, IT IS NOT ANNULLED, UNLESS HE ANNULS IN RESPECT OF GRAPES TOO. IF SHE VOWS, 'ḲONAM IF I TASTE FIGS' AND 'IF I TASTE GRAPES', THEY ARE TWO DISTINCT VOWS.[5]

GEMARA. Who is the author of our Mishnah?—R. Ishmael. For it was taught: *Her husband may confirm it, or her husband may make it void:*[6] if she vows, '*Ḳonam*, if I taste these figs and grapes', and he [the husband] confirms [the vow] in respect of figs, the whole vow is confirmed; [87*b*] but if he annulled it in respect of figs, it[7] is not annulled, unless he annuls in respect of the grapes too: this is R. Ishmael's opinion. R. Akiba said: Behold, it is written,

retain the 'last clause' (v. n. 6) and this bracketed passage, present, on the view of Asheri, a conflated text.]

(1) Since he was alive when the garments were rent, that rending is invalid. (2) So the text as emended by BaḤ. (3) Hence cancelling or modifying the action, as the case may be. (4) If one commits blasphemy or practises idolatry, and immediately, within the period of utterance, retracts, his retraction is unavailing. If a woman accepts *ḳiddushin* or a divorce, and immediately thereafter withdraws her consent, such withdrawal is invalid. (5) And each can be annulled or confirmed without the other. (6) Num. XXX, 14. (7) [*a*. Either the whole vow; or *b*. the part he did not annul (Ran); v. p. 270, n. 5.]

her husband may [yeḳimennu] *confirm it or her husband may annul it* [yeferenu]: just as *yeḳimennu* implies *mimmennu* [part of it],[1] so *yeferenu* means part thereof.[2] And R. Ishmael?[3]—Is it then written, he shall annul [part] thereof? And R. Akiba?[4]—Annulment is assimilated to confirmation: just as confirmation [denotes a part] thereof, so annulment too [denotes a part] thereof. R. Ḥiyya b. Abba said in R. Joḥanan's name: These are the views of R. Ishmael and R. Akiba. But the Sages maintain: Confirmation is assimilated to annulment: just as in the case of annulment, that which he annulled is void, so also in respect to confirmation, that which he confirmed is confirmed.[5]

IF SHE VOWS, 'ḲONAM, IF I TASTE FIGS' [AND 'IF I TASTE GRAPES, etc.']. Raba said: Our Mishnah agrees with R. Simeon, who ruled: He must say 'I swear' to each one separately.[6]

MISHNAH. [IF THE HUSBAND DECLARES,] 'I KNOW THAT THERE WERE VOWS, BUT DID NOT KNOW THAT THEY COULD BE ANNULLED', HE MAY ANNUL THEM [NOW]. [BUT IF HE SAYS:] 'I KNOW THAT ONE CAN ANNUL, BUT DID NOT KNOW THAT THIS WAS A VOW,' R. MEIR RULED: HE CANNOT ANNUL IT, WHILST THE SAGES MAINTAIN: HE CAN ANNUL.[7]

(1) *Yeḳimennu* is taken as a contraction of *yaḳim mimmenu*, 'he shall confirm part of it'. (2) Though *yeferenu* itself cannot bear that meaning, it is nevertheless so rendered by analogy with *yeḳimennu*. Hence if he annulled part thereof, the entire vow is annulled. (3) How does he justify his view? (4) And how does he dispose of this objection? (5) On this reading, the Sages regard it as axiomatic that part of a vow can be annulled, and by analogy rule likewise for confirmation. Hence the statement of the Mishnah, that if he annulled the vow in respect of figs it is not annulled, must mean that the vow is not *entirely* void; the conflict in the Baraitha must also be interpreted on the same lines. But in the Tosefta it appears that if one annulled only part thereof the entire vow remains valid. Consequently the reading of some editions is preferable: But the Sages maintain, just as in the case of annulment, even that part which he annulled is not void; so is confirmation too—even that which he confirmed is not confirmed (Ran). (6) V. *supra* p. 211, n. 3; so here too, only if she says 'If I taste' for each separately, is it regarded as two distinct vows. (7) V. *supra* 79a for notes.

GEMARA. But the following contradicts this: [*Or if he smote him with any stone, wherewith a man may die,*] *seeing him not* [... *then the congregation shall restore him to the city of his refuge*]:[1] this excludes a blind man;[2] that is R. Judah's view. R. Meir said: It is to include a blind person![3]—[88*a*] Raba answered: In each case [the ruling follows] from the context.[4] R. Judah reasons: Concerning a murderer it is written, *As when a man goeth into a wood with his neighbour, etc.*,[5] implying whoever can go into a 'wood', and a blind person too can enter a wood. Now, should you say that '*seeing him not*' teaches the inclusion of the blind, that could be deduced from '*a wood*'. Hence '*seeing him not*' must exclude the blind. But R. Meir maintains: It is written, [*Whoso killeth his neighbour*] *without knowing*,[6] [which implies] whoever that can know, whereas a blind person cannot know. Now, should you say that '*seeing him not*' excludes

(1) Num. XXXV, 23f. (2) Who is not exiled to the refuge cities for manslaughter. (3) In Deut. XIX, 5, it is stated, *as when a man goeth into a wood with his neighbour, etc.* This implies that the unwitting murderer must have known where his victim was, but that he killed him unintentionally. If, however, he did not know of his presence, the law of exile is inapplicable. Now a blind person does not see his victim; nevertheless, owing to the greater keenness of his other faculties he senses the presence of the victim, though not knowing exactly where he is. R. Judah maintains that the partial knowledge of the blind is regarded as full knowledge, and would be sufficient for the law to operate. Consequently, when Scripture states, '*seeing him not*', which implies that he might however have seen him, it must teach the exclusion of the blind. R. Meir's view is that partial knowledge is in itself not regarded as complete knowledge; hence, without any verse one would assume that a blind person is excluded. Consequently, '*seeing him not*' cannot exclude the blind, since for that no verse is necessary, but must be translated, 'though not seeing him', i.e., though unable to see him, and the verse extends the law to the blind. Thus this contradicts the Mishnah, for there R. Meir rules that since he possessed the partial knowledge that a husband can annul vows, he is regarded as having possessed the complete knowledge, and therefore cannot annul after the day of hearing. Likewise R. Judah here is opposed to the Sages in the Mishnah, by whom R. Judah is meant, when they are in opposition to R. Meir (Rashi). Ran, Asheri and Tosaf. give different interpretations. (4) So cur. edd. Ran reads: In this case (*sc.* of a murderer) the ruling follows from the context. (5) Deut. XIX, 5. (6) Ibid. 4; i.e., by throwing a stone without knowing where it will fall.

the blind, that would follow from, '*without knowing*'. Consequently, '*seeing him not*' must teach the inclusion of the blind.[1]

MISHNAH. IF A MAN IS UNDER A VOW THAT HIS SON-IN-LAW SHALL NOT BENEFIT FROM HIM,[2] AND HE DESIRES TO GIVE MONEY TO HIS DAUGHTER, HE MUST SAY TO HER, 'THIS MONEY IS GIVEN TO YOU AS A GIFT, PROVIDING THAT YOUR HUSBAND HAS NO RIGHTS THEREIN, [FOR ONLY THAT IS YOURS] WHICH YOU MAY PUT TO YOUR PERSONAL USE.'[3]

GEMARA. Rab said: We learnt this only if he says to her, 'WHICH YOU MAY PUT TO YOUR PERSONAL USE.' But if he says, 'Do what you please,' the husband acquires it.[4] Samuel said: Even if he declares, 'Do what you please,' the husband has no rights therein. R. Zera demurred to this: [88b] With whom does this ruling of Rab agree? With R. Meir, who said: The hand of a woman is as the hand of her husband.[5] But the following contradicts it: How is a partnership formed in respect of an alley way?[6] One [of the residents] places there a barrel [of wine] and declares, 'This belongs to all the residents of the alley way': and he transfers ownership to them through his Hebrew slave, male or female, his adult son or daughter, or his wife.[7] But if you say, her husband acquires it, the '*erub*[8] has not left the husband's possession?[9]— Raba replied: Although R. Meir said, The hand of a woman is

(1) Thus their dispute does not centre on the question whether partial knowledge is as full knowledge or not, and hence has no bearing on our Mishnah. (2) The text is uncertain. (3) Lit., 'put into your mouth.' (4) For since she is able to put it to *any* use, her rights are automatically transferred to her husband. (5) I.e., she has no independent rights, v. Ḳid. 23*b*. (6) By a legal fiction a partnership was formed by all the Jewish residents of an alley in respect thereto, that it might rank as a private domain, and carrying therein be permitted on the Sabbath. This was effected by placing in it some food of which all the residents became joint-owners, v. 'Er. 73*b*. (7) Who accept it from him on behalf of the residents. (8) Lit., 'mixture', 'combination', the technical term for the thing deposited (v. Glos.). (9) And that law is contained in an anonymous Mishnah, the author of which is R. Meir.

as the hand of her husband, he agrees in respect to 'partnership',[1] that since his object is to transfer it to others, she can acquire it from her husband. Rabina objected before R. Ashi: The following can acquire it on their behalf: his adult son or daughter, his Hebrew slave, male or female. But the following can not acquire it on their behalf: his son or daughter, if minors, his Canaanite slave, male or female, and his wife![2]—But, said R. Ashi, the Mishnah[3] holds good [only] when she possesses a court in that alley way,[4] so that since she can acquire part ownership [in the *'erub*] for herself,[5] she can also acquire it on behalf of others.

MISHNAH. BUT EVERY VOW OF A WIDOW AND OF HER THAT IS DIVORCED... SHALL STAND AGAINST HER.[6] HOW SO? IF SHE DECLARED, 'BEHOLD, I WILL BE A NAZIRITE AFTER THIRTY DAYS', EVEN IF SHE MARRIED WITHIN THE THIRTY DAYS, HE CANNOT ANNUL IT. [89*a*] IF SHE VOWS WHILE UNDER HER HUSBAND'S AUTHORITY, HE CAN DISALLOW HER. HOW SO? IF SHE DECLARED, 'BEHOLD! I WILL BE A NAZIRITE AFTER THIRTY DAYS,' [AND HER HUSBAND ANNULLED IT], EVEN THOUGH SHE WAS WIDOWED OR DIVORCED WITHIN THE THIRTY DAYS, IT IS ANNULLED. IF SHE VOWED ON ONE DAY, AND HE DIVORCED HER ON THE SAME DAY AND TOOK HER BACK ON THE SAME DAY, HE

(1) *Shittuf.* The technical term for the partnership created for the purposes of the Sabbath law. (2) The reference is the same as above. This shews that the wife, having no powers of acquisition apart from her husband, cannot be the medium of transference, and thus contradicts the Mishnah just quoted. This difficulty arises in any case, but Rabina adduces it here to refute the distinction posited by Raba. (3) In 'Er. (4) E.g., if she had inherited it before marriage, and the groom had written a deed renouncing all rights therein. (5) Because that is in the husband's own interest, for carrying is forbidden in the alley unless every resident—and the wife ranks as one in her own rights, since she possesses a court—is part owner of the *'erub*, whereas the other teaching (a Baraitha) refers to the case where she has no court of her own. (6) Num. XXX, 10.

CANNOT ANNUL IT. THIS IS THE GENERAL RULE: ONCE SHE HAS GONE FORTH AS HER OWN MISTRESS [EVEN] FOR A SINGLE HOUR, HE CANNOT ANNUL.

GEMARA. It was taught: If a widow or a divorced woman declares, 'Behold! I will be a nazirite when I marry,' and she marries,—R. Ishmael said: He [the husband] can annul. R. Akiba ruled: He cannot annul. (And the mnemonic is YeLaLY).[1] If a married woman declares, 'Behold! I will be a nazirite when I am divorced,' and she is divorced: R. Ishmael ruled: He cannot annul;[2] R. Akiba said: He can annul.[3] R. Ishmael argued: Behold, it is said, *But every vow of a widow, and of her that is divorced . . . shall stand against her,*[4] implying that the [incidence of] the vow must be in the period of widowhood or divorce.[5] [But] R. Akiba maintains: It is written, *with whatever she hath* bound *her soul,*[4] implying that the *binding* of the vow must be [created] in the period of widowhood or divorce.[6]

R. Ḥisda said: Our Mishnah agrees with R. Akiba.[7] Abaye said: It may agree even with R. Ishmael: in the Mishnah she made herself dependent upon a time factor; the period may end without her being divorced or the period may end without her being married;[8] but in the Baraitha she made the vow dependent upon marriage.[9]

(1) I.e., in the clause just quoted, R. Ishmael rules Y*afer*, he may annul; R. Akiba: L*o* *yafer*, he cannot annul. In the next clause it is the reverse; R. Ishmael says, L*o* *Yafer;* and R. Akiba: Y*afer*. (2) The husband's annulment whilst she is married is invalid after divorce. (3) Thus in both cases R. Ishmael maintains that the woman's status when the vow is to take effect is the deciding factor, and R. Akiba holds that it depends on her status when she vows. (4) Num. XXX, 10. (5) And that in that case it '*shall stand against her*', i.e., it cannot be annulled, proving that the *incidence* of the vow is what matters. (6) I.e., that she *makes* the vow then, and that in that case her husband cannot annul. (7) Since in both clauses of the Mishnah the matter is determined by the time when the vow was made. (8) Adopting the reading of BaḤ. v. Ran. (9) If she is unmarried, and vows to be a nazirite when she marries, there must be a change of status between the making of the vow and its incidence; in that case R. Ishmael rules that we regard the latter. But if she merely postpones the incidence of the vow, she may bear the same status when the vow becomes

'This is the general rule,' taught with respect to a betrothed maiden,[1] is to extend the law to where the father accompanied the [betrothed] husband's messengers, or the father's messengers accompanied the [betrothed] husband's messengers,—that in the case of a betrothed maiden her vows are annulled by her father and husband.[2] 'THIS IS THE GENERAL RULE,' taught in the chapter,[3] 'Now these are the vows,' is meant to extend [the law] to where the father delivered her to her [betrothed] husband's messengers, or where the father's agents delivered her to the messengers of the [betrothed] husband, [and it teaches] that the husband cannot annul [vows] made [by her] previously.[4]

MISHNAH. THERE ARE NINE MAIDENS WHOSE VOWS[5] STAND:[6] [i] A BOGERETH WHO [VOWED] AND IS AN ORPHAN;[7] [ii] A MAIDEN [WHO VOWED] AND [THEN] BECAME A BOGERETH AND IS AN ORPHAN; [89b] [iii] A NA'ARAH WHO IS NOT YET A BOGERETH, AND IS AN ORPHAN;[8] [iv] A BOGERETH [WHO

operative as when it is made; there R. Ishmael may admit that we regard the time of making the vow.

(1) *Supra* 71a. Whenever a general rule is stated, it is always meant to add to the specific case actually given. (2) When the father gives over his daughter to the messengers of the husband to escort her to her new home, she is regarded as a *nesu'ah*, and has passed out of her father's authority. But if he or his messengers accompany her, together with her husband's messengers, she is yet under his authority, and he still shares the power to annul with her husband. On this home-taking ceremony v. Keth. 48*b*. (3) I.e., in the present Mishnah, which forms part of Chapter XI. (4) I.e., vows made before her home-coming. Having passed out of her father's authority, (v. n. 2) she is her own mistress until she enters her husband's home, and if she vowed in the interval, he cannot annul. (5) 'Maidens' is not used here in the restricted sense of *na'arah*, but means girls and women in general who were betrothed while still in the stage of *na'arah*. (6) I.e., they cannot be annulled. (7) The reference is to 'an orphan during her father's lifetime,' i.e., one who was married with *nissu'in*, and then widowed or divorced. Even if she is still a minor, her father no longer has any authority over her, so she is called 'an orphan during her father's lifetime.' (8) So Asheri: A *na'arah* who vowed before becoming a *bogereth*, and was orphaned (and is still not a *bogereth*). [These three belong to

VOWED] AND WHOSE FATHER DIED;[1] [v] A NA'ARAH [WHO VOWED] AND IS NOW A BOGERETH AND WHOSE FATHER DIED;[1] [vi] A NA'ARAH WHO IS NOT YET A BOGERETH AND WHOSE FATHER DIED; [vii] A MAIDEN WHOSE FATHER DIED, AND AFTER HER FATHER DIED SHE BECAME A BOGERETH;[2] [viii] A BOGERETH[3] WHOSE FATHER IS ALIVE; [ix] A MAIDEN TURNED BOGERETH, WHOSE FATHER IS ALIVE.[4] R. JUDAH SAID: ALSO ONE WHO MARRIED HIS DAUGHTER WHILST A MINOR, AND SHE WAS WIDOWED OR DIVORCED AND RETURNED TO HIM [HER FATHER] AND IS STILL A NA'ARAH.

GEMARA. Rab Judah said in Rab's name: These are the words of R. Judah. But the Sages say: The vows of three maidens stand: [i] a bogereth; [ii] an orphan; and [iii] an orphan during her father's lifetime.[5]

MISHNAH. [IF SHE VOWS,] 'ḲONAM THAT I BENEFIT NOT FROM MY FATHER OR YOUR FATHER IF I PREPARE AUGHT FOR YOU,'[6] OR, 'ḲONAM THAT I BENEFIT NOT FROM YOU, IF I PREPARE AUGHT FOR MY FATHER OR YOUR FATHER,' HE CAN ANNUL.

GEMARA. It was taught: [If she vows, '*Ḳonam*] that I benefit not from my father or your father, if I prepare aught for you,'

the group of maidens whose vows cannot be annulled because they are orphans (as defined).]

(1) [She made a vow as *na'arah*, lost her father and is still a *na'arah*. These three belong to the group of maidens whose vows cannot be annulled because they have no fathers.] (2) [She lost her father, vowed, and then became a *bogereth*.] (3) I.e., who vowed as a *bogereth*. (4) I.e., who vowed as a *na'arah*, but comes to enquire about annulment when she is a *bogereth*. [These three belong to the group of maidens whose vows cannot be annulled because they have reached the status of *bogereth*.] (5) V. p. 275, n. 7. There is actually no conflict, R. Judah's nine being included in the Sages' three. R. Judah's enumeration is merely in greater detail, and intended to sharpen his disciples' minds (T. J. *a.l.*). (6) Lit., 'for thy mouth'.

—R. Nathan said: He cannot annul;[1] the Sages maintain: He can annul.[2] 'May I be removed from Jews,[3] if I minister to you,' —R. Nathan said: He cannot annul: the Sages rule: He can annul.

A man once vowed not to benefit from the world if he should marry before having studied *halachah*:[4] he ran with ladder and cord,[5] yet did not succeed in his studies. Thereupon R. Aḥa son of R. Huna came and led him into error,[6] and caused him to marry; [90*a*] then daubed him with clay[7] and brought him before R. Ḥisda.[8] Said Raba: Who is so wise as to do such a thing if not R. Aḥa son of R. Huna, who is [indeed] a great man? For he maintains: Just as the Rabbis and R. Nathan disagree in reference to annulment, so also with respect to absolution.[9] But R. Papi said: The disagreement is only in respect to annulment, R. Nathan holding that the husband cannot annul unless the vow has already become operative, for it is written, *Then the moon shall be confounded*;[10] whilst the Rabbis maintain: The husband can annul even before the vow takes effect, as it is written, *He maketh void the* intentions *of the*

(1) He does not regard it as a vow of self-denial, for she can refrain from doing anything for her husband. (2) Since she is in duty bound to serve her husband. (3) Cf. p. 279, n. 7. (4) Laws. For a discussion of the full meaning of the term *halachah* v. Weiss, *Dor*. I, 70. (5) נפא is the ladder by which one ascends the palm tree to gather its dates; תוביל‍א is the cord whereby its branches are pulled down, to facilitate gathering whilst one stands on the ground.—The expression is metaphorical: he made every possible effort. (6) By making him believe that if he married the vow would not be valid. (7) I.e., his garments. To show him that the services of other people were indispensable: he would straightway need someone to clean his garments (Ran). (8) For absolution. (9) V. *supra* 89*b*. R. Nathan maintains that since the vow is not yet operative, he cannot annul, whilst the Rabbis hold that he can annul it though as yet inoperative. So with reference to absolution: in R. Nathan's view, one can be absolved from his vow only when it is in effect etc. For that reason he caused him to marry first, and did not have the vow annulled immediately. (10) Isa. XXIV, 23; Heb. וחפרה הלבנה. This is merely quoted as a sign. וחפרה is similar to והפרה (*and he shall disallow her*), whilst הלבנה is connected with בנה to build, and thus, by a play on words, the phrase is translated: and he shall disallow her, when the edifice (of the vow) be erected, i.e., when the vow is operative, but not before. [It is however omitted from MS.M.]

crafty.[1] But as for absolution, all agree that a Sage cannot permit anything until the vow is operative, for it is written, *He shall not break his word.*[2]

Shall we say that the following supports him? [If he vows,] '*Ḳonam* that I benefit not from So-and-so, and from anyone from whom I may obtain absolution for him,' he must obtain absolution in respect of the first, and then obtain absolution in respect of the second.[3] But if you say, absolution may be granted even before the vow takes effect, surely he can be absolved in whatever order he pleases![4]—And who knows whether this one is first and that the other is the second?[5]

Shall we say that this supports him: [If he vows,] '*Ḳonam* that I benefit not from So-and-so, and behold! I will be a nazirite if I be absolved therefrom'; he must be absolved of his vow, and then of his naziriteship.[6] But if you say, absolution may be granted before the vow takes effect, if he wishes, let him first be absolved of his vow;[8] and if he wishes, let him first be absolved of being a nazirite?—This agrees with R. Nathan.[7]

Rabina said: Meremar told me: Thus did your father say in R. Papi's name: The controversy is only in reference to annulment, but in respect to absolution all agree that he [the Sage] may grant it even before the vow is operative,[8] because it is

(1) Job V, 12, i.e., even when a vow is as yet merely an intention, not having taken effect, it can be annulled. (2) Num. XXX, 3: Rashi translates: he (the Rabbi) shall not break (i.e., grant absolution for) his *vow*, i.e., as long as it is only a word, which has not yet taken effect. Asheri observes: from this we deduce, *he* (who vowed) may not break his word, but another (*sc.* a Sage) may break it, i.e., grant absolution, but that is only when '*he must* do *according to all that proceedeth out of his mouth,*' viz., when the vow is operative. (3) I.e., the Sages who became subject to the vow on account of having granted absolution. (4) Lit., 'if he wishes, he can be absolved of this one first, and if he wishes, he can be absolved of the other first.'—Thus this supports R. Papa's contention. (5) I.e., indeed that is so: 'first' and 'second' need not refer to the order in which he vowed, but to the order of absolution. (6) Here it is explicitly stated that he can only be absolved of being a nazirite after absolution of his vow, when his conditional vow to be a nazirite has taken effect. (7) I.e., R. Abba b. R. Huna may be correct in asserting that this is a matter of dispute, and this Baraitha is taught according to R. Nathan. (8) The reverse of what was said above.

written, '*He shall not break his word,*' [90*b*] intimating that no act had yet taken place.[1]

An objection is raised: [If he vows,] '*Ḳonam* that I benefit not from So-and-so, and from anyone from whom I obtain absolution for him'; he must be absolved in respect of the first, and then obtain absolution in respect of the second. But why so? Let him be absolved in whichever order he pleases![2]—Who knows which one is first or which one is second?[3]

An objection is raised: [If he vows,] '*Ḳonam* that I benefit not from So-and-so, and behold! I will be a nazirite if I be absolved therefrom': he must be absolved of his vow, and then of his naziriteship. But why so? If he wishes, let him first be absolved of his vow, and if he wishes, let him first be absolved of being a nazirite! This is indeed a refutation.

MISHNAH. AT FIRST IT WAS RULED THAT THREE WOMEN MUST BE DIVORCED AND RECEIVE THEIR KETHUBAH:[4] SHE WHO DECLARES: 'I AM DEFILED TO YOU';[5] OR 'HEAVEN IS BETWEEN YOU AND ME';[6] AND 'MAY I BE REMOVED FROM JEWS.'[7] BUT SUBSEQUENTLY, TO PREVENT HER FROM CONCEIVING A PASSION FOR ANOTHER[8] TO THE INJURY OF HER HUSBAND,[9] THE RULING WAS AMENDED THUS: SHE WHO

(1) V. p. 278, n. 2; the vow was not yet operative, and we deduce that the Sage can cause him, by absolution, to break his word. So Ran. Rashi: thus asserting that the act (*sc.* of R. Abba b. R. Huna, v. 89*b* end) was unnecessary. (2) V. p. 278, n. 4. (3) V. p. 278, n. 5. (4) V. Glos. (5) I.e., unfaithful. (6) I.e., her husband is impotent—a thing that, apart from herself, can be known only to Heaven. (7) Including her own husband. By this vow she shewed that cohabitation was unbearable to her, and therefore could demand to be divorced and receive her *Kethubah*. (8) Lit., 'casting her eyes at another man.' (9) [מקלקלת על בעלה. A difficult phrase. According to the rendering adopted, the meaning is: She will purposely make one of these declarations in order to obtain her freedom against his will. Ran explains: She may go to a place where nothing is known of her vow and marry there. He seemed to have taken this phrase as denoting: She will act unseemly (whilst still) with her husband, and as referring only to the declaration 'May I be removed from Jews'.]

DECLARED, 'I AM DEFILED UNTO YOU,' MUST BRING PROOF: 'HEAVEN IS BETWEEN ME AND YOU'—THEY SHOULD ENGAGE IN PRAYER,[1] AND 'MAY I BE REMOVED FROM JEWS'—HE [THE HUSBAND] MUST ANNUL HIS PORTION,[2] AND SHE SHALL MINISTER TO HIM, WHILST REMAINING REMOVED FROM JEWS.

GEMARA. The scholars propounded: If she declared to her husband, 'I am defiled to you,'[3] may she eat of *terumah?*[4]—R. Shesheth ruled: She may eat thereof, so as not to cast a stigma upon her children.[5] Raba said: She may not eat, for she can eat *ḥullin*.[7] Raba said: Yet R. Shesheth admits that if she was widowed,[6] she may not eat: is his reason aught but that she should not cast a stigma upon her children? But if she was widowed or divorced [and she ceases to eat of *terumah*], it will be said, It is only now that she was seduced.[8]

R. Papa said, Raba tested us: If the wife of a priest was forcibly ravished,[9] does she receive her *Kethubah* or not? Since forcible seduction in respect to a priest is as voluntary infidelity in respect to an Israelite, she does not receive her *Kethubah;*[10] or perhaps she can plead, 'I personally am fit;[11] [91*a*] it is only the man whose field has been ruined?'[12] And we answered him, It is [taught in] our

(1) That his impotency might cease (Tosaf.) [Lit., 'They should act by way of a request'. Ran: attempts should be made to placate the wife. Rashi: the husband should be asked to agree to a divorce.] (2) I.e., as far as he personally is concerned. (3) This refers to the wife of a priest. (4) If it is true, she certainly must not. Yet the Mishnah in its second recension ruled that she must first prove it. Now the question arises, Do we disbelieve her in all respects, in which case she may eat of *terumah*, or only in respect of a divorce? (5) If she refrains, it will be assumed that she told the truth, in which case her children may be bastards. (6) None will observe that she consistently refrains from eating *terumah* and no aspersions will be cast upon her children. (7) Rashi and Tosaf. read: or divorced. (8) Thus her refraining leaves the honour of her children unaffected. (9) If the wife of an Israelite is seduced: if voluntarily, she becomes forbidden to him; if forcibly, she remains permitted. But the wife of a priest is forbidden in both cases. (10) As is the case of an Israelite's wife who committed adultery of her own free will. (11) Having been forcibly ravished, she has committed no wrong. (12) I.e., it is *his* sanctity, not *my* wrong-doing, that prohibits me to him.

Mishnah: [SHE WHO DECLARES,] 'I AM DEFILED TO YOU,' RECEIVES HER KETHUBAH. Now to whom does this refer? Shall we say, to the wife of an Israelite: if of her own free will, does she receive her *Kethubah?* Whilst if by force, is she forbidden to her husband?[1] Hence it must refer to the wife of a priest: now, if of her own free will, does she receive the *Kethubah?* Is she of less account[2] than the wife of an Israelite, [who sinned] voluntarily? Hence it must surely mean by force; and it is stated that she receives her *Kethubah*.

The scholars propounded: What if she declares to her husband, 'You have divorced me'?[3]—R. Hamnuna said: Come and hear: SHE WHO DECLARES, 'I AM DEFILED TO YOU': Now even according to the later Mishnah,[4] which teaches that she is not believed, it is [only] there that she may lie, in the knowledge that her husband does not know;[5] but with respect to 'You have divorced me,' of [the truth of] which he must know, she is believed, for there is a presumption [that] no woman is brazen in the presence of her husband.[6] Said Raba to him: On the contrary, even according to the first Mishnah, that she is believed, it is [only] there, because she would not expose herself to shame;[7] but here it may happen that she is stronger [in character] than her husband,[8] and so indeed be brazen.

R. Mesharsheya objected: 'HEAVEN IS BETWEEN ME AND YOU,' as ruled by the early Mishnah, refutes Raba's view; for here it involves no shame for her, yet it is stated that she is believed? —Raba holds that there, since she cannot avoid declaring whether the emission is forceful or not, were it not as she said, she would not make the charge.[9]

But let 'HEAVEN IS BETWEEN US,' as ruled by the later Mish-

(1) Surely not! and there is no need to divorce her. (2) I.e., is her sin of less account? (3) Is she believed in spite of his denial, or may it be a ruse to gain her freedom? (4) I.e., the Mishnah as it was subsequently amended. (5) Whether her statement is true. (6) I.e., she would not be brazen enough to tell such a lie in his presence, wherefore she is believed. (7) If she had not actually been ravished. (8) So Ran. Rashi: her husband might have ill-treated her; she has conceived a strong passion for (another) man. (9) I.e., since it is a charge of extreme delicacy and unpleasantness, she would not make it if it were untrue.

nah, refute R. Hamnuna's view; for here she knows that her husband knows,[1] yet it is taught that she is not believed?—R. Hamnuna maintains that here too she would argue to herself, 'Granted that he knows that cohabitation has taken place, does he know whether the emission is forceful'?[2] Therefore she may be lying.

A certain woman was accustomed to rise [in the morning] and wash her husband's hands whenever intimacy had taken place. One day she brought him water to wash. 'But,' exclaimed he, 'nothing has taken place to-day'! 'If so,' she rejoined, [it must have been] 'one of the gentile [91*b*] perfume sellers[3] who were here to-day; if not you, perhaps it was one of them.' Said R. Naḥman: She had conceived a passion for another, and her declaration has no substance.[4]

A certain woman shewed displeasure with her husband. Said he to her, 'Why this change now?' She replied, 'You have never caused me so much pain through intimacy as to-day.' 'But there has been none to-day!' he exclaimed. 'If so,' she returned, [it must have been] 'the gentile naphtha sellers who were here to-day; if not you, perhaps it was one of them.' Said R. Naḥman: Disregard her; she had conceived a passion for another.

A certain man was closeted in a house with a [married] woman. Hearing the master [her husband] entering, the adulterer broke through a hedge and fled.[5] Said Raba: The wife is permitted; had he committed wrong, he would have hidden himself [in the house].[6]

A certain adulterer visited a woman. Her husband came, whereupon the lover went and placed himself behind a curtain before the door.[7] Now, some cress was lying there, and a snake [came and ate] thereof; the master [her husband] was about to eat of

(1) Whether the charge is true or not. (2) Surely not, for only the woman can feel that. (3) Lit., 'dealers in aloe'. (4) I.e., she is disbelieved. The reference here is to the wife of a priest; v. p. 280, n. 9. For if she were the wife of an Israelite, she would not be forbidden to him even if it were true. Ran. (5) [In the presence of the husband ('Aruch).] (6) That the husband should remain in ignorance of his presence. (7) So Ran. 'Aruch: and placed himself in a concealed arch by the gate.

the cress, unknown to his wife. 'Do not eat it,' warned the lover, 'because a snake has tasted it.' Said Raba: The wife is permitted: had he committed wrong, he would have been pleased that he should eat thereof and die, as it is written, *For they have committed adultery, and blood is in their hands.*[1] Surely that is obvious?—I might think that he had committed wrong, and as for his warning, that is because he prefers the husband not to die, so that his wife may be to him as *Stolen waters are sweet, and bread eaten in secret is pleasant;*[2] therefore he teaches otherwise.

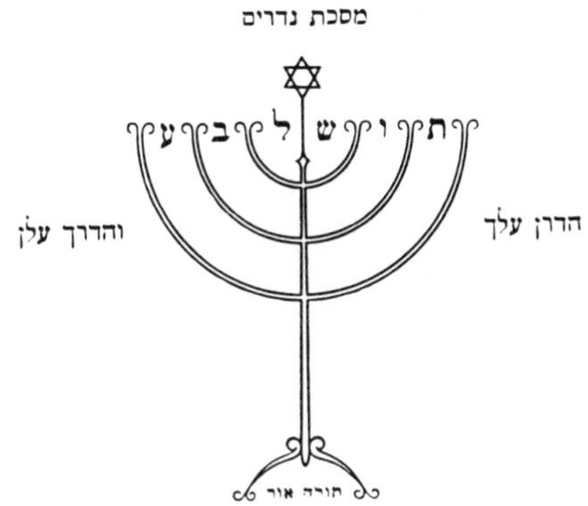

(1) Ezek. XXIII, 37. (2) Prov. IX, 17. Though this Tractate ends with a number of stories referring to adultery, these are not to be taken as reflecting general conditions. The strong opposition to unchastity displayed by the Prophets and the Rabbis, as well as the practice of early marriage, would have conduced to higher moral standards. V. *J.E.* art. 'Chastity'.

GLOSSARY

INDEX OF SCRIPTURAL REFERENCES

GENERAL INDEX

TRANSLITERATION OF HEBREW LETTERS

ABBREVIATIONS

GLOSSARY

'AM HA-AREẒ pl. *'amme ha-areẓ'*. Lit., 'people of the land', 'country people'; the name given in Rabbinic literature to (*a*) a person who through ignorance was careless in the observance of the laws of Levitical purity and of those relating to the priestly and Levitical gifts. In this sense opposed to *ḥaber*, q.v.; (a) an illiterate or uncultured man, as opposed to *talmid ḥakam*.

ARUS. The technical term for a husband of a betrothed woman, when *erusin* (q.v.) has taken place; v. ARUSAH.

ARUSAH. A betrothed woman after *erusin* (q.v.); v. ARUS.

ASMAKTA: 'Reliance.' An assurance that one will pay or forfeit something in the case of the non-fulfilment of a certain condition which, however, he is confident that he will fulfil.

BARAITHA (Lit., 'outside'); a teaching or a tradition of the Tannaim that has been excluded from the Mishnah and incorporated in a later collection compiled by R. Ḥiyya and R. Oshaiah, generally introduced by 'Our Rabbis taught', or, 'It has been taught'.

BERERAH. (Lit., 'choice'); the selection retrospectively of one object rather than another as having been designated by a term equally applicable to both.

BETH DIN (Lit., 'house of law or judgment'); a gathering of three or more learned men acting as a Jewish court of law.

BOGERETH. A girl from the age of twelve years and a half plus one day and onwards.

CUTHI, CUTHEAN. A member of the sect of Samaritans by whom Northern Israel was repopulated after the dispersal of the ten tribes.

DENAR. *Denarius*, a silver or gold coin, the former being worth one twenty-fourth (according to others one twenty-fifth) of the latter.

'ERUB (Lit., 'mixture'); a quantity of food, enough for two meals, placed (*a*) 2000 cubits from the town boundary, so as to extend the Sabbath limit by that distance; (*b*) in a room or in a courtyard to enable all the residents to carry to and fro in the courtyard on Sabbath.

ERUSIN (Lit., 'betrothal'); a formal betrothal, which cannot be annulled without a bill of divorce.

GET. A deed or legal document; when used without further specification denotes generally a writ of divorce.

GEZERAH SHAWAH (Lit., 'equal cut'); the application to one subject of a rule already known to apply to another, on the strength of a common expression used in connection with both in the Scriptures.

ḤABER. 'Fellow', 'associate', opp. to *'am ha-arez* (q.v.); one scrupulous in the observance of the law, particularly in relation to ritual cleanness and the separation of the priestly and Levitical dues.

HABDALAH ('separation'): a blessing recited on the termination of Sabbaths and Festivals, thanking God for the distinction He has made between holy days and week days.

ḤADASH ('new'); the new cereal crops, which may not be eaten before the waving of the 'sheaf' (*'omer*); v. Lev. XIII, 10-14.

HALACHAH (Lit., 'step', 'guidance'), (*a*) the final decision of the Rabbis, whether based on tradition or argument, on disputed rules of conduct; (*b*) those sections of Rabbinic literature which deal with legal questions, as opposed to the *Aggadah*.

ḤALIZAH (Lit., 'drawing off'); the ceremony of taking off the shoe of the brother of a husband who has died childless. (V. Deut. XXV, 5-9.)

ḤALLAH. The portion of the dough which belongs to the priest (v. Num. XV, 20 et seq.); in the Diaspora this is not given to the priest but burnt.

ḤASID ('pious'). A pious man; at one time possibly a designation of a member of a particularly pious and strictly observant sect.

HEFḲER. Property which has no owner: a renunciation of ownership in favour of all and sundry.

HEḲDESH. Any object consecrated to the Sanctuary.

ḤELEB. The portion of the fat of a permitted domestic animal which may not be eaten; in sacrifices that fat was burnt upon the altar.

ḤEREM, pl. *ḥaramim* ('devoted'). Property devoted to the use of the priests or the Temple; when used in vows it denotes that benefit shall be prohibited from the person or thing so designated.

ḤULLIN (Lit., 'profane'). Ordinary unhallowed food, as opposed to *terumah*, q.v.; unconsecrated objects, as opposed to *heḳdesh*, q.v.

ḤUPPAH (Lit., 'canopy'). The bridal chamber; the entrance of a bride into the bridal chamber, whereby the marriage was completed; v. ḲIDDUSHIN.

KARETH (Lit., 'cutting off'). Divine punishment for a number of sins for which no human penalty is specified. Sudden death is described as '*kareth* of days'; premature death at sixty as '*kareth* of years'.

KETHUBAH (Lit., 'a written document'). (*a*) A wife's marriage settlement which she is entitled to recover on her being divorced or on the death of her husband. The minimum settlement for a virgin is two hundred *zuz*, and for a widow remarrying a hundred *zuz;* (*b*) the marriage contract specifying the mutual obligations between husband and wife and containing the amount of the endowment and any other special financial obligations assumed by the husband.

ḲIDDUSH ('Sanctification'). A benediction recited at the beginning of Sabbath and Festivals, thanking God for having sanctified them; v. HABDALAH.

ḲIDDUSHIN ('sanctification'). (*a*) The act of affiancing or betrothal; (*b*) the money or article given to effect the betrothal.

KIL'AYIM. (*a*) Diverse seeds sown together, which is forbidden; (*b*) the prohibited mixture of wool and linen in garments.

KOR. A measure of capacity = thirty *se'ahs* (q.v.).

LULAB. The palm-branch used in the ceremony of the Feast of Tabernacles (v. Lev. XXIII, 40).

MADDIR. He who vows that his neighbour should not benefit from him; his neighbour is then called the *muddar*.

MIḲWEH (Lit., 'a gathering [of water]'); a ritual bath containing not less than forty *se'ahs* of water.

MIN pl. *minim* (Lit., 'kind,' 'species'); (*a*) a heretic; (*b*) a member of the sect of the early Jewish-Christians.

MISHNAH (repetition). The collection of oral laws edited by R. Judah ha-Nasi.

MUDDAR; v. MADDIR.

MUMḤE. Skilled, expert; a person recognised as a fully qualified judge.

NA'ARAH. A girl between the age of twelve years and a day and twelve years and a half plus one day, when she becomes a *bogereth*; q.v.

NEBELAH, p. *nebeloth* (carrion); an animal slaughtered in any manner other than that prescribed by Jewish ritual law; the least deviation therefrom, e.g., if the knife has the slightest notch, renders the animal *nebelah*.

NESU'AH. A married woman after home-taking (*nissu'in*, q.v.), whereby the marriage is completed in the sense that cohabitation is permitted; opposed to *arusah*, q.v., with whom cohabitation is yet prohibited.

NEZIROTH. Vows of naziriteship.

NEZIRUTH. Naziriteship, the state of being a nazirite.

NIDDAH. A woman in the period of her menstruation.

NISSU'IN. The ceremony of home-taking, which completes the marriage; v. NESU'AH,

NOTHAR ('left over'); portions of sacrifices left over after the prescribed time within which they must be eaten.

'ORLAH ('uncircumcised'); applied to newly-planted trees for a period of three years during which their fruits must not be eaten (v. Lev. XIX, 23ff).

PARASANG. A Persian mile, about 4000 yards.

PE'AH ('corner'); the corner of a field that is being reaped, which must be left for the poor (v. Lev. XIX, 9ff).

PERUṬAH. The smallest copper coin, equal to one-eighth of an *issar* or one-sixteenth of a *dupondium*, or one-one hundred and ninety-second part of a *zuz*.

PIGGUL (Lit., 'abhorred'); flesh of the sacrifice which the officiating priest has formed the intention of eating at an improper time. V. Lev. VII, 18.

SE'AH. Measure of capacity, equal to six *ḳabs*.

SELA'. Coin, equal to four *zuz* or denarii (one sacred, or two common, sheḳels).

SHEḲEL. Coin or weight, equal to two denarii. The sacred *sheḳel* was twice the value of the common *sheḳel*.

SHEMA' (Lit., 'hear'); the Biblical verse, 'Ḥear, O Israel,' etc. (Deut. VI, 4); also the three sections (Deut. VI, 5-9; Deut. XI, 13-20; Num. XV, 37-41) wḥich are recited after this verse in the morning and evening prayers.

SOFERIM ('scribes'); title of the pre-Tannaitic teachers, beginning with Ezra (v. Ezra VII, 11).

SUKKAH. Booth, esp. the festive booth for Tabernacles (Lev. XXIII, 34ff), the roof of which must be made of something that grows from the ground, e.g., reeds or branches.

TANNA (Lit., 'one who repeats' or 'teaches'); (*a*) a Rabbi quoted in the Mishnah or Baraitha (q.v.); (*b*) in the Amoraic period, a scholar whose special task was to memorize and recite Baraithas in the presence of expounding teachers.

ṬEBEL. Produce, already at the stage of liability to the levitical and priestly dues (v. *Terumah*), before these have been separated.

TEFILLIN. Phylacteries; small cases containing passages from Scripture and affixed to the forehead and arm during the recital of morning prayers, in accordance with Deut. VI, 8.

TEḤUM. The boundary beyond which one must not walk on the Sabbath, which is 2000 cubits without the town limits; this can be extended by another 2000 cubits by means of an *'erub*, q.v.

ṬEREFAH (Lit., 'torn'); (*a*) an animal torn by a wild beast; (*b*) any animal suffering from a serious organic disease, whose meat is forbidden even if it had been ritually slaughtered.

TERUMAH. 'That which is lifted or separated'; the heave-offering given from the yields of the yearly harvests, from certain sacrifices, and from the *sheḳels* collected in a special chamber in the Temple (*terumah ha-lishkah*). *Terumah gedolah* (great offering): the first levy on the produce of the year given to the priest. (V. Num. XVIII, 8ff.) Its quantity varied according to the generosity of the owner, who could give one-fortieth, one-fiftieth, or one-sixtieth of his harvest. *Terumath ma'aser* (heave-offering of the tithe): the heave-offering given to the priest by the Levite from the tithes he receives (V. Num. XVIII, 25ff).

TORAH (Lit., 'teaching', 'learning', 'instruction'); (*a*) the Pentateuch (Written Law); (*b*) the Mishnah (Oral Law); (*c*) the whole body of Jewish religious literature.

YABAM. The brother of a married man who dies childless; the widow is called YEBAMAH. V. ḤALIẒAH.

ZAR (Lit., 'stranger'); an Israelite, as opposed to a priest, who may not eat of *terumah* or perform certain acts in connection with sacrifices.

ZUZ. A coin the value of a *denarius;* v. DENAR.

SCRIPTURAL REFERENCES

SCRIPTURAL REFERENCES

GENERAL INDEX*

A

Aaron, dough of, 31, 36, 244.
Abbreviations of vows. *See* Vows.
Abdominal trouble, 64.
Abraham, 90, 93, 95f, 97ff.
Absolution in vows. *See* Vows, regret in, *and* annulment of.
Acco, 86f, 242.
Accentuation, 113ff.
Acquisition, mode of, 149.
Adar, 201f.
Adereth, S., 233.
Adultery, 282f.
Agent, status of, 229.
Aggadoth, 106f, 113.
'*Am-haarez*, 37, 56, 261f.
Amos, 119f.
Analogy, deduction by, 4, 8, 15, 245.
Anecdotes, 155ff, 196, 213f.
Angels as term for Rabbis, 57f.
– ministering, 97.
Anger personified, 95.
Apikora, 66f.
Artisan, 91.
Aruch, 73, 157, 282.
Asceticism, 22, 23.
Asmakta, 78f.
Astrology, 96.
Atonement, Day of, 98, 173, 202, 251.

B

Babylonia, 64, 146, 167.
Bacher, 57, 64.
Baḥja Ibn Paḳuda, 197.
Bald, 87.
Ban, 15ff, 56, 59, 158. *See also* Ḥerem.
– qualification for lifting, 18f.
Bar Cochba revolt, 213.
Barley for sheaf-waving, 114.
Basket, 195.
Bathing, 249f.
Baths, 15.
– ritual, 129, 238.
Bed, mourners'. *See* Mourners'.
– in vows. *See* Vows.
Beets, 154.
Belshazzar, 196f.
Benediction, 155, 174f, 253.
Ben Eleasa, 159f.
Bererah, 233.
Berliner, A., 113.
Beth din, 56.
– ha-Midrash, 154.
– Hillel, 25f, 74f, 80f, 220, 226, 244.
– Horon, gift of, 139, 147ff.
– Shammai, 25f, 74f, 79f, 81, 220, 226, 243, 245.
Betrothals, 84f, 194, 216ff, 269. *See also Ḳiddushin.*
Bible, 107, 114. *See also* Scripture.
Bird-sacrifice, 106f, 108.
Black-haired, 87.
Blasphemy, 269.
Blau, 118.
Blind, 87, 206, 271f.
Bogereth, 122, 216, 223ff, 230, 275f.
Book of Life, 62.
Büchler, 23, 46, 155.

* An Index of Rabbinical Names will be provided in the special Index Volume to be published on completion of the translation of the entire Talmud.

C

D

E

F

T

Torah, study of, 97, 173f, 197.
– vowing by. *See* Vows.
Tradesman, 92.
Trading affected by vows. *See* Vows.
Trespass, law of, 105f.
Trustees, 91.
Turnusrufus, 157.

U

Ugliness, 157f.
Urge, Evil, 98, 127.
– Good, 98.
Utterance as time minimum, 269.

V

Vows, 1ff.
– abbreviations of, 2ff, 8ff, 15ff, 20.
– abbreviations of inexplicit, 10ff.
– against benefit from seafarers etc. *See* Seafarers.
– annulment of, 4, 8, 36, 55f, 61ff, 188, 191, 202f, 216ff, 236ff, 239, 242.
– annulment of partial, 74ff, 210f, 269f.
– as sin, 243.
– beds in, 177.
– betrothed maiden's, 216ff.
– by God, 65.
– by joint owners, 142ff.
– by Torah, 37f.
– confirmation of, absolution from, 220f, 247.
– deafness factor in, 229f.
– double modification of, 26.
– exchanged objects in, 145, 180.
Vows, food in, 151ff, 160ff, 169ff, 180, 187, 195, 202.
– formulas of annulment of, 244.
– garments, 175.
– greater stringency of, 35, 45, 49.
– houses in, 176f, 179.
– husband's annulment of, 249f.
– incentive, 60ff.
– incidence of, 9f.
– in error, 60, 73f, 208, 212.
– invalid, 36f, 42, 55.
– invalidated by Sages, 60ff, 242ff, 255.
– loans in, 136f.
– mother in, 37.
– neighbours in, 100ff, 121ff, 132ff, 137f.
– of exaggeration, 60, 70ff.
– of self-denial, 249ff, 254f.
– of the righteous, 20f.
– of the wicked, 20.
– of woman waiting for *yabam*, 232ff.
– opening for absolution from, 204ff.
– place factor in, 199.
– popular usage in, 151.
– pre-*nesu'in*, 228.
– prohibition of making, 63.
– purchases in, 136f.
– regret in, 18, 55f, 65ff, 74 *et passim*.
– revoked in advance, 67f.
– Sabbath in. *See* Sabbath.
– specified, 50f.
– substitute formulas of, 1ff, 24ff.
– the nine maidens, 275f.
– time factor in, 190ff, 193ff, 199f, 201f, 241, 274.
– towns in, 179.
– trading affected by, 90.

TRANSLITERATION OF HEBREW LETTERS

א (in middle of word)	= '
ב	= b
ו	= w
ח	= ḥ
ט	= ṭ
כ	= k
ע	= '
פ	= f
צ	= ẓ
ק	= ḳ
ת	= th

Full particulars regarding the method and scope of the translation are given in the Editor's Introduction in the Yebamoth volume (Nashim, Vol. I).

ABBREVIATIONS

Ab.	Aboth.
'Aruch	Talmudic Dictionary by R. Nathan b. Jehiel of Rome (d. 1106).
Asheri	R. Asher b. Jeḥiel (1250-1327).
'A.Z.	'Aobdah Zarah.
b.	ben, bar: son of.
B.B.	Baba Bathra.
BaḤ.	Bayith Ḥadash, Glosses by R. Joel b. Samuel Sirkes (1561-1640).
Ber.	Berakoth.
B.M.	Baba Meẓi'a.
Cur. ed(d).	Current edition(s).
Dor	*Dor Dor Wedoreshaw* by I. H. Weiss (2nd. ed.).
Doroth	*Doroth Harishonim* by I. Halevy.
'Ed. 'Eduy.	'Eduyyoth.
'Er. 'Erub.	'Erubin.
E.V.	English Version.
Giṭ.	Giṭṭin.
Glos.	Glossary.
Graetz.	Graetz. H., *Geschichte der Juden* (4th ed.).
Ḥag.	Ḥagigah.
Ḥan.	Ḥananeel b. Ḥushiel of Kairwan (c. 990-1050).
Ḥul.	Ḥullin.
Ḥ.M.	Ḥoshen ha-Mishpaṭ.
J.Jer.	Jerushalmi, the Jerusalem Talmud.
Jast.	M. Jastrow's Dictionary of the Targumim, the Talmud Bible and Yerushalmi, and the Midrashic Literature.
J.E.	Jewish Encyclopedia.
Kel.	Kelim.
Ket. Keth.	Kethuboth.
Ḳid.	Ḳiddushin.
Kil.	Kil'ayim.
Maharsha	R. Samuel Eliezer Halevi Edels (1555-1631).
Men.	Menaḥoth.
M.Ḳ.	Mo'ed Ḳaṭan.
MS.M.	Munich Codex of the Talmud.
Naz.	Nazir.
Pes.	Pesaḥim.
R.	Rab, Rabban, Rabbenu, Rabbi.
Ran	Rabbi Nissim b. Reuben of Gerondi (14th century).
Rashal	Notes and Glosses on the Talmud by R. Solomon Luria (d. 1573).

Rashi	Commentary of R. Isaac Yizḥaḳi (d. 1105).
Sanh.	Sanhedrin.
Sheb.	Shebi'ith.
Shebu.	Shebu'oth.
Sheḳ.	Sheḳalim.
Sonc. ed.	English Translation of the Babylonian Talmud, Soncino Press, London.
Soṭ.	Soṭah.
Strashun	Annotations by Samuel Strashun (1794-1872) in the Wilna editions of the Talmud.
Suk.	Sukkah.
T.A.	*Talmudische Archäologie*, by S. Krauss.
Ta'an.	Ta'anith.
Tem.	Temurah.
T.J.	Talmud Jerusalemi.
Tosaf.	Tosafoth.
Tosef.	Tosefta.
Ṭoho.	Ṭoharoth.
Wilna Gaon	Notes by Elijah of Wilna (1720-1797) in the Wilna editions of the Talmud.
Yeb.	Yebamoth.
Zeb.	Zebaḥim.

NAZIR

TRANSLATED INTO ENGLISH

WITH NOTES, GLOSSARY

AND INDICES

BY

RABBI B. D. KLIEN, B. A.

CONTENTS

INTRODUCTION

Nazir or Neziroth, as it is also sometimes known, is the fourth treatise of Seder Nashim, and deals with the laws regulating naziriteship. The assumption of nazirite vows, the different types of naziriteship, the observance and breach of the accompanying obligation to abstain from wine, shaving the hair, and contact with the dead, and the order of sacrifice on contact with the dead and on the completion of a nazirite's term, are all discussed. Little not narrowly relevant to these topics will be found in these pages, and the tractate contains but few haggadic passages.

The destruction of the Temple in 70 C.E. and the consequent cessation of the sacrificial system, precluded the nazirite vow from being properly terminated and so naziriteship was no longer undertaken; but the inclusion of the treatise in the order Nashim instead of Kodashim, whether as an antidote to Giṭṭin and Soṭah (v. fol. 2*a*) or because of its resemblance to Nedarim (v. Soṭah 2*a*) led to its provision with an adequate Gemara in both the Babylonian and the Jerusalem Talmud. In Geonic times, however, in common with Nedarim and Kodashim in general, the treatise was neglected, so that its text lacks the finish and excellent state of preservation of other talmudic treatises, whilst the absence of a commentary by Rashi, embodying traditional interpretations, increases the difficulties of the student. The commentary in the standard editions of the Talmud, bearing Rashi's name, is a much glossed one, ascribed to his son-in-law RIBaN (R. Judah b. Nathan); the Tosafoth issued from the school of R. Perez b. Elijah of Corbeil (13th cent.). RIBaN notes a number of resemblances in style between our treatise and the Jerusalem Talmud (v., e.g., fol. 32*a*), and in this connection it should be remarked that the placing of Nazir between Giṭṭin and Soṭah on fol. 2*a*, follows the order of the treatises in the Palestinian Talmud and not in the Babylonian Talmud.

Of individual cases of naziriteship, the Bible records few—Samson and Absalom naturally spring to mind. Our tractate affords ample evidence, however, of the existence of numerous nazirites in Maccabaean and later times, whilst the naziriteship of Helena, the illustrious proselyte Queen of the Adiabene, should be noted, for it is to her residence in Jerusalem which its observance entailed that we may no doubt trace the many stories of herself and her family preserved elsewhere in the Talmud.

Naziriteship, with its ascetic obligations, found little favour in Pharisee circles, as is evidenced by the implied disapproval of Simeon the Just (v. fol. 4*b*), and the later statement of R. Eleazar ha-Ḳappar (fol. 19*a*) that the nazirite is indeed a sinner. It is not impossible that many of the ascetic sects that flourished in the early centuries of the current era, began as nazirite groups. Little positive evidence of this can, however, be found in our treatise. A brief summary of the contents follow.

CHAPTER I. Assumption of the vow and its duration. The various circumlocutory ways in which naziriteship was undertaken should be noted as instancing the extreme reluctance to utter a direct vow, observed throughout rabbinic literature. The Samson nazirite and the life-long nazirite are also defined.

CHAPTER II. Continues the themes of the first chapter, and discusses whether it is possible to undertake a naziriteship, limited to part only of the nazirite duties.

CHAPTER III. The procedure of polling at the close of naziriteship and when uncleanness intervenes is described.

CHAPTER IV. The annulment of naziriteship by appeal to a Sage, a husband's rights over his wife's nazirite vows, and a father's power to impose nazirite vows on his son are here discussed. In this Chapter there occurs an *Haggadic* passage dealing with the importance of motive in action.

CHAPTER V. Other aspects of the incidence of nazirite vows are examined, and reference is made to the situation that arose when the destruction of the Temple rendered impossible the completion of nazirite vows previously undertaken.

CHAPTER VI discusses the duties of the nazirite in greater detail and the steps that must be taken in the event of a breach of observance of the oath.

Chapter VII. When a nazirite may knowingly break his vow, and unwitting breaches of the same.

Chapter VIII. Deals with uncertain breaches of the vow.

Chapter IX. Gentiles cannot become nazirites, women and slaves can. The last Mishnah discusses whether or not the prophet Samuel was a nazirite.

The translation was prepared jointly by my brother, Mr. Hyman Klein, M.A., and myself, and many valuable notes were added by him. The whole of the manuscript was read by Mr. Maurice Simon, whose influence will be apparent to all who are acquainted with the fluidity and charm of his prose. To both of these I take this opportunity of expressing my thanks.

Authorities consulted are mentioned in the notes. Occasionally the German translation of Lazarus Goldschmidt and the English translation of the Mishnah by Canon H. Danby were also referred to.

B. D. KLIEN

The Indices of this Tractate have been compiled by Judah J. Slotki, M. A.

NAZIR

CHAPTER I

MISHNAH. ALL THE SUBSTITUTES FOR THE NAZIRITE VOW[1] ARE EQUIVALENT TO NAZIRITE VOWS. IF A MAN SAYS, 'I SHALL BE [ONE],' HE BECOMES A NAZIRITE. [IF HE SAYS,] 'I SHALL BE COMELY, A NAZIRITE, A NAZIK,[2] A NAZIAḤ[2] A PAZIAḤ,' HE BECOMES A NAZIRITE. [IF HE SAYS,] 'I INTEND TO BE LIKE THIS,' OR 'I INTEND TO CURL [MY HAIR],' OR 'I MEAN TO TEND [MY HAIR],' OR 'I UNDERTAKE TO DEVELOP TRESSES,' HE BECOMES A NAZIRITE. [IF HE SAYS,] 'I TAKE UPON MYSELF [AN OBLIGATION INVOLVING] BIRDS,' R. MEIR SAYS HE BECOMES A NAZIRITE, BUT THE SAGES SAY HE DOES NOT BECOME A NAZIRITE.

GEMARA. Seeing that the Tanna[3] is teaching the order Nashim,[4] why does he speak of the nazirite?—The Tanna had in mind the scriptural verse, *Then it cometh to pass if she find no favour in his eyes, because he hath found some unseemly thing in her,*[5] and he reasons thus. What was the cause of the woman's infidelity? Wine. Further, he proceeds, whosoever sees an unfaithful wife in her degradation[6] will take a nazirite's vow and abjure wine.[7]

[How is it that in enunciating the general rule,[8] the Mishnah]

(1) V. Num. VI, 1-22. (2) These 'substitutes' are mutilations of the Hebrew word *nazir*. Cf. *Ned.* 10*b*. (3) V. Glos. (4) Nashim, the third of the six orders of the Mishnah contains the laws pertaining to women. The inclusion of the nazirite regulations appears at first sight incongruous. (5) Deut. XXIV, 1. The verse is quoted in the concluding paragraph of M. Giṭṭin. This suggests that the order of the treatises assumed was Giṭṭin, Nazir, Soṭah, the order of the Jerusalem Talmud. In Soṭ. 2*a*, a different reason is given assuming the order of the Babylonian Talmud, viz.:—Nedarim, Nazir, Soṭah. V. however Tosaf. s.v. מאי. (6) Cf. Num. V, 11-31. (7) For this reason Nazir is followed by Soṭah. (8) I.e., all the substitutes for the nazirite vow, etc.

mentions first 'substitutes' and then gives examples of 'allusions'?[1] —Raba, others say Kadi,[2] said: There is a hiatus [in the Mishnah] and it should read as follows: 'All the substitutes for the nazirite vow are equivalent to nazirite vows, and all allusions to the nazirite vow are equivalent to nazirite vows. The following are allusions. If a man says, "I shall be [one]," he becomes a nazirite [etc.].' Ought not then the substitutes to be enumerated first?[3]—It is customary for the Tanna to explain first what he mentions last. Thus we learn: With what materials may [the Sabbath lamp] be kindled, and with what may it not be kindled?[4] and the exposition begins: It is forbidden to kindle etc. [Again, we learn:] With what materials may [hot victuals] be covered [on the Sabbath,][5] and with what may they not be covered?[6] and the exposition begins: It is forbidden to cover etc. [Again:] What may a woman wear when she goes out [on the Sabbath], and what may she not wear when she goes out?[7] and the exposition begins: She must not go out, etc.

But have we not learnt: With what trappings may an animal go out [on the Sabbath], and with what may it not go out?[8] whilst the exposition begins: The camel may go out etc.; [and again:] Some both inherit and bequeath,[9] and some inherit but do not bequeath. Some bequeath and do not inherit, and some neither inherit nor bequeath,[10] whilst the exposition begins: The following both inherit and bequeath?—The truth is that the Tanna adopts sometimes one method and sometimes the other, [according to circumstances]. In the first set of cases adduced, because the prohibition is a personal one,[11] this personal prohibition is expounded first. On the other hand, in the case of the animal, since the prohibition arises primarily through the animal,[12] those things which are permitted are mentioned first. [2b] With inheritance, again, the basic type of inheritance is dealt with first. Granted all this, [in the case of the

(1) Viz., 'I shall be one' etc. Allusions, Heb. *yadoth;* lit., 'handles', phrases suggesting the nazirite's vow. (2) *Aliter,* others quote the statement anonymously. (3) Cf. Ned. 2*b*ff. (4) Shab. 20*b*. (5) To retain their warmth. (6) Ibid. 47*b*. (7) Ibid. 57*a*. (8) Ibid. 52*b*. (9) I.e., to those from whom they inherit. (10) B.B. 108*a*. (11) He himself is forbidden to do the action. (12) He may not allow the animal to wear the trappings.

nazirite vow] why should not the substitutes be enumerated first? —There is a special reason, viz., that [the rule regarding the efficacy of] the allusions is derived [from the scriptural text] by a process of inference[1] and therefore the Tanna set a special value on it. Then why does he not mention them first?—For opening the subject the Tanna prefers to mention the basic type of vow,[2] but in his exposition, he illustrates the allusions first.

IF A MAN SAYS 'I SHALL BE [ONE],' HE BECOMES A NAZIRITE. But might he not mean, 'I shall keep a fast day'?[3]—Samuel said: We must suppose that a nazirite is passing by [when he makes this declaration]. Are we to infer from this that Samuel is of the opinion that allusions, the significance of which is not manifest,[4] have not the force of a direct statement?[5]—Let me explain. [What Samuel means is that] if a nazirite is passing by, there is no reason to suspect a different intention,[6] but without question, if no nazirite is passing by, we say that he might mean, 'I shall keep a fast day.'[7]

But perhaps his purpose was to free the other from his sacrifices?[8] —[We presume it to be known] that he added mentally ['a nazirite']. If so, it is surely obvious [that he becomes a nazirite]?—It might be thought that we require his utterance and his intention to coincide, and so we are told [that this is not so].

'I SHALL BE COMELY' . . . HE BECOMES A NAZIRITE. Perhaps he means, 'I shall be comely before Him in [the performance of] precepts, as has been taught: [The verse], *This is my God and I will glorify*[9] *Him*[10] means, I will glorify Him in [the performance of]

(1) They are not mentioned explicitly, but are inferred from the redundant sequence of references to the Nazirite vow in Num. VI, 2. V. Ned. 3*a*. (2) Heb. '*Ḳorban*', 'sacrifice', the generic term for every kind of vow. The 'substitutes' are considered essential forms of the vow, the 'allusions' subsidiary forms. (3) Lit., 'I shall be in a fast'. (4) As would be the case if a nazirite did not pass by at the time. (5) Ḳid. 5*a* reports Samuel as holding the opposite. (6) [Although the allusion is not particularly manifest, in accordance with Samuel's view, in Ḳid. *loc. cit.* Cf. Asheri.] (7) And in the absence of an allusion of any likely significance, there is no obligation at all. Cf. Asheri. (8) I.e., defray their cost. His meaning would then be, 'I shall be in his place for the purpose of offering his sacrifices;' cf. Num. VI, 14ff. (9) 'Glorify' and 'comely' are from the same Hebrew root. (10) Ex. XV, 2.

precepts; I shall build an attractive booth,[1] procure a faultless palm-branch,[1] wear elegant fringes, write a mangificent Scroll of the Law and provide it with wrappings of choicest silk?—Samuel said: [We assume that] he takes hold of his hair[2] when he says, 'I shall be comely.'

[Seeing that to become] a nazirite is in a way a sin,[3] can it be termed comely?—[3a] Yes. For even R. Eliezer ha-Ḳappar who says that a nazirite is accounted a sinner, means only the nazirite who has contracted ritual impurity; for, since he must nullify [his previous abstinence][4] in accordance with the rule laid down by the Merciful One, *But the former days shall be void, because his consecration was defiled,*[5] there is a danger that he may break his nazirite vow.[6] But a nazirite who remains ritually clean is not termed a sinner.[7]

I INTEND TO BE LIKE THIS: Granted that he takes hold of his hair, he does not say 'I intend to be through this,'[8] [but only 'like this']?—Samuel said: We suppose that a nazirite is passing by at the time.

I INTEND TO CURL[9] [MY HAIR]. How do we know that this [word MESALSEL] refers to the curling of the hair?—From a remark made by a maidservant[10] of Rabbi's household, who said to a certain man: How much longer are you going to curl [*mesalsel*] your hair? But perhaps [it refers to] the Torah[11] in accordance with the verse, *Extol her* [salseleha] *and she will exalt thee?*[12]—Samuel said: Here, too, we suppose that he takes hold of his hair.

I MEAN TO TEND[13] [MY HAIR]. How do we know that this [word MEKALKEL] refers to the tending of his hair?—From what we

(1) For the Feast of Tabernacles. Cf. Lev. XXIII, 42 and 40. (2) And so the reference is to the naziriteship, when his hair would grow long. (3) Because he denies himself that which the Torah has permitted. (4) The period which elapsed before he became unclean. (5) Num. VI, 12. (6) He may not be able to control his desire for wine for the longer period. (7) Cf. *infra* 19*a*, where the opposite is asserted. (8) The text is uncertain. The meaning would apparently be: I intend to discipline myself through my hair, reading בזה instead of כזה in cur. edd. (9) Heb. *mesalsel*. (10) This maidservant always spoke Hebrew, v. Meg. 18*a*. (11) I.e., he vows to engage in the study of Torah. (12) Prov. IV, 8. (13) Heb. *mekalkel*.

learnt: 'With regard to orpiment,[1] R. Judah said that there must be sufficient to depilate the *kilkul*,'[2] and Rab commented: [This means the hair of] one of the temples.[3] But might it not mean tending the poor, in accordance with the verse, *And Joseph sustained* [wa-yekalkel] *his father and his brothers?*[4]—Samuel said: Here too, we assume that he takes hold of his hair.

'I UNDERTAKE TO DEVELOP[5] TRESSES,'[6] HE BECOMES A NAZIRITE. How do we know that this [word] *shilluaḥ* signifies increase?—From the verse, *Thy shoots* [shelohayik] *are a park of pomegranates.*[7] But perhaps it has the significance of 'removal'[8] in accordance with the verse, *And sendeth* [we-sholeaḥ] *waters upon the fields?*[9] —The occurrence of the word *pera'* [tresses] in connection with the nazirite gives the tanna the clue. It says here, *He shall be holy, he shall let the locks* [pera'] *grow long*,[10] and it says elsewhere regarding an ordinary priest,[11] *Nor suffer their locks* [pera'] *to grow long* [yeshalleḥu].[12] Alternatively, we can say that the *sholeaḥ* used of water,[13] also signifies increase,[14] for when produce is watered it shoots up.

[IF HE SAYS] 'I TAKE UPON MYSELF [AN OBLIGATION INVOLVING] BIRDS,' R. MEIR SAYS HE BECOMES A NAZIRITE. What is R. Meir's reason?—Resh Laḳish said: [In making this vow] he has in mind the birds that are coupled with hair in the scriptural verse, *Till his* hair *was grown long like eagles' feathers, and his nails like* birds' *claws.*[15] R. Meir is of the opinion that a man will

(1) Heb. *sid*, usually lime, here orpiment, used as a depilatory. (2) The transference of this amount from a private to a public domain on the Sabbath constitutes an indictable offence. (3) Shab. 80*b*. (4) Gen. XLVII, 12. (5) Heb. *leshaleaḥ*. (6) Heb. *pera'*. (7) Cant. IV, 13. (8) I.e., he vows to remove his hair. (9) Job V, 10. I.e. transports the waters from field to field (*cf.* the context). (10) Num. VI, 5. (11) I.e., not the High Priest, who is subject to stricter regulations. V. Sanh. 22*b*. (12) Ezek. XLIV, 20. In Sanh. 22*b* this same comparison is made to show that *pera'* means a growth of thirty days' duration (the normal duration of a nazirite vow). Thus whether *shilluaḥ* means 'grow' or 'remove', the nazirite vow is implicit in the word *pera'*. (13) In the verse of Job. (14) [Cur. edd. add in brackets, 'as R. Joseph translated,' referring to the Targum on the Prophets ascribed to R. Joseph. V. B.Ḳ. (Sonc. ed.) p. 9, n. 9. The reading that follows is, however, not found in our Targum.] (15) Dan. IV, 30. It is assumed that he takes hold of his hair, or a nazirite is passing by (Rashi). Cf. below.

refer to one thing when he means something else occurring in the same context,[1] [3b] whilst the Rabbis are of the opinion that a man will not refer to one thing when he means another. R. Joḥanan said: Both [R. Meir and the Rabbis] are agreed that a man will not refer to one thing etc.,[2] and R. Meir's reason is that we take account of the possibility that what he had undertaken was to bring the birds of a ritually unclean nazirite.[3]

But if we are to take [possible meanings] into account, why should we not say that he was undertaking [to bring] a free will offering of birds?—In that event, he would have said, 'I undertake to bring a nest.'[4]

But perhaps he meant: I undertake [to bring] the birds of a leper?[5]—We must suppose that a nazirite passes by at the time. But perhaps it was a ritually unclean nazirite and he desired to free him from his [obligatory] sacrifices?—We must suppose that a ritually clean nazirite passes by at the time.[6]

What [practical] difference is there between them?[7]—There would be a difference [for example] if he should say: I take upon myself [an obligation involving] the birds mentioned in the same context as hair. According to R. Joḥanan, notwithstanding that he says this, he becomes a nazirite if one is passing at the time, but not otherwise;[8] whereas according to R. Simeon b. Laḳish, even though no nazirite passes by at the time [he becomes a nazirite].[9]

(1) Lit., 'he is seized by what is close to it.' E.g., here, he says 'birds' when he means 'hair'. (2) And therefore R. Meir's reason is not the one given by Resh Laḳish. (3) V. Num. VI, 10. [I.e., he undertook to bring such birds should he afterwards become unclean during his proposed naziriteship; hence he becomes a nazirite (Rashi).] (4) As this was the usual manner in which free-will offerings of birds were made. (5) Cf. Lev. XIV, 4. [That is he undertook to bring birds *for* a leper freeing him from his obligatory sacrifices. Asheri.] This question creates a difficulty both for R. Joḥanan and Resh Laḳish (Rashi). (6) And as such a one has not to bring the offering of birds, he must have referred to himself. (7) Between R. Joḥanan and Resh Laḳish. (8) As he may simply be undertaking to bring an offering of birds. (9) [That is, according to R. Meir; v. Rashi and Tosaf. This difference will, however, apply also on the view of the Rabbis, for where he explicitly states . . . 'the birds mentioned in the same context as hair,' the Rabbis would also agree according to Resh Laḳish that he becomes a nazirite; cf. Rashi 2b (top).]

But is there any authority who disputes that a man may refer to one thing and mean another occurring in the same context? Has it not been taught: If a man says, '[By] my right hand,' it is accounted an oath.[1] Now, surely the reason for this is the verse, *When he lifted up his right hand and his left hand unto heaven, and swore by Him who liveth for ever?*[2]—Not so. It is because the expression '[By my] right hand,' is itself an oath, as it has been taught: How do we know that if a man says, '[By] my right hand,' it is accounted an oath? From the verse, *The Lord hath sworn by his right hand.*[3] And how do we know that if a man says, 'By my left hand,' it is accounted an oath? Because the verse continues, *And by the arm of his strength.*[3]

MISHNAH. [IF A MAN SAYS] 'I DECLARE MYSELF A NAZIRITE [TO ABSTAIN] FROM PRESSED GRAPES, OR FROM GRAPE STONES, OR FROM POLLING, OR FROM [CONTRACTING] RITUAL DEFILEMENT,' HE BECOMES A NAZIRITE AND ALL THE REGULATIONS OF NAZIRITESHIP APPLY TO HIM.

GEMARA. The Mishnah is not in agreement with R. Simeon, for it has been taught: R. Simeon says that he does not incur the liabilities [of a nazirite] unless he vows to abstain from everything [that is forbidden to a nazirite], whilst the Rabbis say that even though he vows to abstain from one thing only, he becomes a nazirite.

What is R. Simeon's reason?—Scripture says, [*He shall eat*] nothing *that is made of the grape-vine, from the pressed grapes even to the grape-stone.*[4] And what is the Rabbis' reason?—The verse reads, *He shall abstain*[5] *from wine and strong drink.*[6]

(1) Tosaf. Ned. I; e.g., if he says, 'My right hand that I shall eat this loaf.' (2) Dan. XII, 7; and when he refers to his right hand he means the oath in the same context. (3) Isa. LXII, 8. ['*Arm of his strength*' refers to the left hand; v. Ber. 6a.] (4) The emphasis is laid on the word '*nothing*', so that the vow must expressly include everything. Num. VI, 4. (5) Lit., 'vow to abstain'. (6) Ibid. VI, 3. Thus it is sufficient if his vow refers specifically to wine only. This verse

What does R. Simeon make of the statement, '*He shall abstain from wine and strong drink*'?—He requires it to prohibit wine the drinking of which is a ritual obligation as well as wine the drinking of which is optional. What is this [wine the drinking of which is obligatory]? The wine of *Ḳiddush*[1] and *Habdalah*,[1] [is it not]? [4*a*] But surely here he is bound by the oath taken on Mount Sinai?[2] —We must therefore suppose the following dictum of Raba to be indicated, [viz.:]—[If a man says,] 'I swear to drink [wine]' and later says, 'I wish to be a nazirite,' the nazirite vow operates despite the oath.[3]

And do not the Rabbis also require [this verse] to prohibit wine, the drinking of which is a ritual obligation as well as wine the drinking of which is optional?—If this were its [sole] purpose, only '*wine*' need have been mentioned in the verse! [What is the purport of the addition] of '*strong drink*'! It is to enable us to infer both things.[4] And R. Simeon?[5]—He [will hold] that the reason for the addition of *strong drink* is to guide us in the interpretation of the same expression when used in connection with the Temple service, in the verse, *Drink no wine nor strong drink, thou, nor thy sons with thee.*[6] Just as for the nazirite, only wine is forbidden but not other beverages, so in connection with the Temple service, only wine is forbidden [to the priests], but not other intoxicating beverages. This conflicts with the opinion of R. Judah, for it has been taught:

is made here to refer to the actual taking of the nazirite vow; though from the context it might be thought to be part of the enumeration of objects forbidden the nazirite.

(1) V. Glos. (2) I.e., surely his vow cannot annul obligations in existence since the giving of the law on Mount Sinai, so Rashi. Tosaf. (Rabbenu Tam) replaces the last two sentences by the following: 'Can it be that the wine of *Ḳiddush* and *Habdalah* is indicated? But is he then bound by an oath taken on Mount Sinai?' According to this view there is *no* scriptural obligation to drink wine at *Ḳiddush* and *Habdalah*. This is the view usually accepted. (3) I.e., although this is wine the drinking of which is incumbent on him. (4) Viz.: (i) wine the drinking of which is an obligation is forbidden the nazirite. (ii) though he vows to abstain from one thing only he becomes a nazirite. (5) How will he meet the argument of the Rabbis? (6) The verse was addressed to Aaron as High Priest. Lev. X, 9.

R. Judah said that [a priest] who eats preserved figs from Keilah,[1] or drinks honey or milk, and then enters the Temple, is guilty.[2]

Alternatively,[3] R. Simeon rejects the principle that a prohibition can come into operation when a prohibition [on a different count] is already present,[4] as has been taught: R. Simeon says that a man who eats carrion[5] on the Day of Atonement is not liable [to a penalty for breach of observance of the day].[6]

What do the Rabbis make of the verse, ['*He shall eat*] nothing *that is made of the grape-vine*'?[7]—The Rabbis will tell you that this teaches that [the various kinds of food] forbidden to a nazirite can combine together.[8] R. Simeon, on the other hand, does not require a rule about combination, for it has been taught: R. Simeon says that a mite [of forbidden food] is sufficient [to entail liability] to stripes; a quantity equivalent to an olive is required only where a sacrifice is [the appropriate penalty].

MISHNAH. [IF A MAN SAYS] 'I VOW TO BE LIKE SAMSON,[9] THE SON OF MANOAH, WHO WAS THE HUSBAND OF DELILAH,' OR 'WHO PLUCKED UP THE GATES OF GAZAH,'[10] OR 'WHOSE EYES THE PHILISTINES PUT OUT,'[11] HE BECOMES A NAZIRITE LIKE SAMSON.

(1) A town in the lowlands of Judea, cf. Josh. XV, 44, v. Sanh. (Sonc. ed.) p. 481, n. 6. (2) Of transgressing the prohibition against strong drink in Lev. X, 9. (3) An alternative reason for R. Simeon's opinion that he does not become a nazirite unless he vows to abstain from everything, is being given (Rashi). (4) In other words, an act already prohibited cannot be prohibited on another count. Hence, once his vow to abstain from wine begins to operate, he can no longer become a full nazirite (Rashi). This interpretation considers the statement, 'I declare myself a nazirite (to abstain) from pressed grapes' to consist of two parts in the following order: (i) I vow to abstain from pressed grapes; (ii) I declare myself a nazirite. For other interpretations. v. Tosaf. and Asheri. (5) Heb. *nebelah*, v. Glos. (6) Carrion being already in itself prohibited. (7) V. *supra* p. 7, n. 4. (8) I.e., supposing he eats less of each kind than the minimum size of an olive, yet the *total* quantity consumed is the size of an olive, he is liable to stripes. (9) Samson was a nazirite to a limited extent only. V. next Mishnah. (10) V. Judg. XVI, 3. (11) V. Judg. XVI, 21.

GEMARA. Why must [the Mishnah] specify all these expressions?—All are necessary. For if he were to say, 'I wish to be like Samson,' I might think that some other Samson [was intended], and so we are told [that he must add] 'like the son of Manoah.' Again, if he were to add [only] 'the son of Manoah,' I might think that there is someone else so named, and so we are told [that he must add], 'like the husband of Delilah,' or 'like him whose eyes the Philistines put out.'[1]

MISHNAH. WHAT DIFFERENCE IS THERE BETWEEN A NAZIRITE LIKE SAMSON AND A LIFE-NAZIRITE?[2] A LIFE-NAZIRITE, WHENEVER HIS HAIR BECOMES BURDENSOME, MAY THIN IT WITH A RAZOR AND THEN OFFER THREE ANIMAL SACRIFICES,[3] WHILST SHOULD HE BE RITUALLY DEFILED, HE MUST OFFER THE SACRIFICE [PRESCRIBED] FOR DEFILEMENT.[4] THE NAZIRITE LIKE SAMSON IS NOT PERMITTED TO THIN HIS HAIR SHOULD IT BECOME BURDENSOME, AND IF [RITUALLY] DEFILED, DOES NOT OFFER THE SACRIFICE [PRESCRIBED] FOR DEFILEMENT.

GEMARA. How does the life-nazirite come in here?[5]—There is a hiatus [in the Mishnah], and it should read as follows: If a man says, 'I intend to be a life-nazirite,' he becomes a life-nazirite. What difference is there between a nazirite like Samson and a life-nazirite? A life-nazirite whenever his hair becomes burdensome may thin it with a razor and then offer three animal sacrifices, whilst should he be ritually defiled, he must offer the sacrifice [prescribed] for defilement. The nazirite like Samson is not permitted to thin his hair with a razor should it become burdensome, [4*b*] and if ritually defiled does not offer the sacrifice [prescribed] for defilement.

(1) Thus the first three expressions are *de rigueur*, but for the third equivalents may be used. (2) One who declares himself a nazirite for life. Samson was also a nazirite for life. (3) A nazirite on terminating his abstinence was required to offer three animal sacrifices. V. Num. VI, 13ff. (4) Defilement of a nazirite. Num. VI, 9. (5) Lit., 'who mentioned its name'.

[You say that the nazirite like Samson] does not have to offer the sacrifice [prescribed] for defilement,[1] enabling me to infer that he is subject to the nazirite obligation [which forbids him to defile himself]. Who then is [the author of] our Mishnah, [seeing that] it can be neither R. Judah nor R. Simeon? For it has been taught: R. Judah said that a nazirite like Samson is permitted to defile himself [deliberately, by contact] with the dead, for Samson himself did so; R. Simeon says that if a man declares, '[I intend to be] a nazirite like Samson,' his statement is of no effect, since we are not aware that Samson personally ever pronounced a nazirite vow.[2] [We ask then:] Who [is the author of our Mishnah]? It cannot be R. Judah, for he says that [a nazirite like Samson] may even [defile himself] intentionally, whereas our Mishnah [merely] states [that no sacrifice need be offered] *if* he has become defiled [accidentally]; nor can it be R. Simeon since he says that the vow does not become operative at all!—Actually it is R. Judah [and the nazirite like Samson is permitted to defile himself] but because in referring to the life-nazirite,[3] the Mishnah uses the expression 'SHOULD HE BE [RITUALLY] DEFILED,' the same expression is used in referring to the nazirite like Samson.[4]

May we say that the difference [of R. Judah and R. Simeon] is essentially the same as that of the following Tannaim? For it has been taught: [If a man says,] 'This [food] shall be [as forbidden] for me as a firstling,'[5] R. Jacob says he may not eat it, but R. Jose says he may.[6] May we not say then that R. Judah agrees with R. Jacob in holding that the object [with which the comparison is made,][7] need not itself be one forbidden as the result of a vow, whilst R. Simeon agrees with R. Jose in holding that the object [with which comparison is made] must be one forbidden as the result of a vow?—This is not so. Both [R. Judah and R. Simeon] are agreed that it is necessary for the object [with which comparison

(1) I.e., if he becomes unclean. (2) Tosef. Nazir I, 3. (3) Who is forbidden to defile himself. (4) And the *if* is not to be pressed. (5) The firstlings of clean domestic animals were the perquisite of the priests and could be eaten by them only. V. Num. XVIII, 15. (6) V. Ned. 13*a*. (7) E.g., the firstling or Samson. It is impossible to vow not to eat a firstling as it is holy from birth.

is made] to be one forbidden as the result of a vow, but the case of the firstling is different, since in the verse, [*When a man voweth a vow*][1] *unto the Lord,*[2] [the superfluous words '*unto the Lord*'] include the firstling[3] [as a legitimate object of comparison].

What does R. Jose reply [to this argument]?—He will say that the expression '*unto the Lord*' serves to include the sin-offering and the guilt-offering[4] [but not the firstling]. [We may ask him:] On what ground, then, are the sin-offering and the guilt-offering included rather than the firstling?— [He would reply:] The sin-offering and the guilt-offering are included because they have to be expressly dedicated,[5] but the firstling is excluded since it need not be expressly dedicated. And R. Jacob?—He can rejoin: Firstlings too, are expressly dedicated, for it has been taught: [The members] of our Teacher's household[6] used to say: How do we know that when a firstling is born in a man's flock, it is his duty to dedicate it expressly [for the altar]? Because it says, *The males shalt thou dedicate.*[7] And R. Jose?—He can reply: Granted that it is a religious duty to dedicate it [expressly], yet if he fails to do so, is it not nevertheless sacred?[8]

[It may be said:] In the case of the nazirite, too, is there not a phrase '*unto the Lord*'?[9]—This is required for the purpose taught [in the following passage]: Simon the Just[10] said: In the whole of my life, I ate of the guilt-offering of a defiled nazirite [only once].[11]

(1) From this phrase we infer that the object used for comparison must be itself prohibited as the result of a vow. V. Ned. 13*a*. (2) Num. XXX, 3. (3) Since it must be dedicted *unto the Lord* by the owner. (4) Being obligatory, they might be thought not to count as things dedicated by a vow. (5) Lit., 'they are seized by a vow'. Although the obligation to offer a sin-offering does not result through a vow, yet the animal to be used must be dedicated by the owner, 'This is my sin-offering.' (6) Probably R. Gamaliel III son of R. Judah ha-Nasi I (called simply Our Teacher) cf. *Halikoth 'Olam* I, 3. (7) Deut. XV, 19. (8) And so the firstling must be excluded as an object of comparison. (9) Num. VI, 2. And so should it not be possible to vow to become a nazirite like Samson? (10) High Priest circa 300 B.C.E., v. however Aboth (Sonc. ed.) p. 2, n. 1. (11) He feared that nazirites, after defilement, would regret their vows because of the inevitable prolongation. As the sacrifice would then retrospectively prove to have been unnecessary, he refused to eat of it.

This man who came to me from the South country, had beauteous eyes and handsome features with his locks heaped into curls. I asked him: 'Why, my son, didst thou resolve to destroy such wonderful hair?' He answered: 'In my native town, I was my father's shepherd, and, on going down to draw water from the well, I used to gaze at my reflection [in its waters]. Then my evil inclination assailed me, seeking to compass my ruin,[1] and so I said to it, "Base wretch! Why dost thou plume thyself on a world that is not thine own, for thy latter end is with worms and maggots. I swear[2] I shall shear these locks to the glory of Heaven!"' Then I rose, and kissed him upon his head, and said to him: 'Like unto thee, may there be many nazirites in Israel. Of such as thou art, does the verse say, *When a man shall clearly utter a vow, the vow of a nazirite to consecrate himself* unto the Lord.'[3]

But was not Samson a nazirite [in the ordinary sense]?[4] Surely the verse states, *For the child shall be a nazirite unto God from the womb!*[5]—It was the angel who said this.

How do we know that [Samson] did defile himself [by contact] with the dead? Shall I say, because it is written, *With the jawbone of an ass have I smitten a thousand men,*[6] but it is possible that he thrust it at them without touching them? But [we know it] again from the following, *And smote thirty men of them and took their spoil.*[7] But it is possible that he stripped them first and slew them afterwards?—It says clearly [first], *And he smote,* [and then,] *And took.* But it is still possible that he [merely] wounded them mortally[8] [before stripping them]!—[We must say], therefore, that it was known by tradition [that he did come into contact with them].

Where does it state [in the Scriptures] that a life-nazirite [may thin his hair]?—It has been taught: Rabbi said that Absalom was

(1) Lit., 'drive me from the world'. (2) Lit., 'by the (Temple) service', a common form of oath at this period. (3) Num. VI, 2. [The story has a parallel in the familiar Narcissus story, Ovid, *Metamorphoses*, III, 402ff; but its moral in endowing the youth with the power of self-mastery is evidently superior.] (4) I.e., was not his naziriteship the result of a vow? (5) Judg. XIII, 5. (6) Judg. XV, 16. (7) Judg. XIV, 19. (8) [Defilement is communicated only after the last breath of life is gone.]

a life-nazirite, for it says, *And it came to pass at the end of forty years that Absalom said to the king: I pray thee, let me go and pay my vow which I have vowed unto the Lord in Hebron.*[1] He used to cut his hair every twelve months, for it says, [*And when he polled his head,*] *now it was at every year's* [yamim] *end* [*that he polled it*],[2] [5*a*] and the meaning of the word '*yamim*' here is decided by its meaning when used in connection with houses in walled cities;[3] just as there it means twelve months,[4] so here it means twelve months. R. Nehorai said: [Absalom] used to poll every thirty days. R. Jose said: He used to poll on the eve of each Sabbath, for princes usually poll on the eve of each Sabbath.

[We have said that] Rabbi's reason [for interpreting '*yamim*' as a year] is because of its occurrence in connection with houses in walled cities. But has not Rabbi himself said that '*yamim*' [in that connection] means not less than two days?[5]—The only reason that he uses the comparison at all[6] is because of the reference to the heaviness [of Absalom's hair],[7] and two days' growth is not heavy.[8]

Why should it not be two years, in accordance with the verse, *And it came to pass at the end of two full years?*[9]—From a text containing '*yamim*' without mention of '*years*' conclusions may be drawn concerning another text containing '*yamim*' without mention of '*years*';[10] but no conclusion can be drawn here from this verse where there is mention of '*years*'.

Why should it not be thirty days, for there is a verse, *but a whole month?*[11]—From a text mentioning '*yamim*' without '*months*', conclusions may be drawn concerning another text mentioning

(1) The verse following states that Absalom vowed to serve the Lord. This, together with the known length of his hair, leads to the conclusion that he was a life-nazirite. II Sam. XV, 7. (2) II Sam. XIV, 26; *yamim* usually means 'days'. (3) V. Lev. XXV, 29. (4) Since the word 'year' is used explicitly in the same connection. (5) V. 'Ar. 31*a*, where he infers from this text that redemption cannot take place before the second day, though it may take place any time within the year. (6) The *Gezerah shawah* (v. Glos.). (7) V. II Sam. XIV, 26. (8) Hence the comparison must be with *yamim* in the sense of year, which it also bears in this passage; v. n. 4. (9) Lit., 'two years of *yamim*', Gen. XLI, 1. (10) E.g., from Lev. XXV, 29 to II Sam. XIV, 26. (11) Lit., 'a month of *yamim*', Num. XI, 20.

'yamim' without *'months'*,[1] but this verse affords no indication since *'months'* are mentioned therewith.

Why should not the inference be made from *mi-yamim yamimah* [*'from days to days'*]?[2]—Conclusions may be drawn concerning a text containing *'yamim'*, from another [text] containing *'yamim'*, but not from one containing *'yamimah'*.

But what is the difference [between *'yamim'* and *'yamimah'*]? Have not the school of R. Ishmael taught that in the verses, *And the priest shall* come again,[3] *Then the priest shall* come in,[3] *'coming again'* and *'coming in'* mean one and the same thing?[4]—Inference [from non-identical expressions] is permissible where there is no identical expression [on which to base the inference], but where an identical expression exists, the inference must be drawn from the identical expression.[5]

Another reply [to the suggestion that inference be made from *'yamimah'*]: How do we know [with certainty] that [they went] once every three months? May not the four times per annum have occurred alternately at intervals of four months and of two months?[6]

'R. Nehorai said: [Absalom] used to poll every thirty days.' What is his reason?—[Ordinary] priests [poll every thirty days][7] because [their hair] becomes burdensome, and so here it would become burdensome [after thirty days].[8]

'R. Jose said: He polled on the eve of each Sabbath, [etc.]' What difference then was there between him and his brothers?[9]—When a festival occurred in mid-week, his brothers polled, but he did not do so. Alternatively, his brothers [if they wished] could poll on Friday morning, but he could not do so until the late afternoon.

(1) V. *supra* p. 14, n. 10. (2) The reference is to Jephthah's daughter, visited by the Israelitish maidens *'four days in the year'*, i.e., apparently, at equal intervals of three months. Judg. XI, 40. (3) Lev. XIV, 39-44, referring to an infected house. (4) For purposes of inference, v. Hor. (Sonc. ed.), p. 57, n. 11. How much more so then with words so similar as *'yamim'* and *'yamimah'*! (5) I.e., since there is another context where the word *'yamim'* occurs, we learn from that and not from *'yamimah'*. (6) It is impossible therefore to give an exact value to *'yamimah'*. (7) V. Ta'an. 17*a*. (8) And Absalom polled when his hair became heavy. II Sam. XIV, 26. (9) Since all princes poll weekly.

What were the forty years referred to [by Absalom]?[1]—R. Nehorai, citing R. Joshua, said that it means 'forty years after [the Israelites] had demanded a king.'[2] It has been taught: The year in which they demanded a king, was the tenth year [of the principate of] Samuel the Ramathean.[3]

MISHNAH. A NAZIRITE VOW OF UNSPECIFIED DURATION [REMAINS IN FORCE] THIRTY DAYS.

GEMARA. Whence is this rule derived?—R. Mattena said: The text reads *He shall be* [yihyeh] *holy,*[4] and the numerical value[5] of the word *yihyeh* is thirty.[6] Bar Pada said: [The duration of the vow] corresponds to the number of times that parts of the root *nazar* are found in the Torah,[7] viz., thirty less one.[8] Why does not R. Mattena derive [the number of days] from the [occurrences of the various] parts of *nazar*?—He will tell you that [some of] these are required for teaching special lessons. [Thus the verse,] *He shall abstain* [yazzir] *from wine and strong drink,*[9] is required to prohibit wine the drinking of which is a ritual obligation as well as wine the drinking of which is optional;[10] [whilst the verse,] *Shall clearly utter a vow, the vow of a nazirite to consecrate himself,*[11] teaches that one nazirite vow can be superimposed on another.[12] [5b] To which Bar Pada can reply: Is there not even one [recurrence of a part of *nazar*] that is not needed for a special lesson? Since this one may be used for computation, all may be used for computation.[13]

We have learnt: A NAZIRITE VOW OF UNSPECIFIED DURATION [REMAINS IN FORCE] THIRTY DAYS. Now, this fits in

(1) In II Sam. XV, 7. (2) V. I Sam. VIII, 5. (3) V. Seder 'Olam XIV. (4) Num. VI, 5. (5) *Gematria*, v. Sanh. (Sonc. ed.), p. 121, n. 4. (6) יהיה Y = 10; H = 5; Y = 10; H = 5. In Hebrew, as in Greek, the letters have numerical values. (7) I.e., in the section on the nazirite vow. Num. VI, 1ff. Parts of the root *nadar* are included in the computation, but the *nazar* of verse 7 is omitted since it does not mean '*separation*', but '*crown*'. (8) V. *infra*. (9) Num. VI, 3. (10) V. *supra* p. 8. (11) Ibid. VI, 2. (12) If he repeats the vow, he becomes a nazirite twice. (13) As well as for teaching special lessons.

well enough with the view of R. Mattena, but how can it be reconciled with Bar Pada's view?[1]—Bar Pada will tell you that because [the period of the vow closes with] the thirtieth day, on which the nazirite polls and brings his sacrifices, [the Mishnah] says thirty [days].

We have learnt: If a man says, 'I declare myself a nazirite,' he polls on the thirty-first day.[2] Now, this fits in well enough with the view of R. Mattena, but how is it to be reconciled with Bar Pada's view?—Bar Pada will say: Consider the clause which follows, [viz.:] Should he poll on the thirtieth day, his obligation is fulfilled. We see, then, that the second clause [of this Mishnah] lends support to his view, whilst the original clause [must be read] as though it contained the word [I declare myself a nazirite for thirty] 'whole' [days].[3] Does not this second clause need to be reconciled with R. Mattena's view?[4]—He considers part of a day equivalent to a whole day.[5]

But have we not learnt: '[Should someone say,] "I intend to be a nazirite for thirty days," and poll on the thirtieth day, his obligation is not fulfilled'?[6]—[We presume that] he said, 'whole days'.

We have learnt: If a man undertakes two naziriteships, he polls for the first one on the thirty-first day, and for the second on the sixty-first day.[6] This fits in well enough with the view of R. Mattena [6a] but how is it to be reconciled with Bar Pada's view?—Bar Pada will say: Consider the clause which follows, [viz.:] If, however, he should poll for the first on the thirtieth day, he can poll for the second on the sixtieth day. Thus the second clause lends support to his view, whilst the original clause [must be read] as though it contained the words 'whole days'.

Is not R. Mattena in conflict with this second clause?[7]—R. Mattena can reply: This must be interpreted in the light of the next clause, which says that the thirtieth day counts as belonging

(1) According to which the period should be 29 days. (2) V. *infra* 16a. (3) And therefore he polls on the 31st day. (4) According to which the polling should be on the thirty-first day. (5) Thus though he polls on the thirtieth day, he has kept thirty days of naziriteship. (6) *Infra* p. 53. (7) Cf. n. 4.

to both periods.[1] This is taken to signify then that part of a day is equivalent to a whole day. But has he [the Tanna] not stated this once already?[2]—It might be thought that this is only true for one naziriteship but not for two, and so we are told [that it is also true for two].[3]

We have learnt: Should he poll on the day prior to the sixtieth, he has fulfillied his obligation, since the thirtieth day is included in the [required] number.[4] Now, this fits in well enough with the view of R. Mattena, but for Bar Pada what necessity is there [for this statement], since he says that [the normal duration] is thirty days less one?—He will say: This is the very passage on which I rely for my opinion.

We have learnt: If a person says, 'I intend to be a nazirite' and contracts ritual defilement on the thirtieth day, the whole period is rendered void.[4] Now, this fits in well enough with the view of R. Mattena, but does it not conflict with that of Bar Pada?—[6*b*] Bar Pada will say: Consider the subsequent clause [which reads]: R. Eliezer says: Only the [next] seven days are void.[5] Now if you assume that thirty days are necessary [as the minimum period of nazirite separation], should not all be void?[6] [R. Mattena, however, will reply:] R. Eliezer is of the opinion that part of a day is equivalent to the whole.[7]

We have learnt: [If a man says] 'I intend to be a nazirite for one hundred days,' and contracts ritual defilement on the hundredth day, the whole period is rendered void. R. Eliezer said that only thirty days are rendered void.[8] Now, if we assume[9] that R. Eliezer considers part of a day to be equivalent to a whole day, surely only seven days should be annulled?[5] Again [on the other hand] if we

(1) As end of the first and beginning of the second naziriteship. (2) As an inference from another clause of the same Mishnah (v. *supra*, p. 17); what necessity is there then for this latter clause? (3) That one part of the day belongs to one and the other to the second period. (4) *Infra* p. 53. (5) Since he is unable to offer his nazirite sacrifices until he has been sprinkled with the ashes of the red heifer on the third and seventh days. V. Num. XIX, 1ff. (6) Because the defilement takes place while the vow is still in force. (7) Hence when the defilement takes place, the vow is no longer in force. (8) *Infra* p. 53. (9) As does R. Mattena.

assume[1] that he does not regard part of the day as equivalent to a whole day, should not the whole period be annulled?[2]—In point of fact, we do not regard part of a day as equivalent to a whole day. In that case, why is not the whole period annulled?—Said Resh Laḳish: R. Eliezer's reason is as follows: Scripture says, *And this is the law of the nazirite,* [on the day] *when the days of his consecration are fulfilled.*[3] Thus the Torah expressly declares that if he contracts ritual defilement on the day of fulfilment, the law for a nazirite vow [of unspecified duration] is to be applied to him.[4]

May we say [that the difference between R. Mattena and Bar Pada] is the same as that between the following Tannaim? [For it was taught:] From the verse, *Until the days be fulfilled,*[5] I can only infer that the vow must continue in force at least two days,[6] and so the text adds, *He shall be holy; he shall let the locks grow long,*[7] and hair does not '*grow long*' in less than thirty days. This is the view of R. Josiah. R. Jonathan, however, said that this [reasoning] is unnecessary, for we have the text, *Until the days* be fulfilled.[7] What days then are those which have to be '*fulfilled*'? You must say the thirty days [of the lunar month].[8] May we assume that R. Mattena agrees with R. Josiah, and Bar Pada with R. Jonathan?—R. Mattena can maintain that both [authorities] agree that thirty days is the necessary period and the point at issue between them is whether the word '*until*' [preceding a number] signifies the inclusion or exclusion [of the last unit of that number].[9] R. Josiah is of the opinion that in the term '*until*' [the last unit] is not included,[10] whereas R. Jonathan is of the opinion that by the use of '*until*', [the last unit] is included.[11]

(1) As does Bar Pada. (2) For then the naziriteship is not complete until the close of the hundredth day and defilement during the naziriteship nullifies the whole preceding period. (3) Num. VI, 13. (4) I.e., he is to be a nazirite again for 30 days, [i.e., not more and not less, irrespective of the question whether or not part of the day is equivalent to a whole day (Tosaf.).] (5) Ibid. 5. (6) 'Two' being the minimum to which the plural '*days*' could be applied. (7) Num. VI, 5. (8) An ordinary lunar month contains 29 days, a '*full*' month 30 days. (9) I.e., whether e.g. 'until 30' means 30 or 29. (10) And the number thirty is derived by means of the rest of the verse, '*He shall let the locks grow long*'. (11) And the number thirty is obtained from '*Until the days be fulfilled*'.

The Master stated: What days then are those which have to be '*fulfilled*'? You must say, The thirty days [of a lunar month]. But could it not be a week[1]—[In the case of] a week, what deficiency is there to make up? [7*a*] Could it then not be a year?[2]—Are these reckoned in days? Surely the Rabbis of Caesarea[3] have said: How do we know that a year is not reckoned in days? Because Scripture says, *months of the year:*[4] [this signifies that] months are counted towards years but not days.

MISHNAH. IF HE SAYS, 'I INTEND TO BE A NAZIRITE FOR ONE LONG [PERIOD,' OR] 'I INTEND TO BE A NAZIRITE FOR ONE SHORT [PERIOD],' THEN EVEN [IF HE ADDS, 'FOR AS LONG AS IT TAKES TO GO] FROM HERE TO THE END OF THE EARTH,' HE BECOMES A NAZIRITE FOR THIRTY DAYS.

GEMARA. Why is this so? Has he not said, 'from here to the end of the earth'?[5]—His meaning is: For me this business is as lengthy as if it would last from here to the end of the earth.

We have learnt: [If a man says,] 'I wish to be a nazirite as from here to such and such a place,' we estimate the number of days' journey from here to the place mentioned, and if this is less than thirty days, he becomes a nazirite for thirty days; otherwise he becomes a nazirite for that number of days.[6] Now why should you not say in this case also that [his meaning is]: For me, this business seems as if it would last from here to the place mentioned?[7]—Raba replied: We assume that [when he made the declaration] he was setting out on the journey.[8] Then why should he not [observe a naziriteship of thirty days] for each *parasang*?[9]—R. Papa said: We

(1) Lit., 'a Sabbath', i.e., six working days completed by the Sabbath to make a week. (2) And the ordinary year may be considered 'deficient' by the side of a leap year. (3) [On the Rabbis of Caesarea v. Lieberman, S. *The Talmud of Caesarea*, pp. 9ff.] (4) Ex. XII, 2. (5) And he should be a nazirite for life. (6) *Infra* p. 23. (7) And his naziriteship should in any case not extend beyond thirty days. (8) The presumption is, then, that the journey and the length of naziriteship are connected. (9) A Persian mile.

speak of a place where they do not reckon [distances] in *parasangs*. Then let him [observe a naziriteship] for every stage [on the road]; for have we not learnt that [a man who says,] 'I intend to be a nazirite as the dust of the earth,' or 'as the hair of my head,' or 'as the sands of the sea,' becomes a life-nazirite, polling every thirty days?[1]—This [principle][2] does not apply to [a nazirite vow in which] a definite term is mentioned,[3] and this has indeed been taught [explicitly]: [A man, who says,] 'I intend to be a nazirite all the days of my life,' or 'I intend to be a life-nazirite,' becomes a life-nazirite,[4] but even [if he says] 'a hundred years,' or 'a thousand years,' he does not become a life-nazirite,[5] but a nazirite for life.[6]

Rabbah said: Hairs are different [from *parasangs* or stages], since each is separate from the others.[7]

In the case of days, do we not find the verse, *And there was evening and there was morning, one day?*[8]—There it is not because [days] are discrete entities [that the verse says *one day*] but to inform us that a day with the night [preceding it] together count as a day,[9] though they are really not discrete entities.

Raba said: Why raise all these difficulties? The case [in which he says 'FROM HERE TO THE END OF THE EARTH'] is different, because he has already said: I INTEND TO BE A NAZIRITE FOR ONE [SINGLE PERIOD].

MISHNAH. [IF A MAN SAYS] 'I INTEND TO BE A NAZIRITE, PLUS ONE DAY,' OR 'I INTEND TO BE A NAZIRITE, PLUS AN

(1) *Infra* p. 23. (2) That he has to observe a succession of periods of naziriteship, polling at the end of each period. (3) E.g., from here to such and such a place. (4) And polls every thirty days. (5) Having mentioned a definite term. (6) I.e., he keeps one long naziriteship during which he can never poll. Tosef. Naz. I, 3. (7) But distance is continuous. Hence if he mentions hairs, he is understood to mean a succession of short naziriteships, but if he mentions a distance, one long one. (8) And so distance in terms of days is also discrete, yet the Mishnah quoted above confines the naziriteship to a single period, and not to a succession equal in number to the number of days. (9) For the reckoning of Sabbaths and Festivals.

HOUR,' OR 'I INTEND TO BE A NAZIRITE, ONCE AND A HALF,' HE BECOMES A NAZIRITE FOR TWO [PERIODS].

GEMARA. What need is there [for the Mishnah] to specify all these cases?[1]—They are all necessary. For had it mentioned only, 'I INTEND TO BE A NAZIRITE, PLUS ONE DAY,' [it might have been thought] that here only do we apply the rule that 'there is no naziriteship for a single day,' and so he must reckon two [periods], whereas [when he says] 'I INTEND TO BE A NAZIRITE, PLUS AN HOUR,' he is to reckon thirty one days. So this case is mentioned explicitly. [7*b*] Again if it had simply added, '[I INTEND TO BE A NAZIRITE] PLUS AN HOUR,' [it might have been thought that he must count two periods] because he was [clearly] not speaking with precision,[2] whereas the expression 'ONCE AND A HALF' is precise, and it might therefore have been thought that he should not reckon two [periods].[3] And so we are told that in each case, he becomes a nazirite for two periods.

MISHNAH. [IF A MAN SAYS,] 'I INTEND TO BE A NAZIRITE FOR THIRTY DAYS PLUS AN HOUR,' HE BECOMES A NAZIRITE FOR THIRTY-ONE DAYS, SINCE THERE IS NO NAZIRITESHIP FOR HOURS.

GEMARA. Rab said: This applies[4] only when he says, 'thirty-one days,' but if he says, 'thirty days plus one day,' he becomes a nazirite for two periods.[5] Rab follows R. Akiba whose method it was to lay stress on superfluities of expression, as we have learnt: [If a man sells a house, the sale includes] neither the cistern nor the cellar, even though he inserted the depth and the height [in the deed of sale]; he must, however, purchase for himself a right-of-

(1) One would be enough, and we could infer the others. (2) Since naziriteships are reckoned in days only. (3) But forty-five days. (4) The assumption of the Mishnah that a man can become a nazirite for thirty-one days. (5) See last Mishnah and Gemara.

way.[1] This is the opinion of R. Akiba, but the Sages say that he need not purchase a right-of-way for himself.[2] R. Akiba does admit, however, that if he explicitly excludes [pit and cellar], he does not have to purchase a right-of-way.[3]

MISHNAH. [8*a*] [IF A MAN SAYS,] 'I INTEND TO BE A NAZIRITE AS THE HAIRS OF MY HEAD, OR THE DUST OF THE EARTH, OR THE SANDS OF THE SEA,' HE BECOMES A LIFE-NAZIRITE, POLLING EVERY THIRTY DAYS. RABBI SAID THAT SUCH A MAN DOES NOT POLL EVERY THIRTY DAYS;[4] THE MAN WHO POLLS EVERY THIRTY DAYS IS THE ONE WHO SAYS, 'I UNDERTAKE NAZIRITESHIPS[5] AS THE HAIR ON MY HEAD, OR THE DUST OF THE EARTH, OR THE SANDS OF THE SEA.' [IF HE SAYS,] 'I INTEND TO BE A NAZIRITE AS THE CAPACITY OF THIS HOUSE, OR AS THE CAPACITY OF THIS BASKET,' WE INTERROGATE HIM. IF HE SAYS THAT HE HAS VOWED ONE LONG PERIOD OF NAZIRITESHIP, HE BECOMES A NAZIRITE FOR THIRTY DAYS, BUT IF HE SAYS THAT HE HAS VOWED WITHOUT ATTACHING ANY PRECISE MEANING [TO HIS STATEMENT], WE REGARD THE BASKET AS THOUGH IT WERE FULL OF MUSTARD SEED, AND HE BECOMES A NAZIRITE FOR THE WHOLE OF HIS LIFE.[6] [IF HE SAYS,] 'I INTEND TO BE A NAZIRITE, AS FROM HERE TO SUCH AND SUCH A PLACE,' WE ESTIMATE THE NUMBER OF DAYS' [JOURNEY] FROM HERE TO THE PLACE MENTIONED. IF THIS IS LESS THAN THIRTY DAYS, HE BECOMES A NAZIRITE FOR THIRTY DAYS; OTHERWISE HE BECOMES A NAZIRITE FOR THAT NUMBER OF DAYS. [IF HE SAYS], 'I INTEND TO BE A NAZIRITE, AS THE NUMBER OF

(1) I.e., He does not retain a right-of-way to the cistern and cellar, unless he explicitly reserves it for himself. (2) Since the sale does not include the cistern and cellar, he may be presumed to have reserved a right of way to them. (3) The insertion of this superfluous clause is taken by R. Akiba to indicate that he wished to retain a right of way; v. B.B. 64*a*. (4) But becomes a nazirite for life and may never poll. (5) נְזִירוֹת. (6) (*a*) One naziriteship for every grain of mustard, [or, (*b*) one long naziriteship during which he can never poll].

DAYS IN A SOLAR YEAR,' HE MUST COUNT AS MANY NAZIRITESHIPS AS THERE ARE DAYS IN THE SOLAR YEAR. R. JUDAH SAID: SUCH A CASE ONCE OCCURRED, AND WHEN THE MAN HAD COMPLETED [HIS PERIODS], HE DIED.

GEMARA. WE REGARD THE BASKET AS THOUGH IT WERE FILLED WITH MUSTARD SEED, AND HE BECOMES A NAZIRITE FOR THE WHOLE OF HIS LIFE. But why [mustard seed]? Surely we could regard it as though it were full of cucumbers or gourds, and so provide him with a remedy?[1]—Hezekiah said: This is a matter on which opinions differ, the author [of our Mishnah] being R. Simeon, who has affirmed that people do undertake obligations in which the use of an ambiguous formula results in greater stringency than the use of a precise one.[2] For it has been taught: [If a man has said,] 'I intend to be a nazirite provided this heap [of grain] contains a hundred *kor*,[3] and on going to it, he finds that it has been stolen or lost, R. Simeon declares him bound [to his vow] since whenever in doubt as to a nazirite's liabilities, we adopt the more stringent ruling.[4] R. Judah, however, releases him since whenever in doubt as to a nazirite's liabilities, we adopt the more lenient ruling.[5]

R. Johanan said: It is even possible that [the author of the Mishnah] is R. Judah. For in the case just mentioned, the man has possibly not entered into a naziriteship at all [if there were not one hundred *kor* in the heap],[6] whereas in this case [mentioned in the Mishnah,] he does at any rate enter into a naziriteship.[7] On what grounds can he be released from it?[8] But why not regard the basket as though it were full of cucumbers and gourds, and so provide

(1) [By enabling him to poll at the end of every thirty days (according to (*b*) p. 23, n. 6).] (2) As here, the reference to a basketful without specifying its contents, results in naziriteship for life. (3) A dry measure; v. Glos. (4) So that, as we are not certain that the heap contained less than 100 *kor*, he must observe the naziriteship. (5) Tosef. Naz. II, 2. (6) And therefore we do not declare him a nazirite lest he should eventually bring profane animals into the sanctuary, v. *infra* p. 102. (7) For some period of time, whatever the basket is regarded as containing. (8) And therefore he must be a nazirite for life.

him with a remedy?[1] — Such an idea ought not to cross your mind, for he has undertaken one [unbroken] naziriteship,[2] [8b] R. Judah agreeing with Rabbi, as we have learnt: RABBI SAID THAT SUCH A MAN DOES NOT POLL EVERY THIRTY DAYS. THE MAN WHO POLLS EVERY THIRTY DAYS IS THE ONE WHO SAYS, 'I UNDERTAKE NAZIRITESHIPS AS THE HAIR OF MY HEAD, OR THE DUST OF THE EARTH, OR THE SANDS OF THE SEA.'

Is it then a fact that R. Judah agrees with Rabbi? Have we not learnt: [IF HE SAYS,] 'I INTEND TO BE A NAZIRITE AS THE NUMBER OF DAYS IN A SOLAR YEAR,' HE MUST COUNT AS MANY NAZIRITESHIPS AS THERE ARE DAYS IN THE SOLAR YEAR. R. JUDAH SAID: SUCH A CASE ONCE OCCURRED, AND WHEN THE MAN HAD COMPLETED [HIS PERIODS], HE DIED? Now if you say that this man, [by using this formula,][3] undertook [consecutive] naziriteships,[4] we can understand why [R. Judah says that] when he finished,[5] he died. But if you say that he undertook a single naziriteship,[6] could it ever be said of such a man that he had 'COMPLETED'?[7] Moreover, could [R. Judah] possibly agree with Rabbi, seeing that it has been taught: R. Judah said: [If a man says,] 'I intend to be a nazirite, as the number of heaps of the fig crop,[8] or the number of ears [in the field] in the Sabbatical year,'[9] he must count naziriteships as the number of heaps of the fig crop, or the number of ears [in the field] in the Sabbatical

(1) I.e., let him keep as many naziriteships as the basket will contain gourds or cucumbers. The questioner imagines that in R. Judah's view he becomes a life-nazirite, who can poll every thirty days, cf. *supra*, p. 21, n. 4. (2) And if he brings his sacrifices at the termination of the number of days that the basket would contain gourds or cucumbers, he may be bringing profane animals into the sanctuary, as his naziriteship may be of longer duration. Thus he becomes a nazirite for life, during which he can never poll. (3) 'I intend to be a nazirite, etc.' (4) 365 naziriteships, each of thirty days duration. (5) At the end of thirty years. (6) He would then mean, 'I undertake to be a nazirite for the number of the sun's days, i.e., for ever.' (*Rashi*). [Alternatively: If you say he undertook a single naziriteship (i.e. of 365 days duration) could it be said of him that he had completed the amount of naziriteships required by the Rabbis, in support of whose view R. Judah cites the incident; v. Tosaf.] (7) He could never bring sacrifices. (8) *Aliter:* paths of the fig-gatherers, v. Kohut, *Aruch.* (9) *Aliter:* field-paths in the Sabbatical year.

year?[1]—[Where he explicitly mentions the word] 'number', it is different.

But does Rabbi make a distinction where the word 'number' [is used]? Has it not been taught: [If a man says,] 'I intend to be a nazirite as the number of days in a solar year,' he must count as many naziriteships as there are days in the solar year; if [he says] 'as the days of a lunar year,' he must count as many naziriteships as there are days in a lunar year. Rabbi said that this does not hold unless he says, 'I undertake *naziriteships* as the number of days in the solar year or as the number of days in the lunar year'?[2]—R. Judah agrees with Rabbi on one point, and differs from him on the other. He agrees with him on one point, viz: that what is undertaken is a [single] naziriteship,[3] but differs from him on the other, for whilst R. Judah distinguishes between [the cases] where the word 'number' is mentioned and where it is omitted, Rabbi does not so distinguish.

Our Rabbis taught: [A man who says,] 'I wish to be a nazirite all the days of my life,' or 'I wish to be a life-nazirite,' becomes a life-nazirite. Even if he says a hundred years, or a thousand years, he does not become a life-nazirite, but a nazirite for life.[4]

Our Rabbis taught: [If a man says,] 'I wish to be a nazirite plus one,' he must reckon two [naziriteships]. [If he adds,] 'and another,' he must reckon three, and if he then adds 'and again', he counts four. Surely this is obvious?—It might be thought that the words 'and again' refer to the whole [preceding number], making six in all, and so we are told that this is not so.

Our Rabbis taught: [When a man says,] 'I wish to be a nazirite,' Symmachos affirmed [that by adding] *hen,*[5] [he must reckon] one; *digon,*[6] two; *trigon,*[6] three; *tetragon,*[6] four; *pentagon,*[6] five [naziriteships].[7]

(1) Tosef. Naz. I. Whereas Rabbi holds that in such a case he would have to count only as many days as there are heaps of figs. (2) Tosef. Naz. I. And, according to Rabbi, the same would be the case if he omitted the word 'number', the important thing being the use of the term, 'nazirite' or 'naziriteships'. (3) I.e., when he says, 'I intend to be a nazirite as the capacity of this house'. (4) Tosef. Naz. I, 3, and *supra* p. 21. (5) Gr. ἕν, once. (6) The last syllable is probably a Hebraisation of χως Thus *digon* — διχως — twice; and so on. V. Kohut, *Aruch*. (7) Tosef. Naz. I.

Our Rabbis taught: A house that is round, or *digon*,[1] or *trigon*,[1] or *pentagon*,[1] does not contract defilement through the plague [of leprosy]. One that is *tetragon*[1] does. What is the reason?—For Scripture, both in the latter part and in the earlier part of the passage [dealing with the leprosy of houses], puts *walls* [in the plural][2] instead of *wall* [in the singular], thus making four walls in all.[3]

(1) Here we have the normal meaning, two-sided, and so on. (2) Lev. XIV, 39, and 37. (3) Cf. Neg. XII, 1.

NAZIR

CHAPTER II

MISHNAH. [9*a*] [IF A MAN SAYS,] 'I INTEND TO BE A NAZIRITE [AND ABSTAIN] FROM DRIED FIGS AND PRESSED FIGS', BETH SHAMMAI SAY THAT HE BECOMES A NAZIRITE [IN THE ORDINARY SENSE],[1] BUT BETH HILLEL SAY THAT HE DOES NOT BECOME A NAZIRITE. R. JUDAH SAID: EVEN THOUGH BETH SHAMMAI DID AFFIRM [THAT THE FORMULA IS OF SOME EFFECT], THEY MEANT ONLY WHERE HE SAID,[2] 'THEY ARE [FORBIDDEN] TO ME, AS IS A SACRIFICE.'[3]

GEMARA. [IF A MAN SAYS,] 'I INTEND TO BE A NAZIRITE [AND ABSTAIN] FROM DRIED FIGS AND PRESSED FIGS', BETH SHAMMAI SAY THAT HE BECOMES A NAZIRITE: But why? Does not the Divine Law say, *nothing that is made of the* grape-vine?[4] —Beth Shammai adopt the view of R. Meir, who said that a man does not make a declaration without meaning something,[5] whilst Beth Hillel adopt the view of R. Jose that a man's intentions are to be gathered from[6] the concluding portion of his statement [equally with the first portion], and [in consequence] the vow here carries with it its annulment.[7]

But surely Beth Shammai also agree that the vow here carries with it its annulment?—We must therefore say, that Beth Shammai adopt the view of R. Meir, who said that a man does not make a

(1) I.e., he must abstain from wine and grapes. (2) I.e., he added (Rashi). [Tosaf: '. . . . as if he said'; Asheri: '. . . . where he *intended*']. (3) They then become forbidden, but he does not become a nazirite even according to Beth Shammai. (4) Num. VI, 4, which would show that naziriteship applies only to wine etc. (5) Even though taken altogether his words are meaningless, and we therefore select that part which has a meaning and hold him to it. (6) Lit., 'a man is held by'. (7) Lit., 'its door' for escape; by his concluding remarks, he has withdrawn from his nazirite vow.

declaration without meaning something, and so immediately he utters the words 'I INTEND TO BE A NAZIRITE', he becomes a nazirite, and in adding '[AND ABSTAIN] FROM DRIED FIGS AND PRESSED FIGS', his purpose is to obtain release[1] [from his vow], and Beth Shammai [reject this] in accordance with their general principle that there can be no release from [vows made for] sacred purposes, and since there can be no release from [vows made for] sacred purposes, there can be no release from naziriteship. Beth Hillel, on the other hand, agree with R. Simeon, as we have learnt:[2] R. Simeon declared him free[3] [of obligation], since his offering was not undertaken in the customary manner:

[*9b*] Our Mishnah is not in agreement with the following tanna. For it has been taught: R. Nathan said that Beth Shammai declare him both to have vowed [to abstain from figs] and to have become a nazirite, whilst Beth Hillel declare him to have vowed [to abstain from figs], but not to have become a nazirite. [Here,] Beth Shammai agree with R. Meir[4] and R. Judah,[5] and Beth Hillel with R. Jose.[6]

According to another report, R. Nathan said that Beth Shammai declare him to have vowed [to abstain from figs], but not to have become a nazirite, whilst Beth Hillel declare him neither to have vowed, nor to have become a nazirite. [Here,] Beth Shammai agree with R. Judah, and Beth Hillel with R. Simeon.[7]

We have learnt elsewhere: A man who says, 'I undertake to bring a meal-offering of barley-flour,' must [nevertheless] bring one of wheaten flour.[8] If he says, 'of coarse meal,' he must [nevertheless] bring fine meal. If, 'without oil and frankincense,' he must [nevertheless] add oil and frankincense; 'of half a tenth,' he must offer a whole tenth; 'of a tenth and a half', he must offer two tenths. R.

(1) Lit., 'to ask for remission'. (2) In connection with one who vowed to bring a meal-offering of barley flour; v. *infra*. (3) From bringing the offering, since a meal-offering could be brought only of wheaten flour. (4) That a man does not make a declaration without meaning something. (5) Of our Mishnah. (6) That a man's intention may be gathered from the concluding portion of his statement, and not like R. Simeon; cf. n. 7. (7) That a vow must be undertaken in the customary manner. (8) Which alone was permissible for a meal-offering, v. Lev. II, 1: *And when anyone bringeth a meal-offering unto the Lord, his offering shall be of fine flour; and he shall pour oil upon it and put frankincense thereon.*

Simeon declared him free [of obligation], since his offering was not undertaken in the customary manner.[1]

Who is the Tanna [who asserts that] if anyone undertakes to bring a meal-offering of barley-flour, he must bring one of wheaten flour?—Hezekiah replied: The matter is a subject of controversy, [the Tanna here] representing Beth Shammai. For have not Beth Shammai averred that when a man says ['I intend to be a nazirite and abstain] from dried figs and pressed figs,' he becomes a nazirite? So too, if he says 'of barley-flour', he must bring one of wheaten-flour. R. Joḥanan, on the other hand, replied that it is possible to maintain that [the passage quoted] represents the views of both [Beth Shammai and Beth Hillel] and that it refers to a man who says, 'Had I known that such vows are not made, I should not have vowed in this wise, but in the [correct] manner'.

Hezekiah said: The rule just laid down applies only where he said 'of barley', but if he says 'of lentils',[2] he need bring nothing at all. [Can this be so?] Consider: To whom does Hezekiah ascribe the Mishnah [containing this ruling]? To Beth Shammai! Now lentils in regard to a meal-offering, are as dried figs to a nazirite, and there Beth Shammai declare him to be a nazarite?[3] Hezekiah relinquished that opinion.[4] Why did he relinquish it?—[5]Raba said: Because he found that Mishnah difficult to understand. Why does it say 'barley' and not 'lentils'?[6] And so Hezekiah concluded that Beth Shammai's assertion was what R. Judah [maintained it to be].[7]

(1) M. Men. 103*a*. (2) There was an obligatory offering of barley for the '*Omer* but no offering of lentils at all (v. Lev. XXIII, 10ff.). (3) And so here he ought to bring a meal-offering of wheaten flour if he says 'of lentils'. (4) That the Tanna of the Mishnah of Men. 103*a* is Beth Shammai. [He will consequently accept the explanation of R. Joḥanan (Tosaf.).] (5) He could still have maintained that the Mishnah of Men. represents the view of Beth Shammai, and retract from the second statement holding that the ruling applies even if the man said 'of lentils'! (6) If the view of Beth Shammai is that we hold a man to the first portion of his vow, then even if he says, 'I intend to offer a meal-offering of lentils', he should be obliged to bring one of wheaten flour. (7) [The text is in disorder, and the interpretations suggested are many and varied. It appears to be best understood on the basis of Rashi's interpretation of R. Judah's statement in *our* Mishnah, viz., that he actually added, THEY ARE

R. Johanan, on the other hand, affirmed that [the rule of the Mishnah is applicable] even if he says 'of lentils'. But was it not R. Johanan who averred that [he only brings the offering if] he affirms: Had I known that such vows are not made, I should not have vowed in this wise, but in the [correct] manner?[1]—He[2] was arguing on Hezekiah's premises. You relinquished your former opinion,[3] because [the *Mishnah*] does not mention [the case] 'of lentils'. But might it not be a case of progressive argument, viz, not only is it true that when he says, 'of lentils' he must bring a proper meal-offering, since we may hold that he is there repenting [of his vow], and so we lay stress upon the opening portion of his statement, but even if he says 'of barley', where we could take it as certain that his intention is: If it can become consecrated after the manner of the *'Omer* meal-offering,[4] [10a] or the meal-offering of the faithless wife,[5] then I desire it to become consecrated, but not otherwise—even there we are told that he must bring one of wheaten flour.[6]

MISHNAH. IF HE SAYS, 'THIS HEIFER IS SAYING I SHALL BECOME A NAZIRITE IF I RISE,'[7] OR 'THIS DOOR IS SAYING I

FORBIDDEN TO ME AS IS A SACRIFICE (v. *supra* p. 28, n. 2). On this view, even according to Beth Shammai, where he vowed to bring a meal-offering from barley, he would not be obliged to bring one of wheat unless he, e.g., explicitly stated that had he known that such vows are not made, he would have vowed in the correct manner, as R. Johanan (*supra* p. 30), but while such a plea would be accepted if he vowed barley because it could have been a bona-fide error, it could not be admitted if he undertook to offer 'lentils'. Granted this, the Mishnah in Men. can represent the views of both Beth Hillel and Beth Shammai, as R. Johanan stated, hence the reason for Hezekiah relinquishing his former opinion (v. p. 30, n. 4).]

(1) [A plea which is not admitted if he vowed to bring 'lentils', v. n. 4.] (2) [R. Johanan, in affirming that the ruling is applicable even if he says 'of lentils'.] (3) [V. *supra* p. 30, n. 4.] (4) Which was of barley, v. Lev. XXIII, 10ff. (5) This was also barley, v. Num. V, 15. (6) I.e. although his vow has a certain meaning even if taken at face value, and there is no need for us to emphasise the first clause to the exclusion of the second, yet we do so. (7) Apparently this is taken as a clumsy way of saying: 'If I do not make this cow get up, I vow abstinence from its flesh.'

SHALL BECOME A NAZIRITE IF I OPEN', BETH SHAMMAI SAY THAT HE BECOMES A NAZIRITE, BUT BETH HILLEL SAY THAT HE DOES NOT BECOME A NAZIRITE. R. JUDAH SAID: EVEN THOUGH BETH SHAMMAI DID AFFIRM [THAT THE FORMULA WAS OF SOME EFFECT], IT WAS ONLY WHERE HE SAYS:[1] 'THIS HEIFER SHALL BE [FORBIDDEN] TO ME AS IS A SACRIFICE, IF IT SHOULD STAND UP [OF ITSELF]'.

GEMARA. Is it possible for a heifer to talk?—Rami b. Ḥama replied: [The Mishnah] here, refers to where a heifer lay crouching before him, and he said, 'This heifer thinks that it is not going to stand up. I intend to be a nazirite [and abstain] from its flesh, if it stands up of its own accord,' and it then arose of its own accord. Beth Shammai now apply their customary view and Beth Hillel their customary view. Beth Shammai who affirm that [in spite of his saying], 'from dried figs and pressed figs', he becomes a nazirite, assert here that [even] when he says 'from its flesh', he becomes a nazirite, whilst Beth Hillel declare that he does not become a nazirite.

But have not Beth Shammai asserted this once, already?—Raba replied: A second and a third time[2] [did they repeat it]. R. Ḥiyya, too, taught it a second and a third time, and so did R. Oshaia teach it a second and a third time, and they are all necessary statements. For if the rule had been stated merely in the case of dried figs and pressed figs, [it might have been argued] that Beth Shammai were of the opinion there that his words take effect and he becomes a nazirite because [figs and] grapes can be confused,[3] whereas flesh and grapes cannot be confused. Similarly had it been affirmed regarding flesh [it might have been argued] that Beth Shammai were of the opinion in this instance that he becomes a nazirite, because flesh and wine [are naturally associated],[4] but it would not apply to dried figs and pressed figs, and so this case also is given explicitly. Again, had it been affirmed in these two cases

(1) Cf. *supra* p. 28, n. 2. (2) The case of the DOOR. (3) So that when he said figs he may have meant grapes. (4) And when he spoke of the one, he thought of the other.

[only, it might have been argued] that only in these cases was Beth Shammai's assertion to be applied, whilst as concerns the door, they would defer to Beth Hillel.[1] Further, had only the door been referred to, [it might have been argued] that only in this case do Beth Hillel dissent, but in the other two they defer to Beth Shammai, and so we are told that this is not so.

[Nevertheless,] said Raba, does the Mishnah say if [the cow] rises of its own accord?[2]—But, said Raba, we must explain thus: The heifer, for example, is recumbent before him, and he says, 'I undertake to bring it as a sacrifice'.

This is all very well as regards the heifer which can be offered as a sacrifice but can a door be sacrificed?[3]—Raba therefore [corrected himself and] said: The heifer, for example, is recumbent before him,[4] [10*b*] and he says, 'I undertake a nazirite-vow [to abstain] from wine if it does not stand up,' and it then stood up of its own accord. In Beth Shammai's opinion, the substance[5] of this man's vow lay in his intention to cause [the heifer] to rise by force,[6] and this he did not do,[7] whereas Beth Hillel are of the opinion that [the vow was made] because [the heifer] was recumbent,[8] and it has risen.[9]

If this is [the meaning of the Mishnah], how is the subsequent clause to be understood, viz.: R. JUDAH SAID: EVEN THOUGH BETH SHAMMAI DID AFFIRM [THAT THE FORMULA WAS OF SOME EFFECT], IT WAS ONLY WHERE HE SAYS, 'AND SHALL BE FORBIDDEN TO ME AS A SACRIFICE ETC.'? Does [his vow]

(1) Because there is no association between a door and grapes. (2) Whilst admitting the necessity of restating the principle in our Mishnah, Raba objects to the explanation of Rami b. Ḥama on the ground that the word 'rises' might mean with the help of others, whereas according to Rami b. Ḥama the vow is effective only when the heifer rises of its own accord. (3) Since the case of the door in the Mishnah is parallel to that of the heifer, any explanation applying to the heifer must hold good if the door is substituted. (4) And appears as if it will never rise, even if force is used. (5) Lit., 'the obligation'. (6) Lit., 'with his hand'. The word 'stand up' being taken to mean 'stand up through me'. (7) He therefore becomes a nazirite. (8) And can only take effect if it remains recumbent. (9) He does not therefore become a nazirite.

then, attach to the heifer at all?[1]—[It must be] therefore, that he said, for example, 'I undertake a nazirite vow [to abstain] *from its flesh* if it should not stand up,' and it then stands up of its own accord. In Beth Shammai's opinion, the substance of this man's vow is his intention to cause [the heifer] to rise by force, and this he has not done, whereas according to Beth Hillel, the substance of his vow lies in the fact that [the heifer] was recumbent, and it has risen.[2]

But are Beth Hillel of the opinion that if [the heifer] does not stand up, [the man] becomes a nazirite? Have they not said that [by a vow to abstain] from flesh, he does not become a nazirite?[3] —They were arguing on the premises of Beth Shammai. In our opinion, he does not become a nazirite even if [the heifer] should not stand up, but you who say that he does become a nazirite[4] should at least admit that the substance of his vow lay in the fact that [the heifer] was recumbent, and it has since risen. Beth Shammai reply that this is not so, and the substance of the man's vow lay in his intention to cause [the heifer] to rise by force, and this he has not done.[5]

MISHNAH. [11a] IF A CUP OF WINE DULY TEMPERED[6] IS OFFERED TO A MAN, AND HE SAYS, 'I INTEND TO BE A NAZIRITE IN REGARD TO IT,' HE BECOMES A NAZIRITE. ON ONE OCCASION A CUP OF WINE WAS OFFERED TO A WOMAN ALREADY INTOXICATED AND SHE SAID, 'I INTEND TO BE A NAZIRITE IN REGARD TO IT.' THE SAGES RULED THAT ALL THAT SHE MEANT WAS TO FORBID IT TO HERSELF, AS A SACRIFICE [IS FORBIDDEN].

(1) The words 'it is forbidden to me as a sacrifice' imply that the heifer itself was the object of the vow, whereas in Raba's explanation it is the heifer's not standing up which is the condition for the operation of the man's naziriteship, and he has no intention of attaching any sanctity to the heifer. (2) But if it did not rise he would be a nazirite. (3) Even as in the case of a vow to abstain from pressed figs, v. *supra* p. 32. (4) Where he says simply, 'I undertake to be a nazirite (and abstain) from flesh.' (5) And so he becomes a nazirite. (6) Wine in ancient times was never drunk neat.

GEMARA. You cite a case to disprove [the rule]! You begin by saying that HE BECOMES A NAZIRITE, and then quote the case of the woman [who does not become a nazirite], from which I should conclude that [by means of this formula] he forbids to himself only this [cup that is offered to him] but is allowed to drink other wine? —There is a hiatus [in the Mishnah], which should read: 'If a cup of wine duly tempered is offered to a man, and he says "I undertake a nazirite vow [to abstain] from it", he becomes a nazirite.' If, however, he was [already] intoxicated when he said 'I intend to be a nazirite [and abstain] from it', he does not become a nazirite,[1] (since he is accounted as having merely forbidden it to himself as a sacrifice is forbidden. If you should object that he ought to have said so [unambiguously], [the reply is] that he thought they would bring a fresh one and importune him, and so he thought, 'I will say something to them which will leave them in no doubt [as to my intention]). ON ONE OCCASION, TOO, A WOMAN [ALREADY INTOXICATED etc.].

MISHNAH. [IF A MAN SAYS,] 'I DECLARE MYSELF A NAZIRITE, ON CONDITION THAT I CAN DRINK WINE, OR CAN HAVE CONTACT WITH THE DEAD', HE BECOMES A NAZIRITE, AND ALL THESE THINGS ARE FORBIDDEN HIM. [IF HE SAYS,] 'I WAS AWARE THAT THERE IS SUCH A THING AS NAZIRITESHIP BUT I WAS NOT AWARE THAT A NAZIRITE IS FORBIDDEN TO DRINK WINE', HE IS BOUND [TO HIS VOW].[2] R. SIMEON, HOWEVER, RELEASES HIM.[3] [IF HE SAYS,] 'I WAS AWARE THAT A NAZIRITE IS FORBIDDEN TO DRINK WINE,[4] BUT I IMAGINED THAT THE SAGES WOULD GIVE ME PERMISSION, SINCE I CANNOT DO WITHOUT WINE', OR 'SINCE I AM A SEXTON',[5] HE IS RELEASED.[6] R. SIMEON, HOWEVER, BINDS HIM [TO HIS VOW].[7]

(1) His intention being to cease from drinking. (2) I.e. he becomes a full nazirite. (3) He does not become a nazirite at all, R. Simeon being of opinion that a nazirite vow is not effective unless it comprises all the things forbidden to a nazirite, v. *supra* 3*b*. (4) [Add, 'or that a nazirite may have no contact with the dead.'] (5) [And therefore thought the Rabbis would permit me to come in contact with the dead.] (6) He does not become a nazirite at all. (7) He becomes a full nazirite.

GEMARA. Why does R. Simeon not dissent from the first ruling [also]?—R. Joshua b. Levi said: R. Simeon did in fact dissent from the first ruling also. Rabina said: In the opening clause, R. Simeon does not dissent, because the condition [there attached to the vow][1] is contrary to an injunction of the Torah, and whenever a condition is contrary to an injunction of the Torah, it is void.[2] R. Joshua b. Levi, on the other hand, considered that the words ON CONDITION here are equivalent to 'except'.[3]

It has been taught in support of Rabina's view: If he said, 'I declare myself a nazirite, on condition that I may drink wine, or have contact with the dead,' he becomes a nazirite and all these things are forbidden to him, since the condition he lays down is contrary to an injunction of the Torah; and whenever a condition is contrary to an injunction of the Torah, it is void.[4]

[IF HE SAYS] I WAS AWARE THAT A NAZIRITE IS FORBIDDEN TO DRINK WINE [etc.]: In the preceding clause,[5] we find it is [the Rabbis] who bind him [to his vow] and R. Simeon who releases him [and why is it not the same here]?—Here, too, it should read: [The Rabbis] bind him whilst R. Simeon releases.

Alternatively, you need not reverse the text, [11*b*] [and we may explain thus]. In the first clause, where he makes a nazirite vow [to abstain] from one thing[6] only, according to the Rabbis, who hold that [the nazirite vow takes effect] even though he forswears one thing only, he becomes a nazirite and [the things forbidden to a nazirite] are forbidden to him; whereas according to R. Simeon who holds that [the nazirite vow does not take effect] until he forswears all of them, [all the things forbidden to a nazirite] are permitted to him. In the subsequent clause where he forswears all, and desires release as regards one thing, according to the Rabbis who declare him to be a nazirite even though he forswears one thing only, if he desires release as regards one only, he is released

(1) That he should be allowed to touch a dead body or drink wine. (2) And therefore the vow stands. (3) Hence the vow was not all-inclusive, and therefore R. Simeon regards it as null. (4) Tosef. Naz. II, 1. (5) Where he says he did not know that wine is forbidden. (6) I.e., one of the things forbidden a nazirite, e.g. wine.

[from all]; according to R. Simeon who requires him to forswear them all, he cannot obtain release from one, until he obtains release from all. This is the reason we have the reading [in the second clause]: R. SIMEON BINDS HIM.

Yet another solution is possible. The controversy concerns vows [broken] under pressure,[1] and the difference [between R. Simeon and the Rabbis] is the same as that between Samuel and R. Assi [in the following passage]. For we have learnt: Four types of vows were remitted by the Sages,[2] incentive vows,[3] vows of exaggeration,[4] inadvertent vows[5] and vows [broken] under pressure.[6] And [commenting thereon] R. Judah said: 'R. Assi ruled that it was necessary with these four types of vow to seek remission from a Sage. When I told this to Samuel, he said to me, The Tanna says that the Sages *have* remitted them, and you say that they must still be asked to remit them!' The Rabbis agree with Samuel,[7] R. Simeon with R. Assi.[8]

MISHNAH. [SHOULD A MAN SAY,] 'I DECLARE MYSELF A NAZIRITE AND I UNDERTAKE TO POLL A NAZIRITE',[9] AND SHOULD HIS COMPANION, HEARING THIS, SAY: 'I TOO, AND I UNDERTAKE TO POLL A NAZIRITE', THEN, IF THEY ARE CLEVER THEY WILL POLL EACH OTHER; OTHERWISE THEY MUST POLL OTHER NAZIRITES.

GEMARA. The question was propounded: If his companion, on hearing [his vow], says [simply]: 'I TOO', what are the consequences? Does [the remark] 'I TOO' embrace the whole of the

(1) Viz., his inability to live without wine. (2) I.e., without the need of remission being asked for. (3) E.g., 'I vow . . . if I pay more', made during bargaining to show himself in earnest. (4) E.g., 'I vow . . . if there were not a million people there', the number being obviously exaggerated. (5) E.g., 'I vow . . . if I was there,' and he later remembers that he was there. (6) E.g., through illness. V. Ned. 20*b*. (7) Since it is impossible for a nazirite to be a sexton, the vow is null of itself and he is not a nazirite. (8) Though he cannot be a nazirite, the vow must be remitted by a Sage. (9) I.e., enable a nazirite to poll by providing his sacrifices.

original statement,[1] or does it embrace only half of it? If it should be decided that it embraces only half of the statement, is this to be the first half or the second half?—Come and hear: [AND HIS COMPANION, HEARING THIS, SAYS:] I TOO, AND I UNDERTAKE TO POLL A NAZIRITE, THEN IF THEY ARE CLEVER THEY WILL POLL EACH OTHER. From the fact that he is made to say both 'I TOO' and 'I UNDERTAKE', it may be inferred that 'I TOO' has reference to half of the statement only.

Quite so: it has reference to half of the statement only, but is this the first half or the second half?—This follows from the same [passage]. For since he is made to say 'AND I UNDERTAKE TO POLL'[2] it follows that 'I TOO' has reference to the first half.

R. Huna, the son of R. Joshua said to Raba: How can we be sure that this is so? May we not suppose that 'I TOO' really refers to the whole statement, and that the additional 'AND I UNDERTAKE', merely confirms his undertaking? For if you do not admit this, [what do you make of] the subsequent [Mishnah] that reads: [Should a man say:] 'I undertake half the polling of a nazirite', and should his companion, hearing this, say: 'I too, I undertake half the polling of a nazirite'?[3] Are there here two sections to which he can be referring? We can only suppose that there he is merely repeating 'I have undertaken this obligation', and in this case too [it is possible] that he is merely repeating 'I have undertaken this obligation.' Raba replied: How now! If you are prepared to say that in the first [Mishnah the words 'I UNDERTAKE ETC.'] are of importance, but not in the subsequent one, then they are repeated in the subsequent one—unnecessarily, it is true—because they are included in the first one where it is important,[4] but if you maintain that it is of importance neither in the first [Mishnah] nor in the subsequent one, would it be included unnecessarily in both?

R. Isaac b. Joseph citing R. Joḥanan said: If a man instructs his representative [12a] to go and betroth for him a wife, without specifying any woman, he becomes [in the meanwhile] forbidden

(1) I.e., both (i) 'I wish to be a nazirite,' and (ii) 'I undertake to poll a nazirite.' (2) And not merely 'I TOO'. (3) Mishnah *infra* 12b. (4) I.e., the second Mishnah repeats the phrasing of the first, for the sake of parallelism.

[to marry] any woman in the world, since it is presumed that the messenger carries out his commission, and since he did not specify [the woman], he does not know which he betrothed for him.[1]

Resh Laḳish raised an objection against R. Joḥanan [from the following]: If a dove of an indeterminate pair[2] should fly away into the air, or amongst those sin-offerings that have to be killed,[3] or if one of the pair should perish, a partner is to be taken for the other one.[4] [This implies that] with a determinate pair there is no remedy;[5] though all other pairs [in the world] would be valid.[6] Now why should this be so? Should we not say of each one, perhaps this is one [that flew away]?[7]—He replied: I spoke of a woman who is stationary and you raise objections from prohibited things that are mobile![8] Should you argue further that here too the woman may be mobile, for it is possible that he may have met her in the street and betrothed her, [the cases are still different] for the woman returns to her customary place, but can the same be said of the bird-pair?

Raba said: R. Joḥanan would admit that a woman who has [among her unmarried relatives] neither daughter, daughter's daughter, nor son's daughter; neither mother nor maternal grandmother, nor sister, although she may have a sister who was divorced after [the representative was sent]—such a woman would be permitted to him,[9] because at the time that he gave his instructions, [the sister] was still married, and when a person appoints a deputy, it is [to perform] something that is possible at the time,[10] but for

(1) Any woman may therefore be a relative, of a forbidden degree of kinship, of his betrothed wife. (2) A pair of doves of which it has not yet been determined which is to be the sin-offering and which the burnt-offering. (3) V. Kin. I, 2. (4) The pair is then to be determined in the usual way; Kin. II, 1. (5) Since it is not known which is the survivor. (6) We assume that a random pair does not contain the missing dove, as we are guided by the majority. (7) [And could not be offered except on behalf of the owner who originally determined it.] (8) Where the objects are stationary (קבוע), a majority is not considered decisive, but any minority is as potent as the majority (cf. Sanh. [Sonc. ed.] p. 531, n. 4) and so there is an even chance that any woman is a near kinswoman of his betrothed wife. (9) I.e., to betroth before the deputy returns. (10) Here, to betroth an unmarried woman.

something that is not possible at the time he does not appoint a deputy.[1]

We have learnt: [SHOULD A MAN SAY:] 'I DECLARE MYSELF A NAZIRITE, AND I UNDERTAKE TO POLL A NAZIRITE,' AND SHOULD HIS COMPANION, HEARING THIS, SAY: 'I TOO, AND I UNDERTAKE TO POLL A NAZIRITE,' THEN, IF THEY ARE CLEVER, THEY WILL POLL EACH OTHER; OTHERWISE THEY MUST POLL OTHER NAZIRITES. Now this [suggestion][2] is all very well as regards the latter, since the former had become [a nazirite] first,[3] but as to the former, was the latter a nazirite [when he made his vow]?[4] [12b] It follows therefore that he must have meant: 'If I should find one who is a nazirite, I shall poll him'; and so here too, perhaps he means: 'If you find one who is divorced, [you can] betroth her on my behalf'?—We may put [our maxim] thus. A person can appoint a deputy only for a commission that he himself can execute at the moment, but he cannot appoint him for a commission that he himself cannot execute at the moment [but can only do later].

But is that so? Come and hear: If a man says to his agent,[5] 'You are to declare void any vows that my wife makes from the present moment until the time I return from such-and-such a place,' and he does so, it might be imagined that they become void, but Scripture says: Her husband *may let it stand, or* her husband *may make it void.*[6] This is the opinion of R. Josiah. R. Jonathan said: In all circumstances do we find that a man's representative is equivalent to himself.[7] Now, [R. Josiah's] reason derives from the statement of the Divine Law, Her husband *may let it stand, or* her husband *may make it void,* and but for this, the agent would be able to declare them void, whereas where [the husband] himself is concerned, it has been

(1) Hence the deputy could not possibly have betrothed the other sister. (2) Viz., that they should poll each other. (3) Lit., 'since the former was in his presence'; and so his vow to poll a nazirite can be understood as applying to the former. (4) How then can his vow apply to the latter, if we accept Raba's contention that a man can appoint an agent only for something which is possible at the time. (5) A person left by a man in charge of his household while he is away. (6) Num. XXX, 14. (7) Ned. 72*b*.

taught: Should a man say to his wife, 'All the vows that you may make from the present moment until I return from such-and-such a place are to stand,' this is of no effect. [Should he say,] 'They are to be void,' R. Eliezer declares them void, but the Sages say that they are not void.[1] Now assuming that R. Josiah agrees with the Rabbis that he himself could not make them void, [we nevertheless find that] had not the Divine Law said, *Her husband may let it stand or her husband may make it void,* the agent could have declared them void?[2]—It is possible that he agrees with R. Eliezer that [the husband] can make them void [in advance]. If that is so, why does he trouble to appoint a deputy? Why does he not declare them void himself?—He fears that [at the moment of departure][3] he might forget, or be angry, or be too busy.

MISHNAH. [SHOULD A MAN SAY,] 'I UNDERTAKE THE POLLING OF HALF A NAZIRITE,'[4] AND HIS COMPANION, HEARING THIS, SAY 'I, TOO; I UNDERTAKE THE POLLING OF HALF A NAZIRITE,' THEN, ACCORDING TO R. MEIR, EACH MUST POLL A NAZIRITE COMPLETELY, BUT THE SAGES SAY: EACH POLLS HALF A NAZIRITE.

GEMARA. Raba said: All agree that if he says, 'I undertake half the *sacrifices*[4] of a nazirite,' he is obliged to bring only half the sacrifices;[5] if he says 'I undertake the sacrifices of half a nazirite,' he must bring a complete set of sacrifices, since partial naziriteship is impossible.[6] Where they differ is when the phraseology of the Mishnah [is used].[7] R. Meir considers that as soon as he says 'I

(1) Ned. 72*a*. (2) Which seems to show that a man can appoint an agent for something which cannot be done at once but can be done later. (3) Until then, he wishes to retain his option of declaring his wife's vows void or not, at his pleasure. (4) I.e., to bring half the sacrifices accompanying the polling of a nazirite. (5) Because there is no ambiguity. (6) The phrase 'half a nazirite' is meaningless and must therefore be replaced by 'a nazirite', since it is presumed that he intended to undertake a real obligation. (7) Here the actual obligation, which is to provide sacrifices, is not mentioned explicitly but must be inferred.

undertake [to poll]' he becomes liable to the complete sacrifice of naziriteship, and when he [afterwards] specifies half a naziriteship, it is no longer within his power [to limit his obligation].[1] The Rabbis, on the other hand, look upon it as a vow accompanied by its own modification.[2]

MISHNAH. [SHOULD A MAN SAY,] 'I UNDERTAKE TO BECOME A NAZIRITE WHEN I SHALL HAVE A SON,' AND A SON BE BORN TO HIM, HE BECOMES A NAZIRITE. IF THE CHILD BORN BE A DAUGHTER, OR SEXLESS, OR AN HERMAPHRODITE, HE DOES NOT BECOME A NAZIRITE. SHOULD HE SAY, 'WHEN I SHALL HAVE A CHILD,' THEN EVEN IF IT BE A DAUGHTER, OR SEXLESS, OR AN HERMAPHRODITE, HE BECOMES A NAZIRITE.

[13*a*] SHOULD HIS WIFE MISCARRY, HE DOES NOT BECOME A NAZIRITE. R. SIMEON SAID: [IN THIS CASE] HE MUST SAY, 'IF IT WAS A VIABLE CHILD, I AM A NAZIRITE OBLIGATORILY; OTHERWISE I UNDERTAKE A NAZIRITESHIP VOLUNTARILY.'[3] SHOULD [HIS WIFE] LATER BEAR A CHILD,[4] HE THEN BECOMES A NAZIRITE. R. SIMEON SAID: HE SHOULD SAY, 'IF THE FIRST WAS A VIABLE CHILD, THE FIRST [NAZIRITESHIP] WAS OBLIGATORY, AND THE PRESENT ONE WILL BE VOLUNTARY, OTHERWISE, THE FIRST ONE WILL HAVE BEEN VOLUNTARY, AND THE PRESENT ONE IS OBLIGATORY.'

GEMARA. For what purpose are we told this?[5]—Because of the subsequent clause, viz.:—IF IT BE A DAUGHTER, OR SEXLESS, OR AN HERMAPHRODITE, HE DOES NOT BECOME A NAZIRITE. But is not this obvious?—It might be thought that his

The position of the word 'half' is no longer decisive, since no other position yields more sense. Accordingly, its significance must be determined.

(1) Limitation is now only possible on application to a Sage, and so he must bring a complete sacrifice. (2) And therefore only the modified vow comes into operation and it is sufficient for him to bring half the sacrifices. V. *supra* p. 28, n. 7. (3) And in either case he becomes a nazirite. (4) After her miscarriage. (5) That if a son is born, he becomes a nazirite.

meaning was 'If I beget a child'[1] and so we are told that this is not so.

SHOULD HE SAY 'WHEN I SHALL HAVE A CHILD' etc.: But is not this obvious?—It might be thought that he only meant the child that is reckoned amongst men,[2] and so we are told [that any child is meant].

SHOULD HIS WIFE MISCARRY HE DOES NOT BECOME A NAZIRITE. The author of this statement is the R. Judah of the heap of grain.[3]

R. SIMEON SAID: HE SHOULD SAY, 'IF THE CHILD WAS VIABLE, THEN I AM A NAZIRITE OBLIGATORILY; OTHERWISE I UNDERTAKE NAZIRITESHIP VOLUNTARILY.' R. Abba put the following question to R. Huna: Should a man say, 'I undertake to become a nazirite when I shall have a son', and his wife miscarries, and he set aside a sacrifice,[4] and then his wife gave birth [to a son],[5] what is the law?[6] From whose standpoint [was this problem propounded]? If from the standpoint of R. Simeon, what problem is there? Does not R. Simeon say that wherever there is a doubt in questions concerning naziriteship we adopt the more stringent ruling?[7]—It must therefore be from the standpoint of R. Judah, who maintains that in questions concerning naziriteship, if there is a doubt the more lenient ruling is adopted. The query then is whether [the animal] became sacred or not.[8] But what [practical] difference can it make [which it is]?[9]—[There would be the question of] whether he might shear it, or work with it.[10] The problem was unsolved.

(1) The Hebrew word בן, 'son', is a denominative of בנה 'to beget children', and might be used for any child (Rashi). (2) I.e., a son through whom the family is propagated. (3) V. *supra* 8a. (4) To bring at the end of his proposed naziriteship. (5) As a result of the same confinement. (6) I.e., what about the sacrifice between the time it was set aside, and the time the second child was born. The question is made clearer anon. (7) So that the husband was a nazirite in law, and the sacrifice properly set aside from the first. (8) [Does the birth of the second child prove that the first was the result of the same pregnancy and consequently not premature and viable, or do we assume that it was the result of a *later* pregnancy and thus premature and non-viable?] (9) Since it is now sacred. (10) In the interval between the birth of the first and second child, as no benefit might be derived from sacred property.

Ben Reḥumi put the following question to Abaye: [Should a man say,] 'I undertake to become a nazirite when I shall have a son,' and his companion, hearing this, add 'And I undertake likewise,' what would be the law? Is the reference to his words[1] or to him himself?[2] Should your finding be that the reference is to him himself, then if a man should say, 'I undertake to become a nazirite when I shall have a son,' and his companion, hearing this, add 'I too', what would be the law? Is the reference to himself,[3] or does he mean, 'I am as much your good friend as you are yourself'?[4] Should your finding be that whenever the other is present [13b] he would be ashamed [to refer to himself],[5] then if a man should say, 'I undertake to be a nazirite when so-and-so has a son,' and his companion, hearing this, add 'I too,' what would be the law? Would it be said then that because the other is not present he is referring to himself,[6] or does he mean, 'I am as good a friend to him as you are'?[7]

The problem was left unsolved.

MISHNAH. [IF A MAN SAYS,] 'I INTEND TO BE A NAZIRITE [NOW] AND A NAZIRITE WHEN I SHALL HAVE A SON', AND BEGINS TO RECKON HIS OWN [NAZIRITESHIP], AND THEN HAS A SON BORN TO HIM, HE IS TO COMPLETE HIS OWN NAZIRITESHIP] AND THEN RECKON THE ONE ON ACCOUNT OF HIS SON. [IF HE SAYS,] 'I INTEND TO BE A NAZIRITE WHEN I SHALL HAVE A SON, AND A NAZIRITE [ON MY OWN ACCOUNT]', AND HE BEGINS TO RECKON HIS OWN [NAZIRITESHIP] AND THEN HAS A SON BORN TO HIM, HE MUST INTERRUPT HIS OWN [NAZIRITESHIP], RECKON THE ONE ON ACCOUNT OF HIS SON, AND THEN COMPLETE HIS OWN.

(1) I.e., 'I also undertake to become a nazirite when *I* have a son'. (2) The former, i.e., I also undertake to become a nazirite when *you* have a son'. (3) The latter, meaning, 'I too shall be a nazirite when *I* have a son'. (4) I.e., 'I too shall be a nazirite when *you* have a son'. (5) And he must have meant, 'I shall be a nazirite when *you* have a son.' (6) I.e., 'I too shall be a nazirite when I have a son.' (7) I.e., 'I too shall be a nazirite when so-and-so has a son.'

GEMARA. Raba put the following question. If he should say, 'I wish to be a nazirite[1] after twenty days time,' and then 'For one hundred days commencing now', what would be the law? Seeing that these hundred days will not be complete in twenty, are they to be inoperative [for the time being][2] or, seeing that there will remain sufficient time afterwards[3] for the hair to grow long,[4] do they come into operation [immediately]?[5]

Why does [Raba] not [first] raise the question of a [second] naziriteship of short duration?[6] It is a problem within a problem that he has raised: [14*a*] Suppose it is decided that with a short naziriteship, since only ten days remain,[7] these ten days would certainly not be reckoned,[8] [what are we to say] of a naziriteship of a hundred days?[9] Seeing that eighty remain, would these [eighty days] be reckoned[8] or not?

And again, suppose it is decided that [the naziriteship] [in this case] operates [immediately], what would be the law if he were to say 'I wish to be a nazirite after twenty days time' and then 'I wish to be a life nazirite now',[10] would this become operative [at once] or not?[11] And again, supposing it is decided that in all these cases, since it is possible to secure release,[12] they become operative [at once],[13] what would be the law if he were to say 'I wish to become

(1) An ordinary naziriteship of thirty days. (2) I.e., till thirty days after the twenty. (3) At the termination of the ordinary naziriteship. (4) A nazirite could not poll until his hair had grown for thirty days. (5) He will count twenty days, observe an ordinary naziriteship of thirty days, and then count eighty days to complete the naziriteship of one hundred days. (6) 'I wish to be a nazirite after twenty days', and then, 'An (ordinary) nazirite commencing now.' (7) If it is interrupted by a naziriteship after twenty days. (8) As completing the first naziriteship by adding them to the twenty days, since ten days do not allow for the hair to grow long and therefore this naziriteship does not commence until the other one is finished. (9) Is it on the same footing as the short one, or does it commence at once? (10) Though a life-nazirite polls every thirty days, the naziriteship is continuous and cannot be interrupted. Thus once the life-naziriteship operates it is impossible for the ordinary naziriteship to take effect. (11) I.e., shall the life-naziriteship be suspended until the ordinary naziriteship has been observed, or does it become operative and he must obtain release from the other naziriteship. (12) From the naziriteship which is to become operative in twenty days time. (13) And he must secure

a nazirite like Samson in twenty days time', and then 'I wish to be an ordinary nazirite now'? In this case, since release cannot be secured,[1] would it become operative or not?

If he were to say, 'I desire to be as Moses on the seventh of Adar,'[2] what [would his meaning be]?[3]

Of these [questions], decide the first, [For it was taught: Should a man say] 'I wish to be a nazirite after twenty days time,' and then 'For a hundred days from now,' he reckons twenty days, and then thirty days, and then eighty days to complete the first naziriteship.[4]

[SHOULD HE SAY, 'I WISH TO BE A NAZIRITE WHEN I SHALL HAVE A SON, AND A NAZIRITE ON MY OWN ACCOUNT etc.']

If he contracts ritual defilement[5] during the period [of naziriteship] on account of his son, R. Joḥanan said: This renders void [the first[6] period as well], but Resh Laḳish said: It is not void. 'R. Joḥanan said that it becomes void,'—because [the whole] is one long period of naziriteship; 'but Resh Laḳish said that it is not void,'—since his own naziriteship, and the one on account of his son are distinct.

[14b] If he contracts ritual defilement during the period that he is leprous,[7] R. Joḥanan said: This renders void [the earlier period of naziriteship]; but Resh Laḳish said: It is not void. 'R. Joḥanan said that it becomes void,'—since he is in the midst of his period of naziriteship,[8] 'but Resh Laḳish said that it is not void,'—because the period of leprosy and the naziriteship are distinct.

And it is necessary [to have both these controversies on record]. For if only the first[9] were recorded, [we might say that] there R.

release from the naziriteship which was to have operated after twenty days.

(1) A nazirite like Samson could never be freed from his vow, since Samson could not be freed. (2) Supposed to be the date of the birth and death of Moses, v. Ḳid. 38a. (3) *Either* 'As after the death of Moses on the seventh of Adar'; when presumably many nazirite vows were made by the Israelites, *or*, 'As after the birth of Moses on the seventh of Adar', a festive occasion. (4) Tosef. Nazir II. (5) With the dead. (6) The period counted before his son's naziriteship came into operation. (7) One who becomes leprous during his naziriteship completes it when the leprosy is cured. (8) As is proved by the fact that when he recovers from his leprosy he completes his period. (9) Relating the naziriteship on account of his son.

Johanan was of the opinion that [the first period] becomes void because the same term, naziriteship, applies to both, whereas in the other he would agree with Resh Lakish that the nazirite period and the leprosy are distinct. Similarly had only the other [regarding leprosy] been recorded, [we might suppose that] only there did Resh Lakish hold [the two periods to be distinct], whereas in the first he would agree with R. Johanan. Thus the necessity [for recording both controversies] is demonstrated.

If he becomes unclean on a day [during the period that] his hair is growing,[1]—Rab said: This does not render void [the earlier period]; this even according to R. Johanan who said [above] that the [earlier period] does become void, for this is only so [when the uncleanness is incurred] during the naziriteship itself, but not during the period his hair is growing which is merely the complement of the naziriteship.[2] Samuel, on the other hand, said: It does render void [the earlier period]; and this even according to Resh Lakish who said [above] that [the earlier period] does not become void, for whereas there, there are two distinct naziriteships, here[3] there is but one naziriteship.[4]

R. Hisda said: All would agree that should his hair be still unshorn[5] when the blood [of his sacrifice had been sprinkled],[6] he would have no remedy.[7] With whose opinion does this statement accord? It cannot be with that of R. Eliezer,[8] for seeing that in his opinion polling estops [him from drinking wine, the uncleanness][9] is still prior to the '*fulfilment of his* [*consecration*]'[10] and [the whole period] should become void![11] Nor can it accord with the Rabbis, seeing that they say that the polling does not estop [him

(1) If he had his hair polled by force, his naziriteship is not interrupted thereby and he completes his period. If this is less than thirty days, he must nevertheless allow his hair to grow for thirty days. The additional days constitute the 'period that his hair is growing'. (2) And not an integral part of it. (3) When he allows his hair to grow after having been polled by force. (4) The additional days are an integral part of naziriteship and not a mere complement. (5) Lit., 'hallowed', cf. Num. VI, 11. (6) And he became unclean. (7) In regard to polling and wine drinking—so it is assumed at present. (8) V. *infra* 47a. (9) He cannot drink wine after polling (10) Cf. Num. VI, 13. (11) Cf. ibid. 12, and he begins a new period at the end of which he finds the remedy.

from drinking wine]![1]—In point of fact, it does accord with the opinion of the Rabbis, the phrase, 'he would have no remedy', meaning, 'he would have no means of fulfilling the precept of polling [in purity]'.

R. Jose son of R. Ḥanina said: A nazirite whose period is completed, is scourged for contracting ritual defilement,[2] but not for polling or for [drinking] wine. Why is he scourged for ritual defilement? [Assuredly] because Scripture says, All *the days that he consecrateth himself unto the Lord [he shall not come near to a dead body]*,[3] thus including the days after fulfilment equally with the days before fulfilment! But in that case, for polling too he should be liable to scourging seeing that the All-Merciful Law says, All *the days of his naziriteship there shall come no razor upon his head*,[4] thereby including the days after fulfilment equally with the days before fulfilment. Again, All *the days of his naziriteship shall he eat nothing that is made of the grape-vine*,[5] should also include the days after fulfilment equally with the days before fulfilment?—[15a] [Defilement] is different, for the All-Merciful Law says, *And he defile his consecrated head*,[6] showing that [the penalty for defilement lies] wherever the naziriteship depends on the head.[7]

An objection was raised: A nazirite who has completed his period is forbidden to poll, or drink wine, or have contact with the dead. Should he poll or drink wine, or have contact with the dead he is to receive the forty stripes. [This is] a refutation of R. Jose son of R. Ḥanina.

MISHNAH. [SHOULD A MAN SAY,] 'I UNDERTAKE TO BECOME A NAZIRITE WHEN I SHALL HAVE A SON, AND TO BE A NAZIRITE FOR ONE HUNDRED DAYS [ON MY OWN ACCOUNT],' AND A SON BE BORN TO HIM BEFORE THE EXPIRATION OF

(1) And defilement after the termination of his period does not affect the naziriteship. (2) Before offering his sacrifices. (3) Num. VI, 6. (4) Ibid. VI, 5. (5) Num. VI, 4. (6) Num. VI, 9. (7) I.e., as long as his head is unpolled, though the 'days of his consecration are fulfilled'.

SEVENTY DAYS, HE LOSES NONE OF THIS PERIOD;[1] BUT IF AFTER SEVENTY DAYS, THESE SEVENTY DAYS ARE VOID, SINCE THERE CAN BE NO POLLING FOR LESS THAN THIRTY DAYS.[2]

GEMARA. Rab said: The seventieth day itself is reckoned as part of both periods.[3]

We learnt: IF [A SON] BE BORN TO HIM BEFORE THE EXPIRATION OF SEVENTY DAYS, HE LOSES NONE OF THIS PERIOD. Now if you assume that [the day of birth] is reckoned as part of both periods, [not only does he not lose but] he actually profits![4] —Strictly speaking there should have been no mention of the period before the seventieth day,[5] but because it says in the subsequent clause [of the Mishnah], that [birth] after the seventieth day renders these seventy days void, the period before the seventieth day is mentioned in the first clause.

Come [then] and hear the subsequent clause: 'IF IT BE BORN AFTER THE SEVENTIETH DAY,[6] THE SEVENTY DAYS ARE VOID' —The meaning of 'AFTER' is, after [the day] after [the seventieth day].[8] You say then that [a birth on] the day after [the seventieth day] itself,[9] would not render void [the previous period]. But if this is so, why should we be told that if the birth occurs *before* the seventieth day none of the period is lost, seeing that the same is

(1) I.e., He counts a naziriteship of thirty days on account of his son, and then completes the hundred days on his own account. (2) And since there are not thirty days left over from the first naziriteship, the whole of it becomes void, and he has to start his one hundred days over again. (3) So that on the one hand seventy days of his own naziriteship are completed, and on the other he need only reckon twenty-nine more days for the naziriteship following the birth of his son. The same will of course be true of the last day of this naziriteship, when he must again commence the remainder of his own (Rashi). (4) For each of the days between the naziriteships counts as two. (5) Because there is no manner of doubt as to what the law should be and he does in fact gain. (6) I.e., as we should suppose on the seventy-first. (7) Whereas if Rab be right, a birth on the seventy-first day should not render void the previous period, since reckoning both ways, thirty days remain. (8) I.e., The seventy-second day, which on any reckoning would not leave more than twenty-nine. (9) I.e., seventy-first day.

true [of a birth occurring] on the day after the seventieth day?—It is consequently to be inferred that 'AFTER' means [the day] after literally, and thus the Mishnah unquestionably [contradicts] Rab.

Whose authority was Rab following in making this assertion? Shall we say it was Abba Saul, [in connection with whom] we have learnt: If a man bury his dead three days before a festival, the enactment of seven days' [full mourning] ceases to apply to him. If eight days before the festival, the enactment of thirty days [half-mourning] ceases to apply, and he may trim his hair on the eve of the festival. Should he, however, fail to trim his hair on the eve of the festival, he is not permitted to do so afterwards [until the thirty days' half-mourning elapse]. [15*b*] Abba Saul said: Even if he should fail to trim his hair before the festival, he is permitted to do so afterwards, for just as the observance of three days [before the festival] causes the enactment of seven days [full mourning] to lapse, so the observance of seven days [full-mourning before the festival] causes the enactment of thirty days [half-mourning] to lapse. Now, Abba Saul's reason is surely that the seventh day is reckoned as part both of [the full-mourning] and of [the half-mourning]![1]—Possibly Abba Saul only makes this avowal in connection with the periods of the seven days'[2] mourning which are a rabbinic enactment, whereas he would not do so in connection with naziriteship, a scriptural enactment?[3] It must therefore be that Rab follows R. Jose, for it has been taught: R. Jose said that a woman, 'on the wait' for gonorrhoenic issue,[4] on whose behalf [the paschal lamb] has been slaughtered and [its blood] sprinkled, on the second day [of her waiting], and who later [in the same day] observes an issue, may not eat [of the passover],[5] and does not

(1) In the same way as Rab reckons the 70th day twice over. (2) The argument applying with greater force to the period of half-mourning. (3) Hence Rab cannot appeal to his authority. (4) V. Lev. XV, 25ff. Should a woman observe issue *after* her menstrual period, she becomes unclean until evening. From that time she is 'on the wait', and if there is an issue on the second day, she becomes unclean for seven days. A third day certifies her as gonorrhoeic, and she must then bring a sacrifice after purification; v. Sanh. (Sonc. ed.) p. 577, n. 1. Whilst unclean she must not eat the flesh of sacrifices. (5) For she is now unclean for seven days.

have to prepare the second passover.[1] Now R. Jose's reason is surely because in his opinion, part of the day counts as a whole day, so that she becomes unclean only from the moment [of observing the issue] and thereafter.[2]

Is this indeed R. Jose's opinion?[3] Has it not been taught: R. Jose said that a sufferer from gonorrhoea who has observed unclean issue on two occasions, and on whose behalf [the paschal lamb] has been slaughtered and [its blood] sprinkled 'on the seventh day [of his impurity], and similarly a woman, on the wait' for gonorrhoeic issue on whose behalf [the paschal lamb] has been slaughtered and [its blood] sprinkled— if they afterwards observe an unclean issue, then even though they render unclean couch and seat[4] retrospectively, they are not obliged to offer the second passover?[5] —[The uncleanness] is retrospective only by enactment of the Rabbis. This is indeed evident, for if it were scriptural, on what grounds would they be exempt from the second passover?[6] [No!][7] In point of fact it would be possible for the uncleanness [to be retrospective] in biblical law also, the concealed impurity[8] of gonorrhoea not being reckoned a ban [to the offering of the passover].

R. Oshaya, too, is of the opinion that the retrospective incidence is rabbinic in origin,[9] for it has been taught:[10] R. Oshaia said that one who observes a gonorrhoeic issue on his seventh day, renders void the preceding [seven days]. R. Joḥanan said to him: Only that day itself becomes void. But consider! [What is R. Joḥanan saying?] If it renders void at all, it should render all [seven days] void, otherwise it should not render void even the same day?— Read therefore: [R. Joḥanan said that] it does not even render void

(1) On the 14th day of the following month, Iyar; v. Num. IX, 9ff. (2) She was fit to offer the Passover, although she cannot now eat it. Adopting the reading of Tosaf., Asheri and others. (3) That she becomes unclean only from that moment. (4) Cf. Lev. XV, 4. (5) Since they render unclean couch and seat retrospectively, the day must count as belonging wholly to the unclean period! (6) Since they were already unclean when the paschal lamb was killed. (7) This would afford no proof. (8) Lit., 'impurity of the abyss', a technical term for an impurity of which there is no sign until its issue. (9) In the opinion of R. Jose. (10) [*Var. lec.*: For R. Oshaia said].

the same day. [fol. 16a]. [R. Oshaia] replied: You have on your side R. Jose, who said that the uncleanness is incident [according to the Scripture] from the moment [of observation] and thereafter. Now was it not R. Jose who said that the uncleanness was retrospective? We see therefore that the retrospective incidence must [in his opinion] be rabbinic.[1]

Now seeing that R. Jose is of the opinion that part of a day counts as a whole day, how is it ever possible for there to be a certified[2] female sufferer from gonorrhoea to offer the [prescribed] sacrifice, for if the issue is observed in the second half of the day, then the first half of the day counts as the period of 'waiting'?[3]—It is possible either if she should have continual issue for three days, or alternatively, if she observes the issue on each of the three days shortly after sunset, so that there is no part of the day that can be reckoned [as a period of cleanness].

(1) Otherwise he would be contradicting himself. (2) One who has observed an issue on three successive days. (3) During which she has been clean, and being clean part of the day, she is considered to have been clean all day.

NAZIR

CHAPTER III

MISHNAH. IF A MAN SAYS, 'I INTEND TO BE A NAZIRITE', HE POLLS ON THE THIRTY-FIRST DAY, BUT SHOULD HE POLL ON THE THIRTIETH DAY, HIS OBLIGATION IS FULFILLED. [IF, HOWEVER, HE SAYS] 'I INTEND TO BE A NAZIRITE FOR THIRTY DAYS,' AND POLLS ON THE THIRTIETH DAY, HIS OBLIGATION IS NOT FULFILLED. IF A MAN UNDERTAKES TWO NAZIRITESHIPS, HE POLLS FOR THE FIRST ONE ON THE THIRTY-FIRST DAY, AND FOR THE SECOND ON THE SIXTY-FIRST DAY. IF, HOWEVER, HE SHOULD POLL FOR THE FIRST ON THE THIRTIETH DAY, HE CAN POLL FOR THE SECOND ON THE SIXTIETH DAY, WHILST SHOULD HE POLL ON THE DAY PRIOR TO THE SIXTIETH, HE HAS FULFILLED HIS OBLIGATION; FOR THIS WAS THE TESTIMONY THAT R. PAPAIAS BORE CONCERNING ONE WHO UNDERTAKES TWO NAZIRITESHIPS, VIZ., THAT IF HE SHOULD POLL FOR THE FIRST ON THE THIRTIETH DAY, HE IS TO POLL FOR THE SECOND ON THE SIXTIETH DAY, WHILST SHOULD HE POLL ON THE DAY PRIOR TO THE SIXTIETH DAY, HE HAS FULFILLED HIS OBLIGATION, THE THIRTIETH DAY COUNTING TOWARDS THE REQUIRED NUMBER. IF A MAN SAYS, 'I INTEND TO BE A NAZIRITE,' AND CONTRACTS RITUAL DEFILEMENT ON THE THIRTIETH DAY, HE RENDERS VOID THE WHOLE PERIOD. R. ELIEZER SAYS: ONLY THE SEVEN DAYS ARE VOID. [IF HE SAYS,] 'I INTEND TO BE A NAZIRITE FOR THIRTY DAYS,' AND CONTRACTS RITUAL DEFILEMENT ON THE THIRTIETH DAY, THE WHOLE PERIOD IS VOID. [IF HE SAYS,] 'I INTEND TO BE A NAZIRITE FOR ONE HUNDRED DAYS,' AND CONTRACTS RITUAL DEFILEMENT ON THE HUNDREDTH DAY, HE RENDERS VOID THE WHOLE PERIOD. R. ELIEZER SAYS: ONLY THIRTY DAYS ARE VOID. IF HE CONTRACTS DEFILEMENT ON THE HUNDRED AND FIRST DAY,

THIRTY DAYS ARE VOID. R. ELIEZER SAYS: ONLY SEVEN DAYS ARE VOID.

GEMARA. IF A MAN SAYS, 'I INTEND TO BE A NAZIRITE' AND CONTRACTS RITUAL DEFILEMENT ON THE THIRTIETH DAY, HE RENDERS VOID THE WHOLE PERIOD. R. ELIEZER SAYS: ONLY THE SEVEN DAYS ARE VOID. [16*b*] R. Eliezer is of the opinion that any [defilement contracted] after the 'fulfilment' [of the period] renders only seven days void.[1]

[IF HE SAYS,] 'I INTEND TO BE A NAZIRITE FOR THIRTY DAYS,' AND CONTRACTS RITUAL DEFILEMENT ON THE THIRTIETH DAY, THE WHOLE PERIOD IS VOID. Here, R. Eliezer does not dissent because [we assume that] the man said, 'whole days'.[2]

[IF HE SAYS,] 'I INTEND TO BE A NAZIRITE FOR A HUNDRED DAYS,' AND CONTRACTS RITUAL DEFILEMENT ON THE HUNDREDTH DAY, HE RENDERS VOID THE WHOLE PERIOD. R. ELIEZER SAYS: ONLY THIRTY DAYS ARE VOID. All this may be taken [in two ways,] according as we follow Bar Pada or R. Mattena as explained above.[3]

MISHNAH. IF A MAN MAKES A NAZIRITE VOW WHILST IN A GRAVEYARD, THEN EVEN IF HE REMAINS THERE FOR THIRTY DAYS, THESE ARE NOT RECKONED,[4] AND HE DOES NOT HAVE TO BRING THE SACRIFICE [PRESCRIBED] FOR RITUAL DEFILEMENT. IF HE LEAVES[5] IT AND RE-ENTERS,[6] [THE PERIOD][7] IS RECKONED, AND HE MUST BRING THE SACRIFICE [PRESCRIBED] FOR DEFILEMENT. R. ELIEZER SAID: NOT [IF HE RE-ENTERS] ON THE SAME DAY, FOR IT SAYS, BUT THE FORMER DAYS

(1) V. *supra* 6*b*. (2) And the thirty are not yet completed. (3) According to R. Mattena a naziriteship whose duration is not specified lasts thirty days, whilst Bar Pada says that it lasts twenty-nine days. The full discussion of the *Mishnah* occurs above, fols. 5*b*-7*a*. (4) I.e., the naziriteship does not begin. (5) [And submits to the process of purification.] (6) After becoming clean, v. *infra*. (7) He is considered an ordinary nazirite from the time he becomes clean until he re-enters the graveyard.

SHALL BE VOID,[1] [IMPLYING] THAT THERE MUST BE 'FORMER DAYS'

GEMARA. It has been stated: If a man makes a nazirite vow whilst in a graveyard, then according to R. Joḥanan the naziriteship takes effect, but according to Resh Laḳish it does not take effect. R. Joḥanan says: The naziriteship does take effect because he considers it merely to be suspended and in readiness, so that whenever he becomes ritually clean, it commences to operate; whereas Resh Laḳish holds that, the naziriteship does not take effect; if he repeats [the vow] later [when he is clean], it will commence to operate, but not otherwise.

R. Joḥanan raised an objection to Resh Laḳish [from the following]: IF A MAN MAKES A NAZIRITE VOW WHILST IN A GRAVEYARD, THEN EVEN IF HE REMAINS THERE FOR THIRTY DAYS, THESE ARE NOT RECKONED, AND HE DOES NOT HAVE TO BRING THE SACRIFICE [PRESCRIBED] FOR RITUAL DEFILEMENT. [This implies, does it not,] that it is only the sacrifice [prescribed] for ritual defilement that he does not have to bring, but [the vow] does take effect?—He replied: [Not so;] he does not come within the scope of the law, either of ritual defilement or of the sacrifice.

An objection was again raised by him [from the following]: If a man is ritually defiled, and vows to become a nazirite, he is forbidden to poll, or to drink wine, or to touch a dead body. Should he poll, or drink wine, or touch a dead body, he is to receive the forty stripes.[2] If now you admit that [the vow] takes effect, then we see why he receives the forty stripes; but if you say that it does not take effect, why should he receive the forty stripes?—[17*a*] We are dealing here with the case in which he left [the graveyard] and re-entered it.[3]

A [further] objection was raised by him [as follows]: The only difference between a person ritually defiled who makes a nazirite

---

(1) Num. VI, 12.   (2) Tosef. Naz. II, 9.   (3) When he had become clean and repeated the vow.

vow, and a ritually clean nazirite who becomes unclean, is that the former reckons his seventh day [of purification] as part of his period [of naziriteship], whereas the latter does not reckon his seventh day [of purification] as part of his [new] period. If now you assume that [the vow of the unclean person] does not take effect, how is [the seventh day] to be counted [in his period]?—Mar b. R. Ashi said: Both [R. Joḥanan and Resh Laḳish] agree that [the vow] does take effect; where they differ is whether there is [to be a penalty of] stripes.[1] R. Joḥanan is of the opinion that since [the vow] takes effect, he suffers the penalty of stripes, but Resh Laḳish is of the opinion that there is no penalty of stripes, although [the vow] does take effect.

R. Joḥanan raised an objection to Resh Laḳish [from the following]: IF A MAN MAKES A NAZIRITE VOW WHILST IN A GRAVEYARD, THEN EVEN IF HE SHOULD REMAIN THERE FOR THIRTY DAYS, THESE ARE NOT RECKONED, AND HE DOES NOT HAVE TO BRING THE SACRIFICE [PRESCRIBED] FOR RITUAL DEFILEMENT. [This implies, does it not,] that it is only the sacrifice prescribed for ritual defilement that he does not have to bring, but he does suffer stripes?—Strictly speaking, it should have stated that he does not receive stripes, but since it was requisite in the subsequent clause to mention that where HE LEAVES [THE GRAVEYARD] AND RE-ENTERS, THE [PERIOD] IS RECKONED, AND HE MUST BRING THE SACRIFICE [PRESCRIBED] FOR DEFILEMENT, the initial clause, too, mentions that he need not bring the sacrifice [prescribed] for ritual defilement.[2]

Come and hear: The only difference between a ritually defiled person who makes a nazirite-vow, and a ritually clean nazirite who becomes unclean, is that the former reckons his seventh day [of purification] as part of his period [of naziriteship], whereas the latter does not reckon his seventh day as part of his period. [Does not this imply] that as regards stripes, they are on a par?—He[3] replied: Not so. Where they are on a par is as regards polling.

(1) [For contracting defilement whilst making his vow in the graveyard.] (2) Thus making the two clauses symmetrical in form. (3) Resh Laḳish.

[You aver, then,] that the latter receives stripes,[1] but the former does not do so. Why is this not mentioned?—The [Baraitha] is referring to that which is serviceable[2] to him, not to that which is to his detriment.[3]

Come and hear: Whosoever was ritually defiled and vowed to be a nazirite is forbidden to poll, or to drink wine. If he should poll, or drink wine, or come into contact with the [human] dead, he is to receive the forty stripes? This is undeed a refutation.[4]

Raba enquired: If a man vows to be a nazirite whilst in a graveyard, what is the law? Has he to be [in the graveyard] a certain time[5] for him to be liable to stripes, or not?

What are the circumstances? If he was told not to make a nazirite vow, why should any length of stay be necessary? What is the reason why no length of stay [in the graveyard] is necessary for the [ritually clean] nazirite [to be liable to stripes]? It is because he was forewarned;[6] and here too he was forewarned! [17*b*] We must suppose, therefore, that he entered [the graveyard] in a box, or a chest, or a portable turret,[7] and his fellow came and broke away the covering.[8] [The question then arises] whether [the rule requiring] a certain length of stay[9] was only laid down with reference to [defilement within] the Temple precincts, but not outside,[10] or whether there is no distinction.[11] The problem was unsolved.

R. Ashi raised the following question: If a man vows to become a nazirite whilst in a graveyard, is he required to poll or not? Is polling required only of a ritually clean nazirite who has contracted ritual defilement, because he has defiled his consecration,[12] and not of a ritually unclean person who makes a nazirite vow, or is there

(1) For defilement. (2) To know when to commence the naziriteship. (3) To receive stripes. (4) Of Resh Laḳish (5) A minimum period. V. Shebu. 17*a*. (6) Of the prohibition against defiling himself. (7) And therefore did not contract uncleanness when in the graveyard, being in a separate place. (8) After he had vowed to become a nazirite. (9) Viz., sufficient for prostration. V. Shebu. 17*a*. (10) To cases not connected with the Temple, e.g., when a nazirite becomes unclean inside the graveyard. (11) And therefore in the graveyard also a certain length of stay is required. (12) V. Num. VI, 9.

no difference [between the two]?—Come and hear: IF A MAN MAKES A NAZIRITE VOW WHILST IN A GRAVEYARD, THEN EVEN IF HE REMAINS THERE FOR THIRTY DAYS, THESE ARE NOT RECKONED, AND HE DOES NOT HAVE TO BRING THE SACRIFICE [PRESCRIBED] FOR RITUAL DEFILEMENT. [This implies, does it not,] that it is only the sacrifice prescribed for ritual defilement that need not be brought, but that polling is necessary!—[That is not so.] The statement is made as a reason [for something else]. The reason that he need not bring the sacrifice prescribed for ritual defilement is that polling is unnecessary.[1]

Come and hear: The only difference between a ritually defiled person who makes a nazirite vow and a ritually clean nazirite who contracts ritual defilement is that the former reckons his seventh day [of purification] as part of his period [of naziriteship], whereas the latter does not reckon his seventh day as part of his [new] period. Surely, then, as regards polling both are on the same footing?—No! Where both are on the same footing is as regards stripes. In the case of polling, [you aver that] one polls and the other does not. Then why not mention this?—The seventh day is mentioned, and includes all observances dependent upon it.[2]

Come and hear: I am only told here[3] that the period of his ritual defilement is not reckoned [in the days of his naziriteship]. How do we know [that the same is true] of the period of declared leprosy?[4] This can be derived from an analogy [between the two]. Just as after the period of ritual defilement he is required to poll and bring a sacrifice, so after the period of declared leprosy he is required to poll and bring a sacrifice; and so just as the period of ritual defilement is not reckoned, the period of declared leprosy ought not to be reckoned.—Not so! For in the case of the period of defilement, it may be because this renders void the former reckoning[5] that it is not reckoned, whereas the period of declared

(1) The problem therefore remains. (2) The seventh day is counted as part of his naziriteship because he need not bring a sacrifice, and he does not bring a sacrifice since he does not poll. (3) In Num. VI, 12. (4) Cf. Lev. XIII, 3ff. (5) The period of naziriteship counted before defilement.

leprosy does not render void the former reckoning,[1] and therefore it should itself be reckoned.—I will put the argument differently. Seeing that 'a nazirite in a graveyard',[2] whose hair is ripe for polling,[3] does not count [the days spent in the graveyard as part of his naziriteship], surely the period of declared leprosy, when his hair is not ripe for polling,[4] should not be counted.[5] Now surely polling as a result of his defilement is meant?[6]—No! the reference may be to polling [after observing the nazirite vow] in ritual purity.[7] This is indeed evident. [18*a*] For if you assume that polling as a result of the defilement is intended, does he not have to poll after the period of declared leprosy?[8]—No, [this does not constitute proof, for] the reference is to the polling on account of the naziriteship.[9]

Come and hear: The verse, *And he defile his consecrated head*[10] refers to a ritually clean [nazirite] who contracts ritual defilement; it enjoins on such a one to remove his hair and sacrifice bird-offerings, but [by implication] exempts one, who vows to become a nazirite at a graveside, from removing his hair and sacrificing bird-offerings. For you might argue *a fortiori:* if the ritually clean

(1) The period counted before leprosy. (2) I.e., one who made the vow of naziriteship in a graveyard. (3) For he will poll automatically at the end of the seven days of purification, just as a ritually clean nazirite polls at the end of his naziriteship. This is the initial interpretation of the argument as understood by the Gemara. (4) There is no definite period at which he has to poll, but he must wait until he recovers from the disease. (5) The whole of the above paragraph is a quotation from Sifre on Num. VI, 12. (6) I.e., surely the phrase 'whose hair is ripe for polling' means that he must poll as a result of his defilement in the graveyard, so that R. Ashi's question is answered in the affirmative. (7) So that the argument is: Seeing that 'a nazirite in a graveyard' whose hair will be ripe for polling after he has purified himself and observed the period of his naziriteship, does not count etc., surely the leper, whose hair is not ripe for polling as part of his naziriteship because he must poll on recovery from his disease before he commences to count the naziriteship, ought not to count etc. (8) So that the two cases are exactly analogous, and we cannot call one 'ripe for polling' and the other 'not ripe for polling'. (9) The defiled nazirite has to poll because he is a nazirite, whereas the leper polls because he was a leper. There would thus still be room for the argument even if the meaning were that 'a nazirite in a graveyard' must poll. (10) Num. VI, 9.

[nazirite] who contracts ritual defilement must remove his hair and sacrifice bird-offerings, all the more must one who commenced [his naziriteship] whilst defiled remove his hair and sacrifice bird-offerings; therefore the text says expressly, *'And he defile his consecrated head'*, [implying] that only the ritually clean [nazirite] who contracts ritual defilement is required by Scripture to remove his hair and sacrifice bird-offerings, but not the person who vowed to become a nazirite at a graveside. This proves then [that the latter is exempt].

Who is the author of the following dictum, taught by the Rabbis, [*viz.*,] The only difference between a ritually defiled person who makes a nazirite vow, and a ritually clean nazirite who contracts ritual defilement, is that the former reckons his seventh day [of purification] as part of his period [of naziriteship],[1] whilst the latter does not reckon his seventh day as part of his [new] period? —R. Ḥisda said: It is Rabbi, for Rabbi has said that the naziriteship [after defilement] does not recommence until the eighth day of purification, for if you were to say it is R. Jose son of R. Judah, surely he holds that the naziriteship [after defilement] begins to operate on the seventh day of purification.

Where are these opinions of Rabbi and R. Jose son of R. Judah [to be found]?—It has been taught: *And he shall hallow his head that same day;*[2] Rabbi says [that this refers to] the day on which he offers his sacrifices,[3] but R. Jose son of R. Judah says [it refers] to the day on which he polls.[4]

And who is the author of the teaching that, 'A nazirite who contracts ritual defilement many times brings a single sacrifice only'?[5]—R. Ḥisda said: It is R. Jose son of R. Judah, who has said that the naziriteship [after defilement] recommences on the seventh day of purification. Thus the case [contemplated] could arise if he were to contract defilement on the seventh day [of purification][6]

(1) I.e., the seventh day is counted as the first day of his thirty days of naziriteship. (2) Num. VI, 11. (3) The eighth day after the occurrence of the defilement. (4) The seventh day after the occurrence of the defilement. (5) Ker. II, 3. (6) After he has bathed.

and then again on the seventh day after that,[1] nevertheless since there was no period when he could have brought his sacrifice,[2] he need offer one sacrifice only [for both defilements]. According to Rabbi, however, if he contracted ritual defilement on the seventh day and then again on the seventh day,[3] the whole is one long period of ritual defilement,[4] whilst if we suppose he contracts ritual defilement upon the eighth day and again upon the eighth day, then there is a point of time [on each occasion] when he could bring his sacrifice.[5]

What is Rabbi's reason [for his opinion]?—The verse says [first], *And make atonement for him that he sinned by reason of the dead,*[6] and then, *And he shall hallow his head.*[7] And what does R. Jose son of R. Judah [say to this]?—If this is its intention, the text should read simply, '*And he shall hallow his head*'. [18*b*] What is the purpose of [the additional phrase], '*that day*'? Since it cannot refer to the eighth day,[8] we may take it as referring to the seventh day. And Rabbi? He can say that the purpose of the phrase '*that day*' is to tell us that even if he should fail to bring his sacrifices [the naziriteship commences].

Now what compelled R. Ḥisda to ascribe the authorship of this dictum to R. Jose son of R. Judah? Why should he not have interpreted it as referring to where he became unclean on the eighth night,[9] and ascribed the authorship to Rabbi?[10] Are we to understand from the fact that he does not ascribe the authorship to Rabbi, that in his opinion the night [before the day that his sacrifice is due] is not regarded as belonging to the preceding period?[11]

(1) After the occurrence of the *second* defilement, so that this is a separate defilement. But if he became unclean on the sixth day, it would be the same defilement. (2) Which has to be brought on the 8th day. (3) After the occurrence of the second defilement. (4) Hence we cannot say 'many times' as in the passage quoted. (5) And he must bring a sacrifice for each period of defilement. (6) Num. VI, 11. (7) Hence the naziriteship is to recommence *after* the offering of the sacrifice, which took place on the eigth day. (8) For if it did, it would be superfluous. (9) I.e., the night preceding the eigth day. (10) So that the defilements are separate, though in regard to sacrifices they would be considered one, seeing that no sacrifice can be brought at night. (11) Lit., 'wanting time'. Although the sacrifice cannot be brought till the next day.

—R. Adda b. Ahaba replied: One thing depends on the other. If we hold that the night [before the day his sacrifice is due] is regarded as belonging to the preceding period, then, since he can offer his sacrifice only in the morning, the naziriteship does not begin to operate until the morning;[1] whereas if the night [before the day his sacrifice is due] is not regarded as belonging to the preceding period, the naziriteship after purification [from defilement] begins in the evening.[2]

Our Rabbis taught:[3] If [a nazirite][4] contracts defilement on the seventh day [of purification], and then he again contracts defilement on the seventh day [following], he is only required to offer one sacrifice. If he contracts defilement on the eighth day, and then once more on the eighth day [following], he is required to offer a sacrifice for each [defilement]. He begins to reckon [the new naziriteship] immediately;[5] this is the opinion of R. Eliezer, but the Sages say: He is required to offer but one sacrifice for all [the defilements] so long as he has not yet offered his sin-offering.[6] If he has brought his sin-offering and then contracts defilement, and again offers his sin-offering and again contracts defilement, he is required to furnish a [full] sacrifice for each defilement. If he has furnished his sin-offering, but not his guilt-offering, he [nevertheless] commences to reckon [the new naziriteship]. R. Ishmael, the son of R. Johanan b. Beroka said: Just as his sin-offering estops him [from commencing to reckon the new naziriteship], so does his guilt-offering.

Now, all is in order according to R. Eliezer, for the verse says, *And he shall hallow his head* that same *day*,[7] even though he may not yet have provided the sacrifices. [And likewise] the Rabbis [explain]

(1) So that there would still be only one defilement. (2) And he would have to bring, according to Rabbi, a sacrifice for each defilement. (3) [So Rashi; cur. edd., read, 'The text (states)'. This term, however, would not have the same meaning here as elsewhere in the Talmud where the reference is to a text previously cited; v. Asheri.] (4) Who became unclean. (5) Though he has not yet offered his sacrifices. (6) The sacrifice of a nazirite who had become unclean consisted of two doves, one a sin-offering, the other a burnt-offering, and also a he-lamb as a guilt-offering. V. Num. VI, 10-12. (7) Num. VI, 11.

'*that* [*day*]', [implying], even though he may not yet have provided the *guilt-offering*.[1] But what does R Ishmael, the son of R. Joḥanan b. Beroḳa make of the words '*that* [*day*]'?—He will reply: [His naziriteship commences] '*that* [*day*]', even though he may not yet have provided the burnt-offering. And the Rabbis?—They do not consider it necessary to have an excluding phrase for [permission to dispense with] the burnt offering, since it is [brought] simply as a gift.[2]

What is the Rabbis' reason [for stating that the guilt-offering is no bar]?—It has been taught: What is the implication of the verse, *And he shall consecrate unto the Lord the days of his Naziriteship, and shall bring a he-lamb of the first year for a guilt-offering?*[3] Since we find that all other guilt-offerings mentioned in the Torah are a bar [to atonement so long as they are not brought], it might have been thought that this one is also a bar, [19*a*] and so the text says, '*And he shall consecrate . . . and shall bring* [*a guilt-offering*]' implying that even though he may not yet have brought [the guilt-offering], he is to consecrate. R. Ishmael, son of R. Joḥanan b. Beroḳa said: '*And he shall consecrate . . . and shall bring*'. When does he consecrate? *After* he has brought.[4]

Who is the Tanna of the following [teaching] taught by the Rabbis: 'If a woman undertakes a nazirite vow, and contracts ritual defilement, and then her husband declares [her vow] void, she must bring the sin-offering of a bird, but not the burnt-offering of a bird'?—R. Ḥisda replied: It is R. Ishmael.[5] How comes [R. Ishmael] to this ruling?—If he holds that the husband nullifies [his wife's vow],[6] then she should not be required to bring the sin-offering of a bird, whilst if he holds that the husband only terminates[7] [the vow],[8] why should she not be required to bring the

(1) But the new naziriteship cannot commence till he has brought the others. (2) [And not to effect atonement, as the other sacrifices, v. Zeb. 7*b*.] (3) Num. VI, 12. (4) The naziriteship begins anew after he has brought the guilt-offering. (5) [Who, in contradistinction to the Rabbis, holds that the burnt-offering is not brought as a mere gift, but specifically as a sacrifice of a nazirite, and since her naziriteship is void, she brings no sin-offering.] (6) Lit., 'uproots', i.e., that his action is retrospective and the vow has never been valid. (7) Lit., 'cuts off'. (8) When he disallows it; until then it was effective.

burnt-offering of a bird as well?—Actually he is of the opinion that a husband nullifies [his wife's vow], and he further agrees with R. Eleazar ha-Ḳappar. For it has been taught: R. Eleazar ha-Ḳappar, Berabbi,[1] said: Why does the Scripture say, *And make atonement for him, for that he sinned by reason of the soul.*[2] Against what 'soul' did he then sin? It can only be because he denied himself wine.[3] If then this man who denied himself wine only is termed a sinner, how much more so is this true of one who is ascetic in all things!

But the verse is referring to an unclean nazirite,[4] whilst we are applying it even to a ritually clean nazirite?—R. Eleazar ha-Ḳappar[5] is of the opinion that a ritually clean nazirite is also a sinner, and the reason that Scripture teaches this [lesson in connection] with a defiled nazirite is that he repeats his sin.[6]

IF HE LEAVES IT AND RE-ENTERS, THE DAYS ARE RECKONED. It is stated that they are reckoned.[7] Does then the naziriteship begin to operate merely because he has left [the graveyard]?[8]—Samuel said: [We are speaking of] where he has left it, been sprinkled [a first and] a second time and bathed.[9] But [are we to infer that] if he re-enters, then only are they reckoned, whilst if he does not re-enter, they are not reckoned?—The argument is progressive. Not only [do they count] if he leaves, but [they count] also if he re-enters [immediately after purification].[10]

R. Kahana and R. Assi asked Rab: Why have you not explained

(1) [Or 'Berebi'. Designation by which Bar Ḳappara is known in order to distinguish him from his father who bore the same name. The meaning of the title is uncertain: (*a*) a compound of 'house', *be*, and '*rabbi*', i.e., belonging to the school of an eminent teacher (Jast.), or (*b*) a compound of 'son', '*bir*', and '*rabbi*', 'a son of a scholar', i.e., 'a scholar', v. *J.E.* III, 52.] (2) נפש, E.V.: 'dead'. Num. VI, 11. (3) And so the woman must bring the sin-offering because she wished to deny herself wine. (4) The section of which it forms part begins (Num. VI, 9), *If any man die suddenly upon him*, so that he become defiled, . . . *he shall bring two turtle doves*, of which one was a sin-offering brought because, . . . *he sinned by reason of the soul*. (5) Cf., however, *supra* 3*a*, where R. Eleazar ha-Ḳappar is reported as saying that a ritually clean nazirite is not a sinner. (6) For the period before defilement is void and he must now recommence to count thirty days. (7) So that he must bring the sacrifices of a nazir who becomes unclean. (8) For he is still unclean. (9) I.e., undergone the purification rites. V. Num. XIX, 19. (10) In which case we might think that he is as at first.

[the Mishnah] to us in this manner?—He replied: I was under the impression that you did not require [to be told].

R. ELIEZER SAID: NOT IF HE DOES SO ON THE SAME DAY, FOR IT SAYS, AND THE FORMER DAYS SHALL BE VOID, IMPLYING THAT THERE MUST BE FORMER DAYS. 'Ulla said: R. Eliezer was referring only to a ritually defiled person who makes a nazirite vow, but a ritually clean nazirite who contracts ritual defilement, makes [his naziriteship] void, even on the first day.[1] [19b] Raba added: R. Eliezer's reason[2] is that the text continues, *Because his consecration was defiled,*[3] i.e., because he undertook the naziriteship during defilement.

Abaye raised an objection [from the following]. [If a man says,] 'I wish to be a nazirite for one hundred days,' and contracts ritual defilement at the very beginning of them, it might be held that this makes void [the naziriteship], but the text reads, *'And the former days shall be void'*; there must first be *'former days'*, and here there are no former days. If he contracts ritual defilement at the end of the hundred days, it might be held that this makes void [the naziriteship], but the text reads, *'And the former days shall be void'*, implying that there are later days too, and here there are no days to come. If he contracts ritual defilement on the ninety-ninth day, it might be held[4] that he should not make void the naziriteship, but the text reads, *And the former days shall be void,* implying that there must be days to come, and here there are both former days[5] and days to come. Now it cannot be said that we are dealing with a ritually defiled person who makes a nazirite vow, since the account begins, '"I wish to be a nazirite for a hundred days," and he contracts defilement at the very beginning of them,' and yet it says that former *days* are necessary.—This indeed is a refutation [of 'Ulla].

R. Papa asked Abaye: Regarding the days that are required, is

(1) When there are no 'former days'. (2) For making a distinction between one who undertook the naziriteship in purity, and an unclean person who undertakes a naziriteship, where we require *'former days'*. (3) Num. VI, 12. (4) Since there is only one day to come and not *'days'*. (5) Viz., part of the ninety-ninth and the hundredth.

it sufficient if one has passed and [the defilement occurs when] the second begins, or must two pass, and [the defilement occur when] the third has begun?—[Abaye] had no information on the subject, so [Rab Papa] went and asked Raba. He replied: The text reads they *shall fall away.*[1]

Both the word *'days'*, and the [plural] form, *'they shall fall away'* are needed,[2] for if the Divine Law had used the word *'days'* and not the form *'they shall fall away'*, it might have been held that it is sufficient if one day has passed, and the second begun,[3] and so the Divine Law wrote *'they shall fall away'*. And if it had used the form *'they shall fall away'*, and not [the plural] *'days'*, it might have been held that even one day is sufficient, and so the Divine Law uses the word *days.*

MISHNAH. IF A MAN VOWS A NAZIRITESHIP OF LONG DURATION AND COMPLETES IT AND THEN ARRIVES IN THE LAND [OF ISRAEL], BETH SHAMMAI SAY THAT HE IS A NAZIRITE FOR THIRTY DAYS, BUT BETH HILLEL SAY THAT HIS NAZIRITESHIP COMMENCES AGAIN AS AT FIRST. IT IS RELATED THAT QUEEN HELENA,[4] WHEN HER SON WENT TO WAR,[5] SAID: 'IF MY SON RETURNS IN PEACE FROM THE WAR, I SHALL BE A NAZIRITE FOR SEVEN YEARS.' HER SON RETURNED FROM THE WAR, AND SHE OBSERVED A NAZIRITESHIP FOR SEVEN YEARS. AT THE END OF THE SEVEN YEARS, SHE WENT UP TO

(1) Meaning that two complete days must have passed. So Rashi. (2) [The text could have read 'And he shall hallow his head on that day apart from the previous days' (Tosaf.)] (3) Because part of a day is like the whole. The reading of Rashi and the BaḤ has been adopted. Our printed text reads: It might have been held that it is necessary for two days to have passed and the third begun, and so the Divine Law used the form *'they shall fall away'*. Thus the inference conflicts with the usually accepted interpretation of Raba's reply. The objection to it is that the Gemara above appears to imply that the two phrases are weak forms needing to be strengthened by the appearance of both. The printed text, on the other hand, at the last treats 'days' as a strong form. (4) Queen of the Adiabene, *circa* 40 C.E., Mother of Izates. V. Josephus *Ant.* XX, 2-4. (5) Possibly the war of the restoration of Artabanus as King of Parthia. *Ibid.* 3.

THE LAND [OF ISRAEL][1] AND BETH HILLEL RULED THAT SHE MUST BE A NAZIRITE FOR A FURTHER SEVEN YEARS. TOWARDS THE END OF THIS SEVEN YEARS, SHE CONTRACTED RITUAL DEFILEMENT, AND SO ALTOGETHER SHE WAS A NAZIRITE FOR TWENTY-ONE YEARS. R. JUDAH SAID: SHE WAS ONLY A NAZIRITE FOR FOURTEEN YEARS.[2]

GEMARA. The first clause reads: BETH SHAMMAI SAY [HE] IS A NAZIRITE FOR THIRTY DAYS, BUT BETH HILLEL SAY THAT HIS NAZIRITESHIP COMMENCES AGAIN AS AT FIRST. May we say that the ground on which they differ is that Beth Shammai are of the opinion [Rabbis declared] foreign lands [to be unclean] on account of their soil, [20a] whilst Beth Hillel are of the opinion that it was on account of the air also?[3]—No! All are agreed that the enactment was because of the soil, but Beth Shammai are of the opinion that we penalise[4] him by [the imposition of] a naziriteship of normal length, whilst Beth Hillel are of the opinion that he is penalised from the very commencement of his naziriteship.

IT IS RELATED THAT QUEEN HELENA etc.: The question was asked: [Does R. Judah agree that] she contracted impurity, in which case his statement concurs with Beth Shammai's opinion,[5] or does he deny that she contracted impurity, in which case his statement concurs with Beth Hillel's opinion?[6]—

Come and hear: SHE WENT UP TO THE LAND [OF ISRAEL], AND BETH HILLEL RULED THAT SHE MUST OBSERVE NAZIRITESHIP FOR A FURTHER SEVEN YEARS ETC. Now if you assume that she did contract impurity, and that [R. Judah] concurs with Beth Shammai, then the text should read: R. Judah said: She was a nazirite for fourteen years and thirty days, instead of [simply]

(1) Also recorded by Josephus 2, 5. (2) V. the Gemara, *infra*. (3) Hence according to Beth Hillel the defilement which he has contracted by being on a foreign land is much more severe. (4) For incurring a defilement instituted by the Rabbis though not recognised by the Torah. (5) That only thirty days are required, the second seven years being due to the impurity. (6) That seven years are required, the fourteen being made up of the original seven, and the seven imposed because of absence from Palestine.

fourteen years! There has also been taught in the same sense: R. Judah quoting R. Eliezer said that the implication of the verse, *And this is the law of the Nazirite* [on the day *when the days of his separation are fulfilled*][1] is: the Torah says that if he contracts ritual defilement on the day of his fulfilment, he is to be given the law of a nazirite.[2]

MISHNAH. WHERE TWO GROUPS OF WITNESSES GIVE EVIDENCE CONCERNING A MAN, ONE SAYING THAT HE VOWED TWO NAZIRITESHIPS[3] AND THE OTHER THAT HE VOWED FIVE, BETH SHAMMAI SAY THAT THE EVIDENCE IS CONFLICTING [IN TOTO], AND NO NAZIRITESHIP OPERATES AT ALL, BUT BETH HILLEL SAY THAT 'FIVE' INCLUDES 'TWO', SO THAT HE BECOMES A NAZIRITE FOR TWO PERIODS.

GEMARA. The Mishnah disagrees with the following Tanna. For it has been taught: R. Ishmael, the son of R. Joḥanan b. Beroḳa, said that Beth Shammai and Beth Hillel did not dispute that five included two where there are two groups of witnesses one saying five and one two. Where they differed was when of a single pair of witnesses, one says five and the other two, Beth Shammai averring that this is conflicting evidence, whilst Beth Hillel maintained that [here also], five includes two.

Rab said: All are agreed that where [the witnesses] enumerate [the evidence is conflicting]. R. Ḥama said to R. Ḥisda: What does this mean? It cannot mean that one says it was five and not two, and the other it was two and not five, for they plainly contradict each other. And if again it means that one says, [he vowed] a first and a second time, and the other a third, fourth and fifth time. [20b] [we may ask,] what need is there for the se-

(1) Num. VI, 13. (2) The implication is probably that R. Judah does require a nazirite who becomes defiled in his last day to observe thirty more days, so we are entitled to make an inference from the brief form 'fourteen years' as is done in the text. (3) So Tosaf. Rashi renders 'years of naziriteship'.

cond to repeat [the first two]?[1] Seeing that [the second witness] testifies to the more stringent ones,[2] then he certainly testifies to [the first two] that are less stringent?[3]—In the West[4] they maintain that where there is enumeration, there is no conflicting [of evidence].[5]

(1) There is still no conflict, although there is enumeration, for seeing that, etc. (2) To the existence of a third, fourth, and fifth naziriteship. (3) In this paragraph, the reading of Tosaf. has been adopted. [According to printed texts, render: 'Why was it necessary to state this; seeing that Rab ruled to this effect in a more stringent case, would he not rule likewise in a less stringent one?' The stringent case referred to is where the enumeration is made by *two groups* of witnesses, in which case Rab ruled (in a passage which Rashi cites from J. Sanh. V) that the evidence is conflicting.] (4) I.e., in Palestine, cf. J. Sanh. V, 2. (5) He is therefore required to observe two naziriteships, Rab's opinion being wrong. The second witness is not really contradicting the first, and thus there are two witnesses to the first two naziriteships.

NAZIR

CHAPTER IV

MISHNAH. SHOULD A MAN SAY, 'I INTEND TO BE A NAZIRITE,' AND HIS COMPANION OVERHEAR AND ADD 'I TOO,' [AND THE NEXT REPEAT] 'I TOO', ALL BECOME NAZIRITES. IF THE FIRST IS RELEASED [FROM HIS VOW],[1] ALL ARE [AUTOMATICALLY] RELEASED, BUT IF THE LAST ONE IS RELEASED, HE ALONE BECOMES FREE, THE OTHERS REMAINING BOUND [BY THEIR VOWS]. IF HE SAYS, 'I INTEND TO BE A NAZIRITE,' AND HIS COMPANION OVERHEARS AND ADDS, 'LET MY MOUTH BE AS HIS MOUTH AND MY HAIR AS HIS HAIR,' HE [ALSO] BECOMES A NAZIRITE. [IF HE SAYS,] 'I INTEND TO BE A NAZIRITE,' AND HIS WIFE OVERHEARS AND ADDS, 'I TOO,' HE CAN DECLARE HER [VOW] VOID,[2] BUT HIS OWN REMAINS BINDING. [IF A WOMAN SAYS,] 'I INTEND TO BE A NAZIRITE,' AND HER HUSBAND OVERHEARS AND ADDS, 'I TOO,' HE CANNOT DECLARE [HER VOW] VOID.[3] [IF HE SHOULD SAY IN CONVERSATION WITH HIS WIFE,] 'I INTEND TO BE A NAZIRITE. WHAT ABOUT YOU?' AND SHE ANSWER 'AMEN,' HE CAN DECLARE HER [VOW] VOID, BUT HIS OWN REMAINS BINDING. [BUT IF SHE SHOULD SAY,] 'I INTEND TO BE A NAZIRITE. WHAT ABOUT YOU?' AND HE ANSWER, 'AMEN,' HE CANNOT DECLARE [HER VOW] VOID.[3]

GEMARA. Resh Lakish was [once] seated in the presence of R. Judah the Prince,[4] and discoursed as follows: [They become nazirites by saying 'I too,'] only if they all attach their vows

(1) Under certain conditions release can be obtained from a vow on application to an authorised Rabbi. V. Ned. 78*a*. (2) The husband has the power of confirming or declaring void his wife's vow's *'on the day that he hears them'*—v. Num. XXX, 9. (3) For by attaching his vow to hers, he incidentally confirms her vow. (4) *Nesi'ah*; R. Judah II.

within the interval of a break in conversation.[1] And how much is the length of such an interval? The time sufficient for a greeting. And how much is this? The time taken by a disciple to greet his master.[2] [R. Judah] said to him: You do not allow a disciple any further opportunity.[3]

[21a] The same principle[4] is taught in the following passage: If a man says, 'I intend to be a nazirite' and his companion overhear and delay long enough to make a break in conversation and then add, 'I too,' he himself is bound [by his vow], but his companion is free. The length of a break in conversation is the time taken by a disciple to greet his master.[5]

May we say that the following [passage] corroborates [Resh Lakish's statement]? [For the Mishnah says:] SHOULD A MAN SAY, 'I INTEND TO BE A NAZIRITE,' AND HIS COMPANION OVERHEAR AND ADD 'I TOO,' [AND THE NEXT REPEAT] 'I TOO,' [ALL BECOME NAZIRITES];[6] and carries the series no further?[7] —Do you expect the Tanna to string together a list like a pedlar [crying his wares]?[8] Then why should he not mention ['I too']

(1) I.e., the normal interval between the remarks of two persons holding a conversation. Lit., 'within the time sufficient for (the next) remark.' The point of Resh Lakish's statement is that we do not consider the remark 'I too' as being like one of the 'allusions' of the beginning of the first chapter, but its validity depends solely on its being obviously a reference to the original vow. Hence it must follow it, as though they were part of the same conversation. (2) I.e., to say the three words, *Shalom 'aleka Rabbi;* 'Peace unto Thee, Master'. (3) Both to greet his master and say 'I too', ואני (one word), if he wishes to. According to Rashi, R. Judah agreed with Resh Lakish, but other commentators consider that he disagreed with Resh Lakish and allowed four words as the interval in this case. (4) According to the other commentators: To the same effect as Resh Lakish, as opposed to R. Judah. (5) Tosef. Naz. III, 1. (6) Which would show that only two can attach themselves. (7) The argument is: If the Tanna merely desired to state that any number of persons can become nazirites by saying 'I too', he should not have stopped after two. Since he does stop, he must have had a different aim, viz., to fix the length of the interval that can elapse and the formula still be valid. The interval is naturally that of a break in conversation. (8) Although the expression 'I too', is repeated only twice, there may be no limit to the number of persons who could become nazirites in this manner.

once only and leave us to infer the rest?[1]—He could very well have done so, but because in the clause that follows he says: IF THE FIRST IS RELEASED [FROM HIS VOW] ALL ARE [AUTOMATICALLY] RELEASED, BUT IF THE LAST ONE IS RELEASED, HE ALONE BECOMES FREE, THE OTHERS REMAINING BOUND [BY THEIR VOWS], thus [using a phrasing which] implies that there is a person [or persons] in between, he mentions 'I too,' twice [in the opening clause].[2]

The question was propounded: Does each link up with his immediate predecessor, or do they all link up with [the utterance of] the first? The practical issue involved is whether the process can be continued indefinitely. If each links up with his immediate predecessor, then it would be possible to continue indefinitely,[3] but if they all link up with the first one, the process could not continue for longer than the space of a break in conversation.[4] What then is the law?—Come and hear: SHOULD A MAN SAY, 'I INTEND TO BE A NAZIRITE,' AND HIS COMPANION OVERHEAR AND ADD 'I TOO,' [AND THE NEXT REPEAT] 'I TOO'; without going further; and so we can infer that they all link up with the first,[5] for if it be the case that each links up with his immediate predecessor, why should not the phrase 'I too' be repeated many more times?—Do you expect the Tanna to string together a list like a pedlar [crying his wares]? Then let him mention ['I too'] once, and indicate all the rest in this manner?[6]—Since he continues: IF THE FIRST IS RELEASED [FROM HIS VOW] ALL ARE [AUTOMATICALLY] RELEASED, BUT IF THE LAST ONE IS RELEASED, HE ALONE BECOMES FREE, THE OTHERS REMAINING BOUND

(1) Viz. That it is possible for any number to become nazirites by saying 'I too'. (2) To provide the extra person in between the first and the last. (3) Since any number of persons could become nazirites by each saying 'I too' within the specified interval after his immediate predecessor's declaration, 'I too'. (4) I.e., within the specified interval after the first person's declaration, 'I intend to be a nazirite.' (5) So that not more than two persons can say 'I too', consecutively and became nazirites. (6) I.e., since the Tanna does not wish to give a long list, why should he mention even as many as two persons. All the information is contained in the first statement that by saying 'I too' it is possible to become a nazirite.

[BY THEIR VOWS; thus using a phrasing] which implies that there are persons in between, he therefore mentions 'I too' twice [in the first clause].[1]

Come and hear: IF THE FIRST IS RELEASED [FROM HIS VOW] ALL ARE RELEASED; [it follows that] only [on the release of] the first are the others released, but not [on the release of] an intermediate one, and so we can infer that they all link up with the first one![2]—I can reply that actually each links up with his immediate predecessor, and the reason [why the first is mentioned] is that [the Tanna] desired to say that 'ALL ARE RELEASED', and if he had stated this in connection with the intermediate one there would have remained the first one unreleased; therefore he preferred to mention in this connection the first.[3]

Come and hear: IF THE LAST ONE IS RELEASED, HE ALONE BECOMES FREE, THE OTHERS REMAINING BOUND [BY THEIR VOWS]. [Now the reason for this is presumably because] there are no others following him,[4] but if the second one, who is followed by others, [were released,] these would also become free,[5] and so we can infer that each links up with his immediate predecessor! —In point of fact, I can argue that they all link up with the first, and that the expression 'THE LAST' [as used by the Tanna] refers to those in between [also], but because he speaks [in the preceding clause] of 'THE FIRST', he refers to the others as 'THE LAST'.[6]

Come and hear [the following passage] where it is taught explicitly: If the first is released they all become free; if the last is released he alone becomes free, the rest remaining bound; if an intermediate one is released, those following him also become free, but those

(1) Thus indicating the person in between the first and the last. (2) For otherwise all those who had spoken after any one of the intermediate ones should be released with that one. (3) But in point of fact if any one of the others is released, all the succeeding ones are released. (4) There are in existence several readings of the text at this point. We have adopted that of Tosaf., which keeps very close to the usual printed text. (5) The Mishnah is taken to mean: Only if it is the last one who is released, do all the others remain bound by their vows. (6) But his intention is to exclude only the first.

preceding him remain bound. This shows conclusively that each links up with his immediate predecessor.[1]

[IF HE SAYS,] 'I INTEND TO BE A NAZIRITE' AND HIS COMPANION OVERHEARS AND ADDS, 'LET MY MOUTH BE AS HIS MOUTH AND MY HAIR AS HIS HAIR,' [HE ALSO BECOMES A NAZIRITE]: Simply because he says, 'LET MY MOUTH BE AS HIS MOUTH AND MY HAIR AS HIS HAIR,' does he become a nazirite?[2] [21b] Does not this conflict with the following passage? [It has been taught that if a man says,] 'Let my hand be a nazirite,' or 'Let my foot be a nazirite,' his words are of no effect. [But if he says,] 'Let my head be a nazirite,' or 'let my liver be a nazirite,' he becomes a nazirite. The rule is: If the organ is one upon which life depends, he becomes a nazirite![3]—Rab Judah replied: [In the Mishnah] he is presumed to say, 'Let my mouth be as his mouth as regards wine,' or 'my hair as his hair as regards shearing.'[4]

[IF A WOMAN SAYS,] 'I INTEND TO BE A NAZIRITE,' AND HER HUSBAND OVERHEARS AND ADDS, 'I TOO,' HE CANNOT DECLARE [HER VOW] VOID: The question was propounded: Does the husband nullify[5] or does he only terminate [the vow]?[6] The difference is of importance for deciding the case of a woman who vows to be a nazirite and whose companion overhears and says, 'I too,' and whose husband subsequently hears of the matter and declares her vow void. If it be decided that he nullifies [her vow], her companion is also set free,[7] but if it be decided that he merely terminates [the vow], she herself will be released, and her companion will remain bound [to the vow]. What, then, is the law?

Come and hear: [IF A WOMAN SAYS,] 'I INTEND TO BE A NAZIRITE,' AND HER HUSBAND OVERHEARS AND ADDS, 'I TOO,' HE

(1) The Gemara frequently attempts to obtain a ruling from a Mishnah even though a Baraitha states explicitly what is required. (2) Which would seem to show that if he says, 'My mouth is a nazirite,' he is a nazirite. (3) But it is possible to live without hair or mouth—hence the conflict. Tosef. Naz. III, 1. (4) Thus expressly referring to the obligations of a nazirite. The statement is now very similar to the 'allusions' of Chapter I. (5) Lit., 'uproot'. (6) I.e., is it as though the vow had never been made, or is the vow only cancelled from the time it is declared void? V. Num. XXX, 7ff. (7) Since the words 'I too' have no object of reference.

CANNOT DECLARE [HER VOW] VOID. Now, should you suppose that the husband terminates [the vow], he ought to be able to declare his wife's [vow] void, whilst remaining bound himself.[1] It surely follows, therefore, [from the fact that he cannot do so] that a husband nullifies [his wife's vow]?[2]—Not at all! Strictly speaking, the husband [in general] only terminates [the wife's vow,] and here by rights he should be able to declare her vow void,[3] and the reason why he cannot do so is because his saying, 'I too,' is equivalent to saying, 'I confirm it for you,'[4] and so if he [later] seeks to have the confirmation revoked,[5] he can then declare [his wife's vow] void,[6] but not otherwise.

Come and hear: If a woman undertakes a nazirite vow and sets aside the requisite animal [for the sacrifice] and her husband subsequently declares [the vow] void, then, if the animal was one of his own, it can be put to pasture with the herd,[7] but if it was one of hers, the sin-offering is to be left to die [etc.].[8] Now, should you suppose that the husband nullifies [the vow, the animal] should become profane?[9] It surely follows, therefore, that the husband [merely] terminates [the vow]?[10]—In point of fact, we can maintain that the husband nullifies [the vow], but [the animal remains sacred] for this reason. Since she no longer requires atonement,[11] [the case] is similar to that of a sin-offering whose owner has died, and it is a tradition that sin-offerings whose owners have died are left to die.

(1) She would be free hereafter, whilst he would remain a nazirite. Because the termination, while freeing her, in no wise affects the force of his 'I too'. (2) And so he cannot declare his wife's vow void, for by so doing, he would incidentally retract his own vow, which is forbidden. (3) Since the termination of her naziriteship does not affect his own naziriteship. (4) Once the husband has confirmed his wife's vow, he can no longer declare it void; v. Num. XXX, 16. (5) By applying to a Sage. (6) And he himself will remain a nazirite. (7) I.e., it ceases to be sacred and may be returned to the fold. (8) I.e., it is still sacred, v. *infra* 24*a*. (9) For the naziriteship is null, and the animal was set aside in error, v. *infra* 31*a*. (10) And the animal is actually a sin-offering, but cannot be offered since the woman is no longer a nazirite. (11) For she has ceased to be a nazirite; thus Rashi and the printed text. Tosaf. and other MSS. read: 'Since she requires atonement,' i.e., because she denied herself wine (v. *supra* 19*a*).

Come and hear: If a woman undertakes a nazirite vow and then drinks wine or is defiled by a corpse, she is to receive forty stripes.[1] What exactly are the circumstances? If her husband has not declared [the vow] void, would it have been necessary to tell us this?[2] Obviously, then, her husband must have declared [the vow] void.[3] Now if you suppose that the husband nullifies [the vow], why should she receive forty stripes?[4] It surely follows, therefore, that the husband [only] terminates [the vow]?[5]—In point of fact, we can maintain that the husband really nullifies [the vow], but [in this case] because we are told in the clause that follows: If her husband declares it void without her being aware of it, and she drinks wine or is defiled by a corpse, she does not receive the stripes;[6] [22a] we are also taught in the first clause that, [if her husband does not annul her naziriteship,] she does receive [stripes].[7]

Come and hear: If a woman undertakes a nazirite vow and contracts ritual defilement, and then her husband declares [the vow] void, she is to bring a bird as a sin-offering, but not one as a burnt-offering.[8] Now if you suppose that the husband terminates [the vow], she ought also to bring a bird as a burnt-offering?[9] —What then would you have us think? That [the husband] nullifies [the vow]? Then she ought not to bring a bird as a sin-offering either?[10]—That is so. Here, however, we are being given the opinion of R. Eleazar ha-Ḳappar, for it has been taught: R. Eleazar ha-Ḳappar Berabbi said: [It may be asked,] Why does Scripture say, [*And make atonement for him*] *for that he sinned by reason of the soul?*[11] For against what soul has he sinned? [The reply is,] however, that because he denied himself wine, he is called a sinner. If then

(1) *Infra* 23a. (2) Viz., that she receives stripes. For she is no different from any other nazirite. (3) After his wife drank wine. (4) For we now see that she was not really a nazirite when she violated the rules of naziriteship. (5) And though she is no longer a nazirite, she must receive stripes for drinking wine when she was a nazirite. (6) *Infra* 23a. (7) Though here it is obvious. (8) A nazirite who contracts defilement must bring one bird as a burnt offering and one as a sin-offering, (cf. Num. VI, 10, 11); v. *supra* 19a. (9) For the husband does not affect the period before his declaration that the vow is to be void. (10) Since she was not really a nazirite when she violated her vow. (11) For notes v. *supra* p. 64.

this man who denied himself wine only is called a sinner, how much more so is this true of one who is ascetic in all things![1]

Come and hear the following where it is taught explicitly: If a woman vows to be a nazirite and her companion overhears and says, 'I too,' and then the husband of the first woman declares [her vow] void, she is released [from her vow] but her companion remains bound.[2] From this it follows that the husband terminates [the vow].[3] R. Simeon however says[4] that where [her companion] says to her, 'I undertake the same [obligation] as you,' both become free.

[22*b*] Mar Zuṭra, the son of Rab Mari said: The same problem is raised here as was raised by Rami b. Ḥama.[5] For Rami b. Ḥama wished to know the effect of saying, 'Let these [victuals] be, as far as I am concerned, as the flesh of [this] peace-offering.'[6] Does a man, in thus linking one thing with another, refer to the original state [of the subject of comparison],[7] or to its ultimate state?[8]

But surely [the two cases] do not bear comparison?[9] For when

(1) Thus she must bring a sin-offering even though the husband nullifies the vow, because she had denied herself wine. (2) Tosef. Naz. III, 5. (3) Continuation of the cited Baraitha. (4) Since otherwise both women should become free together. (5) I.e., whether the vow of the second woman remains binding or not depends, not on the precise force of the husband's declaration that a vow is void, but on the alternatives enunciated by Rami b. Ḥama. (6) This might not be eaten before its blood was sprinkled on the altar, but could be eaten afterwards. (7) Here, the flesh before the sprinkling of the blood; so that the victuals indicated would also become forbidden. This problem is treated differently in Ned. 11*b* (q.v.). (8) After the sprinkling of the blood, when the flesh may be eaten. Similarly in the case of the second woman the problem is:—Did she contemplate the original state of the first woman, so that she remains a nazirite, or did she also consider the possibility of the husband declaring the vow void, when her own would also become void. As the Baraitha says that her vow remains binding we may also infer that in Rami b. Ḥama's case the original state was meant and the victuals are forbidden. The word צננא used to convey the idea of a final state is usually taken from the root meaning 'cold', i.e., 'when it had cooled down'. L. Goldschmidt suggests that it may be derived from a Syriac word '*zenana*' meaning the savour of roast meat,' and refers to the time when the flesh is prepared for food. (9) And therefore the solution of the one problem obtained from the Baraitha, does not give the solution of the other.

he says in that case, 'Let these [victuals], as far as I am concerned, be as the flesh of this peace-offering,' [the fact remains that] even though once the blood is sprinkled, this may be eaten outside [the Temple precincts, yet it] is still sacred.[1] In our case, on the other hand, if we suppose that she has the ultimate state in mind, then the husband [of the first woman] has declared [the vow] void![2]

Some consider that our problem and that of Rami b. Ḥama are undoubtedly identical.[3]

If [a woman] says to her [companion], 'I intend to be a nazirite in your wake,'[4] what would the law be? Does 'in your wake' [mean,] 'I intend to follow in your wake in every respect,' so that she becomes free, or does it refer to her [companion's] condition before her husband declared [the naziriteship] void, so that she remains bound?

Come and hear: If a woman vows to be a nazirite and her husband overhears and adds, 'I too,'[5] he cannot declare [her vow] void. Now should you assume that when he says, 'I intend to follow in your wake,'[6] he has in mind the original situation,[7] why should he not be able to declare her [vow] void, whilst allowing his own to remain? Does it not follow, therefore, that what he refers to is the situation with all its developments, and so [it is only when] he himself [is involved that he] cannot declare [the vow] void,[8] but where

(1) For it may be eaten for a limited period only, viz.: two days and one night (v. Zeb. V, 7), and so the victuals might also be subject to this restriction. Hence whichever of the alternatives enunciated by Rami is adopted, there is a restriction on the victuals. (2) And the vow of the second will not operate. But she must have meant something by the vow, and we are therefore *forced* to conclude that she had only the original state in mind. Thus the solution of this problem given by the Baraitha affords no clue to the solution of Rami's problem. (3) These do not consider the distinction drawn above decisive, for the woman may have considered it sufficient if she abstained from wine until the husband of the first one declared the vow void, and so once more we have two alternatives. (4) And then the vow of the other is declared void. (5) This is taken to be the same as 'in your wake', for since the husband can declare her vow void and the outcome of her vow is in his power, he would be referring to her ultimate as well as her present state. (6) And all the more if he says, 'I too', to his wife. (7) And he himself is not affected by any change in her vow. (8) Since he would be freeing himself.

[another] woman says, 'I intend to follow in your wake,' she would also be freed?[1]—This is not the case. In point of fact, he may be referring to the original situation, but in this case, when he says, 'I too,' it is as though he says, 'I confirm it for you,' and so if he consults [a wise man] in order to have his ratification upset, he will be able to declare [her vow] void, but not otherwise.

[IF HE SHOULD SAY IN CONVERSATION WITH HIS WIFE,] 'I INTEND TO BE A NAZIRITE, WHAT ABOUT YOU'[2] AND SHE ANSWER 'AMEN,' HE CAN DECLARE HER [VOW] VOID, BUT HIS OWN REMAINS BINDING: The following passage seems to contradict this statement. [If a man says to his wife,] 'I intend to be a nazirite. What about you?'[3] if she answers 'Amen,' both become bound [to their vows],[4] but otherwise both are free, because he made his vow contingent on hers?[5]—Rab Judah replied: You should [emend the Baraitha to] read, He can declare her [vow] void, but his own remains binding.

Abaye said: It is even possible to leave the reading intact. The Baraitha supposes him to say to her, 'I intend to be a nazirite with you,' thus making his vow contingent on her vow;[6] [23*a*] whilst our Mishnah supposes him to say to her, 'I intend to be a nazirite. What about you?'[7] And so he may declare her [vow] void but his own remains binding.

MISHNAH. IF A WOMAN UNDERTAKES A NAZIRITE VOW AND THEN DRINKS WINE OR IS DEFILED BY A CORPSE,[8] SHE IS TO RECEIVE FORTY [STRIPES]. IF HER HUSBAND DECLARES IT VOID WITHOUT HER BEING AWARE OF IT, AND SHE DRINKS WINE OR IS DEFILED BY A CORPSE, SHE DOES NOT RECEIVE THE FORTY [STRIPES]. R. JUDAH SAID: ALTHOUGH [IT MAY BE A FACT THAT] SHE DOES NOT RECEIVE THE FORTY [STRIPES],

(1) If the husband annuls the first woman's vow. (2) Lit., 'I intend . . . and thou . . .' (3) Lit., 'I intend . . . and thou.' (4) But our Mishnah empowers him to declare her vow void. (5) Tosef. Naz. III. (6) Thus he cannot declare her vow void, for he would be nullifying his own at the same time. (7) Thus his own naziriteship is independent of hers. (8) Intentionally.

SHE SHOULD RECEIVE THE STRIPES INFLICTED FOR DISOBEDIENCE.[1]

GEMARA. Our Rabbis taught: [In the verse,] *Her husband hath made them void; and the Lord will forgive her,*[2] Scripture is speaking of a woman whose husband has declared her [vow] void without her knowledge,[3] [intimating] that she requires atonement and forgiveness. When R. Akiba reached this verse, he wept: 'For if one who intended to take swine's flesh and by chance takes lamb's flesh[4] stands in need of atonement and forgiveness, how much more so does one who intended to take swine's flesh and actually took it, stand in need thereof'?[5]

A similar inference may be made [from the verse], *Though he know it not, yet is he guilty and shall bear his iniquity.*[6] If of one who intends to take lamb's flesh and by chance takes swine's flesh, for instance in the case of [one who ate] a slice of fat concerning which it was uncertain whether it was of the permitted or the forbidden kind,[7] the text says, *'and shall bear his iniquity'*, how much more so [is this true] of one who intended to take swine's flesh and actually took it.

Isi b. Judah interpreted [the verse], *Though he know it not, yet is he guilty and shall bear his iniquity,* [as follows]. If of one who intends to take lamb's flesh and takes swine's flesh for instance in the case of [one who eats one of] two slices[8] of fat one of which is forbidden fat and the other permitted fat, the text says, *and shall bear his iniquity,* how much more so [is this true] of one who intended to

(1) These were administered at the discretion of the court and are Rabbinical in origin. (2) Num. XXX, 13. (3) Since the same words in verse 9 refer to a woman who knows that her husband has declared her vow void. (4) I.e., the woman who thought to drink wine during her naziriteship, but was not really a nazirite. (5) Tosef. Naz. III, 6. (6) Lev. V, 17, with reference to the offering of a guilt-offering. (7) Heb. *Ḥeleb*, 'suet'. Animal fat used in the sacrificial rite. This fat might not be eaten even in the case of ordinary animals. (8) Isi b. Judah holds that this guilt-offering was not brought if he ate a slice concerning which it was doubtful whether it was permitted or forbidden fat, but only if he ate one of two slices and did not know if it was the permitted or the forbidden slice.

take swine's flesh and actually took it. For this let them grieve that are fain to grieve.

But what need is there for all these cases?[1] — They are all necessary. For if we had only been told about the woman, [we might have thought] that atonement and forgiveness are necessary there,[2] because from the very beginning her intention was to do that which is forbidden, whereas with the slice concerning which it is uncertain whether it is forbidden or permitted fat, where his intention was to do that which is permitted,[3] [we might have thought] that atonement and forgiveness are not necessary. If, on the other hand, we had only been told about the latter, [we might have thought] that it is because there is a definite prohibition involved,[4] whereas the woman whose husband has declared her [vow] void and whose act is [consequently] permitted, should not require atonement and forgiveness. Again, if we had only been told of these two cases, we might have thought that in these two cases atonement and forgiveness suffice, since the presence of something forbidden is not definite, whereas with two slices of which one is forbidden and one permitted fat, where the presence of something forbidden is definite, atonement and forgiveness do not suffice.[5] We are therefore told that there is no difference.

Rabbah b. Bar Ḥana, quoting R. Joḥanan, said:[6] The verse, *For the ways of the Lord are right, and the just do walk in them; but transgressors do stumble therein*,[7] may be illustrated by the following example. Two men roast their paschal lambs.[8] One eats it with the intention of fulfilling the precept[9] and the other eats it with the inten-

(1) R. Akiba's interpretation of the nazirite woman and the two cases of one who may have eaten forbidden fat. (2) The passage in Lev. V, 17, says that a guilt-offering must be brought for '*atonement*' and the offender will be '*forgiven*'. (3) He thought it was the permitted kind of fat. (4) For the slice might in fact be forbidden fat. (5) And there must also be expiation. A guilt-offering could be brought only to make as atonement for an unintentional transgression. (6) The whole passage from here to the next Mishnah occurs again in Hor. 10*b*-11*b*; for fuller notes v. Hor. (Sonc. ed.), p. 73. (7) Hosea XIV, 10. (8) The passover was to be eaten as the final course of the evening meal when the guests had already eaten their fill. (9) To eat the passover offering. V. Ex. XII, 8.

tion of having an ordinary meal. To the one who eats it to fulfil the precept [applies], '*And the just do walk in them,*' but to the one who eats it to have an ordinary meal [applies], '*but transgressors do stumble therein*'. Resh Lakish remarked to him: Do you call such a man wicked? Granted that he has not fulfilled the precept in the best possible manner, he has at least carried out the passover rite. Rather should it be illustrated by two men, each of whom had his wife and his sister staying with him. One chances upon his wife and the other chances upon his sister. To the one who chances upon his wife [applies], '*And the just do walk in them*', and to the one who chances upon his sister [applies], '*but transgressors do stumble therein*'.

But are the cases comparable? We speak [in the verse] of one path, whereas here [in the example given] there are two paths.[1] Rather is it illustrated by Lot when his two daughters were with him.[2] To these [the daughters], whose intention it was to do right,[3] [applies], '*the just do walk in them*', whereas to him [Lot] whose intention it was to commit the transgression [applies], '*but transgressors do stumble therein*'.

But perhaps it was his intention also to do right?—[Do not think this for a moment, for][4] R. Johanan has said: The whole of the following verse indicates [Lot's] lustful character. *And Lot lifted up*[5] is paralleled by, *And his master's wife lifted up her eyes upon;*[6] '*his eyes*' is paralleled by, *for she hath found grace in my eyes*[7] '*and beheld*' is paralleled by, *And Shechem the son of Ḥamor beheld her;*[8] '*all the kikar ['plain'] of the Jordan*' by *For on account of a harlot, a man is brought to a kikar ['loaf'] of bread;*[9] and '*for it was well watered everywhere*' by, *I will go after my lovers, that give me my bread and my water, my wool and my flax, mine oil and my drink.*[10]

But [Lot] was the victim of compulsion?[11]—It has been taught

(1) Each has done a different act. (2) After the destruction of Sodom. V. Gen. XIX, 32. (3) Viz., to preserve the human species, for they imagined that the rest of mankind had perished. V. Gen. XIX, 31. (4) Inserted from 'En. Jacob. (5) Gen. XIII, 10. (6) E.V., '*cast*' *her eyes;* Potiphar's wife to Joseph. Gen. XXXIX, 7. (7) E.V., '*For she pleaseth me well*'; Samson of the Philistine woman. Jud. XIV, 3. (8) Gen. XXXIV, 2. (9) Prov. VI, 26. (10) Hosea II, 7. 'Watered' and 'drink' are from the same root. (11) His daughters first made him drunk.

on behalf of R. Jose son of R. Ḥoni that the dot[1] over the letter *waw* [='*and*'] in the word *U-bekumah* ['*and when she arose*'][2] occurring in [the story of] the elder daughter, is to signify that it was her lying down that he did not notice, but he did notice when she arose. But what could he have done, since it was all over?— The difference is that he should not have drunk wine the next evening.

Raba expounded as follows: What is the significance of the verse, *A brother offended is harder to be won than a strong city;* [23*b*] *And their contentions are like the bars of a castle?*[3] '*A brother offended is harder to be won than a strong city*', refers to Lot who separated from Abraham,[4] '*And their contentions are like the bars of a castle*', for he gave rise to contentions [between Israel and Ammon][5] for *An Ammonite or a Moabite shall not enter into the assembly of the Lord.*[6]

Raba and some say R. Isaac, expounded as follows: What is the significance of the verse, *He that separateth himself seeketh his own desire and snarleth against all sound wisdom?*[7] '*He that separateth himself seeketh his own desire*' refers to Lot. '*And snarleth* [yithgale'] *against all sound wisdom*', tells us that his disgrace was published [*nithgaleh*][8] in the Synagogues and Houses of Study, as we have learnt: An Ammonite and a Moabite[9] are forbidden [in marriage] and the prohibition is perpetual.[10]

'Ulla said: Both Tamar[11] and Zimri[12] committed adultery. Tamar committed adultery and gave birth to kings and prophets.[13] Zimri

(1) One of the *puncta extraordinaria*. V. *Ges. K. Grammar*, sec. 5*n*. (2) '*And the first born went in and lay with her father; and he knew not when she lay down,*' nor '*when she arose*'. Gen. XIX, 33. (3) Prov. XVIII, 19. (4) Thereby offending him. V. Gen. XIII, 11. (5) Corrected from Hor. 10*b*. Thus Moab and Ammon, Lot's descendants, were barred from intermarriage with Israel because Lot offended Abraham. [The text here reads: 'like bolts and the palace.' I.e., the contentions constitute the bolts which bar the admission of Ammon and Moab into the house of Israel—the palace.] (6) Deut. XXIII, 4. (7) Prov. XVIII, 1. (8) A play on the Hebrew roots indicated. (9) But not an Ammonite woman or a Moabite woman. (10) Yeb. 76*b*. (11) With her father-in-law, Judah. V. Gen. XXXVIII, 14. (12) With the Midianitish woman. V. Num. XXV, 14. (13) David and his descendants were of the tribe of Judah; Amos and Isaiah are traditionally said to have been of the tribe of Judah. V. Soṭ. 10*b*.

committed adultery and on his account many tens of thousands of Israel perished.[1]

R. Naḥman b. Isaac said: A transgression performed with good intention is better than a precept performed with evil intention.[2] But has not Rab Judah, citing Rab, said: A man should always occupy himself with the Torah and [its] precepts, even though it be for some ulterior motive,[3] for the result will be that he will eventually do them without ulterior motive?[4]—Read then: [A transgression performed with good intention is] as good as a precept performed for an ulterior motive, as it is written, *Blessed above women shall Jael be, the wife of Heber the Kenite. Above women in the tent shall she be blessed,*[5] and by '*women in the tent*', Sarah, Rebecca, Rachel and Leah are meant.[6]

R. Joḥanan said: That wicked wretch [Sisera] had sevenfold intercourse [with Jael] at that time, as it says, *At her feet he sunk, he fell, he lay;* etc.[7] But she derived pleasure from his intercourse? —R. Joḥanan said:[8] All the favours of the wicked are evil to the righteous, for it says, *Take heed to thyself that thou speak not to Jacob either good or bad.*[9] Now [that he was not to speak] bad we can understand, but why was he not to speak good? Thus it may properly be inferred that the good of such a one is an evil.

The above text [states]: Rab Judah, citing Rab, said: A man should always occupy himself with the Torah and [its] precepts, even though it be for some ulterior motive, for the result will be that he will eventually do them without ulterior motive. For as reward for the forty-two sacrifices which the wicked Balak offered,[10] he was privileged to be the progenitor of Ruth, for R. Jose son of

(1) In the plague; v. Num. XXV, 9. (2) For an example see below. (3) לשמה, 'for its own sake'. (4) An example of this occurs below. (5) Jud. V, 24. (6) The word '*tent*' occurs in connection with each of these (Tosaf.). Rashi omits Rebecca and says that the reference is to the fact that each of the other three gave their handmaidens to their husbands with ulterior motive. (7) The words '*he sunk*', '*he fell*', occur three times each, and the words '*he lay*' once. Jud. V, 27. (8) *Var. lec.*: R. Joḥanan said R. Simon b. Yoḥai said (Hor. 10*b*). (9) Gen. XXXI, 29. (10) On the occasion of Balaam's attempt to curse Israel. V. Num. XXIII-XXIV.

R. Ḥanina has said that Ruth was descended from[1] Eglon, [the grandson of Balak,][2] king of Moab.

R. Ḥiyya b. Abba, citing R. Joḥanan, said: How do we know that the Holy One, blessed be He, does not withhold the reward even for a decorous expression? The elder daughter [of Lot] called her son Moab[3] and so the All-Merciful One said [to Moses]:[4] *Be not at enmity with Moab, neither contend with them in battle.*[5] Only war was forbidden, but they might be harassed. The younger daughter, on the other hand, called [her son's] name Ben-Ammi[6] and so it says, *Harass them not, nor contend with them.*[7] They were not to be harassed at all.

R. Ḥiyya b. Abin said: R. Joshua b. Korḥa said: A man should always be as alert as possible to perform a precept, for as reward for anticipating the younger by one night, the elder daughter [of Lot] [24*a*] was privileged to appear in the genealogical record of the royal house of Israel, four generations[8] earlier.

MISHNAH. IF A WOMAN MAKES A NAZIRITE VOW AND SETS ASIDE THE REQUISITE ANIMAL [FOR THE SACRIFICE] AND HER HUSBAND SUBSEQUENTLY DECLARES [THE VOW] VOID, THEN, IF THE ANIMAL WAS ONE OF HIS OWN, IT CAN BE PUT TO PASTURE WITH THE HERD,[9] BUT IF IT WAS ONE OF HERS, THE SIN-OFFERING IS TO BE LEFT TO DIE, THE BURNT-OFFERING IS TO BE OFFERED AS AN [ORDINARY] BURNT-OFFERING, AND THE PEACE-OFFERING IS TO BE OFFERED AS AN [ORDINARY] PEACE-OFFERING. THIS [LAST], HOWEVER, MAY BE EATEN FOR ONE DAY [ONLY],[10] AND REQUIRES NO LOAVES.[11] IF SHE HAS A LUMP SUM OF MONEY[12] [SET ASIDE

(1) Lit., 'the granddaughter of', cf. Tosaf. (2) Inserted from Hor. 10*b*. (3) Lit., 'of my father'. (4) Inserted from Hor. 10*b*. (5) Deut. II, 9. (6) Lit., 'son of my people'. A less shameless appellation. (7) Deut. II, 19. (8) Obed, Jesse, David and Solomon through Ruth; while Rehoboam was a son of Naamah, the Ammonitess. (9) I.e., it ceases to be sacred and may be returned to the fold. (10) Until midnight, the period allowed for a nazirite offering (v. Zeb. V, 6); whereas an ordinary peace-offering could be eaten for two days and a night. (V. Ibid. V, 7). (11) Whereas a nazirite offering does require them. V. Num. VI, 15. (12) I.e., if the sums to be spent on the separate sacrifices were still unspecified.

FOR THE PURCHASE OF SACRIFICES], IT IS TO BE USED FOR FREE-WILL OFFERINGS;[1] IF EARMARKED MONEY,[2] THE PRICE OF THE SIN-OFFERING IS TO BE TAKEN TO THE DEAD SEA;[3] THE USE OF IT IS FORBIDDEN, BUT INVOLVES NO MALAPPROPRIATION;[4] FOR THE SUM SET ASIDE FOR THE BURNT-OFFERING, A BURNT-OFFERING IS TO BE PROVIDED, THE USE OF WHICH INVOLVES MALAPPROPRIATION;[5] WHILST FOR THE SUM SET ASIDE FOR THE PEACE-OFFERING, A PEACE-OFFERING IS TO BE PROVIDED, WHICH MAY BE EATEN FOR ONE DAY [ONLY] AND REQUIRES NO LOAVES.[6]

GEMARA. Who is the Tanna [of our Mishnah, who intimates] that the husband is not liable for the wife's [sacrifices]?[7]—R. Ḥisda said: It is the Rabbis, for if you suppose it is R. Judah [then since he is liable,] why should [the animals] be sent to pasture with the herd?[8] For it has been taught: R. Judah says: A man [who can afford to do so] must offer the rich man's sacrifice[9] on his wife's behalf, as well as all other sacrifices for which she may be liable. For thus does he write to her [in the marriage settlement, viz. :I shall pay] every claim you may have against me from before up to now.[10]

Raba said: It may even be R. Judah. [The reply to R. Ḥisda's

(1) Burnt-offerings, whose hides became the perquisite of the priests. (2) I.e., divided into portions for the separate sacrifices. (3) 'Taken to the Dead Sea' is the usual Talmudic mode of saying, 'not applied to any useful purpose.' (4) I.e., there is no penalty. For the rules regarding the unauthorised use of sacred property, v. Lev. V, 15. (5) Heb. *me'ilah*, the diversion of sacred or priestly things to secular or lay uses. E.V. uses 'trespass', but 'mal-appropriate' expresses better the sense of the Hebrew word (cf. *N.E.D.*). (6) Thus earmarked money is treated in the manner prescribed for sacrifices. (7) By declaring that if she sets aside his animals without his consent, they do not remain sacred at all. (8) They ought to remain sacred, because she had the right to take them. (9) Where the kind of sacrifice to be offered depends upon a man's means. V. e.g., Lev. V, 7. (10) This clause is taken as referring to sacrifices for which she may have become liable after the betrothal. This shows that in R. Judah's opinion the husband is liable. Other versions read instead of the last sentence: For thus does she write (in the receipt for her marriage-settlement when she claims it after divorce): And every claim that I may have had against you before now (is hereby discharged).

objection being that the husband] is liable only for something which she needs, but not for something which she does not need.[1]

Another version [of the above discussion is as follows]. Who is the Tanna [of our Mishnah]?—R. Ḥisda said: It is R. Judah,[2] [the husband, however,] being liable only for something that she needs, but not for something that she does not need.[3] For if it were the Rabbis [do they not say that] he is not liable for her [sacrifices] at all?[4] The only possible interpretation of the liability [implicit in the Mishnah][5] would be that he transferred [the animals] to her, but on transference it becomes her own property.[6] [24*b*] Raba said: It may even be the Rabbis, for even when he transfers it to her [his intention is] to provide something which she needs, but he does not transfer it to provide something she does not need.[7]

IF IT WAS ONE OF HERS, THE SIN-OFFERING IS TO BE LEFT TO DIE, THE BURNT-OFFERING IS TO BE OFFERED: Where did she get it from, seeing that it has been affirmed that whatever a woman acquires becomes her husband's?—R. Papa replied: She saved it out of her housekeeping money.[8] Another possibility is that it was given to her by a third person with the proviso that her husband should have no control over it.

THE BURNT-OFFERING IS TO BE OFFERED AS AN [ORDINARY] BURNT-OFFERING, AND THE PEACE-OFFERING IS TO BE OFFERED [etc.]. Samuel said to Abbahu b. Ihi: 'You are not to sit down[9] until you explain to me the following dictum: 'The four

(1) And his annulment of her vow shows that there was no need for her sacrifice, which thereby loses its sanctity. (2) Who says that a man must offer a rich man's sacrifice for his wife. (3) And therefore when the husband declares the vow void, the animals lose their sanctity. (4) What need therefore for the rule? She cannot make his animal sacred at all. (5) Which in saying that the animals are sent to pasture only if the husband declares her vow void, implies that if he does not declare it void, they become sacred. (6) And this case is considered in the second clause of the Mishnah: 'BUT IF IT WAS ONE OF HERS.' Thus this interpretation on the view of the Rabbis is impossible. (7) The transference is thus provisional, and this case is not the same as that of the second clause. (8) Lit., 'scraped it off her dough.' (9) [Lit., 'sit on your legs,' with reference to their custom of sitting on the ground with the legs crossed under them, v. *Oraḥ Mishor*, a.l.]

rams that do not require loaves [as an adjunct of the sacrifice] are the following:—his, hers, and those after death and after atonement!'[1]—[He explained as follows:] 'Hers' is the one referred to [in our Mishnah]. 'His' is referred to in the following [Mishnah]: For we learnt: A man is able to impose a nazirite vow on his son, whereas a woman cannot impose a nazirite vow on her son. Consequently, if [the lad] polls himself [within the period of his naziriteship] or is polled by his relatives, or if he protests[2] or his relatives protest on his behalf, then if a lump sum was set aside, it is to be used to provide free-will offerings, and if earmarked monies, the price of the sin-offering is to be taken to the Dead Sea, [the use of it is forbidden, but involves no malappropriation];[3] for the price of the burnt-offering, a burnt-offering is to be provided and this can involve malappropriation, whilst for the price of the peace-offering, a peace-offering is to be provided which may be eaten for one day only and requires no loaves.[4] Whence do we know [this of] 'the one after death'?—For we have learnt: Should a man set aside money for his nazirite offerings, the use of it is forbidden but involves no malappropriation since it may all be expended on the purchase of a peace-offering.[5] If he should die, monies not earmarked are to be used for providing freewill-offerings, whilst with regard to earmarked monies, the price of the sin-offering is to be taken to the Dead Sea, the use of it is forbidden but involves no malappropriation; for the price of the burnt-offering, a burnt-offering is to be provided, and this does involve malappropriation; whilst for the price of the peace-offering, a peace-offering is to be provided, which may be eaten for one day [only] and requires no loaves.[6]

[That] 'the one after atonement' [requires no loaves] we learn by a process of reasoning. For the reason that the 'one after death'

(1) 'After atonement' means an animal that was lost and replaced and then found. The others are explained below. (2) Even if he does not poll. (3) Added with R. Akiba Eger (d. 1837) from the Mishnah text *infra* 28*b*. (4) *Infra* 28*b*. For the various terms used see our Mishnah (24*a*) and notes. (5) A peace-offering could not be malappropriated until after the ritual sprinkling of its blood, v. Me'il, 6*b*. For the other offerings extra money could be provided. (6) Me'il III, 2.

does not [require loaves] is because it is not eligible for the purposes of atonement,[1] but then neither is the 'one after atonement' eligible for the purpose.[2]

But are there no more? What of the following [passage that Levi taught]:[3] All other peace-offerings of a nazirite, not slaughtered in the prescribed manner[4] are fit [for the altar], but they do not count as fulfilment of their owner's obligation;[5] they may however be eaten for one day [only],[6] and do not require loaves or [the gift of] the shoulder[7] [to the priest]?[8]—The enumeration [of Samuel] includes [animals offered] in the prescribed manner but omits those not [offered] in the prescribed manner.

['If he should die,] and have a lump sum of money it is to be used for providing free-will offerings'.[9] [25a] But money for a sin-offering is included in it?[10]—R. Johanan said: This is a traditional rule[11] relating to the nazirite. Resh Lakish said: The Torah says, [in the verse] *Whether it be any of their vows or any of their freewill offerings.*[12] This indicates that anything left over from [money subscribed for] vowed offerings is to be spent on freewill-offerings.[13]

Now if we accept the view of R. Johanan who says that this ruling concerning the nazirite is traditional, we can understand why it [applies only to] a lump sum of money and not to earmarked money.[14] But on Resh Lakish's view that it is derived from the verse, *Whether it be any of their vows, or any of their freewill offerings,* why should it apply only to money in a lump sum? Surely it should also apply to earmarked monies?—Raba replied: You cannot maintain that the reference is also to specific monies, for a Tanna of the School of R. Ishmael has already given a [different] decision [as follows]: The verse, *Only thy holy things which thou hast and thy*

(1) For the owner is dead and no further atonement is necessary. (2) Because the atonement has already been made, and so here too loaves are not required. (3) So BaH, cf. Men. 48b. (4) The prescribed peace-offering for a nazirite is a ram of the second year. (5) And he must offer another beast. (6) V. *supra* p. 85, n. 10. (7) V. Num. VI, 19. (8) V. Tosef. Naz. IV. (9) Quoted from Mishnah Me'il, cited above. (10) Should not this be 'taken to the Dead Sea'? (11) Lit., 'a *halachah*'. (12) Lev. XXII, 18. (13) And here there is money left over from the naziriteship money. (14) For presumably the tradition mentioned one and not the other.

vows,[1] speaks of the offspring and substitutes[2] of sacred animals. What is to be done with them? *Thou shalt take* [*them*] *and go unto the place which the Lord shall choose.*[1] It might be thought [from this] that they are to be taken to the Temple and kept without food and drink until they perish, but Scripture continues, *And thou shalt offer thy burnt-offerings, the flesh and the blood,*[3] as much as to say, as you do with the burnt-offering so do with its substitute,[4] as you do with the peace-offering so do with its offspring [and substitutes]. It might further be thought that the same applies to the offspring [and substitutes] of a sin-offering and the substitute of a guilt-offering,[5] but the text states *'only'* [precluding these].[6] The above is the opinion of R. Ishmael. R. Akiba says that it is unnecessary [to use this argument for the guilt-offering], for it says, *It is a guilt-offering,*[7] which shows that it retains its status.[8]

[The above passage] states: 'It might be thought that they are to be taken to the Temple and kept without food and drink until they perish, but Scripture continues, *And thou shalt offer thy burnt-offerings, the blood and the flesh.*' But why [should one think this]; seeing that only in regard to the sin-offering is there a traditional teaching that it is left to perish?[9]—Were it not for the verse, it might have been thought that the offspring of the sin-offering [may be allowed to perish] anywhere, [25*b*] whilst the offspring of other sacred animals [are left to perish] in the Temple only;[10] hence we are told that they are not [left to perish at all].

It also states above: It might further be thought that the same applies to the offspring [and substitutes] of sin-offerings and the

(1) Deut. XII, 26. The words in themselves are superfluous. (2) Substitution of a sacrifice was not allowed, and if it was attempted both animals became sacred, v. Lev. XXVII, 33. (3) Deut. XII, 27. (4) I.e., sacrifice it in the same way. 'Offspring' is not mentioned in connection with the burnt-offering or guilt-offering because these are males. (5) That they be offered as guilt-offerings or sin-offerings. (6) The particle רק, only, is one of the particles invariably considered to indicate a limitation of the rule that follows it. (7) Lev. V, 19. (8) The word הוא 'it is', is emphatic in the Hebrew. Hence if money is ear-marked for a sin-offering etc., it cannot be used for voluntary offerings, but must be used in the manner described in the Mishnah. (9) Tem. 21*b*. (10) Since it says, '*Thou shalt take* (*them*) etc.'

substitute of a guilt-offering, but the text states *'only'* precluding [these]. But what need is there of a verse, for there is a traditional ruling that the offspring of a sin-offering is to perish?—That is so; but the verse is required for the guilt-offering.

But for the guilt-offering, too, there is a traditional ruling viz., that wherever [an animal] if intended as a sin-offering, is left to perish, if intended as a guilt-offering it is allowed to pasture [until a blemish appears]?[1]—If we had only the traditional ruling, it might be thought that the traditional ruling [is indeed so], but [nevertheless] should someone sacrifice [the animal] he would incur no guilt by so doing; hence the verse tells us that if someone should sacrifice it, he has transgressed a positive precept.[2]

'R. Akiba says that it is unnecessary [to use this argument for the guilt-offering] for it says, *It is a guilt-offering*, which shows that it retains its status.' What need is there of the verse, since we have it as a traditional ruling that wherever [an animal] if intended as a sin-offering is left to perish, if intended as a guilt-offering, it is to pasture [until a blemish appears]?—That is so, and the verse is only necessary for [the case described by] Rab. For R. Huna, citing Rab, said: If a guilt-offering which had been relegated to pasture[3] [until a blemish appears] was slaughtered as a burnt-offering, it is a fit and proper [sacrifice].[4] This is true only if it was [already] relegated, but not otherwise, for the verse says, *'It is [a guilt-offering,'* implying] that it retains its status.[5]

The master said [above]: 'This is a traditional ruling[6] concerning the nazirite.' Are there then no other spheres [in which it applies]? Has it not been taught: 'And all others[7] required by the Torah

(1) When it would be sold and the money devoted to sacred purposes. (2) Viz.: that only the others are to be sacrificed and not this one. A prohibition inferred from a positive command, as here, is called a positive precept. (3) Lit., 'was transferred (from the category of guilt-offering) to pasture.' (4) And the flesh may be burnt on the altar. (5) As a guilt-offering and if offered as a burnt-offering, the flesh is not fit for the altar. (6) That no account is taken of the presence of money that should have gone to purchase a sin-offering, but the whole of the money if in a lump sum is utilised for freewill-offerings. (7) As well as the nazirite.

to offer a nest of birds,[1] [26a] who set aside money for this purpose and then desire to use it to provide an animal[2] as sin-offering, or as burnt-offering can do so. Should such a one die and leave a lump sum of money, it is to be used to provide freewill-offerings'?[3]—He mentions the nazirite, meaning also [to include] those required to offer birds whose case is similar,[4] but excluding [the following case]. For it has been taught: If a man, under an obligation to offer a sin-offering, says, 'I undertake to provide a burnt-offering,' and sets aside money saying, 'This is for my obligation,' should he then desire to provide from it either a sin-offering or a burnt-offering he must not do so.[5] Should he die and leave a lump sum of money, it is to be taken to the Dead Sea.[6]

R. Ashi said: In the statement[7] that moneys earmarked must not be used [for freewill-offerings], you should not presume [the meaning to be] that he said, 'This [portion] is for my sin-offering, this for my burnt-offering, and this for my peace-offering,' for even if he says simply, '[All] this is for my sin-offering, burnt-offering and peace-offering,' it counts as earmarked money.[8] Others say that R. Ashi said. Do not presume that he must say, '[All] this is for my sin-offering, burnt-offering and peace-offering,' for even if he says, '[All] this is for my obligation,' it is regarded as earmarked money.[9]

Raba said: Though we have said that a lump sum of money is to be used for freewill-offerings, yet if the money for the sin-offering becomes separated from the rest,[10] all is regarded as earmarked.

(1) E.g., a leper who must offer on recovery a sin-offering and a burnt-offering, and may provide birds if he cannot afford animals; v. Lev. XIV, 21ff. (2) If they become more affluent. (3) Thus the ruling applies to these as well as to the nazirite. (4) Since their obligation to provide both a sin-offering and a burnt-offering springs from a single source, and they are not separate obligations. (5) Here the obligations are separate. What he must do is to add more money and buy both animals at the same time (Tosaf.). (6) The traditional ruling does not apply here, and there is now no remedy since a sin-offering cannot be brought after death. Tosef. Me'il. I, 5. (7) In the various texts quoted above. (8) And must not be used for freewill-offerings. (9) And the sums required are regarded as unspecified only if he put them aside without stating their purpose. (10) E.g., if sufficient for a sin-offering is lost, the rest is to be used as to half for a peace-offering and half for a burnt-offering.

[26*b*]. It has been taught in agreement with Raba: [If a nazirite says,] 'This is for my sin-offering and the remainder for the rest of my nazirite obligations,' [and then dies,] the money for the sin-offering is to be cast into the Dead Sea, and the rest is to be used, half to provide a burnt-offering, and half, a peace-offering.[1] The law of malappropriation applies to the whole of it,[2] but not to any separate part of it.[3] [If he says,] 'This is for my burnt-offering and the remainder for the rest of my nazirite obligations,' [and then dies,] the money for the burnt-offering is to be used for a burnt-offering and it can suffer malappropriation, whilst the rest is to be used to provide freewill-offerings and can suffer malappropriation.[4]

Rab Huna, citing Rab, said that [our rule][5] applies only to money, but animals would be regarded as earmarked.[6] R. Naḥman added that the animals that would be regarded as earmarked would only be unblemished animals, but not blemished ones.[7] [Three] bars of silver, on the other hand, would be counted as earmarked.[8] R. Naḥman b. Isaac, however, considered even bars of silver as unspecified,[9] but not [three] piles of timber.[10]

R. Shimi b. Ashi asked R. Papa: What is the reason [for the distinctions made] by these Rabbis?[11] Is it that they interpret

(1) In agreement with Raba. (2) Since the money for the burnt-offering can suffer malappropriation. (3) Since the money for the peace-offering may be in the part used, and a peace-offering does not suffer malappropriation. (4) Adopting an emendation of the Wilna Gaon after the text of Tosef. Me'il. I, 5. Our texts read: 'The law of malappropriation applies to the whole of it, but not to any part of it.' This cannot be the case since all the rest is to be used for freewill burnt-offerings which suffer malappropriation. (5) Regarding the disposition of a lump sum of money. (6) Even if they were not the animals that a nazirite must bring (v. Tosaf. and Asheri for various explanations of the distinctions). Possibly the reason is that it can be assumed that he intended to exchange each one for one of the animals suitable for his sacrifice. (7) He would have to sell these first in order to purchase others, and would not think of them in terms of animals but in terms of money. (8) He would not sell the silver to buy animals, in order not to lose on the two transactions, but would await his opportunity to barter for animals. (9) They are easily convertible into money at a very small loss, and would therefore naturally be thought of in terms of money. (10) Which would not be sold, in order to avoid loss, but bartered for animals. (11) Rab, R. Naḥman and R. Naḥman b. Isaac.

'money',[1] as meaning neither animals, nor bars of silver, nor piles of timber [as the case may be]? For if so, they should also say 'money' but not birds.[2] Should you reply that they do make this distinction too, how comes R. Ḥisda to say that birds[3] do not become earmarked except [when earmarked] by the owner at their purchase, or by the priest at their preparation,[4] seeing that our tradition is that only money [is regarded as unspecified]?—[27a] He replied: But on your own argument [that all these are unspecified], how are we to explain [the following] which we learnt: R. Simeon b. Gamaliel said that if [a nazirite] brings three animals and does not say explicitly [what they are for], the one which is fit to be a sin-offering shall be offered as a sin-offering,[5] the one fit to be a burnt-offering[6] shall be offered as a burnt-offering and the one fit for a peace-offering[7] shall be offered as a peace-offering?[8] Now why should this be so? Do you not say that animals are not regarded as earmarked?[9]—[R. Shimi b. Ashi][10] rejoined: [The explanation is this.[11] In R. Hisda's case] the reason[12] is because the All-merciful has said, *And she shall take [two turtle doves, the one for a burnt-offering and the other for a sin-offering]*,[13] and also, *And [the priest] shall take [the one for a sin-offering and the other for a burnt-offering*[14] showing that they can be earmarked] either when the

(1) In the phrase, 'money in a lump sum,' occurring in our Mishnah and the other texts. (2) I.e., they should regard birds as specified. (3) Lit., 'nests', i.e., the pair of birds brought as offerings; cf. e.g., Lev. XII, 8. (4) But not by the mere purchase. Hence if the owner dies, the pair is indeterminate and becomes a freewill-offering in the cases considered, contrary to the assumption that this is true only of money. (5) The ewe lamb; v. Num. VI, 14. (6) The one year old male lamb. (7) The two year old ram. (8) *Infra* 45a. (9) Surely therefore we must regard them as earmarked and take the expression 'money' as excluding all else from being regarded as unspecified. (10) So Asheri. According to Rashi, R. Papa is still speaking; but v. Yoma 41a where the statement following is attributed to R. Shimi b. Ashi. (11) R. Shimi now assumes that unless there has been explicit earmarking, everything is unspecified, and he therefore goes on to explain why R. Hisda allows the priests to earmark the birds and the reason for R. Simeon b. Gamaliel's statement. (12) That it is possible for the priest to sacrifice the birds even if the owner does not specify them, although birds are otherwise specified. (13) Lev. XII, 8. (14) Lev. XV, 30.

owner takes them or when the priest offers them. [In R. Simeon b. Gamaliel's case] too [27*b*] would it be possible to say that the one that should be the sin-offering is to be the burnt-offering, seeing that one is female and the other male?[1]

R. Hamnuna raised an objection: Do we really say that an animal which has a blemish is regarded as unspecified? Come [then] and hear [the following]: What are the circumstances in which a man is permitted to poll at the expense of his father's naziriteship? Suppose his father had been a nazirite and had set apart the money for his nazirite sacrifices and died, and [the son then] said, 'I declare myself a nazirite on condition that I may poll with my father's money,'[2] [then he may do so].[3] If he leaves unspecified moneys, they fall to [the Temple treasury to provide] freewill-offerings. If there were animals set apart, the sin-offering is left to die, the burnt-offering is to be offered as a burnt-offering, and the one for a peace-offering is to be offered as a peace-offering.[4] Is not this the case even if the animal is blemished?[5]—No; only if it is without blemish. But if a blemished one is unspecified, why is 'money' mentioned?[6] The text ought to read: If he left a blemished animal, it is to be used to provide freewill-offerings?[7]—That is precisely what it means. For a blemished animal is made sacred purely in respect of the price it will bring; and this price is [included in] 'money'.

Raba raised an objection. [It has been taught: The expression] his *offering*[8] [signifies] that he can discharge his obligation with his

(1) And so formal earmarking is not necessary, but in all other cases it is necessary and without it they are regarded as unspecified. Thus R. Shimi b. Ashi disagrees with the Rabbis mentioned above. Maim. *Yad Neziruth* IX, 5, also rules in agreement with this interpretation of R. Shimi's views. (2) I.e., buy the sacrifices that must be offered on polling with my father's money. (3) The quotation is incomplete. V. the Tosef. and cf. *infra* 30*b*. (4) Tosef. Naz. III, 9. (5) Viz., that it is left to die or to be used to provide a burnt-offering or a peace-offering, as the case may be. How then does R. Naḥman (R. Hamnuna's contemporary) distinguish between blemished and unblemished animals? (6) In the opening clause of the Baraitha. (7) This is a finer distinction than the one between animals and money. (8) Used with reference to the sacrifice a ruler must bring if he sins in error, Lev. IV, 23.

own offering but not with that of his father. It might be thought [that this means merely] that an obligation with regard to a serious offence cannot be discharged with an offering set aside by his father for a less serious offence or *vice versa,* whereas he could discharge an obligation entailed by a less serious offence, with an offering set aside by his father for a similar offence, or [an obligation] entailed by a more serious offence, with [an offering set aside for] a similar offence. Hence Scripture repeats the words, his *offering,*[1] [to show that] he can discharge an obligation with his own offering but not with that of his father [even in this instance]. Again, it might be supposed that [the rule that] he cannot discharge an obligation with his father's offering applies only if it is an *animal* set aside by his father albeit for an offence of a similar degree of gravity, since [there is a similar rule] that a man cannot make use of his father's [nazirite] *animal* for polling in respect of [his own] naziriteship,[2] but that he could discharge his obligation with *money* set aside by his father, and even [transfer it] from a serious offence to one less serious or *vice versa,* for a man can make use of his father's [nazirite] money for polling in respect of [his own] naziriteship, [28*a*] always provided that it is a lump sum and not earmarked money.[3] Hence Scripture repeats the expression his *offering*[4] [a third time, to show] that he can discharge his obligation with his own offering, but not with that of his father [even in this instance]. It might be thought, further, [that we can only lay down] that he is unable to discharge an obligation with money set aside by *his father,* albeit for an offence of equal gravity, but that he could discharge his obligation with an offering he himself has set apart, [even transferring it] from a less serious to a more serious offence, or *vice versa*. Hence Scripture uses the expression, *his offering . . . for* his *sin,*[5] to show that the offering must be for the particular sin. It might be argued, again, that [we can only lay down that] he cannot discharge his obligation

(1) Used also with reference to the goat brought as a sacrifice by one of the common people who sins in error, Lev. IV, 28. (2) V. *infra* 30*a*. (3) Ibid. (4) Used also with reference to the lamb brought as a sacrifice by one of the common people who sins in error, Lev. IV, 32. (5) '*He shall bring for his offering a goat . . . . for his sin which he hath sinned.*' Lev. IV, 28.

with an *animal* which he has set apart for himself whether for an equally serious offence or for an offence of a different degree of gravity, since [we know that] if he sets aside an animal [to make atonement] for [the offence of eating] forbidden fat,[1] and [by mistake] sacrifices it for [the offence of eating] blood, or *vice versa*, he has not been guilty of malappropriation and [consequently] has not procured atonement;[2] but [we might think] that he could discharge his obligation with *money* which he set aside for himself whatever be the degree of gravity of the offence, since [we know that] if he set aside money for himself [to make atonement] for [the offence of eating] forbidden fat, and used it [by mistake] for [the offence of eating] blood, or *vice versa*, he is guilty of malappropriation and [consequently] does procure atonement,[3] and so Scripture says, *for* his *sin*[4] to show that the offering must be for the particular sin [even in such circumstances].[5] Now this passage refers simply to an animal.[6] Surely this includes even a blemished one?[7]—Not at all. One without blemish is meant. But if a blemished animal is regarded as not earmarked, why go on to speak of money set aside by his father when it could speak of an animal which has a blemish [instead]?[8]—That is precisely [what is meant], for the only use [of such an animal for sacrificial purposes] is for the price it will bring, and this price is 'money'.

(1) Heb. *Ḥeleb*. (2) He is guilty of malappropriation if he transfers an object in error from sacred to profane use. This cannot be done with animals intended for the altar, but only with objects intended for general temple use. Since an animal intended for the altar cannot be transferred from sacred to profane use, it cannot possibly become his again, and so once he sets aside an animal for the offence of eating forbidden fat, he cannot gain possession of it in order to use it to atone for his offence of eating blood. (3) For malappropriating sacred money renders it his and it can now be used for any purpose he likes; v. note 2. (4) Lev. IV, 28. The phrase used is the same as that from which the last inference was drawn. Rashi uses the verse in Lev. IV, 26, 'as concerning his sin'; but the parallel quotation in Ker. 27*b* is identical with this. (5) And so, although the transference in error was valid, he is unable to transfer it at will. This Baraitha occurs also in Ker. 27*b*. (6) In mentioning that a nazirite cannot poll with his father's animal. (7) And so we see that a blemished animal is regarded as specific. (8) And so make the distinction finer.

MISHNAH. IF ONE OF THE KINDS OF BLOOD[1] HAS BEEN SPRINKLED ON HER BEHALF, [THE HUSBAND] CAN NO LONGER ANNUL [THE VOW].[2] R. AKIBA SAYS, IF EVEN ONE OF THE ANIMALS HAS BEEN SLAUGHTERED ON HER BEHALF, HE CAN NO LONGER ANNUL [THE VOW]. THE ABOVE IS TRUE ONLY IF SHE IS POLLING[3] [AFTER OBSERVING THE NAZIRITESHIP] IN PURITY, BUT IF SHE IS POLLING AFTER RITUAL DEFILEMENT, HE CAN [STILL] ANNUL [THE VOW], BECAUSE HE CAN SAY, 'I CANNOT TOLERATE AN UNSEEMLY WIFE.'[4] RABBI[5] SAYS THAT HE CAN ANNUL [HER VOW] EVEN IF SHE IS POLLING [AFTER OBSERVING THE NAZIRITESHIP] IN PURITY, SINCE HE CAN AVER THAT HE CANNOT TOLERATE A WOMAN WHO IS POLLED.

GEMARA. Our Mishnah does not agree with R. Eliezer, for R. Eliezer says that polling is a bar [to the drinking of wine],[6] and since she has not polled, she is forbidden wine, and so since she is [still] unseemly, he is able to annul [her vow]. [28*b*] Our Tanna [on the other hand] takes the view that as soon as the blood is sprinkled on her behalf, she is permitted to drink wine and as a result she is no longer unseemly, whilst R. Akiba is of the opinion that even though the animal has only been slaughtered, he is no longer able to annul [her vow] since destruction of sacred property [would result].[7]

R. Zera objected: But why [should there necessarily be destruction of sacred property, in such a case]? Could not the blood be sprinkled as though it were some other [sacrifice],[8] when it would be permitted to eat the flesh? For has it not been taught: If the lambs prepared for the Festival of Assembly[9] were slaughter-

(1) I.e., the blood of one of the sacrifices. (2) And her hair must be shorn. (3) I.e., bringing the sacrifices at the polling. (4) A teetotaller. This is based on the verse in Zach. IX, 1, *'New wine shall make the maids flourish.'* (5) Some versions read R. Meir. (6) No wine may be drunk until after polling. (7) For the flesh could not be eaten. R. Akiba, however, would admit her right to drink wine after the sprinkling of the blood. (8) Lit., 'be sprinkled not in its own name.' (9) Pentecost.

ed as though they were a different sacrifice, or before or after the proper time,[1] the blood is to be sprinkled and the flesh can be eaten. Should [the mistake] occur on a Sabbath, [the blood] is not to be sprinkled, but if [notwithstanding] it is sprinkled, [the sacrifice] is acceptable, but the portions belonging to the altar must be roasted after dark?[2]—The reply is this. If it were the burnt-offering or the peace-offering that had been slaughtered,[3] this [procedure] could be followed, but [the Mishnah] assumes that the sin-offering was slaughtered first [as could in fact happen], for we have learnt: If [the nazirite] polls after [the sacrifice] of any one of the three, his duty is performed.[4]

THE ABOVE IS TRUE ONLY IF SHE IS POLLING [AFTER OBSERVING THE NAZIRITESHIP] IN PURITY, BUT IF SHE IS POLLING AFTER RITUAL DEFILEMENT, HE CAN [STILL] ANNUL [THE VOW], BECAUSE HE CAN SAY, 'I CANNOT TOLERATE AN UNSEEMLY WIFE.' RABBI SAYS THAT HE CAN ANNUL [HER VOW] EVEN IF SHE IS POLLING [AFTER OBSERVING THE NAZIRITESHIP] IN PURITY, SINCE HE CAN AVER THAT HE CANNOT TOLERATE A WOMAN WHO IS POLLED. The first Tanna [does not allow this objection] because she can wear a wig, but Rabbi considers that [the husband] will not be satisfied with a wig because of the dirt [it collects].[5]

MISHNAH. A MAN IS ABLE TO IMPOSE A NAZIRITE VOW ON HIS SON,[6] BUT A WOMAN CANNOT IMPOSE A NAZIRITE

(1) [In the absence of a fixed calendar there was always the possibility of the festival sacrifice being offered on a day earlier or later, and this Baraitha explains the procedure to be followed should such an incident occur.] (2) And thus we see that an animal slaughtered as though it were some other sacrifice need not be destroyed, but can be eaten. (3) On behalf of the nazirite woman. (4) And so if the husband is allowed to annul the vow, this sin-offering would have to be destroyed, as is asserted by R. Akiba, like all sin-offerings the owners of which no longer stand in need of atonement. *Infra* 45*a*. (5) And so in order not to provoke ill-feeling between them, the husband should be allowed to annul the vow and save her from polling. (6) Until what age will be discussed in the Gemara.

VOW ON HER SON. IF[1] [THE LAD] POLLS HIMSELF OR IS POLLED BY HIS RELATIVES, OR IF HE PROTESTS OR HIS RELATIVES PROTEST ON HIS BEHALF, THEN IF [THE FATHER] HAD SET ASIDE AN ANIMAL [FOR THE SACRIFICE], THE SIN-OFFERING IS LEFT TO DIE, THE BURNT-OFFERING IS TO BE OFFERED AS AN [ORDINARY] BURNT-OFFERING, AND THE PEACE-OFFERING IS TO BE OFFERED AS AN [ORDINARY] PEACE-OFFERING. THIS [LAST], HOWEVER, MAY BE EATEN FOR ONE DAY [ONLY], AND REQUIRES NO LOAVES. IF HE HAD UNSPECIFIED MONIES, THEY FALL [TO THE TEMPLE TREASURY] TO PROVIDE FREE-WILL-OFFERINGS: WHILST WITH REGARD TO EARMARKED MONIES, THE PRICE OF THE SIN-OFFERING IS TO BE TAKEN TO THE DEAD SEA, IT BEING NEITHER PERMISSIBLE TO USE IT, NOR POSSIBLE TO MALAPPROPRIATE IT; FOR THE PRICE OF THE BURNT-OFFERING, A BURNT-OFFERING IS TO BE PROVIDED AND THIS CAN SUFFER MALAPPROPRIATION, WHILST FOR THE PRICE OF THE PEACE-OFFERING, A PEACE-OFFERING IS TO BE PROVIDED, WHICH MAY BE EATEN FOR ONE DAY ONLY AND REQUIRES NO LOAVES.

GEMARA. A man can [subject the son to a nazirite vow], but not a woman. Why?—R. Johanan said: It is a [traditional] ruling with regard to the nazirite.[2] R. Jose son of R. Ḥanina, [29*a*] citing Resh Laḳish, said: So as to train him to [carry out his] religious duties.[3] If so, why should not a woman also be able to do so?—[Resh Laḳish] holds that it is a man's duty to train his son to [carry out his] religious duties, but not a woman's duty to train her son.[4]

Now on R. Johanan's view that it is a [traditional] ruling with regard to the nazirite vow, we can understand why he can do this with his son but not with his daughter,[5] but according to Resh

(1) [So Tosaf. and Asheri, omitting כיצד ('how?') in our texts which Bertinoro however explains: How (shall the offerings be treated) if the lad polls himself, etc.?] (2) And requires no other justification. A tradition has the force of a Biblical injunction. (3) I.e., it is Rabbinic in its origin. (4) And so she has not the power to impose upon him an obligation involving the offering of sacrifices. (5) For the tradition was only known with regard to sons.

Laḳish, ought not the same to be true of a daughter?—He holds that it is his duty to train his son, but not to train his daughter.

Now on R. Joḥanan's view that it is a [traditional] ruling with regard to the nazirite, we can understand why he can impose naziriteship [on his son], but not [ordinary] vows;[1] but on Resh Lakish's view, why should he not be able [to impose ordinary] vows too?—[The Mishnah] argues progressively.[2] Not only is it his duty to train [his son] by [imposing upon him] vows, which do not make him unseemly, but it is even his duty to impose a naziriteship, although this will make him unseemly.

Now on R. Joḥanan's view that it is a [traditional] ruling with regard to the nazirite, we can understand how it teaches: IF HE PROTESTS OR HIS RELATIVES PROTEST ON HIS BEHALF [THE NAZIRITESHIP IS VOID];[3] but on Resh Laḳish's view, as cited by R. Jose son of R. Ḥanina, have relatives the power to tell [the father] not to instruct [the son] in religious duties?—He holds that [the son] objects to any training which is undignified.[4]

Now on R. Joḥanan's view that it is a [traditional] ruling with regard to the nazirite, we can understand why [the boy] is permitted to poll,[5] although [this means] rounding [the corners of the head];[6] but on Resh Laḳish's view as cited by R. Jose son of R. Ḥanina that it is in order to train him to [carry out his] religious duties, he would be [transgressing] in rounding [the corners of his head]?[7]—[Resh Laḳish] holds that the rounding of the whole head[8] is [prohibited only by] a rabbinic enactment,[9] and since training is [a duty] imposed by the Rabbis, [the duty as to] training imposed by the Rabbis can overrule the rabbinic enactment against rounding [the whole head].

(1) The Mishnah mentions only naziriteship and not other vows. (2) And the inference that he cannot impose ordinary vows is wrong. (3) This being part of the tradition. (4) On account of the need to shave his head. And so the relatives can protest on his behalf. (5) On completing the term of naziriteship. (6) Which is otherwise forbidden; v. Lev. XIX, 27. (7) [Which vitiates the whole value of the training.] (8) Which is the manner in which a nazirite polls. (9) The Scriptural verse says that '*the corners*' are not to be rounded, and this is taken to mean the corners *by themselves*, but not in conjunction with the rest of the head.

Now on R. Johanan's view that it is a [traditional] ruling with regard to the nazirite, we can understand why [the boy] is allowed to poll and offer the sacrifices [of a nazirite]; but on the view of Resh Lakish as cited by R. Jose son of R. Hanina that it is in order to train him to [carry out his] religious duties, he would be bringing profane [animals] into the Temple court?[1] — [Resh Lakish] holds that [the prohibition against the bringing of] ordinary animals into the Temple-court is not Scriptural.[2]

Now on R. Johanan's view that it is a [traditional] ruling with regard to the nazirite, we can understand why if he contracts ritual defilement, he may bring an offering of a pair of birds, which the priest will eat after pinching off [the head];[3] but on Resh Lakish's view, as cited by R. Jose son of R. Hanina, he will be eating carrion?[4] — [Resh Lakish] agrees with R. Jose son of R. Judah that fowl do not require to be [ritually] slaughtered in Torah law, and considers that [the prohibition against bringing] non-sacred [fowl] into the Temple court is not Scriptural.[5]

Is this in fact R. Jose's opinion? Has it not been taught: R Jose son of R. Judah said: Whence do we infer that a sin-offering of fowl, brought in a doubtful case [of childbirth][6] is not to be eaten?[7] From the verse, *And of them that have an issue, whether it be a man or a woman.*[8] Woman is here compared to man.[9] Just as a man is required to bring an offering for [a transgression],[10] which has

(1) I.e., offer profane animals on the altar, for as he is not a nazirite the animals do not become sacred. This is forbidden. (2) And is therefore permitted in this instance. (3) Birds offered as sacrifices were not slaughtered ritually with a knife, but the priest pinched off their heads with his thumb nail. (4) Since there was no obligation to offer birds, these birds are not really an offering and should be killed in the usual way. (5) There is a controversy on this point in Hul. 27*b*. (6) After childbirth, or even a miscarriage, a mother was required to offer certain sacrifices, including a bird as sin-offering (v. Lev. XII, 6). In this Baraitha R. Jose son of R. Judah explains what is to happen if there is a doubt as to a birth (i.e., a true miscarriage) having taken place (cf. also Ker. I, 2). (7) Although after certain childbirth it was eaten. (8) Lev. XV, 33. (9) I.e., cases in which a man (as well as a woman) is required to furnish an offering, with the case in which only a woman can do so, viz.: childbirth. (10) When the Torah prescribes an offering for some offence, e.g., the eating of forbidden

certainly been committed so must the woman bring an offering for [a childbirth] which has certainly occurred;[1] and just as there is an offering to be brought by a man after a doubtful [transgression], so must an offering be brought by a woman after a doubtful [childbirth]. Again, just as a man brings [an offering of] the same kind in a case of doubtful [transgression] as he does after a certain one,[2] so must a woman bring [an offering of] the same kind after a doubtful [childbirth] as she does after a certain one.[3] [Shall we] then [infer further that] just as [in a doubtful case] a man brings an offering that is eaten,[4] so is the offering brought by the woman to be eaten? [29*b*] You cannot say so. Whilst this applies in the case of a man where only one forbidden act is involved,[5] you cannot argue that this should also be the case with a woman where two forbidden acts are involved. Now what are the two forbidden acts referred to? Are they not the prohibition against the eating of carrion,[6] and the prohibition against the entry of profane [sacrifices] into the Temple court?[7]

R. Aḥa, the son of R. Iḳa [however] demurred [to this inference[8] being drawn], for it is surely possible that [the eating was forbidden][9] because it would appear as though two *rabbinic* enactments were being trangsressed.[10]

fat, it is understood that there is to be no doubt that an offence was committed. Where a doubt existed a different offering, the guilt-offering, was prescribed (v. Lev. V, 17).

(1) I.e., Lev. XII, 6, which describes the offering, is referring to a certain and not a doubtful childbirth. (2) Viz., an animal (and not a bird) in both cases if the offence is, e.g., the eating of forbidden fat. (3) Including a sin-offering of a bird in both cases. (4) [The flesh of a guilt-offering for a doubtful transgression was eaten, v. Zeb. 54*b*.] (5) If he was not in fact guilty, a profane animal was sacrificed on his behalf. This the Tanna of the Baraitha considers is forbidden. (6) The bird, having its neck pinched, is carrion, pinching being only permitted to a true sacrificial bird. (7) And thus we see that R. Jose considers both these acts forbidden by the Torah, in contradiction to the statement attributed to him above. (8) That the above acts are forbidden by the Torah. (9) Our text has, instead of this inserted phrase, 'She is liable', which gives no sense. We have therefore followed all the commentators and omitted it. (10) I.e., the eating of the bird brought by the woman was forbidden not because the comparison with the guilt-offering brought by the man did not extend

Can we say that [the controversy between R. Joḥanan and Resh Laḳish] is the same as that between [the following] Tannaim? [For it has been taught:] Rabbi says that he can impose a nazirite vow on his son until his majority;[1] but R. Jose son of R. Judah says, [only] until he reaches the age of making vows [for himself].[2] Now surely [the controversy between R. Joḥanan and Resh Laḳish] is the same as [that between these] Tannaim, Rabbi considering it to be a [traditional] ruling with regard to the nazirite, so that though [the son] may have reached the age of making vows [for himself, the father] can still impose a [nazirite] vow on him until he attains his majority, whereas R. Jose son of R. Judah who asserts [that he can do so only] until [the son] reaches the age of making vows [for himself] is of the opinion that [the father may impose a naziriteship] in order to train him to [carry out his] religious duties, and, now that he has passed out of his [father's] control,[3] there is no longer an obligation [to train him]?[4]—I will tell you; not at all. Both [Rabbi and R. Jose son of R. Judah may] agree that this is a [traditional] ruling with regard to the nazirite. Where they differ is about [the vows of] one who can discriminate[5] [but] who has not quite reached manhood. Rabbi considers that [a youth] who can discriminate [but] who has not quite reached manhood is [permitted to make vows] only by enactment of the Rabbis and so the right granted by the Torah [to the parent][6] overrules the Rabbinical right [of the youth];[7] whereas R. Jose son of R. Judah considers that [a youth] who can discriminate [but] who has not quite reached manhood, has a Scriptural right [to make vows].[8]

to cover it, but because *two* enactments of the Rabbis were involved, and this outweighs the analogy with the guilt-offering.

(1) Lit., 'until two hairs appear', i.e., until there is definite evidence that he has reached puberty, usually after the end of the thirteenth year. (2) I.e., between the twelfth and thirteenth birthdays, when he understands the significance of a vow. (3) For he can now make his own vows. (4) And therefore he cannot impose one. (5) I.e., who realises the significance of a vow. (6) To impose a naziriteship. A *halachah* or traditional ruling has the force of a scriptural enactment. (7) To make vows himself. (8) And when he reaches this age, his father can no longer impose a naziriteship upon him.

Alternatively, it may be that both [Rabbi and R. Jose son of R. Judah] would agree that [the father may impose a naziriteship] in order to train him to [carry out his] religious duties, and that [the right of a youth,] who can discriminate [but] who has not quite reached manhood, [to make vows] is Rabbinic. Rabbi, on the one hand, holds that [the parent's duty] to train, which is itself Rabbinic, overrules [the right of the youth,] who can discriminate [but] who has not quite reached manhood, [to make vows for himself] which is also Rabbinic;[1] whilst R. Jose son of R. Judah, who says [that the father's right lasts only] until [the lad] reaches the age of making vows, holds that the Rabbinic duty to train [the lad] does *not* set aside [the right of a youth] who can discriminate [but] who has not quite reached manhood [to make his own vows, although this is also Rabbinic].[2]

Can we say that [the controversy between] the above Tannaim[3] is the same as that between the following Tannaim?[4] For it has been taught: It is related that R. Ḥanina's father once imposed a nazirite vow upon him and then brought him before R. Gamaliel. R. Gamaliel was about to examine him to discover whether or not he had reached his majority[5]—according to R. Jose[6] it was to discover whether he had reached the age of making vows[7]—when [the young Ḥanina] said to him, 'Sir, do not exert yourself to examine me. If I am a minor, then I am a nazirite because of my father's [imposition], whilst if I am an adult,[8] I undertake it on my own account.' Thereupon R. Gamaliel rose and kissed him upon his head, and said, 'I am certain that this [lad] will be a religious leader[9] in Israel.' It is said that in a very short space of time, he became in fact a religious leader in Israel.[10]

(1) And the father can impose a naziriteship until the boy is thirteen. (2) And when the boy reaches the age of making vows, the father's right to impose a naziriteship ceases. (3) Rabbi and R. Jose son of R. Judah. (4) This is put as a question although the answer in this case is not negative. This is not uncommon (Asheri). (5) Lit., 'produced two hairs', as a sign of puberty. On this view, he was thirteen years old at the time. (6) I.e., R. Jose son of R. Judah. V. Tosaf. (7) The boy was only twelve years old according to R. Jose. (8) In regard to making vows. (9) Lit., will render *halachic* decisions.' (10) Tosef. Nid. V.

Now on R. Jose son of R. Judah's view that [the father's control lasts only] until [the boy] reaches the age at which he can make vows [for himself], we can understand why he should have said, 'If I am a minor,[1] I shall be [a nazirite] because of my father's [action, and so on].' But on Rabbi's view that [it lasts] until manhood, [of what value was the statement], 'whilst if I am an adult, I undertake it on my own account,' [30a] seeing that he was still under his father's control?[2]—[Rabbi will reply that] he really said, 'I intend to be one on my father's account [if he still has the right to impose it],[3] and on my own account [otherwise].' Now if he had in fact reached manhood at that time, his own naziriteship would take effect; if [he reached manhood] after [observing the naziriteship], he would have observed his father's naziriteship.[4] But suppose he reaches [manhood] during this period, what is to happen then?[5] Now on R. Jose son of R. Judah's view that [the father's right lasts] until the age at which he can make vows [for himself], all will be well,[6] but on Rabbi's view that [the right lasts] until he reaches manhood, how will you explain what happened?[7]—In point of fact, on Rabbi's view no other solution is possible,[8] than that he should observe [naziriteships] both on the father's account and on his own account.[9]

MISHNAH. A MAN CAN POLL [WITH OFFERINGS DUE FOR] HIS FATHER'S NAZIRITESHIP.[10] BUT A WOMAN CANNOT

(1) It is here supposed that all the young R. Ḥanina meant was, 'If I cannot yet make vows myself,' no special significance attaching to his use of the word 'minor'. (2) So that although he could make vows himself, his father could still impose a naziriteship on him. (3) I.e., 'minor' means 'under my father's control.' (4) This is the explanation of R. Ḥan. quoted in Tosaf. (5) For his father's naziriteship will automatically lapse on his reaching manhood; v. Tosef. Naz. III. (6) For on his reaching the age of making vows, vows imposed by his father beforehand are unaffected, and manhood is a long way off. (7) I.e., how do you account for the acceptance by Rabban Gamaliel of the double vow without further ado, since R. Ḥanina might reach manhood during the naziriteship. (8) If the boy does not wish to be examined. (9) I.e., observe a naziriteship of sixty days, instead of thirty, so that all contingencies are covered. (10) I.e., may purchase the sacrifices due on polling with money set apart for his father's sacrifices.

DO SO. WHERE, FOR EXAMPLE, A MAN'S FATHER HAD BEEN A NAZIRITE, AND HAS SET APART A LUMP SUM OF MONEY FOR [THE SACRIFICES OF] HIS NAZIRITESHIP AND DIED AND [THE SON THEN] SAID, 'I DECLARE MYSELF A NAZIRITE ON CONDITION THAT I MAY POLL WITH MY FATHER'S MONEY,' R. JOSE SAID THAT THESE MONEYS ARE TO BE USED FOR FREEWILL-OFFERINGS AND THAT SUCH A MAN CANNOT POLL AT THE EXPENSE OF HIS FATHER'S NAZIRITESHIP. WHO CAN DO SO? HE WHO WAS A NAZIRITE TOGETHER WITH HIS FATHER, AND WHOSE FATHER HAD SET APART A LUMP SUM OF MONEY FOR HIS NAZIRITE [SACRIFICES] AND DIED. [ONLY] SUCH A MAN CAN POLL AT THE EXPENSE OF HIS FATHER'S NAZIRITESHIP.[1]

GEMARA. Why [cannot a woman poll with her father's money]?—R. Johanan said: It is a [traditional] ruling with regard to the nazirite.[2] Surely this is obvious and so what purpose does [the ruling] serve, for a son inherits his father but a daughter does not do so?[3]—It is not necessary, except in the case where he had a daughter only.[4] It might have been thought that the tradition received was that [all] heirs [could poll][5] [30*b*] and so the ruling tells us [that this is not so].

The question was asked: Do the Rabbis differ from R. Jose or not;[6] and if it should be decided that they differ, whether with the first clause [only] or with the subsequent clause also?[7] Come and hear: In what circumstances was it said that a man may poll at the expense of his father's naziriteship? Where his father who had been

(1) Many MSS. (v. Tosaf.) reverse these two examples, making R. Jose permit him to poll if he becomes a nazirite afterwards, but not if he is a nazirite together with his father. In the parallel passage Tosef. Naz. III, there is the same MS. confusion. Cf. also *supra* 27*b*, and *infra* 30*b*. (2) No justification is therefore needed. (3) And so she could not obtain the money. For the rules of inheritance, v. Num. XXVII, 6ff. (4) In such a case the daughter inherits (ibid.). (5) So that where there was no son, the daughter could poll. (6) The problem arises because of the wording of our *Mishnah*. If no one differs from R. Jose, why say 'R. Jose said'? (7) I.e. do they permit the son to poll in both cases, or do they permit the one R. Jose forbids and *vice versa*.

a nazirite set apart money for [the sacrifices of] his naziriteship and died, and [the son then] said, 'I declare myself a nazirite on condition that I may poll with my father's money,' he [the son] is permitted to poll with his father's money. But where both he and his father were nazirites together, and his father set apart money for [the sacrifices of] his naziriteship and died, the money is to be used for freewill-offerings. The above is the opinion of R. Jose.[1] R. Eliezer,[2] R. Meir and R. Judah said: Just such a one may poll with his father's money.[3]

Rabbah raised the problem: Suppose [the nazirite] has two sons, both nazirites,[4] what is the law? Did the tradition state [simply] that there is a *halachah*,[5] so that the one who was first [to become a nazirite] may poll, or did it state [that the son may use the money because it is his] inheritance and so they divide it?

Raba raised the problem: Suppose [the sons were] the first-born[6] and another, what would the law be? Was the tradition received as a *halachah* and [the first-born] is therefore not entitled to receive for polling the same proportion as he receives [of the rest of the estate], or is [the money for the nazirite sacrifices, part of his] inheritance, and just as he takes a double portion there, so also is it with the [money for] polling?

Should it be decided that [the money for the nazirite sacrifices is part of] the inheritance, so that [the first-born] receives for polling in proportion to what he receives [of the rest of the estate], does [the first-born] receive a double portion only when [the money] is

(1) The opinion here ascribed to R. Jose is not that of our version of the Mishnah, but is that of the MS. versions. One or other must be emended, for consistency (v. Tosaf.). (2) Our text, R. Eliezer, is a common scribal error for R. Eleazar b. Shamua, the colleague of the other Rabbis mentioned. (3) Tosef. Naz. III, 9. Hence, (*a*) these Rabbis differ from R. Jose, (*b*) the difference covers both cases, for the 'Just such a one' is emphatic. So Rashi. Tosaf., Maim. *Yad.* (*Neziruth* VIII, 15), and most other commentators, however, consider that in the opinion of these Rabbis he may use his father's money under all circumstances. (4) And then dies, leaving money for sacrifices. (5) A ruling. Viz.: that it is possible for the son to use the money left by his father for his own naziriteship, no reason being given as to why he may do so. (6) Who is entitled to a double portion of the heritage. V. Deut. XXI, 17.

profane, but not when it becomes sacred,[1] or is there no difference, seeing that he has acquired [a double portion] for polling?[2]

Suppose his father was a life-nazirite[3] and he an ordinary nazirite, or his father an ordinary nazirite and he a life-nazirite, what would the law be?[4] Was the *halachah* received only with regard to ordinary naziriteships,[5] or is there no difference?[6]

Should it be decided that [such is the case] here [because] both the naziriteships[7] were discharged in ritual purity,[8] [then] R. Ashi raised a [further] problem. Suppose his father were an unclean nazirite[9] and he a clean nazirite,[10] or his father were a clean nazirite[11] and he an unclean nazirite,[12] what would be the law? The problem was unsolved.

(1) I.e., he receives two thirds of the money left towards his own nazirite sacrifices, but after the animals have been slaughtered and sacrificed he must return part of the sacred meat to his brother, so that each obtains just half of the meat which is to be eaten.—This question is raised because except for unslaughtered peace-offerings a first-born does not obtain a double portion of the sacred animals left at his father's death. (2) And so he will also keep a double portion of the meat. (3) And he put aside money for his naziriteship and died. (4) I.e., may the son use the money for his own naziriteship or not? (5) And he may not use the money. (6) And he may use the money. (7) Of the father and of the son. (8) And there is no distinction between the kind of naziriteship undertaken. (9) And he had set aside money to buy the sacrifices required for purification (v. Num. VI, 10), and then died. (10) I.e., may the son use the money towards the sacrifices he must offer on completing his naziriteship. (11) And he had set aside money for the sacrifices and then died. (12) I.e., may the son use the money towards the sacrifices of an unclean nazirite.

NAZIR

CHAPTER V

MISHNAH. BETH SHAMMAI SAY THAT CONSECRATION IN ERROR IS [EFFECTIVE] CONSECRATION, [31*a*] BUT BETH HILLEL SAY THAT IT IS NOT EFFECTIVE. FOR EXAMPLE, IF SOMEONE SAYS, 'THE BLACK BULL THAT LEAVES MY HOUSE FIRST SHALL BE SACRED,' AND A WHITE ONE EMERGES, BETH SHAMMAI DECLARE IT SACRED, BUT BETH HILLEL SAY THAT IT IS NOT SACRED. [OR IF HE SAYS,] 'THE GOLD DENAR THAT COMES INTO MY HAND FIRST SHALL BE SACRED,' AND A SILVER DENAR CAME TO HIS HAND BETH SHAMMAI DECLARE IT SACRED, WHILST BETH HILLEL SAY THAT IT IS NOT SACRED. [AGAIN, IF HE SAYS,] 'THE CASK OF WINE THAT I COME ACROSS FIRST SHALL BE SACRED,' AND HE COMES ACROSS A CASK OF OIL, BETH SHAMMAI DECLARE IT SACRED, BUT BETH HILLEL SAY THAT IT IS NOT SACRED.

GEMARA. BETH SHAMMAI SAY THAT CONSECRATION, etc.: Beth Shammai's reason is that they compare original consecration[1] with secondary consecration.[2] Just as substitution, even when made in error, is effective,[3] so [original] consecration, even when made in error, is effective. Beth Hillel, however, contend that this is true only of substitution,[4] but that no consecration in error can take effect in the first instance.

But suppose, according to Beth Shammai, someone says, 'This [animal] is to replace that [one] at midday,' it would surely not become a substitute [immediately] from that moment, but only

(1) Consecration of a profane object. (2) Lit., 'final consecration'. If anyone substitutes a profane animal for one already sacred, the substitution is not effective, but the profane animal becomes sacred too (v. Lev. XXVII, 10). Substitution is termed 'secondary consecration'. (3) V. Tem. 17*a*. (4) Since one animal was already sacred.

when midday arrives, and so here too, [surely, consecration should not take effect] until the condition [under which it was made] becomes realized?[1]—R. Papa replied: The reason that [the word] 'FIRST' was mentioned by him was [simply] to indicate that one [of his black oxen] which should emerge first.[2]—But the text says, 'the black bull,' and surely it contemplates the case where he may have only the one?[3]—In the case considered, he is assumed to have two or three.[4] Beth Hillel, however, contend that if this [was his intention][5] it should have said, '[The black bull] that leaves earliest.'[6]—Raba of Barnesh[7] said to R. Ashi; Is this [called] consecration in error? It is surely intentional consecration?[8]—[He replied:] Quite so, but [it is called consecration in error] because at first the expression he used gave a wrong impression.[9]

Is it indeed Beth Shammai's opinion that consecration in error is not effective consecration?[10] Have we not learnt: If a man, who vows to be a nazirite, sets aside an animal [for the sacrifice], and [then] applies to the Sages [for absolution from his vow] and they release him, [the animal] goes forth and pastures with the flock.[11] Beth Hillel said to Beth Shammai: Do you not admit that this is a case of consecration in error,[12] and yet [the animal] goes forth and pastures with the flock?[13] Whence[14] it follows [does it not] that

(1) But not where the stipulation was not fulfilled, as, e.g., a white bull emerged and not a black one. Thus the comparison with substitution is not borne out. (2) R. Papa rejects the explanation of Beth Shammai's opinion given above, and says that even on Beth Shammai's view, it is the black bull that emerges first which becomes sacred. In other words we do not set aside his statement because a white bull emerged first, as 'FIRST' may be understood as applying to the black oxen only (Tosaf.). (3) In which case, he could not mean 'the first of the black bulls.' (4) I.e., unless he has two or three black bulls, the question of one bull becoming sacred does not arise. (5) Viz., that the first black bull to emerge should become sacred, irrespective of whether others came out before it. (6) [שיצא בראשון, lit., 'at first', which may also denote the first (black bull) that leaves.] (7) [Near Sura, v. Obermeyer, *Die Landschaft Babylonien*, p. 296.] (8) For on R. Papa's view, he intended to make the first black bull to emerge sacred. (9) For he appears to mean that the black bull must come out before any other bull. (10) As is maintained by R. Papa. (11) I.e., it ceases to be holy. (12) For when he consecrated the animal he believed himself liable, whilst his subsequent release showed that he was not. (13) *Infra* 31*b*. (14) From Beth Hillel's remark.

Beth Shammai hold consecration in error to be effective?—No; Beth Hillel were mistaken. They took the reason for Beth Shammai's view[1] to be that consecration in error is effective, but the latter replied that [the consecration is effective] not because it was consecration in error, but because at first the expression he used gave a wrong impression.[2]

But is it Beth Shammai's opinion that consecration in error is not effective? Come [then] and hear: If [some people] were walking along the road [31*b*] and [saw] someone coming towards them, and one said, 'I declare myself a nazirite if it is So-and-so,' whilst another said, 'I declare myself a nazirite if it is not So-and-so,' [and a third man,] 'I declare myself a nazirite if one of you is a nazirite,' [a fourth, 'I declare myself a nazirite] if neither of you is a nazirite,' [a fifth, 'I declare myself a nazirite] if both of you are nazirites,' [and a sixth, 'I declare myself a nazirite] if all of you are nazirites,' Beth Shammai say that all [six] of them are nazirites.[3] Now this is a case of consecration in error,[4] and yet [the Mishnah] teaches that all of them are nazirites?—From this it certainly follows that Beth Shammai are of the opinion that consecration in error is effective, but not from the other.[5]

Abaye said: You should not assume that [the declaration] was made in the morning.[6] We speak here of a case where it was already midday, and he then said, 'The black bull that *left* my house first [to day] shall be sacred,'[7] and when informed that a white one left [first], he remarked, 'Had I known that a white one left, I should not have said black.'[8] But how can you say that it refers to what took place at midday,[9] seeing that the text reads: THE GOLD

(1) That the first black bull is sacred. (2) I.e., he really meant that bull to be sacred, but appeared to be saying something else. (3) Mishnah, *infra* 32*b*. q.v. (4) Since they become nazirites whether or no their conditions are fulfilled. (5) I.e., not from our own Mishnah, which is only apparently but not really a case of consecration in error, as explained by R. Papa and R. Ashi. (6) I.e., that when the man said, 'The black bull etc.' he was referring to a future event and not a past one. (7) [Vocalizing יָצָא instead of יֵצֵא.] (8) The case is now analogous to substitution in error, and Beth Shammai's reason will be that they infer consecration in error from substitution in error. (9) I.e., to a past event.

DENAR THAT COMES?[1]—Read, 'that has come.'[2] [But the text also reads,] THE CASK OF WINE THAT I COME ACROSS?[1]—Read, 'that I came across.'[2]

R. Ḥisda said: Black [oxen] amongst white [ones] spoil the herd.[3] White [patches] on black [oxen] are a blemish.

We have learnt: [IF SOMEONE SAYS,] 'THE BLACK BULL THAT IS THE FIRST TO LEAVE MY HOUSE [SHALL BE SACRED,' AND A WHITE ONE EMERGES, BETH SHAMMAI DECLARE] IT SACRED. Now when a person consecrates, he does so with an ill grace,[4] and yet Beth Shammai say that [the white bull] is sacred?[5] Do you suggest then that a person consecrates with a good grace?[6] [If so, how can we explain the following clause: IF HE SAYS,] 'THE GOLD DENAR THAT COMES INTO MY HAND FIRST [SHALL BE SACRED],' AND A SILVER DENAR CAME TO HIS HAND, BETH SHAMMAI DECLARE IT SACRED?[7]—Do you submit, then, that a person consecrates with an ill grace? [Consider then the following: IF HE SAYS,] 'THE CASK OF WINE THAT I COME ACROSS FIRST [SHALL BE SACRED],' AND HE COMES ACROSS A CASK OF OIL, BETH SHAMMAI DECLARE IT SACRED; and yet oil is superior to wine?—That raises no difficulty, for it was taught with reference to Galilee where wine is superior to oil. But the first clause [of our Mishnah] seems to contradict R. Ḥisda?—R. Ḥisda will reply: My statement[8] referred to Carmanian[9] oxen.

R. Ḥisda also used to say: A black ox for its hide, a red one for its flesh, a white one for ploughing.[10]

(1) 'Left' and 'will leave' have the same consonants in Hebrew but are pronounced differently (v. p. 112, n. 7); but in these cases, the past has different consonants from the future and so cannot be confused with it. (2) I.e., change the reading. Instead of יעלה read עלה and instead of תעלה read עלתה. (3) Because black oxen are inferior to white ones. (4) Lit., 'malevolent eye'. He does not wish anything more than he has specified to become sacred. (5) And so white bulls must be worth less than black ones. (6) Lit., 'benevolent eye'. (7) Thus he is satisfied to give a silver coin instead of a gold one, but had he consecrated with a good grace, the silver would not become sacred. (8) That white oxen are better than black. (9) Carmania, a province of Persia, the oxen of which were generally employed for ploughing. (10) I.e., each kind is most suitable for the purpose mentioned. Thus in respect to its hide, a black ox is superior to a white one. [V. Lewysohn, *Zoologie*, p. 131.]

But R. Ḥisda said that black [oxen] amongst white ones spoil the herd?[1]—He said that with reference to Carmanian oxen.

MISHNAH. IF A MAN VOWS TO BE A NAZIRITE AND THEN SEEKS RELEASE FROM A SAGE[2] BUT IS FORBIDDEN [TO ANNUL HIS VOW], HE CAN RECKON [THE NAZIRITESHIP] FROM THE TIME THAT THE VOW WAS MADE.[3] IF HE SEEKS RELEASE FROM A SAGE AND IS ABSOLVED AND HAS AN ANIMAL SET ASIDE [FOR A SACRIFICE], IT GOES FORTH TO PASTURE WITH [THE REST OF] THE HERD.[4] BETH HILLEL SAID TO BETH SHAMMAI: DO YOU NOT ADMIT THAT HERE WHERE THE CONSECRATION IS IN ERROR,[5] [THE ANIMAL] GOES FORTH TO PASTURE WITH THE HERD?[6] BETH SHAMMAI REPLIED: DO YOU NOT ADMIT THAT IF A MAN IN ERROR CALLS THE NINTH [ANIMAL], THE TENTH,[7] OR THE TENTH THE NINTH, OR THE ELEVENTH THE TENTH, EACH BECOMES SACRED?[8] BETH HILLEL RETORTED: IT IS NOT THE ROD THAT MAKES THESE SACRED,[9] FOR SUPPOSE THAT IN ERROR HE PLACED THE ROD UPON THE EIGHTH OR UPON THE TWELFTH, WOULD THIS HAVE ANY EFFECT? [THE FACT IS] THAT SCRIPTURE WHICH HAS DECLARED THE TENTH TO BE SACRED, HAS ALSO DECLARED SACRED THE NINTH [32a] AND THE ELEVENTH.[10]

GEMARA. Who can the author of [the first paragraph of] our Mishnah be? For it [agrees] neither with R. Jose nor with the Rabbis. For it has been taught: If a man vows [to be a nazirite] and transgresses a rule of his naziriteship, his case is not examined,[11]

(1) Yet here he says that their hides are superior. (2) It is presumed that he had drunk wine in the interval. (3) I.e., presumably, his transgression has not affected the validity of the period past. (4) I.e., it ceases to be holy. (5) Because his release shows that no sacrifice was necessary. (6) And so no consecration in error should be effective. (7) During tithing of cattle; cf. Lev. XXVII, 32. (8) Thus consecration in error is effective. (9) I.e., it is not his error in striking the wrong animal with the tithing rod that makes it sacred. (10) If they are struck in error; v. *infra* for source. (11) Should he desire to be released from his vow.

unless he [first] observes in [nazirite] abstinence as many days as he has passed in indulgence.[1] R. Jose said that thirty days are enough.[2] Now if [the author] be the Rabbis, [the case also of] naziriteship for a long period offers difficulty,[3] whilst if it be R. Jose, [the case of] naziriteship for a short period offers difficulty?[4]—It may be maintained either that [the author] is R. Jose, or that [the authors] are the Rabbis. It may be maintained that [the author] is R. Jose, by supposing that [the Mishnah refers] to a long period of naziriteship [only],[5] and [the Baraitha] to a short period of naziriteship [as well].[6] It can also be maintained that [the authors] are the Rabbis, in which case we must read [in the Mishnah] not, 'FROM THE TIME THAT THE VOW WAS MADE,'[7] but 'equal [to the period which has elapsed] since the vow was made.'[8]

IF HE SEEKS RELEASE FROM THE SAGES, AND THEY ABSOLVE HIM etc.: R. Jeremiah said: From [the opinion of] Beth Shammai we can infer that of Beth Hillel. Do not Beth Shammai assert that consecration in error is effective and yet when it becomes clear[9] that the nazirite vow is not valid, [the animal] goes forth to pasture with the herd? So too, for Beth Hillel. Although they say that

(1) I.e., the number of days which have elapsed between his transgression and his seeking for absolution. (2) Tosef. Ned. I; i.e., if his period of transgression was longer than thirty days, he is made to keep a naziriteship of thirty days, before being released. (3) The Mishnah allows him to reckon in all cases the days of his transgression as part of his naziriteship, whilst the Rabbis do not do so. (4) They would conflict in regard to the short period in the manner explained in the previous note. In regard to the long period they would not conflict, since R. Jose allows him to reckon all the period of transgression, which is more than thirty days, and it could be argued that this is all that the Mishnah means. The text adopted here is that of Tosaf.; Asheri, Maim. and most other commentators, agreeing with the quotation in Ned. 20a. Our printed text, which reads that the short period offers a difficulty for the Rabbis and the long period for R. Jose, assumes a reading of the Tosefta which would agree with most MSS. of the Tosef. (Ned. I, 11) and with the Jerusalem Talmud (J. Naz. V, 4), but requires an argument at once more complicated and subtle. (5) There being no conflict with R. Jose's view, as explained in the previous note. (6) In this case only does R. Jose require the whole of the period of transgression to be counted afresh. (7) Which implies that the period when there was transgression forms part of the naziriteship and so conflicts with the view of the Baraitha. (8) Mishnah and Baraitha now agree. (9) By the release that was granted.

substitution in error is effective substitution, this is only true where the original consecration remains,[1] but where the original consecration is revoked,[2] [the consecration resulting from] the substitution is also revoked.[3]

The Master said: 'DO YOU NOT ADMIT THAT IF HE CALLS THE NINTH THE TENTH, etc.' It has been stated: In the case of the tithe, R. Naḥman said that [this is the rule only] if this is done in error, not if it is done intentionally.[4] R. Ḥisda and Rabbah b. R Huna, however, said that [it is certainly the rule] if it is done in error, and all the more so if it is done intentionally.[5]

Raba said to R. Naḥman: According to you who assert that [it is the rule only] if it is done in error and not if done intentionally, when Beth Shammai asked Beth Hillel, DO YOU NOT ADMIT THAT IF HE CALLED THE NINTH THE TENTH, THE TENTH THE NINTH, OR THE ELEVENTH THE TENTH, THAT ALL THREE ARE SACRED? and Beth Hillel were silent,[6] why could they not have answered that the case of tithes is different since these[7] cannot be made sacred intentionally?[8]—R. Shimi b. Ashi replied: The reason that they did not do so is because of an *a fortiori* argument that might be based on this [by Beth Shammai].[9] For [Beth Shammai might have argued that] if tithes that cannot be consecrated [out of turn] intentionally can be so consecrated in error, then ordinary consecration that can be done intentionally should certainly take effect [in error].[10] This [argument], however, would be unsound, for [ordinary] consecration depends entirely upon the intention of the owner.[11]

(1) I.e., when the first animal for which the second is substituted is not afterwards declared profane. (2) [E.g., owing to the remission of the naziriteship for which the animal was reserved.] (3) I.e., the animal substituted also becomes profane. (4) If he intentionally strikes the ninth animal as though it were the tenth, it does not become sacred. (5) I.e., in either case the animal becomes sacred. (6) I.e., they found no flaw in the argument itself, but were compelled to reply that it is only in this case that Scripture has declared consecration in error effective. (7) I.e., the ninth or eleventh animal. (8) And since they did not say this, it follows that even if he strikes the ninth animal intentionally, it becomes sacred. (9) If it is assumed that the cases are comparable. (10) And Beth Hillel do not admit that consecration in error is effective. (11) Whereas a man is bound to tithe his animals, and so the rules applying in the one case

MISHNAH. IF A MAN VOWS TO BE A NAZIRITE AND ON GOING TO BRING HIS ANIMAL [FOR THE SACRIFICE] FINDS THAT IT HAS BEEN STOLEN, THEN IF HE HAD DECLARED HIMSELF A NAZIRITE BEFORE THE THEFT OF HIS ANIMAL,[1] HE IS [STILL] A NAZIRITE, [32b] BUT IF HE HAD DECLARED HIMSELF A NAZIRITE AFTER THE THEFT OF HIS ANIMAL, HE IS NOT A NAZIRITE.[2] IT WAS ON THIS POINT THAT NAHUM THE MEDE FELL INTO ERROR WHEN NAZIRITES ARRIVED [IN JERUSALEM] FROM THE DIASPORA AND FOUND THE TEMPLE IN RUINS.[3] NAHUM THE MEDE SAID TO THEM, 'HAD YOU KNOWN THAT THE TEMPLE WOULD BE DESTROYED, WOULD YOU HAVE BECOME NAZIRITES?' THEY ANSWERED, 'NO,' AND SO NAHUM THE MEDE ABSOLVED THEM.[4] WHEN, HOWEVER, THE MATTER CAME TO THE NOTICE OF THE SAGES THEY SAID: WHOEVER DECLARED HIMSELF A NAZIRITE BEFORE THE DESTRUCTION OF THE TEMPLE IS A NAZIRITE, BUT IF AFTER THE DESTRUCTION OF THE TEMPLE, HE IS NOT A NAZIRITE.

GEMARA. Rabbah said: The Rabbis overruled R. Eliezer and laid down [the law] in accordance with their own views. For we have learnt: It is permitted to grant release on the ground of improbable contingencies;[5] this is the opinion of R. Eliezer, but the Sages forbid this.[6]

Rabbah[7] said further: Although the Rabbis said that improbable contingencies cannot be made the grounds for release, yet conditions involving improbable contingencies can be made a ground for release. For example, it would have been possible to say to

need bear no resemblance to those applying in the other. Hence R. Naḥaman cannot be refuted from this (Tosaf.).

(1) I.e., the three animals which a nazirite offers on completing his vow. (2) As his vow had been made under a misapprehension. (3) The nazirite vow was binding until the sacrifices had been offered. (4) As the vow had been made under a misapprehension. (5) I.e., the grounds for release need not have been anticipated at the time the vow was entered into. (6) Mishnah, Ned. IX, 1. Here in Nazir, on the other hand, R. Eliezer's view is not quoted, showing that it was not considered permissible to rely on it under any circumstances whatsoever. (7) Our text, in error, has Raba.

them: Suppose someone had come and said to you[1] that the Temple would be destroyed, would you have uttered your vow?

R. Joseph said: Had I been there, I should have said to them:[2] Is it not written, *The temple of the Lord, the temple of the Lord, the temple of the Lord, are these,*[3] which points to [the destruction of] the first and second temples?[4]—Granted that they knew it would be destroyed, did they know when this would occur?[5]

Abaye objected: And did they not know when? Is it not written, *Seventy weeks are determined upon thy people, and upon thy holy city?*[6] —All the same, did they know on which day?[7]

MISHNAH. IF [PEOPLE] WERE WALKING ALONG THE ROAD AND [SAW] SOMEONE COMING TOWARDS THEM, AND ONE SAID, 'I DECLARE MYSELF A NAZIRITE IF IT IS SO-AND-SO,' WHILST ANOTHER SAID, 'I DECLARE MYSELF A NAZIRITE IF IT IS NOT SO-AND-SO,' [AND A THIRD MAN,] 'I DECLARE MYSELF A NAZIRITE IF ONE OF YOU IS A NAZIRITE,' [A FOURTH, 'I DECLARE MYSELF A NAZIRITE] IF NEITHER OF YOU IS A NAZIRITE,' [A FIFTH, 'I DECLARE MYSELF A NAZIRITE] IF BOTH OF YOU ARE NAZIRITES,' [AND A SIXTH, 'I DECLARE MYSELF A NAZIRITE] IF ALL OF YOU ARE NAZIRITES.' BETH SHAMMAI SAY THAT ALL [SIX] OF THEM ARE NAZIRITES, BUT BETH HILLEL SAY THAT ONLY THOSE WHOSE WORDS WERE NOT FULFILLED, ARE NAZIRITES.[8] R. TARFON SAID: NOT ONE OF THEM IS A NAZIRITE. IF [THE PERSON APPROACHING] TURNED

(1) When you were about to declare yourselves nazirites. (2) To those who contended that the destruction of the Temple, being an event which could not have been foreseen, could not be used as a ground for release (Asheri). (3) Jer. VII, 4. (4) Since it indicates that there would be three temples. Thus the destruction was foretold and could have been anticipated. (5) And so they could not anticipate it. (6) Dan. IX, 24. This prophecy was uttered at the beginning of the seventy years captivity in Babylon. From the restoration to the second destruction is said to have been 420 years, making in all 490, i.e., seventy weeks of years. (7) And since they did not know, they expected to offer their sacrifices before the destruction. (8) This is explained in the Gemara.

AWAY SUDDENLY[1] [WITHOUT BEING IDENTIFIED], HE[2] IS NOT A NAZIRITE. R. SIMEON SAYS: HE SHOULD SAY, 'IF I WAS RIGHT,[3] I AM A NAZIRITE OBLIGATORILY, OTHERWISE I WISH TO BE A NAZIRITE, VOLUNTARILY.'

GEMARA. Why should the ones whose words were not fulfilled become nazirites?[4]—Rab Judah replied: Read, 'those whose words were fulfilled.' [33a] Abaye replied: We suppose him to have added, for example, 'even if it be not So-and-so I intend[5] to be a nazirite,' the meaning of the phrase HIS WORDS WERE NOT FULFILLED [used in the Mishnah] being, his first words were not fulfilled but his later ones were.[6]

IF [THE PERSON APPROACHING] TURNED AWAY SUDDENLY [WITHOUT BEING IDENTIFIED] HE IS NOT A NAZIRITE etc.: The reason [that he is not a nazirite] is because the other turned away, which would show that had the other come before us, he would become a nazirite. Who is the author [of this opinion]?[7] [34a] Should you say it is R. Tarfon, would he become a nazirite? For since he did not know at the time he uttered the nazirite vow whether it was So-and-so or not, would the naziriteship have become operative [at all]? For have we not been taught: R. Judah on behalf of R. Tarfon said that not one of them[8] is a nazirite because naziriteship is not intended except when assumed unequivocally?[9] —It must, therefore, be R. Judah [who indicated this in connection] with the heap of grain. For it has been taught: [If a man says,] 'I declare myself a nazirite, provided that this heap of grain contains one hundred *kor*,' and then finds that [the heap] has been stolen or is lost, R. Simeon binds [him to a naziriteship], whilst R. Judah frees him [from the vow].[10]

(1) Lit., 'he shuddered back'. (2) I.e., one whose naziriteship was contingent on the identity of the person approaching. (3) In my identification. (4) According to Beth Hillel. (5) [Read איהוי for אי הוי.] (6) And so he becomes a nazirite. (7) There is no Gemara on 33b, this page being taken up with Tosaf. (8) One of those, mentioned in our Mishnah, who undertook a naziriteship if the person approaching were So-and-so. (9) Tosef. Naz. III. (10) Thus in R. Judah's view unless the vow is free from all doubt it does not become operative.

R. Simeon holds that since, had it not been stolen, it might have been found to contain one hundred *kor*, in which case he would have become a nazirite, he must now also become a nazirite. Here,[1] too, since, had the other come before us and we had known that it was So-and-so, he would have become a nazirite, now [that the other has not come] he also becomes a nazirite.

MISHNAH. IF [ONE MAN] SAW A KOY[2] AND SAID, 'I DECLARE MYSELF A NAZIRITE IF THAT IS A BEAST OF CHASE,' [AND ANOTHER] 'I DECLARE MYSELF A NAZIRITE IF THAT IS NOT A BEAST OF CHASE,' [A THIRD SAID] 'I DECLARE MYSELF A NAZIRITE IF THAT IS CATTLE,' [A FOURTH SAID,] 'I DECLARE MYSELF A NAZIRITE IF THAT IS NOT CATTLE,' [A FIFTH SAID,] 'I DECLARE MYSELF A NAZIRITE IF THAT IS BOTH A BEAST OF CHASE AND CATTLE,' [AND A SIXTH SAID,] 'I DECLARE MYSELF A NAZIRITE IF THAT IS NEITHER BEAST OF CHASE NOR CATTLE.' [THEN A SEVENTH SAID,] 'I DECLARE MYSELF A NAZIRITE IF ONE OF YOU IS A NAZIRITE,' [AN EIGHTH SAID,] 'I DECLARE MYSELF A NAZIRITE IF NOT ONE OF YOU IS A NAZIRITE,' [WHILST A NINTH SAID,] 'I DECLARE MYSELF A NAZIRITE IF YOU ARE ALL NAZIRITES,' THEN ALL OF THEM BECOME NAZIRITES.

GEMARA. In one [Baraitha] it is taught that nine [can become] nazirites,[3] and in another that nine naziriteships [can be undertaken].[4] Now there would be nine nazirites if, for example, a

Tosef. Naz. II. Cf., however, Ned. 19*a*, where the view of R. Judah here, and R. Judah on behalf of R. Tarfon and held by R. Ashi to be identical.

(1) I.e., in the Mishnah. (2) The Rabbis were uncertain whether the *Koy*, an animal permitted for food, should be considered of the genus cattle, בהמה, or a beast of chase, חיה. V. Aruch s.v. כוי. [It is generally taken as a cross between a goat and some species of gazelle; v. Lewysohn, *op. cit.* p. 115.] (3) By using different formulae and making the vow contingent on the *Koy* being a beast of chase or cattle. (4) I.e., one man can undertake nine naziriteships by using different formulae with reference to the *Koy*.

number of men referred to [the *Koy*] one after another;[1] but how is it possible for nine naziriteships [to be undertaken] by one man? There could indeed be six, as enumerated in our Mishnah,[2] but how could the other three be undertaken?—R. Shesheth replied: He could say,[3] 'I declare myself a nazirite and undertake the naziriteships of you all.'[4]

(1) As described in our Mishnah. (2) For the first six formulae could all be uttered by one man. (3) Referring to nine men who had each undertaken a naziriteship in the manner of the Mishnah. (4) I.e., 'I undertake a naziriteship for each one of you who is a nazirite.'

NAZIR

CHAPTER VI

MISHNAH. THREE THINGS ARE FORBIDDEN TO A NAZIRITE, VIZ.:—RITUAL DEFILEMENT, POLLING, AND PRODUCTS OF THE VINE. ALL PRODUCTS OF THE VINE CAN BE RECKONED TOGETHER[1] WHILST THERE IS NO PENALTY UNLESS HE EATS AN OLIVE'S BULK OF GRAPES, [34*b*] [OR,] ACCORDING TO THE EARLIER MISHNAH,[2] UNLESS HE DRINKS A QUARTER [OF A LOG][3] OF WINE. R. AKIBA SAID THAT THERE IS A PENALTY EVEN IF HE SOAKS HIS BREAD IN WINE AND ENOUGH [IS ABSORBED] TO MAKE UP ALTOGETHER[4] AN OLIVE'S BULK.[5]

THERE IS A SEPARATE PENALTY FOR WINE, FOR GRAPES, FOR ḤARZANIM AND FOR ZAGIM.[6] R. ELEAZAR B. AZARIAH SAID: THERE IS NO PENALTY [IN THE CASE OF THE LAST TWO SPECIES] UNLESS HE EATS TWO ḤARZANIM AND ONE ZAG.

BY ḤARZANIM AND ZAGIM ARE MEANT THE FOLLOWING. ACCORDING TO R. JUDAH, ḤARZANIM MEANS THE OUTER PORTION [OF THE GRAPE],[7] ZAG THE INNER PORTION,[8] BUT R. JOSE SAID: THAT YOU MAY NOT ERR, [THINK OF] THE ZOG [BELL] OF AN ANIMAL,[9] OF WHICH THE OUTER PART IS TERMED

(1) To form a total of an olive's bulk in the case of solids, or as the earlier Mishnah has it, a quarter of a *log* in the case of fluids, for the consumption of which there is a penalty, viz. stripes. (Meiri's interpretation of a very difficult passage). (2) [Or *'First Mishnah'*, a collection of *Halachoth* the compilation of which began according to Geonic accounts as early as Hillel and Shammai; v. Sanh. (Sonc. ed.) p. 163, n. 7.] (3) A quarter of a *log* is between 50 and 60 c.c. (= the bulk of one and a half average-sized eggs). (4) I.e., along with the bread. (5) According to R. Akiba, an olive's bulk (less than 10 c.c.) carries with it a penalty in the case of liquids. (6) There is no need to consume more than one variety to incur the penalty. All four species are mentioned in Num. VI, 3-4, *ḥarzanim* being usually translated *'pressed grapes'* and *zag*, *'grape-stone'*, following the opinion of R. Judah given later in the Mishnah. (7) The skin. (8) The stone. (9) The bell suspended at the animal's neck.

THE ZOG [HOOD],[1] AND THE INNER PART THE 'INBAL [CLAPPER].

GEMARA. THREE THINGS ARE FORBIDDEN TO A NAZIRITE, VIZ.:—RITUAL DEFILEMENT etc.: Products of the vine are [forbidden] but not the vine itself, so that our Mishnah differs from R. Eleazar, for it has been taught: R. Eleazar said that even leaves and shoots [of the vine] are included [in the things forbidden to a nazirite].

Some draw the inference[2] from the subsequent clause, viz.:—WHILST THERE IS NO PENALTY UNLESS HE EATS AN OLIVE'S BULK OF GRAPES. GRAPES only [carry a penalty] but not the vine itself, so that our Mishnah differs from R. Eleazar, for it has been taught: R. Eleazar said that even leaves and shoots are included.

In what [essentially] does the difference [between R. Eleazar and the Rabbis of our *Mishnah*] lie?—R. Eleazar interprets [certain scriptural passages as consisting of] 'amplifications and limitations,'[3] whilst the Rabbis interpret [them as] general statements and specifications.[4] R. Eleazar [argues as follows:] *He shall abstain from wine and strong drink*[5] is a limitation,[6] whilst, Nothing *that is made of the grape-vine*[7] is an amplification. When a limitation is followed by an amplification all things are embraced.[8] What then does the amplification serves to include [here]? Everything [coming from the vine],[9] and what does the limitation exclude? Only the twigs.

The Rabbis, on the other hand, [argue as follows:] '*He shall*

(1) And so, too, *zag* of a grape is its skin. (2) That our Mishnah and R. Eleazar differ. (3) *Ribbni u-Mi'uṭ*. I.e., as consisting of clauses that amplify and clauses that restrict. (4) *Kelal u-feraṭ*. The significance of these technical terms will become clearer in the argument set out below. For a full explanation of these terms, v. Shebu. (Sonc. ed.) p. 12, n. 3. (5) Num. VI, 3. (6) The things prohibited are confined to the things mentioned. (7) Num. VI, 3. Lit., *Of* everything *that is made . . . he shall not eat*. (8) I.e., the scope, in this case of the prohibition, is as wide as possible, the restriction serving merely to exclude some one thing, here the twigs. (9) And so also the leaves and the shoots.

abstain from wine and strong drink' is a specification;[1] '[*He shall eat*] *nothing that is made of the grape-vine'* is a general statement; *'from the pressed grapes even to the grape-stone'*[2] is again a specification. When we have a specification, a generalisation, and a [second] specification, only what is similar to the specification may be adjudged [to be within the scope of the prohibition]. In the specification fruit[3] and fruit refuse[4] are particularised, and so whatever is fruit[5] or fruit refuse [is prohibited].[6] Should you object that in the specification ripe fruit is particularised, and so only what is ripe fruit [is prohibited],[7] the reply is that [in this view] nothing would be left implicit in Scripture, everything being explicitly mentioned.[8] Fresh grapes and dried grapes are mentioned, as are also wine and vinegar. It follows that the inference must be drawn not in the latter form,[9] but in the first form. Again, seeing that we finally include everything [similar to fruit or fruit refuse], for what purpose is *'from pressed grapes even to the grape-stone'* mentioned [separately from the other specification]?[10] To tell us that wherever a specification is followed by a general statement it is not permissible to extend [the terms of the specification] so as to include only whatever is similar to it, but the general statement widens the scope of the specification,[11] unless Scripture indicates the specification in the manner in which it is indicated in the case of the nazirite.[12]

The Master said: 'In the specification fruit and fruit refuse are particularised, and so whatever is fruit or fruit refuse [is prohibited].' 'Fruit' means grapes, but what is 'fruit refuse'?—Vinegar. What is meant by 'Whatever is fruit'?—Unripe grapes. And by 'whatever is fruit refuse'?—R. Kahana said that this serves to include worm-eaten grapes.[13] [And what is the significance of]

(1) Of the things forbidden. (2) Num. VI, 4; the concluding half of the last verse quoted. (3) Grapes and wine. (4) Vinegar. (5) Including unripe grapes. (6) Worm-eaten grapes. (7) And thus unripe grapes would be excluded. (8) I.e., there is no form of ripe fruit different from those mentioned in the verses quoted. (9) Restricted to ripe fruit. (10) I.e., why does not the whole specification precede the generalisation. (11) And includes also things not similar to the specification. (12) With the general statement interrupting it. (13) That went bad before they ripened.

'even *to the grape-stone'?*[1]—Rabina said that this serves to include the intermediate part.[2]

The Master said: 'Should you object that in the specification raw ripe fruit is particularised, and so only what is ripe fruit [is prohibited], the reply is that [on this view] nothing would be left implicit in Scripture, everything being explicitly mentioned. Fresh grapes and dried grapes are mentioned, as are also wine and vinegar. It follows that the inference must be drawn not in the latter form, but in the first form. Again, seeing that we finally include everything [similar to fruit or fruit refuse], for what purpose is *from pressed grapes even to the grape-stone* mentioned [separately from the other specification]? To tell us that wherever a specification is followed by a general statement it is not permissible to extend [the terms of the specification] as as to include only whatever is similar to it, but the general statement widens the scope of the specification, unless Scripture indicates the specification [35a] in the manner in which it is indicated in the case of the nazirite.'

Now, R. Eleazar b. Azariah utilises the clause, *'from the pressed grapes even to the grape-stone'* for the inference that there is no penalty unless he eats two pressed grapes and one grape-stone.[3] Where does he find a [second] specification?[4]—He will agree with R. Eleazar who interprets [the passage as a clause that] amplifies [followed by a clause] that limits.[5] Alternatively, it can be argued that he agrees with the Rabbis, for [he might say] if [the sole object of this clause were the inference] of R. Eleazar b. Azariah, the Torah could have included, *'from the pressed grapes even to the grape-stone'* with the other items specified.[6] Why then does it appear after the general statement? To show that the text is to be construed as a general statement followed by a specification.

But why should not this be its sole object?[7]—If this were so, the verse should have read either 'pressed grapes and grape-stones'

(1) In Num. VI, 3. (2) What remains of the flesh after the wine has drained off. (3) V. our Mishnah *supra*. (4) To be able to continue the argument as the Rabbis do. (5) In R. Eleazar's argument no second specification is needed. (6) In the verse preceding. (7) Leaving no room for R. Eleazar b. Azariah's further ruling.

[with both words in the plural] or 'pressed grape and grape-stone' [with both in the singular]. The reason why the All-merciful says, *'from the pressed grapes even to the grape-stone'* can only be that we should both interpret as a general statement followed by a specification and infer [that there is no penalty] unless he eats two pressed-grapes and one grape-stone.

Now R. Eleazar interprets [the text as consisting of] a clause that amplifies and a clause that limits. Where then does he find [in the Scripture the typical example of] specification, general statement and second specification?—R. Abbahu said that he finds it in the following verse. *If a man deliver unto his neighbour an ass, or an ox, or a sheep,*[1] is a specification; *or any beast* is a generalisation; *to keep* is a further specification,[2] and so we may infer only what is similar to the specification.[3]

Raba said that [R. Eleazar] could find one in the following verse. *And if [his offering] be* of *[the flock]*[4] is a specification, *the flock* a general statement, and *[whether of] the sheep, [or of] the goats* a further specification, and so we may infer only what is similar to the specification.[5]

Rab Judah of Diskarta[6] asked Raba: Why should not [R. Eleazar] find it in the following verse? *[Ye shall bring your offering] of*[7] is a specification, *the cattle* [beasts] a general statement, and *[of] the herd [or of] the flock* a further specification, and so only what is similar to the specification can be inferred?[8]—He replied: This is not a clear case, for if [he inferred it] from there it could be argued that [in the expression] *'the cattle'*, [35b] cattle includes beasts of chase.[9]—[Rab Judah] retorted: Could beasts of chase be included

(1) As a bailment. Ex. XXIII, 9. (2) For it excludes beasts of prey which cannot be 'kept', i.e. guarded. (3) Domestic animals of any kind and also poultry. (4) Lev. I, 10. The inference depends on the Hebrew construction which could have read 'And if flock', so that the expression '*of* the flock' does limit the choice permitted. (5) In this example it is not clear from the verse what is excluded. An animal that had been worshipped as a deity would be forbidden as a sacrifice, but the commentators differ as to whether Raba could have had this in mind. (6) [Deskarah, sixteen parasangs N.E. of Bagdad, Obermeyer *op. cit.* p. 146.] (7) Lev. I, 2. (V. note 4). (8) Viz.: domestic clean animals, though the age would be immaterial. (9) And so the second specification is in any case necessary to exclude these, and we cannot use it to derive the method of specification etc.

in 'cattle' [in this instance]? For *'the herd and the flock'*[1] are mentioned, making in fact a specification, a general statement, and a specification, and only what is similar to the specification can be inferred![2]

How do we know that [the rule] is correct?[3]—It has been taught: *And thou shalt bestow the money for whatsoever thy soul desireth*[4] is a general statement, *for oxen or for sheep or for wine or for strong drink* a specification, and *or for whatsoever thy soul asketh of thee* a further general statement, making a general statement, a specification and a second general statement. Only what is similar to the specification may be inferred,[5] and so because the specification particularises the product of that which is itself a product,[6] whose sustenance is drawn from the earth,[7] whatever is a product of a product-bearing species that draws its sustenance from the earth [may be purchased].[8]

Seeing that when there is a general statement, a specification, and a general statement, we infer whatever is similar to the specification, what is then the function of the second general statement? It is to add whatever resembles the things specified.[9] Again, seeing that when there is a specification, a general statement, and a specification, what is similar to the specification is inferred, what is the purpose of the second specification?—But for its presence it would be said that it is a case of general statement being added to the [first] specification.[10] Further, seeing that both when there are two general statements [separated by] a specification and when

(1) Which are domestic clean animals and not beasts of chase, and their mention serves to exclude beasts of chase. (2) Thus beasts of chase would be automatically excluded by the operation of the rule, so that the rule can be applied. (3) Viz.: that when there is more than one specification, whatever is similar can be inferred (Rashi). (4) Deut. XIV, 26, referring to money converted from the second tithe. (5) Thus the presence of a second generalisation alters the rule that applies when there is a single clause of each kind. The same is taken to be true when there is a second specification. (6) Mineral substances are thus excluded. (7) In contrast to fish. (8) E.g., poultry also. (9) Without the second general statement, only the things actually specified would be included in the scope of the subject under discussion. (10) [In which case the rule is that even things that do not resemble the specification are included.]

there are two specifications [separated by] a general statement, what is similar to the specification is inferred, what then is the difference between the two cases?—It is that whereas in the former case we include even things that resemble the specification in one respect only,[1] in the latter case we include only what resembles [the specification] in two respects, but not what resembles it in one respect.[2]

Seeing that when a specification is followed by a general statement, the general statement supplements the specification, all things being included, and again when a limitation is followed by an amplifying clause, this amplifies to the fullest extent, all things being included, what then is the difference between [the two cases]? —The difference is that whereas in the case of a specification followed by a general statement, both shoots and leaves [say],[3] would be included, in the case of a limitation followed by an amplifying clause, only the shoots, but not the leaves [would be included].[4]

R. Abbahu said: R. Joḥanan said that what is permitted is not reckoned together with what is forbidden[5] in the case of any prohibition of the Torah with the exception of the prohibitions of the nazirite where the Torah says explicitly, [*Neither shall he drink*] *that which is soaked in grape-juice*.[6] [36a] Ze'iri said: Another [exception] is leaven which it is prohibited to burn [on the altar].[7] According to whom [will Ze'iri infer this? Evidently] after the manner of R. Eleazar who interprets the particle *kol* [any].[8] But then should not another exception be leaven [on passover]?[9]—Quite so. But

(1) E.g., in the case of the second tithe we do not also require the thing purchased to be attached to the soil and so exclude poultry. (2) And so, for example, vine shoots are not forbidden the nazirite although they may be edible. (3) This is not referring to any particular case, but is simply an illustration of how the difference might arise. (4) V. Shebu. (Sonc. ed.) p. 12, n. 3. (5) I.e., there is no penalty unless a full olive's bulk of the forbidden food is consumed. Thus half an olive's bulk of forbidden fat and half of permissible meat would entail no penalty. (6) E.V. '*liquor*'. Num. VI, 3. Hence an olive's bulk of, e.g., bread soaked in wine carries the penalty. (7) Lev. II, 11. (8) Ibid. '*any* leaven' as a sign that even in combination it is forbidden, with the full penalty for transgression. (9) For here R. Eleazar explicitly makes this interpretation of *kol*. (v. Pes. 43b), and so why does not Ze'iri mention it.

[Ze'iri wished to indicate his] dissent from the opinion of Abaye that the burning of even less than an olive's bulk counts as an offering,[1] and so he [incidentally] tells us that the burning of less than an olive's bulk does not count as an offering.[2]

As R. Dimi was once sitting and repeating the above reported decision [of R. Johanan][3] Abaye raised the following objection. [A Mishnah says:] If part of a stew of *terumah*[4] containing garlic and oil of *hullin*[5] is touched by a [defiled person who] had bathed that day,[6] the whole is rendered unfit [to be eaten].[7] If part of a stew of *hullin* containing garlic and oil of *terumah* is touched by a [defiled person who] had bathed that day, only that part that was touched becomes unfit [to be eaten].[8] Now, in discussing this it was asked why the part touched should become unfit[9] and Rabbah b. Bar Hanah quoting R. Johanan replied: The reason is that a layman[10] would be scourged for eating an olive's bulk.[11] Surely this [36b] is because permitted food combines with forbidden?[12]—[R. Dimi] replied: No! [What R. Johanan means] by an olive's bulk is that an olive's bulk [of actual *terumah*][13] would be consumed during the time taken to eat a *peras*.[14] [Abaye objected:] Is then the time taken to eat a *peras* [reckoned] as a meal by the Torah?[15]—[R.

(1) So that even if the total bulk burnt is less than an olive, there is a penalty. V. Men. 58*a*. (2) Although not all the olive's bulk need be leaven. That leaven on passover is another exception we are expected to infer. (3) That what is permitted does not combine with what is forbidden. (4) The priestly heave-offering (v. Glos.). It had to be kept in ritual purity. (5) 'Profane food' i.e. not *terumah*. (6) And would become ritually pure after sunset. Although counted as clean for many purposes he could still defile *terumah*. (7) Including the garlic and the oil, which are regarded as though absorbed in the *terumah*. (8) Teb. Y. II, 3. (9) Seeing that *hullin* predominates. (10) A non-priest who is forbidden to eat *terumah*. (11) Thus the predominance of *hullin* does not take away the sacred character of the *terumah* contained in the mixture. (12) Seeing that scourging is the penalty for eating an olive's bulk of the mixture. (13) Not of the mixture. (14) *Lit.* 'piece', a piece of bread equal in size to four average eggs. This interval constitutes a single meal (Ker. III, 3). Since the quantity of *terumah* contained in the amount of stew eaten in this interval was an olive's bulk, there would be a penalty of scourging for a layman. [According to Maimonides, *Yad*, *Erubin* I, 9, *peras* is equal to three average 'eggs']. (15) So that stripes would be inflicted even if other food is taken in the same interval.

Dimi] replied: It is. Then, [Abaye asked], why do the Rabbis differ from R. Eleazar as regards Babylonian *kutaḥ?*[1] — [R. Dimi] replied: Let Babylonian *kutaḥ* alone,[2] since there is no olive's bulk [of leaven] consumed in the time it takes to eat a *peras*. For if a man does gulp down [a large quantity] at once, we disregard such a fancy as being quite exceptional,[3] whilst if one merely dips [other food] into it, you will not find an olive's bulk [of the leaven] consumed in the time taken to eat a *peras*.[4]

He [Abaye] raised objection against [R. Dimi's ruling from the following passage]. [It has been taught:] If two [spice] mortars, one containing *terumah* and the other *ḥullin* stood near two pots, one containing *terumah* and the other *ḥullin*, and [the contents of] the first pair fell into the other pair,[5] both [dishes] may be eaten,[6] for we assume that *ḥullin* fell into *ḥullin* and *terumah* into *terumah*. Now if it is a fact that the consumption of an olive's bulk within the time taken to eat a *peras* is [prohibited by] the Torah, why do we make this assumption?[7] — But if, [granting your view, replied R. Dimi] permitted and forbidden foods combine, how again could the assumption be justified?[8] The fact is that no argument can be based on the *terumah* of spices, [for its sanctity is the result] of a rabbinic enactment.[9]

(1) A preserve of sour milk, bread crusts and salt used as a source. R. Eleazar considered it to be prohibited on Passover by the Torah, so that its consumption entailed a penalty, whilst the Rabbis considered it to be forbidden only by rabbinic decree; v. Pes. 43*a*. (2) For if indeed permitted and forbidden foods combined, you would be still harder put to it to explain why the Rabbis would not consider it forbidden by the Torah-law! (So the text in Pes. 44*a*). (3) Because ordinary people do not use it as a food, his eccentric eating of it is not treated as eating to entail a penalty. (4) And so it is only forbidden by rabbinic decree. (5) Without it being known which was tipped into which. (6) I.e., the dish of *ḥullin* may still be eaten by a layman. (7) Since a mixture of *ṭerumah* and *ḥullin* would be forbidden in Torah-law, our doubt concerning the dishes should be resolved (as it always is in cases of Torah-law) in the stricter sense, and both declared *terumah*. (8) For then the doubt would certainly be concerned with Torah-law, so that both dishes should be forbidden. (4) The Torah does not require *terumah* to be separated from spices. Hence the doubt concerns only what is forbidden by the Rabbis and so is resolved in the more lenient sense.

He [Abaye] raised a [further] objection. [It has been taught:] If two baskets, one containing *terumah* and the other *ḥullin* stood near two vessels,¹ one of *terumah* and the other of *ḥullin* and the former pair were tipped into the latter, both are permitted, for we assume that *ḥullin* fell into *ḥullin* and *terumah* into *terumah*.² Now if it is a fact that an olive's bulk consumed within the time taken to eat a *peras* is [prohibited by] the Torah, how can we make such an assumption? [37a] On my view that what is permitted and what is forbidden combine [in general], this will offer no difficulty, for it may be taken for granted that *ḥullin* predominated;³ whereas on your view [that there is a prohibition whenever] an olive's bulk is consumed within the time taken to eat a *peras*, what difference would the predominance of *ḥullin* make?⁴—[R. Dimi] replied: Do not seek to argue from *terumah* at the present time, for [its sanctity] is rabbinic.⁵

Abaye asked [R. Dimi]: What ground is there for assuming that the purpose of the phrase 'soaked in'⁶ is to indicate that what is permitted and what is forbidden combine,⁷ for may not its purpose be to indicate that the taste is equivalent to the substance itself?⁸

(1) *Heb. Sa'in*, plural of *Sa'ah*, a large dry measure, here assumed to contain grain. (2) Tosef. Ter. VI, 15. (3) So that there would no longer be a Torah-prohibition, for the predominance of the *ḥullin* causes the *terumah* to lose its identity in Torah-law. This argument could not be used of spices since its flavour which permeates the whole dish is too strong to become neutralised. (4) For it is unlikely that the Baraitha is assuming that there was so little in the baskets that a *peras* of the mixed contents afterwards contained less than an olive's bulk of the contents of one of them. The Torah-doubt would therefore remain. (5) After the destruction of the Temple and the depopulation of Judea, many scriptural precepts, including the separation of tithes and *terumah* were still observed by the people, although not strictly binding on them in Torah-law. (6) V. *supra* p. 128, n. 6. (7) In the case of the nazirite prohibitions only, as asserted by R. Dimi quoting R. Johanan. V. *supra* 35a, end. (8) I.e., anything flavoured with a forbidden substance is equally forbidden, even as the forbidden substance itself. [That is, provided the forbidden substance consisted originally of the size of an olive. This requirement distinguishes Abaye's principle from the one reported by R. Dimi in virtue of which what is permitted combines with what is forbidden, even though the latter is less in size than an olive's bulk.]

(Is not this curious? First Abaye is perplexed by R. Dimi's statement[1] and points out all the above contradictions, and then he suggests that perhaps, after all, the flavour is equivalent to the substance![2]—After [R. Dimi] had answered him,[3] he went on to suggest that perhaps its purpose is to indicate that the taste is equivalent to the substance itself.)[4] For it has been taught: The phrase 'soaked in' makes the taste equivalent to the substance itself, so that if [the nazirite] soaked grapes in water and this acquired the taste of wine, there would be a penalty [for drinking it].[5] From this case, an inference may be drawn applicable to all prohibitions of the Torah. For seeing that in the case of the nazirite where the prohibition is not permanent,[6] where he is not forbidden to derive any benefit [from wine],[7] and where he may even have the prohibition removed,[8] the taste was declared to be equivalent to the substance, then in the case of mixed seeds in the vineyard[9] where the prohibition is permanent, where it is forbidden to derive any benefit from them, and where there is no way in which the prohibition can be removed it surely follows that the flavour is to be equivalent to the substance itself. The same argument applies to *'Orlah*[10] which has two [of these properties].[11]—[R. Dimi] replied:[12] The above represents the view of the Rabbis, whereas R. Abbahu, in making his statement [on behalf of R. Joḥanan],[13] was following the opinion of R. Akiba.

(1) And considers that the same should be true of all prohibitions, not merely the nazirite prohibition. (2) Thus rejecting the inference *in toto!* (3) All the questions he put to him. (4) The bracketed passage is an interjection. (5) And so why does not R. Joḥanan make the same inference as the author of this Baraitha? The rest of the paragraph contains the concluding portion of the Baraitha. (6) But lasts as long as the naziriteship, which may be as little as thirty days. (7) He may, for example, sell it. (8) By giving sufficient grounds for this to a Sage. (9) It was forbidden to sow grain between the vines, v. Deut. XXII, 9. (10) The fruit of a tree during its first three years after planting, v. Lev. XIX, 23. (11) The prohibition is permanent, and it is forbidden to derive any benefit from it, but after the 3rd year the fruit may be eaten.—This ends Abaye's argument. (12) [So *Var. lec.* Cur. edd.: 'A certain scholar said to him'.] (13) *Supra* 35*b*, that permitted and forbidden foods combine in the case of the nazirite prohibition.

To what [statement of] R. Akiba [does this refer]? Shall I say that it is the [dictum of] R. Akiba to be found here [in our Mishnah] where we learn: R. AKIBA SAID THAT THERE IS A PENALTY EVEN IF HE SOAKS HIS BREAD IN WINE AND ENOUGH [IS ABSORBED] TO COMBINE INTO AN OLIVE'S BULK;[1] But whence [do you know that the olive's bulk includes the bread eaten]?[2] May it not mean that the wine alone must be an olive's bulk! And should you object that the statement would then be obvious?[3] [To this we may reply] that its object is to indicate dissent from the opinion of the first Tanna[4] [that there is no penalty] unless he drinks a quarter [of a *log*] of wine! It must therefore be the [statement of] R. Akiba to be found in the following *Baraitha* where it is taught: R. Akiba said that a nazirite who soaks his bread in wine and eats an *olive's bulk of the bread and wine* is liable [to the penalty].

R. Aḥa, the son of R. Iwia, asked R. Ashi: Whence will R. Akiba, who interprets the phrase 'whatever is soaked in' as implying that permitted and forbidden foods combine, derive the rule that the taste is equivalent to the substance itself?[5]—He can derive it from [the prohibition of] meat and milk [seethed together],[6] for there is no more than the mere taste in that case[7] and yet it is forbidden, whence we may infer that the same is true here.[8] The Rabbis do not allow this inference to be made from meat and milk because it is an anomalous [prohibition].[9]

What constitutes its anomaly? Shall I say it is the fact that each constituent is permitted separately, while the combination is forbidden? Surely also in the case of mixed [seeds][10] each constituent is permitted separately and the combination is forbidden![11]—It is,

(1) *Supra* 34b. (2) To enable us to infer that permitted and forbidden foods combine. (3) In which case there would have been no point in having it in the Mishnah. (4) The Tanna of the 'earlier Mishnah' mentioned in our Mishnah. (5) It is assumed that R. Akiba admits this rule. (6) V. Ex. XXIII, 19. (7) Since the meat by itself is forbidden owing to the taste of the milk it absorbed. (8) I.e., that water having the taste of wine is forbidden the nazirite. (9) And so cannot be made the basis of a general rule. (10) The planting of mixed seeds in a vineyard, v. Deut. XXII, 9. (11) So that milk and meat are not unique in this respect.

therefore, the fact that if soaked in milk all day long, [the meat] remains permitted, and yet on seething it becomes forbidden.[1]

Must not R. Akiba, too, agree that [the seething together of] meat and milk is an anomalous [prohibition]?[2]—It must therefore be [37b] that he derives the rule from the [necessity for] scalding the vessels of a Gentile.[3] For the All-Merciful Law has said, *Everything that may abide the fire [ye shall make go through the fire etc.]*[4] telling us that they are [otherwise] forbidden. Now the scalding of a Gentile's vessels [must be done] because the mere taste is forbidden, and so here too, the same is true.

Then why should not the Rabbis also infer this rule from the scalding of a Gentile's vessels?—[Rab Ashi] replied: There [too] the prohibition is anomalous for everywhere else in the Torah whatever imparts a worsened flavour is permitted,[5] whereas in the case of the scalding of a Gentile's vessels a worsened [flavour][6] is forbidden.

Must not R. Akiba agree that this case is anomalous?[7]—R. Huna b. Ḥiyya replied: According to R. Akiba, the Torah only forbade utensils that had been used [by a gentile] on the same day, in which case the flavour is not detrimental.[8] And the Rabbis?—They considered that even with a pot that had been used on the same day it was impossible for the flavour not to be slightly detrimental.

R. Aḥa, the son of R. Iwia, said to R. Ashi: The Rabbis' opinion should throw a certain light on the views of R. Akiba. For the Rabbis say that [the phrase] 'whatever is soaked in' has as its object to indicate that the taste is equivalent to the substance itself, and [further] that a rule may be derived from this applicable

(1) Thus it is not the taste but the seething that is at the root of the prohibition. (2) From which no analogies can be drawn. (3) Before they can be used by Jews. (4) Referring to the vessels captured by the Jews during the campaign against Midian. Num. XXXI, 23. The scalding prescribed causes the sides of the vessel to exude forbidden flavours that may have been absorbed. (5) And consequently does not cause what is permitted to become forbidden. For the derivation of this rule v. A.Z. 67*b*. (6) Any flavour exuded from the sides of a cooking-utensil not properly scalded of course worsens the food. (7) And so how can it form the basis of our rule. (8) And we may properly infer that the flavour of a forbidden substance is forbidden.

to all prohibitions of the Torah. And so, ought not R. Akiba also, who interprets this same [phrase] 'whatever is soaked in' as implying that what is permitted combines with what is forbidden, infer [further] from it a rule applicable to all prohibitions of the Torah?[1]—[R. Ashi] replied: [He does not do so] because the nazirite and the sin-offering[2] are dealt with in two verses [of Scripture] from which the same inference[3] is possible, and whenever there are two verses from which the same inference is possible no other cases may be inferred.[4]

The nazirite [passage] is the one just explained.[5] What is [the inference from] sin-offering?—It has been taught: [The verse] *Whatsoever [food] shall touch the flesh thereof*[6] *shall be holy*[7] might be taken to imply that [it becomes holy] even if none [of the sin-offering] is absorbed by it.[8] Scripture [however] says the flesh *thereof*, [this indicates that it becomes sacred] only when it absorbs from its flesh;[9] *'it [then] shall be holy', [that is,* have the same degree of sanctity] as [the sin-offering] itself.[10] If the latter is ritually unfit [to be eaten][11] the other becomes unfit also, whilst if it is still permitted, the other is also permitted, only under the same conditions of stringency [as the sin-offering].[12]

(1) Whereas R. Joḥanan, who is following the opinion of R. Akiba, expressly confines the rule to nazirite prohibitions only; v. *supra* 35*b*. (2) This is explained immediately below. (3) Viz.: That a permitted and a forbidden substance combine. (4) Ordinarily a rule is derived from a single passage. If another passage occurs from which *exactly the same rule* would follow, it can only be because there is in fact no rule, and both the cases are exceptional; v. Sanh. (Sonc. ed.) p. 458, n. 9. (5) *Whatever is soaked in* ... Num. VI, 3. (6) I.e. of the sin-offering. (7) Lev. VI, 20. (8) The meaning is: It might have been taken as implying this if the word *flesh* had not been used. (9) In which case the permitted and forbidden foods have combined. R. Akiba's deduction now follows. [The text of cur. edd. is difficult. A better reading is preserved in the Sifra a.l. 'till it absorbs', omitting the words, 'into its flesh.] (10) The sin-offering could be eaten only 'by the males of the priesthood, within the hanging of the court, the same day and evening until midnight'. (M. Zeb. V, 3; Singer's *P.B.* p. 12). For other meats there were other, often less stringent regulations. (Ibid.). (11) E.g. because it is after midnight. (12) See note 10.

What can the Rabbis [say to this argument]?[1]—They will contend that both verses are necessary.[2] For if the All-Merciful had inscribed only the verse relating to the sin-offering it would have been said that we have no right to infer from it the case of the nazirite, for we could not infer anything about the nazirite from [regulations applying to] sacrificial meats.[3] Again, had the All-Merciful inscribed only the verse relating to the nazirite, it could have been argued that no rule can be derived from the nazirite, since the prohibitions in his case are very severe indeed for he is forbidden even the skin of the grape. On this ground we should have been able to infer nothing. [Thus both verses are necessary.]

What is R. Akiba's reply [to this argument]?—He will reply that both verses are certainly not necessary. Granted that had the All-Merciful inscribed only the verse relating to the sin-offering, we could not have deduced the case of the nazirite because what is profane cannot be inferred from [regulations applying] to sacrificial meats,[4] yet the All-Merciful could have inscribed only the verse relating to the nazirite, and the case of the sin-offering could have been deduced from this, since [in any case] all other prohibitions of the Torah are inferred from the nazirite prohibition.[5] And the Rabbis?—They [can] reply that while the [verse relating to] sin-offering [tells us] that permitted and forbidden foods combine, we cannot infer from [regulations applying to] sacrificial meats any rule concerning profane food,[6] [whereas] when the phrase

(1) If the verses relating to nazirite and sin-offering both lead to the same inference how do they establish their rule about taste and substance? (2) I.e. That it is in fact impossible to infer the rule from either one of the passages taken alone, since its presence would have been put down to other properties of the sin-offering or the nazirite, which are really irrelevant as far as the rule is concerned. (3) Since no rule about profane things can be inferred from sacred ones. This is a general principle. (4) So that the inference that could be drawn from the sin-offering is admittedly not *exactly* the same as that drawn from the nazirite prohibitions. (5) By the Rabbis. For no mention of the sin-offering is made in the Baraitha (*supra* 37a). Thus this verse would be altogether superfluous, and the principle of 'two verses from which the same inference can be drawn' can be applied. (6) And so this principle is confined to sacred meats.

'whatever is soaked in' tells us that the taste is equivalent to the substance itself, a rule is inferred from this applicable to all prohibitions of the Torah. And R. Akiba?—He considers that both verses are intended to tell us that what is permitted combines with what is forbidden, so that these are two verses from which the same inference can be made, and when two verses occur from which the same inference can be made, no other cases may be inferred.[1]

R. Ashi said to R. Kahana: How are we to explain the following, where it is taught: '[The verse] *Nothing that is made of the grape-vine, from the pressed grapes even to the grape-stone,*[2] teaches that the things forbidden to a nazirite can combine together'?[3] For seeing that it is possible, according to R. Akiba, for what is permitted to combine with what is forbidden, need we be told that the same is true of two species of forbidden substances?—[R. Kahana] replied: What is permitted [combines with] what is forbidden only [if they are eaten] together, whereas two species of forbidden substances combine even [if eaten] consecutively.

Now R. Simeon [38*a*] does not require the principle of combination.[4] What interpretation does he put on the verse, '*Nothing that is made etc.*'?—He requires it for the rule that one cannot become a nazirite without undertaking explicitly to abstain from all the things [that are forbidden a nazirite].[5]

R. Abbahu, quoting R. Eleazar, said: In none of the instances in the Torah requiring a quarter [of a *log*][6] does what is permitted combine with what is forbidden, with the exception of the quarter [of a *log*] of the nazirite, where the Torah uses the phrase 'soaked in'.[7] What is the difference between R. Johanan[8] and R. Eleazar? —It is that the former includes solid foods,[9] the latter liquids only but no other things.

(1) And that is why R. Akiba confines the principle to the nazirite prohibitions. (2) Num. VI, 4. (3) So that provided an olive's bulk is consumed there is a penalty, even if the quantity of each constituent is less than this. (4) Because in his opinion there is a penalty even for a minute quantity of any *one* of the things forbidden the nazirite. V. *supra* 4*a*. (5) *Supra* 3*b*. (6) E.g., The quarter-*log* of blood that spreads defilement throughout a tent; Cf. *infra* 54*a*. (7) Num. VI, 3. (8) Who uses the term 'all the prohibitions of the Torah' instead of 'all quarters (of a *log*) in the Torah'. *Supra* 35*b*. (9) In the scope of the application of the principle.

R. Eleazar said that there are ten quarters [of a *log*][1] and R. Kahana knew for a fact[2] that five [involved] red [liquids][3] and five white.[4] For the five red ones [there is the following mnemonic]:[5] A nazirite and a celebrant of the passover who delivered judgment in the sanctuary and died. 'A nazirite' indicates the quarter [*log*] of wine [entailing a penalty] for the nazirite [who drinks it].[6] 'A celebrant of the passover' refers to the following dictum quoted by Rab Judah on behalf of Samuel viz:—Each of these four cups[7] should contain sufficient [undiluted wine] to make a quarter of a *log* [of diluted wine].[8] 'Who delivered judgment' [refers to the law that] one who has partaken of a quarter of a *log* of wine must not render a decision.[9] 'In the sanctuary' [refers to the law that a priest] who drinks a quarter of a *log* of wine and then enters the sanctuary renders himself liable to death-penalty.[10] 'And they died' [indicates the following teaching]: For it has been taught, whence do we infer that a quarter of a *log* of blood taken from two corpses renders unclean the contents of a tent? Because it is said, *Neither shall he go to any dead body.*[11]

The five white [fluids are indicated in the following mnemonic]: The cake of a nazirite or a leper who were disqualified on the Sabbath. 'The cake' [signifies] the quarter of a *log* of oil for the cake;[12] 'of a nazirite', the quarter of a *log* of oil [that must be brought] by a nazirite;[13] 'or a leper,' the quarter of a *log* of water [that must be used] for a leper.[14] 'Disqualified' [indicates] what

(1) In ten instances the quantity of fluid required by the Law is a quarter of a *log*. (2) Lit., 'held in his hand'. (3) Wine or blood. (4) Water or oil. (5) Each term of the mnemonic indicates one of the instances. (6) Mishnah *supra* 34*b* (7) That must be partaken of at the passover meal; v. Pes. X, 1. (8) Wine was usually diluted with three parts of water, v. Pes. 108*b*. (9) Inferred from the juxtaposition of the forbidding of wine to priests about to enter the sanctuary (Lev. X, 9) and the statement that a priest's duty is to '*teach* (lit., 'render decisions for') the children of Israel'. (Ibid. V, 11). (10) M. Ker. III, 3, inferred from Lev. X, 9. (11) Lev. XXI, 11. Heb. '*nafshoth*' in the plural, and so two or more corpses, v. Sanh. 4*a*. (12) I.e., the unleavened portion of the thank-offering, which required half of what was brought for the whole thank-offering. V. Lev. VII, 12 and Men. 89*a* (Tosaf). (13) Num. VI, 15. (14) Lev. XIV, 5.

we have learnt: Other ritually defiled liquids render the body unfit[1] if a quarter of a *log* [is partaken of].[2] 'On the Sabbath' [indicates] what we have learnt: For all other liquids [the legal quantity][3] is a quarter of a *log*, and for all waste liquids [the legal quantity] is a quarter of a *log*.

But is there no instance other than [the ten mentioned, requiring a quarter of a *log*?] There is surely the case: 'With a quarter [of a *log* of water] the hands of one person, and even of two may be washed [before food]'![4]—Disputed cases are not included.[5]

But we have [also the following case]: He brought an earthenware phial and poured into it half a *log* of water from the laver.[6] According to R. Judah it was only a quarter of a *log*'?[7]—Disputed cases are not included.

But we have [also the following]: 'How much water must be poured [into the chamber-pot]?[8] As little as one pleases. R. Zakkai said: It must be a quarter of a *log*'.[9]—Disputed cases are not included.

But there is also the ritual-bath?[10]—[There are ten cases] besides this one, for the Rabbis [subsequently] disallowed this quantity.[11]

[38*b*] WHILST THERE IS NO PENALTY UNLESS HE EATS AN OLIVE'S BULK OF GRAPES etc.:] The first Tanna[12] does not put all the things forbidden a nazirite on the same footing as drinking,[13] whereas R. Akiba, because of the verse *Nor eat fresh grapes nor*

(1) I.e., ritually unclean. (2) V. Me'il. 17*b*. [There the reading is 'all liquids'. Our text is difficult to explain; cf. Bertinoro on Miḳ. X, 7.] (3) The removal of which from a public to a private domain carries with it a penalty for breach of the Sabbath. (4) Yad. I, 1. (5) This is not a unanimous opinion, R. Jose contending that each person requires a quarter of a *log* (ibid.). (6) The Mishnah is describing the preparation of the 'bitter waters' to be drunk by a faithless wife. V. Lev. V, 17. (7) Sotah II, 2. (8) To enable one to say one's prayers in the same room. (9) Ber. 25*b*. (10) A ritual-bath containing a quarter of a *log* might be used for dipping small vessels such as needles to remove ritual defilement; v. Pes. 17*b*. (11) And enacted that only a full-size ritual-bath containing 40 *seahs* was to be used even for needles. V. Ḥag. 21*b*. (12) I.e. the 'earlier Mishnah' of our text, which prescribes a different legal quantity for drinking (viz.: a quarter of a *log*) than for eating. (13) And so in other cases an olive's bulk entails a penalty. Thus the first Tanna makes no use of the arguments of R. Akiba given later at all.

dried,[1] says that just as in eating an olive's bulk [entails a penalty], so for all the prohibitions[2] an olive's bulk [is sufficient to entail a penalty].

THERE IS A SEPARATE PENALTY FOR WINE etc. Our Rabbis taught: [The verse,] *'Nor eat fresh grapes nor dried'* indicates that there is a penalty for [eating] the one by itself, and a penalty for [eating] the other by itself.[3] From here a rule may be derived applicable to all prohibitions of the Torah.[4] Just as here where we have a single species [grapes] known by two different names [fresh and dried], each entails a distinct penalty, so wherever we find a single species known by two different names, each entails a penalty distinct from the other. In this way, new wine and grapes are included.[5]

Abaye said: For eating pressed-grapes [the nazirite] is scourged twice;[6] For eating grape-stones he is scourged twice; for eating both pressed-grapes and grape-stones he is scourged three times.

Raba[7] said: He is scourged once only [in the first two cases] since we do not scourge for [breach of] the prohibition expressed in general terms.

R. Papa raised an objection: [It is taught] R. Eleazar said that a nazirite who drank wine all day long would be scourged once only. If, however, he was warned, 'Do not drink', and again 'Do not drink', [and so on], there would be a penalty for each [warning]. If he ate fresh grapes, dried grapes, pressed-grapes, grape-stones, and squeezed a cluster of grapes and drank [the liquor] he would be scourged five times.[8] Now if [Abaye is right] he should

(1) Num. VI, 3, the first half of which is the prohibition against drinking. (2) Including drinking. (3) So that in eating both together there will be a double penalty. (4) Tosaf. has the preferable reading 'all prohibitions of the nazirite'. (5) Although the first can be obtained simply by squeezing the second, a nazirite who partakes of both is scourged twice. (6) The general prohibition contained in the verse, *'He shall eat nothing that is made of the grape-vine'* is held by Abaye to add one scourging to the total number entailed by eating forbidden substances. (7) In Pes. 41*b*, where this controversy also oc curs, the names are interchanged, Raba's appearing before the statement here attributed to Abaye. V. D.S. *a.l* (8) Tosef. Naz. IV, 1. (Here there is a variation based on the Mishnah *infra* 42*a*).

be scourged six times, including once on account of '*He shall eat nothing* [*that is made of the grape-vine*]'?—[Abaye replied:] He mentioned some and omitted others.[1] But what other [count] is omitted, that the one referred to[2] should have been omitted?[3]—He omitted, *He shall not break his word.*[4] Had this last, however, been the only one, it would not have been considered an omission,[5] [as it could be argued that R. Eleazar] mentioned only [those prohibitions] that are not found elsewhere, whereas this one is found in connection with ordinary vows too.[6]

Rabina of Paraziḳia[7] said to R. Ashi: But he has in any case omitted the intermediate portion of the grape![8]—But said R. Papa[9] [in reply to the various arguments advanced]: Five is not actually mentioned [in the Baraitha].[10] But [R. Papa] [39*a*] quoted the passage in contradiction [of Abaye] because of the five [scourgings], and if five is not mentioned in it, why did he quote it as a contradiction?—R. Papa said [to himself]: I imagined that [Abaye's opinion] was not a tradition [he had received], and so he would retract [on hearing my quotation], for I did not know that it was a tradition and that he would not retract.[11]

R. ELEAZAR B. AZARIAH SAID etc.: R. Joseph said: In agreement

(1) I e. 'five' does not represent the total number of counts, but there are five scourgings in addition to others on counts not mentioned. (2) Viz., The general prohibition '*He shall eat nothing etc.*' (3) It is assumed that the Tanna would not ordinarily omit one count only. (4) Num. XXX, 3. There would be stripes for breach of this injunction also. (5) And so its omission cannot be used as a counter argument against Raba (Tosaf). *Aliter* 'This is not an omission at all, for R. Eleazar etc.' so that the original contradiction remains. (6) There is thus a good reason for its omission, and so no objection to its being the only one omitted. (Tosaf.) (7) [Or Paraziḳa, Farausag, near Bagdad, Obermeyer, p. 269. *Var. lec.* Raba of Paraziḳia, v. B.B. (Sonc. ed.) p. 15.] (8) The pulp, which entails a separate penalty, (v. *supra*, 34*b* near end). This would be present in the squeezed cluster, so that there should be six counts apart from the other two. (9) [*Var. lec.* Rabina; cf. n. 7.] (10) The correct reading is '. . . he would be scourged on each count', so that both Abaye and Raba can interpret it to suit their opinions. Incidentally the objection of Rabina of Paraziḳia is also disposed of. (11) Instead he tried to explain away the Baraitha as quoted, and so R. Papa explained that there was in fact no contradiction.

with whom is the rendering in the Targum[1] as *'from the kernels even unto the skins'*?[2] — In agreement with the opinion of R. Jose.[3]

MISHNAH. A NAZIRITESHIP OF UNSPECIFIED DURATION LASTS THIRTY DAYS.[4] SHOULD [THE NAZIRITE] POLL HIMSELF OR BE POLLED BY BANDITS,[5] THIRTY DAYS ARE RENDERED VOID.[6] A NAZIRITE WHO POLLS HIMSELF, NO MATTER WHETHER HE USES A SCISSORS OR A RAZOR, OR WHO TRIMS [HIS HAIR] HOWEVER LITTLE, INCURS A PENALTY.

GEMARA. [The Academy] wished to know whether the growth of the hair takes place at the roots or at the tips.[7] [The knowledge] is of importance for the case of a nazirite polled by bandits who left enough [of each hair] for the end to be curled in towards the root.[8] If [the hair] grows at the roots the consecrated part has been removed,[9] but if it grows at the tips, then the part he consecrated is still there.[10]

Judge from the live nit found at the root of a strand [of hair], for if it were true that the growth is at the root ought it not to be found at the tip?[11] — The growth may well be at the tip, but the nit, being alive, continually moves down [towards the root].

Judge[12] from a dead nit [that is found] at the end of a strand [of

(1) V. Targum Onkelos on Num. VI, 4. (2) Instead of *from the 'pressed-grapes (skins) even to the grape-stone* as our versions have. (3) V. Our Mishnah. (4) This statement is repeated here (from *supra* 5*a*) to explain the rule of the next sentence. (5) Before bringing his sacrifices. (6) So that he should have a nazirite's poll when his sacrifices are offered and the vow terminated. (7) I.e., Does the growth of the hair result from new portions emerging from beneath the scalp, so that the part at first in contact with the scalp is afterwards found at a distance from it; or does this part remain where it is, and the growth take place in the visible part of the hair? (8) I.e., a seven-days growth, v. *infra* 39*b*. (9) And so this nazirite would have to observe a further thirty days as enjoined in the Mishnah. (10) And he may proceed to bring his sacrifices and poll in the ordinary manner. In this argument it is taken for granted that a nazirite consecrates the hair on his head at the time of his vow. (11) Assuming that the nit stays on the same point of the strand all the time. (12) Lit., 'come and hear'.

hair], for if it were true that the growth takes place at the end, ought it not to be found near the root?—There again [it may well be] because it has no power [to grasp the hair][1] that it slides more and more along it.

Judge from the pigtails of heathens[2] that loosen near the root after growing [for some time]![3]—There too, [it may well be] because of its being creased by his lying on it that it grows loose.[4]

Judge from the *sekarta*[5] for the wool grows fresh again underneath [the marking], and this is something which we learned [in a Mishnah];[6] further when old men dye their beards, these grow white again [39*b*] at the roots.[7] From this we can justly infer that hair increases at the roots. This proves it.

But it has been taught [as follows]: A nazirite polled by bandits who left sufficient [of each hair] for the end to be curled inwards towards the root is not required to render void [his naziriteship].[8] Now if it is true that the hair grows from beneath, why should he not render it void?—It is here assumed that they polled him after the termination [of his naziriteship], and the author is R Eliezer in whose opinion whatever happens after the termination of the naziriteship renders void only seven days,[9] his reason being that he applies the same rule to polling in ritual purity[10] as to polling after defilement. Just as in polling after defilement seven days become void,[11] so in polling in ritual purity seven days are to be-

(1) Now that it is dead. (2) [Heb. *belorith* (etym. obscure), a heathen fashion of growing locks from the crown of the head hanging down in plaits at the back; v. Krauss, *TA* I, 645.] (3) So that new hair must have appeared near the roots. (4) And not because new hair has grown. (5) A red paint with which the tenth animals were marked during tithing, v. Bek. IX, 7 (58*a*). (6) The Mishnah (Bek. IX, 7) would not have suggested marking with *sekarta* if the markings were to become hidden shortly afterwards by a new growth. Mishnaic verification is always preferable to a mere argument. (7) So that the same is true of human hair as of sheep's wool. (8) But may proceed to bring his sacrifices and poll in the ordinary manner. (9) This view is stated in connection with a nazirite who contracted defilement after the termination of his period. V. *supra*. Mishnah and Gemara 16*a*. (10) I.e. polling *after the termination of the vow* in ritual purity. Before the termination, in both cases thirty days become void according to R. Eliezer; Ibid. (11) Viz.: the seven days during which he is unclean.

come void; and the Rabbis knew for a fact that every seven days enough hair grows for the tip to be curled inwards towards the root.[1]

A NAZIRITE WHO POLLS HIMSELF, NO MATTER WHETHER HE USES A RAZOR OR A SCISSORS,[2] OR WHO TRIMS [HIS HAIR] HOWEVER LITTLE INCURS A PENALTY: Our Rabbis taught: [From the word] *razor,*[3] I only know [that he is forbidden to use] a razor. How do I know that if he pulls [his hair] out, or plucks it [with tweezers] or trims it however little [he is equally culpable]? The verse continues, *He shall be holy, and shall let the locks of the hair of his head grow long.*[4] The above is the opinion of R. Josiah, whereas R. Jonathan said that *'razor'* implies razor only, and if he plucks [his hair] or pulls it out, or trims it but a little there is no penalty.[5] But it says, *He shall be holy etc.?*[6]—This is to tell us that if he removes it with a razor, he has transgressed both a positive and a negative precept.[7]

Another [Baraitha] taught: 'Razor' tells me only [that he is forbidden to use] a razor. How do I know that if he pulls out [his hair], or plucks it, or trims it but a little [he is equally culpable]? The verse reads, *[A razor] shall not come upon his head.*[8] Now seeing that we are finally [intended] to include all means [of removing the hair], why are we told that A razor *shall not come upon his head?* This is because we should not otherwise be able to infer that the final polling must be done with a razor.[9] For it is impossible to derive

(1) So that if this amount was already left by the bandits, he need not wait at all. (2) In the Mishnah the order is, 'scissors or razor'. (3) '*There shall no razor come upon his head*' (Num. VI, 5)—of the nazirite. (4) Indicating that the objection is to removing the hair and not simply to the use of a razor, as the means of removing it. (5) It is not even forbidden to do this according to R. Jonathan (v. Tosaf.). (6) Implying at least that it is forbidden to remove his hair by any means, even if there is no penalty (see previous note). (7) I.e., the implication is also a razor only, the prohibition of its use being merely strengthened. (8) Interpreted, omitting the first word *'razor'*, as 'he shall not remove (the hair) of his head'. (9) At the termination of the naziriteship; v. Num. VI, 18, where the instrument to be used for polling is not mentioned, and so we infer it from the mention of the razor earlier in the passage.

this from the leper[1] [40a], since we could not argue to the less stringent[2] from the more stringent[3] and impose [on the former] greater stringency.[4] Rabbi said: This argument is unnecessary.[5] For the text [can be] read, *A razor shall not come upon his head until [the days of his naziriteship] are fulfilled,*[6] so that the Torah says explicitly that after fulfilment, polling is to be carried out only with a razor.

But it [also] says, *A razor shall not come upon his head?*[7]—This is to provide for a penalty on two counts.[8]

R. Ḥisda said that stripes are incurred by [removing] one hair; [the completion of his naziriteship] is held up if two hairs [remain];[9] [the naziriteship] does not become void unless the greater part of his hair is removed by a razor.

[Are we to understand that] a razor only [is meant by R. Ḥisda] but no other method? Is it not taught 'How do we know that all other methods of removing [the hair are equally forbidden] etc.'? —You must therefore say [in R. Ḥisda's dictum] 'removed as though by a razor.'[10]

Likewise has it been taught: A nazirite who pulls out [his hair], or plucks it, or trims it but a little [incurs a penalty, but he][11] does not render void [the previous period] unless [he shaves] the greater part of his head with a razor.[12] R. Simeon b. Judah in the name of R. Simeon said: Just as two hairs [if they are left] hold up [the termination of the naziriteship], so also [the removal of] two hairs renders void [the previous period].[13]

(1) Who is also required to poll; v. Lev. XIV, 8-9. (2) The nazirite who polls only his head. (3) The leper who must shave his wholy body. (4) Requiring a razor to be used, because the leper uses a razor. It might well be that a nazirite could use any means for removing his hair. (5) Viz.: The argument that because the word razor is *superfluous* in v. 5, polling in v. 18 means with a razor. (6) By altering the punctuation in v. 5, which concludes '*Until the days of his naziriteship are fulfilled he is holy to the Lord*'. (7) Implying equally that a razor only is forbidden during the naziriteship. (8) There is a penalty for removing the hair, and a second penalty if a razor is used during the naziriteship. (9) The polling is invalidated thereby, and the procedure at the termination cannot continue as long as these remain. (10) I.e. close to the scalp. (11) Added from the Tosef. agreeing with the reading of the various commentators. (12) Thus the Baraitha agrees with R. Ḥisda. (13) Tosef. Naz. IV, 2.

We learn elsewhere: There are three who must poll, and whose polling is a religious duty,the nazirite, the leper, and the levites.[1] If any one of them polled without a razor, or left behind two hairs, his act is invalid.[2]

The Master said, 'There are three who must poll and whose polling is a religious duty.' Surely this is obvious?[3] It might have been thought that they are simply required to remove their hair, and even smearing it with *nasha*[4] [is valid] and so we are told that this is not so.[5]

It is [also] stated, 'If any one of them polled without a razor etc.' Now we can grant this in the case of a nazirite where there is written, *There shall no razor come upon his head,*[6] and of the levites where there is written, *And let them cause a razor to pass over all their flesh,*[7] but how do we know that a leper must use a razor? Should you reply that this can be inferred from the levites [by the following argument, viz.] The levites require to poll, and the polling must be performed with a razor, and so I will infer of the leper who is required to poll that the polling must be performed with a razor; [your argument] can be refuted. For although it is true of the levites [that they must use a razor, this may be] because they had to be offered as a wave-offering,[8] which is not the case with the leper. You will therefore attempt to infer it from the nazirite.[9] But [it may be asked] although it is true of the nazirite, [this may be] because his sacrifice must be accompanied by cakes,[10] whereas a leper's does not require this. It being thus impossible to infer what is required from one by itself, you will try to infer it from both together in the following way. You will infer it [using the above

(1) When first appointed to office the levites had to poll. V. Num. VIII, 7. (2) Neg. XIV, 4. (3) For in each case there is a verse requiring them to poll. (4) Or *nesa,* a plant the sap of which was used as a depilatory. [Others regard it as a poisonous drug. Krauss, *op. cit.* I, 642, takes *nasa* as a variant of *nasam* mentioned in Neg. X, 10.] (5) But that a razor is essential. (6) Num. VI, 5. From this it is inferred that only a razor may be used at the final polling. V. *supra.* (7) Num. VIII, 7. (8) V. Num. VIII, 11. To refute an argument of the above kind, it is sufficient to show some difference however trivial between the procedure to be followed in both cases. (9) By an argument similar in the above. (10) V. Num. VI, 15.

argument] from the levites. [To the objection] that although it is true of the levites [this may be] because they had to be offered as a wave-offering, [you will reply that] the nazirite will show [that this cannot be the reason].[1] [To the objection that] although it is true of the nazirite [this may be] because his sacrifice must be accompanied by cakes, [you will reply that] the levites show [that this cannot be the reason].[2] The argument thus goes round; what applies to one side does not apply to the other; and what applies to the other side does not apply to the one side. What they have in common is that they both require to poll[3] and this polling must be done with a razor, and so I will infer with regard to the leper[4] who is also required to poll that his polling must be done with a razor.

Said Raba of Barnesh[5] to R. Ashi: But can it not be objected that another common property of [the levites and the nazirite] is [40b] that their sacrifice could not be offered in poverty,[6] whereas the sacrifice of a leper could be offered in poverty?[7]

Raba b. Mesharsheya said to Raba: This Tanna first asserts that [the rule of the nazirite] could not be deduced from that of the leper[8] because we must not argue to the less stringent from the more stringent in order to impose on it the same stringency, and then he goes on to say that [the case of the leper itself] should be inferred by argument,[9] whereas in fact we are not able to infer it

(1) For a nazirite was not required to be offered as a wave-offering yet had to use a razor. (2) For although the same was not true of the levites, yet they had to use a razor. (3) And it must be this common property that determines the other common property, viz.: that a razor must be used. (4) Lit., 'add to them the leper . . .' (5) [Near Matha Meḥasia, a suburb of Sura; Obermeyer *op. cit.* p. 297]. (6) A nazirite or a levite who could not afford the necessary sacrifices was given no alternative but had to wait until he could do so. (7) For a leper who was poor, special sacrifices of doves were permitted (v. Lev. XIV, 21ff.). Hence the leper is less stringent than either of the others, and so should perhaps not be obliged to use a razor for his ritual shaving. (8) Thus assuming that a leper certainly has to use a razor (v. *supra* 39*b* end). Raba b. Mesharsheya is here taking it for granted that the two Baraithas to which he makes reference form a single text. (9) For the gathering together of the three cases, nazirite, leper, and levites, into a single Baraitha is an indication that the case that is not explicit is deducible from those that are.

from any argument![1]—[Raba] replied: The former discussion is based on the view of the Rabbis,[2] the latter on that of R. Eliezer,[3] for we have learnt:[4] Whilst there is no penalty[5] unless he plucks out [the hair] with a razor. R. Eliezer said that even if he plucks it with tweezers or with a *rohitni*[6] he incurs a penalty.[7]

What is the reason of the Rabbis?[8] It has been taught: Why does Scripture mention his *beard?*[9] Because we find elsewhere[10] the verse, *Neither shall they shave off the corners of their beards,*[11] it might be thought that this applies even to [a priest who is] a leper. We are therefore told [that the leper must shave] *'his beard'.*[12] Whence [do we know] that he must use a razor?—It has been taught: [The verse,] *Neither shall they shave off the corners of their beards*[13] could mean that even if they shaved it with scissors there would be a penalty, and so we are told [elsewhere], *Neither shalt thou* mar [*the corners of thy beard*].[14] [This last verse alone] could mean that even if he plucks it out with tweezers or a *rohitni* there is a penalty, and so we are told, *Neither shall they shave the corners of their beards.* How [do we make the inferences from these verses]? The kind of shaving that also mars [the beard] is with a razor.[15]

But how does it follow?[16] For may it not well be that even if [the

(1) Since the argument from the levites or the nazirite fails completely. Even to an argument from the common properties there is the objection of Raba of Barnesh. How then, Raba b. Mesharshaya asks, is the sequence of the two Baraithas to be explained? (2) Who do in fact deduce that a leper must use a razor from an independent source. V. *infra.* (3) Who deduces that a leper must use a razor from the nazirite obligation to do so. V. *infra* 41*a*. (4) This Mishnah is quoted simply in order to show the existence of a controversy between R. Eliezer and the Rabbis, the Baraithas adduced to expound the sources of the controversy being anonymous. (5) For rounding the corners of the head. (6) *Rohitni*, usually a plane, here appears to mean some instrument for removing single hairs, since it is compared to a tweezers. V. Jastrow s.v. (7) Mak. 20*a*. (8) I.e., what is their source for the case of the leper? (9) In Lev. XIV, 9, of the leper, for we already know that he must shave *'all his hair'.* (10) Of the priests. (11) Lev. XXI, 5. (12) Even if he is a priest. (13) Lev. XXI, 5. (14) Of ordinary Israelites, not priests. Here the word '*mar*' is used and a scissors does not 'mar'. (15) And since what is forbidden the ordinary person is prescribed for the leper, as is inferred in the previous Baraitha, a leper can, nay *must*, use a razor. (16) That he *must* use the razor.

leper] uses tweezers or a *rohitni* he has carried out his religious duty, the purpose of the verse[1] being to tell us that even if he uses a razor there is no penalty?—I will explain. If you assume that even if he uses tweezers or a *rohitni* he has carried out his religious duty, the verse should have remained silent on the subject[2] and I should have argued as follows. Seeing that a nazirite, who has done what is forbidden,[3] is nevertheless obliged [to use a razor], then [the leper] who is here doing a religious duty[4] should certainly [be allowed to use a razor]. [41*a*] Moreover, should you assume that if he uses tweezers or a *rohitni* he has carried out his religious duty, then because a razor is not mentioned explicitly [it should be entirely forbidden][5] in accordance with the dictum of Resh Laḳish who has said that wherever we find both a positive command and a prohibition[6] then, if it is possible to observe both[7] well and good, otherwise the positive command is to override the prohibition.[8]

And what is R. Eliezer's reason?[9]—It has been taught: Why does Scripture mention *'his head'?*[10]—Since it says in connection with the nazirite, *There shall no razor come upon his head*[11] it might be thought that this is true even of a nazirite who becomes a leper. We are therefore told that [the leper must shave] his head.[12]

(1) Which says that the leper must *shave*, and also that he must shave his beard, and not simply that he must remove the hair. (2) Not using the word '*shave*'. (3) By becoming defiled; *aliter*, by becoming a nazirite at all, in accordance with the opinion of R. Eleazar ha-Ḳappar, v. *supra* 19*a*. (4) He was not responsible for his leprosy, so that the act of purification is purely a religious duty, not an expiation. (5) I.e., even if the word '*shave*' had been used without the additional use of the expression 'his *beard*' we should not have made the inference that he is allowed to use a razor because of the dictum of Resh Laḳish now given. (6) I.e., a command to do something (e.g., the leper is told to shave his beard) forbidden under certain circumstances. (7) I.e., carry out the positive command without transgressing the other. (8) The positive command must be fulfilled at all costs. (9) I.e., what is his source for the law that a leper must use a razor, since he holds that the prohibition of marring his beard applies to all instruments, there is no proof that a leper is *obliged* to use a razor. (10) Of a leper, seeing it has already said he must shave all his hair. Lev. XIV, 9. (11) Num. VI, 5. (12) And we see also that it must be with a razor, since it is this that is explicitly forbidden the nazirite.

How does it follow?[1] May it not well be that even if he uses tweezers or a *rohitni* he has carried out his religious duty? And should you object that the razor should not have been mentioned,[2] [the answer would be that] this tells us that [the leper] may use even a razor; for I might have thought that because a nazirite who uses a razor[3] incurs a penalty, so does a leper[4] who uses a razor incur a penalty, and so we are told that this is not so?[5]—If you assume that a leper who uses tweezers or a *rohitni* has carried out his religious duty, then because a razor is not mentioned explicitly [in his case, it should be forbidden entirely], in accordance with the dictum of Resh Lakish.[6]

What interpretation do the Rabbis put on [the mention of] *'his head'?*[7]—They require it to override the prohibition against rounding [the corners of the head], as it has been taught: [The verse] *Ye shall not round the corners of your heads*[8] might mean that the same is true of a leper, and we are therefore told [that he must shave] *'his head'*.

But this[9] can be deduced from [the mention of] *'his beard'*. For it has been taught: Why does Scripture mentions *his beard?* Since it says, *Neither shall they shave off the corners of their beards,*[10] it might be thought that even [a priest who is] a leper may not do so. And we are therefore told [that the leper must shave] *'his beard'*. Now why should it be necessary to mention both *'his head'* and *'his beard'?*[11]—It is necessary. For had the All-Merciful mentioned *'his beard'* and not *'his head'* it might have been thought that the rounding of the whole head is not considered [as infringing the prohibition against] rounding,[12] and so the All-Merciful Law also

(1) That he is *obliged* to use the razor. (2) In Num. VI, 5, in connection with the nazirite, seeing that all things are forbidden him. (3) During his naziriteship. (4) [Who is also a nazirite.] (5) But there is still no proof that he *must* use a razor. (6) V. *supra* p. 149. (7) Since they already know that a leper may use a razor. (8) Which applies to all persons. Lev. XIX, 27. (9) Viz. the fact that the injunction to the leper to shave overrides any prohibition that might otherwise prevent him from so doing. (10) Lev. XXI, 5; of the priests. (11) Seeing that either case could be inferred from the other. (12) I.e., that shaving the head is permitted even to an ordinary person, only the rounding of the corners without the rest of the head being forbidden because it was a

mentions *'his head'*.[1] [41*b*] Again, had *'his head'* been mentioned and not *'his beard'* I would have understood that two things are implied, first that the positive command [to shave] overrides the prohibition, and secondly that the rounding of the whole head is considered [to infringe the prohibition against] rounding, but there would still remain [the question], how do we know that a razor must be used?[2] And so the All-Merciful Law mentions *his beard*.[3]

And whence does R. Eliezer learn that a positive command overrides a prohibition?—He infers it from the [command to wear] twisted cords. For it has been taught: *Thou shalt not wear a mingled stuff, [linen and wool together]*;[4] [42*a*] but nevertheless, *Thou shalt make thee twisted cords of them*.[5]

The Master said: 'If any one of them polled without a razor, or left behind two hairs, his act is invalid.'[6] R. Aḥa the son of R. Iḳa said: This implies that Torah-law accepts [the principle that] the majority[7] counts as the whole.[8] In what way [does this follow]? —From the fact that the All-Merciful reveals in the case of the nazirite that, *On the seventh day he shall shave it*,[9] [for we infer that] here only [is his duty unfulfilled] until the whole [has been shaved],[10] whilst elsewhere the majority counts as the whole.

R. Jose son of R. Ḥanina demurred to this: But this [verse] is speaking of a defiled nazirite?[11]

heathen practice. Whether this is in fact the case is discussed *infra* 57*b*-58, both sides of the question receiving arguments in its favour.

(1) Enabling us to infer that even the shaving of the whole head is also forbidden an ordinary person. (2) For there the expression *'rounding'* is used, and in fact 'rounding' is forbidden even if no razor is used. (3) In this case the expression is *'shave'* which has been shown (*supra* 40*b*) to imply the use of a razor. (4) Deut. XXII, 11. The next quotation is the beginning of the next verse. (5) From the juxtaposition of the two laws it is inferred that the second is to be carried out even at the cost of transgressing the first. A further discussion of this point will be found *infra* (58*a-b*). (6) *Supra* 40*a*. (7) Or the larger portion. (6) I.e., is legally equivalent to the whole. (9) Num. VI, 9. This sentence is a superfluous repetition of the previous one, *'He shall shave his head on the day of his cleansing'*, and is therefore taken as indicating that the whole head must be shaved (10) Because here we have a special indication that the larger portion is insufficient (11) Whereas according to the Baraitha, even a clean nazirite who leaves two hairs standing has not shaved effectively.

In the West[1] they laughed at this [objection]. Consider, [they said]. That a defiled nazirite is required to use a razor [in shaving his head] is inferred from a ritually pure nazirite.[2] [It stands to reason then that] we can now infer the rule of the ritually pure nazirite from the defiled nazirite, viz. that just as when the latter leaves two hairs standing his act is invalid, so when the former leaves two hairs standing his act is invalid.

Abaye propounded [the following question]: What [would be the Law] if a nazirite shaved and left two hairs standing, and then when his head showed a new growth shaved off [those two hairs], would this hold up [the termination of the naziriteship] or not?

Raba propounded [the following question]: What [would be the law] if a nazirite shaved, leaving two hairs standing,[3] and then shaved one and one fell out?[4]

R. Aḥa of Difti[5] asked Rabina: Has Raba any doubt in the case where hair is shaved one at a time?[6]—[He replied], We must say then, [the question arises if] one fell out and he shaved the other.[7]

He then replied:[8] Here is no polling, for here is no hair.

But if there is no hair here, then polling has been performed?[9] —The meaning is: Although there is no hair left, the duty to poll has not been validly observed.[10]

MISHNAH. A NAZIRITE MAY SHAMPOO [HIS HAIR] AND PART IT [WITH HIS FINGERS] BUT MAY NOT COMB IT.[11]

(1) I.e., the Palestinian Academies. [The reference elsewhere is to R. Jose b. Ḥanina. Here it may be to R. Eleazar. V. Sanh. 17*b*.] (2) The razor mentioned in Num. VI, 5, refers to an undefiled nazirite. (3) So that the polling is invalid and must be repeated on the remaining two hairs. (4) So that he had not polled two hairs validly. (5) [Dibtha below the Tigris, S.E. Babylon, Obermeyer, *op. cit.* 197.] (6) There would finally remain two as in the present instance, and the polling of one would, R. Aḥa assumes, certainly complete the polling. (7) Thus when he commenced the final polling, there were not two hairs left, but one. (8) I.e., Raba answered his own problem (v. the parallel text in B.Ḳ. 105*a*). (9) For he is only required to poll what is actually there. (10) Since there were not two hairs when he started. He should therefore poll again later (v. Asheri and Maimonides, *Yad Neziruth*, VIII, 7); Rashi, here, does not require him to poll again. (11) I.e., may not use a comb, because hair will come out.

GEMARA. HE MAY SHAMPOO [HIS HAIR] AND PART IT [WITH HIS FINGERS]. Who is the author of this opinion?—It is R. Simeon who says a breach of the law which is not intended is allowed.[1] BUT HE MAY NOT COMB IT; here we come round to the opinion of the Rabbis.[2] [Are we then to understand that] the first clause is by R. Simeon and the next one by the Rabbis?—Rabbah replied: The whole is by R. Simeon, [for] a man who combs his hair intends to remove loose strands.[3]

MISHNAH. R. ISHMAEL SAID: HE IS NOT TO CLEANSE IT WITH EARTH BECAUSE IT CAUSES THE HAIR TO FALL OUT.

GEMARA. The Academy wished to know whether we read 'because *it* causes the hair to fall out,' or 'because of [the kinds of earth that] cause the hair to fall out.' Where would a practical difference arise? In the case where there is a variety of earth that does not cause it to fall out. If you say that we read 'because *it* causes it to fall out,' then wherever we know that it does not cause it to fall out, it could be used. But if you say 'because of [the kinds of earth that] cause it to fall out' that he may not use any kind at all! This was left undecided.

MISHNAH. A NAZIRITE WHO HAS DRUNK WINE ALL DAY LONG HAS INCURRED A SINGLE PENALTY ONLY. IF HE WAS TOLD 'DO NOT DRINK,' 'DO NOT DRINK' AND HE DRANK,[4] HE HAS INCURRED A PENALTY FOR EACH [WARNING].

FOR POLLING ALL DAY LONG HE INCURS ONE PENALTY ONLY. IF HE WAS TOLD, 'DO NOT POLL,' 'DO NOT POLL' AND HE DID POLL,[4] HE HAS INCURRED A PENALTY FOR EACH [WARNING].

(1) Provided that the act he is doing is permitted, he is not made to refrain because he may unintentionally also do something forbidden (v. Shab. 50*b*). So here, although hairs may detach themselves even if he uses only his fingers, we do not forbid him to use them. (2) For here too it is not his intention to detach hairs. (3) And this is forbidden. (4) After each warning.

FOR DEFILING HIMSELF [BY CONTACT] WITH THE DEAD ALL DAY LONG HE INCURS ONE PENALTY ONLY. IF HE WAS TOLD, 'DO NOT DEFILE YOURSELF,' 'DO NOT DEFILE YOURSELF,' AND HE DID DEFILE HIMSELF,[1] HE HAS INCURRED A PENALTY FOR EACH [WARNING].

GEMARA. [42b] It was stated: Rabbah, citing R. Huna, said: Scripture [speaking of the nazirite] makes the comprehensive statement, *He shall not make himself unclean;*[2] when it adds, *He shall not enter* [*by a dead body*],[3] [its intention is] to utter a [separate] warning against defilement [by contact] and a [separate] warning against entering [a tent],[4] but not against defilement [by contact] from two scources [at the same time].[5] R. Joseph, however, said: By God! R. Huna said that even for defilement [by contact] from two sources [at the same time there are separate penalties]. For R. Huna has said that a nazirite, standing in a cemetery, who was handed the corpse of his own [relative] or some other corpse, and touched it incurs a penalty.[6] Now why should this be so? Is he not actually being defiled all the time?[7] It follows therefore that R. Huna must have said that even for defilement [by contact] from two sources [he is to receive separate penalties].

Abaye raised an objection from the following. [A Baraitha teaches:] 'A priest,[8] carrying a corpse on his back, who was handed the corpse of his own [relative] or some other corpse and touched it, might be thought to have incurred a penalty,[9] but the text says, *Nor profane* [*the sanctuary*][10] [prescribing a penalty] for one not already profaned [and thus] excluding this man who is already

(1) After each warning. (2) Num. VI, 7. (3) E.v. *'come near to'*, Num. V, 6. (4) Containing a dead body. So that a nazirite, duly warned, who enters a covered place containing a corpse and actually touches the corpse is scourged twice. (5) I.e., for touching two corpses at the same time he is scourged only once, even if warned against each separately. (6) I.e., a penalty for touching the corpse. (7) By being in the cemetery. (8) Some versions (including Tosaf. and Asheri) read 'a nazirite'. (9) I.e., a further penalty for the second contact. (10) Of the High Priest. Lev. XXI, 12; so our text. Tosaf. and others read the verse, 'to profane himself' (Ibid. 4) spoken of an ordinary priest. In either case it is presumed that the same is true of the nazirite.

profaned?[1]—[R. Joseph] replied: But our Mishnah should cause you the same perplexity, for we learn [there], FOR DEFILING HIMSELF [BY CONTACT] WITH THE DEAD ALL DAY LONG HE INCURS ONE PENALTY ONLY. IF HE WAS TOLD, 'DO NOT DEFILE YOURSELF,' 'DO NOT DEFILE YOURSELF,' AND HE DID DEFILE HIMSELF, HE HAS INCURRED A PENALTY FOR EACH [WARNING]. But why should this be so? Is he not already defiled? We can therefore only conclude that [the Mishnah and the Baraitha] contradict each other.[2]

[Abaye retorted:] There is no difficulty [in reconciling the Mishnah and the Baraitha]. The latter assumes that there is concatenation,[3] the former that there is no concatenation.

Is then defilement through concatenation a Torah enactment? Has not R. Isaac b. Joseph said: R. Jannai said that defilement through concatenation was held to be effective only as it affects *terumah* and sacrificial meats,[4] but not the nazirite or a celebrant of the passover?[5] Now, if as you assert, it is a Torah [defilement], why should there be this difference?[6]—There concatenation of one man with another is meant;[7] in our case concatenation of the man with the corpse.[8]

'But not against defilement [by contact] from two sources [at the same time,'[9] said Rabbah] because he is actually defiled already. But in the case of defilement [by contact] and entering [a

(1) Whereas according to R. Joseph there should be an extra penalty. Hence the contradiction. (2) And I, says R. Joseph, agree with the Mishnah which is more important. (3) I.e., that the person and the two corpses are in contact at the same time, and that is why there is no extra penalty. Where there is contact at different times there is an additional penalty. (4) I.e., a person defiled through concatenation (in what way is explained below) is forbidden to eat *terumah* (v. Glos.) or sacrificial meats for seven days, as though there had been direct contact with the corpse. (5) These observe defilement for one day only. (6) Hence concatenation is not a Torah enactment, and why should there be the difference between the Mishnah and the Baraitha. (7) I.e., a man touching a second man in contact with a corpse. Here the defilement for seven days instead of one is rabbinic. (8) If he then touches a second corpse there is no further defilement and so no further penalty. (9) The Torah does not prescribe two scourgings in such a case, v. *supra*.

tent containing a corpse] is he not also already defiled?[1]—R. Joḥanan replied: In the latter case [he is supposed to enter] a house [whilst undefiled];[2] in the former, [which takes place] in the open [there cannot be two penalties].[3]

[43a] But even [on entering] a house, as soon as his hands are inside he becomes unclean,[4] so that when he has gone right in he is already unclean?[5]—As a matter of fact, said R. Eleazar, if he put his hands together and entered there would be [a penalty only] for defilement but none for entering, but if he drew himself up[6] and entered, defilement and entering occur at the same moment.

But it is impossible for his nose not to go in first?—As a matter of fact, said Raba, if he introduces his hand[7] there would be [a penalty] for defilement and not for entering, but if he introduces his body,[8] defilement and entering are simultaneous.

But it is impossible for his toes not to enter first?—R. Papa therefore said: It is supposed that he entered in a box, or a chest, or a turret,[9] and his fellow came and broke away the covering,[10] so that defilement and entering are simultaneous. Mar b. R. Ashi said: It is supposed that he entered whilst the other lay dying,[11] and whilst he was sitting there the spirit departed so that defilement and entering were simultaneous.

Our Rabbis taught: *To profane himself*[12] signifies that until the

(1) Why then does Rabbah say that he is to receive two scourgings in this case? (2) So that he both enters the house of the dead and becomes defiled at the same instant. Hence both prohibitions are transgressed together. (3) Because he becomes unclean by the first contact and then no further penalty can lie for contact or entering a tent of the dead. (4) Defilement is supposed to pervade the whole of the interior of a house containing a corpse, and so any organ introduced has touched the source of defilement. (5) And thus even with a house there can be no additional penalty for entering. (6) I.e., kept his hands at his sides. (7) Or any other organ. Asheri reads here 'head'. (8) Keeping his head and arms well back. (9) Being in a separate domain he would not then become unclean. (10) Making the interior of the box part of the interior of the tent. [It is assumed that he too helped in the removal of the covering, or otherwise he would incur no penalty (Asheri)]. (11) [As a priest he had no right to enter a house where a person lay dying, v. *infra* (Asheri)]. (12) Spoken of the priests in connection with the prohibition against defiling themselves with the dead other than near kin, Lev. XXI, 4.

time that the other dies [he is permitted to remain with him].[1] Rabbi said that, *When they die*[2] signifies that he may be in contact with them until they die.

What is the difference between these two [alternative reasons]?[3] —R. Johanan said that they differ only as to the texts selected.[4] Resh Lakish said: They differ as regards the rule for a dying man. The one who takes the text *'To profane himself'* considers a dying man [as profanation],[5] whilst the one who takes, *'When they die'*, says that [there is no prohibition] until he is dead, and so none in the case of one who is dying.

Now, according to the one who derives [the law] from *'to profane himself'*, is there not the text, *'When they die'?*[6]—He requires this for [the following inference] of Rabbi. For it has been taught: Rabbi said that *'When they die'* he is forbidden to defile himself, but he may defile himself [by association with them] when they are suffering from leprosy[7] or an issue.[8]

But does not the one who derives [the law] from *'when they die'* also require it for this inference?—If this is [its sole purpose], the text should read 'When dead'. Because it says *'When they die'* we infer both things.

Now according to the one who derives [the law] from *'When they die'*, is there not the verse, *'to profane himself'?*[9]—*'To profane himself'* signifies the following, viz:—that one who is not profaned [incurs a penalty] but not the one who is already profaned.[10]

But does not the one who derives [the law] from *'to profane himself'* also require it for this inference?—If this were its sole purpose, the text should read 'to profane'. Because it reads, *'to profane himself'* we infer both things.

(1) I.e., only the actual profanation is forbidden. (2) Spoken of the nazirite prohibition against defilement even with near kin. Num. VI, 7. (3) I.e., what difference in law results. (4) Lit., 'the implications of the phrases in need of interpretation'. There is no practical difference. (5) For most people who are dying do die and so actual defilement is very probable. The risk therefore counts as profanation. (6) What is his interpretation of the latter verse? (7) V. Lev. XIII, 1ff. (8) Gonorrhoea, v. Lev. XV, 1ff. (9) What is his interpretation of it? (10) Cf. *supra* 42b.

An objection was raised. [We have learnt:] A man does not spread defilement until his life departs. Not even one whose arteries are severed or who is in the throes of death does so.[1] Now according to the one who bases the rule on '*to profane himself*',[2] does it not say here that they do not spread defilement?[3] —Defilement is not spread until the life departs, but there is profanation already.[4]

[43*b*] R. Ḥisda, citing Rab, said: [A priest] if his father was decapitated, must not defile himself for him, For what reason? The text says *for his father*,[5] meaning when he is whole and not when he is defective.[6] R. Hamnuna said to him: In that case, suppose [the father] were travelling through the valley of 'Araboth[7] and robbers cut off his head, would you also maintain that [the son] is not to defile himself for him?[8] —He replied: You raise the question of a *meth miẓwah!*[9] Seeing that we consider it his duty [to defile himself under such circumstances] to strangers,[9] how much more so is this true of his father!

But is this considered a *meth miẓwah?* Has it not been taught: A *meth miẓwah* is [a corpse] with none to bury him. Were he able to call and others answer him,[10] he is not a *meth miẓwah;*[11] and here this man has a son?[12] —Because they are travelling on the road, it is as though he had none to bury him.

An objection was raised [from the following]: [It has been taught,] *For her may he defile himself*[13] signifies that he may defile

---

(1) Oh. I, 6. (2) To include a dying man as profanation, as the Rabbis interpret this verse in the opinion of Resh Laḳish. (3) Contradicting Resh Laḳish. (4) A priest is accordingly forbidden to come in contact with the dying. (5) Although the priest is forbidden to defile himself for the dead yet he may defile himself for near relatives such as his father, Lev. XXI, 2. (6) If the head is severed from the body, even though it is beside it, the corpse is considered defective. (7) A valley in Babylonia, notorious for its robber bands. (Jast.). (8) R. Hamnuna assumes rightly that R. Ḥisda would not deny this. (9) A corpse whose burial is a religious duty, v. Glos. *Infra* 44*a*. (10) I.e., if he has relatives to provide for his burial. (11) And a priest must not defile himself by undertaking his burial. (12) Who could arrange for other people to bury his father. If, then, he is allowed to do so himself it must be because decapitation does not matter; which contradicts R. Ḥisda. (13) Of the spinster sister of a priest, Lev. XXI, 3.

himself for her herself but not for one of her limbs; for he may not defile himself for a limb cut off [even] from his father[1] whilst still alive; but he may search for a bone the size of a barleycorn.[2] Now what means 'he may search for a bone the size of a barleycorn'? Surely that if there is a small part missing [he may nevertheless defile himself]?[3]—No. The author of that statement is R. Judah. For it has been taught: R. Judah said that he may defile himself for her, but not for her limbs; for he is forbidden to defile himself for limbs severed from his father whilst still alive; but he may defile himself for limbs severed from his father after death.

But R. Kahana taught amongst [the Baraithas of] R. Eliezer b. Jacob [the following one]: *'For her may he defile himself,'* but he must not defile himself for limbs, thus excluding an olive's bulk of [the flesh of] a corpse, or an olive's bulk of *neẓel,*[4] or a spoonful of *raḳab.*[4] It might be thought that he is also forbidden to defile himself for the spinal column, or the skull, or the greater part of the bodily frame [of his sister's corpse][5] or the majority [of its bones],[5] but since it is written, *and say unto them,*[6] it follows that Scripture has permitted you an additional defilement. [44a] It might be thought [further] that he is not to defile himself for the spinal column, or the skull, or the greater part of the bodily frame or the majority of the bones of the other [relations],[7] but I will tell you [why that is not so]. His sister is distinguished [from strangers] by the fact that her body depends on him [for its burial], and he is required to defile himself for the spinal column, or the skull, or the greater part of its bodily frame or the majority [of its bones], and so in all cases where the body depends on him [for burial], he is required to defile himself, for its spinal column, or its skull, or the

(1) Who is a closer relation. (2) I.e., if he is engaged in burying his father he may search for any parts missing to restore them to the corpse. (3) And since no other opinion is mentioned, it is to be presumed that no-one disagrees with the statement; and thus R. Ḥisda is contradicted. (4) V. Mishnah *infra* 49b. (5) Each of these counts as a whole corpse for the purposes of defilement in a tent. (6) Lev. XXI, 1. The phrase is superfluous, for the verse begins, *Speak unto the priests* .... (7) Mentioned in the verse before the one dealing with his spinster sister.

greater part of its bodily frame, or the majority [of its bones]. [This contradicts Rab, does it not?][1]—The author of this [Baraitha] too is R. Judah, whereas Rab agrees with the following Tanna. For it has been taught: The story is told that the father of R. Isaac [the priest][2] died at Ginzaḳ[3] and he was informed three years later. He went and asked R. Joshua b. Elisha and the four Elders with him,[4] and they replied: *For his father*[5] when he is whole, but not when he is defective.[6]

MISHNAH. THREE THINGS ARE FORBIDDEN THE NAZIRITE, VIZ:—DEFILEMENT, POLLING AND PRODUCTS OF THE VINE. DEFILEMENT AND POLLING HAVE A STRINGENCY NOT POSSESSED BY PRODUCTS OF THE VINE IN THAT DEFILEMENT AND POLLING RENDER VOID [THE PREVIOUS PERIOD], WHEREAS [PARTAKING OF] PRODUCTS OF THE VINE DOES NOT DO SO. PRODUCTS OF THE VINE HAVE A STRINGENCY NOT POSSESSED BY DEFILEMENT OR POLLING IN THAT PRODUCTS OF THE VINE PERMIT OF NO EXCEPTION FROM THE GENERAL PROHIBITION,[7] WHEREAS DEFILEMENT AND POLLING ARE ALLOWED AS EXCEPTION FROM THE GENERAL PROHIBITION IN THE CASE WHERE POLLING IS A RELIGIOUS DUTY,[8] OR WHERE THERE IS A METH MIẒWAH[9]. DEFILEMENT ALSO HAS

(1) For according to this Baraitha, too, he is permitted to defile himself for a part of the body, in contradiction to the statement made by R. Ḥisda in the name of Rab. The Baraithas of R. Eliezer b. Jacob were highly esteemed and that is why this one is quoted, although the reply may seem obvious. It would now be necessary to show some other Baraitha agrees with Rab. (2) *Var. lec.* R. Zadok the priest. [V. Tem. XII. Hyman, *Toledoth*, I, p. 202 gives preference to our text, since R. Zadok was present at his father's death.] (3) [Ganzaḳa, N.W. of Persia; v. A.Z. (Sonc. ed.) p. 165, n. 5.] (4) Whether he might personally arrange his removal to the family sepulchre (Rashi). (5) Lev. XXI, 2. (6) After three years he would undoubtedly be defective. Thus this Baraitha agrees with Rab. (7) I.e. under no circumstances is a nazirite ever permitted to drink wine. (8) As when a nazirite becomes a leper and then recovers from the disease. (9) A corpse without relatives to provide for its burial must be buried by the first person who can do so, be he nazirite, priest, or even High Priest; cf. *infra* 47a *seq*.

A STRINGENCY NOT POSSESSED BY POLLING, IN THAT DEFILEMENT RENDERS VOID THE WHOLE OF THE PRECEDING PERIOD,[1] AND ENTAILS THE OFFERING OF A SACRIFICE, WHEREAS POLLING RENDERS VOID ONLY THIRTY DAYS AND DOES NOT ENTAIL A SACRIFICE.

GEMARA. Why should not defilement also permit of no exception from the general prohibition, in virtue of the following *a fortiori* argument from wine? Seeing that wine which does not render void [the previous period] permits of no exception from the general prohibition, then defilement which does render void [the previous period] should certainly not permit of an exception from the general prohibition?—The text says, *Nor defile himself for his father or for his mother,*[2] signifying that it is only for his father or for his mother that he is forbidden to defile himself, whereas he is required to defile himself for a *meth mizwah*.

Then why should not wine permit of an exception from the general prohibition because of the following *a fortiori* argument from defilement? Seeing that defilement, which renders void [the previous period], permits of an exception from the general prohibition, then wine which does not render void [the previous period] should certainly permit of an exception from the general prohibition?—The verse says, *He shall abstain from wine and strong drink,*[3] thus forbidding wine that should be drunk as a ritual obligation[4] as well as wine that he might drink from choice.[5]

Then why should not wine render void the whole [of the previous period] because of the following *a fortiori* argument from defilement? Seeing that defilement which permits of an exception from the general prohibition renders void [the previous period], then wine which permits of no exception should certainly render void [the preceding period]?—The verse says, *But the former days shall*

(1) However long it should be. (2) Lev. XXI, 11; although referring to the High Priest, the same applies to the nazirite. (3) Num. VI, 3; wine is mentioned specifically to tell us that it is to permit of no exception. (4) E.g. if the person had sworn to drink wine before becoming a nazirite, he must not do so notwithstanding. (5) Cf. *supra* 3b.

be void because his consecration was defiled,[1] signifying that defilement renders void, but wine does not do so.

Why should not polling render void the whole [of the previous period][2] because of the following *a fortiori* argument from defilement? Seeing that defilement, the agent of which is not subjected to the same [penalty] as the patient,[3] renders void the whole [of the previous period], then polling where the agent is subject to the same penalty as the patient,[4] should certainly render void the whole [of the preceding period]?—The verse says, *But the former days shall be void because his consecration was defiled*[5] signifying that defilement renders void the whole [of the preceding period], but polling does not do so.

Why should not the agent be subject to the same [penalty] as the patient in the case of defilement, because of the following *a fortiori* argument from polling? Seeing that in the case of polling, where only thirty days are rendered void, the agent is subject to the same [penalty] as the patient, then in the case of defilement where the whole [of the preceding period] is rendered void, the agent should certainly be subject to the same [penalty] as the patient?—The verse says, *And he defile* his *consecrated head*[6] signifying [that the penalty is only] for him who defiles his [own] consecrated head.

Then polling should not result in the agent being subject to the same [penalty] as the patient, because of the following *a fortiori* argument from defilement. Seeing that in the case of defilement, where the whole [of the preceding period] is rendered void, the agent is not subject to the same [penalty] as the patient, then in the case of polling, which does not render void the whole [of the preceding period], the agent should certainly not be subject to the same [penalty] as the patient?—The verse says, *There shall no razor come upon his head,*[7] and can be read as signifying that he shall not make it come himself, and that no other shall make it come either.[8]

(1) Num. VI, 12. (2) Instead of only thirty days. (3) There is no penalty attached to one who defiles a nazirite. (4) Both are scourged, v. *infra.* (5) Num. VI, 12. (6) Ibid. 9. (7) Ibid. 5. (8) The verb is written defectively and may therefore be read as an active mood instead of a passive one. There is now

Polling should not permit of an exception from the general prohibition because of the following *a fortiori* argument from wine. Seeing that wine which does not render void [the preceding period] permits of no exception from the general prohibition, then polling which does render void [the preceding period] should certainly permit of no exception?—The All-Merciful mentions both his hair and his beard.[1]

Then polling should not render void any [of the preceding period] because of the following *a fortiori* argument from wine. Seeing that wine which permits of no exception does not render void, polling which does permit of an exception from the general prohibition should certainly not render void?—We require a sufficient growth of hair and this would be lacking.[2]

Why should not wine render void thirty days because of the following *a fortiori* argument from polling? Seeing that polling, which permits of an exception from the general prohibition, renders void [thirty days], then wine which permits of no exception from the general prohibition should certainly do so?—Is not the only reason[3] because there must be a sufficient growth of hair? After wine his hair is still intact.[4]

MISHNAH. [44b] HOW WAS [THE RITE OF] THE POLLING AFTER DEFILEMENT [PERFORMED]? HE WOULD BE SPRINKLED ON THE THIRD AND SEVENTH DAYS,[5] POLL ON THE SEVENTH DAY AND BRING HIS SACRIFICES ON THE EIGHTH DAY. IF HE

no agent mentioned who 'causes it to come upon his head' and so whoever uses the razor on the nazirite is also a transgressor. [This follows Rashi's reading. Asheri seems to have had a smoother text which simply took '*razor*' as subject of '*come upon his head*', thus making no distinction as to who passes the razor over the nazirite.]

(1) In Lev. XIV, 9, whence is derived that the leprous nazirite must poll, v. *supra* 41a. (2) After he had once polled illegitimately. Hence he must render thirty days void, before terminating the naziriteship. (3) Why polling renders void thirty days. (4) And so there is no point in requiring him to render any period void. (5) After defilement, with water mixed with ashes of the red heifer, v. Num. XIX.

POLLED ON THE EIGHTH DAY,[1] HE WOULD BRING HIS SACRIFICES ON THAT SAME DAY. THIS IS THE OPINION OF R. AKIBA. R. TARFON ASKED HIM: WHAT DIFFERENCE IS THERE BETWEEN THIS [NAZIRITE] AND A LEPER?[2] HE REPLIED: THE PURIFICATION OF THIS MAN DEPENDS ON THE [LAPSE OF SEVEN] DAYS [ONLY], WHEREAS THE PURIFICATION OF A LEPER DEPENDS [ALSO] ON HIS POLLING,[3] AND HE CANNOT BRING A SACRIFICE UNLESS THE SUN HAS SET UPON HIM [AFTER HIS RITUAL BATH].[4]

GEMARA. Did [R. Tarfon] accept this answer or not?[5]—Come and hear: Hillel[6] learnt: If [the nazirite] polled on the eighth day, he was to bring his sacrifices on the ninth. Now if you assume that he accepted the answer, should he not bring his sacrifices on the eighth day?[7]—Raba said: This creates no difficulty,[8] for the one

(1) Instead of the seventh. (2) A leper who polled on the eighth day instead of the seventh was required to wait until the ninth day before offering his sacrifices. [V. Sifra on Lev. XIV, 9, where this, R. Akiba's view in the case of the leper is stated. According to some texts, however, R. Akiba is of the opinion that the leper could bring his sacrifices on the same day (v. Malbim, a.l.). On this reading, adopted by Rashi, Maimonides, and others, the Mishnah is to be interpreted thus: SAID R. TARFON TO HIM, IF SO WHAT IS THE DIFFERENCE BETWEEN THE NAZIRITE AND THE LEPER (SINCE BOTH ARE IN THIS RESPECT ALIKE). HE REPLIED, (THEY DIFFER IN THIS:) THE PURIFICATION OF THIS MAN DEPENDS ON THE LAPSE OF SEVEN DAYS (ONLY)—i.e., he becomes clean on the seventh day even if he did not poll—WHEREAS THE PURIFICATION OF A LEPER DEPENDS ALSO ON HIS POLLING (v. n. 6); AND (THERE IS A FURTHER DIFFERENCE IN THAT A NAZIRITE) DOES NOT BRING A SACRIFICE UNLESS THE SUN HAS SET UPON HIM (AFTER HIS RITUAL BATH)—i.e., whenever he immersed whether on the seventh or eighth day, he brings the sacrifice only on the *following* day, whereas the leper who immersed on the eighth day may bring the sacrifice on the *same* day, since he has been declared by the Torah clean as a result of the first polling and immersion, v. Lev. XIV, 8.] (3) He does not take a ritual bath until after the polling (Lev. XIV, 8); the nazirite took it before. (4) Until evening he is a *ṭebul yom* (v. Glos.) and so cannot bring sacrifices. (5) I.e., does he now agree with R. Akiba, or does he still contend that the nazirite who polls on the eighth day must wait like the leper until the ninth before bringing his sacrifices? (6) The Amora of that name; not the Patriarch Hillel. (7) So that unless R. Tarfon still disagreed with R. Akiba there would be no author for this Baraitha of Hillel. (8) Even if R. Tarfon agreed with R. Akiba.

case[1] assumes that he bathed on the seventh day, and the other[2] that he did not bathe on the seventh day.[3]

Abaye said: I came across the colleagues of R. Nathan b. Hoshaia, seated [at their studies] and reporting the following [teaching]. [Scripture says,] *And come before the Lord unto the door of the tent of meeting and give them unto the priest.*[4] When is he to come?[5] If he has bathed and waited until after sunset he may [come], but if he has not bathed and waited until after sunset he may not do so. Thus we see [they said] that [this Tanna] is of the opinion that a *ṭebul yom*[6] after gonorrhoea is still like a sufferer from gonorrhoea.[7] I [Abaye] then said to them: If that is so,[8] then in the case of a defiled nazirite where we find the verse, *He shall bring two turtle doves . . . to the priest to the door of the tent of meeting*[9] [we should also say] that he is to come only if he has bathed and waited until after sunset.[10] [45*a*] Now where were the Gates of Nicanor[11] situated? At the entrance to [the camp of] the Levites[12] [were they not]? And

(1) That of the Mishnah which permits him to offer his sacrifices on the eighth day. (2) The Baraitha which compels him to wait until the ninth day. (3) And could not bring sacrifices before sunset on the day he bathed (the eighth day), and so had to wait until the ninth day. (4) Lev. XV, 14. Referring to the sacrifices of one who has recovered from an unclean issue. V. 13 requires him to bathe on the seventh day after the cessation of the issue. (5) I.e., when is he permitted to enter the Temple precincts again? (6) V. Glos. (7) And so could not enter the Temple mount to give his sacrifices to the priest. Further, on the Eve of Passover it would be forbidden to slaughter a Paschal lamb on his behalf and he would have to wait until the second Passover (v. Ker. 10*a*). (8) I.e., if the reason just given is in fact the Tanna's reason for requiring him to wait until after sunset. (9) Num. VI, 10. In this context, too, the previous verse requires him to bathe first. (10) And so a nazirite after defilement should also be forbidden to enter the temple mount in just the same way as one who has recovered from gonorrhoea is forbidden to do so. (11) It was to the Gates of Nicanor, which separated the Women's Court from the rest of the Temple precincts, that the sacrifices were brought. [The Nicanor Gate was situated on the West of the Women's Court, and was an entrance to the Inner Court. For a full discussion of the apparent discrepancies between the Talmudic sources and Josephus on the situation of the Nicanor Gate, v. Buchler, *JQR*, 1898, 687ff, and Hollis, F. J., *The Archaeology of Herod's Temple*, pp. 180ff.] (12) The division of the encampment of the Israelites in the wilderness into three camps of varying degrees of sanctity, viz.: (i) The Camp of Israel, (ii) The Camp of the

yet it has been taught: One who is defiled by a corpse is allowed to enter the camp of the Levites; and not merely one defiled by a corpse, but even the corpse itself [may enter there], for it says, *And Moses took the bones of Joseph with him;*[1] the meaning of *with him* is 'in his own section', i.e. in the camp of the Levites.[2] It must therefore be,[3] said Abaye, that a *ṭebul yom* after gonorrhoea is not like a sufferer from gonorrhoea,[4] but in spite of this, because he still lacks atonement, he is not to enter [into the Temple precincts].[5] For seeing that the reference is to the Camp of the Levites,[6] why is it called [in the verse], *'the Tent of Meeting'?* To tell us that just as one who lacks atonement might not enter there,[7] so one who lacks atonement may not enter the Camp of the Levites.[8]

Levites, (iii) The Camp of the Divine Presence, was transferred to the Temple at Jerusalem, the three divisions being known by the same names (v. Sifre Num. I, 1).

(1) Ex. XIII, 19. (2) Thus the nazirite even before purification could enter the Camp of the Levites, which makes the above deduction after the fashion of the colleagues of R. Nathan b. Hoshaya absurd. (V. Tosef. Kelim Ḳamma, I, 7.) (3) What follows is the text and version of Tosaf. That of Rashi is given below, note 8. (4) And might have a Paschal lamb slaughtered on his behalf. (5) I.e., he is forbidden to enter the Camp of the Levites to give his sacrifices to the priest, not because he is treated as though he were still suffering from the issue, but because he is lacking in atonement, i.e., has not yet offered the necessary sacrifices. And although, in general, a person lacking in atonement was not forbidden to enter the Camp of the Levites, but only the Camp of the Divine Presence, here for the reason to be given immediately entry even into the Camp of the Levites is forbidden until after sunset. (6) For the sacrifices had only to be taken as far as the Gates of Nicanor in the Camp of the Levites. (7) The proof is given below. (8) Whereas the nazirite is not considered lacking in atonement since his defilement arose from external causes (contact with the dead) and not from internal ones (leprosy or issue). Thus far the version of Tosaf. Rashi reads as follows: '(The colleagues of R. Nathan replied): As a matter of fact, a *ṭebul yom* after gonorrhoea does count as a sufferer from gonorrhoea, whilst even in the case you mention (of the nazirite) he should not enter (the Camp of the Levites, although a corpse itself might do so) because he lacks atonement. For if it is only the Camp of the Levites that is in question (i.e., if in any case the defiled nazirite can enter the Camp of the Levites and has to penetrate no further), why is it referred to in the verse as '*the Tent of Meeting*' (which is part of the Camp of the Divine Presence)? To tell us that just as one who lacks atonement may not enter (the latter place), so he may

How is it known in that case?[1]—It has been taught: *He shall be unclean,*[2] includes also a *ṭebul yom; his uncleanness is yet upon him*[3] includes also one who lacks atonement.

MISHNAH. HOW WAS [THE RITE OF] POLLING IN RITUAL PURITY[4] PERFORMED? HE WOULD BRING THREE ANIMALS, A SIN-OFFERING, A BURNT-OFFERING, AND A PEACE-OFFERING, SLAUGHTER THE PEACE-OFFERING AND POLL THEREAFTER. THIS IS THE OPINION OF R. JUDAH. R. ELEAZAR SAID: HE WOULD POLL ACTUALLY AFTER THE SIN-OFFERING, FOR IN ALL CASES [THE SACRIFICE OF] THE SIN-OFFERING TAKES PRECEDENCE.[5] BUT IF HE POLLED AFTER [THE SLAUGHTER] OF ANY ONE OF THE THREE HIS OBLIGATION WOULD BE DISCHARGED.[6]

R. SIMEON B. GAMALIEL SAID: IF HE BROUGHT THREE ANIMALS WITHOUT SPECIFYING [WHAT THEY WERE FOR],[7] THE ONE SUITABLE FOR A SIN-OFFERING[8] WAS TO BE SACRIFICED AS A SIN-OFFERING, FOR A BURNT-OFFERING[9] AS A BURNT-OFFERING, AND FOR A PEACE-OFFERING[10] AS A PEACE-OFFERING.

GEMARA. Our Rabbis taught: [When it says], *And the nazirite shall shave* at the door of the tent of meeting,[11] Scripture is speaking

not enter the Camp of the Levites'. It will be observed that apart from the obvious difference at the beginning, Tosaf. does not consider a defiled nazirite as coming within the category of 'lacking atonement' whilst Rashi does.

(1) I.e., how do we know that one who lacks atonement is forbidden to enter the Camp of the Divine Presence? (2) Num. XIX, 13; this refers to a person defiled by a corpse who has not bathed; and in the context he is forbidden to enter the Sanctuary. The use of the future tense in the verb is taken as a sign that even a *ṭebul yom* must not enter there. (3) Ibid. The inference is from the redundancy of these words. (4) At the termination of the naziriteship; v. Num. VI, 14ff. (5) V. Zeb. 90*a*. (6) I.e., the opinions of R. Judah and R. Eleazar give the normal procedure, but a variation in the order would not invalidate the polling. (7) Cf. *supra* 28*b*. (8) A ewe-lamb in its first year. (9) A he-lamb in its first year. (10) A two-year old ram. (11) Num. VI, 18.

of the peace-offering[1] of which it is said, *And kill it* at the door of the tent of meeting.[2] You say that Scripture is speaking of the peace-offering, but may it not mean literally 'at the door of the tent of meeting'?[3] I will explain. If that were its meaning, it would show contempt [for the Sanctuary]. R. Josiah said: It is unnecessary [to rely on a mere assertion].[4] For the Torah says, *Neither shalt thou go up by steps upon Mine Altar,*[5] and how much more so should it be forbidden to show contempt.[6]

R. Isaac said: This argument is unnecessary.[7] For the verse continues, *And shall take the hair of his consecrated head and put it on the fire [which is under the sacrifice of peace-offerings)*,[8] referring to one who needs only to take it and put it [on the fire], and thus excluding [the case contemplated],[9] where he would need to take it, fetch it,[10] and put it [on the fire].

Another version [of R. Isaac's dictum].[11] R. Isaac said: Scripture is there[12] speaking of the peace-offering. You say it is speaking of the peace-offering, but may it not mean literally 'at the door of

(1) I.e., the nazirite is to shave after the slaughter of the peace-offering. (2) Lev. III, 2. (3) And so be referring to the place, not the time of polling. (4) We can infer directly from the Torah that a disdainful proceeding is not to be allowed, and need not rely on our feelings on the subject. (5) 'That thy nakedness be not uncovered there', Ex. XX, 23. (6) We have given our printed text as interpreted by the early commentators (Rashi, Asheri). In Sifre Num. Sect. 34 (in VI, 18), the words 'R. Josiah said: It is unnecessary' are lacking. Recent Talmud editions insert in square brackets an alternative text from the Midrash Rabbah on Numbers, beginning with 'R. Josiah said: Scripture is speaking etc.' There is also a version of the Wilna Gaon (v. Ed. Romm, Marginal Annotations), concluding, 'This is the opinion of R. Josiah'. All these alternatives make what our text gives as two opinions, one opinion. (7) I.e., it is unnecessary to make use of the argument that to shave at the door of the tent of meeting would show contempt. (8) Num. VI, 18. (9) I.e., that the nazirite should shave at the door of the tent of meeting. (10) From where he shaved to the place where the nazirites used to broil the peace-offering. It follows then that the first half of the verse cannot be taken literally as referring to place, but must be referring to time, viz.: after the slaughter of the peace-offering. [The chamber where the Nazirites broiled their peace-offering was situated on the South East of the women's court, Mid. II, 6.] (11) This is the version in Sifre (ibid.). (12) In Num. VI, 18, *And the nazirite shall shave at the door* etc.

the tent of meeting'? The verse continues, *And shall take the hair of his consecrated head* [etc.], signifying that he shaved where he broiled [the peace-offering].[1]

Abba Ḥanan, on behalf of R. Eliezer, said: '*And the nazirite shall shave at the door of the tent of meeting*' signifies that whenever the door of the tent of meeting is not open,[2] he is forbidden to shave.

R. Simeon [of] Shezuri said: '*And* the nazirite *shall shave at the door of the tent of meeting*', but not a female nazirite, [45*b*] lest the young priests become assailed by temptation through her.[3] [R. Simeon's colleagues] said to him: The case of the faithless wife[4] disproves your point, for there it is written, *And* [*the priest*] *shall set her before the Lord*,[5] and we are not afraid lest the young priests be assailed by temptation, through her.[6] He replied: [The woman nazirite] pencils [her eyebrows] and applies rouge, whilst [the faithless wife] uses neither pencil nor rouge.[7]

MISHNAH. HE THEN TOOK THE HAIR OF HIS CONSECRATED HEAD AND THREW IT UNDER THE CAULDRON.[8] IF HE SHAVED IN THE 'PROVINCE'[9] HE DID NOT THROW IT UNDER THE CAULDRON: THE ABOVE REFERS ONLY TO POLLING IN

(1) Asheri pertinently points out that there is no Scriptural proof that the broiling was not to take place at the door. (2) פתח, 'door' means 'opening'. Abba Ḥanan prefers an interpretation as near as possible to the literal one, if the literal one itself cannot be used. (3) The female nazirite was therefore required to poll in private, but not a male nazirite. [R. Simeon, according to Tosaf. understood 'door' in the literal sense, and consequently differs from the Mishnah Mid. II, 6, which provides for the polling a special chamber, v. *supra* p. 168, n. 10). (4) Or *Soṭah*, v. Num. V, 11ff. (5) Num. V, 16. The hair was uncovered during the ceremony of administering the 'bitter waters'. V. 17. (6) The purpose of the verse cannot be therefore to require a woman nazirite to poll in private. In fact, she need not do so. (7) And is therefore not attractive. R. Simeon retained his opinion that a woman nazirite was to poll in private, and a male in public. (8) In which his peace-offering was being prepared. (9) I.e., outside the Temple precincts, he did not have to bring the hair into the temple. Thus the Babylonian version of the Mishnah. The Jerusalem version reads here also, 'he threw it under'

RITUAL PURITY.[1] WHEREAS IN POLLING [AFTER] RITUAL DEFILEMENT HE DID NOT CAST IT UNDER THE CAULDRON; R. MEIR SAID: ALL [NAZIRITES] THREW IT UNDER THE CAULDRON WITH THE SOLE EXCEPTION OF A DEFILED NAZIRITE [WHO POLLED] IN THE 'PROVINCES'.

GEMARA. HE THEN TOOK THE HAIR OF HIS CONSECRATED HEAD. Our Rabbis taught: He then took the broth,[2] put it along with the hair of his consecrated head and threw it under the cauldron containing the peace-offering. But if he threw it under the cauldron containing the sin-offering or the guilt-offering, his obligation would also be discharged.

But is there a guilt-offering in the case of a ritually pure nazirite?[3] —Raba replied: It means that if a ritually defiled nazirite threw it under the pot of the guilt-offering, his obligation would be discharged.

How do we know this?[4]—Raba replied: The verse says, '*Which is under the sacrifice of the peace-offerings*', signifying that part of its sacrifice should be underneath it.[5]

'But if he threw it under the cauldron containing the sin-offering [or the guilt-offering] his obligation would also be discharged.' Why?[6]—The verse says, '*The sacrifice of*,' thereby including the sin-offering and the guilt-offering.[7]

But have you not made use of the words '*the sacrifice of*' for [the rule concerning] the broth?—If that is its whole significance the verse should have said, 'Of the broth of the peace-offerings.' Why then does it say '*the sacrifice of*'? Clearly to include the sin-offering and the guilt-offering.

But perhaps its whole significance is this inference of the sin-

(1) At the termination of the naziriteship. (2) Of the peace-offering. (3) The sacrifices mentioned (*supra* 45a) are sin-offering, burnt-offering, peace-offering. (4) That the broth had also to be cast under the cauldron. (5) The inference is from the superfluous words '*the sacrifice of*': showing that the fire was beneath the sacrifice itself, and not merely beneath the pot. (6) I.e., why not say that the peace-offering only is meant, since it is mentioned explicitly. (7) Although it should preferably be the peace-offering.

offering and the guilt-offering?[1] —If so, the verse should have read 'the peace-offering or the sacrifice'. Why does it say, *'the sacrifice of the peace-offering'?* We are thus entitled to infer both things.

Our Rabbis taught: All [nazirites] threw [their hair] beneath the cauldron with the exception of a defiled nazirite who polled in the 'province', because his hair had to be buried.[2] This is the opinion of R. Meir. R. Judah said: Ritually clean [nazirites] whether in the one place or the other[3] threw it under; ritually defiled nazirites whether in the one place or the other[3] did not throw it under, whilst the Sages said: None threw it under the cauldron excepting a clean [nazirite who polled] in the sanctuary, because [the polling] had then been properly done in the prescribed manner.[4]

MISHNAH. HE EITHER BOILED OR HALF-BOILED[5] THE PEACE-OFFERING. THE PRIEST THEN TOOK THE BOILED SHOULDER OF THE RAM,[6] AN UNLEAVENED CAKE FROM THE BASKET, AND AN UNLEAVENED WAFER, PLACED THEM ON THE NAZIRITE'S HANDS[7] AND WAVED THEM. AFTER THIS, THE NAZIRITE WAS ALLOWED TO DRINK WINE AND DEFILE HIMSELF FOR THE DEAD. [46a] R. SIMEON SAID THAT AS SOON AS ONE KIND OF BLOOD[8] HAD BEEN SPRINKLED ON HIS BEHALF THE NAZIRITE COULD DRINK WINE AND DEFILE HIMSELF FOR THE DEAD.[9]

GEMARA. Our Rabbis taught: *And after that the nazirite may drink wine*[10] means after [the performance of] all that has to be done.[11]

(1) And not the rule concerning the broth. (2) V. Tem. 34a. (3) Whether in the Temple or in the 'province'. (4) Tosef. Naz. IV, 5. (5) [שולק. So Rashi; according to Tosaf. the word denotes 'overdone'.] (6) [The Mishnah does not mention the *'breast'* and the *'shoulder'*, Num. VI, 20), as it deals only with such rites as are distinct to the peace-offering of the nazirite; v. Petuchowski, a.l.] (7) V. Num. VI, 19. (8) I.e., the blood of any one of the three sacrifices. (9) He did not have to wait until the whole rite was completed. (10) Num. VI, 20. (11) I.e., all the rites of the preceding verses.

This is the opinion of R. Eliezer, but the Sages said that [it means] after any single act.[1]

What is the Rabbis' reason?—In this verse it is written, '*And after that the nazirite may drink wine*,' whilst in the preceding verse occur the words, After *he has shaven his consecrated head*,[2] and so just as there ['*after*'] means after the single act, here too it means after a single act.

But may it not mean after both acts?[3]—If that were so, there would be no need for the similarity of phrase.[4]

Rab said: The rite of 'waving' in the case of the nazirite is indispensable.[5]

Whose opinion does this follow? Shall I say that of the Rabbis? Surely, since the Rabbis do not consider polling indispensable, the 'waving' is certainly not so![6] It must therefore be that of R. Eliezer. But then it is obvious, for R. Eliezer has said that [the verse[7] means] 'after all that has to be done'?—It might be thought that since in the matter of atonement it is merely a non-essential feature[8] of the [sacrificial] rite,[9] it is also not indispensable here, and so we are told [by Rab that this is not so].[10] [46b] But is it in fact indispensable? Has it not been taught: *This is the law of the nazirite*[11] [signifies] whether he has hands or not?[12]—But then, when we are taught: '*This is the law of the nazirite*' signifies whether he has hair or not,[13] would this also mean that [polling] can be dispensed with?[14] Are we not taught further: A bald nazirite, say Beth

(1) After even the first of the acts, viz.: the sprinkling of one kind of blood (Tosaf.). (2) Num. VI, 19. (3) I.e., after the polling of the preceding verse, as well as the sacrifice. (4) The *Gezerah Shawah*, v. Glos. For it would have been more natural for the verse to have said simply 'and then he may drink etc.' instead of 'and after etc.' (5) Lit., 'holds up' the nazirite from wine and defilement. (6) V. Num. VI, 19-20, for the 'waving' follows the polling. (7) '*And after that the nazirite may drink wine*' ibid. 21. (8) Although part of the normal procedure; v. Yoma 5*a*. (9) Lit., 'relics of a precept'. (10) And that it is here indispensable, in the view of R. Eliezer. (11) Num. VI, 21. (12) Tosef. Naz. I, 6. The meaning is here assumed to be, 'if he has no hands, the waving-rite can be omitted', so that even if he has hands it does not prevent him from drinking wine before it has taken place. (13) Tosef. Naz. I, 6. (14) By the same argument as before, assuming that if he has no hair the ceremony of shaving need not be performed.

Shammai, need not pass a razor over his head, whereas Beth Hillel say that he must pass a razor over his head;[1] and Rabina has explained that Beth Shammai's 'need not' signifies that he has no remedy,[2] whilst in Beth Hillel's view there is a remedy?[3]

The above interpretation [by Rabina of the Baraitha] agrees with that of R. Pedath. For R. Pedath has said that Beth Shammai [in this Baraitha] and R. Eliezer hold the same opinion. The [dictum of] R. Eliezer referred to [is the following]. It has been taught: If [the leper] has no [right] thumb or great toe[4] he can never become clean. This is the opinion of R. Eliezer. R. Simeon said that [the blood] should be put on their place and this would be valid, whilst the Sages said that it should be put on his left [thumb and great toe] and this would be valid.[5]

Another version.[6] Raba[7] said: The rite of 'waving' in the case of the nazirite is indispensable.

Whose opinion does this follow? Shall I say that of R. Eliezer? It would be obvious. Since R. Eliezer said that [the nazirite cannot drink wine until] after [the completion of] all that has to be done! Therefore it must be that of the Rabbis. But seeing that the Rabbis say that polling [itself] is not indispensable, certainly the 'waving' [which follows polling] can be dispensed with?

But can it be dispensed with? Has it not been taught: *'This is the law of the nazirite'* signifies whether he has hands or no?[8]—But

(1) Tosef. Naz. I, 7 and Yoma 61*b* with the ascriptions reversed. Nazir contains a number of such passages both tannaitic and of later date (e.g. *supra* 38*b*. Abaye and Raba reversed in Pes. 41*b*). Cf. Tosaf. Men. 58*b*, s.v. ואיכא. (2) Since he can never shave, he will never be able to drink wine. (3) He can perform the motions of the rite—pass a razor over his head—although the actual shaving is impossible. And so above the true interpretation is that he must do what is possible consistent with his lack of hands, e.g., use his arms. But the 'waving' can by no means be dispensed with. (4) One of the rites to be performed during the purification of the leper was the sprinkling of blood of the sacrifice on his *right* thumb and great toe; Lev. XIV, 14. (5) Neg. XIV, 9. (6) Of the dictum attributed above to Rab, and of the discussion round it. (7) Our printed text has Rab. But all the commentators appear to have had Raba, not Rab. (8) The ceremony must be performed, and thus is indispensable. Here the interpretation is the reverse of what it was in the earlier version.

then when we are taught: *'This is the law of the nazirite'* signifies whether he has hair or no, would this also mean that [polling] is indispensable?[1] Have we not been taught further: A bald nazirite, say Beth Shammai, need not pass a razor over his head whilst Beth Hillel say that he must pass a razor over his head?[2] —R. Abina replied: 'Must' according to Beth Hillel signifies that he has no remedy,[3] whereas according to Beth Shammai he has a remedy.

This interpretation [of the Baraitha by R. Abina] differs from that of R. Pedath.[4]

MISHNAH. SHOULD HE POLL AFTER ONE OF THE SACRIFICES AND THIS BE FOUND INVALID,[5] HIS POLLING IS INVALID[6] AND HIS SACRIFICES[7] DO NOT COUNT: [THUS][8] SHOULD HE POLL AFTER THE SIN-OFFERING, WHICH WAS NOT OFFERED AS SUCH,[9] AND THEN OFFER THE OTHER SACRIFICES UNDER THEIR CORRECT DESIGNATIONS, HIS POLLING IS INVALID AND [NONE OF] HIS SACRIFICES COUNTS FOR HIM. [SIMILARLY], SHOULD HE POLL AFTER THE BURNT-OFFERING OR THE PEACE-OFFERING, WHICH HAVE NOT BEEN OFFERED AS SUCH, AND THEN OFFER THE OTHER SACRIFICES UNDER THEIR CORRECT DESIGNATION, HIS POLLING IS INVALID AND [NONE OF] HIS SACRIFICES COUNTS FOR HIM. R. SIMEON SAID:

(1) I.e., whether he has hair or not, shaving must be done. (2) So that the act of polling is not indispensable according to Beth Hillel, and consequently the waving should also be considered not indispensable. (3) For he has no hair to shave, and therefore can never terminate his naziriteship. Similarly the wave-offering is indispensable. (4) For according to R. Abina, Beth Shammai allow him a remedy, whereas R. Pedath (v. *supra*) says that they do not allow him a remedy. (5) As explained later in the Mishnah (Rashi); or by the blood being upset before the sprinkling, or the sacrifice becoming defiled (Tosaf.). (6) And he must wait thirty days according to the Rabbis, or seven according to R. Eliezer before bringing fresh sacrifices; v. Mishnah *supra 39a*. (7) Other sacrifices offered after the polling. (8) The word 'thus' is added by Rashi, who considers what follows explanatory of the opening phrase of the Mishnah. Tosaf. considers it a new section, explaining the first clause differently; (v. note 5). (9) But was sacrificed as a peace-offering instead.

THAT PARTICULAR SACRIFICE DOES NOT COUNT,[1] BUT HIS OTHER SACRIFICES DO COUNT.

SHOULD HE POLL AFTER ALL THREE SACRIFICES AND ONE OF THEM BE FOUND VALID, HIS POLLING IS VALID AND HE HAS [ONLY] TO BRING THE OTHER SACRIFICES.

GEMARA. R. Adda b. Ahaba said: This [Mishnah] tells us that R. Simeon is of the opinion that a nazirite who polls after offering a voluntary peace-offering has fulfilled his religious obligation.[2] Why is this so? Because the verse says, *And put it on the fire which is under the sacrifice of peace-offerings,*[3] and not '*his* peace-offerings'.[4]

MISHNAH. [47*a*] IF [A NAZIRITE] ON WHOSE BEHALF ONE KIND OF BLOOD[5] HAS BEEN SPRINKLED BECOMES UNCLEAN, R. ELIEZER SAID EVERYTHING IS RENDERED VOID,[6] WHILST THE SAGES SAID: HE IS TO BRING HIS REMAINING SACRIFICES AFTER PURIFICATION. THEY SAID TO [R. ELIEZER]: IT IS RELATED OF MIRIAM OF TARMOD[7] THAT ONE KIND OF BLOOD WAS SPRINKLED ON HER BEHALF WHEN SHE WAS TOLD THAT HER DAUGHTER WAS DANGEROUSLY ILL. SHE WENT AND FOUND HER DEAD,[8] AND THE SAGES TOLD HER TO OFFER HER REMAINING SACRIFICES AFTER PURIFICATION.

GEMARA. The Mishnah says: R. ELIEZER SAID EVERYTHING IS RENDERED VOID. But R. Eliezer has said that whatever occurs after the fulfilment [of the nazirite period] renders void seven

(1) Where the burnt-offering or peace-offering was sacrificed under an incorrect designation (Rashi); they count as *voluntary* peace-offerings (v. Zeb. 2*a*), but for the purpose of liberating the nazirite must be replaced by other animals. [A sin-offering, however, sacrificed under an incorrect designation is entirely disqualified, v. Zeb. ibid.] (2) Since R. Simeon's dictum refers to a nazirite who polled after a voluntary-offering (v. previous note). (3) Num. VI, 18. (4) Hence any peace-offering is valid. (5) I.e., the blood of one of the three sacrifices. (6) Explained in the Gemara. (7) A nazirite. *Tarmod* or *Tadmor* Palmyra. (V. I Kings, IX, 18). (8) Thus becoming accidentally unclean.

days?[1]—Rab replied: By 'IS RENDERED VOID' here, R. Eliezer means 'renders his sacrifices void'.[2] This is also clear from the sequel, viz:—WHILST THE SAGES SAID: HE IS TO BRING HIS REMAINING SACRIFICES AFTER PURIFICATION.[3] IT IS RELATED FURTHER, OF MIRIAM OF TARMOD, THAT ONE KIND OF BLOOD WAS SPRINKLED ON HER BEHALF WHEN SHE WAS TOLD THAT HER DAUGHTER WAS DANGEROUSLY ILL. SHE WENT AND FOUND HER DEAD, AND THE SAGES TOLD HER TO OFFER THE REMAINING SACRIFICES AFTER PURIFICATION. This proves it.[4]

(1) *Supra* 16*a-b*. If then 'EVERYTHING' means the nazirite period, R. Eliezer is contradicting himself. (2) I.e., the sacrifice the blood of which had been sprinkled is invalid and must be replaced, in accordance with R. Eliezer's view that the whole termination ceremony of the nazirite hangs together; v. *supra* 46*a*. (3) The words in cur. edd. 'This proves it' are to be deleted. (4) That the point at issue was only the validity of the first sacrifices.

NAZIR

CHAPTER VII

MISHNAH. A HIGH PRIEST AND A NAZIRITE MAY NOT DEFILE THEMSELVES [BY CONTACT] WITH THEIR [DEAD] RELATIVES, BUT THEY MAY DEFILE THEMSELVES WITH A METH MIẒWAH.[1]

IF THEY WERE WALKING BY THE WAY AND FOUND A METH MIẒWAH, R. ELIEZER SAYS THAT THE HIGH PRIEST SHOULD DEFILE HIMSELF BUT NOT THE NAZIRITE, BUT THE SAGES SAY: THE NAZIRITE SHOULD DEFILE HIMSELF BUT NOT THE COMMON PRIEST.[2] R. ELIEZER SAID TO THEM: RATHER SHOULD THE PRIEST, WHO DOES NOT OFFER A SACRIFICE ON DEFILEMENT, DEFILE HIMSELF, THAN THE NAZIRITE WHO MUST OFFER A SACRIFICE ON DEFILEMENT.[3] THEY REPLIED: RATHER SHOULD THE NAZIRITE WHOSE CONSECRATION IS NOT PERMANENT,[4] DEFILE HIMSELF, THAN THE PRIEST WHOSE CONSECRATION IS PERMANENT.[5]

GEMARA. It is clear that as between a High Priest and a nazirite, the one [authority][6] is of the opinion that the High Priest is of superior sanctity,[7] and the other[8] that the nazirite is of superior sanctity.[9]

As between [a High Priest] anointed with the anointing oil,[10]

(1) I.e., a corpse without relatives at hand to bury it; v. Glos. (2) Some versions read 'High Priest'. The argument is not affected. (3) V. Num. VI, 9ff. (4) It lapses at the end of the period of his naziriteship, or he can obtain release from his vow by application to a sage (Tosaf.). (5) It is a result of his birth. (6) I.e., the Sages. (7) I.e., if both come upon a corpse which has no relatives to bury it, the nazirite must defile himself in order to bury it. (8) R. Eliezer. (9) And the High Priest must bury the corpse. (10) V. Ex. XXX, 30. The High Priest ceased to be consecrated with this oil in the days of Josiah (c. 620 B.C.E.); v. Hor. 12*a* and Yoma 52*b*. After this, consecration took place by investing the priest with the garments of a High Priest.

[47b] and [one consecrated by wearing] the additional garments,[1] the former is of superior sanctity,[2] for the former must offer the bullock brought for breach of any of '*all the* commandments',[3] but the latter cannot offer it.[4]

As between an anointed [High Priest] who has been superseded,[5] and one consecrated by [wearing] the additional garments,[6] the latter is of superior sanctity,[7] for he performs the Temple service, whilst the former is not permitted to perform the Temple service.[8]

As between one superseded on account of a [nocturnal] mishap,[9] and one superseded on account of a deformity,[10] the former is of superior sanctity,[11] for he will be fit to perform the Temple service on the morrow, whilst the one superseded on account of his deformity is not fit to perform the Temple service.[12]

The question was propounded: As between [the High Priest] anointed for a war,[13] and the deputy [High Priest],[14] which is of superior sanctity? Does the [High Priest] anointed for war take precedence, because he is qualified to go to war, or does the deputy take precedence, because he is qualified to perform the Temple service?[15] — Come and hear: For it has been taught: The only difference between a [High Priest] anointed for war and a deputy is that if they were both walking by the way and encountered a *meth*

(1) The High Priest wore eight garments and the common priest four. V. Ex. XXVIII. (2) And if both encounter a corpse, the latter must bury it. (3) V. Lev. IV, 2ff. (4) V. Hor. 11*b*. (5) If the High Priest could not officiate on the Day of Atonement, another priest was appointed to his office for that day only. As soon as the former was able to perform his duties, the latter was superseded. (6) And who is the regular High Priest. (7) And the former must defile himself if the latter is the only other person present and they encounter a corpse. (8) Having officiated as High Priest, he was not allowed to act as a common priest, nor could he officiate as High Priest whilst the other lived, as this would cause jealousy, v. Hor. 12*b*. (9) Lev. XV, 16. (10) Lev. XXI, 17. (11) And the latter must defile himself in the event of both meeting with a corpse. (12) Until the deformity disappears. (13) V. Deut. XX. (14) *Segan*, who deputised for the High Priest if he was unable to perform the Temple service on the Day of Atonement. On *Segan*, v. Sanh. (Sonc. ed.) p. 97, n. 1. (15) But once a priest had been anointed for war, he could no longer take part in the Temple service.

mizwah, the [High Priest] anointed for war is to defile himself, but not the deputy. But has it not been taught: A [High Priest] anointed for war takes precedence of a deputy?—Mar Zuṭra replied: As far as saving his life is concerned,[1] the [High Priest] anointed for war has a superior claim for many [people] depend upon him,[2] but as regards defilement, the deputy is of superior sanctity, as has been taught: R. Ḥanina b. Antigonus said that the reason the office of deputy to the High Priest was created,[3] was that should any disqualification happen to him [the High Priest], he can enter and minister in his stead.

[Now Eliezer and the Sages] differ only as regards a High Priest and a nazirite walking together, but each one by himself would be required to defile himself.[4] How is it known that this is so?—Our Rabbis have taught: To what does the passage, *Neither shall he go in to any dead body,*[5] refer? It can hardly be to strangers, since this could be inferred *a fortiori* [by the following argument]. Seeing that a common priest, who is allowed to contract defilement in the case of kinsmen, is forbidden to do so in the case of strangers,[6] the High Priest who is not permitted to contract defilement in the case of kinsmen should certainly not be permitted to do so in the case of strangers. It follows that the passage refers to kinsmen, [and when therefore the text says,] *Nor for his father*[7] is he permitted to defile himself, [we infer that] he is permitted to defile himself in the case of a corpse [the burial of] which is a religious duty. [48*a*] [The words,] *Nor for his mother*[7] form the basis of the *Gezerah shawah* used by Rabbi. For it has been taught: Rabbi said: In the case of a nazirite, *when they die,*[8] he is not allowed to defile himself on their account, but he may defile himself [if they are unclean] through [leprous] plague or unclean issue. But this covers the

(1) Should both be in danger. (2) For he is to go to war on their behalf. (3) This saying occurs also in Yoma 39*a*, where the reading is: 'R. Ḥanina, the priestly deputy, said that the reason the deputy stands at his (the High Priest's) right is that . . .' on the whole passage v. Hor. (Sonc. ed.) pp. 97ff. (4) If they came upon a corpse whose burial is a religious duty. (5) Lev. XXI, 11. (6) V. Lev. XXI, 2 and 3. (7) Since this part of the verse is superfluous. Lev. XXI, 11. (8) Num. VI, 7. Referring to a nazirite's relatives.

nazirite only. How are we to infer the same for a High Priest? As follows: There is no need for the expression, *his mother*[1] in the case of the High Priest, and Scripture need not have mentioned this, since the same may be derived from the following *a fortiori* argument. Seeing that though a common priest may defile himself on account of his brother by the same father,[2] yet a High Priest may not defile himself on account of his father,[3] then if a common priest may not defile himself on account of his brother by the same mother,[4] surely [it follows that] a High Priest may not defile himself on account of his mother. Since this can be inferred by a process of reasoning, why does Scripture mention '*his mother*' in connection with the High Priest? It is available for purpose of comparison and to set up a *Gezerah shawah* [from like expressions]. The phrase '*his mother*' occurs in connection with the nazirite and the phrase '*his mother*' occurs in connection with the High Priest, and so just as in the case of the nazirite it is to his mother [etc.], '*when they die*' that he is forbidden to defile himself, but not when they are unclean through leprosy or unclean issue, so in the case of the High Priest, it is to his mother [etc.], when they die that he is forbidden to defile himself, but not when they are unclean through leprosy or unclean issue.

We have thus found the sanction for a High Priest.[5] How is the same known of a nazirite? It has been taught: From the passage, *All the days that he separateth himself unto the Lord, he shall not come near to a [dead]*[6] *body [nefesh]*,[7] it might be concluded that even the body [*nefesh*] of an animal is intended, the word [*nefesh*] being used as in the verse, *And he that smiteth [the* nefesh *of] a beast.*[8] Therefore Scripture says, '*he shall not come near to a* dead *body,*' indicating that a human body [*nefesh*] is being referred to. R. Ishmael says: It is unnecessary [to argue in this manner]. Since it

(1) Lev. XXI, 11. A High Priest may not defile himself for his mother's corpse. (2) But not the same mother. (3) Though a father is nearer kin than a brother. (4) But not the same father. (5) I.e., that a High Priest must defile himself for a corpse the burial of which is a religious duty. (6) Some authorities omit the word '*dead*' from the Talmud text, since the assumed inference would only follow if it were lacking in the Bible. (7) Num. VI, 6. (8) Lev. XXIV, 18.

says, *'he shall not come'*, Scripture is referring to bodies which cause defilement merely on *coming* [under the same roof].[1] [Futher], *for his father, or for his mother,*[2] he may not defile himself, but he may defile himself for a *meth mizwah*. But even if this [expression] did not occur, I could infer it as follows: Seeing that a High Priest whose consecration is permanent may defile himself for a *meth mizwah*, then surely a nazirite whose consecration is not permanent[3] may defile himself?[4] But this inference is not valid. For if it is true in the case of a High Priest, it may be because he is not required to offer a sacrifice as a consequence of his defilement, whereas a nazirite must offer a sacrifice as a consequence of his defilement, [and it might be objected that] since he must offer a sacrifice in consequence of his defilement,[5] he may not defile himself for a *meth mizwah*. And so Scripture says, *'He shall not make himself unclean for his father, or for his mother'*, [implying], 'but he may make himself unclean for a *meth mizwah*'. But perhaps [the correct inference is that] he may not defile himself for his father or for his mother, but he may defile himself for other corpses?[6] This follows by an argument *a fortiori*. Seeing that a common priest who may defile himself for his kinsmen is forbidden to defile himself for other dead,[7] then a nazirite who may not defile himself for kinsmen is surely forbidden to defile himself for other dead. [48b] And so why does Scripture say, *'for his father, or for his mother'?* For his father or for his mother he is forbidden to defile himself, but he may defile himself for a *meth mizwah*. But even if this[8] were not written, I could infer it as follows: A general prohibition[9] is stated for the High Priest, and a general prohibition[10] is stated for the nazirite, and so just as, though there is a general prohibition for

(1) This applies to human corpses. Animal corpses defile only if touched or carried. (2) Num. VI, 7. (3) But only for as long as he has undertaken to be a nazirite, or until he seeks release at the hands of a Sage. (4) And the phrase, *'For his father etc.'* is unnecessary to teach that he may defile himself for a corpse whose burial is a religious duty. (5) V. Num. VI, 9ff. (6) I.e., non-kinsmen whose death he would not mourn so much. (7) V. Lev. XXI, 1. (8) The phrase *'For his father or for his mother'*. (9) *'Neither shall he go in to* any *dead body'*; Lev. XXI, 11. (20) *'He shall not come near to* a *dead body'*. Num. VI, 6.

the High Priest, he is forbidden to defile himself for his father, but he may defile himself for a *meth miẓwah*, so when there is a general prohibition for the nazirite [it signifies that] he may not defile himself for his father but he may defile himself for a *meth miẓwah*.[1] But it is possible to argue in another direction. A general prohibition is stated for the common priest,[2] and a general prohibition is stated for the nazirite, and so just as, though there is a general prohibition stated for the common priest, he may defile himself for his father, so too though there is a general prohibition stated for the nazirite he may defile himself for his father. Scripture therefore says, '*He shall not make himself unclean for his father, or for his mother,*' but he may make himself unclean for a *meth miẓwah*.

But surely this is needed to tell us [the plain fact] that he may not defile himself for his father?[3] — In point of fact, '*for his father*' tells us that he may not defile himself for his father;[4] '*for his brother*'[5] he may not defile himself but he may defile himself for a corpse [the burial of] which is a religious duty; '*or for his mother*'[5] is used to form the basis of a *Gezerah shawah* after the manner of Rabbi;[6] whilst '*or for his sister*'[5] is required for the following [teaching]. For it has been taught: For what purpose is '*for his sister*' mentioned?[7] If a [nazirite] was on his way to slaughter his Paschal lamb, or to circumcise his son and he heard that a near kinsmen had died, it might be thought that he ought to defile himself. It therefore says, '*He shall not make himself unclean*'. But it might [then] be thought he should not defile himself for a *meth miẓwah*. The text therefore adds, '*for his sister*', [implying that] for his sister he is forbidden to defile himself, but he may defile himself for a *meth miẓwah*.

R. Akiba said:[8] ['*Nefesh*'] '*body*' refers to strangers; '*dead*' to

---

(1) And '*For his father* etc.' is superfluous.   (2) '*There shall none defile himself for the dead amongst the people*'; Lev. XXI, 1.   (3) And it is not meant merely to provide the ground for the inference, that a nazirite may defile himself for a corpse whose burial is a religious duty.   (4) And since he may not defile himself for his father, he may not for his brother, since the father is nearer kin.   (5) Num. VI, 7.   (6) *Supra* 48*a*.   (7) For since he may not defile himself for his father, he may not for his sister.   (8) R. Akiba is interpreting Num. VI, 6 and 7, in a different manner to R. Ishmael.

kinsmen, *'For his father or for his mother'* [teaches that] he is forbidden to defile himself for these, but he may defile himself for a *meth mizwah*. *'For his brother'* [tells us] that if he be both High Priest and a nazirite, it is for his brother that he is forbidden to defile himself, but he may defile himself for a corpse [the burial of] which is a religious duty. *'For his sister'* [is required] as has been taught: 'If a man was on his way to slaughter his Paschal lamb or circumcise his son etc.'

Whence does R. Akiba derive the lesson learnt by Rabbi from the *Gezerah shawah?*—He will reply: Since it has been said that if he be both High Priest and a nazirite it is for his brother that he is forbidden to defile himself but he may defile himself for a *meth mizwah*,[1] what difference does it make whether he is simply High Priest or High Priest and a nazirite.[2]

And whence does R. Ishmael derive the rule about a High Priest who is a nazirite?[3]—Since the All-Merciful allows [the breach of] a single prohibition in connection with a *meth mizwah*, what does it matter whether there is only one prohibition or two?

[In that case] for what purpose is *for his sister* required?[4]—You might assume that in connection with a *meth mizwah* the All-Merciful permitted [the defilement of] a nazirite and a priest because this is an offence which is merely prohibited, but where the neglect of circumcision and the Paschal lamb entailing *kareth*[5] is involved, [the nazirite or priest] should not defile himself for a *meth mizwah*[6] and so we are told [that he should].

[49a] On the view of R. Akiba, seeing that whether he be simply a High Priest or whether he be a High Priest who is also a nazirite, we can infer from *'for his brother'* [that he may defile himself for a neglected corpse], what is the purpose of *'for his father and for his*

(1) So that the inference, *when they die*, but not when they have plague also refers to the kinsmen of a nazirite who is High Priest. (2) In either case he is not forbidden to touch them if they have leprosy or unclean issue. (3) That he may defile himself to bury a neglected corpse. (4) If a nazirite must defile himself to bury a neglected corpse, he must also defile himself for this purpose even when on his way to slaughter his paschal lamb. (5) V. Glos. (6) When about to slaughter his paschal lamb.

mother'?—They are both necessary. For were only his father mentioned, it might be thought that the reason why he may not defile himself for him is that there is merely a presumption [of paternity],[1] whereas for his mother who we know bore him, he should defile himself. Again, if the All-Merciful had mentioned his mother, it might be thought that he may not defile himself for his mother because her children['s descent] is not reckoned through her,[2] whereas for his father, since it has been affirmed, *'by their families, by their fathers' houses'*,[3] it might be said that he should defile himself. We are therefore told [that he may defile himself for neither].

[On the view of R. Akiba] what is the purpose of *'Neither shall he go in to any dead body'?*[4]—[49*b*] *'To any'* excludes strangers;[5] *'dead'* excludes kinsmen, *'body'* [*nafshoth*] excludes a quarter [of a *log*] of blood coming from two corpses, [and informs us] that it renders unclean by being under a covering [with it], as it is written, *'neither shall he go in to any dead body* [*nafshoth*]*'*.[6]

MISHNAH. THE NAZIRITE MUST POLL FOR [DEFILEMENT CONTRACTED FROM] THE FOLLOWING SOURCES OF DEFILEMENT: FOR A CORPSE, OR AN OLIVE'S BULK OF [THE FLESH OF] A CORPSE, OR AN OLIVE'S BULK OF NEẒEL,[7] OR A LADLEFUL OF CORPSE-MOULD,[8] OR THE SPINAL COLUMN, OR THE SKULL, OR ANY LIMB [SEVERED] FROM A CORPSE OR ANY LIMB [SEVERED] FROM A LIVING BODY THAT IS STILL PROPERLY COVERED WITH FLESH,[9] OR A HALF-ḲAB[10] OF BONES, OR A HALF-LOG[10] OF BLOOD, WHETHER [THE DEFILEMENT IS CON-

(1) His wife may have committed adultery. (2) But through the male line. (3) Num. I, 2. From this verse the inference is drawn that descent is counted in the male line; v. B.B. 109*b*. (4) Lev. XXI, 11. Said of the High Priest. (5) I.e., that he may not defile himself by touching their corpses. (6) The Hebrew has the plural of *nefesh*, indicating two corpses. The *nefesh* is identified with the blood (v. Deut. XII, 23) hence R. Akiba's inference; v. Sanh. (Sonc. ed.) pp. 12 and 14. (7) Coagulated corpse-dregs; v. *infra* 50*a*. (8) The earth of a decomposed body. (9) Sufficient flesh for the limb to have maintained itself when attached to the body. (10) V. Glos. for these measures.

TRACTED] FROM CONTACT WITH THEM, FROM CARRYING THEM, OR FROM OVERSHADOWING[1] THEM; FOR [DEFILEMENT CONTRACTED FROM] A BARLEY-GRAIN'S BULK OF BONE, WHETHER BY CONTACT OR CARRYING. ON ACCOUNT OF THESE, A NAZIRITE MUST POLL AND BE SPRINKLED ON THE THIRD AND SEVENTH DAYS; SUCH [DEFILEMENT] MAKES VOID THE PREVIOUS PERIOD, WHILST HE DOES NOT BEGIN TO COUNT ANEW [HIS NAZIRITESHIP] UNTIL HE HAS BECOME CLEAN AND BROUGHT HIS SACRIFICES.

GEMARA. Our Rabbis taught: After the demise of R. Meir, R. Judah said to his disciples, 'Do not allow the disciples of R. Meir to enter here, for they are disputatious and do not come to learn Torah, but come to overwhelm me with citations from tradition.' Symmachus forced his way through and entered. He said to them, 'Thus did R. Meir teach me: The nazirite must poll for [defilement contracted from] the following sources of defilement: for a corpse, or for an olive's bulk of [the flesh of] a corpse.' R. Judah was wroth and said to them, 'Did I not tell you not to allow the pupils of R. Meir to enter here, because they are disputatious? If he must poll for an olive's bulk of [the flesh of] a corpse, then certainly he must poll for the corpse itself![2] [50*a*] R. José commented: People will say, 'Meir is dead, Judah is angry, José is silent, what is to become of the Torah?' And so R. José explained: It was only necessary [to mention the corpse itself explicitly] for the case of a corpse that has not an olive's bulk of flesh upon it.—But it can still be objected: If [the nazirite] must poll for a [single] limb, then surely he must poll for the whole [skeleton]!—It must therefore be as R. Joḥanan explained [elsewhere],[3] that it was only necessary [to mention the corpse itself]

(1) This type of defilement is caused by being, either under the same roof as, or perpendicularly above or below, the source of defilement; cf. Num. XIX, 14ff. (2) And this does not require explicit mention. (3) The reference here is thought to be to Oh. II, 1, dealing with defilement by overshadowing, where the same phrase occurs. But the only occurrence of this statement of R. Joḥanan is found in Ḥul. 89*b*, with reference to our Mishnah; v. Tosaf. Naz. and Ḥul.

for the case of an abortion in which the limbs were not bound together by the sinews, and here too it refers to an abortion in which the limbs are not bound together by the sinews.[1]

Raba said: It is only necessary [to mention the corpse itself] for the case where there is the greater part[2] of the frame [of a corpse][3] or the majority [of its bones],[3] which do not amount altogether to a quarter [*ḳab*] of bones.[4]

FOR AN OLIVE'S BULK OF [THE FLESH OF] A CORPSE, OR AN OLIVE'S BULK OF NEẒEL: And what is NEẒEL? The flesh of a corpse that has coagulated, and liquid secretion [from a corpse] that has been heated [and has congealed].[5]

What are the circumstances? If it be not known to belong to [the corpse], what does it matter if it has coagulated?[6] Whilst if we know that it pertains to [the corpse], then even though it has not coagulated [it should defile]!—R. Jeremiah replied: [Secretion] of uncertain origin is referred to. If it coagulates, it is [cadaverous] secretion,[7] otherwise it may be phlegm or mucus.[8]

Abaye inquired of Rabbah: Is there [defilement through] corpse-dregs in the case of [defilement caused by] animals[' corpses], or not?[9] Was the tradition only that corpse-dregs coming from man [defile], but not corpse-dregs coming from animals, or is there no difference?[10] According to the opinion that the uncleanness is of the heavier type[11] only until [the animal is unfit to be eaten by] a stranger,[12] and is then of the lighter type[13] until [it is unfit to be

(1) A single limb of such an abortion not containing an olive's bulk of flesh, would not convey defilement, but the whole does. (2) The greater part being equivalent to the whole. (3) V. *infra* 52*b* for the explanation of these terms. (4) And but for the fact that it constitutes the greater part of the frame of the corpse it would not convey defilement. (5) [*Neẓel* is thus derived from נצל 'to separate', cf. Gen. XXXI, 9 (Rashi); Petuchowski connects it with נזל 'to flow', 'melt away'.] (6) It should not convey defilement. (7) And causes defilement. (8) Which do not defile. (9) This question has no bearing on the nazirite, who does not lose any of his period for defilement caused by an animal corpse. (10) And animal corpse-dregs also defile. (11) Defiling man by contact or carrying. (12) V. Bek. 23*b*. A Jew may not eat the flesh of an animal which dies of itself, but may give it to a stranger; v. Deut. XIV, 21. (13) Defiling food only but not man.

eaten by] a dog,[1] there is no difficulty,[2] but according to the opinion that the uncleanness remains of the heavier type until [it is unfit to be eaten by] a dog, what answer can be given?[3]—Come and hear: If he melted [unclean fat] with fire, it remains unclean, but if in the sun,[4] it becomes clean. Now if you assume [that the animal remains unclean] until [it is unfit to be eaten by] a dog, then even if [the fat has been melted] in the sun, it should also [remain unclean]![5]—It only melts after it has decomposed in the sun, and since it has decomposed it is [nothing but] dust.[6]

We have learnt elsewhere: Any jet of liquid [poured from a clean to an unclean vessel] is clean[7] save only [a jet of] thick honey[8] and heavy batter.[9] [50*b*] Beth Shammai say: Also one of a porridge of grist or beans, because [at the end of its flow] it springs back.[10]

Rammi b. Ḥama asked: Is there [transference of defilement through] a jet in the case of foodstuffs,[11] or does [transference of defilement through] a jet not apply to foodstuffs? Do we say [that the principle applies to thick honey and batter] because they contain liquor,[12] whereas [foodstuffs] contain no liquor,[13] or is it perhaps because they are compact masses[14] and [foodstuffs] are also compact masses?[15]—Raba replied: Come and hear: A whole piece of fat[16] from a corpse, if melted, remains unclean, but if it was in

(1) After which it ceases to defile. (2) For corpse-dregs are unfit to be eaten by a human being. (3) For corpse-dregs are fit to be eaten by a dog. (4) When it becomes corpse-dregs. (5) It is assumed that though the sun turns the fat into corpse-dregs, it is still fit to be eaten by a dog. (6) And unfit for a dog. Hence it becomes clean. (7) I.e., it does not convey defilement from the unclean to the clean vessel. (8) *Aliter:* The honey of Zifim; (cf. Josh. XV, 24). V. Soṭ. 48*b*. (9) So the *Aruch*. (10) Being thick liquids, they have such elasticity that when he ceases to pour out the liquid, the lower end of the jet, which has touched the unclean vessel, springs back into the upper vessel. M. Maksh. V. 9. (11) Viz., if he melted some solid food, e.g., fat, and poured it from a clean to an unclean vessel. (12) And it is the presence of the liquor which causes the jet to shrink backwards. (13) Whence they would not transfer defilement from the lower end of the jet to the upper end. (14) And so transfer defilement; in the same way as any solid becomes wholly unclean even if part of it is defiled. (15) And transfer defilement. (16) Of an olive's bulk.

pieces[1] and they were melted, it remains clean.[2] Now if you assume [that the principle of transference of defilement through] a jet does not apply to foodstuffs, [then even if it be] whole and then melted it should become clean![3]—R. Zera commented: I and Mar, son of Rabina, interpreted [the above teaching as follows]: It refers to where at the time of melting, the column of fire ascended to the mouth of the vessel[4] and [the fat] coagulated whilst it was all together.[5]

Rabina said to R. Ashi: Come and hear [the following]: Beth Shammai say: Also one of a porridge of grist or of beans, because [at the end of its flow] it springs back![6]—What does this prove? In the other cases[7] it may be the fact that they are compact masses [which causes defilement] though here it is because of the liquor.[8]

OR A LADLEFUL OF CORPSE-MOULD: And what is its size?—Hezekiah said: The palm of the hand full. R. Joḥanan said: The hollow of the hand[9] full.

It has been taught: The [measure of the] ladleful of corpse-mould mentioned is, from the bottom of the fingers upwards.[10] So R. Meir. The Sages say [it means] the hollow of the hand full.[11] Now R. Joḥanan at least agrees with the Rabbis; but with whom does Hezekiah agree, neither with R. Meir, nor with the Rabbis? —I will tell you. The palm of the hand full and from the joints of

(1) Each smaller than an olive. When smaller than an olive, unclean flesh loses its defiling property. (2) Though now solidified to one piece larger than an olive's bulk. Tosaf. Oh. IV, 3. (3) Whilst being melted, the fat would move from side to side of the vessel and so there would be less than an olive's bulk of the fat in one spot, if the jet of liquid fat be not counted as joined together. (4) And the vessel was at rest when heated so that the fat was heated all together. (5) Without moving from its original position, so Rashi. Tosaf. and Asheri give the following reading: 'It refers to where at the time of melting a column [of fat] rose and sublimed at the mouth of the vessel'. In either case there is no *flow*. (6) It is now assumed that the Rabbis disagree with Beth Shammai only as regards grist and beans, but accept his criterion of springing back. This occurs in the presence of a liquid only. (7) I.e., thick honey and batter. (8) And the Rabbis disagree as to the criterion. Beth Shammai say it is liquor and the Rabbis, perhaps, the fact that it is a compact mass. (9) Formed by bending the fingers to touch the wrist. (10) I.e., presumably towards the tips of the fingers. (11) Tosef. Oh. II, 2.

the fingers upwards is the same measure.[1]—R. Shimi b. Adda said to R. Papa: How is it known that 'from the joints of the fingers and upwards' means towards the tips? Perhaps it means lower down the hand[2] when [the measure] is the palm of the hand full?[3] This was not solved.[4]

[51a] Our Rabbis taught: What type of corpse produces corpse-mould [that can defile]? A corpse buried naked in a marble sarcophagus or on a stone floor is a corpse which produces corpse-mould. If it is buried in its shroud, or in a wooden coffin, or on a brick floor, it is a corpse which does not produce corpse-mould [that can defile].[5]

'Ulla said: Corpse-mould [to defile] must come from flesh and sinew and bone. Raba raised [the following] objection to 'Ulla. [It has been taught:] Corpse-mould derived from flesh is clean. This implies that if it be from bones it is unclean, even though there be no flesh present?—Say rather as follows: Corpse-mould derived from flesh is clean, unless there be bone in the flesh. But there are no sinews!?[6]—It is impossible that there should be flesh and bones without sinews.

Rab Samuel[7] b. Abba said that R. Joḥanan said: Two corpses buried together act as *gilgelin*[8] to each other. R. Nathan [son of R. Oshaia][9] raised the following objection. [It has been taught that corpse-mould] derived from two corpses is unclean?—Said Raba, [we suppose that] each was buried separately and decayed and together formed a ladleful of corpse-mould.[10]

Rabbah b. Bar Ḥanah said that R. Joḥanan said: If a man cut [the corpse's] hair and buried it with it, it acts as *gilgelin* [and the resultant mould does not defile].

(1) And he agrees with R. Meir. (2) Upwards in the direction of the shoulder. (3) And there is no difficulty for Hezekiah. (4) These words occur in the printed texts, but are omitted by Tosaf. and others. (5) For the resultant mould will be mixed with fragments of cloth, wood, or brick, since these crumble. Tosef. Oh. II, 2. (6) And 'Ulla said all three are necessary. (7) *Var. lec.* Shaman. (8) A covering or girdle, lit., 'wrappers'; so that the corpse-mould which results does not defile, just as it does not when the corpse is buried in a shroud. (9) Inserted from BaḤ. (10) In such a case, the joint mixture causes defilement; but if buried together, the resultant mould does not defile.

We have learnt elsewhere: Every part of a corpse is unclean except the teeth, the hair and the nails; but whilst still attached [to the corpse], they are all unclean.[1] Hezekiah propounded: What is the law in the case of hair long enough to be polled,[2] and nails long enough to be pared?[3] Do we say that anything which is fit to be cut is as though already cut,[4] or perhaps they are after all still attached?[5] —But cannot the question be resolved from [the dictum of] Rabbah b. Bar Ḥanah?[6] The reason [that the hair acts as *gilgelin*] is because he cut it, but if he does not cut it, it does not?[7] He [Rabbah b. Bar Ḥanah] might have meant this: If he cut it, it acts as *gilgelin;* but if he did not cut it, he was in doubt [as to its effect].[8]

R. Jeremiah propounded: What is the law regarding corpse-mould coming from the heel?[9] Does our tradition specify corpse-mould derived from a whole corpse, but not corpse-mould resulting from [the decomposition of] the heel, or is there no difference? —Come and hear: R. Nathan son of R. Oshaia learnt that corpse-mould derived from two corpses is unclean. Now if you assume that what comes from the ḥeel is not [counted as corpse-mould], then, if we look to the one [corpse], [the mould in the mixture] may have been taken from the heel, and if to the other, it may have been taken from the heel?[10] —Where the whole corpse has decayed and [the corpse-mould] has been taken from the heel, there it would certainly be [counted as corpse-mould],[11] but here the question is when one limb[12] has decomposed and [the mould] has been taken from the heel. This was left unsolved.

R. Jeremiah propounded: Does a fetus in a woman's womb act as *gilgelin* or not? Since a Master has affirmed that a fetus counts

(1) Oh. III, 3. (2) Hair that is long and would have been polled had not death intervened. (3) Does the resultant corpse-mould defile?—So Rashi. According to Tosaf. the question is: Is the hair unclean or not? (4) And prevents the formation of corpse-mould. (5) And count as part of the body. (6) 'If he *cut* the hair and buried it, it acts as *gilgelin*'. (7) Thus attached hair counts as part of the corpse. (8) And this was the very question of Hezekiah. (9) The lower part of the body. (10) And the resulting mixture should not defile, if corpse-mould from the heel does not. (11) This is shown by R. Nathan's dictum. (12) One of the lower limbs.

as the thigh of its mother, is it therefore part of her body and so does not act as *gilgelin*, or perhaps since it would eventually leave [the womb], does it count as separated from her? Should you decide that since a fetus will eventually leave [the womb], it is separate from her, [51*b*] what would be the law regarding semen in a woman's womb? Do we say that because it has not yet formed [into an embryo] it counts as part of her body,[1] or perhaps seeing it has come from elsewhere, it is not [part of the body]?[2]

R. Papa propounded: What about excrement? Seeing that one cannot exist without food, is it part of one's life,[3] or perhaps this too comes from elsewhere?[4]

R. Aḥa son of R. Iḳa propounded: What about his skin?[5]

R. Ḥuna b. Manoah propounded: What about his phlegm and his mucus?

R. Samuel b. Aḥa said to R. Papa: If now you assume that all these mentioned act as *gilgelin*, how can there be corpse-mould which defiles?—If he was given to drink water from [the Well of] the Palm Trees,[6] depilated with *nasha*,[7] and was steeped in the [hot] springs of Tiberias.[8]

Abaye said: We hold a tradition that a corpse that has been ground to powder does not come under [the law of] corpse-mould. The following was propounded: If it were ground and then decayed, what would be the law? Is the reason [that corpse-mould defiles] solely because flesh and bones and sinews are present, and here they are present, or do we require it [to have become corpse-mould] as in its original form, and this has not occurred? This was left unsolved.

'Ulla b. Ḥanina learned: A defective corpse[9] does not come under [the law of] corpse-dust,[10] nor does it acquire the soil on

(1) And does not act as *gilgelin*. (2) And acts as *gilgelin*. (3) And so does not act as *gilgelin*. (4) And not being part of the body acts as *gilgelin*. (5) Does it act as *gilgelin* or not? *Rashi* translates: What about his spittle? (6) A violent purgative; v. Shab. 110*a*. (7) A natural depilatory, v. *supra* p. 164, n. 4. (8) To remove the skin. (9) One lacking a member. (10) When it decays, a ladleful of its corpse-dust does not defile by 'overshadowing'.

which it lies,[1] nor does it help to make an area into a graveyard.[2] The following objection was raised. [We have learnt:] No! Because you say this[3] of a corpse to which [the law concerning] 'the greater part,' 'a quarter [*kab*]' and 'a ladleful of corpse-mould' applies, would you say it of a living body to which [the laws concerning] 'the greater part,' 'a quarter [*kab* of bones]' and 'a ladleful of corpse-mould' do not apply?[4] What are the circumstances?[5] [Surely,] that one limb has decayed.[6] And similarly[7] in the case of a corpse, even if one member [has decomposed, the law of] corpse-dust applies?[8]—Does it say, 'whereas in the case of a corpse [the law of corpse-dust applies]'?[9] What we are told is that there are corpses to which [the law of] corpse-dust applies,[10] but there are no living bodies to which [the law of] corpse-dust applies.

Raba propounded: If [a man's limb] decayed whilst he was alive and he then died,[11] what would the law be?[12] Does the tradition specify corpse-mould which decayed when he was dead, or perhaps it is enough that he is now dead?—Come and hear [the following]. [We have learnt:] No! Because you say this of a corpse to which [the laws concerning] 'the greater part', 'a quarter [*kab* of bones]' and 'a ladleful of corpse-mould' apply, would you say it of a living body etc. The reason [that the law of corpse-mould does not apply to a living body] is because it is alive, from which we infer that if he died [the law of] corpse-mould would apply.[13]—Does it say, 'whereas if he died [the law of corpse-mould applies]'? What we are told is that there are corpses to which [the law of] corpse-mould

(1) Lit., 'take possession'. If a complete corpse is unearthed, the soil round about it must be removed with the body; v. *infra* Mishnah 64*b*. (2) Lit., 'It has not (the law of) the area of a cemetery'. If three complete corpses are found together, the place where they are found must be converted into a graveyard. Ibid. (3) That an olive's bulk of its flesh defiles by 'overshadowing'. (4) V. 'Ed. VI, 3. (5) Under which the law of corpse-mould does not apply to a living body. (6) I.e., only part of the body. (7) Since the cases are parallel. (8) Contradicting 'Ulla b. Ḥanina's teaching. (9) Which would imply that the comparison was exact. (10) Viz., whole bodies. (11) And the body crumbled into corpse-dust, together with the limb which decayed during his lifetime. (12) Does the law of corpse-dust apply or not? (13) Thus Raba's question is answered in the affirmative.

applies, but there are no living bodies to which [the law of] corpse-mould applies.[1]

Raba propounded: What is the law concerning a defective[2] ant?[3] Does the tradition specify [a certain] size[4] and this is wanting, or does it specify a [separate] creature[5] and this it is?—[52*a*] R. Judah of Disḳarta[6] replied: Judge from the following. [It has been taught: From the verse, *Whosoever doth touch*] *them* [. . . *shall be unclean*],[7] it might be thought that this is [only if he touches] whole [reptiles], and so Scripture says, [*And upon whatsoever any*] *of them* [. . . *doth fall*].[8] From '*of them*' [alone] it might be thought that part of them [defiles], and so Scripture says '*them*'. How are [the texts to be] reconciled? [He is not unclean] unless he touches a part of one equivalent to a whole one and the Sages estimated this to be the size of a lentil, since the sand-lizard[9] at its first formation[10] is of the size of a lentil. Hence it follows that tradition specifies [a certain] size.[11] R. Shemaya demurred: The reason that we require a [particular] size, so that if it is not the size of a lentil it does not defile, is because there is no life in it,[12] but when there is life in it, [it may be that] no [minimum size is required].[13] It is this question that is being put to you.[14]

THE BACKBONE AND THE SKULL: The question was propounded: Does the Mishnah say the backbone *and* the skull,[15] or does it say perhaps the backbone *or* the skull?[16]—Raba replied: Come and hear: A backbone that has been stripped of most of its ribs[17] is clean,[18] but if it is in the grave, even though it is broken in

(1) And the question remains. (2) One lacking a limb. (3) Does he receive stripes for eating it or not?—V. Mak. 13*a*. (4) That the creature eaten must be the size of an ant. (5) That what is eaten must be a separate creature. (6) V. *supra* p. 126, n. 6. (7) Lev. XI, 31. Referring to dead reptiles. (8) Ibid. 32. '*Of*' meaning even 'part of'. (9) One of the reptiles which defile; v. Ibid. 30. (10) But if less, it does not defile. (11) For the sand-lizard is the size of a lentil when whole. (12) As in the case of the dead sand-lizard. (13) But only that the creature should be alive. (14) And R. Judah of Disḳarta has not answered this. (15) That both must be in the room for the nazirite to poll. (16) And he must poll if only one is there. (17) Cf. the Tosef. where the reading is probably, 'vertebrae'. (18) I.e., it does not defile through 'overshadowing'.

pieces or separated [into parts], it is unclean,[1] because of the grave.[2] Now the reason [that the backbone is clean] is that it has been stripped, but if it were not stripped, it would be unclean,[3] and so may we [not] infer from this that the correct reading is, either the backbone *or* the skull?—Does it say, 'But if etc.'?[4] What we are told is that when [the backbone is] stripped, it is clean;[5] but the other case[6] still remains doubtful.

Come and hear: R. Judah says: Six things were declared unclean by R. Akiba and clean by the Sages, and R. Akiba retracted his opinion. It is related that a basket full of [human] bones was taken into the Synagogue of the Tarsians[7] and placed in the open air.[8] Then Theodos, the Physician, together with all the physicians, entered, and said that there was not the backbone of a single corpse there.[9] The reason [that it was declared clean] is that there was not a backbone from a single [corpse], but had there been either a backbone or a skull from a single [corpse],[10] a nazirite would have been required to poll because of it, whence it follows that we read in our Mishnah, either the backbone *or* the skull?—The case was put strongly. Not only was there not the backbone and skull of a single corpse, but there was not even the backbone of a single corpse or the skull of a single corpse.

Judge[11] from the enumeration [of the six things]: And what are the six things that R. Akiba declared unclean and the Sages clean? A limb set up[12] from two corpses, a limb set up [from bones sever-

(1) And defiles if 'overshadowed'. (2) Which joins the pieces together. Tosef. Oh. II, 3. (3) Though the backbone alone is mentioned in the Tosefta. (4) Adopting reading of Asheri. (5) Perhaps even when the skull is there too. (6) Stripped and the skull removed. (7) Other renderings are, 'weavers', 'bronze-workers'; v. *Aruch* and A.Z. 17*b*. [We find a synagogue of Tarsians in Jerusalem, Tiberias and Lydda. According to Krauss, *Synagogale Altertümer*, p. 201, they are identical with the synagogues of Alexandrians, who had brought over with them, to Palestine, the industry in Tarsian carpets—an industry which flourished greatly in Egypt; v. also *TA*. II, 625.] (8) I.e., under an opening in the roof, to prevent it conveying uncleanness by 'overshadowing'. (9) And so it could not convey defilement by 'overshadowing'. Tosef. Oh. IV, 2. (10) And a nazirite had 'overshadowed' it. (11) Lit., 'come and hear'. (12) I.e., made by taking one bone from one corpse and another bone from a second corpse.

ed] from two living men, and a half-*kab* of bones taken from two corpses, a quarter [*log*] of blood taken from two [corpses], a barley-corn's bulk of bone broken into two parts, the backbone and the skull.[1] [52*b*] Now if you assume that either the backbone *or* the skull [alone is unclean] there would [surely] be seven things there? —When [the number six] was mentioned,[2] it referred to all those things where the majority differed from him, but excluded [the case of] a barley-corn's bulk of bone, since it is an individual who differed from him,[3] for we have learnt: If a barley-corn's bulk of bone is divided into two, R. Akiba declares it unclean and R. Joḥanan b. Nuri clean.[4]

Alternatively, [the number six] referred to members coming from a corpse, but it did not refer to [the case of] a member [severed] from a living being.[5]

Alternatively, [the number six] referred to all those [cases] where a nazirite must poll because of 'overshadowing' them, but excludes [the case of] a barley corn's bulk of bone,[6] since he need not.

Alternatively, [the number six] referred to all those [cases] from which he retracted, but excludes [the case of] a quarter [*log*] of blood, from which he did not retract. For Rabbi said to Bar Ḳappara, 'Do not include [the case of] a quarter [-*log*] of blood amongst the retractions, for R. Akiba had that as a [traditional][7] teaching, and furthermore the verse, *Neither shall he go in to any dead body,*[8] supports him.—R. Simeon says: All his life he declared [a quarter-*log* of blood from two corpses] unclean, whether he retracted after his death, I do not know.[9]—A Tanna taught that [R. Simeon's] teeth grew black because of his fasts.[10]

(1) This enumeration appears to be a digest of Oh. II, 6 and 7, or Tosef. 'Ed. I, 6; but is not quite identical with either. (2) In the text there occurs here the following mnemonic for the alternative methods of arriving at the number six: 'The mnemonic is: An individual who polls and another'. (3) In which case the norm is in accordance with R. Akiba. (4) Oh. II, 7. (5) This excludes the case of a limb set up from bones severed from two living beings: Tosaf. reads here: 'Only those cases relating to corpses are included (in the six), not those relating to living bodies'. (6) V. our Mishnah. (7) So Asheri. (8) Lev. XXI, 11; v. *supra* 38*a*. (9) Tosef. Oh. IV, 2. (10) To atone for the not quite respectful reference to his teacher. Cf. Ḥag. 22*b*.

Come and hear: It has been taught: Beth Shammai say that a quarter [-*kab*] of bones, be they any of the bones, whether from two [limbs] or from three,[1] [is sufficient to cause defilement by overshadowing]. And Beth Hillel say, a quarter [-*kab* of bones] from a [single] corpse [is required], [and these bones must be derived] from [those bones which form] the greater part [of a skeleton] either in frame[2] or in number.[3] R. Joshua asserted: I can make the statements of Beth Shammai and Beth Hillel one.[4] For [when] Beth Shammai say 'from two [limbs] or from three,' [they mean] either from two shoulders and one thigh, or from two thighs and one shoulder, since this is the major part of a man's structure in height, whilst Beth Hillel say [the quarter *kab* must be taken] from the corpse, [viz.] from the greater part either in structure[5] or in number, for this [numerical majority] is to be found in the joints of the hands and feet.[6] Shammai says even a [single] bone, from the backbone *or* from the skull [defiles by overshadowing]![7] —Shammai is different, as he takes the more stringent view.[8]

Can one infer from this that Shammai's[9] reason is that he takes the stricter view, but the Rabbis would require both backbone and skull?—No! For the Rabbis may only disagree with Shammai concerning a single bone coming from the backbone or the skull, but where these are complete one alone [may be sufficient].

Rammi b. Ḥama propounded: What is the law in the case of a quarter [-*kab*] of bones [coming] from the backbone and the skull?

(1) I.e., the quarter-*kab* must contain parts of more than one bone. Some (e.g. Maimonides to 'Ed. I, 7) interpret: from two corpses or from three. (2) Lit., 'building' i.e. those bones which go towards forming the greater part of the frame, e.g., the shoulder and thigh bones. (3) A body contains 248 bones, whence the greater part in number is 125 bones. V. Mak. (Sonc. ed.) p. 169, n. 5. (4) So that the two schools refer to different things and their opinions are not mutually exclusive. (5) This is the shoulder and thigh. (6) I.e., the bones in the hands and feet form the greater number of bones in the body, without being so important that they form the major part of the structure. (7) Thus backbone *or* skull is meant. This should solve the reading in the Mishnah. Part of this *Baraitha* occurs as a Mishnah, 'Ed. I, 7. (8) He holds that even a single bone defiled, hence does not require both the skull and backbone, but the Rabbis may disagree. (9) The printed text reads in error 'Beth Shammai'.

When [our Mishnah] stated that a half-*ḳab* of bones [is required], was it only where there are present [bones] from its other limbs [too], but since [the bones] from the backbone and skull are treated more seriously, even a quarter [-*ḳab*] of bones [is sufficient], or perhaps there is no difference?[1]—Raba replied: Come and hear: [We learnt:] THE BACKBONE AND THE SKULL.[2] Now if you assume that a quarter [-*ḳab*] of bones coming from the backbone and the skull is to be taken more seriously,[3] it should state 'for a quarter [-*ḳab*] of bones coming from the backbone etc.'?[4]—[53*a*] But it was Raba himself who said that [special mention] was required only for a backbone and a skull containing less than a quarter [-*ḳab*] of bones?[5]—After hearing R. Akiba's opinion, [he altered his own opinion].[6]

Come and hear: Shammai says, even a single bone, from the backbone or from the skull [defiles by 'overshadowing']![7]—Shammai is different, for he takes the much more stringent view.[8]

Can we infer from this that Shammai's reason[9] is that he is strict, but according to the Rabbis [there is no defilement by 'overshadowing'] unless there is a half-*ḳab* of bones?—Perhaps the Rabbis only disagree with Shammai where there is a single bone,

(1) And even here a half-*ḳab* is necessary. The Wilna Gaon deletes the last sentence as an interpolation based on false premises. He asserts that the query is whether a quarter-*ḳab* of bones from the skull or backbone conveys uncleanness by overshadowing, even as a quarter-*ḳab* derived from the great part of a skeleton either in frame or in number, and connects with Oh. II, 1 *q.v.* (2) According to Rashi the Tosef. quoted at foot of 52*a* is referred to. Tosaf. thinks it is our Mishnah, whilst the Wilna Gaon refers it to Oh. II, 1. (3) R. Elijah of Wilna reads: is unclean. (4) For this is less than a whole skull and includes it. (5) And how can he infer from the mention of the backbone and skull that a quarter *ḳab* of bones from the backbone and skull does not defile. (6) And the reply to Rammi b. Hama was given before he heard it. This last phrase is authenticated by the MSS. but its meaning is obscure. The Wilna Gaon reads: (That statement of Raba's was) in accordance with the view of Beth Shammai; a reading in keeping with his text. (7) The rule for these being more stringent, as seen from Shammai's ruling, a quarter of a *ḳab* should suffice according to the Rabbis. (8) But the Rabbis disagree. (9) That a single bone suffices.

but where there is a quarter [-*ḳab*] of bones even the Rabbis agree [that this is sufficient].

R. Eliezer said: The Elders of an earlier generation [were divided]. Some used to say that a half-*ḳab* of bones and a half-*log* of blood [is required] for everything,[1] whilst a quarter [-*ḳab*] of bones and a quarter [-*log*] of blood is not sufficient for anything. Others used to say that even a quarter [-*ḳab*] of bones and a quarter [-*log*] of blood [is enough] for everything. The Court that came after them said that a half-*ḳab* of bones and a half-*log* of blood [is the quantity] for [making unclean] everything, a quarter [-*ḳab*] of bones and a quarter [-*log*] of blood [is sufficient] in the case of *terumah*[2] and sacred meats,[3] but not in the case of a nazirite or one preparing the paschal lamb.[4] But surely the compromise of the third [opinion] is no [true] compromise?[5]—R. Jacob b. Idi replied: They had it as a tradition deriving from Haggai, Zechariah and Malachi.

ON ACCOUNT OF THESE A NAZIRITE MUST POLL: The word THESE,[6] in the first clause serves to exclude a barley-corn's bulk of bone, for touching or carrying which he must [poll] though not for overshadowing it. The word THESE in the next clause serves to exclude a rock overhanging a grave.[7]

OR A HALF-ḲAB OF BONES: [53*b*] [We see that] only if there is a half-*kab* of bones [must the nazirite poll], but not if there is a quarter [-*ḳab*] of bones. What are the circumstances? For if we assert that there are amongst them bones of a barley-corn in size, then we can give as the reason [that the nazirite must poll, the presence of] a barley-corn's bulk of bone?—The reference is to where [the bone] was crushed into powder.

OR ANY LIMB [SEVERED] FROM A CORPSE OR ANY LIMB

(1) I.e., conveys defilement by 'overshadowing' in all cases. (2) V. Glos. (3) After being under the same roof with a quarter-*ḳab* of bones, a man may not eat *terumah* or sacred meats. (4) These are not rendered unclean so as to cause the nazirite to lose the period already counted, or to prevent the passover celebrant from offering the paschal lamb. (5) And cannot be accepted as the final decision; for it is not arrived at by logical argument, but by accepting part of each of the other opinions; v. Rashi. (6) I.e., but no others. (7) Although he becomes unclean by touching the stone, he need not poll; cf. Shab. 82*b*.

[SEVERED] FROM A LIVING BODY THAT IS STILL PROPERLY COVERED WITH FLESH: What are the consequences if sufficient flesh is not attached [and a nazirite is defiled by touching or carrying such a bone]?[1]—R. Johanan said that the nazirite is not required to poll because of them. Resh Lakish said that the nazirite must poll because of them. R. Johanan said that the nazirite is not required to poll because of them, for it says in the first [Mishnah],[2] only ANY LIMB [SEVERED] FROM A CORPSE OR ANY LIMB [SEVERED] FROM A LIVING BODY THAT IS STILL PROPERLY COVERED WITH FLESH, [implying] 'but not otherwise'; whilst Resh Lakish said that he must poll, since this case is not mentioned in the subsequent [Mishnah].[3] [To the argument of Resh Lakish] R. Johanan will reply that whatever can be inferred from the rule [of our Mishnah] is not mentioned in the subsequent [Mishnah]. But what of the half-*kab* of bones [mentioned in our Mishnah] which implies that only half a *kab* of bones [can defile] but not a quarter [-*kab*] of bones, and yet the subsequent [Mishnah] mentions [explicitly] that a quarter [-*kab*] of bones [do not defile]?—In that instance were a quarter [-*kab*] of bones not [mentioned], I should have thought that he need not [poll] even [if defiled] through contact with it or carrying it, and so the Mishnah had to mention the [case of a] quarter [-*kab*] of bones [in order to teach] that it is only for overshadowing them that the nazirite is not required to poll.[4]

But what of the half-*log* of blood [mentioned in our Mishnah], from which it may be inferred that only [if the nazirite is defiled by 'overshadowing'] a half-*log* of blood, [is he required to poll] but not by a quarter [-*log*] of blood, and yet the subsequent [Mishnah] mentions [explicitly that] a quarter [-*log*] of blood [does not defile]? —In that case, the purpose [of mentioning it in the next Mishnah] is to dissent from the view of R. Akiba, for R. Akiba has stated that a quarter [-*log*] of blood coming from two corpses conveys defilement by overshadowing.[5]

(1) It is assumed that the bone has not the bulk of a barley-corn. (2) *Supra* 49*b*. (3) *Infra* 54*a*, where the kinds of defilement for which the nazirite need not poll are enumerated. (4) But he must poll if he touches it or carries it. (5) *Supra* 38*a*; 49*b*. And so we are told that a nazirite is not required to poll for defilement

How are we to picture this limb [severed] from a corpse? For if it has a bone of a barley-corn's bulk, what is R. Joḥanan's reason [for saying that a nazirite need not poll if he touches it], whilst if it has not a bone of a barley-corn's bulk, what is Resh Laḳish's reason [for saying that the nazirite must poll if he touches it]? —Resh Laḳish will reply that in point of fact it has not a bone of a barley-corn's bulk, and in spite of this, the All-Merciful has included it [amongst the things which cause defilement]. For it has been taught: [The verse,] *And whosoever in the open field toucheth one that is slain with a sword, or one that dieth of himself* [. . . *shall be unclean seven days*,[1] has the following significance]. '*In the open field*' refers to one who overshadows a corpse. '*One that is slain*'[2] refers to a limb [severed] from a living body which is in such condition that [if attached to the body] it could have been restored. '*A sword*' signifies that this is of the same [degree of defilement][3] as the slain body. '*Or one that dieth of himself*' refers to a limb severed from a corpse. '*Or a bone of a man*' refers to a quarter [-*ḳab*] of bones. '*Or a grave*' refers to a close grave;[4] [54*a*] for a Master said that defilement breaks through [the ground] and ascends, and breaks through [the ground] and descends.[5] [Thus far defilement by 'overshadowing' has been discussed,] whilst as regards [defilement by] contact, Rab Judah said that it has been taught: [The verse], *And upon him that touched the bone, or the slain*[6] [etc.] [has the following significance]. '*The bone*' refers to a barley-corn's bulk of bone. '*Or the slain*' refers to a limb severed from a living body which is not in such condition that [if attached to the body] it could have been restored. '*Or the dead*' refers to a limb severed from a corpse. '*Or the grave*' refers, said Resh Laḳish, to the grave, [of those buried] before the revelation [at Sinai].[7]

conveyed by a quarter-*log* of blood. [Asheri and others omit 'for R. Akiba . . . by overshadowing', the reference being to R. Akiba's view given *infra* 56*b* that a nazir must poll for coming in contact with a quarter-*log* of blood.]

(1) Num. XIX, 16. (2) Lit., 'that which is severed'. (3) If used to slay a person. (4) I.e., one in which there is no hollow space of a handbreadth between the corpse and the roof of the grave. (5) So that any one walking above or beneath such a grave is accounted as 'overshadowing' it and becomes unclean. Cf. Oh. VII, 1. (6) Num. XIX, 18. (7) Lit., 'before the Word'. I.e.,

Now what is meant by 'a limb [severed] from a corpse'? For if it has a bone of a barley-corn's bulk, it is [covered by the rule concerning] one who touches a bone! — We must therefore suppose that it has not a bone of a barley-corn's bulk, and in spite of this the All-Merciful Law has included it [amongst the things whose contact defiles].

R. Johanan, on the other hand, will say that in point of fact [the limb severed from a corpse] has [a barley-corn's bulk of bone] in it, and if [the verse] is unnecessary for teaching [that the limb defiles by] contact,[1] you can use it to teach[2] [that it defiles through] carrying.[3]

AND BE SPRINKLED ON THE THIRD AND SEVENTH DAYS AND IT MAKES VOID etc.: The question was propounded: When the Mishnah teaches UNTIL HE HAS BECOME CLEAN, does it refer to the seventh day, meaning until after sunset, so that the author is R. Eliezer,[4] or does it perhaps refer to the eighth day, the words UNTIL HE HAS BECOME CLEAN, meaning until he has brought his sacrifices, so that it gives the view of the Rabbis? — Judge[5] from the following. Since it teaches in the subsequent [Mishnah] that he commences to count *immediately* [after purification],[6] it follows that UNTIL HE HAS BECOME CLEAN in the first [Mishnah][7] means, until he has brought his sacrifices, and the ruling is that of the Rabbis who assert that naziriteship after purification does not operate until the eighth day.

the bodies of Israelites buried before the revelation, though they do not defile by 'overshadowing', are treated like bodies of gentiles that defile at least by contact.

(1) For we already know this from the rule of one who touches a bone. (2) [In accordance with the principle of Talmudic hermeneutics to apply a Biblical statement superfluous in respect of its own law to some other subject.] (3) And we cannot infer from this that a limb which has not a bone of a barley-corn's bulk defiles a nazirite who touches it. (4) The controversy concerns the question whether the naziriteship after purification commences immediately or whether it does not begin until the necessary sacrifices have been offered; v. *supra* 18*b*. (5) Lit., 'come and hear'. (6) With reference to the defilements for which a nazirite need not poll; *infra* 54*b*. (7) Where it does not say 'immediately'.

MISHNAH. BUT FOR [DEFILEMENT CAUSED BY] SEKAKOTH [OVERHANGING BOUGHS][1] OR PERA'OTH [PROTRUDING BRICKS][2] OR A [FIELD THAT IS A] BETH PERAS,[3] OR LAND OF THE GENTILES[4] OR THE GOLEL [COVERING STONE] OR DOFEK [SIDE STONES] OF A TOMB,[5] OR A QUARTER [-LOG] OF BLOOD, OR A TENT [IN WHICH IS A CORPSE],[6] OR A QUARTER [-KAB] OF BONES, OR UTENSILS THAT HAVE BEEN IN CONTACT WITH A CORPSE, OR [THE DEFILEMENT OF A LEPER'S] TALE OF DAYS[7] OR HIS PERIOD OF DECLARED LEPROSY;[8] FOR ALL THESE THE NAZIRITE IS NOT REQUIRED TO POLL. HE MUST, HOWEVER, BE SPRINKLED ON THE THIRD AND SEVENTH [DAYS], [54b] WHILST [THE UNCLEANNESS] DOES NOT RENDER VOID THE FORMER PERIOD,[9] BUT HE COMMENCES TO RESUME COUNTING [HIS NAZIRITESHIP] IMMEDIATELY [AFTER PURIFICATION] AND THERE IS NO SACRIFICE.[10] [THE SAGES] SAID IN FACT[11] THAT THE DAYS OF

(1) Under which there is a source of defilement, the exact branch being unknown. Such a branch would defile by 'overshadowing', and the person becomes unclean because of the doubt that has arisen. (2) The meaning is *mutatis mutandis*, the same as in previous note. (3) A field in which a grave has been ploughed becomes a *beth peras*, and renders unclean through contact for a distance of half a furrow of one hundred cubits in each direction. *Peras* = Half. (4) V. *supra* 19*b*. (5) According to Rabbenu Tam, 'the tombstone and the side stones on a grave'. [The tombs in ancient times were closed by means of large stones in order to protect them against the ravenous jackals (v. *J.E.* XII, p. 188). According to Levy the *golel* was an upright stone put up at the entrance of every niche or chamber כוך (v. B.B. (Sonc. Ed.) pp. 422ff, for illustrations) into which the bodies were deposited; and the *dofek* is the buttressing stone which was placed in front of the *golel* to prevent it from falling. For other views v. Krauss *TA*. II, pp. 488ff.] (6) According to Tosaf. the meaning is 'a quarter-*log* of blood or a quarter-*kab* of bones in a tent.' (7) V. Lev. XIV, 8. (8) According to Rashi; the period during which he offers his sacrifices for purification after the tale of days; v. Lev. XIV, 9ff. (9) I.e., the period before defilement. (10) I.e., the sacrifice prescribed for a nazirite after defilement. (11) באמת Lit., 'In truth did they say'. Rashi remarks that this phrase denotes a halachah received by Moses at Sinai. V. B.M. 60*a*. Cf., however, below (56*b*) where this is derived by interpretation of the verses. [Rosenthal, F., *Hoffmann Festschrift*, p. 40, explains the phrase as the latin *vero* = 'in fact'; and here is used to affirm the view that only the days of defilement of a male or female

[DEFILEMENT OF] A MALE OR FEMALE SUFFERER FROM GONORRHOEA[1] AND THE DAYS THAT A LEPER IS SHUT UP[2] ARE RECKONED [AS PART OF THE NAZIRITESHIP].

GEMARA. By SEKAKOTH is meant a tree that overhangs the ground and by PERA'OTH protrusions from a fence.[3]

OR LAND OF THE GENTILES: The question was propounded: Did [the Rabbis] enact that the land of the Gentiles [causes defilement] because of the air,[4] or did they, perhaps, enact only because of the soil?[5]—Come and hear: HE MUST, HOWEVER, BE SPRINKLED ON THE THIRD AND SEVENTH [DAYS]. Now if you suppose that it was [declared unclean] because of the air, what need is there for sprinkling?[6] Does it not follow then that it was because of the soil?—No. In point of fact, it may have been because of the air, and when the Mishnah teaches [that he must be sprinkled] it refers to the other instances. This indeed appears to be the case, since UTENSILS THAT HAVE BEEN IN CONTACT WITH A CORPSE are mentioned. Do such utensils necessitate sprinkling?[7] Thus it follows from this that [sprinkling] applies to the remainder only.[8]

[55*a*] Can we say [that the controversy about the air of a foreign country] is the same as that between the following Tannaim? [It

sufferer from gonorrhoea and the days that a leper is shut up are reckoned, but not the days of the leper's tale and his period of declared leprosy. This affirmation was necessary in view of the suggestion *supra* 56*b* that even in the latter case the days should be reckoned.]

(1) Cf. Lev. XV. (2) Cf. Lev. XIII, 4ff. (3) Oh. VIII, 2, and Tosef. Oh. IX, 4. (4) So that entering the atmosphere of a foreign country renders unclean. For the time when this enactment was promulgated, v. *Shab.* 15*a*. (5) And one who does not touch the soil remains clean. (6) Defilement from the air would be mild and would not necessitate sprinkling. (7) In many instances they do not. [Vessels that come in contact with the dead do not communicate defilement to man so as to render him a principal source of uncleanness. The only question arises in case of metal vessels which, according to some authorities, become as grave a source of uncleanness as the dead itself. V. Tosaf. a.l.] (8) I.e., to those to which we know it applies on other grounds. Thus the air of the lands of the gentiles may defile and the Mishnah affords no evidence about it.

has been taught:] If a person enters a foreign country in a box, or a chest, or a portable turret, Rabbi declares him unclean, while R. Jose son of R. Judah declares him clean. Is not this because Rabbi holds that [the uncleanness of the lands of the Gentiles][1] is because of the air[2] and R. Jose son of R. Judah holds that it is because of the soil?[3] — No. Both would agree that [foreign countries defile] because of the soil. The latter, however, holds that a tent in motion is still counted a tent,[4] whilst the former holds that a tent in motion does not constitute a tent.[5] But have we not been taught: R. Jose son of R. Judah says that if a chest is full of utensils and someone throws it in front of a corpse in a tent, it becomes unclean,[6] whilst if it were there already [in the tent], it remains clean?[7] — It must therefore be that both [Rabbi and R. Jose son of R. Judah agree that foreign countries defile] because of the air. The latter holds that since [travelling in a chest] is not common the Rabbis did not intend the enactment to apply [to such a case],[8] whilst the former holds that although it is unusual, the Rabbis intended the enactment to apply to it. It has been taught to the same effect:[9] A person who enters a foreign country in a box, or a chest, or a portable turret remains clean, whilst [if he enters] in a carriage, or a boat, or a ship with a mast,[10] he becomes unclean.[11]

Alternatively,[12] [Rabbi and R. Jose son of R. Judah] may dis-

(1) [It is suggested that the uncleanness of the land of gentiles was decreed in the days of Alcimus in order to stem the tide of immigration from Palestine that had set in as a result of his persecutions, v. Weiss, *Dor* I, 105.] (2) And even in a chest, he touches the air. (3) And since he has not touched the soil, he is clean. (4) And protects whatever is inside from defilement from outside. (5) And whatever is inside is accounted as having contact with the ground and becomes unclean. (6) Together with its contents. (7) Which proves that R. Jose b. R. Judah does not consider that a tent in motion affords protection from defilement. (8) And so the person inside remains clean. (9) That the reason R. Jose declares him clean is that this method of travelling is uncommon. (10) [אסקריא. So Jast.; or better, 'sailing boat', v. Krauss *TA*. II, p. 341, who connects it with Grk. *ἱστοκεραία*.] (11) Tosef. Oh. XVIII, 2. (12) It is now assumed: (i) That the enactment was because of the soil. (ii) That a tent in motion affords protection from defilement. (iii) When a chest full of utensils is thrown in front of a corpse, it becomes unclean because it ceases to have the character of a tent, protecting from defilement, and is treated as a utensil.

agree here on the question [whether a man travelling in a chest was declared unclean] for fear lest he put out his head or the greater part of his [body].[1] It has been taught to this effect. R. Jose son of R. Judah says, a person who enters a foreign country in a box, or a chest, or a portable turret is clean until he puts out his head or the greater part of his [body].

BUT HE COMMENCES TO RESUME COUNTING [IMMEDIATELY etc.]: R. Ḥisda said: It was taught [that the days of declared leprosy are not counted] only in the case of a short naziriteship,[2] but in the case of a long naziriteship[3] they also help to discharge [the days of his naziriteship]. R. Sherabya objected: HE COMMENCES TO RESUME COUNTING IMMEDIATELY AND DOES NOT ANNUL THE PREVIOUS PERIOD.[4] What are the circumstances? For if it is speaking of a short naziriteship, he requires [thirty days] growth of hair,[5] [55*b*] and so it surely refers to a long naziriteship, and yet it teaches that HE COMMENCES TO COUNT IMMEDIATELY?—[R. Sherabya] put the question and answered it himself. [The Mishnah is speaking] of a naziriteship of, say, fifty days, of which he had observed twenty [days] when he became leprous. He must then poll for his leprosy [when he is healed] and observe a further thirty days of the nazirite [obligation], in which case he has a [thirty days] growth of hair.[6]

Rami b. Ḥama raised the following objection:[7] [We have learnt:] A nazirite, who was in doubt whether he had been defiled[8] and in doubt whether he had been a declared leper,[9] [56*a*] may eat sacred

(1) When he would become unclean because of 'overshadowing' the soil. (2) Of thirty days duration. (3) Longer than thirty days when even if the period of leprosy is counted, thirty days still remain. (4) It is clear from this that there has been a break in the counting. (5) And so must ignore what has gone before and count thirty days. (6) The days of declared leprosy cannot then be counted since he would not have thirty days left. (7) To refute R. Ḥisda's statement. (8) On the day he became a nazirite. (9) On the day that he became a nazirite, having perhaps been healed the same day. A nazirite who becomes unclean must poll on becoming clean, and a leper shaves his body twice on recovering. Since this nazirite may not have been unclean nor may he have been a leper, he cannot shave his head during the period of his naziriteship. He must therefore count the full period before shaving because of

meats after sixty days,[1] and drink wine and touch the dead after one hundred and twenty days.[2] In connection with this passage it has been taught: This is only true of a short naziriteship, but in the case of a naziriteship of [say,] a year, he may eat sacred meats [only] after two years, and drink wine and touch the dead after four years.[3] Now if you suppose that the days [of declared leprosy] help to discharge his [naziriteship], then three years and thirty days should be enough?[4]

R. Ashi raised the following objection:[5] I am only told that the days of his defilement are not reckoned in the number [of days of his naziriteship]. How do we know [that the same is true] of the days of his declared leprosy? This follows by analogy. [After] the days of defilement, he must poll and bring an offering, and [after] the days of his declared leprosy, he must poll and bring an offering. Whence we should infer that just as the days of his defilement are not reckoned in the number [of days of his naziriteship], so the days of his declared leprosy are not reckoned in the number! No! If you say this of the days of his defilement, where the previous days[6] are rendered void because of them, would you also say it of the days of his declared leprosy where the previous days are not rendered void because of them? I can argue then in the following manner. Seeing that a nazirite [who undertakes his naziriteship] at the graveside, whose hair is ripe for polling because of his naziriteship, does not count [the time spent at the grave] in the number [of days of his naziriteship],[7] surely the days of his declared leprosy

the doubt, and allow a similar period to pass before the second and third shaving. Since he may have been both a leper and unclean because of touching a dead body, he must count a fourth period for his naziriteship in purity.

(1) When he will have shaved twice for his leprosy. (2) After polling once for his defilement and again on terminating his naziriteship; v. *infra* 59b. (3) Tosef. Naz. VI, 1. (4) The third polling taking place after two years and thirty days, thirty days being the time for a growth of hair and the rest of the year will be coincident with the time of his leprosy. Since this is not the case, it follows that the days of his leprosy are not reckoned towards the naziriteship. (5) To refute R. Ḥisda. (6) The period of naziriteship counted before defilement. (7) I.e., he does not poll for his defilement, but begins his naziriteship after leaving the grave and becoming clean and then polls on completing his naziriteship.

when his hair is not ripe for polling because of the naziriteship[1] should not be counted. In this way we may only infer that the period of his declared leprosy [may not be counted]. How do we know that [the same is true] of his tale of days?[2] This follows by analogy. [56*b*] Just as [after] the days of his declared leprosy he must poll,[3] so [after] his tale of days [he must poll],[4] and so, just as the days of his declared leprosy are not reckoned in the number [of days of his naziriteship], so his tale of days [are not counted]. It might be thought that the same is true of the days that he is shut up,[5] and this too could be derived by analogy. A declared leper defiles both couch and seat,[6] and during the days that he is shut up, he defiles both couch and seat. And so if you infer that the days of his declared leprosy are not counted in the number [of days of his naziriteship], neither should the days when he is shut up be counted in the number. But this is not so. If it is true of the days of his declared leprosy [that the days are not counted], it is because [after] his declared leprosy, he must poll and bring an offering and therefore they are not counted, whereas since [after] the days that he is shut up he does not need to poll nor need he bring an offering, therefore they can be counted in the number [of days of his naziriteship]. From these arguments [the Rabbis] inferred that the days of [the leper's] telling and the days of his declared leprosy are not counted in the number [of days of his naziriteship], but the days [of defilement] of a male or female sufferer from gonorrhoea, and the days when a leper is shut up are counted.[7]

Now one of the arguments mentioned is: 'No! If you say this of the days of his defilement where the previous days are rendered void because of them, would you also say it of the days of his declared leprosy [where the previous days are not rendered void]'.

(1) He has to poll because he was a leper; cf. *supra* 17*b*. (2) The seven days that he 'tells' on recovery; v. Lev. XIV, 8. (3) Lev. XIV, 8. (4) Ibid. v. 9. (5) A doubtful case of leprosy is isolated for seven days; v. Lev. XIII, 4-6. (6) V. Lev. XV, 4, for this type of defilement. (7) The whole of the last paragraph occurs in Sifre to Num. VI, 12. R. Ashi now proceeds with his objection.

What kind [of naziriteship is referred to]? Should it be a short naziriteship,[1] then we require a [thirty days] growth of hair and there is not such a growth.[2] Thus it must be a long naziriteship [which is referred to] and yet it says that they are not reckoned in the number [of days of the naziriteship]. From this it follows [that the period of declared leprosy is never counted].[3] This proves it.

MISHNAH. R. ELIEZER[4] SAID ON BEHALF OF R. JOSHUA THAT EVERY DEFILEMENT [CONVEYED] BY A CORPSE FOR WHICH A NAZIRITE MUST POLL ENTAILS A LIABILITY FOR ONE ENTERING THE SANCTUARY[5] [WHILST THUS DEFILED], AND EVERY DEFILEMENT [CONVEYED] BY A CORPSE FOR WHICH A NAZIRITE IS NOT REQUIRED TO POLL DOES NOT ENTAIL A LIABILITY FOR ONE ENTERING THE SANCTUARY [WHILE SO DEFILED]. R. MEIR SAID: SUCH [DEFILEMENT] SHOULD NOT BE LESS SERIOUS THAN [DEFILEMENT THROUGH] A REPTILE.[6]

GEMARA. Did R. Eliezer receive this [statement] in the name of R. Joshua?[7] Did he not receive it in the name of R. Joshua b. Memel, as has been taught: R. Eliezer[8] said: When I went to 'Ardacus[9] I found R. Joshua b. Pethar Rosh[10] sitting and expound-

(1) And we are told that the period before the declared leprosy is counted, but not the period of leprosy. (2) If we reckon the days before leprosy. (3) Thus R. Ḥisda's statement is refuted. (4) [Read with J. 'R. Eleazar (b. Shammua)', a disciple of R. Akiba. R. Eliezer b. Hyrcanus the teacher of R. Akiba could not have reported a teaching in the name of R. Joshua a disciple of his disciple. V. also n. 10 and p. 201 n. 1.] (5) The Temple precincts. The liability is a sacrifice, if the offence is committed unwittingly. (6) R. Meir's argument is: Since there is a penalty for entering the Temple after defilement by a reptile, although the person so defiled does not have to be sprinkled on the third and seventh days, then in the case of defilement by a corpse for which a nazirite need not poll, just as he need not after defilement by a reptile, there should be a penalty on entering the Temple, for in this case he must be sprinkled on the third and seventh days. (7) R. Joshua b. Ḥananiah (c. 100 C.E.). (8) [*Var. lec.* R. Eleazar.] (9) Identified with Damascus (Jast.). [Or, with Ard a-Suḳ near the source of the Jordan (Horowitz I. S. *Palestine*, p. 78).] (10) [*Var. lec.* 'b. Pethora'; 'b. Bathyra'. V. Zuckermandel *Tosefta* p. 290.]

ing points of law in the presence of R. Meir. [One of them was as follows.] Every defilement [conveyed] by a corpse for which a nazirite must poll entails a penalty for entering the Sanctuary, and every defilement [arising] from a corpse for which a nazirite is not required to poll, does not entail a penalty for entering the Sanctuary. [R. Meir] said to him: Such [defilement] should not be less stringent than [defilement by] a reptile? I then asked [R. Joshua b. Pethar Rosh], 'Are you at all versed in [the sayings of] R. Joshua b. Memel?' He replied, 'I am'. Thus did R. Joshua b. Memel tell me in the name of R. Joshua: Every defilement [arising] from a corpse for which a nazirite must poll, entails a penalty for entering the Sanctuary, and every defilement [arising] from a corpse for which a nazirite is not required to poll, does not entail a penalty for entering the Sanctuary.[1] Thus we see that it was in the name of R. Joshua b. Memel that [R. Eliezer] received it?—They replied:[2] From this it follows that whenever a tradition is transmitted through three [men], the first and the last [name] are mentioned, whilst the middle [name] is not mentioned.[3]

R. Naḥman b. Isaac said: We, too, have learned to the same effect: Naḥum the Scribe[4] said, This was transmitted to me from R. Measha, who received it from his father, who received it from 'the Pairs',[5] who received it from the Prophets as a tradition [handed] to Moses on Mt. Sinai: If a man who has sown his field with two varieties of wheat collects them on one threshing floor,[6] he need leave [only] one *pe'ah*,[7] but if he collects them on two threshing floors,[8] he must leave two *pe'ahs*.[9] Now here, Joshua and

(1) Tosef. Naz. V, 3. Tos. Oh. IV, 7. (2) [Asheri and Tosaf. omit 'they replied'.] (3) Thus in our Mishnah though the tradition was received from R. Joshua through R. Joshua b. Memel and R. Eliezer, only the first and last of these is mentioned. (4) Heb. לבלר = *libellarius*. (5) *Zugoth* (Pairs), from Jose B. Jo'ezer and Jose B. Joḥanan to Hillel and Shammai; v. Aboth (Sonc. ed.) p. 3, n. 8. (6) I.e., does not keep them separate. (7) *Pe'ah*. The corner of the field that was left for the poor. V. Lev. XXIII, 22. (8) Thus treating them as two separate crops. (9) Pe'ah II, 6. The text here has been emended after all the commentators to agree with the Mishnah in Pe'ah. The text, which is supported by the MSS., quotes instead Pe'ah III, 2, as the tradition of Naḥum: If a man sowed dill or mustard seed in two or three separate places, he must leave *pe'ah* from each.

Caleb are not mentioned [between Moses and the Prophets]. Thus it follows from this [that intermediate names may be omitted].

MISHNAH. R. AKIBA SAID: I ARGUED IN THE PRESENCE OF R. ELIEZER[1] AS FOLLOWS. SEEING THAT A BARLEY-CORN'S BULK OF BONE WHICH DOES NOT DEFILE A MAN BY 'OVERSHADOWING', COMPELS A NAZIRITE TO POLL SHOULD HE TOUCH IT OR CARRY IT, THEN SURELY A QUARTER [-LOG] OF BLOOD WHICH DEFILES A MAN BY 'OVERSHADOWING', SHOULD CAUSE A NAZIRITE TO POLL IF HE TOUCHES IT OR CARRIES IT?[2] HE REPLIED: 'WHAT NOW, AKIBA! TO ARGUE FROM THE LESSER TO THE GREATER IS NOT PERMITTED IN THIS INSTANCE.' WHEN I AFTERWARDS WENT AND RECOUNTED THESE WORDS TO R. JOSHUA, HE SAID TO ME, 'YOUR ARGUMENT WAS SOUND, BUT [IN THIS CASE] THIS HAS BEEN DECLARED AS A FIXED HALACHAH.[3]

GEMARA. [57*a*] The question was propounded: Was it [the law concerning] a barley-corn's bulk of bone[4] that was a *halachah* and that of the quarter [-*log*] of blood [that was being derived] by argument, and [this is what is meant by saying that] an argument from the lesser to the greater is not permitted in the case of a *halachah?*[5] Or, was it [the law concerning] a quarter [-*log*] of blood[6] that was a *halachah*, while [the law concerning] a barley-corn's bulk of bone [was simply used] for the argument, and [this is what is meant by] saying that an argument from the lesser to the greater is not permitted in the case of a *halachah?*[7]—Come and hear: [It

(1) R. Eliezer b. Hyrcanus. In the last Mishnah by R. Eliezer, R. Eleazar b. Shammua is meant. V. *supra* p. 208, n. 4. (2) Yet the Mishnah 54*a* counts the quarter-*log* of blood as one of the things for which a nazirite need not poll. (3) As a tradition from Sinai and no inference may be drawn. (4) Viz., that a nazirite must poll if he touches a bone of that size. (5) And this was the reason that R. Akiba's argument was not accepted. (6) Viz., that it defiles by 'overshadowing'. (7) I.e., no new properties may be added by an argument to what is traditionally known.

has been taught: The rulings concerning] a barley-corn's bulk of bone is a *halachah;* [the rulings of] a quarter [-*log*] of blood [can be derived] by an argument; but an argument from the lesser to the greater is not permitted in the case of a *halachah.*[1]

(1) Thus the first alternative is meant.

NAZIR

CHAPTER VIII

MISHNAH. TWO NAZIRITES TO WHOM SOMEONE SAYS, 'I SAW ONE OF YOU DEFILED, BUT I DO NOT KNOW WHICH OF YOU IT WAS,' MUST [BOTH] POLL[1] AND BRING SACRIFICES [PRESCRIBED] FOR DEFILEMENT AND SACRIFICES [DUE ON TERMINATING A NAZIRITESHIP] IN PURITY,[2] [AND ONE OF THEM] MUST SAY, 'IF I AM UNCLEAN, THE SACRIFICES FOR DEFILEMENT ARE MINE, AND THE SACRIFICES IN PURITY ARE YOURS, WHILST IF I AM THE ONE WHO IS CLEAN, THE SACRIFICES IN PURITY ARE MINE AND THE SACRIFICES FOR DEFILEMENT ARE YOURS.' THEY MUST THEN COUNT THIRTY [MORE] DAYS[3] AND BRING SACRIFICES IN PURITY AND [ONE OF THEM] MUST SAY, 'IF I AM THE ONE WHO WAS UNCLEAN, THE SACRIFICES FOR DEFILEMENT WERE MINE, THE SACRIFICES IN PURITY WERE YOURS, AND THESE ARE MY SACRIFICES IN PURITY, WHILST IF I WAS THE ONE WHO WAS CLEAN, THE SACRIFICES IN PURITY WERE MINE, THE SACRIFICES FOR DEFILEMENT WERE YOURS, AND THESE ARE YOUR SACRIFICES IN PURITY.'

GEMARA. The Mishnah says: TWO NAZIRITES TO WHOM SOMEONE SAYS, 'I SAW ONE OF YOU DEFILED, BUT I DO NOT KNOW WHICH OF YOU IT WAS [etc.]: Now why [is this necessary]?[4] For whence do we derive all [the laws concerning] doubtful defilement [arising] in a private domain?[5] [Is it not] from [the regulations regarding] a faithless wife?[6] [Whence it may be in-

(1) When both have completed their periods of naziriteship. (2) One set of each kind of sacrifice. (3) The usual period of naziriteship. (4) Why should either of them have to take account of the possibility that he has become unclean? (5) Viz.: That cases of doubtful defilement in a private domain are treated as if definitely unclean. (6) Cf. Num. V, 11ff. The woman is regarded

ferred that] just as in the case of a faithless wife [only] the lover and his mistress are together,[1] so in every case of doubtful defilement in a private domain [the defilement is assumed to be definite] only if there were but two persons present, whereas in the present instance, the two nazirites and the one standing near[2] make three, so that it becomes [the same as] a case of doubtful defilement in a public domain [and the rule is:] Every case of doubtful defilement in a public domain remains clean?[3]—Rabbah son of R. Huna replied: [The Mishnah assumes that the third person] says, 'I saw a source of defilement thrown between you?[4] R. Ashi commented: This is also indicated [in the language of the Mishnah] [57*b*] for it says: BUT I DO NOT KNOW WHICH OF YOU IT WAS, which proves [that he was not in their company].[5]

THEY MUST POLL AND BRING [etc.]: But why [should they be allowed to poll]? Perhaps they are not unclean and they will [nevertheless] have rounded [the corners of the head]?[6]—Samuel replied: [The Mishnah is speaking] of a woman or a minor.[7]

Why does he not regard [the Mishnah] as speaking of an adult [male nazirite], the rounding of the whole head not being considered [an infringement of the prohibition against] rounding?[8]—Since he does not do so, it follows that Samuel holds that the rounding of the whole head is considered [an infringement of the prohibition against] rounding.

Mar Zuṭra taught this exposition of Samuel with reference to a subsequent Mishnah [which reads]: A nazirite who was in doubt whether he had been defiled and in doubt whether he had been a

as having defiled her marital relationship and must undergo the ordeal of the bitter waters though there is no evidence of unfaithfulness; v. Soṭ. 28*b*.

(1) Proceedings involving the drinking of bitter waters can be taken against a faithless wife only if there is no eye-witness of unfaithfulness; v. Num. V, 13, and Soṭ. 2*b*. (2) Who asserts that he saw one of them become unclean. (3) And so each nazirite should regard himself as clean and need bring no sacrifice for defilement. (4) And the third person was at a distance, so that the conditions for a private domain were fulfilled. (5) For otherwise it should have read: 'And I have forgotten which of you it was'. (6) Which is forbidden except to a nazirite or a leper; v. Lev. XIX, 27. (7) For whom there is no prohibition against rounding. (8) Cf. *supra* 41*a*.

certified leper may eat sacred meats after sixty days [etc.][1] and must shave four times.[2] [But why?][3] Will he not have marred [the corners of his beard]?[4]—Samuel replied: [The Mishnah is speaking] of a woman or a minor.[5]

R. Huna said: One who rounds [the head of] a minor is guilty.[6] R. Adda b. Ahabah said to R. Huna: Then who shaves your [children's heads]?—He replied: Ḥoba.[7] [Rab Adda exclaimed:] Does Ḥoba wish to bury her children?[8] During the whole of R. Adda b. Ahabah's lifetime, none of R. Huna's children survived.[9]

Seeing that both [R. Huna and R. Adda] hold that rounding the whole head is [an infringement of the rule against] rounding,[10] wherein do they differ?[11]—R. Huna holds that [the verse,]*Ye shall not round the corners of your heads, neither shalt thou mar the corners of thy beard,*[12] [signifies] that to whomsoever marring is applicable,[13] rounding is applicable, and since marring does not apply to women, rounding, too, does not apply to them.[14] R. Adda b. Ahabah, on the other hand, holds that both he who rounds and he who is rounded are included [in the prohibition],[15] the one who rounds

(1) *Infra* 59*b*; v. *supra* 55*b* for relevant notes. (2) 'And drink wine and have contact with the dead after one hundred and twenty days', which occurs in the Mishnah is here contracted to 'shave four times' after the Baraitha quoted on page 60*a*. (3) Inserted with BaḤ, i.e., why may he shave in case of doubt? (4) And this is forbidden (v. Lev. XIX, 27) unless he is actually a leper. The reading we have adopted is that of Rashi and Tosaf. Our printed text has: 'Will he not have rounded?' in which case there is no difference between Mar Zuṭra and the earlier statement. On our reading the point of Mar Zuṭra's statement is that we are without definite evidence of Samuel's opinion on the subject of rounding the whole head. (5) Who have no beards. (6) Of transgressing the command not to round. (7) The wife of R. Huna, who, being a woman, was not commanded not to round. (8) If the rounding of a child's head is forbidden, it is also forbidden for a woman to round it. (9) Although R. Adda himself would have allowed the children's heads to be rounded even by a man (v. *infra*), his unfortunate forecast proved true during his lifetime. (10) For the point at issue was whether this was permitted in the case of a minor, but both agreed that it is forbidden with an adult. Why does the one permit a woman to round a child and the other not allow it. (11) What is the point at issue? (12) Lev. XIX, 27. (13) I.e. men who have beards. (14) I.e., There is no penalty even if a woman rounds an adult. But a man may not round a minor. (15) I.e., '*Ye shall not round*' refers to both.

being compared to the one who is rounded, [to the effect that] wherever the one who is rounded is guilty, the one who rounds is also guilty. Hence, since a child is not punishable[1] and so is not guilty [of the offence of rounding], he who rounds [the child] is also not guilty.[2]

Can we say that [the question of] rounding the whole head is the subject of [controversy between] Tannaim? For our Rabbis have taught: Why does Scripture mention *his head?*[3] Since it says, *ye shall not round the corners of your heads,*[4] [58*a*] it might be thought that the same is true of a leper, therefore Scripture says *'his head'*.[5] And another [Baraitha] taught: Why does Scripture mention *'his head'?*[3] Since it says with reference to the nazirite, *There shall no razor come upon his head,*[6] it might be thought that the same is true of a nazirite who becomes a leper, therefore Scripture says *'his head'*.[7] Now surely there is here a difference of opinion between Tannaim [on the question of rounding the whole head]. The [Tanna] who refers [*'his head'*] to the nazirite holding that the rounding of the whole head does not count as rounding,[8] and that the purpose of the text[9] is to override the prohibition and positive command [incumbent on the nazirite],[10] whilst the other [Tanna] holds that the rounding of the whole head does count as rounding[11] and the purpose of the verse is to override a simple prohibition![12] —Said Raba: [It may be that] both [Tannaim] agree that the rounding of the whole head does not count as rounding, and the

(1) For any offence. (2) Hence even an adult may round a child. Thus when R. Adda said that Ḥoba should not poll the children, he was arguing on R. Huna's premises. (3) Of the leper; although it has already said that he must shave all his hair; Lev. XIV, 9. (4) Speaking of all persons. Lev. XIX, 27. (5) The leper must even shave his head. (6) Num. VI, 5. (7) Even a nazirite must shave his head if he becomes a leper. Cf. the somewhat different discussion of these two Baraithas, *supra* 41*a*. (8) And so no special permission is required to round the head of a leper on shaving him. (9) *'His head'*. (10) Viz.: *There shall no razor come upon his head* (Num. VI, 5) and, *He shall let the locks of the hair of his head grow long* (Ibid.). In spite of these verses, the leprous nazirite is to shave his head. (11) And it might be thought that even an ordinary leper must not round his head. (12) I.e., one which has no accompanying positive command to the same effect.

purpose of the verse [according to the latter Tanna][1] is [to permit rounding] where he first rounds [the corners only] and then shaves [the rest of the head]. Since he would not be guilty if he shaved it all at the same time, he is not guilty if he first rounds [the corners] and then shaves [the rest].[2]

But could Scripture possibly intend this?[3] Has not Resh Laḳish said that wherever we find a positive command and a prohibition [at variance], then if it is possible to observe both, well and good, otherwise the positive command overrides the prohibition?[4]—We must therefore say that both [Tannaim] agree that the rounding of the whole head counts as rounding [the corners], and that the authority who utilises the verse ['*his head*' to prove that a positive command] may override both a prohibition and a positive command, infers that a simple prohibition [can be overridden] from [the command to wear] twisted cords. For the verse says, *Thou shalt not wear a mingled stuff,*[5] and it has been taught [in explanation of this]: *Thou shalt not wear a mingled stuff,* [*wool and linen together*], but nevertheless, *Thou shalt make thee twisted cords*[6] of them.

Why does not the one who infers this [rule][7] from '*his head*' infer it from '*twisted cords*'?—He will reply that [the latter] is required for [the following dictum of] Raba. For Raba noted the following contradiction. It is written, *And that they put with the fringe of each corner,* [*i.e.,*] of the same [material] as the corner[8] must there be *a thread of blue.*[9] Yet it is [also] written *wool and linen together.*[10]

(1) Who uses it to allow rounding in the case of an ordinary leper. (2) I.e., the verse tells us that even if he shaves his head without avoiding the transgression of the prohibition against rounding, there is no penalty. (3) Viz.: to permit infringement of a prohibition when it can be avoided. (4) And here, if rounding the whole head is not an infringement, he should shave the whole head at once. (5) Deut. XXII, 11. (6) The next verse. The inference is that fringes of wool may be placed on a linen garment, the prohibition of the preceding verse notwithstanding. (7) That a positive command overrides a simple prohibition. (8) This is inferred from the redundant '*each corner*'. Since we know from the preceding phrase that the fringes are to be on the corners, Raba concludes that the fringes must be of the same material as the garment. (9) Num. XV, 38. (10) Deut. XXII, 11, followed by *Thou shalt make thee twisted cords,* implying apparently that fringes must be made of wool and linen only.

How are these to be reconciled? Wool and linen discharge [the obligation to provide fringes] both for [garments of] their own species,[1] and also for other species,[2] but other kinds [of material] discharge [this obligation] only for [garments of] the same species but not for [garments of] a different species.[3]

And whence does the Tanna who utilises *'his head'* for [the inference that a positive command overrides] a simple prohibition learn that the positive command[4] overrides both a prohibition and a positive command?[5]—He infers it from [the expression] *'his beard'*.[6] For it has been taught: Why does Scripture mention *'his beard'*?[7] Since it says,[8] *neither shall they shave off the corners of their beard,*[9] it might be thought that the same is true of a priest who is a leper, and so Scripture says *'his beard'*.[10]

Why does not the [Tanna] who utilises *'his head'* for [teaching that] the positive command and prohibition [can be overruled by a positive command] infer it from [the words] *'his beard'*?—But according to your view[11] when we have the rule elsewhere [58*b*] that a positive command cannot override a prohibition accompanied by a positive command, let it be inferred from the [case of a leprous] priest that it *can* override?[12] [To this you reply] that we can make no inference from the [case of a leprous priest], [because] the case of the priest is different since the prohibition [overridden] does not apply to all people equally.[13] So, too, we are unable to infer the nazirite [leper] from the priest [leper] since the prohi-

(1) Wool and linen. (2) Wool fringes may be put on a silk or linen garment. (3) Silk fringes do not count as fringes if put on a woollen garment. (4) In the case of the leper. (5) If the nazirite becomes leprous he may shave his head on recovering. (6) Lev. XIV, 9, of a leper. (7) Since he must shave the whole of his body. (8) Of the priests. (9) Lev. XXI, 5. This is the prohibition. The positive command is contained in the next verse. *They shall be holy unto their God.* (10) Even a priest must shave his beard if he is a leper. (11) That we make the inference from *'his beard'*, so that the case of the leprous nazirite can be deduced from that of the leprous priest. (12) For your question assumes that there is no difference between this case and others. (13) It refers to priests but not to ordinary Israelites. A prohibition which applies to all equally must be considered of greater force and, therefore, if accompanied by a positive command, it cannot be overruled.

bition [overridden in the case of the priest] does not apply equally to all people.[1]

Now to what use does the [Tanna] who utilises [the phrase] *'his head'* for the nazirite [leper], put [the phrase] *'his beard'?*[2]—He requires it for [the following] that has been taught:[3] [From the verse] *Neither shall they* shave off *the corners of their beard,*[4] it might be thought that even if he shaved it with a scissors, he would be guilty, and so Scripture says [elsewhere], *neither shalt thou* mar [*the corners of thy beard*].[5] If it had [only written] *'neither shalt thou* mar' it might have been thought that if he plucked it out with tweezers or a *rohitni,*[6] he would be guilty, and so Scripture says, *'neither shalt they* shave off *the corners of their beard'.* What sort of shaving also mars? I should say that this is [shaving with] a razor.[7]

Now according to the other tanna who utilises the phrase, *'his head'* for [overriding] a simple prohibition, why is it necessary to write both *'his head'* and *'his beard'?* [For since the expression *'his head'*] can be understood as implying the overriding of a simple prohibition[8] and it can be understood also as implying the overriding of a prohibition accompanied by a positive command,[9] it can be applied indifferently to both,[10] and both could be inferred?[11] —The priest [leper] cannot be inferred from the nazirite [leper],

(1) But anyone can become a nazirite and so the nazirite prohibition is of greater force, and a rule which applies to priests cannot be taken as applying to nazirites. (2) For the priest leper can be inferred from the nazirite leper. (3) Our text repeats here the Baraitha about a priest leper quoted before: Why does Scripture mention *'his beard'*? Because it says, *neither shall they shave off the corners of their beard,* it might be thought that the same is true of a priest who is a leper, and so Scripture says *'his beard'*. And how do we know that this must be done with a razor? It has been taught: This passage appears to have been omitted by all the commentators and so we omit it with the BaḤ. (4) Lev. XXI, 5. (5) Lev. XIX, 27 of an ordinary Israelite. Scissors do not mar. (6) V. Glos. (7) And the phrase, *'his beard'* teaches us that the leper too must shave with a razor; Cf. *supra* 40*b*. (8) By inference from the verse, *'ye shall not round the corners of your head'* as in the first Baraitha *supra*. (9) From the nazirite as in the second Baraitha. (10) I.e., seeing that the method of inference is the same in both cases, we should have inferred both. (11) What need is there of *'his beard'*? The priest-leper can be inferred from the nazirite-leper.

since the latter can secure release [from his nazirite vow].[1] The nazirite [leper] cannot be inferred from the priest [leper], since the [latter] prohibition does not apply equally to all people.[2] [Finally,] we cannot infer from these a rule for other cases,[3] since the previously mentioned objections could be raised.[4]

Rab said: A man may thin [the hair of] his whole body with a razor. An objection was raised. [It has been taught:] One who removes [the hair of] the armpits or the private parts is to be scourged?[5]—This [refers to removal] by a razor whereas the other of [Rab refers to removal] by a scissors. But Rab also mentions a razor?—[He means closely] as though with a razor.

R. Ḥiyya b. Abba, citing R. Joḥanan said: One who removes [the hair of] the armpits or of the private parts is to be scourged. An objection was raised. [It has been taught:] Removal of hair is not [forbidden] by the Torah, but only by the Soferim?[6]—What he too meant by scourging is [scourging inflicted] by the Rabbis.[7] [59a] Others say [that the above argument took the following form]. R. Ḥiyya b. Abba, citing R. Joḥanan, said: One who removes [the hair of] the armpits or the private parts is to be scourged because of [infringing the prohibition] *neither shall a man put on a woman's garment.*[8] An objection was raised. [We have been taught:] Removal of hair is not [forbidden] by the Torah, but

(1) By applying to a sage. And since the prohibition is not a permanent one, it might be thought that only here can a positive command override a prohibition accompanied by a positive command but not in the case of a priest-leper. (2) But only to priests, whereas anyone can become a nazirite. Hence if the fact that a priest-leper may shave were taught, it would not be possible to infer in the case of a nazirite-leper that the prohibition and positive command to let his hair grow are overruled by the positive command for a leper to shave. (3) Lit., 'we cannot infer other cases from them'. I.e., that in all cases a positive command overrides a prohibition accompanied by a positive command. (4) Viz.: That the case of the nazirite and the priest are special instances and cannot be generalised. (5) For infringing the prohibition against a man appearing as a woman; v. *infra*. (6) Lit. 'by the Scribes' (v. Sanh., Sonc. ed., p. 360, n. 7). Why then does R. Joḥanan say that the penalty is scourging. (7) I.e. not the statutory 39 stripes, but a scourging prescribed at the discretion of the Rabbis for transgressing a non-Biblical law. (8) Deut. XXII, 5. It was customary only for women to shave the hair of the body.

only by the Soferim?—That statement [of R. Johanan] agrees with the following Tanna. For it has been taught: One who removes [the hair of] the armpits or the private parts infringes the prohibition, *neither shall a man put on a woman's garment.*

What interpretation does the first Tanna[1] put on [the verse] *'neither shall a man put on a woman's garment'?*—He requires it for the following that has been taught: Why does Scripture say, *A woman shall not wear that which pertaineth unto a man* [etc.]?[2] If merely [to teach] that a man should not put on a woman's garment, nor a woman a man's garment, behold it says [of this action] *this is an abomination*[3] and there is no abomination here![4] It must therefore mean that a man should not put on a woman's garment and mix with women, nor a woman a man's garment and mix with men. R. Eliezer b. Jacob says: How do we know that a woman should not go to war bearing arms? Scripture says, *'A woman shall not wear that which pertaineth unto a man.'* [The words] *'Neither shall a man put on a woman's garment,'* [signify] that a man is not to use cosmetics as women do.

R. Naḥman said that a nazirite is permitted [to remove the hair of his armpits],[5] but this is not the accepted ruling.

The Rabbis said to R. Simeon b. Abba: We have seen that R. Joḥanan has no [hair in his armpits].[6] [R. Simeon] said to them: It has fallen out because of his old age.

A certain man was sentenced to scourging before R. Ammi, and when his armpits became bared,[7] he noticed that they were not shaven. R. Ammi said to them: Let him go free. This man must be a member of the [learned] fraternity.[8]

Rab asked R. Ḥiyya whether [it was permitted] to shave[9] [the

(1) Who holds that the removal of this hair is not forbidden by the Torah. (2) *Ibid.* (3) The end of the verse reads: *'whosoever doeth these things is an abomination to the Lord'*. This word, *'abomination'*, is used of forbidden intercourse. (4) The mere act of putting on the garments is not wrong. (5) At the same time as he shaves his head when he would in any case be unattractive. (6) How is it possible, if the removal is forbidden. (7) As he was stripped to receive the punishment. (8) As the fact that his armpits were unshaven proved. (9) With scissors.

armpits]. He replied: It is forbidden. [Rab] then asked: But it grows?[1] He replied: Son of great ancestors,[2] there is a limit. If it continues to grow [beyond this] it falls out.

Rab asked R. Ḥiyya whether [it was permitted] to scratch [the armpits to remove the hair]. He replied: It is forbidden. [To the further question] whether he might [scratch] through his garment,[3] he replied that it was permitted. Some say that he asked him whether he might [scratch] through his garment during prayers[4] and he replied that it was forbidden; but this is not the accepted ruling.[5]

MISHNAH. [59*b*] IF ONE OF THEM DIES;[6] R. JOSHUA SAID THAT [THE OTHER] SHOULD SEEK SOME THIRD PERSON[7] PREPARED TO UNDERTAKE A NAZIRITE-VOW TOGETHER WITH HIM, AND SAY: 'IF I WAS DEFILED, YOU ARE TO BE A NAZIRITE IMMEDIATELY, BUT IF I WAS CLEAN, YOU ARE TO BECOME A NAZIRITE AT THE END OF THIRTY DAYS.' THEY THEN COUNT THIRTY DAYS AND BRING SACRIFICES FOR DEFILEMENT AND SACRIFICES [DUE ON TERMINATING A NAZIRITESHIP] IN PURITY AND [THE FIRST ONE] SAYS, 'IF I AM THE ONE WHO WAS DEFILED, THE SACRIFICES FOR DEFILEMENT ARE MINE AND THE SACRIFICES IN PURITY ARE YOURS, WHILST IF I AM THE ONE WHO REMAINED CLEAN, THE SACRIFICES IN PURITY ARE MINE AND THE SACRIFICES AFTER DEFILEMENT ARE [SACRIFICES OFFERED] IN DOUBT.'[8] THEY THEN COUNT [A FURTHER] THIRTY DAYS AND BRING [ONE SET OF] THE SACRIFICES IN PURITY AND [THE FIRST ONE] SAYS, 'IF I AM THE

(1) Uncomfortably long, and one should be allowed to remove it for the sake of comfort without transgressing the prohibition. (2) Lit., 'Son of princes'. A favourite appellation of Rab, used by his uncle R. Ḥiyya. (3) I.e. whether he might scratch on top of his shirt, without touching the bare flesh. (4) To remove a source of irritation. It is forbidden to touch the bare skin during prayers. (5) I.e. scratching through a garment is allowed. (6) One of the two men mentioned in the last Mishnah 57*a*. (7) Lit. 'someone from the street'. (8) Its flesh would be interred and not eaten, as is the case with a sacrifice brought for certain defilement; v. *supra* 29*a*.

ONE WHO WAS DEFILED, THE SACRIFICE FOR DEFILEMENT [OFFERED PREVIOUSLY] WAS MINE AND THE SACRIFICE IN PURITY WAS YOURS, AND THIS IS MY SACRIFICE IN PURITY, WHILST IF I WAS THE ONE WHO REMAINED CLEAN, THE SACRIFICE IN PURITY WAS MINE AND THE SACRIFICE AFTER DEFILEMENT [WAS OFFERED] IN DOUBT AND THIS IS YOUR SACRIFICE IN PURITY.

BEN ZOMA SAID TO [R. JOSHUA]: WHO WILL LISTEN TO [THIS MAN] AND UNDERTAKE A NAZIRITE-VOW TOGETHER WITH HIM? WHAT HE MUST DO IS TO BRING[1] A BIRD AS A SIN-OFFERING AND AN ANIMAL AS A BURNT-OFFERING AND SAY, 'IF I WAS DEFILED, THE SIN-OFFERING IS PART OF MY DUE[2] AND THE BURNT-OFFERING IS A VOLUNTARY OFFERING, WHILST IF I REMAINED CLEAN, THE BURNT-OFFERING IS PART OF MY DUE AND THE SIN-OFFERING [A SACRIFICE OFFERED] IN DOUBT.' HE MUST THEN COUNT THIRTY DAYS AND BRING THE SACRIFICES IN PURITY AND SAY, 'IF I WAS DEFILED, THE FORMER BURNT-OFFERING WAS A VOLUNTARY ONE AND THIS IS THE OBLIGATORY ONE, WHILST IF I REMAINED CLEAN, THE FORMER BURNT-OFFERING WAS THE OBLIGATORY ONE AND THIS THE VOLUNTARY ONE. THESE [OTHERS] ARE THE REST OF MY SACRIFICES.' R. JOSHUA RETORTED: THE RESULT WILL BE THAT THIS [NAZIRITE] WILL BRING HIS SACRIFICES HALF AT A TIME![3] THE SAGES, HOWEVER, AGREED WITH BEN ZOMA.

GEMARA. But let him bring them [half at a time]?[4]—Rab Judah citing Samuel said: R. Joshua only said this in order to sharpen [the wits of] the students.[5]

(1) On completing his naziriteship. (2) He must offer the sin-offering because he cannot commence to count the naziriteship in purity until it is sacrificed, if he had been in fact defiled. The other sacrifices can be dispensed with in the circumstances; v. *supra* 18*b*. (3) If he was in fact clean, his burnt-offering will have been brought thirty days before the other sacrifices. (4) I.e., What is the point of R. Joshua's objection to the procedure of Ben Zoma. (5) It was not a real objection. R. Joshua merely wanted the students to learn not to forbear from raising an objection because it may have no basis.

R. Naḥman[1] said, What would R. Joshua do with the intestines to prevent them decomposing?[2]

MISHNAH. A NAZIRITE WHO WAS IN DOUBT WHETHER HE HAD BEEN DEFILED AND IN DOUBT WHETHER HE HAD BEEN A CONFIRMED[3] LEPER, MAY EAT SACRED MEATS AFTER SIXTY DAYS,[4] AND DRINK WINE AND TOUCH THE DEAD AFTER ONE HUNDRED AND TWENTY DAYS,[5] SINCE POLLING ON ACCOUNT OF [LEPROUS] DISEASE OVERRIDES [THE PROHIBITION AGAINST] THE POLLING OF THE NAZIRITE ONLY WHEN [THE LEPROSY] IS CERTAIN, BUT WHEN IT IS DOUBTFUL IT DOES NOT OVERRIDE IT.[6]

GEMARA. [60*a*] A Tanna taught: [The procedure laid down in the *Mishnah*] applies only in the case of a short naziriteship,[7] but in the case of a naziriteship of [, say,] a year, he may eat sacred meats [only] after two years, and drink wine and touch the dead after four years.[8] It has been taught further in connection with this: He must poll four times.[9] At the first polling he brings a pair of birds, a bird as a sin-offering, and an animal as a burnt-offering.[10] At the second [polling] he brings a bird as a sin-offering and an animal as a burnt-offering. At the third he [again] brings a bird

(1) Both Rashi and Tosaf. have: 'R. Naḥman b. Isaac'. (2) If we were to do as R. Joshua suggests, the fat of the intestines (which must be offered on the altar) would decompose whilst *both* nazirites were being shaved prior to the waving. Surely, this is as great an objection as the bringing of the sacrifices at different times. R. Naḥman points out that not merely is there no technical objection to the procedure of Ben Zoma but R. Joshua's cannot even be considered preferable. *Tosaf.* (3) מוחלט 'confirmed': a person afflicted with leprosy who, on the first examination or after the period of confinement, is declared by the priest to be a leper; v. Lev. XIII, 45ff. (4) I.e., after counting two nazirite periods of thirty days. (5) After four nazirite periods. V. *supra* 55*b* for relevant notes. (6) But the period of naziriteship must be observed before polling; v. *Gemara* following. (7) Of thirty days duration. (8) Tosef. Naz. VI, 1. (9) At the end of each thirty days or year. (10) The purpose of the offerings will be explained immediately.

as a sin-offering and an animal as a burnt-offering. At the fourth he brings the sacrifice [due on terminating the naziriteship] in purity.

It has just been said: 'At the first polling he brings etc.' [In this way] whatever the facts are he offers the correct [sacrifice]. For if he was certainly a leper but was not defiled, the pair of birds are [in discharge of] his obligation,[1] the bird as a sin-offering [is a sacrifice offered] in doubt and is to be buried, and the burnt-offering is a free-will offering. He cannot however be shaved [a second time] seven days hence,[2] for perhaps he is not a confirmed leper and the All-Merciful has said [of the nazirite], *There shall no razor come upon his head until [the days] be fulfilled.*[3] If, on the other hand, he was not certainly a leper but he was defiled, then the bird as a sin-offering is [in discharge of] his obligation,[4] the pair of birds, being prepared without [the Temple court][5] are not [in the category of] profane [animals] brought into the Temple-court,[6] whilst the animal as a burnt-offering is a freewill-offering. Finally, if he was neither a leper nor defiled, then the pair of birds are [in any case] prepared without [the Temple-court],[7] the bird as a sin-offering is to be buried, and the animal as a burnt-offering is [in discharge of] his obligation [as a clean nazirite].[8]

But surely he requires a guilt-offering?[9]—[The author of this Baraitha] is R. Simeon who says that he brings one and makes a stipulation.[10]

At the second and third polling a pair of birds is unnecessary

(1) V. Lev. XIV, 2. (2) The normal period of separation between the two pollings of a leper; Lev. XIV, 9. (3) Num. VI, 5. He must therefore wait another whole period before he can shave the second time. Hence he can eat sacred meats only after two periods have elapsed. (4) Ibid. 10. (5) Lev. XIV, 5 *seq*. (6) And so can be offered even though he may not have been a leper. (7) And so can be offered even if he is not a leper. (8) This permits him to poll and the other sacrifices can be brought later. (9) After the second polling on recovery from leprosy (Lev. XIV, 10). Until it was brought he could not eat sacred meats. (10) V. Men. 105*a*. He stipulates that if a guilt-offering is not due, the animal is to be a voluntary peace-offering. Since the author is R. Simeon, there was no need to mention the guilt-offering.

for these have been prepared.[1] What [doubt] is there [remaining]? That perhaps he was actually a confirmed leper?[2] [Because of this he offers] one [of the two birds as a sin-offering,][3] for the doubt on account of the tale of days[4] and one for the doubt on account of defilement.[5]

At the fourth polling he brings the sacrifice in purity and stipulates [60*b*] that if he was actually a [clean] nazirite,[6] the first burnt-offering was [in discharge of] his obligation and the present one is a freewill-offering, whilst if he was defiled and a confirmed leper, the first burnt-offering was a freewill-offering and this one is [in discharge of] his obligation and the other [animals] are the rest of his sacrifice.

[A nazirite] who was in doubt whether he had been defiled but certainly been a confirmed leper, may eat sacred meats after eight days,[7] and may drink wine and touch the dead after sixty-seven days.[8] One who was in doubt whether he had been a confirmed leper but had certainly been defiled, may eat sacred meats after thirty-seven days,[9] and may drink wine and touch the dead after seventy-four days. One who was certainly defiled and certainly a confirmed leper may eat sacred meats after eight days, and may drink wine and touch the dead after forty-four days.[10]

R. Simeon b. Yoḥai was asked by his disciples: May a ritually

(1) At the first polling. (2) When he must now bring sacrifices due after his tale of days; Lev. XIV, 9. (3) Brought at the second and third pollings. (4) The seven days that must be counted between the two pollings of a nazirite, but which have here become a whole period. (5) The burnt-offering is brought on each occasion in case he should have completed his naziriteship in purity. (6) And was never a leper nor unclean. (7) Since the shaving for leprosy may take place immediately he is seen to be clean and he has still to wait eight days. (8) For he must wait thirty days after the second polling for leprosy before he may shave on account of the doubt whether he was defiled, and then he counts thirty days for his naziriteship in purity. (9) As a defiled nazirite, he polls on becoming clean at the end of seven days and then again for his clean naziriteship after thirty days. Since he may have been a leper, these two pollings now count for the leprosy and as he was certainly unclean he can poll after seven days for the uncleanness and again after thirty days for his clean naziriteship. (10) Seven for the leprosy, seven for the defilement and thirty for the clean naziriteship; Tosef. *Naz.* VI, 2.

clean nazirite who was a leper poll once only[1] and have it reckoned for both purposes?[2]—He replied: He cannot poll in this way.[3] They then asked him: Why?—He replied: If both [the nazirite and the leper polled] in order that it should grow again,[4] or both [polled] in order to remove [the hair],[5] your suggestion would be sound, but as it is the nazirite [polls] to remove [the hair] and the leper [polls] to let it grow again. [They then said:] Granted that it should not count [for both pollings] after the period of confirmed leprosy, let it still count [for both] after his tale of days?[6]—He replied: If both were required to poll before the sprinkling of the blood [of the sacrifice], your suggestion would be sound, but here the leper polls before the sprinkling of the blood[7] and the nazirite after the sprinkling of the blood.[8] [They next suggested that though the one polling] should not count both for the days of his leprosy and his naziriteship, yet it ought to count for the days [both] of his leprosy and of his defilements.[9] [R. Simeon, however,] said to them: If both [polled] before bathing, your proposal would be sound, but the defiled [nazirite polls] after bathing[10] and the leper before bathing.[12]

[Another version of the discussion is as follows.][13] They said to him: You have given a good reason why it should not count [both] for his tale of days and for his naziriteship, but why should not [one polling] count for his period of confirmed leprosy as well as for his defilement, since in both cases [the polling] is to allow [the hair] to grow?—He replied: In the case of a ritually clean nazirite

(1) If the termination of his naziriteship and his recovery from the disease coincided. (2) This is really an objection to the Mishnah which requires him to poll four times, i.e., separately for each contingency. (R. Asher.) (3) And he must poll twice. (4) I.e., if both were required to remove the hair a second time as the leper must. (5) With no subsequent obligation to let it grow. (6) Since after the tale of days (Lev. XIV, 9), the leper also polls to remove his hair. (7) He shaves on the seventh day and offers the sacrifice on the eighth day, (Lev. XIV, 9-10). (8) V. Num. VI, 16-18. (9) I.e., when the end of leprosy and defilement coincide. (10) *He shall shave his head on the day of his cleansing* (Num. VI, 9) i.e., after bathing. (11) V. Lev. XIV, 9. (12) Tosef. *Naz.* V, 4, where the arguments are transposed in part. (13) So Tosaf. and R. Asher consider the next passage.

who is a leper, [the purpose of] the one [polling][1] is for [the hair] to grow again and the other[2] is to remove [the hair], whilst in the case of a defiled nazirite who is a leper, the latter [polling takes place] before bathing and the former after bathing.

[61*a*] R. Ḥiyya taught [the following differences: The leper polls] before bathing, [the unclean nazirite] after bathing; the former before the sprinkling of the blood, the [clean nazirite] after the sprinkling of the blood.

SINCE POLLING ON ACCOUNT OF [LEPROUS] DISEASE etc. Rami b. Ḥama propounded: Are the four pollings required[3] for carrying out a religious duty,[4] or whether they are merely in order to remove defiled hair?[5] The practical issue is whether this may be removed with *nasha.*[6] For if we say that they are a religious duty it would not be permitted to treat [the hair] with *nasha,* whereas if their purpose is simply the removal of defiled hair, treatment with *nasha* would be permitted. What, then, is the law?—Raba replied: Come and hear: And he is required to undergo four pollings.[7] Now if you assume that their purpose is simply the removal of defiled hair, three [pollings] alone should suffice.[8] Hence you may prove that they are [all] a religious duty. This proves it.

(1) Viz., the polling because of the confirmed leprosy. (2) Viz., the polling after the naziriteship. (3) For a nazirite who was both doubtfully a leper and doubtfully defiled. (4) I.e., whether each one is a religious duty requiring a razor. (5) And only the polling of a clean nazirite requires a razor. (6) A plant depilatory, v. *supra* p. 146, n. 4. (7) The Baraitha cited above. (8) For only the first three pollings are because of the doubtful leprosy and defilement. The fourth is certainly an ordinary polling of a clean nazirite. Hence since the Baraitha makes no distinction between them, they must all be equally a religious duty.

NAZIR

CHAPTER IX

MISHNAH. GENTILES HAVE NO [COMPETENCE FOR] NAZIRITESHIP,[1] BUT WOMEN AND SLAVES[2] HAVE. THE NAZIRITE VOW IS MORE STRINGENT IN THE CASE OF WOMEN THAN IN THE CASE OF SLAVES, FOR A MAN CAN COMPEL HIS SLAVE [TO BREAK HIS VOW][3] BUT HE CANNOT COMPEL HIS WIFE [TO DO SO].

GEMARA. The Mishnah teaches that GENTILES HAVE NO [COMPETENCE FOR] NAZIRITESHIP [etc.]. How do we know this?—For our Rabbis taught: [Scripture says] *Speak unto the children* of Israel,[4] but not to Gentiles; *and say unto them,* thereby including slaves.[5]

But what need is there of a verse,[6] seeing that there is a principle that every precept incumbent on women is also incumbent on slaves?[7]—Raba replied: [Naziriteship] is different [from other laws]. For there is a verse, [*When a man voweth a vow*] *to bind* his *soul with a bond,*[8] which thus refers to one who is his own master[9] and excludes slaves who are not their own masters.[10] Now because [slaves] are not their own masters it might be thought that they are precluded from making nazirite-vows[11] and so we are told [this is not so].

(1) I.e., if a gentile undertakes to be a nazirite, the vow is of no effect. (2) [I.e., non-Jewish slaves who, after having submitted to circumcision and the prescribed ablution, are subject to the fulfilment of certain precepts.] (3) As long as the slave belongs to him. (4) Num. VI, 2; opening the chapter on naziriteship. (5) 'Israel' is not repeated, and thus we infer that others than Israelites can undertake naziriteship, i.e., slaves also. (6) To allow slaves to undertake naziriteship. (7) Women are explicitly allowed to become nazirites (Num. VI, 2). For the principle, v. Chag. 4*a*. (8) Num. XXX, 3 which lays down that vows are binding. (9) Lit., 'whose soul (person) belongs to himself'. (10) A slave's vows are not binding. (11) Since they are also a kind of vow.

The Master stated: '*Speak unto the children of Israel* but not to Gentiles.' But does the mention of Israel always exclude Gentiles?[1] Is there not written in connection with '*Arakin*,[2] *Speak unto the children of Israel*,[3] and yet it has been taught: 'Israelites can vow '*Arakin* but not Gentiles. It might be thought that [Gentiles] cannot be the subject of '*Arakin* vows either,[4] but the verse says *A man*'?[5]—[Naziriteship] is different, for here there is a verse, *He shall not make himself unclean for his father or his mother*,[6] which shows that [the passage] is referring to such as have a [legal] father,[7] and thus excluding Gentiles who have no [legal] father. In what respect have Gentiles no father? Shall I say it is as regards inheritance?[8] Surely R. Ḥiyya b. Abin, citing R. Joḥanan has said that a Gentile inherits his father in Torah-law, for there is a verse, *Because I have given Mount Seir to Esau for an [inheritance]*![9]—You must therefore mean that such as are bound to honour their fathers [are referred to].[10] But does it say *Honour thy father* in connection with nazirites?[11] —We must therefore say that the verse, '*He shall not make himself unclean for his father or his mother*' shows that only those to whom [the laws of] defilement apply [can assume naziriteship] [61*b*] but not gentiles to whom [the laws of] defilement do not apply.

How do we know that [the laws of] defilement do not apply to them?—The verse says, *But the man that shall be unclean and shall not purify himself, that soul shall be cut off from the midst of the* ḳahal

(1) From the scope of the scriptural passage in which it occurs. (2) Vows of valuation, v. Lev. XXVII. (3) Lev. XXVII, 1. (4) I.e., that an Israelite cannot vow to give the valuation of a Gentile. (5) Ibid. v. 2; '*When a man shall clearly utter a vow of persons unto the Lord according to thy valuation*'. Thus we see that '*Israel*' in v. 1 does not exclude Gentiles entirely from the scope of the chapter, but only disqualifies them from vowing '*Arakin*. Similarly, since the word '*man*' also occurs in connection with naziriteship (Num. VI, 2), Gentiles should not be wholly excluded from naziriteship. (6) Num. VI, 7. (7) Viz.: Jews, who in all matters belong to their fathers' family, Gentiles, on the other hand, are held in Jewish law to count descent from the mother. (8) I.e., that a Gentile should not inherit his father. (9) E.V. 'possession'. Deut. II, 5. (10) V. Num. VI, 7. And since a Gentile is not bound by the commandment, he cannot become a nazirite. (11) That you hold Gentiles to be excluded from the scope of the chapter.

[*assembly*],[1] referring to such as form a *kahal* and excluding [gentiles] who do not form a *kahal*.[2]

How does it follow [that the laws of defilement do not apply to gentiles]? Perhaps [all that is meant is that] he is not liable to *kareth* [excision],[3] but [the laws of] defilement do apply [to him]?[4]—Scripture says, *And the clean person shall sprinkle upon the unclean*,[5] [teaching that] whoever can become clean,[6] becomes unclean, and whoever cannot become clean does not become unclean.[7]

But perhaps we may say that while [the laws of] purification do not apply to [gentiles], yet [the laws of] defilement do apply?[8]—Scripture says, *But the man that shall be unclean and shall not purify himself*.[9]

R. Aḥa b. Jacob said: [Naziriteship] is different,[10] for here there is a verse, *And ye may make them an inheritance for your children after you*.[11] [From this we learn that] to whomsoever [the laws of] inheritance [of slaves] apply, to him [the laws of] defilement apply, and to whomsoever [the laws of] inheritance [of slaves] do not apply, to him [the laws of] defilement do not apply.[12]

If that is the reason [that gentiles cannot become nazirites],[13] then slaves too should not be able [to become nazirites]?[14]—In point of fact, said Raba, [the following is the reason that gentiles are wholly excluded from naziriteship].[15] It is quite permissible in

(1) Num. XIX, 20. (2) The term '*kahal* is used of Jews only. (3) If he enters the Temple whilst defiled; for the word *kahal* is used in the phrase referring to excision. On *kareth* v. Glos. (4) I.e., he can become unclean and defile others. (5) Num. XIX, 19. (6) I.e., by undergoing the purification rites. [These rites are specially prescribed for the congregation of the children of Israel. V. Num. XIX, 9.] (7) And since a gentile cannot undergo the purification rites, he does not become unclean. (8) I.e., having become unclean, he can defile others and remains unclean himself, but he cannot become clean again. (9) Num. XIX, 20. Implying that wherever there can be no purification, there is no defilement. (10) From '*Arakin*. And when we said that gentiles have no legal father, it was in respect of slaves. (11) Lev. XXV, 46. Referring to gentile slaves. A gentile cannot bequeath his slaves in Torah-law; v. Giṭ. 38*a*. (12) And since the laws of defilement do not apply to gentiles, they cannot become nazirites. (13) Viz., that they cannot bequeath their slaves to their heirs. (14) For the laws of inheritance do not apply to slaves. A slave's property becomes his master's. (15) Although the mention of '*children of Israel*' does not necessarily exclude gentiles from the scope of a scriptural passage.

the case of *'Arakin* [to argue thus:] when it says, *'the children of Israel'* [it implies that] Israelites can vow *'Arakin* but not gentiles. I might go on to infer from this that [gentiles] cannot be the subject of *'Arakin* vows either,[1] Scripture [therefore] says *'a man'*.[2] [But you cannot similarly argue] here, [in the case of naziriteship as follows: The words *'children of Israel'* imply that] Israelites can undertake nazirite-vows and bring the offering [due on terminating the naziriteship], but not gentiles.[3] I might go on to infer from this that [gentiles] cannot become nazirites at all. Scripture [therefore] says *'man'*.[4] For I will say such an argument is inadmissable[5] since [the exclusion of gentiles] from [bringing the nazirite] offering is not inferred from this [verse], but from elsewhere, [as has been taught:] R. Jose, the Galilean said, [the verse] *for a burnt-offering*[6] serves to exclude [a gentile] from [bringing] the nazirite-offerings.[7]

Why not argue [as follows: The words *'children of Israel'* imply that] Israelites can undertake life-naziriteships but not gentiles. I might go on to infer from this that [gentiles] cannot undertake [ordinary] nazirite-vows either,[8] Scripture [therefore] says *'man'*?[9] —R. Johanan replied: Is the life-nazirite mentioned [in Scripture]?[10]

Why not argue [as follows: The words *children of Israel* imply that] Israelites can impose nazirite-vows upon their children, but not gentiles. I might go on to infer from this that [gentiles] cannot become nazirites [at all], Scripture [therefore] says *'man'*?[11] —But

(1) I.e., that gentiles are wholly excluded from the scope of the passage dealing with *'Arakin*. (2) And gentiles may be the subject of an *'Arakin* vow though they cannot make such a vow. (3) Thus the mention of *'children of Israel'* excludes gentiles from the scope of the nazirite passage. (4) Num. VI, 2. The mention of *'man'* now partially includes gentiles within the scope of the passage. They can become nazirites, but may not bring the offerings due on terminating the naziriteship. (5) I.e., it is impossible to utilise the words *'children of Israel'* merely in order to exclude gentiles from bringing the nazirite offerings. (6) Lev. XXII, 18. (7) V. Men. 73*b*. Thus the words *'children of Israel'* must wholly exclude gentiles from naziriteship. (8) I.e., gentiles are wholly excluded from the scope of the nazirite passage. (9) They can become ordinary nazirites. (10) We learnt about it from the case of Absalom (*supra* 4*b*). Hence the verse cannot be referring to the life-nazirite at all. (11) They can themselves undertake nazirite-vows but cannot impose them upon their children.

R. Johanan has said that this is a [traditional] ruling with regard to the nazirite![1]

Why not argue [as follows: The words *'children of Israel'* imply that] Israelites can poll [with the offerings due] for their father's nazirite-sacrifices,[2] but not gentiles. [62a] I might go on to infer from this that [gentiles] cannot become nazirites [at all], Scripture [therefore] says *man?*—But it has been stated: R. Johanan said, This is a [traditional] ruling with regard to the nazirite.[3]

Now if it is a fact [that *'man'* includes gentiles],[4] what need is there for the expression, *When* a man *shall clearly utter a vow . . . according to thy valuation*[5] occurring in connection with *'Arakin?* For consider! *'Arakin* are compared [in this verse] with vows, as it says, *When a man shall clearly* utter a vow . . . *according to thy valuation,*[5] and it has been taught in connection with vows: Scripture mentions the word *man*[6] in order to include gentiles, who are allowed to vow vowed-offerings[7] and freewill-offerings,[8] just as Israelites do.[9] What need then is there for the verse, *'When a* man *shall clearly utter'* in connection with *'Arakin?*[10]—In point of fact, this [word] *'man'* is required for the inclusion of [a

(1) *Supra* 28*b*. Hence, Scripture cannot be referring to this ruling. (2) *Supra* 30*a*. (3) Hence Scripture cannot be referring to it and the words, *'children of Israel'*, must entirely exclude gentiles from undertaking naziriteships. (4) The upshot of the previous discussion is a vindication of the assertion that *'man'* usually includes gentiles. It is only because it cannot possibly have that meaning in connection with naziriteship, that it is not so interpreted there. Hence the *Gemara* now enquires whether gentiles would not have been included for the purposes of *'Arakin* even without *'man'* being mentioned. (5) Lev. XXVII, 2. (6) V. Lev. XXII, 18. *Whoever he be* (*lit., a man, a man*) . . . *that bringeth his offering, whether it be of their vows* etc. The reference in the following discussion is to vowing sacrifices for the altar. [The text adopted follows BaH. Cur. edd. read: Scripture should have mentioned (only) 'a man' why does it state *'a man, a man'*. Though the reading is supported by the parallel passages, it hardly fits in with the trend of the passage where the word *'man'* in itself is taken to include gentiles.] (7) Heb. נדר. (8) Heb. נדבה. The difference between a vowed-offering and a freewill offering is this. The former, if it dies or is lost, must be replaced, but the latter need not be replaced. (9) Cf. *Tem.* 2*b*. (10) For *'Ar.* are covered by the interpretation of Lev. XXII, 18 in the Baraitha.

youth] who can discriminate but has not quite reached manhood.[1]

This is all very well [if we accept the view of] the authority[2] who considers that a youth who can discriminate but has not quite reached manhood has a Scriptural right [to make vows],[3] but [if we accept the view of] the authority[4] who considers this right to be rabbinic, what need is there for, *When a* man *shall clearly utter* [*etc.*]?[5] It serves to include a gentile [youth] who can discriminate but has not quite reached manhood.[6]

This is all very well if we accept the view of the authority[7] who argues [as follows: The words *'children of Israel'* imply that] Israelites can be the subject of *'Arakin* vows but not gentiles. I might go on to infer from this that [gentiles] cannot vow *'Arakin*, Scripture [therefore] says *man*.[8] If, however, we accept the view of the authority[9] who argues [as follows: The words *children of Israel* imply that] Israelites can vow *'Arakin* but not gentiles. I might go on to infer from this that [gentiles] cannot be the subject of *'Arakin*, Scripture [therefore] says *man*: [our difficulty remains]. For seeing that even a baby a month old can be the subject of an *'Arakin* vow, what need is there of, *'when* [*a man*] *shall clearly utter'?*[10]—R. Adda b. Ahaba replied: Its purpose is to bring within the scope of the rule an adult gentile who although he is an adult [cannot make even ordinary vows, if he] cannot discriminate.[11]

Now what need is there of [the phrase,] *'when* [*a man*] *shall clearly utter'* mentioned in connection with the naziriteship? For seeing that the naziriteship is compared with [ordinary] vowing[12] what need is there of *'when* [*a man*] *shall clearly utter'?*—It serves to include

(1) He too may make vows. V. *supra* 29*b*. (2) R. Jose b. R. Judah. V. *supra* 29*b*. (3) This right is then inferred from the word *'man'* in Lev. XXVII, 2. (4) R. Judah the Prince (Ibid.). (5) I.e., We are still without a use for the word *'man'* in this verse. (6) R. Judah the Prince also agreeing that his right to make vows is Scriptural. (7) R. Judah; V. *'Ar.* 5*b*. (8) Thus permitting gentile youths who have not yet reached manhood to make *'Arakin* (and other) vows. (9) R. Meir. *Ibid.* (10) For it can no longer refer to gentile youths since no gentile can make an *'Arakin* vow. (11) The inference being: Only a gentile who knows what he is uttering can make even ordinary vows (Tosaf.). (12) V. Ned. 3*a*. And *'shall clearly utter'* already occurs in connection with vows in Lev. XXVII, 2.

allusions the significance of which is not manifest.[1] For it has been stated: Abaye said that allusions whose significance is not manifest have the force of a direct statement, whilst Raba said that they have not the force of a direct statement.[2] Now if we accept Abaye's view, there is no difficulty,[3] but if we accept Raba's view what can we reply?[4]—In point of fact *'when [a man] shall clearly utter'* is necessary for R. Tarfon's case. For it has been taught: R. Judah on behalf of R. Tarfon said that not one of these people[5] is a nazirite, because naziriteship is not intended except when assumed unequivocally.[6] This is all very well if we accept the view of R. Tarfon, but [if we accept the view of] the Rabbis what can you reply?[7]—In point of fact it is necessary for [the following] which has been taught: Annulment of vows has no foundation[8] and is without [Scriptural] support.[9] R. Eliezer says that it has [Scriptural] support, for Scripture says twice *'when [a man] shall clearly utter'?*[10] one signifies a distinct binding expression,[11] and one a distinctness [which opens the way] to annulment.[12]

MISHNAH. [62b] [THE NAZIRITE-VOWS OF] SLAVES ARE MORE STRINGENT THAN [THOSE OF] WOMEN; FOR HE CAN DECLARE VOID THE VOWS OF HIS WIFE, BUT HE CANNOT DECLARE VOID THE VOWS OF HIS SLAVES. IF HE DECLARES HIS WIFE'S [VOW] VOID, IT IS VOID FOR EVER, BUT IF HE DECLARES HIS SLAVE'S VOW VOID, HE BECOMES FREE AND MUST COMPLETE HIS NAZIRITESHIP.[13]

(1) V. *supra* 2a-b. (2) And the vow fails to take effect. (3) The interpretation will be: The vow must be uttered clearly or it is of no effect. (4) I.e., what use does he make of the phrase 'to utter clearly?' (5) Who vow nazariteships of the form. If the person approaching is So and so, I will become a nazirite. (6) V. *supra* 34a. (7) I.e., what use do they make of '*shall clearly utter*'? (8) Lit., '*fly in the air*'. (9) I.e., the possibility of annulling vows is purely a traditional law. (10) Once in Lev. XXVII, 2 of '*Arakin* and once in Num. VI, 2 of nazirite vows. (11) I.e., once the vow is clearly undertaken, it remains binding. (12) If annulment is sought, the vow ceases to be binding. (13) Thus our text, and so Maimonides (*Mishnah Commentary a.l.* and *Yad. Neziruth.* II, 18). Raabad however, reads 'and he afterwards becomes free, then he must complete his vow'.

GEMARA. Our Rabbis taught: What can his master compel him [to disregard]? [The vow of] Naziriteship, but not [other] vows, or [vows involving] *'Arakin*.[1]

Why this difference in the case of the nazirite-vow?—The *All-Merciful* has said, *To bind his soul with a bond*,[2] showing that only those who are their own masters[3] are referred to, and excluding slaves, who are not their own masters. But if this is the reason, the same should be true of [other] vows?[4]—R. Shesheth replied: We suppose here[5] that a cluster of grapes lay before [the slave].[6] In the case of vows, where if this [cluster] becomes prohibited to him, others will not become prohibited, [his master] cannot compel him [to eat this one]. But in the case of a nazirite-vow, if this one becomes forbidden,[7] all others become forbidden; and that is why he can compel him [to eat it].[8]

But do not [ordinary] vows[9] include the possibility that there is available only the one cluster of grapes in question, so that if he does not eat it he will grow weak[10] [and yet the vow takes effect]?—Raba therefore said: We suppose that a pressed grape lay before him.[11] In the case of vows, he is prohibited from eating that one only, and so [his master] cannot compel him [to break his vow]. But in the case of the nazirite-vow where he is also prohibited from eating others, he can compel him [to break his vow].

But do not [ordinary] vows include the possibility that there is available only the one pressed grape in question, so that if he does not eat it he will grow weak [and yet the vow takes effect]?—Abaye therefore replied: [The Baraitha really means] what is his master obliged to compel him [to disregard]? [The vow of] naziriteship,[12]

(1) Tosef. Naz. VI, where 'oaths' replaces '*Arakin*', for which v. Glos. (2) Num. XXX, 3 of ordinary vows. (3) V. *supra* p. 228, n. 9. (4) Seeing that the passage in which the verse occurs refers to ordinary vows. (5) In the Baraitha which distinguishes nazirite-vows from other vows. (6) And his vow, nazirite or ordinary, was made with reference to that bunch of grapes. (7) I.e. if the nazirite-vow does become operative. (8) [So as to have his strength unimpaired.] (9) As referred to in the Baraitha. (10) And so injure his master. (11) [It is assumed that abstention from the pressed grape cannot affect his strength (Asheri)]. (12) If he does not wish it to take effect.

but he does not [even] have to compel him [to disregard ordinary] vows or oaths.[1] This is because the verse says [*If any one swear*] *to do evil or to do good.*[2] Just as doing good is a voluntary undertaking, so must the doing of evil be a voluntary undertaking, the doing of evil to others being thereby excluded, since he has not the right [to harm others].[3]

MISHNAH. SHOULD [THE SLAVE] FLEE FROM [HIS MASTER'S] PRESENCE,[4] R. MEIR SAID THAT HE MUST NOT DRINK WINE, BUT R. JOSE SAID THAT HE MAY.

GEMARA. Is it possible that [R. Meir and R. Jose] differ in regard to the following dictum of Samuel? For Samuel has said: Should a man renounce ownership of his slave, he becomes free, no deed of emancipation being required. Does R. Meir agree with Samuel[5] and R. Jose differ from him?—No; both hold this opinion of Samuel.[6] But the one who says he should drink considers that since he is ultimately to return to his master, he ought to drink in order not to grow emaciated. The other, who says that he should not drink considers that he should feel the pangs of deprivation in order that he should return [to his master].

MISHNAH. [63*a*] IF A NAZIRITE POLLS AND THEN DISCOVERS THAT HE WAS DEFILED, THEN IF THE DEFILEMENT IS DEFINITE [THE NAZIRITESHIP] IS RENDERED VOID, BUT IF IT IS A DEFILEMENT OF THE DEPTH,[7] IT IS NOT RENDERED VOID. BEFORE POLLING, HOWEVER, EITHER [TYPE OF DEFILE-

(1) These being automatically of no effect. (2) Lev. V, 4. (3) And since a slave's vows harm his master, they are inoperative. (4) Run away after making a nazirite-vow. (5) And assume that the owner despairs of the slave's return and thus renounces his ownership. The slave being free must therefore complete his naziriteship (v. previous Mishnah). (6) And do not consider the owner to have renounced his possession of the slave. (7) טומאת התהום. A particular type of uncertain defilement, defined later in the Mishnah.

MENT] RENDERS [THE NAZIRITESHIP] VOID. [THE LAW REGARDING 'DEFILEMENT OF THE DEPTH' IS] AS FOLLOWS. IF HE GOES DOWN INTO A CAVERN TO BATHE, AND A CORPSE IS FOUND FLOATING AT THE MOUTH OF THE CAVERN,[1] HE IS [DEFINITELY] UNCLEAN. IF IT IS FOUND EMBEDDED IN THE FLOOR OF THE CAVERN,[2] THEN IF HE WENT IN MERELY TO REFRESH HIMSELF HE REMAINS CLEAN,[3] BUT IF IT WAS TO PURIFY HIMSELF AFTER DEFILEMENT THROUGH CONTACT WITH THE DEAD HE REMAINS UNCLEAN,[4] BECAUSE WHERE THE STATUS QUO IS ONE OF DEFILEMENT THE DEFILEMENT REMAINS, BUT WHERE IT IS ONE OF PURITY, HE REMAINS CLEAN, THIS BEING THE PRESUMPTION [IN EACH CASE].[5]

GEMARA. How do we know this?[6]—R. Eliezer said: A verse reads, *And if any man die very suddenly beside him*,[7] *'beside him'* signifying that it is evident to him.[8] Resh Laḳish said: A verse reads, *If* [*any man* . . .] *shall be unclean by reason of a dead body or be on the road, afar off*,[9] signifying that [the uncleanness] must be like a road. Just as a road is visible, so must uncleanness be visible.

If these be correct,[10] what of the following where we learnt: 'Defilement of the depth' is such [defilement] as is not known even to a single person living anywhere in the world. If, however, it is known to someone living even at the end of the world, it is not

(1) The cavern is a tent for the purposes of defilement. Although the corpse was discovered after he left the cavern, the defilement is regarded as a certain one, the doubt having arisen in a private domain (v. *supra* 212*f*). (2) This is the ordinary case of defilement of the depth, the source of defilement being 'below ground'. V. Gemara below. (3) To the extent that if he does not discover the incident until after polling, there is no effect on the naziriteship. But if he discovers it earlier, then he is unclean. (4) Definitely unclean, for the purposes of our Mishnah. (5) Lit., 'the matter has feet'; i.e., a basis of support. (6) Viz. that defilement of the depth does not necessarily render void a naziriteship. (7) Num. VI, 9, on the defilement of a nazirite. (8) Defilement of the depth, as described in the Mishnah, is not evident to him, for he could not know of the corpse's existence beneath the floor of the cavern. (9) E.V. 'In a journey'. Num. IX, 10 of the second passover. Defilement of the depth was treated leniently as regards celebrants of the passover also. (10) Viz., that the regulations concerning 'defilement of the depth' are deduced from Scripture.

defilement of the depth.[1] Now on [Resh Laḳish's] view that [defilement] should be [visible] like a road, there is no difficulty,[2] but on [R. Eleazar's] view that it must be evident to him, what matters it if there is someone at the end of the world who knows of it? Further, there is the following: If a man finds a corpse lying [buried] across the road,[3] he becomes unclean in respect of *terumah*,[4] but remains clean as regards naziriteship and celebration of the passover.[5] But what is the difference?[6]—We must therefore say that [the rule of] defilement of the depth is known by tradition.[7]

BEFORE POLLING, HOWEVER, etc.: Who is the author [of the Mishnah]?[8]—R. Joḥanan replied: R. Eliezer, who considers that polling estops [him from drinking wine].[9]

Rami b. Ḥama propounded: What would be the law if [the nazirite] became unclean during the fulfilment of [his naziriteship], but discovered this after the fulfilment.[10] Is it [the moment of] discovery that is important,[11] and this occurred after fulfilment, or not,[12] the practical difference being [the period that is] to be rendered void?[13] [63*b*] Raba replied: Come and hear: BEFORE POLLING, HOWEVER, EITHER [TYPE OF DEFILEMENT RENDERS IT VOID]. How are we to undersand this? If he discovered [the defilement] during the period of fulfilment would it be necessary to tell us [that the naziriteship is void]?[14] It follows that after fulfilment is meant. Hence [discovery after fulfilment renders void].

(1) Tosef. Zabim II, 5. (2) The fact that one man knows of it is enough to make it 'visible' for legal purposes. (3) I.e., a defilement of the depth, it being uncertain whether the man overshadowed it. (4) V. Glos. (5) Ibid. (6) If he is clean, he is clean for all things. Otherwise he is unclean for all things. (7) And tradition confines the leniency only to naziriteship and the passover. (8) Which implies that the naziriteship is over only after the *polling*, even if the sacrifices have been offered. (9) *Supra* 14*b*. (10) After counting the whole period of the naziriteship but before the termination (sacrifices or polling according to the Rabbis or R. Eliezer). (11) And he counts as unclean henceforth. (12) And he is unclean retrospectively. (13) Uncleanness after fulfilment renders a shorter period void than uncleanness during the period; v. *supra* 16*a-b*. (14) For there is no question that defilement of the depth counts as ordinary defilement as regards the future. It is only retrospectively that concessions are made to nazirites and celebrants of the passover.

The question, however, still remains whether the whole [period] is rendered void or only seven [days].

But on whose [view is this question asked]?[1] Shall I say on the Rabbis' view? It is obvious that the whole period becomes void! Whilst on R. Eliezer's view any [defilement contracted] after fulfilment renders only seven days void?—The reply is [that R. Eliezer said] this of one who actually becomes unclean after fulfilment, whereas here [the defilement of the depth] occurred before the fulfilment.[2] [Do we then say that the whole is rendered void] or is this case different since discovery did not come until after fulfilment?—The same passage [answers this question too]. For it says: EITHER [TYPE OF DEFILEMENT] RENDERS IT VOID, making no distinction between them.[3]

Our Rabbis taught: If a man finds a corpse lying across the road,[4] he becomes unclean in respect of *terumah*,[5] but remains clean in respect of the nazirite-vow and celebrating the passover.[6] This is only true if there was no room for him to pass [without actually walking over the corpse], but if there was room for him to pass, he remains clean even in respect of *terumah*.[7] [Further], it is only true[8] if [the corpse] was found whole, but if it was found [with its limbs] broken or dislocated, even though there was no room to pass[9] we conceive that he may perhaps have passed between the pieces.[10] If, however, [the corpse] was in a grave, then, even if [its

(1) The Gemara here interrupts the argument to analyse the question. (2) If it is the time of defilement that is important, then the whole period may be rendered void. Hence the question is asked of R. Eliezer and not of the Rabbis. (3) And thus the defilement is retrospective, there being no half measures. Except for the nazirite who has entirely completed his naziriteship and the passover celebrant who did not learn of the incident soon enough to prevent the sacrifice of the passover-offering, defilement of the depth is true defilement. (4) I.e., if the corpse is found buried after he has passed, making defilement of the depth. V. *infra*. (5) V. Glos. And may not eat it. (6) Retrospectively only; v. *infra*. (7) Since there is now a genuine doubt occurring in a public place as to whether he did become defiled. (8) That he is unclean as regards *terumah*. (9) Had he walked straight on. But it is assumed that there is nowhere an unbroken line of pieces stretched across the road. (10) I.e. walked irregularly and not straight on, therefore he remains clean.

limbs were] broken or dislocated, he becomes unclean because the grave unites it. [Further,] we say this[1] only of one who was walking on foot, but if he was carrying a load or riding, he becomes unclean,[2] because it is possible for one walking on foot to avoid either touching [the corpse] or making it vibrate,[3] or overshadowing it, but it is impossible for one carrying a load or riding to avoid either touching it or making it vibrate or overshadowing it. [Further,] this ruling[4] applies only to a 'defilement of the depth', but if it was a known [source of] defilement, all three become unclean. A defilement of the depth is one which is not known to anyone [living even] in any part of the world. If, however, someone [living even] at the other end of the world knows about it, it is not [regarded as] a defilement of the depth.[5] If [the corpse] was hidden in straw or in pebbles, it counts as a defilement of the depth,[6] [but if] in the sea or by darkness or in a cleft of the rocks, this does not count as a defilement of the depth.[7] 'Defilement of the depth' was held to apply only in the case of a corpse.[8] [THE LAW REGARDING DEFILEMENT OF THE DEPTH IS] AS FOLLOWS. IF HE GOES DOWN: A [dead] reptile when floating, does not defile.[9] For it has been taught: If there is a doubt concerning a [source of defilement] floating in a vessel or on the earth,[10] it is treated as clean. R. Simeon said that in a vessel [the doubtful object] is treated as unclean, whilst on the earth it is treated as clean.[11]

[64a] What is the first Tanna's reason?[12]—R. Isaac b. Abudimi said: Scripture says, [*Ye shall not make yourselves abominable*] *with any swarming thing that swarms,*[13] signifying no matter where it swarms,[14]

(1) That he remains clean in the case of a dislocated corpse. (2) And may not eat *terumah*. (3) By stepping on some object which will move the corpse. (4) That there is a difference between *terumah* and the others. (5) But as a certain source of defilement. (6) For it is possible that new straw was blown across it and pebbles rolled against it and nobody knew of its existence. (7) Since someone has probably looked in and seen the corpse. (8) Tosef. Zabim II, 5. (9) I.e. if there is a doubt as to whether a floating reptile was touched, we assume that it was not touched. (10) A pool in the ground. (11) Tosef. Toharoth V, 4. (12) I.e., what is the source of his opinion? (13) Lev. XI, 43, continuing *Neither shall ye defile yourselves with them.* (14) Even on the surface of water.

and says further, *'On the earth'*.[1] How are these verses to be reconciled? Where there is no doubt that he touched it he is [always] unclean, but if there is a doubt he remains clean.[2]

And what is R. Simeon's reason?—'Ulla said: Scripture says, *Nevertheless a fountain* [... *shall be clean*][3] and continues [*But he who toucheth their carcase*] *shall be unclean.*[4] How are we to reconcile these? Whilst floating in a vessel [a doubtful object] is treated as unclean, but on the earth it is treated as clean.

Our Rabbis taught: Where there are doubts concerning any [source of defilement] that is carried[5] or dragged along, the objects are regarded as unclean, because it is as though they are at rest,[6] but where the doubt concerns things that are thrown,[7] they are treated as clean, with the exception of an olive's bulk of a corpse, one who overshadows a source of defilement, and all [other] things that propagate defilement upwards as well as downwards.[8] [This last expression] serves to include sufferers from gonorrhoea, male and female.[9]

Rami b. Hama propounded: What is the law concerning a corpse[10] lying in a vessel floating on the surface of the water. Is the vessel the criterion,[11] or the corpse?[12] Should it be decided that the vessel is the criterion,[13] what would be the law if the [fragment of]

(1) Ibid v. 44. *Neither shall ye defile yourselves with any manner of swarming thing that moveth upon the earth.* (2) In the case where the reptile was floating. (3) Lev. XI, 36. This signifies that even if there is a (dead) reptile in the fountain, there would be no defilement. (4) Ibid. Signifying whatever the circumstances. (5) Or 'suspended' (Tosef. and Maimonides, *Yad Aboth ha-Tumeoth*, XIV, 3). (6) Since they are in contact with the ground or the person carrying them all the time. (7) The doubt being whether it brushed against the person in transit. (8) Tosef. Zabim III, 8. In these cases, the defilement being of a more stringent type, even doubts as to projectiles are sufficient to render unclean. The corpse defiles in a tent i.e., upwards. (9) The gonorrhoeic sufferer defiles anything pressing on him from above even if it is not in direct contact with him. (10) Maimonides, *Aboth ha-Tumeoth* XIV, 4 reads 'reptile'. (11) And the corpse is at rest in the vessel. The doubt is as to whether it was touched, the person concerned being in no doubt that he did not overshadow it. (12) Which is floating. Tosaf. read 'Or the water' which is moving. The problem is whether this is a floating source of defilement or not. (13) So that in cases of doubt, uncleanness is assumed.

a corpse was lying on a [dead] reptile?[1] Seeing that the latter defiles only until evening and the former for seven days, are we to consider it as though it were lying in a vessel,[2] or should it perhaps be considered a compact source of defilement?[3] Should it be decided [further] that this is considered as though it were lying in a vessel, and therefore is treated as though defilement were certain, what would be the law if a [dead] reptile were lying on a floating animal carcase? Seeing that both defile only until evening, are they to be regarded as a compact source of defilement, or should we consider rather that of the one an olive's bulk is necessary,[4] whilst of the other a lentil's bulk is sufficient? [Further] what would be the law if one reptile lay on the other? Here certainly the measure is the same,[5] but perhaps, seeing that they are distinct, we should regard it as lying in a vessel? Again, should it be decided that in the case of one reptile lying on another, it is regarded as though it lay in a vessel because the [two reptiles] are distinct, what would be the law regarding a reptile floating on a liquefied animal carcase?[6] Seeing that it has been liquefied is it to be regarded as liquid,[7] or do we perhaps say that after all it is [now] a solid?[8] [Again], should you decide that it is a solid, what would be the law regarding a reptile [floating] on an effusion of semen? Should you decide that the latter, because it originates by detachment [from the human body] is a solid, what would be the law regarding a reptile floating on Water of Cleansing,[9] that was floating on the surface of [ordi-

(1) Here, and in the other cases below, the second object is to be taken as floating on the surface of water. Maimonides reads here 'A reptile lying on a corpse'. There are many, not particularly important variations, in the readings of questions that follow; v. Marginal notes of the Wilna Gaon. (2) So that in cases of doubt, uncleanness is assumed. (3) I.e., as one source floating on water. Then, provided it is certain that there was no overshadowing, cleanness will be assumed. (4) Of the carcase, an olive's bulk must be present before defilement ensues. This 'measure', and the 'lentil's bulk' for reptiles are Rabbinic traditions. (5) I.e., for both a lentil's bulk is sufficient to defile. (6) That had afterwards coagulated. (7) So that the reptile is really floating on the water. (8) Lit., 'a food', the generic word for solids. (9) I.e., the water containing the ashes of the Red Heifer, which also defiled by contact. V. Num. XIX, 1 *seq*.

nary] water?[1]—We do not know. All these problems remain unsolved.

[64b] R. Hamnuna said: A nazirite or a celebrant of the passover who walks over a grave of the depth on his seventh day [of purification after defilement][2] is clean,[3] the reason being that defilement of the depth is not potent enough to render void [the naziriteship or the passover]. Raba objected: IF IT WAS TO PURIFY HIMSELF AFTER DEFILEMENT[4] THROUGH CONTACT WITH THE DEAD HE REMAINS UNCLEAN, BECAUSE WHERE THE STATUS QUO IS ONE OF DEFILEMENT THE DEFILEMENT REMAINS, BUT WHERE IT IS ONE OF PURITY HE REMAINS CLEAN?[5]—[R. Hamnuna] replied: I admit you are right in the case of a nazirite who needs polling.[6] Raba [then] said to him: And I admit you are right in the case of a celebrant of the passover who has completed all preliminaries.[7] Abaye said [to Raba]: But has he not still to wait for the sun to set?[8]—He replied: The sun sets of its own accord.[9]

Abaye, too, gave up this opinion, for it has been taught: If it is on the day of fulfilment,[10] she must bring [a further sacrifice], but if during fulfilment she need not bring one.[11] It might be thought that she is not required to bring [a sacrifice] for a birth occurring during the fulfilment, but must bring one for a birth occurring

(1) Would the Water of Cleansing, thickened by the ashes, count as a solid, and so as a vessel, or not? (2) When sunset would make him clean. (3) Provided that he does not learn of the incident until the naziriteship is done with; v. our Mishnah. (4) That he entered the cave containing a grave of the depth. (5) And the Mishnah is speaking of the seventh day of purification after defilement, and so contradicts R. Hamnuna. (6) The unclean nazirite does not complete his purification until he has polled. That is why the presumption of uncleanness is considered to be still present on the seventh day of purification. (7) And thus has a presumption of purity. (8) The purification is not really complete until sunset even in the case of a celebrant of the passover. (9) He himself has nothing more to do. (10) The reference is to a miscarriage occurring within the term of purification after childbirth, viz. 41 days for a male child and 81 days for a female child. V. Lev. XII, 1 ff. The period of purification and all other obligations follow a miscarriage as well as a normal birth. (11) The reason is explained below.

after the fulfilment,[1] and discharge her obligation for both births,[2] and so Scripture says, *And when the days of her purification are fulfilled,*[3] which signifies that if it occurs on the day of fulfilment she must bring [a sacrifice] but not if it occurs during the fulfilment. [Whereon] R. Kahana explained that the difference[4] was due to the fact that she needed to bring a sacrifice.[5] Now, in the other case, has she not still to wait for the sun to set?[6]—Abaye replied: the sun sets of its own accord.[7]

MISHNAH. IF A MAN FINDS A CORPSE FOR THE FIRST TIME[8] LYING IN THE USUAL POSITION,[9] HE MAY REMOVE IT TOGETHER WITH THE SOIL THAT IT OCCUPIES.[10] [IF HE FINDS] TWO, HE MAY REMOVE THEM TOGETHER WITH THE GROUND THEY OCCUPY. IF HE FINDS THREE, THEN IF THE DISTANCE BETWEEN THE FIRST AND THE LAST IS FROM FOUR TO EIGHT CUBITS,[11] THIS IS A GRAVEYARD SITE.[12] [65a] HE MUST THEN SEARCH BEYOND FOR A DISTANCE OF TWENTY CUBITS.[13] IF HE FINDS A SINGLE [CORPSE] AT THE END OF TWENTY CUBITS, HE MUST SEARCH BEYOND FOR ANOTHER TWENTY

(1) I.e. after the term of fulfilment, reckoning from the first birth, but before the term of fulfilment reckoning from the subsequent one, for which as we have been told no sacrifice is needed. (2) I.e., bring two sacrifices, one for the first birth and one for the third. (3) Lev. XII, 6 continuing, *She shall bring a lamb* etc. (4) Between the case where the second birth occurs on the day of fulfilment and she is required to bring a second sacrifice, and that where the third birth occurs after the first fulfilment and she is not required to bring a sacrifice. (5) In the latter case, she was still unclean at the time of the third birth, owing to the intervention of the second one, and so the first sacrifice was not yet due. She is therefore considered to be within the period of fulfilment. Not so in the former case. (6) Before she becomes clean, and fit to eat of sacrifices. (7) Thus we see that Abaye does not regard the necessity of waiting for sunset as interfering with the presumption of cleanness. (8) Without previously having found a corpse in the same spot, and without knowing that it was there. (9) Prostrate: the only way Jews were buried. (10) For reburial elsewhere, v. Gemara. (11) Which is an indication that he has stumbled on an old burial vault. (12) The bodies must not be removed, but have to be reburied where found. (13) For other vaults.

CUBITS. THE REASON[1] IS THAT THERE IS [NOW] A PRESUMPTION,[2] WHEREAS IF HE HAD FOUND IT FIRST, HE WOULD HAVE BEEN ABLE TO REMOVE IT TOGETHER WITH THE SOIL IT OCCUPIES.[3]

GEMARA. Rab Judah said: IF A MAN FINDS, but not if [he knows] it is to be found there;[4] A CORPSE, but not one who had been killed;[5] LYING, but not seated;[6] IN THE USUAL POSITION, but not with its head lying between its thighs.[6] 'Ulla b. Ḥanina taught: A defective corpse[7] does not acquire the ground it occupies, nor does it help to form a graveyard site.

Why does not [the law of the Mishnah] apply to all these?—Because we say that perhaps it is [the body of] a heathen.[8]

If he finds two [corpses] with the head of one beside the feet of the second, and the head of the second beside the feet of the first, they do not acquire the soil which they occupy and do not help to form a graveyard site.[9] If he finds three [corpses] one of which was known to be there while the others [were found] for the first time, or if two [were found] for the first time and two were known [to be there] they do not acquire the soil they occupy[10] and do not form a graveyard site.

It is related that R. Yeshobab once searched [a certain spot] and found two [bodies] which were known to be there and one

(1) That he must continue to search if he finds one only. (2) That the field is a graveyard site; since twenty cubits would not be an abnormal distance between two vaults; cf. *supra* p. 237, n. 5. (3) Oh. XVI, 3. On the measurements v. B.B. (Sonc. ed.) p. 426 and notes. (4) In that case he may not remove it (Tosaf.). (5) In which case it is assumed that it was buried there for convenience and not that there was an old cemetery there. (6) Jewish bodies were always buried prostrate; hence this cannot be an old Jewish cemetery. In these last three cases, he removes the body for reburial elsewhere. (7) A corpse lacking a member essential to life. (Tosef. Oh. XVI, 2). (8) Hence the site is not declared a Jewish cemetery and the bodies can be removed for burial elsewhere. (9) Jews were not buried in this manner. (10) Thus our text and Rashbam in B.B. 101*b*; but this as it stands contradicts our Mishnah, and it is therefore better to read with Tosef. Oh. XVI, 2 'Or if one (was found) for the first time and two were known, they *are* entitled to the ground they occupy, but do not form a graveyard site'.

[which was discovered] for the first time, and he wanted to declare them a graveyard site.[1] R. Akiba said to him: All your trouble was for nothing. [The Rabbis] did not declare a graveyard site save where three [corpses] were known to be there, or three [were found] for the first time.[2]

[IF HE FINDS] TWO, HE MAY REMOVE THEM TOGETHER WITH THE SOIL THEY OCCUPY: Where is this law of the soil [a corpse] occupies to be found?[3]—R. Judah said: The verse says, *Thou shalt carry me out of Egypt*,[4] [signifying] carry with me [some Egyptian soil].[5] And what is the quantity of earth] which it occupies?—R. Eleazar[6] explained that he takes the loose earth[7] and digs up three finger-breadths of the virgin soil.[8]

The following objection was raised. [It has been taught:] And what quantity [of earth] are we to understand by 'the ground which it occupies?' R. Eleazar b. R. Zadok explained that he takes the chips [of the coffin][9] and the lumps of earth,[10] discarding what certainly [did not belong to the body] and leaving whatever was doubtful [for removal].[11] The remainder adds together to form the major part of the structure of the corpse, the quarter [*ḳab*] of bones and the spoonful of corpse-mould?[12]—[R. Eleazar] agrees with the following Tanna. For it has been taught: What quantity of [earth is meant by] 'the ground which it occupies?' R. Joḥanan,[13] citing Ben 'Azzai, said: He takes the loose earth and digs up three finger-breadths of virgin soil.

(1) This would entail examining for twenty cubits. (2) And whilst they may not be removed, they do not form a graveyard site. V. Tosef. Oh. XVI, 2 where the last paragraph occurs with variations. (3) [So *Aruch*; cur. edd. 'What means the ground it occupies'?] (4) Gen. XLVII, 30; spoken by Jacob to Joseph. (5) Interpreting the verse, 'carry with me of Egypt'. (6) R. Eleazar b. Pedath. Our texts have in error R. Eleazar b. R. Zadok. (7) Formed through the decomposition of the body. (8) This being the depth to which any blood etc., coming from the body would penetrate. (9) Which was usually of stone (Tosaf.). *Aliter* The chips of spices put in with the body; cf. II Chronicles XVI, 14. (10) Into which the decomposing corpse congealed. (11) When the body was removed. Hence the part to be removed contained no virgin soil, contrary to the opinion of R. Eleazar. (12) Required to propagate uncleanness in a tent. (V. *supra* 49*b*, 50*a*). Tosef. Oh. II, 2 with variations. (13) R. Joḥanan b. Nuri.

HE MUST THEN SEARCH BEYOND IT: [65*b*] Raba said: If he searched, [found a corpse][1] and removed it, searched [again and found another] and removed it, [and then] searched [again] and found [a third corpse], he must not remove this one [for reburial] with the other two,[2] nor the other two [for reburial] with this one.[3]

Others say that Raba said: As permission had been given to remove [the others],[4] he may remove them [all].[5] But why should not [the field] become a graveyard site?[6]—Resh Lakish said: [The Rabbis] seized upon any pretext to declare the Land of Israel clean.[7]

Suppose he searched [beyond it][8] for twenty cubits [in one direction only][9] and did not find [another corpse], what is the law?[10]—R. Monashya b. Jeremiah, citing Rab, replied: This is the graveyard site.[11] What is the reason [that we say this?][12]—Resh Lakish said: They seized on any pretext to declare the Land of Israel clean.

MISHNAH. EVERY DOUBTFUL CASE OF [LEPROUS] DISEASE[13] ENCOUNTERED FOR THE FIRST TIME BEFORE UN-

(1) For the first time. (2) Since the region is now revealed as a graveyard site. (3) Once removed legally they need not be brought back. (4) I.e., since the removal of the two was legal. (5) The third corpse counts as newly found. (6) Since three bodies have been uncovered in it. (7) I.e. in order to declare a region in the land of Israel clean, the least pretext was considered sufficient. Rashi suggests another rendering, viz.: 'They found a rib and declared the Land of Israel clean'; i.e., the Jews on entering Palestine found a human rib buried and thereupon declared the whole of the rest of Palestine clean, no further search after graveyard sites being necessary. Hence any pretext to avoid declaring parts of Palestine unclean will do. (8) Referring to the Mishnah that he must search beyond the three corpses found to a distance of twenty cubits. (9) Tosaf. v. next note. (10) Must he search in other directions or not? (Tosaf.). *Aliter*. Do these three alone form a graveyard site or not? (Rashi). *Aliter:* If he has searched in all directions and found nothing, must he search more thoroughly and dig more deeply? (Asheri). (11) But no other part of the field. (12) I.e., why are we not stricter in our requirements? (13) Referring to a doubt that has arisen as to whether an affected spot has spread or not (v. Lev. XIII), e.g., two persons are examined by a priest and have different-sized

CLEANNESS HAS BEEN ESTABLISHED[1] IS CLEAN.[2] AFTER UNCLEANNESS HAS BEEN ESTABLISHED DOUBTFUL CASES ARE UNCLEAN.[3]

GEMARA. How do we know this?[4]—Rab Judah citing Rab, said: The verse says, *to pronounce it clean, or to pronounce it unclean.*[5] Scripture mentions cleanness first.[6] In that case even after uncleanness has been established, doubtful cases should be clean?[7] —We must therefore say that this dictum of Rab, quoted by R. Judah was uttered in connection with the following.[8] [A Mishnah says:] If the bright spot[9] appears before the white hair,[10] he is unclean, but if the white hair appears before the bright spot he is clean. If there is a doubt, he is unclean. R. Joshua said: It is doubtful.[11] What is meant by 'it is doubtful'?—Rab Judah[12] replied: It is doubtful and [consequently] clean.[13] May it not mean that it is doubtful and [consequently] unclean?—Rab Judah citing Rab said: The verse says, *to pronounce it clean, or to pronounce it unclean;*[14] Scripture mentions cleanness first.[15]

MISHNAH. A PERSON SUFFERING FROM A FLUX IS EX-

areas of disease. The following week both areas are the size of the larger of the two and the priest is uncertain which one has increased, v. Neg. V, 4.

(1) Lit., 'so long as he has not become bound to the uncleanness'. Before the patient has been declared unclean. (2) Both men remain clean. (3) If a similar doubt arises as to whether the diseased part has diminished in size. (4) That there is any difference between the two cases quoted in the Mishnah. (5) Lev. XIII, 59, concluding the chapter on the symptoms of leprous disease. (6) Hence doubtful cases should also be regarded as clean. (7) Thus there is no ground for basing the distinction on this verse. (8) And the law of the Mishnah is not derived from a verse, but follows from the fact that in the first case there is no presumption of uncleanness and in the second case there is. (9) Of leprous disease, v. Lev. XIII, 2. (10) The symbol of uncleanness. Ibid. v. 3. (11) Neg. IV, 11. The word rendered 'doubtful' is the technical term for 'dim' used of a diseased spot, (v. Lev. XIII, 6). For a discussion of the reading here v. Tosaf. Sanh. 87*b*, s.v. (12) Parallel passages (Sanh. 87*b*) have Rabbah. (13) I.e., it is considered to have become dim and is therefore clean. (14) Lev. XIII, 59. (15) The disease is to be pronounced clean

AMINED REGARDING SEVEN THINGS,[1] BEFORE THE PRESENCE OF GONORRHOEA HAS BEEN ESTABLISHED,[2] VIZ.:—WITH REGARD TO FOOD,[3] DRINK, BURDENS,[4] LEAPING,[5] SICKNESS, A VISION[6] OR AN IMPURE THOUGHT.[7] ONCE GONORRHOEA IS ESTABLISHED, HE IS NO LONGER EXAMINED. [FLUX RESULTING] FROM AN ACCIDENT[8] TO HIM, DOUBTFUL [FLUX],[9] AND HIS ISSUE OF SEMEN ARE UNCLEAN, FOR THERE IS A PRESUMPTION [OF UNCLEANNESS].[10]

IF A MAN GIVES ANOTHER A BLOW FROM WHICH HE WAS EXPECTED TO DIE AND HE PARTIALLY RECOVERED AND THEN GREW WORSE AND DIED [THE OTHER] IS LIABLE [FOR MURDER]. R. NEHEMIAH EXEMPTS HIM SINCE THERE IS A PRESUMPTION [IN HIS FAVOUR].[11]

GEMARA. How do we know this?[12]—R. Nathan said: The verse says, *And of the gonorrhoeic*[13] *that have the issue,*[14] [*whether it be a man or a woman*].[15] [The male] at his third experience of issue is compared to the female.[16] But have we not been taught: R. Eliezer says: At the third [issue] we examine him but not at the fourth?[17]—In point of fact they disagree on [the question

unless it certainly has the symptoms of uncleanness described in that chapter.

(1) To determine whether any of these seven things was not the cause of the flux, as it would not then be evidence of gonorrhoea. (2) I.e., before there has been a flux on three occasions, v. Zabim II, 2. (3) Whether he had eaten too much. (4) Whether he had carried heavy loads. (5) Any kind of strain through physical exercise might cause flux. (6) The sight of two people in coition. (7) A similar thought. (8) I.e., after one of the seven things mentioned. (9) See the Gemara. (10) V. Zabim II, 2. (11) The recovery creates a presumption that death was not caused by the blow. [Maim. *Yad.*, *Rozeah*, IV, 5 explains contrariwise: The fact that he ultimately died creates a presumption that death was caused by the blow, the last clause being thus explanatory of the views of the Rabbis.] (12) That after gonorrhoea is established, he is not questioned as to possible causes. (13) E.V. '*And of them*'. Indicating the first issue. (14) Expressed in Heb. by the *nota accusativi*, '*eth*'. Indicating the second issue. (15) Indicating the third issue; Lev. XV, 33. (16) Who becomes gonorrhoeic whatever the cause. Hence at the third issue gonorrhoea is established whatever its cause. (17) And on the present interpretation of the verse, he is not examined for the third issue.

of stressing the particle] 'the'.[1] R. Eliezer lays stress on [the particle] 'the', whilst the Rabbis do not do so.

[FLUX RESULTING] FROM AN ACCIDENT TO HIM, DOUBTFUL FLUX: [66a] Raba said: Do not suppose [that the meaning of 'doubtful flux' is] that there is a doubt whether there was an issue or not. In point of fact, the issue must be a certain one,[2] the doubt being whether it was due to an issue of semen[3] or whether it was caused by [a separate gonorrhoeic] attack.[4] Once uncleanness has been established, if there is a doubt, he is unclean.[5]

HIS ISSUE OF SEMEN IS UNCLEAN: In what respect [is the semen unclean]? For if it be in respect of touching it,[6] how is it worse than the issue of semen of a clean person?[7]—It must therefore mean that the semen of a sufferer from gonorrhoea defiles through being carried. But who is known to hold the view that the issue of semen of a sufferer from gonorrhoea defiles if carried? For if you say that it is the following Tanna, as has been taught: 'R. Eliezer says that the issue of semen of a sufferer from gonorrhoea does not defile if carried, whilst R. Joshua says that it does defile if carried, because it is impossible that it should not be diluted with gonorrheic fluid'—even R. Joshua only says this[8] because it is diluted with gonorrhoeic fluid, but not when it is undiluted?[9]—In point of fact, said R. Adda b. Ahabah, [the purpose of the Mishnah is] to lay down that [subsequent gonorrhoeic issue] is not ascribed to [the prior flow of semen].[10]

(1) The Hebrew particle governing the accusative. This particle can be omitted and so its presence is taken by R. Eliezer to indicate another issue before the comparison is made of man with woman. (2) Examination must show the presence of gonorrhoeic matter. (3) When it only adds one day to his period of counting. (4) When he would have to begin to count his seven clean days over again, (v. Lev. XV, 13). (5) And the gonorrhoeic matter is ascribed to an attack of gonorrhoea and not to the issue of semen. (6) That one who touches the semen of a sufferer from gonorrhoea becomes unclean. (7) Which also renders unclean by contact. Lev. XV, 16, 17. (8) Viz.: That the semen defiles if carried. (9) Which is the case contemplated by the Mishnah. The question still remains, why does the Mishnah say that the semen of a sufferer from gonorrhoea is unclean? (10) As would be the case for twenty-four hours after an emission of semen in the case of a normal person; v. Zabim II, 3.

R. Papa tried to argue with Raba that this[1] was because the flow resulted from his weakness [following the gonorrhoea].[2] Raba said to him: Have we not learnt: A proselyte defiles if subject to a gonorrhoeic flow immediately after conversion?[3]—He replied: There cannot be greater sickness than this.[4]

We must say in fact[5] that [to what extent semen of a sufferer from gonorrhoea defiles] is a controversy of Tannaim. For it has been taught: The semen of a sufferer from gonorrhoea defiles for twenty-four hours[6] if carried. R. Jose however, says; for the whole of the same day.[7]

Wherein does their controversy lie?[8]—In respect of the point raised by Samuel. For Samuel noted the following contradiction. It is written, *If there be among you any man that is not clean by reason of that which chanceth him by night* [etc.][9] and it is written [further], *when evening cometh on he shall bathe himself in water.*[10] The one who says twenty-four hours infers this from *when evening cometh on*,[11] and the other infers it from, '*that which chanceth him by night*'.[12] Now

(1) The reason that it is not ascribed to the issue of semen once gonorrhoea is established. (2) And was due to the gonorrhoea and not a consequence of the emission of semen. (3) Zabim II, 3; If an issue of semen preceded conversion and gonorrhoeic flow followed, it is not ascribed to the emission, but counts as a first gonorrhoeic flow. (4) The emotional effect of the conversion is sufficient sickness to occasion the flow, but does not render it nugatory as the seven things of the Mishnah do (Rashi). Tosaf. achieves better sense by omitting 'he replied', and making the whole part of Raba's objection, viz.: 'Can there be greater weakness than that which results from the emotional effect of conversion?' and yet the flow is considered unclean. Hence R. Papa's reason is not correct. (5) Although R. Adda attempted to argue to the contrary. (6) I.e., If the semen issues within twenty-four hours of the gonorrhoeic flow. (7) If it comes before the evening; here there is no mention of dilution of the semen by gonorrhoeic fluid. Thus these Tannaim differ from R. Eliezer and R. Joshua, and the Mishnah represents their opinion, that the semen renders unclean if carried. (8) The controversy of R. Jose and the other Tanna. (9) Deut. XXIII, 11. Interpreted as meaning: If he should chance to have an emission of semen during the day, consequent on a gonorrhoeic issue during the previous night. (10) Ibid. v. 12. (11) Which indicates that though night has already fallen he still remains unclean; i.e., until the end of the period of twenty-four hours. (12) Which he interprets as meaning, 'until nightfall'; but as soon as night has fallen he becomes clean and an emission will not then defile, if carried.

to the one who infers it from *'when evening cometh on,'* [it may be objected] it is written, *'that which chanceth him by night'?*—He will reply that it is customary for an emission to occur at night.[1]

MISHNAH. SAMUEL WAS A NAZIRITE IN THE OPINION OF R. NEHORAI, AS IT SAYS, AND THERE SHALL NO RAZOR [MORAH] COME UPON HIS HEAD.[2] IT SAYS WITH REFERENCE TO SAMSON, AND [NO] RAZOR [MORAH][3] AND IT SAYS WITH REFERENCE TO SAMUEL, AND [NO] RAZOR [MORAH]; JUST AS MORAH IN THE CASE OF SAMSON [IS USED OF] A NAZIRITE,[4] SO [WE SHOULD SAY] MORAH IN THE CASE OF SAMUEL [IS USED OF] A NAZIRITE. R. JOSE OBJECTED: BUT HAS NOT MORAH REFERENCE TO [FEAR[5] OF] A HUMAN BEING? R. NEHORAI SAID TO HIM: BUT DOES IT NOT ALSO SAY, AND SAMUEL SAID; 'HOW CAN I GO? IF SAUL HEAR IT HE WILL KILL ME'[6] [WHICH SHOWS] THAT HE WAS IN FACT AFRAID OF A HUMAN BEING?[7]

GEMARA. Rab said to his son Ḥiyya: [66*b*] Snatch [the cup] and say grace.[8] So also did R. Huna say to his son Rabbah. Snatch [the cup] and say grace.

Does this mean that it is better to say the blessing [than to make the responses]? Has it not been taught: R. Jose says that he who responds, 'Amen', is greater than he who says the blessing, and R. Nehorai said to him: I swear[9] that this is so. In proof of this, [it may be noted] that the ordinary soldiers begin a battle but the picked troops gain the victory?[10]—There is a difference of opinion

(1) But there is no particular significance in the use of the word *night*. (2) I Sam. I, 11. (3) Judges XIII, 5. *'And no razor shall come upon his head'*. (4) Ibid. *'for the child shall be a nazirite unto God'*. (5) Reading מורה as מורא (fear) from ירא the verb having adopted a ל"ה ending. Jast. s.v. מורה II interprets from a root מר meaning 'authority'. (6) I Sam. XVI, 2. (7) Lit., 'flesh and blood'. Hence *morah* cannot mean 'fear' or Hannah's prediction would have been false. It must therefore mean 'a razor'. (8) You be the one who takes the cup of wine to say the grace, and let the others answer, 'Amen' to your blessings. (9) Lit., 'by heaven'. (10) A reference to the Roman practice of saving the veteran

between Tannaim on this matter. For it has been taught: Both the one who says the blessing and the one who responds, 'Amen', are included [in this verse].[1] Nevertheless, [reward] is given first to the one who says the blessing.

R. Eleazar,[2] citing R. Ḥanina, said: The disciples of the sages increase peace throughout the world, as it is said, *And all thy children shall be taught of the Lord; and great shall be the peace of thy children.*[3]

soldiers until the enemy's resistance had been weakened by the less experienced soldiers. We see then that the one who completes the blessing by responding is greater.

(1) Ps. XXXIV, 3, *'O magnify the Lord with me, and let us exalt His name together'.* (Rashi). (2) V. Yeb. 122*b*. (3) Isa. LIV, 13.

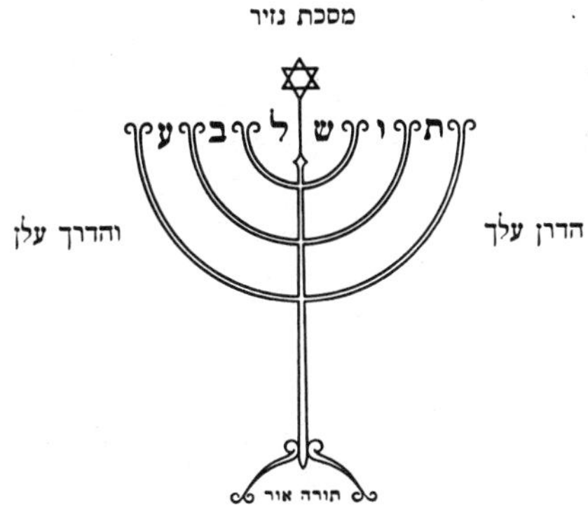

GLOSSARY

INDEX OF SCRIPTURAL REFERENCES

GENERAL INDEX

TRANSLITERATION OF HEBREW LETTERS

ABBREVIATIONS

GLOSSARY

'ARAKIN. (Lit., 'values'): the valuation set by the priest on persons or objects dedicated to the Sanctuary. (V. Lev. XXVII).

BARAITHA. (Lit., 'outside'); a teaching or a tradition of the Tannaim that has been excluded from the Mishnah and incorporated in a later collection compiled by R. Ḥiyya and R. Oshaiah, generally introduced by 'Our Rabbis taught', or 'It has been taught'.

GEZERAH SHAWAH. (Lit., 'equal cut'): the application to one subject of a rule already known to apply to another, on the strength of a common expression used in connection with both in the Scriptures.

HABDALAH. (Lit., 'separation'): the blessing (usually made over wine) by which the Sabbath or any other holy day is ushered out.

ḲAB. Measure of capacity equal to four *logs* or one-sixth of a *se'ah*.

KARETH. (Lit., 'cutting off'): divine punishment for a number of sins for which no human penalty is specified. Sudden death is described as '*kareth* of days', premature death at sixty as '*kareth* of years'.

ḲIDDUSH. (Lit., 'sanctification'): the blessing (usually made over wine) by which the Sabbath or any other holy day is ushered in.

KOR. A measure of capacity equal to 30 *se'ahs*.

LOG. A liquid measure equal to a quarter of a *ḳab* (q.v.), or the space occupied by six eggs, c. 549 cubic centimetres.

METH MIẒWAH. (Lit., 'a dead [body] which is a commandment'): a corpse lying unattended with nobody to arrange for its burial. The duty of burying it devolves upon whomsoever discovers it, even if he be a Nazirite or a High Priest.

NEBELAH. (pl. *nebeloth*): an animal slaughtered in any manner other than that prescribed by Jewish ritual law; the least deviation therefrom, e.g., if the knife has the slightest notch, renders the animal *nebelah*.

ROHITNI. (Lit., 'a carpenter's plane'): an instrument for cropping close the hair of the beard.

TANNA. (Lit., 'one who repeats' or 'teaches'): (*a*) a Rabbi quoted in the Mishnah or Baraitha; (*b*) in the Amoraic period, a scholar whose special task was to memorize and recite Baraithas in the presence of expounding teachers.

ṬEBUL YOM. (Lit., 'bathed during the day'): a person who has bathed to cleanse himself at the end of the period of his defilement, but who must wait until sunset to regain his ritual purity (Lev. XXII, 7).

TERUMAH. 'That which is lifted or separated'; the heave-offering given from the yields of the yearly harvests, from certain sacrifices, and from the *sheḳels* collected in a special chamber in the Temple (*terumah ha-lishkah*). *Terumah gedolah* (great offering): The first levy on the produce of the year given to the priest. (V. Num. XVIII, 8ff). Its quantity varied according to the generosity of the owner, who could give one-fortieth, one-fiftieth, or one-sixtieth of his harvest. *Terumath ma'aser* (heave-offering of the tithe): the heave-offering given to the priest by the Levite from the tithes he receives (v. Num. XVIII, 25ff).

SCRIPTURAL REFERENCES

SCRIPTURAL REFERENCES

GENERAL INDEX*

A

Aaron, 8.
Abraham, 83.
Absalom, 13ff.
Academy, 142, 153.
A fortiori, 59, 116, 161ff, 179f.
Adiabene, 66.
Adultery, 83f, 184.
Agent, 40. *See also* Deputy.
'Allusions' in vows. *See* Vows.
Ambiguity in vows. *See* Vows of imperfectly specified duration.
Amen, 70, 79, 252f.
Ammon, 83.
Ammonite, 83.
Amos, 83.
'Amplifications and limitations', 123, 126.
Analogy, deduction by, 58, 103f, 206f. *See also Gezerah shawah.*
Anecdote, 13.
Animals, consecration of. *See* Consecration.
Ant, 193.
'Araboth, 158.
'Arakin, 229, 231ff, 235.
'Ardacus, 208.
Argument, progressive, 31, 101.
Aristobulus, 204.
Artabamus, 66.
Aruch, 120, 187, 194. *See also* Kohut.
Asceticism, 64, 76f.
Atonement, Day of, 9, 178.

B

Babylon, 118.
Bagdad, 126, 141.
Balaam, 84.
Balak, 84f.
Bandits, 142f.
Barnesh, 111, 147f.
Bath, ritual, 139, 164.
Bell, 122.
Belorith, 143.
Beth peras, 202.
Beth Hillel, 28ff, 32ff, 66ff, 110ff, 173f, 196.
– Shammai, 28ff, 32ff, 66ff, 110ff, 172ff, 187f, 196.
Betrothal by deputy, 38f.
Birds in Nazirite vow. *See* Vows.
Blood, eating, 97.
– defilement, 138, 184, 202, 210.
– sprinkling, 98f, 171, 175.
Booth, 4.
Büchler, 165.
Bull, 110f.
Burial, 50, 158, 245.

C

Caesarea, the Rabbis of, 20.
Caleb, 210.
Camps, the three, 165f.
Carmania, 113f.
Carrion, 9, 102f.
Cauldron, 169ff.
Cemetery, 154, 192. *See also* Graveyard.
Childbirth, 102f.
Combination of minima. *See* Minima.
Combing. *See* Hair.

* An Index of Rabbinical Names will be provided in the special Index Volume to be published on completion of the translation of the entire Talmud.

H

I

Israel, 83, 85.
– land of, 66f, 247.
Issue. *See* Flux.
Izates, 66.

J

Jackals, 202.
Jael, 84.
Jastrow, 148, 158, 204, 208, 252.
J.E., 64, 202.
Jephthah, 15.
Jerusalem, 117, 165.
Josephus, 66, 67.
Joshua, 209.
Judea, 131.

K

Ḳab, 184, 192, 195.
Ḳahal, 230.
Kareth, 183, 230.
Keilah, 9.
Kelal u-feraṭ, 123.
Ḳiddush, 8.
Kilkul, 5.
Kohut, 25, 26. *See also* Aruch.
Kor, 24, 119f.
Koy, 120f.
Krauss, 143, 146, 194, 202, 204.
Kutaḥ, 130.

L

Leah, 84.
Leaven, 128f.
Leper, 92, 138, 145ff, 164, 173, 202f, 214ff, 223ff.
– sacrifice of, 223ff.
Leprosy, 27, 46f, 58f, 157, 166, 180, 202, 205f, 247.
Levites, 146f.
– camp of, 166.
Levy, 202.
Lewysohn, 113, 120.
Libellarius, 209.
Lieberman, S., 20.
Liquids, red, 138.
– white, 138f.
Loaves as adjuncts of sacrifices, 85f, 88f, 100.
Loq, 122, 137ff, 184, 195.
Lot, 82f, 85.

M

Maidservant of Rabbi, 4.
Maim., 95, 115, 152, 164, 196, 234, 241, 242, 249.
Malachi, 198.
Malappropriation, 86, 88, 93, 97, 100.
Manoaḥ, 9.
Matha Meḥasia, 147.
Meat and milk, 133f.
Me'ilah. *See* Malappropriation.
Mekalkel, 4.
Mesalsel, 4.
Meth mizwah, 158, 160f, 177ff, 244ff.
Milk, 9.
Mingling of sexes, 220.
– of stuffs, 216f.
Minima, combination of, 9, 122, 129ff. *See also* Olive.
Miriam of *Tarmod*, 175f.
Miscarriage, 42f.
Mnemonic, 138.
Moab, 85.
Moabite, 83.
Moses, 46, 209f.
Mourning, 50.
Mucus, 186, 191.
Murder, 249.

N

Narcissus, 13.
Nasha, 146, 191, 227.

O

P

Vows of wife, 40f, 63f, 70, 74ff, 79f, 85ff, 98f.
– of women, 235. *See also* Nazirite, woman as.
– remission of, 37, 70ff, 79, 111.
– substitutes for, 1ff.
– utterance as factor in, 3.

W

Warning as legal factor, 153ff.
Waters of cleansing, 242f.
– the bitter, 139, 169, 213.
Waving, 171ff.
Weiss, 204.
West as term for Palestine, 69, 152.
Wicked and righteous, 81ff.
Wig, 99.
Wilna Gaon, 93, 168, 197.
Wine, 1, 4, 8f, 16, 34f, 64, 98 *et passim*.
– of *Habdalah*, 8.
Wine, of *Ḳiddush*, 8.
– whose drinking is obligatory, 8, 16.
– whose drinking is optional, 8, 16.
Witnesses, 68.

Y

Yadoth in vows. *See* Vows, 'allusions' in.
Yamim, discussion of, 14f.

Z

Zagim, 122.
Zechariah, 198.
Zimri, 83.
Zog, 122f.
Zuckermandel, 208.
Zugoth, 209.

TRANSLITERATION OF HEBREW LETTERS

א (in middle of word)	= '
ב	= b
ו	= w
ח	= ḥ
ט	= ṭ
כ	= k
ע	= '
פ	= f
צ	= ẓ
ק	= ḳ
ת	= th

Full particulars regarding the method and scope of the translation are given in the Editor's Introduction to Seder Neziḳin (Baba Ḳamma, Vol. I).

ABBREVIATIONS

Ant.	*Antiquities* by Flavius Josephus.
'Ar.	'Arakin.
Asheri.	R. Asher b. Jeḥiel (1250–1327).
A.Z.	'Abodah Zarah.
B.B.	Baba Bathra.
b.	*ben, bar,* son of.
BaḤ.	*Bayith Ḥadash,* Glosses by R. Joel b. Samuel Sirkes (1561–1640).
Bek.	Bekoroth.
Ber.	Berakoth.
B.Ḳ.	Baba Ḳamma.
B. M.	Baba Meẓi'a.
Cur. ed.(d)	Current edition(s).
D.S.	*Diḳduḳe Soferim,* by R. Rabbinowicz.
Dor.	*Dor Dor Wedoreshaw,* by I. H. Weiss (2nd ed.).
'Ed.	'Eduyyoth.
E.V.	English Versions of the Bible.
Giṭ.	Giṭṭin.
Glos.	Glossary.
Ḥag.	Ḥagiga.
Hor.	Horayoth.
Ḥul.	Ḥullin.
J.	Jerusalem (Jerushalmi); J.T., Jerusalem Talmud.
Jast.	M. Jastrow's *Dictionary of the Targumim, the Talmud Babli and Yerushalmi, and the Midrashic Literature.*
J.E.	*Jewish Encyclopaedia.*
Ker.	Kerithoth.
Ḳid.	Ḳiddushin.
Kin.	Kinnim.
Maim.	Moses Maimonides (1135–1204).
Mak.	Makkoth.
Meg.	Megillah.
Me'il.	Me'ilah.
Men.	Menaḥoth.
Miḳ.	Miḳwaoth.
Naz.	Nazir.
Ned.	Nedarim.
Neg.	Nega'im.
Nid.	Niddah.
Oh.	Ohaloth.

ABBREVIATIONS

Oraḥ Mishor	Novellae on Nazir by Joḥanan b. Meir Kremnitzer (17th Century).
P.B.	The Authorised Daily Prayer Book, S. Singer.
Pes.	Pesaḥim.
R.	Rab, Rabban, Rabbenu, Rabbi.
Rashi	Commentary of R. Isaac Yiẓḥaḳi (d. about 1105).
Sanh.	Sanhedrin.
Shab.	Shabbath.
Sheb.	Shebi'ith.
Shebu.	Shebu'oth.
Sonc. ed.	English Translation of the Babylonian Talmud, Soncino Press, London.
Soṭ.	Soṭah.
TA.	*Talmudische Archäologie*, by S. Krauss.
Ta'an.	Ta'anith.
Tem.	Temura.
Ter.	Terumoth.
Tosaf.	Tosafoth.
Tosef.	Tosefta.
Wilna Gaon	Notes by Elijah of Wilna (1720-1797) in the recent printed editions of the Talmud.
Yad.	*Yad Haḥazakah*, by Moses Maimonides.
Yeb.	Yebamoth.
Zeb.	Zebaḥim.

SOṬAH

TRANSLATED INTO ENGLISH

WITH NOTES, GLOSSARY

AND INDICES

BY

THE REV. DR A. COHEN, M. A., PH. D.

CONTENTS

INTRODUCTION

The Gemara offers a homiletic explanation why this Tractate follows immediately on Nazir, in the same way that the Biblical chapters on the two themes adjoin, viz., it teaches that whoever witnesses a suspected woman in her disgrace should withhold himself from wine (2*a*). The moral was thereby drawn that intemperance tends to weaken the power of resistance to temptation and leads to lewdness.

The name of the Tractate, Soṭah, is derived from the verb *saṭah* in Numbers V, 12, *If any man's wife go aside* (*sisṭeh*). The *Soṭah* is a woman who, suspected by her husband of infidelity, has to submit to the ordeal of drinking the bitter water to establish her innocence. The main subject treated in the Tractate is accordingly the Scriptural section Numbers V, 12-31, which is examined in the closest detail.

The Tractate Soṭah is important for the reason that it is the only source of information at our disposal relating to the ordeal of the bitter water as practised by the Hebrews. Josephus (*Ant.* III, xi, 6) merely summarises the law as it is found in the Bible. The Scriptures give no instance of the ordeal being carried out, although some commentators detect a reference to it in Psalm CIX, 18, *He clothed himself also with cursing as with a garment, and it came into his inward parts like water.*

It would be hazardous to argue from the silence of the earlier Hebrew literature that the ritual described in Numbers V was not put into operation. As with the other Semitic peoples, the legislation had to provide for the contingency of a husband suspecting his wife's chastity without there being definite evidence that she had been unfaithful to him. The Code of Hammurabi prescribes: 'If the wife of a man her husband has accused her, and she had not been caught in lying with another male, she shall swear by God and shall return to her house. If a wife of a man on account of another male has had the finger pointed at her, and has not been caught in lying with another male, for her husband she shall plunge into the holy river' (§§ 131, 132). According to this law, mere suspicion on the husband's part could be overcome by the woman taking an oath, and she is given the right to separate from him and go back to her father's house. But if her conduct had caused a scandal, she is forced to go through the ordeal of being cast into the river and if she sank it was regarded as proof of guilt.

An indication that the Hebrews resorted to the ordeal of the bitter water for the purpose may perhaps be found in what is narrated in Exodus XXXII, 20 where we are informed that Moses made the people drink water in which had been sprinkled the powdered metal of the golden calf. As stated in the Talmud the object may have been to distinguish the innocent from the guilty, the latter being harmfully affected by this otherwise quite innocuous potion.

The principal points of law in connection with a *Soṭah* which are treated in the Tractate are as follows: The husband is obliged to give his wife due warning that she must not associate with the man who has aroused his jealousy (2*a*). One witness is accepted that she had disregarded the warning, provided he does not testify that she committed adultery in which case the ordeal would not be applied (3*b*). There is a difference of opinion whether it is obligatory on the husband to make his wife undergo the test if she has excited his jealousy (3*a*).

The next questions considered are the minimum length of time in which she secludes herself with the man to justify the suspicion that intimacy may have occurred (4*a*); what form the husband's warning must take (5*b*); and her position with regard to *ḥaliẓah* and the levirate-marriage if the husband died before the ordeal took place (5*b*-6*a*).

It is claimed that though she be guilty, the water would not affect her if the witnesses who could prove misconduct were abroad and unable to testify against her, or if she possessed personal merit, or if her husband cohabited with her prior to the test (6*a*, 7*a*).

The accused woman had to bring a meal-offering to the Temple; and the disposal of the offering is discussed if it became defiled, or the husband died, or witnesses arrived to give evidence of misconduct, before she drank the water (6*b*).

There follows a detailed account of the procedure adopted for the carrying out of the text. She appears before the local Court, and then before the Great Sanhedrin in Jerusalem who solemnly charge her to make confession if she is guilty so as to avoid the unnecessary obliteration of the Divine Name which is part of the ceremony. If she pleads guilty she is divorced forthwith; but if she protested her innocence she is taken to the East Gate of the Temple, her garments are rent, her hair is loosened, her ornaments are removed and a common rope tied around her breasts (7*a*, *b*). Two women are not permitted to undergo the ordeal simultaneously (8*a*).

The meal-offering was then presented to the priest (14*a*, *b*), and the water prepared by mingling it with dust from the floor of the Temple (15*b*). If there was no dust there, what may be used as a substitute is considered (16*a*), also how much dust suffices, and it is insisted that the dust must be poured upon the water and not *vice versa* (16*b*).

After that comes the description of the scroll, what is written upon it, the writing materials used (17*a*), the oath of innocence which she swore (18*a*), and the waving and disposal of the meal-offering (19*a*). It is debated whether she drinks the water before or after the sacrifice of the meal-offering.

The Talmud then proceeds to point out that she is forced to drink the water if she refuses to do so after the writing on the scroll had been obliterated (19*b*), and what is to be done with the scroll and meal-offering if she refuses before the obliteration takes place (20*a*, *b*).

The effect of drinking the water is described (20*b*, 21*a*), and how her merit may suspend the consequences (23*a*). What is to be done with the meal-offering if it became defiled is discussed (22*b*, 23*a*).

Circumstances are enumerated in which the ordeal is not administered but the woman is to be divorced forthwith (23*b*, 24*a*, 25*a*), and also circumstances in which a Court of Law can give her the necessary warning in place of the husband (24*a*, *b*, 27*a*).

The question is raised whether a husband can retract his warning (25*a*), and it is maintained that the warning against seclusion holds good even when the man is organically defective or a gentile (26*b*). The ordeal is not applied if the husband or wife is blind, lame, armless or dumb (27*a*, *b*). The paramour is affected by the water as well as the woman (28*a*). Finally there is a section dealing with the evidence of misconduct which bars the application of the ordeal. (31*a*-32*a*).

The foregoing is a summary of the points of law on the *Soṭah* as they are treated in the first six chapters of the Tractate. In this portion other Halachic matters of an extraneous character are dealt with, chief among them being some legal differences between a man and woman (23*a*, *b*) and the various degrees of defilement with holy and non-holy foods (29*a*-30*b*).

With Chapter VII the Tractate enters upon a fresh field of discussion. Beginning with the statement that the Scriptural passages which form part of the ceremony of the ordeal may be recited in any language (32*b*), the Mishnah enumerates other rites and prayers which may be similarly rendered in any language as well as those which can only be spoken in Hebrew. The Gemara thereupon deals at length with the manner in which the priestly benediction was to be pronounced in the Temple and the Synagogue (38*a*-40*b*), how the High Priest rendered his Scriptural recital and benediction on the Day of Atonement (40*b*-41*a*), how the king read his portion on the Feast of Tabernacles (41*a*, *b*), and how the priest designated to accompany the army made his declaration on the field of battle (42*a*). The last mentioned point inaugurates a discussion on the right of exemption from military service (43*a*-44*b*). Lastly there is a full treatment of the law of the heifer whose neck was to be broken when a dead body was found (44*b*-47*b*).

It will thus be seen that the Tractate is rich in Halachic material; but it also abounds in valuable Aggadic references. Biblical narratives relating to important personages and incidents are expounded and embellished. Noteworthy among them are: the history of Samson (9*b*, 10*a*), Judah (10*a*, *b*), Absalom (10*b*, 11*a*), Miriam (11*a et seq.*), the slavery in Egypt and the release (11*a*-12*b*), the childhood of Moses (12*a*, *b*), the burial of Jacob (13*a*), the conveyance of Joseph's bones from Egypt (13*a*, *b*), the burial of Moses

(13*b*, 14*a*), the song at the Red Sea (30*b*, 31*a*), the crossing of the Jordan and the blessings and curses on Mount Gerizim and Mount Ebal (33*b*-34*a*, 35*b*, 36*a*, *b*, 37*a*, *b*), the sending of the twelve spies (34*b*, 35*a*), the smiting of Uzzah (35*a*), Joseph and Potiphar's wife (36*b*), Goliath (42*b*), Phineas (43*a*), and Elisha and the bears (46*b*, 47*a*). They supply excellent examples of the manner in which the Scriptural stories were elaborated for popular edification.

In addition there are many passages which elucidate the views of the Rabbis on religious and ethical questions. We find striking utterances on the futility of secret sin (3*a*), the destructive effect of marital infidelity (3*b*), the harmfulness of pride (4*b*-5*b*), on the *Shechinah* abiding with a happily married couple (17*a*), the evil of flattery (41*b*, 42*a*), and the duty of forming an escort (46*b*). Certain important doctrines of Jewish theology are stressed, viz. divine retribution (8*b*), the Imitation of God as the rule of living (14*a*), and the superioritiy of the service of God from love over the service from fear (31*a*). Other subjects of interest dealt with are the seven types of Pharisees (22*b*), a probable reference to Jesus of Nazareth (47*a*), reforms instituted by John Hyrcanus (47*a*-48*a*), the *Bath Ḳol* (48*b*), the *Shamir* (48*b*) and the civil war between Aristobulus and Hyrcanus (49*b*).

The concluding section of the Tractate describes with impressive vividness the state of deterioration into which the Jewish people sank in the period immediately before and after the fall of the Temple. Owing to the prevalence of murder the ceremony of breaking the heifer's neck was discontinued, and Rabban Joḥanan b. Zakkai suspended the ordeal because of the spread of immorality (47*a*, *b*). Justice became perverted with dire effects upon the life of the people (47*b*). With the destruction of the Sanctuary the great Rabbis passed away, demagogues rose to power, and scholarship was despised. The sad plight of the populace leads to a description of the terrible conditions which will obtain before the advent of the Messiah; and the plaintive refrain is repeated, 'Upon whom is it for us to rely? Upon our Father Who is in heaven'.

The deep note of pessimism on which the Mishnah closes was unjustified. The haunting fear that Israel was doomed to a continuous decline was disproved by events. Eminent scholars arose to fill the place of those who had gone. Chastened by suffering the people renewed their delight in, and loyalty to, the Torah. The fall of the Temple and State did not write the word *finis* to the story of the Jewish people; and nothing contributed so largely to their survival as the devotion to the study of the Torah as it is embodied in the Talmud.

A. COHEN

The Indices of this Tractate have been compiled by Judah J. Slotki, M. A.

SOṬAH

CHAPTER I

MISHNAH. [2a] IF ONE WARNS[1] HIS WIFE [NOT TO ASSOCIATE WITH A CERTAIN MAN], R. ELIEZER SAYS: HE WARNS HER ON THE TESTIMONY OF TWO WITNESSES,[2] AND MAKES HER DRINK [THE WATER OF BITTERNESS] ON THE TESTIMONY OF ONE WITNESS[3] OR HIS PERSONAL TESTIMONY. R. JOSHUA SAYS: HE WARNS HER ON THE TESTIMONY OF TWO AND MAKES HER DRINK ON THE TESTIMONY OF TWO.

HOW DOES HE WARN HER? IF HE SAYS TO HER IN THE PRESENCE OF TWO, DO NOT CONVERSE WITH THAT MAN, AND SHE CONVERSED WITH HIM, SHE IS STILL PERMITTED TO HER HUSBAND[4] AND PERMITTED TO PARTAKE OF THE HEAVE-OFFERING.[5] SHOULD SHE HAVE ENTERED A PRIVATE PLACE WITH HIM AND STAYED WITH HIM A TIME SUFFICIENT FOR MISCONDUCT TO HAVE OCCURRED, SHE IS FORBIDDEN TO HER HUSBAND[6] AND FORBIDDEN TO PARTAKE OF THE HEAVE-OFFERING. IF [HER HUSBAND] DIED,[7] SHE PERFORMS THE CEREMONY OF ḤALIẒAH[8] BUT CANNOT CONTRACT A LEVIRATE MARRIAGE.

GEMARA. Now that the Tanna has finished [Tractate] Nazir, what is his reason for continuing with [Tractate] Soṭah?[9]—It is according to the view of Rabbi; for it has been taught: Rabbi says,

(1) Lit., 'is jealous of', i.e., he gives her a warning because he feels jealous. (2) There must be two witnesses that he had warned her in their presence; otherwise he cannot require her to drink the water of bitterness. (3) That she had secluded herself with the man, after due warning had been given. (4) Lit., 'to her house'. Marital relations may continue. (5) If her husband is a priest. The heave-offering could be eaten by any member of the priest's household who was ritually clean; Num. XVIII, 8ff. (6) Forthwith, before the water is drunk. (7) Before she had undergone the ordeal. (8) V. Glos. (9) What is the association of ideas between the subject of the Nazirite and the woman suspected of infidelity?

Why does the section of the Nazirite adjoin that of the suspected woman?[1] To tell you that whoever witnesses a suspected woman in her disgrace should withhold himself from wine.[2] But [the Tanna in the Mishnah] should treat of [Tractate] Soṭah first and afterwards that of Nazir![3] — Since he treated of [Tractate] Kethuboth [marriage-settlements] and dealt with the theme, '*He who imposes a vow upon his wife*',[4] he next treated of [Tractate] Nedarim [vows]; and since he treated of [Tractate] Nedarim, he proceeded to treat of [Tractate] Nazir which is analogous to Nedarim,[5] and then continues with Soṭah for the reason given by Rabbi.

IF ONE WARNS HIS WIFE. As an accomplished fact[6] it is allowable, but as something still to be done it is not. Consequently our Tanna holds that it is forbidden to give a warning.[7]

R. Samuel b. R. Isaac said: When Resh Laḳish began to expound [the subject of] Soṭah, he spoke thus: They only pair a woman with a man according to his deeds;[8] as it is said, *For the sceptre of wickedness shall not rest upon the lot of the righteous.*[9] Rabbah b. Bar Ḥanah said in the name of R. Joḥanan: It is as difficult to pair them as was the division of the Red Sea; as it is said, *God setteth the solitary in families: He bringeth out the prisoners into prosperity!*[10] But it is not so; for Rab Judah has said in the name of Rab: Forty days before the creation of a child, a *Bath Ḳol*[11] issues forth and proclaims, The daughter of A is for B;[12] the house of C is for D; the field of E is for F! — There is no contradiction, the latter dictum referring to a first marriage and the former to a second marriage.

R. ELIEZER SAYS, HE WARNS HER ON THE TESTIMONY OF

(1) In Num. V and VI. (2) Immoderate use of wine is a source of immorality. v. Ber. 63*a*. (3) That being the order in which they are dealt with in Scripture. (4) The opening words of Keth. VII. (5) A man becomes a nazirite by imposing a vow upon himself. (6) This is derived from the addition of the definite article, the literal sense being: he who warns, i.e., he who has given a warning. (7) Different views are taken on this question; v. p. 8. (8) Only if his actions are righteous does he have a faithful wife. (9) Ps. CXXV, 3. (10) Ibid. LXVIII, 7. The first clause refers to marriage-making, the second to the release of prisoners. Therefore the two are declared identical as regards difficulty. (11) V. Glos. (12) Since the marriage is ordained even before birth, it cannot be dependent upon a man's conduct.

TWO WITNESSES etc. So far only do [R. Eliezer and R. Joshua] differ, viz. in the matter of warning and seclusion, but in the matter of misconduct [they agree] that one witness is believed.[1] We similarly learn in the Mishnah: If one witness says, I saw that she committed misconduct, she does not drink the water.[2] Whence is it derived according to Torah-law that one witness is believed? As our Rabbis taught: *And there be no witness against her*[3]—the text refers to two witnesses.[4] But perhaps it is not so and even one [suffices]! There is a teaching to declare, *One witness shall not rise up against a man.*[5] [2b] From the fact that it is stated, '[A] witness[6] *shall not rise up against a man*', do I not know that one is intended? Why is there a teaching to declare '*one witness*'?[7] This establishes the rule that wherever it is stated '*witness*', it signifies two unless the text specifies '*one*'; and [in the case under discussion] the All-Merciful declares that when there are not two witnesses against her but only one, *and she has not been violated,*[8] she is forbidden [to her husband].[9] Now the reason for that[10] is because it is written, *One witness shall not rise up against a man*. Were it however not so [stated], I might have supposed that '*witness*' in the verse relating to a suspected woman means one.[11] But if there be not even one witness against her, why should she then be prohibited [to her husband]?—[The verse, *One witness* etc.] is necessary, because otherwise it might have occurred to me to suppose that '*there be no witness*

(1) [After due warning had been given and seclusion taken place]. And without drinking the water she leaves her husband's house and does not receive what would normally have been due to her under the marriage-contract. (2) *Infra* 31*a*. (3) Num. V, 13. (4) I.e., wherever Scripture uses the word *witness*, even in the singular, it denotes two. (5) Deut. XIX, 15. (6) And not *witnesses*. (7) The word *one* is superfluous if a single witness is intended, since it would have been sufficient to state *a witness*. (8) But consented to the act. Num. V, 13. The English Version translates the verb *she be not taken in the act;* but the Rabbis understood it in the sense that she was not forced to misconduct and was a consenting party. Cf. the use of the same verb in Deut. XXII, 28. If she had been violated, she was exempt from the ordeal. (9) *Infra* 31*b*. [This proves that in the matter of misconduct one witness is believed, as otherwise whence is it known that she was not violated?] (10) For maintaining that the term '*witness*' in the case of the *Soṭah* denotes two. (11) 'And there be no witness against her' means not even one.

against her' means, he is not believed against her. He is not believed against her! What, then, [does the text] want unless there are two witnesses?[1] Let the Scriptural text be silent on the point [and not mention it at all], since the rule could have been deduced by analogy from the occurrence of the word *dabar*[2] in the verse relating to civil actions, and I would know that it applies to every case of testimony mentioned in the Torah!—It was necessary [for Scripture to have mentioned it], because otherwise it might have occurred to me to suppose that the matter is different in the case of a suspected woman inasmuch as there was some basis for the charge, seeing that he had warned her and she had been secluded [with the man]; consequently one witness should be believed against her. But how is it possible to say [that if the Torah had not specified that *'witness'* always means two, I might have supposed that the intention of *'there be no witness against her'* was] that he is not believed against her and she is permitted to her husband? Surely from what is written, *'and she had not been violated'*,[3] it is implied that she is forbidden to him! It was necessary [for Scripture to have mentioned this], because otherwise it might have occurred to me to suppose that [the evidence against her] is not believed unless there are two witnesses,[4] and [that the verse means] that she had not been violated on the evidence of two witnesses. We are consequently taught [that one witness is believed].

R. JOSHUA SAYS: HE WARNS HER ON THE TESTIMONY OF TWO etc. What is R. Joshua's reason? Scripture states *'against her'* —i.e., *'against her'* [in the matter of misconduct][5] but not in the matter of warning, *'against her'* [in the matter of misconduct] but

(1) What is the purpose of the words if the meaning of *there be no witness* indicates only one and that his evidence is not accepted? (2) In connection with infidelity the text has *he hath found some unseemly matter* (dabar) *in her* (Deut. XXIV, 1), and in connection with civil actions *At the mouth of two witnesses, or at the mouth of three witnesses, shall a matter* (dabar) *be established* (ibid. XIX, 15). By the rule of *Gezerah Shawah*, analogy of expression, the principle of the latter with regard to the number of witnesses required is also applied to the former. (3) Therefore it is maintained that misconduct has occurred with her consent. (4) In a charge of misconduct. (5) One witness is sufficient; but for warning and seclusion two are necessary.

not in the matter of seclusion. R. Eliezer, [on the other hand] says, '*Against her*' [in the matter of misconduct] but not in the matter of warning only. Perhaps, however, '*against her*' does mean, and not in the matter of seclusion!—Seclusion is compared to 'defilement' [misconduct], for it is written, *and he kept close and she be defiled.*[1] But warning also is compared to 'defilement', for it is written, *and he be jealous of his wife and she be defiled!*[2]—The All-Merciful excluded this by the phrase '*against her*'.[3] But what leads you to this conclusion?[4]—It is obvious that seclusion is more serious [than warning] because she is forthwith prohibited to her husband as with 'defilement'. On the contrary, warning is more serious since it is the root cause [of her seclusion rendering her forbidden to her husband]![5]—If there was no seclusion, would there have been any warning?[6] But if there was no warning, what effect would seclusion have?—Nevertheless seclusion is the more serious since it is the beginning of 'defilement'.

Our Mishnah does not agree with the following Tanna. For it has been taught: R. Jose son of R. Judah says in the name of R. Eliezer: He who warns his wife does so on the testimony of one witness or his personal testimony, and makes her drink [the water of bitterness] on the testimony of two witnesses. The Sages replied, According to the view of R. Jose son of R. Judah, there is no purpose in the matter.[7] What is the reason of R. Jose son of R. Judah?—Scripture states '*against her*'—i.e. '*against her*' [in the matter of misconduct] but not in the matter of seclusion. Perhaps, however, '*against her*' means: and not in the matter of warning?—Warning is compared to 'defilement', for it is written, *and he be jealous of his wife and she be defiled*. But seclusion is also compared to 'defilement', for it is written, *and he kept close and she be defiled?*

(1) Num. V, 13. (2) Ibid. 14. (3) The phrase '*against her*' was explained above as relating only to misconduct. (4) That '*against her*' excludes the idea that warning is to be compared to misconduct, and that only seclusion is to be likened to it. (5) Without previous warning she would not be prohibited to her husband because of seclusion. (6) There must have been seclusion to cause jealousy and consequently a warning. (7) In requiring the husband's personal testimony, since, as the Gemara will explain, it may be false.

—That refers to a length of time sufficient for 'defilement' to have occurred.[1]

[It was stated above:] 'The Sages replied, According to the view of R. Jose son of R. Judah, there is no purpose in the matter'. What does this mean?—There may be times when he did not warn her and he claims that he did warn her.[2] Is there, then, according to our Mishnah any purpose in the matter, since there may be times when she had not been secluded with the man and the husband claims that she had been secluded?[3]—R. Isaac b. Joseph said in the name of R. Joḥanan, [Read] also according to the view of R. Jose son of R. Judah, there is no purpose in the matter. 'Also according to the view of R. Jose son of R. Judah' [you say]; is there, then, no question with respect to our Mishnah? On the contrary, according to our Mishnah there is foundation [for the charge], but in the other case [the view of R. Jose son of R. Judah] there may be no foundation![4]—But if the teaching is reported, it must be in this form: R. Isaac b. Joseph said in the name of R. Joḥanan: 'According to the view of R. Jose son of R. Judah, and also according to our Mishnah, there is no purpose in the matter.'

R. Ḥanina of Sura said: Nowadays a man should not say to his wife, 'Do not be secluded with So-and-so', lest we decide according to R. Jose son of R. Judah who said, A warning [is effective] if given on [the husband's] personal testimony. If she then secluded herself with the man, since we have not now the water for a suspected woman to test her, the husband forbids her to himself for all time.

Resh Laḳish said: What is the meaning of the term *Ḳinnui?*[5] A matter which causes hatred [*Ḳin'ah*] between her and others.

(1) So that if the time of seclusion was insufficient, she is not required to drink the water. (2) So what purpose is there in requiring the husband's unsupported evidence? (3) The Mishnah compels the woman to drink the water on the unsupported evidence of the husband. (4) According to the Mishnah there must have been warning on the testimony of two witnesses, so there is some foundation for the charge; but according to R. Jose the husband can give her warning on his uncorroborated testimony which might be groundless. (5) That is the term used in Num. V, 14, *'he be jealous'*.

Consequently he holds that the warning can be on [the husband's] personal testimony; and since not everybody knows that he gave her a warning and they say, 'What has happened that she holds herself aloof?' they will proceed to cause hatred against her. R. Jemar b. Shelemia said in the name of Abaye: [*Ḳinnui* means] a matter which causes hatred between husband and wife. Consequently he holds that the warning must be on the testimony of two witnesses and everybody is aware that he gave her a warning,[1] and it is he who proceeds to cause hatred against her. [3a] Conclude that they hold that it is forbidden to give a warning;[2] but according to him who says that it is permissible to give a warning, what is the meaning of *Ḳinnui?*—R. Naḥman b. Isaac said: *Ḳinnui* means nothing but 'warning;' and thus Scripture states, *Then the Lord warned* [wa-yeḳanna] *his land.*[3]

It has been taught: R. Meir used to say, If a person commits a transgression in secret, the Holy One, Blessed be He, proclaims it against him in public; as it is said, *And the spirit of jealousy came upon him;*[4] and the verb *'abar* [came upon] means nothing but 'proclaiming', as it is said, *And Moses gave commandment, and they caused it to be proclaimed throughout the camp.*[5] Resh Laḳish said: A person does not commit a transgression unless a spirit of folly [*sheṭuth*] enters into him; as it is said, *If any man's wife go aside.*[6] [The word is] written [so that it can be read] *sishṭeh.*[7]

The School of R. Ishmael taught: Why does the Torah believe one witness in the case of a suspected woman? Because there was some basis for the charge, seeing that he had warned her and she had secluded herself with the man, and one witness testifies that she had 'defiled' [misconducted] herself. R. Papa said to Abaye, But the warning is mentioned in the text *after* the seclusion and misconduct?[8]—He replied to him, *We'abar* [means] there had

(1) Since the witnesses are likely to talk of it to others. (2) Because they explain *Ḳinnui* in the sense of hatred, and it is not allowed to create hatred. (3) Joel II, 18. (E.V. '*Then the Lord was jealous for his land*'.) (4) Num. V, 14. (5) Ex. XXXVI, 6. (6) Num. V, 12. The word for '*go aside*' is *sisṭeh.* (7) I.e., act in folly. (8) The matter of seclusion and misconduct is mentioned in Num. V, 12f. and the warning from jealousy in verse 14.

already come upon him.[1] But can that interpretation be also applied to, *And every armed man of you will pass over?*[2]—In that passage, since it is written, *And the land will be subdued before the Lord, then afterward ye shall return,*[3] it follows that the reference is to the future; but here, if it should enter your mind that we follow the order of the text [and *we'abar* signifies '*will come*'], of what use is a warning after misconduct and seclusion had taken place?

The School of R. Ishmael taught: A man does not warn his wife unless a spirit[4] enters into him; as it is said, '*And the spirit of jealousy came upon him and he be jealous of his wife*'. What is the meaning [of the word] '*spirit*'?—The Rabbis declare, It is a spirit of impurity;[5] but R. Ashi declares, It is a spirit of purity.[6] Reasonable is the view of him who declares that it is a spirit of purity, because it was taught: *And he be jealous of his wife*—this is voluntary[7] in the opinion of R. Ishmael; but R. Akiba says, It is obligatory. It is well if you say that it means a spirit of purity, then everything is right; but if you say that it means a spirit of impurity, is it voluntary or obligatory for a man to introduce a spirit of impurity into himself!

[To turn to] the main text: *And he be jealous of his wife*—this is voluntary in the opinion of R. Ishmael; but R. Akiba says, It is obligatory. *For her he may defile himself*[8]—this is voluntary in the opinion of R. Ishmael; but R. Akiba says, It is obligatory. *Of them shall ye take your bondmen for ever*[9]—this is voluntary in the opinion of R. Ishmael; but R. Akiba says, It is obligatory. R. Papa said to Abaye—others declare it was R. Mesharsheya who said to Raba: Is this to say that R. Ishmael and R. Akiba differ in this way throughout the Torah, one maintaining that [a precept] is voluntary and the other that it is obligatory?—He replied,

(1) [ועבר is treated as pluperfect.] (2) Num. XXXII, 21 where the same word, *we'abar*, occurs. (3) Ibid. 22. (4) Introduced into him by God to warn him of what had occurred. (5) An instigation by Satan. (6) Which revolts against immorality. (7) The husband can ignore the matter if he so wishes. (8) Lev. XXI, 3. Does it mean *he may* or *he should;* and similarly with the other instances discussed. (9) Ibid. XXV, 46.

They only differ here over texts: *And he be jealous of his wife*—it is voluntary in the opinion of R. Ishmael; but R. Akiba says, It is obligatory. What is the reason of R. Ishmael?—He holds the same view as that of the following teacher. It has been taught: R. Eliezer b. Jacob says, Since the Torah declares, *Thou shalt not hate thy brother in thine heart,*[1] it is possible to think that this applies also in such a circumstance;[2] therefore there is a text to say, *And the spirit of jealousy came upon him and he be jealous of his wife.*[3] And [what is the reason of] R. Akiba?—The word '*jealous*' occurs a second time in the verse.[4] And [how does] R. Ishmael [explain the repetition of *jealous*]?—Since it was necessary to write, *And she be defiled* and afterwards *and she be not defiled*, the Torah wrote *and he be jealous of his wife.*[5] This is in agreement with the teaching of the School of R. Ishmael; for it was taught in the School of R. Ishmael: Wherever a Scriptural passage is repeated, it is only repeated because of some new point contained therein. [Similarly] '*For her he may defile himself*'—this is voluntary in the opinion of R. Ishmael; but R. Akiba says, It is obligatory. What is the reason of R. Ishmael?—Since it is written, *Speak unto the priests the sons of Aaron and say unto them, There shall none defile himself for the dead among his people,*[6] it was likewise necessary to write, *For her he may defile himself.* And [from where does] R. Akiba [learn that a priest may so defile himself]?—He derives it from, *Except for his kin;*[7] what then is the purpose of, *For her he should defile himself?* [It is to indicate that] it is obligatory. And [how does] R. Ishmael [explain the addition of these words]?—'*For her*' he may defile himself but not for any of her limbs.[8] [3*b*] [What reply does] R. Akiba [make to this explanation]?—If that were the sole intention,

(1) Ibid. XIX, 17. (2) That a husband may overlook his wife's seclusion with another man and not warn her. (3) He interprets the words as meaning: if the spirit of jealousy came upon him and he wishes to warn his wife. (4) He understands the second clause as *he should be jealous* and warn her. (5) The words are repeated because of the two contingencies mentioned and no such deduction is to be drawn as R. Akiba suggests. (6) Lev. XXI, 1. (7) Ibid. 2. (8) An amputated limb of a body defiles in the same way as the whole body. V. Nazir 43*b*.

the All-Merciful should have written *'for her'* and then stop; what is the purpose of the words *'he should defile himself'?* Deduce therefrom.[1] [How does] R. Ishmael [meet this argument]?—Since the Torah wrote *'for her'*, it likewise wrote *'he may defile himself'*. This is in agreement with the teaching of the School of R. Ishmael; for it was taught in the School of R. Ishmael: Wherever a Scriptural passage is repeated, it is only repeated because of some new point contained therein. [And similarly,] *Of them shall ye take your bondmen for ever*[2]—this is voluntary in the opinion of R. Ishmael; but R. Akiba says, It is obligatory. What is the reason of R. Ishmael? —Since it is written, *Thou shalt save alive nothing that breatheth,*[3] it was likewise necessary to write, *'Of them shall ye take your bondmen for ever'*, in order to indicate that if a man belonging to any other Gentile people has intercourse with a Canaanite woman[4] and begets a son by her, it is permissible to purchase him as a slave. For it has been taught: Whence is it that if a man belonging to any other Gentile people has intercourse with a Canaanite woman and begets a son by her, it is permissible to purchase him as a slave? There is a text to declare, *Moreover of the children of the strangers that do sojourn among you, of them shall ye buy.*[5] It is possible to think that also if a Canaanite had intercourse with a woman belonging to any other Gentile people and he begets a son by her, it is permissible to purchase him as a slave; therefore there is a text to declare, *Which they have begotten in your land*[6]—from those born in your land[7] and not from those who dwell in your land.[8] And [from where does] R. Akiba [learn this rule]?—He derives it from, *'Of them shall ye buy'*; what then is the purpose of, *'Of them ye shall take your bondmen for ever'?* [It indicates that] it is obligatory. And [how does] R. Ishmael [explain the addition of these words]?—*'Of them'* [he may purchase] but not of your brethren. [From where does]

(1) That it is obligatory. (2) Lev. XXV, 46. (3) Deut. XX, 16. (4) The woman belonged to the seven nations which had to be exterminated. (5) Lev. XXV, 45. (6) Ibid. I.e. the original natives of Canaan. (7) [Whose father belongs to another land.] (8) [I.e., the original natives of Canaan]. It is to be noted that descent is traced through the father, whereas in the case of a Jew descent is traced through the mother.

R. Akiba [derive this rule]?—It is deduced from the mention of '*your brethren*' at the end of the verse, *But over your brethren the children of Israel ye shall not rule, one over another, with rigour.*[1] [How does] R. Ishmael [meet this argument]?—Since the Torah wrote '*But over your brethren*', it likewise wrote '*of them*'. This is in agreement with the teaching of the School of R. Ishmael; for it was taught in the School of R. Ishmael: Wherever a Scriptural passage is repeated, it is only repeated because of some new point contained therein.

R. Ḥisda said: Immorality in a house is like a worm in the sesame plant. Further said R. Ḥisda: Anger in a house is like a worm in the sesame plant. Both these statements refer to a woman, but in the case of a man there is no objection.[2] Further said R. Ḥisda, At first, before Israel sinned [against morality], the *Shechinah* abode with each individual; as it is said, *For the Lord thy God walketh in the midst of thy camp.*[3] When they sinned, the *Shechinah* departed from them; as it is said, *That he see no unclean thing in thee and turn away from thee.*[4]

R. Samuel b. Naḥmani said in the name of R. Jonathan: Whoever performs one precept in this world, it precedes him for the world to come; as it is said, *And thy righteousness shall go before thee;*[5] and whoever commits one transgression in this world, it clings to him and precedes him for the Day of Judgment, as it is said, *The paths of their way are turned aside; they go up into the waste and perish.*[6] R. Eleazar says: It attaches itself to him like a dog; as it is said, *He hearkened not unto her, to lie by her, or to be with her*[7]—*to lie by her* in this world, *or to be with her* in the world to come.

We learn elsewhere: It is a proper conclusion that if the first evidence [that the woman had secluded herself with the man], which does not prohibit her [to her husband] for all time,[8] is not established by fewer than two witnesses, is it not right that the final evidence [that she had misconducted herself] which prohibits her to him for all time, should not be established by fewer than

(1) Lev. XXV, 46. (2) This opinion is contradicted by popular proverbs quoted in the Talmud, viz., 'He among the full-grown pumpkins and his wife among the young ones' (*infra*, p. 45), and 'He who gives vent to his anger destroys his house' (Sanh. 102*b*). (3) Deut. XXIII, 15. (4) Ibid. (5) Isa. LVIII, 8. (6) Job VI, 18. (7) Gen. XXXIX, 10. (8) Because the water may prove her innocent.

two witnesses! Therefore there is a text to state, '*And there be no witness against her*', [implying that], whatever [evidence] there may be against her [is believed, even if it be only one witness]. And with respect to the first evidence [about her seclusion with the man, that one witness suffices may be argued by] *a fortiori* reasoning as follows: If the final evidence [regarding misconduct], which prohibits her to her husband for all time, is established by one witness, is it not proper that the first evidence, which does not prohibit her to him for all time, should be established by one witness! Therefore there is a text to state, *Because he hath found some unseemly matter in her,*[1] and elsewhere it states, *At the mouth of two witnesses, or at the mouth of three witnesses shall a matter be established;*[2] as the '*matter*' mentioned in this latter case must be confirmed by the testimony of two witnesses, so also here [in the case of the suspected woman] the '*matter*' must be confirmed by the testimony of two witnesses.[3] Is this deduction to be drawn from the words, '*Because he hath found some unseemly matter in her*'? It ought to be derived from '*against her*'—i.e., '*against her*' [in the matter of misconduct] but not in the matter of warning, '*against her*' [in the matter of misconduct] but not in the matter of seclusion![4]—He also says similarly[5] [and his teaching is to be cited as follows]: Therefore there is a text to state '*against her*' [in the matter of misconduct] but not in the matter of warning, '*against her*' [in the matter of misconduct] but not in the matter of seclusion; and whence is it that merely in a case of misconduct, where there had been no warning or seclusion, one witness is not believed? It is stated here, '*Because he hath found some unseemly matter in her*', and elsewhere it states, '*At the mouth of two witnesses, or at the mouth of three witnesses, shall a matter be established*'; as in the '*matter*' mentioned in the latter case two witnesses are required, so also here [where there has been misconduct without warning and seclusion] two witnesses are required.

(1) Deut. XXIV, 1. (2) Ibid. XIX, 15. (3) *Infra* 31a-b. (4) V. *supra* p. 5. (5) The teacher in the Mishnah accepts the deduction from '*against her*' and uses the argument from the occurrence of the word '*matter*' for another purpose. He had been quoted wrongly and the Gemara proceeds with the correct form of the teaching.

Our Rabbis have taught: Which is the 'first testimony'? Evidence of seclusion, and the 'final testimony' is evidence of 'defilement' [misconduct]. [4a] And how long is the duration in the matter of seclusion? Sufficient for misconduct, i.e., sufficient for coition, i.e., sufficient for sexual contact, i.e., sufficient for a person to walk round a date-palm. Such is the view of R. Ishmael; R. Eliezer says: Sufficient for preparing a cup of wine;[1] R. Joshua says: Sufficient to drink it; Ben Azzai says: Sufficient to roast an egg; R. Akiba says: Sufficient to swallow it; R. Judah b. Bathyra says: Sufficient to swallow three eggs one after the other; R. Eleazar b. Jeremiah says: Sufficient for a weaver to knot a thread; Ḥanin b. Phineas says: Sufficient for a woman to extend her hand to her mouth to remove a chip of wood [from between the teeth]; Pelemo says: Sufficient for her to extend her hand to a basket and take a loaf therefrom. Although there is no proof for this [last opinion] there is an indication, viz., *For on account of a harlot, to a loaf of bread.*[2] What is the purpose of all these definitions?—They are necessary; because if we were only taught sufficient for misconduct, I would have thought that it meant sufficient time for her misconduct and her submission;[3] therefore it is defined as sufficient for coition.[4] If, however, it were only taught sufficient for coition, I would have thought that it meant sufficient time for completed coition; therefore it is defined as sufficient for sexual contact. If, further, we had only been taught sufficient for sexual contact, I would have thought that it meant sufficient time for sexual contact and her submission; therefore it is defined as sufficient for misconduct. And how much is the time sufficient for sexual contact? Sufficient for a person to walk round a date-palm.

In contradiction of the above [I quote the following]: *And be kept close*[5]—but how long is the duration in the matter of seclusion we have not heard. Since, however, it states '*and she be defiled*', deduce that it is time sufficient for misconduct, i.e., sufficient for coition,

(1) By diluting it with water. (2) Prov. VI, 26. This is the literal rendering of the Hebrew. (3) I.e., that he should make improper advances and induce her to submit. (4) Consequently she must have secluded herself with the intention of committing misconduct. (5) Num. V, 13.

i.e., sufficient for sexual contact, i.e., sufficient for a date-palm to rebound.[1] Such is the view of R. Eliezer; R. Joshua says: Sufficient for preparing a cup of wine; Ben Azzai says: Sufficient to drink it; R. Akiba says: Sufficient to roast an egg; R. Judah b. Bathyra says: Sufficient to swallow it.[2] Now it is assumed that walking round a date-palm and the rebound of a date-palm are identical [in length of time, and the question thus arises:] R. Ishmael said above, 'Sufficient for a person to walk round a date-palm', and R. Eliezer disagreed with him; and here R. Eliezer says, 'Sufficient for a date-palm to rebound'!—Abaye said, 'Walking round' means on foot, and 'rebound' means by the force of the wind. R. Ashi asked, How is 'rebound' to be understood? Does it mean that the palm is blown in one direction and then in its opposite, or perhaps that it is blown in one direction and then in its opposite and finally returns to its original position?—The question remains unanswered.

R. Eliezer said above: 'Sufficient for preparing a cup of wine', and here he says, 'Sufficient for a date-palm to rebound'!—They are alike in duration. R. Joshua said above, 'Sufficient to drink it', and here he says, 'Sufficient for preparing a cup of wine'!—Say [that the correct version is], Sufficient for preparing a cup of wine and drinking it. But why not say rather that they are alike in duration?—If so, he would agree with R. Eliezer's view.[3] Ben Azzai said above 'Sufficient to roast an egg', and here he says, 'Sufficient to drink [a cup of wine]'!—They are alike in duration. R. Akiba said above, 'Sufficient to swallow [a roasted egg]', and here he says, 'Sufficient to roast an egg'!—Say [that the correct version is], Sufficient to roast an egg and swallow it. But why not say rather that they are alike in duration?—If so, he would agree with Ben Azzai's view. R. Judah b. Bathyra said above, 'Sufficient to swallow three eggs one after the other', and here he says, 'Sufficient to swallow [one roasted egg]'!—He spoke in accordance with the view of R. Akiba who said that we fix as the duration a length

(1) After having been bent by the wind. (2) Tosef. Soṭ. I, 2. (3) That cannot be, because he gives a different definition, and so it is impossible to think them alike in duration.

of time sufficient to roast and swallow an egg, [and with reference to this he said,] 'speak rather only of the duration of swallowing', that is 'sufficient time to swallow three eggs one after the other', for that is the same as roasting and swallowing [one egg][1].

'R. Eleazar b. Jeremiah says, Sufficient for a weaver to knot a thread'. R. Ashi asked, Does this mean two ends which are distant or near?[2]—The question remains unanswered.

'Ḥanin b. Phineas said, Sufficient for a woman to extend her hand to her mouth to remove a chip of wood'. R. Ashi asked, Does this mean wedged tightly [between the teeth] or not?—The question remains unanswered.

'Pelemo said: Sufficient for her to extend her hand to a basket and take a loaf therefrom'. R. Ashi asked, Is it [a loaf] which is wedged in tightly or not, a new or old [basket],[3] a hot or cold [loaf],[4] [4b] wheaten or of barley,[5] soft or hard-baked?—The question remains unanswered.

R. Isaac son of R. Joseph said in the name of R. Joḥanan: Each of the teachers defined the duration [of coition] from his own experience. But they included Ben Azzai who was unmarried!—If you wish I can say that he had married and separated [from his wife],[6] or that he had heard it from his master, or that *The secret of the Lord is with them that fear him.*[7]

R. 'Awira expounded, sometimes in the name of R. Ammi and at other times in the name of R. Assi: Whoever eats bread without previously washing the hands is as though he had intercourse with a harlot; as it is said, *For on account of a harlot, to a loaf of bread.*[8]

(1) [Why introduce at all the act of roasting, seeing that the act of swallowing by itself can afford a suitable standard for defining the duration?] (2) I.e., does it include the time spent in bringing the threads together as well as tying them? (3) In a new basket the ends of straws protrude and catch in the loaves, so that it takes longer to get one out. (4) A warm loaf has to be drawn out with greater care and therefore takes longer. (5) A wheaten loaf is smoother and has to be grasped more firmly; and similarly with one which is soft-baked. (6) The passage in Yeb. 63b does not make it clear whether Ben Azzai was censured for remaining a bachelor or for having married and not begetting children. (7) Ps. XXV, 14. The knowledge was revealed to him. (8) Prov. VI, 26. (E.V. '*For on account of a harlot a man is brought to a loaf of bread*'). [As

Raba said: [On that interpretation] the verse, '*For on account of a harlot, to a loaf of bread*' should have read, 'On account of a loaf of bread, to a harlot'! But, said Raba, [the meaning is:] Whoever has intercourse with a harlot will in the end go seeking a loaf of bread.

R. Zeriḳa said in the name of R. Eleazar: Whoever makes light of washing the hands [before and after a meal] will be uprooted from the world. R. Ḥiyya b. Ashi said in the name of Rab: With the first washing [before the meal] it is necessary to lift the hands up; with the latter washing [after the meal] it is necessary to lower the hands. There is a similar teaching: Who washes his hands [before the meal] must lift them up lest the water pass beyond the joint,[1] flow back and render them unclean. R. Abbahu says: Whoever eats bread without first wiping his hands is as though he eats unclean food; as it is stated, *And the Lord said, Even thus shall the children of Israel eat their bread unclean.*[2]

And[3] what means, *And the adultress hunteth for the precious life?* —R. Ḥiyya b. Abba said in the name of R. Joḥanan: Every man in whom is haughtiness of spirit will in the end stumble through an [unfaithful] married woman; as it is said, '*And the adultress hunteth for the precious life*'. Raba said: [On that interpretation] the word '*precious*' should have been 'haughty'! Furthermore the verse should have read, [The haughty soul] hunteth [the adultress]! But, said Raba, [the meaning is:] Whoever has intercourse with a married woman, even though he had studied Torah, of which it is written, *It is more precious than rubies,*[4] i.e., above a High Priest who enters into the innermost part of the Sanctuary, she will hunt him to the judgment of Gehinnom.[5]

R. Joḥanan said in the name of R. Simeon b. Yoḥai: Every man in whom is haughtiness of spirit is as though he worships idols; it

much as to say that the disregard of one Rabbinic precept leads to the disregard of another.]

(1) When washing the hands for a meal, the water should reach the second joint of the fingers; Ḥul. 106*a*. The hands beyond the joint having been left unwashed are deemed unclean. (2) Ezek. IV, 13. (3) The Gemara now continues the discussion of Prov. VI, 26 quoted above. (4) Prov. III, 15. מפנינים. (5) לפני ולפנים, a play upon the word מפנינים, v. n. 4.

is written here, *Every one that is proud in heart is an abomination to the Lord,*[1] and it is written elsewhere, *Thou shalt not bring an abomination into thine house.*[2] R. Johanan himself said: He is as though he had denied the fundamental principle;[3] as it is said, *Thine heart be lifted up and thou forget the Lord thy God,* etc.[4] R. Ḥama b. Ḥanina said: He is as though he had broken all the laws of sexual morality;[5] it is written here, *Every one that is proud in heart is an abomination to the Lord,* and it is written elsewhere, *For all these abominations,* etc.[6] 'Ulla said: He is as though he had erected an idolatrous altar; as it is said, *Cease ye from man whose breath is in his nostrils;*[7] *for wherein* [bammeh] *is he to be accounted of?*[8]—read not *bammeh* but *bamah* [an idolatrous altar].

What means, *Hand to hand, he shall not escape punishment?*[9] Rab said: Whoever has intercourse with a married woman, though he proclaim the Holy One, blessed be He, to be Possessor of heaven and earth as did our father Abraham, of whom it is written, *I have lift up mine hand unto the Lord, God Most High, Possessor of heaven and earth,*[10] he will not escape the punishment of Gehinnom. The students of the School of R. Shila objected: [On that interpretation] the phrase '*Hand to hand* etc.' should have read, 'Of my [God's] hand will not escape punishment'! But, said they of the School of R. Shila, [the meaning is:] Though he received the Torah as did our teacher Moses, of whom it is written, *At his right hand was a fiery law unto them,*[11] he will not escape the punishment of Gehinnom. R. Johanan objected: [On that interpretation] the phrase '*Hand to hand*' should have read 'Hand from hand'![12] But, said R. Johanan, [5*a*] [the meaning is:] Though he practise charity in secret,[13] concerning which it is written, '*A gift in secret pacifieth anger,*[14] he will not escape the punishment of Gehinnom.

(1) Prov. XVI, 5. (2) Deut. VII, 26, the reference being to an idolatrous image. (3) Viz., the existence of God. (4) Ibid. VIII, 14. (5) Enumerated in Lev. XVIII. (6) Lev. XVIII, 27. (7) Understood in the sense: who is proud. (8) Isa. II, 22. (9) Prov. XVI, 5. (10) Gen. XIV, 22. (11) Deut. XXXIII, 2. (12) Since the interpretation implies that the adulterer receives from, and does not give to. (13) He gives from '*hand to hand*'. (14) Prov. XXI, 14.

Whence is there a prohibition for the haughty of spirit?—Raba said in the name of Ze'iri: *Hear ye, and give ear; be not proud.*[1] R. Naḥman b. Isaac said: [It is derived] from this passage, *Thine heart be lifted up, and thou forget the Lord thy God,*[2] and it is written, *Beware lest thou forget the Lord thy God.*[3] This is in accord with what R. Abin said in the name of R. Elai; for R. Abin said in the name of R. Elai: Wherever it is stated '*Beware*' '*lest*' and '*Do not*' the reference is to a prohibition.

R. 'Awira expounded, sometimes he said it in the name of R. Assi and at other times in the name of R. Ammi: Every man in whom is haughtiness of spirit will in the end be reduced in rank; as it is said, *They are exalted, there will be reduction of status;*[4] and lest you think that they remain in existence, the text continues, '*And they are gone*'. If, however, he changes [and becomes humble], he will be gathered [to his fathers] in his due time like our father Abraham; as it is said, *But when they are lowly, they are gathered in like all*[5]—i.e., like Abraham, Isaac and Jacob in connection with whom the word '*all*' is used.[6] If not, *They are cut off as the tops of the ears of corn.*[7] What means '*as the tops of the ears of corn*'? R. Huna and R. Ḥisda [explain it]. One says that it means like the awn of the grain, and the other that it means like the ears themselves. This is quite right according to him who says that it means like the awn of the grain, since it is written '*as the tops of the ears of corn*'; but according to him who says that it means like the ears themselves, what signifies '*as the* tops *of the ears of corn*'?—R. Assi said, and it was similarly taught in the School of R. Ishmael: It is like a man who enters his field; he gleans the tallest ears.

With him also that is of a contrite and humble spirit.[8] R. Huna and R. Ḥisda [explain it]. One says that it means the contrite is with Me, and the other that I [God] am with the contrite. The more probable view is in accord with him who holds the meaning to be I am with the contrite; for behold, the Holy One, blessed be He, ignored all the mountains and heights and caused His *Shechinah* to

(1) Jer. XIII, 15. (2) Deut. VIII, 14. (3) Ibid. 11. (4) Job XXIV, 24. (5) Ibid. (6) V. Gen. XXIV, 1, XXVII, 33 and XXXIII, 11. (7) Job *loc. cit.* (8) Isa. LVII, 15.

abide upon Mount Sinai, but did not elevate Mount Sinai [up to Himself].

R. Joseph said: Man should always learn from the mind of his Creator; for behold, the Holy One, blessed be He, ignored all the mountains and heights and caused His *Shechinah* to abide upon Mount Sinai, and ignored all the beautiful trees and caused His *Shechinah* to abide in a bush.[1]

R. Eleazar also said: Every man in whom is haughtiness of spirit is fit to be hewn down like an *Asherah*[2]. It is written here, *The high ones of stature shall be hewn down,*[3] and elsewhere it is written, *And ye shall hew down their Asherim.*[4] Further said R. Eleazar, Every man in whom is haughtiness of spirit, his dust will not be disturbed [for the Resurrection]; as it is said, *Awake and sing, ye that dwell in the dust*[5]—it is not said 'ye that lie in the dust', but, '*ye that dwell* [shokne] *in the dust*', i.e., each one who during his lifetime made himself a neighbour [*shaken*] to the dust [by his humility]. Further said R. Eleazar: Over every man in whom is haughtiness of spirit the *Shechinah* laments; as it is said, *But the haughty he knoweth from afar.*[6]

R. Awira expounded, and according to another version it was R. Eleazar: Come and see that the manner of the Holy One, blessed be He, is not like the manner of human beings. The manner of human beings is for the lofty to take notice of the lofty and not of the lowly; but the manner of the Holy One, blessed be He, is not so. He is lofty and He takes notice of the lowly, as it is said, *For though the Lord be high, yet hath he respect unto the lowly.*[7]

R. Ḥisda said, and according to another version it was Mar 'Uḳba: Every man in whom is haughtiness of spirit, the Holy One, blessed be He, declares, I and he cannot both dwell in the world; as it is said, *Whoso privily slandereth his neighbour, him will I destroy; him that hath an high look and a proud heart will I not suffer*[8]—read not

(1) Ex. III, 2. Similarly should man associate with the humble. (2) An object of idolatrous worship. (3) Isa. X, 33. (4) Deut. VII, 5. (5) Isa. XXVI, 19. 'Ye that *lie* in the dust' would apply to all mortals. (6) Ps. CXXXVIII, 6. The Hebrew word translated *knoweth*, ידע, is understood in the sense of punish, cf. Jud. VIII, 16. (7) Ibid. (8) Ps. CI, 5.

'*him*' [I cannot suffer], but '*with him*'[1] I cannot [dwell]. There are some who apply this teaching to those who speak slander; as it is said, '*Whoso privily slandereth his neighbour, him will I destroy*'.

R. Alexandri said: Every man in whom there is haughtiness of spirit, even the slightest wind will disturb;[2] as it is said, *But the wicked are like the troubled sea.*[3] If the sea, which contains so many quarters of a *log*,[4] is ruffled by the slightest wind, how much more so a human being who contains but one quarter of a *log*.[5]

R. Ḥiyya b. Ashi said in the name of Rab: A disciple of the Sages should possess an eighth [of pride].[6] R. Huna the son of R. Joshua said: [This small amount of pride] crowns him like the awn of the grain. Raba said: [A disciple of the Sages] who possesses [haughtiness of spirit] deserves excommunication, and if he does not possess it he deserves excommunication.[7] R. Naḥman b. Isaac said: He should not possess it or part of it; is it a trifling matter concerning which it is written, *Every one that is proud in heart is an abomination to the Lord!*[8]

Hezekiah said: A man's prayer is not heard unless he makes his heart [soft] like flesh; as it is said, *And it shall come to pass, that from one new moon to another, shall all flesh come to worship, etc.*[9] R. Zera said: Concerning flesh it is written, *And it is healed;*[10] but it is not written concerning man, *And he is healed.*

R. Joḥanan said: The word for man [*adam*] indicates dust, blood and gall;[11] the word for flesh [*basar*] indicates shame, stench and worm. Some declare that [instead of 'stench' we should have the word] *Sheol*, since its initial letter corresponds.[12]

R. Ashi said: Every man in whom is haughtiness of spirit will

(1) Involves a slight change in the vocalization. (2) [The smallest disappointment is liable to discomfit him.] (3) Isa. LVII, 20. (4) A liquid measure, equal to the contents of six eggs. (5) This was considered the minimum quantity of blood in the body essential to life. (6) He should have a little pride to maintain his self-respect. (7) To have too much is bad, and also too little because it prevents a Rabbi from exercising his authority. (8) Prov. XVI, 5. (9) Isa. LXVI, 23. (10) Lev. XIII, 18. Hence only one whose heart is soft like flesh will be healed, and not a man in his full pride. (11) The initials of these words in Hebrew form *adam*. (12) The initial of the word for 'stench' is *samek*, whereas the second letter in *basar* is similar in form to that of '*Sheol*'.

in the end be degraded; as it is said, [5b] *For a rising and for a scab,*[1] and *se'eth* ['rising'] means nothing else than elevation, as it is said, *Upon all the high mountains, and upon all the hills that are* nisdoth [*lifted up*].[2] *Sappaḥath* ['scab'] means nothing else than attachment; as it is said, *Attach me, I pray thee, into one of the priests' offices, that I may eat a morsel of bread.*[3]

R. Joshua b. Levi said: Come and see how great are the lowly of spirit in the esteem of the Holy One, blessed be He, since when the Temple stood, a man brought a burnt-offering and received the reward of a burnt-offering, a meal-offering and he received the reward of a meal-offering; but as for him whose mind is lowly, Scripture ascribes it to him as though he had offered every one of the sacrifices; as it is said, *The sacrifices of God are a broken spirit.*[4] More than that, his prayer is not despised; as it continues: *A broken and a contrite heart, O God, thou wilt not despise.*

R. Joshua b. Levi further said: He who calculates his ways in this world will be worthy to behold the salvation of the Holy One, blessed be He; as it is said, *To him that ordereth his way will I shew the salvation of God*[5]—read not *we-sam* [that ordereth] but *we-sham* [who calculates] his way.[6]

HOW MUST HE WARN HER? etc. This is self-contradictory. You declare, IF HE SAYS TO HER IN THE PRESENCE OF TWO, DO NOT CONVERSE WITH THAT MAN—consequently conversation is the equivalent of seclusion.[7] He then proceeds to teach, AND SHE CONVERSED WITH HIM, SHE IS STILL PERMITTED TO HER HUSBAND AND PERMITTED TO PARTAKE OF THE HEAVE-OFFERING—consequently conversation is nothing!—Abaye said, This is what he means: [If he said to her,] Do not converse, and she conversed with him, Do not converse, and she secluded herself with him, that is nothing; [but if he said to her,] Do not be secluded

(1) Lev. XIV, 56 interpreted as: having first been elevated, he will become something superfluous among men, and therefore esteemed as nothing. (2) Isa. II, 14. (3) I Sam. II, 36. The Hebrew for the verb *attach* resembles the word for *scab*, v. Shebu, 6b. (4) Ps. LI, 19. (5) Ibid. L, 23. (6) He calculates the loss incurred in fulfilling a precept against the reward it will bring him, v. Aboth, II, 1. (7) Since it justifies a warning from the husband.

with him, and she conversed with him, she is still permitted to her husband and permitted to partake of the heave-offering. Should she have entered a private place with him and stayed a time sufficient for misconduct to have occurred, she is forbidden to her husband and forbidden to partake of the heave-offering.

IF [HER HUSBAND] DIED, SHE PERFORMS THE CEREMONY OF ḤALIẒAH. Why so? Let her also contract a levirate marriage! —R. Joseph said: Scripture declared, *And when she is departed out of his house, she may go and be another man's wife*[1]—she may marry '*another*' man but not her brother-in-law.[2] Abaye said to him, According to your argument, *Ḥaliẓah* also should be unnecessary! He replied to him, If the husband is living, is not a *Geṭ* required?[3] So here likewise *Ḥaliẓah* is necessary.[4] Another version is: R. Joseph said: The All-Merciful declared, *And when she is departed out of his house, she may go and be another man's wife*, so as not to destroy his house;[5] and you argue, let her also contract a levirate marriage![6] Abaye said to him, According to your argument, she should never marry again so as not to destroy another man's house!—He replied to him, [6*a*] Do we compel any other man to marry her [as in the case of a brother-in-law where it is a duty]! Another version is: R. Joseph replied, The text calls [the second husband] '*another*', because he is not the equal of the first husband, since the latter removes wickedness from his house [by divorcing his wife] whereas the other introduces wickedness into his house [by marrying such

(1) Deut. XXIV, 2. (2) ['*Another*' excludes the brother-in-law whose marriage to her is but a continuation, so to speak, of her first marriage. The derivation is based on the superfluous word '*another*' which is taken to refer to a case where the wife was charged with an '*unseemly thing*' and her husband died. The meaning of the verse would accordingly be as follows: *If she found no favour .... because he hath found some unseemly thing, he shall write her a bill of divorcement. When she departs out of his house* (whether on his death or on divorce) *and she goeth and becometh another man's wife*, implying she can become the wife only of *another* man but not the brother-in-law.] (3) Despite her misconduct. Ibid. 3 mentions, *and write her a bill of divorcement*. The technical term for this document is *Geṭ*. (4) [The brother-in-law taking the place of the dead husband.] (5) V. *supra* p. 11 where it is taught that the wife's immorality destroys the husband's house. (6) And perhaps destroy the brother-in-law's house.

a woman]; and you argue, let her also contract a levirate marriage! Abaye said to him, According to your argument, if she does marry another man and he died without issue, she may not contract a levirate marriage since the text calls him '*another*'![1] — While living with the second husband she may have been of spotless reputation! Raba said, It is an *a fortiori* argument:[2] if she is forbidden to [her husband] to whom she is [otherwise] allowed, how much more so to [her brother-in-law] to whom she is [normally] forbidden! Abaye said to him, According to your argument, if a High Priest betrothed a widow and he died and had a brother who was an ordinary priest, she may not marry him, since if she becomes forbidden to one to whom she is [otherwise] allowed, how much more so to one to whom she is [normally] forbidden![3] [You say,] 'If she becomes forbidden' — she is actually forbidden;[4] 'to one to whom she is allowed' — he is forbidden [to marry her]! But [ask rather as follows: According to Raba's argument] if the wife of a priest had been violated and he died, and he had a brother who was disqualified,[5] she may not marry him, since if she is forbidden to [her husband][6] to whom she is [otherwise] allowed, how much more so to one to whom she is [normally] forbidden![7] — A woman who had been violated is permitted to a non-priest and the prohibition does not apply in his case.[8]

MISHNAH. THE FOLLOWING[9] ARE PROHIBITED TO PARTAKE OF THE HEAVE-OFFERING:[10] SHE WHO SAYS, 'I AM UN-

(1) [And how can we compel the brother-in-law to marry her?] (2) [To forbid her to the brother-in-law.] (3) As wife of his brother. The conclusion is false, because such a levirate marriage is permissible. (4) A High Priest is not allowed to marry a widow; Lev. XXI, 14. (5) From the priesthood because he was the issue of another marriage which was illegal. (6) A priest could not continue to live with his wife after she had been violated. (7) The argument is false, because the man disqualified from the priesthood could marry his childless brother's widow if she had been violated. (8) I.e., a non-priest was not obliged to divorce his wife who was the victim of violation. (9) Wives of priests. (10) For all time, even if the woman be a priest's daughter (v. Bertinoro).

CLEAN TO THEE';[1] WHEN WITNESSES CAME [AND TESTIFIED] THAT SHE HAD MISCONDUCTED HERSELF;[2] SHE WHO SAYS, 'I REFUSE TO DRINK [THE WATER]'; WHEN THE HUSBAND IS UNWILLING TO MAKE HER DRINK [THE WATER]; AND WHEN THE HUSBAND COHABITED WITH HER ON THE JOURNEY.[3]

GEMARA. R. Amram said: The following did R. Shesheth tell us and enlighten our eyes from our Mishnah:[4] In the case of a suspected woman where the witnesses against her are in a far-distant land,[5] the water does not prove her.[6] What is the reason? Because Scripture states, *And be kept close and she be defiled and there be no witness against her*[7]—this is when there is nobody who knows anything against her, thus excluding the case when there are men who know something against her.[8] And he enlightened our eyes from our Mishnah where it is taught: WHEN WITNESSES CAME [AND TESTIFIED] THAT SHE HAD MISCONDUCTED HERSELF. When did the witnesses come? If we say that they came before she drank the water, she is an adulteress;[9] consequently they could only have come after she had drunk the water. This is quite right if you say that the water does not prove her,[10] then all is clear; but if you say that [in such a circumstance] the water does prove her, the water may demonstrate retrospectively that the witnesses were false![11]—R. Joseph said to him, Still I maintain that the water does prove her, and answer that some merit she possesses causes the water to suspend its effect.[12]

(1) She admits misconduct. (2) Even if she had successfully come through the ordeal, v. Gemara. (3) To Jerusalem, where alone the ordeal was carried out. V. Mishnah p. 30. (4) He found support for his teaching in the statement of the Mishnah. (5) And unable to appear before a Court to give evidence that she misconducted herself. (6) It has no effect, though she be guilty. (7) Num. V, 13. (8) '*No witness*' is now interpreted literally, and not as before, viz., only one witness. (9) As the result of their evidence; [consequently she is forbidden to partake of the heave-offering, v. Yeb. 44*b*]. (10) If there are witnesses of her misconduct who have not testified. (11) Because, if she came through successfully, her reputation is cleared. [Why then should she be prohibited to partake of the heave-offering for all time?] (12) This point is discussed immediately. If this view is accepted, the water does not affect her although the witnesses are true.

In what do [R. Joseph and R. Shesheth] differ?—In the matter of her becoming ill, according to the teaching of Rabbi. For we learn: Rabbi says: Merit [in the woman] causes the water of bitterness to suspend its effect, and she never bears a child or thrives, but she gradually grows ill and finally dies through that death.[1] R. Shesheth is of the opinion that both in the view of Rabbi and of the Rabbis she grows ill;[2] and R. Joseph is of the opinion that in the view of Rabbi she grows ill but in the view of the Rabbis she does not.[3]

R. Shimi b. Ashi raised an objection: R. Simeon says, Merit does not cause the water of bitterness to suspend its effect; and if you say that merit does cause the water of bitterness to suspend its effect, you discredit the water in the case of all the women who drink it and defame the pure woman who drank it, since people will say, They were unclean, only their merit caused the water to suspend its effect upon them.[4] But if it is so,[5] then through [the teaching], 'Where the witnesses against her are in a far-distant land', you likewise defame the pure women who drank and people will say, They were unclean, only the witnesses against them are in a far-distant land!—[The reply to R. Shimi is:] You quote R. Simeon; but as R. Simeon holds that merit does not cause the water to suspend its effect, he similarly holds that the existence of witnesses does not cause it to suspend its effect.

Rab raised an objection: The following have their meal-offerings destroyed:[6] [*6b*] She who says, 'I am unclean'; and when witnesses came [and testified] that she had misconducted herself.[7] When did

(1) Through her belly swelling and her thigh falling (Num. V, 27). The passage is cited from *infra* 22*b*. (2) And the Sages only disagree with him on the question whether she dies. In any case, if she does not grow ill, it cannot be attributed to her merit but to the fact that there are witnesses who have not given evidence. (3) So that on either view, if the water has no effect, it is due to her merit. (4) Also quoted from *infra* 22*b*. (5) Viz., that the existence of absent witnesses causes the water not to take effect. (6) V. Num. V, 15 for this offering. In the cases mentioned, it is not burnt upon the altar or redeemed by payment in money of its value, but destroyed by fire. (7) Quoted from *infra* p. 144.

the witnesses come? If I say that they came before the offering was hallowed,[1] then it can become non-holy?[2] Consequently they could only have come after it had been hallowed. This is quite right if you say that the water proves her;[3] consequently she is qualified to have [the flour] hallowed and offered on her behalf, and since it was hallowed from the commencement, it is certainly holy[4] and for that reason her meal-offering is destroyed. But if you say that the water does not prove her, it becomes evident retrospectively that the hallowing was from the commencement in error,[5] and therefore [the flour] becomes non-holy![6]—Rab Judah of Disḳarta[7] said: Suppose that [after the hallowing] she committed adultery within the Temple-precincts,[8] since it was hallowed from the commencement, it is certainly holy! R. Mesharsheya objected: But do not the priestly novitiates accompany her?[9]—Rab Judah [meant,] She committed adultery with one of these novitiates. R. Ashi[10] said: Suppose it was necessary for her to relieve herself, do you think that the priestly novitiates hang on to her headgear![11] R. Papa said: The matter is certainly as we originally explained;[12] and when you argue, [The offering] becomes non-holy, [the answer is that the rule by which the offering is destroyed] is a decree of the Rabbis lest it should be said, we may take [the flour] out of the ministering vessel for secular use.

R. Mari raised an objection: If her offering became ritually defiled before it became hallowed in the vessel, behold it is like all meal-offerings[13] and is redeemed; but if [it became defiled]

(1) By the priest placing the flour in one of the ministering vessels. (2) By being redeemed; so why does the Mishnah say it is destroyed? (3) And she drank the water before witnesses testified. (4) Even after the witnesses gave evidence. (5) Since witnesses proved her guilty and the ordeal was unnecessary. (6) And does not even have to be redeemed since the hallowing was based on an error. (7) [Deskarah, 16 miles N.E. of Bagdad; Obermeyer, *Die Landschaft Babylonien*, p. 116.] (8) And witnesses came to testify concerning this act of infidelity. (9) So that adultery could not occur there. (10) Who rejects the thought that she could be guilty with one of the novitiates. (11) When she retired to relieve herself. Consequently she could have the opportunity with another than the novitiates. (12) That the witnesses came concerning the first act of infidelity. (13) Which became defiled before being hallowed.

is trusted.[1] If a husband is trusted in the matter of his wife during menstruation where the penalty is excision,[2] how much more so in the matter of his wife under suspicion in connection with which there is a mere prohibition.[3] And [how do] the Rabbis [meet this argument]?—The same reasoning establishes [their view]: in the case of a wife during menstruation where the penalty is excision, since it is so stringent, the husband is trusted; but in the case of a wife under suspicion where [cohabitation] is a mere prohibition, since there is no stringent [penalty] for him, he is not trusted. But does R. Judah derive his view from *a fortiori* reasoning? He surely derives it from a Scriptural text; for it has been taught: *Then shall the man bring his wife unto the priest*[4]—according to the Torah it is the husband who has to bring his wife; but said the Sages, They assign to him two disciples of the Sages lest he cohabit with her on the journey. R. Jose says: By *a fortiori* reasoning [it is deduced] that a husband is trusted with her. If a husband is trusted in the matter of his wife during menstruation where the penalty is excision, how much more so in the matter of his wife while under suspicion in connection with which there is a mere prohibition. [The Sages] replied to him, No; if you argue [that he may be trusted] in the case of his wife during menstruation to whom he will have a right [on her recovery], will you argue so in the case of his wife under suspicion when he may never have a right to her![5] It further states, *Stolen waters are sweet*, etc.![6] R. Judah says: According to the Torah it is the husband who has to bring his wife; as it is said, *Then shall the man bring his wife!*[7]—At first he argued his view to [the Sages] by *a fortiori* reasoning; but when they refuted it, he then quoted the text to them. But R. Judah's opinion is the same as that of the first Tanna![8]—There is a point of difference

(1) In this matter of cohabitation and witnesses are unnecessary. (2) *Kareth* v. Glos. Lev. XX, 18. A husband may occupy the same room as his wife while she is in that condition and he is trusted not to cohabit. (3) Without any penalty attached thereto, v. Yeb. 11*b*. (4) Num. V, 15. (5) If she is proved guilty, he must divorce her. Consequently the temptation is greater in the latter case. (6) Prov. IX, 17. (7) [R. Judah thus derives his ruling from a Scriptural text and not from *a fortiori* reasoning?] (8) Quoted at the end of the last paragraph who cites Num. V, 15.

between them, viz., [the continuation], 'But, said the Rabbis' etc.[1]

MISHNAH. THEY BRING HER UP TO THE GREAT COURT OF JUSTICE WHICH IS IN JERUSALEM, AND [THE JUDGES] SOLEMNLY CHARGE HER IN THE SAME WAY THAT THEY CHARGE WITNESSES IN CAPITAL CASES[2] AND SAY TO HER, 'MY DAUGHTER, WINE DOES MUCH, FRIVOLITY DOES MUCH, YOUTH DOES MUCH, BAD NEIGHBOURS DO MUCH.[3] DO IT[4] FOR THE SAKE OF HIS GREAT NAME WHICH IS WRITTEN IN HOLINESS SO THAT IT MAY NOT BE OBLITERATED BY THE WATER.'[5] AND THEY RELATE TO HER MATTERS WHICH NEITHER SHE NOR ALL THE FAMILY OF HER FATHER'S HOUSE IS WORTHY TO HEAR.[6]—IF SHE SAID, 'I HAVE MISCONDUCTED MYSELF', SHE GIVES A QUITTANCE FOR HER MARRIAGE-SETTLEMENT[7] AND DEPARTS;[8] BUT IF SHE SAYS, 'I AM PURE', THEY BRING HER UP TO THE EAST GATE WHICH IS BY THE ENTRANCE OF NICANOR'S GATE[9] WHERE THEY GIVE SUSPECTED WOMEN THE WATER TO DRINK, PURIFY WOMEN AFTER CHILDBIRTH AND PURIFY LEPERS.[10] A PRIEST SEIZES HER GARMENTS[11]—IF THEY ARE RENT THEY ARE RENT, AND IF THEY BECOME UNSTITCHED THEY ARE UNSTITCHED—UNTIL HE UNCOVERS HER BOSOM,[12] AND HE UNDOES HER HAIR. R. JUDAH SAYS: IF HER BOSOM WAS BEAUTIFUL HE DOES NOT UNCOVER IT,

(1) With which R. Judah disagrees. (2) V. Sanh. 37*a*. (3) I.e., there may be some excuse for your behaviour. (4) Confess if you are guilty, and so make the ordeal unnecessary which includes the use of the Divine Name. (5) V. Num. V, 23. (6) Instances of persons in Israel's history who confessed their guilt. (7) I.e., she admits misconduct in writing and the forfeiture of the sum due to her under the marriage-settlement. (8) After being formally divorced. (9) Two gates of Corinthian bronze presented to the Temple by an Alexandrian named Nicanor. They were located between the Court of Israelites and the Court of women. V. Nazir (Sonc. ed.) p. 165, n. 11. (10) I.e., the place where such persons, who are not allowed through uncleanness to enter the Temple-precincts, bring their purificatory offerings. (11) At the neck. (12) Lit., 'heart'.

AND IF HER HAIR WAS BEAUTIFUL HE DOES NOT UNDO IT. —IF SHE WAS CLOTHED IN WHITE, HE CLOTHES HER IN BLACK. IF SHE WORE GOLDEN ORNAMENTS [7b] AND NECKLACES, EAR-RINGS AND FINGER-RINGS, THEY REMOVE THEM FROM HER IN ORDER TO MAKE HER REPULSIVE. AFTER THAT [THE PRIEST] TAKES A COMMON ROPE[1] AND BINDS IT OVER HER BREASTS.[2] WHOEVER WISHES TO LOOK UPON HER COMES TO LOOK WITH THE EXCEPTION OF HER MALE AND FEMALE SLAVES, BECAUSE HER HEART IS MADE DEFIANT THROUGH THEM. ALL WOMEN ARE PERMITTED[3] TO LOOK UPON HER, AS IT IS SAID, THAT ALL WOMEN MAY BE TAUGHT NOT TO DO AFTER YOUR LEWDNESS.[4]

GEMARA. Whence is this?[5]—R. Ḥiyya b. Gamda said in the name of R. Jose b. Ḥanina: From the analogous use of the word '*law*'. It is written here, *And the priest shall execute upon her all this law;*[6] and elsewhere it is written, *According to the tenor of the law which they shall teach thee.*[7] As in this latter case it is [the Court of] seventy-one,[8] so also in the former it is [the Court of] seventy-one.

AND [THE JUDGES] SOLEMNLY CHARGE HER etc. I quote in contradiction: Just as they solemnly charge her not to drink,[9] so they solemnly charge her to drink, saying to her, 'My daughter, if the matter is clear to thee that thou art pure, rely upon thy purity and drink; because the water of bitterness is only like dry powder which is placed upon living flesh. If there is a wound, it penetrates and goes through [the skin]; and if there is no wound, it has no effect.[10]—There is no contradiction; here [they charge her

(1) The Palestinian Gemara explains it as 'an Egyptian cord' which is used because she followed the immoral practices of Egypt. More probably it means a cord made of twisted strips of the bark of the palm-tree. It was the commonest form of rope and used here as a mark of contempt. (2) To prevent her clothing from falling down. (3) Interpreted in the Gemara to mean that they should as a duty look. (4) Ezek. XXIII, 48. (5) That the water must be administered by the great Court in Jerusalem. (6) Num. V, 30. (7) Deut. XVII, 11. The reference is here to the Supreme Court. (8) V. Sanh. **14*b*** and 86*a*. (9) If guilty, but make confession. (10) Quoted from Tosefta Soṭah I, 6.

not to drink] before [the writing on] the scroll is blotted out,[1] and there [they charge her to drink] after it has been blotted out.[2]

AND SAY TO HER etc. Our Rabbis have taught: He tells her narratives and incidents which occurred in the early writings;[3] for instance, *Which wise men have told and have not hid it [from their fathers]*,[4] namely Judah confessed and was not ashamed; what was his end? He inherited the life of the world to come. Reuben confessed and was not ashamed; what was his end? He inherited the world to come. And what was their reward? What was their reward [you ask]! It was as we have just mentioned. But [the meaning is], What was their reward in this world? *Unto them alone the land was given, and no stranger passed among them.*[5] It is quite right with Judah; we find that he confessed, for it is written, *And Judah acknowledged them, and said, She is more righteous than I.*[6] Whence, however, is it that Reuben confessed?—As R. Samuel b. Naḥmani said in the name of R. Joḥanan: What means that which is written, *Let Reuben live and not die; and this for Judah?*[7] All the years that the Israelites were in the wilderness, Judah's bones[8] kept turning in his coffin until Moses arose and begged mercy for him. He said before Him, Lord of the Universe, who caused Reuben to confess? It was Judah,[9] [as it is stated], '*And this for Judah*'; immediately [after Moses prayed], '*Hear, Lord, the voice of Judah*', each limb entered its socket.[10] But [the angels] would not permit him to enter the heavenly Academy;[11] [so Moses prayed], '*And bring him in unto his people*'. He was unable to discuss the theme which the Rabbis were then debating; [so Moses prayed], '*With his hands let him contend for himself*'.[12] He was still not able to secure a decision in accordance with the traditional practice; [so Moses prayed], '*Be*

(1) Num. V, 23, so that the Divine Name may not be obliterated in vain. (2) To encourage her to go through the ordeal if she is convinced of her innocence. (3) The Pentateuch. (4) I.e., they confessed, Job XV, 18. (E.V. '*Which wise men have told from their fathers and have not hid it*'). (5) Ibid. 19. (6) Gen. XXXVIII, 26. (7) Deut. XXXIII, 6f. (8) According to tradition, the bones of all Jacob's sons were carried out of Egypt. (9) When he confessed, Reuben followed his example. (10) Of the skeleton and ceased rolling about. (11) Where the Torah is studied. (12) May he be able to prevail in the debate.

an help against his adversaries'.[1] It is quite right that Judah confessed so that Tamar should not be burnt; but why did Reuben confess? Surely R. Shesheth has declared, Consider him shameless who [publicly] specifies his sins!—[Reuben confessed] so that his brothers should not be suspected [of his offence].

IF SHE SAID, 'I HAVE MISCONDUCTED MYSELF' etc. Is it to be concluded from this that a quittance is written out?[2]—Abaye said, Read [in our Mishnah]: [The document of the marriage-settlement] is torn. Raba replied to him, But the Mishnah mentions A QUITTANCE! But, said Raba, we deal here with places where they do not write a document for a marriage-settlement.[3]

BUT IF SHE SAYS, 'I AM PURE', THEY BRING HER UP TO THE EAST GATE. 'THEY BRING HER UP'? [8a] But she is already there![4] —They lead her up[5] and lead her down, for the purpose of wearying her.[6] For it has been taught, R. Simeon b. Eleazar says: The Court causes the witnesses to be taken from place to place that their mind may become confused and they retract [their evidence, if false].[7]

WHERE THEY GIVE SUSPECTED WOMEN THE WATER TO DRINK etc. This is quite right in the case of suspected women; because it is written, *And the priest shall set the woman before the Lord.*[8] Likewise is it with lepers; because it is written, *And the priest that cleanseth him shall set the man .... before the Lord.*[9] But why a woman after childbirth? Is it to say because they come to stand by their offerings; for it has been taught: A person's offering is not sacrificed until he stands by it? If so, it should also apply to men and women with a running issue![10]—It does indeed also apply to them, and the Tanna [in the Mishnah] only specifies one of them.[11]

(1) V. B.M. 86*a*. (2) The question whether a quittance is given or the document of the marriage-settlement torn is discussed in B.B. 170*b*. (3) This was sometimes not done because there was an established rule about the amount due to a wife from her husband, v. B.M. (Sonc. ed.) p. 107, n. 4. (4) V. Mishnah p. 30. (5) The Temple-mount to be charged by the judges, then lead her to the bottom, and finally up again. (6) So that she may be more disposed to confess. (7) V. Sanh. 32*b*. (8) Num. V, 18. (9) Lev. XIV, 11. (10) Ibid. XV, 14, 29. (11) Who do not enter the Temple precincts owing to a condition of defilement, and consequently stand at Nicanor's gate.

Our Rabbis have taught: They do not give two suspected women the water to drink at the same time, so that the heart of one should not become defiant because of the other.[1] R. Judah says: It is not from this reason, but Scripture declares, [*The priest shall cause*] *her* [*to swear*][2]—her alone. And for the first Tanna it is likewise written '*her*'![3]—The first Tanna is R. Simeon who expounds the reason of Scriptural texts[4] and [here] he states the reason: What is the meaning of '*her*'? Her alone, so that the heart of one should not become defiant because of the other. What difference is there, then, between them?—The difference between them is the case of a woman who is trembling.[5] But even if [a woman] is trembling, may we give her the water to drink [simultaneously with another woman] when, behold, we may not perform precepts in bundles?[6] For we have learnt: They do not give two suspected women the water to drink at the same time, nor purify two lepers at the same time, nor bore the ears of two slaves at the same time,[7] nor break the necks of two calves at the same time,[8] because we may not perform precepts in bundles!—Abaye said, but others declare it was R. Kahana: There is no contradiction; the latter case referring to one priest,[9] the other to two priests.

A PRIEST SEIZES HER GARMENTS. Our Rabbis have taught: *And let the hair of the woman's head go loose.*[10] I only have here mention of her head; whence is it derived that it applies to her body?[11] The text states, '*the woman's*'.[12] If so, what is the object of the text declaring, '*And let the hair of the head go loose*'? It teaches that the priest undoes her hair.[13]

R. JUDAH SAYS, IF HER BOSOM WAS BEAUTIFUL etc. Is this

(1) One may be guilty and the other not. The first may refuse to confess because the other does not confess. (2) Num. V, 19. V. Ned. 73*a*. (3) So why does he give his own reason? (4) V. B.M. 115*a*. (5) And therefore we cannot say she is defiant, and on the view of the first Tanna, as explained, she might be submitted to the ordeal at the same time with another suspected woman. (6) Each must have separate attention. (7) Ex. XXI, 6. (8) Deut. XXI, 1 ff. (9) Administering the water to two women, when it would be performing a precept in bundles. (10) Num. V, 18. (11) That he uncovers her bosom, as stated in the Mishnah. (12) And not merely '*the hair of her head*'. (13) And unravels the locks.

to say that R. Judah is afraid of impure thoughts being aroused and the Rabbis do not fear this? Behold we have heard the opposite opinion of them; for it has been taught: In the case of a man [who is to be stoned] they cover him with one piece of cloth in front, and in the case of a woman with two pieces, one in front and one behind, because the whole of her is considered nudity. This is the statement of R. Judah; but the Sages say, A man is stoned naked but a woman is not stoned naked![1]—Rabbah answered, What is the reason here?[2] Lest she go forth from the Court innocent, and the priestly novitiates become inflamed through her, whereas in the other case she is stoned. Should you reply that it may cause them to be inflamed by another woman, Raba[3] declared, We have learnt a tradition that the evil impulse only bears sway over what a person's eyes see. Raba asked, Is it, then, that R. Judah contradicts himself and the Rabbis do not contradict themselves? But, said Raba, R. Judah does not contradict himself as we have just explained[4] [8b], and the Rabbis likewise do not contradict themselves. What is the reason here?[5] Because [it is written], *That all women may be taught not to do after your lewdness.*[6] In the other case [of stoning], however, there cannot be a severer warning than that.[7] Should you argue, Let both be inflicted upon her,[8] R. Naḥman said in the name of Rabbah b. Abbuha: The text states, *Thou shalt love thy neighbour as thyself*[9]—choose for him [or her] a light death. Is this to say that Mishnaic teachers disagree [with respect to this teaching] of R. Naḥman?[10]—No; everybody is in agreement with R. Naḥman's teaching, but they differ here on the following point: [the Rabbis] hold that disgrace is worse than physical pain, and [R. Judah] holds that physical pain is worse than disgrace.[11]

(1) V. Sanh. 45*a*. (2) That R. Judah is against the exposure of her bosom. (3) In the parallel passage in Sanh. 45*a* the name is Rabbah. (4) The case of a suspected woman is not analogous to that of a woman who is to be stoned. (5) That the Rabbis do not scruple to disgrace the suspected woman, whereas in the case of the woman who is stoned they do. (6) Ezek. XXIII, 48. (7) Viz., the stoning itself; therefore the Rabbis are against the exposure of the body. (8) Disgrace as well as death by stoning. (9) Lev. XIX, 18. (10) That when R. Judah says a woman is stoned naked except for a loin-cloth in front and behind he evidences disagreement with R. Naḥman. (11) Therefore the

IF SHE WAS CLOTHED IN WHITE etc. It has been taught: If black garments became her, they clothe her in mean garments.

IF SHE WORE GOLDEN ORNAMENTS etc. This is obvious. Since she has to be made repulsive how much more is it necessary to do this![1] — What you might have thought is that with these ornaments upon her, the disgrace would be greater; as the proverb declares, 'Stripped naked, yet wearing shoes'. Therefore we are taught [that all ornaments must be removed].

AFTER THAT [THE PRIEST] TAKES A COMMON ROPE etc. R. Abba asked R. Huna, Does [the absence of] a common rope invalidate the ceremony of a suspected woman? If the purpose is that her garments should not slip down from her, then a small belt would also suffice; or is it perhaps as the Master said, 'She girded herself with a belt [to adorn herself] for him,[2] therefore the priest takes a common rope and binds it over her breasts', and consequently [its absence] does invalidate the ceremony? — He replied, You have [the reason stated:] After that he takes a common rope and binds it over her breast so that her garments should not slip down from her.

WHOEVER WISHES TO LOOK UPON HER COMES TO LOOK etc. This is self-contradictory! You say, WHOEVER WISHES TO LOOK UPON HER COMES TO LOOK; consequently it makes no difference whether they be men or women. Then it is taught: ALL WOMEN ARE PERMITTED TO LOOK UPON HER — hence women are [permitted] but men are not! — Abaye answered, Explain it[3] as referring to women. Raba said to him, But the Mishnah states, WHOEVER WISHES TO LOOK UPON HER COMES TO LOOK! But, said Raba, [the meaning is:] WHOEVER WISHES TO LOOK UPON HER COMES TO LOOK, it makes no difference whether they be men or women; but women are obliged[4] to look upon her, as it is said, '*That all women may be taught not to do after your lewdness*'.

former believe that a woman about to die would prefer to be clothed although it may involve a more protracted death, while R. Judah takes the opposite view, v. Sanh. (Sonc. ed.) pp. 294-5.

(1) Why, then, does the Mishnah mention it? (2) Her paramour; v. *infra* p. 38. (3) The phrase, WHOEVER WISHES etc. (4) The word מותרות, 'are per-

MISHNAH. IN THE MEASURE WITH WHICH A MAN MEASURES IT IS METED OUT TO HIM. SHE ADORNED HERSELF FOR A TRANSGRESSION; THE HOLY ONE, BLESSED BE HE, MADE HER REPULSIVE. SHE EXPOSED HERSELF FOR A TRANSGRESSION; THE HOLY ONE, BLESSED BE HE, HELD HER UP FOR EXPOSURE. SHE BEGAN THE TRANSGRESSION WITH THE THIGH AND AFTERWARDS WITH THE WOMB; THEREFORE SHE IS PUNISHED FIRST IN THE THIGH AND AFTERWARDS IN THE WOMB,[1] NOR DOES ALL THE BODY ESCAPE.

GEMARA. R. Joseph said: Although the measure[2] has ceased, [the principle] IN THE MEASURE has not ceased.[3] For R. Joseph said, and similarly taught R. Ḥiyya: From the day the Temple was destroyed, although the Sanhedrin ceased to function, the four modes of execution[4] did not cease. But they did cease! —[The meaning is:] The judgment[5] of the four modes of execution did not cease. He who would have been condemned to stoning either falls from a roof [and dies] or a wild beast tramples him [to death]. He who would have been condemned to burning either falls into a fire or a serpent stings him. He who would have been condemned to decapitation is either handed over to the [Gentile] Government[6] or robbers attack him. He who would have been condemned to strangulation either drowns in a river or dies of a quinsy.[7]

It has been taught: Rabbi[8] used to say, Whence is it that in the measure with which a man measures it is meted out to him? As it is said, *By measure in sending her away thou dost contend with her.*[9] I have here only a *se'ah;*[10] whence is it to include a *triḳab* and half

mitted', is apparently derived here from the root תרה 'to warn'; hence 'are warned, obliged'.

(1) V. Num. V, 21 f. (2) Meted out by a Jewish Court of Justice. (3) Referring to Divine retribution. (4) V. Sanh. 90*a*. (5) Through Divine intervention. (6) Which executes him by the sword. (7) V. Sanh. (Sonc. ed.) p. 236. (8) [The parallel passage in Sanh. 100*a* has 'R. Meir']. (9) Isa. XXVII, 8. (10) The word for *by measure* is connected by Rabbi with *se'ah*, a dry measure of which a *triḳab* (equals three *ḳab*) is a half. *Se'ah* is taken as representing a very serious offence.

a *triḳab*, a *ḳab* and half a *ḳab*, a quarter, an eighth, a sixteenth and a thirtysecond part of a *ḳab?* There is a text to state, *For all the armour of the armed man in the tumult.*[1] And whence is it that every *perutah*[2] reckons together into a great sum? There is a text to state, *Laying one thing to another to find out the account.*[3] Thus we find in the case of a suspected woman that in the measure with which she measured it was meted out to her. She stood at the entrance of her house to display herself to the man; therefore a priest sets her by the Nicanor-gate and displays her disgrace to all. She wound a beautiful scarf about her head for him; therefore a priest removes her headgear and places it under her feet. She beautified her face for him; therefore [9a] her face is made to turn green in colour.[4] She painted her eyes for him; therefore her eyes protrude. She plaited her hair for him; therefore a priest undoes her hair. She signalled to him with her finger; therefore her finger-nails fall off. She girded herself with a belt for him; therefore a priest takes a common rope and ties it above her breasts. She thrust her thigh towards him; therefore her thigh falls. She received him upon her body; therefore her womb swells. She gave him the world's dainties to eat; therefore her offering consisted of animal's fodder.[5] She gave him costly wine to drink in costly goblets; therefore a priest gives her water of bitterness to drink in a potsherd. She acted in secret; and *He that dwelleth in the secret place of the Most High*[6] directed His face against her [to punish her], as it is said, *The eye also of the adulterer waiteth for the twilight, saying, No eye shall see me.*[7] Another version is: She acted in secret; the All-present proclaims it in public, as it is said, *Though his hatred cover itself with guile, his wickedness shall be openly shewed before the congregation.*[8]

Since [the teaching that even the slightest sin is punished] is

(1) Isa. IX, 4, E.V. 5. The Hebrew words for *'armour'* סאון and *'armed man'* סואן are likewise connected with *se'ah*. (2) A small coin, here representing a minor offence which is not overlooked for punishment. (3) Eccl. VII, 27. (4) This, and the protruding of the eyes, are the effect of drinking the water; v. Mishnah 20*a*. (5) Barley meal, Num. V, 15. (6) Ps. XCI, 1. (7) Job XXIV, 15. *No eye* etc. is explained in the sense, God will not observe me. (8) Prov. XXVI, 26.

derived from '*Laying one thing to another to find out the account*', why do I require '*For all the armour of the armed man in the tumult*'?—That [the punishment is] according to measure. But since that is derived from '*For all the armour of the armed man in the tumult*', why do I require '*By measure in sending her away thou dost contend with her*'?—It is in accord with the teaching of R. Ḥinena b. Papa; for R. Ḥinena b. Papa said: The Holy One, blessed be He, does not exact punishment of a nation until the time of its banishment into exile, as it is said, '*By measure in sending her away*, etc'. But it is not so; for Raba has said: Why are three cups mentioned in connection with Egypt?[1] One which she drank in the days of Moses; one which she drank in the days of Pharaoh-Necho;[2] and one which she is destined to drink with her allies! Should you reply that they passed away, and these are different [Egyptians],[3] behold it has been taught: R. Judah said: Minyamin, an Egyptian proselyte, was a colleague of mine among the disciples of R. Akiba; and Minyamin, the Egyptian proselyte, told me, 'I am an Egyptian of the first generation,[4] and I married an Egyptian woman of the first generation; I will marry my son to an Egyptian woman of the second generation so that my grandson may be permitted to enter the Community'![5]—But if the above statement was made it was made as follows: R. Ḥinena b. Papa said: The Holy One, blessed be He, does not exact punishment of a king until the time of his banishment into exile, as it is said, '*By measure in sending her away*, etc'. Amemar applied this teaching of R. Ḥinena b. Papa to the following: What means the text, *For I the Lord change not; therefore ye, O sons of Jacob, are not consumed*'?[6] '*I the Lord change not*'—I have not smitten a people and repeated it;[7] '*therefore ye, O sons of Jacob, are not consumed*'—that is

(1) The word '*cup*' occurs three times in Gen. XL, 11, and is a symbol of calamity. (2) When Egypt was defeated by Babylon (Jer. XLVI, 2). The third '*cup*' refers to the Messianic era. The conclusion is, therefore, that punishment is not exacted of a nation only at the time of banishment. (3) The original Egyptians had disappeared and their land was inhabited by a different race. (4) That means, he had been personally converted to Judaism and was not the son of a proselyte. (5) V. Deut. XXIII, 9, E.V. 8. This proves that the original Egyptians are considered as still extant. (6) Mal. III, 6. (7) The Hebrew word for '*change*' שנה also means 'repeat'.

what is written, *I will spend Mine arrows upon them*[1]—Mine arrows will be spent, but [the sons of Jacob] will not cease.

R. Hamuna said: The Holy One, blessed be He, does not exact punishment of a man until his measure [of guilt] is filled; as it is said, '*In the fullness of his sufficiency he shall be in straits*, etc'.[2] R. Ḥinena b. Papa expounded: What means the text, *Rejoice in the Lord, O ye righteous; praise is comely for the upright?*[3] Read not *praise is* na'wah ['*comely*'], but *praise is* neweh ['*a habitation*']. This alludes to Moses and David over whose works [in erecting a Sanctuary] their enemies had no power.[4] Of [the Temple planned by] David, it is written, *Her gates are sunk in the ground.*[5] With regard to Moses the Master said, After the first Temple was erected, the Tent of Meeting was stored away, its boards, hooks, bars, pillars and sockets. Where [were they stored]?—R. Ḥisda said in the name of Abimi: Beneath the crypts of the Temple.

Our Rabbis have taught: The suspected woman[6] set her eyes on one who was not proper for her; what she sought was not given to her[7] and what she possessed was taken from her;[8] because whoever sets his eyes on that which is not his is not granted what he seeks and what he possesses is taken from him. [9*b*] We thus find it with the primeval serpent [in the Garden of Eden] which set its eyes on that which was not proper for it; what it sought was not granted to it and what it possessed was taken from it. The Holy One, blessed be He, said, I declared, Let it be king over every animal and beast; but now, *Cursed art thou above all cattle and above every beast of the field.*[9] I declared, let it walk with an erect posture; but now it shall go upon its belly. I declared, Let its food be the same as that of man; but now it shall eat dust. It said, I will kill Adam and marry Eve; but now, *I will put enmity between thee and the woman, and between thy seed and her seed.*[10] Similarly do we find it with Cain, Korah, Balaam, Doeg, Ahitophel, Gehazi, Absalom,

(1) Deut. XXXII, 23. (2) Job XX, 22. (3) Ps. XXXIII, 1. (4) I.e., the enemies of Israel did not profit by any of the materials when the Temple was destroyed. (5) Lam. II, 9. (6) Who is guilty. (7) She is not allowed to marry her lover. (8) She dies if she drinks the water, and is divorced with loss of her settlement if she confesses. (9) Gen. III, 14. (10) Ibid. 15.

Adonijah, Uzziah and Haman, who set their eyes upon that which was not proper for them; what they sought was not granted to them and what they possessed was taken from them.

SHE BEGAN THE TRANSGRESSION WITH THE THIGH etc. Whence is this? Shall I say because it is written, *When the Lord doth make thy thigh to fall away and thy belly to swell?*[1] But it is likewise written, *Her belly shall swell and her thigh shall fall away!*[2]—Abaye said: When [the priest] utters the curse, he first curses the thigh and then curses the belly; but when the water produces its effect it does so in its normal order, viz., the belly first and then the thigh. But also in connection with the curse, it is written, *Make thy belly to swell and thy thigh to fall away!*[3]—That is what the priest informs her, viz., that it affects her belly first and then the thigh so as not to discredit the water of bitterness.[4]

MISHNAH. SAMSON WENT AFTER [THE DESIRE OF] HIS EYES; THEREFORE THE PHILISTINES PUT OUT HIS EYES, AS IT IS SAID, AND THE PHILISTINES LAID HOLD ON HIM, AND PUT OUT HIS EYES.[5] ABSALOM GLORIED IN HIS HAIR; THEREFORE HE WAS HANGED BY HIS HAIR. AND BECAUSE HE COHABITED WITH THE TEN CONCUBINES OF HIS FATHER, THEREFORE HE WAS STABBED WITH TEN LANCES, AS IT IS SAID, AND TEN YOUNG MEN THAT BARE JOAB'S ARMOUR COMPASSED ABOUT.[6] AND BECAUSE HE STOLE THREE HEARTS, THE HEART OF HIS FATHER, THE HEART OF THE COURT OF JUSTICE, AND THE HEART OF ISRAEL, AS IT IS SAID, SO ABSALOM STOLE THE HEARTS OF THE MEN OF ISRAEL,[7] THEREFORE THREE DARTS WERE THRUST THROUGH HIM, AS IT IS SAID, AND HE TOOK THREE DARTS IN HIS HAND, AND THRUST THEM THROUGH THE HEART OF ABSALOM.[8]—IT[9] IS THE SAME IN CONNECTION

(1) Num. V, 21. '*Thigh*' is mentioned first. (2) Ibid. 27. Here '*thigh*' is mentioned second. (3) Ibid. 22. (4) If the effects were produced in the reverse order. (5) Judg. XVI, 21. (6) And slew Absalom, II Sam. XVIII, 15. (7) Ibid. XV, 6. (8) Ibid. XVIII, 14. (9) The principle of measure for measure.

WITH THE GOOD. MIRIAM WAITED A SHORT WHILE FOR MOSES, AS IT IS SAID, AND HIS SISTER STOOD AFAR OFF;[1] THEREFORE ISRAEL WAS DELAYED FOR HER SEVEN DAYS IN THE WILDERNESS, AS IT IS SAID, AND THE PEOPLE JOURNEYED NOT TILL MIRIAM WAS BROUGHT IN AGAIN.[2] JOSEPH EARNED MERIT BY BURYING HIS FATHER AND THERE WAS NONE AMONG HIS BROTHERS GREATER THAN HE; AS IT IS SAID, AND JOSEPH WENT UP TO BURY HIS FATHER, ETC.,[3] AND THERE WENT UP WITH HIM BOTH CHARIOTS AND HORSEMEN.[4] WHOM HAVE WE GREATER THAN JOSEPH SINCE NONE OTHER THAN MOSES OCCUPIED HIMSELF WITH HIS BURIAL? MOSES EARNED MERIT THROUGH THE BONES OF JOSEPH AND THERE WAS NONE IN ISRAEL GREATER THAN HE, AS IT IS SAID, AND MOSES TOOK THE BONES OF JOSEPH WITH HIM.[5] WHOM HAVE WE GREATER THAN MOSES SINCE NONE OTHER THAN THE OMNIPRESENT OCCUPIED HIMSELF [WITH HIS BURIAL], AS IT IS SAID, AND HE BURIED HIM IN THE VALLEY?[6] NOT ONLY CONCERNING MOSES DID THEY SAY THIS, BUT CONCERNING ALL THE RIGHTEOUS, AS IT IS SAID, AND THY RIGHTEOUSNESS SHALL GO BEFORE THEE, THE GLORY OF THE LORD SHALL BE THY REARWARD.[7]

GEMARA. Our Rabbis have taught: Samson rebelled [against God] through his eyes, as it is said, *And Samson said unto his father, Get her for me, because she is pleasing in my eyes;*[8] therefore the Philistines put out his eyes, as it is said, *And the Philistines laid hold on him and put out his eyes.*[9] But it is not so; for behold it is written, *But his father and his mother knew not that it was of the Lord!*[10] — When he went [to choose a wife] he nevertheless followed his own inclinations.[11]

(1) Ex. II, 4. (2) Num. XII, 15. (3) Gen. L, 7. (4) Ibid. 9. (5) Ex. XIII, 19. (6) Deut. XXXIV, 6. (7) Isa. LVIII, 8. The verb translated '*shall be thy rearward*' seems to be taken here in its literal sense, *shall gather thee* sc. to thy fathers. (8) Judg. XIV, 3. (9) Ibid. XVI, 21. (10) Ibid. XIV, 4. (11) And not the will of God.

It has been taught: Rabbi says: The beginning of his [Samson's] degeneration occurred in Gaza; therefore he received his punishment in Gaza. 'The beginning of his [Samson's] degeneration was in Gaza', as it is written, *And Samson went to Gaza, and saw there an harlot* etc.;[1] 'therefore he received his punishment in Gaza,' as it is written, *And they brought him down to Gaza.*[2] But behold it is written, *And Samson went down to Timnah!*[3]—Nevertheless the beginning of his degeneration occurred in Gaza.[4]

And it came to pass afterward, that he loved a woman in the valley of Sorek, whose name was Delilah.[5] It has been taught: Rabbi says: If her name had not been called Delilah, she was fit that it should be so called. She weakened[6] his strength, she weakened his heart, she weakened his actions. 'She weakened his strength', as it is written, *And his strength went from him.*[7] 'She weakened his heart', as it is written, *And when Delilah saw that he had told her all his heart.*[8] 'She weakened his actions' since the *Shechinah* departed from him, as it is written, *But he wist not that the Lord had departed from him.*[9]

'*And when Delilah saw that he had told her all his heart*'. How did she know this?[10] R. Ḥanin said in the name of Rab: Words of truth are recognisable. Abaye said: She knew that this righteous man would not utter the Divine Name in vain; when he exclaimed, *I have been a Nazirite unto God,*[11] she said, Now he has certainly spoken the truth.

And it came to pass, when she pressed him daily with her words, and urged him.[12] What means '*and urged him*'? R. Isaac of the School of R. Ammi said: At the time of the consummation, she detached herself from him.

Now therefore beware, I pray thee, and drink no wine nor strong drink, and eat not any unclean thing.[13] What means '*any unclean thing*'? Furthermore, had she [Samson's mother] up to then eaten unclean things?

(1) Judg. XVI, 1. (2) Ibid. 21. (3) Ibid. XIV, 1. (4) He lawfully married the woman in Timnah but not the woman in Gaza. (5) Ibid. XVI, 4. (6) *Dildelah*, a play on her name. (7) Ibid. 19. (8) Ibid. 18. (9) Ibid. 20. (10) He had previously told her several falsehoods; so how did she know that he had now spoken the truth? (11) Ibid. 17. (12) Ibid. 16. (13) Ibid. XIII, 4.

R. Isaac of the School of R. Ammi said: [She had hitherto eaten] things forbidden to a Nazirite.

But God clave the hollow place that is in Lehi.[1] R. Isaac of the School of R. Ammi said: He [Samson] lusted for what was unclean;[2] therefore his life was made dependent upon an unclean thing.[3]

And the spirit of the Lord began, etc.[4] R. Ḥama b. Ḥanina said: Jacob's prophecy became fulfilled, as it is written, *Dan shall be a serpent in the way.*[5]

To move him in Mahaneh-Dan.[6] R. Isaac of the School of R. Ammi said: This teaches that the *Shechinah* kept ringing in front of him like a bell;[7] it is written here *to move him* [lefa'amo] *in Mahaneh-Dan,* and it is written elsewhere *A golden bell* [pa'amon] *and a pomegranate.*[8] *Between Zorah and Eshtaol*[9]—R. Assi said: Zorah and Eshtaol are two great mountains, and Samson uprooted them and ground one against the other.

And he shall begin to save Israel.[10] R. Ḥama b. Ḥanina said: [10*a*] The oath of Abimelech became void, as it is written, *That thou wilt not deal falsely with me, nor with my son, nor with my son's son.*[11]

And the child grew, and the Lord blessed him.[12] Wherewith did He bless him?—Rab Judah said in the name of Rab: With his physique which was like that of other men but his manly strength was like a fast-flowing stream.[13]

And Samson called unto the Lord, and said, O Lord God, remember me, I pray Thee and strengthen me, I pray Thee, that I may be at once avenged of the Philistines for my two eyes.[14] Rab said: Samson spoke before the Holy One, blessed be He, Sovereign of the Universe,

(1) Judg. XV, 19. (2) Philistine women. (3) The ass's jawbone (*leḥi*) out of which he drank in his thirst. (4) Ibid. XIII, 25. (5) Gen. XLIX, 17. This prophecy alluded to Samson who was of the tribe of Dan. (6) The word in Judg. XIII, 25 for *'move'* is commonly used of striking a bell. (7) To direct him where he was to go. (8) Ex. XXVIII, 34. (9) Judg. XIII, 25. (10) Ibid. 5. The word *'begin'* (יחל) is connected with a similar root (חלל) meaning *become void.* (11) Gen. XXI, 23. The alliance between the Israelites and Philistines ended in the time of Samson. (12) Judg. XIII, 24. (13) The point underlying this piece of Rabbinic hyperbole is that it was through Samson's inordinate passion for Philistine women that he came in contact with their people and brought about Israel's release from their power. (14) Ibid. XVI, 28.

Remember on my behalf the twenty[1] years I judged Israel, and never did I order anyone to carry my staff from one place to another.

And Samson went and caught three hundred foxes.[2] Why just foxes? —R. Aibu b. Nagari said in the name of R. Ḥiyya b. Abba: Samson declared, Let [the animal] come which turns backward[3] and exact punishment of the Philistines who went back on their oath.[4]

It has been taught: R. Simeon the Pious said: The width between Samson's shoulders was sixty cubits, as it is said, *And Samson lay till midnight, and arose at midnight and laid hold of the doors of the gate of the city, and the two posts, and plucked them up, bar and all, and put them upon his shoulders;*[5] and there is a tradition that the gates of Gaza were not less than sixty cubits [in width]. *And he did grind in the prison house.*[6]

R. Joḥanan said: '*Grind*' means nothing else than [sexual] transgression; and thus it is stated, *Then let my wife grind unto another.*[7] It teaches that everyone brought his wife to him to the prison that she might bear a child by him [who would be as strong as he was]. R. Papa said: That is what the proverb tells, 'Before the wine-drinker [set] wine, before a ploughman a basket of roots.'

R. Joḥanan also said: Whoever is faithless, his wife is faithless to him; as it is said, *If mine heart have been enticed unto a woman, and I have laid wait at my neighbour's door;*[8] and it continues, *Then let my wife grind unto another, and let others bow down upon her.* That is what the proverb tells, 'He among the full-grown pumpkins and his wife among the young ones'.

R. Joḥanan also said: Samson judged Israel in the same manner as their Father in heaven; as it is said, *Dan shall judge his people as One.*[9] R. Joḥanan also said: Samson was called by the name of the Holy One, blessed be He; as it is said, *For the Lord God is a sun and a shield.*[10] According to this argument, [his name] may not be

(1) Some edd. read 'twenty-two' in error; v. ibid. 31. (2) Judg. XV, 4. (3) When a fox is hunted, it does not run ahead but in a roundabout course. (4) Between Isaac and Abimelech; v. *supra*. (5) Ibid. XVI, 3. (6) Ibid. 21. (7) Job XXXI, 10. (8) Ibid. 9. (9) Gen. XLIX, 16, the *One* being God. (10) Ps. LXXXIV, 12, E.V. 11. The word for *sun* is *shemesh* which is the basis of Samson's name, *Shimshon*.

erased![1]—The intention is that [his name] was typical of the name of the Holy One, blessed be He;[2] as the Holy One, blessed be He, shields the whole world, so Samson shielded Israel during his generation.

R. Johanan also said: Balaam was lame in one leg, as it is said, *And he went* shefi;[3] Samson was lame in both legs, as it is said, *An adder in the path.*[4]

Our Rabbis have taught: Five were created after the likeness of Him Who is above, and all of them incurred punishment on account of [the feature which distinguished] them: Samson in his strength, Saul in his neck,[5] Absalom in his hair,[6] Zedekiah in his eyes, and Asa in his feet. 'Samson [was punished] in his strength', as it is written, *And his strength went from him.*[7] 'Saul [was punished] in his neck', as it is written, *Saul took his sword and fell upon it.*[8] 'Absalom [was punished] in his hair', as we shall have occasion to explain later. Zedekiah [was punished] in his eyes, as it is written, *They put out the eyes of Zedekiah.*[9] Asa [was punished] in his feet, as it is written, *But in the time of his old age he was diseased in his feet;*[10] and Rab Judah said in the name of Rab, *Podagra* [gout] attacked him.

Mar Zuṭra, son of R. Naḥman, asked R. Naḥman, What is *Podagra* like?—He answered, Like a needle in living flesh. How did he know this?—Some say he suffered from it himself; others say that he heard it from his teacher;[11] and others declare, *The secret of the Lord is with them that fear Him, and He will shew them His covenant.*[12]

Raba expounded: Why was Asa punished? Because he imposed forced labour[13] upon the disciples of the Sages, as it is said, *Then King Asa made a proclamation unto all Judah; none was exempted.*[14] What

(1) As it is forbidden to erase the Divine Name. (2) The word *sun* is not God's Name but a simile. (3) Num. XXIII, 3. (E.V. '*To a bare height*'). The Hebrew word is explained as '*lame*'. (4) Gen. XLIX, 17. The word for *adder* is *shefifon* which looks like a duplicated form of *shefi* from the root שוף, 'to dislocate'. (5) Cf. I Sam. X, 23. (6) Cf. II Sam. XIV, 26. There is no Biblical reference in connection with Zedekiah and Asa. (7) Judg. XVI, 19. (8) I Sam. XXXI, 4. The sword passed through his neck. (9) II Kings XXV, 7. (10) I Kings XV, 23. (11) His teacher was a Rabbi named Samuel who was a physician. (12) Ps. XXV, 14. The information was revealed to him by God. (13) In the public service. (14) I Kings XV, 22.

means '*none was exempted*'?—Rab Judah said in the name of Rab: Even the bridegroom from his chamber and the bride from her canopy.

It is written, *And Samson went down to Timnah*,[1] and it is written, *Behold, thy father-in-law goeth up to Timnah!*[2] R. Eleazar said: Since in the case of Samson he was disgraced there, it is written in connection with it '*went down*;' but in the case of Judah, since he was exalted in it,[3] there is written in connection with it '*goeth up*'. R. Samuel b. Naḥmani said: There are two places named Timnah; one [was reached] by going down and the other by going up. R. Papa said: There is only one place named Timnah; who came to it from one direction had to descend and from another direction had to ascend, as, e.g., Wardina, Be Bari and the market-place of Neresh.[4]

She sat in the gate of Enaim.[5] R. Alexander said: It teaches that she [Tamar] went and sat at the entrance [of the hospice] of our father Abraham, to see which place all eyes ['*enaim*] look. R. Ḥanin said in the name of Rab: It is a place named Enaim, as it states, *Tappuah and Enam.*[6] R. Samuel b. Naḥmani said: [It is so called] because she gave eyes to her words.[7] When [Judah] solicited her, he asked her, 'Art thou perhaps a Gentile?' She replied, 'I am a proselyte'. 'Art thou perhaps a married woman?' She replied, 'I am unmarried'. 'Perhaps thy father has accepted on thy behalf betrothals?'[8] She replied, 'I am an orphan'. 'Perhaps thou art unclean?' She replied, 'I am clean'.

And he planted a tamarisk tree in Beer-sheba.[9] Resh Laḳish said: It teaches that he [Abraham] made an orchard and planted in it all kinds of choice fruits. R. Judah and R. Nehemiah [differ in this

(1) Judg. XIV, 1. (2) Gen. XXXVIII, 13. Why does one text say '*down*' and the other '*goeth up*'? (3) Perez was born there from whom David was descended. (4) Towns in Babylonia situated on mountain slopes on the east bank of the Euphrates, v. Obermeyer, *op. cit.*, p. 309. (5) Gen. XXXVIII, 14. (6) Josh. XV, 34. Enam is identified with Enaim. (7) Tamar gave convincing replies to Judah's questions as to whether she was permitted to him. (8) [And thou thus belongest to another man.] (9) Gen. XXI, 33. The explanation 'hospice' is obtained by taking each letter of the word אשל '*tamarisk-tree*', and making them the initials of three Hebrew words meaning 'eating, drinking, lodging'.

matter]; one said that it was an orchard and the other that it was a hospice. It is right according to him who said that it was an orchard, since it is written *'and he planted'*; but according to him who said that it was a hospice, what means *'and he planted?'* —It is similarly written, *And he shall plant the tents of his palace,* etc.[1]

And he called there on the name of the Lord, the Everlasting God.[2] Resh Lakish said: Read not *'and he called'* [10*b*] but 'and he made to call', thereby teaching that our father Abraham caused the name of the Holy One, blessed be He, to be uttered by the mouth of every passer-by. How was this? After [travellers] had eaten and drunk, they stood up to bless him; but, said he to them, 'Did you eat of mine? You ate of that which belongs to the God of the Universe. Thank, praise and bless Him who spake and the world came into being'.

When Judah saw her, he thought her to be an harlot; for she had covered her face.[3] Because she had covered her face he thought her to be an harlot!—R. Eleazar said: She had covered her face in her father-in-law's house;[4] for R. Samuel b. Naḥmani said in the name of R. Jonathan: Every daughter-in-law who is modest in her father-in-law's house merits that kings and prophets should issue from her. Whence is this? From Tamar. Prophets [issued from her], as it is written, *The vision of Isaiah the son of Amoz,*[5] and kings [issued from her] through David; and R. Levi has said: This is a tradition in our possession from our fathers that Amoz and Amaziah[6] were brothers.

When she was brought forth.[7] Instead of *muẓeth* the verb should have been *mithwaẓẓeth!*[8] R. Eleazar said: [The verb in the text implies] that after her proofs[9] were found, Samael[10] came and

(1) Dan. XI, 45. (2) Gen. l.c. (3) Ibid. XXXVIII, 15. (4) So that Judah had never seen it and did not recognise her. (5) Isa. I, 1. (6) King of Judah, and since he was a descendant of David and Amoz was his brother, it is true that prophets and kings issued from Tamar. (7) Gen. XXXVIII, 25. (8) The verbal form used in the text could be translated *'was found'*, and the alternative suggested would have clearly indicated *'brought forth'*. (9) The signet, cord and staff. (10) Angel of evil, later identified with Satan.

removed them, and Gabriel[1] came and restored them. That is what is written, *For the Chief Musician, the silent dove of them that are afar off. Of David, Michtam*[2]—R. Joḥanan said: At the time when her proofs were removed, she became like a silent dove. '*Of David*', '*Michtam*'—[that means] there issued from her David who was meek [*mach*] and perfect [*tam*] to all. Another explanation of '*Michtam*' is: his wound [*makkah*][3] was whole [*tammah*], since he was born already circumcised. Another explanation of '*Michtam*' is: just as in his youth [before he became king] he made himself small in the presence of anyone greater than himself to study Torah, so was he the same in his greatness.[4]

She sent to her father-in-law, saying, By the man whose these are, am I with child.[5] She ought to have told [the messenger] plainly![6]—R. Zuṭra b. Tobiah said in the name of Rab—another version is, R. Ḥama b. Bizna said in the name of R. Simeon the Pious; and still another version is, R. Joḥanan said in the name of R. Simeon b. Yoḥai: Better for a man to cast himself into a fiery furnace rather than shame his fellow in public. Whence is this? From Tamar.[7]

Discern, I pray thee.[8] R. Ḥama b. Ḥanina said: With the word '*discern*' [Judah] made an announcement to his father, and with the word '*discern*' an announcement was made to him. With the word '*discern*' he made an announcement—*Discern now whether it be thy son's coat or not;*[9] and with the word '*discern*' an announcement was made to him—*Discern, I pray thee, whose are these.*[8] The word '*na*' ['I pray thee'] is nothing else than an expression of request. She said to him, 'I beg of thee, discern the face of thy Creator and hide not thine eyes from me'.[10]

And Judah acknowledged them, and said, She is more righteous than I.[11] That is what R. Ḥanin b. Bizna said in the name of R. Simeon the

(1) One of the four Archangels. (2) Ps. LVI, 1. (3) I.e., the place where there should have been a wound after circumcision. (4) After he became king, he humbled himself to study. So he was meek and perfect. (5) Gen. XXXVIII, 25. (6) That Judah was the father of her child. Why the circumlocution? (7) She risked being burnt to death rather than publicly shame Judah. (8) Ibid. (9) Ibid. XXXVII, 32. (10) That is how '*Discern, I pray thee*' is explained. (11) Ibid. XXXVIII, 26.

Pious: Joseph who sanctified the heavenly Name in private[1] merited that one letter should be added to him from the Name of the Holy One, blessed be He, as it is written, *He appointed it in Joseph for a testimony.*[2] Judah, however, who sanctified the heavenly Name in public merited that the whole of his name should be called after the Name of the Holy One, blessed be He.[3] When he confessed and said, *She is more righteous than I*, a *Bath Ḳol*[4] issued forth and proclaimed, 'Thou didst rescue Tamar and her two sons from the fire. By thy life, I will rescue through thy merit three of thy descendants from the fire'. Who are they? Hananiah, Mishael and Azariah.[5] '*She is more righteous than I*'—how did he know this?[6] A *Bath Ḳol* issued forth and proclaimed, 'From Me came forth secrets.'[7]

And he knew her again no more.[8] Samuel the elder, father-in-law of R. Samuel b. Ammi said in the name of R. Samuel b. Ammi: Having once known her,[9] he did not separate from her again. It is written here, '*And he knew her again no more* [*Yasaf'*], and elsewhere it is written, *With a great voice unceasing* [*Yasaf*].[10]

ABSALOM GLORIED IN HIS HAIR etc. Our Rabbis have taught: Absalom rebelled [against his father] through his hair, as it is said, *There was none to be so much praised as Absalom for his beauty . . . And when he polled his head, now it was at every year's end that he polled it because the hair was heavy on him therefore he polled it, he weighed the hair of his head at two hundred shekels, after the king's weight.*[11] It has been taught that [*the king's weight*] was the weight with which the men of Tiberias and Sepphoris weigh. Therefore he was hanged by his hair, as it is said, *And Absalom chanced to meet the servants of David. And Absalom rode upon his mule, and the mule went under the*

(1) When he resisted Potiphar's wife. (2) Ps. LXXXI, 6, E.V. 5. Here in the Hebrew the letter *'he'*, one of the letters of the Tetragrammaton, is added to Joseph's name יהוסף. (3) The four letters of the Tetragrammaton occur in Judah's name יהודה. (4) V. Glos. (5) See Dan. III. (6) Since she might have cohabited with other men. (7) V. Mak. 23*b*. (8) Gen. XXXVIII, 26. (9) That she was righteous. (10) Deut. V, 19. The two verbs are really distinct, but the Rabbi connected them both with the root אסף and accordingly explained the phrase in Gen. as *'and he knew her again without ceasing'*, v. Sanh. 17*a*.. (11) II Sam. XIV, 25f.

thick boughs of a great oak, and his head caught hold of the oak, and he was taken up between the heaven and the earth; and the mule that was under him went on.[1] He took a sword and wished to cut himself loose;[2] but it was taught in the School of R. Ishmael, At that moment Sheol was split asunder beneath him.[3]

And the king was much moved, and went up to the chamber over the gate, and wept; and as he went, thus he said, O my son Absalom, my son, my son Absalom! would God I had died for thee, O Absalom, my son, my son.[4] *And the king covered his face, and the king cried with a loud voice, O my son Absalom, O Absalom my son, my son.*[5] Why is '*my son*' repeated eight times? Seven to raise him from the seven divisions of Gehinnom; and as for the last, some say to unite his [severed] head to his body and others say to bring him into the World to Come.

Now Absalom in his lifetime had taken and reared up.[6] What means '*had taken*'?—Resh Laḳish said: He had made a bad purchase for himself.[7] *The pillar which is in the king's dale*, etc.—R. Ḥanina b. Papa said: In the deep plan of the King of the Universe;[8] [11*a*] as it is written, *I will raise up evil against thee out of thine own house.*[9] Similarly it is stated, *So he sent him* [Joseph] *out of the vale of Hebron.*[10] R. Ḥanina b. Papa said: [The meaning is:] It was through the deep plan of that righteous man [Abraham] who had been buried in Hebron; as it is written, *Know of a surety that thy seed shall be a stranger in a land that is not theirs.*[11]

For he said, I have no son.[12] Had he, then, no sons? Behold it is written, *And unto Absalom there were born three sons and one daughter!*[13] —R. Isaac b. Abdimi said: [His meaning was] that he had no son fit for the kingship. R. Ḥisda said: There is a tradition that whoever

(1) II Sam. XVIII, 9. (2) The first half of this sentence is omitted in some edd. (3) So that had he cut through his hair he would have fallen into Sheol. (4) Ibid. XIX, 1. E.V. XVIII, 33. (5) Ibid. 5, E.V. 4. (6) Ibid. XVIII, 18. (7) The verb signifies both took and purchased. The meaning appears to be that his conduct resulted in his having to buy a monument to preserve his memory instead of his succeeding his father; hence it was a bad bargain for him. (8) The word '*dale*' means 'deep', and '*king*' is applied to God Who had decided that this should happen as a punishment for his sin with Bath-sheba. (9) Ibid. XII, 11. (10) Gen. XXXVII, 14. Here '*vale*' is also explained as deep plan. (11) Ibid. XV, 13. (12) II Sam. l.c. (13) Ibid. XIV, 27.

burns his neighbour's produce will not leave a son to succeed him; and he [Absalom] had burnt [the produce] of Joab, as it is written, *Therefore he said unto his servants, See, Joab's field is near mine, and he hath barley there; go and set it on fire. And Absalom's servants set the field on fire.*[1]

IT IS THE SAME IN CONNECTION WITH THE GOOD. MIRIAM etc. Is this like [the other cases mentioned]? There she waited a short while [for Moses], here [the Israelites waited for her] seven days?[2]—Abaye said: Read that in connection with the good [the principle of measure for measure] does not apply. Raba said to him, But the Mishnah teaches IT IS THE SAME IN CONNECTION WITH THE GOOD! But, said Raba, the Mishnah must be understood thus: It is the same in connection with the good that there is the same measure; nevertheless the measure in the case of the good is greater than the measure in the case of punishment.[3]

And his sister stood afar off.[4] R. Isaac said: The whole of this verse is spoken with reference to the *Shechinah: 'and stood'*, as it is written, *And the Lord came and stood* etc.[5] '*His sister*', as it is written, *Say unto wisdom, thou art my sister.*[6] '*Afar off*', as it is written, *The Lord appeared from afar unto me.*[7] '*To know*', as it is written, *For the Lord is a God of knowledge.*[8] '*What*', as it is written, *What doth the Lord require of thee?*[9] '*Done*', as it is written, *Surely the Lord God will do nothing.*[10] '*To him*', as it is written, *And called it Lord is peace.*[11]

Now there arose a new king etc.[12] Rab and Samuel [differ in their interpretation]; one said that he was really new, while the other said that his decrees were made new. He who said that he was really new did so because it is written '*new*'; and he who said that his decrees were made new did so because it is not stated that [the former king] died and he reigned [in his stead].

(1) II Sam. 30. (2) So how does the principle of measure for measure apply? (3) The reward for a good deed exceeds the actual merit of an action and is not merely a *quid pro quo* as with a wrong deed. (4) Ex. II, 4. (5) I Sam. III, 10. (6) Prov. VII, 4. Wisdom is an emanation from God. (7) Jer. XXXI, 3. (8) I Sam. II, 3. (9) Deut. X, 12. (10) Amos III, 7. (11) Judg. VI, 24. The Hebrew word '*it*' is the same as '*to him*'. (12) Ex. I, 8.

Who knew not Joseph—he was like one who did not know [Joseph] at all.

And he said unto his people, Behold the people of the children of Israel.[1] A Tanna taught: He [Pharaoh] originated the plan first, and therefore was punished first. He originated the plan first, as it is written, *And he said unto his people;* therefore he was punished first, as it is written, *Upon thee, and upon thy people, and upon all thy servants.*[2]

Come, let us deal wisely with him[3]—it should have been *with them!* —R. Ḥama b. Ḥanina said: [Pharaoh meant,] Come and let us outwit the Saviour of Israel. With what shall we afflict them? If we afflict them with fire, it is written, *For, behold the Lord will come with fire,*[4] and it continues, *For by fire will the Lord plead* etc.[5] [If we afflict them] with the sword, it is written, *And by His sword with all flesh.*[6] But come and let us afflict them with water, because the Holy One, blessed be He, has already sworn that he will not bring a flood upon the world; as it is said, *For this is as the waters of Noah unto Me,* etc.[7] They were unaware, however, that He would not bring a flood upon the whole world but upon one people He would bring it; or alternatively, *He* would not bring [the flood] but they would go and fall into it. Thus it says, *And the Egyptians fled towards it.*[8] This is what R. Eleazar said: What means that which is written, *Yea, in the thing wherein they zadu [dealt proudly] against them?*[9] In the pot in which they cooked were they cooked. Whence is it learnt that '*zadu*' means cooking?—Because it is written, *And Jacob sod* [wa-yazed] *pottage.*[10]

R. Ḥiyya b. Abba said in the name of R. Simai: There were three in that plan,[11] viz. Balaam, Job[12] and Jethro. Balaam who

(1) Ex. 9. (2) Ibid. VII, 29. (3) Ibid. I, 10. The Hebrew is literally *with him.* (4) Isa. LXVI, 15. (5) Ibid. 16. (6) Ibid. Some edd. quote as the proof text, *With his sword drawn in his hand* (Num. XXII, 23). (7) Isa. LIV, 9. (8) Ex. XIV, 27. So the Hebrew literally. (9) Ibid. XVIII, 11. The verb '*they dealt proudly*' resembles in form another with the meaning '*they cooked*' זדו. (10) Gen. XXV, 29. (11) To destroy Israel through the decree: *Every son that is born ye shall cast in the river,* Ex. I, 22. (12) Various opinions are expressed in the Talmud regarding the age in which he lived. According to one view he was born in the year that Jacob settled in Egypt and died at the time of the Exodus, v. B.B. 15*a*-*b*.

devised it was slain; Job who silently acquiesced was afflicted with sufferings; Jethro, who fled, merited that his descendants should sit in the Chamber of Hewn Stone,[1] as it is said, *And the families of scribes which dwelt at Jabez; the Tirathites, the Shimeathites, the Sucathites. These are the Kenites that came of Hammath, the father of the house of Rechab;*[2] and it is written, *And the children of the Kenite, Moses' father-in-law* etc.[3]

And fight against us and get them up out of the land[4]—it should have read 'and we will get us up!'[5]—R. Abba b. Kahana said: It is like a man who curses himself and hangs the curse upon somebody else.

Therefore they did set over him taskmasters[6]—it should have read 'over them'!—It was taught in the School of R. Eleazar b. Simeon, It indicates that they brought a brick-mould and hung it round Pharaoh's neck; and every Israelite who complained that he was weak was told, 'Art thou weaker than Pharaoh?'

Missim [*'taskmasters'*]—i.e., something which forms [*mesim*].[7] *'To afflict him with their burdens'*—it should have read 'them'!—The [meaning is] to afflict Pharaoh with the burdens of Israel.[8]

And they built for Pharaoh store cities [miskenoth].[6] Rab and Samuel [differ in their interpretation]; one said, [They were so called] because they endangered [*mesakkenoth*] their owners,[9] while the other said because they impoverished [*memaskenoth*] their owners,[10] for a master has declared that whoever occupies himself with building becomes impoverished.[11]

Pithom and Raamses[6]—Rab and Samuel differ [in their interpretation];[12] one said, Its real name was Pithom, and why was it called

(1) In the Temple where the Sanhedrin met. (2) I Chron. II, 55. The various names are understood in the sense that they were eminent scholars. (3) Judg. I, 16; v. Sanh. (Sonc. ed.) p. 722. (4) Ex. I, 10. (5) I.e., we will be driven out of the land. (6) Ibid. 11, the text is literally *him*. (7) Viz., bricks, referring to the brick-mould which Pharaoh had to wear. (8) He had to carry the brick-mould as the pattern for the Israelites to work upon. (9) Led to the destruction of the Egyptians. (10) When they were spoiled by the Israelites before the Exodus. (11) [According to this dictum the interpretation '*memaskenoth*' is general in its application and has no particular reference to the Egyptians. Some edd. accordingly omit the last sentence.] (12) They agreed that only one store city was built.

Raamses? Because one building after another collapsed [*mithroses*]. The other said that its real name was Raamses, and why was it called Pithom? Because the mouth of the deep [*pi tehom*] swallowed up one building after another.

But the more they afflicted him, the more he will multiply and the more he will spread abroad[1]—it should have read 'the more they multiplied and the more they spread abroad'!—Resh Laḳish said: The Holy Spirit announced to them. 'The more he will multiply and the more he will spread abroad'.

And they were grieved [wa-yakuẓu] *because of the children of Israel*[1]—this teaches that they were like thorns [*koẓim*] in their eyes.

And the Egyptians made the children of Israel to serve [11b] *with rigour* [*parek*].[2] R. Eleazar said: [It means] with a tender mouth [*peh rak*];[3] R. Samuel b. Naḥmani said: [It means] with rigorous work [*perikah*]. *And they made their lives bitter with hard service, in mortar and in brick* etc. Raba said: At first it was in mortar and in brick; but finally it was in all manner of service in the field. *All their service wherein they made them serve with rigour.*[4] R. Samuel b. Naḥmani said in the name of R. Jonathan: They changed men's work for the women and the women's work for the men; and even he who explained [*parek*] above as meaning 'with tender mouth' admits that here it means 'with rigorous work'.

R. 'Awira expounded: As the reward for the righteous women who lived in that generation were the Israelites delivered from Egypt. When they went to draw water, the Holy One, blessed be He, arranged that small fishes should enter their pitchers, which they drew up half full of water and half full of fishes. They then set two pots on the fire, one for hot water and the other for the fish, which they carried to their husbands in the field, and washed, anointed, fed, gave them to drink and had intercourse with them among the sheepfolds, as it is said, *When ye lie among the sheepfolds* etc.[5] As the reward for '*When ye lie among the sheepfolds*', the Israelites merited the spoliation of the Egyptians, as it is said, *As the wings*

(1) Ex. 12. So the Hebrew literally. (2) Ibid. 13. (3) They induced the Israelites to work by using smooth words to them. (4) Ibid. 14. (5) Ps. LXVIII, 14, E.V., 13.

of a dove covered with silver, and her pinions with yellow gold.[1] After the women had conceived they returned to their homes; and when the time of childbirth arrived, they went and were delivered in the field beneath the apple-tree, as it is said, *Under the apple-tree I caused thee to come forth* [from thy mother's womb] etc.[2] The Holy One, blessed be He, sent down someone from the high heavens who washed and straightened the limbs [of the babes] in the same manner that a midwife straightens the limbs of a child; as it is said, *And as for thy nativity, in the day thou wast born thy navel was not cut, neither wast thou washed in water to cleanse thee.*[3] He also provided for them two cakes, one of oil and one of honey, as it is said, *And He made him to suck honey out of the rock, and oil* etc.[4] When the Egyptians noticed them, they went to kill them; but a miracle occurred on their behalf so that they were swallowed in the ground, and [the Egyptians] brought oxen and ploughed over them, as it is said, *The ploughers ploughed upon my back.*[5] After they had departed, [the Israelite women with their babes] broke through [the earth] and came forth like the herbage of the field, as it is said, *I caused thee to multiply as the bud of the field;*[6] and when [the babes] had grown up, they came in flocks to their homes, as it is said, *And thou didst increase and wax great and didst come with ornaments*[7]—read not *with ornaments* [ba'adi 'adayim] but *in flocks* [be'edre 'adarim]. At the time the Holy One, blessed be He, revealed Himself by the Red Sea, they recognised Him first, as it is said, *This is my God and I will praise Him.*[8]

And the king of Egypt spake to the Hebrew midwives etc.[9] Rab and Samuel [differ in their interpretation]; one said they were mother and daughter, and the other said they were daughter-in-law and mother-in-law. According to him who declared they were mother and daughter, they were Jochebed and Miriam; and according to him who declared they were daughter-in-law and mother-in-law,

(1) Ps. LXVIII, 14, E.V., 13. The dove is often used by the Rabbis as a symbol of Israel. (2) Cant. VIII, 5. That is how the verb is interpreted here. (3) Ezek. XVI, 4. There was no midwife present to cut the navel-string, nor was ordinary water used. (4) Deut. XXXII, 13. (5) Ps. CXXIX, 3. (6) Ezek. XVI, 7. (7) Ibid. (8) Ex. XV, 2. The word '*this*' implies that He had been previously seen; therefore it must have been by the former babes. (9) Ibid. I, 15.

they were Jochebed and Elisheba.[1] There is a teaching in agreement with him who said they were mother and daughter; for it has been taught: '*Shiphrah*'[2] is Jochebed; and why was her name called Shiphrah? Because she straightened [*meshappereth*] the limbs of the babe. Another explanation of *Shiphrah* is that the Israelites were fruitful [*sheparu*] and multiplied in her days. '*Pu'ah*' is Miriam; and why was her name called Puah? Because she cried out [*po'ah*] to the child[3] and brought it forth. Another explanation of *Pu'ah* is that she used to cry out through the Holy Spirit[4] and say, 'My mother will bear a son who will be the saviour of Israel'.

And he said, When ye do the office of a midwife to the Hebrew women etc.[5] What means '*obnayim*'?[6] R. Ḥanan said: He entrusted them with an important sign and told them that when a woman bends to deliver a child, her thighs grow cold like stones ['*abanim*'].[7] Another explains [the word '*obnayim*'] in accordance with what is written, *Then I went down to the potter's house, and, behold, he wrought his work on the wheels.*[8] As in the case of a potter, there is a thigh on one side, a thigh on the other side and the wooden block in between, so also with a woman there is a thigh on one side, a thigh on the other side and the child in between.

If it be a son, then ye shall kill him.[9] R. Ḥanina said: He entrusted them with an important sign, viz., if it is a son, his face is turned downward and if a daughter, her face is turned upward.[10] *But the midwives feared God, and did not as the king of Egypt spoke to them.*[11] Instead of *alehen* ['*to them*'] we should have had '*lahen*'![12]—R. Jose son of R. Ḥanina said: It teaches that he solicited them for immoral intercourse,[13] but they refused to yield.

(1) She was Aaron's wife (Ex. VI, 23). (2) Ibid. I, 15. (3) Rashi explains: she uttered soothing words which induced the child to come forth. She blew a charm into the mother's ear and brought forth the child (Jast.). (4) I.e., the prophetic gift. (5) Ibid. 16. (6) This word in the verse is translated *birthstool*. (7) By means of this symptom they would be able to detect a mother who tried to conceal a birth. (8) Jer. XVIII, 3. The word for *wheels* is '*obnayim*'. (9) Ex. I, 16. (10) At the time of birth (Nid. 31*a*). (11) Ibid. 17. (12) The latter is the more usual form since no direct speech follows. (13) The preposition '*el*, which occurs in the text, is employed in this sense.

But saved the men children alive—A Tanna taught: Not only did they not put them to death, but they supplied them with water and food.[1] *And the midwives said unto Pharaoh, Behold the Hebrew women are not as the Egyptian women* etc.[2] What means *ḥayoth?*[3] If it is to say they were actually midwives,[4] do you infer that a midwife does not require another midwife to deliver her child!—But [the meaning is] they said to him, This people are compared to an animal [*ḥayyah*]—Judah [is called] *a lion's whelp;*[5] of Dan [it is said] *Dan shall be a serpent;*[6] Naphtali [is called] *a hind let loose;*[7] Issachar *a strong ass;*[8] Joseph *a firstling bullock;*[9] Benjamin *a wolf that ravineth.*[10] [Of those sons of Jacob where a comparison with an animal] is written in connection with them, it is written: but [in the instances where such a comparison] is not written, there is the text, *What was thy mother? A lioness; she couched among lions* etc.[11]

And it came to pass, because the midwives feared God, that He made them houses.[12] Rab and Samuel [differ in their interpretation]; one said they are the priestly and Levitical houses, and the other said they are the royal houses. One who says they are the priestly and Levitical houses: Aaron and Moses; and one who says they are the royal houses: for also David descended from Miriam, as it is written, *And Azubah died, and Caleb took unto him Ephrath, which bare him Hur,*[13] and it is written, *Now David was the son of that Ephrathite* etc.[14]

And Caleb the son of Hezron begat children of Azubah his wife and of Jerioth; and these were her sons: Jesher and Shobab and Ardon.[15] '*The son of Hezron*'? He was the son of Jephunneh![16]—[It means] that he was a son who turned [*panah*] from the counsel of the spies. Still, he was the son of Kenaz, as it is written, *And Othniel the son of Kenaz, Caleb's younger brother, took it!*[17]—Raba said: He was the stepson of Kenaz. [12a] There is also evidence for this, since it is written,

(1) The text does not state, 'they did not kill'; therefore '*saved alive*' is so explained. (2) Ex. I, 19. (3) The word in this verse translated *lively*. (4) That is the significance the word has in Rabbinic Hebrew. (5) Gen. XLIX, 9. (6) Ibid. 17. (7) Ibid. 21. (8) Ibid. 14. (9) Deut. XXXIII, 17. (10) Gen. XLIX, 27. (11) Ezek. XIX, 2. (12) Ex. I, 21. (13) I Chron. II, 19. (14) I Sam. XVII, 12. (15) I Chron. II, 18. (16) V. Num. XIII, 6. (17) Judg. I, 13.

[*And Caleb the son of Jephunneh*] *the Kenizzite.*[1] Conclude, therefore, that Azubah is identical with Miriam; and why was her name called Azubah? Because all men forsook her [*'azabuhah*] at first.[2] *'Begat!'*[3] But he was married to her!—R. Joḥanan said: Whoever marries a woman for the name of heaven,[4] the text ascribes it to him as though he had begotten her. *'Jerioth'*—[she was so named] because her face was like curtains.[5] *'And these were her sons'*—read not *baneha* [her sons] but *boneha* [her builders].[6] *'Jesher'* [he was so called] because he set himself right [*yishsher*].[7] *'Shobab'*—[he was so called] because he turned his inclination aside [*shibbeb*].[8] *'And Ardon'*—[he was so called] because he disciplined [*radah*] his inclination. Others say, Because his face was like a rose [*wered*].

And Ashhur the father of Tekoa had two wives, Helah and Naarah.[9] Ashhur is identical with Caleb; and why was his name called Ashhur? Because his face was blackened [*hushḥeru*] through his fasts.[10] *'The father'*—he became a father to her.[11] *'Tekoa'*—he fixed [*taḳa'*] his heart on his Father in heaven.[12] *'Had two wives'*—[this means] Miriam became like two wives. *'Helah and Naarah'*—she was not both Helah and Naarah, but at first she was Helah [an invalid] and finally Naarah [a young girl].[13] *And the sons of Helah were Zereth, Zohar and Ethnan.*[14] *'Zereth'*—[Miriam was so called]—because she became the rival [*ẓarah*] of her contemporaries [in beauty]. *'Zohar'*—because her face was [beautiful] like the noon [*ẓoharayim*]. *'Ethnan'*—because whoever saw her took a present [*'ethnan*] to his wife.[15]

And Pharaoh charged all his people.[16] R. Jose son of R. Ḥanina said:

(1) Josh. XIV, 6, and not the son of Kenaz. (2) She was an invalid so that nobody would marry her. (3) The Hebrew text could be translated: and Caleb begat Azubah. (4) From a pious motive, as in this case where through illness Miriam remained unmarried. (5) She also is identified with Miriam. Through illness her face was pale like the colour of curtains (*yeri'oth*). (6) Through them she attained the dignity of motherhood. (7) Viz., Caleb escaped the error of the other spies. (8) From following the rest of the spies. (9) I Chron. IV, 5. (10) He mortified himself to resist joining the other spies. (11) To Miriam who, on account of illness, required constant attention. (12) For will-power not to join in the evil report. (13) I.e., she recovered and became young in appearance. (14) I Chron. IV, 7. (15) His passion was aroused by the sight of Miriam. (16) Ex. I, 22.

He imposed the same decree upon his own people.[1] R. Jose son of R. Ḥanina also said: He made three decrees: first, '*if it be a son, then ye shall kill him*'; then '*every son that is born ye shall cast into the river*'; and finally he imposed the same decree upon his own people.

And there went a man of the house of Levi.[2] Where did he go? R. Judah b. Zebina said that he went in the counsel of his daughter. A Tanna taught: Amram was the greatest man of his generation; when he saw that the wicked Pharaoh had decreed '*Every son that is born ye shall cast into the river*', he said, In vain do we labour. He arose and divorced his wife.[3] All [the Israelites] thereupon arose and divorced their wives. His daughter said to him, 'Father, thy decree is more severe than Pharaoh's; because Pharaoh decreed only against the males whereas thou hast decreed against the males and females. Pharaoh only decreed concerning this world whereas thou hast decreed concerning this world and the World to Come.[4] In the case of the wicked Pharaoh there is a doubt whether his decree will be fulfilled or not, whereas in thy case, though thou art righteous, it is certain that thy decree will be fulfilled, as it is said, *Thou shalt also decree a thing, and it shall be established unto thee!*[5] He arose and took his wife back; and they all arose and took their wives back.

And took to wife[2]—it should have read 'and took back'![6] R. Judah b. Zebina said:—He acted towards her as though it had been the first marriage; he seated her in a palanquin, Aaron and Miriam danced before her, and the Ministering Angels proclaimed, *A joyful mother of children.*[7]

A daughter of Levi.[2] How is this possible! She was one hundred and thirty years old, and he calls her '*a daughter*'! (For R. Ḥama b. Ḥanina said: This[8] refers to Jochebed whose conception occurred

(1) To kill the male children, because the astrologers had warned him that a boy was soon to be born who would overthrow him. (2) Ex. II, 1. (3) Since all the male children to be born would be killed, and the primary object of marriage was the procreation of sons. (4) The drowned babes would live again in the Hereafter; but unborn children are denied that bliss. (5) Job XXII, 28. (6) His wife, according to the story just related. (7) Ps. CXIII, 9. (8) 'The daughter of Levi'.

during the journey [to Egypt] and her birth between the walls;[1] as it is said, *Who was born to Levi in Egypt*[2]—her birth occurred in Egypt but her conception did not occur there.)[3]—Rab Judah said: [She is called '*a daughter*'] because the signs of maidenhood were reborn in her.[4]

And the woman conceived and bare a son.[5] But she had already been pregnant three months![6]—R. Judah b. Zebina said: It compares the bearing of the child to its conception; as the conception was painless so was the bearing painless. Hence [it is learnt] that righteous women were not included in the decree upon Eve.[7]

And when she saw him that he was good.[5] It has been taught: R. Meir says: His name was *Ṭob* [good]; R. Judah says: His name was Ṭobiah; R. Nehemiah says: [She foresaw that he would be] worthy of the prophetic gift; others say: He was born circumcised; and the Sages declare, At the time when Moses was born, the whole house was filled with light—it is written here, *And when she saw him that he was good*, and elsewhere it is written, *And God saw the light that it was good.*[8]

She hid him three months.[5] [She was able to do this] because the Egyptians only counted [the period of her pregnancy] from the time that she was restored [to youth], but she was then already pregnant three months.

And when she could not longer hide him[9]—why? She should have gone on hiding him!—But whenever the Egyptians were informed that a child was born, they would take other children there so that it should hear them [crying] and cry with them; as it is written, *Take us the foxes, the little foxes etc.*[10]

She took for him an ark of bulrushes[9]—why just bulrushes? R. Eleazar said: Hence [it is learnt] that to the righteous their money is dearer

(1) I.e., just as the caravan arrived at Egypt. (2) Num. XXVI, 59. The Torah mentions that the Israelites numbered seventy who came to Egypt, whereas there are only sixty-nine names in the list. Hence this statement about Jochebed. (3) From that time one hundred and thirty years had elapsed. (4) Although so old, she became young in form and appearance. (5) Ex. II, 2. (6) Viz., before she was restored to youth, as will be explained. (7) That she would bear children in pain (Gen. III, 16). (8) Gen. I, 4. (9) Ex. II, 3. (10) Cant II, 15.

than their body;[1] and why so?—That they should not stretch out their hand to robbery.[2] R. Samuel b. Naḥmani says: [She selected them] because they are a soft material which can withstand both soft and hard materials.[3]

And daubed it with slime and with pitch[4]—A Tanna taught: The slime was inside and the pitch outside so that that righteous child should not smell the bad odour.

And she put the child therein and laid it in the reeds [*suf*][4]—R. Eleazar said: In the Red [*suf*] Sea; R. Samuel b. Naḥmani said: [12b] It means reeds, as it is written, *The reeds and flags shall wither away.*[5]

And the daughter of Pharaoh came down to bathe at the river.[6] R. Joḥanan said in the name of R. Simeon b. Yoḥai: It teaches that she went down there to cleanse herself of her father's idols;[7] and thus it says, *When the Lord shall have washed away the filth of the daughters of Zion* etc.[8] *And her maidens walked along etc.*[9] R. Joḥanan said: The word for '*walk*' means nothing else than death; and thus it says, *Behold I am going to die.*[10] *And she saw the ark among the reeds.*[6] When [the maidens] saw that she wished to rescue Moses, they said to her, 'Mistress, it is the custom of the world that when a human king makes a decree, though everybody else does not obey it, at least his children and the members of his household obey it; but thou dost transgress thy father's decree!' Gabriel came and beat them to the ground.

And sent her handmaid to fetch it[6]—R. Judah and R. Nehemiah [differ in their interpretation]; one said that the word means 'her hand' and the other said that it means 'her handmaid'. He who said that it means 'her hand' did so because it is written *ammathah;*[11] he who said that it means 'her handmaid' did so because the text

(1) She selected bulrushes because of their cheapness, although hard wood would have been better for the welfare of the child. (2) They are frugal in expenditure upon their comforts so as not to be tempted to dishonesty for the gratification of their needs. (3) Hard wood would be more easily split, whereas bulrushes yield under pressure. (4) Ex. II, 3. (5) Isa. XIX, 6. (6) Ex. II, 5. (7) Since immersion is part of the ceremony of conversion, it is assumed that she became a proselyte. (8) Isa. IV, 4. (9) Ex. II, 5. (10) Gen. XXV, 32. (11) The text could be read either as *amathah* 'her maid' or *'ammathah* 'her arm'. The Targum of Onḳelos renders by 'her arm'.

has not *yadah* [her hand]. But according to him who said that it means 'her handmaid', it has just been stated that Gabriel came and beat them to the ground![1]—He left her one, because it is not customary for a king's daughter to be unattended. But according to him who said that it means 'her hand', the text should have been *yadah!*—It teaches us that [her arm] became lengthened; for a master has said, You find it so[2] with the arm of Pharaoh's daughter and similarly with the teeth of the wicked, as it is written, *Thou hast broken* [*shibbarta*] *the teeth of the wicked,*[3] and Resh Laḳish said, Read not *shibbarta* but *shirbabta* [thou has lenghtened].[4]

She opened it and saw the child[5]—it should have been '*and saw*'. R. Jose b. R. Ḥanina said: She saw the *Shechinah* with him.[6]

And, behold, the boy wept[5]—he is called a '*child*' and then a '*boy*'!—A Tanna taught, He was a child but his voice was like that of a grown boy; such is the view of R. Judah. R. Nehemiah said to him, If so, you have made our master Moses into one possessed of a blemish;[7] but it teaches that his mother made for him a canopy [such as is used at the marriage] of boys[8] in the ark, saying, 'Perhaps I may not be worthy [to be present at] his marriage-canopy'.

And she had compassion on him and said, Of the Hebrews' children is this.[5] How did she know it?—R. Jose b. R. Ḥanina said: Because she saw that he was circumcised. '*Is this*'—R. Joḥanan said, It teaches that she unwittingly prophesied that '*this*' one will fall [into the river] but no other will fall.[9] That is what R. Eleazar said, What means the text, *And when they shall say unto you, Seek unto them that have familiar spirits and unto the wizards, that chirp and that mutter?*[10] They foresee and know not what they foresee; they mutter and know not what they mutter. They saw that Israel's saviour would be

(1) Therefore they were all dead; so how could the princess send her handmaid? (2) [The lengthening of a limb, v. Meg. 15*b*.] (3) Ps. III, 8. (4) [The reference is to Og, King of Bashan, v. Ber. 54*b*.] (5) Ex. II, 6. The text is literally: she saw him the child. (6) The suffix *hu* (him) is explained as God and the particle *eth* as 'with' and not the sign of the accusative: 'she saw Him with the child'. (7) His voice would be abnormal, and this disqualified a Levite from the Temple-ministry. (8) [Or. 'canopy of youth', i.e., a bridal canopy.] (9) Because on that day the decree to drown the males was rescinded. (10) Isa. VIII, 19.

punished through water; so they arose and decreed, *Every son that is born ye shall cast into the river.*[1] After they had thrown Moses [into the water], they said, 'We do not see that sign any longer';[2] they thereupon rescinded their decree. But they knew not that he was to be punished through the water of Meribah.[3] That is what R. Ḥama b. Ḥanina said, What means the text, *These are the waters of Meribah, because they strove?*[4] These are [the waters] about which Pharaoh's magicians saw and erred; and concerning this Moses said, *Six hundred thousand footmen* etc.[5] Moses said to Israel, 'On my account were all of you delivered [from drowning by the edict of Pharaoh]'.

R. Ḥanina b. Papa said: That day[6] was the twenty-first of Nisan,[7] and the Ministering Angels spoke before the Holy One, blessed be He, 'Lord of the Universe! Shall he who will utter a song to Thee by the Red Sea on this day be punished on this day?' R. Aḥa b. Ḥanina said: That day was the sixth of Sivan,[8] and the Ministering Angels spoke before the Holy One, blessed be He, 'Lord of the Universe! Shall he who will receive the Torah on Mount Sinai on this day be punished on this day?' It is quite right according to him who said that it was the sixth of Sivan, for then it occurred three months [after his birth]; for a master has said, Moses died on the seventh of Adar[9] and was born on the seventh of Adar, and from the seventh of Adar to the sixth of Sivan is three months. But according to him who said that it was the twenty-first of Nisan, how could it have been?[10]—That year was a leap year;[11] the greater part of the first [Adar] and the greater part of the last [Nisan] and a full month in between.[12]

Then said his sister to Pharaoh's daughter, Shall I go and call thee a nurse of the Hebrew women?[13] Why just *'of the Hebrew women'?*—It teaches

(1) Ex. I, 22. (2) Indicating that the peril to Pharaoh was averted by this action. (3) [And that this was the meaning of the sign they had seen.] (4) Num. XX. 13. (5) Ibid. XI, 21. *Footmen* is in Hebrew *ragli* which can also mean 'for my sake'. (6) [On which Moses was cast into the Sea.] (7) The first month in the Jewish year. It was on that day later on that the Egyptians were drowned. (8) The third month, the date of the Revelation. (9) The twelfth month. (10) The difference between the two dates is only one month and fourteen days. (11) When a thirteenth month is inserted between Adar and Nisan. (12) This gives in round figures the three months required. (13) Ex. II, 7.

that they handed Moses about to all the Egyptian women but he would not suck. He[1] said, Shall a mouth which will speak with the *Shechinah* suck what is unclean! That is what is written, *Whom will He teach knowledge* etc.?[2]—To whom will He teach knowledge and to whom will He make the message understandable? *To them that are weaned from the milk, and drawn from the breasts.*

And Pharaoh's daughter said unto her, Go etc.[3] R. Eleazar said: It teaches that she went quickly like a young woman.[4] R. Samuel b. Naḥmani said: [She is called] *the maid* [*'almah*] because she made the words secret.[5]

And Pharaoh's daughter said unto her, Take this child away.[6] R. Ḥama b. Ḥanina said: She prophesied without knowing what she prophesied—*Heliki* ['take away']—behold what is thine [*ha sheliki*].

And I will give thee thy wages.[6] R. Ḥama b. Ḥanina said: Not enough that the righteous have their loss restored to them but they also receive their reward in addition.

And Miriam the prophetess, the sister of Aaron, took etc.[7] The *'sister of Aaron'* and not the sister of Moses!—R. Amram said in the name of Rab, and according to others it was R. Naḥman who said in the name of Rab: It teaches that she prophesied while she yet was the sister of Aaron only[8] [13*a*] and said, 'My mother will bear a son who will be the saviour of Israel'. When Moses was born, the whole house was filled with light; and her father arose and kissed her upon her head, saying 'My daughter, thy prophecy has been fulfilled'; but when they cast him into the river, her father arose and smacked her upon her head, saying, 'Where, now, is thy prophecy!' That is what is written, *And his sister stood afar off to know what would be done to him*[9]—what would be the fate of her prophecy.

JOSEPH EARNED MERIT etc. Why the difference that first it is written, *And Joseph went up to bury his father, and with him went up all the servants of Pharaoh* etc.,[10] followed by, *And all the house of Joseph,*

(1) Some authorities explain 'He' as referring to God. (2) Isa. XXVIII, 9. (3) Ex. II, 8. (4) The word in the verse *'almah* 'maid' is connected with its analogous root in Aramaic which means 'to be vigorous'. (5) *'Alam* means 'to hide'; she did not disclose her relationship to the child. (6) Ex. II, 9. (7) Ibid. XV, 20. (8) Before Moses' birth. (9) Ibid. II, 4. (10) Gen. L, 7.

and his brethren, and his father's house,[1] and in the sequel it is written, *And Joseph returned into Egypt, he and his brethren,*[2] followed by, *And all that went up with him to bury his father?*—R. Joḥanan said: At first, before [the servants of Pharaoh] beheld the glory of the Israelites, they did not treat them with respect;[3] but in the sequel, when they beheld their glory, they treated them with respect. For it is written, *And they came to the threshing-floor of Atad;*[4] but is there a threshing-floor for brambles?—R. Abbahu said: It teaches that they surrounded Jacob's coffin with crowns like a threshing-floor which is surrounded with a hedge of brambles, because the sons of Esau, of Ishmael and of Keturah also came. A Tanna taught: They all came to wage war [against the Israelites]; but when they saw Joseph's crown hanging upon Jacob's coffin, they all took their crowns and hung them upon his coffin. A Tanna taught: Sixty-three crowns were hung upon Jacob's coffin.

And there they lamented with a very great and sore lamentation.[5] It has been taught: Even the horses and asses [joined in the lamentation]. When [the cortège] arrived at the Cave of Machpelah, Esau came and wished to prevent [the interment there], saying to them, *Mamre, Kiriath-arba, the same is Hebron*[6]—now R. Isaac has said, *Kiriath-arba* [is so called] because four couples [were buried there], viz. Adam and Eve, Abraham and Sarah, Isaac and Rebekah, and Jacob and Leah—[Jacob] had buried Leah in his portion and what remains belongs to me'. They replied to him, 'Thou didst sell it'. He said to them, 'Granted that I sold my birth-right, but did I sell my plain heir's right!' They replied, 'Yes, for it is written, *In my grave which I* [Jacob] *have digged for me*',[7] and R. Joḥanan has said in the name of R. Simeon b. Jehozadak: The word *kirah* [dig] means nothing else than 'sale' [*mekiraḥ*], and thus in the coast-towns they use *kirah* as a term for 'sale'.—He said to them, 'Produce a document

(1) Gen. L, 8. (2) Ibid. 14. The order of the procession is now reversed. (3) And proceeded in front of them. (4) Ibid. 10. As a common noun *'atad'* means 'brambles'. (5) Gen. L, 10. (6) Ibid. XXXV, 27. *Kiriath—'arba* is literally 'the burial of four'. He claimed that only four couples were to be buried there, and demanded the one remaining sepulchre for himself. The explanatory remark of R. Isaac is interpolated into Esau's words. (7) Ibid. L, 5.

[of sale] for me'. They replied to him, 'The document is in the land of Egypt. Who will go for it? Let Naphtali go, because he is swift as a hind'; for it is written, *Naphtali is a hind let loose, he giveth goodly words*[1]—R. Abbahu said: Read not '*goodly words*' [imre shefer] but *imre sefer* [words of a document]. Among those present was Ḥushim, a son of Dan, who was hard of hearing; so he asked them, 'What is happening?' They said to him, '[Esau] is preventing [the burial] until Naphtali returns from the land of Egypt'. He retorted, 'Is my grandfather to lie there in contempt until Naphtali returns from the land of Egypt!' He took a club and struck [Esau] on the head so that his eyes fell out and rolled to the feet of Jacob. Jacob opened his eyes and laughed; and that is what is written, *The righteous shall rejoice when he seeth the vengeance; he shall wash his feet in the blood of the wicked.*[2] At that time was the prophecy of Rebekah fulfilled, as it is written, *Why should I be bereaved of you both in one day?*[3] Although the death of the two of them did not occur on the one day, still their burial took place on the same day.—But if Joseph had not occupied himself with [Jacob's burial], would not his brethren have occupied themselves with it? Behold it is written, *For his sons carried him into the land of Canaan!*[4]—They said [among themselves], 'Leave him [to conduct the interment]; for the honour [of our father] will be greater [when it is conducted] by kings than by commoners'.

WHOM HAVE WE GREATER THAN JOSEPH etc.? Our Rabbis have taught: Come and see how beloved were the commandments by Moses our teacher; for whereas all the Israelites occupied themselves with the spoil, he occupied himself with the commandments, as it is said, *The wise in heart will receive commandments* etc.[5] But whence did Moses know the place where Joseph was buried?—It is related that Serah, daughter of Asher, was a survivor of that generation. Moses went to her and asked, 'Dost thou know where Joseph was buried?' She answered him, 'The Egyptians made a metal coffin for him which they fixed in the river Nile so that its

(1) Gen. XLIX, 21. (2) Ps. LVIII, 11. (3) Gen. XXVII, 45. (4) Ibid. L, 13. It is not stated that Joseph did this. (5) Prov. X, 8.

waters should be blessed'. Moses went and stood on the bank of the Nile and exclaimed, 'Joseph, Joseph! the time has arrived which the Holy One, blessed be He, swore, "I will deliver you", and the oath which thou didst impose upon the Israelites[1] has reached [the time of fulfilment]; if thou wilt shew thyself, well and good; otherwise, behold, we are free of thine oath'. Immediately Joseph's coffin floated [on the surface of the water]. Be not astonished that iron should float; for, behold, it is written, *As one was felling a beam, the axe-head fell into the water* etc. *Alas, my master, for it was borrowed. And the man of God said, Where fell it? And he shewed him the place. And he cut down a stick and cast it in thither, and made the iron to swim.*[2] Now cannot the matter be argued by *a fortiori* reasoning—if iron floated on account of Elisha who was the disciple of Elijah who was the disciple of Moses, how much more so on account of Moses our teacher! R. Nathan says: He was buried in the sepulchre of the kings; and Moses went and stood by the sepulchre of the kings and exclaimed, 'Joseph! the time has arrived which the Holy One, blessed be He, swore "I will deliver you", and the oath which thou didst impose upon the Israelites has reached [the time of fulfilment]; if thou wilt shew thyself, well and good; otherwise, behold, we are free of thine oath'. At that moment, Joseph's coffin shook, and Moses took it and carried it with him. All those years that the Israelites were in the wilderness, those two chests, one of the dead and the other of the *Shechinah*,[3] proceeded side by side, and passers-by used to ask, 'What is the nature of those two chests?' They received the reply, 'One is of the dead and the other of the *Shechinah*'. 'But is it, then, the way of the dead to proceed with the *Shechinah*?' They were told, [13*b*] 'This one [Joseph] fulfilled all that was written in the other'.[4] But if Moses had not occupied himself with him, would not the Israelites have occupied themselves with him? Behold, it is written, *And the bones of Joseph which the children of Israel brought up out of Egypt buried they in Shechem!*[5]

(1) To carry Joseph's bones out of Egypt (Exod. XIII, 19). (2) II Kings VI, 5f. (3) *Aron* means in Hebrew both an ark and a coffin. It here refers to the Ark of the Covenant. (4) The Ark contained the tables of the Decalogue. (5) Josh. XXIV, 32.

Furthermore, if the Israelites had not occupied themselves with him, would not his own sons have done so? And, behold, it is written, *And they became the inheritance of the children of Joseph!*[1] —They[2] said [to one another], 'Leave him; his honour will be greater [when the burial is performed] by many rather than by few'; and they also said, 'Leave him; his honour will be greater [when the burial is performed] by the great rather than by the small'.

Buried they in Shechem.[1] Why just in Shechem?—R. Ḥama son of R. Ḥanina said, From Shechem they stole him,[3] and to Shechem we will restore what is lost. The following verses are contradictory: it is written, *And* Moses *took the bones of Joseph with him,*[4] and it is written, *And the bones of Joseph which* the children of Israel *brought up*[5] etc.!—R. Ḥama son of R. Ḥanina said: Whoever performs a task without finishing it and another comes and completes it, Scripture ascribes it to the one who completed it as though he had performed it. R. Eleazar said: He[6] is likewise deposed from his greatness; for it is written, *And it came to pass at that time that Judah went* down.[7] R. Samuel b. Naḥmani said: He also buries his wife and children; for it is written, *Shua's daughter, the wife of Judah, died* etc.,[8] and it is written, *But Er and Onan died.*[9]

Rab Judah said in the name of Rab: Why was Joseph called 'bones' during his lifetime?[10] Because he did not interfere to safeguard his father's honour when [his brothers] said to him, *Thy servant our father*[11] and he made no reply to them. Rab Judah also said in the name of Rab, and others declare that it was R. Ḥama son of R. Ḥanina: Why did Joseph die before his brothers? Because he gave himself superior airs.

And Joseph was brought down to Egypt.[12] R. Eleazar said: Read not '*was brought down*' but '*brought down*', because he brought Pharaoh's astrologers down from their eminence.[13] *And Potiphar, an officer of*

(1) Josh. XXIV, 32. (2) Joseph's sons. (3) His brothers. Cf. Gen. XXXVII, 12. (4) Ex. XIII, 19. (5) Josh. XXIV, 32. (6) Viz., he who does not finish his undertaking. (7) Gen. XXXVIII, 1, i.e. descended from his greatness, because he began to rescue Joseph but did not complete it. (8) Ibid. 12. (9) Ibid. XLVI, 12. They were Judah's sons. (10) Cf. L, 25. (11) Ibid. XLIV, 31. (12) Ibid. XXXIX, 1. (13) He interpreted the dreams which baffled them.

Pharaoh's bought him, Rab said: He bought him for himself;[1] but Gabriel came and castrated him,[2] and then Gabriel came and mutilated him [*pera'*], for originally his name is written Potiphar but afterwards Potiphera.[3]

WHOM HAVE WE GREATER THAN MOSES etc. *And the Lord said unto me, Let it suffice thee.*[4] R. Levi said: With the word '*suffice*' [Moses] made an announcement and with the word '*suffice*' an announcement was made to him. With the word '*suffice*' he made an announcement: '*Suffice you*';[5] and with the word '*suffice*' an announcement was made to him: '*Let it suffice thee*'. Another explanation of '*Let it suffice* [rab] *thee*' is, Thou hast a master [*rab*], viz., Joshua.[6] Another explanation of '*Let it suffice thee*' is, That people should not say, How severe the Master is and how persistent the pupil is.[7] And why so? In the School of R. Ishmael it was taught, According to the camel is the burden.[8]

And he said unto them, I am an hundred and twenty years old this day.[9] Why does the text state '*this day?*' [The meaning is], This day are my days and years completed.[10] Its purpose is to teach you that the Holy One, blessed be He, completes the years of the righteous from day to day, and from month to month; for it is written, *The number of thy days I will fulfil.*[11] *I can no more go out and come in*[9]—what means '*go out and come in*'? If it is to be understand literally, behold it is written, *And Moses was an hundred and twenty years old when he died; his eye was not dim, nor his natural force abated;*[12] it is also written, *And Moses went up from the plains of Moab unto mount Nebo;*[13] and it has been taught: Twelve steps were there, but Moses mounted them in one stride!—R. Samuel b. Naḥmani said in the name of R. Jonathan: [It means] to '*go out and come in*' with words of Torah, thus indicating that the gates of wisdom were closed against him.

(1) For an immoral purpose, being inflamed by Joseph's beauty. (2) The word Hebrew for '*officer*' also means eunuch. (3) Cf. Gen. XLI, 45. (4) Deut. III, 26. (5) Num. XVI, 3. (6) The meaning is that his leadership was coming to an end and Joshua was about to succeed him. (7) Do not petition Me more, lest the people make reflections on My nature. (8) God is stricter with the righteous because their faith will stand the test. (9) Deut. XXXI, 2. (10) It was his birthday. (11) Ex. XXIII, 26. (12) Deut. XXXIV, 7. (13) Ibid. 1.

And Moses and Joshua went, and presented themselves in the tent of meeting.[1] A Tanna taught: That was a Sabbath when two teachers [gave discourses] and the authority was taken from one to be transferred to the other. It has further been taught: R. Judah said: Were it not for a Scriptural text, it would be impossible to utter the following. Where did Moses die? In the portion of Reuben, for it is written, *And Moses went up from the plains of Moab unto mount Nebo,* and Nebo was located in the portion of Reuben, for it is written, *And the children of Reuben built ... and Nebo* etc.[2]—It was called Nebo because three prophets [*nebi'im*] died there, viz. Moses, Aaron, and Miriam.—And where was Moses buried? In the portion of Gad, for it is written, *And he provided the first part for himself* etc.[3] Now what was the distance between the portion of Reuben and that of Gad? Four *mil.*[4] Who carried him those four *mil?* It teaches that Moses was laid upon the wings of the *Shechinah,* and the Ministering Angels kept proclaiming, *He executed the justice of the Lord, and His judgments with Israel,*[5] and the Holy One, blessed be He, declared, *Who will rise up for Me against the evil-doers? Who will stand up for Me against the workers of iniquity?*[6]

Samuel[7] said [that God declared], *Who is as the wise man? and who knoweth the interpretation of a thing?*[8] R. Joḥanan said [that God declared], *Where shall wisdom be found?*[9] R. Naḥman said [that God announced], *So Moses died there* etc.[10] Semalyon[11] said, *So Moses died there,* the great Sage of Israel.[12]

It has been taught: R. Eliezer the Elder said: Over an area of twelve *mil* square, corresponding to that of the camp of Israel, a *Bath Ḳol* made the proclamation, '*So Moses died there*', the great Sage

(1) Deut. XXXI, 14. (2) Num. XXXII, 37f. (3) Deut. XXXIII, 21. It continues, *For there was the lawgiver's portion reserved.* (4) A *mil* equalled 2,000 cubits, or 3,000 feet. (5) Ibid. (6) Ps. XCIV, 16. I.e., now that Moses is dead. (7) The Rabbi of that name. (8) Eccl. VIII, 1. (9) Job XXVIII, 12. (10) Deut. XXXIV, 5. (11) Rashi explains it as the name of a wise man. Others take it as the designation of an angel who made the proclamation, v. *Aruch.* (12) [רבא ספרא. Lit., 'the Great Scribe'. Moses is so designated because he wrote the Torah (Maharsha). Krauss, S., (*Hagoren*, VII, p. 32ff) attempts to connect this appellation with the mythological idea of a heavenly Scribe by the side of the Deity determining the fate of nations and individuals].

of Israel. Others declare that Moses never died; it is written here, '*So Moses died there*', and elsewhere it is written, *And he was there with the Lord.*[1] As in the latter passage it means standing and ministering, so also in the former it means standing and ministering.

And He buried him in the valley in the land of Moab over against Beth-peor.[2] R. Berechyah said: Although [Scripture provides] a clue within a clue, nevertheless *no man knoweth of his sepulchre.*[2] The wicked Government once sent to [14*a*] the governor[3] of Beth-peor [the message], 'Shew us where Moses is buried'. When they stood above, it appeared to them to be below; when they were below, it appeared to them to be above. They divided themselves into two parties; to them who were standing above it appeared below, and to those who were below it appeared above. This is in fulfilment of what is said, '*No man knoweth of his sepulchre*'. R. Ḥama son of R. Ḥanina said: Even Moses our teacher does not know where he is buried; it is written here, '*No man knoweth of his sepulchre*', and it is written elsewhere, *And this is the blessing wherewith Moses the man of God blessed.*[4] R. Ḥama son of R. Ḥanina also said: Why was Moses buried near Beth-peor? To atone for the incident at Peor.[5]

R. Ḥama son of R. Ḥanina further said: What means the text, *Ye shall walk after the Lord your God?*[6] Is it, then, possible for a human being to walk after the *Shechinah;* for has it not been said, *For the Lord thy God is a devouring fire?*[7] But [the meaning is] to walk after the attributes of the Holy One, blessed be He. As He clothes the naked, for it is written, *And the Lord God made for Adam and for his wife coats of skin, and clothed them,*[8] so do thou also clothe the naked. The Holy One, blessed be He, visited the sick, for it is written, *And the Lord appeared unto him by the oaks of Mamre,*[9] so do

(1) Ex. XXXIV, 28. The word *there* is common to both verses. (2) Deut. XXXIV, 6. (3) This is Rashi's explanation of the word *gasṭera*. Goldschmidt, accepting it, identifies it with the latin *quaestor;* but Jastrow and Krauss render 'camp', connecting it with *castra*. (4) Ibid. XXXIII, 1. The word '*man*' is common to both passages. (5) V. Num. XXV, 1ff. (6) Deut. XIII, 5. (7) Ibid. IV, 24. (8) Gen. III, 21. (9) Ibid. XVIII, 1. Since the preceding verses deal with Abraham's circumcision, it is deduced that the occasion was when he was recovering.

thou also visit the sick. The Holy One, blessed be He, comforted mourners, for it is written, *And it came to pass after the death of Abraham, that God blessed Isaac his son,*[1] so do thou also comfort mourners. The Holy one, blessed be He, buried the dead, for it is written, *And He buried him in the valley,*[2] so do thou also bury the dead.

'*Coats of skin*'—Rab and Samuel [differ in their interpretation]; one said that it means a material that grows from the skin, and the other a material from which the [human] skin derives pleasure.[3]

R. Simlai expounded: Torah begins with an act of benevolence[4] and ends with an act of benevolence. It begins with an act of benevolence, for it is written, *And the Lord God made for Adam and for his wife coats of skin, and clothed them;*[5] and it ends with an act of benevolence, for it is written, '*And He buried him in the valley*'.

R. Simlai expounded: Why did Moses our teacher yearn to enter the land of Israel? Did he want to eat of its fruits or satisfy himself from its bounty? But thus spake Moses, 'Many precepts were commanded to Israel which can only be fulfilled in the land of Israel. I wish to enter the land so that they may all be fulfilled by me'. The Holy One, blessed be He, said to him, 'Is it only to receive the reward [for obeying the commandments] that thou seekest? I ascribe it to thee as if thou didst perform them'; as it is said, *Therefore will I divide him a portion with the great, and he shall divide the spoil with the strong; because he poured out his soul unto death, and was numbered with the transgressors; yet he bare the sins of many, and made intercession for the transgressors.*[6] '*Therefore will I divide him a portion with the great*'—it is possible [to think that his portion will be] with the [great of] later generations and not former generations; therefore there is a text to declare, '*And he shall divide with the strong*', i.e., with Abraham, Isaac and Jacob who were strong in Torah and the commandments. '*Because he poured out his soul unto death*'—because

(1) Gen. XXV, 11. (2) Deut. XXXIV, 6. (3) I.e., wool and linen respectively. (4) [*Gemiluth ḥasadim*, lit., 'doing deeds of loving kindness'. The inner meaning of the phrase is 'making good', 'requiting'—a making good to man for the goodness of God and it is connected with tenderness and mercy to all men and all classes. V. J. Pe'ah. IV.] (5) Gen. III, 21. (6) Isa. LIII, 12.

he surrendered himself to die, as it is said, *And if not, blot me, I pray thee* etc.[1] '*And was numbered with the transgressors*'—because he was numbered with them who were condemned to die in the wilderness. '*Yet he bare the sins of many*'—because he secured atonement for the making of the Golden Calf. '*And made intercession for the transgressors*'—because he begged for mercy on behalf of the sinners in Israel that they should turn in penitence; and the word *pegi'ah* ['*intercession*'] means nothing else than prayer, as it is said, *Therefore pray not thou for this people, neither lift up cry nor prayer for them, neither make intercession to Me.*[2]

(1) Ex. XXXII, 32. (2) Jer. VII, 16. [It is suggested that the application of these verses to Moses was a tacit parrying of the use made of that passage by Christian apologists. V. Moore, *Judaism III*, p. 166, n. 254.]

SOṬAH

CHAPTER II

MISHNAH. [THE HUSBAND] BRINGS HER MEAL-OFFERING[1] IN A BASKET OF PALM-TWIGS AND PLACES IT UPON HER HANDS IN ORDER TO WEARY HER. WITH ALL OTHER MEAL-OFFERINGS, THE BEGINNING AND END OF THEIR [SACRIFICE] ARE IN MINISTERING VESSELS; BUT WITH THIS, ITS BEGINNING IS IN A BASKET OF PALM-TWIGS AND ITS END IN A MINISTERING VESSEL. ALL OTHER MEAL-OFFERINGS REQUIRE OIL AND FRANKINCENSE, BUT THIS REQUIRES NEITHER OIL NOR FRANKINCENSE. ALL OTHER MEAL-OFFERINGS CONSIST OF WHEAT, BUT THIS CONSISTS OF BARLEY. THE MEAL-OFFERING OF THE 'OMER[2], ALTHOUGH CONSISTING OF BARLEY, WAS IN THE FORM OF GROATS; BUT THIS WAS IN THE FORM OF COARSE FLOUR. RABBAN GAMALIEL SAYS: AS HER ACTIONS WERE THE ACTIONS OF AN ANIMAL, SO HER OFFERING [CONSISTED OF] ANIMAL'S FODDER.

GEMARA. It has been taught: Abba Ḥanin says in the name of R. Eliezer: What is the purpose [of placing the basket upon her hands]? In order to weary her so that she may retract.[3] If the Torah has such consideration[4] for them who transgress His will, how much more so for them who perform His will. But whence is it [known that the object of this regulation is] to show consideration; perhaps it is to avoid [the Divine Name on] the scroll being obliterated? —He is of the opinion [14b] that she is first given the water to drink and then the offering is sacrificed,[5] so that if it be [suggested that

(1) Num. V, 15. (2) Lev. II, 14. The Talmud (Men. 68*b*) argues that it consisted of barley. (3) And confess, if guilty. (4) In its endeavour to make the woman avoid the serious consequences of drinking the water. (5) This question is discussed *infra* 19*a*. The effects of the water take place only after the offering of the meal-offering.

the reason is] because of the scroll, [the writing] has already been obliterated.

WITH ALL OTHER MEAL-OFFERINGS etc. The following is quoted in contradiction: How is the procedure of meal-offerings? A man brings a meal-offering from his house[1] in silver or golden baskets, places it in a ministering vessel, hallows it in a ministering vessel, adds to it its oil and frankincense, and carries it to a priest who carries it to the altar and brings it near unto the south-west corner opposite the point of the altar's horn, and that suffices. He then moves the frankincense to one side [of the vessel], takes a handful [of the flour] from a place where its oil is abundant, sets it in a ministering vessel, hallows it in a ministering vessel, gathers its frankincense and places it on the top thereof, and sets it upon the altar and fumigates it in a ministering vessel. He next salts [the handful of flour] and sets it upon the fire. When the handful has been offered, the remainder may be eaten, and the priests are allowed to mix it with wine, oil and honey, and are only forbidden to make it leaven.[2] Now here it is taught that [meal-offerings are brought only] in silver or golden baskets![3]—R. Papa said: The correct version [of the Mishnah] is: in vessels which are proper to be used as ministering vessels. It therefore follows that a basket of palm-twigs is not proper to be used as a vessel. This would not agree with the view of R. Jose son of R. Judah; for it has been taught: As regards a ministering vessel of wood, Rabbi disqualifies it but R. Jose son of R. Judah allows it!—If you wish you may say that it is in accord even with the view of R. Jose son of R. Judah, because he is referring to [wooden vessels which are] valuable, but does he say that with regard to [wooden vessels which are] inferior![4] Does R. Jose son of R. Judah not hold with the text, *Present it now unto thy governor?*[5]

'Places it in a ministering vessel and hallows it in a ministering vessel'. Is the conclusion to be drawn from this that the ministering

(1) To the Temple-court. (2) V. Tosefta Men. I, 16f. The whole passage is explained anon. (3) And not in ministering vessels as taught in the Mishnah. (4) E.g., of palm-twigs. (5) Mal. I, 8. The context is a denunciation of offering inferior animals. The same rule applies to vessels used in the Temple.

vessels only hallow when such is the intention![1]—The correct version is: places it in a ministering vessel in order to hallow it in a ministering vessel. 'Adds to it its oil and frankincense'; as it is said, *He shall pour oil upon it, and put frankincense thereon.*[2] 'And carries it to a priest'; for it is written, *And he shall bring it to Aaron's sons* etc.[3] 'Who carries it to the altar'; for it is written, *And he shall bring it unto the altar.*[4] Brings it near unto the south-west corner opposite the point of the altar's horn, and that suffices'. Whence is this?—For it is written, *And this is the law of the meal-offering: the sons of Aaron shall offer it before the Lord, before the altar;*[5] and it has been taught: '*Before the Lord*'—it is possible [to think that this means] on the west [side of the altar],[6] therefore the text declares, '*Before the altar*'.[7] If [Scripture only had] '*before the altar*', it is possible [to think that this means] on the south side, therefore the text declares, '*Before the Lord*'. So what was the procedure? He sets it on the south-west corner opposite the point of the altar's horn, and that suffices. R. Eleazar says: It is possible [to think that the meaning is] he sets it on the west of the horn or the south of the horn; but you can answer, Wherever you find two texts, one self-confirmatory and confirming the words of the other, whereas the second is self-confirmatory but annuls the words of the other, we abandon the latter and accept the former. Thus when you emphasize '*before the Lord*' on the west [side of the altar],[8] you annul '*before the altar*' on the south side;[9] but when you emphasize '*before the altar*' on the south side,[8] you confirm '*before the Lord*' on the west side.[8] What, then, is the procedure? He brings it on the south of the horn. But how do you confirm it?[10]—R. Ashi

(1) On this there is a difference of opinion, one being that the vessels automatically hallow their contents, v. Men. 7a. (2) Lev. II, 1. This is done by the person who presents the offering. (3) Ibid. 2. (4) Ibid. 8. (5) Ibid. VI, 7, E.V. 14. (6) Since this side faced the Holy of Holies which was located in the west of the Temple-area. (7) Lit., '*before the face of the altar*'. I.e., the face of the altar which was towards the south. [Since the north side of the altar was designated '*the side*' ירך, i.e., the rear (v. Lev. I. 11) the *face* of the altar must denote the south side.] (8) V. note 6. (9) V. note 7. (10) If the meal-offering is to be brought to the south side of the altar, it is not opposite the entrance of the Sanctuary, which is on the West.

said: This Tanna holds that the whole of the altar stood in the north.[1]

What means 'and that suffices'?[2]—R. Ashi said: It was necessary [to mention this], because otherwise it may have occurred to me to say that the bringing of the meal-offering itself [to the altar without the ministering vessel] is required. Consequently we are informed [that the contrary is the correct procedure]. But say that it is really so [and the ministering vessel is not necessary]!—The text states, *And it shall be presented unto the priest, and he shall bring it unto the altar*[3]—as the presentation to the priest is in a [ministering] vessel, so also the bringing to the altar must be in a [ministering] vessel.

'He then moves the frankincense to one side [of the vessel]', so that none of it may be included in the handful taken of the meal-offering; as we have learnt: If, when he took a handful, there came into his hand a pebble or particle of salt or grain of frankincense, it is disqualified.[4] 'Takes a handful [of flour] from a place where its oil is abundant'—whence is this? For it is written, *Of the fine flour thereof and of the oil thereof;*[5] *of the bruised corn thereof and of the oil thereof.*[6] 'Sets it in a ministering vessel and hallows it in a ministering vessel'—for what purpose, since he has already hallowed it once?—It is analogous to the case of blood: although the knife[7] hallows it in the animal's neck, [the priest] again hallows it in a ministering vessel;[8] so here, too, there is no difference. 'Gathers its frankincense and places it on the top thereof'; for it is written, *And all the frankincense which is upon the meal-offering.*[9] 'And sets it upon the altar [15a] and fumigates it in a ministering vessel'. He fumigates it in a ministering vessel' [you say]![10]—The correct version is: and sets it upon the altar in a ministering vessel to fumigate it.

(1) Of the Temple-area. So that the south of the altar faced the entrance of the Sanctuary and is thus described as *'before the Lord'*. (2) What else could he think was necessary? (3) Lev. II, 8. (4) As not being a complete handful. (5) Ibid. 2. (6) Ibid. 16. (7) Which is regarded as a utensil of the Sanctuary. (8) I.e., the basin in which the blood is received. (9) Lev. VI, 8, E.V. 15. (10) [Surely the fumigation does not take place at this stage! Rashi deletes the words 'in a ministering vessel', as the question is concerned only with the act of fumigation].

He next salts [the handful of flour] and sets it upon the fire'; for it is written, *And every oblation of thy meal-offering shalt thou season with salt.*[1] 'When the handful has been offered, the remainder may be eaten'. Whence is this?—For it is written, *And the priest shall burn the memorial of it* etc.,[2] and it is written, *And that which is left of the meal-offering shall be Aaron's and his sons'.*[3] 'When the handful has been offered etc.'—this[4] is differently explained by two teachers; for it has been reported: From what time does the taking of the 'handful' render the eating of the remainder permissible? R. Ḥanina says, When the fire takes hold of it; R. Joḥanan said, When the fire burns the greater part of it. 'And the priests are allowed to mix it with wine, oil and honey'—for what reason? The text states, *By reason of the anointing,*[5] i.e., as a mark of eminence, in the same manner as kings take their food. 'And are only forbidden to make it leaven'; for it is written, *It shall not be baked with leaven, their portion*[6]—R. Simeon b. Laḳish says: [It means] that even their portion must not be baked with leaven.

WITH ALL OTHER MEAL-OFFERINGS etc. But do all other meal-offerings[7] require oil and frankincense? Behold, there is the meal-offering of the sinner concerning which the All-Merciful said, *He shall put no oil upon it, neither shall he put any frankincense thereon!*[8]—This is what he intends: All other meal-offerings require oil and frankincense, and consist of wheat in the form of fine flour; but the meal-offering of the sinner, although it does not require oil and frankincense, consists of wheat in the form of fine-flour; the meal-offering of the *'omer,* although it consists of barley, requires oil and frankincense and is in the form of groats; but this one [of the suspected woman] does not require oil and frankincense, and consists of barley in the form of coarse flour.

It has been taught: R. Simeon said: It is right that the meal-offering of a sinner should require oil and frankincense, so that a sinner should not gain;[9] why, then, are they not required? That his

(1) Lev. II, 13. (2) Ibid. 16. (3) Ibid. 10. (4) The meaning of the term *offered* used in this connection. (5) Num. XVIII, 8. Anointing occurred at the induction of a priest and a king. (6) Lev. VI, 10. (7) With the exception of that of the suspected woman. (8) Ibid. V, 11. (9) By being spared the cost of these ingredients.

offering should not be luxurious. It is also right that an ordinary sin-offering[1] should require drink-offerings, so that a sinner should not gain; why, then, are they not required? That his offering should not be luxurious. The sin-offering of a leper, however, and his trespass-offering do require drink-offerings because they are not due to sin. But that is not so; for, behold R. Samuel b. Naḥmani said in the name of R. Jonathan: On account of seven faults does the plague of leprosy occur etc.![2]—In this case he received atonement [of his sin] by the plague[3] he suffered; and when he brings an offering, it is only to allow him to participate in what is holy.[4] According to this conclusion, the sin-offering of a Nazirite should require drink-offerings, since it is not due to a sin! He holds with R. Eliezer ha-Ḳappar who said, A Nazirite is also a sinner.[5]

RABBAN GAMALIEL SAYS, AS etc. It has been taught: Rabban Gamaliel[6] said to the Sages: Learned men, permit me to explain this allegorically.[7] [15b] He had heard R. Meir say, She fed him with the dainties of the world; therefore her offering is animal's fodder.[8] Then said he to him, You may be right about a rich woman, but what of a poor woman! But [the reason is], As her actions were the action of an animal, so her offering [consisted of] animal's fodder.

MISHNAH. [THE PRIEST] TAKES AN EARTHENWARE BOWL AND POURS HALF A LOG OF WATER INTO IT FROM THE LAVER. R. JUDAH SAYS: A QUARTER [OF A LOG]. JUST AS [R.

(1) Lit., 'sin-offering of (forbidden) fat', because the words *ye shall eat neither fat nor blood* (Lev. III, 16) are followed by Chap. IV which deals with the sin-offering. (2) Enumerated in 'Ar. 16*a*, v. Shebu. 8*a*. (3) Suffering, according to the Rabbis, is a means of atonement. (4) The offerings were purificatory in their intention, and unlike an ordinary sin-offering, which is brought in expiation. (5) Because he abstained from wine. V. Naz. 22*a*. (6) [Apparently Gamaliel III, the son of R. Judah ha-Nasi, a contemporary of R. Meir; v. Chayes. Z.H., *notes;* and Lauterbach, *JQR* (N.S.), I, p. 514, where the whole passage is discussed. V. also Wahrmann, *Untersuchungen*, I, p. 26ff.] (7) כמין חמר For the term here used, v. Lauterbach *op. cit.* I 291ff., 503ff, especially p. 509 and Ḳid. 22*b*. (8) V. *supra* p. 75.

JUDAH] REDUCES THE AMOUNT OF WRITING,[1] SO HE REDUCES THE QUANTITY OF WATER. [THE PRIEST] ENTERS THE TEMPLE AND TURNS RIGHT. THERE WAS A PLACE THERE A CUBIT SQUARE IN EXTENT WITH A MARBLE TABLET, TO WHICH A RING WAS ATTACHED. HE LIFTS THIS OUT, TAKES SOME DUST FROM BENEATH IT WHICH HE PUTS [INTO THE BOWL] JUST SUFFICIENT TO BE VISIBLE ABOVE THE WATER; AS IT IS SAID, AND OF THE DUST THAT IS ON THE FLOOR OF THE TABERNACLE THE PRIEST SHALL TAKE, AND PUT IT INTO THE WATER.[2]

GEMARA. A Tanna taught: [The priest takes] a new earthenware bowl—such is the opinion of R. Ishmael. What is R. Ishmael's reason?[3]—He derives it from the common use of the word '*vessel*' [here and in the law] of a leper. As with the latter new earthenware was required, so here likewise was new earthenware required. Whence is it that there [with a leper it must be new]?—For it is written, *And the priest shall command to kill one of the birds in an earthen vessel over running water*[4]—as it must be running water which has not been previously used, so also it must be a vessel which has not been previously used. According to this argument, as there [with a leper] it had to be running water, so also here [with a suspected woman] it had to be running water!—In the view of R. Ishmael that is indeed so; for R. Johanan said the water from the laver[5] was according to R. Ishmael spring-water, and the Sages declare that it can be ordinary water. It may, however, be objected [to this argument] that as with a leper it is necessary to have cedar wood, hyssop and scarlet,[6] [so are these required with the water of bitterness]![7]—Rabbah said: The text mentions *in an earthen vessel,*[8] i.e., a vessel to which I referred previously.[9]

(1) V. next Mishnah, p. 87. (2) Num. V, 17. (3) For requiring a *new* bowl. (4) Lev. XIV, 5. (5) [Which water was used for the water of bitterness.] (6) V. ibid. 4. (7) The Torah does not require these things, and so the analogy is false. (8) [And not 'he shall take a vessel and put in it etc.'] (9) Viz., in the law of the leper. Hence it is established that a new vessel is also necessary in the ceremony of the water of bitterness.

Raba said: [The Rabbis in our Mishnah] did not teach [that a used vessel may be employed] except when its exterior is not blackened [by smoke]; but if its exterior is blackened it is unfit for use. What is their reason?—It is analogous to the water: just as the water must not be changed in appearance,[1] so also the vessel must not be changed in appearance. Raba asked, How is it if the earthenware had been blackened and re-whitened by being passed through the furnace again? Do we say that since it has once been rejected, it remains rejected; or perhaps, since it has been restored, it is suitable?—Come and hear: 'R. Eleazar says: If a man twisted cedar wood, scarlet and hyssop into a cord for the purpose of carrying his bundle on his back, they are unfit [to be used in the ceremony of purification];' and yet they are here again smoothed out![2] But in that case we suppose that [some of the material] has been peeled off.[3]

[THE PRIEST] ENTERS THE TEMPLE AND TURNS RIGHT etc. For what reason? Because a Master has declared, All the turns which thou dost make must only be to the right.

THERE WAS A PLACE THERE A CUBIT etc. Our Rabbis have taught: '*And of the dust that is* etc.'—it is possible to think that [the priest] may prepare [dust] from outside and bring it in; therefore there is a text to state, '*On the floor of the tabernacle*'. If '*on the floor of the tabernacle*', it is possible to think that he may dig for it with an axe; therefore there is a text to state '*that is*'. How was it done? If [dust] is there, take of it; if none is there, put some there [and take of it]. Another [Baraitha] taught: '*And of the dust that is*'—this teaches that he prepares some from outside and brings it in. '*On the floor of the tabernacle*'—Issi b. Judah says: It includes the floor [16a] [of the Tabernacle] in Shiloh, Nob, Gideon and the permanent Temple; Issi b. Menaḥem says: It is unnecessary [to include the permanent Temple];[4] if in the case of a minor defile-

(1) Although they do not insist on running water, it must not be discoloured by dirt. (2) When they are disconnected. So by analogy the earthenware cannot be made fit for use by re-whitening. (3) While it was used as a cord; therefore the restoration is not complete. But in the case of the vessel there is complete restoration and so it is allowed. (4) In Jerusalem.

ment[1] Scripture does not differentiate [between the temporary Tabernacle and the permanent Temple], in the case of the defilement of a married woman[2] how much more so [is it unnecessary to differentiate]. Why, then, does the text state *'on the floor of the tabernacle'*? He may not take it from the midst of a heap.[3]

The following question was asked: If there is no dust, how is it about putting ashes there? According to the view of Beth Shammai, the question does not arise because they said that we never find ashes called dust; but the question does arise according to the view of Beth Hillel because they said that we do find ashes called dust.[4] How is it then? Although the word *'dust'* is used, it is here written *'on the floor of the tabernacle'*;[5] perhaps, however, the phrase *'on the floor of the tabernacle'* is intended to be understood according to the interpretation of Issi b. Judah and Issi b. Menaḥem?[6] —Come and hear: for R. Joḥanan said in the name of R. Ishmael: In three places the *halachah* crushes the Scriptural text under heel:[7] the Torah states *with dust,*[8] whereas the *halachah* allows [the blood to be covered] with anything; the Torah states *no razor,*[9] whereas the legal decision is [that a Nazirite may not shave] with anything; the Torah states *a book,*[10] whereas the legal decision [allows] any [form of document]. Now if this[11] is so, it should also have been enumerated!—He taught [some instances] and omitted others. What else, then, did he omit?[12]—He omitted [the shaving] of a leper;[13] for it has been taught: *And it shall be on the seventh day tha*

(1) I.e., entrance into the Temple-precincts while ritually unclean. This is not an offence punished by a Court with death. (2) Which is a capital crime. (3) It must first be scattered on the floor. [In contradiction to the second Baraitha cited which permits the bringing in dust from elsewhere and putting it forthwith into the water]. (4) This matter, with reference to covering the blood after slaughter of an animal, is discussed in Ḥul. 88*b*. (5) So it is impossible to think that ashes could be meant. (6) If these words intend the inclusion of temporary Sanctuaries and the Temple, then *'dust'* could here signify ashes. (7) I.e., practice goes beyond the letter of the Torah. (8) Lev. XVII, 13. (9) Num. VI, 5. (10) So literally, of a letter of divorcement (Deut. XXIV, 1). (11) The use of ashes instead of dust. (12) [He would not in enumeration just stop short at one point.] (13) This refers to the second act of shaving. The leper was shaved twice; see Lev. XIV, 8 and 9.

he shall shave all his hair—that is a generalization; *off his head and his beard and his eyebrows*—that is a particularization; *even all his hair he shall shave off*[1]—that is again a generalization. Now [the rule of exegesis is]: when there is a general proposition, followed by the enumeration of particulars, and this is followed by a general proposition, include only that which resembles the particulars.[2] As the particulars refer to a part [of the body] where the hair grows and is visible, so every place where the hair grows and is visible [comes within the scope of the law]. What does it include? It includes the hair on the private part. What does it exclude? It excludes that of the arm-pit and the whole body [which is normally covered]. The *halachah*, however, is: he shaves himself as smooth as a gourd.[3] For we have learnt: When [the priest] comes to shave the leper, he passes a razor over all his flesh;[4] and it continues,[5] On the seventh day he shaves[6] the second shaving after the manner of the first.[7] R. Naḥman b. Isaac said: [R. Joḥanan] enumerated instances where the *halachah* crushes the Scriptural text under heel; but here it crushes a Rabbinical te ching[8] under heel.[9] R. Papa said: [R. Joḥanan] enumerated instances where the *halachah* crushes the Scriptural text under heel and overthrows it; but here it crushes the text under heel and extends it.[10] R. Ashi said: According to whom is this teaching [that only the visible parts of the body are to be shaved]? It is R. Ishmael who expounds [the Torah] by the rule of generalization and particularization.[11] [16*b*] According to whom [is the teaching that he must be shaved the second time] as smooth as a gourd? It is R. Akiba who expounds [the Torah] by the rule of amplification and limitation; for it has been taught: '*And*

(1) Lev. XIV, 9. (2) V. Shebu (Sonc. ed.) p. 13, n. 3. (3) I.e., all over his body. (4) Neg. XIV. 2. (5) Ibid 3. (6) [This is a reading of Rashi which is preferable to that of the cur. edd: '*on the seventh day he shall shave*', as this is a quotation of Neg. XIV. 3.] (7) Over all the body. (8) [A teaching derived from Rabbinic exegesis. MS.M. reads 'Midrash'; v. Chajes, Z.H. ntes.] (9) And therefore R. Joḥanan's list of three cases is complete. (10) [By shaving the whole body the demands of the text are not set aside but extended.] (11) He elaborated thirteen rules of interpretation, and that quoted above is one of them. [And so according to R. Ishmael in whose name the above enumeration was reported by R. Joḥanan the list is complete].

it shall be on the seventh day that he shall shave all his hair'—that is an amplification; *'off his head and his beard and his eyebrows'*—that is a limitation; *'even all his hair he shall shave off'*—that is again an amplification. Now [the rule of exegesis is]: Where there is an amplification, followed by a limitation, and this is followed by an amplification, the amplification applies to the whole. In which respect is there an amplification? It includes all the body [to be shaved]. In which respect is there a limitation? It excludes the hair which grows inside the nostril. How is it, then, with our original question [whether ashes may be used when there is no dust]?—Come and hear: For R. Huna b. Ashi said in the name of Rab: If there is no dust there, he brings decayed herbage and hallows it!—But this is no proof. Decayed herbage may indeed be [called] dust but not ashes.

JUST SUFFICIENT TO BE VISIBLE ABOVE THE WATER. Our Rabbis have taught: Three things must be visible, viz., the dust in the ceremony of the suspected woman, the ashes in the ceremony of the red heifer[1] and the spittle in the ceremony of *Ḥaliẓah*.[2] They said in the name of R. Ishmael, Also the blood of the bird.[3] What is R. Ishmael's reason?—Because it is written, *And shall dip them in the blood of the bird* etc.;[4] and it has been taught: *'in the blood'*—it is possible [to think that they must be dipped] in blood and not in water; therefore the text declares '[*over the running*] *water*'. If Scripture [had only mentioned] *'water'*, it would be possible [to think that they must be dipped] in water and not in blood; therefore the text declares *'in the blood'*. What, then, was the procedure? He brings water in which the blood of the bird is recognisable. What is the quantity? A quarter [of a *log*]. And [why is this instance not included in their enumeration by] the Rabbis?—That is part of the subject-matter; for thus said the All-Merciful, Dip in blood and water.[5] [How is this argument met by] R. Ishmael?—In that case, the All-Merciful should have written, 'And he shall dip in them'; so why [is it stated] in blood and in water? That [the blood] must be

(1) Num. XIX. (2) V. Glos. (3) Used in the purificatory rites of a leper. (4) Lev. XIV, 6. (5) So long as there is some blood in the water, even if it cannot be distinguished.

recognisable. And [how is this argument met by] the Rabbis?—If the All-Merciful had written, 'And he shall dip in them', I might have imagined [that he was to dip] in each separately; therefore He wrote 'in blood and in water' to indicate that they must be mixed. [How does] R. Ishmael [answer this point]? That they are to be mixed [is learnt from] another verse; it is written, *And kill one of the birds in an earthen vessel over running water.*[1] [How do] the Rabbis [answer this point]?—If [we had to learn it] from that passage, we might have thought that he is to kill it near a vessel, press the jugular veins,[2] and receive the blood in another vessel. Hence we are informed [by this verse that the killing must be done over the vessel containing the water].

R. Jeremiah asked R. Zera, How is it if [the bird] was so big that [its blood] effaced [all trace of] the water, or if it was so small that [all trace of its blood] was effaced by the water? He answered, Have I not told thee not to take thyself beyond the legal decision?[3] The Rabbis estimated [the quantity of a quarter of a *log*] by a free bird;[4] and this is never so big that [its blood] should efface [all trace of] the water, nor so small that [all trace of its blood] should be effaced by the water.

Our Rabbis have taught: If he put the dust [in the bowl] before the water, it is invalid; but R. Simeon allows it. What is the reason of R. Simeon?—Because it is written, *And for the unclean they shall take of the dust of the burning of the sin-offering;*[5] and it has been taught: R. Simeon said: Was it dust and not ashes? The text changes the expression to indicate that a conclusion was to be drawn from it by the rule of analogy: it is mentioned here '*dust*', and there [in the ceremony of the suspected woman] it is also mentioned '*dust*'; as in the second instance the dust had to be placed over the water,[6] so also here the dust had to be placed over the water; and further, as it is valid here if he put the dust on before the water, so also there [in

(1) Lev. XIV, 5. (2) So that no blood escapes while carrying it to the other vessel. (3) Not to raise questions about exaggerated points in connection with the decisions. (4) Such as flies in and out of a house. [A swallow; v. Lewysohn *Zoologie*, p. 206ff]. (5) Num. XIX, 17. The text has the word for *dust*, not 'ashes'. (6) As stated in Num. V, 17.

the ceremony of the suspected woman] it is valid if he put the dust on before the water.[1] Whence is this derived there [in the rite of the red heifer]?—There are two texts: it is written *thereto*,[2] consequently the ashes are first; and it is written *running water in a vessel*, consequently the water is first. So what was the procedure? He can put either in first. [How is this interpretation answered by] the Rabbis?[3]—'*In a vessel*'—precisely so;[4] '*thereto*'—that they are to be mixed. But say rather that '*thereto*' means precisely so;[5] and '*in a vessel*' means that the water must be poured directly into the vessel from the spring![6]—As we find that everywhere it is the qualifying element which is on top,[7] so also here[8] the qualifying element must be on top.

MISHNAH. [17a] WHEN HE COMES TO WRITE THE SCROLL, FROM WHAT PLACE DOES HE WRITE? FROM IF NO MAN HAVE LAIN WITH THEE[9] . . . BUT IF THOU HAST GONE ASIDE, BEING UNDER THY HUSBAND ETC.[10] HE DOES NOT, HOWEVER, INCLUDE, THEN THE PRIEST SHALL CAUSE THE WOMAN TO SWEAR,[11] BUT CONTINUES WITH, THE LORD MAKE THEE A CURSE AND AN OATH . . . AND THIS WATER THAT CAUSETH THE CURSE SHALL GO INTO THY BOWELS AND MAKE THY BELLY TO SWELL, AND THY THIGH TO FALL AWAY.[12] HE DOES NOT, HOWEVER, INCLUDE, AND THE WOMAN SHALL SAY, AMEN, AMEN. R. JOSE SAYS, HE MAKES NO OMISSIONS.[13] R. JUDAH SAYS, HE

(1) As explained anon. (2) Ibid., *running water shall be put thereto*. (3) Who declare that the rite is invalid if the dust is placed in the bowl before the water. (4) I.e., the water must be poured in first. (5) The water to be poured on the ashes. (6) It must be *running water*, and not poured from another vessel. (7) [In the case of a suspected woman, and of a leper, the qualifying elements—i.e., the dust which gives the water of bitterness its efficacy and the blood of the bird—must be placed on top as indicated by the plain meaning of the Scriptural texts: Num. V, 17, and Lev. XIV, 6.] (8) With the ashes of the red heifer. (9) Num. V, 19,—'*be thou free from this water of bitterness*'. (10) Ibid. 20,—[This is taken to imply a curse; v. *infra*]. (11) Ibid. 21. (12) Ibid. 22. (13) And the whole Scriptural passage is included.

WRITES NONE OF ALL THIS EXCEPT, THE LORD MAKE THEE A CURSE AND AN OATH ETC. AND THIS WATER THAT CAUSETH THE CURSE SHALL GO INTO THY BOWELS ETC. AND DOES NOT INCLUDE, AND THE WOMAN SHALL SAY, AMEN, AMEN.

GEMARA. On what point do they differ?—They differ in [the interpretation of] the following verse, *And the priest shall write these curses in a book.*[1] R. Meir[2] is of the opinion that *curses* denotes [the passages which are] actually curses;[3] *the curses*[4] is to include the curses which result from the benedictions;[5] '*these*' is to exclude the curses in Deuteronomy;[6] '*the these*' is to exclude instructions [given to the officiating priest] and the responses of *Amen* [made by the woman]. R. Jose agrees with all that has been stated, except that he interprets the particle '*eth*[7] as indicating the inclusion of instructions and responses, whereas R. Meir draws no deductions from the occurrences of the particle '*eth*. R. Judah, on the other hand, expounds all the above points as implying limitation; '*curses*' denotes [the passages which are] actually curses; '*the curses*' is to exclude the imprecations which result from the benedictions; '*these*' is to exclude the imprecations in Deuteronomy; '*the these*' is to exclude instructions and responses. What is the difference that R. Meir interprets the definite article [in *the curses*] as implying amplification and the definite article [in *the these*] as implying limitation?—When the definite article occurs in connection with amplification[8] it also denotes amplification, and when it occurs in connection with limitation[9] it also denotes limitation. But R. Meir

(1) Num. V, 23. (2) Who is the author of the anonymous statement in the Mishnah, v. Sanh. 86*a*. (3) '*The Lord make thee etc.*', verse 20. (4) According to Hebrew idiom, '*these curses*' is literally 'the curses the these'. (5) [I.e., '*if no man have lain with thee . . . be thou free*' implies that '*if thou hast gone aside . . . be thou not free*']. (6) If the text of Num. V, 23 had read 'and the priest will write the curses in a book' it might have been understood as referring to the curses in Deut. XXVIII, 16ff. (7) The sign of the accusative before '*these curses*'. (8) The phrase '*and the priest will write*' is a general statement—an amplification. (9) '*These*' is a limited term.

does not accept the rule that an affirmative is to be deduced as the corollary of a negative![1]—R. Tanḥum said: It is written *hinnaḳi*.[2]

R. Akiba expounded: When husband and wife are worthy, the *Shechinah* abides with them; when they are not worthy fire consumes them.[3] Raba said: [The fire which results] from the woman is severer than that from the man.[4] What is the reason? In the case of the former [the letters *aleph* and *shin*] are consecutive, but not in the case of a man.[5]

Raba said: Why does the Torah command that dust should be provided for [the ceremony of] a suspected woman? If she be innocent, there will issue from her a son like our father Abraham, of whom it is written, *Dust and ashes;*[6] and if she be not innocent, she reverts to dust.[7]

Raba expounded: As a reward for our father Abraham having said, '*I am but dust and ashes*', his descendants were worthy to receive two commandments, viz., the ashes of the red heifer and the dust [of the ceremony] of a suspected woman. But there is likewise dust for the covering of the blood![8]—In this case [the use of dust is merely] the completion of the commandment without any advantage [to the performer].[9]

Raba expounded: As a reward for our father Abraham having said, *I will not take a thread nor a shoelatchet,*[10] his descendants were

(1) How then does he consider verse 20 to imply a curse, v. Ḳid. 61a-62a and Shebu. 36a. (2) '*Be free*' in Num. V, 19. Since the word is defectively spelt without the *mater lectionis*, and the Hebrew letter *he* closely resembles the letter *ḥeth*, it might be taken to mean 'be strangled'; and so an imprecation is mentioned and it has not to be deduced as a corollary, v. Shebu (Sonc. ed.) p. 213, n. 6. (3) The letters of the word for 'husband' are *aleph*, *yad* and *shin*, and for 'wife' *aleph*, *shin* and *he*. The *yod* and *he* form the Divine Name; but if omitted, only *aleph* and *shin* are left which form the word *esh* 'fire'. (4) I.e. a bad wife is more destructive of domestic happiness than a bad husband. (5) The first and second letters of the word for 'woman' or 'wife' form *esh;* but in the word for 'husband' or 'man' they are the first and third letters. (6) Gen. XVIII, 27. (7) Dies from the effect of the water. (8) Of a slaughtered animal (Lev. XVII, 13). (9) Whereas the dust in the ceremony of the ordeal helps to restore the confidence of a husband in his wife or punishes immorality and the ashes of the red heifer serve to cleanse the unclean. (10) Gen. XIV, 23.

worthy to receive two commandments, viz., the thread of blue[1] and the thong of the phylacteries. It is right in the case of the thong of the phylacteries, for it is written, *And all the peoples of the earth shall see that thou art called by the name of the Lord,*[2] and it has been taught: R. Eliezer the Elder says: This refers to the phylactery worn upon the head;[3] but what is [the advantage to him who performs the law] of the thread of blue?—It has been taught: R. Meir used to say, Why is blue specified from all the varieties of colours? Because blue resembles [the colour of] the sea, and the sea resembles [the colour of] heaven, and heaven resembles [the colour of] the Throne of Glory, as it is said, *And they saw the God of Israel and there was under His feet as it were a paved work of sapphire stone, and as it were the very heaven for clearness,*[4] and it is written, *The likeness of a throne as the appearance of a sapphire stone.*[5]

MISHNAH. HE WRITES NEITHER ON A [WOODEN] TABLET NOR ON PAPYRUS NOR ON [17*b*] DIFTERA[6] BUT ON A [PARCHMENT] SCROLL, AS IT IS SAID, IN A BOOK.[7] NOR DOES HE WRITE WITH A [PREPARATION OF] GUM OR VITRIOL[8] OR WITH ANYTHING WHICH INDENTS [THE PARCHMENT] BUT WITH INK,[9] AS IT IS SAID, AND BLOT OUT[10]—WRITING WHICH IS CAPABLE OF BEING BLOTTED OUT.

GEMARA. Raba said: A scroll for a suspected woman which one wrote at night is invalid. What is the reason? An analogy is drawn between two passages where the word '*law*' occurs: here it

(1) On the fringes of the garment (Num. XV, 38). (2) Deut. XXVIII, 10. (3) Hence its advantage to him who performs the precept. (4) Ex. XXIV, 10. (5) Ezek. I, 26. [And he who fulfils the precept is blessed, as it were, with the Divine Presence (Rashi).] (6) Animal's hide prepared with salt and flour but not with gallnut. It was consequently more absorptive than fully prepared parchment. V. Krauss, *TA. II*, 262, v. Giṭ. (Sonc. ed.) p. 87, n. 2. (7) Num. V, 23. The book was then in the form of a scroll. (8) [*Ḳanḳantun*, v. Giṭ. (Sonc. ed.) p. 10, n. 8.] (9) It was really black paint, consisting of lampblack mixed with oil. V. Krauss, *op. cit., III*, 148ff., v. Giṭ. (Sonc. ed.) p. 70, n. 9. (10) Num. V, 23.

is written, *And the priest shall execute upon her all this law,*[1] and elsewhere it is written, *According to the tenor of the law which they shall teach thee, and according to the judgment.*[2] As judgment [could only be delivered] in the daytime,[3] so a scroll for a suspected woman [could only be written] in the daytime. If he wrote the text not in its proper order,[4] it is invalid; for it is written, *And he shall write these curses*[5]—just as they are written [in the Scriptural text]. If he wrote it before she took the oath upon herself, it is invalid; as it is said, *He shall cause her to swear* and after that, *He shall write.*[6] If he wrote it in the form of a letter,[7] it is invalid—'*in a book*' said the All-merciful. [18*a*] If he wrote it on two folios it is invalid; the All-merciful spoke of one '*book*' and not of two or three books. If he wrote one letter and blotted it out [with the water of bitterness] and then wrote another letter and blotted it out[8] it is invalid; for it is written, *And the priest shall execute upon her* all *this law.*[1]

Raba asked: How is it if he wrote two scrolls for two suspects and blotted them in one vessel of water? Do we only require that the writing should be expressly for each case? That we have here; or perhaps it is also necessary to have obliteration expressly for each case! If, furthermore, you conclude that we also require obliteration expressly for each case, how is it if he obliterated them in two vessels and then mixed them? Do we only require that the obliteration should be expressly for each case? That we have here; or perhaps each of the women does not drink the water prepared for her! If, furthermore, you conclude that [this renders the rite invalid because] each of the women does not drink the water prepared for her, how is it if he again divided the water into two parts [after having mixed it]? Is there or is there not a retrospective differentiation?[9]—The questions remain unanswered.

(1) Num. V, 30. (2) Deut. XVII, 11. (3) This was the rule of judicial procedure; v. Sanh. 32*a*. (4) [Lit., 'backward'; probably as an incantation, v. Blau, *Das altjüdische Zauberwesen*, pp. 146ff.] (5) Num. V, 23. (6) Ibid. 19 and 23. (7) I.e., without first tracing lines to secure evenness of script, as is required with a scroll of the Law, v. Giṭ. (Sonc. ed.) p. 20, n. 3. (8) He did not write out the text in full before obliterating it. (9) *Bererah* v. Glos. Do we regard the water now divided as being differentiated and identical with the original quantities of water?

Raba asked: How is it if he made her drink through a straw or tube? Is that to be regarded as a mode of drinking or not?—The question remains unanswered. R. Ashi asked: How is it if some of the water was spilt or remained over? The question remains unanswered.

R. Zera said in the name of Rab: Why are two oaths mentioned in connection with a suspected woman?[1] One [was imposed] before [the writing on] the scroll was blotted out and the other after it was blotted out. Raba demurred, They are both written [in the Scriptural text] before [the inscription on] the scroll was obliterated! But, said Raba, with one oath a curse was connected[2] and not with the other. What was the formula of the oath with which a curse was connected?—R. Amram said in the name of Rab: 'I make thee swear that thou hast not misconducted thyself, for if thou hast, may [the curses] befall thee.' Raba asked: [In this wording] the curse and the oath are distinct![3] But, said Raba, [the formula is], 'I make thee swear that if thou hast misconducted thyself, may [the curses] befall thee'.[4] R. Ashi asked: [In this wording] there is a curse but no oath! But, said R. Ashi, [The formula is], 'I make thee swear that thou hast not misconducted thyself; and that if thou hast, may [the curses] befall thee'.

MISHNAH. TO WHAT DOES SHE RESPOND 'AMEN, AMEN'? AN 'AMEN' OVER THE CURSE AND AN 'AMEN' OVER THE OATH; AN 'AMEN' WITH RESPECT TO THIS MAN[5] AND AN 'AMEN' WITH RESPECT TO ANY OTHER MAN;[6] AN 'AMEN' THAT I DID NOT GO ASTRAY AS A BETROTHED MAIDEN OR MARRIED WOMAN [18*b*] OR [A CHILDLESS WIDOW] WAITING FOR MY BROTHER-IN-LAW'S [DECISION WHETHER HE WOULD MARRY ME] OR TAKEN TO HIS HOUSE,[7] AND AN 'AMEN' THAT I HAVE

(1) V. Num. V, 19, 21. (2) Verse 21 where the phrase *oath of cursing* occurs. (3) [The oath here is not connected with the curse, but relates to the wife's fidelity.] (4) [The oath relates only to the wife's conduct and is not connected with the curse.] (5) Who is the cause of the ordeal. (6) With whom she may have associated without her husband's knowledge. (7) For the purpose of marriage, but before its consummation.

NOT MISCONDUCTED MYSELF AND IF I HAVE MAY [THE CURSES] BEFALL ME. R. MEIR SAYS: ONE 'AMEN' IS THAT I HAVE NOT MISCONDUCTED MYSELF AND THE OTHER 'AMEN' THAT I WILL NOT MISCONDUCT MYSELF.

ALL AGREE THAT A MAN CANNOT MAKE A STIPULATION WITH HER IN RESPECT OF THE TIME BEFORE SHE WAS BETROTHED[1] OR AFTER SHE IS DIVORCED. IF SHE SECLUDES HERSELF WITH ANOTHER MAN[2] AND MISCONDUCTS HERSELF AND SUBSEQUENTLY [HER HUSBAND] TAKES HER BACK, HE CANNOT MAKE A STIPULATION WITH HER [IN RESPECT OF THIS].[3] THIS IS THE GENERAL RULE: HE CANNOT MAKE A STIPULATION WITH HER IN RESPECT OF ANY ACT OF COHABITATION WHICH DOES NOT RENDER HER PROHIBITED TO HIM.

GEMARA. R. Hamnuna said: [A childless widow] waiting for her brother-in-law's [decision whether he would marry her] who acted immorally is forbidden to her levir.[4] Whence is this? Since the Mishnah teaches: [A CHILDLESS WIDOW] WAITING FOR MY BROTHER-IN-LAW'S [DECISION WHETHER HE WOULD MARRY ME] OR TAKEN TO HIS HOUSE. This is quite right if you say that she is prohibited [to her brother-in-law] then he can make a stipulation with her;[5] but if you say that she is not prohibited to him,[6] how can he make a stipulation with her; for we have learnt: THIS IS THE GENERAL RULE: HE CANNOT MAKE A STIPULATION WITH HER IN RESPECT OF ANY ACT OF COHABITATION WHICH DOES NOT RENDER HER PROHIBITED TO HIM! In the West,[7] however, they said, The legal decision is not in agreement with R. Hamnuna. But whose [then] is the teaching concerning [A CHILDLESS WIDOW] WAITING FOR HER BROTHER-IN-LAW OR

(1) That she had never acted immorally. (2) After being divorced, and the divorce was not on account of misconduct because in that event there could be no re-marriage. (3) In respect of what she may have done after the divorce. (4) Because she is regarded as a wife who was unfaithful to her husband. (5) In respect of her conduct before he married her; and if she was immoral, he may not marry her. (6) For immorality before marriage. (7) The Palestinian Schools.

TAKEN TO HIS HOUSE?—It is R. Akiba's; for he said, No betrothal can take effect in cases which are subject to a mere negative prohibition,[1] and he regards her[2] act as equal to an incestuous union.[3]

R. Jeremiah asked: Can he make a stipulation in connection with a first marriage[4] or her marriage with his brother?[5]—Come and hear: THIS IS THE GENERAL RULE: HE CANNOT MAKE A STIPULATION WITH HER IN RESPECT OF ANY ACT OF COHABITATION WHICH DOES NOT RENDER HER PROHIBITED TO HIM. Consequently when it would render her prohibited to him he can make a stipulation with her. Draw that conclusion.[6]

R. MEIR SAYS: ONE 'AMEN' IS THAT I HAVE NOT MISCONDUCTED MYSELF etc. It has been taught: When R. Meir declares, AND THE OTHER 'AMEN' THAT I WILL NOT MISCONDUCT MYSELF, it does not imply that if she in the future misconducts herself, the water affects her now; but should she later misconduct herself, the water will bestir and affect her.

R. Ashi asked: Can a man make a stipulation with regard to remarriage?[7] [Do we argue] that for the present she is not prohibited to him [and therefore he cannot make a stipulation with her], or that it may happen that he will divorce and remarry her [and therefore can make a stipulation]?—Come and hear: ALL AGREE THAT A MAN CANNOT MAKE A STIPULATION WITH HER IN RESPECT OF THE TIME BEFORE SHE WAS BETROTHED OR AFTER SHE IS DIVORCED. IF SHE SECLUDES HERSELF WITH

(1) Without carrying with them the death penalty or of *kareth*. There is such a prohibition in connection with a childless widow's marriage (v. Deut. XXV, 5) v. Yeb. 10*b*. (2) The childless widow who acted immorally. (3) [And therefore forbidden to her brother-in-law just as a wife who misconducted herself is forbidden to her husband.] (4) When he had remarried her after divorcing her can he make her swear that she had been faithful to him during their first marriage? (5) After he had gone through the levirate-marriage with her, can he make her swear that she had not misconducted herself whilst living with his brother? (6) In both of the contingencies mentioned immorality would render her prohibited; so he can make the stipulation. (7) Since R. Meir interprets 'Amen' as referring to what may occur in the future, suppose a husband makes a condition that his wife shall not misconduct herself if he divorces her and remarries her, and after remarriage she is unfaithful?

ANOTHER MAN AND MISCONDUCTS HERSELF AND SUBSEQUENTLY [HER HUSBAND] TOOK HER BACK, HE CANNOT MAKE A STIPULATION WITH HER [IN RESPECT OF THIS]. Hence if he takes her back and she then misconducts herself, he can make a stipulation [in respect of this]. Draw that conclusion.[1]

Our Rabbis have taught: *This is the law of jealousy*[2]—it teaches that a woman may drink [the water of bitterness] and do so again.[3] R. Judah says: '*This*'[4] indicates that a woman does not drink and do so again. R. Judah said: It happened that Neḥonia the well-digger[5] testified before us that a woman had drunk [the water of bitterness] and had done so a second time. We accepted his testimony as relating to two husbands but not one husband. The Sages, however, declared that a woman does not drink and do so again, whether it be in respect of one husband or two husbands. But for the first Tanna [cited above] it is likewise written '*This*'![6] And for the latter Rabbis [cited above] it is likewise written '*the law of*'![7]—Raba said: In the case of the same husband and the same paramour none differ that a woman does not drink and do so again, [19*a*] for it is written '*This*'. In the case of two husbands and two paramours none differ that a woman drinks and does so again, for it is written '*the law of*'. Where they differ is in the case of the same husband and two paramours, or two husbands and the same paramour. The first Tanna holds that '*the law of*' indicates the inclusion of them all, and '*This*' indicates the exclusion of the case of the same husband and the same paramour. The Rabbis hold that '*This*' indicates the exclusion of them all, and '*the law of*' indi-

(1) That such a stipulation is permissible. (2) Num. V, 29. The text is literally 'law of jealousies', which is taken to mean: the law is to be applied in every instance of suspicion. (3) If suspected a second time. (4) The word has an exclusive meaning, and equals this is the only time the woman undergoes the ordeal. (5) [V. B.Ḳ. (Sonc. ed.) p. 287. He however could not have testified before R. Judah who lived about 200 years later. The text must accordingly be connected with the parallel passage in J. Soṭah II, where the reading is Nehemia of Shiḥin testified in the name of R. Akiba v. Hyman, A *Toledoth*, p. 924.] (6) He permits a woman to drink a second time; why does he not interpret '*This*' is an exclusive sense? (7) Why do they not understand this as not permitting the second ordeal?

cates the inclusion of the case of two husbands and two paramours. R. Judah holds that '*This*' is to exclude two cases and '*the law of*' is to include two cases. '*This*' is to exclude two cases, viz., the same husband and the same paramour, and the same husband and two paramours; '*the law of*' is to include two cases, viz., two husbands and the same paramour, and two husbands and two paramours.

SOṬAH

CHAPTER III

MISHNAH. HE[1] TAKES HER MEAL-OFFERING OUT OF THE BASKET OF PALM-TWIGS AND PLACES IT IN A MINISTERING VESSEL AND SETS IT UPON HER HAND; AND THE PRIEST PLACES HIS HAND UNDER HERS AND WAVES IT.[2]

HAVING WAVED IT, HE BROUGHT A HANDFUL [TO THE ALTAR], FUMIGATED IT, AND THE REMAINDER WAS EATEN BY THE PRIESTS. HE [FIRST] GIVES [HER THE WATER OF BITTERNESS] TO DRINK, AND THEN SACRIFICES HER MEAL-OFFERING. R. SIMEON SAYS: HE SACRIFICES HER MEAL-OFFERING AND THEN GIVES HER TO DRINK, AS IT IS SAID, AND AFTERWARD SHALL MAKE THE WOMAN DRINK THE WATER;[3] BUT IF HE GAVE HER TO DRINK AND THEN SACRIFICED HER MEAL-OFFERING IT IS VALID.

GEMARA. R. Eleazar said to R. Joshiah his contemporary:[4] You shall not sit down[5] until you have explained the following: Whence is it that the meal-offering of a suspected woman requires to be waved? 'Whence have we it? It is written in connection therewith, *And shall wave*'![6] — But [my question is], whence [is it that it has to be done] with [the co-operation of] the owner?'[7] — It is derived from the analogous use of the word '*hand*' in connection with the peace-offering. Here it is written, '*The priest shall take out of the woman's hand*', and there it is written, *His own hands shall bring*.[8] As in this present case it refers to the priest [who waves

(1) According to Rashi it is the husband; other commentators declare it is the priest. (2) The offering, forward and backward, and up and down. (3) Num. V, 26. (4) This is added to distinguish him from an earlier Rabbi of that name. (5) Lit., 'sit on your legs', v. Nazir (Sonc. ed.) p. 87, n. 9. (6) Ibid. 25. (7) In this instance, the suspected woman; and the verse declares, *The priest shall take the meal-offering of jealousy out of the woman's hand and shall wave*, Ibid. (8) Lev. VII, 30.

the offering of the suspected woman], so there it refers to the priest;[1] and as there [in the waving of the peace-offering] the owner [holds it during the rite] so here the owner [holds it]. What, then, was the procedure?—[The priest] places his hand under the hands of the owner and waves.

HAVING WAVED IT, HE BROUGHT A HANDFUL . . . HE [FIRST] GIVES [HER THE WATER OF BITTERNESS] TO DRINK, AND THEN SACRIFICES HER MEAL-OFFERING. But he has already offered it![2]—This is what is intended:[3] What is the procedure in connection with meal-offerings? He waves, brings a handful [to the altar], fumigates it and the remainder is eaten by the priests. As to the giving of the water to drink, on this R. Simeon and the Rabbis differ; because the Rabbis hold that he gives her to drink and then sacrifices her meal-offering, whereas R. Simeon holds that he sacrifices her meal-offering and then gives her to drink, as it is said, '*And afterwards shall make the woman drink*'.

BUT IF HE GAVE HER TO DRINK AND THEN SACRIFICED HER MEAL-OFFERING IT IS VALID. [19*b*] Our Rabbis taught: *And when he hath made her drink*[4]—what does this intend to tell us since it has already been stated, *And he shall make the woman drink?*[5] [It informs us] that if [the writing on] the scroll has been obliterated and she says, 'I refuse to drink', they exert influence upon her and make her drink by force. Such is the statement of R. Akiba. R. Simeon says: '*And afterwards shall make the woman drink*'—what does this intend to tell us since it has already been stated, '*And he shall make the woman drink*'? [It informs us] that it only takes place after all the rites mentioned above have been carried out, thus indicating that three things prevent [the giving of the water to drink]: [the priest] must have offered the handful, [the writing on] the scroll must have been blotted out, and [the woman] must have taken the

(1) Who performs the act of waving although it is not explicitly mentioned. (2) Since the Mishnah stated, HE BROUGHT A HANDFUL (TO THE ALTAR), FUMIGATED IT. (3) This Mishnah is describing the order of the sacrifice without any reference to whether it comes before or after the drinking of the water. (4) Num. V, 27. (5) Ibid. 24. In the consonantal text the two verbs look the same, but there is a grammatical difference.

oath. '[The priest] must have offered the handful'—R. Simeon is consistent with his opinion when he said that the priest sacrifices her meal-offering and then gives her to drink. '[The writing on] the scroll must have been blotted out'—[obviously so], for what else could he give her to drink![1]—R. Ashi said: No, it is necessary [to mention this for the case where] a trace of the inscription is recognisable.[2] '[The woman] must have taken the oath.' [This means] merely she does not drink, but they write the scroll for her [before she takes the oath]? But Raba has said: If he wrote the scroll for a suspected woman before she took the oath, what he did was invalid!—[R. Simeon] mentioned this[3] unnecessarily. On what, then, do they differ?—There are three verses: first *'he shall make the woman drink'*, second *'and afterward shall make drink'*, and third *'and when he hath made her drink'*. The Rabbis hold that the first phrase is required for the subject-matter, i.e., he gives her to drink and then sacrifices her meal-offering; the phrase *'and afterward shall make drink'* is necessary [to cover the case where] a trace of the inscription is recognisable; and the third phrase indicates that if [the writing on] the scroll has been obliterated and she says 'I refuse to drink', they exert influence upon her and make her drink by force. R. Simeon, on the other hand, holds that *'and afterward shall make drink'* is required for the subject-matter, i.e., he sacrifices her meal-offering and then gives her to drink. The first phrase is to indicate that if he first gave her to drink and afterward sacrificed her meal-offering it is valid; and the third phrase denotes that if [the writing on] the scroll has been obliterated and she says 'I refuse to drink', they exert influence upon her and make her drink by force. The Rabbis, however, do not hold that the text opens with [a commandment which is only valid as] an accomplished fact.[4]

Does R. Akiba hold that they give her to drink by force? Surely

(1) Since the writing was an essential ingredient of what she drank. (2) R. Simeon insists on total obliteration. (3) That she first takes the oath before drinking; for it must have been done before the scroll was written. (4) A Biblical precept states what is or is not to be done, not that something should not be done but, if accomplished, it is allowed to stand. For this reason they reject R. Simeon's explanation of the first phrase.

it has been taught: R. Judah says: They insert iron tongs into her mouth, so that if [the writing on] the scroll has been obliterated and she says 'I refuse to drink', they exert influence upon her and make her drink by force. R. Akiba says: Do we require anything else than to prove her, and is she not actually proved![1] But so long as the priest has not offered the handful, she can retract;[2] and when he has offered the handful, she cannot retract!—But, even on your reasoning, the teaching is inconsistent. It states: 'When he has offered the handful, she cannot retract', but is she not actually proved![3] [You must perforce say] that there is no contradiction; as one case is where she retracts through trembling and the other where she retracts through defiance;[4] and this is what he means: when [she retracts] through defiance she does not drink at all; but when it is through trembling, so long as the priest has not offered the handful she is able to retract, since [the writing on] the scroll had not yet been obliterated, or even if it had been obliterated because the priests acted illegally in obliterating it; but if he had offered the handful, in which case the priests acted legally in obliterating it, she is unable to retract.[5] [20a] But R. Akiba [nevertheless] contradicts himself; he declared above that it was the obliteration [of the inscription] which prevents [her from retracting], and here he declares that [the offering of the] handful prevents her!—There are two Tannaim [who take opposite sides on this question] in the view of R. Akiba.

The question was asked, How is it if she said, 'I refuse to drink' through defiance and she retracts and says 'I am willing to drink'? Is it that since she said, 'I refuse to drink' she admitted 'I am unclean', and having presumed herself to be unclean, she is unable to retract; or perhaps, since she says 'I am willing to drink', she evidences that she first spoke in terror?—The question remains unanswered.

(1) Her refusal to drink is interpreted as an admission of guilt. R. Akiba is therefore against force being used. (2) And admit guilt, and so avoid force. (3) By refusing to drink before the handful was offered. (4) Only in the latter is the refusal considered an admission of guilt. (5) [Similarly R. Akiba in stating in the first Baraitha that she is given to drink by force refers to the case when it is through trembling.]

Samuel's father said: It is necessary to put something bitter into the water. What is the reason? Scripture declares, *The water of bitterness*[1]—i.e., [water] which had been previously made bitter.

MISHNAH. IF, BEFORE [THE WRITING ON] THE SCROLL HAD BEEN BLOTTED OUT, SHE SAID 'I REFUSE TO DRINK', HER SCROLL IS STORED AWAY[2] AND HER MEAL-OFFERING IS SCATTERED OVER THE ASHES.[3] HER SCROLL IS NOT VALID TO BE USED IN GIVING ANOTHER SUSPECTED WOMAN TO DRINK. IF [THE WRITING ON] THE SCROLL HAS BEEN BLOTTED OUT AND SHE SAID 'I AM UNCLEAN', THE WATER IS POURED AWAY AND HER MEAL-OFFERING IS SCATTERED IN THE PLACE OF THE ASHES.[4] IF [THE WRITING ON] THE SCROLL HAD BEEN BLOTTED OUT AND SHE SAID 'I REFUSE TO DRINK', THEY EXERT INFLUENCE UPON HER AND MAKE HER DRINK BY FORCE.

SHE HAD SCARCELY FINISHED DRINKING WHEN HER FACE TURNS GREEN, HER EYES PROTRUDE AND HER VEINS SWELL;[5] AND IT IS EXCLAIMED, 'REMOVE HER THAT THE TEMPLE-COURT BE NOT DEFILED'.[6] IF SHE POSSESSED A MERIT, IT [CAUSES THE WATER] TO SUSPEND ITS EFFECT UPON HER. SOME MERIT SUSPENDS THE EFFECT FOR ONE YEAR, ANOTHER FOR TWO YEARS, AND ANOTHER FOR THREE YEARS. HENCE DECLARED BEN AZZAI, A MAN IS UNDER THE OBLIGATION TO TEACH HIS DAUGHTER TORAH, SO THAT IF SHE HAS TO DRINK [THE WATER OF BITTERNESS], SHE MAY KNOW THAT THE MERIT SUSPENDS[7] ITS EFFECT. R. ELIEZER SAYS:

(1) Num. V, 18. (2) It was not destroyed because the inscription included the Divine Name. (3) Of the Temple-offerings. (4) This was a special Court in the Temple where the refuse of sacrifices was destroyed. (5) Literally, she becomes filled with veins. (6) The reason is discussed in the Gemara. (7) [MS.M.: 'suspended'. In the absence of such a knowledge, the woman who passed through the ordeal unscathed may be led to doubt the efficacy of the water of bitterness searching out sin, and thus indulge in further immoral practices. By realising however that merit has suspended the effects, she would pause and be in constant dread of the fate hanging over her.]

WHOEVER TEACHES HIS DAUGHTER TORAH TEACHES HER OBSCENITY. R. JOSHUA SAYS: A WOMAN PREFERS ONE ḲAB[1] AND SEXUAL INDULGENCE TO NINE ḲAB[2] AND CONTINENCE. HE USED TO SAY, A FOOLISH PIETIST, A CUNNING ROGUE, A FEMALE PHARISEE, AND THE PLAGUE OF PHARISEES[3] BRING DESTRUCTION UPON THE WORLD.

GEMARA. Rab Judah declared that Samuel said in the name of R. Meir: When I studied Torah with R. Akiba, I used to put vitriol[4] into the ink and he said nothing to me; but when I went to R. Ishmael, he said to me, 'My son, what is thy occupation?' I answered, 'I am a scribe'.[5] He told me, 'My son, be careful, because thy work is the work of Heaven; if thou omittest a single letter or addest a single letter, thou dost as a consequence destroy the whole world'.[6] I said to him, 'There is an ingredient which I put into the ink, and its name is vitriol'. He asked me, 'May we put vitriol into ink? The Torah has said, *He shall blot out*,[7] i.e., writing which can be blotted out!' What did [R. Ishmael] intend to tell [R. Meir] that the latter answered him in that manner?[8]—[R. Meir] meant, Obviously, I am skilled in the rules of defective and *plene* spelling;[9] but I even have no reason to fear lest a fly should come and settle upon the crownlet of the letter D and obliterate it so that it makes it look like the letter R.[10] There is an ingredient which I put into the ink, and its name is vitriol. But it is not so; for it has been taught: R. Meir said: When I studied Torah with R. Ishmael, I used to put vitriol into the ink and he said nothing to me; but when I went to R. Akiba, he forbade it to me! Here is an inconsistency in [the order of the Rabbis upon whom R. Meir] attended, and an inconsistency in [the name of the Rabbi who] forbade it. It is quite right, there is no inconsistency in [the order of the

(1) Metaphorical for a scanty livelihood. (2) Luxurious style of living. (3) All these phrases will be explained in the Gemara. (4) V. *supra* p. 90, n. 8. (5) Of Torah-scrolls for use in the Synagogue. (6) Such an error might turn a phrase into blasphemy. (7) Num. V, 23. (8) By mentioning the use of vitriol. (9) I.e., the use of vowel letters which are sometimes added and sometimes omitted. (10) [Changing, e.g., ד׳ אחד *'the Lord is one'* into אחר 'another'.]

Rabbis upon whom R. Meir] attended; he first went to R. Akiba, but when he was unable [to follow his arguments],[1] he went to R. Ishmael. After having studied[2] with him, he returned to R. Akiba whose reasoning he was then able to grasp. But there is an inconsistency in [the name of the Rabbi who] forbade it!—That is a difficulty.

It has been taught: R. Judah says: R. Meir used to declare that for all [kinds of script] we may put vitriol into the ink [20*b*] except only for the portion concerning the suspected woman. R. Jacob says in his [R. Meir's] name, Except the portion of the suspected woman [written] in the Temple.[3] What is the difference between them?—R. Jeremiah said: The point between them is [whether it is permissible] to blot out from the Torah [-scroll the passage required for the rite of the water of bitterness];[4] and these teachers [differ on the same issue] as the following teachers, for it has been taught: Her scroll is not valid to be used in giving another suspected woman to drink. R. Aḥi b. Joshiah says: Her scroll is valid to be used in giving another suspected woman to drink.[5] R. Papa said: Perhaps it is not so; the first teacher only gives his opinion there because [the scroll] was designated for Rachel and cannot therefore be re-designated for Leah, but since the text of the Torah-scroll is written without reference to any individual, we may obliterate [the passage]. R. Naḥman b. Isaac said: Perhaps it is not so; R. Aḥi b. Joshiah only gives his opinion there in the case of a scroll which was written for the purpose of the curses; but with a Torah-scroll which is written for the purpose of study, we may not obliterate [the passage]. Does not, then, R. Aḥi b. Joshiah accept what we learnt: If a man wrote [a document] to divorce his wife but changed his mind, and then met a man who

(1) Which, through lack of knowledge, were beyond his comprehension. (2) [Lit., 'learned Gemara'. On the term Gemara v. B.M. (Sonc. ed.) p. 206, n. 6. Here it denotes the summary of Tannaitic teachings preserved in early Mishnas and Baraithas; v. *Epistle of Sherira Gaon*, p. 44.] (3) Specially prepared for the ordeal. (4) According to R. Jacob it is not permissible, and consequently one may use vitriol for writing that portion in the Torah-scroll. (5) The point here also is whether the scroll must be expressly written for the ordeal.

resided in the same city[1] and said to him, 'My name is identical with yours and my wife's name identical with your wife's name', it is invalid [as a document] wherewith to divorce?[2]—They answer, There [in connection with divorce] the All-Merciful declared, *He shall write for her*[3]—we require that it should be written expressly for her; here likewise [it is stated], *Shall execute upon her*[4]— what is intended by the word *'execute'?* The obliteration [of the writing].[5]

SHE HAD SCARCELY FINISHED DRINKING WHEN HER FACE etc. Whose [teaching] is this?[6]—It is R. Simeon's, because he said that [the priest] sacrifices her meal-offering and then gives her to drink,[7] since the water does not affect her so long as her meal-offering is not sacrificed, as it is written, *A meal-offering of memorial, bringing iniquity to remembrance.*[8] But cite the continuation [of the Mishnah]: IF SHE POSSESSED A MERIT, IT [CAUSES THE WATER] TO SUSPEND ITS EFFECT UPON HER—this accords with the view of the Rabbis; because if [it be supposed that it accords with the view of] R. Simeon, behold he has declared, Merit does not cause the water of bitterness to suspend its effect![9]—R. Ḥisda said: Whose is it, then? It is R. Akiba's, because he said: He sacrifices her meal-offering and then gives her to drink, and on the question of [the effect of] merit he agrees with the Rabbis.

AND IT IS EXCLAIMED, 'REMOVE HER' etc. What is the reason? —Perhaps she dies. Is this to say that a corpse is forbidden in the camp of the Levites?[10] But it has been taught: One who is defiled through contact with a corpse is permitted to enter the camp of the Levites; and not only did they say this of one who is defiled through contact with a corpse but even the corpse itself [may be taken there], as it is said, *And Moses took the bones of Joseph with*

(1) The name of the city is inserted in the document. (2) The second woman, since it must be written expressly for the woman who is to be divorced, v. Giṭ. 24*a*. (3) Deut. XXIV, 1. (4) Num. V, 30. (5) Only the obliteration, but not the writing, must be expressly for the woman who is being tried. (6) That the water takes effect as soon as she drinks it. (7) V. *supra* 19*a*. (8) Ibid. 15. (9) V. *supra* p. 25. Consequently the above teaching cannot be R. Simeon's. (10) The Court of the Levites in the Temple where the Court of Women and the Nicanor Gate (v. *supra* p. 30, n. 9.) were located.

him[1]—'*with him*', i.e., in his division![2]—Abaye said: [The reason is] lest she become menstruant.[3] Is this to say that a sudden fright brings on [menstruation]?—Yes, for it is written, *And the queen was exceedingly grieved,*[4] and Rab said, [It means] that she became menstruant. But we have learnt: Trembling holds back [the menstrual] flow!—Fear holds it back but a sudden fright brings it on.

IF SHE POSSESSED A MERIT etc. Whose teaching is our Mishnah? It is not that of Abba Jose b. Ḥanan, nor of R. Eleazar b. Isaac of Kefar Darom, nor of R. Ishmael; for it has been taught: If she possess a merit, it suspends [the effect of the water] for three months, sufficiently long for pregnancy to be recognisable. Such is the statement of Abba Jose b. Ḥanan; R. Eleazar b. Isaac of Kefar Darom says: For nine months, as it is stated, *Then she shall be free and shall conceive seed,*[5] and elsewhere it declares, *A seed shall serve him, it shall be related*[6]—i.e., a seed which is fit to be related.[7] R. Ishmael says: For twelve months, and although there is no proof of this, yet there is some indication; because it is written, *Wherefore, O king, let my counsel be acceptable unto thee, and break off thy sins by righteousness, and thine iniquities by showing mercy to the poor;* [21a] *if there may be a lengthening of thy tranquillity,*[8] and it is written, *All this came upon king Nebuchadnezzar,*[9] and it is written, *At the end of twelve months!*[10]—[The teaching is] certainly R. Ishmael's and he found a verse which mentions [the period] and repeats it; for it is written, *Thus saith the Lord: For three transgressions of Edom.*[11] But why [was it said] that although there is no proof of this, yet there is some indication?[12]—It may be different with heathens upon whom [God] does not execute judgment immediately.

AND ANOTHER FOR THREE YEARS etc. What sort of merit? If I answer merit of [studying] Torah, she is [in the category] of one

(1) Ex. XIII, 19. (2) Which was the camp of the Levites. (3) As the result of her agitation. (4) Est. IV, 4. (5) Num. V, 28. (6) Ps. XXII, 31. (7) Viz., at birth, and so the period of nine months is required. Rashi explains differently. (8) Dan. IV, 24. (9) Ibid. 25. (10) Ibid. 26. (11) Amos I, 11. The respite of a year is trebled and this period corresponds to that given in the Mishnah. (12) The texts quoted did afford proof!

who is not commanded and fulfils![1]—Rather must it be merit of [performing] a commandment. But does the merit of performing a commandment protect as much as that?—Surely it has been taught: The following did R. Menaḥem son of R. Jose expound: *For the commandment is a lamp and Torah is light*[2]—the verse identifies the commandment with a lamp and Torah with light; the commandment with a lamp to tell thee that as a lamp only protects temporarily, so [the fulfilment of] a commandment only protects temporarily; and Torah with light to tell thee that as light protects permanently, so Torah protects permanently; and it states, *When thou walkest it shall lead thee* etc.[3]—'*when thou walkest it shall lead thee*', viz., in this world; '*when thou sleepest it shall watch over thee*', viz., in death; *and when thou awakest it shall talk with thee,* viz., in the Hereafter. Parable of a man who is walking in the middle of the night and darkness, and is afraid of thorns, pits, thistles, wild beasts and robbers, and also does not know the road in which he is going. If a lighted torch is prepared for him, he is saved from thorns, pits and thistles; but he is still afraid of wild beasts and robbers, and does not know the road in which he is going. When, however, dawn breaks, he is saved from wild beasts and robbers, but still does not know the road in which he is going. When, however, he reaches the cross-roads, he is saved from everything.[4] Another explanation is: A transgression nullifies[5] [the merit of] a commandment but not of [study of] Torah; as it is said, *Many waters cannot quench love!*[6]—Said R. Joseph: A commandment protects and rescues[7] while one is engaged upon it; but when one is no longer engaged upon it, it protects[8] but does not rescue. As for [study of] Torah, whether while one is engaged upon it or not, it protects and rescues. Raba demurred to this: According to this reasoning, did not Doeg and Ahitophel engage upon [study of] Torah; so

(1) The duty of Torah-study is not obligatory upon a woman; therefore she cannot acquire so much merit even if she does so, v. A.Z. 3*a*. (2) Prov. VI, 23. (3) Ibid. 22. (4) The commandment is the torch, Torah the dawn, and death the cross-roads. (5) Lit., 'extinguishes'. (6) Cant. VIII, 7. This shows that a commandment has no great protective powers. (7) 'Protects' from sufferings and 'rescues' from the urge of the evil inclination. (8) The merit of its fulfilment can thus protect the woman against the effects of the water.

why did it not protect them?[1]—But, said Raba, while one is engaged upon [study of] Torah, it protects and rescues, and while one is not engaged upon it, it protects but does not rescue. As for a commandment whether while one is engaged upon it or not, it protects but does not rescue.

Rabina said: It is certainly merit of [the study of] Torah [which causes the water to suspend its effect]; and when you argue that she is in the category of one who is not commanded and fulfils, [it can be answered] granted that women are not so commanded, still when they have their sons taught Scripture and Mishnah and wait for their husbands until they return from the Schools,[2] should they not share [the merit] with them?

What means 'the cross-roads' [in the parable related above]? —R. Ḥisda said: It alludes to a disciple of the Sages and the day of his death. R. Naḥman b. Isaac said: It alludes to a disciple of the Sages and his fear of sin.[3] Mar Zuṭra said: It alludes to a disciple of the Sages when the tradition cited by him is in accord with the *halachah*.[4] Another explanation is: A transgression nullifies [the merit of] a commandment but not of [study of] Torah. R. Joseph said: R. Menaḥem son of R. Jose expounded that verse[5] as though [it were interpreted] from Sinai, and had Doeg and Ahitophel expounded it [similarly], they would not have pursued David, as it is written, *Saying, God hath forsaken him,* etc.[6] What verse did they expound?[7]—*That he see no unclean thing in thee* etc.[8] They did not know, however, that a transgression nullifies [the merit of] a commandment but not of [study of] Torah.[9]

(1) [This is used in a loose sense. The question is the Torah should have 'rescued' them (Tosaf. of Sens.] (2) These were often a distance from the home and involved a long absence. V. Ber. 17*a*. (3) His study of Torah imbues him with a fear of sin which withholds him from transgression. His clear conscience serves him well at the time of death. (4) This is proof that he had studied correctly and the consciousness of this also calms his mind at the end of his life. (5) Viz., Prov. VI, 23. (6) Ps. LXXI, 11, i.e., David because of his sin with Bathsheba, and so they imagined they could pursue him with impunity. (7) To support them in their view. (8) Deut. XXIII, 15, E.V. 14. The continuation is: *and turn away from thee*. Now the phrase '*unclean thing*' usually means an immoral act, and it was so understood by Doeg and Ahitophel. (9) And David was still protected

What means *He would utterly be contemned?*[1]—'Ulla said: Not like Simeon the brother of Azariah nor like R. Joḥanan of the Prince's house[2] but like Hillel[3] and Shebna. When R. Dimi came[4] he related that Hillel and Shebna were brothers; Hillel engaged in [study of] Torah and Shebna was occupied in business. Eventually [Shebna] said to him, 'Come, let us become partners and divide [the profits]'. A *Bath Ḳol*[5] issued forth and proclaimed, *If a man would give all the substance of his house* etc.[6]

[21*b*] HENCE DECLARED BEN AZZAI: A MAN IS UNDER THE OBLIGATION TO TEACH . . . R. ELIEZER SAYS: WHOEVER TEACHES HIS DAUGHTER TORAH TEACHES HER OBSCENITY. Can it enter your mind [that by teaching her Torah he actually teaches her] obscenity!—Read, rather: as though he had taught her obscenity. R. Abbahu said: What is R. Eliezer's reason?—Because it is written, *I wisdom have made subtilty my dwelling*,[7] i.e., when wisdom enters a man subtilty enters with it.

And what do the Rabbis[8] make of the words '*I wisdom*'?—They require them in accordance with the teaching of R. Jose son of R. Ḥanina; for R. Jose son of R. Ḥanina said: Words of Torah only remain with him who renders himself naked[9] on their behalf; as it is said, '*I wisdom have made nakedness my dwelling*'. R. Joḥanan said: Words of Torah only remain with him who makes himself like one who is as nothing, as it is said, *Wisdom shall be found from nothing*.[10]

R. JOSHUA SAYS: A WOMAN PREFERS etc. What does he intend?—He means that a woman prefers one *ḳab* and sensuality with it to nine *ḳab* with continence.

HE USED TO SAY, A FOOLISH PIETIST etc. What is a foolish

by his zeal in Torah-study. This is the exposition of R. Menaḥem son of R. Jose.

(1) Cant. VIII, 7. (2) Simeon studied while supported by his brother, and R. Joḥanan was subsidised by R. Judah II, the Prince. Each, therefore, forfeited some of the merit which accrued from his study. (3) Who studied in the direst poverty; v. Yoma 35*b*. (4) From Palestine to Babylon. (5) V. Glos. (6) Cant. VIII, 7. Hillel, unlike the others named, declined to barter the merit he earned by devotion to Torah. (7) Prov. VIII, 12. Subtilty is not desirable in a woman. (8) Those who disagree with R. Eliezer. (9) He neglects everything else, and is therefore destitute. The Hebrew word for '*subtilty*' is connected with a root meaning 'to be naked'. (10) *Sic.*, Job XXVIII, 12.

pietist like?—E.g., a woman is drowning in the river, and he says, 'It is improper for me to look upon her and rescue her'. What is the cunning rogue like?—R. Johanan says: He who explains his case to the judge before the other party to the suit arrives.[1] R. Abbahu says: He who gives a poor man a *denar* to bring his possessions to the total of two hundred *zuz*;[2] for we have learnt; He who possesses two hundred *zuz* may not take gleanings, forgotten sheaves, the produce of the corner of the field, or the poor tithe;[3] but should he lack one *denar* of the two hundred [*zuz*], even if a thousand persons give him [the gleanings, etc.] simultaneously, he may accept.[4] R. Assi said in the name of R. Johanan: [A cunning rogue is] he who gives advice to sell an estate which is inconsiderable;[5] for R. Assi said in the name of R. Johanan: If the male-orphans sold an inconsiderable estate before [the daughters established their claim at a Court], their act of selling is legal. Abaye said: [A cunning rogue is] he who gives advice to sell property in accordance with the view of Rabban Simeon b. Gamaliel; for it has been taught: [If a man said], 'My property is for you and after you for So-and-so', and the first person went and sold it and ate up [the proceeds], the second man can recover from the purchaser. Such is the statement of Rabbi; Rabban Simeon b. Gamaliel says: The second only receives what the first left.[6] R. Joseph b. Ḥama said in the name of R. Shesheth: He who induces others to follow in his ways.[7] R. Zerika said in the name of R. Huna: He who is lenient with himself[8] and strict with others. 'Ulla said: He [22a] who learnt Scripture and Mishnah but did not attend upon Rabbinical scholars.[9]

It has been reported, If one has learnt Scripture and Mishnah

(1) Such an action is illegal; v. Shebu. 31a. (2) In order to prevent him from taking advantage of the law, so that he can retain the produce for his own kinsfolk. (3) V. Lev. XXIII, 22, Deut. XXIV, 19. (4) Pe'ah VIII, 8. (5) The law of inheritance is that where the estate is small, the daughters inherit 'and the sons can go begging' (B.B. 140a). (6) Cf. Keth. 95b; and B.B. 137a. (7) By hypocritically pretending to be pious. (8) In the interpretation of the Law. (9) To attain higher learning in Torah. He thus makes a pretence of a scholarship which he really does not possess.

but did not attend upon Rabbinical scholars, R. Eleazar says he is an *'Am ha-areẓ;*[1] R. Samuel b. Naḥmani says he is a boor; R. Jannai says he is a Samaritan;[2] R. Aḥa b. Jacob says he is a magician.[3] R. Naḥman b. Isaac said, The definition of R. Aḥa b. Jacob appears the most probable; because there is a popular saying: The magician mumbles and knows not what he says; the tanna[4] recites and knows not what he says.

Our Rabbis taught: Who is an *'Am ha-areẓ?* Whoever does not recite the *Shema'*[5] morning and evening with its accompanying benedictions; such is the statement of R. Meir. The Sages say, Whoever does not put on the phylacteries. Ben Azzai says, Whoever has not the fringe upon his garment.[6] R. Jonathan b. Joseph says, Whoever has sons and does not rear them to study Torah. Others say, Even if he learnt Scripture and Mishnah but did not attend upon Rabbinical scholars, he is an *'Am ha-areẓ*. If he learnt Scripture but not Mishnah, he is a boor; if he learnt neither Scripture nor Mishnah, concerning him Scripture declares, *I will sow the house of Israel and the house of Judah with the seed of man and with the seed of beast.*[7]

My son, fear thou the Lord and the king, and mingle not with them that are given to change.[8] R. Isaac said: They are the men who learn legal decisions.[9] This is self-evident![10]—[It is not, because] you might have supposed [that the text meant], they who repeat a sin, and that it is according to the teaching of R. Huna; for R. Huna said: When a man commits a transgression and repeats it, it becomes to him something which is permissible. Therefore he informs us

(1) Lit., 'people of the earth'; the description of those Jews who are careless about religious duties. (2) And his bread and wine must not be used by an observant Jew. (3) Who deceives the people. (4) V. Glos., s.v. Tanna (*b*). (5) V. Glos. For the benedictions, V. Singer *P.B.* pp. 39ff, 96ff. (6) V. Num. XV, 37ff [Zeitlin, S. (*JQR* (NS) XXIII, p. 58) sees in this an allusion to the early Jewish Christians who, as is known from the N.T. and the early Church Fathers, objected to the *Shema'*, phylacteries and fringes.] (7) Jer. XXXI, 27. (8) Prov. XXIV, 21. The word for *'that are given to change'* is *shonim* from *shanah* which in later Hebrew means 'learn' or 'repeat'. (9) And do not study with the scholars to understand their scope and derivation from Scripture. (10) So why is it mentioned?

[that this is not the intention of the text]. A Tanna taught: The Tannaim[1] bring destruction upon the world. How can it occur to you to say that they bring destruction upon the world! Rabina said: Because they decide points of law from their teachings.[2] It has been similarly taught: R. Joshua said: Do they destroy the world? Rather do they cultivate the world, as it is said, *As for the ways, the world is for him!*[3] But [the reference is to] those who decide points of law from their teachings.

A FEMALE PHARISEE etc. Our Rabbis have taught: A maiden who gives herself up to prayer,[4] a gadabout widow,[5] and a minor whose months are not completed[6]—behold these bring destruction upon the world. But it is not so; for R. Joḥanan has said: We learnt fear of sin from a maiden [who gave herself up to prayer] and [confidence in] the bestowal of reward from a [gadabout] widow! Fear of sin from a maiden—for R. Joḥanan heard a maiden fall upon her face and exclaim, 'Lord of the Universe! Thou hast created Paradise and Gehinnom; Thou hast created righteous and wicked. May it be Thy will that men should not stumble through me'. [Confidence in] the bestowal of reward from a widow—a certain widow had a Synagogue in her neighbourhood; yet she used to come daily to the School of R. Joḥanan[7] and pray there. He said to her, 'My daughter, is there not a Synagogue in your neighbourhood?' She answered him, 'Rabbi, but have I not the reward for the steps!'[8]—When it is said [that they bring destruction upon the world] the reference is to such a person as Joḥani the daughter of Reṭibi.[9] What means 'a minor whose months are not completed'?

(1) Who only report teachings without giving their derivations, cf. Glos. *s.v.* (*b*), and *supra* p. 103, n. 2. (2) [The Baraithas and Mishnas which they memorized without knowing perfectly the reasoning on which they were based.] (3) *Sic.*, Hab. III, 6. In Meg. 28*b* this is explained: Read not *halichoth* 'ways', but *halachoth* 'legal decisions', i.e., as for him (who studies) legal decisions, the world exists on account of him. (4) In the J. Talmud there is a variant: 'gives herself up to fasting'. We seem to have here an expression of disapproval of conventual life. (5) Her chastity is open to suspicion. (6) Explained below. (7) Where Services were held. (8) I.e., for the extra distance she walked to attend the Services. (9) She was a widow who by witchcraft made childbirth difficult for a woman and then offered prayer for her.

—They explained it thus: It refers to a disciple who rebels against the authority of his teachers. R. Abba said: It refers to a disciple who has not attained the qualification to decide questions of law and yet decides them; for R. Abbahu declared that R. Huna said in the name of Rab, What means that which is written, *For she hath cast down many wounded, yea, all her slain are a mighty host?*[1] *'For she hath cast down many wounded'*—this refers to a disciple who has not attained the qualification to decide questions of law and yet decides them; *'yea, all her slain are a mighty host'*—this refers to a disciple who has attained the qualification to decide questions of law and does not decide them. [22b] At what age [is he qualified]?—At forty.[2] But it is not so, for Rabbah decided questions of Law![3] —[He did so only in a town where the Rabbis] were his equals.[4]

AND THE PLAGUE OF PHARISEES etc. Our Rabbis have taught: There are seven types of Pharisees: the *shikmi* Pharisee, the *nikpi* Pharisee, the *ḳizai* Pharisee, the 'pestle' Pharisee, the Pharisee [who constantly exclaims] 'What is my duty that I may perform it?', the Pharisee from love [of God] and the Pharisee from fear. The *shikmi* Pharisee—he is one who performs the action of Shechem.[5] The *nikpi* Pharisee—he is one who knocks his feet together.[6] The *ḳizai* Pharisee—R. Naḥman b. Isaac said: He is one who makes his blood to flow against walls.[7] The 'pestle' Pharisee—Rabbah b. Shila said: [His head] is bowed like [a pestle in] a mortar. The

(1) Prov. VII, 26. (2) Tosaphoth explains this to mean after forty years of study. It may, however, be connected with the statement in Ab. V, 24, At forty for understanding. (3) He died at the age of forty; v. R. H. 18*a*. (4) Since they were not his superiors in learning, he decided questions although less than the requisite age. [Tosaf. *s.v.* שוין explains that Rabbah surpassed all other scholars in his town, and the restriction applies only where there are others equal in learning to the young scholar. For further notes on the passage, v. A.Z. (Sonc. ed.) p. 101.] (5) Who was circumcised from an unworthy motive (Gen. XXXIV). The J. Talmud (Ber. 14*b*) explains: who carries his religious duties upon his shoulder (*shekem*), i.e., ostentatiously. (6) He walks with exaggerated humility. According to the J. Talmud: He says, Spare me a moment that I may perform a commandment. (7) In his anxiety to avoid looking upon a woman he dashes his face against the wall. The J. Talmud explains: calculating Pharisee, i.e., he performs a good deed and then a bad deed, setting one off against the other.

Pharisee [who constantly exclaims] 'What is my duty that I may perform it?'—but that is a virtue!—Nay, what he says is, 'What further duty is for me that I may perform it?'[1] The Pharisee from love and the Pharisee from fear—Abaye and Raba said to the tanna [who was reciting this passage], Do not mention 'the Pharisee from love[2] and the Pharisee from fear'; for Rab Judah has said in the name of Rab: A man should always engage himself in Torah and the commandments even though it be not for their own sake,[3] because from [engaging in them] not for their own sake, he will come [to engage in them] for their own sake. R. Naḥman b. Isaac said: What is hidden is hidden, and what is revealed is revealed; the Great Tribunal will exact punishment from those who rub themselves against the walls.[4]

King Jannai[5] said to his wife, 'Fear not the Pharisees and the non-Pharisees but the hypocrites who ape the Pharisees; because their deeds are the deeds of Zimri[6] but they expect a reward like Phineas'.[7]

MISHNAH R. SIMEON SAYS: MERIT DOES NOT CAUSE THE WATER OF BITTERNESS TO SUSPEND ITS EFFECT, AND IF YOU SAY THAT MERIT DOES CAUSE THE WATER OF BITTERNESS TO SUSPEND ITS EFFECT, YOU DISCREDIT THE WATER IN THE CASE OF ALL THE WOMEN WHO DRINK IT AND DEFAME THE PURE WOMAN WHO DRANK IT, SINCE PEOPLE WILL SAY,

(1) As though he had fulfilled every obligation. (2) [Abaye and Raba understood 'love' and 'fear' to denote love of the rewards promised for the fulfilment of precepts and fear of punishment for transgressing them. In J. Ber., however, they are both taken in reference to God —i.e., love of God and fear of Him.] (3) From pure and disinterested motives. (4) In simulated humility. Others render: who wrap themselves in their cloaks. The meaning is that hypocrisy is of no avail against the Judge Who reads the heart. (5) Alexander Jannaeus. For his advice, given on his death-bed to his wife Salome, v. Josephus, *Ant.* XIII, XV, 5. (6) Num. XXV, 14. (7) Ibid. 11ff. [He probably had in mind the treacherous act by a group of Zealots—not Pharisees—in resisting foreign assistance—Demetrius Eucerus, King of Syria—in their struggle with Alexander Jannaeus. Josephus, *op. cit.* XIII, 13, 5. V. Klausner, היסטוריה II, 128.]

THEY WERE UNCLEAN, ONLY THEIR MERIT CAUSED THE WATER TO SUSPEND ITS EFFECT UPON THEM. RABBI SAYS: MERIT CAUSES THE WATER OF BITTERNESS TO SUSPEND ITS EFFECT, AND SHE NEVER BEARS A CHILD OR THRIVES, BUT SHE GRADUALLY GROWS ILL AND FINALLY DIES THROUGH THAT DEATH.[1]

IF HER MEAL-OFFERING BECAME DEFILED BEFORE IT BECAME HALLOWED IN THE [MINISTERING] VESSEL, BEHOLD IT IS LIKE ALL MEAL-OFFERINGS [SIMILARLY DEFILED] AND CAN BE REDEEMED;[2] BUT IF [IT BECAME DEFILED] AFTER IT HAD BEEN HALLOWED IN THE [MINISTERING] VESSEL, BEHOLD IT IS LIKE ALL MEAL-OFFERINGS [SIMILARLY DEFILED] AND IS DESTROYED. THE FOLLOWING HAVE THEIR MEAL-OFFERINGS DESTROYED: [23*a*] SHE WHO SAYS, 'I AM UNCLEAN TO THEE',[3] WHEN WITNESSES CAME [AND TESTIFIED] THAT SHE HAD MISCONDUCTED HERSELF, SHE WHO SAYS 'I REFUSE TO DRINK', WHEN THE HUSBAND REFUSES TO LET HER DRINK, AND WHEN HER HUSBAND COHABITED WITH HER ON THE JOURNEY [TO JERUSALEM]. FURTHERMORE, THE MEAL-OFFERINGS OF ALL WOMEN MARRIED TO PRIESTS ARE DESTROYED.[4] THE MEAL-OFFERING OF THE DAUGHTER OF AN ISRAELITE[5] WHO IS MARRIED TO A PRIEST IS DESTROYED. BUT THE MEAL-OFFERING OF A PRIEST'S DAUGHTER WHO IS MARRIED TO AN ISRAELITE IS EATEN. WHAT [DIFFERENCES ARE THERE IN LAW] BETWEEN A PRIEST AND A PRIEST'S DAUGHTER? THE MEAL-OFFERING OF A PRIEST'S DAUGHTER IS EATEN BUT THE MEAL-OFFERING OF A PRIEST IS NOT EATEN.[6] A PRIEST'S DAUGHTER MAY BECOME DECLASSED,[7] BUT A PRIEST DOES NOT BECOME DECLASSED.[8] A PRIEST'S DAUGHTER MAY RENDER HERSELF

(1) Caused by the symptoms described in Num. V, 27. (2) By paying its value into the Temple treasury. (3) To her husband through infidelity. (4) Although not defiled. The law of Lev. II, 3 does not apply, v. Gemara. (5) A non-priest. (6) V. Lev. VI, 16. (7) By contracting an illegal marriage. Even after divorce or in widowhood she loses her privileges. (8) Permanently by contracting an illegal marriage. After divorce or his wife's death he regains his privileges.

UNCLEAN BY CONTACT WITH THE DEAD, BUT A PRIEST MAY NOT RENDER HIMSELF UNCLEAN BY CONTACT WITH THE DEAD. A PRIEST EATS OF THE MOST HOLY [CLASS OF OFFERINGS],[1] BUT A PRIEST'S DAUGHTER MAY NOT EAT OF THE MOST HOLY.

WHAT [DIFFERENCES ARE THERE IN LAW] BETWEEN A MAN AND A WOMAN? A MAN RENDS HIS CLOTHES AND LOOSENS HIS HAIR,[2] BUT A WOMAN DOES NOT REND HER CLOTHES AND LOOSEN HER HAIR. A MAN MAY VOW THAT HIS SON WILL BECOME A NAZIRITE, BUT A WOMAN MAY NOT VOW THAT HER SON WILL BECOME A NAZIRITE.[3] A MAN MAY BE SHAVED ON ACCOUNT OF THE NAZIRITESHIP OF HIS FATHER,[4] BUT A WOMAN CANNOT BE SHAVED ON ACCOUNT OF THE NAZIRITESHIP OF HER FATHER. A MAN MAY SELL HIS DAUGHTER,[5] BUT A WOMAN MAY NOT SELL HER DAUGHTER. A MAN MAY GIVE HIS DAUGHTER IN BETROTHAL,[6] BUT A WOMAN MAY NOT GIVE HER DAUGHTER IN BETROTHAL. A MAN IS STONED NAKED, BUT A WOMAN IS NOT STONED NAKED.[7] A MAN IS HANGED,[8] BUT A WOMAN IS NOT HANGED. A MAN IS SOLD FOR HIS THEFT,[9] BUT A WOMAN IS NOT SOLD FOR HER THEFT.

GEMARA. Our Rabbis taught: The meal-offerings of all women who had married into the priesthood are to be destroyed.[10] How is this? In the case of the daughter of a priest, Levite or Israelite who had married a priest, her meal-offering is not eaten because he has a share in it,[11] nor is it treated as a holocaust[12] because she[13] has a share in it; but the handful is offered separately and the

(1) A sin-offering or guilt-offering. (2) When declared a leper (Lev. XIII, 45). (3) V. Nazir 28*b*. (4) I.e., in the event of his father's death, he can go through the ceremony described in Num. VI, 18, v. Nazir 30*a*. (5) As a bondwoman (Ex. XXI, 7). (6) Without her consent when she is a minor. (7) V. Sanh. 44*b*. (8) After capital punishment (Deut. XXI, 22). (9) Ex. XXII, 2. (10) And not eaten by the priests. (11) The flour belongs to him, and so the offering in fact comes under the law of Lev. VI, 16. (12) Which is the way the meal-offering of a priest is treated (13) Who is a non-priest.

remainder separately. But there is to be applied here the rule that whatever sacrifice has a portion thereof treated as 'offerings made by fire' comes under the law of *ye shall not burn!*[1] —R. Judah, son of R. Simeon b. Pazi said: They are burnt as fuel,[2] in accordance with the statement of R. Eliezer; for it has been taught: R. Eliezer says, *For a sweet savour*[3] thou mayest not bring it [upon the altar] but thou mayest bring it as fuel. This is right for R. Eliezer who holds this opinion; but what is there to say as regards the Rabbis who do not hold this opinion?—[They declare that] it is to be treated according to the view of R. Eleazar b. Simeon; for it has been taught: R. Eleazar b. Simeon says: The handful[4] is offered separately and the remainder is scattered upon the place of the ashes. [23*b*] And even the Rabbis only differ from R. Eleazar b. Simeon in the matter of the meal-offering brought by a sinner from among the priests which is something to be offered [in its entirety],[5] but even here[6] the Rabbis admit.[7]

[THE MEAL-OFFERING] OF THE DAUGHTER OF AN ISRAELITE WHO IS MARRIED etc. What is the reason?—Because Scripture declared, *And every meal-offering of the priest shall be wholly burnt; it shall not be eaten*[8]—'*of the priest*' but not of a priest's daughter.[9]

A PRIEST'S DAUGHTER MAY BECOME DECLASSED, BUT A PRIEST DOES NOT BECOME DECLASSED. Whence have we this? —Because Scripture declared, *He shall not profane his seed among his*

(1) Lev. II, 11. In this verse the word *mimmennu* 'of it' appears to be superfluous, and the deduction is drawn that the parts of a sacrifice which are designated as not to be burnt upon the altar must not be burnt upon it. How, then, can it be stated that 'the remainder' is to be burnt separately? (2) Upon the altar but not as part of the sacrifice. (3) Ibid. 12. (4) Of a meal-offering for a sin brought by a priest. Lev. VI, 16 speaks of a freewill-offering. (5) According to the Rabbis, this sin-offering is to be dealt with in the same manner as the ordinary meal-offering of the priest and burnt in its entirety without the handful being first removed and offered. (6) With the meal-offering of a priest's wife which is not something to be wholly offered, since this is treated like a non-priest. (7) That the remainder is not to be offered, but should be scattered. (8) Lev. VI, 16. (9) Consequently if the woman is a priest's wife but not a priest's daughter her offering is destroyed.

people[1]—his seed may become profaned,[2] but he himself cannot become profaned.

A PRIEST'S DAUGHTER MAY RENDER HERSELF UNCLEAN etc. What is the reason?—Scripture declared, *Speak unto the priests the sons of Aaron*[3]—'*the sons of Aaron*' but not the daughters of Aaron.

A PRIEST EATS OF THE MOST HOLY—for it is written, *Every male among the children of Aaron shall eat of it.*[4]

WHAT [DIFFERENCES ARE THERE IN LAW] BETWEEN A MAN etc. Our Rabbis taught: [*He is a leprous*] *man.*[5] I have here only mention of a man; whence is it [that the law applies to] a woman? When it states, *And the leper in whom* [*the plague is*],[6] behold here are two.[7] If so, what does the word '*man*' indicate? [It is to be applied] to the subject-matter of what follows, viz., it is a man who rends his clothes etc. [but not a woman].

A MAN MAY VOW THAT HIS SON WILL BECOME A NAZIRITE, BUT A WOMAN CANNOT VOW THAT HER SON WILL BECOME A NAZIRITE. R. Joḥanan said: This is a legal decision [traditionally handed down] in connection with a Nazirite.[8]

A MAN MAY BE SHAVED ON ACCOUNT OF THE NAZIRITESHIP OF HIS FATHER, BUT A WOMAN CANNOT BE SHAVED ON ACCOUNT OF THE NAZIRITESHIP OF HER FATHER. R. Joḥanan said: This is a legal decision [traditionally handed down] in connection with a Nazirite.[9]

A MAN MAY GIVE HIS DAUGHTER IN BETROTHAL, BUT A WOMAN CANNOT GIVE HER DAUGHTER IN BETROTHAL. Because it is written, *I gave my daughter unto this man.*[10]

A MAN MAY SELL HIS DAUGHTER, BUT A WOMAN MAY NOT SELL HER DAUGHTER. Because it is written, *And if a man sell his daughter.*[11]

A MAN IS STONED NAKED etc. What is the reason?—*And stone him*[12]—what means '*him*'? If I say that it means him and not her,

(1) Lev. XXI, 15. (2) As the result of an illegal marriage. (3) Ibid. 1. (4) Ibid. VI, 11. (5) Ibid. XIII, 44. (6) Ibid. 45. (7) Since these words are otherwise redundant after the preceding verse. (8) V. Nazir 28*b*. (9) V. Nazir 30*a*. (10) Deut. XXII, 16. The subject is '*the damsel's father*'. (11) Ex. XXI, 7. (12) Lev. XXIV, 14.

behold it is written, *Then shalt thou bring forth that man or that woman!*[1] But [the meaning is] *'him'* without his clothing but not her without her clothing.

A MAN IS HANGED etc. What is the reason?—Scripture declared, *And thou hang him on a tree*[2]—*'him'* but not her.

A MAN IS SOLD FOR HIS THEFT, BUT A WOMAN IS NOT SOLD FOR HER THEFT. What is the reason?—Scripture declared, *Then he shall be sold for his theft*[3]—*'for his theft'* but not for her theft.

(1) Deut. XVII, 5. (2) Ibid. XXI, 22. (3) Ex. XXII, 2. E.V. 3.

SOṬAH

CHAPTER IV

MISHNAH. A BETROTHED MAIDEN AND A CHILDLESS WIDOW WAITING FOR HER BROTHER-IN-LAW [TO DECIDE WHETHER HE WILL MARRY HER] DO NOT DRINK [THE WATER OF BITTERNESS][1] AND DO NOT RECEIVE WHAT IS DUE UNDER THE MARRIAGE-SETTLEMENT; AS IT IS SAID, WHEN A WIFE, BEING UNDER HER HUSBAND, GOETH ASIDE,[2] THUS EXCLUDING A BETROTHED MAIDEN AND A CHILDLESS WIDOW WAITING FOR HER BROTHER-IN-LAW. A WIDOW WHO HAD MARRIED A HIGH PRIEST,[3] A DIVORCED WOMAN OR A ḤALUẒAH[4] WHO HAD MARRIED AN ORDINARY PRIEST, AN ILLEGITIMATE [24*a*] OR A NETHINAH[5] WHO HAD MARRIED AN ISRAELITE, AND AN ISRAELITE'S DAUGHTER WHO HAD MARRIED AN ILLEGITIMATE OR A NATHIN DO NOT DRINK [THE WATER OF BITTERNESS] AND DO NOT RECEIVE WHAT IS DUE UNDER THE MARRIAGE-SETTLEMENT.

THE FOLLOWING DO NOT DRINK AND DO NOT RECEIVE THE MARRIAGE-SETTLEMENT: SHE WHO SAYS 'I AM UNCLEAN', WHEN WITNESSES CAME [AND TESTIFIED] THAT SHE HAD MISCONDUCTED HERSELF, AND SHE WHO SAYS 'I REFUSE TO DRINK'. WHEN HER HUSBAND IS UNWILLING TO LET HER DRINK, OR WHEN HER HUSBAND COHABITED WITH HER ON THE JOURNEY [TO JERUSALEM], SHE RECEIVES THE MARRIAGE-SETTLEMENT BUT DOES NOT DRINK. IF THE HUSBANDS DIED BEFORE [THE WOMEN] DRANK, BETH SHAMMAI DECLARE THAT THEY RECEIVE THE MARRIAGE-SETTLEMENT BUT DO

(1) In the event of seclusion with another man after receiving due warning. (2) Num. V, 29. (3) All the marriages enumerated here are illegal. (4) V. Glos. (5) A descendant of the Gibeonites (Josh. IX) with whom Israelites were not allowed to intermarry. An illegitimate was debarred under the law of Deut. XXIII, 3, E.V. 2.

NOT DRINK, AND BETH HILLEL DECLARE THAT THEY EITHER DRINK OR DO NOT RECEIVE THE MARRIAGE-SETTLEMENT.

[A WIFE] WHO WAS PREGNANT BY A FORMER HUSBAND OR WAS SUCKLING A CHILD BY A FORMER HUSBAND[1] DOES NOT DRINK AND DOES NOT RECEIVE THE MARRIAGE-SETTLEMENT. SUCH IS THE STATEMENT OF R. MEIR; BUT THE RABBIS DECLARE THAT HE IS ABLE TO SEPARATE FROM HER AND TAKE HER BACK AFTER THE PERIOD [OF TWO YEARS]. A WOMAN INCAPABLE OF CONCEPTION,[2] ONE TOO OLD TO BEAR CHILDREN, AND ONE WHO IS UNFIT TO BEAR CHILDREN[3] DO NOT RECEIVE THE MARRIAGE-SETTLEMENT AND DO NOT DRINK.[4] R. ELIEZER SAYS: HE IS ABLE TO MARRY ANOTHER WIFE[5] AND HAVE OFFSPRING BY HER. AS FOR ALL OTHER WOMEN, THEY EITHER DRINK OR DO NOT RECEIVE THE MARRIAGE-SETTLEMENT.

THE WIFE OF A PRIEST DRINKS AND IS PERMITTED TO HER HUSBAND.[6] THE WIFE OF A EUNUCH[7] DRINKS. THROUGH [SECLUSION WITH] ALL PERSONS FORBIDDEN TO HER IN MARRIAGE[8] JEALOUSY [NECESSITATING THE ORDEAL] IS ESTABLISHED WITH THE EXCEPTION OF A MINOR[9] AND ONE NOT A MAN.[10]

IN THE FOLLOWING CASES A COURT OF LAW CAN GIVE WARNING:[11] WHEN THE HUSBAND IS A DEAF-MUTE OR HAS BECOME INSANE OR IS IMPRISONED. NOT FOR THE PURPOSE OF MAKING HER DRINK DID THEY SAY THIS, BUT TO DISQUALIFY HER IN CONNECTION WITH THE MARRIAGE-SETTLE-

(1) Under Rabbinic Law, a pregnant woman who had been divorced or widowed should not marry for two years This Mishnah deals with the case where she married within that period and her husband became jealous of her. (2) Lit., 'ram-like', v. Keth. 11*a*. (3) This refers to a woman who lost the capability of bearing by taking some drug and not just barren or too old to bear children. (4) Because marriage with such as these is forbidden to one who has no children. (5) In addition to her; he therefore regards such a marriage as valid. (6) If proved innocent. (7) Who became so after marriage. (8) E.g., her father or brother. (9) Under the age of nine years. (10) Explained in the Gemara. (11) Instead of the husband, when they have cause to suspect the wife.

MENT. R. JOSE SAYS: ALSO TO MAKE HER DRINK; WHEN HER HUSBAND IS RELEASED FROM PRISON HE MAKES HER DRINK.

GEMARA. [In the instances enumerated by the Mishnah, the husband] does not let her drink, but he may give her a warning.[1] Whence is this learnt?—Our Rabbis taught: *Speak unto the children of Israel and say*[2]—[the addition of '*and say*'] is to include a betrothed maiden and a childless widow waiting for her levir in the law respecting the warning. Whose is [the teaching of] our Mishnah?—It is R. Jonathan's; for it has been taught: *Being under thy husband*[3] excludes a betrothed maiden. It is possible to think that we are also to exclude a childless widow; therefore the text repeats the word '*man*'.[4] Such is the statement of R. Joshiah. R. Jonathan says: '*Being under thy husband*' excludes a childless widow. [It is possible to think that] we exclude a childless widow waiting for her levir but not a betrothed maiden; therefore there is a text to declare, *When a wife, being under her husband, goeth aside*,[5] thus excluding a betrothed maiden. One teacher[6] considers a betrothed maiden as more bound to him since the marriage ensues through him and they stone her on his account;[7] whereas the other teacher considers that a childless widow is more bound to [her brother-in-law] since the nuptial surrender is not lacking.[8] What, then, does R. Jonathan make of the repetition of the word '*man*'?—He requires it to include the wife of a deaf-mute man, the wife of an imbecile, and the wife of [24*b*] a weak-minded man.[9] And what does R. Joshiah make of the phrase '*being under her husband*'?—He requires it to draw an analogy between a husband and wife and between a wife and husband.[10]

(1) Not to associate with the man, in order to deny her right to the marriage-settlement if she disobeyed. (2) Num. V, 12. (3) Ibid. 19. (4) In verse 12 *any man's wife* is literally: a man, a man, his wife. The addition of the word '*man*' is taken to include the case of a childless widow, waiting for her levir. (5) Ibid. 29. (6) R. Jonathan. (7) If she is unchaste (Deut. XXII, 24). (8) By the death of her husband she *ipso facto* becomes the wife of her brother-in-law if he wishes to take her, and an act of cohabitation constitutes a marriage. (9) V. *infra* 27*a*. (10) This is likewise expounded *infra* 27*a*.

Now the reason [given why a betrothed maiden is excluded] is because these Scriptural texts occur, otherwise I would have said that a betrothed maiden must drink; but when R. Aḥa b. Ḥanina came from the South he brought this teaching with him: *Besides thine husband*[1]—i.e., when intercourse with a husband had preceded intercourse with a paramour and not when intercourse with a paramour had preceded intercourse with a husband![2]—Rami b. Ḥama said, [It is necessary to rely upon the texts] for such a contingency as when the fiancé had had intercourse with her in her father's house.[3] Similarly with a childless widow the texts would be required for the contingency as when the brother-in-law had had intercourse with her in her father-in-law's house;[4] but can you call her a childless widow waiting for her levir'? [In such circumstances], surely she is his legal wife; for Rab has said, He[5] has acquired her [as his wife] in every respect![6]—It is as Samuel said, He has only acquired her for the objects mentioned in the Scriptural portion.[7] If that is so, are we to say that Rab agrees with R. Joshiah[8] and Samuel with R. Jonathan?[9]—Rab can reply, I even agree with R. Jonathan, because from the fact that it was necessary for the text to exclude her,[10] it follows that she is his legal wife. [25*a*] Similarly Samuel can reply, I even agree with R. Joshiah, because from the fact that it was necessary for the text to include her, it follows that she is not his wife at all.

The question was asked, Does a woman who transgresses [the Jewish] ethical code[11] require to be warned in order to make her

(1) Num. V, 20. (2) Consequently a betrothed maiden is excluded from the law. (3) Before marriage. (4) After her husband's death. (5) The levir. (6) By cohabitation. If, e.g., he is a priest, she partakes of the heave-offering. (7) Deut. XXV, 5-10, viz., to be his brother's heir and free himself from the ceremony of *Ḥaliẓah;* but cohabitation would not constitute a marriage to give her the right to partake of the heave-offering if he was a priest. (8) Who says that a childless widow waiting for her levir drinks, and that can arise in the case where the cohabitation occurred in her father's house. (9) Who holds that she does not drink, for cohabitation does not constitute full marriage. (10) A childless widow who cohabited with her brother-in- law. (11) And thereby shows an indifference for public opinion; such a woman is put away without recovering her *kethubah*, v. Keth. 72*a*.

lose her marriage-settlement or does she not require it? Do we say that since she transgresses the ethical code she does not require to be warned; or perhaps warning is necessary because she may reform?—Come and hear: A BETROTHED MAIDEN AND A CHILDLESS WIDOW WAITING FOR HER BROTHER-IN-LAW[1] DO NOT DRINK AND DO NOT RECEIVE WHAT IS DUE UNDER THE MARRIAGE-SETTLEMENT. [In these instances the man] does not let her drink but he may give her warning. But for what purpose [does he warn her]? Is it not to make her lose her marriage-settlement![2]—Abaye said: No; [the purpose is] to prohibit her to himself [in marriage]. R. Papa said: [The purpose is] to make her drink when she is married;[3] as it has been taught: We may not warn a betrothed maiden with the object of making her drink while she is betrothed; but we may warn a betrothed maiden with the object of making her drink when she is married.

Raba said: Come and hear: A WIDOW WHO HAD MARRIED A HIGH PRIEST, A DIVORCED WOMAN OR A ḤALUẒAH WHO HAD MARRIED AN ORDINARY PRIEST, AN ILLEGITIMATE OR A NETHINAH WHO HAD MARRIED AN ISRAELITE, AND AN ISRAELITE'S DAUGHTER WHO HAD MARRIED AN ILLEGITIMATE OR A NATHIN DO NOT DRINK AND DO NOT RECEIVE WHAT IS DUE UNDER THE MARRIAGE-SETTLEMENT. They do not drink but they receive a warning. But for what purpose? If [you answer] to make them prohibited to the husband, behold they are already prohibited;[4] rather must it be to make them lose the marriage-settlement!—Rab Judah of Diskarta[5] said: No; [the purpose is] to prohibit her to the paramour as to the husband; as we learn: Just as she is prohibited to the husband so is she prohibited to the paramour.[6]

R. Ḥanina of Sura said; Come and hear: IN THE FOLLOWING CASES A COURT OF LAW CAN GIVE WARNING: WHEN THE

(1) These too had transgressed the ethical code by their act of seclusion. (2) Consequently, without warning she would not lose it. (3) If she secluded herself with a man after marriage, then the warning which the husband gave her for a previous action, while she was betrothed, is still valid. (4) Since such a marriage is contrary to law. (5) V. *supra* p. 26, n. 7. (6) V. *infra* 27*b*.

HUSBAND IS A DEAF-MUTE OR HAS BECOME INSANE OR IS IMPRISONED. NOT FOR THE PURPOSE OF MAKING HER DRINK DID THEY SAY THIS BUT TO DISQUALIFY HER IN CONNECTION WITH THE MARRIAGE-SETTLEMENT. Conclude from this that she does require to be warned! That conclusion is to be drawn. But why did not [the other Rabbis] draw the inference from this passage?—[They thought] perhaps it is different in the circumstance where she had no cause at all to be afraid of her husband.[1]

The question was asked, If a woman transgresses [the Jewish] ethical code and the husband desired to retain her, may he do so or may he not? Do we say that the All-Merciful depends upon the husband's objection [to her conduct],[2] and in this case he does not object; or, perhaps, since [a husband normally] objects, he must object [and divorce her]?—Come and hear: IN THE FOLLOWING CASES A COURT OF LAW CAN GIVE WARNING: WHEN THE HUSBAND IS A DEAF-MUTE OR HAS BECOME INSANE OR IS IMPRISONED. Should you maintain that if the husband desired to retain her he may do so, can the Court of Law do something of which the husband may not approve?[3]—As a general rule, when a woman transgresses the ethical code, [the husband] is agreeable [to the warning].

The question was asked, If a husband retracted his warning, is the warning retracted or not?[4] Do we say that the All-Merciful depends upon the husband's warning and here the husband retracted it; or perhaps since he already gave a warning he is unable to withdraw it?—Come and hear: IN THE FOLLOWING CASES A COURT OF LAW CAN GIVE WARNING: WHEN THE HUSBAND IS A DEAF-MUTE OR HAS BECOME INSANE OR IS

(1) Since he was incapacitated; but in normal circumstances, they imagined that she would lose her marriage-settlement without a warning. (2) Because Scripture declares, *'and he be jealous of his wife'*. If he is not jealous, is her conduct to be overlooked? (3) The Court, representing the husband, would thereby involve him in an act which was contrary to his wish, and this is not legally possible, v. Keth. 11*a*. (4) [Assuming that the husband may retain a wife who transgresses the ethical code, the question still arises whether he can retract or not in the case where he had given her a warning.]

IMPRISONED. Should you maintain that if a husband retracted his warning his warning is retracted, can we[1] perform an action which the husband may come and retract![2]—As a general rule, a man agrees with the opinion of a Court of Law.[3]

Come and hear: And they assign to him two disciples of the Sages lest he cohabit with her on the journey.[4] Should you maintain that if a husband retracted his warning the warning is retracted, let him then withdraw it and cohabit with her!—Why are disciples of the Sages specified? Because they are learned men, so that if he wishes to cohabit with her, they say to him, 'Withdraw your warning and cohabit with her'.[5]

Come and hear: R. Joshiah said: Three things did Ze'ira tell me as emanating from the men of Jerusalem:[6] If a husband retracted his warning the warning is retracted; if a Court of Law wished to pardon an elder who rebelled [against their decision] they may pardon him; and if the parents wished to forgive a stubborn and rebellious son[7] they may forgive him.[8] When, however, I came to my colleagues in the South, they agreed with me in respect of two but did not agree with me in respect of the rebellious elder, so that disputes should not multiply in Israel. Deduce therefrom that if a husband retracted his warning the warning is retracted. Draw that conclusion.

In this connection R. Aḥa and Rabina differ. One said that [the warning can be] retracted before seclusion but not after seclusion, and the other said that also after seclusion it can be retracted. The more probable view is that of him who said that it cannot be retracted. Whence is this learnt?—[It is to be inferred] from the answer which the Rabbis gave to R. Jose; for it has been taught: R. Jose says: By *a fortiori* reasoning [it is deduced] that a husband is trusted with her. If a husband is trusted in the matter of his

(1) I.e., the Court. (2) And then offer an affront to the court. (3) But if he wishes to retract he may do so. (4) V. *supra* 7a. (5) This is a reply to the question. The husband indeed can withdraw, and that is the very reason why disciples of the Sages are specified. (6) [Rashi: who was of the men of Jerusalem]. (7) Cf. Deut. XXI, 18ff. (8) For further notes v. Sanh. (Sonc. ed.) p. 585.

wife during menstruation where the penalty is excision, how much more so in the matter of his wife while under suspicion in connection with which there is a mere prohibition! [The Rabbis] replied to him, No; if you argue [that he may be trusted] in the case of his wife during menstruation to whom he will have a right [on her recovery], will you argue so in the case of his wife while under suspicion when he may never have a right to her![1] Now if you maintain that [a warning may be] retracted after seclusion, then it can happen that he may again have a right to her; because if he so desire, he can retract his warning and cohabit! Therefore deduce from this that after seclusion it cannot be retracted. Draw that conclusion.

IF THE HUSBANDS DIED BEFORE [THE WOMEN] DRANK, BETH SHAMMAI etc. On what point [do the two Schools] differ? —Beth Shammai are of opinion that a bond which is due for redemption is considered as having been redeemed;[2] [25b] whereas Beth Hillel are of opinion that a bond which is due for redemption is not considered as having been redeemed.[3]

[A WIFE] WHO WAS PREGNANT BY A FORMER HUSBAND etc. R. Naḥman said in the name of Rabbah b. Abbuha: The dispute[4] is in connection with a barren woman and one too old to bear children; but as for a woman incapable of conception, all agree that she does not drink and does not receive her marriage-settlement, as it is said, *Then she shall be free and shall conceive seed*[5] —i.e., one whose way it is to conceive seed, thus excluding one whose way is not to conceive seed.

(1) V. *supra* 7a. (2) If the bond was on the security of the borrower's property, then at the time of the redemption the property is considered as automatically passing into the possession of the creditor pending payment. By analogy, the widow is automatically entitled to her marriage-settlement on the husband's death and the onus is upon the heirs to prove that she had forfeited it by producing witnesses that she had committed adultery. (3) As the creditor must first establish his right to the debtor's property, so the widow must prove her right to the marriage-settlement by drinking the water, since she is under suspicion; for fuller notes v. Shebu. (Sonc. ed.) p. 298, n. 5. (4) Viz., R. Eliezer says, He is able to marry another wife and have offspring by her. (5) Num. V, 28.

An objection was raised: 'If a man gives a warning to his betrothed or to his brother's childless widow, should she seclude herself [with the other man] before the marriage, she does not drink and does not receive her marriage-settlement'.[1] [26a] '[A wife] who was pregnant by a former husband or was suckling a child by a former husband does not drink and does not receive the marriage-settlement.'[2] Such is the statement of R. Meir; because R. Meir says, A man may not marry a woman who is pregnant by a former husband or is suckling a child by a former husband, and if he married her he must let her go and never take her back; the Sages, on the other hand, say, He must let her go, but when the time arrives when he may marry her[3] he marries her. 'If a youth married a barren woman or one too old to bear, and he did not previously have a wife and children, she does not drink and does not receive the marriage-settlement. R. Eliezer says: He is able to marry another wife and have offspring by her'.[4] But 'if a man gives a warning to his betrothed or to his brother's childless widow and she secluded herself after marriage, she either drinks or does not receive the marriage-settlement. If the wife is pregnant or suckling a child by himself,[5] she either drinks or does not receive the marriage-settlement. And if a youth married a barren woman or one too old to bear, and he already had a wife and children, she either drinks or does not receive the marriage-settlement. The legal wife of an illegitimate,[6] the legal wife of a *Nathin*, the wife of a proselyte or freed slave, and a woman incapable of conception either drink or do not receive the marriage-settlement.[7] Here the woman incapable of conception is specified [among the woman who are required to drink]! It is a refutation of R. Naḥman.[8]

R. Naḥman can reply, [That which I stated above is a difference

(1) V. Tosef. Soṭah V, 4. (2) Ibid. 6. (3) I.e., after the lapse of two years from the birth of the child. (4) Tosef. ibid. 5. The last sentence occurs in the Mishnah p. 120, and instead the Tosef. reads: R. Eliezer says, He is able to separate from her and take her back after a time. (5) I.e., by the husband who gives her warning. (6) Viz., a woman who was competent to marry such a man, and she secluded herself after warning. (7) Tosef. ibid. 1-4. (8) He asserted above, 'All agree that she does not drink'.

between] Tannaim, whereas I agree with the following Tanna. For it has been taught: R. Simeon b. Eleazar says: A woman incapable of conception does not drink and does not receive the marriage-settlement, as it is said, *Then she shall be free and shall conceive seed*[1]—i.e., one whose way is to conceive seed, thus excluding one whose way is not to conceive seed.[2] What, then, do the Rabbis make of the phrase '*Then she shall be free and shall conceive seed*'? They require it in accordance with the following teaching: '*Then she shall be free and conceive seed*'—so that if she had been barren, she now becomes visited.[3] Such is the statement of R. Akiba. R. Ishmael said to him, In that case, all barren women will seclude themselves and be visited, and since this one did not seclude herself she will be the loser![4] If so, what is the purpose of '*Then she shall be free and shall conceive seed*'? If she formerly bore children in pain she will now bear with ease; if formerly girls she will now give birth to boys; if formerly short she will now bear tall children; if formerly dark she will now have fair children.

'The legal wife of an illegitimate [either drinks or does not receive the marriage-settlement]'—this is self-evident![5]—What you might have said was that disqualified [members of the Community] should not be multiplied.[6] Therefore he informs us [that such a marriage is treated like any other].

'The wife of a proselyte or freed slave and a woman incapable of conception [either drink or do not receive the marriage-settlement]'—this is self-evident!—What you might have said was, *Speak unto the children of Israel*[7]—but not to proselytes. Therefore he informs us [that proselytes are included in the law]. Or as an alternative answer, *And say*[8] is to be interpreted as including [the wife of a proselyte, etc.].

THE WIFE OF A PRIEST DRINKS etc. This is self-evident!—What

(1) Num. V, 28. (2) Tosef. ibid. 4. (3) The Biblical term used of barren women who conceive. (4) By remaining loyal to her husband and avoiding all suspicion a barren woman will continue sterile! (5) Since her marriage is legal. (6) The purpose of the Torah cannot be to restore harmony between such a couple, since the offspring of the union would be disqualified from membership in the Community. (7) Num. V, 12. (8) Ibid.

you might have said was, *And she had not been violated*[1]—then she is prohibited [to her husband];[2] hence if she had been violated she is permitted to him; but this woman [being the wife of a priest] is prohibited to him even if she had been violated, and consequently she does not drink. Therefore he informs us [that she does undergo the ordeal].

AND IS PERMITTED TO HER HUSBAND. This is self-evident! —R. Huna said: [This refers to a case where] she becomes ill.[3] But if she becomes ill, the water has proved her [guilty]!—[It refers to a case where] she becomes ill in other limbs.[4] What you might have said was that she had committed adultery, and the fact that the water did not affect her in the usual way was due to her having acted immorally under force and as such she is prohibited to a priest. Therefore he informs us [that she is permitted to her husband].

THE WIFE OF A EUNUCH DRINKS. This is self-evident!—What you might have said was, *Besides thine husband*[5] declared the All-Merciful, and this man [being a eunuch] does not come within the category [of husband]. Therefore he informs us [that he is considered to be her husband for the law of the ordeal].

THROUGH [SECLUSION WITH] ALL PERSONS FORBIDDEN TO HER IN MARRIAGE JEALOUSY IS ESTABLISHED. This is self-evident! [26*b*]—What you might have said was, The phrase *'and she be defiled'* occurs twice[6]—once with respect to the husband and the other with respect to the paramour[7]—but it only applies when she becomes prohibited [to the paramour] by this act of adultery; but where she was in any event forbidden to him, conclude that she is not [barred from marrying him]. Therefore he informs us [that she has to undergo the ordeal although the paramour was forbidden to her in any case and if guilty she cannot marry her paramour].

WITH THE EXCEPTION OF A MINOR etc. A *man*[8] declared the All-Merciful, not a minor.

(1) Num. V, 13; i.e., she had been a consenting party. (2) V. *supra 2b*. (3) After drinking the water. (4) Not those enumerated in Num. V, 22. (5) Ibid. 20. (6) Ibid. 13f. (7) She must be divorced by her husband and is not allowed to marry her paramour. V. Mishnah p. 135. (8) *Lie with her carnally*, Num. V, 13.

AND ONE NOT A MAN. Whom does this exclude? If I answer that it is to exclude one whose flesh is wasted,[1] behold Samuel has said: A warning [against seclusion] can be given in connection with a man who is wasting and he disqualifies for partaking of the heave-offering![2] (A warning [against seclusion] can be given in connection with him—this is self-evident!—What you might have said was, *'And a man lie with her carnally'* declared the All-Merciful and such a one does not come within that category; therefore he informs us [that seclusion with him does bring the woman within the scope of the law]. And he disqualifies for partaking of the heave-offering—that is self-evident!—What you might have said was, *He shall not profane his seed*[3] declared the All-Merciful—one who had *'seed'* can profane,[4] but one who had no *'seed'* cannot profane; therefore he informs us [that he can profane].[5]) If, on the other hand, it is to exclude a gentile, behold R. Hamnuna has said: A warning [against seclusion] can be given in connection with a gentile and he disqualifies for partaking of the heave-offering! (A warning [against seclusion] can be given in connection with him—this is self-evident!—What you might have said was, The phrase *'and she be defiled'* occurs twice—once with respect to the husband and the other with respect to the paramour—but it only applies when she becomes prohibited [to the paramour] by this act of adultery; but where she was in any event forbidden to him,[6] conclude that she is not [warned against seclusion]. Therefore he informs us [that a warning can be given with respect to a gentile]. And he disqualifies for partaking of the heave-offering—this is self-evident!—What you might have said was, *And if a priest's daughter be married unto a stranger*[7] declared the All-Merciful, i.e., when there was a legal marriage-status, but not when there is no legal marriage-status. Therefore he informs us [that a gentile]

(1) Tosef. Bek. V, 4, identifies the term with *he who hath his stones broken* in Lev. XXI, 20. (2) If he married a priest's daughter when he was so afflicted, she loses the right to eat of the heave-offering. (3) Lev. XXI, 15. (4) A priest's daughter by marriage. (5) Consequently a person who is so afflicted is regarded as 'a man' and cannot be intended by the Mishnah. (6) He being a gentile. (7) Lev. XXII, 12.

does disqualify her. This is in agreement with R. Johanan who said in the name of R. Ishmael: Whence is it that a gentile or a slave who had intercourse with a priest's daughter or Levite's daughter or an Israelite's daughter disqualifies her [for the heave-offering]? As it is said, *But if a priest's daughter be a widow, or divorced*[1]—only in the case of a man where her widowhood or divorce [is legally recognised],[2] thus excluding a gentile or slave where her widowhood or divorce is not [legally recognised].)[3] What, then, [does the phrase AND NOT A MAN] exclude?—R. Papa said: It excludes an animal, because there is not adultery in connection with an animal.[4]

Raba of Parazika[5] asked R. Ashi, Whence is the statement which the Rabbis made that there is no adultery in connection with an animal?—Because it is written, *Thou shalt not bring the hire of a harlot or the wages of a dog* etc.;[6] and it has been taught: The hire of a dog[7] and the wages of a harlot[8] are permissible, as it is said, *Even both these*[9]—the two [specified in the text are abominations] but not four.[10]

What is the purpose [of the Scriptural phrase] *carnally?*[11]—It is required for this teaching: '*Carnally*' to the exclusion of something else. What means 'something else'?—R. Shesheth said: It excludes the case where he warned her against unnatural intercourse. Raba said to him, [It excludes the case where he warned her against] unnatural intercourse? It is written, *As lying with womankind!*[12] But, said Raba, it excludes the case where he warned her against contact of the bodies.[13] Abaye said to him, That is

(1) Lev. XXII, 13. (2) Does she return to her father's house and eat the heave-offering. (3) Therefore a gentile cannot be intended by the Mishnah. (4) She would not be prohibited to her husband for such an act. (5) Farausag near Bagdad v. B.B. (Sonc. ed.) p. 15, n. 4. He is thus distinguished from the earlier Rabbi of that name. (6) Deut. XXIII, 19. (7) Money given by a man to a harlot to associate with his dog. Such an association is not legal adultery. (8) If a man had a female slave who was a harlot and he exchanged her for an animal, it could be offered. (9) *Are an abomination unto the Lord* (ibid.). (10) Viz., the other two mentioned by the Rabbis. (11) In Num. V, 13, since the law applies to a man who is incapable. (12) Lev. XVIII, 22. The word for '*lying*' is in the plural and is explained as denoting also unnatural intercourse. (13) With the other man, although there is no actual coition.

merely an obscene act [and not adultery], and did the All-Merciful prohibit [a wife to her husband] for an obscene act? But, said Abaye, it excludes the case where he warned her against external contact. This is quite right according to him who maintains that by sexual contact is to be understood insertion[1] inasmuch as external contact is not regarded, and consequently the Scriptural phrase is intended to exclude the latter; but according to him who maintains that sexual contact is the external contact what is there to say?—Certainly [the Scriptural phrase is intended to exclude the case where] he warned her against contact of the bodies; and should you argue that the All-Merciful made it depend upon the husband's objection [to such conduct] and behold the husband did object,[2] therefore he informs us [that the phrase *'carnally'* is to exclude this].

Samuel said: Let a man marry [27*a*] a woman of ill-repute rather than the daughter of a woman of ill-repute, since the former comes from pure stock and the latter from impure stock.[3] R. Johanan, however, said: Let a man marry the daughter of a woman of ill-repute rather than a woman of ill-repute, since the former is presumably chaste whereas the latter is not. An objection was raised: One should marry a woman of ill-repute!—Raba said: Can you possibly think that [the meaning is that] he should marry [a woman of ill-repute who is such] at the outset? But the statement should take this form: 'If a man married [a woman of ill-repute']; and similarly [read] 'the daughter of a woman of ill-repute'.[4] But the legal decision is: Let a man marry the daughter of a woman of ill-repute rather than a woman of ill-repute; because R. Taḥlifa, the son of the West,[5] recited in the presence of R. Abbahu, If a woman is an adulteress, her children are legitimate since the majority of the acts of cohabitation are ascribed to the husband.

R. Amram asked: How is it if she was excessively dissolute?[6]

(1) Which is legally equal to complete coition. (2) As evidenced by his warning. (3) [As it is not known with whom the mother had relation.] (4) [Since the Baraitha has to be amended in any case we might just as well amend 'a woman' into 'the daughter of a woman etc.'.] (5) I.e., the Palestinian. (6) Are the children legitimate?

According to him who maintains that a woman only conceives immediately before her period the question does not arise, because [the husband] may not know [when this is] and does not watch her; but the question does arise according to him who maintains that a woman only conceives immediately after the time of her purification. How is it then? Does he watch her since he knows when this occurs; or perhaps this is of no account since she is excessively dissolute?[1] The question remains unanswered.

IN THE FOLLOWING CASES A COURT OF LAW etc. Our Rabbis taught: '*Man*'—why does Scripture repeat the word?[2] To include the wife of a deaf man, the wife of an imbecile, the wife of a weak-minded man, and cases where the husband has gone on a journey to a distant country or is imprisoned, that a Court of Law can give them warning to disqualify them in connection with the marriage-settlement. It is possible [to think that the warning] is also to make them drink; therefore there is a text to say, *Then shall the man bring his wife.*[3] R. Jose says: It is also to make the woman drink so that when the husband is released from prison he makes her drink.[4] On what do they differ?—The Rabbis are of the opinion that we require that the same man who '*warned*' her must '*bring*' her,[5] whereas R. Jose is of the opinion that we do not require that the same man who '*warned*' her must '*bring*' her.[6]

Our Rabbis taught: *When a wife, being under her husband, goeth aside*[7]—this is to compare a husband with a wife and a wife with a husband. For what practical purpose?—R. Shesheth said: Just as he does not make her drink if he is blind, as it is written, *And it be hid from the eyes of her husband,*[8] so she does not drink if she is blind. R. Ashi said: Just as a woman who is lame or armless does not drink, for it is written, [27b] *And the priest shall set the woman*

(1) And she may deceive him although he is careful to watch her. (2) In the Hebrew text of Num. V, 12. (3) Ibid. 15. (4) V. *supra* 24a. (5) To the ordeal, and only the husband can bring her. (6) And so he gives the Court power to warn her for the purpose of the ordeal. (7) Num. V, 29. (8) Ibid. 13. He presumably could see.

before the Lord . . . and put the meal-offering in her hands,[1] so he does not make her drink if he is lame or armless. Mar son of R. Ashi said: Just as a dumb woman does not drink, for it is written *And the woman shall say Amen, Amen,*[2] so he does not make her drink if he is dumb.

(1) Num. V, 18. (2) Ibid. 22.

SOṬAH

CHAPTER V

MISHNAH. JUST AS THE WATER PROVES HER SO THE WATER PROVES HIM;[1] AS IT IS SAID, 'AND SHALL ENTER' TWICE.[2] JUST AS SHE IS PROHIBITED TO THE HUSBAND[3] SO IS SHE PROHIBITED TO THE PARAMOUR;[4] AS IT IS SAID, DEFILED ... AND IS DEFILED.[5] THIS IS THE STATEMENT OF R. AKIBA. R. JOSHUA SAID: THUS USED ZECHARIAH B. HAḲAẒAB TO EXPOUND.[6] RABBI SAYS: THE WORD 'DEFILED' OCCURS TWICE IN THE SCRIPTURAL PORTION,[7] ONE REFERRING [TO HER BEING PROHIBITED] TO THE HUSBAND AND THE OTHER TO THE PARAMOUR.

ON THAT DAY,[8] R. AKIBA EXPOUNDED, AND EVERY EARTHEN VESSEL, WHEREINTO ANY OF THEM FALLETH, WHATSOEVER IS IN IT SHALL BE UNCLEAN,[9] IT DOES NOT STATE ṬAME [IS UNCLEAN] BUT YIṬMA',[10] I.E. TO MAKE OTHERS UNCLEAN. THIS TEACHES THAT A LOAF WHICH IS UNCLEAN IN THE SECOND DEGREE[11] MAKES [WHATEVER IT COMES IN CONTACT WITH] UNCLEAN IN THE THIRD DEGREE. R. JOSHUA SAID: WHO WILL REMOVE THE DUST

(1) Her paramour. (2) Num. V, 24, 27. (3) He must divorce her if she is guilty. (4) He is not allowed to marry her. (5) Ibid. 29. The *and* is redundant; it is therefore employed by R. Akiba for an exegetical purpose. (6) He similarly explained the redundant *and*. (7) In verses 14 and 29. It also occurs in verse 13; but that is expounded in a different connection. V. fol. 2*b*, p. 5. (8) When the preceding was taught. It was the important occasion when R. Eleazar b. Azariah was appointed Principal of the School in place of Rabban Gamaliel II. V. Ber. 27*b et seq*. (Rashi). V. 'Ed. (Sonc. ed.). Introduction p. XI. [Geiger, *Lesestücke aus der Mischnah*, p. 37: on the same day on which the previous teachings were presented.] (9) Lev. XI, 33. The reference is to unclean creeping things. (10) Since the text was unpointed, R. Akiba read the word as *yeṭamme'*, i.e., 'makes (others) unclean'. (11) The vessel becomes unclean first and then defiles the loaf in it.

FROM THINE EYES, R. JOḤANAN B. ZAKKAI, SINCE THOU SAYEST THAT ANOTHER GENERATION IS DESTINED TO PRONOUNCE CLEAN A LOAF[1] WHICH IS UNCLEAN IN THE THIRD DEGREE ON THE GROUND THAT THERE IS NO TEXT IN THE TORAH ACCORDING TO WHICH IT IS UNCLEAN![2] IS NOT R. AKIBA THY PUPIL?[3] HE ADDUCES A TEXT IN THE TORAH ACCORDING TO WHICH IT IS UNCLEAN, VIZ., 'WHATSOEVER IS IN IT SHALL BE UNCLEAN'.

ON THAT DAY R. AKIBA EXPOUNDED, AND YE SHALL MEASURE WITHOUT THE CITY FOR THE EAST SIDE TWO THOUSAND CUBITS ETC.[4] BUT ANOTHER TEXT STATES, FROM THE WALL OF THE CITY OUTWARD A THOUSAND CUBITS ROUND ABOUT.[5] IT IS IMPOSSIBLE TO SAY THAT IT WAS A THOUSAND CUBITS SINCE IT HAS BEEN ALREADY STATED 'TWO THOUSAND CUBITS'; AND IT IS IMPOSSIBLE TO SAY THAT IT WAS TWO THOUSAND CUBITS SINCE IT HAS BEEN ALREADY STATED 'A THOUSAND CUBITS'! HOW WAS IT THEN? A THOUSAND CUBITS FOR THE SUBURB[6] AND TWO THOUSAND CUBITS FOR THE SABBATH-LIMIT.[7] R. ELIEZER THE SON OF R. JOSE THE GALILEAN SAYS: A THOUSAND CUBITS FOR THE SUBURB AND TWO THOUSAND CUBITS FOR FIELDS AND VINEYARDS.[8]

ON THAT DAY R. AKIBA EXPOUNDED, THEN SANG MOSES AND THE CHILDREN OF ISRAEL THIS SONG UNTO THE LORD AND SPAKE, SAYING.[9] THERE WAS NO NEED FOR THE WORD 'SAYING', SO WHY WAS IT ADDED? IT TEACHES THAT THE ISRAELITES RESPONDED TO EVERY SENTENCE AFTER MOSES, IN THE MANNER OF READING

(1) [Even in holy food like that of the heave-offering.] (2) (Even in common food.) (3) [He was not the pupil of R. Joḥanan b. Zakkai, but of his disciple R. Eliezer b. Hyrcanus, yet he is so described on account of his eminence. (Maim.).] (4) Num. XXXV, 5, defining the limits of the cities of refuge. (5) Ibid. 4. (6) Open spaces for cattle. (7) Beyond the city an additional space was included equal to the extreme point one was allowed to proceed to from an inhabited spot on the Sabbath, viz., 2000 cubits. This latter space was inclusive of the suburb. (8) This was also inclusive of the suburb. (9) Ex. XV, 1.

HALLEL,[1] 'I WILL SING UNTO THE LORD, FOR HE HATH TRIUMPHED GLORIOUSLY,[2] ON THAT ACCOUNT IS THE WORD 'SAYING' MENTIONED. R. NEHEMIAH SAYS: IN THE MANNER OF READING THE SHEMA'[3] AND NOT HALLEL.

ON THAT DAY R. JOSHUA B. HYRCANUS EXPOUNDED: JOB ONLY SERVED THE HOLY ONE, BLESSED BE HE, FROM LOVE; AS IT IS SAID, THOUGH HE SLAY ME, YET WILL I WAIT FOR HIM.[4] AND SHOULD IT BE STILL DOUBTFUL WHETHER THE MEANING IS 'I WILL WAIT FOR HIM' OR 'I WILL NOT WAIT',[5] THERE IS ANOTHER TEXT TO DECLARE, TILL I DIE I WILL NOT PUT AWAY MINE INTEGRITY FROM ME.[6] THIS TEACHES THAT WHAT HE DID WAS FROM LOVE. R. JOSHUA [B. ḤANANIAH] SAID: WHO WILL REMOVE THE DUST FROM THINE EYES, R. JOḤANAN B. ZAKKAI, SINCE THOU HAST BEEN EXPOUNDING ALL THY LIFE THAT JOB ONLY SERVED THE ALL-PRESENT FROM FEAR, AS IT IS SAID, THAT MAN WAS PERFECT AND UPRIGHT, AND ONE THAT FEARED GOD, AND ESCHEWED EVIL![7] DID NOT JOSHUA, THE PUPIL OF THY PUPIL,[8] TEACH THAT WHAT HE DID WAS FROM LOVE?[9]

GEMARA. [The Mishnah states: SO THE WATER PROVES] HIM. Whom? If I say that it is the husband, what has the husband done? Should you reply [28*a*] that if there be sin in him[10] the water proves him, [it may be asked] should there be sin in him on his own account does the water prove her for her own sin, and behold it has been taught: *And the man shall be free from iniquity,*

(1) This will be explained in the Gemara. *Hallel*, lit., 'praise', is the name given to Pss. CXIII- CXVIII, cf. Suk. III, 10. (2) Ex. XV, 1. (3) V. Glos. The method of recital is explained in the Gemara. (4) Job XIII, 15. (5) There is a variant in the text which gives the alternative translation. V. R.V. margin. (6) Ibid. XXVII, 5. (7) Ibid. I, 1. (8) He was the pupil of Akiba. (9) [Büchler, *Sin and Atonement*, p. 140, suggests this controversy to have arisen in connection with the discussion whether the book of Job should be included in the Canon.] (10) By having cohabited with her after she had secluded herself with the other man.

and that woman shall bear her iniquity,[1] i.e., so long as the husband is free from iniquity the water proves his wife, but if the husband is not free from iniquity the water does not prove his wife!—Should [the Mishnah, on the other hand, refer] to the paramour, it should have used the same phraseology as in the continuation, viz., 'Just as she is prohibited to the husband so is she prohibited to the paramour'![2]—It certainly refers to the paramour; but in the first clause since it uses the word 'HER' it uses the word 'HIM', and in the continuation since it used the word 'HUSBAND' it used the word 'PARAMOUR'.

AS IT IS SAID 'AND SHALL ENTER' TWICE. The question was asked, Does [the teacher in the Mishnah] mean 'shall enter *and* shall enter' or 'and shall enter and shall enter'?[3]—Come and hear: JUST AS SHE IS PROHIBITED TO THE HUSBAND SO IS SHE PROHIBITED TO THE PARAMOUR; AS IT IS SAID, DEFILED ... AND IS DEFILED.[4] But it is still questionable whether [the teacher in the Mishnah] draws the conclusion from the repetition of '*defiled*' or from the conjunction in '*defiled* ... and *is defiled*'!—Come and hear: Since he states in the continuation, RABBI SAYS: THE WORD DEFILED OCCURS TWICE IN THE SCRIPTURAL PORTION, ONE REFERRING TO THE HUSBAND AND THE OTHER TO THE PARAMOUR, it follows that it is R. Akiba who expounds the conjunction '*and*'. Consequently for R. Akiba there are six texts [containing the phrase '*and shall enter*'][5]—one for the command regarding her[6] and one for the command regarding him;[7] one for the action regarding her and one for the action regarding him;[8] one for the notification[9] regarding her and one for the notification regarding him. For Rabbi,[10] on the other hand, there

(1) Num. V, 31. (2) And state, 'so the water proves the paramour'. (3) I.e., is the inference drawn from the redundant *and* or from the repetition of the word? (4) Similarly in the first clause the deduction is drawn from the redundant *and*. (5) In verses 22, 24 and 27, the conjunction '*and*' duplicating each. (6) Verse 24, where God decreed that the water should have the effect of proving her. (7) The paramour. (8) Verse 27, where the assurance is given that the water would take effect. (9) Of the priest, in verse 22. (10) Who draws no conclusion from '*and*'.

are three texts—one for the command, one for the action and one for the notification.[1] But whence does Rabbi derive the teaching: JUST AS THE WATER PROVES HER SO THE WATER PROVES HIM?—He derives it from [the following teaching]: For it has been taught: *And make the belly to swell and the thigh to fall away,*[2] i.e., the belly and thigh of the paramour. You say it is the belly and thigh of the paramour; perhaps it is not so, but the belly and thigh of the adulteress! Since it is stated *and* her *belly shall swell and* her *thigh shall fall away,*[3] here it is clearly the belly and thigh of the adulteress which are referred to; so how am I to explain '*and make the belly to swell and the thigh to fall away*'? It refers to the belly and thigh of the paramour. And the other?[4]—It indicates that the priest informs her that [the water] affects the belly first and then the thigh so as not to discredit the water of bitterness.[5] And the other?[6]—If that were so, it should have been written 'her belly and her thigh'; what means 'belly and thigh' [without specification]? Conclude that the reference is to the paramour. But am I to suppose that [the phrase without specification] is intended only for this?[7]—If that were so, it should have been written 'his belly and his thigh'; what means 'belly and thigh'? Draw two inferences therefrom.[8]

R. JOSHUA SAID, THUS USED ZECHARIAH etc. Our Rabbis taught: Why is it mentioned three times in the Scriptural portion *if she be defiled,*[9] *she be defiled,*[10] and *she is defiled?*[11] One [to make her prohibited] to the husband, one to the paramour, and one for partaking of the heave-offering. This is the statement of R. Akiba. R. Ishmael said: It is an *a fortiori* conclusion; if a divorced woman,[12] who is allowed to partake of the heave-offering, is prohibited [to

(1) As regards the woman only in each instance. (2) Num. V, 22. The pronoun '*thy*' in the E.V. does not occur in the Hebrew. Therefore the reference is taken to be the paramour. (3) Ibid. 27. (4) I.e., how does R. Akiba explain the phrase '*and make the belly etc.*'? (5) V. *supra* 9b. (6) How does Rabbi meet this argument? (7) To teach that it refers to the paramour. (8) That it refers to the paramour and also that it indicates the order in which the effect of the water is felt. (9) Num. V, 27. (10) Ibid. 14. (11) Ibid. 29. (12) Viz., a priest's daughter who had been married to a non-priest, v. Lev. XXII, 13.

marry into] the priesthood, how much more must a woman who is prohibited from partaking of the heave-offering[1] be prohibited [to marry into] the priesthood![2] For what purpose[3] is it stated *and she be defiled . . . and she be not defiled?*[4] If she be defiled, why should she drink; and if she be not defiled, why does he make her drink! Scripture informs you that in a doubtful case she is prohibited. From this you can draw an analogy [with respect to the defilement caused] by a creeping thing:[5] if in the case of a suspected woman, where the effect is not the same should the act be in error or in presumption, under compulsion or of free will,[6] there is the consequence [of being prohibited] when there is a doubt as when there is certainty; how much more so must there be the consequence [of defilement] in a case of doubt as in a case of certainty with a creeping thing where the effect is the same whether [the contact was] in error or in presumption, or whether it was under compulsion or of free will! [28*b*] And from the position you have taken up[7] [proceed to draw the following deductions]: As [the case of doubt in connection with] the suspected woman can only occur in a private domain [where seclusion takes place],[8] so [the case of doubt in connection with] a creeping thing can only occur [when the contact takes place] in a private domain.[9] And as [the case in connection with] a suspected woman is a matter where there is a rational being to be interrogated,[10] so [in the case of doubt in connection with] a creeping thing it must be a matter where there is a rational being to be interrogated.[11] Hence [the Rabbis] said, Where there is a rational being to be interrogated, should a doubtful [case of defilement] occur in a private domain it is regarded as unclean, but should it occur in a public place as

(1) Because of suspected adultery. (2) This will be explained anon. (3) The exposition that follows is independent of the preceding. (4) Num. V, 14. (5) Viz., when it is doubtful whether defilement has been caused. (6) If the woman acted in error or under force, she does not undergo the ordeal. (7) Viz., drawing the above analogy. (8) As distinct from a public place. (9) If the doubt occurred about contact in a public place, there is no defilement. (10) As to whether she had misconducted herself or not. (11) There must have been a person present who can be questioned about the probability of the contact having taken place.

clean; and when there is no rational being to be interrogated whether it occurs in a private domain or in a public place a doubtful [case of defilement] is regarded as clean.[1]

R. Akiba dealt above with [the woman being prohibited to partake] of the heave-offering, and R. Ishmael answers him with a statement about the priesthood![2] And further, whence does R. Akiba derive [the rule that the suspected woman cannot marry into] the priesthood? Should you answer that with reference to [this rule about] the priesthood a Scriptural text is not necessary, [29a] since a woman about whom there is a doubt whether she is immoral is treated like an immoral woman,[3] then [for the rule about] the heave-offering a Scriptural verse should likewise be unnecessary, since a woman about whom there is a doubt whether she is immoral is treated like an immoral woman![4]—But according to R. Akiba, there are four texts [where the word '*defiled*' occurs][5]—one [to prohibit the woman] to the husband, one to the paramour, one to the priesthood and one for the heave-offering. Whereas according to R. Ishmael there are [only] three texts[6]—one [to prohibit her] to the husband, one to the paramour, and one for the heave-offering; and [the prohibition] regarding the priesthood he deduces by *a fortiori* reasoning. Whence, however, does R. Ishmael [know] that a text is required for the heave-offering and that [the prohibition] regarding the priesthood is to be deduced by *a fortiori* reasoning; perhaps [a text] is required as regards the priesthood and the heave-offering is permitted to her![7]—He can reply to you, This is proved by the analogy of the husband and paramour: just as [the prohibition] respecting husband and para-

(1) Thus the end of the cited Baraitha. (2) Into which an adulteress cannot marry. The reply was quite irrelevant to the issue. (3) '*A harlot*' (Lev. XXI, 7) whom a priest may not marry. (4) And if a priest's daughter loses the right to eat of the heave-offering though lawfully married to a non-priest (Lev. XXII, 12), how much more must she forfeit it if she is immoral; v. Yeb. 68*a*. (5) In Num. V, 17, 28 and 29. In the last verse it is preceded by '*and*', which is understood as the duplication of the term. (6) He does not expound '*and*'. (7) Why does he not apply one occurrence of the word '*defiled*' to the matter of the priesthood instead of the heave-offering?

mour is in force already during the lifetime [of the husband],[1] so also [the prohibition] respecting the heave-offering is likewise to come into force during his lifetime, to the exclusion of that respecting the priesthood which comes into effect after death.[2] R. Akiba, on the other hand,[3] does not accept the analogy of the husband and paramour; and even if he accepted it, a teaching which is deducible by *a fortiori* reasoning Scripture took the trouble to write down.[4]

R. Giddal said in the name of Rab: The [difference between] a case where there is a rational being to be interrogated and one where there is no rational being to be interrogated is derived from the following texts: *And the flesh that toucheth any unclean thing shall not be eaten*[5]—when the thing is certainly unclean it may not be eaten; hence when there is a doubt whether it is unclean or clean it may be eaten. Consider now the continuation: *And as for the flesh, all that is clean shall eat [sacrificial] flesh*[6]—[A man who is] certainly clean may eat, but when there is a doubt whether he is unclean or clean he may not eat![7] Is not, then, the conclusion to be drawn from this that in one case there is a rational being to be interrogated and not in the other?[8] The statement of R. Giddal in the name of Rab was necessary, and it was also necessary to derive [the rule of defilement caused by a creeping thing] from the case of the suspected woman; for if [it had only been based on] the teaching of Rab, I would have said that the rule was the same whether [the defilement occurred] in a private domain or a public

(1) She is forbidden to the paramour whilst the husband is yet alive. (2) During the husband's lifetime she cannot in any way marry into the priesthood since a priest may not marry a divorcee; the prohibition is consequently to refer here to after the husband's death, that even then a priest may not marry the suspected woman. Since the analogy does not apply, the text cannot be applied to this prohibition. (3) Who bases the prohibition of marriage with a priest on a text. (4) So the fact that the rule could be arrived at by deduction does not obviate R. Akiba's contention that it is based on a text. (5) Lev. VII, 19. (6) Ibid., *sic.* (7) Contrary conclusions are drawn from the verse. (8) The clause '*and as for flesh* etc.' speaks of a man who is the object of uncleanness and a rational being to be interrogated; whereas the former '*and the flesh that toucheth* etc.' refers to where there is no rational being to be interrogated.

place; therefore it was also necessary to derive it from the case of a suspected woman.[1] If, further, it [had been derived solely] from the case of the suspected woman, I would have said that the rule[2] only applied when that which was touched and that which touched it were both rational beings.[3] So it is necessary [to have Rab's teaching].[4]

ON THAT DAY R. AKIBA EXPOUNDED, AND EVERY EARTHEN VESSEL etc. Since it has no [basis in Scripture according to which it is unclean],[5] why should it be unclean?—Rab Judah said in the name of Rab, It has none from the Torah, but it has one as a deduction from *a fortiori* reasoning: If a *ṭebul yom*,[6] who is allowed with non-holy food,[7] disqualifies[8] the heave-offering,[9] how much more so must a loaf unclean in the second degree, which is disqualified in the case of non-holy food,[10] render the heave-offering unclean in the third degree! It can, however, be objected, This[11] applies to a *ṭebul yom* because he may be a source of primary defilement.[12] [But it may be answered,] You can draw [the necessary conclusion] [29b] from a *ṭebul yom* [who was defiled] by a creeping thing.[13] [Should it be objected that] it applies [only] to a *ṭebul yom* [who was defiled] by a creeping thing because he

(1) From which it is learnt that the rule is not the same in both localities. (2) About a doubtful case of defilement being regarded as unclean. (3) As happens with the suspected woman. (4) That it is sufficient if the object touched is a rational being for a doubtful case to be unclean. It is not required that the defiling agent should also be a rational being. (5) As R. Joḥanan declares in the Mishnah; and yet he held it to be defiled. (6) Lit., 'bathed during day', i.e., an unclean person who has undergone immersion but awaits sunset before he regains his state of purity. V. Lev. XXII, 7. (7) And does not defile it. (8) [פסול This term denotes the last degree of uncleanness which cannot communicate defilement to any other object coming into contact with it.] (9) By touching it so that it may not be eaten by a priest, v. Yeb. 74*b*. (10) [If a creeping thing touches an object which in turn comes into contact with non-holy food, the latter, which is in the second degree of uncleanness, is disqualified; v. Lev. XI, 33.] (11) The disqualifying of the heave-offering. (12) Lit., 'father of defilement'. By, e.g., having touched a corpse or by himself being a leper. *Ṭebul yom* cannot thus be made the basis of deduction. (13) He is then unclean in the first degree but not a source of primary cause of defilement. A creeping thing is a primary source of defilement.

belongs to that category in which there may be a primary source of defilement],[1] the case of an earthenware vessel proves [the contrary].[2] [And should it be objected that] it applies to an earthenware vessel because its interior space renders unclean,[3] the case of *ṭebul yom* proves [the contrary].[4]

Thus the original reasoning [by *a fortiori*] holds good, since the characteristic [of the *ṭebul yom*] is unlike the characteristic [of the earthenware vessel][5] and *vice versa;*[6] the point they have in common is that they are allowed with non-holy food but disqualify the heave-offering.[7] How much more, then, must a loaf unclean in the second degree, which disqualifies in the case of non-holy food, disqualify the heave-offering! ANOTHER GENERATION,[8] however, might object, What is the point common to them both? That in each there is a characteristic which makes for severity![9] But R. Johanan does not raise an objection on the ground that there is in each a characteristic which makes for severity.[10]

It has been taught: R. Jose said: Whence is it that with sacrificial food there is disqualification with the fourth degree of defilement? It is a deduction [from a *fortiori* reasoning]: If one lacking atonement,[11] who is permitted with the heave-offering,[12] is dis-

(1) [A man who touches a dead body becomes a primary source of uncleanness. This does not apply to foodstuffs.] (2) Since it can never be a primary source of defilement and yet defiles the heave-offering by contact. (3) Without actual contact, v. Lev. XI, 33. (4) Because he obviously cannot defile except by direct contact and yet he disqualifies the heave-offering by touching it. (5) Since the latter unlike the former defiles by its interior space. (6) The former, unlike the latter, being possibly a primary source of defilement. (7) [This is difficult to explain, since an earthenware vessel does disqualify non-holy food (v. Lev. XI, 33ff). Rashi suggests another reading which is not free from difficulty. Tosaf. of Sens explains the reference to be to a broken earthenware vessel which in respect of non-holy food communicates no defilement.] (8) Which would not regard this as unclean. (9) In the law relating thereto, viz., the *ṭebul yom* can be a primary source of defilement and the interior space of an earthenware vessel can render unclean. (10) Because the characteristic of severity is peculiar to each and not common to both. (11) E.g., a leper on his recovery, (v. Lev. XIV, 9ff). The seventh day the sacrifice had not yet been offered, and he may not partake of sacrificial food until this has been done. (12) And does not disqualify it by his touch.

qualified as regards sacrificial food[1], how much more does the third degree, which is disqualified with the heave-offering,[2] create a fourth degree of defilement with sacrificial food! We learnt [the rule about] a third degree of defilement with sacrificial food from the Torah and a fourth degree from *a fortiori* reasoning;[3] whence have we it from the Torah that there is a third degree with sacrificial food?—As it is written, *And the flesh that toucheth any unclean thing shall not be eaten*[4]—do we not deal here with [flesh] that touched something unclean in the second degree?[5] And the All-Merciful declared, '*It shall not be eaten*'. A fourth degree [is derived] from *a fortiori* reasoning as we stated above.

R. Joḥanan said: I do not understand the Master's[6] reason[7] since its refutation is by its side, viz., food which is made unclean by contact with a *ṭebul yom* proves [the contrary], inasmuch as it is disqualified in the case of heave-offering but does not create a fourth degree of defilement with sacrificial food. For it has been taught: Abba Saul said, A *ṭebul yom* is unclean in the first degree as regards sacrificial food to create two further degrees of defilement[8] and one degree of disqualification.[9] R. Meir says: He creates one further degree of defilement and one of disqualification. The Sages say: Just as he disqualifies food or liquids of the heave-offering,[10] so he disqualifies sacrificial food and drinks.[11] To this R. Papa demurred: Whence is it that R. Jose holds the same view as the

(1) I.e., he disqualifies it by his touch. (2) As proved on *a fortiori* reasoning, *supra*. (3) [Once the third degree is derived from the Torah, it is possible to employ the *a fortiori* reasoning in regard to the fourth degree. Were it not so, we should have required the *a fortiori* reasoning for the third degree only.] (4) Lev. VII, 19. (5) Since '*unclean thing*' means that which had been rendered unclean by something else. The flesh was accordingly unclean in the third degree. (6) V. Nazir (Sonc. ed.) p. 64, n. 1. (7) R. Jose's argument as given in the preceding paragraph with respect to a fourth degree with holy food. (8) What touches him is unclean in the second degree and what this touches is unclean in the third. (9) If the heave-offering was touched by the object unclean in the third degree it would become disqualified but would not create a fourth degree. (10) But does not create any further degree of defilement. (11) [Without creating a further degree of defilement. Whereas, adopting R. Jose's arguments the food touched by the *ṭebul yom* should on *a fortiori* reasoning produce here a disqualification in the fourth degree.]

Rabbis? Perhaps he holds the same view as Abba Saul who says [that the *ṭebul yom*] creates two further degrees of defilement and one of disqualification!—If it enter your mind that he holds the same view as Abba Saul, let him [deduce the rule about] a fourth degree of defilement with sacrificial food from the case of food that is rendered unclean by contact with a *ṭebul yom* [as follows]: If a *ṭebul yom* is himself allowed with non-holy food,[1] and yet you say that food which is unclean through him creates a fourth degree with sacrificial food, [30*a*] then that which is unclean in the third degree through contact with what is unclean in the second degree —the second degree which is itself forbidden in the case of non-holy food[2]—must all the more create a fourth degree with the holy![3] And should you reply [as stated above], 'It can, however, be objected, It applies to a *ṭebul yom* because he may be a primary source of defilement', behold he [R. Jose] derived his argument from one lacking atonement and [he] did not raise this objection.[4]

R. Assi said in the name of Rab — another version is Rabbah b. Issi said in the name of Rab —, R. Meir, R. Jose, R. Joshua, R. Eleazar and R. Eliezer all hold the view that what is unclean in the second degree does not create a third degree with non-holy food. R. Meir—for we have learnt: Everything that requires immersion in water according to the statement of the scribes[5] defiles the holy, disqualifies the heave-offering, and is permitted with the non-holy and with the tithe. Such is the statement of R. Meir; but the Sages prohibit in the case of the tithe.[6] R. Jose—as

(1) And does not disqualify it. (2) Non-holy food can become unclean in the second degree. (3) [The advantage of this deduction consists in that it is more direct than that of R. Jose, which involves a second *a fortiori* reasoning to prove that there is a disqualification in the third degree in the case of the heave-offering (v. p. 145, n. 3) Tosaf.] (4) I.e., that one lacking atonement is different since he may be a primary source of defilement. The reason R. Jose did not raise this objection is evidently because he is no longer regarded as unclean, and the same applies to a *ṭebul yom*. Consequently R. Jose cannot be said to agree with Abba Saul, but must agree with the Rabbis, hence the question of R. Joḥanan. (5) Viz., things which, according to the Torah, are clean, but the Rabbis take a stricter view. (6) To be eaten; v. Parah, XI, 5.

we have stated above; for if it were so,[1] then let him derive a fourth degree with the heave-offering and a fifth with the sacrificial food.[2] R. Joshua—for we have learnt: R. Eliezer says: He who eats food unclean in the first degree is unclean in the first degree; [if he eats] food unclean in the second degree he is unclean in the second degree; and similarly with the third degree. R. Joshua says: He who eats food unclean in the first or second degree is unclean in the second degree; [if he eats food unclean] in the third degree, he is unclean in the second degree as regards the sacrificial food but not unclean in the second degree as regards the heave-offering. This[3] is said of non-holy food which was prepared in the purity of the heave-offering.[4] [This means, does it not,] 'When it is in the purity of the heave-offering' but not when it is in the purity of the sacrificial food?[5] Conclude, then, that he holds that [normally] what is unclean in the second degree does not create a third degree with the non-holy. R. Eleazar — for it has been taught: R. Eleazar says, The following three are alike: the first degree of defilement in the case of the sacrificial food, the non-holy and the heave-offering; it creates two further degrees of defilement and one of disqualification with the sacrificial food;[6] it creates one further degree of defilement and one of disqualification with the heave-offering;[7] and it creates one degree of disqualification with the non-holy.[8] R. Eliezer—for we have learnt: R. Eliezer says: *Ḥallah*[9] may be taken from [dough] which is pure on account of that which is defiled. How is this? There are two portions of dough, one pure and the other defiled. He takes a quantity sufficient for

(1) That there was a third degree of defilement with the non-holy. (2) From his own *a fortiori* reasoning cited above. (3) That food in the third degree renders the one eating it unclean in respect of sacrificial food. (4) I.e., when a priest took upon himself that even the non-holy food he ate should be in the same state of purity as the heave-offering. But ordinary non-holy food cannot become unclean in the third degree. (5) [As non-holy food cannot be raised to the level of purity of sacrificial food. Rashi reads: 'but not when it is ordinary non-holy food'. This is also the reading of MS.M.] (6) There is thus a fourth degree of defilement. (7) There is then a third degree. (8) And so there is no third degree with the non-holy. (9) Part of the dough presented to the priest; v. Num. XV, 17-21.

ḥallah[1] from the dough from which its *ḥallah* had not been removed,[2] and places a piece less than the size of an egg[3] in the centre [of the defiled dough] so that [it may be considered that *ḥallah*] had been taken from the mass [of the defiled dough]. [30*b*] The Sages, however, forbid this. And it has also been taught: [The quantity[4] may be] equal to the size of an egg.—[Now the schoolmen] held that both [these teachings][5] refer to dough which is unclean in the first degree, and that non-holy food from which *ḥallah* had not yet been taken is not like *ḥallah*.[6] Is it not, then, to be supposed that they differ on this point: One[7] holds that a second degree of defilement does not create a third with the non-holy,[8] whereas the others hold that it does create a third degree with the non-holy?[9] R. Mari b. R. Kahana said, All agree that a second degree of defilement does not create a third with the non-holy; but here they differ with regard to non-holy food from which *ḥallah* had yet to be taken. One holds that it is like *ḥallah*;[10] the other holds that it is not like *ḥallah*. If you like I can say that all agree that non-holy food from which *ḥallah* had yet to be taken is not like *ḥallah* and a second degree of defilement does not create a third with the non-holy; and here they differ on whether it is permitted to apply the laws of defilement to non-holy food in the land of

(1) One twenty-fourth of the whole in the case of an individual and half of that proportion in the case of a baker. (2) The pure dough. (3) A quantity less than the size of an egg cannot communicate defilement. (4) [According to R. Eliezer.] (5) [The one that holds that the quantity should be less than the size of an egg as well as the other, that it may be the size of an egg.] (6) I.e., like heave-offering in respect of the law of defilement. [But is treated like non-holy, both on the view of R. Eliezer and the Rabbis. For this reason even if the quantity placed between the two doughs is of the size of an egg it does not communicate the defilement in the second degree, which it contracts from the defiled dough to the pure one, since there is no third degree with non-holy.] (7) R. Eliezer. (8) [For this reason he allows in the second teaching a quantity of the size of an egg; and the reservation in the first teaching is merely as a precaution lest the piece of dough may come in contact with impure dough after the *ḥallah* has been designated.] (9) This shews that R. Eliezer holds that there is no third degree with non-holy food. (10) The Rabbis consider that it can create a third degree.

Israel.[1] One[2] holds that it is permitted to apply the laws of defilement to non-holy food in the land of Israel, the others hold that it is prohibited.[3]

ON THAT DAY R. AKIBA EXPOUNDED, [AND YE SHALL MEASURE] etc. On what do they[4] differ?—One holds that the regulations concerning the Sabbath-limit are an institution of the Torah,[5] whereas the other holds they are an institution of the Rabbis.

Our Rabbis taught: On that day R. Akiba expounded: At the time the Israelites ascended from the Red Sea, they desired to utter a song; and how did they render the song? Like an adult who reads the *Hallel* [for a congregation][6] and they respond after him with the leading word.[7] [According to this explanation] Moses said, *'I will sing unto the Lord'* and they responded, *'I will sing unto the Lord'*; Moses said, *'For He hath triumphed gloriously'* and they responded, *'I will sing unto the Lord'*. R. Eliezer son of R. Jose the Galilean declares, Like a minor who reads the *Hallel* [for a congregation], and they repeat after him all that he says.[8] [According to this explanation] Moses said, *'I will sing unto the Lord'* and they responded, *'I will sing unto the Lord'*; Moses said, *'For He hath triumphed gloriously'* and they responded, *'For He hath triumphed gloriously'*. R. Nehemiah declares: Like a school-teacher[9] who recites[10] the *Shema'* in the Synagogue, viz., he begins first and they respond after him.[11] On

(1) In Ber. 47b R. Meir defines an *'Am ha-arez* (v. *supra* p. 110) as one who does not eat his non-holy food in a condition of ritual purity; but the Rabbis give a different definition. (2) R. Eliezer. (3) [And their concern is with the piece of dough placed between the two doughs which, though less than the size of an egg, can yet contract defilement.] (4) R. Akiba and R. Eliezer, son of R. Jose of Galilee. (5) R. Akiba takes this view; and therefore, according to him, the Torah had to make provision for the Sabbath-limit in the cities of refuge. (6) He acts as Precentor and his rendering is on their behalf so that they may thereby fulfil their duty to recite it. (7) Lit., 'heads of chapters'. According to a statement in Suk. 38a, the response consisted of the word Hallelujah. (8) Since he was a minor, his rendering would not exempt them from saying every word. (9) Whose class was usually in the Synagogue and so he acted as Precentor. (10) The word *pores* is lit., 'divide', and its exact meaning is disputed. V. Elbogen, *Der jüdische Gottesdienst*, pp. 514ff and the references cited there. (11) Elbogen takes this to mean that the Precentor and Congregation read the verses

what do they differ?—R. Akiba holds that the word *'saying'* [1] refers to the first clause;[2] R. Eliezer son of R. Jose the Galilean holds that *'saying'* refers to every clause; and R. Nehemiah holds that *'and spake'* indicates that they sang all together *'and saying'* that Moses began first.

Our Rabbis taught: R. Jose the Galilean expounded: At the time the Israelites ascended from the Red Sea, they desired to utter a song; and how did they render the song? The babe lay upon his mother's knees and the suckling sucked at his mother's breast; when they beheld the *Shechinah,* the babe raised his neck and the suckling released the nipple from his mouth, and they exclaimed, *This is my God and I will praise Him;*[3] as it is said, *Out of the mouths of babes and sucklings hast thou established strength.*[4] R. Meir used to say, Whence is it that even the embryos in their mothers' womb uttered a song? As it is said, [31a] *Bless ye the Lord in the Congregations, even the Lord, from the fountain of Israel.*[5] But these could not behold [the *Shechinah*]!—R. Tanḥum said: The abdomen became for them a kind of transparent medium and they did behold it.

ON THAT DAY R. JOSHUA B. HYRCANUS EXPOUNDED, JOB ONLY SERVED etc. But let him see how the word *'lo'*[6] is spelt; if it is written with *lamed* and *aleph* then it means 'not', and if with *lamed* and *waw* then it means 'for Him'![7] But is the meaning 'not' wherever the spelling is *lamed* and *aleph?* Can it apply to: *In all their affliction there was affliction to Him?*[8] [The word *'lo', 'to Him'*] is spelt *lamed* and *aleph,* but does it here also signify 'not'! And should you say that here too [it means 'not'], behold it continues with:

alternately. Rashi's explanation is: he reads the benedictions preceding the *Shema'* which they repeat after him and then they read the *Shema'* in unison. According to this explanation, Moses and the Israelites were divinely inspired so that they independently sang the same words in unison.

(1) In Ex. XV, 1. (2) *'I will sing unto the Lord'*, and that only was the Israelite's response. (3) Ibid. 3. (4) Ps. VIII, 3. E.V. 2. (5) Ibid. LXVIII, 27, E.V. 26. *'From the fountain'* indicates those who were still in the womb. (6) In Job XIII, 15. (7) So how could the Mishnah state that there is a doubt about the meaning? (8) Isa. LXIII, 9.

And the angel of His presence saved them![1] But sometimes it has one meaning and at other times the other meaning.

It has been taught: R. Meir says: It is declared of Job *one that feared God,*[2] and it is declared of Abraham *thou fearest God;*[3] just as 'fearing God' with Abraham indicates from love, so 'fearing God' with Job indicates from love. Whence, however, have we it in connection with Abraham himself [that he was motived by love]? As it is written, *The seed of Abraham who loved Me.*[4] What difference is there between one who acts from love and one who acts from fear?—The difference is that indicated in this teaching: R. Simeon b. Eleazar says: Greater is he who acts from love than he who acts from fear, because with the latter [the merit] remains effective for a thousand generations but with the former it remains effective for two thousand generations. Here it is written, *Unto thousands of them that love Me and keep My commandments*[5] and elsewhere it is written, *And keep His commandments to a thousand generations.*[6] But in this latter passage it is likewise written, '*With them that love Him and keep His commandments to a thousand generations!* —In the first verse cited [the word '*thousand*'] is attached [*to them that love Me,*] whereas in the second verse [cited the word '*thousand*'] is attached [to *keep His commandments*].[7]

Two disciples were once sitting in the presence of Raba. One said to him, In my dream they read to me, *O how great is Thy goodness which Thou hast laid up for them that fear Thee.*[8] The other said to him, In my dream they read to me, *But let all those that put their trust in Thee rejoice, let them ever shout for joy, because Thou defendest them; let them also that love Thy name be joyful in Thee.*[9] He replied to them, Both of you are completely righteous Rabbis, but one is actuated by love and the other by fear.

(1) These words prove that '*lo*' in the preceding clause cannot mean 'not'. (2) Job I, 1. (3) Gen. XXII, 12. (4) Isa. XLI, 8, *sic*. (5) Ex. XX, 6. '*Thousands*' is interpreted as generations, and the plural indicates at least two thousand. (6) Deut. VII, 9. (7) So in the former the motive is love, in the latter fear of punishment. (8) Ps. XXXI, 20. (9) Ibid. V, 12.

SOṬAH

CHAPTER VI

MISHNAH. IF A MAN WARNED HIS WIFE AND SHE SECLUDED HERSELF [WITH ANOTHER MAN], EVEN IF HE HEARD [THAT SHE HAD DONE SO] FROM A FLYING BIRD,[1] HE DIVORCES HER AND GIVES HER THE MARRIAGE-SETTLEMENT.[2] SUCH IS THE STATEMENT OF R. ELIEZER. R. JOSHUA SAYS: [HE DOES NOT DO THIS] UNTIL WOMEN WHO SPIN BY MOONLIGHT DISCUSS HER.[3]

IF ONE WITNESS SAID, I SAW THAT SHE COMMITTED MISCONDUCT, SHE DOES NOT DRINK THE WATER.[4] NOT ONLY THAT, BUT EVEN A SLAVE, MALE OR FEMALE,[5] IS BELIEVED ALSO TO DISQUALIFY HER FOR THE MARRIAGE-SETTLEMENT. HER MOTHER-IN-LAW, HER MOTHER-IN-LAW'S DAUGHTER, HER ASSOCIATE-WIFE,[6] HER SISTER-IN-LAW[7] AND HER STEP-DAUGHTER[8] ARE BELIEVED, NOT TO DISQUALIFY HER FOR

(1) It was only a vague rumour that came to his ears. [The rumour was concerning (*a*) seclusion only (Rashi); (*b*) misconduct (Maim.).—'A FLYING BIRD' may denote a talking bird, a parrot (v. Maim. and Strashun.] (2) He gives this to her if he was unwilling for her to drink the water, (Rashi). [According to this interpretation the husband, if he wishes, can make her drink even on the strength of a vague rumour, even as he can on the evidence of one witness to the seclusion, according to R. Eliezer. Rashbam, however, holds that a vague rumour is not on par with one witness and the husband therefore, though he cannot make her drink, must put her away and give her the marriage-settlement. (V. Tosaf. Sens): Similarly on the view of Maimonides (v. n. 1) the divorce is compulsory, though in the absence of real evidence of misconduct she does not forfeit the marriage settlement.] (3) Her behaviour had given rise to public scandal. (4) One witness is accepted and she is divorced besides losing the marriage-settlement. V. *supra* 2*a*. (5) Whose evidence is not accepted in an ordinary case. (6) The husband had more than one wife. (7) Viz., the wife of her husband's brother whom she was due to marry if she was left a childless widow. (8) All these are presumably ill-disposed towards her, and their evidence would not have been accepted in any other kind of charge.

THE MARRIAGE-SETTLEMENT BUT THAT SHE SHOULD NOT DRINK.

IT[1] IS A PROPER CONCLUSION THAT IF THE FIRST EVIDENCE [THAT THE WOMAN HAD SECLUDED HERSELF WITH THE MAN], WHICH DOES NOT PROHIBIT HER [TO HER HUSBAND] FOR ALL TIME,[2] IS NOT ESTABLISHED BY FEWER THAN TWO WITNESSES, IS IT NOT RIGHT THAT THE FINAL EVIDENCE [THAT SHE HAD MISCONDUCTED HERSELF] WHICH PROHIBITS HER TO HIM FOR ALL TIME, SHOULD NOT BE ESṬABLISHED BY FEWER THAN TWO WITNESSES! THEREFORE THERE IS A TEXT TO STATE, AND THERE BE NO WITNESS AGAINST HER,[3] I.E., WHATEVER [EVIDENCE] THERE MAY BE AGAINST HER [IS BELIEVED, EVEN IF IT BE ONLY ONE WITNESS]. AND WITH RESPECT TO THE FIRST EVIDENCE [ABOUT HER SECLUSION WITH THE MAN, THAT ONE WITNESS SUFFICES MAY BE ARGUED BY] A FORTIORI REASONING AS FOLLOWS: IF [31b] THE FINAL EVIDENCE [REGARDING MISCONDUCT], WHICH PROHIBITS HER TO HER HUSBAND FOR ALL TIME, IS ESTABLISHED BY ONE WITNESS, IS IT NOT PROPER THAT THE FIRST EVIDENCE, WHICH DOES NOT PROHIBIT HER TO HIM FOR ALL TIME, SHOULD BE ESTABLISHED BY ONE WITNESS! THEREFORE THERE IS A TEXT TO STATE, BECAUSE HE HATH FOUND SOME UNSEEMLY MATTER IN HER,[4] AND ELSEWHERE IT STATES, AT THE MOUTH OF TWO WITNESSES, OR AT THE MOUTH OF THREE WITNESSES, SHALL A MATTER BE ESTABLISHED;[5] AS THE 'MATTER' MENTIONED IN THIS LATTER CASE MUST BE CONFIRMED BY THE TESTIMONY OF TWO WITNESSES, SO ALSO HERE [IN THE CASE OF THE SUSPECTED WOMAN] THE 'MATTER' MUST BE CONFIRMED BY THE TESTIMONY OF TWO WITNESSES.

IF ONE WITNESS SAYS THAT SHE MISCONDUCTED HERSELF AND ANOTHER WITNESS SAYS THAT SHE DID NOT,[6] OR IF A

(1) V. *supra* 3b. (2) Because the water may prove her innocent. (3) Num. V, 13. (4) Deut. XXIV, 1. (5) Ibid. XIX, 15. (6) At the time of seclusion.

WOMAN SAYS [OF HER] THAT SHE MISCONDUCTED HERSELF AND ANOTHER WOMAN SAYS THAT SHE DID NOT, SHE DRINKS THE WATER. IF ONE WITNESS SAYS THAT SHE MISCONDUCTED HERSELF AND TWO SAY THAT SHE DID NOT, SHE DRINKS THE WATER. IF TWO SAY THAT SHE MISCONDUCTED HERSELF AND ONE SAYS THAT SHE DID NOT, SHE DOES NOT DRINK IT.

GEMARA. [Why does the teacher in the Mishnah use] the Scriptural text, *'Because he hath found some unseemly matter in her'?* He should have used [the teaching]: *'Against her'*—i.e., *'against her'* [in the matter of misconduct] but not in the matter of warning, *'against her'* [in the matter of misconduct] but not in the matter of seclusion![1]—He does also intend to say this: Therefore there is a text to state *'against her'*—i.e., *'against her'* [in the matter of misconduct] but not in the matter of warning, *'against her'* [in the matter of misconduct] but not in the matter of seclusion. Whence, however, have we it that one witness is not believed in an ordinary charge of infidelity where there was neither warning nor seclusion? Here [in connection with infidelity] the word *'matter'* occurs and it also occurs [in the law of evidence]; as with the latter [a charge is established] by two witnesses so [is the former established] by two witnesses.

IF ONE WITNESS SAYS THAT SHE MISCONDUCTED HERSELF. The reason [why one witness is not accepted] is because there is another who contradicts him; but where nobody contradicts him one witness is believed. Whence have we this rule? Because our Rabbis have taught: *'And there be no witness against her'*—the text refers to two witnesses. You say that it refers to two witnesses; but perhaps it is not so and even one [suffices]! There is a teaching to declare, *One witness shall not rise up against a man* etc.[2] From the fact that it is stated, '[A] *witness shall not rise up against a man,'* do I not know that one is intended? Why is there a teaching to declare *'one witness'?* This establishes the rule that wherever it is stated *witness*, it signifies two unless the text specifies *'one'*; and [in the

(1) For notes v. *supra* 3b. (2) Deut. XIX, 15.

case under discussion] the All-Merciful declares that when there are not two witnesses against her but only one, *'and she has not been violated,'* she is forbidden [to her husband].[1]

But since, according to the Torah one witness is believed, how is it possible for another to contradict him? Surely 'Ulla has said: Wherever the Torah accepts the testimony of one witness, he is regarded as two, and the evidence of one is of no account when opposed by two![2]—But, said 'Ulla, read the Mishnah as, 'She does not drink';[3] and R. Isaac similarly declared that she does not drink, but R. Ḥiyya said that she does drink. The view of 'Ulla creates a difficulty against the statement of R. Ḥiyya![4]—There is no difficulty; one statement refers to evidence given simultaneously[5] and the other when one witness follows the other.[6]

We learnt: IF ONE WITNESS SAYS THAT SHE MISCONDUCTED HERSELF AND TWO SAY THAT SHE DID NOT, SHE DRINKS THE WATER. Consequently if there was one [against her] and one [for her], she would not drink; this is a refutation of R. Ḥiyya!—R. Ḥiyya can reply, And according to your view [that she does not drink] consider the next clause: IF TWO SAY THAT SHE MISCONDUCTED HERSELF AND ONE SAYS THAT SHE DID NOT, SHE DOES NOT DRINK IT. Consequently if there was one [against her] and one [for her], she would drink! But the whole [of this section of Mishnah] refers to disqualified witnesses,[7] and it is R. Nehemiah's teaching; for it has been taught: R. Nehemiah says: 'Wherever the Torah accepts the testimony of one witness, [the decision] follows the majority of persons [who testify]', so that two women against one man is identical with two men against one man. But there are some who declare that wherever a com-

(1) For notes v. *supra 3b*. (2) So that the evidence of the first witness, being accepted by the Torah, must stand though it is contradicted by another. (3) Instead of 'she drinks the water', and she is held to be guilty. (4) If the Torah accepts one witness, why should she drink the water? (5) If it is contradictory it is not accepted. (6) If one witness had testified and been accepted, another cannot come subsequently and offer contradictory evidence. (7) Viz., women and slaves; and it teaches that two witnesses of this class can discredit the evidence of a competent witness.

petent witness came [and testified] first, even a hundred women are regarded as equal to one witness[1]; [32a] and with what circumstance are we dealing here?[2] For example, if it was a woman who came first [and testified]; and R. Nehemiah's statement is to be construed thus: R. Nehemiah says: 'Wherever the Torah accepts the testimony of one witness, [the decision] follows the majority of persons [who testify]', so that two women against one woman is identical with two men against one man, but two women against one man is like half and half.[3] Why, then, have we two teachings concerning disqualified witnesses?[4] What you might have said was that when we follow the majority of persons [who testify] it is for taking the severer view, but to take the lenient view we do not follow [the majority]. Therefore [the Mishnah] informs us [of one case where the accused must drink and one where she does not drink, and in each the majority is followed].

(1) And they cannot upset his testimony. (2) When the Mishnah teaches: IF ONE WITNESS . . . AND TWO SAY etc. (3) One witness against one witness; if they testified simultaneously the evidence is not accepted. (4) In these last two clauses of the Mishnah which have been explained as referring to the evidence of women and slaves.

SOṬAH

CHAPTER VII

MISHNAH. THE FOLLOWING MAY BE RECITED IN ANY LANGUAGE: THE SECTION CONCERNING THE SUSPECTED WOMAN,[1] THE CONFESSION MADE AT THE PRESENTATION OF THE TITHE,[2] THE SHEMA',[3] THE 'PRAYER',[4] THE GRACE AFTER MEALS,[5] THE OATH CONCERNING TESTIMONY[6] AND THE OATH CONCERNING A DEPOSIT.[7]

THE FOLLOWING ARE RECITED IN THE HOLY TONGUE:[8] THE DECLARATION MADE AT THE OFFERING OF THE FIRST-FRUITS,[9] THE FORMULA OF ḤALIẒAH,[10] THE BLESSINGS AND CURSES,[11] THE PRIESTLY BENEDICTION,[12] THE BENEDICTION OF THE HIGH PRIEST,[13] THE SECTION OF THE KING,[14] THE SECTION OF THE CALF WHOSE NECK IS BROKEN,[15] AND THE ADDRESS TO THE PEOPLE BY THE PRIEST ANOINTED [TO ACCOMPANY THE ARMY] IN BATTLE.[16]

WHENCE IS IT THAT THE DECLARATION MADE AT THE OFFERING OF THE FIRST-FRUITS [MUST BE IN HEBREW]? [IT IS STATED], AND THOU SHALT ANSWER AND SAY BEFORE THE LORD THY GOD,[17] AND ELSEWHERE IT IS STATED, AND THE LEVITES SHALL ANSWER AND SAY;[18] AS THE LATTER MUST BE IN THE HOLY TONGUE,[19] SO MUST THE FORMER BE IN THE HOLY TONGUE.

(1) The exhortation addressed to her by the priest (Num. V, 19ff). (2) Deut. XXVI, 13ff. (3) V. Glos. (4) 'The Eighteen Benedictions' recited twice daily. V. *P.B.* pp. 44ff. (5) *Op. cit.* pp. 280ff. (6) Against the withholding of evidence (Lev. V, 1ff.). (7) That it had not been misappropriated if the bailee declares that it had been stolen or is missing. (8) Hebrew. (9) Deut. XXVI, 9ff. (10) Ibid. XXV, 9. (11) Ibid. XXVII, 15ff. (12) Num. VI, 24ff. (13) V. *infra,* Mishnah p. 198. (14) V. *infra,* Mishnah p. 202. (15) Deut. XXI, 7f. (16) Ibid. XX, 3ff. (17) Ibid. XXVI, 5. (18) Ibid. XXVII, 14. (19) This will be demonstrated in the Gemara.

WHENCE IS IT THAT THE FORMULA OF ḤALIẒAH [MUST BE IN HEBREW]? [IT IS STATED], AND SHE SHALL ANSWER AND SAY,[1] AND ELSEWHERE IT IS STATED, 'AND THE LEVITES SHALL ANSWER AND SAY'; AS THE LATTER MUST BE IN THE HOLY TONGUE, SO MUST THE FORMER BE IN THE HOLY TONGUE. R. JUDAH SAYS: [IT IS DERIVED FROM THE TEXT], AND SHE SHALL ANSWER AND SAY THUS[2] —I.E., SHE MUST SAY IT IN THIS LANGUAGE.

HOW WERE THE BLESSINGS AND CURSES [PRONOUNCED]? WHEN ISRAEL CROSSED THE JORDAN AND CAME TO MOUNT GERIZIM AND MOUNT EBAL WHICH ARE BY SAMARIA, (THIS IS IN THE VICINITY OF SHECHEM WHICH IS IN THE VICINITY OF THE TEREBINTHS OF MOREH, AND IT IS SAID, ARE THEY NOT BEYOND JORDAN ETC.[3] AND ELSEWHERE IT STATES, AND ABRAM PASSED THROUGH THE LAND UNTO THE PLACE OF SHECHEM UNTO THE TEREBINTH OF MOREH;[4] AS THE TEREBINTH OF MOREH MENTIONED IN THIS LATTER VERSE IS SHECHEM, SO THE TEREBINTH OF MOREH MENTIONED IN THE FORMER VERSE IS SHECHEM.) SIX TRIBES ASCENDED THE SUMMIT OF MOUNT GERIZIM, SIX TRIBES ASCENDED THE SUMMIT OF MOUNT EBAL, AND THE PRIESTS AND LEVITES WITH THE ARK WERE STATIONED BELOW IN THE CENTRE, THE PRIESTS SURROUNDING THE ARK, THE LEVITES [SURROUNDING] THE PRIESTS, AND ALL ISRAEL ON THIS SIDE AND THAT SIDE; AS IT IS SAID, AND ALL ISRAEL, AND THEIR ELDERS AND OFFICERS, AND THEIR JUDGES STOOD ON THIS SIDE THE ARK AND ON THAT SIDE ETC.[5] THEY TURNED THEIR FACES TOWARDS MOUNT GERIZIM AND OPENED WITH THE BLESSING: 'BLESSED BE THE MAN THAT MAKETH NOT A GRAVEN OR MOLTEN IMAGE',[6] AND BOTH PARTIES[7] RESPOND 'AMEN'. THEY THEN TURNED THEIR FACES TOWARDS MOUNT EBAL AND OPENED WITH THE CURSE: 'CURSED BE THE MAN

(1) Ibid. XXV, 9. (2) He attaches the word '*thus*' to what precedes. (3) Deut. XI, 30. The verse ends with: *beside the terebinths of Moreh.* (4) Gen. XII, 6. (5) Josh. VIII, 33. (6) The reverse of Deut. XXVII, 15. (7) On the two mounts.

THAT MAKETH A GRAVEN OR MOLTEN IMAGE', AND BOTH PARTIES RESPOND 'AMEN'. [SO THEY CONTINUE] UNTIL THEY COMPLETE THE BLESSINGS AND CURSES. AFTER THAT THEY BROUGHT THE STONES,[1] BUILT THE ALTAR AND PLASTERED IT WITH PLASTER, AND INSCRIBED THEREON ALL THE WORDS OF THE TORAH IN SEVENTY LANGUAGES,[2] AS IT IS SAID, VERY PLAINLY.[3] THEN THEY TOOK THE STONES[4] AND WENT [32b] AND SPENT THE NIGHT IN THEIR PLACE.[5]

GEMARA. Whence have we it that the section concerning the suspected woman [may be recited in any language]?—As it is written, *And the priest shall say unto the woman*[6]—in whatever language he speaks.

Our Rabbis taught: They explain to her in any language she understands for what reason she is about to drink the water, in what [sort of vessel] she drinks, why she had misconducted herself and in what manner she had misconducted herself. For what reason she is about to drink the water—because of [her husband's] warning and her subsequent seclusion. In what [sort of vessel] she drinks—in a potsherd.[7] Why she had misconducted herself—because of levity and childishness. And in what manner she had misconducted herself—whether in error or deliberately, under compulsion or of free will. But why all this? So as not to discredit the water of bitterness.[8]

THE CONFESSION MADE AT THE PRESENTATION OF THE TITHE. Whence have we it that this [may be recited in any language]?—As it is written, *And thou shalt say before the Lord thy God, I have put away the hallowed things out of mine house*,[9] and the deduction is to be drawn from the analogous use of the word '*say*'

(1) V. Deut. XXVII, 2ff. (2) The total number of languages in the world as the Rabbis thought. (3) Ibid. 8. (4) After the sacrifices had been offered, the altar was taken to pieces. (5) Viz., in Gilgal where they were again set up (Josh. IV, 20). (6) Num. V, 21. (7) V. *supra* p. 38. (8) So that if she had offended in error or under compulsion and the water did not affect her, she should not think there would have been no effect if she had offended deliberately or of her free will. (9) Deut. XXVI, 13.

in connection with the suspected woman that it may be in whatever language he speaks. R. Zebid said to Abaye, But let the deduction be drawn from the analogous use of the word '*say*' in connection with the Levites[1] [as follows]: As there it means that it must be in the holy tongue so here it must be in the holy tongue! —[He answered], We deduce [the meaning of] an unqualified use of '*say*' from another occurrence of an unqualified use of '*say*', but we do not deduce [the meaning of] an unqualified use of '*say*' from a passage where the expression '*answer and say*' occurs.[2]

It has been taught: R. Simeon b. Yoḥai said: A man should recount what is to his credit in a low voice and what is to his discredit in a loud voice. That he is to recount what is to his credit in a low voice [is learnt] from the confession made at the presentation of the tithe, and what is to his discredit in a loud voice from the declaration made at the offering of the first-fruits.[3] But should one recount what is to his discredit in a loud voice? Surely R. Johanan has said in the name of R. Simeon b. Yoḥai: Why was it instituted that the 'prayer'[4] should be recited softly? So as not to put transgressors to shame;[5] for behold, Scripture made no distinction as to the place of a sin-offering or burnt-offering![6]—Do not read [in R. Simeon's statement] 'his discredit' but 'his trouble';[7] as it has been taught: *And he shall cry, Unclean, unclean*[8] —it is necessary [for the leper] to make his trouble known to the multitude so that the multitude may pray on his behalf; and thus everybody to whom a calamity has occurred should make it known to the multitude so that the multitude may pray on his behalf.

(1) V. ibid. XXVII, 14 and Mishnah p. 157. (2) Viz., in connection with the Levites. Consequently the analogy is drawn with the reference to the suspected woman and not the Levites. (3) In the former he tells how he had done his duty (V. Deut. XXVI, 13f.) and in that connection the unqualified '*say*' occurs. In the latter he tells of his humble ancestry (ibid. 5ff.) and in that connection '*answer and say*', i.e., say aloud, occurs. (4) V. *supra* p. 157, n. 4. (5) Who confess their sins in the course of prayer. (6) They were offered on the same side of the altar, and an onlooker would not be able to tell which offering was being sacrificed. (7) In the declaration made over the first-fruits, the allusion was to the vicissitudes of the patriarch; and such should be spoken aloud. (8) Lev. XIII, 45.

The [above] text states: 'R. Johanan said in the name of R. Simeon b. Yoḥai: Why was it instituted that the 'prayer' should be recited softly? So as not to put transgressors to shame; for, behold, Scripture made no distinction as to the place of a sin-offering or burnt-offering.' But it is not so, for there is a difference in the treatment of the blood. The blood of a sin-offering [was applied] above [the red line which ran round the altar], whereas the blood of a burnt-offering [was applied] below it!—Only the priest would know that. There is, however, the difference that for a sin-offering a female animal was sacrificed and for a burnt-offering a male!—Being covered by the fat tail [the sex would not be recognised]. That is quite right with a female lamb, but what of a female goat?[1]—In that case the man brought the shame upon himself, because he should have offered a lamb but offered a goat. What, however, of the sin-offering brought for idolatry when only a goat suffices![2]—In that case let him experience shame so that he may receive atonement.

THE SHEMA'. Whence have we it that this [may be recited in any language]? As it is written, *Hear, O Israel*[3]—in any language you understand.

Our Rabbis taught: *The Shema'* must be recited as it is written.[4] Such is the statement of Rabbi but the Sages say, In any language. What is Rabbi's reason?—Scripture declares, *And [these words] shall be*,[5] i.e., they must remain as they are. And [what is the reason of] the Rabbis?—Scripture declares, '*Hear, O Israel*'—in any language you understand. But for the Rabbis it is likewise written, '*And [these words] shall be*'![6]—That indicates that one may not read it in the wrong order.[7] And whence does Rabbi derive the rule that one may not read it in the wrong order?—From the fact that the text uses '*these words*' and not merely 'words'. And the Rabbis?[8]—They draw no inference from the use of '*these words*' instead of 'words'. But for Rabbi it is likewise written, '*Hear*'!—He requires

(1) Which has no fat tail. (2) V. Num. XV 27, 29. (3) Deut. VI, 4. The word for '*Hear*' also means 'understand'. (4) Only in Hebrew. (5) Ibid. 6. (6) Why do they not explain them: they must remain as they are? (7) V. *supra* p. 91. (8) What do they derive from the use of '*these words*'?

that for the rule: Make audible to your ears what you utter with your lips.[1] And the Rabbis?—They agree with him who said that if one has not recited the *Shema'* audibly he has fulfilled his obligation. It is possible to say that Rabbi holds [33a] that the whole Torah may be read in any language; for if you maintain that it may be read[2] only in the holy tongue, wherefore had the All-Merciful to write *'And [these words] shall be'?*—It is necessary because itis written *'Hear'*.[3] It is likewise possible to say that the Rabbis hold that the whole Torah must be read in the holy tongue; for if you maintain that it can be read in any language, wherefore had the All-Merciful to write the word *'Hear'?*—It is necessary because it is written *'And [these words] shall be'*.[4]

THE 'PRAYER'. [It may be recited in any language because] it is only supplication, and one may pray in any language he wishes. But may the 'prayer' be recited in any language? Behold Rab Judah has said: A man should never pray for his needs in Aramaic. For R. Joḥanan declared: If anyone prays for his needs in Aramaic, the Ministering Angels[5] do not pay attention to him, because they do not understand that language!—There is no contradiction, one referring to [the prayer] of an individual and the other to that of a Congregation.[6] And do not the Ministering Angels understand Aramaic? Behold it has been taught: Joḥanan, the High Priest, heard a *Bath Ḳol*[7] issue from within the Holy of Holies announcing, 'The young men who went to wage war against Antioch[8] have been victorious.'[9] It also happened with Simeon the Righteous[10]

(1) I.e., the *Shema'* must be recited audibly. (2) In the synagogue (Rashi). (3) If he were of the opinion that the Torah can only be read in Hebrew, it would necessarily apply to the *Shema'*. Why, then, should he draw a conclusion from *shall be?* He does so to oppose the inference which the Rabbis draw from *Hear*. (4) Which might otherwise be taken to indicate that the *Shema'* must be read in Hebrew. (5) Who convey the petitions to the Throne of Glory. (6) With the latter, the help of the angels is not required. (7) V. Glos. This is evidently the incident related by Josephus (Ant. XIII, X, 3) of John Hyrcanus. (8) [Antiochus Cyzicenus, over whom the children of John Hyrcanus were victorious, v. *loc. cit.*, and Derenbourg, *Essai*, p. 47.] (9) This and the following announcements were made in Aramaic, so the angels must have understood it. (10) Possibly the High Priest Simon, son of Boethus, also called Cantheras,

that he heard a *Bath Ḳol* issue from within the Holy of Holies announcing, 'Annulled is the decree which the enemy intended to introduce into the Temple'. Then was Caius Caligula[1] slain and his decrees annulled. They noted down the time [when the *Bath Ḳol* spoke] and it tallied.[2] Now it was in Aramaic that it spoke!—If you wish I can say that it is different with a *Bath Ḳol*, since it occurs for the purpose of being generally understood;[3] or if you wish I can say that it was Gabriel who spoke; for a Master has declared, Gabriel came and taught [Joseph] the seventy languages.[4]

THE GRACE AFTER MEALS. [That this may be recited in any language is derived from] the text, *And thou shalt eat and be full, and thou shalt bless the Lord thy God*[5]—in any language wherein thou utterest a benediction.

THE OATH CONCERNING TESTIMONY. [That this may be uttered in any language is derived from] the text, *And if any one sin, in that he heareth the voice of adjuration*[6]—in whatever language he hears it.

THE OATH CONCERNING A DEPOSIT. [That this may be uttered in any language] is derived from the analogous use of the phrase '*if any one sin*' in the oath concerning testimony.[7]

THE FOLLOWING ARE RECITED IN THE HOLY TONGUE: THE DECLARATION MADE AT THE OFFERING OF THE FIRST-FRUITS, THE FORMULA OF ḤALIẒAH, etc. down to: WHENCE IS IT THAT THE DECLARATION MADE AT THE OFFERING OF THE FIRST-FRUITS [MUST BE IN HEBREW]? [IT IS STATED], AND THOU SHALT ANSWER AND SAY BEFORE THE LORD THY GOD, AND ELSEWHERE IT IS STATED, AND THE LEVITES SHALL ANSWER AND SAY; AS THE LATTER MUST BE IN THE HOLY TONGUE, SO MUST THE FORMER BE IN THE

as Josephus describes him (*op. cit.* XIX, VI, 2). [For other views v. *HUCA* VIII-IX, p. 300.]

(1) The name is corrupted in the text. He ordered that his statue should be placed in the Temple and worshipped (Josephus, *War* II, X, 1.) (2) With the time of Caligula's assassination. (3) And Aramaic was the vernacular of the period. (4) V. *infra*. Gabriel was exceptional; but the other angels were ignorant of Aramaic. (5) Deut. VIII, 10. (6) Lev. V, 1. (7) V. ibid. 21.

HOLY TONGUE. But whence have we it of the Levites themselves [that they used Hebrew]?—It is derived from the analogous use of the word *'voice'* in connection with Moses. Here it is written *with a loud voice*,[1] and elsewhere it is written, *Moses spake and God answered him by a voice*;[2] as in the latter passage it was in the holy tongue, so also in the other passage it means in the holy tongue.

WHENCE IS IT THAT THE FORMULA OF ḤALIẒAH etc. What, then, do the Rabbis make of the word *'thus'*?[3]—They require it to indicate that each act[4] invalidates [the ceremony by its omission]. And R. Judah?[5]—From the use of *'Kakah'* instead of *koh*.[6] And the Rabbis?—They draw no inference from the use of *'Kakah'* instead of *koh*. [33*b*] What, then, does R. Judah make of the phrase *'and she shall answer and say'*?[7]—He requires it for the purpose of deducing that the Levites [must pronounce the blessings and curses] in the holy tongue.[8] But let him derive that from the analogous use of the word *'voice'* in connection with Moses!—He had learnt [from his teacher] to draw an inference from the analogous use of the word *'answer'* but not from *'voice'*.[9] It has been similarly taught: R. Judah says: Wherever [in Scripture the words] *'thus'*, both in the form of *'koh'* and *'kakah'*, or *'answer and say'* occur, [what has to be spoken] must only be in the holy tongue. The word *'koh'* is found in *'Thus ye shall bless'*,[10] *'kakah'* in connection with *Ḥaliẓah*, and *'answer and say'* with the Levites.

HOW WERE THE BLESSINGS AND CURSES [PRONOUNCED]? WHEN ISRAEL CROSSED THE JORDAN etc. Our Rabbis taught:

(1) Deut. XXVII, 14. (2) Ex. XIX, 19. (3) Upon which R. Judah bases the teaching that the formula must be in Hebrew. (4) Mentioned in Deut. XXV, 9, viz., loosing the shoe, spitting in his face, and pronouncing the formula. (5) From where does he derive this teaching? (6) Both words signify *'thus'*; and since the text has the longer form, he takes it as an indication that the formula must be in Hebrew and also that the omission of an act invalidates the ceremony. (7) Since he does not follow the Rabbis in basing upon it the rule that the formula must be in Hebrew. (8) Since the phrase *'answer and say'* occurs in Deut. XXVII, 14. (9) [No inference can be drawn from the analogous use of a word (a *Gezerah shawah*, v. Glos.) which has not been received on tradition from a teacher.] (10) Num. VI, 23, the priestly benediction which must be in Hebrew.

Are they not beyond Jordan?[1] [This means] on the other side of the Jordan and beyond; such is the statement of R. Judah. *Behind the way of the coming cf the sun*[2]—the place where the sun dawns.[3] *In the land of the Canaanites which dwell in the Arabah*[2]—i.e., mount Gerizim and mount Ebal where the Cutheans[4] dwell. *Over against Gilgal*[2]—[this means] near Gilgal.[5] *Beside the terebinths of Moreh*[2]—[this means] Shechem. Elsewhere it states, *And Abram passed through the land unto the place of Shechem unto the terebinth of Moreh;*[6] as the terebinth of Moreh mentioned in this latter verse is Shechem, so in the former verse it means Shechem.

It has been taught:[7] R. Eleazar son of R. Jose said: In this connection I proved the Samaritan Scriptures[8] to be false. I said to them, 'You have falsified your Torah[9] but you gained nothing thereby.[10] You declare that '*the terebinths of Moreh*' means Shechem; we too admit that '*the terebinths of Moreh*' means Shechem. We learnt this by an inference from analogy;[11] but how have you learnt it!'[12]

R. Eleazar said: '*Are they not beyond the Jordan*'? [This means] near the Jordan; because if it signified on the other side of the Jordan and beyond, is it not written, *And it shall be when ye are passed over Jordan!*[13] '*Behind the way of the coming of the sun*'—[this means] the

(1) Deut. XI, 30. This might have been interpreted as close to the other side of the Jordan. (2) Ibid.; '*coming*' is usually understood as 'setting', but it is here explained as 'coming up, rising'. (3) [The East. The phrase means accordingly: Far away from the Eastern bank of the Jordan where the Israelites were at the time towards the West. The term אחרי as distinct from אחר denotes 'greatly separated'.] (4) Samaritans, so called because they were brought by Sargon, King of Assyria, from Cuthea, to take the place of the exiled Israelites. (5) [Not the Gilgal east of Jericho, but another place of that name identified with Juleijil, east of Mt. Gerizim; v. p. 166, n. 3. (6) Gen. XII, 6. (7) As Rashi remarks, the words 'it has been taught' should be deleted, as it is the continuation of the Baraitha, v. Sifre, *a.l.* (8) For *sifre* 'Scriptures' we must read with the J. Talmud *Sofre* 'scribes, learned men'. (9) The Samaritan recension of the Pentateuch. In Deut. XI, 30 it adds 'over against Shechem' which does not appear in the Hebrew version. (10) I.e., your addition of the words was unnecessary. (11) *Gezerah shawah* (v. Glos.). (12) By tampering with the text. (13) Ibid. XXVII, 4. This is explained: as soon as you have passed over; therefore it must have been a place close to the Jordan.

place where the sun sets.[1] *'In the land of the Canaanites'*—i.e., the land of the Hivites. *'Which dwell in the Arabah'*—but do they not dwell among mountains and hills![2] *'Over against Gilgal'*—but they could not see Gilgal![3]—R. Eliezer b. Jacob says: Scripture has here only the intention of pointing out to them the route for the second [part of the journey] as it had pointed out to them the route for the first [part of the journey].[4] *'The way'*—[this means], Proceed along the high-road and not through fields and vineyards. *'Which dwell'*—[this means], Pass through inhabited territory and not through deserts. *'In the Arabah'*—[this means], Pass through the plain and not through mountains and hills.

Our Rabbis taught: How did Israel cross the Jordan? Each day [during the journey in the wilderness] the ark journeyed behind two standards,[5] but on this day [of crossing] it journeyed in front; as it is said, *Behold, the ark of the covenant of the Lord of all the earth passeth over before you.*[6] Each day the Levites carried the ark, but on this day the priests carried it; as it is said, *And it shall come to pass, when the soles of the feet of the priests that bear the ark of the Lord* etc.[7]—It has been taught: R. Jose says: On three occasions the priests carried the ark: when they crossed the Jordan, when they walked round Jericho,[8] and when they deposited it in its place.[9]—[34*a*] When the feet of the priests were dipped in the water, the water flowed backward; as it is said, *And when they that bore the ark were come unto the Jordan . . . that the waters which came down from above stood and rose up in one heap.*[10] What was the height of the water? Twelve *mil* by twelve *mil* in accordance with the dimensions

(1) [The West, and the verse means far away from the Western towards the Eastern bank of the Jordan.] (2) *Arabah* signifies the plain. (3) They lived at a distance from it; so why is this mentioned? [Rashi, who seems to have another and preferable text, explains the question: 'but they (these places) are far from Gilgal'—Gilgal being East of Jericho (v. p. 165, n. 5), why then mention it, cf. also Rashi on Deut. XI, 30.] (4) When Israel left Egypt a pillar of fire and cloud directed them; but this ceased on the death of Moses. Scripture therefore gives them directions, and its purpose is not to explain the location of Gerizim and Ebal. (5) Of the tribes; v. Num. X, 11ff. (6) Josh. III, 11. (7) Ibid. 13. (8) Ibid. VI, 6. (9) In Solomon's Temple (I Kings VIII, 3). (10) Josh. III, 15f.

of the camp of Israel.[1] Such is the statement of R. Judah; and R. Eleazar b. Simeon said to him, According to your explanation, which is swifter, man or water? Surely water is swifter; therefore the water must have returned and drowned them![2] It rather teaches that the waters were heaped up like stacks to a height of more than three hundred *mil*, until all the kings of the East and West saw them; as it is said, *And it came to pass, when all the kings of the Amorites, which were beyond Jordan westward, and all the kings of the Canaanites, which were by the sea, heard how that the Lord had dried up the waters of Jordan from before the children of Israel until they were passed over, that their heart melted, neither was there spirit in them any more, because of the children of Israel.*[3] And also Rahab the harlot said to Joshua's messengers, *For we have heard how the Lord dried up the water of the Red Sea* etc.;[4] and it continues, *And as soon as we heard it, our hearts did melt neither did there remain any more* etc.[5]

While they were still in the Jordan, Joshua said to them, Know why you are crossing the Jordan; it is on condition that you disinherit the inhabitants of the land from before you; as it said, *Then ye shall drive out all the inhabitants of the land from before you* etc.[6] If you do this, well and good; otherwise the water will return and drown you [*othekem*].[7]—What means '*othekem*'? Me and you.—While they were still in the Jordan, Joshua said to them, *Take you up every man of you a stone upon his shoulder, according unto the number of the tribes of the children of Israel* etc.;[8] and it continues, *That this may be a sign among you, that when your children ask in time to come, saying, What mean ye by these stones?* etc.[9] It was to be a monument for the children that their fathers had crossed the Jordan. While they were still in the Jordan, Joshua said to them. *Take you hence out of the midst of the Jordan, out of the place where the priests' feet stood firm, twelve stones, and carry them over with you, and lay them down in the*

(1) *supra* p. 71. So that as soon as the last Israelite had crossed over, the waters returned. (2) If the water rose to twelve *mil* only to subside again, they would not have been able to traverse a sufficient distance to escape the returning water. (3) Josh. V, 1. (4) Ibid. II, 10. (5) Ibid. 11. (6) Num. XXXIII, 52. (7) This is an unusual Hebrew form, and is taken as a combination of *othi*, 'me' and *ethkem* 'you'. (8) Josh. IV, 5. (9) Ibid. 6.

lodging place, where ye shall lodge this night etc.[1] It is possible [to think that they were to deposit them] in any lodging place; therefore there is a text to state, '*Where ye shall lodge this night*'.

R. Judah[2] said: Abba Ḥalafta, R. Eliezer b. Mathia and Ḥananiah b. Hakinai stood upon those stones and estimated that each was equal to about forty *se'ah*.[3] There is a tradition that the weight which a man can raise upon his shoulder is a third of the weight he can carry;[4] so from this you may calculate what was the weight of the cluster of grapes,[5] as it is said, *And they bare it upon a staff between two*.[6] From the fact that it is stated *upon a staff* do I not know that it [was carried] between two? Why, then, is there a text to state '*between two*'? [It means] on two staffs. R. Isaac said: [It means] a series of balancing poles.[7] How was it? Eight [spies] carried the grape-cluster,[8] one carried a pomegranate, one carried a fig, and Joshua and Caleb did not carry anything. If you wish I can say [that they did not carry anything] because they were the most distinguished of them,[9] or alternatively that they did not have a share in the plan.[10]

R. Ammi and R. Isaac the smith differ in opinion. One said, According to the statement of R. Judah,[11] [34*b*] they crossed over in the formation of their encampment, and according to the statement of R. Eleazar b. Simeon[12] they crossed over in single file.[13] The other said, According to the statement of both teachers they crossed over in the formation of their encampment. One teacher was of the opinion that man was swifter, and the other that water was swifter.[14]

(1) Josh. IV, 3. (2) The reading should be: R. Jose. (3) The *se'ah* was a measure of capacity; so what is here meant is a weight equal to that of forty *se'ah* of wheat. (4) When others help to set it upon his shoulder. Consequently the weight of each was 120 *se'ah*. (5) Carried by the spies. (6) Num. XIII, 23. (7) For four couples of carriers. (8) [The weight of which would have been on this calculation 960 *se'ahs*, that is 8 times 120.] (9) And so it was beneath their dignity. (10) The bringing of the fruit was part of the plan to discourage the community. They would judge from its size what must be the stature of the inhabitants. (11) That the water was twelve *mil* in height. (12) That the height was over three hundred *mil*. (13) The time of crossing was much longer; consequently the heap of water had to be of greater height. (14) For that reason

Send for thee men[1]—Resh Laḳish said: ['*For thee*' means] from thine own mind;[2] because does anybody choose a bad position for himself?[3] That is what is written, *And the thing pleased me well*[4]—Resh Laḳish said: It pleased me [Moses] well but not the All-Present.

That they search the land for us[5]—R. Ḥiyya b. Abba said: The spies aimed at nothing else than discrediting the land of Israel. Here it is written, *That they may search* [*we-yaḥperu*] *the land for us*, and elsewhere it is written, *Then the moon shall be confounded* [*we-ḥaferah*] *and the sun ashamed* etc.[6]

And these were their names: of the tribe of Reuben, Shammua the son of Zaccur.[7] R. Isaac said: It is a tradition in our possession from our forefathers that the spies were named after their actions, but only with one has it survived with us: *Sethur the son of Michael.*[8] [He was named] Sethur because he undermined [*sathar*] the works of the Holy One, blessed be He; and Michael [was so named] because he suggested that God [*el*] was weak [*mak*].[9] R. Johanan said: We can also explain [the name] Nahbi the son of Vophsi.[10] [He was named] Nahbi because he hid [*hiḥbi*] the words[11] of the Holy One, blessed be He; and Vophsi [was so named] because he stepped over [*pasa'*] the attributes[12] of the Holy One, blessed be He.

And they went up by the South and he came unto Hebron[13]—it should have read 'and they came'!—Raba said: It teaches that Caleb held aloof from the plan of the spies and went and prostrated himself upon the graves of the patriarchs, saying to them, 'My fathers, pray on my behalf that I may be delivered from the plan of the spies'. (As for Joshua, Moses had already prayed on his behalf;

they suggest different heights for the water to enable the people to escape.

(1) Num. XIII, 2. So the Hebrew literally. (2) I.e., the plan did not emanate from God but from Moses. (3) Would God have sanctioned a plan which He knew was to end in disaster? (4) Deut. I, 23. (5) Ibid. 22. The word for *search* is here given the meaning 'confound'. (6) Isa. XXIV, 23. (7) Num. XIII, 4. (8) Ibid. 13. (9) Lit., 'he made himself to be weak'—a reverential avoidance of a disparaging reference to God. He was the man who said, 'Even the master of the house cannot remove his furniture from there' (*infra* 35a). (10) Ibid. 14. (11) Did not truthfully report them. (12) He misrepresented them. (13) Ibid. 22. So the Heb. literally.

as it is said, *And Moses called Hoshea the son of Nun Joshua,*[1] [meaning], May Jah save thee [*yoshi'aka*] from the plan of the spies.) That is the intention of what is written, *But My servant Caleb, because he had another spirit with him.*[2]

And there were Ahiman, Sheshai and Talmai[3]—Ahiman [was so named because he was] the strongest [*meyuman*] of them; Sheshai because he made the earth like pits [*sheḥithoth*];[4] Talmai because he made the earth like furrows [*telamim*]. Another explanation:[5] Ahiman built 'Anath, Sheshai built Alash, and Talmai built Telbesh.[6] *The children of Anak*—[they are so called] because they wore the sun as a necklace [*ma'aniḳin*] owing to their stature.

Now Hebron was built seven years[3]—what means '*was built*'? If I say that it means actually built, is it possible that a man constructs a house for his younger son before his elder son; as it is written, *And the sons of Ham: Cush and Mizraim?*[7]—But [the intention is], it was seven times more productive than Zoan. There is no worse stony ground in all the land of Israel than Hebron, and that is why they bury the dead there; and there is none among all the countries superior to the land of Egypt, as it is said, *Like the garden of the Lord, like the land of Egypt;*[8] and there is no place superior to Zoan in all the land Egypt, as it is written, *For his princes are at Zoan.*[9] Nevertheless Hebron was seven times more productive than Zoan. But was Hebron stony ground; behold it is written, *And it came to pass at the end of forty years, that Absalom said unto the king, I pray thee, let me go [and pay my vow ... in Hebron]*;[10] and R. Iwya—another version is, Rabbah b. Bar Ḥanan—said: He went to fetch lambs from Hebron; and there is also a teaching: [The best] rams are

(1) Num. XIII, 16. (2) Ibid. XIV, 24. It continues: *I will bring him into the land whereinto he went,* viz. Hebron. V. Josh. XIV, 14. (3) Num. XIII, 22. (4) Through his heavy tread. (5) These words should be deleted, and do not occur in the parallel passage Yoma 10*a*. (6) [Identified by Obermeyer (*op. cit.* pp. 102-3) with 'Anah, Alusa and Telbeth, three fortified island-towns on the Northern Euphrates.] (7) Gen. X, 6. Canaan was the youngest of his sons and Mizraim the second. (8) Ibid. XIII, 10. (9) Isa. XXX, 4. (10) II Sam. XV, 7.

from Moab and lambs from Hebron!—From that very fact [it is proved that the land was stony]; because the soil is thin it produces pastures[1] and the cattle grow fat there.

And they returned from spying out the land . . . [35a] *and they went and came.*[2] R. Joḥanan said in the name of R. Simeon b. Yoḥai, It compares the going to the coming back; as the coming back was with an evil design, so the going was with an evil design.[3] *And they told him and said, We came* etc.,[4] and it continues, *Howbeit the people are strong.*[5] R. Joḥanan said[6] in the name of R. Meir, Any piece of slander, which has not some truth in the beginning, will not endure in the end.[7]

And Caleb stilled [*wa-yahas*] *the people concerning Moses*[8]—Rabbah said, [It means] that he won them over [*hissithan*] with words. When Joshua began to address them, they said to him, 'Would this person with the lopped-off head[9] speak to us!' [Caleb] said [to himself], If I address them [in the same strain as Joshua], they will answer me in like manner and silence me; so he said to them, 'Is it this alone that Amram's son has done to us!'[10] They thought that he was speaking to censure Moses, so they were silent. Then he said to them, 'He brought us out of Egypt, divided the Red Sea for us and fed us with manna. If he were to tell us, Prepare ladders and ascend to heaven, should we not obey him! *Let us go up at once and possess it* etc.'[11]

But the men that went up with him said, We will not be able etc.[12]—R. Ḥanina b. Papa said: A grievous statement did they make at that moment, viz. *For they are stronger than we*—read not *than we*—

(1) It does not yield any other produce. (2) Num. XIII, 25f. (3) They planned at the outset to bring back a discouraging report. (4) Ibid. 27. (5) Ibid. 28. (6) The Gemara inserts here: mnemonic—*truth, alone, interment.* These are key-words to assist in remembering the sequence of the passages treated. (7) On that account the report opened with a true description of the land's fertility. (8) Ibid. 30. I.e., he silenced them to hear something about Moses. E.V. '*before*'. (9) An allusion to the fact that he was childless. What interest could he have in the conquest since he had no children to possess the land! (Rashi). (10) He chose his words that the people should imagine he was against Moses, and so they would listen to him. 'Alone' in this sentence is the key-word of the mnemonic. (11) Ibid. (12) Ibid. 31.

but *than He*;[1] as it were even the master of the house cannot remove his furniture from there.[2]

It is a land that eateth up the inhabitants thereof.[3] Raba expounded: The Holy One, blessed be He, said, I intended this for good[4] but they thought it in a bad sense. I intended this for good, because wherever [the spies] came, the chief [of the inhabitants] died, so that they should be occupied [with his burial] and not inquire about them.[5] (Others say that Job died then and the whole world was occupied with mourning for him.) But they thought it in a bad sense: *It is a land that eateth up the inhabitants thereof.*[6]

And we were in our own sight as grasshoppers, and so we were in their sight.[7] R. Mesharsheya said, The spies were liars. As regards '*we were in our own sight as grasshoppers*', very well; but how could they know that '*so we were in their sight*'? But it is not so;[8] for when [the inhabitants] held their funeral-meal[9] they ate it beneath cedar trees, and when [the spies] saw them they climbed the trees and sat there. Then they heard them say, 'We see men like grasshoppers in the trees'.

And all the congregation lifted up their voice and wept.[10] Rabbah said in the name of R. Johanan: That day was the ninth of Ab;[11] and the Holy One, blessed be He, said, They are now weeping for nothing, but I will fix [this day] for them as an occasion of weeping for generations.

But all the congregation bade them stone them with stones,[12] and it continues, *And the glory of the Lord appeared in the tent of meeting.* R. Ḥiyya b. Abba said: It teaches that they took stones and hurled them against Him Who is above.[13]

(1) [מִמֶּנּוּ instead of מִמֶּנוּ, a difference of pronounciation in the Babylonian Masora, in order to distinguish between the 1st. masc. plur and 3rd. sing, v. *Ges. K.* (1910) para. m, n. 1, and cf. Ibn Ezra on Ex. I, 9.] (2) Even God is powerless against them. (3) Num. XIII, 32. (4) Viz., that many Canaanites die there. Hence the word 'interment' in the mnemonic. (5) This is how the spies were able to return unmolested. (6) This fate would befall the Israelites if they settled there. (7) Ibid. 33. (8) The spies did not lie in this matter. (9) After burying the dead, as mentioned above. (10) Ibid. XIV, 1. (11) Fifth month. On that date the two Temples were destroyed, and the day is observed as a fast. (12) Ibid. 10. (13) The word '*them*' includes God.

Even those men that did bring up an evil report of the land died by the plague.[1] R. Simeon b. Laḳish said: They died an unnatural death.[2] R. Ḥanina b. Papa said: R. Shila of Kefar Temarthah expounded; It[3] teaches that their tongue was elongated and reached down to their navel, and worms issued from their tongue and penetrated their navel and from their navel they penetrated their tongue. R. Naḥman b. Isaac said: They died of croup.[4]

When[5] the last of the Israelites ascended from the Jordan, the waters returned to their place; as it is said, *And it came to pass, when the priests that bore the ark of the covenant of the Lord were come up out of the midst of the Jordan, and the soles of the priests' feet were lifted up unto the dry ground, that the waters of Jordan returned unto their place, and went over all its banks, as aforetime.*[6] Consequently the ark and its bearers and the priests were on one side [of the Jordan] and the Israelites on the other![7] The ark carried its bearers and passed over [the river]; as it is said, *And it came to pass, when all the people were clean passed over, that the ark of the Lord passed over, and the priests, in the presence of the people.*[8] On that account was Uzza punished, as it is said, *And when they came unto the threshing-floor of Chidon, Uzza put forth his hand to hold the ark.*[9] The Holy One, blessed be He, said to him, 'Uzza, [the ark] carried its bearers; must it not all the more [be able to carry] itself!'

And the anger of the Lord was kindled against Uzzah; and God smote him there for his error [shal] etc.[10] R. Joḥanan and R. Eleazar [differ on the interpretation of the word '*shal*']. One said [that it means]

(1) Num. XIV, 37. (2) That is the meaning of '*by the plague*'. (3) The definite article in '*the plague*' shows that it was not an ordinary epidemic. (4) It was regarded as the severest form death could take (Ber. 8*a*) and was the fate of the slanderer (Shab. 33*b*). (5) After this long digression there is resumed the narrative of the crossing of the Jordan. (6) Josh. IV, 18. (7) The text is understood in the same sense that the priests who carried the ark dipped their feet in the Jordan and the waters remained parted so long as the feet were kept there. When the Israelites had crossed, the priests lifted their feet out of the water, stepping back upon the bank. They were consequently on the other side; so how did they get over? (8) Ibid. 11. Note that the ark '*passed over*', and was not carried over. (9) I Chron. XIII, 9. (10) II Sam. VI, 7.

on account of the act of error [*shalu*];[1] the other said [that it means] he relieved himself in its presence.[2]

And there he died by[3] *the ark of God*. R. Johanan said: Uzzah entered the World to Come, as it is stated *'with the ark of God'*—as the ark endures for ever, so Uzzah entered the World to Come.

And David was angry, because the Lord had broken forth upon Uzzah.[4] R. Eleazar said: His face was changed [so that it became in colour] like a cake baked upon the coals [*ḥararah*]. Are we to infer from this that wherever *wa-yiḥar* occurs it has this meaning?—In other passages the word *'af'* [anger] is added but here it is not added.

Raba expounded: Why was David punished?[5] Because he called words of Torah 'songs', as it is said, *Thy statutes have been my songs in the house of my pilgrimage.*[6] The Holy One, blessed be He, said to him, 'Words of Torah, of which it is written, *Wilt thou set thine eyes upon it? It is gone,*[7] thou recitest as songs! I will cause thee to stumble in a matter which even school-children know.' For it is written, *But unto the sons of Kohath he gave none, because the service of the sanctuary* etc.;[8] and yet [David] brought it in a waggon.

And he smote of the men of Beth-Shemesh, because they looked into the ark.[9] God smote them because they looked into the ark! R. Abbahu and R. Eleazar [differ in their interpretation]; one said that they went on reaping while they prostrated themselves [before the ark];[10] the other said that they also used this [disrespectful] language to it, [35b] 'Who embittered thee that thou wast thus embittered,[11] and what has come upon thee that thou art now appeased?'

(1) [שלוֹ, error, neglect, cf. Ezra IV, 12.] (2) *Shal* is connected with the root *nashal* 'to drop off'. (3) Lit., 'with'. (4) II Sam. VI, 8. '*Angry*' is '*wa-yiḥar*' lit., 'be kindled'. The explanation is intended to avoid the thought that David was angered against God. (5) That Uzzah died through him. (6) Ps. CXIX, 54. When he fled from his enemies, he entertained himself by treating Scriptural passages as songs. He thus made a profane use of them. (7) Prov. XXIII, 5—i.e., the Torah is beyond human understanding. (8) Num. VII, 9. The ark had to be carried upon the shoulders of the Levites. (9) I Sam. VI, 19. (10) [The phrase ראו בארון, is taken to signify '*they gazed at the ark*' with unbecoming interest, v. Driver, S.R., *Samuel, a.l.*] (11) And didst not release thyself from the Philistines.

Even He smote of the people seventy men and fifty thousand men.[1] R. Abbahu and R. Eleazar [differ in their interpretation]; one said that there were only seventy men [smitten] each of whom was the equal of fifty thousand men, while the other said that there were fifty thousand men [smitten] each of whom was equal to the seventy who constituted the Sanhedrin.

And it was so, that when they that bore the ark of the Lord had gone six paces, he sacrificed an ox and a fatling,[2] and it is also written, [*They sacrificed*] *seven bullocks and seven rams!*[3]—R. Papa said in the name of Samuel: [The two passages are reconciled by supposing that] at each pace an ox and a fatling [were offered] and at each six paces seven bullocks and seven rams. R. Ḥisda said to him, On your theory you filled the whole of the land of Israel with high places! But, said R. Ḥisda, at each six paces an ox and a fatling [were offered] and at each six sets of six paces seven bullocks and seven rams.

[In one place the name of the threshing-floor] is written Chidon [and in another] Nacon![4]—R. Joḥanan said: At first [it was called] Chidon and afterwards Nacon.[5]

In consequence [of what is related in the Scriptures], you must conclude that there were three sets of stones: one which Moses caused to be erected in the land of Moab, as it is said, *Beyond Jordan, in the land of Moab, began Moses to declare* etc.,[6] and elsewhere it states, *Thou shalt write upon the stones all the words of this law* [*very plainly*],[7] and the inference is drawn from the use of the analogous word [that as in the latter passage stones were employed, they were similarly employed in connection with what is narrated in the first passage]. The second set was that which Joshua caused to be erected in the midst of the Jordan, as it is said, *And Joshua set up twelve stones in the midst of Jordan.*[8] The third set was that which

(1) I Sam. VI, 19. [In M.T. the particle ו (*'and'*) is missing.] (2) II Sam. VI, 13. (3) I Chron. XV, 26. (4) Cf. II Sam. VI, 6 with I Chron. XIII, 9. (5) *Chidon* means 'a spear', an appropriate name for the place where Uzzah lost his life; *Nacon* means 'established', and alludes to the fact that the ark was established there. (6) Deut. I, 5. The Hebrew for *'declare'* is *be'er*. (7) Ibid. XXVII, 8. The Hebrew for *'plainly'* is *ba'er*. (8) Josh. IV, 9.

he caused to be erected in Gilgal, as it is said, *And those twelve stones which they took.*[1]

Our Rabbis taught: How did the Israelites inscribe the Torah?—R. Judah says: They inscribed it upon the stones, as it is stated, '*Thou shalt write upon the stones all the words of this law* etc.' After that they plastered them over with plaster. R. Simeon said to him, According to your explanation, how did the nations of that period learn the Torah![2] —He replied to him, The Holy One, blessed be He, endowed them with exceptional intelligence; and they sent their scribes who peeled off the plaster and carried away [a copy of the inscription]. On that account was the verdict sealed against them [to descend] to the pit of destruction, because it was their duty to learn [Torah] but they failed to do so. R. Simeon says: They inscribed it upon the plaster and wrote below, *That they teach you not to do after all [their abominations]*.[3] Hence you learn that if they turn in penitence they would be accepted. Raba b. Shila said: What is R. Simeon's reason?—Because it is written, *And the peoples shall be as the burnings of lime*[4]—i.e., on account of the matter of the plaster.[5] And [how does] R. Judah [explain this verse]?—[Their destruction will be] like plaster—as there is no other remedy for plaster except burning, so there is no other remedy for those nations [who cleave to the abominations] except burning. According to whom [is the following teaching] which has been taught: *And thou carriest them away captive*[6]—this is to include Canaanites who reside outside the land [of Israel] so if they turn in penitence they will be accepted. [36*a*] According to whom is this?—According to R. Simeon.

Come and see how many miracles were performed on that day. Israel crossed the Jordan, came to mount Gerizim and mount Ebal

(1) Josh. IV, 20. (2) Since the inscription was covered with plaster. (3) Deut. XX, 18. The command to destroy was limited to those of the seven nations who resided in Canaan. Those of them who lived outside its borders could survive by giving up their abominable practices. (4) Isa. XXXIII, 12. The word for '*lime*' is the same as for *plaster*. (5) The nations will be destroyed because they neglected to pay heed to the teachings inserted on the plaster. (6) Deut. XXI, 10.

[thus traversing a distance of] more than sixty *mil*, no creature was able to withstand them and whoever withstood them was immediately panic-stricken; as it is said, *I will send My terror before thee, and will discomfort all the people to whom thou shalt come*, etc.,[1] and it states, *Terror and dread falleth upon them . . . till Thy people pass over, O Lord.*[2] This alludes to the first advance [of Israel in the days of Joshua]; and '*Till the people pass over which Thou hast gotten*'[2] alludes to the second advance [in the days of Ezra]. Conclude from this that the Israelites were worthy that a miracle should be performed on their behalf during the second advance as in the first advance, but sin caused [it to be withheld].

After that they brought the stones, built the altar, and plastered it with plaster, and inscribed thereon all the words of the Torah in seventy languages; as it is said, *Very plainly.*[3] Then they sacrificed burnt-offerings and peace-offerings, ate and drank and rejoiced, pronounced the blessings and the curses,[4] packed up the stones, and came and lodged in Gilgal; as it is said, *Carry them over with you and lay them down in the lodging place.*[5] It is possible [to think that they were to deposit them] in any lodging place; therefore there is a text to state, *Where ye shall lodge this night,*[5] and then it is written, *And those twelve stones, which they took [out of Jordan, did Joshua set up in Gilgal].*[6]

A Tanna taught: The hornet did not pass over [Jordan] with them; but behold it is written, *And I will send the hornet before thee!*[7] —R. Simeon b. Laḳish said: It stood by the bank of the Jordan and injected a virus [into the Canaanites] which blinded their eyes above and castrated them below; as it is said, *Yet destroyed I the Amorite before them, whose height was like the height of the cedars, and he was strong as the oaks; yet I destroyed his fruit from above and his roots from beneath* etc.[8] R. Papa said: There were two hornets, one in the period of Moses and the other in the period of

(1) Ex. XXIII. 27. (2) Ibid. XV, 16. (3) Deut. XXVII, 8. (4) [Wilna Gaon deletes 'and the curses', and refers the blessings to the Grace after meals, since the blessings and curses on the Mounts were pronounced before the altar was built, v. Mishnah.] (5) Josh. IV, 3. (6) Ibid. 20. (7) Ex. XXIII, 28. (8) Amos II, 9.

Joshua; the former did not pass over [Jordan] but the other did.

SIX TRIBES ASCENDED THE SUMMIT OF MOUNT GERIZIM etc. What means *and* the *half of them?*[1]—R. Kahana said: As they were divided here [on the mounts][2] so were they divided on the stones of the ephod.[3] An objection was raised: The High Priest had two precious stones on his shoulders, one on this side and one on the other side; upon them were inscribed the names of the twelve tribes, six on one stone and six on the other, as it is said, *Six of their names on the one stone, [and the names of the six that remain on the other stone, according to their birth]*.[4] [This indicates that] the second six were to be according to their birth, but the first six were not to be according to their birth; because [the name of] Judah came first, and there were fifty letters, twenty-five on each stone. R. Ḥanina b. Gamaliel says: [36*b*] They were not apportioned upon the stones as they were apportioned in the Book of Numbers[5] but as they were apportioned in the second Book of the Pentateuch.[6] How then [were they arranged]? The sons of Leah in order of seniority [on one stone, and on the other] the sons of Rachel, one on top and the other at the bottom, with the sons of the handmaids in the centre.[7] In that case, how am I to explain '*according to their birth*'? [It means that the inscription was] according to the names which their father called them and not according to the names which Moses called them—Reuben and not Reubeni, Simeon and not Simeoni, Dan and not had-Dani, Gad and not hag-Gadi.[8] This is a refutation of R. Kahana![9] The refutation [is unanswered].

What, then, is the meaning of '*and* the *half of them*'?—It has been

(1) Josh. VIII, 33. The Hebrew has the definite article which seems superfluous. (2) Simeon, Levi, Judah, Issachar, Joseph and Benjamin on Mount Gerizim, and Reuben, Gad, Asher, Zebulun, Dan and Naphtali on Mount Ebal, v. Deut. XXVII, 12-13. (3) Six tribes in the same order on each stone; v. Ex. XXVIII, 9ff. (4) Ibid. 10. (5) V. I, 5ff. (6) V. Ex. I, 2ff. (7) On the one stone were Reuben, Simeon, Levi, Judah, Issachar and Zebulun; on the other Benjamin, Dan, Naphtali, Gad, Asher and Joseph. (8) The latter are the tribal as distinct from the personal names. (9) Who said that the tribes were divided on the stones of the ephod as on the two mounts; and this has been shewn to be incorrect.

taught: 'The half in front of mount Gerizim was larger than that in front of mount Ebal, because [the tribe of] Levi was below [with the ark].'[1] On the contrary, for the reason that Levi was below it must have been smaller![2] —This is what he intends: Although Levi was below [the party on mount Gerizim was still larger] because the sons of Joseph were included with them [and they were very numerous]; as it is said, *And the children of Joseph spake unto Joshua, saying, Why hast thou given me but one lot and one part for an inheritance, seeing I am a great people? . . . And Joshua said unto them, If thou be a great people, get thee up to the forest.*[3] He said to them, 'Go, hide yourselves in the forests that the evil eye[4] may not have sway over you'. They replied to him, 'The evil eye can bear no sway over the seed of Joseph'; for it is written, *Joseph is a fruitful bough, a fruitful bough by a fountain,*[5] and R. Abbahu said, Read not *'ale 'ayin* [by a fountain] but *'ole 'ayin* [overcoming the eye]. R. Jose b. Ḥanina said: [It is derived] from this passage, *And let them grow* [*we-yidgu*] *into a multitude in the midst of the earth*[6]—as the water covers the fish [*dagim*] in the sea so that the [evil] eye bears no sway over them, so the [evil] eye bears no sway over the seed of Joseph.

[It was stated above that on the stones of the ephod] were fifty letters; but there were fifty less one!—R. Isaac said: One letter was added to the name of Joseph, as it is said, *He appointed it in Joseph for a testimony, when he went out over the land of Egypt.*[7] R. Naḥman b. Isaac objected: We require *according to their birth!*[8]—But [the correct explanation is] that throughout the whole Torah Benjamin's name is spelt without the letter *yod* [before the final letter], but here

(1) [The article '*the*' denotes that those who stood on Ebal represented the full contingent of half the tribes. Whereas on Gerizim one of the tribes—Levi—was missing (Maharsha)]. (2) Since Levi should have been among the first six tribes. (3) Josh. XVII, 14f. (4) The personification of envy which causes harm to those who enjoy good fortune. Their numerical strength would excite envy. (5) Gen. XLIX, 22. (6) Ibid. XLVIII, 16, referring to Joseph's sons. (7) Ps. LXXXI, 6. In this verse Joseph's name is spelt with five letters instead of the usual four, v. *supra* p. 50, n. 2. (8) As explained above, viz., the name as given by Jacob; consequently we cannot use the exceptional form of his name as it occurs here.

[on the ephod] it was spelt complete with *yod;* as it is written, *But his father called him Benjamin.*[1]

R. Ḥana[2] b. Bizna said in the name of R. Simeon the Pious: Because Joseph sanctified the heavenly Name in private one letter was added to him from the Name of the Holy One, blessed be He; but because Judah sanctified the heavenly Name in public, the whole of his name was called after the Name of the Holy One, blessed be He. How was it with Joseph [that he sanctified the Name]?—As it is written, *And it came to pass about this time, that he went into the house to do his work.*[3] R. Joḥanan said: This teaches that both [Joseph and Potiphar's wife] had the intention of acting immorally. '*He went into the house to do his work*'—Rab and Samuel [differ in their interpretation]. One said that it really means to do his work; but the other said that he went to satisfy his desires.[4] '*And there was none of the men of the house* etc.'—is it possible that there was no man in a huge house like that of this wicked [Potiphar]!—It was taught in the School of R. Ishmael: That day was their feast-day, and they had all gone to their idolatrous temple; but she had pretended to be ill because she thought, I shall not have an opportunity like to-day for Joseph to associate with me. *And she caught him by his garment, saying* etc.[5] At that moment his father's image came and appeared to him through the window and said, 'Joseph, thy brothers will have their names inscribed upon the stones of the ephod and thine amongst theirs; is it thy wish to have thy name expunged from amongst theirs and be called an associate of harlots?' (As it is written, *He that keepeth company with harlots wasteth his substance.*)[6] Immediately *his bow abode in strength*[7]—R. Joḥanan said in the name of R. Meir: [This means] that his passion subsided. *And the arms of his hands were made active*[7]—he stuck his hands in the ground so that his lust came out from between his finger-nails. '*By the hands of the Mighty One of Jacob*'[7]—Who caused his name to be engraven upon the stones of the ephod but the Mighty One of

(1) Gen. XXXV, 18; here it is spelt with the *yod.* (2) In the parallel passage, *supra* 10*b* the name is Ḥanin. (3) Ibid. XXXIX, 11. (4) I.e., for an immoral purpose. (5) Ibid. 12. (6) Prov. XXIX, 3. (7) Gen. XLIX, 24.

Jacob? *'From thence is the shepherd, the stone of Israel'* [1]—from there was he worthy to be made a shepherd, as it is said, *Give ear, O Shepherd of Israel, Thou that leadest like the flock of Joseph.* [2]

It has been taught: Joseph was worthy that twelve tribes should issue from him as they issued from his father Jacob, as it is said, *These are the generations of Jacob, Joseph;* [3] but his lust came out from between his finger-nails.[4] Nevertheless they[5] issued from his brother Benjamin and were given names on his own account; as it is said, *And the sons of Benjamin: Bela and Becher and Ashbel* etc.[6] [He was called] Bela, because [Joseph] was swallowed up [*nibla'*] among the peoples. [He was called] Becher, because [Joseph] was the first-born [*bekor*] of his mother. [He was called] Ashbel, because God sent [Joseph] into captivity [*sheba'o el*]. [He was called] Gera, because [Joseph] dwelt [*gar*] in lodgings [in a strange land]. [He was called] Naaman, because he was especially beloved [*na'im*]. [They were called] Ehi and Rosh, because [Joseph] is my brother [*aḥi*] and chief [*rosh*]. [They were called] Muppim and Huppim, because [Benjamin said, Joseph] did not see my marriage-canopy [*ḥuppah*] and I did not see his.[7] [He was called] Ard, because [Joseph] descended [*yarad*] among the peoples. Others explain [that he was called] Ard, because [Joseph's] face was like a rose [*wered*].

R. Ḥiyya b. Abba said in the name of R. Joḥanan: At the moment when Pharaoh said to Joseph, *And without thee shall no man lift up his hand* etc.,[8] Pharaoh's astrologers exclaimed, 'Wilt thou set in power over us a slave whom his master bought for twenty pieces of silver!' He replied to them, 'I discern in him royal characteristics.' They said to him, 'In that case he must be acquainted with the seventy languages'. Gabriel came and taught [Joseph] the seventy languages, but he could not learn them. Thereupon [Gabriel]

(1) Gen. XLIX, 24. (1) Ps. LXXX, 2, E.V. 1., *sic*. Hence Israel is called Joseph's flock and he is the shepherd. (3) Gen. XXXVII, 2. (4) As mentioned above, and so his power to beget was diminished. (5) I.e., ten sons, who, added to Joseph's two, made the total of twelve. (6) Ibid. XLVI, 21. (7) The derivation of Muppim has fallen out of the text, but is found in Tanḥuma to Genesis (ed. Buber, p. 206), viz., his mouth (*pi*) was like that of our father, i.e., he learnt Torah from Joseph as from Jacob. (8) Ibid. XLI, 44.

added to his name a letter from the Name of the Holy One, blessed be He, and he learnt [the languages] as it is said, *He appointed it in Joseph*[1] *for a testimony, when he went out over the land of Egypt, where I [Joseph] heard a language that I knew not.*[2] On the morrow, in whatever language Pharaoh conversed with him he replied to him; but when [Joseph] spoke to him in the holy tongue he did not understand what he said. So he asked him to teach it to him; he taught it to him but he could not learn it. [Pharaoh] said to him, 'Swear to me that thou wilt not reveal this';[3] and he swore to him. When [Joseph] later said to him, *My father made me swear, saying,*[4] he remarked to him, 'Go, ask [to be released from] thine oath.'[5] He replied to him, 'I will also ask [to be released from my oath] concerning thee'.[6] Therefore, although it was displeasing to him, [Pharaoh] said to him, *Go up and bury thy father, according as he made thee swear.*[7]

What was it that Judah did?[8]—As it has been taught: R. Meir said: When the Israelites stood by the Red Sea, the tribes strove with one another, each wishing to descend into the sea first. Then sprang forward [37*a*] the tribe of Benjamin and descended first into the sea; as it is said, *There is little Benjamin their ruler*[9]—read not *rodem* [*their ruler*] but *rad yam* [descended into the sea]. Thereupon the princes of Judah hurled stones at them; as it is said, *The princes of Judah their council.*[10] For that reason the righteous Benjamin was worthy to become the host of the All-Powerful,[11] as it is said, *He dwelleth between his shoulders.*[12] R. Judah said to [R. Meir]: That is not what happened; but each tribe was unwilling to be the first

(1) V. p. 179, n. 7. (2) Ps. LXXXI, 6. (3) That he was ignorant of Hebrew, and a king was expected to know every language. (4) Ibid. L, 5, viz., that he should inter his body in Canaan. (5) In Jewish Law only proper authorities could release a man from his oath. Pharaoh did not wish Joseph to leave Egypt to bury his father. (6) I.e., if Pharaoh refused him permission, he would take steps to enable him to disclose the king's ignorance of Hebrew. (7) Ibid. 6. (8) That he sanctified God's Name publicly. (9) Ps. LXVIII, 28, E.V. 27. (10) Ibid. The word for *council* has the same root as the verb 'to stone'; so it is here understood as 'their stoners'. (11) The Temple was erected on the territory of Benjamin, v. Yoma 12*a*. (12) Deut. XXXIII, 12, i.e., God dwells in the land of Benjamin.

to enter the sea. Then sprang forward Nahshon the son of Amminadab[1] and descended first into the sea; as it is said, *Ephraim compasseth me about with falsehood, and the house of Israel with deceit; but Judah yet ruleth with God.*[2] Concerning him it is stated in Scripture,[3] *Save me O God, for the waters are come in unto my soul. I sink in deep mire, where there is no standing* etc.[4] *Let not the waterflood overwhelm me, neither let the deep swallow me up* etc.[5] At that time Moses was engaged for a long while in prayer; so the Holy One, blessed be He, said to him, 'My beloved ones are drowning in the sea and thou prolongest prayer before Me!' He spake before Him, 'Lord of the Universe, what is there in my power to do?' He replied to him, *Speak unto the children of Israel that they go forward. And lift thou up thy rod, and stretch out thy hand* etc.[6] For that reason Judah was worthy to be made the ruling power in Israel, as it is said, *Judah became His sanctuary, Israel his dominion.*[7] Why did Judah become His sanctuary and Israel his dominion? Because *the sea saw [him] and fled.*[8]

It has been taught. R. Eliezer b. Jacob says: It is impossible to declare that Levi [was stationed] below since it is stated that he was above,[9] and it is impossible to declare that he was above since it is stated that he was below;[10] so how was it? The elders of the priests and Levites were below and the rest above. R. Joshiyah said: All [the Levites] who were qualified to serve [as bearers of the ark] were below and the rest above. Rabbi says: Both [the priests and Levites] and also [the Israelites] were standing below.[11] They turned their faces towards mount Gerizim and opened with the blessing, and then towards mount Ebal and opened with the curse; for what means *'al?*[12] It means 'near to'; as it has been taught: *And thou shalt put pure frankincense near* ['al] *each row*[13]—Rabbi says:

(1) He was the prince of the tribe of Judah (Num. VII, 12). (2) Hos. XII, 1. The last words are *rad 'im el*, which are interpreted: he descended (into the sea because his trust was) with God. (3) *Ḳabbalah*, lit., 'tradition', a term used for the Biblical canon other than the Pentateuch, v. B.Ḳ. (Sonc. ed) p. 3, n. 3. (4) Ps. LXIX, 2f. (5) Ibid. 16. (6) Ex. XIV, 15f. (7) Ps. CXIV, 2. The Temple was in the kingdom of Judah. '*His dominion*' is understood as Judah's rule over Israel. (8) Ibid. 3. (9) On Gerizim (Deut. XXVII, 12). (10) Josh. VIII, 33. (11) This seems to be implied in Josh. l.c. (12) In Deut. XXVII, 12, translated '*upon*'. (13) Lev. XXIV, 7.

'Al means 'near to'. You declare that *'al* means 'near to'; but perhaps it is not so and the signification is actually 'upon'? Since it states, *Thou shalt put a veil* 'al *the ark,*[1] conclude that *'al* means 'near to'.

THEY TURNED THEIR FACES TOWARDS MOUNT GERIZIM AND OPENED WITH THE BLESSING etc. Our Rabbis taught: There was a benediction in general and a benediction in particular, likewise a curse in general and a curse in particular.[2] [Scripture states]: *to learn, to teach,* to *observe* and to *do;*[3] consequently there are [37b] four [duties associated with each commandment]. Twice four are eight[4] and twice eight are sixteen.[5] It was similar[6] at Sinai and the plains of Moab; as it is said, *These are the words of the covenant which the Lord commanded Moses* etc.,[7] and it is written, *Keep therefore the words of this covenant* etc.[8] Hence there were forty-eight covenants in connection with each commandment.[9] R. Simeon excludes [the occasion of] Mount Gerizim and Mount Ebal[10] and includes that of the Tent of Meeting in the wilderness.[11] The difference of opinion here is the same as that of the teachers in the following: R. Ishmael says: General laws were proclaimed at Sinai and particular laws in the Tent of Meeting. R. Akiba says: Both general and particular laws were proclaimed at Sinai, repeated in the Tent of Meeting, and for the third time in the plains of Moab. Consequently there is not a single precept written in the Torah in connection with which forty-eight covenants were not made. R. Simeon b. Judah

(1) Ex. XL, 3. The veil was not 'upon' the ark but 'near to', i.e., in front of it. (2) The general blessing or curse was in connection with Deut. XXVII, 26, and the particular blessing or curse for the actions specified in that chapter. (3) Cf. ibid. v. 1 and XI, 19. (4) In connection with every command there is a covenant for each of the four duties. So there were four blessings and four curses pronounced with each precept. (5) Eight blessings and curses with the general commandment and eight with the particular commandments. (6) Viz., there were sixteen blessings and curses implied with the covenants entered into in each of the two places named. (7) Deut. XXVIII, 69, apart from the section at Mt. Gerizim. (8) Ibid. XXIX, 8. (9) Sixteen in each of the three places. (10) Because not all the commandments formed the covenant there. (11) After its erection God spoke to Moses from thence (Lev. I, 1).

of Kefar Acco[1] said in the name of R. Simeon: There is not a single precept written in the Torah in connection with which forty-eight times 603,550[2] covenants were not made. Rabbi said: According to the reasoning of R. Simeon b. Judah of Kefar Acco who said in the name of R. Simeon that there is not a single precept written in the Torah in connection with which forty-eight times 603,550 covenants were not made, it follows that for each Israelite there are 603,550 commandments.[3] What is the issue between them?—R. Mesharsheya said: The point between them is that of personal responsibility and responsibility for others.[4]

R. Judah b. Naḥmani, the lecturer[5] of Simeon b. Laḳish, expounded: The whole section [of the blessings and curses] refers to none other than the adulterer and adulteress. [It states,] *Cursed be the man that maketh a graven or molten image* etc.[6] Does it suffice merely to pronounce *cursed* with such a person![7]—But it alludes to one who has immoral intercourse, and begets a son who goes to live among heathens[8] and worships idols; cursed be the father and mother of this man since they were the cause of his sinning.[9]

Our Rabbis taught: *Thou shalt set the blessing upon Mount Gerizim and the curse* etc.[10] What is the purpose of this text? If it is to teach that the blessing [is to be pronounced] on mount Gerizim and the curse on mount Ebal, it has already been said, *These shall stand upon mount Gerizim to bless the people,*[11] and it continues, *And these shall stand upon mount Ebal for the curse!*[12] But [the purpose is to indicate] that the blessing must precede the curse. It is possible

(1) [Caphare Accho in lower Galilee, mentioned in Josephus, *Wars* II, 20, 6; v. Hildesheimer, *Beiträge*, p. 81.] (2) The number of male Israelites, with each of whom the covenants were made. (3) And forty-eight covenants were made in connection with each of them. (4) If it is held according to the Rabbis that each Israelite is responsible for the conduct of the rest, then the number must be squared to get the total. (5) It was customary for a teacher to impart the lesson to a lecturer who delivered it to the disciples. (6) Deut. XXVII, 15. (7) The penalty is death. (8) [Being the offspring of an adulterous union, he is debarred from the Assembly and cannot marry an Israelite woman.] (9) [And not only with idolatry. His heathen association will lead him to commit the other offences in this section, provoking upon his parents the enumerated curses; v., however, Rashi.] (10) Ibid, XI, 29. (11) Ibid. XXVII, 12. (12) Ibid. 13.

to think that all the blessings must precede the curses; therefore the text states *'blessing'* and *'curse'*, i.e., one blessing precedes a curse and all the blessings do not precede the curses. A further purpose is to draw a comparison between blessing and curse to tell us that as the curse is pronounced by the Levites so the blessing must be pronounced by the Levites; as the curse is uttered in a loud voice so must the blessing be uttered in a loud voice; as the curse is said in the holy tongue[1] so must the blessing be said in the holy tongue; as the curse is in general and particular terms so must the blessing be in general and particular terms; and as with the curse both parties respond with Amen so with the blessing both parties respond with Amen.

MISHNAH. HOW WAS THE PRIESTLY BENEDICTION [PRONOUNCED]? IN THE PROVINCE[2] IT WAS SAID AS THREE BLESSINGS,[3] BUT IN THE TEMPLE AS ONE BLESSING.[4] IN THE TEMPLE THE NAME WAS UTTERED [38a] AS WRITTEN,[5] BUT IN THE PROVINCE IN ITS SUBSTITUTED NAME.[6] IN THE PROVINCE THE PRIESTS RAISE THEIR HANDS IN A LINE WITH THEIR SHOULDERS, BUT IN THE TEMPLE ABOVE THEIR HEADS, EXCEPT THE HIGH PRIEST WHO DOES NOT RAISE HIS HANDS HIGHER THAN THE PLATE.[7] R. JUDAH SAYS: ALSO THE HIGH PRIEST RAISES HIS HANDS HIGHER THAN THE PLATE, AS IT IS SAID, AND AARON LIFTED UP HIS HANDS TOWARD THE PEOPLE AND BLESSED THEM.[8]

GEMARA. Our Rabbis taught: *On this wise ye shall bless*[9]—i.e., in the holy tongue. You say that it means in the holy tongue; but perhaps it is not so and it means in any language! It is stated here, *'On this wise ye shall bless,'* and elsewhere it is stated, *These shall stand*

(1) V. *supra* 33a. (2) I.e., outside the Temple. (3) As divided in Num. VI, 24ff., and after each sentence there was a response of Amen. (4) There was no interruption because the response of Amen was not made in the Temple. (5) The Tetragrammaton *YHWH*. (6) Viz., *Adonai*. (7) Worn on the forehead (Ex. XXVIII, 36). (8) Lev. IX, 22. (9) Num. VI, 23.

to bless the people;[1] as in this latter passage it was in the holy tongue, so also in the former it was in the holy tongue. R. Judah says: [This deduction] is unnecessary, because it states *'on this wise'* [which signifies] that they must pronounce it in this language [as written in Scripture].[2]

Another [Baraitha] taught: *'On this wise ye shall bless'*—i.e., standing. You say that it means standing; but perhaps that is not so and [the benediction may be pronounced] even sitting! It is stated here, *'On this wise ye shall bless,'* and elsewhere it is stated, '*These shall* stand *to bless*'—as here it was standing so in the former passage it was standing. R. Nathan says: [This deduction] is unnecessary; behold it states, *To minister unto Him and to bless in His name*[3]—as [the priest] ministers standing so he blesses standing. Whence is it that the ministering itself [was performed standing]? Because it is written, *To stand to minister.*[4]

Another [Baraitha] taught: *'On this wise ye shall bless'*—i.e., with raising of the hands. You say that it means with raising of the hands; but perhaps that is not so [and the benediction can be pronounced] without raising of the hands! It is stated here, *'On this wise ye shall bless'*, and elsewehere it is stated, '*And Aaron* lifted up *his hands toward the people and blessed them'*;[5] as in this latter passage it was with raising of the hands, so also in the former passage it was with raising of the hands. R. Jonathan raised the question: If [your reasoning is valid], then as in that passage[5] [the benediction was pronounced] by the High Priest, on the new moon[6] and in the service of the Community, so also here it must be the High Priest, on the new moon and in the service of the Community! R. Nathan says: [This deduction] is unnecessary; behold it states, *Him and his sons for ever,*[7] comparing him and his sons—as [the High Priest pronounced the benediction] with raising of the hands, so also his sons with raising of the hands. Furthermore it is written

(1) Deut. XXVII, 12. (2) V. *supra* 33*b*, p. 164. (3) Ibid. X, 8. (4) Ibid. XVIII, 5. (5) Which refers to the special occasion when the Tent of Meeting was dedicated. (6) That day on which the Tabernacle was set up was New Moon, v. Ex. XL, 2. (7) Deut. XVIII, 5.

for ever,[1] and a comparison is drawn between the benediction and ministering.[2]

Another [Baraitha] taught: *'On this wise ye shall bless the children of Israel'*—with the use of the *Shem Hameforash.*[3] You say that it means with the Tetragrammaton; but perhaps that is not so and a substituted name was used![4] There is a text to say, *So shall they put My name*[5]—My name which is unique to Me. It is possible to think that [the *Shem Hameforash* was also used] in places outside the Temple; but it is stated here, *'So shall they put My name'* and elsewhere it is stated, *To put His name there*[6]—as in this latter passage it denotes in the Temple so also in the former passage it denotes in the Temple. R. Joshiah says: [This deduction] is unnecessary; behold it states, *In every place where I cause My name to be remembered I will come unto thee.*[7] Can it enter your mind that every place is intended?[8] But the text must be transposed thus: In every place where I will come unto thee and bless thee will I cause My name to be remembered; and where will I come unto thee and bless thee? In the Temple; there, in the Temple, will I cause My name to be remembered.

Another [Baraitha] teaches: *'On this wise ye shall bless the children of Israel'*—I have here only the children of Israel; whence is it that proselytes, women and enfranchised slaves [are included]? There is a text to state, *Ye shall say unto them*[9]—i.e., to all of them.

Another [Baraitha] teaches: *'On this wise ye shall bless'*—i.e., face to face.[10] You say that it means face to face; but perhaps that is not so and it means the face [of the priests] towards the back [of

(1) He thus answers the argument that the benediction should only be pronounced by the High Priest and on the new moon. (2) I.e., although Deut. XVIII, 5 only mentions ministering and not blessing, yet from the phrase *to minister and to bless* (ibid. X, 8) it is concluded that they are analogous. (3) [Lit., 'the Distinguished Name', synonymous with *Shem Hameyuḥad*, 'the Unique Name' and generally held identical with the Tetragrammaton, uttered as written, v. Sanh. (Sonc. ed.) p. 408, n. 1.] (4) [I.e., as read *Adonai*, v. Tosaf.] (5) Num. VI, 27. (6) Deut. XII, 5. (7) Ex. XX, 24. (8) [That the Divine Presence will come there. Surely this is restricted to the Sanctuary or Temple; v. Rashi.] (9) Num. VI, 23. (10) The priests and people must face one another.

the people]! There is a text to state, *'Ye shall say unto them'*—i.e., like a man who talks to his companion.

Another [Baraitha] teaches: *'On this wise ye shall bless'*—i.e., in a loud voice. But perhaps it is not so and the meaning is softly! There is a text to state, *'Ye shall say unto them'*—like a man who talks to his companion.

Abbaye said, We have a tradition that [the Precentor][1] exclaims *'Kohanim!'* when [at least] two are present but he does not exclaim *'Kohen!'* when only one is there;[2] as it is said, *Ye shall say unto them*—i.e., [at least] unto two. R. Ḥisda said: We have a tradition that [when the Precentor is himself] a *kohen* he exclaims *'Kohanim!'* but a lay-Israelite does not; as it is said, 'Ye *shall say unto them'*—the saying [38*b*] must come from one of their own body. The legal decision is in accord with the view of Abaye and not according to R. Ḥisda.

(Mnemonic:[3] *Desires, for the benediction, platform, in the 'Service', cup, recognise, accepts hospitality, heifer.*)

R. Joshua b. Levi said: Whence is it that the Holy One, blessed be He, desires the priestly benediction? As it is said, *So shall they put My name upon the children of Israel; and I will bless them.*[4] R. Joshua b. Levi also said: Every *kohen* who pronounces the benediction is himself blessed, but if he does not pronounce it he is not blessed; as it is said, *I will bless them that bless thee.*[5] R. Joshua b. Levi also said: Any *kohen* who refuses to ascend the platform[6] transgresses three positive commandments, viz., *'On this wise shall ye bless'*, *'Ye shall say unto them'*, and *'So shall they put My name'*. Rab said: We have to take into consideration that he might be the son of a divorcee or the son of a *Ḥaluẓah*.[7] But [R. Joshua and Rab] are

(1) When calling upon the *Kohanim* (v. Glos., *s.v. Kohen*) in the Synagogue to pronounce the benediction. (2) [But the priest turns his face to bless the people of his own accord; v. *'Atereth Zekenim Sh. 'A. Oraḥ Ḥayyim* 128, 10.] (3) V. p. 171, n. 6. (4) Num. VI, 27. [By blessing the people, the priests place, so to speak, to the delight of God, His name upon them (Rashi)]. (5) Gen. XII, 3. (6) From which the benediction is pronounced. (7) V. Glos. His father may have contracted a marriage which is forbidden to a *kohen*, in which case the son was disqualified.

not at variance, one referring to a case where he ascends [the platform] occasionally,[1] the other to a case where he does not occasionally ascend it.

R. Joshua b. Levi also said: Any *kohen* who does not ascend [the platform] in the 'Service'[2] may not ascend later; as it is said, *And Aaron lifted up his hands toward the people, and blessed them; and he came down from offering the sin-offering and the burnt-offering and the peace-offering.*[3] As in this passage [the benediction occurred] during the 'Service', so here [in the Synagogue] it must be [during the prayers relating to] the 'Service'. But that is not so, seeing that R. Ammi and R. Assi ascended [at a later point in the liturgy]! —R. Ammi and R. Assi had already moved their feet [at the proper point to ascend the platform] but did not reach there [in time]. This is as R. Oshaia taught, [The statement that the *kohen* may not ascend after that point in the liturgy] does not apply except when he had not moved his feet, but if he had moved his feet he may ascend. It has been similarly learnt: If he[4] is confident that he can raise his hands [for the benediction] and resume the prayers [without an error], he is permitted to do so;[5] on arguing in this connection that he surely does not move [his feet],[6] [the reply was] that he shifts a little [to one side]; so also in the present instance, if [a *kohen*] moves a little [to ascend at the right point, it is sufficient].

R. Joshua b. Levi also said: We give the cup of blessing[7] for the recital of the Grace after meals only to one who is of a generous disposition,[8] as it is said, *He that hath a bountiful eye shall be blessed, for he giveth of his bread to the poor*[9]—read not *yeborak* ['*shall be blessed*']

(1) On some of the Festivals and then declines to do so on others; in which case we do not suspect him of being disqualified. (2) I.e., the paragraph of the Eighteen Benedictions referring to the Temple-service. That is the point at which the *kohen* ascends the platform. V. *P.B.* p. 238*a*. (3) Lev. IX, 22. (4) The case is where the Precentor is the only *kohen* in the Synagogue. He is not required to 'raise his hands', because it might confuse him and lead to a mistake in the rendering of the prayers. (5) V. Ber. 34*a*. (6) From the reading desk to ascend the platform, so how can he 'raise his hands'? (7) A cup of wine is used in the recital of Grace. (8) Lit., 'good of eye', the opposite of bad of eye, i.e., envious. (9) Prov. XXII, 9.

but *yebarek* [shall say the Benediction]. R. Joshua b. Levi also said: Whence is it that even the birds recognise those who have a niggardly spirit?[1] As it is said, *For in vain is the net spread in the eyes of any bird.*[2] R. Joshua b. Levi also said: Whoever accepts hospitality of men of niggardly spirit transgresses a prohibition; as it is said, *Eat thou not the bread of him that hath an evil eye, [neither desire thou his dainties]. For as he reckoneth within himself; so is he; eat and drink, saith he to thee, [but his heart is not with thee].*[3] R. Naḥman b. Isaac said: He transgresses two prohibitions, '*Eat thou not*' and '*Neither desire thou*'. R. Joshua b. Levi also said: [The necessity for] the heifer whose neck is to be broken[4] only arises on account of the niggardly of spirit, as it is said, *Our hands have not shed this blood.*[5] But can it enter our minds that the elders of a Court of Justice are shedders of blood! The meaning is, [The man found dead] did not come to us for help and we dismissed him, we did not see him and let him go— i.e., he did not come to us for help and we dismissed him without supplying him with food, we did not see him and let him go without escort.[6]

Adda said in the name of R. Simlai: In a Synagogue where all the worshippers are *kohanim*, they all ascend the platform. For whom, then, do they pronounce the benediction? R. Zera answered, For their brethren [working] in the fields.[7] But it is not so; for Abba the son of R. Minyamin b. Ḥiyya taught: The people who are behind the *kohanim* do not come within the scope of the benediction![8]—There is no contradiction; the former refers to men who are compelled [to be absent] and the latter to men who are not compelled [to be stationed behind the *kohanim*]. But R. Shimi of the Fort of Shiḥori taught, In a Synagogue where all the worshippers are *kohanim*, some ascend [the platform] and the rest respond with Amen!—There is no contradiction; the latter refers

(1) Lit., 'narrow of eye'. Birds avoid such as these. (2) Prov. I, 17. Verse 19 continues, *So are the ways of everyone that is greedy of gain.* (3) Ibid. XXIII, 6f. (4) Cf. Deut. XXI, 1ff. (5) Ibid. 7. (6) A man without escort was liable to be set upon and murdered. (7) Who were prevented by their work from being present. (8) R.H. 35a. So how much more, they who are not present!

to where ten remain [to respond Amen] and the former where ten do not remain.

The [above] text stated: 'Abba the son of R. Minyamin b. Ḥiyya taught, The people who are behind the *kohanim* do not come within the scope of the benediction.' It is obvious that the tall do not create an obstruction for the short,[1] nor does the ark [where the Torah-scrolls are deposited] create an obstruction; but how is it with a partition [within the Synagogue]?—Come and hear: R. Joshua b. Levi said: Even a partition of iron does not divide between Israel and their Father in heaven. The question was asked, How is it with those standing on the side [of the *kohanim*]?—Abba Mar son of R. Ashi said, Come and hear: We have learnt, If he intended to sprinkle[2] in front of him [39*a*] and he sprinkled behind him, or vice versa, the sprinkling is invalid; [but if he intended to sprinkle] in front of him and did so on the sides in front of him, his sprinkling is valid.[3]

Raba son of R. Huna said: When the Torah-scroll is unrolled[4] it is forbidden to converse even on matters concerning the law; as it is said, *And when he opened it all the people stood up*,[5] and standing up signifies nothing else than silence, as it is said, *And I wait because they speak not, because they stand still and answer no more*.[6] R. Zera said in the name of R. Ḥisda: [It may be derived] from this passage, *And the ears of all the people were attentive unto the book of the law*.[7]

R. Joshua b. Levi also said: Any *kohen* who has not washed his hands may not lift them up [to pronounce the benediction]; as it is said, *Lift up your hands in holiness and bless ye the Lord*.[8]

His disciples asked R. Eleazar b. Shammua, 'How have you prolonged your life?' He replied, 'Never have I made use of a Synagogue as a short cut,[9] nor stepped over the heads of the holy

(1) Although the latter are shut out from the view of the *kohanim*, they are not excluded from the benediction. (2) The purifying water to remove the defilement of vessels (v. Num. XIX, 18). (3) Consequently those standing on the side are within the scope of the benediction. (4) For the lection in the Synagogue. (5) Neh. VIII, 5, describing the reading of the Torah to the assembly. (6) Job XXXII, 16. (7) Neh. VIII, 3. (8) Ps. CXXXIV, 2. (9) In Ber. 62*b* it is stated: If one enters a Synagogue not for the purpose of making it a short cut, he may use it in that manner. But R. Eleazar took a stricter view.

people,[1] nor lifted up my hands [as a *kohen*] without first uttering a benediction.' What benediction did he utter?—R. Zera said in the name of R. Ḥisda: '[Blessed art Thou, O Lord our God, King of the Universe] Who hast commanded us with the sanctity of Aaron and hast commanded us to bless Thy people Israel in love'.[2] When he [the priest] moves his feet [to ascend the platform] what does he say?—'May it be pleasing before Thee, O Lord our God, that this benediction wherewith Thou hast commanded us to bless Thy people Israel may be free from stumbling and iniquity.' When he turns his face from the Congregation [to the ark after pronouncing the benediction] what does he say?—R. Ḥisda led R. 'Uḳba forward[3] and the latter explained [that what he says is], 'Lord of the Universe, we have performed what Thou hast decreed upon us;[4] fulfil with us [39*b*] what Thou hast promised us, viz., *Look down from Thy holy habitation, from heaven* etc.'[5]

R. Ḥisda said: The *kohanim* are not permitted to bend their fingerjoints[6] until they turn their faces from the congregation.

R. Zera said in the name of R. Ḥisda: The Precentor is not permitted to exclaim '*Kohanim!*'[7] until the response of Amen [to the preceding benediction] had been completed by the congregation; and the *kohanim* are not permitted to begin the benediction until the announcement [of '*Kohanim!*'] had been completed by the Precentor; and the congregation is not permitted to respond Amen until the benediction had been completed by the *kohanim;* and the *kohanim* are not permitted to begin another section of the bene-

(1) I.e., made his way to his seat by passing through the students who sat on the floor. He either arrived first or sat on the outside. (2) This formula has been adopted in the ritual; *P.B.* p. 238*a*. [Cf. Rashi, Num. VI, 23 (quoting from Midrash): Ye shall not bless them hurriedly and hastily but devoutly and with a perfect heart.] (3) [אדבריה. Rashi (Beẓah. 29*a*), 'took him out for a walk'; R. Ḥananeel (*a.l.*): 'put the words in his mouth'—i.e., prepared the exposition for him. R. 'Uḳba was Exilarch and had his public discourses prepared by R. Ḥisda.] (4) [I.e., although we are not worthy to bless; v. Tiḳḳin *Tefillah.*, *Oẓar ha-Tefilloth*, (Wilna, 1923) p. 941.] (5) Deut. XXVI, 15. (6) The fingers are outstretched during the benediction. (7) On hearing which word they begin to bless the congregation.

diction until the response of Amen had been completed by the congregation [to the preceding].

R. Zera also said in the name of R. Ḥisda: The *kohanim* are not permitted to turn their faces from the congregation until the Precentor begins the paragraph 'Grant peace';[1] nor are they permitted to move their feet and descend until the Precentor has finished 'Grant peace'.

R. Zera also said in the name of R. Ḥisda: The congregation is not permitted to respond Amen until a benediction had been completed by the Precentor; and the reader is not permitted to read in the Torah until the response of Amen [to the preliminary benediction] had been completed by the congregation; and the translator[2] is not permitted to begin the translation until the verse had been completed by the reader; and the reader is not permitted to begin another verse until the translation [of the preceding verse] had been completed by the translator.

R. Tanḥum said in the name of R. Joshua b. Levi: He who is to read the lection from the prophets must first read [a passage] in the Torah.[3] R. Tanḥum also said in the name of R. Joshua b. Levi: He who is to read the lection from the prophets is not permitted to begin his recital until the Torah-scroll is rolled up.[4] R. Tanḥum also said in the name of R. Joshua b. Levi: The Precentor is not permitted to strip the ark bare in the presence of the Congregation because of the dignity of the congregation.[5] R. Tanḥum also said in the name of R. Joshua b. Levi: The congregation is not permitted to depart until the Torah-scroll is removed[6] and deposited in its place. Samuel said: [They may not depart] until [the Pre-

(1) V. *P.B.*, p. 53. (2) In the ancient Synagogue the recital of each verse of the Scriptural section was followed by a translation into the vernacular. (3) This custom is still preserved in the Synagogue, except that the lection from Scripture is read by the Precentor and not the person called up to the reading of the Law. (4) The purpose is that they who are rolling it should not be prevented from listening to the recital. (5) The ark was adorned with hangings, and these must not be removed so long as the worshippers are present. (6) [From the ark. The Scroll was removed from the synagogue after service for safe custody. The words, 'and deposited in its place' are difficult to explain. Rashi does not appear to have had them, nor do they occur in MS.M.]

centor] has gone out.[1] There is no variance between them; the former refers to when there is another exit,[2] the latter to when there is not another exit. Raba said: Bar Ahina explained to me [that the Scriptural basis for this regulation is], *Ye shall walk* after *the Lord your God.*[3]

While the *kohanim* are blessing the people[4] what do the latter say?—R. Zera declared in the name of R. Ḥisda: *Bless the Lord, ye angels of His, ye mighty in strength . . . Bless the Lord, all ye His hosts, ye ministers of His that do His pleasure. Bless the Lord, all ye His works, in all places of His dominion. Bless the Lord, O my soul.*[5] What do they say [during the benediction] in the additional service of the Sabbath?[6]—R. Assi declared: *A Song of Ascents, Behold, bless ye the Lord, all ye servants of the Lord . . . Lift up your hands in holiness and bless ye the Lord.*[7] *Blessed be the Lord out of Zion, Who dwelleth at Jerusalem. Praise ye the Lord.*[8] But they should also say: *The Lord bless thee out of Zion*[9] which occurs in that context!—Judah the son of R. Simeon b. Pazzi answered, Since he commenced with the blessings of the Holy One, blessed be He, he should conclude with His blessings. What do they say in the afternoon-service of a fast-day?[10]—R. Aḥa b. Jacob declared: *Though our iniquities testify against us, work Thou for Thy name's sake . . . O Thou hope of Israel, the Saviour thereof in the time of trouble, why shouldest Thou be as a sojourner in the land . . . Why shouldest Thou be as a man astonied, as a mighty man that cannot save?* etc.[11] [40*a*] What do they say in the concluding service of the Day of Atonement?[12]—Mar Zuṭra declared—according to another version, there is a teaching to this effect—: *Behold, thus shall the man be blessed that feareth the Lord. The Lord shall bless thee out of*

(1) He used to carry the Scroll with him to his house for safe custody. (2) [In which case the congregation can depart through the other exit as soon as the Scroll is removed, even before it leaves the synagogue (Rashi).] (3) Deut. XIII, 5. (4) On week-days according to the old usage. (5) Ps. CIII, 20ff. Each of the Scriptural selections consists of three verses, one for each part of the priestly benediction. (6) According to modern usage the *kohanim* do not utter the benediction on the Sabbath, with the exception of the Day of Atonement which falls on a Sabbath. (7) Ibid. CXXXIV, 1f. (8) Ibid. CXXXV, 21. (9) Ibid. CXXXIV, 3. (10) This is not the modern practice. (11) Jer. XIV, 7ff. (12) This also is omitted in the modern ritual.

Zion, and thou shalt see the good of Jerusalem all the days of thy life. Yea, thou shalt see thy children's children. Peace be upon Israel.[1] Where did they say these verses?—R. Joseph answered: Between each benediction. R. Shesheth answered: At the mention of the Divine Name. R. Mari and R. Zebid differ on this matter; one said, A verse [by the congregation is to be recited] simultaneously with a verse [by the *kohanim*], while the other said, [The congregation recites] the whole for each verse [by the *kohanim*]. R. Ḥiyya b. Abba said: Whoever recites them outside the Temple simply errs.[2] R. Ḥanina b. Papa said: Know that even in the Temple it is unnecessary to recite them; for is there a servant whom one blesses without his listening! R. Aḥa b. Ḥanina said: Know that even outside the Temple it is necessary to recite them; for is there a servant whom one blesses without his face brightening![3]

R. Abbahu said: At first I used to recite them; but when I saw that R. Abba of Acco did not recite them I also did not. R. Abbahu also said: At first I used to think that I was humble; but when I saw R. Abba of Acco offer one explanation and his Amora[4] offer another without his taking exception, I considered that I was not humble. How did R. Abbahu display humility?—The wife of R. Abbahu's Amora said to R. Abbahu's wife, 'My husband has no need of [instruction from] your husband; and when he bends down[5] and straightens himself, he merely pays him respect'.[6] R. Abbahu's wife went and reported this to him, and he said to her, 'Why worry about it? Through me and him the All-Highest is praised'. Further, the Rabbis decided to appoint R. Abbahu as principal [of the Academy]; but when he saw that R. Abba of Acco had numerous creditors [pressing for payment], he said to the Rabbis, 'There is a greater [scholar than I for the office]'.

(1) Ps. CXXVIII, 4ff. (2) They should be said only in the Temple where alone the Tetragrammaton is used, since they are a blessing upon the Divine Name. (3) Therefore the recital of these verses, in acknowledgement, by the congregation is acceptable to God. (4) V. Glos. Who should have conveyed the Rabbi's explanation to the disciples. (5) To receive the teaching from the Rabbi. (6) Because he was highly regarded by the Government. V. *infra* and Ḥag. 14*a*, Sanh. 14*a*.

R. Abbahu and R. Ḥiyya b. Abba once came to a place; R. Abbahu expounded *Aggada*[1] and R. Ḥiyya b. Abba expounded legal lore. All the people left R. Ḥiyya b. Abba and went to hear R. Abbahu, so that the former was upset. [R. Abbahu] said to him: 'I will give you a parable. To what is the matter like? To two men, one of whom was selling precious stones and the other various kinds of small ware. To whom will the people hurry? Is it not to the seller of various kinds of small ware?' Everyday R. Ḥiyya b. Abba used to accompany R. Abbahu to his lodging-place because he was esteemed by the Government; but on that day R. Abbahu accompanied R. Ḥiyya b. Abba to his lodging-place, and still his mind was not set at rest.

While the Precentor recites the paragraph 'We give thanks'[2] what does the congregation say?—Rab declared: 'We give thanks unto Thee, O Lord our God, because we are able to give Thee thanks'. Samuel declared: 'God of all flesh, seeing that we give Thee thanks'. R. Simai declared: 'Our Creator and Creator of all things in the beginning, seeing that we give Thee thanks.' The men of Nehardea[3] declared in the name of R. Simai: 'Blessings and thanksgiving to Thy great Name because Thou hast kept us alive and preserved us, seeing that we give Thee thanks'. R. Aḥa b. Jacob used to conclude thus: 'So mayest Thou continue to keep us alive and be gracious to us; and gather us together and assemble our exiles to Thy holy courts to observe Thy statutes and to do Thy will with a perfect heart, seeing that we give Thee thanks'. R. Papa said: Consequently let us recite them all.[4]

R. Isaac said: Let respect for the congregation be always upon thee; for behold, the *kohanim* had their faces towards the people and their backs towards the *Shechinah*.[5] R. Naḥman said: It is derived from this text: *Then David the king stood up upon his feet and said, Hear me, my brethren and my people*.[6] If [he called them] '*my brethren*' why '*my people*', and *vice versa?*—R. Eleazar said: David

(1) The non-legal part of Rabbinic lore which is the more popular, v. Glos. (2) V. *P.B.* p. 51. (3) A town in S. Babylonia where Rab founded his School. (4) The accepted version combines them all. V. *P.B.* p. 51. (5) I.e., the Ark in which the Torah-Scrolls are kept. (6) I Chron. XXVIII, 2.

told the Israelites, If you listen to me, you are my brethren; if not, you are my people and I will rule you with a rod. The Rabbis said: It is derived from the regulation that the *kohanim* are not permitted to ascend the platform wearing their shoes. This is one of the ten ordinances which R. Joḥanan b. Zakkai instituted. What was the reason? Was it not out of respect for the congregation?—R. Ashi said: No; [the reason] there was lest the shoe-lace become untied and he proceeds to retie it, and people will say, 'He is the son of a divorcee or a *Ḥaluẓah*'.[1]

BUT IN THE TEMPLE AS ONE BLESSING etc. [40*b*] For what reason is this?—Because the response of Amen was not made in the Temple.

Our Rabbis taught: Whence is it that the response of Amen was not made in the Temple? As it is said, *Stand up and bless the Lord your God from everlasting to everlasting.*[2] And whence is it that every benediction must be followed by an expression of praise? As it is said, *And blessed be Thy glorious name which is exalted above all blessing and praise*[3]—i.e., upon every benediction ascribe praise to Him.

MISHNAH. WHAT WAS THE PROCEDURE WITH THE BENEDICTIONS OF THE HIGH PRIEST?[4] THE SYNAGOGUE-ATTENDANT TAKES A TORAH-SCROLL AND HANDS IT TO THE SYNAGOGUE-PRESIDENT. THE SYNAGOGUE-PRESIDENT

(1) Disqualified for priestly service. A derisive taunt at him for his undignified behaviour by stooping on the platform to retie his shoelace. (2) Neh. IX, 5. This was the response to be used in the Temple; not Amen. [No satisfactory reason has so far been given for this regulation. Graetz *MGWJ* 1872, pp. 492ff., suggests that this does not mean that the response Amen was not allowed in the Temple, but that the solemnity of its service, heightened by the pronunciation of the Tetragrammaton as written, demanded a more extensive and impressive formula than the single Amen. V. also Blau, L. *REJ*, XXXIX, p. 188.] (3) Ibid. The word '*above*' is understood as 'upon'. (4) What is described here followed the completion of the rites connected with the sacrifices of the Day of Atonement. The Synagogue referred to was that situated on the Temple Mount.

HANDS IT TO THE DEPUTY[1] AND HE HANDS IT TO THE HIGH PRIEST. THE HIGH PRIEST STANDS, RECEIVES [THE SCROLL] AND READS [THEREIN] AFTER THE DEATH[2] AND HOWBEIT ON THE TENTH DAY.[3] THEN HE ROLLS THE TORAH-SCROLL TOGETHER, PLACES IT IN HIS BOSOM AND EXCLAIMS, 'MORE THAN I HAVE READ BEFORE YOU IS WRITTEN HERE!' THE PASSAGE 'ON THE TENTH DAY', WHICH IS IN THE BOOK OF NUMBERS, HE READS BY HEART,[4] AND HE RECITES EIGHT BENEDICTIONS IN CONNECTION THEREWITH, VIZ., OVER THE TORAH, FOR THE TEMPLE-SERVICE, FOR THE THANKSGIVING, FOR THE PARDON OF SIN, OVER THE TEMPLE, OVER ISRAEL, OVER THE PRIESTS, OVER JERUSALEM, AND THE REST OF THE PRAYER.[5]

GEMARA. Is it to be deduced from this[6] that honour may be paid to a disciple in the presence of his master?—Abaye said: [No]; all this was done for the purpose of honouring the High Priest.

THE HIGH PRIEST STANDS, RECEIVES [THE SCROLL] AND READS etc. [Since it is stated that] he stands, it follows that he had been sitting; but a Master has said, In the Temple-court the kings of the house of David alone were allowed to sit, as it is said, *Then David the king went in, and sat before the Lord, and he said, Who am I?* etc!'[7]—It is as R. Ḥisda declared, [This occurred] in the Court of Women;[8] and here also [with the reading of the High Priest] it was in the Court of Women. An objection was raised: Where did the lection take place? In the Temple-court; R. Eliezer b. Jacob declares it was on the Temple Mount, as it is said, [41a]

(1) *Segan*. Of the High Priest who took his place if he became defiled or incapacitated during the Day of Atonement (Rashi); v. however Sanh. (Sonc. ed.) p. 97, n. 1. (2) I.e., Lev. XVI. (3) Ibid. XXIII, 26-32. (4) Num. XXIX, 7-11, to obviate the necessity of unrolling the Scroll from the former passage in Leviticus. (5) The separate editions of the Mishnah and the J. Talmud omit 'over Jerusalem', and to complete the number eight read 'and over the rest of the prayer'. (6) That the Torah was handed to his inferiors before being delivered to the High Priest. (7) II Sam. VII, 18. (8) A part of the Temple-precincts which was non-holy.

And he read therein before the broad place that was before the water gate.[1] R. Ḥisda said: In the Court of Women.

AND READS [THEREIN] AFTER THE DEATH AND HOWBEIT ON THE TENTH DAY. I quote in contradiction: We may skip a passage in the Prophets but not in the Torah![2]—Abaye said: There is no contradiction; the latter teaching refers to a case where the passage skipped is sufficiently long to interrupt the translator, whereas [in the Mishnah] it is not sufficiently long to interrupt the translator.[3] On this point, however, it has been taught: We may skip a passage in the Prophets but not in the Torah. How much may be skipped [in the reading of the Prophets]? A passage which is not sufficiently long to interrupt the translator. Consequently so far as the Torah is concerned nothing at all [may be skipped]!—But Abaye said: There is no contradiction; the teaching [that we may skip a passage in the reading of the Torah] applies to where there is one theme,[4] the other teaching to where there are two themes. Thus it has been taught: We may skip [a passage] in the Torah where there is one theme and in the Prophets where there are two themes, but in either case only when it is not sufficiently long to interrupt the translator. We may not, however, skip from one Prophetical Book to another; but with a book of the Minor Prophets[5] we may skip [from one to another] except that this may not be done from the end of the Book to its beginning.[6]

THEN HE ROLLS THE TORAH-SCROLL TOGETHER, PLACES IT IN HIS BOSOM etc. Why all this?[7]—So as not to discredit the Torah-Scroll.[8]

THE PASSAGE 'ON THE TENTH DAY', WHICH IS IN THE BOOK OF NUMBERS, HE READS BY HEART. Let him roll up the

(1) Neh. VIII, 3. (2) When read in the Synagogue. (3) While he is translating the last passage from Lev. XVI, it would be possible to turn up chap. XXIII, v. *supra* p. 199, nn. 2-3. (4) As here, since both passages deal with the Day of Atonement. (5) These are regarded as one Book. (6) I.e., it is not allowed to turn back in the reading. (7) Viz., his exclamation, 'More than I have read' etc. (8) The people should not imagine it was a defective Scroll and for that reason he read a portion by heart.

Scroll and recite [the passage]![1]—R. Huna b. Judah said in the name of R. Shesheth: Because we do not roll up a Torah-scroll in the presence of a congregation.[2] Then let another Torah-scroll be brought and read [it therein]!—R. Huna b. Judah said: [No], because it would discredit the first.[3] R. Simeon b. Lakish said: Because we may not pronounce an unnecessary benediction.[4] Do we, then, pay attention to [the reason that it would] discredit [the first Scroll]? Behold, R. Isaac the smith said: When the new moon of Tebeth[5] falls on the Sabbath, three Scrolls are brought: the first for the lection of the [Sabbath] day, the second for [the portion of] the new moon, and the third for [the portion of] *Ḥanukkah!*[6]—When three men [read] in three Scrolls, there is no fear about [a Scroll] being discredited, but when one man [reads] in two Scrolls there is this fear.

AND HE RECITES EIGHT BENEDICTIONS IN CONNECTION THEREWITH etc. Our Rabbis taught: [The High Priest] pronounces a benediction over the Torah just as we do in Synagogue;[7] for the Temple-service, for the thanksgiving,[8] and for the pardon of sin as usual;[9] over the Temple separately,[10] over the priests separately, over the Israelites separately, and over Jerusalem separately.

AND THE REST OF THE PRAYER. Our Rabbis taught: The rest of the prayer consists of petition, song and supplication that Thy people Israel is in need of salvation; and he concludes with, '[Blessed art Thou, O Lord,] Who hearkenest unto prayer.' From this point onward,[11] each individual brings a Torah-scroll from his house and reads therein. For what purpose is this done? To display its beauty in public.[12]

(1) Since he does not read it from the Scroll, why is it left open? (2) In modern practice this is done. (3) People would conclude that it had some defect, and for that reason another was brought. (4) Over the use of the second Scroll. (5) The tenth month. (6) The Feast of Dedication which occurs at the end of Kislev and the beginning of Ṭebeth. Why are not all three portions read from one Scroll? (7) V. *P.B.* p. 147. (8) *Op. cit.*, 50f. (9) [As we have it in the Day of Atonement liturgy (Rashi, Yoma 70).] (10) This and the following benedictions are not in the existing liturgy. (11) I.e., after the High Priest had finished the benedictions. (12) It was considered praiseworthy to possess a beautiful copy of the Torah-scroll.

MISHNAH. WHAT WAS THE PROCEDURE IN CONNECTION WITH THE PORTION READ BY THE KING? AT THE CONCLUSION OF THE FIRST DAY OF THE FESTIVAL [OF TABERNACLES] IN THE EIGHTH,[1] I.E., THE END OF THE SEVENTH,[2] THEY ERECT A WOODEN DAIS IN THE TEMPLE COURT, UPON WHICH HE SITS; AS IT IS SAID, AT THE END OF EVERY SEVEN YEARS, IN THE SET TIME etc.[3] THE SYNAGOGUE-ATTENDANT[4] TAKES A TORAH-SCROLL AND HANDS IT TO THE SYNAGOGUE-PRESIDENT,[5] AND THE SYNAGOGUE-PRESIDENT HANDS IT TO THE [HIGH PRIEST'S] DEPUTY. HE HANDS IT TO THE HIGH PRIEST WHO HANDS IT TO THE KING. THE KING STANDS AND RECEIVES IT, BUT READS SITTING. KING AGRIPPA[6] STOOD AND RECEIVED IT AND READ STANDING, FOR WHICH ACT THE SAGES PRAISED HIM. WHEN HE REACHED, THOU MAYEST NOT PUT A FOREIGNER OVER THEE,[7] HIS EYES RAN WITH TEARS.[8] THEY SAID TO HIM, 'FEAR NOT, AGRIPPA, THOU ART OUR BROTHER, THOU ART OUR BROTHER!' [THE KING] READS FROM THE BEGINNING OF DEUTERONOMY UP TO THE SHEMA',[9] THE SHEMA', AND IT SHALL COME TO PASS IF YE HEARKEN,[10] THOU SHALT SURELY TITHE,[11] WHEN THOU HAST MADE AN END OF TITHING,[12] THE PORTION OF THE KING,[13] AND THE BLESSINGS AND CURSES, UNTIL HE FINISHES ALL THE SECTION. THE KING PRONOUNCES THE SAME BENEDICTIONS AS THE HIGH PRIEST, EXCEPT THAT HE SUBSTITUTES ONE FOR THE FESTIVALS INSTEAD OF ONE FOR THE PARDON OF SIN.

(1) This is explained in the Gemara. (2) The years were arranged in Cycles of seven, the seventh being 'the year of release' (Deut. XV, 1ff). (3) Deut. XXXI, 10. (4) [*Ḥazzan*. There is no certainty either in regard to the original function or rank of the *Ḥazzan*. Here he appears as second to the synagogue president; v. n. 5.] (5) [ראש הכנסת. Identified with the ἀρχισυνάγωγος, the officer who administered the external affairs of the synagogue; v. Krauss, *Synagogale Altertümer* pp. 116ff. and *JE* II, 86.] (6) Agrippa I. His reading occurred in the year 41 C.E. [Others ascribe this incident to Agrippa II. V. Derenbourg, *op. cit.* p. 217, and Büchler, *Priester und der Cultus* pp. 12ff.] (7) Ibid. XVII, 15. (8) Because on his father's side he was not of Jewish descent. (9) I.e., down to ibid. VI, 4. (10) Ibid. XI, 13-25. (11) Ibid. XIV, 22ff. (12) Ibid. XXVI, 12ff. (13) Ibid. XVII, 14ff.

GEMARA. Does it enter your mind [that the Mishnah means] the eighth [day of the Festival]!—Read 'the eighth [year].[1] But why all this?[2]—It is all necessary; for if the All-Merciful had only written *'at the end'*, I might have thought that the reckoning was to be from then[3] although they had not observed a year of release;[4] therefore the All-Merciful wrote in *'the year of release'*. If the All-Merciful had only written *'the year of release'*, I might have thought that this means the end of the year of release;[5] therefore the All-Merciful wrote *'in the set time'*.[6] If He had only written *'in the set time'*, I might have thought that this means at the New Year festival; therefore the All-Merciful wrote *'in the feast of tabernacles'*. And if the All-Merciful had only written *'in the feast of tabernacles'*, I might have thought that this means on the last day of the festival; therefore the All-Merciful wrote *'when all Israel is come'*[7] [41*b*], i.e., the beginning of the Festival.

THE SYNAGOGUE-ATTENDANT TAKES A TORAH-SCROLL AND HANDS IT TO THE SYNAGOGUE-PRESIDENT. Is it to be deduced from this that honour may be paid to a disciple in the presence of his master?[8]—Abaye said: [No]; all this was done for the purpose of honouring the king.

THE KING STANDS AND RECEIVES IT, BUT READS SITTING. KING AGRIPPA STOOD AND RECEIVED IT AND READ STANDING. [Since it is stated that] he stands, it follows that he had been sitting. But a Master has said, In the Temple-court the kings of the House of David alone were allowed to sit; as it is said, *Then David the king went in, and sat before the Lord, and he said* etc.![9]—It is as R. Ḥisda declared: [This occurred] in the Court of Women, and here also [with the reading by the king] it was in the Court of Women.

(1) The word should have the feminine form, not masculine as in the Mishnah, to make it clear that the year and not the day is intended. (2) Viz., the elaborate description of the time when the reading takes place as it is given in Deut. XXXI, 10. (3) From the fortieth year after the Exodus. (4) The observance only began seven years after the land had been divided among the Israelites. (5) I.e., before the eighth year. (6) The word for *'set time'* usually denotes a festival; hence it refers to a festival in the eighth year. (7) Deut. XXXI, 11, referring to the pilgrimage to the Sanctuary which was on the first day. (8) V. *infra* 40*b*. (9) II Sam. VII, 18.

FOR WHICH ACT THE SAGES PRAISED HIM. Since they praised him, it follows that he acted rightly; but R. Ashi has said: Even according to him who maintains that when a *Nasi*[1] forgoes the honour due to him one may avail himself of the permission, when a king forgoes the honour due to him one may not avail himself of the permission; as it is said, *Thou shalt set a king over thee*[2]—that his authority[3] may be over thee!—It is different [with the fulfilment of] a precept.[4]

WHEN HE REACHED 'THOU MAYEST NOT PUT [etc.]'. A Tanna taught in the name of R. Nathan: At that moment[5] the enemies of Israel[6] made themselves liable to extermination, because they flattered Agrippa. R. Simeon b. Ḥalafta said: From the day the fist of flattery prevailed, justice became perverted, conduct deteriorated, and nobody could say to his neighbour, 'My conduct is better than yours'. R. Judah the Palestinian—another version, R. Simeon b. Pazzi—expounded: It is permitted to flatter the wicked in this world, as it is said, *The vile person shall be no more called liberal, nor the churl said to be bountiful*[7]—consequently it is allowed in this world. R. Simeon b. Lakish said: [It may be derived] from this text, *As one seeth the face of God, and thou wast pleased with me.*[8] On this point he is at variance with R. Levi; for R. Levi said: A parable of Jacob and Esau: To what is the matter like? To a man who invited his neighbour to a meal, and the latter perceived that he wished to kill him. So he said to him, 'The taste of this dish of which I am partaking is like the dish I tasted in the king's palace'. The other said [to himself], 'He is acquainted with the king!' So he became afraid and did not kill him.[9] R. Eleazar said: Every man in whom is flattery brings anger upon the world: as it is said, *But they that are flatterers at heart lay up anger.*[10] Not only that, but their

(1) The Chief of the Great Sanhedrin. (2) Deut. XVII, 15. (3) Lit., 'fear'. (4) A king may forgo his honour when fulfilling it. (5) When the Rabbis said, 'Thou art our brother'. (6) An euphemism for Israel. (7) Isa. XXXII, 5. This verse alludes to the Hereafter. (8) Gen. XXXIII, 10. The words were spoken in flattery by Jacob to the wicked Esau. (9) Similarly Jacob's words were not flattery, but spoken with the intention of frightening Esau. (10) Job XXXVI, 13.

prayer remains unheard; as it continues, *They cry not for help when He chasteneth them.*[1] (Mnemonic:[2] *Anger, embryo, Gehinnom, in his hand, menstruant, exile*).

R. Eleazar also said: As for any man in whom is flattery, even the embryos in their mothers' wombs curse him; as it is said, *He that saith unto the wicked, Thou art righteous, peoples shall curse him, nations shall abhor him*[3]—the word *ḳob* ['abhor'] means nothing but 'curse', as it is said, *Whom God hath not cursed;*[4] and *le'om* [nation] means nothing but 'embryo', as it is said, *And the one* le'om [*nation*] *shall be stronger than the other nation.*[5] R. Eleazar also said: Every man in whom is flattery will fall into Gehinnom; as it is said, *Woe unto them that call evil good, and good evil* etc.[6] What is written after that? *Therefore as the tongue of fire devoureth the stubble, and as the dry grass sinketh down in the flame* etc.[7] R. Eleazar also said: Whoever flattereth his neighbour[8] will finally fall into his hand; if he does not fall into his hand, he will fall into the hand of his sons; and if he does not fall into his sons' hand, he will fall into the hand of his grandsons; as it is stated, *And Jeremiah said to Hananiah, Amen; the Lord do so; the Lord perform thy words,*[9] and it is written, [42a] *And when he was in the gate of Benjamin, a captain of the ward was there, whose name was Irijah, the son of Shelemiah, the son of Hananiah; and he laid hold on Jeremiah the prophet, saying, Thou fallest away to the Chaldeans. Then said Jeremiah, It is false; I fall not away to the Chaldeans* etc.,[10] and it continues, *So he laid hold on Jeremiah and brought him to the princes.*[11] R. Eleazar also said: Any community in which is flattery is as repulsive as a menstruant woman; as it is said, '*For the community of flatterers is* galmud'[12]—and in over-sea towns they call a menstruant woman *galmudah*. What means *galmudah?*—She is separated

(1) Because their cry receives no response. (2) V. p. 171, n. 6. The first word refers to what has just preceded. (3) Prov. XXIV, 24. (4) Num. XXIII, 8. (5) Gen. XXV, 23. The context deals with the unborn sons of Rebekkah. (6) Isa. V, 20. (7) Ibid. 24. (8) [*Var. lec.* 'the wicked'] (9) Jer. XXVIII, 6. In the Massoretic text the reading is '*The prophet Jeremiah said, Amen; the Lord* etc.' (10) Ibid. XXXVII, 13f. Note the captain was the grandson of Hananiah. (11) [The M.T. reads '*So I Irijah laid hold* etc.'] (12) Job XV, 34. The usual translation of *galmud* is 'barren'.

[*gemulah da*] from her husband. R. Eleazar also said: Any community in which is flattery will finally go into exile. It is written here, '*For the community of flatterers is* galmud', and elsewhere it is written, *Then shalt thou say in thine heart, Who hath gotten me these, seeing I have been bereaved of my children, and am solitary* [*galmudah*], *an exile and wandering to and fro* etc.[1]

R. Jeremiah b. Abba said: Four classes will not receive the presence of the *Shechinah:* the class of scoffers, the class of flatterers, the class of liars, and the class of slanderers. The class of scoffers, as it is written, *He stretched out His hand against scorners.*[2] The class of flatterers, as it is written, *For a flatterer shall not come before Him.*[3] The class of liars, as it is written, *He that speaketh falsehood shall not be established before Mine eyes.*[4] The class of slanderers, as it is written, *For Thou art not a God that hath pleasure in wickedness; evil shall not sojourn with Thee*[5]—i.e., Thou art righteous, O Lord, evil may not sojourn in Thy habitation.

(1) Isa. XLIX, 21. (2) Hos. VII, 5 *sic.*, i.e., God kept them at a distance. (3) Job XIII, 16. (4) Ps. CI, 7. (5) Ibid. V, 5. The Psalm deals with the evil of slander.

SOṬAH

CHAPTER VIII

MISHNAH. AT THE TIME WHEN THE ANOINTED FOR BATTLE[1] ADDRESSES THE PEOPLE HE SPEAKS IN THE HOLY TONGUE, AS IT IS SAID, AND IT SHALL BE, WHEN YE DRAW NIGH UNTO THE BATTLE, THAT THE PRIEST SHALL APPROACH[2]—I.E., THE ANOINTED FOR BATTLE; AND SPEAK UNTO THE PEOPLE—I.E., IN THE HOLY TONGUE; AND SHALL SAY UNTO THEM, HEAR, O ISRAEL, [YE DRAW NIGH THIS DAY UNTO BATTLE AGAINST YOUR ENEMIES][3]—'AGAINST YOUR ENEMIES' BUT NOT AGAINST YOUR BRETHREN, NOT JUDAH AGAINST SIMEON NOR SIMEON AGAINST BENJAMIN, SO THAT IF YOU[4] FALL INTO THEIR HAND THEY SHALL HAVE MERCY UPON YOU, AS IT IS SAID, AND THE MEN WHICH HAVE BEEN EXPRESSED BY NAME ROSE UP, AND TOOK THE CAPTIVES, AND WITH THE SPOIL CLOTHED ALL THAT WERE NAKED AMONG THEM, AND ARRAYED THEM, AND SHOD THEM, AND GAVE THEM TO EAT AND TO DRINK, AND ANOINTED THEM, AND CARRIED ALL THE FEEBLE OF THEM UPON ASSES, AND BROUGHT THEM TO JERICHO, THE CITY OF PALM TREES, UNTO THEIR BRETHREN; THEN THEY RETURNED TO SAMARIA ETC.[5] AGAINST YOUR ENEMIES DO YOU MARCH, SO THAT IF YOU FALL INTO THEIR HAND THEY WILL HAVE NO MERCY UPON YOU. LET NOT YOUR HEART FAINT; FEAR NOT NOR TREMBLE ETC.[6]—'LET NOT YOUR HEART FAINT' AT THE NEIGHING OF THE HORSES AND THE BRANDISHING OF SWORDS; 'FEAR NOT' BECAUSE OF THE CRASH OF SHIELDS AND THE TRAMP OF THE SOLDIERS' FOOTWEAR;

(1) The priest designated to accompany the army to battle. (2) Deut. XX, 2. (3) Ibid., 3. (4) I.e., any Israelite falls into the hand of another Israelite in battle. (5) II Chron. XXVIII, 15. (6) Deut. XX, 3.

—NOR TREMBLE' AT THE SOUND OF TRUMPETS; 'NEITHER BE YE AFFRIGHTED' AT THE SOUND OF BATTLE-CRIES. FOR THE LORD YOUR GOD IS HE THAT GOETH WITH YOU[1]—THEY COME [RELYING] UPON THE MIGHT OF FLESH AND BLOOD, BUT YOU COME [RELYING] UPON THE MIGHT OF THE ALL-PRESENT. THE PHILISTINES CAME [RELYING] UPON THE MIGHT OF GOLIATH; BUT WHAT WAS HIS FATE? IN THE END HE FELL BY THE SWORD AND THEY FELL WITH HIM. THE AMMONITES CAME [RELYING] UPON THE MIGHT OF SHOBACH;[2] BUT WHAT WAS HIS FATE? IN THE END HE FELL BY THE SWORD AND THEY FELL WITH HIM. BUT WITH YOU IT IS OTHERWISE; 'FOR THE LORD YOUR GOD IS HE THAT GOETH WITH YOU TO FIGHT WITH YOU ETC.' [THIS ALLUDES TO] THE CAMP OF THE ARK.[3]

GEMARA. How does [the author of the Mishnah] prove his point?[4]—He proves it thus: It is stated in this connection '*and speak*', and elsewhere it states, *Moses spake, and God answered him by a voice;*[5] as in the latter passage it was in the holy tongue, so also in the former it was in the holy tongue.

Our Rabbis taught: *The priest shall approach and speak unto the people.*[6] It is possible to think that any priest who so desires [may address them]; therefore there is a text to state, *And the officers shall speak*[7]—as the officers must have been appointed so must the priest have been appointed [for the purpose]. But I might say that it is the High Priest [who addresses them]!—It is analogous to the case of an officer; as an officer has a superior appointed over him,[8] so also the priest [who addresses the people] has a superior appointed over him.[9] But the High Priest likewise [has a superior over him], viz., the king!—He is referring to his service.[10] But I might say that it is the deputy High Priest [who addresses them]![11]—The deputy

(1) Deut. XX, 4. (2) Cf. II Sam. X, 14ff. (3) I.e., the Israelite army which was accompanied by the ark. (4) That the priest addresses the people in Hebrew. (5) Ex. XIX, 19. (6) Deut. XX, 2. (7) Ibid. 5. (8) Viz., the judge whose decisions the officer enforces. (9) Therefore the High Priest is excluded. (10) In the Temple. In this sphere the High Priest is supreme. (11) V. p. 199, n. 1.

High Priest is not considered appointed; as it has been taught: R. Ḥanina, the deputy of the priests,[1] said: For what is the priests' deputy appointed? If any disqualification should occur to the High Priest, he enters and functions in his stead.[2]

'*And shall say unto them, Hear, O Israel*'. Why must he just [open with the words] '*Hear, O Israel*'?—R. Joḥanan said in the name of R. Simeon b. Yoḥai: The Holy One, blessed be He, said to Israel, Even if you only fulfilled morning and evening the commandment to recite the *Shema'*,[3] you will not be delivered into [the enemy's] hand.

'*Let not your heart faint; fear not*' etc. Our Rabbis taught: He addresses them twice: once on the boundary[4] and once on the battle-field. What does he say on the boundary? [42*b*] 'Hear the words of the war-regulations and return home'.[5] What does he say to them on the battle-field? '*Let not your heart faint; fear not, nor tremble, neither be ye affrighted*'. [These four expressions] correspond to the four means adopted by the nations of the world [to terrorise the enemy]: they crash [their shields], sound [trumpets], shout [battle-cries] and trample [with their horses].

THE PHILISTINES CAME [RELYING] UPON THE MIGHT OF GOLIATH etc. Goliath [was so named], said R. Joḥanan, because he stood with affrontery [*gilluy panim*] before the Holy One, blessed be He; as it is said, *Choose you a man for you, and let him come down to me.*[6] The word '*man*' signifies none other than the Holy One, blessed be He, as it is said, *The Lord is a man of war.*[7] The Holy One, blessed be He, declared, Behold, I will bring about his downfall through the hand of a son of man; as it is said, *David was the son of that man of Ephrath.*[8]

R. Joḥanan said in the name of R. Meir: In three places did his mouth trap that wicked man:[9] first, '*Choose you a man for you, and let him come down to me*';[6] second, '*If he be able to fight with me, and*

(1) V. Aboth. (Sonc. ed.) III, 2. (2) But so long as the High Priest could officiate, the deputy ranked as an ordinary priest. (3) V. Glos. This also opens with '*Hear, O Israel*'. (4) Before marching into the enemy's territory. (5) Viz., those who are qualified for exemption. V. ibid. 5ff. (6) I Sam. XVII, 8. (7) Ex. XV, 3. (8) I Sam. XVII, 12. (9) Goliath's words brought calamity upon him.

kill me etc.,'[1] and third, '*Am I a dog, that thou comest to me with staves?*'[2] David likewise replied to him, *Thou comest to me with a sword, and with a spear, and with a javelin;*[3] and he continued, *But, I come to thee in the name of the Lord of hosts, the God of the armies of Israel, which thou hast defied.*[3]

And the Philistine drew near morning and evening.[4] R. Joḥanan said: To make them omit the recital of the *Shema'* morning and evening.

And presented himself forty days.[4] R. Joḥanan said: [The period] corresponds to the forty days in which the Torah was given.[5]

And there went out a champion [benayim] *out of the camp of the Philistines* etc.[6] What means '*benayim*'?—Rab said: That he was built up [*mebunneh*] without any blemish. Samuel said: He was the middle one [*benoni*] of his brothers.[7] In the School of R. Shila they explained, He was made like a building [*binyan*]. R. Joḥanan said: He was the son of a hundred fathers and one mother [*ben nane*].[8] '*Named Goliath of Gath*'—R. Joseph learnt: [He is so described] because all men pressed his mother like a wine-press [*gath*].

The text has *ma'aroth*[9] but we read the word as *ma'arkoth!* R. Joseph learnt: Because all had intercourse [*he'eru*] with his mother. The text has *Harafah* and also *Orpah!*[10]—Rab and Samuel [differ in their interpretation]. One said that her name was *Harafah* and why was she called *Orpah?* Because all had intercourse with her from the rear ['*orfin*]. The other said: Her name was *Orpah;* and why was she called *Harafah?* Because all ground her like a bruised corn [*harifoth*]. Thus it states, *And the woman took and spread the covering over the well's mouth and strewed* harifoth [*bruised corn*] *thereon.*[11] If you like, I can derive [the meaning of *harifoth*] from this verse: *Though thou*

(1) I Sam. XVII, 9. David did kill him. (2) Ibid. 43. (3) Ibid. 45. (4) Ibid. 16. (5) V. Ex. XXIV, 18. [Ginzberg (*Legends*, VI, p. 250) quotes in this connection Philo, who explains the forty days as corresponding to the number of days wherein Israel feasted when they received the law in the wilderness. 'For forty days' said Goliath 'I will reproach them and after that I will fight them'. V., however, Rashi.] (6) I Sam. XVII, 4. (7) The third of four brothers. V. *infra.* (8) *Nana*, Pers. for mother. (9) '*Out of the ranks*', ibid. 23. (10) Cf. II Sam. XXI, 18 and Ruth I, 4. The first is taken as a proper noun and identified with the second. (11) II Sam. XVII, 19.

shouldest bray a fool in a mortar with a pestle among harifoth [*bruised corn*].[1]

These four were born to Harafah in Gath; and they fell by the hand of David, and by the hand of his servants.[2] Who were they?—R. Ḥisda said: Saph, Madon, Goliath and Ishbi-benob.[3] '*And they fell by the hand of David, and by the hand of his servants*', as it is written, *And Orpah kissed her mother-in-law, but Ruth clave unto her.*[4] R. Isaac said: The Holy One, blessed be He, spake, May the sons of the one who kissed[5] come and fall by the hand of the sons of the one who clave.

Raba expounded: As a reward for the four tears which Orpah dropped upon her mother-in-law, she merited that four mighty warriors should issue from her; as it is said, *And they lifted up their voice and wept again.*[6]

The text further has *ḥeẓ* [the arrow] *of his spear* but we read *'eẓ* [the staff] *of his spear!*[7]—R. Eleazar said: [It indicates that] we have not reached half [*ḥaẓi*] the praise of that wicked man.[8] Hence [it is learnt] that it is forbidden to recount the praise of the wicked. Then [Scripture] should not have begun to recount it at all!—[The object] is to proclaim the praise of David [who conquered such a giant].

THE AMMONITES CAME [RELYING] UPON THE MIGHT OF SHOBACH etc. [The name] is written *Shobach* and also *Shofach!*[9]—Rab and Samuel [differ in their interpretation]. One said that his name was *Shofach;* and why was he called *Shobach?* Because he was made like a dove-cote [*shobak*].[10] The other said that his name was Shobach; and why was he called *Shofach?* Because whoever beheld him was [through terror] poured out [*nishpak*] before him like a ewer.

(1) Prov. XXVII, 22. (2) II Sam. XXI, 22. (3) V. ibid. 18, 20 (translated *a man of great stature*), 19 and 16. (4) Ruth I, 14. (5) Goliath and his brothers were sons of Orpah who is identified with Naomi's daughter-in-law. (6) Ibid. '*Again*' denotes that they wept twice, and a tear dropped from each eye on each occasion. (7) In I Sam. XVII, 7. (8) Scripture has not described in full the prowess of Goliath. (9) Cf. II Sam. X, 16 and I Chron. XIX, 16. (10) He was excessively tall.

Their quiver ['ashpah] *is an open sepulchre, they are all mighty men.*[1] Rab and Samuel [differ in their interpretation]; another version is, R. Ammi and R. Assi [differ in their interpretation]. One said, At the time when they shot an arrow they made heaps upon heaps [*ashpatoth*] of slain; and should you say that this was only because they were only skilled in fighting, there is a text to state, *They are all mighty men.*[2] The other said, At the time when they relieved themselves they made heaps and heaps of excrement; and should you say that this was due to disorder of the bowels, there is a text to state, *They are all mighty men.*[3] R. Mari said: Infer from this that whoever has excessive excrement suffers from disorder of the bowels. What is the practical purpose of this?—He should take steps [to cure himself].

Heaviness in the heart of a man maketh it stoop [yashḥennah].[4]—R. Ammi and R. Assi [differ in their interpretation]. One said, [The last word means], let him dismiss it [*yisseḥennah*] from his mind; the other said, [It means], let him talk of it [*yesiḥenah*] with others.

BUT WITH YOU IT IS OTHERWISE etc. Why all this?[5] Because the Name[6] and all His substituted names [43a] were deposited in the ark. Thus it states, *And Moses sent them, a thousand of every tribe, to the war, them and Phinehas*[7]—*'them'* refers to the Sanhedrin; *'Phinehas'* was the [priest] Anointed for Battle; *'with the vessels of the sanctuary'* i.e., the ark and the tablets [of the decalogue] which were in it; *'and the trumpets for the alarm'* i.e., the horns.[8]—A Tanna taught: Not for naught did Phinehas go to the battle [against Midian] but to exact judgment on behalf of his mother's father [Joseph]; as it is said, *And the Midianites sold him into Egypt* etc.[9] Is this to say that Phinehas was a descendant of Joseph? But behold it is written, *And Eleazar Aaron's son took him one of the daughters of Putiel to wife; [and she bare him Phinehas]*![10] Is it not to be supposed,

(1) Jer. V, 16. (2) So it was due to their extraordinary strength. (3) As giants they ate abnormal quantities of food. (4) Prov. XII, 25. (5) Viz., *'For the Lord your God* etc.' and not simply, Your God is with you. (6) The Tetragrammaton. (7) Num. XXXI, 6. (8) [*Shofaroth* (pl. of *Shofar*)—i.e., the instruments which were called in those days *Shofaroth* and not by the biblical term *ḥaẓoẓeroth;* v. Shab. 36*a* (Strashun).] (9) Gen. XXXVII, 36. (10) Ex. VI, 25.

then, that he was a descendant of Jethro who fattened [*piṭṭem*][1] calves for idolatry?—No; [he was a descendant] of Joseph[2] who mastered [*piṭpeṭ*] his passion. But did not the other tribes despise him[3] [saying], 'Look at this son of Puṭi, the son whose mother's father fattened calves for idolatry; he killed a prince in Israel!'[4] But, if his mother's father was descended from Joseph, then his mother's mother was descended from Jethro; and if his mother's mother was descended from Joseph, then his mother's father was descended from Jethro. This is also proved as a conclusion from what is written, '*One of the daughters of Putiel*', from which are to be inferred two [lines of ancestry].[5] Draw this conclusion.

MISHNAH. AND THE OFFICERS SHALL SPEAK UNTO THE PEOPLE, SAYING, WHAT MAN IS THERE THAT HATH BUILT A NEW HOUSE, AND HATH NOT DEDICATED IT? LET HIM GO AND RETURN TO HIS HOUSE ETC.[6] IT IS ALL ONE WHETHER HE BUILT A BARN FOR STRAW, A STABLE FOR CATTLE, A SHED FOR WOOD, OR A STOREHOUSE;[7] IT IS ALL ONE WHETHER HE BUILT, PURCHASED, INHERITED IT OR SOMEBODY HAD GIVEN IT TO HIM AS A PRESENT.[8] AND WHAT MAN IS THERE THAT HATH PLANTED A VINEYARD, AND HATH NOT USED THE FRUIT THEREOF? ETC.[9] IT IS ALL ONE WHETHER HE PLANTED A VINEYARD OR PLANTED FIVE FRUIT-TREES[10] AND EVEN OF FIVE SPECIES;[11] IT IS ALL ONE WHETHER HE PLANTED, BENT[12] OR GRAFTED IT, OR WHETHER HE PURCHASED,

(1) Putiel is explained as 'one who fattened (calves) for a god'. (2) Identified with Putiel. (3) Phinehas. (4) Viz., Zimri (Num. XXV, 7ff). Consequently Phinehas was considered by his contemporaries to have descended from Jethro. V. Sanh. 82*b*. (5) The name Putiel is spelt with a *yod* which is usually the sign of the plural. Hence both the explanations given are possible, viz., Putiel can be identified either with Joseph or Jethro. (6) Deut. XX, 5. (7) For wine, oil, produce etc. (8) So long as it was new to him, he was exempt from service. (9) Ibid. 6. (10) The minimum number to warrant exemption. (11) May be included in the requisite number of plantings. (12) The vine so that the end is embedded in the soil and brings forth a new shoot.

INHERITED OR SOMEBODY HAD GIVEN IT TO HIM AS A PRESENT. AND WHAT MAN IS THERE THAT HATH BETROTHED A WIFE? ETC.[1] IT IS ALL ONE WHETHER HE HAD BETROTHED A VIRGIN OR A WIDOW, OR EVEN A CHILDLESS WIDOW WAITING FOR HER BROTHER-IN-LAW, OR EVEN IF A MAN HEARD THAT HIS BROTHER HAD DIED IN BATTLE,[2] HE RETURNS HOME. ALL THESE HEAR THE PRIEST'S WORDS CONCERNING THE WAR-REGULATIONS AND RETURN HOME; BUT THEY SUPPLY WATER AND FOOD AND REPAIR THE ROADS [FOR THE ARMY].

THE FOLLOWING DO NOT RETURN HOME: HE WHO BUILT A LODGE,[3] A LOGGIA OR A VERANDAH; HE WHO PLANTED FOUR FRUIT-TREES OR FIVE TREES WHICH ARE NOT FRUIT-BEARING; HE WHO TOOK BACK HIS DIVORCED WIFE. IF A HIGH PRIEST MARRIED A WIDOW, OR AN ORDINARY PRIEST MARRIED A DIVORCEE OR A ḤALUẒAH,[4] OR A LAY ISRAELITE MARRIED AN ILLEGITIMATE OR A NETHINAH,[5] OR THE DAUGHTER OF AN ISRAELITE MARRIED AN ILLEGITIMATE OR A NATHIN, HE DOES NOT RETURN HOME.[6] R. JUDAH SAYS: ALSO HE WHO REBUILT A HOUSE UPON ITS FOUNDATIONS DOES NOT RETURN HOME. R. ELIEZER SAYS: ALSO HE WHO BUILT A BRICK-HOUSE IN SHARON[7] DOES NOT RETURN HOME.

THE FOLLOWING DO NOT MOVE FROM THEIR PLACE:[8] HE WHO BUILT A NEW HOUSE AND DEDICATED IT, PLANTED A VINEYARD AND USED ITS FRUIT, MARRIED HIS BETROTHED, OR TOOK HOME HIS BROTHER'S CHILDLESS WIDOW; AS IT IS SAID, HE SHALL BE FREE AT HOME ONE YEAR[9]—'AT HOME,' THIS REFERS TO HIS HOUSE; 'SHALL BE' REFERS TO HIS VINEYARD; 'AND SHALL CHEER HIS WIFE' REFERS TO HIS WIFE; 'WHICH HE HATH TAKEN' IS TO INCLUDE HIS BROTHER'S CHILDLESS WIDOW. THESE DO NOT SUPPLY WATER AND FOOD AND REPAIR THE ROADS [FOR THE ARMY].

(1) Deut. XX, 7. (2) Leaving no offspring, and it is his duty to marry the widow. (3) Lit., 'house of the gate'. (4) V. Glos. (5) V. p. 119, n. 5. (6) Because these are illegal marriages. (7) A place in Palestine which is very sandy; so a house built there does not last long. (8) To join the army and then claim exemption. (9) Deut. XXIV, 5.

GEMARA. Our Rabbis taught: '*And the officers shall speak*'—it is possible to think that this refers to their own words;[1] but when it states, *And the officers shall speak further*,[2] behold this is to be understood as their own words; so how am I to explain '*And the officers shall speak*'? Scripture alludes to the words of the priest Anointed for Battle. So what was the procedure? A priest speaks [the words] and an officer proclaims them [to the army]. One [authority] taught: A priest speaks [the words] and an officer proclaims them; another taught: A priest speaks [the words] and a priest proclaims them; while yet another taught: An officer speaks [the words] and an officer proclaims them!—Abaye said: What, then, was the procedure? From '*when ye draw nigh*' down to '*and the officers shall speak*'[3] a priest speaks and a priest proclaims. From '*and the officers shall speak*' down to '*and the officers shall speak further*'[4] a priest speaks and an officer proclaims. From '*and the officers shall speak*' onwards an officer speaks and an officer proclaims.

WHAT MAN IS THERE THAT HATH BUILT A NEW HOUSE? etc. Our Rabbis taught: '*That hath built*'—I have here only the case where he built; whence is it [that the law applies also to a case where] he purchased, inherited or somebody gave it to him as a present? There is a text to state, *What man is there that hath built a house*.[5] I have here only the case of a house; whence is it that it includes a barn for straw, a stable for cattle, a shed for wood and a storehouse? There is a text to state '*that hath built*'—i.e., whatever [structure be erected]. It is possible to imagine that I am also to include one who built a lodge, loggia or verandah; there is a text to state '*a house*'—as '*house*' implies a place suitable for habitation so every [building for which exemption may be claimed must be] suitable for habitation. R. Eliezer b. Jacob says: [The word] '*house*' [is to be interpreted] according to its usual definition; [and the fact that Scripture does not read] 'and hath

(1) I.e., spoken by the officers and not by the priest. (2) Deut. XX, 8. The addition of '*further*' is the basis of the deduction. (3) I.e., the exhortation in Deut. XX, 3ff. (4) Ibid. 5-7. (5) This is understood as: whatever man built a new house, the present owner of it is exempt.

not dedicated' but *and hath not dedicated it*[1] is to exclude a robber.[2] Is this to say that [this teaching] is not in agreement with that of R. Jose the Galilean?[3] For if it agreed with R. Jose the Galilean, behold he has said, *Fainthearted*[4] i.e., he who is afraid [43*b*] because of the transgressions he had committed![5]—You may even say that it agrees with R. Jose the Galilean, as, e.g., when the man had repented and restored the monetary value. But in that event he becomes the purchaser, and as such returns home!—Since it originally came into his possession as the result of robbery, he does not [return home].

AND WHAT MAN IS THERE THAT HATH PLANTED A VINEYARD? etc. Our Rabbis taught: '*That hath planted*'—I have here only the case where he planted; whence is it [that the law applies also to a case where] he purchased, inherited or somebody gave it to him as a present? There is a text to state, *And what man is there that hath planted a vineyard.* I have here only the case of a vineyard; whence is it that it includes five fruit-trees and even of other kinds [of plantings]? There is a text to state '*that hath planted*'. It is possible to think that I am also to include one who planted four fruit-trees or five trees which are not fruit-bearing; therefore there is a text to state '*a vineyard*'. R. Eliezer says: [The word] '*vineyard*' [is to be interpreted] according to its usual definition; [and the fact that Scripture does not read] 'one hath not used the fruit' but '*and hath not used the fruit thereof*' is to exclude one who bends or grafts [the vine]. But we have the teaching: IT IS ALL ONE WHETHER HE PLANTED, BENT OR GRAFTED IT!—R. Zera said in the name of R. Ḥisda: There is no contradiction, the latter referring to a permitted grafting and the former to a prohibited grafting.[6] What is an instance of this permitted grafting? If I say a young shoot on a young shoot, it follows that he ought to return home on account of [planting] the first young shoot! It must therefore be [grafting] a young shoot on an old stem. But R. Abbahu has said: If he grafted a young shoot on an old stem, the young

(1) The suffix is superfluous. (2) A man who steals a new house is not exempt. (3) Who exempts a sinner; v. *supra* p. 222. (4) Deut. XX, 8. (5) Consequently a robber may return home. (6) Two different species.

shoot is annulled by the old stem and the law of *'orlah*[1] does not apply to it!—R. Jeremiah said: It certainly refers to a young shoot on a young shoot, and [the case of a permitted grafting is where], e.g., he planted the first [stem] for a hedge or for timber; as we have learnt: He who plants for a hedge or for timber is exempt from the law of *'orlah*.[2]

What is the distinction that a young shoot is annulled [when grafted] on an old stem[3] but not [when grafted] on a young shoot?[4] —In the former case if he reconsiders his intention with regard to it, it is incapable of retraction;[5] but in the latter case if he reconsiders his intention with regard to it, it is capable of retraction[6] since it is then analogous to [plants which] grow of themselves;[7] for we have learnt: When they grow of themselves they are liable to *'orlah*. But let him explain [the Mishnah[8] as dealing with] the case of a vineyard belonging to two partners, where each returns home on account of his own [grafting]![9]—R. Papa declared: This is to say that in the case of a vineyard belonging to two partners, the war-regulations do not apply to it.[10] Why, then, is it different with five brothers, one of whom dies in battle,[11] that they all return home?—In the latter illustration we apply the words *'his wife'* to

(1) Lit., 'circumcision', the Law of Lev. XIX, 23 forbidding the enjoyment of the fruit of a tree during the first three years of growth. Since this regulation does not apply to a young shoot grafted on an old stem, it is not regarded as a new planting. (2) And similarly he would not have to return on account of it. (3) And its fruit is not subject to *'orlah*. (4) [Since it has been stated that one returns on account of a young shoot grafted on to another which has been planted for timber.] (5) An old stem can never become young again, consequently the young shoot grafted to it becomes annulled. (6) The planter can change his mind within the first three years, and determine the purpose of the young shoot, originally grafted for timber, to be for fruit, so that it becomes itself subject to *'orlah*. (7) And at the time of their plantation there was no definite purpose in the mind of the planter whether it was for fruit or timber. (8) Which rules that one returns on account of grafting. (9) [Instead of the far-fetched circumstance where the first young shoot was planted for timber.] (10) Lit., 'they do not return on account of it from the army'. The partners do not have exemption for a new planting or grafting which belongs to them jointly, so that the Mishnah cannot deal with such a case. (11) Leaving no offspring so that his wife is due to marry one of his brothers.

each one of them;[1] but in the other we cannot apply the words *'his vineyard'* to each one of them.[2]

R. Naḥman b. Isaac said: [The Mishnah deals with the] case where he grafted[3] a tree into vegetables, and this accords with the view of the teacher responsible for the following teaching: If one bends[4] a tree into vegetables, Rabban Simeon b. Gamaliel allows it in the name of R. Judah b. Gamda of Kefar Acco,[5] but the Sages forbid it. When R. Dimi came [from Palestine to Babylon] he reported in the name of R. Joḥanan, Whose teaching is it?[6] It is that of R. Eliezer b. Jacob. Did not R. Eliezer b. Jacob declare above, The word *'vineyard'* [is to be interpreted] according to its usual definition? So here also *'planted'* [is to be interpreted] according to its usual definition; hence if he planted he does [return home], but if he bends or grafts he does not.[7]

When R. Dimi came he reported that R. Joḥanan said in the name of R. Eliezer b. Jacob: A young shoot less than a handbreadth in height is liable for *'orlah* so long as it appears to be a year old;[8] but this only applies where there are two plants with two other plants parallel to them and one in front.[9] Should, however, the entire vineyard [consist of such shoots], then it is talked about.[10]

When R. Dimi came he reported that R. Joḥanan said in the name of R. Eliezer b. Jacob: A dead body affects four cubits with respect to the recital of the *Shema'*,[11] as it is said, *Whoso mocketh the poor reproacheth his Maker.*[12]

(1) Since it is not determined which one will marry her. (2) Because it belongs to them jointly. (3) [So Rashi. Rabina is answering the question in the Mishnah exempting one who grafts, cur. edd: 'bent'.] (4) [Tosef. Kil. I, has 'grafts'.] (5) [Being a permissible grafting it exempts the owner.] (6) Viz., the statement above: is to exclude one who bends or grafts (the vine). (7) [Even in a permissible case of bending or grafting.] (8) Because if he uses its fruit, it might seem to others that he was doing what was forbidden. (9) Five plants so arranged are considered a vineyard, to which all agree that the law of *'orlah* applies, v. Ber. 35*a*. (10) It is generally known that the vineyard has this peculiarity, and he may use the fruit. (11) It may not be recited within the four cubits. (12) Prov. XVII, 5. To perform a precept near a corpse is to deride it, since it is denied the privilege.

R. Isaac declared that R. Joḥanan said in the name of R. Eliezer b. Jacob: A step-daughter reared with her [step-] brothers is forbidden to marry one of them because she appears to be their sister. But this is not so since the relationship is generally known.[1]

R. Isaac also declared that R. Joḥanan said in the name of R. Eliezer b. Jacob: If gleanings, forgotten sheaves and the corner of the field[2] are gathered into a barn, they become subject to the tithe.[3] 'Ulla said: He only intended this to refer to a rural district, but in the city the fact [that the owner is a poor man who collected the produce from the fields of others] is generally known.

R. Isaac also declared that R. Joḥanan said in the name of R. Eliezer b. Jacob: A shoot which is less than a handbreadth in height does not make the seeds forfeit;[4] but this only applies when there are two plants with two other plants parallel to them and one in front. Should, however, the entire vineyard [consist of such shoots] it does make [the seeds] forfeit.

R. Isaac also declared that R. Joḥanan said in the name of R. Eliezer b. Jacob: [44*a*] A dead body affects four cubits with respect to communicating defilement.[5] Similarly teaches a Tanna: With a fore-court of a burial vault,[6] whoever stands within it is clean, provided there is in it a space of four cubits.[7] Such is the statement of Beth Shammai; but Beth Hillel declare, [A space of] four handbreadths'.[7] When does this[8] apply? If the entrance is from above; but if the entrance is from the side,[9] all agree that [a space of] four cubits [is necessary]. This should be just the reverse![10] On the contrary, when [the entrance is] from the side, he merely steps aside and goes out; but when it is from above it is impossible for

(1) That they have neither father or mother in common. (2) V. Lev. XIX, 9f. and Deut. XXIV, 19. (3) Because people may think that it is the produce of the man's field. (4) Under the law forbidding mixture; v. Deut. XXII, 9. (5) Whoever comes within that distance is rendered unclean. (6) V. B.B. (Sonc. ed.) p. 422 for diagram. (7) V. *op. cit.* p. 423. (8) The more lenient requirement of the School of Hillel. (9) [This means apparently that the sepulchral chambers surrounded the fore-court only on three sides, the fourth side being left open. V. R. Samson of Sens commentary on Oh. *loc. cit.*] (10) Viz., that when the entrance is from the side the requirement should be less strict.

him to avoid forming a cover![1]—But read thus: when does [the statement of Beth Hillel] apply? To [a vault] whose entrance is from the side; but if the entrance is from above [a space of] four cubits [is necessary].[2] Now [the teaching that one is clean who stands therein] only holds good of a fore-court of a burial vault where the partitions [between the graves and the fore-court] are distinctly marked, but a corpse in general affects four cubits.[3]

AND WHAT MAN IS THERE THAT HATH BETROTHED A WIFE? etc. Our Rabbis taught: *'That hath betrothed'*—it is all one whether he betrothed a virgin or a widow or a childless widow waiting for her brother-in-law; and even when there are five brothers, one of whom died in battle, they all return home.[4] [The fact that Scripture does not read] 'and hath not taken' but *'and hath not taken her'* is to exclude a High Priest who married a widow, an ordinary priest who married a divorcee or a *Ḥaluẓah,* a lay Israelite who married an illegitimate or a *Nethinah,* or a daughter of an Israelite married to an illegitimate or a *Nathin.* Is this to say that [this teaching is] not in agreement with R. Jose the Galilean? For if it agreed with R. Jose the Galilean, behold he has said, *'Fainthearted'* i.e., he who is afraid because of the transgressions he had committed![5]—You may even say that it agrees with R. Jose the Galilean, and it is in accord with Rabbah; for Rabbah said: He is certainly not guilty until he has cohabited with her. For what is the reason [of the prohibition] *shall he not take?*[6] So that *he shall not profane* [*his seed*].[7] Hence he does not receive the punishment of lashes[8] until he has cohabited with her.

(1) When he climbs up to get out he may put his hands upon the graves; therefore a larger space should be required since the probability of contracting defilement is greater. (2) [This is the end of the cited Mishnah Oh. XV, 8. What follows is from a Baraitha another version of which is to be found in Tosef. Oh. XV.] (3) [Even according to Beth Hillel, otherwise what need for their ruling in the case of one standing in a fore-court? The Tanna of the cited Mishnah is thus in support of R. Eliezer b. Jacob.] (4) V. *supra* p. 214. (5) If that is so, the men who contracted an illegal marriage should return home. (6) Lev. XXI, 14, referring to the women forbidden in marriage to a High Priest. (7) Ibid. 15. (8) And but for the verse *'and hath not taken her'*, they would not be exempted where there was betrothal.

Our Rabbis taught: [The order of the phrases is] *'that hath built'*, *'that hath planted'*, *'that hath betrothed'*. The Torah has thus taught a rule of conduct: that a man should build a house, plant a vineyard and then marry a wife. Similarly declared Solomon in his wisdom, *Prepare thy work without, and make it ready for thee in the field; and afterwards build thine house*[1]—*'prepare thy work without'*, i.e., a dwelling-place; *'and make it ready for thee in the field'*, i.e., a vineyard; *'and afterwards build thine house'*, i.e., a wife. Another interpretation is: *'prepare thy work without'*, i.e., Scripture; *'and make it ready for thee in the field'*, i.e., Mishnah; *'and afterwards build thine house'*, i.e., Gemara. Another explanation is: *'prepare thy work without'*, i.e., Scripture and Mishnah; *'and make it ready for thee in the field'*, i.e., Gemara; *'and afterwards build thine house,'* i.e., good deeds. R. Eliezer, son of R. Jose the Galilean says: *'Prepare thy work without,'* i.e., Scripture, Mishnah and Gemara; *'and make it ready for thee in the field,'* i.e., good deeds; *'and afterwards build thine house,'* i.e., make research [in the Torah] and receive the reward.

THE FOLLOWING DO NOT RETURN HOME: HE WHO BUILT A LODGE etc. A Tanna taught: If [when rebuilding the house] he adds a row [of fresh bricks] to it, he does return home.[2]

R. ELIEZER SAYS: ALSO HE WHO BUILT A BRICK-HOUSE IN SHARON DOES NOT RETURN HOME. A Tanna taught: [The reason is] because they have to renew it twice in a period of seven years.

THE FOLLOWING DO NOT MOVE FROM THEIR PLACE: HE WHO BUILT A NEW HOUSE AND DEDICATED IT etc. Our Rabbis taught: *A new wife*[3]—I have here only *'a new wife'*; whence is it [that the law applies also to] a widow and divorcee? There is a text to state *'wife'*, i.e., in every case. Why, however, does the text state *'a new wife'?* [It means] one who is new to him, thus excluding the case of a man who takes back his divorced wife, since she is not new to him.

Our Rabbis taught: *He shall not go out in the host*[4]—and it is

(1) Prov. XXIV, 27. (2) It is then regarded as a new house. (3) Deut. XXIV, 5. (4) Ibid.

possible to think that he does not go out in the host, but he supplies water and food and repairs the roads [for the army]; therefore there is a text to state, *'Neither shall he be charged with any business'*. It is possible to think that I am also to include [among those who do not move from their place] the man who built a house but did not dedicate it, or planted a vineyard and did not use its fruit, or betrothed a wife but did not take her; therefore there is a text to state, *'Neither shall he be charged'*—but you may charge others.[1] Since, however, it is written *'Neither shall he be charged'*, what is the purpose of *'He shall not go out in the host'*?[2] So that a transgression of the Law should involve two prohibitions.

MISHNAH. AND THE OFFICERS SHALL SPEAK FURTHER UNTO THE PEOPLE ETC.[3] R. AKIBA SAYS: 'FEARFUL AND FAINTHEARTED' IS TO BE UNDERSTOOD LITERALLY VIZ., HE IS UNABLE TO STAND IN THE BATTLE-RANKS AND SEE A DRAWN SWORD. R. JOSE THE GALILEAN SAYS: 'FEARFUL AND FAINTHEARTED' ALLUDES TO ONE WHO IS AFRAID BECAUSE OF THE TRANSGRESSIONS HE HAD COMMITTED; THEREFORE THE TORAH CONNECTED ALL THESE[4] WITH HIM THAT HE MAY RETURN HOME ON THEIR ACCOUNT.[5] R. JOSE SAYS: A HIGH PRIEST WHO MARRIED A WIDOW, AN ORDINARY PRIEST WHO MARRIED A DIVORCEE OR ḤALUẒAH, A LAY ISRAELITE WHO MARRIED AN ILLEGITIMATE OR NETHINAH, AND THE DAUGHTER OF AN ISRAELITE WHO MARRIED AN ILLEGITIMATE OR A NATHIN—BEHOLD SUCH AN ONE IS 'FEARFUL AND FAINTHEARTED'.[6]

AND IT SHALL BE, WHEN THE OFFICERS HAVE MADE AN END OF SPEAKING UNTO THE PEOPLE,

(1) E.g., who have built a house and not dedicated it or betrothed a woman and not taken her to wife. (2) The former surely includes the latter. (3) Deut. XX, 8. (4) Those who had exemption because of a new house etc. (5) Otherwise anyone who claimed exemption because of sinfulness had to expose himself publicly as a transgressor. (6) The difference in the point of view of R. Jose the Galilean and R. Jose will be explained in the Gemara.

THAT THEY SHALL APPOINT CAPTAINS OF HOSTS AT THE HEAD OF THE PEOPLE.[1] AND AT THE REAR OF THE PEOPLE THEY STATION GUARDS IN FRONT OF THEM AND OTHERS BEHIND THEM, WITH IRON AXES IN THEIR HANDS, AND SHOULD ANYONE WISH TO FLEE, THEY HAVE PERMISSION TO SMITE HIS THIGHS, [44*b*] BECAUSE THE BEGINNING OF FLIGHT IS FALLING,[2] AS IT IS SAID, ISRAEL IS FLED BEFORE THE PHILISTINES, AND THERE HATH BEEN A GREAT SLAUGHTER AMONG THE PEOPLE;[3] AND FURTHER ON IT STATES, AND THE MEN OF ISRAEL FLED FROM BEFORE THE PHILISTINES AND FELL DOWN SLAIN ETC.[4]

TO WHAT DOES ALL THE FOREGOING APPLY? TO VOLUNTARY WARS, BUT IN THE WARS COMMANDED BY THE TORAH[5] ALL GO FORTH EVEN A BRIDEGROOM FROM HIS CHAMBER AND A BRIDE FROM HER CANOPY.[6] R. JUDAH SAYS: TO WHAT DOES ALL THE FOREGOING APPLY? TO THE WARS COMMANDED BY THE TORAH; BUT IN OBLIGATORY WARS[7] ALL GO FORTH, EVEN A BRIDEGROOM FROM HIS CHAMBER AND A BRIDE FROM HER CANOPY.

GEMARA. What is the difference between R. Jose and R. Jose the Galilean?[8]—The issue between them is the transgression of a Rabbinical ordinance.[9] With whom does the following teaching accord: He who speaks between [donning] one phylactery and the other[10] has committed a transgression and returns home under the war-regulations? With whom [does it accord]? With R. Jose the Galilean. Who is the Tanna of the following: Our Rabbis taught:

(1) Deut. XX, 9. (2) The Gemara reverses the wording here. (3) I Sam. IV, 17. (4) Ibid. XXXI, 1. (5) E.g., the conquest of Canaan and the annihilation of the Amalekites (Deut. XXV, 19). (6) The women provided food for the troops. (7) In defence against attack. (8) Since they agree in defining *'faint-hearted'* as one afraid of his sins. (9) R. Jose does not consider this sufficient to warrant exemption; therefore in the Mishnah he instances marriages forbidden by the Torah as the kind of transgression for which exemption may be claimed. (10) Upon the arm and the forehead. It is forbidden to speak between the putting on of the two.

If he heard the sound of trumpets and was terror-stricken, or the crash of shields and was terror-stricken, or [beheld] the brandishing of swords and the urine discharged itself upon his knees, he returns home? With whom [does it accord]? Are we to say that it is with R. Akiba and not R. Jose the Galilean?[1]—In such a circumstance even R. Jose the Galilean admits [that he returns home], because it is written, *Lest his brethren's heart melt as his heart.*[2]

AND IT SHALL BE, WHEN THE OFFICERS HAVE MADE AN END etc. The phrase, BECAUSE THE BEGINNING OF FLIGHT IS FALLING should be, 'because falling is the beginning of flight'! Read [in the Mishnah]: Because falling is the beginning of flight.

TO WHAT DOES ALL THE FOREGOING APPLY? TO VOLUNTARY WARS etc. R. Joḥanan said: [A war] which is [designated] voluntary according to the Rabbis is commanded according to R. Judah,[3] and [a war] which is [designated] commanded according to the Rabbis is obligatory according to R. Judah.[4] Raba said:[5] The wars waged by Joshua to conquer [Canaan] were obligatory in the opinion of all; the wars waged by the House of David for territorial expansion were voluntary in the opinion of all; where they differ is with regard to [wars] against heathens so that these should not march against them. One[6] calls them commanded and the other voluntary, the practical issue being that one who is engaged in the performance of a commandment is exempt from the performance of another commandment.[7]

(1) Since the latter does not understand '*fainthearted*' as relating to physical fear. (2) Deut. XX, 8. (3) They differ in terminology but agree that a bridegroom does not serve. (4) They agree that a bridegroom must serve. (5) Raba explains R. Joḥanan's statement. (6) R. Judah. (7) If it is to be considered a war commanded by the Torah, those engaged in it are exempt from the performance of other commandments.

SOṬAH

CHAPTER IX

MISHNAH. [THE DECLARATION OVER] THE HEIFER WHOSE NECK IS TO BE BROKEN MUST BE IN THE HOLY TONGUE; AS IT IS SAID, IF ONE BE FOUND SLAIN IN THE EARTH... THEN THY ELDERS AND THY JUDGES SHALL COME FORTH.[1] THREE USED TO GO FORTH FROM THE SUPREME COURT IN JERUSALEM; R. JUDAH SAYS: FIVE, AS IT IS STATED, 'THY ELDERS,' I.E., TWO, 'AND THY JUDGES' I.E., TWO, AND SINCE A COURT OF JUSTICE CANNOT CONSIST OF AN EVEN NUMBER, THEY ADD ONE MORE.

IF [THE CORPSE] WAS FOUND HIDDEN IN A HEAP OF STONES, OR HANGING ON A TREE, OR FLOATING UPON THE SURFACE OF THE WATER, THEY DO NOT BREAK [A HEIFER'S NECK], BECAUSE IT IS STATED, 'IN THE EARTH'—AND NOT HIDDEN IN A HEAP OF STONES, NOR HANGING ON A TREE IN A FIELD, NOR FLOATING UPON THE SURFACE OF THE WATER. IF IT WAS FOUND NEAR TO THE FRONTIER, OR A CITY THE MAJORITY OF WHOSE INHABITANTS WERE HEATHENS, OR A CITY IN WHICH THERE IS NO COURT OF JUSTICE, THEY DO NOT BREAK [A HEIFER'S NECK]. THEY ONLY MEASURE[2] THE DISTANCE TO A CITY IN WHICH THERE IS A COURT OF JUSTICE.

GEMARA. How does [the author of the Mishnah] prove his point?[3]—R. Abbahu said: This is what he intends: It is stated, *And they shall answer and say*[4] and elsewhere it is stated, *And the Levites shall answer and say* etc.,[5] as the answering mentioned in this latter passage was in the holy tongue, so here also it was in the holy tongue, and as to the procedure in the ceremony of the heifer

(1) Deut. XXI, 1ff. (2) The distance between the corpse and the nearest city (ibid. 2). (3) That the declaration must be in Hebrew. The verse adduced affords no proof. (4) Ibid. 7. (5) Ibid. XXVII, 14.

whose neck was to be broken—IF ONE BE FOUND SLAIN IN THE EARTH . . . THEN THY ELDERS AND THY JUDGES SHALL COME FORTH. THREE USED TO GO FORTH FROM THE SUPREME COURT IN JERUSALEM; R. JUDAH SAYS: FIVE etc.

Our[1] Rabbis taught: *'Then thy elders and thy judges shall come forth'* —*'thy elders'*, i.e., two, *'and thy judges'*, i.e., two, and since a Court of justice cannot consist of an even number, they add one more; hence there were five. Such is the statement of R. Judah; but R. Simeon says: *'Thy elders,'* i.e., two, and since a Court of Justice cannot consist of an even number, they add one more; hence there were three. But for R. Simeon also it is written *'and thy judges'!* —He requires that for [the teaching that they must be] the most distinguished of thy judges. And [where does] R. Judah [derive the teaching that they must be the most distinguished]?—It follows from *'thy'* in *'thy elders'*.[2] [How does] R. Simeon [meet this argument]?—If the All-Merciful had only written *'elders'*, I might have thought that even old men from the market-place [would suffice]; therefore the All-Merciful wrote *'thy elders'*. If, further, the All-Merciful had only written *'thy elders'*, I might have thought that even [members of] a minor Sanhedrin[3] [would suffice]; therefore the All-Merciful wrote *'and thy judges'* i.e., the most distinguished of thy judges. [Where does] R. Judah [derive the teaching that they must be members of the Supreme Court]?—He draws an analogy between the use of the word *'elders'* here and in the phrase *the elders of the Congregation;*[4] as it there denotes the most distinguished men of the congregation so here also it denotes the most distinguished men of the congregation. If he makes a deduction, then let him deduce the whole from there and what is the necessity of *'and thy judges'!*[5]—But the *'and'* in *'and thy judges'* [denotes that the

(1) On the whole passage, v. Sanh. (Sonc. ed.) pp. 66ff. (2) It would have been sufficient for the text to read: Then elders shall go forth. (3) Consisting of twenty-three members, and not the Great Sanhedrin in Jerusalem of seventy-one members. (4) E.g., in Lev. IV, 15. (5) In Sanh. 3*b* it is argued that Lev. IV, 15 must be interpreted in the sense that five elders are required; that being so, why does not R. Judah use that argument and not *'and thy judges'* for his opinion that five are necessary?

phrase is to be used] for obtaining the requisite number. [How does] R. Simeon [meet this argument]?[1] [45a] He draws no deduction from *'and'*;[2] (for what then does the All-Merciful intend by the phrase?—They are to be the most distinguished of thy judges.)[3] But on this line of argument: *'and they shall come forth'*[4] i.e., two, *'and they shall measure'* i.e., two; according to R. Judah, then, there must be nine and according to R. Simeon there must be seven![5]—[No; the two phrases] are required for the following teaching:[6] *'They shall come forth'*—they and not their agents; *'and they shall measure'*—even if it is found obviously near to a particular city,[7] they must still measure since it is a commandment to carry out the measurement.

Our Mishnah is not in agreement with R. Eliezer b. Jacob; for it has been taught: R. Eliezer b. Jacob says: *'Thy elders'* i.e., the Sanhedrin; *'thy judges'* i.e., the king and High Priest—the king, for it is written, *The king by judgment establisheth the land;*[8] and the High Priest, for it is written, *And thou shalt come unto the priests the Levites, and unto the judge that shall be* etc.[9] The question was asked: Is R. Eliezer b. Jacob only at variance [in defining *'judges'*] as the king and High Priest, but as regards [the number of members of] the Sanhedrin does he agree with R. Judah or R. Simeon; or perhaps he is also at variance on that matter too and requires the whole of the Sanhedrin?—R. Joseph said, Come and hear: If they[10] found a rebellious elder[11] in Beth Pagi,[12] and he rebelled against them,[13] it is possible to think that his act of rebellion is punishable;

(1) Since he only requires three. (2) I.e., he does not expound the analogy. (3) [This passage, which is bracketed in cur. edd., is rightly omitted in some texts.] (4) Deut. XXI, 2. (5) The former obtained the number five from *'thy elders and thy judges'* and now four more are to be added. (6) And are not to be used to add to the number of elders. (7) So that there is no need for measuring. (8) Prov. XXIX, 4. (9) Deut. XVII, 9. *'And'* is understood as 'even'; therefore the priests acted as judges; and since one in particular is specified in *'the judge'* it must be the High Priest. (10) The number of the Great Sanhedrin. (11) One who refused to abide by the decision of the Sanhedrin, Deut. XVII, 8. (12) A place within the walls of Jerusalem. Origen mentions that it was a village inhabited by priests. (13) Against the decision of the local Sanhedrin to whom a disputed point of law was submitted.

therefore there is a text to state, *Then shalt thou arise and get thee up unto the place.*[1] This teaches that the 'place' determines [whether the act of rebellion is punishable].

Now how many of them had gone forth [from the Great Sanhedrin to Beth Pagi]? If I say that only a part of them had gone forth, perhaps they who remain behind are of the same opinion as the accused![2] It is therefore evident that all must go forth. And for what purpose? If for a secular object, was it possible for them all to go? For behold it is written, *Thy navel is like a round goblet, wherein no mingled wine is wanting,*[3] so that should a member have need to go out [from the hall where the Sanhedrin was in session], he may only do so if twenty-three [of his colleagues] remain, corresponding to the number of a minor Sanhedrin, otherwise he may not leave! Obviously, then, [they had gone forth] for a religious object. For what object? Must it not be to measure in connection with the heifer, according to the opinion of R. Eliezer b. Jacob?[4]—Abaye said to [R. Joseph], No; [they may all go forth for such a purpose as] to add to the boundaries of the city [of Jerusalem] or the Temple-courts; as we have learnt: We do not add to the boundaries of the city [of Jerusalem] or the Temple-courts except by a Court of seventy-one.[5] There is a teaching in agreement with R. Joseph: If they[6] met in Beth Pagi, and [an elder] rebelled against them; e.g., they went forth to carry out a measurement in connection with the heifer, or to add to the boundaries of the city [of Jerusalem] or the Temple-courts,[7] it is possible to think that his act of rebellion is punishable; therefore there is a text to state, *Then shalt thou arise and get thee up* [etc.].[1] This teaches that the 'place' determines [whether the act of rebellion is punishable].

(1) Deut. XVII, 8, i.e., the Temple mount, the locale of the Great Sanhedrin. (2) How then could the rebellious elder be condemned? (3) Cant. VII, 3, E.V. 2. This verse is applied to the Sanhedrin, called '*navel*', because it sat in a place which was considered to be the centre of the world. '*Mingled wine*' is defined (Shab. 77*a*) as diluted with two-thirds of water. Hence one third of the Sanhedrin must at least be present at a session. (4) Who, *ex hypothesi*, requires the presence of the entire Sanhedrin. (5) Sanh. I, 5. (6) The Great Sanhedrin. (7) So it is possible that they all went out to do the measuring.

IF [THE CORPSE] WAS FOUND HIDDEN IN A HEAP OF STONES, OR HANGING ON A TREE. Is this to say that our Mishnah agrees with R. Judah and not the Rabbis? For it has been taught: *And hast forgot a sheaf in the field*[1]—this excludes [a sheaf] which was hidden; such is the statement of R. Judah, but the Sages declare that *'in the field'* is to include a hidden sheaf![2]—Rab said, You may even maintain that it agrees with the Rabbis since each case is to be explained in the light of its context. [In connection with the corpse] it is written, *'If one be found slain,'* i.e., wherever it be found; *'in the earth'*, i.e., to the exclusion of one which is hidden. The other case [of the sheaf] is to be explained in the light of the context; for it is written, *'When thou reapest thine harvest in thy field and hast forgot a sheaf'*. There is an analogy between the forgotten sheaf and the harvesting: as the harvesting is visible to all so the forgotten sheaf must be visible to all;[3] and the fact that the All-Merciful wrote *'in the field'* is to include a hidden sheaf. Then let R. Judah likewise draw an analogy between the forgotten sheaf and the harvesting![4]—He actually does so; but [he argues], What is the purpose of *'in the field'?* It is required to include standing-corn which is forgotten.[5] From where, then, do the Rabbis derive the regulation of standing-corn which is forgotten?—They derive it from, *When thou reapest thine harvest in thy field* [*and hast forgot*].[6] And [how does] R. Judah [explain this phrase]?—He requires it for the teaching of R. Abbahu in the name of R. Eleazar; for R. Abbahu said in the name of R. Eleazar: It excludes the case where sheaves were carried [by the wind] into his neighbours' field.[7] And [from where] do the Rabbis [derive this regulation]?—From the fact that Scripture has *'thy field'* and not merely 'the field'. And [what of] R. Judah?—He draws no inference from *'thy field'* as distinct from 'the field'.

(1) Deut. XXIV, 19. (2) The former explains *'in the field'* as lying about upon the surface of the field; the Rabbis understand it as hidden somewhere in the field. (3) And the reaper merely overlooked it. (4) And not maintain that it is excluded. (5) If he forgot to cut down a portion of the corn, this remains for the poor. (6) They connect *'forgot'* with *'thy field'*, so that the forgetting applies also to corn standing in the field. (7) And thinking that they were not his, he left them.

R. Jeremiah asked: How is it if sheaves were carried[1] into his own field? Is the air-space above a field identical with the field or not?—R. Kahana said to R. Papi—another version is, R. Kahana said to R. Zebid, The problem is to be solved from the teaching of R. Abbahu who said in the name of R. Eleazar, 'It excludes the case where sheaves were carried [by the wind] into his neighbour's field,' implying, does it not, that only [when they are carried into] his neighbour's field they are [excluded], but [if the wind drops them] into his own field they are not![2] But according to your reasoning, [it would follow that] if the sheaves were carried into his neighbour's field [and alighted upon a stone, etc.,] they are excluded, but should they lie [upon the ground] they are not;[3] surely we require [the sheaves to be] *'in thy field'*, but they are not there! Rather must they [argue thus:[4] 'It excludes when the sheaves were] in his neighbour's field' even if actually lying upon the ground; and the expression 'carried' is only employed because this could have happened only if they were 'carried' [by the force of the wind].

Come and hear: If he laid hold of a sheaf to convey it into the city, placed it on top of another sheaf belonging to his neighbour and forgot it, the lower is considered to be a forgotten sheaf but not the upper. R. Simeon b. Judah says in the name of R. Simeon: Neither is a forgotten sheaf, the lower because it is hidden and the upper because it is suspended.[5] Hence they only differ as regards the lower, but with respect to the upper they all agree that it is not a hidden sheaf![6]—It is different in this circumstance, because having taken hold of it he has the right to it. If that is so,[7] why use the argument 'placed it on top of another sheaf belonging to his

(1) Some texts read *'afu* (flew) instead of *ẓafu*. The question relates to the circumstance where the sheaves did not fall upon the field but upon a stone or something similar, so that they were suspended above the field. (2) Consequently so long as the sheaves are in his own field, they come within the law of the forgotten sheaf. (3) And come within the law of the forgotten sheaf. (4) With reference to the teaching of R. Abbahu. (5) Not lying upon the ground. (6) This conclusion would therefore answer R. Jeremiah's question. (7) That his having taken hold of it precludes it from being regarded as a forgotten sheaf.

neighbour'? It would have been the same if he had laid it upon the field [of his neighbour]!—That is so; but he used the illustration of 'on top of another sheaf belonging to his neighbour', because of the instance of the lower sheaf [about which there was a difference of opinion]. Why, then, should he use the phrase 'because it is suspended'![1]—Read: because it is like something suspended.[2]

Abaye said: Behold I am like Ben Azzai in the streets of Tiberias.[3] So one of the Rabbis asked Abaye, If there were two corpses, one on top of the other,[4] from which is the measurement taken? [Do we argue that with] two things of the same kind [the lower] is regarded as hidden and with two things of the same kind [the upper] is not regarded as suspended, so that he takes the measurement from the upper; or perhaps with two things of the same kind [the upper] is regarded as suspended and with two things of the same kind [the lower] is not regarded as hidden, so that he takes the measurement from the lower; or perhaps with two things of the same kind [the lower] is regarded as hidden and with two things of the same kind [the upper] is regarded as suspended, so that he takes measurement neither from the lower nor the upper! —He replied to him, [45b] You have it stated, 'If he laid hold of a sheaf to convey it into the city, placed it on top of another sheaf belonging to his neighbour and forgot it, the lower is considered to be a forgotten sheaf but not the upper. R. Simeon b. Judah says in the name of R. Simeon: Neither is a forgotten sheaf, the lower because it is hidden and the upper because it is suspended. Now they were[5] of the opinion that these Tannaim agreed with R. Judah who said, '*In the field*', i.e., to the exclusion of one which is hidden. Do they, then, not differ on this issue: One holds that with two things of the same kind [the lower] is regarded as hidden,

(1) Since it was irrelevant to the issue. (2) It is exempt from the law of the forgotten sheaf because, having been in the owner's hand, it is like something suspended and not lying upon the ground. (3) I.e., in his own town of Pumbeditha he felt as competent to solve difficult problems as did Ben Azzai in his city of Tiberias. (4) The top one is not fully over the other, so that if the measurements are taken from the two a different city would be the nearest in each case. (5) The scholars who thought of solving the question from this Baraitha.

and the other holds it is not regarded as hidden?—No; if they were of the same opinion as R. Judah, they all agree that with two things of the same kind [the lower] is regarded as hidden; but here the difference is the same as that of R. Judah and the Rabbis. The Rabbis here agree with the Rabbis there,[1] and R. Simeon b. Judah agrees with R. Judah.[2] If that is so, why use the argument 'on top of another sheaf belonging to his neighbour'? It would have been the same if he had placed it on the earth or on pebbles!—That is so; but the purpose was to let you know how strong is the position of R. Judah who said that even with two things of the same kind [the lower] is regarded as hidden.

Our Rabbis taught: *'Slain,'* but not strangled,[3] *'slain,'* but not one who is expiring;[4] *'in the land'*, but not hidden in a heap of stones; *'lying'*, but not hanging on a tree; *'in the earth'*, but not floating upon the surface of the water. R. Eleazar says: In all these cases, if the person had been slain, they break the heifer's neck. It has been taught: R. Jose b. Judah said: They asked R. Eleazar, Do you not admit that if he had been strangled and was lying upon a dung-heap,[5] they do not break the heifer's neck?[6] [Yes:] consequently [you must agree that] *'slain'* indicates one who is not strangled; similarly *'in the earth'* indicates one who is not hidden in a heap of stones, *'lying'* one who is not hanging on a tree, *'in the earth'* one who is not floating upon the surface of the water!—[How does] R. Eleazar [meet this argument]?—The word *'slain'* is written redundantly.[7]

IF IT WAS FOUND NEAR TO THE FRONTIER, OR A CITY THE MAJORITY OF WHOSE INHABITANTS WERE GENTILES etc. Because it is written *'be found'*, thus excluding what commonly occurs.[8]

(1) Who maintained that a hidden sheaf came within the law of the forgotten sheaf. (2) Who excludes a hidden sheaf from the law. (3) The Hebrew for slain (*ḥalal*) denotes by the sword. (4) Not actually dead. (5) So the body was not hanging, hidden or floating. (6) For the reason that he was not *'slain'*. (7) It occurs four times in Deut. XXI, 1-9; emphasing that he must be 'slain' and not 'strangled'. (8) It frequently happened that dead bodies were found in such localities.

OR A CITY IN WHICH THERE IS NO COURT OF JUSTICE. Because we require *'the elders of that city'*, and such are not [forthcoming].

THEY ONLY MEASURE THE DISTANCE TO A CITY [IN WHICH THERE IS A COURT OF JUSTICE]. This is obvious! Since he stated: OR A CITY IN WHICH IS NO COURT OF JUSTICE [etc.], I know that they only measure the distance to a city in which there is a Court of Justice!—He thereby informs us what is taught in the following: Whence is it that if it was found near a city in which there is no Court of Justice, they leave [the city out] and measure to [the nearest] city which has a Court of Justice? There is a text to state, *The elders of that city shall take,*[1] i.e., in every case.[2]

MISHNAH. IF [THE CORPSE] WAS FOUND EXACTLY BETWEEN TWO CITIES, BOTH OF THEM BRING TWO HEIFERS [BETWEEN THEM]. SUCH IS THE STATEMENT OF R. ELIEZER;[3] BUT JERUSALEM DOES NOT BRING A HEIFER WHOSE NECK IS TO BE BROKEN. IF THE HEAD WAS FOUND IN ONE PLACE AND THE BODY IN ANOTHER PLACE, THEY CARRY THE HEAD TO THE BODY. SUCH IS THE STATEMENT OF R. ELIEZER.[4] R. AKIBA SAYS: [THEY CARRY] THE BODY TO THE HEAD. FROM WHAT PART [OF THE BODY] DO THEY MEASURE? R. ELIEZER SAYS: FROM THE NAVEL; R. AKIBA SAYS: FROM THE NOSE; R. ELIEZER B. JACOB SAYS: FROM THE PLACE WHERE HE WAS MADE A SLAIN PERSON, FROM THE NECK.

GEMARA. What is R. Eliezer's reason?[4]—He holds that it is possible to make an exact measurement; and the word *'nearest'*[5] holds good of even more than one city.

(1) Deut. XXI, 3. (2) The measurement must always be made and the nearest city containing *'elders'* ascertained. (3) [J. adds: BUT THE SAGES SAY ONLY ONE CITY BRINGS A HEIFER WHOSE NECK IS TO BE BROKEN BUT TWO CITIES DO NOT BRING.] (4) For requiring two heifers if the body is found equidistant between two cities. (5) Deut. XXI, 3.

BUT JERUSALEM DOES NOT BRING A HEIFER WHOSE NECK IS TO BE BROKEN. Because Scripture declares, *To possess it,*[1] and he is of the opinion that Jerusalem was not apportioned among the tribes.

IF THE HEAD WAS FOUND IN ONE PLACE etc. In what do they differ? If I should say that they differ on the question from where the measurement is to be taken, behold since [the author of the Mishnah] states in the sequel: FROM WHAT PART [OF THE BODY] DO THEY MEASURE? it follows that we are not dealing here with the subject of measurement!—R. Isaac said: They differ because of the regulation that a *meth mizwah*[2] acquires his place; and thus he means to say: He acquires his place for burial, and where the head is found in one place and the body in another, they carry the head to the body [and bury it there]. Such is the statement of R. Eliezer; but R. Akiba says, [They carry] the body to the head [and bury it there]. In what do they differ? One is of the opinion that the body is in the place where it fell and the head rolled away, while the other is of the opinion that the head remains in the place where it falls while the body falls some way off.

FROM WHAT PART [OF THE BODY] DO THEY MEASURE? In what do they differ? One is of the opinion that the source of existence is in the nose, while the other is of the opinion that the source of existence is in the navel. Is this to say [that they differ on the same point] as the following teachers: From where is the embryo formed? From the head, and thus it states, *Thou art He that took me* [gozi] *out of my mother's womb,*[3] and it further states, *Cut off* [gozi] *thine hair and cast it away* etc.[4] Abba Saul says: It is from the navel, and its root spreads in all directions [from there]!—You may even say that Abba Saul [agrees with R. Akiba], because Abba Saul's

(1) Deut. XXI, 1. (2) Lit., 'a dead body which is a commandment'; i.e., an unattended corpse, and it is the duty of whoever finds it to be concerned with its burial. The Talmud (B.Ḳ. 81*b*) relates that when Joshua divided out the land, he imposed a condition that a *meth mizwah* should be buried in whatever spot he is found. (3) Ps. LXXI, 6. (4) Jer. VII, 29. On the basis of the similar word in this verse, it is explained in the former as 'the place where my hair grows', i.e., the head.

statement only applies to the formation, that when an embryo is formed it is formed from the centre, but with respect to existence all agree that [its source is] in the nose; for it is written, *All in whose nostrils was the breath of the spirit of life* etc.[1]

R. ELIEZER B. JACOB SAYS: FROM THE PLACE WHERE HE WAS MADE A SLAIN PERSON, FROM THE NECK. What is the reason of R. Eliezer b. Jacob?—Because it is written, *To lay thee upon the necks of the wicked that are slain.*[2]

MISHNAH. WHEN THE ELDERS OF JERUSALEM[3] HAD DEPARTED AND GONE AWAY, THE ELDERS OF THAT CITY[4] TAKE A HEIFER OF THE HERD[5] WHICH HAS NOT DRAWN IN THE YOKE, AND A BLEMISH DOES NOT DISQUALIFY IT. THEY BRING IT DOWN TO A RAVINE WHICH IS STONY[6]—'ETHAN' IS TO BE UNDERSTOOD IN ITS LITERAL SENSE OF 'HARD'—BUT EVEN IF IT BE NOT STONY, IT IS FIT [FOR THE CEREMONY]. THEY THEN BREAK ITS NECK WITH A HATCHET FROM BEHIND.[7] THE SITE MAY NEVER BE SOWN OR TILLED, BUT IT IS PERMITTED TO CARD FLAX AND CHISEL STONES THERE. THE ELDERS OF THAT CITY THEN WASH THEIR HANDS WITH WATER IN THE PLACE WHERE THE HEIFER'S NECK WAS BROKEN AND DECLARE, OUR HANDS HAVE NOT SHED THIS BLOOD, NEITHER HAVE OUR EYES SEEN IT.[8] BUT CAN IT ENTER OUR MINDS THAT THE ELDERS OF A COURT OF JUSTICE ARE SHEDDERS OF BLOOD! [THE MEANING OF THEIR STATEMENT IS], HOWEVER, [THE MAN FOUND DEAD] DID NOT COME TO US [FOR HELP] AND WE DISMISSED HIM WITHOUT SUPPLYING HIM WITH FOOD, WE DID NOT SEE HIM AND LET HIM GO WITHOUT ESCORT.[9] [46a] THEN THE PRIESTS

(1) Gen. VII, 22. (2) Ezek. XXI, 34. (3) The members of the Great Sanhedrin whose duty it was to make the measurement. (4) Which is found to be nearest the corpse. (5) Defined in Parah I, 1 as less than a year old. (6) The word *ethan* (Deut. XXI, 4) is interpreted by Maimonides in the sense given in the E.V. viz., running water. (7) Not in front as in the act of ritual slaughter. (8) Deut. XXI, 7. (9) [In the J. text of the Mishnah and in MS.M. the words

EXCLAIM, FORGIVE, O LORD, THY PEOPLE ISRAEL, WHOM THOU HAST REDEEMED, AND SUFFER NOT INNOCENT BLOOD TO REMAIN IN THE MIDST OF THY PEOPLE ISRAEL.[1] THERE IS NO NEED FOR THEM TO SAY, AND THE BLOOD SHALL BE FORGIVEN THEM;[2] BUT THE HOLY SPIRIT ANNOUNCES TO THEM, 'WHEN YOU ACT THUS, THE BLOOD IS FORGIVEN YOU.'

GEMARA. But that a blemish disqualified a heifer may be deduced by *a fortiori* reasoning from the instance of the [red] cow:[3] if a blemish disqualifies a cow which is not disqualified on account of age,[4] how much more must a blemish disqualify a heifer which is disqualified on account of age!—It is different there, because Scripture stated, Wherein *is no blemish*[5]—a blemish disqualifies [a red cow] but does not disqualify a heifer. According to this argument,[6] the other disqualifications on account of work having been done by it should not apply [to the red cow];[7] why, then, did Rab Judah say in the name of Rab, If a person laid a bundle of sacks upon it,[8] it is disqualified, but with a heifer [it is not disqualified] until it draws [a load]![9]—It is different with a [red] cow, because we derive the meaning of the term *'yoke'* [in connection with a red cow] from its occurrence in connection with a heifer.[10] But let [the deduction that a blemish disqualifies] a heifer be also drawn from the instance of a [red] cow on the basis of a common use of the term *'yoke'*!—Behold the All-Merciful has excluded that

'without . . . food' and 'without escort' are missing, and in the Gemara there it is stated that the reference is not, as maintained by the Babylonian scholars, to the murdered person, but to the murderer. The elders, that is to say, declare that 'he did not come to us and we dismissed him or allowed him to go unpunished.']

(1) Deut. XXI, 8. (2) Ibid. (3) Num. XIX. How can the Mishnah declare that a blemish does not disqualify it? (4) It may be more than a year old. (5) Ibid. 2. (6) That *'wherein'* (*bah*) is a restrictive particle. (7) Since it is merely stated *'upon which never came yoke'* and not, as with the heifer, *'wherewith* (*bah*) *it hath not been wrought and which hath not drawn* (Deut. XXI, 3), the *'wherewith'* restricting it to the heifer. (8) The red cow, and no yoke was placed upon it. (9) Because the text states explicitly *'which hath not drawn'*. (10) And the restrictive word *'wherewith'*, stated with the heifer, is required for another purpose.

by using the word *'wherein'* [*bah*]. But with the heifer it is likewise written *'wherewith'* [*bah*]![1]—This is required to exclude animals destined as sacrifices which are not disqualified by having been used for work; because it might have occurred to you to say, Let us draw a conclusion by *a fortiori* reasoning from the heifer: if a heifer which is not disqualified by a blemish is disqualified by having been used for work, how much more must animals destined as sacrifices, which are disqualified by a blemish, be disqualified by having been used for work! It can, however, be objected: This is right for a heifer because it is also disqualified by an age-limit!—Do you mean to say, then, that there are no animals destined as sacrifices which are disqualified by an age-limit? Hence a text is necessary for those offerings which are disqualified by an age-limit.[2] Is, however, [the regulation that] animals destined as sacrifices are not disqualified by having been used for work derived from here?[3] Surely it is derived from the following: *Blind, or broken, or maimed, or having a wen, or scurvy or scabbed, ye shall not offer these unto the Lord*[4]—these ye shall not offer, but you may offer animals as sacrifices which have been used for work!—[This verse][5] is necessary, because it might have occurred to you to say, This only applies where they have been used for permissible work, but where it was for prohibited work[6] conclude that they are forbidden [as sacrifices]! So it was necessary [to have this verse from which we infer that the animals may be offered even if they had been used for prohibited work]. But it could likewise have been derived from the following: *Neither from the hand of a stranger shall ye offer the bread of your God of any of these*[7]—these you shall not offer, but you may offer animals which have been used for work!—[This verse][5] is necessary, because it might have occurred to you to say, This only applies when they were worked while they were still not designated as sacrifices, but when they were worked after having been designated as sacrifices conclude that they are forbidden! So it was necessary [to have

(1) Cf. p. 236, n. 7. (2) E.g., the lambs offered on the Passover are specified as being *of the first year*, (Num. XXVIII, 19). (3) From the restrictive particle written with the heifer. (4) Lev. XXII, 22. (5) The *'wherewith'* stated with the heifer. (6) E.g., on the Sabbath. (7) Ibid. 25.

this verse from which we infer that even then they are acceptable as offerings].

The above text [teaches]: 'Rab Judah said in the name of Rab: If a person laid a bundle of sacks upon it, it is disqualified; but with a heifer [it is not disqualified] until it draws [a load]'. It is objected: *Yoke*[1]—I have only mention of a yoke; whence is it that there are other [disqualifications on account of] work having been done by it? You may argue by *a fortiori* reasoning: if a heifer which is not disqualified by a blemish is disqualified by having been used for work, how much more must a [red] cow, which is disqualified by a blemish, be disqualified by having been used for various kinds of work! And if you like you may argue:[2] It is stated here *'yoke'* and there [with the heifer] it is stated *'yoke'*, as there the various kinds of work disqualify, so here [with the red cow] the various kinds of work disqualify. But why have this alternative argument?[3]—Because you might reply [as mentioned above], 'It can, however, be objected: This is right for a heifer because it is also disqualified by an age-limit'. Or it might also [be objected] that the case of animals destined as sacrifices proves [the contrary, thus:] a blemish disqualifies them but the fact that they were used for work does not disqualify them. [Therefore the alternative line of reasoning is employed:] It is stated here *'yoke'* and there [with the heifer] it is stated *'yoke'*; as there the various kinds of work [disqualify], so here [with the red cow] the various kinds of work [disqualify].

Now from the same line of reasoning: You may conclude as there [with the heifer it is not disqualified] until it draws [a load], so here [with the red cow it is not disqualified] until it draws [a load]![4]—This is a matter disputed by Tannaim. Some of them deduce it from the instance of the heifer,[5] while others deduce it from [the law of the red] cow itself.[6] For it has been taught: '*Yoke*'—I have mention only of a yoke; whence is it that various kinds of work [disqualify]? There is a text to state, *Upon which never came yoke*[7]—

(1) Num. XIX, 2. (2) Not by *a fortiori* reasoning but from the analogous occurrence of *'yoke'*. (3) Why does not the first suffice? (4) Which refutes Rab Judah. (5) This is the Tanna of the Baraitha cited. He will accordingly not disqualify the cow until it draws. (6) The Tanna who follows. (7) Num. XIX, 2.

i.e., [work] of any sort. If that is so, why is *'yoke'* specified? A yoke disqualifies whether during the time of work or not during the time of work,[1] but the various kinds of work only disqualify during the time of work.[2] But say that *'upon which never came'* is general and *'yoke'* is particular, and where there is a case of general and particular, only what is in the particular is in the general[3]—viz., a yoke only [disqualifies] and nothing else! The phrase *'which'* is inclusive [of various kinds of work], and there is a similar teaching in connection with the heifer as follows: *Yoke*[4]—I have mention only of a yoke; whence is it that various kinds of work [disqualify]? There is a text to state, *'Which hath not been wrought with'*—i.e., [work] of any sort. If that is so, why is *'yoke'* specified? A yoke disqualifies whether during the time of work or not during the time of work, but the various kinds of work only disqualify during the time of work. But say that *'which hath not been wrought with'* is general and *'yoke'* is particular, and where there is a case of general and particular, only what is in the particular is in the general—viz. a yoke [disqualifies] and nothing else![5]—The phrase *'which'* is inclusive [of various kinds of work].

R. Abbahu said: I asked R. Joḥanan, To what extent must there be drawing by a yoke [to constitute a disqualification]?[6]—He replied, The full extent of the yoke. The question was asked, Does this mean its length or breadth? One of the Rabbis, named R. Jacob, answered: The statement of R. Joḥanan was explained to me as indicating drawing by a yoke to the extent of a handbreadth in its breadth. Then [R. Joḥanan] should have said, A handbreadth! —He intended to inform us that the minimum of a yoke [in its breadth] is a handbreadth. For what purpose does he deduce this? —For buying and selling.

(1) If he put the yoke on the animal to ease the load and not for the purpose of drawing it. (2) If, e.g., he put sacks upon it not as a burden, there is no disqualification. Where, however, the sacks were placed as a load there is immediate disqualification, even though the cow did not draw. This is in agreement with Rab Judah. (3) The general rule must be restricted in application to what is contained in the particular. (4) Deut. XXI, 3. (5) This is one of the principles of hermeneutics according to R. Ishmael. V. B.Ḳ., 54a. (6) With a heifer.

R. Johanan b. Saul said: Why does the Torah mention that he should bring a heifer into a ravine? The Holy One, blessed be He, said, Let something which did not produce fruit[1] have its neck broken in a place which is not fertile and atone for one who was not allowed to produce fruit. What [does this last word] 'fruit' mean? If I answer [that it means] offspring, then according to this argument we should not break a heifer's neck if [the man found dead] was old or castrated! Therefore [by 'fruit' must be understood the performance of] commandments.[2]

AND BRING IT DOWN TO A RAVINE WHICH IS STONY—'ETHAN' IS TO BE UNDERSTOOD IN ITS LITERAL SENSE OF 'HARD'. Our Rabbis taught: Whence is it that *'ethan'* means 'hard'? As it is said, [46b] *Strong* [ethan] *is thy dwelling-place, and thy nest is set in the rock;*[3] and it states, *Hear, O ye mountains, the Lord's controversy, and ye enduring foundations* [ethanim] *of the earth.*[4] Others, however, say, Whence is it that *'ethan'* means 'old'? As it is stated, *It is an* ethan *nation, it is an ancient nation.*[5]

THEY THEN BREAK ITS NECK WITH A HATCHET FROM BEHIND. What is the reason [that it is done from behind]?—He derives it by the analogous word 'breaking' [stated] in the case of a bird brought as a sin-offering.[6]

THE SITE MAY NEVER BE SOWN OR TILLED. Our Rabbis taught: *Which is neither plowed nor sown*[7]—this refers to the past; such is the statement of R. Joshiah. R. Jonathan says: It refers to the future. Raba said: Nobody disputes as to the future since it is written, *It shall not be sown;*[8] when they differ as to the past, R. Joshiah argues, Is it written, '*And* it shall not be tilled'[9]? And

(1) A heifer less than a year old could not bring forth young. (2) Which produces a harvest of merit; and he was prevented by his murder from doing this. (3) Num. XXIV, 21. (4) Micah VI, 2. *'Foundations'*, being parallel to *'mountains'*, has a similar meaning. (5) Jer. V, 15. The true meaning here is *'enduring'*, but the word is taken as defined by what follows. (6) Cf. Lev. V, 8 where the Hebrew is 'from the back of the neck'. (7) Deut. XXI, 4. (8) So the Hebrew literally. They all agree that the site may not be sown or tilled after the ceremony has taken place there. (9) Since the text has not this form, it must refer to the past.

R. Jonathan argues, Is it written, 'Which has not been tilled'?[1] And [how does] R. Joshiah [meet R. Jonathan's argument]?—The relative pronoun *'which'* must be understood of the past.[2] And R. Jonathan?—*'Which'* is employed in an inclusive sense.[3]

BUT IT IS PERMITTED TO CARD FLAX AND CHISEL STONES THERE. Our Rabbis taught: *'Which is neither plowed nor sown'*—I have here only sowing; whence is it that the other kinds of agricultural work [are prohibited]? There is a text to state, *'which is neither plowed'*—i.e., [agricultural labour] in any form. If that is so, why is it stated *'nor sown'?*[4] Its purpose is to inform us that as sowing is special since it is connected with the soil itself, so everything which is connected with the soil itself [is forbidden], to the exclusion of carding flax and chiselling stones which are not connected with the soil itself. But argue that *'which is neither plowed'* is general and *'nor sown'* particular, and where there is a case of general and particular, only what is in the particular is in the general—viz. sowing only [is forbidden] but nothing else!—The term *'which'* is employed in an inclusive sense.

THE ELDERS OF THAT CITY THEN WASH THEIR HANDS etc. Our Rabbis taught: *And all the elders of that city, who are nearest unto the slain man, shall wash their hands over the heifer whose neck was broken in the valley,*[5] There was no need to state, *'whose neck was broken'!*[6] Why, then, is *'whose neck was broken'* added? [It signifies], Over the place of the heifer's neck where it was broken. They then declare, *'Our hands have not shed this blood, neither have our eyes seen it'*. But can it enter our minds that [the members of a] Court of Justice shed blood! [The meaning of their statement is], however, [The man found dead] did not come to us for help and we dismissed him without supplying him with food, we did not see him and let him go without an escort.

It has been taught: R. Meir used to say: We may compel a

(1) Consequently it can only refer to the future. (2) Since it would not be used if a command were implied, and the Torah would have stated: 'it shall not be tilled'. (3) To include all kinds of agricultural work, as explained below. (4) Since sowing is included in agricultural labour. (5) Deut. XXI, 6. (6) The words seem redundant.

person to escort [a traveller],[1] because the reward for escorting is limitless; as it is said, *And the watchers saw a man come forth out of the city, and they said unto him, Shew us, we pray thee, the entrance into the city, and we will deal kindly with thee.*[2] It continues, *And he shewed them the entrance into the city.*[3] What was the kindness they did to him? They slew the whole of the city at the edge of the sword, but let that man and his family go.

And the man went into the land of the Hittites, and built a city, and called the name thereof Luz: which is the name thereof unto this day.[4] It has been taught: That is the Luz in which they dye the blue;[5] that is the Luz against which Sennacherib marched without disturbing it,[6] against which Nebuchadnezzar marched without destroying it, and even the Angel of Death has no permission to pass through it, but when the old men there become tired of life[7] they go outside the wall and then die. For is not the matter[8] an *a fortiori* inference? If this Canaanite, who did not utter a word or walk a step,[9] caused deliverance to come to himself and his seed unto the end of all generations, how much more so he who performs the act of escorting by actually going with the person! How did he show them [the way]?—Hezekiah said: He just curved his mouth for them;[10] R. Johanan said: He pointed for them with his finger. There is a teaching in agreement with R. Johanan, viz., Because this Canaanite pointed with his finger, he caused deliverance to come to himself and his seed unto the end of all generations.

R. Joshua b. Levi said: Whoever is on a journey and has no escort should occupy [his mind] with Torah;[11] as it is said, *For they shall be a chaplet of grace unto thy head, and chains about thy neck.*[12] R. Joshua b. Levi also said: Because of the four paces with which Pharaoh

(1) [Or the court compels a town to provide escorts for travellers.] (2) Judg. I, 24. (3) Ibid. 25. (4) Ibid. 26. (5) For the fringes (Num. XV, 38). The purpose of this statement and what follows is to illustrate the words '*which is the name thereof unto this day*', showing that the city survived destruction and still exists. (6) By not plundering it and exiling the inhabitants. (7) Lit., 'their mind becomes loathsome to them'. (8) That the reward for escorting is limitless. (9) It merely states '*he showed them*'. (10) I.e., he made inarticulate sounds. (11) As a means of protection. (12) Prov. I, 9. The Hebrew word for *chaplet* is the same as for 'escort'.

accompanied Abraham, as it is said, *And Pharaoh gave men charge concerning him* etc.,[1] he [was allowed to] enslave the latter's descendants for four hundred years, as it is said, *And shall serve them, and they shall afflict them four hundred years.*[2] Rab Judah said in the name of Rab: Whoever accompanies his neighbour four cubits in a city will come to no harm [when on a journey]. Rabina accompanied Raba b. Isaac four cubits in a city; danger threatened him but he was saved.

Our Rabbis taught: A teacher [accompanies] his pupils until the outskirts[3] of a city; one colleague [accompanies] another up to the Sabbath-limit;[4] a pupil [accompanies] his master a distance without limit.[5] But how far?[6]—R. Sheṣheth said: Up to a *parasang*. This only applies when his master is not a distinguished scholar; but should his master be a distinguished scholar [he accompanies him] three *parasangs*.

R. Kahana once accompanied R. Shimi b. Ashi from Pum-Nahara to Be-Ẓinyatha.[7] When they arrived there, he said to him, 'Is it true what you say, that these palms of Babylon are from the time of Adam?' He answered, 'You have reminded me of something which R. Jose b. Ḥanina said, viz., What means that which is written, *Through a land that no man passed through, and where no man dwelt?*[8] Since no man passed through it, how could anyone dwell there, and since nobody dwelt there how could anyone pass through it! But [the meaning is], A land concerning which Adam decreed that it should be inhabited has become inhabited, and a land concerning which Adam did not so decree has not been inhabited'.[9] R. Mordecai accompanied R. Ashi from Hagronia[10] to Be-Kafi;[11] another version is to Be-Dura.[12]

(1) Gen. XII, 20. (2) Ibid. XV, 13. (3) [I.e., seventy cubits and two thirds beyond the outer range of the houses of the city. V. Ned. 56*a*.] (4) V. p. 136, n. 7. (5) (It is one of those deeds of kindliness to the performance of which no *maximum* is set; v. next note.] (6) [I.e., what *minimum* distance must he accompany his teacher?] (7) [Lit., 'Among the Palms', the former was near the Tigris, the latter was the district of the old city of Babylon, to which Sura belonged and which was rich in palms; cf. Sanh. 96*b* (Obermeyer, *op. cit.* p. 195).] (8) Jer. II, 6. (9) Accordingly Adam must have decreed that those palms should grow there. (10) Outside Nehardea. (11) [Be Kufai. A village four parasangs west of Bagdad, v. Obermeyer, *op. cit.* p. 267.] (12)[Be-Duraja, S.W. of Bagdad.

R. Johanan said in the name of R. Meir: Whoever does not escort others or allow himself to be escorted is as though he sheds blood; for had the men of Jericho escorted Elisha he would not have stirred up bears against the children, as it is said, *And he went up from thence unto Bethel; and as he was going up by the way, there came forth little children out of the city, and mocked him, and said unto him, Go up, thou bald head; go up, thou bald head.*[1] What they said to him was, 'Go up, thou who hast made this place bald for us!'[2] What means *'little children'?*[3]—R. Eleazar said, *Ne'arim* [children] means they were bare [*menu'arim*] of precepts; *'little'* means they were little of faith.[4] A Tanna taught: They were youths [*ne'arim*] but they behaved like little children. R. Joseph demurred to this: But perhaps they were so called after the name of the place; for is it not written, *And the Syrians had gone out in bands, and had brought away captive out of the land of Israel a little maid,*[5] and the question is asked by us *a maid* [*na'arah*] and *little?*[6] And R. Pedath explained, She was a little girl from a place called Ne'uran![7]—In this passage her place is not specified,[8] but in the other their place is specified.[9]

And he looked behind him and saw them, and cursed them in the name of the Lord.[10] What did he see?—Rab said: He actually looked upon them, as it has been taught: Rabban Simeon b. Gamaliel says: Wherever the Sages set their eyes there is either death or calamity.[11] Samuel said: He saw that their mothers had all become conceived

This would be about two hours beyond Be Kafi; (Obermeyer, *op. cit.*, p. 268)]. This is cited to show how far a disciple escorted his teacher.

(1) II Kings II, 23. *'He went up'* implies that he was unaccompanied. (2) He had sweetened the waters in that place (ibid. 19ff.) and so had caused loss to the people of the vicinity who had profited by selling drinkable water. Hence the ill-feeling against him. (3) *'Little'* appears to be superfluous. (4) Because they worried about their livelihood since they could no longer sell water. (5) Ibid. V, 2. (6) *Na'arah* implies that she was young (v. Glos.). (7) Therefore it is suggested that in the other verse *ne'arim* means 'men of Ne'uran'. In Josh. XVI, 7 there is a town called Naarath. (8) It is merely stated *'out of the land of Israel'*, so *Na'arah* could possibly indicate a place name. (9) We gather from the context that the children belonged to Jericho. (10) II Kings II, 24. (11) It was believed that the Rabbis were endowed with this power and the Talmud relates several anecdotes on the subject.

with them on the Day of Atonement.[1] R. Isaac the smith said: He saw that their hair was plaited as with Amorites.[2] R. Joḥanan said: He saw that there was no sap of the commandments in them. But perhaps there would have been such in their descendants![3]—R. Eleazar said: Neither in them nor in their descendants unto the end of all generations.

And there came forth two she-bears out of the wood, and tore forty and two children of them.[4] [47a] Rab and Samuel [differ in their interpretation]; one said it was a miracle, while the other said it was a miracle within a miracle. He who said it was a miracle did so because there was a forest but there were no bears;[5] he who said it was a miracle within a miracle did so because there was no forest nor were there any bears. [But according to the latter interpretation] there need have been [provided] bears but not a forest!—[It was required] because [the bears] would have been frightened.[6]

R. Ḥanina said: On account of the forty-two sacrifices which Balak, king of Moab, offered,[7] were forty-two children cut off from Israel. But it is not so; for Rab Judah has said in the name of Rab: Always should a man occupy himself with Torah and the commandments even though it be not for their own sake,[8] for from [occupying himself with them] not for their own sake he comes to do so for their own sake; because as a reward for the forty-two sacrifices which Balak, king of Moab, offered,[9] he merited that Ruth should issue from him and from her issued Solomon concerning whom it is written, *A thousand burnt-offerings did Solomon offer!*[10] And R. Jose b. Ḥoni said: Ruth was the daughter of Eglon the son of Balak![11]—Nevertheless his desire was to curse Israel.[12]

(1) When cohabitation is forbidden. (2) Lit., 'he saw they had a *belorith*'. They aped heathen manners. On *belorith* v. Sanh. (Sonc. ed.) p. 114, n. 5. (3) So why should they have perished on that account? (4) II Kings II, 24. (5) These were miraculously created for the occasion. (6) If there was no forest provided for them in which they could hide, they would not have dared to attack the children. (7) Num. XXIII, 1, 14, 29. (8) Without the expectation of reward. (9) Although he did not offer them for their own sake. (10) I Kings III, 4. V. Hor. (Son. ed.) p. 75. (11) So this was Balak's reward and not the death of the children. (12) And so he had his reward in the death of these children.

And the men of the city said unto Elisha, Behold, we pray thee, the situation of this city is pleasant, as my lord seeth etc.[1] [But how could it be so] since *'the water is naught and the land miscarrieth'!* What, then, was its pleasantness?—R. Ḥanin said: The favour of a place in the estimation of its inhabitants. R. Joḥanan said: There are three kinds of favour: the favour of a locality in the estimation of its inhabitants, the favour of a woman in the estimation of her husband, and the favour of an article in the estimation of its purchaser.

Our Rabbis taught: Elisha was afflicted with three illnesses: one because he stirred up the bears against the children, one because he thrust Gehazi away with both his hands, and one of which he died; as it is said, *Now Elisha was fallen sick of his sickness whereof he died.*[2]

Our Rabbis have taught: Always let the left hand thrust away and the right hand draw near. Not like Elisha who thrust Gehazi away with both his hands (and not like R. Joshua b. Peraḥiah who thrust one of his disciples away with both his hands).[3] How is it with Elisha? As it is written, *And Naaman said, Be content, take two talents,*[4] and it is written, *And he said unto him, Went not my heart with thee when the man turned again from his chariot to meet thee? Is it a time to receive money, and to receive garments, and oliveyards, and sheep and oxen, and manservants and maidservants?*[5] But had he received all these things? Silver and garments were what he had received!—R. Isaac said: At that time Elisha was engaged [in the study of the Law concerning] the eight kinds of [unclean] creeping things;[6] so he said to [Gehazi], 'You wicked person, the time has arrived for you to receive the reward for [studying the law of] the eight creeping things.'[7] *The leprosy therefore of Naaman shall cleave unto thee and unto thy seed for ever.*[8]

(1) II Kings II, 19. (2) Ibid. XIII, 14. *Sick* and *sickness* denote two, apart from his fatal illness. (3) MSS. and old editions read Jesus the Nazarene. R. T. Herford sees in Gehazi a hidden reference to Paul. Cf. his *Christianity in Talmud and Midrash*, pp. 97ff. (4) II Kings V, 23. (5) Ibid. 26. (6) Name of the Chapter in Mishnah Shabbath, XIV, 1, cf. Lev. XI, 29ff. (7) Referring to the eight kinds of presents he had accepted. That will be his reward in this world so that he may be punished in the Hereafter. For a fuller version v. Sanh. (Sonc. ed.) p. 735. (8) II Kings V, 27. *'For ever'* indicates the World to Come.

Now there were four leprous men[1]—R. Joḥanan said: This refers to Gehazi and his three sons. *And Elisha came to Damascus*[2]—why did he go there?[3]—R. Joḥanan said: He went to induce Gehazi to repent but he refused. He said to him, 'Repent'; but he replied, 'Thus have I received from thee that whoever sinned and caused others to sin is deprived of the power of doing penitence'. What had he done? Some say, He applied a loadstone to the idolatrous image of Jeroboam[4] and suspended it between heaven and earth. Others say, He engraved upon it the Name [of God] so that it used to exclaim, 'I [am the Lord thy God]' and 'Thou shalt have no [other God beside me]'. Still others say, He drove the Rabbis from before him, as it is written, *And the sons of the prophets said unto Elisha, Behold now, the place where we dwell before thee is too strait for us*[5]—hence, up to then it had not been too strait.

What[6] was the incident with R. Joshua b. Peraḥiah?—When King Jannaeus[7] put the Rabbis to death. Simeon b. Shetaḥ was hid by his sister, whilst R. Joshua b. Peraḥiah fled to Alexandria in Egypt. When there was peace,[8] Simeon b. Shetaḥ sent [this message to him]: 'From me, Jerusalem, the Holy city, to thee Alexandria in Egypt. O my sister, my husband[9] dwelleth in thy midst and I abide desolate'. [R. Joshua] arose and came back and found himself in a certain inn where they paid him great respect. He said, 'How beautiful is this *'aksania'*!'[10] One of his disciples[11] said to him, 'My master, her eyes are narrow!' He replied to him, 'Wicked person! Is it with such thoughts that thou occupiest thyself!' He sent forth four hundred horns and excommunicated

(1) II Kings VII, 3. (2) Ibid. VIII, 7. (3) V. Sanh. (Sonc. ed.) p. 734, n. 8. (4) Cf. I Kings XII, 28. (5) II Kings VI, 1. (6) The following paragraph is deleted in censored editions, v. Sanh. (Sonc. ed.) p. 736, n. 2. (7) Alexander Jannaeus, king of Israel from 104 to 78 B.C.E., a persecutor of the Pharisees. The chronological discrepancy is obvious since he lived a century before Jesus, v. however, Sanh. (Sonc. ed.) *loc. cit.* (8) On his death-bed the King advised the Queen to put her confidence in the Pharisees. V. Josephus, *Ant.* XIII, XV, 5. (9) His teacher, R. Joshua. (10) The word means 'inn' and 'female innkeeper'. The Rabbi intended it in the first sense, Jesus in the second. (11) MSS.: 'Jesus'.

him.[1] [The disciple] came before him on many occasions, saying, 'Receive me'; but he refused to notice him. One day while [R. Joshua] was reciting the *Shema'*, he came before him. His intention was to receive him and he made a sign to him with his hand, but the disciple thought he was repelling him. So he went and set up a brick and worshipped it. [R. Joshua] said to him, 'Repent'; but he answered him, 'Thus have I received from thee that whoever sinned and caused others to sin is deprived of the power of doing penitence'. A Master has said: The disciple practised magic and led Israel astray.

It has been taught: R. Simeon b. Eleazar says: Also human nature[2] should a child and woman thrust aside with the left hand and draw near with the right hand.[3]

MISHNAH. IF THE MURDERER WAS DISCOVERED BEFORE THE HEIFER'S NECK WAS BROKEN, IT GOES FREE AND FEEDS WITH THE HERD; BUT IF AFTER THE HEIFER'S NECK WAS BROKEN, IT IS BURIED IN THAT PLACE BECAUSE IT CAME THERE FROM THE OUTSET IN CONNECTION WITH A MATTER OF DOUBT,[4] AND ATONED FOR THE DOUBT WHICH IS NOW GONE. IF THE HEIFER'S NECK WAS BROKEN AND AFTERWARDS THE MURDERER IS DISCOVERED, BEHOLD HE IS EXECUTED.

IF ONE WITNESS SAYS 'I SAW THE MURDERER' AND ONE WITNESS SAYS 'YOU DID NOT SEE HIM';[5] OR IF A WOMAN SAYS 'I SAW HIM' AND ANOTHER WOMAN SAYS 'YOU DID NOT SEE HIM', THEY BREAK ITS NECK. IF ONE WITNESS SAYS 'I SAW HIM' AND TWO SAY 'YOU DID NOT SEE HIM', THEY BREAK ITS NECK. IF TWO SAY 'WE SAW HIM' AND ONE SAYS TO THEM

(1) A horn is blown at the ceremony of excommunication. The large number used on this occasion indicated the extreme severity of the penalty. (2) One must learn to control it so as to avoid extremes. (3) [One must not be too severe in chiding a child or reproving a wife lest they be driven to despair.] (4) The unknown murderer. (5) [I.e., 'I was present with you at the time of the alleged murder and testify that it did not take place.' J. reads 'I did not see it', and similarly in the following clause substitutes the first person for the second.]

'YOU DID NOT SEE HIM', THEY DO NOT BREAK ITS NECK.[1]

WHEN MURDERERS MULTIPLIED THE CEREMONY OF BREAKING A HEIFER'S NECK WAS DISCONTINUED. THAT WAS WHEN ELIEZER B. DINAI, ALSO CALLED TEḤINAH B. PERISHAH, APPEARED;[2] HE WAS AFTERWARDS RENAMED 'SON OF THE MURDERER'. WHEN ADULTERERS MULTIPLIED THE CEREMONY OF THE BITTER WATER WAS DISCONTINUED AND IT WAS R. JOḤANAN B. ZAKKAI WHO DISCONTINUED IT, AS IT IS SAID, I WILL NOT PUNISH YOUR DAUGHTERS WHEN THEY COMMIT WHOREDOM, NOR YOUR BRIDES WHEN THEY COMMIT ADULTERY, FOR THEY THEMSELVES ETC.[3] WHEN JOSE B. JOEZER OF ZEREDAH AND JOSE B. JUDAH OF JERUSALEM DIED, THE GRAPE-CLUSTERS[4] CEASED, AS IT IS SAID, THERE IS NO CLUSTER TO EAT; MY SOUL DESIRETH THE FIRST RIPE FIG.[5]

JOḤANAN THE HIGH PRIEST[6] BROUGHT TO AN END THE CONFESSION MADE AT THE PRESENTATION OF THE TITHE.[7] HE ALSO ABOLISHED THE WAKERS AND THE KNOCKERS[8] [47*b*]. UP TO HIS DAYS THE HAMMER USED TO STRIKE[9] IN JERUSALEM, AND IN HIS DAYS THERE WAS NO NEED TO INQUIRE ABOUT DEMAI.[10]

GEMARA. Our Rabbis taught: Whence is it that if the heifer's neck had been broken, and the murderer is afterwards discovered,

(1) The single witness does not upset the evidence of two, so there is no doubt about the murderer. (2) He was a notorious bandit who committed numerous murders; (v. Josephus, *Ant*. XX, 6, 1; 8, 5.) (3) Hos. IV, 14. (4) Descriptive of Rabbis of exceptional learning. These two Rabbis flourished in the first half of the second cent. B.C.E. and were the first of the *Zugoth* or 'Pairs' of teachers who preserved and passed on the Torah-lore accumulated by the men of the Great Assembly. [Lauterbach. J.Z. (*JQR* VI, p. 32, n. 34) explains this to mean that with his death teachers ceased to act as a body, reporting only such teachings as represented the opinion of the whole group to which they belonged, but began to report rulings of individual teachers.] (5) Micah VII, 1. (6) John Hyrcanus who reigned over Judea from 135 to 104 B.C.E. (7) Cf. Deut. XXVI, 13f. (8) These terms are explained in the Gemara. (9) V. note on the Gemara *infra*. (10) Produce about which there is uncertainty whether it had been tithed. The Gemara will explain what is intended.

they do not set him free? There is a text to state, *And no expiation can be made for the land for the blood that is shed therein, but by the blood of him that shed it.*[1]

IF ONE WITNESS SAYS, 'I SAW THE MURDERER' etc. The reason [why his evidence is not accepted] is because there is somebody who contradicts him; therefore if there is nobody who contradicts him, one witness is believed. Whence is this?—As our Rabbis taught: *And it be not known who hath smitten him*[2]—hence if it be known who had smitten him, even by one person at the other end of the world, they do not break the neck. R. Akiba says: Whence is it that if the Sanhedrin saw a person commit murder, but they do not recognise him, the neck of the heifer is not broken? There is a text to state, *Neither have our eyes seen it;*[3] but [in this case] they had seen it.[4]

Now that you admit that one witness is believed, how is it possible for another individual to contradict him? Surely 'Ulla has said: Wherever the Torah accepts the testimony of one witness, he is regarded as two [witnesses], but the evidence of one is not regarded as the evidence of two![5]—'Ulla can reply to you, Read in the Mishnah: They do not break its neck. Similarly said R. Isaac, Read in the Mishnah: They do not break its neck; but R. Ḥiyya said, Read in the Mishnah: They break its neck. Then R. Ḥiyya is in conflict with the teaching of 'Ulla!—There is no contradiction, one case referring to evidence given simultaneously[6] and the other when one witness follows the others.[7]

The Mishnah declares: IF ONE WITNESS SAYS 'I SAW THE MURDERER' AND TWO SAY 'YOU DID NOT SEE HIM', THEY BREAK ITS NECK. Consequently if there is one against one, they do not break its neck; and this is a refutation of R. Ḥiyya's statement![8]—But according to your own argument, cite the con-

(1) Num. XXXV, 33. (2) Deut. XXI, 1. (3) Ibid. 7. (4) Consequently the ceremony is not performed. (5) But according to the Mishnah, if one is contradicted by one, the former is not accepted and the neck is broken. (6) Then one witness can contradict another. (7) The evidence of the first witness having been accepted is regarded as that of two. (8) He proposed that when one is against one the Mishnah should read: They break its neck.

tinuation: IF TWO SAY 'WE SAW HIM' AND ONE SAYS TO THEM 'YOU DID NOT SEE HIM', THEY DO NOT BREAK ITS NECK. Consequently if there is one against one, they do break its neck![1] But our Mishnah deals entirely with disqualified witnesses,[2] and is in accord with R. Nehemiah who said,[3] Wherever the Torah accepts the testimony of one witness, [the decision] follows the majority of persons [who testify], so that two women against one woman is identical with two men against one man. But there are some who declare that wherever a competent witness came [and testified] first, even a hundred women are regarded as equal to one witness; and with what circumstance are we dealing here? For example, if it was a woman who came first [and testified]; and R. Nehemiah's statement is to be construed thus: R. Nehemiah says: Wherever the Torah accepts the testimony of one witness, [the decision] follows the majority of persons [who testify], so that two women against one woman is identical with two men against one man, but two women against one man is like half and half. Why, then, have we two teachings concerning disqualified witnesses?[4] What you might have said was that when we follow the majority of persons [who testify] it is for taking the severer view, but to take the lenient view we do not follow [the majority]. Therefore [the Mishnah] informs us [of one case where the neck is broken and one where it is not, and in each the majority is followed].

WHEN MURDERERS MULTIPLIED etc. Our Rabbis taught: When murderers multiplied the ceremony of breaking a heifer's neck was discontinued, because it is only performed in a case of doubt; but when murderers multiplied openly, the ceremony of breaking a heifer's neck was discontinued.

WHEN ADULTERERS MULTIPLIED etc. Our Rabbis taught: *And the man shall be free from iniquity*[5]—at the time when the man is free from iniquity, the water proves his wife; but when the man is not free from iniquity, the water does not prove his wife. Why,

(1) Which supports R. Ḥiyya and in apparent contradiction to the first clause. (2) Women and slaves. (3) What follows is quoted from *supra* 31*b et seq.*, q.v. for notes. (4) In the two clauses of our Mishnah which have been explained as referring to the evidence of women and slaves. (5) Num. V, 31.

then, [was it necessary for the Mishnah to add]: AS IT IS SAID, 'I WILL NOT PUNISH YOUR DAUGHTERS WHEN THEY COMMIT WHOREDOM etc'? Should you say that his own iniquity [prevents the water from proving his wife] but the iniquity of his sons and daughters does not, come and hear: 'I WILL NOT PUNISH YOUR DAUGHTERS WHEN THEY COMMIT WHOREDOM, NOR YOUR BRIDES WHEN THEY COMMIT ADULTERY'. And should you say that his sin with a married woman [prevents the water from proving his wife] but not if it was with an unmarried woman, come and hear: 'FOR THEY THEMSELVES GO ASIDE WITH WHORES AND WITH THE HARLOTS etc.' What means *And the people that doth not understand shall be overthrown?*[1] R. Eleazar said: The prophet spoke to Israel, If you are scrupulous with yourselves, the water will prove your wives; otherwise the water will not prove your wives.

When hedonists multiplied, justice became perverted,[2] conduct deteriorated and there is no satisfaction [to God] in the world. When they who displayed partiality in judgment multiplied, the command *Ye shall not be afraid [of the face of man]*[3] became void and *Ye shall not respect [persons in judgment]*[4] ceased to be practised; and people threw off the yoke of heaven and placed upon themselves the yoke of human beings. When they who engaged in whisperings in judgment[5] multiplied, fierceness of [the divine] anger increased against Israel and the *Shechinah* departed; because it is written, *He judgeth among the judges.*[6] When there multiplied [men of whom it is said] *Their heart goeth after their gain,*[7] there multiplied they *who call evil good and good evil.*[8] When there multiplied they '*who call evil good and good evil*', woes[9] increased in the world. When they who draw out their spittle[10] multiplied, the arrogant increased, disciples diminished, and Torah went about [looking] for them who would study it. When the arrogant multiplied, the daughters of Israel began to marry arrogant men, because our generation looks only to the outward appearance. But that is not so; for a Master has

(1) Hos. IV, 14. (2) Judges accepted bribes. (3) Deut. I, 17. (4) Ibid. (5) To influence the judges in favour of one party. (6) Ps. LXXXII, 1, i.e., God is only with honest judges. (7) Ezek. XXXIII, 31. (8) Isa. V, 20. (9) The word *woe* occurs frequently in Isa. V. (10) As a mark of ostentation.

declared, An arrogant person is not acceptable even to the members of his household, as it is said, *A haughty man one abideth not at home*[1]—i.e., even in his own house!—At first they jump round him, but in the end he becomes repugnant to them.

When there multiplied they who forced their goods upon householders,[2] bribery increased as well as miscarriage of justice, and happiness ceased. When there multiplied [judges] who said 'I accept your favour' and 'I shall appreciate your favour', there was an increase of *Every man did that which was right in his own eyes;*[3] common persons were raised to eminence, the eminent were brought low, and the kingdom [of Israel] deteriorated more and more. When envious men and plunderers [of the poor] multiplied, there increased they who hardened their hearts and closed their hands from lending [to the needy], and they transgressed what is written in the Torah, viz., *Beware that there be not* etc.[4] When there multiplied women who had *stretched forth necks and wanton eyes,*[5] [the need] increased for the bitter water but it ceased [to be used]. When receivers of gifts multiplied, the days [of human life] became fewer and years were shortened; as it is written, *But he that hateth gifts shall live.*[6] When the haughty of heart multiplied, dissensions increased in Israel. When the disciples of Shammai and Hillel multiplied who had not served [their teachers] sufficiently, dissensions increased in Israel and the Torah became like two Toroth. When there multiplied they who accepted charity of Gentiles, Israel became on top and they below, Israel went forward and they backward.[7]

WHEN JOSE B. JOEZER DIED etc. What does 'grape-clusters' [*eshkoloth*] mean?—Rab Judah said in the name of Samuel: A man in whom is everything [*ish she-hakol bo*].

JOḤANAN THE HIGH PRIEST BROUGHT TO AN END THE CONFESSION MADE AT THE PRESENTATION OF THE TITHE etc. What was his reason?—R. Jose b. Ḥanina said: Because people were not presenting it according to the regulation; for the All-

(1) Hab. II, 5 *sic*. (2) Judges who compelled them to buy against their will. (3) Judg. XVII, 6. (4) Deut. XV, 9. (5) Isa. III, 16. (6) Prov. XV, 27. (7) A euphemism for the reverse: Israel became below etc. This sentence has fallen out of the text in some modern editions.

Merciful said that they should give it to the Levites [48a] whereas we present it to the priests.[1] Then let them make the confession over the other tithes![2]—Resh Laḳish said: Any household which does not make the confession over the first tithe may not make it over the other tithes. For what reason?—Abaye said: Because Scripture deals with that first;[3] This implies that they had separated it [before proceeding to the other tithes]. But surely it has been taught: He also annulled the confession and decreed in respect of *demai*;[4] because he sent [inspectors] throughout the Israelite territory and discovered that they only separated the great *terumah*[5] but as for the first and second tithes some fulfilled the law while others did not.[6] So he said to [the people], 'My sons, come, I will tell you this. Just as in [the neglect] of the "great *terumah*" there is mortal sin,[7] so with [the neglect] to present the *terumah* of the tithe and with the use of untithed produce there is mortal sin'. He thus arose and decreed for them that whoever purchases fruits from an *'Am ha-areẓ*[8] must separate the first and second tithes therefrom. From the first tithe he separates the *terumah* of the tithe and gives it to a priest, and as for the second tithe he

(1) Deut. XXVI, 13 requires that the first tithe should be given to the Levites; but it is related in Yeb. 86*b* that because the Levites refused to join in the return from Babylon, Ezra punished them by having the tithe transferred to the priests. (2) The second and poor tithes. (3) The Rabbis explain the verse as follows: '*Thou shalt give it unto the Levite*' i.e., the first tithe; '*and unto the stranger*' i.e., the tithe of the poor; '*within thy gates*' i.e., the second tithe. (4) The reason given by R. Jose b. Ḥanina. (5) The part which is separated in the first instance is the 'great *terumah*' or offering for the priests, to distinguish it from the '*terumah* of the tithe', i.e., the tenth part given by the Levite of the tithe he receives, to the priest; then the first tithe is taken from the remainder for the Levites; after that the second tithe is removed to be eaten by the owner in Jerusalem (Deut. XIV, 22ff.); and each third year a tithe is allocated to the poor (ibid. XXVI, 12); v. Glos., s.v. *Terumah*. (6) I. H. Weiss (*Dor* I p. 119) suggests that at that time there was a growing aversion against paying the tithe to the Levites, firstly because their status had changed from the period when the land was apportioned among the tribes and they had no share; and secondly because part of the produce had to be paid as a tax to the Government and the law of the tithe pressed very heavily upon the people. (7) I.e., the penalty involved is death at the hands of Heaven. (8) V. p. 110 n. 1.

should go up and eat it in Jerusalem. With regard to the first tithe and the tithe of the poor[1] whoever demands them from his neighbour has the onus of proving [that they had not been already apportioned]![2]—[Johanan] made two decrees: he abolished the confession [over the presentation of the first tithe] in the case of the *Ḥaberim*[3] and decreed in regard to the *demai*[4] of the '*Amme ha-areẓ*.[5]

HE ALSO ABOLISHED THE WAKERS. What does 'WAKERS' mean?—Reḥabah said: The Levites used daily to stand upon the dais and exclaim, *Awake, why sleepest Thou, O Lord?*[6] He said to them, Does, then, the All-Present sleep? Has it not been stated, *Behold, He that keepeth Israel shall neither slumber nor sleep!*[7] But so long as Israel abides in trouble and the Gentiles are in peace and comfort, the words '*Awake, why sleepest Thou, O Lord*'? [should be uttered].[8]

AND KNOCKERS. What does 'KNOCKERS' mean?—Rab Judah said in the name of Samuel: They used to make an incision on the calf between its horns[9] so that the blood should flow into its eyes.[10] [Johanan] came and abolished the practice because it appeared as though [the animal had] a blemish. There is a Baraitha which teaches: They used to strike [the animal] with clubs as is the practice with idolatry. [Johanan] said to them, How long will you feed the altar with *nebeloth!*[11] [How could he have described the carcasses as] *nebeloth* when they had been properly slaughtered!—Rather

(1) Since they are non-holy and may be eaten by any person. (2) This shows that the people neglected the separation of the tithe to the Levite. (3) The opposite of the '*Amme ha-areẓ*. They were most scrupulous in the allocation of the tithes. The reason for his edict was, as stated, because the tithe was presented to a priest and not a Levite. (4) 'Doubtful produce', corn purchased from a farmer about which there is a doubt whether the tithes had been apportioned. (5) Because he learnt from his inspectors that the law was being neglected. It could therefore be safely assumed that the '*Amme ha-areẓ*, were not observing it. Consequently if one purchased their produce, he had the responsibility of apportioning the tithes. (6) Ps. XLIV, 24. (7) Ibid. CXXI, 4. (8) Since his reign was blessed with peace and prosperity, he felt it was unnecessary for the Levites to use the words. (9) Before it was slaughtered for the altar. (10) To prevent it from seeing what was to happen so that it should not struggle. (11) I.e., animals which died not by the act of ritual slaughter.

[should they be described as] *ṭerefoth*,[1] since the membrane of the brain may have been perforated. He [thereupon] arose and ordained rings for them in the ground.[2]

UP TO HIS DAYS THE HAMMER USED TO STRIKE IN JERUSALEM. On the intermediate days of the Festival.[3]

ALL HIS DAYS[4] THERE WAS NO NEED TO INQUIRE ABOUT DEMAI. As we have explained above.[5]

MISHNAH. WHEN THE SANHEDRIN CEASED [TO FUNCTION], SONG CEASED FROM THE PLACES OF FEASTING; AS IT IS SAID, THEY SHALL NOT DRINK WINE WITH A SONG ETC.[6]

WHEN THE FORMER PROPHETS[7] DIED THE URIM AND THUMMIM[8] CEASED. WHEN [THE SECOND] TEMPLE WAS DESTROYED, THE SHAMIR AND NOPHETH ẒUFIM[9] CEASED, AND MEN OF FAITH DISAPPEARED FROM ISRAEL; AS IT IS SAID, HELP, LORD, FOR THE GODLY MAN CEASETH ETC.[10] RABBAN SIMEON B. GAMALIEL SAYS: R. JOSHUA TESTIFIED THAT FROM THE DAY THE TEMPLE WAS DESTROYED, THERE IS NO DAY WITHOUT A CURSE, THE DEW HAS NOT DESCENDED FOR A BLESSING, AND THE FLAVOUR HAS DEPARTED FROM THE FRUITS. R. JOSE SAYS: THE FATNESS[11] WAS ALSO REMOVED FROM THE FRUITS.

(1) Animals found to possess a disqualification during the examination which followed the act of slaughter. (2) To hold the animals fast so that they should not struggle, and the other methods were discontinued. (3) I.e., work used to be done on those days, which were a semi-festival, and he abolished the practice. (4) [The actual reading in our Mishnah is 'IN HIS DAYS'.] (5) The purchaser had the responsibility of separating the tithe himself, so there was no need to inquire whether the produce had been tithed before the sale. (6) Isa. XXIV, 9. The authority of the Sanhedrin was ended by the Roman General Gabinius in the middle of the first cent. B.C.E. Cf. Josephus, Ant. XIV, v. 4. (7) The phrase is explained in the Gemara. (8) V. Ex. XXVIII, 30. (9) *Shamir* is the name of a worm which tradition relates had the power of splitting the hardest stone. The Gemara will explain *Nopheth Ẓufim*, a phrase occurring in Ps. XIX, 11, lit., 'the droppings of the honeycomb'. (10) Ps. XII, 2. That the second and not the first Temple is intended here is proved in Tosaf. to *Giṭ*. 68*a*. (11) Nourishing quality.

R. SIMEON B. ELEAZAR SAYS; [THE CESSATION OF] PURITY HAS REMOVED TASTE AND FRAGRANCE [FROM FRUITS]; [THE CESSATION OF] THE TITHES HAS REMOVED THE FATNESS OF CORN. BUT THE SAGES SAY: IMMORALITY AND WITCHCRAFT DESTROYED EVERYTHING.

GEMARA. How do we know that the text, [*'They shall not drink wine with a song'*], applies to the time when the Sanhedrin ceased?—R. Huna, son of R. Joshua, said: Because Scripture states, *The elders have ceased from the gate, the young men from their music.*[1]

Rab said: The ear which listens to song should be torn off. Raba said: When there is song in a house there is destruction on its threshold; as it is stated, *Their voice shall sing in the windows, desolation shall be in the thresholds, for He hath laid bare the cedar work.*[2] What means *'for he hath laid bare* ['erah] *the cedar work'?*—R. Isaac said: Is a house panelled with cedar-wood a city [*'irah*]?[3] But [the meaning is] even a house panelled with cedars will be overthrown [*mithro'ea'*].[4] R. Ashi said: Infer from this that when destruction begins, it begins on the threshold; as it is stated, *'Desolation shall be in the thresholds'*. Or if you will, deduce it from here: *And the gate is smitten with destruction.*[5] Mar, son of R. Ashi said: I have personally seen him,[6] and he gores like an ox.

R. Huna said: The singing of sailors and ploughmen is permitted, but that of weavers is prohibited.[7] R. Huna abolished singing, and a hundred geese were priced at a *zuz*[8] and a hundred *se'ahs* of wheat at a *zuz* and there was no demand for them [even at that price];[9] R. Ḥisda came and [ordered R. Huna's edict to be] disregarded, and a goose was required [even at the high price of] a *zuz* but was not to be found.[10] R. Joseph said: When men sing

(1) Lam. V, 14. The elders sat in the gate of the city to judge. (2) Zeph. II, 14. The last clause is understood as: even a cedar house, i.e., even the strongly-built house, will be destroyed. (3) So Maharsha. Rashi explains differently. (4) *Hath laid bare* ('erah) is connected with a root רעע 'to be razed'. (5) Isa. XXIV, 12. (6) The demon of destruction, v. B.K. 21*a*. (7) Singing helps the former in their work, but with the latter it is done out of frivolity. (8) A small coin worth about sevenpence. (9) Through the decline of feasting. (10) The demand for geese had become so great.

and women join in it is licentiousness; when women sing and men join in it is like fire in tow.[1] For what practical purpose is this mentioned?—To abolish the latter before the former.[2]

R. Johanan said: Whoever drinks to the accompaniment of the four musical instruments[3] brings five punishments to the world; as it is stated, *Woe unto them that rise up early in the morning, that they may follow strong drink; that tarry late into the night, till wine inflame them! And the harp, and the lute, the tabret and the pipe, and wine, are in their feasts; but they regard not the work of the Lord.*[4] What is written after this? '*Therefore My people are gone into captivity for lack of knowledge*'—they therefore cause captivity in the world; '*and their honourable men are famished*'—they therefore bring hunger into the world; *and their multitude are parched with thirst*[5]—they therefore cause Torah to be forgotten by its students. *And the mean man is bowed down and the great man is humbled*[6]—they therefore cause humiliation to the haters of God[7]—and '*man*' signifies none other than the Holy One, blessed be He, as it is said, *The Lord is a man of war;*[8] '*and the eyes of the lofty are humbled*'—they therefore cause the humiliation of Israel. And what is written after that? *Therefore* [48b] *Sheol hath enlarged her desire and opened her mouth without measure; and their glory, and their multitude, and their pomp, and he that rejoiceth among them, descend into it.*[9]

WHEN THE FORMER PROPHETS DIED. Who are the former prophets?—R. Huna said: They are David, Samuel and Solomon. R. Naḥman said: During the days of David, they were sometimes successful[10] and at other times unsuccessful; for behold, Zadok consulted it and succeeded, whereas Abiathar consulted it and was not successful, as it is said, *And Abiathar went up.*[11] Rabbah b.

(1) A woman's singing aroused sexual passion. The latter is more serious, because it implies a wilful act on the part of the men to listen to the female voices. (2) If both cannot be suppressed at the same time, the latter should receive more attention as being the worse of the two. (3) Mentioned in the verse to be quoted. (4) Isa. V, 11f. (5) Ibid. 13. (6) Ibid. 15. (7) A euphemism for God Himself. (8) Ex. XV, 3. (9) Isa. V, 14. (10) In obtaining knowledge of the future by consulting the *Urim* and *Thummim*. (11) II Sam. XV, 24. This is explained by the Rabbis: he retired from the priesthood because he received no reply from the *Urim* and *Thummim*.

Samuel objected: [It is written], *And he*[1] *set himself to seek God all*[2] *the days of Zechariah who had understanding in the vision of God.*[3] Was this not by means of the *Urim* and *Thummim?*[4]—No, it was through the prophets.

Come and hear: When the first Temple was destroyed, the cities with pasture land[5] were abolished, the *Urim* and *Thummim* ceased, there was no more a king from the House of David; and if anyone incites you to quote, *And the governor said unto them that they should not eat of the most holy things till there stood up a priest with Urim and Thummim,*[6] reply to him: [It is only a phrase for the very remote future] as when one man says to another, 'Until the dead revive and the Messiah, son of David, comes'!—But, said R. Naḥman: Who are the former prophets? [The term 'former'] excludes Haggai, Zechariah, and Malachi who are the latter [prophets]. For our Rabbis have taught: When Haggai, Zechariah and Malachi died, the Holy Spirit[7] departed from Israel; nevertheless they made use of the *Bath Ḳol.*[8] On one occasion [some Rabbis] were sitting in the upper chamber of Gurya's house in Jericho; a *Bath Ḳol* was granted to them from heaven which announced, 'There is in your midst one man who is deserving that the *Shechinah* should alight upon him, but his generation is unworthy of it'. They all looked at Hillel the elder; and when he died, they lamented over him, 'Alas, the pious man! Alas, the humble man! Disciple of Ezra!' On another occasion they were sitting in an upper chamber in Jabneh; a *Bath Ḳol* was granted to them from heaven which announced, 'There is in your midst one man who is deserving that the *Shechinah* should alight upon him, but his generation is unworthy of it'. They all looked at Samuel the Little;[9] and when he

(1) Uzziah, King of Judah. (2) [M.T. reads 'in the days of'.] (3) II Chron. XXVI, 5. (4) Therefore there were *Urim* and *Thummim* in the days of King Uzziah, contrary to the view of R. Huna. (5) For the Levites; v. Num. XXXV, 2. (6) Ezra II, 63. From this verse it would appear that the *Urim* and *Thummim* continued up to the destruction of the first Temple, contrary to the view of R. Huna. (7) Divine inspiration. (8) V. Glos. (9) A famous pupil of Hillel who died about a decade after the destruction of the second Temple.

died, they lamented over him, 'Alas, the humble man! Alas, the pious man! Disciple of Hillel!' At the time of his death he also said,[1] 'Simeon and Ishmael[2] [are destined] for the sword and their colleagues for death, and the rest of the people for spoliation, and great distress will come upon the nation.' They also wished to lament over R. Judah b. Baba,[3] 'Alas, the pious man! Alas, the humble man!' But the times were disturbed and they could not lament publicly over those who had been slain by the government.

WHEN [THE SECOND] TEMPLE WAS DESTROYED, THE SHAMIR CEASED etc. Our Rabbis taught: With the *Shamir* Solomon built the Temple,[4] as it is said, *And the house, when it was in building, was built of stone made ready at the quarry.*[5] The words are to be understood as they are written;[6] such is the statement of R. Judah. R. Nehemiah asked him, Is it possible to say so? Has it not been stated, *All these were of costly stones . . . sawed with saws!*[7] If that be so, why is there a text to state, *There was neither hammer, nor axe nor any tool of iron heard in the house, while it was in the building?*[8] [It means] that they prepared them outside and brought them within. Rabbi said: The statement of R. Judah is probable in connection with the stones of the Sanctuary, and the statement of R. Nehamiah in connection with [Solomon's] house. For what purpose, then, according to R. Nehemiah, was the *Shamir* necessary?—It was required as taught in the following: We may not write with ink upon these stones,[9] because it is said, *Like the engravings of a signet,*[10] nor cut into them with a knife because it is said, *In their settings;*[11] but he writes with ink upon them, shows the *Shamir* [the written strokes] on the outside, and these split of their

(1) Under the influence of the Holy Spirit. (2) Probably Simeon b. Gamaliel and Ishmael b. Elisha who were put to death after the capture of Jerusalem. See the full discussion in R.T. Herford, *op. cit.*, pp. 129ff. (3) A victim of the Hadrianic persecution. For further notes on this passage, v. Sanh. (Sonc. ed.) p. 46. (4) V. *Giṭ.* (Sonc. ed.) p. 323, n. 2. (5) I Kings VI, 7. The Hebrew is 'perfect stone'. (6) I.e., the stones were naturally in a hewn state, as though they had been cut in a quarry. (7) Ibid. VII, 9 referring to Solomon's house. (8) Ibid. VI, 7 referring to the Temple. (9) On the ephod and High Priest's breastplate. (10) Ex. XXVIII, 11. (11) Ibid. 20. Lit., 'in their fullnesses', i.e., no part of the stones may be cut away.

own accord,[1] like a fig which splits open in summer and nothing at all is lost, or like a valley which splits asunder in the rainy season and nothing at all is lost.

Our Rabbis taught: The *Shamir* is a creature about the size of a barley-corn, and was created during the six days of Creation.[2] No hard substance can withstand it. How is it kept? They wrap it in tufts of wool and place it in a leaden tube full of barley-bran.

R. Ammi said: When the first Temple was destroyed, fringed[3] silk and white glass[4] ceased to be used. There is a teaching to the same effect: When the first Temple was destroyed, fringed silk and white glass and iron chariots ceased to be used. Some say, Also wine-jelly[5] which comes from Senir[6] and resembles cakes of figs.

AND NOFETH ẒUFIM. What means NOFETH ẒUFIM?—Rab said: The fine flour which floats [*ẓafah*] upon the top of a sieve [*nafah*] and resembles dough kneaded with honey and oil. Levi said: It is two loaves attached to [opposite sides of] an oven which keep on swelling until they touch one another.[7] R. Joshua b. Levi said: It is the honey which comes from the hills [*ẓofim*].[8] How is this known?[9]—As R. Shesheth[10] translated:[11] When the bees spring forth and fly in the heights of the world and collect honey from the herbage on the mountains.

We have learnt there:[12] Whatever is poured out[13] is clean with

(1) Through the action of the *Shamir* the stones are split open along the written lines without any part of the stones being cut away. (2) According to Ab. v. 9 it was one of the ten things created in the twilight of the sixth day, before the first Sabbath. (3) Perles, *Etymol. Studien*, p. 51, identifies the word with the Persian *parand* or *barand*. (4) V. B.M. (Sonc. ed.) p. 184, n. 3. (5) Lit., congealed wine; perhaps identical with 'wine mixed with snow (Neg. I, 2). (6) A northern peak of Mt. Hermon mentioned in the Bible as famed for its cypresses. (7) The dough is blessed and so increases in size. The loaves float (*Zaf*) in the space of the oven. (8) There is another reading: *zipya* which Jastrow explains as the inner cells of the honeycomb. (9) That bees gather honey from the hills. (10) [*Var. lec.* 'R. Joseph', v. B.Ḳ. (Sonc. ed.) p, 9, n. 9.] (11) The words '*as bees do*' in Deut. I, 44. (12) Nazir 50*a*. (13) If something is poured from a clean vessel into an unclean vessel, what is in the former is not defiled by the fact that the latter is unclean.

the exception of thick honey and batter.[1] What means *zifim* [thick]?—R. Joḥanan said: Honey used for adulteration [*ziyyef*]; and Resh Laḳish said: It is named after its place, as it is written, *Zif, Telem and Bealoth.*[2] You may similarly quote, *When the Zifites came and said to Saul, Doth not David* etc.[3] What means *Zifites?*—R. Joḥanan said: Men who falsify their words; and R. Eliezer says: They are named after their place, as it is written, *Zif, Telem, and Bealoth.*[2]

AND MEN OF FAITH DISAPPEARED. R. Isaac said: These are men who had faith in the Holy One, blessed be He. For it has been taught: R. Eliezer the Great[4] declares: Whoever has a piece of bread in his basket and says, 'What shall I eat tomorrow?' belongs only to them who are little in faith. And that is what R. Eleazar said, What means that which is written, *For who hath despised the day of small things?*[5] [It signifies,] What is the cause that the tables of the righteous are despoiled in the Hereafter?[6] The smallness [of faith] which was in them, that they did not trust in the Holy One, blessed be He. Raba said: They are the little ones[7] among the children of the wicked of Israel [49*a*] who despoil the verdict upon their fathers in the Hereafter, saying before Him, 'Sovereign of the Universe! Since thou art about to exact punishment of them, why hast Thou blunted their teeth?'[8]

R. Elai b. Jebarekya said: Had it not been for the prayer of David, all Israel would have been sellers of rubbish,[9] as it is stated, *Grant them esteem, O Lord.*[10]

R. Elai b. Jebarekya also said: Had it not been for the prayer of Habakkuk, two disciples of the Sages would have to cover themselves with one garment[11] and occupy themselves with Torah; as

(1) Being thick the outflow connects what is in the two vessels. (2) Josh. XV, 24. (3) Ps. LIV, 2 (in the E.V. it is part of the heading of the Psalm). (4) Eliezer b. Hyrcanus. (5) Zech. IV, 10. (6) They do not receive their full reward. (7) Children who died young. (8) Caused them suffering in this world by our death in childhood. By this plea the bereaved parents are spared punishment. (9) Earning a precarious livelihood. (10) Ps. IX, 21 (E.V. '*Put them in fear*'). ['*Them*' are Israel, and the prayer is that God will bestow on them worldly goods which will secure for them the esteem of the nations.] (11) Through poverty.

it is stated, *O Lord, I have heard the report of Thee and am afraid; O Lord, revive Thy work in the midst of the years*[1]—read not '*in the midst of the years* [*beḳereb shanim*]' but in the drawing together of two [*beḳerub shenayim*].[2]

R. Elai b. Jebarekya also said: If two disciples of the Sages proceed on a journey and there are no words of Torah between them, they are deserving of being burnt with fire; as it is stated, *And it came to pass, as they still went on, that, behold, a chariot of fire* etc.[3] The reason [why the chariot of fire appeared] was that there was discussion [of Torah between them]; hence if there had not been such discussion, they would have deserved to be burnt.

R. Elai b. Jebarekya also said: If two disciples of the Sages reside in the same city and do not support each other in [the study of] the law, one dies and the other goes into exile;[4] as it is stated, *That the manslayer might flee thither, which slayeth his neighbour without knowledge*,[5] and '*knowledge*' means nothing but Torah, as it is stated, *My people are destroyed for lack of knowledge*.[6]

R. Judah, son of R. Ḥiyya said: Any disciple of the Sages who occupies himself with Torah in poverty will have his prayer heard; as it is stated, *For the people shall dwell in Zion at Jerusalem; thou shalt weep no more; He will surely be gracious unto thee at the voice of thy cry; when He shall hear, He will answer thee*,[7] and it continues, *And the Lord will give you bread in adversity and water in affliction*.[8] R. Abbahu said: They also satisfy him from the lustre of the *Sheçhinah*, as it is stated, *Thine eyes shall see thy Teacher*.[9] R. Aḥa b. Ḥanina said: Neither is the veil[10] drawn before him, as it is said, '*Thy teacher shall no more be hidden*.'

RABBAN SIMEON B. GAMALIEL SAYS IN THE NAME OF R. JOSHUA:[11] FROM THE DAY THAT THE TEMPLE WAS DESTROYED,

(1) Hab. III, 2. (2) '*Thy work*' is the study of Torah; and 'drawing together of two' refers to two students sharing one garment. (3) II Kings II, 11. (4) One being the cause of the other's death, he has, so to speak, to flee to a city of refuge; he is exiled. (5) Deut. IV, 42. (6) Hos. IV, 6. (7) Isa. XXX, 19. The people dwelling in Zion symbolise students of Torah. (8) Ibid. 20 *sic*. (9) Ibid. '*Teacher*' is applied to God. (10) Hiding the glory of God from man. (11) The wording in the Mishnah is: R. Joshua testified.

THERE IS NO DAY etc. Raba said: And the curse of each day is severer than that of the preceding, as it is stated, *In the morning thou shalt say, Would God it were even! and at even thou shalt say, Would God it were morning.*[1] Which morning [would they long for]? If I say the morning of the morrow, nobody knows what it will be. Therefore [it must be the morning] which had gone.[2] How, in that case, can the world endure?[3]—Through the doxology recited after the Scriptural reading,[4] and [the response of] 'May His great Name [be blessed]' [which is uttered in the doxology] after studying *Aggada;*[5] as it is stated, *A land of thick darkness, as darkness itself, a land of the shadow of death, without any order.*[6] Hence if there are Scriptural readings, it is illumined from the thick darkness.

THE DEW HAS NOT DESCENDED FOR A BLESSING AND THE FLAVOUR HAS DEPARTED FROM THE FRUITS etc. It has been taught: R. Simeon b. Eleazar says: [The cessation of] purity has removed taste and fragrance [from fruits]; [the cessation of] tithes has removed the fatness of corn. R. Huna once found a juicy date which he took and wrapped in his mantle. His son, Rabbah, came and said to him, 'I smell the fragrance of a juicy date'. He said to him, 'My son, there is purity in thee',[7] and gave it to him. Meanwhile [Rabbah's] son, Abba, came; [Rabbah] took it and gave it to him. [R. Huna] said to [Rabbah], 'My son, thou hast gladdened my heart[8] and blunted my teeth'.[9] That is what the popular proverb says, 'A father's love is for his children; the children's love is for their own children.'

(1) Deut. XXVIII, 67. (2) Because yesterday was less severe than to-day. Therefore they longed for its return. (3) If every day is worse than the preceding day. (4) [*Kidushah-de-Sidra.* Lit., 'the doxology of the order'. This name is given to the passage recited at the conclusion of the morning service which begins 'And a Redeemer shall come unto Zion' (v. *P.B.* p. 73) and which consists of Scriptural verses including the doxology in Hebrew and Aramaic. It was designed according to Rashi to take the place of the daily study of the law which is enjoined upon every Jew. For other explanations v. Abrahams, I., *Companion to the Daily Prayer Book*, p. LXXXIII.] (5) V. p. 197, n. 1. (6) Job X, 22. The word for 'order' is the same as that for the Scriptural reading. (7) For that reason he was able to smell its fragrance. (8) With his purity. (9) By displaying more love for the son than the father, because he gave him the date.

R. Aḥa b. Jacob reared R. Jacob, his daughter's son. When he grew up, [the grandfather] said to him, 'Give me some water to drink'. He replied, 'I am not thy son'.[1] That is what the popular proverb says, 'Rear me, rear me;[2] I am thy daughter's son'.

MISHNAH. DURING THE WAR WITH VESPASIAN[3] THEY [THE RABBIS] DECREED AGAINST [THE USE OF] CROWNS WORN BY BRIDEGROOMS AND AGAINST [THE USE OF] THE DRUM.[4] DURING THE WAR OF QUIETUS[5] THEY DECREED AGAINST [THE USE OF] CROWNS WORN BY BRIDES AND THAT NOBODY SHOULD TEACH HIS SON GREEK. DURING THE FINAL WAR[6] THEY DECREED THAT A BRIDE SHOULD NOT GO OUT IN A PALANQUIN[7] IN THE MIDST OF THE CITY, BUT OUR RABBIS DECREED THAT A BRIDE MAY GO OUT IN A PALANQUIN IN THE MIDST OF THE CITY.

WHEN R. MEIR[8] DIED, THE COMPOSERS OF FABLES CEASED. WHEN BEN AZZAI[9] DIED, THE ASSIDUOUS STUDENTS [OF TORAH] CEASED. WHEN BEN ZOMA[10] DIED, THE EXPOSITORS CEASED.[11] WHEN R. AKIBA[12] DIED, THE GLORY OF THE TORAH CEASED. WHEN R. ḤANINA B. DOSA DIED, MEN OF DEED[13]

(1) He claimed that the duty of honouring parents did not apply to grandparents, although he had been reared by him. (2) And yet I have not the duty of a son. (3) Which ended in the destruction of the second Temple. (4) At wedding festivities. (5) The text has Titus; but Neubauer's *Mediaeval Jewish Chronicles*, II p. 66 has the correct reading. Quietus was a Moorish prince, appointed by Trajan to command the army which overran Babylon in 116 C.E. (6) Rashi explains: when the Temple was destroyed. More probably it refers to the last stand against Rome under Bar Kochba in 135 C.E. (7) In which she was conveyed to her husband's house. (8) He was renowned for his fables. V. Sanh. 38*b*. (9) He was wedded to the Torah. V. *supra* p. 15. (10) He was a famous expositor. V. Ber. 12*b*. (11) [The text of the separately printed Mishnah adds: WHEN R. JOSHUA DIED, GOODNESS DEPARTED FROM THIS WORLD. WHEN R. SIMEON B. GAMALIEL DIED, THE LOCUST CAME AND TROUBLE INCREASED. WHEN R. ELEAZAR B. AZARIAH DIED, WEALTH DEPARTED FROM THE SAGES.] (12) He studied every letter of the Torah and derived ideas from every peculiarity of expression. (13) The phrase has been variously interpreted. V. Büchler, *Some Types of Jewish-Palestinian Piety*, pp. 79ff. He

CEASED. WHEN R. JOSE ḲEṬANTA DIED, THE PIOUS MEN CEASED; AND WHY WAS HIS NAME CALLED ḲEṬANTA? BECAUSE HE WAS THE YOUNGEST[1] OF THE PIOUS MEN.[2] WHEN R. JOḤANAN B. ZAKKAI[3] DIED, THE LUSTRE OF WISDOM CEASED.[4] WHEN RABBAN GAMALIEL THE ELDER DIED, THE GLORY OF THE TORAH CEASED, AND PURITY AND ABNEGATION PERISHED. WHEN R. ISHMAEL B. FABI[5] DIED, THE LUSTRE OF THE PRIESTHOOD CEASED. WHEN RABBI DIED, HUMILITY AND FEAR OF SIN CEASED.[6] R. PHINEAS B. JAIR SAYS: WHEN [THE SECOND] TEMPLE WAS DESTROYED, SCHOLARS[7] AND NOBLEMEN WERE ASHAMED AND COVERED THEIR HEAD,[8] MEN OF DEED WERE DISREGARDED, AND MEN OF ARM AND MEN OF TONGUE[9] GREW POWERFUL. NOBODY ENQUIRES,[10] NOBODY PRAYS [ON THEIR BEHALF], AND NOBODY ASKS.[11] UPON WHOM IS IT FOR US TO RELY? UPON OUR FATHER WHO IS IN HEAVEN. R. ELIEZER THE GREAT SAYS: FROM THE DAY THE TEMPLE WAS DESTROYED, THE SAGES BEGAN TO BE LIKE SCHOOL-TEACHERS,[12] SCHOOL-TEACHERS LIKE SYNAGOGUE-ATTENDANTS, SYNAGOGUE-ATTENDANTS LIKE COMMON PEOPLE, AND THE COMMON PEOPLE [49b] BECAME MORE AND MORE DEBASED; AND THERE WAS NONE TO ASK, NONE TO INQUIRE. UPON WHOM IS IT FOR US TO RELY? UPON OUR FATHER WHO IS IN HEAVEN. IN THE FOOTSTEPS OF THE MESSIAH[13] INSOLENCE WILL INCREASE AND HONOUR DWIN-

explains it as men who devoted their lives to deeds of loving kindness.

(1) I.e., the last of them. There is no other mention of him in Rabbinic literature. (2) [J. B.Ḳ. III, makes him identical with Jose the Babylonian, the son of Aḳabia b. Mahalaliel. V. Derenbourg, *Essai*, p. 483.] (3) His disciples called him 'the lamp of Israel'. V. Ber. 28b. (4) [On the wide sweep of his knowledge embracing the whole gamut of sciences known in his day v. B.B. 134*a*.] (5) Appointed High Priest by Agrippa II in 59 C.E. He was executed in Cyrene after the destruction of the Temple (Josephus, *War* VI, II, 2.). (6) Since Rabbi (Judah I, the Prince) was the redactor of the Mishnah, this paragraph is clearly a later addition. V. Bacher, *Agada der Tannaiten*, II, p. 222, n. 4. (7) *Ḥaberim*, v. Glos. (8) Through the insolence of inferior persons who grew powerful. (9) Demagogues. (10) Concerning Israel's plight. (11) About the welfare of his neighbour. (12) They deteriorated in quality. (13) Just before his advent.

DLE;[1] THE VINE WILL YIELD ITS FRUIT [ABUNDANTLY] BUT WINE WILL BE DEAR;[2] THE GOVERNMENT WILL TURN TO HERESY[3] AND THERE WILL BE NONE [TO OFFER THEM] REPROOF; THE MEETING-PLACE [OF SCHOLARS] WILL BE USED FOR IMMORALITY; GALILEE WILL BE DESTROYED, GABLAN[4] DESOLATED, AND THE DWELLERS ON THE FRONTIER WILL GO ABOUT [BEGGING] FROM PLACE TO PLACE WITHOUT ANYONE TO TAKE PITY ON THEM; THE WISDOM OF THE LEARNED[5] WILL DEGENERATE, FEARERS OF SIN WILL BE DESPISED, AND THE TRUTH WILL BE LACKING; YOUTHS WILL PUT OLD MEN TO SHAME, THE OLD WILL STAND UP IN THE PRESENCE OF THE YOUNG, A SON WILL REVILE HIS FATHER, A DAUGHTER WILL RISE AGAINST HER MOTHER, A DAUGHTER-IN-LAW AGAINST HER MOTHER-IN-LAW, AND A MAN'S ENEMIES WILL BE THE MEMBERS OF HIS HOUSEHOLD;[6] THE FACE OF THE GENERATION WILL BE LIKE THE FACE OF A DOG,[7] A SON WILL NOT FEEL ASHAMED BEFORE HIS FATHER. SO UPON WHOM IS IT FOR US TO RELY? UPON OUR FATHER WHO IS IN HEAVEN.

GEMARA. Rab said: [The decree against the use of a crown] applies only to one made of salt and brimstone,[8] but if made of myrtle or roses it is permitted; and Samuel said: Also one made of myrtle or roses is prohibited, but if made of reeds or rushes it is permitted; and Levi said: Also one made of reeds or rushes is

(1) Jast. renders; the nobility shall be oppressed. In Sanh. 97*a* there is a variant: honour will be perverted; or, according to Jast. the nobility will pervert (justice). (2) Through the spread of drunkenness. (3) These words are omitted in the Talmud ed. of the Mishnah. The meaning is: The Roman Empire will go over to Christianity. V. Herford, *op. cit.*, p. 207. (4) Perhaps Gebal of Ps. LXXXIII, 8, i.e., the Northern part of Mount Seir. [Others: Gaulan, E. of the Sea of Galilee and the Upper Jordan.] (5) Lit., 'scribes'. (6) V. Micah VII, 6. (7) Impervious to shame. [In some editions the whole of this passage beginning 'R. Phineas b. Jair' is introduced with 'Our Rabbis taught', and not as part of the Mishnah.] (8) Rashi explains that it was a crown cut out of a block of salt upon which figures were traced with brimstone.

prohibited. Similarly taught Levi in his Mishnah:[1] It is also prohibited if made of reeds or rushes.

AND AGAINST [THE USE OF] THE DRUM [IRUS]. What means IRUS?—R. Eleazar said: A drum with a single bell.[2] Rabbah b. R. Huna made a tambourine for his son; his father came and broke it, saying to him, 'It might be substituted for a drum with a single bell. Go, make for him [an instrument by stretching the skin] over the mouth of a pitcher or over the mouth of a *kefiz*'.[3]

DURING THE WAR OF QUIETUS THEY DECREED AGAINST [THE USE OF] CROWNS WORN BY BRIDES etc. What means 'crowns worn by brides'?—Rabbah b. Bar Ḥanah said in the name of R. Joḥanan: A [miniature] golden city.[4] There is a teaching to the same effect: What are 'crowns worn by brides'?—A golden city. But one may make a cap for her out of fine wool. A Tanna taught: They also decreed against [the use of] the canopy of bridegrooms. What means 'canopy of bridegrooms'?—Crimson silk embroidered with gold. There is a teaching to the same effect. The canopy of bridegrooms is crimson silk embroidered with gold. But we may make a framework of laths and hang on it anything one desires.

AND THAT NOBODY SHOULD TEACH HIS SON GREEK. Our Rabbis taught: When the kings of the Hasmonean house fought one another,[5] Hyrcanus was outside and Aristobulus within. Each day[6] they used to let down *denarii* in a basket, and haul up for them [animals for] the continual offerings. An old man there, who was learned in Greek wisdom,[7] spoke with them[8] in Greek,[9] saying, 'As long as they carry on the Temple-service, they will never surrender to you'. On the morrow they let down *denarii* in a

(1) His own collection of traditional teachings. (2) Lit., 'mouth'. (3) A vessel of the capacity of three *log*. (4) According to Shab. 59*a* a golden crown designed in the form of Jerusalem. V. Krauss. *Tal. Arch.*, I, p. 662 n. 961. (5) The allusion is to the struggle between the two sons of Alexander Jannaeus. Hyrcanus had the assistance of the Romans who besieged Jerusalem. (6) According to Josephus *Ant.* XIV, II, 2, this demand for animals was for the Passover only. (7) [Sophistry, v. Graetz, *Geschichte*. III, 710ff.] (8) He was in Jerusalem and addressed his words to the besiegers. He spoke in Greek because the people in the city did not understand it. (9) Lit., 'in great wisdom'.

basket, and hauled up a pig.[1] When it reached half way up the wall, it stuck its claws [into the wall] and the land of Israel was shaken over a distance of four hundred parasangs. At that time they declared, 'Cursed be a man who rears pigs and cursed be a man who teaches his son Greek wisdom!' Concerning that year we learnt that it happened that the *'omer*[2] had to be supplied from the gardens of Zarifim and the two loaves from the valley of En-Soker.[3] But it is not so![4] For Rabbi said: Why use the Syrian language in the land of Israel? Either use the holy tongue or Greek! And R. Joseph said: Why use the Syrian language in Babylon? Either use the holy tongue or Persian!—The Greek language and Greek wisdom are distinct.[5] But is Greek philosophy forbidden? Behold Rab Judah declared that Samuel said in the name of Rabban Simeon b. Gamaliel, What means that which is written, *Mine eye affecteth my soul, because of all the daughters of my city?*[6] There were a thousand pupils in my father's house; five hundred studied Torah and five hundred studied Greek wisdom, and of these there remained only I here and the son of my father's brother in Assia![7]—It was different with the household of Rabban Gamaliel because they had close associations with the Government;[8] for it has been taught: To trim the hair in front[9] is of the ways of the Amorites;[10] but they permitted Abtilus b. Reuben[11] to trim his hair in front because he had

(1) In Josephus' version, they took the money but sent up no animals. So the men in Jerusalem 'prayed to God that He would avenge them on their countrymen. Nor did He delay that punishment, but sent a strong and vehement storm of wind that destroyed the fruits of the whole country.' (2) The sheaf of the first fruits and the meal-offering of two tenth parts of an ephah (Lev. XXIII, 10, 13) should consist of produce grown in the vicinity of Jerusalem. But that year the surroundings were devastated and the produce had to be brought from distant places. (3) For further notes on this passage v. B.Ḳ. (Sonc. ed.) pp. 469ff. (4) That it is forbidden to teach Greek. (5) The language is permitted but not the wisdom. (6) Lam. III, 51. (7) So Greek wisdom was studied by Rabban Gamaliel's pupils. Assia was a town east of the lake of Tiberias, v. Sanh. (Sonc. ed.) p. 151, n. 1. (8) An exception was made in their case. (9) Forming a fringe on the forehead and letting the curls hang down over the temples. V. Krauss, *op. cit.*, I. p. 647 n. 845. (10) A heathenish practice which is forbidden. (11) Nothing more is recorded of him in Rabbinic literature.

close associations with the Government. Similarly they permitted the household of Rabban Gamaliel to study Greek wisdom because they had close associations with the Government.

DURING THE FINAL WAR THEY DECREED THAT A BRIDE SHOULD NOT GO OUT IN A PALANQUIN etc. Why?—For reasons of chastity.[1]

WHEN RABBAN JOḤANAN [B. ZAKKAI] DIED, [THE LUSTRE OF] WISDOM CEASED. Our Rabbis taught: When R. Eliezer died, the Torah-scroll was hidden away.[2] When R. Joshua died, counsel and thought ceased.[3] When R. Akiba died, the arms of the Torah ceased and the fountains of wisdom were stopped up. When R. Eleazar b. Azariah died, the crowns of wisdom ceased, because *the crown of the wise is their riches.*[4] When R. Ḥanina b. Dosa died, men of deed ceased. When Abba[5] Jose b. Ḳeṭanta died, the pious men ceased; and why was his name called Abba Jose b. Ḳeṭanta? Because he was the youngest of the pious men. When Ben Azzai died, the assiduous students [of Torah] ceased. When Ben Zoma died, the expositors ceased. When Rabban Simeon b. Gamaliel died, locusts[6] came up and troubles increased. When Rabbi died, troubles were multiplied twofold.

WHEN RABBI DIED, HUMILITY AND FEAR OF SIN CEASED. R. Joseph said to the tanna,[7] Do not include [when reciting this Mishnah] the word 'humility', because there is I.[8] R. Naḥman said to the teacher, Do not include 'fear of sin', because there is I.[9]

(1) There was danger of her being attacked. (2) A tribute to his great learning. (3) He was a protagonist of Judaism against heathen attacks. V. Ḥag. 5*b*. (4) Prov. XIV, 24. He was extremely wealthy. V. Shab. 54*b*. (5) Abba, 'father', was a title of affection given to a number of Rabbis. (6) Some understand this literally; others see a reference to exacting tax-gatherers who despoiled the people. [The reference is said to be to R. Simeon II b. Gamaliel II, (the father of Rabbi) and to the plague of locusts and pestilence that broke out in the year 164 C.E., about the time of his death. V. *Kerem Chemed* IV, p. 220.] (7) Who conveyed his teaching to the students, v. Glos. s.v. (*b*). (8) He claimed to be humble. [V. Hor. (Sonc. ed.) p. 105.] (9) [In the separate printed editions of the Mishnah there follows: R. PHINEAS B. JAIR USED TO SAY: HEEDFULNESS LEADS TO CLEANLINESS; CLEANLINESS LEADS TO PURITY; PURITY LEADS TO ABSTINENCE; ABSTINENCE LEADS TO HOLINESS; HOLI-

NESS LEADS TO HUMILITY; HUMILITY LEADS TO FEAR OF SIN; FEAR OF SIN LEADS TO SAINTLINESS; SAINTLINESS LEADS TO (THE POSSESSION) OF THE HOLY SPIRIT; THE HOLY SPIRIT LEADS TO THE RESURRECTION OF THE DEAD; AND THE RESURRECTION OF THE DEAD COMETH THROUGH ELIJAH OF BLESSED MEMORY, AMEN. On this passage which has been named the Saint's Progress, v. A.Z., 20*b*. (Sonc. ed.) p. 106.]

GLOSSARY

INDEX OF SCRIPTURAL REFERENCES

GENERAL INDEX

TRANSLITERATION OF HEBREW LETTERS

ABBREVIATIONS

GLOSSARY

AGGADA. (Lit., 'tale', 'lesson'); the name given to those sections of Rabbinic literature which contain homiletic expositions of the Bible, stories, legends, folk-lore, anecdotes or maxims.

AMORA. 'Speaker', 'interpreter'; originally denoted the interpreter who attended upon the public preacher or lecturer for the purpose of expounding at length and in popular style the heads of the discourse given to him by the latter. Subsequently (pl. Amoraim) the name given to the Rabbinic authorities responsible for the Gemara, as opposed to the Mishnah or Baraitha (v. Tanna).

BARAITHA. (Lit., 'outside'); a teaching or a tradition of the Tannaim that has been excluded from the Mishnah and incorporated in a later collection compiled by R. Ḥiyya and R. Oshaiah, generally introduced by 'Our Rabbis taught', or 'It has been taught'.

BATH ḲOL (Lit., 'daughter of a voice'); (*a*) a reverberating sound; (*b*) a voice descending from heaven (cf. Dan. IV, 28) to offer guidance in human affairs, and regarded as a lower grade of prophecy.

BERERAH. (Lit., 'choice'); the selection retrospectively of one object rather than another as having been designated by a term equally applicable to both.

GEZERAH SHAWAH. (Lit., 'equal cut'); the application to one subject of a rule already known to apply to another, on the strength of a common expression used in connection with both in the Scriptures.

ḤABER. 'Fellow', 'associate', one scrupulous in the observance of the law, particularly in relation to ritual cleanness and the separation of the priestly and Levitical dues.

ḤALIZAH. (Lit., 'drawing off'); the ceremony of taking off the shoe of the brother of a husband who has died childless. (V. Deut. XXV, 5-9).

ḤALUZAH. A woman who has performed *ḥalizah*.

KARETH. (Lit., 'cutting off'); divine punishment for a number of sins for which no human penalty is specified. Sudden death is described as '*kareth* of days', premature death at sixty as '*kareth* of years'.

KOHEN. A priest, a descendant of Aaron (v. Lev. XXI, XXII).

NA'ARAH. A girl between the ages of twelve years and one day and twelve and a half years plus one day.

SHECHINAH. (Lit., 'abiding [of God]', 'Divine presence'); the spirit of the Omnipresent as manifested on earth.

SHEMA' (Lit., 'hear'); the Biblical verse, '*Hear, O Israel*' etc. (Deut. VI, 4); also the three sections (Deut. VI, 5-9; Deut. XI, 13-20; Num. XV, 37-41) which are recited after this verse in the morning and evening prayers.

TANNA. (Lit., 'one who repeats' or 'teaches'); (*a*) a Rabbi quoted in the Mishnah or Baraitha (q.v.); (*b*) in the Amoraic period, a scholar whose special task was to memorize and recite Baraithas in the presence of expounding teachers.

TERUMAH. 'That which is lifted or separated'; the heave-offering given from the yields of the yearly harvests, from certain sacrifices, and from the *shekels* collected in a special chamber in the Temple (*terumath ha-lishkah*). *Terumah gedolah* (great offering): the first levy on the produce of the year given to the priest. (V. Num. XVIII, 8ff.) Its quantity varied according to the generosity of the owner, who could give one-fortieth, one-fiftieth, or one-sixtieth of his harvest. *Terumath ma'aser* (heave-offering of the tithe): the heave-offering given to the priest by the Levite from the tithes he receives (v. Num. XVIII, 25ff.).

ZOMEM. (pl. *zomemim;*) a witness giving false evidence and who is thus subject to the *lex talionis*. Cf. Deut. XIX, 19.

SCRIPTURAL REFERENCES

NUMBERS

SCRIPTURAL REFERENCES

GENERAL INDEX*

A

Aaron, 58, 60, 65, 71.
Ab, 172.
Abraham, 17f, 47f, 51, 72, 89, 151, 243.
Abrahams, I., 264.
Absalom, 40f, 46, 50ff.
Abtilus b. Reuben, 269.
Academy, heavenly, 32.
— Principal of, 135, 196.
Acco, 196.
Adam, 243.
'*Adam*, discussion of term, 20.
Adonijah, 41.
Adulterers, 249.
Adultery, 185.
— with animals, 131.
Affirmative corrollary of negative, 89.
Aggada, 197, 264.
Agrippa, 202ff.
Ahitophel, 40, 107.
Alash, 170.
Alexandria, 247.
Allegory, 80.
Alusa, 170.
Amen. *See* Benedictions.
Amaziah, 48.
'*Am ha-arez*, 110, 149, 254f.
Amoz, 48.
Amram, 60.
Amplification and limitation, 84f, 88.
'Anah, 170.
Analogy, deduction by, 4, 81f, 86f, 90f, 97, 126, 141f, 159f, 164. *See also Gezerah Shawah.*
'*Anath*, 170.
Angel of Death, 242.
Angels, 162.
Anger, 11, 174.
Antioch, 162.
Apologists, Christian, 74.
Aramaic, 162f.
Aristobulus and Hyrcanus, 268f.
Ark, 166, 173, 194.
Arrogance, 252f.
Aruch, 71.
Asa, 46.
Assia, 269.
Association with other men. *See* Seclusion.
Atonement, Day of, 195, 199f, 245.

B

Babylon, 243, 265.
Bachelor Rabbi, 15.
Bacher, 266.
Balaam, 40, 46, 53.
Balak, 245.
Bar Kochba, 265.
Basket of palm-twigs, 97.
Bath Ḳol, 2, 50, 71, 108, 162f, 259.
Bathsheba, 51.
Be-Dura, 243.
— Duraja, 243.
— Kafi, 243f.
— Kufai, 243.
— Nari, 47.
— Ẓinyatha, 243.
Benedictions, Eighteen. *See* 'Prayer'.
— High Priest's, 157, 186, 198ff.

* An Index of Rabbinical Names will be provided in the special Index Volume to be published on completion of the translation of the entire Talmud.

Sea, Red, 2, 56, 62, 64, 182f.
– Red, Song by the. *See* Moses.
Seclusion, 1, 3ff, 21f, 93f, 125f, 129f.
– after warning, 152f.
– duration of, 13ff.
Segan, 199. *See also* Priest's deputy.
Senir, 261.
Sennacherib, 242.
Sepphoris, 50.
Serah, 67.
Serpent, the, 40.
'Service', the, 190.
Sexes, mingling of, 28.
Shame before Messiah's advent, 267.
– putting one to, 49.
Shamir, 256, 260f.
Sharon, 214, 221.
Sheaf, forgotten, 229ff.
Shebna, 108.
Shechem, 69, 112, 158, 165.
Shechinah, 11, 18f, 43f, 52, 63, 65, 68, 197 *et passim.*
Shema', 110, 137, 149f, 202, 209f, 218, 248.
– language of recital of, 157, 161f.
Shem Hameforash, 188.
Sheol, 51.
Shiḥori, Fort of, 191.
Shiloh, 82.
Shobach, 211.
Simeon the Righteous, 162.
Sinai, 19, 64, 107, 184.
Singer P. B., 110, 157, 190, 193, 194, 197, 201, 264.
Slander, 20, 173, 206.
Slaves, 10, 251.
Solomon, 245, 260.
Son, stubborn and rebellious, 125.
Song of Moses. *See* Moses.
– permissibility of, 257f.
South, 125.
Spies, 168f, 171ff.
Spittle, 252.
Stipulation, 94f.
Stoning, 35, 115.
Students, cessation of, 265.
Sura, 123, 243.
Synagogue, 111, 191ff.
– attendant, 198, 202f, 266.
– president, 198, 202.
Syrian language, 269.

T

Tabernacle, 82f.
Tabernacles, feast of, 202.
Tamar, 47, 49.
Teacher, 149, 243, 266.
Ṭebeth, 201.
Ṭebul yom, 143ff.
Telbesh, 170.
Telbeth, 170.
Temple, 40, 54, 81f, 182f, 186, 188, 199, 260.
– corpse in. *See* Corpse.
– court. *See* Court.
– destruction of, 256, 259, 261, 263f, 265f.
– destruction of effects of, 266.
Tent of Meeting, 40, 184, 187.
Terumah, 254.
Tetragrammaton, 186, 188, 196, 198, 212. *See also* Name.
Texts, exposition of, 34, 49ff, 77 *et passim.*
– implication of, 8ff.
Thread of blue, 90.
Tiberias, 50, 231.
Timnah, 43, 47.
Tithe, 146, 219, 254f, 257.
– confession at bringing of, 157, 159f, 249, 253f.
Torah as protection on journey, 242, 263.

U

V

W

TRANSLITERATION OF HEBREW LETTERS

א (in middle of word)	= '
ב	= b
ו	= w
ח	= ḥ
ט	= ṭ
כ	= k
ע	= '
פ	= f
צ	= ẓ
ק	= ḳ
ת	= th

Full particulars regarding the method and scope of the translation are given in the Editor's Introduction in the Baba Ḳamma volume (Neziḳin, Vol. I).

ABBREVIATIONS

Ab.	Aboth.
Ant.	*Antiquities*, by Flavius Josephus.
'Ar.	'Arakin.
Aruch.	Talmudic Dictionary by R. Nathan b. Jeḥiel of Rome. (d. 1106.)
A.Z.	'Abodah Zarah.
b.	*ben*, *bar*, son of.
B.B.	Baba Bathra.
Bek.	Bekoroth.
Ber.	Berakoth.
Beẓ.	Beẓah.
B.Ḳ.	Baba Ḳamma.
B.M.	Baba Meẓia.
Chajes, Z. H.	Notes by Chajes, Zebi Hirsch b. Meir (1805-1855) in the Wilna Romm edition of the Talmud.
Cur. ed(d).	Current edition(s).
Derenbourg.	Derenbourg, J., *Essai sur l'Histoire et la Géographie de la Palestine.*
Dor	*Dor Dor Wedoreshaw*, by I. H. Weiss (2nd ed.).
'Ed.	'Eduyyoth.
E.V.	English Versions of the Bible.
G.K., Ges. K.	Gesenius-Kautzsch, Hebrew Grammar.
Giṭ.	Giṭṭin.
Glos.	Glossary.
Graetz.	Graetz, H. *Geschichte der Juden* (4th ed.).
Ḥag.	Ḥagigah.
Heb.	Hebrew.
Hildesheimer.	Hildesheimer, H. *Beiträge zur Geographie Palästinas.*
Hor.	Horayoth.
HUCA	Hebrew Union College Annual.
Ḥul.	Ḥullin.
J.	Jerusalem (Jerushalmi); J.T., Jerusalem Talmud.
Jast.	M. Jastrow's *Dictionary of the Targumim, the Talmud Babli and Yerushalmi, and the Midrashic Literature.*
J.E.	*Jewish Encyclopedia.*
JQR.	*Jewish Quarterly Review.*
Ket., Keth.	Kethuboth.
Ḳid.	Ḳiddushin.
Kil.	Kil'ayim.

ABBREVIATIONS

Klausner, J.	היסטוריה ישראלית
Maharsha.	R. Samuel Eliezer ha-Levi Edels (1555-1631).
Maim.	Moses Maimonides (1135-1204).
Meg.	Megillah.
Men.	Menahoth.
MGWJ.	*Monatsschrift für Geschichte und Wissenschaft des Judentums.*
MS.M.	Munich codex of the Talmud.
MSS.	Manuscripts.
M.T.	Massoretic Text of the Bible.
Naz.	Nazir.
Ned.	Nedarim.
Neg.	Nega'im.
Nid.	Niddah.
Oh., Ohal.	Ohaloth.
P.B.	The Authorised Daily Prayer Book, S. Singer.
R.	Rab, Rabban, Rabbenu, Rabbi.
Rashb., Rashbam.	Commentary of R. Samuel b. Meir (d. about 1174).
Rashi.	Commentary of R. Isaac Yiẓḥaḳi (d. 1105).
R.E.J.	*Revue des Etudes Juives.*
R.H.	Rosh Hashanah.
R.V.	Revised Version of the Bible.
San., Sanh.	Sanhedrin.
Shab.	Shabbath.
Shebu.	Shebu'oth.
Sonc. ed.	English Translation of the Babylonian Talmud, Soncino Press, London.
Soṭ.	Soṭah.
Strashun, S.	Notes by Samuel b. Joseph Strashun (1794-1872) in the Wilna Romm edition of the Talmud.
Suk.	Sukkah.
TA.	*Talmudische Archäologie*, by S. Krauss.
Tosaf.	Tosafoth.
Tosaf. of Sens.	Commentary of Samson b. Abraham of Sens, (about 1150-1230) in the Romm edition of Soṭah.
Tosef.	Tosefta.
Wahrmann, N.	*Untersuchungen über die Stellung der Frau im Judentum im Zeitalter der Tannaiten.*
Wilna Gaon.	Notes by Elijah of Wilna (1720-1797) in the recent printed editions of the Talmud.
Yeb.	Yebamoth.